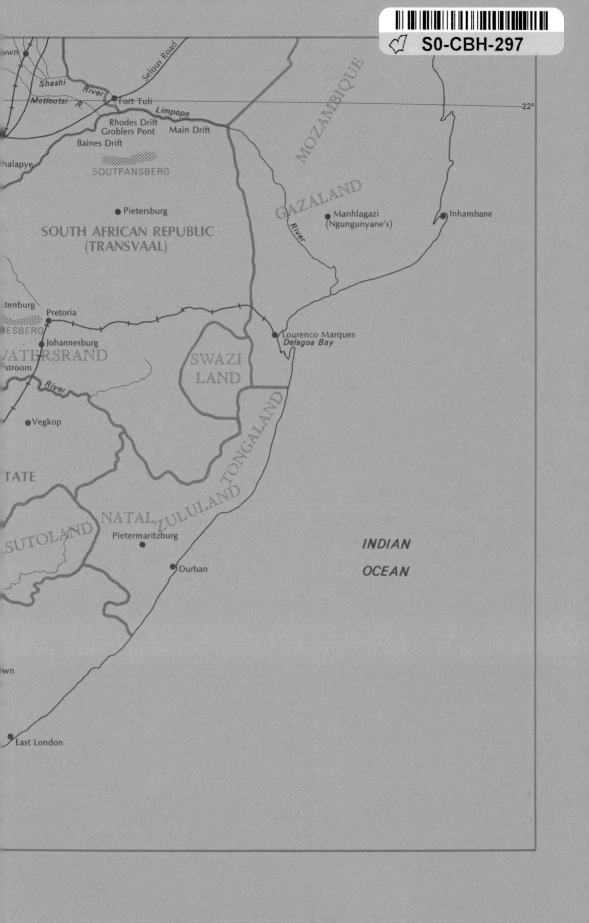

S0-CBH-297

wn

Shashi *River*   Selous Road

Motloutsi *R.*   Fort Tuli

Limpopo   22°

Rhodes Drift
Groblers Pont   Main Drift
Baines Drift

halapye

SOUTPANSBERG

MOZAMBIQUE

Inhambane

GAZALAND

River

• Pietersburg

Manhlagazi
(Ngungunyane's)

SOUTH AFRICAN REPUBLIC
(TRANSVAAL)

tenburg
Pretoria

ESBERG

Johannesburg

Lourenco Marques
Delagoa Bay

WATERSRAND

stroom

SWAZI
LAND

River

• Vegkop

TONGALAND

TATE

NATAL ZULULAND

SUTOLAND

Pietermaritzburg

INDIAN

OCEAN

Durban

wn

• East London

Rhodes in 1890

RHODES AND RHODESIA

The White Conquest of Zimbabwe 1884-1902

ARTHUR KEPPEL-JONES

McGILL-QUEEN'S UNIVERSITY PRESS
Kingston and Montreal, 1983

©McGill-Queen's University Press 1983
Kingston and Montreal
Canada

ISBN 0-7735-0534-2

Reprinted in Canada 1987

Published simultaneously in southern Africa by the
University of Natal Press
Pietermaritzburg, Natal
South Africa

This book has been published with the help of a grant from the Humanities
Federation of Canada, using funds provided by the Social Sciences and Humanities Research Council of Canada.

DESIGN BY Eileen Potts   Queen's Graphic Design Unit
TYPESETTING Howarth & Smith Limited, Toronto
PRINTED in Canada by T.H. Best Printing Company Limited, Toronto

Canadian Cataloguing in Publication Data
    Keppel-Jones, Arthur, 1909-
    Rhodes and Rhodesia : the white conquest of Zimbabwe, 1884-1902

    ISBN 0-7735-0534-2

    1. Zimbabwe – History – 19th century. I. Title.

    DT962.7.K46   968.91'02   C83-098429-1

This edition not for sale in South Africa, South West Africa, Botswana,
Lesotho, Malawi, Mozambique, Swaziland, Zambia and Zimbabwe.

In Memory of Eileen

AUGUSTANA UNIVERSITY COLLEGE
LIBRARY

Lobengula, from a sketch by E.A. Maund, worked up by Ralph Peacock

CONTENTS

At Fort Tuli, 2 July 1890.
Above, Ndebele delegation. Below, Pioneers

ILLUSTRATIONS

All photographs by courtesy of the National archives of Zimbabwe.

MAPS

A settler's place; Dingaan Farm, before 1903

This book is the result of several decades of research and writing. It comes off the press more than six years after it was first submitted to a publisher. These facts are mentioned not as excuses for some of its shortcomings but to draw attention to its essential nature. The main reason for those delays and difficulties is that the book is long and detailed.

It was to provide the details that the book was written. Most works on this subject, as on many others, consist largely of generalizations. These may be sound, but the reader is not able to judge them unless he is given the details on which they are based. This book attempts to supply them. In only one part have I made a concession to the economics of publication: the first chapter is a highly compressed revision of what was a much longer introductory section. I hope it is intelligible as it now stands.

Details must include the actions and thoughts of individual people. For my subject the archives, private collections, and published memoirs, diaries, and letters provide a great stock of this kind of information about the white actors in the drama, but hardly anything about the black ones. Lobengula comes nearest to being an exception, but even he can be seen only through the eyes of aliens. As the subject is the conquest of a preliterate by a literate people, there is no way out of this difficulty. I would have given much to have the same kind of details of the lives and thoughts of the black characters as of the white.

So the book, while it deals with an African country, belongs at least as much to the category of British imperial as to that of African history. Specialists in this field might call it a case of "sub-imperialism." I have made no generalizations about sub-imperialism; I would not have the confidence to do so without having studied, in equal depth, at least half-a-dozen other cases of it. But I hope that, in combination with other such studies, it may provide a basis for generalization of some kind.

To achieve my object it would have been desirable to use, exclusively and exhaustively, primary sources, but this was not possible. Many secondary works were used, almost always to supply facts that were not otherwise available at the time of writing. In some cases I have referred to other historians' theories or explanations in order to discuss them; but as far as possible, so as to reach my conclusions from the contemporary evidence, I avoided reading other general works on the subject while writing my own. Hence what might seem to be some surprising omissions from the bibliography, which is confined to sources and works actually used in the writing of this book.

The names of territories and places, where they occur after the beginning of the colonial period, are the names (with the spellings) used in that period. A glossary gives the equivalents introduced, or restored, after independence.

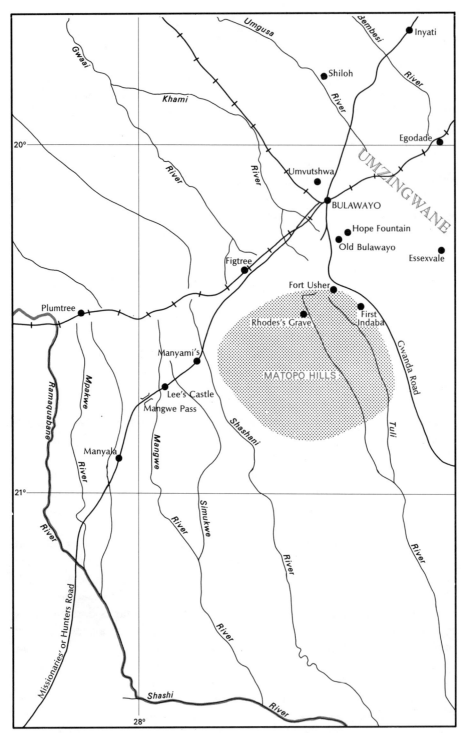

Environs of Bulawayo, 1902

ACKNOWLEDGMENTS

This book could not have been finished or published without a great deal of support. The most fundamental was given by my wife, whose encouragement, faith, and sometimes sacrifice of her interests kept me at the job through many years. The book was to be dedicated to her. As she did not live to see it published it is offered to her memory.

Many friends helped in various ways, by copying documents for me at times when I was not able to do so myself, by offering suggestions and criticisms, and by overcoming many of the obstacles to publication. I thank particularly my colleagues Professors Alan Jeeves, George Rawlyk, and Christopher Youé; Professors John Flint of Dalhousie University, Kenneth Kirkwood of Oxford, George Fortune of the University of Zimbabwe, and my former student Miss Karen Logan. There are many others who have helped in various ways; I hope they will accept my thanks, and understand if I do not mention them all by name.

I owe an immeasurable debt to Queen's University for financial assistance of various kinds, for giving me a research year on full pay, for the congenial conditions of work in the university, and not least for the resources of the Douglas Library. Most of those I have used were acquired specially for my needs. For this I thank, specifically, Mrs. Lin Good. It is through the support of the university, too, that the book has come to be published by the McGill-Queen's University Press. I am grateful to Mrs. Eileen Potts, of the Graphic Design Unit, for all the details of the design.

The materials were collected from various archives and libraries, whose directors and staffs I thank for their help. These were the National Archives of Zimbabwe (called the Central African Archives when I began to work there) and their successive Directors, Messrs. V.W. Hiller, T.W. Baxter, E.E. Burke, and most recently the present Director, Mrs. A. Kamba; the Public Record Office, London; the Bodleian Library, Oxford, and especially its Commonwealth section the Rhodes House Library; the libraries of New College and Christ Church, of the University of Birmingham, of the Royal Commonwealth Society in London and of the University of the Witwatersrand, Johannesburg.

I thank the Marquess of Salisbury for permission to use the papers of the third Marquess; Drs. D.N. Beach and Julian Cobbing for permission to use their unpublished theses, and Mr. and Mrs. W.G.M. Seymour of Pietermaritzburg for allowing me to photocopy and use the papers of F.R. ("Matabele") Thompson.

In addition to the financial support given by Queen's University I have two other, and indispensable, grants to acknowledge. One was from the Canada Council, for the expenses of travel, research, and the collection of material. The other removed the final obstacles. This book has been published with the help of a grant from the Canadian Federation for the Humanities, using funds provided by the Social Sciences and Humanities Research Council of Canada. I am most grateful to these organizations and their officers.

CHAPTER I

The British Advance into the Interior

PRELUDE: HOW THE COMPETITORS MOVED INTO POSITION

On 16 September 1795, the Dutch authorities in Cape Town surrendered their colony to the British. Though it changed hands again and again in the course of the wars, it was destined to remain British thereafter. The significance of the event was apparent at once to the great Portuguese explorer Dr. Francisco Lacerda. "The new possessors of Table Bay (the English)," he wrote, "require careful watching or our want of energy will enable them to extend themselves northwards."[1]

Nothing was further from the minds of the new possessors, then or for many years to come, than extending themselves northwards, but in annexing the Cape they committed themselves to a destiny not of their own designing.

It was only by coincidence that, five days after the Dutch surrender, a meeting at the Castle and Falcon, Aldersgate Street, London, launched the movement that was to become the London Missionary Society;[2] and that three months later Robert Moffat, destined to be one of its most distinguished agents, was born at Ormiston, East Lothian. But each of these events was to contribute to the northward expansion which Lacerda foresaw.

This book is about British operations north of the Limpopo, but these could never have happened without the expansion which brought British control up to the borders of what is now Zimbabwe. Our first concern will be to explain why that movement took place.

The expansion was not, except at a few points, initiated by the British. It was the consequence of two great migrations, one black and one white. Their causes overlapped, each migration was to some extent a cause of the other, and in one way or another the London Missionary Society (LMS) was involved in both.

The black migration was the result of an upheaval, early in the nineteenth century, in Natal. The upheaval was caused by the rise and rivalry of three large political units, the Mthethwa, the Ndwandwe, and the Ngwane, under the chieftainship of Dingiswayo, Zwide, and Sobhuza respectively.[3] In 1818, Dingiswayo having been killed in battle, his position was usurped by Shaka, chief of the Zulu tribe, one of the minor components of the Mthethwa. Using and improving upon the military organization and tactics of his predecessor,

Shaka welded the various elements of the Mthethwa into the Zulu nation, and founded the monarchy which was to loom large in South African history for two generations.

In 1819 Shaka decisively beat the Ndwandwe, thereby setting in motion the great scattering of peoples, the *Mfecane*, [4] which in a few years changed the face of southern Africa. People of both the great language groups, Nguni (mostly on the coastward side of the Drakensberg) and Sotho (in the interior), were involved. The Zulu army became the terror of the whole subcontinent. The vanquished were either absorbed or destroyed, unless they had the luck to escape out of Shaka's reach. Those who did escape fell upon tribes farther a-field, so that Shaka spread devastation both directly and indirectly up and down the coast and inland across the highveld. Many of the people who thus took to the road ended their journey in, or even beyond, Zimbabwe.[5]

Three of the pillaging bands converged in June 1823 upon Dithakong, not far from Robert Moffat's mission station of Kuruman. They were repulsed by the Griquas, a partly Europeanized people of mixed race, who had horses and firearms. Among the horde defeated in that battle was the Fokeng chief Sebetwane, who had adopted for his followers the tribal name of a captured wife, Kololo. These now moved away to the north, settling eventually north of the Zambezi above the Victoria Falls. There they conquered the Lozi kingdom and dominated it for many years.[6]

In the meantime the defeat of the Ndwandwe in 1819, and a more decisive defeat in 1826, had driven many of that people in precipitate flight northwards. Two leaders, Soshangane and Zwangendaba, gathering what followers they could, moved towards Delagoa Bay. Though of more or less common origin, these and other warlords of the migration were rivals, not allies. As they advanced northwards, Soshangane emerged victorious, and was soon in possession of all of Mozambique south of the Zambezi. The Tsonga inhabitants were subjected and partly assimilated. The Portuguese were driven out of the interior and confined to a few precarious toe-holds on the coast and the Zambezi. The kingdom, with its headquarters on the middle course of the Sabi, was called Gaza after the chief's ancestor. The subject peoples were known by the name of the chief himself, and those who fled into the Transvaal came to be called Shangaans.

Soshangane's defeated rival Zwangendaba consoled himself by advancing into the interior country north of the Limpopo, subjecting it to slaughter and devastation, and then moving on across the Zambezi. A solar eclipse is thought to fix the date of the crossing as 19 November 1835.[7]

By that time another great warlord had moved out of Shaka's way. Mzilikazi, chief of a small clan subject to the Ndwandwe, had been driven by the threatened hostility of Zwide to go over to Shaka. The defeat of Zwide in 1819 thus left Mzilikazi on the winning side, and he became one of Shaka's foremost generals. In 1822 he was sent on a cattle-raid against a Sotho clan to the northwest. The enemy was scattered and the cattle taken. But Mzilikazi, who had now resolved to be a great man on his own account, dared to throw down the gauntlet. He refused to hand the cattle over to the king and he defied the messengers who came to demand them.

Shaka almost succeeded in obliterating the rebels, but not quite. With no more than three hundred fighting men, accompanied by women and children, Mzilikazi set out on a march that would take him to the highveld of the eastern Transvaal. During the next few years he and his people made several moves to different parts of that region. The invaded country was swept almost clear of people. Cattle were captured, granaries looted, villages put to the torch, the aged and the infants consigned to the flames, eminent prisoners impaled on sharp stakes. But young women were taken as prizes by the victors, and promising young men were incorporated into the army. Other men were conscripted from time to time as slaves or beasts of burden. The little band of refugees became a great military power on the highveld. As its reputation spread, it drew to itself other refugees from the original homeland, fleeing from the rule of Shaka and then of his brother and assassin, Dingane.[8]

The terrified Sotho gave their enemies a name, *maTebele*, which has been variously interpreted as "wanderers" and as "those who sank out of sight" (behind their great shields); in the Nguni tongue the name became *amaNdebele*. At first there was only one enemy whom Mzilikazi—"Moselekatse" to the Sotho-speaking people—feared: Shaka himself, or Dingane after him. In the winter of 1832, however, a Zulu *impi*[9] sent against Mzilikazi by Dingane was badly mauled. The Ndebele followed up this victory with a devastating punitive raid on a section of the Rolong to their west. The survivors of this attack, as well as the Hurutshe (another Tswana tribe), having fled towards the desert, Mzilikazi in 1833 moved his whole people, bag and baggage, into the delectable Marico valley lately occupied by the Hurutshe.

In that country he seemed to have found both security and a congenial land. There was nothing to fear from his Tswana neighbours. Though Dingane attacked him twice in the valley, both attacks were repulsed. The Griquas and other halfbreeds of the south, who had guns and horses, might be dangerous, but they had no discipline or cohesion. But for the white men, it is hard to say whether the Ndebele would ever have abandoned the Marico district.

They were forced out of it by the Boers, whose appearance on the scene is linked to the series of causes with which this account began: the British conquest of the Cape, the London Missionary Society, and the *Mfecane*. British rule alienated many of the colonists of Dutch stock, and no feature of it gave them more offence than the influence of the missionaries—the LMS in particular. Besides preaching the Gospel within as well as outside the Cape Colony, these men concerned themselves with the interests of slaves, "Hottentots" and "Kaffirs." Out of the tension between the newfangled nineteenth-century

3 The Advance into the Interior

humanitarian notions of the British and the seventeenth-century fundamentalism of the frontiersmen came the white migration, the Great Trek.[10]

Yet there might have been no Trek without Shaka. As the discontented colonists prepared to pull up stakes and trek away from the hated authorities, they sent reconnaissance patrols into the interior to spy out the land. The patrols reported that the country was not only lush, but empty of people. By 1835 the migration across the Orange River had begun.

These emigrants and the Ndebele, recently settled in the Marico valley, were unaware of each other until they met unexpectedly. The Ndebele massacred a Boer party, but were warded off by the next Boer party, which formed a laager (circle of wagons) at Vegkop, in October 1836. Paul Kruger was one of the children in that laager.

The Boers then counter-attacked twice, in February and November 1837, under the leadership of Hendrik Potgieter. Both attacks were successful; the second, a nine days' battle that was not suspended even on Sunday, was decisive. There were three hundred Boers, against an estimated twelve thousand Ndebele in their last great stand. The Boers had the advantage of guns and horses, which enabled them to keep out of spear-range all the time. But it is easy to exaggerate the meaning of this advantage. Potgieter's men had the skills and qualities which the British were to discover in their descendants at the end of the century.

After the battle the whole Ndebele people streamed away over the bushveld horizon to the north. They moved in two separate columns, which were not reunited and reconciled, in the new "Matabeleland," until 1840. There had been charges of treason against Gundwane Ndeweni and other *indunas*, accused of trying to raise the king's eldest son Nkulumane to the throne. Indunas were executed, and Nkulumane himself either put to death or spirited away to Natal; his fate remained a controversial mystery.[11]

Even in their new home the Ndebele were not spared the attentions of Hendrik ("Enteleka") Potgieter. But a Boer expedition in 1847 across the Limpopo, which got as far as the Matopos and fought the Ndebele with varying success, proved to be the last hostile contact between the two peoples. After Potgieter's death there was found among his papers the draft of a treaty, supposedly to confirm an oral agreement with the Ndebele envoys "Mabuyana, Utyotyo and Makwasa," who were sent to make peace after the events of 1847.[12] If an agreement was made at this time it was of no effect and was superseded by another. In any case one of the parties, Potgieter, had at that time no standing in international law which could entitle him to make a treaty. But more would be heard of this document in due course.

By 1847, then, the Ndebele were in firm possession of their new country. It had not been, when they arrived, an uninhabited wilderness. The previous occupants had belonged to the great ethnic and linguistic group, having no common name for itself but called by others the Shona, which had inhabited almost all of the future Zimbabwe for centuries. Successive "empires," those of the Munhumutapa and of the Changamire-Rozvi, had united parts of this population in common political systems at different times, but had all but collapsed by the early nineteenth century. The Rozvi kingdom had been brought to an end, in all but name, by the ravages of Zwangendaba.[13]

In these circumstances power—if that is not too strong a word—devolved upon the lower rank of rulers known as paramount chiefs. These will figure largely in the story that follows, and it is as well that their identities, and the continuity of their dynasties, are easy to recognize. They bore hereditary names or titles such as Mutasa, Makoni, Mangwende, or Chinamhora, in addition to personal names. Inheritance was patrilineal, but the chieftaincy did not pass from father to son in continuous succession. It most commonly passed to the eldest son of the first, then to the sons of the next brother. So long as the Rozvi *Mambos* (emperors) retained their power, they were the arbiters of the disputes to which this system gave rise. As that power declined, palace revolutions and plots became more frequent.

The Shona spoke various dialects, which corresponded to the groups into which the people themselves are conventionally arranged: Manyika, against the eastern mountains; Ndau, south of the Manyika; Zezuru, in the north central region; in the far north a jumble of dialects of varied affinities, but classified together under the name of Korekore; and, in a great belt across the south, Karanga, becoming Kalanga in the west—a group of dialects unintelligible to the Shona, but commonly classified with the various forms of the Shona language.[14]

It was with these last that the Ndebele first came into contact. The invaders, who had fought their way from Natal to the Matopos, and who were an offshoot of Shaka's Zulus, were, naturally, a nation in arms. They seem, however, to have subjected the people west of the Bembesi without much violence. The Ndebele needed grain, which the local Kalanga grew abundantly; the Kalanga accepted the rule of the Ndebele as they had formerly submitted to the Rozvi. This adjustment did not come about altogether peacefully, but followed a few demonstrations of Ndebele power.[15]

The country within a radius of about thirty miles of its future centre, Bulawayo, was occupied intensively by the newcomers. Their relations with the people outside those limits had a different basis. In the course of the migration Mzilikazi had acquired an immense number of cattle. What he needed was people. He therefore took from the Shona-speaking people beyond the Bembesi young people to incorporate in the Ndebele nation, and in return farmed out cattle, of which the Rozvi were in need. The cattle could be recalled at any time, but the children could not. This unequal exchange led to Rozvi attacks on the Ndebele after about 1850, and brought the military aspect of Ndebele society into prominence.

During the next forty years the balance between the civil and the military el-

5 The Advance into the Interior

ements in the nation tilted one way or the other according to circumstances. At some periods there were frequent raids in various directions, of which those to the east and northeast will concern us most. These resulted in the death, subjection, or flight of many of the Shona-speaking people who were within reach of the raiding impis. Those who succeeded in escaping in those directions, like their kinsmen already living there, adopted a way of life that would become familiar to later observers. They perched their villages on the inaccessible granite koppies with which the country abounds, retired to these, or to caves, when attacked, and defended themselves by hurling boulders on their assailants and shooting them with arrows.[16]

The military system of the Ndebele and the predatory character of their society are highly controversial subjects; no more will be said of them here than will give a necessary background to the subject of this book—the white conquest. That Ndebele society developed into something very different from its Zulu antecedent is not surprising, in view of the experiences of the Ndebele during and after their long migration. One peculiarity of the new society was the classification of the people according to their place of origin: *abezansi* (from the south), *abenhla* (from the north), and *amahole* (those recruited from the Shona and Kalanga population.) Most writers have called these classes "castes," a description which Julian Cobbing calls "at best a half-truth." What is clear is that *zansi* ancestry, i.e., descent from Mzilikazi's original followers or others of Nguni origin who joined them, was a source of pride and a sense of superiority; that the *abenhla*, of Sotho origin, were pretty thoroughly assimilated by the Nguni; and that the *amahole*, though in many ways assimilated, were an inferior and despised class.[17]

Shona Village, Chivi's country, about 1890

6 Rhodes and Rhodesia

In the traditional view, the military organization and the civil administrative system of the Ndebele were one and the same thing; the kingdom remained a "nation in arms." This view has been demolished by Julian Cobbing. The change from a predominantly male community, fighting its way for a thousand miles through enemy country, to a settled society that had incorporated many women and children resulted in a distinction between the civil and the military systems. Cobbing consequently challenges the traditional translation of *ibutho* (plural *amabutho*) as "regiment." In this book, nevertheless, I shall continue to use the word "regiment"; firstly, because whenever the *ibutho* figured in relation to the invading Europeans it was as a fighting unit; secondly, because there is no better English word for it. But it can be used only in the light of many qualifications.

Early writers, from T.M. Thomas and E.A. Maund onwards, stated that the regiments, and the country itself, were grouped into four (which may later have become five) "provinces" or "divisions." This idea was repeated by all later writers until attacked by Cobbing, who has argued, mainly on the evidence of the Foster Windram oral interviews, that the theory of the "divisions" arose from a misunderstanding. Their names—*aMhlope, aMnyama, amaKhanda*, and *iGapha*—were the names of Mzilikazi's earliest regiments. During his reign they all died out, after having spawned many other regiments. The memory of the old ones lived on in the members of the new, who thought of their regiments as having a kind of family relationship. But early observers were mistaken when they took these nostalgic memories to mean "provinces" or "divisions."[18]

There is no agreement on the exact number of *amabutho* in existence at any one time; Cobbing has identified forty-two during Mzilikazi's reign, and all agree that about twelve more were added later. There is general agreement that the strength of the army at the end was about 15,000.[19]

Travellers were able to see, and describe, this army on parade when it assembled in January or February for the *Inxwala* ceremony (the "Big Dance") which inaugurated the new year. The soldiers paraded, each regiment with its distinctive shields and headdresses, in a kraal about a quarter of a mile in diameter. They all chanted, in good time, "a monotonous and somewhat solemn accompaniment to a slow dance, the most striking feature of which was the stamp which was given by the whole army at once. The number of men was variously estimated at from seven to ten thousand and that number of men beating time perfectly was impressive." It was a religious ceremony as well as a military review. The king recited "the customary prayer to the spirits of his ancestors for national general prosperity during the year." The ceremony lasted for four or five days.[20]

Mzilikazi died in 1868; in January 1870 his son Lobengula was installed in his place, to the accompaniment of the chants, dances, and feasting of nine thousand soldiers.[21] Most writers have attributed the interregnum of sixteen

7 The Advance into the Interior

months to uncertainty about the succession. It may be that many of the people really believed that the original heir Nkulumane was not dead, but living in Natal; the hereditary regent Mncumbate certainly sent a deputation, including his son Mhlaba, to Natal to find out about this, and to set doubts at rest. Cobbing has pointed out, however, that among the Ndebele the ceremonies following a death, and preceding the distribution of property to the heirs, lasted at least a year in ordinary families and at least two in the royal family. A long interregnum was to be expected, and was provided for by the hereditary regency of Mncumbate's family. In this case the rumour that a rival claimant was alive probably hastened rather than delayed the installation of Lobengula. The Zwangendaba *ibutho*, refusing to accept him, had to be defeated before the new king could be at peace with his subjects.[22]

Lobengula is one of the central characters of this story. Partly because he had been raised to his position by his subjects, whereas in the previous reign it was the nation that owed its existence to the king; partly because there was a "pretender" to whom the discontented could turn; still more, perhaps, because Lobengula was not nearly as rich in cattle as his father had been, so that he had fewer favours to offer, his position was less secure than his father's. This fact had an important effect on his dealings with Europeans.

Though the kings were constantly on the move, each of them had a capital or headquarters, the location of which was changed from time to time. Lobengula at his accession chose a new site, bearing the old name of Gibixhegu, which he changed to Bulawayo. This was "old" Bulawayo, some fourteen miles south of the present city. The move to "new" Bulawayo was made in 1881. This was a bigger place than its predecessor: an oval 800 by 650 yards, housing between fifteen and twenty thousand people. Lobengula, however, spent much time in his "private" kraals, of which Umvutshwa, about seven miles north of the new Bulawayo, will concern us most.[23]

Lobengula was intelligent, well-informed, and a shrewd judge of men. He was born about 1833, in the Transvaal, and at the time of the killings in Matabeleland is said to have been hidden in a grain-bin by the chief induna Gwabalanda until his father's anger had passed. His initial reluctance to be king and his preference for the life of a cattle-farmer may have been genuine, though when he had tasted power he came, like a more famous despot, to enjoy his *métier de roi*. He had an imposing presence when dressed in his scanty traditional costume, though not, foreign visitors thought, in European clothes. After his accession he never wore these.[24]

The respect and awe he inspired in white visitors are important to note. They were due not merely to the fact that he held their lives in his hand, though this would have done much to instil an attitude of deference. He imposed respect by his personality, bearing, and conduct. His word was his bond, his judgments on the whole were just, and he showed a friendly affection for Europeans who were honest and straightforward in their dealings. The combination of power, authority, and kindness, as of a father to his children, in his dealings with them can be sensed in innumerable conversations and incidents. When the great hunter Selous, for instance, reproached him for his unjust decision in the "sea-cow case" of the previous season, the king remained master of the situation: "Houw! that case is finished! dead! what is the use of thinking any more about it? Go and hunt nicely until your heart is white."[25]

He was not bloodthirsty by choice. It was only reluctantly and after much procrastination that he could bring himself to attack the disloyal party in 1870, and even after that battle there was no general proscription. Raids, witchcraft trials, summary justice, and executions were duties imposed upon him by his own peculiar position and the character and situation of his people. Even so, by the end of his reign he was near to losing the allegiance of many of his subjects because of what they regarded as softness to his enemies. Ellerton Fry, the photographer of the Pioneer Column, balanced his qualities neatly: "he was not sufficiently civilised to break his word, and not savage enough to force his people into submission."[26]

In referring to the Pioneer Column we have jumped ahead of our context. In the 1860s, even in 1870, the colonization of the north was not yet even an imperialist dream. To understand the advance of the white men in the wake of the Ndebele we must retrace our steps a few decades.

The invasion of 1890 was the culmination of a steady process of penetration and encroachment on Matabeleland and Mashonaland by aggressive and acquisitive Europeans. The process was complicated, and not to be explained by any simple formula. The only white power that positively desired the territory, Portugal, was swept out of it in the end with little trouble. If the desire was shared by many Englishmen and Boers, it was denounced by the British Colonial Office and aroused no interest in President Paul Kruger. The competitive struggle for the north country was waged by subordinate officials and private adventurers. There were Boers, Portuguese, Englishmen, Americans, and Germans, and their occupations and motives were as varied as their nationalities: missionaries, hunters, traders, scientists, explorers, prospectors, and, only lastly, the official agents of governments.

The Portuguese had frequented Mashonaland since the sixteenth century, but were driven out of it by the operations of Soshangane and Zwangendaba. Some Boer trekkers had crossed the Limpopo on a reconnaissance as early as 1836,[27] and we have seen that Potgieter sent a punitive expedition across it in 1847. This was soon followed up, for reasons connected with a change in the fortunes of the Boers north of the Vaal. In January 1852 Britain by the Sand River Convention recognized the independence of these Boers.[28] The convention was signed with representatives of the "emigrants," not with a state or government, since none existed. The chief Boer signatory was Andries Pretorius; Potgieter, who did not recognize the authority of Pretorius, was not consulted. The omission nearly resulted in civil war, but peacemakers got to work and the leaders were reconciled.

9 The Advance into the Interior

These events were quickly followed by two operations that were to have important consequences for all concerned. Potgieter sent a commission, led probably by J.G.S. Bronkhorst (who had been in the party that crossed the Limpopo in 1836) to Matabeleland to negotiate the treaty foreshadowed in 1847. Before the treaty could be concluded Potgieter died, in December 1852. His son Piet, who was chosen to succeed him as leader in the Soutpansberg, concluded the negotiations the following month.

The other operation, for which Pretorius was responsible, was an attack on the Kwena tribe of the Tswana, under the chief Setshele. The missionary attached to this chief was David Livingstone, son-in-law of Robert Moffat. He and his family were away at the time. The Boer commando looted and destroyed his house. It is unlikely that anything gained by this could have outweighed the unfavourable publicity which Livingstone gave to the event throughout the English-speaking world.[29]

The Volksraad of the republic ratified Potgieter's treaty, but for various reasons, one of which may have been jealousy of the Potgieters, Pretorius was not satisfied with it. He regarded himself as the real head of the executive. He sent Frans Joubert and two of his brothers to negotiate another treaty. This was done on 16 May 1853. The Jouberts were the second white party to reach Mzilikazi in his new country, Potgieter's "commission" having been the first.

The Potgieter treaty, which as Pretorius complained did not bear Mzilikazi's own signature or mark, virtually placed the Ndebele under a Transvaal protectorate. In many of its clauses it curiously foreshadowed the Grobler treaty of 1887, and would be subject to the same criticism. The Pretorius treaty, which must be regarded as the operative one, was in the form of an agreement between equals. It provided for perpetual peace and friendship between the two parties, mutual respect of territories, extradition of criminals, and arbitration of differences. Mzilikazi was to prohibit the arms traffic in his dominions and was to admit hunters to them.[30]

It is not clear what Mzilikazi could expect to gain by prohibiting the arms traffic in his own country, though he shared with the Boers the desire to stop it among the Tswana. He probably did not take this provision seriously. The essence of the treaty in his eyes was the promise of peace with the Transvalers.

The admission of hunters was another matter; by 1854 they were knocking at the door. More precisely, Jan Viljoen and Marthinus Swartz reached the border at the same time as the first missionary party, Robert Moffat and his companion (son of an artisan missionary, but not one himself) Sam Edwards. In spite of Moffat's favourable testimony on their behalf the hunters were not allowed to enter the country, though the ink on the Pretorius treaty was hardly dry.

On Moffat's next visit in 1857 Viljoen was again stopped at the border, but his companion Collins ("wholly given to getting ivory and having little or no command over his tongue in the selection of decent language") was given re-

luctant permission to proceed.[31] It was only after the settlement of the missionaries at Inyati in 1859-60 that Boer and other hunters were regularly admitted.
Even then they were not allowed to go beyond the Ndebele country to Mashonaland. Mzilikazi was afraid of gun-running in that quarter, especially during
the "four years' hard fighting" against the chief Hwata. That chief having been
defeated and captured in 1864, and returned in 1865, superficially submissive,
to his hilltop north of Salisbury, the prohibition was then removed. Jan Viljoen, Piet Jacobs, and their companions were permitted to hunt up to the Umfuli. Sure enough, they sold guns, so were not allowed in again for several
years. But in that season of 1865 they had been followed to the Umfuli by
Henry Hartley and two of his sons.[32]

Hartley, who in 1820 at the age of four had landed in Algoa Bay with his settler parents, subsequently moved to the Transvaal. He acquired his famous
farm in the Magaliesberg about 1841, and by the fifties had begun to make his
great reputation as a hunter. He was admitted to Matabeleland in 1859, and
now to Mashonaland, in the first season in which that country was opened.
Known to white and black alike as the *Oubaas*, he was on excellent terms with
Mzilikazi. It is claimed for him, on good grounds, that he established in 1865
the route from Inyati to the Umfuli that came to be called the Hunters'
Road.[33]

The next five years were the golden age of elephant hunting in Mashonaland. The excitement of the chase can be followed in the books and published
journals of Baines, Leask, Selous, and others, but it must not be forgotten that
most of the hunters were Boers who did not publish their experiences. By 1870
five years of furious hunting had driven most of the elephants back into the habitat of the tsetse fly, so that they could no longer be hunted on horseback.
Hunting them on foot was dangerous, tedious, and much less productive in
relation to the effort expended. In consequence Hartley, Finaughty, and
Leask, for instance, gave up the business at this time.[34] There were others,
such as F.C. Selous, who took it up and hunted on foot, but their operations
were less lucrative.

The discouragement of elephant hunting was one of the smaller trials
inflicted on mankind by the tsetse fly. The most serious was sleeping sickness
or trypanosomiasis, which occurs however only in a few areas and does not appear to have been reported in Zimbabwe. It was to cattle and horses that it
presented a deadly peril as the carrier of nagana. The disease was nearly always fatal, though recovery from it ensured future immunity. Horses, however, were more often the victims of horse-sickness, caused by a virus of which
the carriers were not flies but midges. This was a universal scourge in tropical
Africa, and the rare horses that caught it and recovered—"salted" horses—
were valued and highly priced possessions.

Neither cattle nor horses could survive in tsetse country—a region known as
"the fly." To a people as devoted to cattle as the Ndebele the insect was there-

11 The Advance into the Interior

fore a major nuisance. Mzilikazi might claim the country up to the Zambezi, but his cattle posts, as Moffat reported, did not reach "near half way."[35] Much of Mashonaland was useless to him even as a raiding ground, because the people had no cattle. Where wagons could not go, the missionaries were reluctant to take their families, and traders could not drive a profitable business.

At least the fly (*Glossina morsitans* was the common species in Zimbabwe) was recognized and was known to be the carrier of the disease. In their conflict with the anopheles mosquito men did not yet have the advantage of such knowledge. Malaria was the great killer of people, black or white, who were not acclimatized by generations of contact with it. Year after year missionary and hunting parties were decimated by malaria; all went to their deaths assuming that they had inhaled noxious vapours from marshes. In Europe and America the malaria parasite was being identified during the 1880s. At the same time some researchers were directing attention to the mosquito, but it was the work of Patrick Manson, culminating in 1894, and of Ronald Ross in 1898, with the researches of Bastianelli, Bignami, and Grassi in that year, that at last identified *Anopheles maculipennis* as the culprit. By that time it has sent many people to their graves in Central Africa.[36]

Many of the victims were missionaries. It is now widely believed that Christian missionaries in Africa were harbingers of European imperialism: they "softened up" the Africans for the take-over, called on their metropolitan governments to come in, and afterwards helped them to impose a regime and ideology of white supremacy. Whether or how far this interpretation is true in the Zimbabwean case the reader will judge from the details that follow throughout this book. But there is no doubt that the missionaries—specifically, the London Missionary Society—played a large and almost indispensable part in opening the country to European visitors, if not in the first instance conquerors.

Robert Moffat spent most of his apostolic life at the station of Kuruman, in what after his time became British Bechuanaland. From that place he visited Mzilikazi when the Ndebele were living in the Marico valley. The king at once experienced an infatuation for Moffat ("Moshete") which no simple psychology can explain. It had nothing to do with the missionary's teachings, which Mzilikazi totally rejected. But Moffat in his own way and with reservations reciprocated the king's affection.[37]

Many years later, in 1854, Moffat had occasion—it was meant to be a holiday after the labour of translating the Bible into Tswana—to accompany young Sam Edwards on a journey to the interior, as has already been mentioned. He took the opportunity of paying a visit to his old friend Mzilikazi, who gave him a royal and emotional reception. That paved the way for another visit in 1857, a visit which had far-reaching effects as well as important causes.[38]

David Livingstone, Moffat's son-in-law, was a missionary of the same society, but was not designed by nature for a life of quiet routine. His zeal for travel, and the assistance of a traveler of means, W.C. Oswell, enabled him in 1849 to satisfy the long-cherished ambition of discovering Lake Ngami. There he heard unexpected news of well-watered lands north of the desert. It was known that the Kololo chief Sebetwane lived in that direction, and Sebetwane was a friend of Setshele, with whom Livingstone was stationed. Thus Livingstone was inspired to make more journeys, which in 1851 brought him to Sebetwane's town of Linyanti just before that chief's death.

That experience in turn led to Livingstone's journey (1853-6) from Linyanti to Luanda, back to Linyanti, down the Zambezi (discovering and naming the Victoria Falls), to Quelimane, where he emerged with a mind full of schemes of missionary work, commerce, civilization, the destruction of the slave trade, and possibly a little colonization thrown in. Specifically, he wanted a mission to the Kololo. If the missionaries were to survive, the Kololo would have to move from their fever-stricken marshes to the healthier Batoka plateau. There they would be exposed to raids by the Ndebele. Therefore there would have to be a mission to the Ndebele also; that was what Moffat went up in 1857 to arrange.[39]

The Kololo did not move to the plateau. The Helmore and Price parties, which went to the Kololo country, almost all died at once of malaria.[40] A more important missionary, John Mackenzie, was saved by the lucky chance that he had been given the job of following later with supplies. We shall hear of him again.

Mzilikazi having given permission, Moffat went up once more in 1859, accompanied by his son John Smith Moffat, William Sykes, and Thomas Morgan Thomas. At the end of the year their station was established at Inyati.[41] A permanent European outpost was now placed in Matabeleland, but the evangelizing labours of these patient men (and women) were not destined to bear fruit for many years. On the other hand the station provided a *pied-à-terre* for travellers, and, by being in regular communication with the outside world, did something to encourage European travellers to visit it. Having helped to establish the station, the elder Moffat returned to the south in 1860. As we have seen, the stream of hunters and other visitors began to flow into Matabeleland in that year.

The LMS strengthened its line of communication with Inyati by setting up another station in 1864 at Shoshong, the capital of the Ngwato.[42] This was the largest of the Tswana tribes, and its relations with the Ndebele had worsened ever since their migration through that country in the late thirties. They were the victims of a devastating Ndebele raid in 1863.[43] But after that year open hostilities in the region would involve the Europeans, and would take place along the road which they were using in ever increasing numbers. This was at least one of the reasons why there were few Ndebele raids in that direction after 1863.

If neighbours remain at peace, there is usually an agreement about the posi-

13 The Advance into the Interior

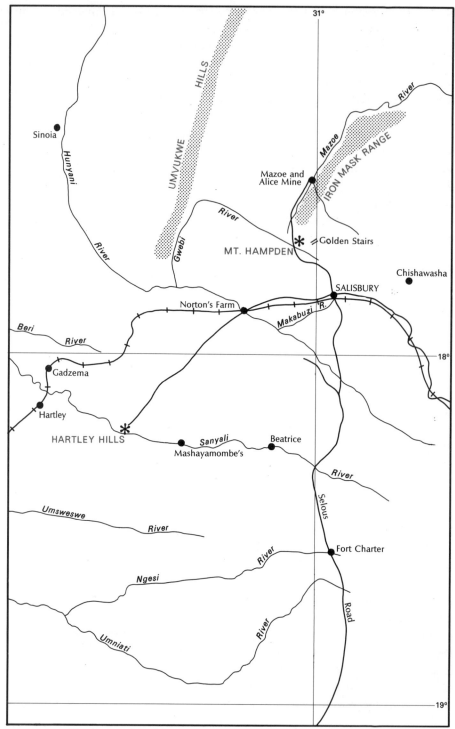

Environs of Salisbury, 1902

14 Rhodes and Rhodesia

tion of their common boundary. In this case there was not. Both the Ndebele kings affected to regard the Ngwato as their "slaves," so that, strictly speaking, no borderline could separate them from their masters. When a British delegation called on Lobengula in 1885 to announce the protectorate over Bechuanaland, the king was offended by the mention of a boundary: "How could Khama speak of a line? He was but a slave of Mzilikazi and had no country."[44]

This point having been made, there was another level of thinking at which a line could be drawn and accepted. At Bulawayo, the line accepted was the Motloutsi; at Shoshong, the Shashi. What lay between these rivers (they had more water in them then than now) was the "disputed territory," whose uncertain status was destined to cause much trouble.

The LMS clung to its foothold in Matabeleland in spite of the apparent hopelessness of its task. The personnel changed. John Smith Moffat left for the south in 1865. T.M. Thomas left the Society and set himself up at Shiloh. Others came and went, and at the end of 1870 the LMS was given a new station at Hope Fountain. By 1882 the men in residence, who were to play their parts in the next decade, were Charles Daniel Helm and David Carnegie, at Hope Fountain, and William Sykes and W.A. Elliot, at Inyati.

The presence of these men in Matabeleland made it a little easier and more natural for other Europeans to visit the country, but they were not the efficient cause of a British invasion and conquest. A much more important factor in this was the discovery of gold. In a sense it was hardly a discovery, since the Portuguese were known to have obtained gold from the interior for centuries. There was, however, a great difference in practical effect between that general information and the discovery of gold reefs in specific places.

On his first hunting trip to the Umfuli in 1865 Hartley noticed what he took, and his Shona informants confirmed, to be old gold workings. They had fallen into disuse since the "Disturbers" had passed over the country a generation before. Back in the Transvaal after the season's hunting, Hartley met the young German scientist Karl Mauch, who for two years had been travelling in the eastern districts of the republic. Mauch had arrived in South Africa with no money, with an irregular training in the natural sciences, and with an insatiable thirst (acquired at the age of fifteen) for African exploration. He accepted with avidity Hartley's invitation to join him on a trip to Mashonaland in 1866.

Though he found evidence of gold in quartz seams in various places, it was still inconclusive. Hartley, Mauch, and the rest of the hunting fraternity returned for the next hunt in the winter of 1867. This time Mauch was left in no doubt. With Hartley he went north from the Umfuli to the banks of the Beri, north of Gadzema. As they returned, Hartley wounded an elephant, which he pursued through the bush. In passing, he noticed several excavations which he took to be old mines, and to which he drew Mauch's attention. Mauch took out his hammer, examined several specimens, and found them to contain gold. Along the Umsweswe and the Sebakwe more old diggings were found, and

15 The Advance into the Interior

gold identified in them. To avoid arousing suspicion, Mauch made his excursions on the excuse of searching for honey, guided by the honey-bird.[45]

As the summer came the hunters turned homeward. On the way out of Matabeleland, on the Tati River, Mauch found more gold. After reaching Hartley's farm he hurried to Pretoria, where in December the *Transvaal Argus* published his account of his discoveries; thence to Natal, where he boarded with the colonial secretary and was received by the lieutenant-governor. The officials as well as the press of the colony, disregarding the difficulties of transportation to and from the remote fields, stimulated the gold fever. The news reached England, where pamphlets such as *To Ophir Direct* raised exaggerated hopes.[46]

By 1868 parties were being made up, in Natal and elsewhere, to go to the Tati goldfield, and behind these came more substantial companies: the Durban Gold Mining Company, the Glasgow and Limpopo Company, the London and Limpopo Mining Company. The latter had some support in the City of London; its chairman was Sir John Swinburne, RN. In 1869 expeditions sent by all these companies—Sir John leading his in person, and with a steam-engine in his equipment—reached the Tati.[47]

Also floated in 1868 was the South African Gold Fields Exploration Company, a subsidiary of the Natal Land and Colonization Company. It was remarkable neither for its capital, its enterprise, nor even for straight dealing with its officers, but for the fact that it employed Thomas Baines as leader of its expedition to the Mashonaland or Northern Goldfields. Baines had been under a cloud since David Livingstone had dismissed him from the Zambezi Expedition of 1858-64 on false charges of peculation made by his brother Charles. A keen and conscientious painter, Baines had put posterity in his debt by the pictures which mark the course of his widespread travels. He was zealous in the service of the company which now sent him to obtain a gold concession. The Ndebele, punning on his name, called him uMsebenzi—"work."

The gold discoveries were made in the last year of Mzilikazi's life. During the interregnum negotiations were in suspense, as the new king had to have a "clean" inheritance. The mining men spent the interval examining the ground and preparing to stake their claims. Baines and his party prospected an area on the Umfuli, selected and marked out a claim, and, as they had been directed there by Hartley, gave his name to the neighbouring hills. Swinburne, who prepared to set up his company on the Tati, tried also to establish a claim to the northern fields, and was not too scrupulous in his rivalry with Baines.

On 9 April 1870 the new king gave a concession, orally, to Baines, and on 29 August 1871 confirmed it in writing. It gave "to Mr. Baines [on behalf of the South African Gold Fields Exploration Company, Limited] full permission to explore, prospect, and dig or mine for gold" in the country between the Gwelo and the Hunyani rivers; and "this my permission includes liberty to build dwelling and store-houses, to erect machinery for crushing rocks or other nec-

16 Rhodes and Rhodesia

essaries, and for the removal of the gold so obtained; and it also includes all lesser details connected with gold-mining." It was made clear in the document that the king's sovereignty over the territory remained intact. Lobengula declined to fix a price for the concession, but left it "to the judgement of Mr. Baines to make me annually, on behalf of the said Company, such presents as might seem proper to him and acceptable to me."

In the meantime, on 29 April 1870, Lobengula had given a written concession to Arthur Levert, who had become the local manager of the London and Limpopo Company when Swinburne had returned to England in the preceding January. The company received a concession for (rather than *of*) the territory between the Shashi and the Ramakwabane rivers, from their sources to their junction. It was to pay the king £60 a year.[48]

The two concessions had very different destinies. There was not much gold on the Tati. The London and Limpopo Company ceased operations in 1875 and went into liquidation. In 1881 Lobengula considered the concession to have lapsed, and gave it to a consortium represented by Sam Edwards, who then carried on the operation for the Northern Light Gold and Exploration Company. This was succeeded in 1888 by the Tati Concession Mining and Exploration Company, which retained its identity thereafter. The Tati Concession was explicitly excluded from the sphere allotted to the British South Africa (BSA) Company.

The South African Gold Fields Company (successor in 1871 to the one with "Exploration" in its name) had no more vitality than its southern competitor, but it owned a much more valuable concession. After the death of Baines in 1875—he died in Durban when about to go north to exploit his goldfield—the company sold the concession to a group of Transvaal speculators, who in turn sold it to the Matabeleland Company. As will be seen, this was one of the concessions ultimately acquired by Rhodes.[49]

Those gold discoveries were to be an important factor in the future imperialist expansion to the north; but, both as a factor in that expansion and as a source of excitement at the time, they were vastly outweighed by the diamond discoveries that occurred at almost the same moment: the first diamond found on the banks of the Orange in 1867, the river diggings on the Vaal, and the "dry diggings" of Kimberley over the next three years. With fortunes to be picked up from the ground in these places, few adventurers were much interested in crushing quartz six or nine hundred miles further into the wilderness.

The diamonds led by a direct sequence of cause and effect to a British advance into the interior.

The area in which they were found was an Alsatia in which the land claims of two Boer republics and many Bantu and Griqua tribes and chiefs conflicted and overlapped. Boundary disputes had been going on for some time before the discoveries; these brought them to a head.

The Transvaal president, M.W. Pretorius (son of Andries), sent the old

17 The Advance into the Interior

hunter Jan Viljoen to see what he could get from Matsheng, chief of the Ngwato, and Mzilikazi; most specifically, the cession of the Tati district to the republic. Viljoen got nothing, but without waiting for his report Pretorius issued a proclamation on 29 April 1868, vastly extending the boundaries of the Transvaal. On the east a corridor was thrown out, one mile on either side of the Pongola and the Maputo, to Delagoa Bay. On the west the boundary was the longitude of Lake Ngami down to the Langeberg. The northern limit of this extension stopped short of the country actually occupied by the Ndebele, but territory subject to the Ndebele, including the Tati district, fell within it. Virtually the whole of the inhabited part of Botswana was "annexed" by this proclamation.

Pretorius was driven to this bold step less by land-hunger or delusions of grandeur than by the desperate financial plight of his state. He had visions of gold and diamonds filling the republican coffers. But the republic was too weak to enforce such claims. Immediate protests by Britain and Portugal forced the president to cancel his proclamation.[50]

The gold of the Tati would not have balanced the republican budget anyway; the diamonds of the "river diggings" might have helped. Pretorius therefore created the district of Bloemhof, extending down the Vaal to its junction with the Harts, and so including what were then the principal river diggings. In June 1870, he got the Volksraad to confer on three of his friends a monopoly of diamond digging for twenty-one years. The outcry from all sides forced Pretorius to abandon this scheme also, but not before the diggers on the spot had set up their own republic with able-bodied seaman Stafford Parker as president.

These events, the claims of the Orange Free State, disputes among Tswana and Griqua chiefs, the intrigues of the schemer David Arnot, other intrigues by some missionaries, and intervention by British authorities who were then just beginning to abandon the policy of "scuttle," led to some of the decisions on which British expansion was to depend. The Transvaal claims having been submitted to arbitration, Lieutenant-Governor Keate of Natal gave his award on 17 October 1871: the western boundary of the Transvaal was pushed back to the Maquassi Spruit, and the area west of it allotted to the Tswana (Rolong and Thlaping) claimants. The award was not concerned with disputes further south, but ten days later, as an indirect result of it, the high commissioner, Sir Henry Barkly, annexed Griqualand West, as shown on modern maps, to the British Crown.[51]

A few days after the annexation, Cecil Rhodes arrived from Natal to seek his fortune on the dry diggings. At the beginning of the previous year, Lobengula had become king of the Ndebele. The paths of these men were still very far from crossing: Bulawayo is seven hundred miles from Kimberley. But the annexation of Griqualand West was one of the decisive steps that would enable and encourage British expansionists to bridge that gap in less than two decades. The road to the north ran along the fringes of the republics. If either of them had annexed any part of that road there would have been no British expansion to the north, because the desert made it impossible to shift the route further west. The decisions of October 1871 had pushed both republics back from the road, and the Union Jack now waved over its southernmost section.

Pretorius had so bungled the Transvaal case that he was forced to resign. His successor, T.F. Burgers, alienated most of the citizens by his religious heresies. When Sir Theophilus Shepstone, in April 1877, annexed the Transvaal to the British Empire they were too demoralized and apathetic to resist. The annexation was intended to promote the South African Confederation which still eluded Lord Carnarvon. Instead, it aroused the latent patriotism of the Transvalers, who rose in revolt at the end of 1880 and after their victory at the Battle of Majuba Hill extorted from Gladstone a restoration within limits ("under the suzerainty of Her Majesty") of their independence.[52] The leader and hero of this revolt was Paul Kruger, who in 1883 became president of the republic. He retained the office as long as the republic existed.

The Convention of Pretoria (2 August 1881), which had restored and restricted its independence, also defined its boundaries. The "Road to the North," or "Missionaries' Road," lay outside them, and the republic could not alter them unilaterally. There was nothing, however, to prevent its citizens from crossing the border and conducting themselves on the other side of it in any way their military superiority might suggest. Intertribal disputes gave them an opening. "Volunteers" went to the help of one chief against another, and in return for their assistance exacted rewards from defeated enemy and grateful ally alike. The outcome of these operations was the setting up in 1882-3 of two independent republics, Stellaland with its capital at Vryburg, and Goshen, with a lair rather than a capital at Rooigrond, astride the border east of Mafeking. The two bands of "freebooters," as the British officials called them, were supplied with ammunition, secret official support, and secure bases, by the Transvaal. The republic's intention to annex the two states at the first convenient opportunity was hardly disguised.[53]

These events had no immediate impact on Lobengula or his people. The first decade of his reign seemed to pass quietly enough, as far as trouble from Europeans was concerned. The stream of travellers from the south flowed more strongly than before, but the danger arising from the discovery of gold seemed to recede. Concessions had been granted, but were not used, or were allowed to lapse. Traders, like James Fairbairn at Bulawayo and George Westbeech at Pandamatenga, settled in the country, to the advantage of buyers and sellers alike. The traders were mostly English. If most of the hunters were Boers, there were still many English in this category. Trading and hunting were often combined: ivory could be got either way. There were also amateurs, gentlemen travellers, bent on exploration or adventure.

Lobengula, like his father, allowed strangers to enter the country by one

19 The Advance into the Interior

route only, the Missionaries' or Hunters' Road through Shoshong; thus channelled, the flow might be controlled. The traveller by this road crossed the disputed territory and several more rivers, up to the Inkwesi, before reaching the first Ndebele outpost. This was the Kalanga village ruled for many years by the Ndebele headman Manyami, who did duty as customs and immigration officer, keeper of the gates, and warden of the marches. At that point the traveller was held up while messengers announced his arrival to the king and brought back, if he was lucky, permission to proceed.

A little further up the road were the house and farm of John Lee, more Boer than Englishman, but also appointed by Mzilikazi, in 1868, and again by Lobengula soon after his accession, as a kind of border officer to deal with white men. Near the house a rocky outcrop known as Lee's Castle was a familiar landmark on the route. During 1884 Lee went away to the south, not returning until 1889. For those five years the farm was occupied by Frederik Greef.[54]

THE STRUGGLE FOR THE SOUTHERN APPROACHES, 1884-1887

At the beginning of 1884 the destiny of Matabeleland and Mashonaland was an open question. Lobengula appeared to be secure against all possible black enemies; of possible white ones, the Portuguese were still showing a "want of energy," the British were six hundred miles away and had no plans of expansion, and the Transvaal was confined within boundaries that it could not alter unilaterally.

By the end of the year these conditions had changed radically; the change marks 1884 as the year in which imperialist expansion to the north effectively began.

The events of 1884 and 1885 resulted in the extension of British control northwards to the 22nd parallel. In the early stages of this development Her Majesty's government was extremely unwilling to undertake any responsibility in those parts. The colonial secretary, Lord Derby, with the acquiescence of his colleagues, would have had no objection to a Transvaal annexation of almost any part of the territory. The new Transvaal president, Paul Kruger, sensing this, led a deputation to England late in 1883, to get Derby to remove the limitations on republican independence that the Convention of Pretoria had imposed.

The Transvalers had accepted that convention in 1881 under protest; thereafter they continued both to protest against the terms and to violate them. Derby might have given Kruger all that he wanted, except independent control of foreign relations, if his resolve had not been stiffened by influences coming from South Africa. The most important of these was the high commissioner, Sir Hercules Robinson, who had come to England specifically for this purpose; next to him, John Mackenzie, who used the missionary and philanthropic network to stir up what Fairfield at the Colonial Office called "an outburst of public opinion." Derby's tactic with the deputation was therefore to refuse to discuss any other matter until agreement was reached on the boundary. The "road to the north" was to remain outside the Transvaal, which was allowed to annex parts, but not the whole, of Stellaland and Goshen.

In return, the South African Republic—its old name was restored—was given almost complete independence. "Suzerainty" was not specifically mentioned, but all that remained of it in practice was Article IV, by which the republic could not conclude a treaty with a foreign state or nation, other than the Orange Free State, or with a native tribe to the east or the west, without the queen's approval.[55] ("There was an unwritten understanding when the delegates were here," the permanent under-secretary, Sir Robert Herbert, thought, "that we would not interfere with their relations with the native tribes to the *north* of the Transvaal.")[56]

By Article II, the republic would appoint commissioners "on the eastern and western borders whose duty it will be strictly to guard against irregularities and all trespassing over the boundaries. Her Majesty's Government will, if necessary, appoint Commissioners in the native territories outside the eastern and western borders of the South African Republic to maintain order and prevent encroachments." We are not concerned with the other terms of the Convention of London, which was signed on 27 February 1884.[57]

The provision for a British commissioner on the western border to maintain order and prevent encroachments was the small seed which grew into the Bechuanaland Protectorate. Indeed, for many months, that provision *was* the protectorate, which had no other legal foundation.[58]

The commissioner would be stationed ("if necessary") outside the border of the South African Republic, but not outside the borders of what was left of Stellaland and Goshen. The first commissioner to be appointed was John Mackenzie, who was regarded by the Boers as the personification of the LMS and all its works, and was accordingly detested.[59] Though the political divisions of Stellaland enabled him to negotiate with one of its factions, and he had no difficulty with the Tswana chiefs, his superiors decided to recall him, after less than four months, in August 1884. Cecil Rhodes, sent in his place, conceded almost everything to the Stellalanders, and in Goshen was treated with contempt by Piet Joubert, Kruger's border commissioner.[60]

The Transvaal seemed to have the ball at its feet. Gladstone's government, preoccupied with other parts of the world, wanted as quickly as possible to hand over the thankless job of policing a semi-desert full of border ruffians to the Cape Colony. But the Cape government—any Cape government—depended on the votes of Afrikaners who were sympathetic to the Transvaal. There was nobody both willing and able to stand up to Kruger and Joubert.

The British South Africans, humiliated by the Boer victory of 1881, tried to fill this gap, but did not by themselves have the necessary power. On 24 September 1884 a large and noisy meeting was held in the Commercial Exchange,

21 The Advance into the Interior

Cape Town. Leading public figures were on the platform. Amid the singing of patriotic songs and the shouting of abuse at the Boer "Freebooters," the meeting passed resolutions warning the imperial government of the "disastrous results to all loyal subjects of Her Majesty throughout South Africa" that would flow from any weakening of its stand on the Transvaal border. Similar meetings were held in other towns of the colony.[61]

They had now become unnecessary. When Rhodes, the Cape politician, dependent on Afrikaner votes, met with nothing but failure and insult in Stellaland and Goshen, he reported that imperial intervention would be necessary. His advice would not in itself have carried much weight, but the intervention was provoked by a series of events between July and September 1884.

Christopher Bethell, a young Englishman in the service of Rolong chief Montshiwa (at Mafeking) was murdered in cold blood by a Transvaler. Bethell happened to have near kinsmen well placed in English society and in both houses of Parliament; his death provoked an outcry in influential quarters.[62] Then Kruger, after some hesitation, took the plunge and signed a proclamation annexing not only what was left of Goshen, but Montshiwa's country as well.[63]

Though he qualified the annexation as "provisional," pending the queen's approval, and justified it as necessary to restore order, the Colonial Office found these proceedings and excuses "amusing for their cool affrontery."[64] The final twist to the lion's tail was more than even Gladstone's government could stand. Kruger was made to withdraw his proclamation. Consultation was begun with the War Office. Sir Charles Warren, who had been in the area several years before, was chosen to lead an expedition. He asked for, and obtained, 4,000 troops. When Mackenzie had gone up as border commissioner, the force at his disposal consisted of four policemen. Though the number was later raised to 100, Warren's army was of a different order.[65]

This decision, which fell into the South African political arena like a bomb and caused some rapid shiftings of position, was caused not only by Kruger's bravado or Bethell's murder. It was caused essentially by Germany. As always, the British government behaved in South Africa with lethargy, parsimony, and occasionally indifference as long as the country was "stewing in its own juice," but was startled into furious activity and reckless expense as soon as a foreign power appeared on the horizon.

The declaration of a German protectorate over the coast of South-West Africa, except for Walvis Bay (annexed by Britain in 1878 and handed over to the Cape in 1884), was announced in Cape Town on 18 August 1884. The British government had been informed of this a few days earlier.[66] The politicians and public of the Cape Colony, who had thought that their manifest destiny was to expand into that country some day, reacted frantically. Many feared that the Germans would reach out from the coast to link up with the Transvaal, and so for ever cut the Cape off from trade and colonization in the interior. Those who had supported Transvaal expansion and opposed British interference now cried out for British control of the north.

The British government had its own reasons for acting. Its purpose was not to promote the trade of the Cape Colony but to preserve southern Africa as a purely British sphere, in which the dominant metropolis would not have to be concerned with the rivalry of other great powers. It was now too late to keep Germany out, but quick action in the interior, followed by a treaty with Germany, would serve almost as well.

It must be noted that the second half of 1884 was the period in which Bismarck suddenly acted as a "Kolonialmensch." Almost the whole of Germany's colonial empire was staked out in late 1884 and early 1885. During that time the West African Conference, which laid down some of the rules for the "scramble," met in Berlin. During the same period Gen. Sir Charles Warren and the four thousand marched up to Stellaland and Goshen, sweeping all opposition aside.

Those turbulent little communities had been the original source of the border troubles, but their suppression did not require anything as formidable as Warren's army. As that army was Britain's answer to the German threat,[67] it had to secure the territory that was thought to be threatened—not merely the "freebooter" republics, but all the Tswana country up to the northern limit of the South African Republic. On 27 January 1885 an order-in-council at last gave the protectorate a solid legal basis, and extended it northwards to the 22nd parallel, westwards to the 20th meridian.[68]

Warren's task, therefore, was not finished when he reached Montshiwa's town of Mafeking. He had to obtain treaties of cession from the chiefs beyond that point, to announce the protectorate to them, and to hold the country until all danger to it had been removed. The treaties were signed, willingly by some chiefs, reluctantly and belatedly by Setshele. The most important of them, and the chief whose affairs impinged most directly on one present subject, was Kgama of the Ngwato.

He had many reasons for accepting the British Protectorate with some enthusiasm. He was continually threatened both by the Boers and by the Ndebele. The latter, indeed, were (wrongly) reported to be attacking his territory while Warren was marching to him. His own claim to the chieftainship was not undisputed. He was a pious Christian, high in the favour of the missionaries. Moreover, the boundaries of his territory were somewhat uncertain. He therefore gladly placed himself under the queen's protection. At the same time he made what Warren called "a magnificent offer" of land for British colonization.[69] As the Colonial Office was not interested in that kind of scheme, and as much of the land in question happened to belong to the Ndebele, the offer was declined. No time was lost in thanking Warren for his valuable services and ordering him to march out of Bechuanaland.[70]

Between 28 September and 1 October 1885 the final arrangements for the territory were made. The part south of the Molopo, where there were white farmers, was annexed to the Crown as the colony of British Bechuanaland; the rest remained a protectorate. Robinson was to receive a new commission as governor of the colony, with an administrator to represent him in it. The administrator, who would also be deputy commissioner for the protectorate, was to be Sidney Shippard, a judge of the Cape High Court and former recorder of Griqualand West.[71]

Meanwhile, in May, Warren had reached the end of his march to the Ngwato country. At Shoshong he realized that an official announcement of the protectorate to Lobengula would be a useful defence of Kgama against attacks from that quarter. He accordingly dispatched Sam Edwards—who was a major in Warren's force—with Lieutenants E.A. Maund and C.E. Haynes to Matabeleland. "Sam" was of course an old hand; Maund was a new one, destined to play a considerable part in the next few years.[72]

Curiously enough, Edwards felt that his knowledge of the language was inadequate. The missionary C.D. Helm was sent for, and after long delay arrived at the king's kraal "at 3:45 p.m. June 27th." At 4:30—this was a military detachment, recording events with precision—Warren's letter was taken to the king. Apart from the visitors, Helm and the trader Dawson were the only people present. Helm translated the letter, which was as follows:

> Shoshong, May 13th, 1885.
> To Lobengula, Chief of the Matabele.
> I have the honour to inform you that Her Majesty the Queen of England has ratified a Protectorate over the Native tribes to the West of the South African Republic, and I send this letter by Major Sam Edwards, who will tell you all the news. I hope that you will live in peace and friendship with the Chiefs and People now under the Protectorate, and that you will give every assistance to Her Majesty's subjects travelling through your territory.
> Charles Warren, Special Commissioner for Bechuanaland

Helm explained the boundaries of the protectorate. The 22nd parallel would be no more intelligible to Lobengula than to Kgama, who complained that "it speaks of a line which has no existence." Kgama's essential complaint, though, was that the line cut across his country. Why was not the whole of it included in the protectorate? The answer to that question was given by Lobengula: "How could Khama speak of a line? He was but a slave of Umsilikazi and had no country." In Edwards's version, Lobengula said, " 'Formerly Khame had no country,' tacitly admitting that he now has." With the British at Shoshong, however, these fine distinctions hardly mattered; the argument was merely an exercise in face-saving.

Lobengula persisted in the belief, which could not be shaken, that the "line" had been devised by Kgama himself. Helm reminded him of an earlier dispute, arising out of the killing of ostriches south of the Motloutsi by a Boer hunter. At that time "a sort of tacit understanding was come to that Macloutsie River should be recognised as the boundary line." Lobengula might well have been content with that, and even have asked the British to confirm it, as Kgama in fact had by no means given up his claim to the line of the Shashi, and more besides. For practical purposes, the dispute was about the strip between the two rivers. For purposes of the higher diplomacy Lobengula took the higher ground: Kgama had no country, but lived and hunted there only on sufferance.

The meeting was adjourned till the following day, when the envoys were received by the king in the company of a few trusted advisers, "Umhlaba, his chief adviser, and the regent if anything happened to the king, Nungu Head Doctor (i.e. doctor of witchcraft), Makwekwe 2nd induna of Gubuluwayo and Mahlahleni, the king's brother. These squatted on the king's left front and we faced them."

The explanations were given over again and the indunas gave the same response as the king: "Has Khame a country? We never knew he had." When the letter in reply to Warren was dictated, the pretence was boldly kept up: "Your letter has come. I thank you for your words. I did not know that Khame had drawn the line of the country. I thank you for telling me this." Here Helm protested at the misinterpretation, but he was stopped short by the indunas: "Are you going to write the King's words, or your own?" And so the letter continued: "I shall ask Khame why he hid it from me. Formerly Khame had no country . . . Khame having drawn the boundary line, where is the country of the Matabele?"

With the British Empire expanding so quickly and so far in his direction, Lobengula might well be worried. His anxiety would have been less if he could have read the mind of the Colonial Office, but greater if he had known the mind of Rhodes.

If one were to believe Mackenzie's apologia (*Austral Africa, Losing It or Ruling It*), one would imagine that Rhodes, up to this point, had been working for the Transvaal. Kruger, who met Rhodes for the first time in January 1885, understood otherwise: "That young man will cause me trouble if he does not leave politics alone and turn to something else." Rhodes's hostility to the "imperial factor" and to Mackenzie and his policy, and his attempt to appease the Transvaal party among the Stellalanders, were all *Realpolitik*. His object was to keep the road to the north open for British, and specifically Cape, expansion; as it was politically necessary to have the support of the Cape Dutch for this, he adapted his methods to that requirement. His immediate object was the same as Mackenzie's, though his methods and his ultimate purpose were different.

Rhodes has already made several appearances in this story. Of his earlier career it is relevant to note that ill health had caused him to emigrate from England in 1870 and to join his eldest brother on a cotton farm in Natal; that he

25 The Advance into the Interior

had moved up to the new diamond fields in the following year; that by 1880 he had taken the lead in forming the De Beers Company—still only one of many companies on the fields; that in the meantime he had kept terms, on and off, at Oriel College, Oxford; that he became a member of the Cape Parliament in 1881; that soon after his election he took his pass BA at Oxford and, thanks to the passage of time, his MA.

His political career coincides precisely with the great age of European imperialism. A few months before Rhodes sailed from England for the first time, to join his brother in Natal, John Ruskin had delivered his inaugural lecture as Slade Professor of Art at Oxford. It is reasonable to assume, as his biographers do, that Rhodes was influenced, directly or indirectly, by the famous appeal:

There is a destiny now possible to us—the highest ever set before a nation to be accepted or refused . . . Or will you, youths of England, make your country again a royal throne of kings; a sceptered isle, for all the world a source of light, a centre of peace . . .

"Vexilla regis prodeunt." Yes, but of which king? There are the two oriflammes; which shall we plant on the farthest islands,—the one that floats in heavenly fire, or that hangs heavy with foul tissue of terrestrial gold? . . .

And this is what she must either do, or perish: she must found colonies as fast and as far as she is able, formed of her most energetic and worthiest men;—seizing every piece of fruitful waste ground she can set her foot on, and then teaching these her colonists that their chief virtue is to be fidelity to their country, and that their first aim is to be to advance the power of England by land and sea: and that, though they live on a distant plot of ground, they are no more to consider themselves disfranchised from their native land, than the sailors of her fleets do, because they float on distant waves.[73]

Rhodes was incapable of using such language, but it precisely expressed his own purpose. In his first will, in 1872, he left his as yet nonexistent fortune to the secretary of state for the colonies, to be used for the extension of the British Empire. His second will in 1877 (the fortune was still to come) provided for "a Secret Society, the true aim and object whereof shall be the extension of British rule throughout the world . . . and especially the occupation by British settlers of the entire Continent of Africa, the Holy Land, the valley of the Euphrates, the Islands of Cyprus and Candia, the whole of South America, the islands of the Pacific not heretofore possessed by Great Britain, the whole of the Malay Archipelago, the seaboard of China and Japan, the ultimate recovery of the United States of America as an integral part of the British Empire, the consolidation of the whole Empire, and finally the foundation of so great a power as to hereafter render wars impossible and promote the best interests of humanity."[74]

Ruskin had said "fruitful waste ground"; Rhodes ignored the restriction. Ruskin had rejected the oriflamme "that hangs heavy with foul tissue of terrestrial gold"; Rhodes said to General Gordon that "it is no use having big ideas if you have not the cash to carry them out." Ruskin, however, did not actually build an empire; Rhodes did.

Viewed from Kimberley, where Rhodes came at the end of 1871 to seek his fortune, the next task of British imperialism seemed to lie obviously at hand: up the Missionaries' Road to the north. Kimberley itself was new-born. Griqualand West was annexed to the Crown a few days before Rhodes's arrival there. Henceforth Kimberley was the fitting-out place and starting-point for northern travellers, their first contact with civilization—of a sort—on their return. The German imperialist Ernst von Weber spent some time at the diggings, and to bolster his argument for German colonization he quoted from articles published in the *Diamond News* in 1873 and 1874, at a time when the Delagoa Bay arbitration was pending: their subject was "the enormous inland territories, of which Delagoa Bay is the natural seaport . . . They have a superfluity of mineral treasures, and could support a population 50 times as large as that of Great Britain."[75]

When in 1881 Griqualand West, annexed to the colony the previous year, sent members to the Cape Parliament, Rhodes was elected for Barkly West. Northern expansion soon became his main political interest. In 1882 he moved for the appointment of a commission to examine the disputed boundary of Griqualand West, and became a member of it himself; he was thus enabled to have a close look at the "freebooters" even before they had proclaimed their two republics. In 1883 he moved, as an amendment to another motion, that the Cape should appoint a resident with the Thlaping chief Mankurwane. This was not done, but Rhodes made his point: "I look upon this Bechuanaland territory as the Suez Canal of the trade of this country, the key of its road to the interior. The House will have to wake up to what is to be its future policy. The question before us really is this, whether this Colony is to be confined to its present borders, or whether it is to become the dominant state in South Africa—whether, in fact, it is to spread its civilisation over the interior."[76]

It was characteristic of him to use, rather disingenuously, a mercenary argument. In future the bait would be gold; now it was trade. What trade was there in that dusty country? The civil commissioner of Kimberley found it impossible to estimate at that time, though when the railway reached Kimberley it would be considerable. Rhodes said that he had consulted three firms, whose names he was not free to reveal, and that one of them gave a figure of £100,000 for its own business.[77]

Fairfield did not believe it: "as to the 'Trade Route,' it is the affair of the Cape—not ours. The people out there know there is very little trade, and that it is diminishing every year by reason of the disappearance of elephants and other similar causes."[78] In later years, as we shall see, the trade along the Missionaries' Road amounted to very little. Rhodes counted on gold, not ivory or skins, to pay for his great venture in the north. In the meantime both he and Mackenzie, in their different ways, had reason to be satisfied with what had been achieved. The road to the north was under British control. The Cape Colony was not shut out of the interior. But the next move in that direction would be a long step. And the South African Republic, with no restriction on its relations with tribes to the north, was not shut out either.

On this point the Colonial Office vacillated. The 22nd parallel just clears the northern reaches of the Limpopo; it was chosen as the northern limit of the protectorate with that fact in mind, so that the protecting power would lie across the path of "freebooters" issuing from any part of the Transvaal. On second thoughts, however, the officials and the secretary of state agreed that the convention and the unwritten understanding that went with it permitted Boer expansion northwards, and that they had no desire to prevent this. Fairfield, in a characteristic minute, urged that if the Boers continued to breed at a prodigious rate, and to incline to a secluded and pastoral life, "we must expect them to spread, and we should only be incurring needless trouble in trying to prevent them"; but that, as settlement even in the northern Transvaal had been receding, he did not in fact think it probable that they would do so![79]

In face of protests both from the South African Republic and from Portugal, the Colonial Office would have been willing to set an eastern limit to the protectorate at the 26th or 27th meridian, *"if it were not for the restlessness of the Germans."*[80] By the time the Germans had agreed to boundaries acceptable to the British, the circumstances of the country in question had changed so radically that the suggested limitation was never adopted.

It was not only the Germans who were restless. Rumours of their territorial ambitions provided a useful stimulus and argument to a varied assortment of men whose vision to the north extended beyond the 22nd parallel. There were two separate objectives here, not always distinguished by their advocates. The larger one was to take possession of—or declare a protectorate over—Lobengula's dominions. The other was to extend the existing protectorate over the rest of Kgama's country, up to the Zambezi, while keeping clear of Matabeleland. For the latter project Kgama himself had given the opening by objecting to the line which cut his country in two. The difficulty about it was that Kgama's conception of his own boundaries did not agree with the views of his neighbours.

According to Maund's report, Kgama claimed not merely the well-known "disputed territory" up to the Shashi, but a great deal more in that direction—well beyond the Ramakwabane, and to the Tuli in the southern sector and the Gwaai in the northern.[81] These, with other debatable lands to the west and northwest, were the claims of the man who "had no country."

The British government preferred not to get involved in disputes of this kind. The Cape government, and some of the Cape colonists, did not care very much whether territories belonged to Kgama or to his neighbours. What worried them were such reports as one from the magistrate at Walvis Bay, who had been confidentially told that "the ultimate aim of the German government is to possess a belt of country stretching from this coast to Zanzibar, so as to cut off our colonies from the interior." At the end of 1885, therefore, the Cape ministry urged upon Her Majesty's government "the necessity for preserving, in the interests of the Empire, outlets for British trade northwards of Bechuanaland to the Zambesi." In January 1886 a new note was struck in the Colonial Office by Hemming: if the Germans got in first, Bismarck would protect them, "and all prospect of expansion for us to the northwards" would be extinguished.[82]

A few weeks later Ralph Williams—still in England, though soon to become British agent in Pretoria—wrote privately to Sir Robert Herbert, urging an arrangement with Lobengula for concessions in the "Mashuna" country; otherwise, he said the Boers were certain to go into it, and the Germans had similar ambitions. Fairfield, predictably, thought Williams "rather feather-headed" because "he looks to the taking over of all the country up to the Zambesi which is ridiculous."[83] Almost at the same moment Robinson was forwarding a petition to the queen from the Cape Town Chamber of Commerce, followed by a similar one from Grahamstown, "that measures are now urgently demanded for securing to British influence the territory stretching from the present limits of the Bechuanaland Protectorate to that great natural line of demarcation, the Zambezi River."[84]

German expansion might be contained by a treaty, as Robinson suggested in his comment on the Cape Town petition; but what of the Boers, who had deliberately been given an opening to the north? At the moment when Warren was arriving at Mafeking on his way up, the Colonial Office received a private letter reporting that a party of Boers had assembled on the Limpopo with the intention of pouncing on "Soochong." Kgama's rival, Kamani, was with them. The expedition had now been abandoned because of horse-sickness, but it was to be undertaken later, perhaps in the coming winter.[85]

Warren's further movements forestalled that action, if it was really intended, but Fairfield's expectation that the Boers would "spread" was nearer the truth than his postscript that they would not. Official reports, private reports, and the orators and framers of petitions continued to ring the changes on the two powers threatening to cut the Cape Colony off from the interior—Germany and the Transvaal. Of the two, the Transvaal was the more serious competitor. In the prolific Afrikaner families every son claimed a farm of three thousand morgen—over six thousand acres—virtually as a birthright. To obtain it he had to trek farther into the interior and take it, if necessary by force. This process had been going on for nearly two centuries. The British annexation of the Transvaal in 1877 occurred at the moment when the available free land of that country was almost exhausted; hence the subsequent thrust into Stellaland, Goshen, and the New Republic (carved out of Zululand). Now, in 1886, the succession of gold discoveries in the Transvaal culminated in the greatest of all, on the Witwatersrand. Foreign fortune-seekers began to pour into the country and to buy farms at fancy prices. For increasing numbers of the old burghers, the time had come to move on.

The urge to go north was, moreover, shared by others. The gold of the Rand was for the big capitalist only, but it had been preceded by the more romantic goldfields of the eastern Transvaal, suitable for the small man. The diamond fields, too, had once swarmed with small men, but their day was over. By 1885 the four chief mines of Kimberley were worked by forty-two companies and fifty-six individual operators.[86] Three years later Rhodes was to succeed in amalgamating them all into one great monopoly. With the boom in the eastern Transvaal collapsing, where was the small man to find his Eldorado? His attention was drawn again, as it had been in the days before Kimberley, to the fabulous riches believed to be waiting for him beyond the Limpopo.

The British occupation of Bechuanaland prepared the way. Imperial law and order and communications now reached almost to Matabeleland. Shippard and his subordinates were no sooner installed than they began to take an official interest in the country beyond them. It is significant that Shippard was recommended for his post by Robinson, that Robinson by 1885 had been closely associated with Rhodes, and that Rhodes had once shared bachelor quarters in Kimberley with Shippard.[87] The administrator and deputy commissioner was well primed in the politics of imperial expansion before he went to Vryburg.

Warren was no friend of Rhodes, but was an imperialist in his own right. The three men he sent as an embassy to Lobengula—Edwards, Maund, and Haynes—all wrote more or less lengthy reports on what they had seen and heard.[88] Maund, especially, submitted a detailed account of the country, its politics, and military organization. Edwards regretted that the envoys had been restricted to the task of informing Lobengula of what had been done to the south. If only he could have been asked to fix a boundary between himself and the English, "I am of opinion . . . he would undoubtedly have given more than either we desire or expect . . . I am convinced that a Commission or any party of Englishmen introduced by an Englishman whom Lobengula knows [such as Sam Edwards?], and who wished to settle in this country, would not only be well received but would obtain from him land to settle on, as long as he knew they would help him defend himself against his enemy the Boer . . . One of the king's brothers, the Induna of a district bordering the Shashani River, stated 'that they all wanted to live at peace now, they were tired of war. We wish the whole country was Government country, and the roads open for intercourse with other tribes'." Then came the usual rumour of Boer intentions; this time it was "Colonel Ferreira" who was raising a mounted force to go into Matabeleland.

The reports were published in the next blue book, for all the world to see. Maund's was supplemented by a private letter, which the Colonial Office sent on to General Brackenbury of the Intelligence Department. That department was preparing a paper on Matabeleland.[89]

At this time John Mackenzie was again working upon public opinion in England. His efforts were effective, though their ultimate results were seldom quite what he had intended. The paper he read to the Society of Arts shows the weakness in his marksmanship. Into an account of Bechuanaland and its recent history he introduced some remarks about "Matabeleland and Mashonaland . . . To the east of Shoshong, and north-east, you have a country which is perhaps the most beautiful and most valuable in South Africa . . . The gold of Mashonaland lies waiting the hand of enterprise and industry." In case the audience should take this to be an argument for immediate annexation, he added, "but I am not at all anxious to open up Mashonaland before the time."[90] The alluring description was one more weight in the scale that Warren, Edwards, Maund, Rhodes, the Chambers of Commerce, and others were helping to bring down in favour of an advance into Matabeleland. The cautionary note was no more than a feather in the opposite scale.

Successive British governments were plied with information and advice, but made no decision about extending the protectorate. In March 1886, Hemming in his minute on the Chamber of Commerce petition again struck the new note: "If, as may be hoped, it is decided to extend the British Protectorate to the Zambesi, the sooner action is taken in the matter the better—otherwise we shall find the Germans there before us."[91] Three months later the secretary of state, Lord Granville, noted that what was proposed, i.e., the northward extension of Bechuanaland, was "really not so much an annexation as a rectification of our frontier, which is shown to be necessary," and that Joseph Chamberlain agreed with this.[92] Then the Liberal cabinet and party were wrecked on the rocks of Home Rule. The Conservative government put the question aside for a time. In August 1887, the new secretary of state, Sir Henry Holland (who became Lord Knutsford the following year), decided against an extension for the present, but asked to be kept informed of any action, or rumours of action, by the Germans or Portuguese in the territory proposed to be protected. He did not mention action by the Boers, but they had already acted when he was writing his minute.

Sir Henry was referring to the northward extension of Kgama's country. The Boers, however, were concerned with Matabeleland. So was Shippard, who continued to receive, and to send on to his superiors, reports and rumours from that country. He received three about the end of 1886. The first was from John Fry, formerly of the detective department in Kimberley, now connected with the mines of the Tati. Fry had been dismissed from the former post for some financial irregularity, but the dismissal was probably unjust, and provoked a weighty protest from the Kimberley community. However that might be, the dismissal led him to seek new pastures in the north. He reported that a party of Boer hunters, with twelve wagons, had just come out of Matabeleland, and that he intended to go there in time for the Big Dance. He was already familiar with the country; some months earlier he had been able to give two members of the Bechuanaland Border Police, travelling to the Victoria Falls, details of the route.[93]

Another of Shippard's reports[94] came from Sergeant-Major W. Bodle, of the same police force, who had gathered at Shoshong a curious rumour. Lobengula was about to hold a meeting of all the Europeans in his country, to discuss "the question of the extension of the British Protectorate to Matabeleland. It is held by some that the Chief is now in favour of such extension, while others contend that he contemplates removing with his people to the northward of the Zambesi and that the meeting is summoned for the purpose of announcing such intention. A report which lacks authority is afloat to the effect that the Agents of the Transvaal have tendered the Chief, as a present or a bribe, a number of cattle and stands of arms to induce him to make the rumoured migration." There would be no profit in speculating on what, if anything, was behind these rumours; their importance lay in their effect on some of the people who received them.

The third of Shippard's reports, from G.L. Pascall, was more specific.[95] Pascall believed that a Boer trek into Mashonaland, via the "Saba" river, was planned for the winter of 1887. His grounds for the belief were that two individuals, whose names he gave, had told him that they would be in the trekking party, and that the "Umzila Kafirs" intended to help the Boers against Lobengula.

John Fry duly went to Matabeleland, and on 21 March 1887, reported again to Shippard.[96] From all he could gather he had gained the impression that Lobengula and his people desired to come under British protection. The great obstacle was the disputed boundary between him and Kgama, so Fry "ventured to suggest" that Shippard might take the initiative in settling this.

Shippard hardly needed the advice. He had been in correspondence with Lobengula, who wrote back to him on 1 March saying that "some of the white people have come in here like wolves, without my permission, and made new roads into my country." On the same day he wrote to Kgama, chiding him about the boundary line: "If you give your country over, and if you take in some of my ground, what will I have to say? I should like to hear your answer at once."[97]

It can be taken as certain that the anxieties of Lobengula and of his subjects increased sharply about the beginning of 1887. Not only was the tide of white travellers flowing more strongly, but many of them were now neither hunters, traders, nor missionaries. Quite a few had official connections with either the British, the Transvaal, or—possibly—the German government. The rumours of Boer movements would be as well known to Lobengula as to Shippard; indeed it was a part of Shippard's duty, as he saw it, to make sure that Lobengula did hear them. One of the king's first steps in reaction to the increasing pressure was to appoint Sam Edwards as a kind of governor of the Tati district, with power to make laws and regulations and also to delegate his authority to others. Edwards was given a written commission, dated 24 February 1887.[98]

It is not likely that the king or many of his subjects wanted to "give the country over" in the manner of Kgama. But if the law officers in London were not quite sure what a protectorate was, Lobengula would be still more confused, and it is possible that what was taken as a request for a protectorate was meant rather as a request for "protection" against Boer invaders, lawless Englishmen, and other disturbers of the Ndebele order. There may also have been a grain of truth in the rumour that Lobengula was planning to move his people across the Zambezi. The idea had been entertained on and off for years, and the Batoka plateau had been ravaged on several occasions, possibly with that need in mind.[99] But there is little evidence to suggest that it was seriously entertained in 1887.

On 29 April Shippard wrote to Lobengula, and at the same time to Kgama, on the lines suggested by Fry: he offered, if the chiefs so desired, to ask the high commissioner to appoint an officer to hear the evidence on both sides and to fix the boundary. Kgama accepted the offer; Lobengula did not.[100]

On 21 May Shippard wrote a long report to Robinson on the "definite and highly advantageous course which hesitation or delay now may render extremely difficult if not impossible hereafter." For, he said.

> I have long known that Mashunaland is beyond comparison the most valuable country South of the Zambesi and in the event of a conflict I regard the conquest of the whole of the Amandebele country by the Boers as absolutely certain . . . I am satisfied not only that Mashunaland contains some of the richest deposits of alluvial gold in the world but that the whole country between the North Eastern boundary of Khama's dominions, the Zambesi, the Umzila Gaza territory and the Limpopo is remarkably fertile and full of mineral wealth of all kinds.
>
> There can be no doubt whatever that the Amandebele country and especially Mashunaland would form a most valuable addition to the British Empire and the necessary complement of a United South Africa under the British flag . . .
>
> I am strongly in favour of annexation wherever practicable in preference to the unsatisfactory transitional device of a Protectorate which imposes great responsibilities without either power or profit; and therefore, while as regards the country north of the Zambesi the extension of a nominal British Protectorate as far as the Southern limit of the Congo State might for the present suffice, I hold that the entire country comprising the present Bechuanaland Protectorate and continued northwards along the 20th meridian East to the Chobe and Zambesi and along the right or southern bank of the Zambesi as far as the Umzila Gaza boundary and thence along the left or northern bank of the Limpopo to Bechuanaland should be annexed as soon as possible to Her Majesty's dominions.

He did not fail to mention such important objects as crushing "the present inhuman slave trade on the Zambesi," abolishing "slavery in its worst and most cruel form," and saving "from impending destruction the ingenious, industrious downtrodden Mashunas." He was prepared to submit "a detailed scheme for carrying it out promptly, peaceably and cheaply."[101]

Robinson does not appear to have sent this report to London; he may have guessed how it would be received there. He had, however, begun, late in 1886, to move in the direction Shippard wanted by proposing an additional magistracy north of the Molopo, and suggesting J.S. Moffat, now magistrate at Taungs, for the post. The suggestion was approved in London; by the end of July 1887, he was able to appoint Moffat assistant commissioner for the protectorate. He was to reside north of the Molopo, but not permanently with any chief; "to influence the chiefs for good"; to be a kind of liaison officer with Lobengula; and possibly to settle the disputed boundary.[102] Moffat was thought to be specially qualified for the latter tasks, as the son of "Moshete" and one of the original band of missionaries at Inyati.

This was an important step to take, but it was not taken until the Transvaal was one jump ahead of the British. As usual, Piet Joubert was the moving spirit; he had begun to look to the north even before the British had thwarted his expansionist policy in the west. He had written to Lobengula in 1882, reminding him of the visit of his (Joubert's) three uncles to Mzilikazi in connection with the Pretorius treaty, and pleading for perpetual friendship between the two peoples. He warned the king about the English: "when an Englishman once has your property in his hands then he is like an ape that has its hands full of pumpkin seeds, if you don't beat him to death he will never let go." Another kind of warning was implied by an account of the sad fate of two chiefs who had defied the republic. Joubert would like to visit Lobengula himself, but would wait "until the stink which the English brought in is first blown away altogether." The letter was accompanied by a cotton blanket for the king and a coloured handkerchief for his "great wife." Maund saw the letter and heard about its reception. "Lobengula," he wrote sarcastically, " . . . was much amused at this costly present which was in good keeping with the letter. His answer was short and to the point. He was very glad to hear they wished to live in peace. He too wished to live in peace and thanked them for the blanket and handkerchief."[103]

In 1886 Joubert found a promising agent for his purpose in P.J. Grobler, a trader for many years at the diamond fields, at Shoshong, and in Matabeleland. Two years earlier his trade at Shoshong had ended in a dispute about what Frank Johnson called "a number of so-called salted horses and a large quantity of gunpowder which latter however would not explode!" According to Shippard's report in 1888, Grobler owed a number of debts at Shoshong, including £341 to Kgama, for "fraudulent horse-dealing." Grobler himself claimed that Kgama owed him thirty oxen but refused to pay; as security for the debt Grobler was retaining a wagon of Kgama's. Whatever the truth may have been, Grobler could no longer trade at Shoshong, and turned his commercial attention to Matabeleland.[104]

Before he left for that country in 1886 Joubert suggested to him that he might sound Lobengula about the possibility of a new treaty with the republic. Grobler did so. Lobengula "expressed a wish to renew the old existing treaties which had been concluded in the 'fifties with Potgieter and Pretorius.''[105] Grobler returned to Pretoria accompanied by an envoy of Lobengula's entrusted with a message to that effect.

In July 1887 Grobler reached the king's kraal again. This time he was commissioned by the president himself, with the approval of the Executive Council, to "renew" the old treaties. Lobengula was uneasy. He spoke of a rumour that the English were about to "overwhelm" the Transvaal, on account of its gold, and that the Boers in turn would overwhelm Matabeleland in their search for a new country. Such a game of musical chairs might have seemed the more credible to the king if he himself had a contingent plan to move north of the Zambezi. It was given further credibility by a letter from Shippard. A merchant had pointed out Grobler and his wagon to Ralph Williams, now British agent in Pretoria, with a warning of his plans. This information was passed through Rhodes and Robinson to Shippard, who wrote to Lobengula about "a large force of men from the Transvaal to invade your country.''[106]

Grobler managed to overcome the suspicions thus sown, so far, at any rate, as on 30 July to get Lobengula's mark to a treaty. It renewed the former treaties of friendship between the republic and Mzilikazi, and provided for perpetual amity and mutual recognition of independence. These, however, were followed by more weighty and specific provisions. Lobengula bound himself to furnish assistance, with troops or otherwise, whenever called upon by an officer of the republic to do so. If the republic should appoint a consul, the king was to give him assistance and protection. He was likewise to assist and protect, and permit to hunt or trade, every Transvaler provided by his government with a pass; nobody who was not so provided would be countenanced by the republican government. The consul would have jurisdiction over all Transvalers in Matabeleland.[107]

Some historians have denied the existence of the treaty. "This document," says Marshall Hole, "bears the stamp of imposture from beginning to end.''[108] The names of the consenting indunas, as spelt on it, are unrecognizable. Lobengula himself denied to Moffat that he had made the treaty—as he later denied to Frederik Grobler that he had made a treaty with Moffat. But the greatest reason for suspicion is the absence of any *quid pro quo* for the vast inroads thus made on the king's independence.

The sequel, however, shows almost conclusively that the marks of Lobengula and some indunas were genuinely affixed; and again almost conclusively that the terms of the agreement could not have been clearly explained to them. The king's subsequent attitude to Grobler and the treaty makes it probable that he regarded it as a mere renewal of friendship with the people of

"Enteleka," (Potgieter), a useful counterweight to the pressure of the mainly British concession-hunters.

By September Grobler, accompanied by two Ndebele indunas, was in Pretoria; by November he had returned to Bulawayo. Though it was widely suspected that his frequent visits had a political purpose,[109] nothing was yet known of the treaty. The republican government was doing its best to keep this secret until it would be too late for such dangerous men as Rhodes to interfere with its operation.

If Rhodes had not appeared to be playing a direct or active part in northern expansion since the occupation of Bechuanaland, it was not that his resolve had weakened. As it was of no use to have "big ideas without the cash to carry them out," he had been devoting his energies to establishing a financial base from which to build an empire when the preparations were complete. The first stage of the operation, the amalgamation of all the holdings in De Beers Mine into one company, was completed in 1887. The next step would be to unite the companies controlling the other mines with his own, a step involving a dramatic struggle with Barney Barnato of the Kimberley Central. This drama was opening as Grobler was receiving Joubert's advice about a treaty with Lobengula. When the king was putting his mark to that treaty, Rhodes was in Europe, getting a loan from the Rothschilds to buy out the Compagnie Française des Diamants du Cap. In this move he was outbidden and apparently defeated by Barnato; but his price was a block of shares in Barnato's company, the weapon with which he won the battle in the end. In the latter part of 1887 the struggle was moving towards a climax.

So was the Transvaal scheme to control Matabeleland, but that was not the only obstacle in Rhodes's way. If he were to annex, develop, and govern provinces through the agency of a company—at this stage it was his De Beer's Company that he had in mind—he must have economic resources as well as political authority. As he wrote to Shippard some months later, "my only fear is that I shall be too late with Lo Bengula as of course if his whole country is given away to adventurers it is no use my stepping in for my Company to assist in the government of a shell, you will see this as clearly as I do."[110] While Grobler had been in Matabeleland on government business, various "adventurers" had indeed been there on business of their own, and it will be necessary to retrace our steps a little to see what they were doing.

Two important parties of concession-hunters visited Lobengula and went into Mashonaland in 1887. One represented the Northern Goldfields Exploration Syndicate, formed by some substantial citizens of Cape Town, including the mayor and several members of Parliament. The leader of its expedition was Frank Johnson, a mere youth, who came of age during the journey.[111] His companions were Maurice Heany (an American), H.J. Borrow, Edward Burnett, and J.A. Spreckley; all, including Johnson, were troopers of the Bechuanaland Border Police who took their discharge from that force to engage in this more promising adventure. As the concession they obtained found its way later, and amicably, into the hands of Rhodes's allies, these men have had a good press and they were all to figure in a favourable light in the history of the next few years. The other party, for reasons which will soon appear, became the villains of the story and have had a bad press. They were J.G. Wood, MLA, of Grahamstown, who conferred the respectability, W.C. Francis, a trader for many years at Shoshong, and Edward Chapman, well known in Matabeleland.[112] Their financial backing appears to have been less substantial than that of the first party.

The Johnson expedition began its business at Shoshong, where Kgama granted the syndicate the sole right to prospect throughout his country; when gold had been found, he would grant a mining concession for an area of 10,000 square miles. The most important business, however, was to be done at Bulawayo, where the haggling was prolonged as Lobengula played for time. " 'Time', said the King, 'was made only for slaves,' therefore there was no hurry. When his heart had found ground for white men to dig, he would remember that they were the first to ask for it."[113] This was more courteous than true. The Baines concession was still in existence, and the Leask group—of which more will be heard in 1888—already had a promise of a concession, sometimes referred to as that same "Baines Concession."

Johnson was persistent in his request for a mining concession in Mashonaland. Lobengula, however, had never heard that there was gold in that country. Later he denied that such rivers as the Hunyani and Mazoe existed, and suggested that the party should return to Cape Town with this information. When he was given a present of numerous articles, including rifles, ammunition, tobacco, scissors, and field-glasses, and was offered £200 a year for a concession, he observed that the company must be very rich and would have no need of more gold.

At last the king's patience was worn out, he gave permission, and the party went on to prospect in the valleys of the Umfuli, the Hunyani, and the Mazoe. The operations were very successful and some gold was brought away. But the subsequent negotiations with Lobengula failed. It may be, as Johnson thought, that the great offence was to bring samples, which would be more likely than mere hearsay to bring in the dreaded miners.[114] In his report to Shippard, however, he put the blame on the activities of the Wood party:

> On the 12th instant [November] I arrived here [Umvutshwa] from Hanyane, and found the state of the country very altered from what it was in July. A panic seemed to have seized the King and Indunas, fearing a rush of gold seekers into the country. I have no hesitation in saying that this state of affairs has been chiefly brought about by the action of Mr. J.G. Woods [sic] and party, who searched for gold when supposed to be hunting.[115]

Both parties were charged with various offences and subjected to the usual in-

37 The Advance into the Interior

timidating trials; Johnson was fined £100 but Wood was acquitted. Johnson got no concession: the king "closed his mouth."

While the Johnson party had been in the country its paths had crossed those of various others. There were many Boer hunters, some of whom were "refused the hunting veld." There was the German Dr. Schultz, the "American expert" Moore, and E.R. Renny-Tailyour, "representing four combined syndicates, at Barberton, Port Elizabeth, London and Hamburg." None of these got a concession. There was "a Boer named Grobbler," and there were Wood, Francis, and Chapman, who were given permission only to hunt in Mashonaland, but who prospected nevertheless.

Wood's diary tells a different story: they were given permission to "proceed on our journey to Mashonaland"; hunting is not mentioned.[116] They were, however, closely watched, and "faced the music" on their return to Bulawayo: "You had no right to look for gold, you must have been spies." Johnson's idea that his own failure was due to the misbehaviour of his rivals was belied by the sequel. Wood was given a concession, but it was for the territory between the Shashi and the Motloutsi, which was included also in Kgama's prospecting (and, subsequently, mining) concession to Johnson. The two parties were committed to opposite sides in the boundary dispute.

Apart from the people actually encountered, the air was thick with rumours of other movements. A Boer commando of 700, destined for Barotseland, was assembling at Rustenburg. A Portuguese official expedition to Mashonaland was leaving Manica. Two other parties were leaving Inhambane and Natal for Lobengula. Some "bastard Portuguese" traders on the Mazoe had been robbed and driven away by the inhabitants the day before Johnson reached the spot.[117]

Whatever the truth of the rumours, the reality was serious enough to arouse Lobengula's fears. If he could not read all the signs, there were white men at hand to read them for him. The concession-hunters, playing for high stakes, were at war with one another; each held a metaphorical dagger behind his back. Three of the local whites, and their associate Thomas Leask of Klerksdorp, held the promise of a concession. As the year wore on the prospect of this became, Johnson thought, "very shaky indeed." By November one of them, James Fairbairn, was being tried on the charge of bringing the white men into the country, and was fined £100.[118] Another of the local men, William Tainton, appeared at first to be helping the Johnson party, but later to be working against it. Wood was on bad terms with his own associates, whose company he bore with a bad grace; Chapman was actually disloyal.[119] The Johnson and Wood parties opposed each other in every way. "The whole country here," wrote Johnson, "is one mass of lies and double dealing—not one man white or black is to be trusted."[120]

Johnson was not an authority on Ndebele politics, but in at least one respect his experience and those of other observers pointed to the same conclusion. At the end of July 1887 the king was discussing Johnson's request for permission to go to Mashonaland with "some 150 indunas, doctors, and big people, all of whom were showing great antagonism to our going in."[121] The very next day the party was allowed to go. By October, when they were on the Mazoe, they got chilling news from the king: on their return they would have to tell him why they went in.[122]

The experiences of others, such as Bishop Knight-Bruce, confirm Johnson's explanation of this change of course: the king's decision and attitude depended on which advisers he was consulting. The 150 indunas, and others, of Johnson's account were the large assembly, the *isikulu*, which reflected the prevailing public opinion that the white men should be kept out. The argument for this course was that they were dangerous. There was plenty of evidence of this. When, for instance, the Johnson and Wood parties, Selous, and others had been gathered together on the Umfuli, the talk round the camp fire had been of "war, and estimating the number of men required to wipe out the Matabele and the best way to come into the country to accomplish this very desirable end."[123] Spies may have reported this discussion to Bulawayo.

The same argument might lead to the opposite conclusion: treat the concession-hunters gently, so as not to give them an excuse to call on the great military power they had behind them. Baines and Swinburne had got concessions, but nothing had come of these. Johnson and Wood, too, might go away quietly if not provoked. This was often the opinion of Lobengula himself, and of some of his most trusted advisers. In important negotiations with strangers he most commonly worked with these, who formed a small inner council.

This council, the *mphakathi*, had no precisely defined membership, but from the references of many observers we can get an approximate idea of its composition. Mhlaba, son and successor of Mncumbate, the "hereditary regent," was one of the most trusted counsellors in the eighties; he must have owed the trust to more than his high rank. He is found presiding over trials and leading the examination of white men accused of offences. Makwekwe, described at different times as second induna of Bulawayo, "head induna," and "spokesman for the Umbiso and Insuku regiments," was often one of the select group; he was generally hostile to the whites. Several of the king's brothers were at times in his confidence, but of them one might say with Napoleon III that "on choisit ses amis; on subit ses frères." One of them, Hlangabeza, Lobengula's only full brother, was "smelt out" and executed early in 1888—ostensibly for causing the king's illness by witchcraft, more probably for being too close to the succession. The *mphakathi* included, however, besides the indunas, the three brothers Nungu, Bosumwane, and Mlugulu, hereditary priests. Europeans always called them the "dance doctors," because of their prominent role in the *inxwala* ceremony. These were the only Ndebele witnesses, though not signatories, of the Moffat treaty, and Moffat thought their concurrence "important, if not indispensable, in any transaction of this kind." The secular indunas could have had no such claim. Some of the most eminent, such as Gampu Sithole, are never mentioned among the select advisers.[124]

Wood, being on bad terms with his companions, kept many of his thoughts to himself—and to his diary. Lobengula might have been surprised to read some of them, typical though they were of the Albany politician: "I am more than ever convinced that this country [Bechuanaland] would suit the requirements of all the native population of the whole of South Africa." The native population having been herded into it, Kaffraria and other desirable lands could then be opened up for white occupation.[125] Mashonaland was in the desirable category: "What I am trying for is a session [sic] of the alluvial ground and five hundred farms for which an annual rent must be paid, should I succeed my object is to offer the farms to Albany and Bathurst farmers."[126]

The mining concession of the Shashi-Motloutsi territory, which was all that he got, hardly lent itself to this kind of scheme. It had also the more serious disadvantage that Kgama gave the mining rights of the same territory, and more, to Johnson. While Johnson was in Matabeleland, Kgama was being prompted by Shippard to have second thoughts about the concession he had given to Johnson's company. Shippard objected to the monopoly given to one group, and to the promise of a mining concession covering 10,000 square miles. Kgama drew back; Johnson sent Heany and Borrow down to Shoshong to clear up the misunderstanding; letters passed continually between Kgama, Shippard, the high commissioner, and the company's secretary in Cape Town. The result was a new concession, agreed upon when Johnson got back to Shoshong in December. His company was to have the first choice in selecting a mining area, and the area was cut down to 400 square miles.[127]

Wood and his party fared better than their rivals with Lobengula; they ran into trouble at Shoshong. Up to this point they had been regarded favourably by both Shippard and Robinson. They carried a letter of recommendation from Shippard. Kgama had refused them a concession on the ground that he had already given the sole prospecting rights to Johnson, but even at that stage he was suspicious of them.

The change in the Wood party's fortunes began with their accepting a concession in the disputed territory from Lobengula. Arrived at Shoshong, Wood had several interviews with Kgama. They began amicably enough, Wood wanting to know where the boundaries of Johnson's concession were. When it appeared that these included the disputed territory, Wood became defiant. "Finally," wrote Johnson, who was at Shoshong at the same time, "Woods [sic] told Khama that he should write that day to Lo Bengulo and demand an impi to protect him on his concession, to which Mr. Hepburn said 'But that Mr. Woods means war,' to which he replied 'Of course it does.' Last night Messrs. Woods and Chapman received official written notice to leave the station within 24 hours, while Francis—who had been trading at Mangwato for 23 years—received a similar notice to leave by next Sunday."[128]

Wood's diary gives only a hasty and compressed account of these events, mentioning however "great prejudice against Chapman and Francis." When he reached Grahamstown, and Johnson Cape Town, each of them wrote to the local paper, setting forth the rival claims of Lobengula and Kgama to the disputed territory. Whatever these might be, Wood had put himself in the wrong with the British authorities by what Moffat, in what was surely an understatement, called his "most ill-advised letter" to Lobengula.[129]

Moffat had been appointed assistant commissioner essentially for the purpose of keeping Lobengula friendly to the English. In September Robinson wrote a letter to him for Moffat to deliver. Among other things he advised the king "to grant no concessions . . . to any Germans, Portuguese or Dutch, but especially not to any Germans who are the most dangerous of all, without consulting Mr. Moffat." The startled Colonial Office reacted quickly to this diplomatic blunder. Robinson, told by cable to remove the offending words, sent the instruction after Moffat by telegram and eventually by Kgama's runners, who covered 150 miles in five days and overtook Moffat at the Tati. So Moffat continued on his way, reached Bulawayo on 29 November, and found Grobler, "a pleasant and intelligent man," still there.[130]

The facts about Grobler's visit, and previous visits, were difficult to establish. Sam Edwards did not believe that Lobengula had made any agreement with the Transvaal—"it would have leaked out." Grobler himself, Moffat wrote, "denies to me that there is any truth in the report that the Transvaal has taken over the Protectorate of Matabeleland." Grobler however admitted to one of the local white men, Moss Cohen, that "some kind of written agreement does exist between Lobengula and the Transvaal," and that his present visit was on government and not private business. Cohen relayed this to Moffat, who then extracted from the king the admission that Grobler's business was the renewal of the old treaty of friendship, but no more. As late as 15 December Moffat was informing Shippard that "reports in newspapers about Transvaal and Lobengula without foundation."[131]

He may have been referring to a report in the *Transvaal Advertiser* to the effect that the Transvaal had declared a protectorate over Matabeleland and that a consul would soon be sent there. Ralph Williams, the British agent in Pretoria, took some trouble to trace that report to its source. It came from a Mr. Cooper, of the firm of Cooper and Beckett, who had learned the facts from the Landdrost of Middelburg. Williams therefore asked Cooper, who was also Reuter's agent, to get official confirmation of the news. Cooper did so: "A Mr. Marais, one of the officials, said 'Oh so it has come out has it,' and Mr. Bok the State Secretary said 'It is true that we are engaged in some negotiations with Lobengula'."

Williams mentioned names, but asked that they be kept absolutely secret.[132] For all his trouble though, his information was no more precise than that which Moffat was to obtain in Matabeleland; Williams's report indeed seemed to be belied by Moffat's. In the course of December, however, more detailed information came to hand. It was not the text of the treaty, but showed how far Kruger might stretch the meaning of that text.

The information came in a private letter "from a gentleman at Pretoria who is well informed respecting Transvaal affairs to a gentleman of high commercial standing at Kimberley," who however was visiting Johannesburg when the letter was written.[133] It was passed on "in the strictest confidence" to Robinson, who suppressed the names of the writer and the recipient. The gentleman from Kimberley appears to have asked his friend in Pretoria for information, on the ground that he intended to invest money in the Tati goldfields, but needed assurance about the political situation there before he did so. The gentleman in Pretoria therefore had a long interview with the president, from whom he learned that Matabeleland, including Tati, "is now officially under the Protection and Sovereignty of this State, and there is a Consul and Resident of this Government appointed and already in office there." The consul was expected to return to Pretoria shortly, bringing with him copies of all concessions granted so far by Lobengula, so that these could be submitted to the government for approval. "One clause of the Convention [i.e., the Grobler treaty] is: that the King shall *not* have the right to grant any concessions or make any contract with anybody whatsoever, without the approval of this Government." Once that approval was given, the concessions would have "great value, as the Government here will then be responsible, that the niggers cannot break them." The president told the gentleman in Pretoria to advise his correspondent to wait a week or two before investing money in the Tati concession, as that concession would then be before him for approval. If it were approved it would be safe. All this information was "*official* and *perfectly reliable.*" The letter was written on 9 December; Grobler had in fact left Bulawayo four days earlier.

According to Fitzpatrick, the gentlemen in Pretoria and Kimberley respectively were Alois Nellmapius and Alfred Beit. Beit of course would have shown the letter to Rhodes (on whose behalf he probably made the enquiry in the first place) and it must have been Rhodes who showed it to Robinson. The high commissioner was in Grahamstown at Christmas, attending the South African Exhibition in honour of the queen's Golden Jubilee. Rhodes and Shippard arrived there unheralded, unnoticed by the local *Journal*, with no time for festivities, and presumably bringing the letter from the "gentleman in Pretoria." The matter was so urgent that the high commissioner was made to attend to it on Christmas day. On the 26th Shippard dispatched the instructions to Moffat.[134]

He asked Moffat to ascertain the truth of the report and to procure a copy of the treaty or agreement. "If there is no truth in these reports, you can point out to Lo Bengula, the risk he runs of troublesome complications with foreign states . . . You can also point out that Her Majesty's Government has no wish either to obtain possession of his country or to interfere with his sovereign rights, and that if he desires to secure himself against insidious attempts or open aggression without losing his independence, this result might be attained if he could induce Her Majesty's Government to conclude with him a treaty similar to that recently entered into by Zambili, a copy of which is enclosed."

Zambili, the queen regent of Tongaland, was in an even more exposed position than Lobengula. The British annexation of Zululand in 1887 left Tongaland the only independent native territory between the British and the Portuguese possessions, a territory accordingly coveted by the Transvaal and Germany; and when the Portuguese tried to impose their rule on Zambili she "considered herself English" and asked for a British protectorate. This was not yet declared, but on July 6 her representatives signed an agreement with the governor of Natal, by which she undertook not to enter into any negotiations with any state without the previous knowledge and sanction of the high commissioner.[135] The vital paragraph of the subsequent treaty with Lobengula was identical with that of the Zambili treaty.

Lobengula did not "consider himself English"—or Boer; he was alarmed by the crowd of concession-hunters and by the signs that more was being read into his treaty with Grobler than the mere "renewal of friendship" that he had intended; he was so reluctant to put his mark to any more documents that Moffat for a time regarded the attempt as hopeless.

In spite of the bonds between their fathers, Lobengula was a little suspicious of Moffat, and he had doubts about committing himself to the English. Moffat said of the Ndebele that "they may like us better, but they fear the Boers more"; they knew about Majuba. Why did the British give up the Transvaal without a struggle, if it were not that the Boers were too strong for them? Grobler had used this argument for all it was worth, but Renny-Tailyour had been able to turn even the abandonment of the Transvaal to good account. It was given up, he said, because the Queen would not have unwilling subjects; nor, therefore, would she declare a protectorate over Lobengula against his will.[136]

Kgama had wanted a protectorate, but this was a sore point with the Ndebele. That the slave without a country should be sheltered behind the Union Jack and the border police was a rankling grievance, for which the chain of responsibility ran from Moffat through Shippard or Warren to the high commissioner. The great queen, however, was represented by a different set of men in Natal: the governor, and most notably the Shepstone family. When Renny-Tailyour and Boyle, representing the group of interests revolving round Lippert, arrived in Matabeleland some weeks before Moffat, they brought a letter from "Offy" Shepstone, then in Swaziland, conveying a friendly message to Lobengula from his uncle the Swazi king; and an old Swazi induna, Silas Mdhluli, to deliver it. By this means they gave Lobengula, intentionally or not, the impression that they had an official status.

There appeared then to be two separate missions from the queen, and of the

43 The Advance into the Interior

two Lobengula preferred the one that had no connection with Bechuanaland. He would like to be protected and to have a British resident in his country, but from Natal, and preferably one of the sons of "Somtseu." All this was explained in a letter composed in great secrecy, most of it before Moffat's arrival, and dispatched to "Offy" Shepstone about the middle of December. The letter was passed on, through official channels in Natal, to Robinson.[137]

It took Moffat some time to discover why he was making no progress with the king. When he did discover the reason he was able to convince Lobengula that the government would not send two missions unknown to each other. Renny-Tailyour and Boyle had insisted on secrecy, but his, Moffat's, mission had been given the fullest publicity. He was thus the only channel of communication with the queen.

This point having been made, Lobengula was prepared to accept a treaty on the lines of the precedent set in Zambili's case. It ran as follows:

> The chief Lo Bengula, Ruler of the tribe known as the Amandebele, together with the Mashuna and Makalaka, tributaries of the same, hereby agrees to the following articles and conditions:-
>
> That peace and amity shall continue for ever between Her Britannic Majesty, Her subjects, and the Amandebele people; and the contracting chief Lo Bengula engages to use his utmost endeavours to prevent any rupture of the same, to cause the strict observance of this treaty, and so to carry out the spirit of the treaty of friendship which was entered into between his late father, the Chief Umsiligaas with [sic] the then Governor of the Cape of Good Hope in the year of our Lord 1836.
>
> It is hereby further agreed by Lo Bengula, Chief in and over the Amandebele country with its dependencies as aforesaid, on behalf of himself and people, that he will refrain from entering into any correspondence or treaty with any Foreign State or Power to sell, alienate, or cede, or permit or countenance any sale, alienation or cession of the whole or any part of the said Amandebele country under his chieftainship, or upon any other subject, without the previous knowledge and sanction of Her Majesty's High Commissioner for South Africa.
>
> In faith of which I, Lo Bengula, on my part have hereunto set my hand at Gubulawayo, Amandebeleland, this eleventh day of February, and of Her Majesty's reign the fifty-first.
> Lo Bengula.

The elements had worked for Moffat: cloud prevented the Ndebele from seeing an eclipse of the sun which occurred on that day.[138]

As the news of the treaty reached Shippard, Robinson, the Colonial Office, Pretoria, and Lisbon it provoked varied reactions. Shippard was uneasy because the document did not bear the marks of the consenting indunas, and because it was unilateral in form. Would it be advisable to get a new treaty in place of it? No, thought Robinson; reopening the question would only arouse suspicion. The three "dance doctors" were present and consenting, even if their marks were not on the paper. In London, the unilateral form appeared to be an advantage, disposing of one of the first questions to be raised—"to what extent Her Majesty's Government ought to be committed to defence of Lobengula in case of attack?" It was not committed; there was no protectorate. The absence of the indunas' marks raised another question, to which Fairfield had found an answer: "The fact that the Treaty was not signed by the Indunas would be an additional reason for giving it the go-by." Without wasting time on further correspondence, he would "negative the whole thing at once." Why make trouble with the Portuguese, who claimed the territory?

Hemming disagreed. Portugal's claims were "altogether shadowy, and need not be regarded." Robinson was satisfied with the treaty; it should not be rejected without consultation with him. And there was the new mood of the public: "Government would be likely to incur much blame when it became known that they had hastily rejected an agreement entailing little responsibility, but which gave them a hold over what may prove a very valuable territory."[139]

Protests were to be expected from Portugal ("need not be regarded") and from the South African Republic. How could Moffat's treaty be defended to Kruger, whose earlier treaty must surely prevail over a later one?

This was a question for the Foreign Office; indeed, for a decision by Lord Salisbury himself. His decision was based on somewhat tortuous reasoning. Article IV of the London Convention permitted the Transvaal to conclude treaties with "native tribes" to the north of the republic, but not with any "State or Nation" other than the Orange Free State. Matabeleland was so highly organized that it must be regarded, if not as a state, then at any rate as a nation, rather than a tribe. The Grobler treaty was therefore *ultra vires* and of no effect.[140]

This point having been settled to the satisfaction of the Colonial Office—no one there dared to cross swords with Lord Salisbury—Robinson was given authority to ratify the treaty, which was accordingly gazetted in Cape Town on 25 April. The expected protests followed. The Portuguese government protested against the inclusion of the "Mashuna and Makalaka" tributaries, whose territory it claimed; it reserved its rights. In conversation with the British minister in Lisbon, however, De Barros Gomes showed little hope of beating Britain on the ground she had chosen. He was concerned rather to stop the British advance at the Zambezi, so that Portugal's dream of a transcontinental empire might still be realised north of the river.[141]

When Williams on 16 May officially informed Kruger of the treaty, the president protested on the spot and said that he would send a written reply to the high commissioner. For some reason the formal protest was not written until 30 November, by which time the chances of its influencing the course of events were even slighter than in May. Three of Kruger's arguments could as easily have been used at the earlier date: the earlier treaty (Grobler's) invalidated the later (Moffat's); Moffat's did not bear the marks of indunas; the treaty conflicted with the spirit (Kruger could have said the "unwritten understanding") of the London negotiations of 1884. A fourth point, that Lobengula denied (to Frederik Grobler) having signed the Moffat treaty, had not come to hand in May.[142]

In June Robinson suggested that Portugal, Germany, and the Transvaal be informed that the country between the Limpopo and the Zambezi, west of the Portuguese province of Sofala and east of the 20th meridian, was now regarded by Her Majesty's government as a British sphere of influence. This concept, envisaged by articles 6 and 9 of the General Act of the Berlin West African Conference in 1885, had been used officially in the Anglo-German treaty of that year. A sphere of influence did not, in international law, exclude any power that had not recognized it by treaty; nor did it require the "effective occupation" which the Berlin act imposed in the case of annexations—only on the coast, and not even there for protectorates. But a state claiming a sphere of influence thereby, at the least, warned other states off the ground and made it known that their intrusion would be an unfriendly act. The Foreign Office, through the Colonial Office, on 24 July 1888, authorized Sir Hercules Robinson to inform President Kruger of the British claim to a sphere of influence in both Lobengula's and (beyond the protectorate) Kgama's countries.[143]

By that date, however, the interest of outsiders in those countries had developed beyond the point reached when Moffat obtained his treaty.

NOTES CHAPTER I

1 R.F. Burton, *The Lands of Cazembe: Lacerda's Journey to Cazembe in 1798*, p.20.
2 Richard Lovett, *The History of the London Missionary Society, 1795-1895*, vol. I, ch.I.
3 These and other unfamiliar proper names are briefly identified in the index; African, Afrikaans, and Dutch common nouns in the glossary.
4 "The crushing," in the Nguni languages; in Sotho, *Difaqane*.
5 For the rise of Shaka and the migrations of his defeated enemies, see M. Wilson and L.M. Thompson, ed., *The Oxford History of South Africa*, vol. I, pp.336-51, 391-405; A.T. Bryant, *Olden Times in Zululand and Natal*; J.D. Omer-Cooper, *The Zulu Aftermath*.
6 The stages of Sebetwane's journey were recorded by Livingstone: I. Schapera, ed., *Livingstone's Private Journals, 1851-1853*, pp.18-22.
7 Bryant, *Olden Times*, pp.471-2; Omer-Cooper, *Zulu Aftermath*, pp.65-7.
8 The most thoroughly researched account of these Ndebele movements is in Julian Cobbing, "The Ndebele Under the Khumalos" (thesis, University of Lancaster), pp.15-38. See also Bryant, *Olden Times*, ch.42; Omer-Cooper, *Zulu Aftermath*, ch. 9; Peter Becker, *The Path of Blood: The Rise and Conquests of Mzilikazi*; William F. Lye, "The Ndebele Kingdom South of the Limpopo River," *Journal of African History*, x, 1 (1969), pp.100-1.
9 *Impi* meant a military party or expeditionary force of any size.

10 The best general history of the Trek is still Eric A. Walker, *The Great Trek* (which Walker with justification regarded as his best book). There is a large literature on the subject in Afrikaans, mostly specialized. A symposium of articles, still authoritative, was published as *Die Groot Trek: Gedenkuitgawe van die Huisgenoot*, December 1938.

11 In R. Foster Windram, "Matabele Traditions" (records of oral interviews), (National Archives of Zimbabwe, WI 8/1/2) evidence of Ntabeni, pp.1, 5, 15-16, 29, 41-2, 68-9; (WI 8/1/1) evidence of Siatcha, pp.1-3; Ginyalitshe, pp.1-5, 8, 26; Mvutu and Posela, pp.1-3; Ngungu (Mkandhla), pp.1-4; Ncupela, pp.2-3. To avoid confusion, in this and subsequent note references to the Foster Windram collection (though not in the text) the names of the witnesses will be spelt as in that source. See also R. Summers and C.W. Pagden, *The Warriors*, p.71; Omer-Cooper, *Zulu Aftermath*, pp.146-8; Becker, *Path of Blood*, pp.181-5. *Induna* meant an officer, military or civil, for which there is no exact equivalent in English.

12 For Potgieter's part in all these events see Carol Potgieter and N.H. Theunissen, *Kommandant-Generaal Hendrik Potgieter*. See also J.I. Rademeyer, *Die Land Noord van die Limpopo*, p.13; H.S. Pretorius and D.W. Kruger, eds., *Voortrekker-Argiefstukke, 1829-1849*, pp.160-1. Another explanation of the name *Enteleka* (Hendrik) is a derivation from ntheleka, the attacker. (Summers and Pagden, *Warriors*, pp.64-5).

13 For the brief account of the Shona which follows I have used, in addition to specific references given in other notes, many articles scattered through the volumes of *Native Affairs Department Annual* (*NADA*), and also: Hilda Kuper and A.J.B. Hughes, *The Shona and the Ndebele of Southern Rhodesia*; Eric Stokes and Richard Brown, ed., *The Zambesian Past*; Charles Bullock, *The Mashona*; F.W.T. Posselt, *Fact and Fiction*; D.N. Beach, "Historians and the Shona Empires," parts I and II (Henderson Seminar Papers nos.19 and 20); Edward A. Alpers, "Dynasties of the Mutapa-Rozwi Complex," *Journal of African History*, XI, 2 (1970). Unfortunately this book had been finished before the appearance of Dr. Beach's most important work, *The Shona and Zimbabwe, 900-1850*.

14 In this connection see "The Unification of the Native Languages" in *NADA*, 1955, pp.114-19.

15 The extent of the killing is difficult to establish. Reports and traditions vary with the source, so that some deponents (e.g. Umzila Mandoropa, p.1, in Foster Windram WI 8/1/1) say that few were killed, while others (e.g. Nkani, p.1 in ibid.) say that many were. The people of the former witness, when Mzilikazi arrived in the country, had not fought but had "joined him." Possibly almost all the killing was of those who attempted to resist. For this whole passage I have followed D.N. Beach, "Ndebele Raiders and Shona Power," *Journal of African History*, XV, 4 (1974), pp.633-51.

16 J.P.R. Wallis, ed., *The Matabele Journals of Robert Moffat, 1829-60*, vol. I, p.241.

17 Cobbing, "Ndebele under the Khumalos," pp.32, 117. For the older view, see e.g., A.J.B. Hughes, *Kin, Caste and Nation Among the Rhodesian Ndebele*; N.M.B. Bhebe, "Some Aspects of Ndebele Relations with the Shona in the Nineteenth Century," *Rhodesian History*, IV (1973); Omer-Cooper, *Zulu Aftermath*, pp.147-50.

18 Cobbing's interpretation is given in his article "The Evolution of the Ndebele Ama-

butho," *Journal of African History*, XV, 4 (1974), pp.607-31, and in a slightly revised form in ch. III of "Ndebele under the Khumalos." With these compare Bhebe, "Ndebele Relations with the Shona," pp.31-2; Summers and Pagden, *Warriors*, pp.139-54; Posselt, *Fact and Fiction*, pp.175-8; R. Summers, "The Military Doctrine of the Matabele," in *NADA*, 1955, pp.7-15.

19 Summers and Pagden, *Warriors*, pp.25, 28, 36-42, 160; E.A. Maund in Command Papers, United Kingdom, C4643, no.34, encl.8; Frank Johnson's Journal (National Archives of Zimbabwe, JO 3/3/2), 5 June 1887; Political Papers of John Smith Moffat (typescript in National Archives), 5 December 1888 and 15 September 1890. But Thomas Maxwell in Diary (National Archives MA 1/2) reckons the strength of the army as 8,000.

20 Evidence of Ntabeni in Foster Windram (WI 8/1/2), p.38; Colonial Office, correspondence with High Commissioner for South Africa, CO 417/19/6973, pp.589-96; cf. David Carnegie, *Among the Matabele*, ch. 5; Summers and Pagden, *Warriors*, p.92.

21 T.M. Thomas, *Eleven Years in Central South Africa*, pp.227-40; Wallis, *Journals of Robert Moffat*, vol. I, p.265; Posselt, *Fact and Fiction*, p.39.

22 In Foster Windram (WI 8/1/2), evidence of Ntabeni, pp.7-8, 31-2, 70, 79; (WI 8/1/1) evidence of Ngungu (Mkandhla), pp.5-7; evidence of Ncupela, pp.2-3; evidence of Mvutu and Posela, pp.1-2; J.P.R. Wallis, ed., *The Northern Goldfields Diaries of Thomas Baines*, vol. III, p.683; Edward C. Tabler, *The Far Interior: Chronicles of Pioneering in the Matabele and Mashona Countries, 1847-1879*, p.374; F.W.T. Posselt, "Nkulumana: The Disputed Succession," in *NADA*, 1923, pp.29-42; W.A. Carnegie, "Brief Notes on Lobengula and his People," in *NADA*, 1933, p.14. Nkulumane (real or pretended) was said to have died at Pugeni (WI 8/1/1, evidence of Ndakama, p.1; Ngungu, p.7). Cobbing points out that disloyalty to Lobengula extended to many other *amabutho*, and that the king's leniency in not punishing these also was to cause trouble throughout his reign (see his thesis "Ndebele under the Khumalos," pp.273-81). The real Nkulumane was almost certainly dead; the pretender, Kanda, was being used by his employer Sir Theophilus Shepstone as an agent of Natal politics.

23 Oliver Ransford, *Bulawayo, Historic Battleground of Rhodesia*, pp.33-9, 46, 50; Tabler, *Far Interior*, p.31; Wallis, *Diaries of Thomas Baines*, vol. II, pp.314, 328, 337, 543; vol. III, p.703; Thomas, *Central South Africa*, pp.240-1; Jeannie M. Boggie, *First Steps in Civilizing Rhodesia*, p.278; Edward C. Tabler, *Pioneers of Rhodesia*, s.v. Halyet.

24 Edward C. Tabler, *Zambezia and Matabeleland in the Seventies*, p.77. Modern readers will be interested to know that Lobengula did not want his soldiers to smoke, because their lungs would then be full of smoke and they would not be able to run; and that he wanted the young men, *amajaha*, to drink milk, not beer. (Evidence of Ntabeni in Foster Windram, WI 8/1/2, p.57.)

25 F.C. Selous, *Travel and Adventure in South-East Africa*, p.156; Colonial Office Confidential Print, Africa, South, CO 879/30/369 no.64, encl. Lobengula was regarded as a clever judge, but not as a soldier like his father. After the fight against the rebels in 1870 he never again went into battle with his army. (Evidence of Siatcha, p.11, in Foster Windram, WI 8/1/1.)

26 Reminiscences of Ellerton Fry (National Archives FR 1/4/1).

27 P.J. van der Merwe, *Nog Verder Noord*, is a minute study of the evidence bearing on this trip.

28 G.W. Eybers, ed., *Select Documents Illustrating South African Constitutional History*, pp.357-9.

29 The true explanation of this event is given by D.C. McGill in "A History of the Transvaal, 1852-1864" (thesis, University of Cape Town), pp.349-73. I owe this reference to the late Professor J.S. Marais. Livingstone's *Missionary Travels and Researches in South Africa*, pp.133-4, gives his side of the story. See J.A.I. Agar-Hamilton, *The Native Policy of the Voortrekkers*, pp.207-9.

30 Potgieter and Theunissen, *Potgieter*, pp.256-61; Rademeyer, *Limpopo*, pp.17-18; J.S. du Plessis, *Die Ontstaan en Ontwikkeling van die Amp van die Staatspresident in die Zuid-Afrikaansche Republiek (1858-1902)*, in *Archives Yearbook for South African History*, 1955 (I), pp.91-3; F.A.F. Wichmann, *Die Wordingsgeskiedenis van die Zuid-Afrikaansche Republiek, 1838-1860*, in *Archives Yearbook for South African History*, 1941 (II), p.121.

31 Wallis, *Journals of Robert Moffat*, vol. II, p.111.

32 Tabler, *Pioneers of Rhodesia*, s.v. Viljoen, Jacobs, Hartley.

33 R.H. Thackeray, "Henry Hartley, African Hunter and Explorer," *Journal of the Royal African Society*, 37 (1938), pp.283-97; cf. pp.273-6.

34 Tabler, *Pioneers of Rhodesia*, s.v. Hartley, Finaughty, Leask.

35 Wallis, *Journals of Robert Moffat*, vol. I, p.241. By 1886 the fly was almost unknown at the Falls and Pandamatenga (C4956, no.4, encl.).

36 Paul F. Russell, *Man's Mastery of Malaria*, ch.2, 3.

37 Wallis, *Journals of Robert Moffat*, vol. I, pp.3-31.

38 Ibid., vol. I, Third Journey.

39 The development of these plans can be followed in both of Livingstone's books (*Missionary Travels and Researches in South Africa* and *Narrative of an Expedition to the Zambesi and its Tributaries*).

40 There are many accounts of this; e.g., Edwin W. Smith, *Great Lion of Bechuanaland*, ch.4, 5.

41 Wallis, *Journals of Robert Moffat*, vol. II, Fifth Journey.

42 The Ngwato frequently moved their principal town, for reasons of sanitation, defence or water supply. It had been at Shoshong from about 1770 to 1817, then at Serowe, then back to Shoshong about 1840. (A. Sillery, *Founding a Protectorate*, p.202; *The Bechuanaland Protectorate*, p.117.)

43 John Mackenzie, *Ten Years North of the Orange River*, ch.14; W.D. Mackenzie, *John Mackenzie: South African Missionary and Statesman*, pp.69-95.

44 Maund Papers, University of the Witwatersrand, B45a. See below, pp.55-6.

45 Dr. A. Petermann, *Mittheilungen aus Justus Perthes' Geographischer Anstalt*, Ergänzungsband VIII (1873-4), no.37 (Carl Mauchs Reisen im Innern von Süd-Afrika, 1865-72), pp.26-7; E. Mager, *Karl Mauch, Lebensbild eines Afrikareisenden*, pp.94-7. Both these works present a favourable picture of Mauch, the man, which is buttressed by carefully selected and edited portions of his writings. When the complete text of his journals became available in recent years a different Mauch was revealed: "a man plagued by emotionalism, always willing to accept, seldom giving and utterly incapable of getting along with anyone for long"; to which may be added "his

aptitude for self-pity . . . and his capacity for hate, be it for an individual or for a foreign nation as a whole." See F.O. Bernhard, "Discoverer of Simbabye: The Story of Karl Mauch," *Rhodesiana*, 21, pp.19-35 and 22, pp.28-44.

46 Mager, *Mauch*, pp.97-8.

47 Tabler, *Pioneers of Rhodesia*, s.v. London and Limpopo Mining Company, Swinburne; *The Far Interior*, pp.291, 300-3, 308-14.

48 Tabler, *Pioneers of Rhodesia*, s.v. London and Limpopo Mining Company, Swinburne; Wallis, *Diaries of Thomas Baines*, vol. ii, pp.317, 340, 543, 556-8; vol. iii, pp.695-6.

49 Tabler, *Pioneers of Rhodesia*, s.v. London and Limpopo Mining Company, S.A. Goldfields Exploration Company, D. Francis, S. Edwards; CO 417/14/11043, pp.593 ff.

50 G.M. Theal, *History of South Africa from 1795 to 1872*, vol. v, pp.16-23; E.A. Walker, *A History of Southern Africa*, p.332, and *Historical Atlas of South Africa*, p.18; D.W. Kruger, *Die Weg na die See*, pp.78-182.

51 Walker, *History of Southern Africa*, pp.332-40; Theal, *South Africa*, vol. iv, ch.77, 78, 79; vol. v, ch.84, 85; J.A.I. Agar-Hamilton, *The Road to the North*, ch.4, 5, 6. Sir Philip Wodehouse was both governor of the Cape Colony and high commissioner for South Africa. The latter office, created in 1847, was the imperial government's agency for dealing with territories outside the Cape Colony. Thus, after the Cape got responsible government in 1872, the governor acted on, but the high commissioner independently of, the advice of the colonial ministers. In this history we are concerned with this two-faced officer in his wider capacity.

52 There is a large body of writing on this subject. See, e.g., D.M. Schreuder, *Gladstone and Kruger*, and C.W. de Kiewiet, *The Imperial Factor in South Africa*.

53 Agar-Hamilton, *Road to the North*, ch.9-13.

54 Wallis, *Diaries of Thomas Baines*, vol. i, p.27; vol. ii, pp.325-6, 552, 562-3, 573; Tabler, *Far Interior*, see index s.v. Lee; *Pioneers of Rhodesia*, s.v. Lee.

55 Schreuder, *Gladstone and Kruger*, ch.7; Kenneth O. Hall, *Imperial Proconsul: Sir Hercules Robinson and South Africa, 1881-1889*, especially ch.4; W.D. Mackenzie, *Mackenzie*, ch.10, 11; A. Sillery, *John Mackenzie of Bechuanaland*, ch.9; CO 879/23/301, p.4.

56 CO 417/5/9382, p.19.

57 The text is in C3914; also in Eybers, *South African Constitutional History*, pp.469-74, and in Schreuder, *Gladstone and Kruger*, appendix. For the negotiations, Agar-Hamilton, *Road to the North*, ch.12; D.W. Kruger, *Paul Kruger*, vol. ii, ch.2 (a chapter headed "Triomf in Engeland").

58 CO 417/1/12074, p.234; C4194, no.30, encl.4. For the concept of the protectorate, Claire Palley, *The Constitutional History and Law of Southern Rhodesia, 1888-1965*, pt. i, ch.4. The notions entertained in the Colonial Office at this time appear in the minutes on the Bechuanaland files, passim. From this point it is appropriate to call Botswana by what was to be its official name, Bechuanaland.

59 CO 417/1/8280, p.104, Derby's minute; and 14184, p.452, Derby's minute. For Mackenzie's role in Bechuanaland see Anthony J. Dachs, "Missionary Imperialism—the Case of Bechuanaland," *Journal of African History*, xiii, 4 (1972), pp.647-58, and A. Sillery, *Mackenzie*, passim. For the period of Mackenzie's commissionership, ibid., ch.10, 11.

60 The Colonial Office files, Confidential Prints and Blue Books for 1884 cover all these events at length. See also Agar-Hamilton, *Road to the North*, ch.13, 14, 15; John Mackenzie, *Austral Africa, Losing it or Ruling it*, books II and III; W.D. Mackenzie, *Mackenzie*, ch.12, 13; J.G. Lockhart and C.M. Woodhouse, *Rhodes*, ch.6; Basil Williams, *Cecil Rhodes*, ch.8.

61 CO 417/2/16441, pp.93-4; *Cape Times* and *Cape Argus* of 25 September 1884 (enclosed in CO 417/2/17955, pp.99-113). Reports of many other meetings, resolutions and petitions are scattered through C4213, C4275, C4310.

62 C4251, no.12, p.10; no.18, p.13; CO 417/1/9445, p.92; Palley, *Constitutional History*, p.85, n.5. At this point it may be useful to explain that when a dispatch from the high commissioner reached the Colonial Office, it passed through the hands of several officials before it reached the permanent under-secretary, and after him the secretary of state. Each in turn wrote a minute expressing his opinion. In almost every case it was the officials who formulated the policy and composed the reply; the political head merely added "I agree," or "So proceed." The minutes of Edward Fairfield, A.W.L. Hemming, John Bramston and their colleagues—all strictly confidential—give the best insight we have into the mind of the Colonial Office and the reasons for its decisions.

63 CO 417/2/18877, pp.152-3; Agar-Hamilton, *Road to the North*, pp.352-4, Krüger, *Kruger*, vol. II, pp.69-72.

64 CO 417/2/18878, p.155.

65 CO 417/3/18625, p.357; C4224, nos.1, 2, 3.

66 C4190, C4262 and CO 879/21/274 and 22/286 deal with the German protectorate and the correspondence preceding it. The protectorate—like the British one in Bechuanaland—came to life by stages; the first announcement reached Cape Town on 24 April 1884 (CO 879/21/274, no.63); CO 417/1/14068, pp.447-50).

67 CO 417/5/10789, p.47; C4432, no.1. See Hall, *Imperial Proconsul*, pp.233-4.

68 CO 417/2/303, p.351. See A. Sillery, *Founding a Protectorate*, pp.40-1. Characteristically, the order-in-council of 27 January merely provided for jurisdiction under the Foreign Jurisdiction Acts. That jurisdiction equals protectorate was a proposition made apparent by a gazette extraordinary in Cape Town on 23 March.

69 CO 417/5/9591, p.100.

70 CO 417/5/11085, p.116.

71 C4643, nos.22, 30; CO 417/6/13816, p.83; 14353, pp.392-5; 14667, p.396; 16112, p.400; CO 417/7/17263, p.137; A. Sillery, *Founding a Protectorate*, p.43.

72 Maund papers, B45a; C4643, no.34, encl.

73 E.T. Cook and Alexander Wedderburn, eds., *The Complete Works of John Ruskin*, vol. XX, p.42.

74 Lockhart and Woodhouse, *Rhodes*, pp.69-70. In a "confession of faith," undated, in RH Mss Afr. t 1, no.17, Rhodes wrote: "I contend that we are the first race in the world, and that the more of the world we inhabit the better it is for the human race."

75 CO 879/21/274, no.1, encl. The population of Great Britain in 1881 was 29,710,000.

76 "Vindex," *Cecil Rhodes: His Political Life and Speeches, 1881-1900*, p.62.

77 Ibid., p.63; Agar-Hamilton, *Road to the North*, p.234.

78 CO 417/4/7677, p.332.

79 CO 417/12/2999, p.801; 9/18849, p.327; 4/6686, pp.304-5; 8/8597, p.265.

80 CO 417/7/1084, p.491. My italics.

81 CO 417/9/4386, pp.245-6, and map annexed.

82 CO 417/7/1084, p.491.

83 CO 417/12/2999, p.806.

84 CO 417 10/3646, p.233 and 5494, p.338.

85 CO 417/9/4474, pp.150-4.

86 Lockhart and Woodhouse, *Rhodes*, p.108.

87 This is not to say that Robinson, as is sometimes assumed, was a mere tool of Rhodes. Interviewed in March 1895 (*Cape Times* weekly edition, 8 November 1897, obituary of Lord Rosmead), Robinson said "the truth is, I saw Northern Expansion before I ever saw Rhodes." See also Hall, *Imperial Proconsul*, ch.4 (and other chapters, passim).

88 C4653, no.34, encl.

89 CO 417/9/4386, p.239.

90 Journal of the Society of Arts, 5 March 1886 (encl. in CO 417/12, p.615). Among many pleas from non-official sources for the annexation of Mashonaland, the missionary William Sykes in 1878 (LMS Papers, LO 6/1/5, Sykes on 21 June 1878) and Frank Mandy in 1887 (CO 417/14/6072, pp.54-69) may be quoted.

91 CO 417/10/5494, p.338.

92 CO 417/11/19302, p.370.

93 CO 417/13/3035, p.127; C4956, no.4, encl. For the question of Fry's dismissal, CO 417/6/15647, pp.255 ff.; CO 879/24/317, no.18, encl.

94 CO 417/13/2356, p.85.

95 CO 417/13/2357, p.89.

96 C5237, no.5, encl., pp.22-3.

97 Ibid.

98 C5237, no.7, encl., p.23.

99 Political Papers of J.S. Moffat, 19 November 1887 (from notebook) and 6 March 1888, 26 September 1888, 29 April 1891.

100 C5237, no.5, encl.

101 Cape Archives, *Bechuanaland* 95/140, quoted in Rademeyer, *Limpopo*, pp.155-7.

102 CO 417/11/19302, p.370; C5237, no.20, p.33. Under European rule the locative Taung had become Taungs.

103 CO 879/30/369, no.90, encl., pp.212-3; CO 417/9/4386, pp.254-5. In this report Maund quoted from the letter, not quite accurately. For Joubert's uncles, see above, p.10.

104 Journal of Frank Johnson (JO 3/3/2), 19 July 1887; CO 879/30/369, no.40, encl., p.71; no.84, encl., p.197; Rademeyer, *Limpopo*, p.52; C5918, no.36, p.130.

105 Rademeyer, *Limpopo*, p.52. My translation.

106 National Archives, Lobengula papers (LO 1/1/1), Shippard to Lobengula, 29 April 1887.

107 Rademeyer, *Limpopo*, pp.51-4; Political Papers of J.S. Moffat, Moffat to Shippard, 6 October 1888; CO 879/30/369, no.13, encl., pp.22-4.

108 H. Marshall Hole, *The Making of Rhodesia*, p.61.

109 E.g., CO 417/16/20063, p.85; CO 417/19/3642, p.182. For Lobengula's ignorance of the contents of the document, CO 879/30/369, no.101, encl. 2, pp.230-2.

52 Rhodes and Rhodesia

110 RH Mss Afr. t 5, ff. 442-5.

111 Johnson's manuscript Journal is in the National Archives, JO 3/3/2. The account in his memoirs, *Great Days*, is based partly on the Journal, but draws also on a not always reliable memory. Johnson had landed in Cape Town as a penniless immigrant; his interest in the interior dated from his dropping in by chance to the great meeting on 24 September 1884; he had enlisted in Warren's expedition and then in the BB Police.

112 Wood's manuscript Journal is in National Archives (WO 1/2/1-8). Edward Chapman was not related to the hunter James Chapman.

113 Johnson's Journal, 15 May 1887. The original grant by Kgama is in Johnson Papers (JO 3/1/1). See also CO 417/16/20062, pp.60-74; 20063, pp.80-95; 22645, pp.378-409; 22646, p.413; 23249, p.517; CO 417/21/11562, pp.50-9.

114 Johnson's Journal, 13 November 1887; Diary of George Westbeech (National Archives WE 1/2/1), p.56.

115 C5363, no.7, pp.40-2.

116 Wood's Journal, under date 12 June 1887, but referring to 14 June 1887.

117 Johnson's Journal, 11 October 1887, and February-March, passim.

118 Ibid., 19 November 1887; C5363, no.7, encl. In his Journal Johnson says the fine was £102.

119 Wood's Journal, 1 September 1887.

120 Johnson's Journal, 12 November 1887.

121 Ibid., 26 June and 28 July 1887.

122 Ibid., 12 November 1887.

123 Ibid., 31 August 1887.

124 For some of the members of the inner council at different times see Cobbing, "Ndebele under the Khumalos," pp.57, 60, 61. For "smelling out" see Glossary.

125 Wood's Journal, 19 May 1887.

126 Ibid., 10 October 1887.

127 CO 417/15/17090, pp.526-36; 18579, pp.747-9; CO 417/16/20062, pp.60-74; 20063, pp.77-95; 22645, pp.378-412; 22646, pp.413 ff.; 23249, pp.517 ff.; CO 417/19/2931, pp.95 ff.; 3641, pp.156 ff.; Johnson's Journal, 16 December 1887.

128 Johnson's Journal, 16 December 1887. Lobengula Papers, Wood, Francis and Chapman to Lobengula, 15 December 1887. A certified copy of the Wood Concession is in Wood Papers, WO 1/1/1.

129 CO 417/19/4024, p.326. On 27 December 1887, the Grahamstown *Journal* reported that "Mr. Jos. Wood, M.L.A., writes from Shoshong that he has received from the Matabele King the long sought-for concession of mining rights over 4000 square miles in Mashonaland for 99 years," etc. On 5 January 1888, the same paper published an ecstatic report of the "simply unlimited gold in the Wood-Francis-Chapman Concession." The reports show, among other things, that you can't believe all that you read in the papers. For the controversy about the rights to the disputed territory, see the *Cape Argus* (weekly edition), 3 February 1888, and the Grahamstown *Journal*, 11 February 1888 and 10 March 1888 (letter from "Old Trader").

130 CO 417/16/19570, p.33; CO 417/17/24158, p.106; CO 417/19/4081, pp.375-9.

131 Political Papers of J.S. Moffat, 19 November, 3 December and 5 December 1887; CO 417/19/4024, p.326.

132 CO 417/16/22188, pp.317-20. There was another report in the same paper about the

slaughter of a number of Ndebele who had failed to prevent Selous and others from prospecting in Mashonaland, but Moffat cannot have been referring to this. (Dawson Papers in National Archives, DA 1/1/1, 22 November 1887.) Selous gave the lie to this story and thought it might have come from the widow of T.M. Thomas (CO 417/19/3645, pp.195 ff., a cutting from the *Cape Times* of 25 January 1888).

133 CO 417/19/4080, pp.359-63; 4024, p.426.

134 CO 417/19/4080, pp.365-8. Ralph Williams, in *How I Became a Governor*, pp.157-8, tells (in 1913) a story of Grobler's wagon, loading in Pretoria for the journey to Bulawayo, being pointed out to him, with information about Grobler's business; of a telegram he (Williams) sent to Rhodes, and of the consequent instructions sent urgently to Moffat. Rhodes's biographers repeat this story. Williams, however, dates the event "one day, in either 1887 or 1888, I forget which." His telegram would have prompted an *earlier* message from Shippard (see above, p.33), but Shippard's Boxing Day dispatch to Moffat begins by referring to information received "from a non-official, but well-informed source in the Transvaal." This cannot have been a telegram from Williams. Robinson, in sending copies of the documents to London, included Shippard's dispatch immediately after the letter from the "gentleman in Pretoria." The identity of the "gentlemen" is given by Fitzpatrick in the introduction to the popular edition (1900) of *The Transvaal from Within*, p.xiv, quoted by R.I. Lovell in *The Struggle for South Africa, 1875-1899*, p.137.

135 CO 879/26/344, no.18, pp.27-8.

136 CO 879/29/358, no.13, encl.

137 Ibid. Somtseu was the Zulu name of Sir Theophilus Shepstone.

138 CO 417/19/6019, pp.526-7; also in C5524, no.6, p.14. The date 1888 was omitted. For Moffat's account see CO 417/19/6873, pp.606-8, and Political Papers of J.S. Moffat, 11 February 1888. Shippard had drawn up another treaty when he heard that Moffat was on his way down with this one. Shippard's draft has a long preamble referring to the treaty of 1836, which it confirms; otherwise it is similar to Moffat's. It was forgotten until acquired by the National Archives on loan from W.A. Carnegie, who gave permission for it to be transcribed by J.P.R. Wallis. See Political Papers, as above.

139 CO 417/19/5633, pp.482-7; 6019, pp.520-8; 6974, pp.613-6, 623-5; CO 879/29/358, no.5.

140 CO 879/29/358, no.4.

141 CO 879/29/358, nos.14, 15; CO 417/20/10094, p.371; C5524, no.20, p.24.

142 C5524, no.24, encl.; CO 879/30/369, no.101, encl., pp.228-30. Lobengula's denial of the Moffat treaty to F. Grobler bears some marks of casuistry: "as Moffat asked me to enter into a treaty, which I refused, Moffat thereupon said that I must at all events answer that I refused it." The refusal to enter into treaties was precisely the substance of the Moffat treaty (ibid., p.230).

143 CO 879/29/358, nos.30, 32, 36, 38; Palley, *Constitutional History*, pp.3-9; S.E. Crowe, *The Berlin West African Conference, 1884-5*, ch.6.

CHAPTER 2

The Rudd Concession and Its Enemies

Outside the royal kraal of Bulawayo stood the "white men's camp." There the wagons of travellers, hunters, and would-be concessionaires were outspanned, varying in numbers according to the season. There was also a small permanent white population of traders and jacks-of-all-trades, some living at the camp, others normally out in the country but coming in from time to time.

C.D. Rudd described these old hands succinctly as "a rum lot." Moffat annotated his list of them with such remarks as "rather an intelligent man—but utterly demoralized"; "a moral invertebrate"; "has some sense left, and is not so saturated with Kafir beer as most." Thomson longed to have in the country a class of men "who observe Sunday, lead pure and honourable lives and abstain from *fornication* and conduct business upon sound and honourable principles." Bishop Knight-Bruce was told that nine-tenths of the European deaths in the country were due directly or indirectly to drink.[1]

Not an edifying picture, but not unusual on the remote periphery of the European world. That the men should take to themselves African wives and raise coloured families was fair enough, and if some were polygamous that was only the custom of the country. It is harder to judge charitably a man who "got rid of" his African concubine and children before returning to England to marry respectably. As for the demon drink, the missionaries were harsh judges, frontier conditions must be allowed for, and the Ndebele were far from sharing Kgama's hatred of the traffic. "Those Gazaland queens," Ivon Fry recollected in his old age, "used to drink gin like water."[2]

The chief trader in Bulawayo in the seventies and eighties was James Fairbairn, whose ledger book contains the accounts of the king and virtually every European visitor to the town in those decades. James Dawson was Fairbairn's partner. They had a store, while George Arthur ("Elephant") Phillips conducted his business from a wagon. Phillips, originally more hunter than trader, was constantly on the move. He formed a partnership with George Westbeech, who in the early seventies established himself at Pandamatenga, then the terminus of wagon travel in the direction of the Victoria Falls, and for a time monopolized the trade of Barotseland. Remote as he was from the European world, Westbeech ("a gentleman by birth and education") was a worthy representative of it, held in high regard by Lobengula, Lewanika, missionaries, and travellers alike. Phillips managed the Bulawayo end of his business.

Thomas Leask, whom we have met before on hunting trips in the early days, can hardly count as a Matabelelander. He gave up hunting when the elephants retreated into "the fly," settled in the Transvaal as the principal merchant of Klerksdorp—indeed the biggest in the southern Transvaal—and his store became a regular fitting-out place for interior travellers. Westbeech at one time was in his debt; Leask was generous in his handling of this, and Westbeech generous in his acknowledgment.[3]

If Lobengula and his advisers feared the importunate concession hunters now flocking into the country, their anxiety was shared by the old hands, who thought they had a better claim than the johnny-come-latelys to its mineral wealth. In 1881 the four here mentioned—Leask, Fairbairn, Westbeech, and Phillips—made an agreement to share equally any concession they might get from Lobengula. They got one in 1884 for the territory between the Gwelo and the Hunyani—the very thing that Baines's company had got and had since sold to another group. Three years later Johnson reported this grant as "very shaky," but the grantees sent in "a practical miner" to prospect, and refused to give up hope. Fairbairn and Phillips had the advantage of continuous contact with Lobengula. Fairbairn had the custody of the elephant seal, a kind of Great Seal of the Realm which was affixed to documents which the king signed with his mark.[4] Phillips was described by Moffat as "a shadow that follows the King in all his movements. He knows everybody and everything in the country."

How these men obtained a new concession for themselves and their partners, and why Lobengula gave it, can only be guessed. Westbeech, travelling south early in July 1888, met the party of "Matabele" Wilson going up. He gave them a letter to the king, recommending the bearers, but saying that "as a friend of the King and one who had also been a friend of his dead father, Moselikatsi, he hoped that the King would not give away to anyone the concession that had been granted to Philips, Fairbairn and himself." When this letter was delivered, the wagons from the south were beginning to arrive for the season. The old hands must have felt a sense of urgency, and the king may have clutched at a means of warding off the horde of strangers: better the devil you know.

On 14 July the king's mark and the elephant seal were affixed to a new concession: "I Lo Bengula King of the Amandebele hereby grant to Thomas Leask, George Arthur Phillips, George Westbeech and James Fairbairn the sole right to dig for Gold and other minerals in my country to the exclusion of all others except those to whom I have already granted such rights, and that on the condition that I receive one half share of the proceeds of the work carried on by them—on the same principle as my own people work for me." Bowen

Rees (of the LMS) and James Dawson signed as witnesses, and Charles D. Helm (LMS, Hope Fountain) as interpreter.[5]

Westbeech, on trek in the Transvaal, died three days later without knowing of this concession, his share of which was credited to his estate. Fairbairn, travelling south to take the document to Leask, met Moffat on the Mpakwe river and showed it to him. Moffat wrote to Leask, congratulating him, wishing him success, and assuring him that "the agreement is good" and that "Lobengula is to be trusted when he puts his mark to an agreement of this kind." The agreement was certainly good—on the face of it, a concession to end all concessions.[6] Yet it was not strong enough to stand against the pressure that was now to be exerted.

The men who had obtained mining concessions up to this time were, financially speaking, small men. What turned a mere nuisance into a mortal danger to the Ndebele was the taking over of the small men's grants by rich and powerful companies, and the appearance on the scene of new competitors, likewise rich and powerful.

The Wood, Francis, and Chapman syndicate hardly survived its return to Grahamstown. Amid mutual and public recriminations, Francis and Chapman broke away and decided to go north again, seeking a new concession for themselves. Wood held Lobengula's concession for the disputed territory, for what it was worth. An English engineer whom he met in Kimberley, Henry Pauling, took the concession to the Baron d'Erlanger in London, who had an interest in the Caisse des Mines of Paris. With this support behind him, Erlanger agreed to take over the concession if it was proved to be valid and if the ground was really auriferous. He sent Pauling back to visit the territory, taking Wood with him, and to report on these points.[7]

Johnson's company made over its grant to the London financiers George Cawston and Lord Gifford, who formed the Bechuanaland Exploration Company to exploit it. They also formed the Exploring Company to seek a concession from Lobengula, and for this purpose employed E.A. Maund as their agent.[8]

At the beginning of May 1888 Cawston approached the colonial secretary, Lord Knutsford, explaining his intention to obtain a mining concession in Matabeleland, and asking for the government's support. He was told that such support was in the discretion of the high commissioner, and that "Her Majesty's government would give no countenance to any concession or agreement unless it were concluded with the knowledge of, and approved by, that officer." Cawston was able to satisfy the secretary of state of his own financial standing and that of his associates, and Knutsford had no objection to the choice of Maund as agent. This correspondence was published in the next blue book and therefore stood, inconveniently as it proved, in the record.

It was a curious, and for Maund a fortunate, coincidence that he and Pauling happened to be fellow passengers in the *Garth Castle* and that Pauling was a garrulous man who told Maund all his business. He would shoot any man, so he said, who interfered with him in his concession; after all, that country was beyond the reach of civilized government, and one must fend for oneself. The tight-lipped Maund allowed Pauling to believe that he was a hunter, and tried to impress upon his principals the importance of keeping their own business secret.[9] For this purpose they had the right agent; Maund's operations are sometimes difficult for the historian to unravel.

His detailed reports of Matabeleland in 1885 and 1888, though in some important respects misleading, include also a good deal of correct and useful information; but these reports did not involve his own interests. His weakness was an inflated sense of his own importance; with that went an inability to abstain from political interference in any confrontation that he happened to run into. He represented the Exploring Company, whose interest was exclusively in Matabeleland, not the Bechuanaland Exploration Company which had taken over Kgama's concession to Johnson. At Shoshong, however, he thought it his duty to arrange for the defence of that place against the Boers. On the other hand he was reported to have told Kgama that the government intended to take over the disputed territory, and to have offered to assist him in preventing this. At the same time he tried to get Kgama to cede the whole of his country. He borrowed garments, razors, pipe and tobacco, and tried to borrow money, from various people at Shoshong. He told a captain of the Transvaal artillery "the exact number and disposition of the men we are leaving here." While at Shoshong he purported to be a correspondent of *The Times*. "I had to convey to Mr. Maund our self-invited guest," wrote Shippard, "a hint to go as I could not possibly write my report while he was prying into everything." Before he left he threatened Shippard "that he would report me to 'his people' at home who had great influence with Her Majesty's Government."

A thin-skinned man would have taken to heart the telegram that some of this news called forth: "Carry out our instructions and leave Khama's country immediately." Not so Maund. From Bulawayo he reported his extremely favourable reception by the king, and also that Moffat "wishes me in no way to make out that I am an official (for the good of the country I would I were). But has not prevented me from saying I came out from Great Men in England . . . with the approval of 'the powers that be'."[10]

In the race to Bulawayo Maund was well ahead of Pauling, but behind many others. The ultimate winner, Rhodes, had long been absorbed in the business of amalgamating the diamond interests, a drama which reached its climax in March 1888. Rhodes having won control of Barnato's company, the Kimberley Central, Barnato acknowledged defeat. All that remained was to settle the terms of the trust deed for the new company, De Beers Consolidated Mines. That proved difficult. Barnato insisted on a company limited to diamond mining, whereas Rhodes intended to use De Beers as his instrument for "winning the north." At the end of an all-night argument in Jameson's cottage, Barnato gave up: "Some people have a fancy for one thing, and some for another. You have a fancy for making an empire. Well, I suppose I must give it to you." The trust deed therefore enabled De Beers not only to mine diamonds and other minerals, but to conduct banking operations, build railways, annex and govern territory, and raise an army.[11]

De Beers, with a virtual monopoly of the world's diamonds, had the resources for empire-building. As Rhodes wrote to Shippard, however, "it is no use my stepping in for my Company to assist in the government of a shell." If the imperial operation were to pay for itself, as the shareholders might reasonably demand, the company must have mining rights in the country it hoped to annex. A concession must be obtained from Lobengula.

Rhodes had not waited to finish the De Beers business before taking this next step. He had chosen John Fry as his agent to get the concession. Fry was to be well rewarded if he got it, or even if he "did the spadework" for a success by others. About the exact terms of his contract with Rhodes the evidence is conflicting. What is certain is that he got no concession; his efforts can hardly count as "spadework" for the Rudd Concession; he returned to Kimberley to die of cancer in November; his lawyer mysteriously "lost" the document recording the contract; his son Ivon tried vainly to get Rhodes to acknowledge it, but received nothing, and nursed the grievance into his old age.

Fry, or someone associated with him, had been indiscreet. On 16 March 1888 Maurice Heany, travelling south from his prospecting work, wrote to Dawson in Bulawayo with the news that Fry "is coming up your way as an agent of Cecil Rhodes—Rhodes is said to have a grand scheme on with regard to Loben's country—some view of purchasing the whole box of tricks and a big thing generally . . . *for the present let this be confidential.*"[12] It is unlikely that Dawson kept the secret; his partner Fairbairn, in "purchasing the whole box of tricks" for his own group four months later, must have known the kind of competition he was facing. Long before Fry had given up, however, Rhodes had begun to employ other agents.

It was high time. Not only were the agents of Cawston, Gifford, Erlanger, Lippert, and other financiers hurrying to the north, but the South African Republic was taking steps to assert its rights under Grobler's treaty, in disregard of Moffat's. On 26 April the appointment of Grobler as consul to Matabeleland was gazetted in the Transvaal *Staatscourant*. He set out from Pretoria with the materials for a wood-and-iron house to be assembled at Bulawayo, arranged for his wife to follow him, travelled by his old route avoiding Kgama's country, and placed a pont on the Limpopo at Baines Drift to improve communications for the future. As the site of the pont was between the Shashi and Motloutsi tributaries, the route beyond the Limpopo ran through the disputed territory.

Grobler reached Bulawayo in June and presented his credentials. Lobengu-

AUGUSTANA UNIVERSITY COLLEGE
LIBRARY

la's account of the interview was taken down and translated by Helm on 24 August:

> Piet Grobelaar came here a month or two ago. I asked him what he had come for. He said he had brought me the old treaty which was made with Enteleka (Hendrik Potgieter) by Umsiligaas. He said it shows where the boundary is between the Boers and the Matabele. It says that all the country where Khama, Sechele, Gasietsiwe and others, as far south as Marico live, belongs to the Matabele. Grobelaar said he had come to live here, in accordance with that treaty. I asked him why no one had come to live with my father in accordance with this treaty. I said, if anybody came, then let the man come who was said to have been promised by Enteleka and who is sent by him. I asked what was meant by his coming to live here. He said, "I came here to look after people who trouble you." I said, "I do not want you here. It is not necessary, and you need not bring your wife here, as you say you are going to do." I said, "I hear you have been telling your Government that I am under the Transvaal." He said, "That is not true, but it is true that Moffat has been telling people you are now under the British Government." I told him to go.[13]

Some allowance must be made for Lobengula's adapting his words to the audience; this account was what Helm would have wanted to hear. In substance it was probably true, and it reveals an interesting aspect of Grobler's diplomacy. He appealed, not to his own treaty, but to Potgieter's, as if his own had been no more than a "renewal" of an old treaty of friendship, as he had claimed when it was signed. But the old treaty of friendship was the one made by Pretorius; Potgieter's, which resembled Grobler's much more closely, had never in fact come into force.

That Grobler, far from being discouraged, stuck to his plan of going down to the Limpopo to fetch his wife, may suggest that Lobengula had received him less coldly than he claimed to have done. By Grobler's own account, the king had appealed to the republic to protect him against the English concession-hunters. The evidence could equally mean no more than that Grobler was a loyal public servant determined to carry out his instructions at all costs.

The cost proved to be heavy, and it was levied not by Lobengula but by Kgama.

Francis and Chapman, like Grobler, were in Kgama's bad books. In the previous December they, together with Wood, had signed the injudicious letter to Lobengula appealing for an impi to support them. Kgama had also an older grudge against Francis, that he had persistently imported liquor in defiance of Kgama's law. The chief had expelled both men from his country. They now entered it again, on their journey to Bulawayo to seek a new concession. At Shoshong they were arrested and brought before Kgama; the missionary Hepburn acted as interpreter, unnecessarily, as both prisoners spoke Tswana fluently. They professed not to know the charge against them, and by Chapman's account, Hepburn refused to allow them to ask questions. They were dispatched under escort to Moffat, who was then at Mafeking.

Chapman, having ascertained from the lone white policeman in the party that the prisoners were not in his charge, gave the escort the slip and crossed the Limpopo into the Transvaal. When the rest of the party reached Setshele's, that old chief, never on good terms with Kgama, released Francis. He, too, crossed the river.

Both men acted openly and did their best to avoid trouble with the British authorities. They had gone openly—or, as Shippard put it, "had the effrontery" to go—to Shoshong. Now each wrote to Shippard, telling his own version of the story and expressing a willingness to appear before the administrator whenever called upon to do so. They also avowed their intention of continuing on their way to Matabeleland, but by a direct route from the Transvaal, avoiding Kgama's country.[14]

Thus they reached Grobler's pont from the south, at the same moment as Grobler, together with companions who had waited for him at the Shashi, was approaching it from the north. Kgama knew about the movements of Francis and Chapman. He sent a regiment commanded by his half-brother Mokhuchwane to arrest them when they got to his side of the river. Mokhuchwane was young and inexperienced, and his men, as was the Ngwato custom, belonged to the same age-set as himself. Hearing that Grobler, another *persona non grata*, was in the neighbourhood, Mokhuchwane divided his force, one detachment going to the pont and the other veering to the left to meet Grobler.

The encounter with Grobler occurred on Sunday, 8 July. While the evidence afterwards submitted was conflicting, the main outlines of the event emerged quite clearly. After preliminaries which included some fisticuffs and the firing of shots, the Boers succeeded in disarming the first small body of Ngwato to reach them. Mokhuchwane with the bulk of his force then arrived, and both sides laid down their rifles for a parley, the Boers however having revolvers still concealed on their persons. Grobler demanded reparation for the insult and injury in the form of cattle, to the value, Shippard estimated, of £1,500. Mokhuchwane agreed to this demand without any intention of honouring it; he intended to use the negotiation as an opportunity to seize the Boers. He gave the order to do so; rifles were hastily picked up, shots were fired, and Grobler was wounded in the leg. The Boers drove their assailants off and continued their journey to the pont, taking the wounded to safety on the Transvaal side. Sixteen days later, before medical help could arrive, Grobler died there.

On 7 July, the day before the fight with Grobler, the other Ngwato detachment had arrived at the pont, to find Francis and Chapman's wagons already on the north bank. They towed these away from the river and guarded them, but on the 9th were frightened away by rifle fire from the other bank; the wagons were then taken back to the Transvaal side.

Robinson heard of Grobler's death in a telegram from Kruger. He expressed regret and promised an enquiry. Kruger's demand for a joint Anglo-

Transvaal enquiry, and Robinson's insistence on a purely British one to which the republic could send observers, were based on opposing views about the territory in which the incident had occurred. Kruger claimed that it was Lobengula's; Robinson could not concede that point, the boundary question still being unresolved. Kruger believed that the site of the action was north of the 22nd parallel, and so outside the protectorate; Shippard believed that Heany with his prismatic compass had shown it to be south of that parallel. There was a further dispute about an eastern limit of the protectorate: Kruger placed this at 27 degrees east, whereas the British government had put it, rather vaguely, at "about 29°20'." By one reckoning the fight had been outside, by the other within, the protectorate. So the enquiry was held by Shippard, from 29 August to 7 September, with Piet Joubert in attendance as observer for his government. The Boers had an enquiry of their own, on their side of the river.[15]

Soon after Grobler's death his brother Frederik had set out for Bulawayo to fetch the dead man's belongings. When he crossed the pont it was in the company of Francis and Chapman, who were able at last to carry out their mission. The party crossed the disputed territory without interference. Another important person was with them—the great induna Gampu Sithole. Gampu had fled in December 1887, after being detected in an "illicit intrigue" with Lobengula's favourite daughter. The princess had tried to escape too, in the wagon of V.P. Swinburne, but had been caught and brought back. Moffat, hearing of Gampu's return, thought he would be put to death. He was not; it was probably a promise of forgiveness that encouraged him to return. On the other hand the king could not have heard the rumour which Newton reported to the high commissioner: that an expedition was being prepared in the Transvaal to attack and kill Lobengula and enthrone Gampu in his place.

Gampu was forgiven, but from the king's point of view he arrived in bad company. Chapman, riding ahead with young John Lee, reached Bulawayo at the same time, 22 August, as Moffat. After an interview with the king he was, says Moffat, "very subdued." He and Francis were dismissed without a concession. Their partisanship in the boundary question was not the kind of support that Lobengula wanted. As he had written to Francis's partner Clark at Shoshong, "That about Francis calling the Matabele 'impi' am I Francis' boy that he should say so."[16]

Frederik Grobler, playing the same card, fared no better than his travelling companions. He tried "to take up, as a matter of offence against Khama, the fact that the skirmish with Grobelaar took place on this side Motloutsie." Lobengula would have none of it. Grobler then talked wildly of raising his own force in the Transvaal—five hundred men, or three thousand if necessary—whether the government approved or not, to attack the Ngwato. Before six months were over, he said, "Khame would be the late Khame."

Frederik Grobler, Moffat wrote, "has not the suavity or the education of his late brother; he cannot speak English, but he may have more commonsense, and, for our sakes, I could have wished that the other had lived. He was doing our work for us most completely."[17]

In his grief it was natural that Grobler, for all his "commonsense," should be belligerent. It is natural also that Afrikaner historians should see the sinister hand of perfidious Albion in the murderous affair that cost the life of the consul.[18] Yet Moffat's remark rings true; if there were any evidence of British instigation of the attack, which there is not, it would suggest that Shippard did not know his business.

Grobler's death did not put an end to Transvaal ambitions of northern expansion. For the time being, however, the pressure on Lobengula came chiefly from British concession-hunters. Rhodes, to counter this, had paid a quick visit to England in the middle of the year and laid some of his plans before Lord Knutsford. Though Knutsford was noncommittal, Gifford and Cawston scented danger. "Rhodes seen Secretary of State for Colonies," they cabled to Maund, who had arrived in Cape Town; "object is anticipate you Lobengula. Proceed immediately to Matabeleland . . . "[19]

Rhodes, for his part, proceeded immediately to Cape Town. "Home Government," he reported to Shippard, "appeared favourable but unfortunately I had no concession to work on."[20] Fry having failed to get one, Rhodes selected a cunningly balanced team of agents for a new attempt. The leader of the team, C.D. Rudd, had been a close business associate of Rhodes since the early days of Kimberley, his collaborator in the De Beers amalgamation, and his right-hand man in the new Transvaal venture, the Gold Fields of South Africa Company. F.R. ("Matabele") Thompson had farmed in Griqualand West (where his father had been murdered before his eyes in the rebellion of 1878), had been Rhodes's secretary when he was deputy commissioner in Bechuanaland in 1884, and at other times inspector of native locations and the reorganizer of the De Beers Compounds. He was chosen for his familiarity with African customs and with the Tswana language. The qualifications of the third member of the team, J.R. Maguire, were less obviously relevant. He was a Fellow of All Souls and a member of the English bar, at which he had never felt the need to practise. Rhodes had known him at Oxford. His positive contribution to the venture—there were a few on the debit side—was to couch the concession document in the turgid language of the Inns of Court.

These three, together with two other white men, one coloured, one American Negro, and two African servants, set out from Kimberley in two wagons on 15 August. Inquisitive onlookers were told that it was a hunting trip. Unlike most hunters, these carried £5,000 in specie, and for a hunting trip it had curiously official associations.[21]

On his return from England Rhodes had laid his plans before the high commissioner. Robinson's confidential dispatch of 21 July to Knutsford had shown how far he had fallen under the spell:

Mr. Rhodes informs me that he has in the New Trust Deed of the Consolidated Diamond Mining Company taken powers to enable the Company to embark in undertakings of the kind referred to, and his plan is to endeavour to obtain from Lo Bengula and his indunas a concession of the parts of Matabeleland and Mashonaland which are not in the occupation or use of the Natives, and to provide for the protection of the Natives in the parts reserved for them, as well as for the development and government of the unoccupied territories surrendered to the Company by a Royal Charter somewhat similar to that granted some years ago to the Borneo Company . . . It appears to me that, looking to the reputed wealth of Matabeleland and its tributaries, the country is sure sooner or later to fall under the influence of some civilized power, and that a scheme such as that designed by Mr. Rhodes might possibly provide for the security of Native rights and interests, as well as for the beneficial development of the resources of the waste lands by British Capital, without entailing on British taxpayers the burden which would be imposed on them by the annexation of the country, and its formation into a Crown Colony.

Mr. Rhodes considers also, and I think with reason, that the extension of British interests in the interior of South Africa by a chartered company with Cape associations would be more in unison with the Africander sentiment than if the same result were attempted by the establishment of another inland Crown Colony.

Knutsford's reply, though not hostile to the scheme, was not altogether encouraging: the government could not favour one company against another, and a royal charter was unlikely.[22]

Before receiving the reply, Robinson had given Rudd a letter recommending him and his party to Lobengula. At Vryburg the hunting party had discussions with the assistant commissioner, F.J. (afterwards Sir Francis) Newton, who then wrote to Moffat, not only recommending the travellers to him but arguing in favour of Rhodes's getting a footing in Matabeleland. They had hoped to meet Shippard at the Limpopo-Notwani junction, but he was away at Baines Drift for the enquiry. They missed Kgama at Shoshong for the same reason. What was worse, he had left instructions that his people were not to part with any grain in his absence. Thompson, however, showed Mrs. Hepburn the letter from Robinson to Lobengula; Kgama's deputy, Seretse, then agreed to the sale of grain to travellers bearing a letter "from the Queen." How that would have upset Maund!

The Motloutsi and the Shashi were crossed without ceremony, but at the Tati there was bad news. Lobengula had "posted a notice at Tati refusing admittance to his country to Concessionists or hunters and had given orders to his regiments on the road to stop the White man." "So we said"—according to Rudd—"we were going to see Moffat officially . . . I then wrote a letter to Moffat asking him to arrange that we should not be detained longer than necessary, and sent it on by special runner." They *were* going to see Moffat, and they had a letter for him from the other assistant commissioner; perhaps that amounted to "seeing him officially."[23]

The party did not wait at the Tati for a reply. They went on to Manyami's, the effective frontier outpost where all travellers had to wait for permission to enter the country. Rudd and Thompson interviewed the local chief ("and a wretched old creature he was with any amount of cheek"), paid him the ten shillings he demanded, with a present for his messengers, and resumed the journey the following morning. The next day they met the runners with Moffat's reply. "It appears that the King was not pleased at our passing Tati in the face of his notice, and also at our writing to Moffat and not direct to him. So we outspanned and had breakfast and have now written direct to Lobengula."

This time, if Thompson's version is correct, the prevarication was more serious: "Rudd decided, against my advice, to write a letter to [the king] and send it on by messenger. In this letter he stated that we were not 'needy adventurers,' nor had we come to the Country to beg from the king, or to ask anything of him."

The king appears to have said, on receiving the letter, "Oh they are now in the country—let them come on." On 20 September they reached Bulawayo, and went the further two miles to the Umguza river where the king then happened to be.[24]

He could not have been glad to see them. For many months the stream of concession-hunters, Transvaal emissaries, and British officials known to have close links with Kgama, magnified in the popular mind by rumours of white impis preparing to invade, had been inflaming the fear and resentment of the Ndebele people. The young soldiers were straining at the leash, begging to be let loose on the white men. The king and the older indunas, with a better knowledge of the power confronting them, did everything possible to hold these passions in check.

Impis were sent out to the traditional raiding grounds. Three regiments crossed the Zambezi and were reported to have "wiped out" the people from whom Selous had recently made his famous and hair-raising escape. They also recovered and brought back some of his lost possessions. It was a curious achievement for men thirsting for European blood; but the king at least had a high regard for Selous. This expedition, like others in that direction, may have been intended to clear the way for a possible future Ndebele migration.

Earlier in the season an impi had been to the Umfuli, apparently to the same people whose chief, the "wizard of Chitungwiza," by being the incarnation of Chaminuka, had invited attack in 1883. Again, as on that occasion, the men and the old women were massacred, and the young women, boys, and cattle captured. Altogether there were thirteen raids in 1888.[25]

The spears were thus washed and the military spirit partly appeased, but the white peril had not been conjured away. Half-hearted attempts were made to keep the foreigners out. The only Europeans allowed into Mashonaland that year were G.W.H. Knight-Bruce, bishop of Bloemfontein, the German traveller Count Schweinitz, and his companion Dunn. They were curious exceptions. A mission in Mashonaland had never been allowed by Lobengula, but Knight-Bruce had no intention of poaching on the LMS ground in Matabeleland. Permission for him to go in was accordingly refused for some time, then rather ambiguously given. The bishop's explanation was probably right: "We walked with him back to his kraal. Fortunately it was practically empty . . . He was in a different humour to what I had seen him in before. I attributed it to a great degree to his being alone." As for Count Schweinitz, he was neither British nor Boer, and Lobengula had narrowly missed receiving Robinson's message that the Germans were the most dangerous of all. Moffat knew all about that. He asked Helm to advise Lobengula not to let Schweinitz go out by the Zambezi, or to "make such observations as will facilitate, at some future date, an inroad on Mashonaland from that side." He hoped that Mrs. Helm, a German, would forgive him.[26]

The notice prohibiting entry was posted at the Tati, and the king asked Sam Edwards "to tell all Hunters and Gold seekers arriving there not to trouble themselves to come any farther as there was neither game nor gold in his country any more."[27] The prohibition was only partly enforced.

Some of the hunters and gold seekers, not liking the temper of the regiments, departed for the south: Frank Mandy, farm manager in the Cape Colony for C.J. Jones (MLA for Port Elizabeth) and formerly a trader in Matabeleland; Frederik Greef, who looked after John Lee's farm at the Mangwe and had been involved in the Grobler affray; Ernst Hassforther, a German associated with Eduard Lippert; and of course Francis and Chapman, whose failure with the king was sufficient reason for them to go. John Fry had left because he was dying, and his son followed him for that reason.

By October, when Maund arrived, there were however many others who were staying the course: Rudd, Maguire, and Thompson; Renny-Tailyour, Frank Boyle, and Reilly, representing Lippert; Alexander Boggie, "Matabele" Wilson, and J. Cooper-Chadwick, representing a somewhat shadowy Johannesburg syndicate, with which the name of H.B. Hampson of Kimberley is associated; a few minor characters, and of course the old hands. There were also the missionaries with their families.[28]

While the king was using all his resources of procrastination in dealing with these men, Shippard, having finished the Grobler enquiry, decided to visit Lobengula himself. From the Tati he wrote to Moffat to ask whether the king would receive him. The reply lacked warmth: "the Administrator must best know himself whether he would come or not"; he might come on with no more than four white men and one wagon. Early the next morning this was modified into a clear invitation; significantly, the bearer of this message to Moffat was the induna Lotshe Hlabangana, the strongest advocate in the king's entourage of friendly relations with the whites.

The news of Shippard's approach precipitated a crisis. "A day or two after a report was brought to the Chief that an impi of white men was coming into the country consisting of 53 wagons, a cannon and a large number of people." All the white men were therefore summoned to a meeting with the indunas, at which the king was not present. He may not have believed the rumour. To Helm, after the meeting, he was "as friendly as usual." By staying away he kept some room to manoeuvre while allowing the steam to blow off.[29]

The steam blew for three hours. The indunas accused Moffat of having an impi. That was why Rudd and his party had arrived so soon after Moffat himself—they had come on ahead to let him know that the impi was on its way. "They said there was no use denying it, as they had seen it with their own eyes." The news had spread everywhere. George Martin, the Inyati trader, reported that "the men at the Umbezweni Kraal ran out at him and another man with him, pulled off their hats and beat their horses, and drove them back. They talk of a white 'impi', which they assert is coming." The missionary Bowen Rees, "in coming through, passed a village, where the people ran out crying 'Beat the white man': but on telling them that they came from here (Inyati), they were more quiet. He says that no one will work in the fields from fear of the white 'impi', which they say is coming: and one woman asked him, whether, when it came, 'it would kill children so high,' or 'so high,' giving different heights, apparently those of her own children."

After the meeting Helm tried to reassure the king. "I told him that people had evidently seen the Administrator's 3 wagons and water cart and perhaps some other wagons that were at Tati at the time and the escort of His Honour and exaggerated them into 53 wagons and a troop of men. I told him that the Administrator as such always travelled with an escort even in his own country and that he would naturally coming so far have an escort of police (15) the Captain, Secretary, cook etc. But that I was perfectly sure that no English impi was on its way. For the English"—the next eight years being mercifully hidden from Helm's view—"don't make raids like that."[30]

As Shippard and his police escort advanced into Matabeleland they were subjected to an interesting though unpleasant display of public opinion. While they waited at the Semokwe river for Moffat's reply an armed force watched over them. This was joined by another regiment, the Impande, which offered serious provocation: "In passing our encampment they jeered at us, taunting and insulting us, and in their war dances some of them ran out stabbing at us and poising assegais, shouting out that they would soon make an end of us when they came into our camp." A little later the whole regiment "came marching down straight towards us, though they did not enter the enclosure. They danced, yelled, howled at us, and insulted us in every way they could, some of them going so far as to stab at me with their assegais close to my fence and within a few feet of me."

The purpose of this behaviour was obvious. The young soldiers had been forbidden by the king to attack the white men, but defending themselves against attack would be a different question. If only this little "impi" could be provoked to fight, the army could "make a breakfast" of all the whites in the country. Shippard and Goold-Adams, who commanded the escort, understood the situation, and "our men behaved throughout with admirable coolness, and looked at the dancing savages with the most stolid indifference."

The king's mobile residence, the wagon captured on an expedition to Lake Ngami, was then parked at the Umguza river. For a whole day—before Shippard's arrival there—the Imbizo regiment had been "trying to persuade Lo Bengula to let them massacre all the White men in Matabeleland." He offered them an alternative: they could go to Kimberley and massacre the whites there. Another regiment had asked permission to kill their present indunas, who were "old women and cowards," and elect others. Permission was refused. Lobengula, if he did not look at them with stolid indifference, needed iron nerves and all of his powers of command in a situation as threatening in its own way as that which Shippard and his men had faced. It would have been easier in the short run to let the young men have their way. But there was also the long run: "You want to drive me into the lion's mouth," he told them.[31] In resisting these demands the king drew support from among the older indunas, and the older men in general.

Shippard's visit had a calming effect. He had not, after all, brought an impi. He was quite clearly the queen's representative; in the king's presence he sat on his chair, not on the ground. He was able to give Lobengula an authoritative account of the Grobler incident which he had been investigating. The king paid him the unusual if not unique honour of sending all the principal indunas to greet him at his camp. The Grobler treaty was discussed, Lobengula insisting that Grobler had described it as merely a renewal of the old treaty of friendship. In reply to the question why, then, another was needed, Grobler had said that only a copy of it survived, the original having been lost. Lobengula gave his version of the visit of Frederik Grobler. Shippard warned him against the danger threatening from the Transvaal. He explained also that when the protectorate was declared, the British authorities had not known where the Ndebele boundary was. They had no intention of infringing that. Their desire to have the boundary between the Ndebele and the Ngwato fixed arose purely from the need to preserve peace; if the Ndebele preferred not to fix it, the matter would be dropped.

All this was very satisfactory, but there were other statements and actions of Shippard's that cannot be passed over so lightly. It was easy to score the diplomatic point that the Boers wanted to take land, whereas the English, the nation of shopkeepers, were interested in mining and trade but not in land. Kgama, who was under their protection, had not been deprived of a single acre. The English did not want Lobengula's land; they wanted him to rule his kingdom in peace as a friendly ally, and to protect people who came to trade and to mine.

This was clever, but not honest. Shippard himself had been urging upon the

James Fairbairn and
James Dawson

F.R. ("Matabele") Thompson

Official visit to Lobengula, October 1888. Left to Right: D. Carnegie,
C.D. Helm, J.S. Moffat, Sir Sidney Shippard, Major H. Goold-Adams

69 The Rudd Concession

high commissioner the annexation—no mere protectorate—of the whole country up to the Zambezi. Though he said that if the government "should decide on maintaining and strengthening its hold on the country between the Zambezi and the Limpopo, the best course would, in my opinion, be to support the authority of Lo Bengula," the closing words of his report had a different implication: "For my own part I can see no hope for this country save through the purifying effects of war."[32] He was in the confidence of Rhodes, and it was not two months since he had received Rhodes's letter about the importance of getting a mining concession because "it is no use my stepping in for my Company to assist in the government of a shell, you will see this as clearly as I do." The letter had been even more explicit than that: "I am quite aware you cannot act freely with [Rudd], but in case he lays the ground work the objects are the same as though he does not know our big ideas, he will try and obtain what he desires for our Companies whose trust deeds I shall use for the objects I have in view . . . If we get Matabeleland we shall get the balance of Africa. I do not stop in my ideas at Zambezi and I am willing to work with you for it."[33]

Rhodes did want Lobengula's land, and he had enlisted Robinson, Shippard, Newton, and Moffat in his cause. The timing of Shippard's visit to Lobengula, in relation to the operations not only of Rudd, Maguire, and Thompson, but of their rivals, was no accident.

That Robinson was committed to Rhodes's plans was suspected by Cawston even in June. The high commissioner's letter commending the Rudd party to Lobengula would not by itself prove the point, but the proof would not be long in coming. Newton's letter to Moffat was the next piece of official support. The day after Rudd and his companions arrived at the Umguza they "had a long talk" with Moffat, who immediately wrote a confidential dispatch to Shippard, arguing that "it would be infinitely better if gold matters could be in the hands of one great corporation and so get rid of a swarm of mischievous meddlers who may, or may not, be amenable to Government authority."

The missionaries were involved too. The day after the discussion with Moffat the Rudd group had a pleasant talk with Helm, which was continued on later occasions and narrowed down to "business matters." It was Helm who, on 27 September, first explained to the king the nature of Rudd's business. Helm, Thompson wrote in his diary, "is our man, and . . . has worked through thick and thin in our interests." A fortnight later Helm was writing to the LMS directors that "it seems to me that unless the Chief comes to some arrangement with a strong company to work the Mashona gold fields and keep out others, there will be a rush there soon and things will come to a climax."[34]

Neither Moffat nor Helm knew of Rhodes's "big ideas"; in preferring one big corporation to a "swarm of mischievous meddlers" they may indeed have been thinking only in terms of "gold matters" and the peace of the realm. It is strange, though, that neither of them should at this stage have mentioned the Leask concession, which Helm had interpreted and Moffat approved not three months before. There is no record of a protest by either of them—or by Fairbairn or Phillips, who were on the spot—against any further concession, the "sole right" having already been granted.

On 27 October, after more than a month at Umvutshwa, Maguire wrote to Newton about the difficulty of discovering what the rival concession-hunters were doing or had obtained. "The only thing we have learnt for certain," he wrote, "is that Fairbairn has got a written concession, but we do not know exactly what it contains, it is probably pretty general but rendered valueless by the promise of an absurd proportion of the gold won to the Chief." How Maguire could know that it was "pretty general" (it was exclusive) and involved "an absurd proportion" (in fact, 50 per cent) without knowing the details, is a mystery. It was in Phillips's and Fairbairn's interest to tell him.

Of course it was in the interest of the Rudd party, whose own exclusive concession was only three days away when Maguire wrote, to feign ignorance of an earlier grant which on the face of it was a bar to the later one. Yet the evidence shows that the ignorance was not feigned. On 1 November Rudd, two days out on his rush to take his concession to Rhodes, wrote to Thompson and Maguire in Bulawayo that "the most important thing with [Phillips] is to wheedle out of him what Leask's concession *is*." Why did such information have to be "wheedled" out of men whose obvious interest was to disclose it? Maund, whether because of his skill at "prying into everything" or because he drew upon his imagination to fill the gaps, appears to have been better informed. "On their own showing," he said of the Leask group, they "have the soundest position in the country." If their concession was valid—surely Moffat could have told him that it was—he thought it not politic to ask Lobengula for another, but advisable rather to merge the Cawston interests with Leask's.[35]

On his way back to Johannesburg Rudd saw Leask in Klerksdorp. He reported at once to Rhodes that Leask, when he saw "Fairbairn's concession," was "so disgusted . . . that he pitched it away and has not seen it since, but that he will find it and send me a copy. It provides for half of the *gross produce* to go to the King, and this alone renders it commercially valueless." Rudd, or Leask, was misquoting: the words in the document were "one half share of the proceeds of the work." Still, this expression was a little ambiguous, and it may well be that Leask thought it a bad proposition as a mere mining concession.

It had, however, another use. Moffat pointed out to Leask—and he may have given Fairbairn and Phillips the same advice earlier—that while their concession was good they did not have the resources to work it. Rhodes's agents represented Big Business. If they got a concession, they would need to acquire the earlier one also to give complete security to their own; Fairbairn and his friends would be well advised not to interfere with Rhodes now, but to try to sell him their concession for a good price later. Leask made the opening moves of this game immediately after seeing Rudd.[36]

If neither Moffat nor Helm was directly involved in Rhodes's schemes, the positions of Shippard and Robinson were more compromising. It must be borne in mind that Rhodes at this time was both a private member of Parliament and a great mining magnate. Had he held office, and used his official position to push his imperial schemes forward, it would have been legitimate for the high commissioner and the deputy commissioner to give them official support. Instead, Rhodes was a private businessman looking for gold mines in competition with other private businessmen. Knutsford had told Rhodes that the government could not favour one company over another. Shippard took care, in speaking to Lobengula, to dissociate the Crown from all private interests; but actions speak louder than words.

It might be thought that Shippard was merely emphasizing official neutrality when he told the king "that any concession seeker who says he is asking for mineral grants on behalf of the Queen's Government is speaking falsely"[37]— until it is realised that Maund and Renny-Tailyour, but not Rudd, came close to claiming just that.

Rudd was offering Lobengula arms and ammunition as the price of a concession. Rudd, Rhodes, Shippard, and everyone else familiar with South African affairs knew the kind of outcry that would be raised when the deal became public. When the outcry came they were ready with their defence: that the Ndebele were far less dangerous with rifles than with assegais. It is therefore significant that when Matabele Wilson and Boggie went over to visit Shippard on the very evening of his arrival at Umvutshwa, one of the things he asked them was: " 'Was the native most dangerous with the assegai or the gun.' We told him," Wilson wrote, "that a Matabele was no good with a gun, but with the assegai he was a thing to fear."[38] They could not have known what a handle they were giving to their rivals with this remark. The significance of the conversation, however, lies in the interest which Shippard took in that question at that time.

As Rudd's negotiations dragged on, Shippard made his departure on 23 October. Rudd's son Frank and his friend Denny, who had joined the party on the journey up, departed with the administrator, who arranged to wait at the Motloutsi for Rudd to overtake him. In the event, Rudd caught up with Shippard a few miles further south. "Goold-Adams caught sight of me, and both he and Shippard gave me a hearty shout of welcome and called out to me to come into the wagon, which I did." Rudd joined the official party for "a champagne lunch in honour of the occasion . . . the thermometer standing at 112° in the coolest place we could find."[39]

In case it be thought that a champagne lunch was only the proper way for official and unofficial Englishmen to celebrate their meeting in the desert, it is right to point out that there were then other Englishmen in that neighbourhood who did not share the lunch, but were being escorted southwards by the police. They were Wood and Pauling.

Pauling, having travelled from Cape Town to Grahamstown and then to the

Transvaal with Wood, learned by degrees that the professional job he had come to do was complicated by political questions. The ground he was to inspect was "disputed territory"; the imperial secretary forbade him, in writing, to enter it; Wood, on the other hand, refused to give Erlanger and Company an extension of time in which to take up their option. Wood also assured Pauling that there was nothing to prevent their entering Lobengula's country by a direct route from the Transvaal. As Kruger forbade them to use Grobler's pont, they crossed the Limpopo further down. At the Mangwe the frontier guard ordered them to stop. On the day that Shippard left for the south the king sent him a letter asking him, if he met Wood, to "take him away out of my ground." Shippard accordingly compelled Wood and Pauling to return south by way of Shoshong under a police escort. At Shoshong they were interrogated by Shippard in the presence of Kgama, Hepburn, Bishop Knight-Bruce, and others. Wood was again accused of trying to provoke war between Kgama and Lobengula, and was required to sign a document binding himself under surety of £2,000 to stay out of Lobengula's territory until the boundary was settled. As he refused to do so, he was escorted further to Mafeking. There, being now on British soil, he was offered the alternative of signing the recognizance or being charged under the high commissioner's proclamation of 1886, which provided for the removal of potential disturbers of the peace. He signed. Pauling, however, had been allowed to go to Pretoria by a direct route from Shoshong.[40]

Wood may have been the danger to peace that Shippard, Kgama, and Lobengula believed him to be. He was certainly a difficult travelling companion: on the previous journey his diary had been full of grievances against Francis and Chapman; on this one, against Pauling. Yet the removal and even arrest of Wood is one of a series of events that throw an interesting light on the relation of the imperial authorities in South Africa to Rhodes. Francis and Chapman had been arrested by Kgama at Shoshong, and had been in danger of another arrest when they crossed the Limpopo at the pont. Frank Johnson had got the promise of a concession from Kgama, only to find it reduced in size at Shippard's request. Shippard realised that the expulsion of Wood could not be justified unless the Bechuanaland Exploration Company were also kept out of the disputed territory: it was accordingly ordered to keep out. P.L. van der Byl, a former member of the Cape Legislative Council, had asked the imperial government's approval for a plan of his own to develop the whole trans-Limpopo country; he was told that, as many Europeans had obtained a footing there, his project of taking over the whole country could not be entertained.[41] No such objection was raised in Rhodes's case.

It was one thing to arrest Joseph Wood or to reject van der Byl's proposal; it was another to provoke George Cawston and Lord Gifford, vc. On 14 December 1888, Gifford wrote a biting letter to the Colonial Office: " . . . My Company would also be pleased to learn under what authority Sir Hercules Robinson has countenanced a Mr. Rudd entering into this territory . . . From information received by last mail, it is alleged . . . that the authorities are also supporting in an indirect manner a syndicate of certain other persons in an attempt to gain all Mashonaland . . . I would point out that the High Commissioner appears to have endeavoured to upset our concession from the beginning . . . and my Company think that these facts ought to be brought to the notice of Lord Knutsford, in order to show the treatment that is being extended to Khama and my Company, who throughout have acted in a straightforward, open manner."[42]

Gifford's complaint came too late. The Rudd Concession had been granted six weeks before; unofficial news of it was reaching the Colonial Office at the moment that Gifford was writing, and he and Cawston were shortly to negotiate with Rhodes a merging of their respective interests.

Robinson, Shippard, and even Moffat had compromised their official positions, and were to compromise them further, by their support of Rhodes. It is easier, however, to blame them for this than to show what they ought to have done in the circumstances. The partition of Africa by European powers was then rapidly accelerating. These men were right in believing that the only alternative for Matabeleland to British rule was annexation by another power; its continued independence was not only not envisaged, but was not a real possibility. The nearest possible approach to it was the kind of independence the Ngwato preserved under British protection. That solution was in the missionary tradition, dating from the strong but unsuccessful advocacy of John Philip in relation to the Xhosa and the Griquas, followed by the French missionaries in the case of Basutoland and Mackenzie in Bechuanaland.

Matabeleland, however, was a different case. After thirty years in that country the LMS had made, at the most, a dozen converts, and the men in the field were not expecting many more while the predatory militarist régime survived. Bishop Knight-Bruce found it "hard not to agree with Mr. Selous, that nothing will be done with them without a war."[43] Sympathy for the poor downtrodden Shona, and other victims of Ndebele bloodlust, was perhaps not entirely hypocritical, and served to rationalize a desire to destroy the Ndebele hegemony. As to how this destruction was to come about, and what was to follow it, the missionaries were not very clear. Some of them, such as John Mackenzie (following the example of Livingstone) believed that European colonists, carefully selected, would be a good civilizing influence in Africa; they thought it possible to avoid the consequences of colonization which they deplored in the Cape Colony. They thought also that there was room for colonists: the missionaries had seen what every traveller reported, large areas of fertile country once cultivated, now depopulated.

If this was the missionary view, and if even Mackenzie thought that British rule offered the only hope for the trans-Limpopo peoples, it was natural enough for Robinson and Shippard to take up the cause of expansion as a patriotic duty. They had reason to know that such plans aroused no enthusiasm in the Colonial Office. There, the prospect of Boer expansion to the Zambezi, or of the Portuguese occupation of Manicaland, had been accepted (before the Moffat treaty) with equanimity, even with detached amusement: "we have recently heard that the Transvaal Government intend to occupy it. If they do it will be interesting to see what steps Portugal will take to defend her claims."[44] Portuguese claims were not to be acknowledged, but it was only German expansion that, by this time, gave the British government (the Foreign Office more than the Colonial Office) any anxiety; it was believed to affect the balance of power in Europe.

If action depended on Downing Street, the Union Jack would not fly beyond the Limpopo. But here was Rhodes, the unofficial empire-builder, ready to plant it there at his own expense. He was the kind of man who could not be diverted from his chosen course: he reached his goal, if not by one means, then by another. If imperial expansion into Central Africa was desired, Rhodes was the man to achieve it. He was also persuasive, and both Robinson and Shippard had often been subjected to his cogent arguments. So they did what they thought they could, not too indiscreetly, to forward his plans and to recommend them to the imperial government, almost forgetting that Rhodes was still a private businessman competing with other businessmen.

Gifford's letter to the Colonial Office might have been a warning signal of the danger lurking in this policy. It had, however, no direct sequel, because in that case the competing interests were soon merged. This indeed was Rhodes's method of converting a private into a public operation and relieving his official friends of some embarrassment: remove the element of competition by absorbing or eliminating the competitors. At the end of 1888, however, none had yet been eliminated, and the officials continued on a course which conflicted with their duty but from which they could not easily turn back.

Specifically, what they had done was to smooth the way for Rudd and to hinder some of his rivals. The practical effect of these actions must not be exaggerated. Wood, having incurred Lobengula's displeasure, was not a serious competitor. Almost all the arrests and prohibitions related to attempts to work in the disputed territory, which was afterwards found to contain no gold; quite apart from the Rhodes plans, it was reasonable to forbid operations which could have induced two groups of capitalists to espouse opposite sides in the boundary dispute. As for the assistance to Rudd, it had consisted chiefly, so far, of demonstrations of official friendliness calculated to remove some doubts from Lobengula's mind. Shippard had done nothing positively to commend Rudd's cause to the king, who could still have refused a concession to Rudd without incurring the open displeasure of the imperial authorities.

Negotiating with Lobengula was a slow business. He had many other affairs to attend to. The dry heat of October precedes what ought to be the rainy season, so that the king had to spend time in the goat kraal on the magical rites to "make rain." The death of one of his wives or children naturally interrupted business. The impatient Europeans had to pass much time at whist, chess, and backgammon, and in visits to one another. The king, for his part, had to weigh, over and over again, the probable advantages against the probable dangers in accepting Rudd's offer. Whatever his decision, it had to be made with an eye to public opinion.

The young soldiers, *amajaha*, would have been relieved to see all the white men turned out of the country and all concessions refused. The chief danger in this course, as the king and many of the older indunas believed, was that it would remove the principal obstacle to a Boer invasion, even if it did not provoke a British one.[45] The available evidence, ranging from Potgieter's battles to Majuba, suggested that in a military sense the Boers were more dangerous than the British. They appeared to be more dangerous also in their aims: they were farmers seeking land, and there was the example of Bechuanaland to support Shippard's argument that the British were interested only in gold and trade. If a handful of miners, such as could be seen at the Tati, would commit the British to keeping the Boers at bay, to let them in might be the wisest course.

Rudd was asking not merely for mining rights, but for the *sole* right to prospect and mine in Lobengula's kingdom. To grant this would mean to exclude the "swarm of mischievous meddlers," which in one way would be a gain. On the other hand there was something to be said for allowing rivalries to continue: that way, the rivals would have to compete for the king's favours. Such points as these must have been discussed at length in Lobengula's meetings with his leading indunas.

That the balance was eventually tipped in Rudd's favour was due largely, if not almost exclusively, to an argument on another plane. Rudd offered to pay, for the concession he wanted, a price which the other competitors could not match: a thousand Martini-Henry breech-loading rifles, a hundred thousand rounds of "suitable ball cartridges," an armed steamboat on the Zambezi (or, if this was not wanted, £500), and a regular payment of £100 on the last day of each lunar month. The money was not important, but the arms and ammunition were passionately desired. Maund in 1885 had reported the number of breech-loading rifles and carbines in the possession of the Ndebele at between six and eight hundred. Most of the six to seven thousand rounds of ammunition they had formerly possessed had been damaged by water two years earlier.[46] Whatever the Wilsons and Boggies might think about "the Matabele being no good with a gun," neither Lobengula nor his subjects doubted that firearms were the key to survival in these dangerous times. Rudd offered them on a large scale; the king did not yet know that while Rudd could, his rivals, even if they had offered to, probably could not, actually deliver them.

As the sequel very soon proved, even this weighty argument would not have prevailed if the king and the indunas had understood even a few of the hidden implications in the document he signed. In a general way, he certainly sensed the danger. As he had said to Helm, "the Boers are like the lizard, they dart about quickly, but the English proceed more cautiously. Did you ever see a chameleon catch a fly? The chameleon gets behind the fly and remains motionless for some time, then he advances very slowly and gently, first putting forward one leg and then another. At last, when well within reach, he darts out his tongue and the fly disappears. England is the chameleon and I am that fly."[47]

It did not necessarily appear, however, that the way to thwart the chameleon was to refuse a concession to Rudd. The document which Maguire had drawn up in legal language was explained to the king, several times and at length, by Helm. As the document itself did not describe the operations to which it would give rise, the grantees offered a description. They "explained to the Chief," Helm wrote, "that what was deemed necessary to get out the gold was to erect dwellings for their overseers, to bring in and erect machinery—use wood and water. They promised that they would not bring more than 10 white men to work in his country, that they would not dig anywhere near towns, etc., and that they and their people would abide by the laws of his country and in fact be his people. But these promises were not put in the concession." Rudd did not record this promise at the time, but a message of his to Lobengula, four months later, could have referred to something of the kind: "I am sending up a few workmen to commence looking for gold, but not many at first until you give us leave." In his report to the imperial secretary Rudd stated that "besides what appears on the face of the agreement, certain verbal undertakings were given to the king by me, as for instance that any white miners engaged in the country by me should be bound to fight in defence of the country if called upon; also, that I should not introduce any white employé or machinery until the first instalment of rifles had been delivered."[48]

Early on the morning of 30 October Rudd and his companions went to the king's kraal to continue discussions that had broken off the previous day. More than a hundred indunas, but not the king, were present at this *indaba*. They "began a lot of new questions, especially as to *where* we wanted to mine. We told them we wanted the whole country. They said 'No, take the part this side of the Tati, you have seen that.' I said 'No, we must have Mashonaland, and right up to the Zambezi as well—in fact, the whole country.' They said 'Where is Mashonaland, and where is the Zambezi?' One old chap pointed south and said 'The Zambezi must be there.' "

After more procrastination and displays of geographical ignorance, Rudd and Thompson played their trump card, announcing that the negotiations were at an end. No, said the indunas, "sit down again." It was agreed that Thompson and one induna, Lotshe, should report the discussion to Lobengula, who was close at hand. Lotshe, the foremost advocate of the concession, was thus the only induna with the king when he made his decision, though it appears that two others, Makwekwe and Sikhombo, influenced it. He still hesitated. Thompson asked the rhetorical question, "Who gives a man an assegai if he expects to be attacked by him afterwards?" It was a good point; a few moments later Lobengula said, "Bring me the fly-blown paper and I will sign it."

Thompson, "assuming as careless a manner as I could," walked out to call Rudd, Maguire, and Helm. After another delay the king put his mark to the document. "As he did so," Thompson records, "Maguire, in a half-drawling, yawning tone of voice, without the ghost of a smile said to me, 'Thompson, this is the epoch of our lives.' "[49] Rudd, Maguire, and Thompson signed as principals, and Helm and Dreyer (an employee of the Rudd party) as witnesses. Helm also wrote the endorsement: "I hereby certify that the accompanying document has been fully interpreted and explained by me to the Chief Lobengula and his full Council of Indunas and that all the Constitutional usages of the Matabele Nation had been complied with prior to his executing same." The king would not allow the indunas to sign. According to Rudd, he thought it unnecessary, as they had all discussed the matter and agreed to the grant. Yet, if the king had any qualms about what he was doing, one would have expected him to want the indunas to share the responsibility. He may have felt that without their marks the grant would be easier to repudiate.

By the concession Lobengula granted and assigned

> unto the said grantees their heirs representatives and assigns jointly and severally the complete and exclusive charge over all metals and minerals situated and contained in my Kingdoms Principalities and dominions together with full power to do all things that they may deem necessary to win and procure the same and to hold collect and enjoy the profits and revenue if any derivable from the said metals and minerals subject to the aforesaid payment and *Whereas* I have been much molested of late by divers persons seeking and desiring to obtain grants and concessions of Land and Mining rights in my territories I do hereby authorise the said grantees their heirs representatives and assigns to take all necessary and lawful steps to exclude from my Kingdoms Principalities and dominions all persons seeking land metals minerals or mining rights therein and I do hereby undertake to render them such needful assistance as they may from time to time require for the exclusion of such persons and to grant no concessions of land or mining rights from and after this date without their consent and concurrence.

The Tati Concession was specifically excluded from the grant. Half of the rifles and cartridges were to be ordered from England immediately, the other half when mining operations had begun. If at any time the monthly payment of £100 fell three months in arrear, "the grant shall cease and determine from the date of the last made payment."[50]

While the grantees were given the power to exclude others seeking either land or mining rights, their own concession was for mining only; there was no grant of land. The price paid seems trivial in comparison with the half share in the Leask contract; yet the heirs and assigns of the grantees so interpreted the right to "do all things that they deem necessary to win and procure the same" (so as to include fighting wars and governing the country) that there was, in fact, no profit for many years. This however was not foreseen, and it may be conceded that the grant was cheaply bought.

The concession was granted to Rudd, Maguire, and Thompson, but they were only agents. The distinction between agents and principals was at first a fine one. The syndicate that financed the expedition consisted of Rhodes, Rudd, and Thompson; as Thompson was a civil servant, and therefore a poor man, his share of the capital came from an overdraft guaranteed by Rudd. This arrangement was good enough for the concession-hunting trip, but would not do for the traffic in armaments, not to mention gold-mining and all things necessary to win and procure the same. Immediately after the granting of the concession the grantees therefore, by what must have been the prearranged plan, "in order to avoid subsequent misunderstanding or complications in case of the death of one or more of them . . . did renounce all right title or interest they might have in or to the said concession . . . by virtue of the grant itself or their signatures thereto and they ceded and made over absolutely all their right title and interest therein to the Gold Fields Company Cecil John Rhodes and the said Charles Dunell Rudd." Three weeks earlier Rudd had made a private written agreement with Thompson, by which the latter was to receive half of Rudd's share in the concession, in return for paying a corresponding share of the expenses and for undertaking to remain in Matabeleland for four months at most. Rhodes was to "settle with" Maguire as Rudd did with Thompson.[51]

In the meantime both Thompson and Maguire were expected to earn their reward by further labours. Within hours of the king's signing the document Rudd and Dreyer were on their way south by mule cart—the fastest conveyance on the road—to take it to Rhodes. Thompson and Maguire were left behind to defend the concession against the attacks that were sure to come.

As Rudd and Dreyer sped along they passed the slower travellers ahead of them—Bishop Knight-Bruce, Frank Rudd, and Denny, Wood and Pauling with the policemen, and then Shippard and Goold-Adams. After the champagne lunch they left the officials behind, drove on in the cool of the evening and cut short their nights to make better time. Their haste was almost in vain. The Lemoen Pan, on which all travellers relied for water, was found to be dry. A piece of paper fixed to a thorn tree by Ivon Fry told them that there was water two miles to the southeast. In the search for this they lost their way in the bush. Rudd dropped his bag of money, the concession, and his other papers into an ant-bear hole, leaving a letter for the administrator with instructions for finding them, and also a farewell letter to his wife. He was almost too exhausted to go on when the barking of dogs drew the attention of their Tswana owners who were encamped near by. They rescued and restored both Rudd and Dreyer and brought in the mules and the cart.

After this narrow escape the buried possessions were recovered and the journey continued. Shippard and others were again encountered and passed on the road. "We drove through the night," Rudd reported at one point, "in stretches of two hours with one and a half hour intervals." On 17 November the travellers reached Mafeking; two days later, with the help of horses provided by the postal contractor, they drove into Kimberley, and handed the concession to Rhodes. It was just twenty days since the signing. Rudd noted with pride that his speed made a record that would not be broken until the railway was extended. He and Rhodes then boarded the train for Cape Town, where they presented themselves to the high commissioner on 21 November.

Robinson "was very pleased to hear the result of our mission and raised no difficulty as to the guns."[52] Rhodes and Rudd understood that this complacency about the guns would not be widely shared. There were few subjects about which white South Africans were more sensitive than this. It is true that the trade in guns was the chief bait drawing labourers to the diamond fields, but its consequences were written large in recent history. The Kimberley guns had been the original cause of the Langalibalele rebellion, which had thrown Bishop Colenso into a new controversy and caused Natal to be put under a "Jamaican constitution." The Cape Parliament had passed a Disarmament Act, and to enforce it had waged a disastrous war in Basutoland. That territory had consequently been disannexed by the Cape and placed directly under the Crown. The Free State government had tried to seize arms from labourers returning across that republic from Kimberley, with the result that they now travelled in gangs and forcibly resisted arrest.

Robinson, whether from naiveté or bravado (neither of which would have been in character, so that his motive is hard to establish), wanted the concession in all its details to be published at once. Rhodes, however, "was afraid that some agitation against the guns might be got up by the Transvaal and Bond party, and that it was safer not to publish until the guns were in Bechuanaland."[53] On the other hand it was necessary to announce the fact of the concession, in order to warn rivals off the ground. A bowdlerized version was therefore drawn up by Rudd, approved by Rhodes and Robinson, and published in the *Cape Times* and *Cape Argus* on 24 November. According to this, the price of the monopoly was "the valuable consideration of a large monthly payment in cash, a gunboat for defensive purposes on the Zambesi, and other services." Much was made of the endorsement by Helm, and the "great favour" with which the concession was viewed by "all the local missionaries." Both papers carried editorials emphasizing the power of Lobengula and the advantage from his point of view of using one great responsible body to keep "freebooters" out and so preserve his independence. Matabeleland, said the *Cape Times*, "is not in a position in which it is necessary for any power—British or Republican—to step in." "We also," Rudd wrote, "drafted a letter from me to the government enclosing copy of concession for their information—this also Bower and the Governor doctored up into suitable form. The Governor has been most cordial and will do all he can, but seems to funk Knutsford a little and thinks he is in with the Bechuanaland people." A useful addition to the press release was a notice by Lobengula, appearing in the *Cape Times* two days later, "that all the mining rights in Matabeleland, Mashonaland, and adjoining territories of the Matabele Chief have been already disposed of, and all concession-seekers and speculators are hereby warned that their presence in Matabeleland is obnoxious to the chief and people . . . "[54]

Rhodes and Rudd did not tarry long in Cape Town; when the news broke in the *Cape Times* they were in the train on their way back to Kimberley. Yet, after all that Rudd had done, Robinson waited till 5 December to inform the Colonial Office, and then did so by letter, not by telegram—"possibly," as Hyatt drily suggests, "from reasons of economy."

The real reasons for his procrastination were two: the rifles and the involvement of officials, neither of which would make good reading in Downing Street. Thompson, in his autobiography, boasts that "not one of the white men at Bulawayo had an inkling of our success." This may have been true on 30 October. But it was only two days later that Matabele Wilson entered in his diary:. "We hear to-day that Rudd's party offered the King 1000 rifles, and a £100 per month for the mineral rights of the country." (Rudd attributed the leak to "the breach of confidence on the part of that swine Sam Edwards.")[55] Six weeks later the news reached Knutsford through Gifford and Cawston, and on 17 December he cabled to Robinson: "Is there any truth in report grant of mining concession over the whole of Matabeleland to Rudd, in consideration of monthly payment of £100, and 1000 Martini-Henry rifles? If rifles part of consideration, as reported, do you think there will be danger of complications arising from this?"[56]

By this time the high commissioner's dispatch, with a copy of the concession enclosed, was on its slow way to England, but Knutsford's question demanded a reply. The substance of the reply—sent, like the previous dispatch, by sea— was the enclosed minute by Shippard. The administrator's first anxiety was to show that "no Government officer or representative had anything to do with the concession in question," a point which he laboured with corroborative detail: "the actual signing . . . took place, as I understand, three days after the departure of Mr. Moffat, the assistant commissioner, and more than a week after I had left Umgusa River on my return from Matabeleland." As Knutsford had not raised the question of Shippard's or Moffat's role in the business, the anxious disclaimer does not look like evidence of a clear conscience.

The main burden of the minute, however, was a reply to Knutsford's question about the rifles. Shippard noted that Bishop Knight-Bruce and Hepburn (of Shoshong) were strongly opposed to the supply of firearms to the Ndebele, while Helm was in favour of it; he, Shippard, was "inclined to agree" with Helm.[57] His reason for doing so was the remarkable theory for which we have

already seen him seeking confirmation: that the Ndebele would be less dangerous with rifles in their hands than with assegais. There was, indeed, evidence
that the musketry of untrained men is ineffective, but the proponents of this
view seem to have overlooked the possibility that the Ndebele riflemen might
improve with experience. Could the *amajaha* (as Hepburn suggested) not carry
assegais as well as rifles?

Whatever the Rudd party might think of such questions, the fatal flaw in
their arguments was that they were not consistent. In the same minute Shippard tried to allay fears for the safety of the Ngwato by reporting that "Mr.
Rudd would, I understand, be prepared to give arms and ammunition to Khama, also for defensive purposes, and the relative positions of the Chiefs would
thus remain unchanged." Are we to understand that the purpose of this generosity was to prevent Kgama from having an unfair advantage over Lobengula?
Again, Shippard argued that it would be politically inexpedient to deny rifles
to Lobengula while allowing Kgama and other chiefs to acquire them—an argument which assumes the efficacy of the rifles. And Thompson, when recording his final rhetorical question to Lobengula ("who gives a man an assegai?"), goes on to say, "for rifles would then be the best defence they could
have." In a previous dispatch to the high commissioner, though not in this
minute, Shippard had revealed the great anxiety of Kgama about this arming
of the Ndebele; as a directly interested party, he at least was under no illusions
about its probable consequences.[58]

The argument cannot of course be taken seriously, but it was the best that
Rudd and Rhodes could produce. In case it should fail to convince, they had a
second one, as disingenuous as the first. This, too, appeared in Shippard's minute and in Robinson's covering dispatch. It was that if Rudd were not allowed
to send the rifles through Bechuanaland he would take them by a direct route
from the Transvaal. Alternatively, if Rudd were not to offer firearms to Lobengula, "our refusal would merely have the effect of throwing him, so to
speak, into the arms of the Transvaal Boers."

That there was no way of preventing Rudd, a British subject, from gun-running was an expression of helplessness that would have interested Wood, Francis, Chapman, and the Bechuanaland Exploration Company. And, though
there were gun-runners among the Boers, one of the few certainties of the situation was that Kruger's government would never have countenanced this operation.

Whatever the risk that the imperial government would obstruct Rhodes's
course in some way, the obstruction would be a slow business. In the meantime, the danger to the concession in Matabeleland itself was immediate. We
have seen that Wilson heard about it two days after Rudd had left. As the rumour circulated it provoked bitter reactions among the crowd of rival agents
who saw their hopes dashed. "Some of them I do not blame," Wilson wrote,
"for wanting something for themselves, as they have wasted a part of their

lives in this country trying to get something, while others have just come up, others again at a considerable expense, to find that after months and maybe years of waiting, the whole of the fruit has been picked."[59]

Maund's immediate reactions were characteristic: he refused to believe that the concession was genuine, and the note of self-congratulation, self-praise, mock modesty ("with all humbleness"), and triumph in his letters to Gifford was struck more stridently than ever. His theory was that Rudd had offered the rifles but not received a concession; he had been told that a concession would be discussed after the rifles had arrived. Maund's advice to Gifford would apply equally to this imaginary situation and to the true one: the imperial government must be persuaded to prevent the passage of the rifles. As Rudd would certainly make claims to a concession, they must be exposed as false. On the positive side Maund had been trying for a concession of the Mazoe valley; this involved the assertion of Lobengula's, and the denial of Portugal's, sovereignty there.[60]

Out of these considerations emerged a plan for Maund to take two Ndebele envoys to England. It has generally been assumed that Maund himself proposed this plan, and that Lobengula agreed to discuss a Mazoe concession after the party had returned. In his controversy with Marshall Hole nearly forty years later Maund attacked this assumption: "The suggestion came directly from the King, who was urged by his Indunas to send Envoys to the Queen. At first I absolutely refused, which angered Lobengula, and only his speaking of my Mazoe request made me reluctantly consent. Neither I nor any white man had any part in suggesting it."[61]

His letter to Gifford at the time was a little more ambiguous, While he affirmed that "this mission was put on me *nolens volens*," there is much in the letter that suggests otherwise: "The king when he sent messengers out for me to come into his country told Sam Edwards that even his business must wait until he had seen me . . . I am bound to carry it through and it will be everything in the world to you . . . By this move I have entirely *non-plussed* every Concession party who have come in and got the whip hand of them all . . . We have this trump card in our hand if I am enabled to play it . . . Thus, if I can carry this mission through I am not only absolute master of the position but it will be the means of solving a difficult political problem . . . I cannot conceive *why*, but he [Lobengula] seems to have the most implicit confidence in me, and, seeing that, I am morally bound to do all in my power to further his and his people's wish in sending these men so far for the sole object of benefiting his country, especially, as in so doing, I am furthering your business for which I was sent out and which now I believe will be brought to a successful issue."[62]

While it is clear from this that Maund was mistaken in claiming that he had "reluctantly consented," his absurd boasting does not necessarily prove that all his statements were untrue. It is possible that the idea of sending envoys to England was first mentioned, perhaps casually, by Lobengula, and that Maund thrust himself forward as the man who could ensure their favourable reception. That Maund played a positive part was certainly the impression of Matabele Wilson, who wrote in his diary at the time: "I am sure that the idea did not originate with the king. He must have been told something of the power of England, and what England could do for him, and how his people would be received, and as Maund had been up here once before as Lieutenant in Sir Charles Warren's expedition, when he was entrusted with some commission for the king, the king evidently thinks he has something to do with Government at the present time." All the evidence confirms Maund's belief in his influence with Lobengula. "Well Wilson," he said before leaving, "I do not know what your business is up here, but I can tell you, that if it is after concessions, you will be doomed to disappointment, as the King will not grant any concessions until after my return from England, neither would Rudd, nor forty thousand Rudds get one while I am away."[63] It is very probable—though the evidence is less direct—that to Lobengula he claimed a similar influence with his own government. Moffat was convinced at the time that Maund, in spite of warnings to the contrary, was trying to represent himself as an officer of that government.

However this might be, there can be no doubt that Lobengula welcomed the opportunity of a direct communication with the queen, by-passing her local representatives. He chose two envoys, Babayane and Mshete, to accompany Maund, entrusting them with an unwritten message which they were not to divulge to anyone along the way. Some months later Bosumwane told Moffat the message: "There are so many people who come here and tell me that they are sent by the Queen. Go and see if there is a Queen and ask her who is the one whom she has really sent." Another of the priestly brothers, Mlugulu, reported the message in similar words to David Carnegie. It is probable that the envoys were instructed, further, to deny to the queen that Lobengula had "given away his country" to Rudd, or even to repudiate the Rudd concession altogether. While the evidence for this comes mainly from Maund, who was an interested party and unreliable, the sequel shows that his assertions are likely to have been correct.[64]

Though Maund was sure that the envoys would make this denial, he professed not to know the words of the oral message. He was, however, the bearer of another message, a written one, as follows:

I, Lo Bengula, King of the Amantabele, hearing that the Portuguese wrongfully claim and purpose giving away rights belonging to me and my people on the Zambesi, do hereby declare that my boundaries go down from beyond the Sabi river and embrace the river Mazoe with all its tributaries down to the Kangudzi river. My territory extends also on the north side of the Zambesi, forming a large trace from a line north from the mouth of the Guay river to the Kafue river thence to its junction with the Zambesi, embracing the Guanga, a large river. The southern bank of the Zambesi is all my people's country to Tete.

I cannot therefore understand how the Portuguese, who have never been to me, can claim the Zambesi river, as I hold the country on either side, and have a fleet of boats on this river for the passage of my people and impis. Neither can I understand how they dare sell my country on the Mozoe [*sic*] river.

I send two of my headmen to England to the Queen, to ask how these things can be. To ask for protection.

I mean by this to be defended against my enemies.

The letter was "signed for Lo Bengula" by Maund, interpreted by Tainton, witnessed by Helm and Colenbrander, and the elephant seal affixed.[65]

In the composition of this, Maund was obviously more than an amanuensis. Its essential purpose was to assert Lobengula's sovereignty over the Mazoe valley, which was where Maund hoped to get a concession. As will be seen later, others who were interested in the same region were trying to get it from the Portuguese. Maund and Lobengula had a common interest in frustrating them.

All the disappointed concession-hunters had a common interest in frustrating Rudd. Thus Renny-Tailyour, who represented Lippert, agreed that his colleague Colenbrander should accompany Maund and the envoys to England as an interpreter. Johann Colenbrander was a Natal frontiersman who had played an adventurous part in the commotions of Zululand after the defeat of Cetshwayo. He had been taken into Lippert's party on account of his command of the Zulu language and his experience of the Zulu people.[66] So, with Lobengula's blessing, Maund, Colenbrander, Babayane, and Mshete set out on the journey that would take them—if the many pitfalls on the way could be avoided—to London. They left in December 1888 and did not return until the following August. During their absence the battle of the concession raged in Matabeleland.

Copies of the Cape papers with their circumspect reports of the concession made their way slowly northwards. The Maund party saw them at Shoshong, where the two envoys hotly denied that the king had "given away the country" in the manner described.

By the middle of January the first report reached Bulawayo in the form of a letter to Reilly, one of Renny-Tailyour's party. He read this to the king in the presence of Helm, Phillips, and Tainton, but not of Maguire and Thompson. Either then or shortly afterwards Tainton (one of the old hands, who often acted as interpreter) produced the Cape press report and translated it to Lobengula, with a gloss of his own. According to Tainton the king "had in fact sold his country, [and] the Grantees could if they so wished bring an armed force into the country; depose him and put another chief in his place; dig anywhere, in his kraals, gardens and towns."

Lobengula was surprised to hear this, as well he might be; though such plans did exist in the minds of Rhodes and others, the language of the "fly-blown paper" could hardly be stretched to imply them. To the disappointed concession-hunters, however, any means would justify the end. Reilly and Tainton were supported by the rest against Maguire and Thompson, while the missionaries did what they could to see fair play. The king asked Helm to read the copy of the concession which had been entrusted to his keeping. He did so, and denied that it bore any of the implications that Tainton had found in it. The king professed to believe that Rudd had asked only "to dig one hole," and here was a document saying that he had given away the whole country.

Tainton then (Helm having refused) drew up at Lobengula's dictation a notice which was published in the *Bechuanaland News and Malmani Chronicle* of 2 February 1889:

> I hear it is published in the newspapers that I have granted a Concession of the Minerals in *all* my country to CHARLES DUNELL RUDD, ROCHFORD [*sic*] MAGUIRE, and FRANCIS ROBERT THOMPSON.
>
> As there is a great misunderstanding about this, all action in respect of said Concession is hereby suspended pending an investigation to be made by me in my country.
>
> (Signed) LOBENGULA[67]

When the Big Dance was over a meeting of the indunas and the Europeans was summoned. As the trend of the talk was to upset the concession, and as neither Thompson, Maguire, nor Helm was present, Wilson objected to the holding of the meeting without them. Helm and Thompson were accordingly sent for—Maguire was away on other business—and on 11 March a series of gruelling indabas began. The king, as usual on such occasions, was not present, but remained accessible in the background. The indunas questioned Helm and Thompson, various white men expressed their views of the concession, and tempers rose as the argument proceeded for "six mortal hours" in the hot sun on one day, for ten on another.[68]

The attack on the concession was led, not by the indunas, but by the local residents Tainton and Usher, the trader Moss Cohen, the American concession-hunter Henry Clay Moore, and William Mzisi, a Mfengu from the Cape Colony who had acquired a position of influence in the king's entourage.

The main question at issue was the extent and implications of the grant to Rudd. The white opposition maintained that it gave the grantees "all the minerals in the country, all the lands, wood, water, in fact that the country and all it contained had been given." Thompson, supported by the missionaries, denied that anything but minerals was involved. Mzisi, however, who had been at the diamond fields, insisted that mining could not be done by one or two white men; it would take thousands. "You say you do not want any land, how can you dig for gold without it, is it not in the land? And by digging into the land is not that taking it, and do not those thousands make fires? Will not that take wood?"

It is difficult to believe that when Lobengula had put his mark to the concession he had not known what it contained, since Helm had explained the document fully more than once. What he had probably not fully understood was the difference in effect among literate peoples between the written and the spoken word. The oral promises that were not written into the document would have seemed to the king, who was "not civilised enough to break his word," as much a part of the agreement as the words on the paper. Thompson had over-reached himself in the use of picturesque Bantu idiom and of other glosses which had served a useful purpose in October. Now, in March, he was again and again confronted with his own "words":

> On the question being put to Thompson if they had or had not when applying for the Concession said "We have no cattle, sheep or goats and all we want is a place to dig" he answered the affirmative. And also "was it not agreed that you were to bring the things which you say you will give and then we shall show you where you can dig?" Again the answer was Yes.
> "How then is it that this writing says you have got the right to dig in the whole of our country and that the king can give no one else a piece of ground to dig in without your consent?" Then followed a long discussion as to what was meant, but the words of the document were inexorable and not to be perverted into meaning anything else than what appeared plainly on the surface. Thompson made reference to a verbal agreement, but it was maintained that any such agreement was worthless while a written one in express terms existed.[69]

It was of course the white opponents of the concession who brought this last argument to bear.

Helm as well as Thompson was put in the dock. He had withheld "the bad news" from the king. White visitors came to him before going to the king. Kgama's men came to him without going to the king at all. All letters passed through his hands—naturally, since he acted as postmaster, but the Ndebele were not familiar with postal organization. He prevented the traders from giving good prices for cattle. (More sophisticated peoples have the same habit of finding scapegoats for economic disorders.) At one point he was ordered to "leave the teaching and join the traders," which upset him. It afterwards appeared that this was not to be taken seriously. "I then spoke to the Induna of Bulawayo," Helm wrote, "and took him to task for what he said, he was friendly and jolly as ever and said, Those were only my words. It is only scolding (*telisa*)." The king himself told Elliot that no importance need be attached to it—that the Ndebele always kick a man when they think he is down.

Elliot and Rees, the missionaries at Inyati, having played no part in the Rudd business, were regarded as relatively impartial. On the fourth day of the proceedings they were called in and asked whether in any other country the sole mining rights could be bought for a similar sum. "Only one answer is possible to that question, and we gave it—'No!' " As Helm disagreed, the Ndebele concluded that one of the opinions must be dishonest. The missionaries went together to the king to try to convince him, without much success they thought, that there could be differences of opinion among honest men.[70]

The indabas were not the only strain to which Thompson was subjected. He and Maguire suffered continually from petty annoyances and sometimes from serious accusations and threats. When to these were added the perpetual anxiety about the concession, and the deprivations of life in the wilds which Maguire especially found it hard to bear, the strain approached the breaking point.

Maguire cleaned his false teeth in what happened to be a sacred spring, and let some drops of eau-de-cologne fall into it: he was accused of poisoning the spring. He was accused also of other forms of witchcraft, such as riding at night on a hyena. But he occasionally found relief by travelling away on business. In December he put one of the terms of the concession into effect by going down to the border, with an impi and the king's approval, to turn a rival party away. It was the party of the Austral Africa Company under Alfred Haggard, who was painfully astonished by this treatment.[71]

Maguire's next excursion, which enabled him to escape the indabas in March, was to go down to meet the Kimberley doctors, Leander Starr Jameson and Rutherfoord Harris, who had arrived at the border with the first consignment of rifles and ammunition.

Two very important characters thus make their appearance in our story. Each in his own way was destined to bear a heavy responsibility for several major disasters to the peace of South Africa and the freedom and unity of its white, if not of its black, peoples. Both began their careers as physicians in Kimberley—Jameson in 1878 and Harris in 1882. In that small society they were naturally thrown into close association with Rhodes. Jameson's association with him was very close. For some years they shared a wood-and-iron bungalow, in which they carried on endless but mostly unrecorded conversations about Rhodes's "big ideas." Like Rhodes, Jameson was and remained a bachelor. Harris, even if he had not married, could never have had the same intimate relationship with Rhodes.

Harris's chief claim to notoriety is his irresponsible handling of the communications between Cape Town and Jameson before the Jameson Raid, but that, as we shall see, was quite in character. Jameson's assessment of Harris was that he was "as thick as they are made."

Jameson was not exactly a pillar of wisdom himself, but he was not without brains. His intelligence, such as it was, was misdirected and circumscribed, but the main root of his follies was a mercurial temperament. After drinking a glass of sherry at the age of six, he is said to have exclaimed, "Now I feel as if I could go and do everything." That is what we shall see him trying to do. He never understood either his own limitations or those imposed by circumstances. But on this, his first important journey in Rhodes's service, there were no obstacles for him to surmount; they had been removed by others.

The "passage of arms," as Maund called it, had been accomplished by curious means. There was in force in the Cape Colony an Act, No. 13 of 1877, which among other things forbade the sale, barter, or gift of firearms and ammunition to any person belonging to one of the native tribes beyond the colonial boundaries, except with the written permission of the colonial secretary, the secretary for native affairs, or some person authorized by either of them. The mere removal or conveyance of such articles across the boundaries was similarly prohibited. The penalty for infringement could be a fine of £500, imprisonment with or without hard labour up to five years, or both fine and imprisonment. No wonder, then, that Rhodes, excusing himself on 14 February to Thompson for not coming himself to Bulawayo as requested, wrote: "I saw clearly that if I left the guns would never have got through so with great difficulty I have managed to get them through the Colony and Bechuanaland . . . If I had left when desired not a single gun would ever have got through."

How was it done? In August Merriman asked a question about it in the Cape House of Assembly. Sprigg, the prime minister, sent the acting high commissioner a memorandum including the information available to his government, and asking for further information from Shippard. It appeared that Rutherfoord, a Cape Town merchant, had obtained a permit from the resident magistrate, Cape Town, to remove the rifles to Kimberley. That was a straightforward operation; the border had not been crossed. At Kimberley, however, the consignment was within Rhodes's personal domain. The sidings and warehouses of De Beers were as useful then as they were to be seven years later, when a still larger armament was to be smuggled into Johannesburg.

On 10 January George Musson and H. Ware took each of them a parcel of 250 rifles over the border, and the remaining 500 were taken on 5 March by Messrs. Hill and Paddon. The permits for these operations were obtained, not from any Cape official, but from *the Administrator of British Bechuanaland* and his subordinate the resident magistrate of Vryburg. Proof was submitted that the rifles taken across the border by these men were the same as had been consigned to Kimberley by Rutherfoord. Sprigg wanted to know the further history of this merchandise; the only source of information was Shippard.

Shippard's reply to the acting high commissioner, Smyth, provoked from someone in the Colonial Office a large exclamation mark in the margin. It reveals more than it conceals: "I should be glad to know with what object the Cape Ministers are instituting enquiries into matters which do not appear to affect the interests of the Cape Colony. I am not at present prepared to furnish the information desired by them. If Your Excellency wishes to confer with me personally on the question raised by Ministers' memorandum I will proceed to Cape Town." Smyth thought this reply unreasonable. Shippard went to Cape

Town and there was more correspondence on the subject. Shippard feigned ignorance; there were no records in British Bechuanaland to show where these rifles had gone; permits were often given to traders; if the destination was the protectorate, there was no way of knowing if the goods had been taken to a point further north; and so on. "This minute," Sprigg wrote at the end of the correspondence," is of course merely an evasion of the question at issue." In the Colonial Office Graham commented: "Sir Gordon Sprigg evidently thinks that the rifles . . . were meant for Lobengula (hinc illae lacrymae) and I daresay he isn't far wrong."[72]

Once the first consignment was safely over the border, Jameson and Harris, like Rudd before them, set out on a "hunting trip" to the north, collected the goods somewhere along the way, and so arrived at the Ndebele border post, Manyami's, and were met by Maguire.

It was understood on both sides that the acceptance of the rifles by Lobengula would confirm the concession. That the £100 which Thompson had paid him each month was not seen in the same light shows the relative importance in the transaction of the "large monthly payment in cash" and the "other services." In March the king, knowing that the rifles were on the way, gave orders that they should be stopped at Manyami's. Leaving the two doctors in charge of them there, Maguire returned to Umvutshwa, where he was soon followed by Jameson. This was Jameson's first visit to Matabeleland and his first encounter with the king. The visit was brief, as he arrived on 2 April, and on the 12th passed the border post on his way out. The dates of the movements, during April, of the characters in the drama are important for their bearing on the repudiation of the concession. While Jameson was at Umvutshwa, Harris remained at the border in charge of the rifles. When he was relieved it was by Wilson, who was thus revealed as having gone over to the Rhodes party. That was not surprising. Wilson, Boggie, and Cooper-Chadwick represented a shadowy syndicate whose secretary did not even reply to their letters. Wilson was disgusted by the crude manoeuvres of what he called the "white oppositionists," had adopted a detached position from the beginning, and was easily recruited by Jameson.

The gain was balanced by a loss, not to the Rhodes party but to its representation in Matabeleland. When Jameson went out Maguire, unable to stand the strain any longer, slipped away and went with him. Maguire in turn was followed by a slave boy of Lobengula's to whom he, Maguire, had shown some kindness. Efforts were made to bring both the runaways back. The slave boy was captured, but a party led by William File, a Xhosa who had been Thompson's interpreter, failed to catch up with Maguire. Thompson had been accused of complicity in the slave boy's escape. As he had denied that the boy had gone with Maguire, he was in serious trouble when it was proved that the boy had done so. By sending File after Maguire he had tried to prove his good faith, but the manner of Maguire's going inevitably reflected upon Thompson.[73]

Rutherfoord Harris, relieved at the border by Wilson, visited Umvutshwa after Jameson had left. Harris and Thompson were then the only representatives of the Rhodes interests left with the king, and Thompson was under a cloud. Moffat was away, but was returning; he reached Umvutshwa on 29 April. The interval between the departure of Jameson, Maguire, and Wilson and the arrival of Moffat was used by the "oppositionists" to commit Lobengula to a formal repudiation of the Rudd concession.

A small opposition conclave held a series of meetings with the king. It consisted of Phillips, Fairbairn, Dawson, Cohen, and Usher; there may have been others present, though certainly none of the pro-concession party. There was some double-dealing here. At the end of January Rhodes had been in the Transvaal and "settled" with Leask, Fairbairn, and Phillips, who ceded their concession to Rhodes and Rudd. Leask retained a one-tenth interest in it and was given a one-tenth interest in the Rudd Concession, as well as £2,000 in cash. Fairbairn and Phillips got each an "allowance" of £300 a year. The negotiation was carried out in Johannesburg by Fairbairn, who then got Leask's approval. Yet here he was in April, with his crony Phillips, at the centre of a conspiracy to get the concession repudiated. It is difficult to understand what they hoped to gain by this. Cohen and Usher, who held no good cards, had everything to gain.[74]

A notice was drawn up, in Dawson's handwriting, and the draft of a letter to the queen, cancelling the Rudd concession. The style and spelling of the draft evidently did not satisfy some of those present, as the letter in its final form was of better literary quality though similar in substance. It briefly recounted the misunderstanding about the concession. Then, "I have since had a meeting of my Indunas, and they will not recognise the paper, as it contains neither my words nor the words of those who got it." The king reported that he had demanded the original document, which had not yet been returned to him, and complained of Maguire's leaving without permission. "I write to you that you may know the truth about this thing, and may not be deceived." The elephant seal was affixed. Phillips, Cohen, and Fairbairn signed as witnesses and Usher as interpreter. The letter was dated 26 April 1889, and was taken to Cape Town by Boyle, of Renny-Tailyour's party. It reached London on 18 June.[75]

Moffat did not reach Umvutshwa until 29 April. If he had been there it might have been difficult to communicate with the queen otherwise than through him; at the least, an attempt to do so would have weakened the effect of the letter in London. As it was, the high commissioner and his subordinates were by-passed and the missionaries ignored; they were all under suspicion of collusion with Rhodes. Complaints at the time and later, as by Marshall Hole, of the breach of protocol were naive; if the regular channels had been used a letter of this kind might never have reached its destination.

As it was, attempts to discredit the letter were made as soon as the news of it leaked out. Harris wrote to Lord Knutsford complaining that the letter had been written while Moffat was in the country, yet without his knowledge. Harris was stretching a point there, unless he was ignorant of the date, which is probable. Thompson, in his autobiography, claims that he "induced two of the conspirators to sign a written document to the effect that the letter had been faked, and was not authorised by Lobengula. I sent this statement to the Colonial Office, through Sir Hercules Robinson, and asked him to add a certificate of my standing and antecedents."[76]

Marshall Hole, in a letter to Maund many years later, pointed out that in 1889 Fairbairn was the custodian of the elephant seal. As the mark of an illiterate could easily be forged, the seal was the only evidence of authenticity, and it was in the possession of an interested party. "Fairbairn admitted to Dr. Harris and Dr. Jameson in my presence that he had concocted this letter from notes given to him by Lobengula, and in a letter which he sent later to Dr. Harris he denied all knowledge of the letter. Yet at that time he had the Seal in his possession."[77] Fairbairn had good reason for his prevarication "later," but the rest of Hole's argument tends to confirm rather than deny the genuineness of the letter. Every secretary "concocts" letters from "notes," and the author of the notes was evidently Lobengula.

That the king really wanted to repudiate the concession is suggested by at least two facts: he refused then, and continued for years to refuse, to accept the rifles; and less than four months later he repeated his repudiation in a form which left no room for doubt.

One reason for his change of front was certainly the difference between what the concessionaires had promised orally and the inexorable "words of the document." There were other reasons too, which struck Wilson at the time: "I personally am inclined to think that the King knows the contents of the document exactly, but that he is trying to wriggle out of it, and keep what he has got. He has granted concession[s] before, and obtained money and goods in return, without the concessionaires taking any more trouble about it (with the exception of Tati). This time the King evidently thinks that he has got people to deal with who will not allow the thing to escape, and do something with it, so hence all this trouble to frighten Rudd's party out of it. Or it may be only to please the chiefs and people." Referring to the rifles, Wilson again speculated with insight: "I often wonder if the King thinks those things, and a few sovereigns he gets every month, is the price of his country and his throne and maybe his own life. Time will tell."[78]

Probably for these reasons, Lobengula told the queen that the concession was cancelled. Nevertheless the initiative in the matter had been taken, and the goad applied, by the white "oppositionists." Buying off that kind of opposition would present no great difficulty to Rhodes. The real Ndebele opposition, the object of which was to preserve the independence of the country and not merely to divide the spoils more widely, could not be overcome by the same means. Lobengula knew that the means used, in the last resort, would be military, and that his army was not likely to resist them successfully. His policy was therefore to postpone the evil day by dividing the white interests where possible, yielding a little at one time to the whites, at another to the clamour of his own subjects, and always procrastinating.

Some of the indunas supported this policy, in varying degrees; most would probably have preferred a firmer line with the whites. This was also the dominant opinion in the regiments, which differed only in the degree of their xenophobia. The indunas who thought it wiser to conciliate the Europeans were therefore in the same difficulty as the king. They had to go through the motions of resistance to white demands if they were not to lose all credit with their followers.

Thus it was the Regent Mhlaba who put to Elliot and Rees the question whether the mineral rights of any other country could be bought as cheaply as Rudd had bought them, and got the negative answer. It was Makwekwe, second induna of Bulawayo, who led the attack on Helm ("White men Helm is your chief: there he is"), told him to leave the teaching and join the traders, and afterwards, jolly and friendly as ever, said, "those were only my words." Makwekwe, however, was at heart less friendly than he professed to be. Perhaps, as "spokesman" for both the Imbizo and Insuka regiments, he found it politic to conform his views to theirs; he became one of the most vocal advocates of resistance.

Yet Makwekwe had been one of the three indunas who advised the king to sign the Rudd concession. The others were Sikhombo, hereditary second induna of the Izinkondo regiment and brother-in-law of the king, and Lotshe, commander of the Induba regiment. Lotshe was at all times the foremost advocate of cooperation with the whites. Sikhombo's advocacy may be partly explained by his being "a finished orator, but not a warrior."[79]

It was often remarked by observers that the Shona captives who became warriors, the *amahole*, were the fiercest enemies of the white invaders. While this is the attitude to be expected of janissaries and the like, it is doubtful whether such a distinction can be made among Lobengula's subjects. The evidence bears out Renny-Tailyour's statement that the Imbizo, Ingubo, and Insuka regiments were "the most headstrong and unruly in the country." Of these, the first two were the only purely *zansi* regiments formed by Lobengula, Imbizo being the crack regiment of the whole army and Ingubo the king's bodyguard; Insuka was apparently mixed *abezansi* and *abenhla*.[80]

On 11 June all the white men connected with the Rhodes party—and this included such as Moffat—were ordered away from Umvutshwa because the Imbizo regiment was coming to speak to Lobengula. Wilson heard that they were coming "for the express purpose to ask the King if he has sold the country for guns, they say the King, if he has done so, has given away in a breath what has taken them years to obtain, and that the white men shall never have it. The fact that the King has sent the white men away, shows that he is afraid of his own power and inability [*sic*] to save them.''

At the beginning of July the alarm sounded again. This time it was all three ''headstrong and unruly'' regiments—Imbizo, Ingubo, and Insuka—who came it was said, ''to ask leave to kill all the whites, and also the old Indunas who were favouring them. Luckily, mixing up the latter in their kind intentions, completely foiled any chance they had, by so exasperating these Indunas that they persuaded the King to take precautions to overcome the young men, and to speak to them in a manner not to be misunderstood.'' Lobengula kept them all in hand and no one was molested.[81]

A reply to the letter of 26 April—not to mention the messages taken by Maund and the envoys—was still awaited. After the dispatch of that letter the king, feeling perhaps that he was now less likely to be compromised, allowed the 500 rifles and the ammunition to be brought in from the border. He did not ''receive'' them; they remained in Wilson's charge at Umvutshwa, where he built a store to house them. On 18 May Dreyer, who had been Rudd's companion in 1888, arrived with the second half of the armament.[82] Lobengula did not touch any of it until the bitter time when the Rudd concession had become irrelevant in comparison with more pressing dangers.

In the meantime the concession had been denounced. The real authors of this policy, Rudd's rivals, hoped to fill the vacuum thus created, but Maund had not boasted in vain when he said that no concession would be granted until he returned. John Lee, who was a British subject but half Afrikaner by birth, a Matabelelander by residence, and a Transvaler in sentiment, returned to the country in June.[83] Together with Streeter, whose background was similar to Lee's, he approached the king for a concession, but in vain. Moffat called both men ''undisguised renegades.'' Harris employed a Koranna who had been in the service of Selous, and could understand Afrikaans, as a spy in the Boers' camp. He reported that Lee and Streeter, who had been in Pretoria, were to present a kind of ultimatum to Lobengula, requiring him to declare whether he was on the English or the Dutch side.[84] If this question was asked, it was apparently not answered, and no consequences followed from the refusal. The time was not yet ripe for a move from the Transvaal.

As will be seen presently, the moves which would decide the fate of Matabeleland were being made elsewhere during these months. The most powerful financial interests were being amalgamated, and the less powerful were being bought and their protesting voices silenced. Reports of these events, and pieces of evidence sometimes difficult to interpret, were beginning to filter through to Umvutshwa.

It had not taken Rhodes long to discover that the Leask concession could be used as evidence against the validity of his own. In December he had written to Rudd, then back in the Transvaal, that ''I think it important to settle with

Leask." By the end of January, as we have seen, he had done so. Sam Edwards, on holiday in Port Elizabeth, had heard about this from Rhodes when he passed through Kimberley. He wrote to Dawson on 27 February to let him know. On 11 March, the day before the indabas began, Wilson noted in his diary: "Post arrived. I hear that Phillips and Fairbairn have been settled with . . . Moore has also an offer made him. Maund is also squared."[85]

Wilson, Boggie, and Cooper-Chadwick had by then decided to break with their own syndicate, which had ceased to answer their letters, and there could be no doubt which syndicate they would find it best to join. At the beginning of April, when Jameson reached Umvutshwa, he was able to enlist Wilson as superintendent of the rifles. Some vague promise of a reward must then have been made. It fell to Thompson to translate this into something more specific. Rudd wrote to Maguire on 11 April, enclosing a joint power of attorney to him and Thompson, signed by Rudd "for self and C.J. Rhodes." This was to enable them—in the event Thompson, since Maguire had fled—to "square" such people as Moore and Tainton. It "should be used with great caution and only if absolutely necessary and it should not be known that you have it." In June, accordingly, Thompson made a proposal to the Wilson party. Ignoring some terms which would not have become operative, it amounted to this, as recorded by Wilson: "we should obtain 20 miles square, something like 400 square miles of country on the halves, Rhodes' party to pay all expenses of working it, and to undertake to float it, the expenses coming off the flotation, we to pay the rate of £3 per month to the concessionaires. That we go and select our ground the same time as Rhodes' people come into the country. We go in on equal footing with them, they not to take any undue advantage of us." On 26 July Thompson, having shown the power of attorney to Wilson, signed a document to this effect.

Rudd's letter had virtually invited Thompson to make just this kind of arrangement with Moore. Wilson and his colleagues, however, did not hold the kind of cards that would justify such generous treatment; indeed, they held no cards at all. In April, moreover, the policy of encouraging sub-concessions had been favoured as a kind of insurance against failure to consolidate the main concession. By June (as will be seen) the imperial government had virtually committed itself to the grant of a charter based on that concession; sub-concessions were no longer favoured by Rhodes and his associates. On 14 June Maguire, from the safety of London, wrote to Thompson accordingly. Pledges of course had to be carried out, but "if to satisfy them you have to sign anything you would of course be very careful to keep the document in your own possession." The operative part of this sentence was underlined in pencil, presumably by Thompson. To extricate himself from an impossible position he asked Boggie to return the document so that the date on it could be altered to 2 April.

At that date the power of attorney had not yet been given. "This," Wilson wrote, "has certainly opened our eyes to the fact that there is something wrong somewhere." He advised Boggie not to give up the paper, sorry as he was that Thompson "has got himself into trouble with Rhodes about it." There is no direct evidence that the date was in fact altered, but the three men did not get their 400 square miles. In the later amalgamation they received 25,000 shares, and we are given the tantalizing information that Boggie gave away 5,000 of these "to some relation of Thompson's who was supposed to have helped him over."[86]

Early in July Renny-Tailyour returned to Bulawayo from the south, and was invited to go on to Umvutshwa to see the king. "He had turned away a lot of white men, including Moffat, so allowing me to visit him was a great favour and shows his liking for us. I have had three interviews with him and given him a lot of presents." Though the king would not "talk business" until his envoys returned, he promised to "talk nicely to us" then. This was appropriate treatment for a known rival of Rudd. Lobengula did not know that Renny-Tailyour had already changed sides. "At present," however, "to declare openly to work with Rhodes would destroy any chance we have got; we are not opposing him, but working independently for our own hand, and at the right time can come in with them before the King." Renny-Tailyour did not even give Reilly, an employee of his own party, "any hint that we were coquetting with them at the Rand, but Dr. Harris proclaimed it from the house tops, or rather from the waggon boards, that we were all one." It was well to be circumspect. Fairbairn was by this time out of favour at court for consorting too openly with the Rhodes party.[87]

It was not long before the king learned that, from his point of view, there was "something wrong somewhere." Usher, one of the few remaining unreconciled oppositionists, produced a copy of the *Cape Argus* weekly edition of 26 June, from which he translated to Lobengula the news of an amalgamation of Rhodes's interests with others, and of the expectation of a royal charter for the amalgamated company. Moffat, asked by the king to give his own interpretation of two passages, refused to do so except in the presence of the man who had shown him the paper. When Usher was brought in ("as I expected"), Moffat was "very glad of the opportunity of unmasking the author of the little plot." That Moffat should regard the reading of news from the *Cape Argus* as a plot shows how far Her Majesty's assistant commissioner had identified his duty to the Crown with his support of Rhodes's interests. "Your Government," said Lobengula, "would surely not do a thing like that without consulting me." No, said Moffat, "they will be sure to speak to you first," but he could say nothing more definite as his government had not yet informed him about the matter.[88]

This conversation took place on 1 August. Information of a sort was then at hand, as four days later Mshete and Babayane, with Maund and Colenbrander, arrived at Umvutshwa.

1 Political Papers of J.S. Moffat, 24 September 1890; LMS Papers (LO 6/1/4), from Thomson, 24 July 1876; Bishop Knight-Bruce in C.E. Fripp and V.W. Hiller, eds., *Gold and the Gospel in Mashonaland, 1888*, p.18; Rudd in ibid., p. 186. See also the papers of F.R. ("Matabele") Thompson: Diary, 12 November 1888; 16 November 1888; 9 December 1888; 22 February 1889; 6 March 1889. (See Bibliography. The copies of these papers at Queen's University have been arranged conveniently and the pages numbered. Reference will be made to these numbers in the relevant notes that follow, as in this example for the above entries: Queen's, pp.8, 10, 15, 40, 119, 133.)

2 Dawson Papers (DA 1/1/1), Heany to Dawson, 16 March 1888; Reminiscences of Ivon Fry (National Archives, FR 2/2/1).

3 Edward C. Tabler, *Pioneers of Rhodesia*, s.v. Fairbairn, Leask, Phillips, Westbeech; J.P.R. Wallis, ed., *The Southern African Diaries of Thomas Leask, 1865-70*, Introduction, *passim*; Dawson Papers (DA 1/1/1), Westbeech to Dawson, 4 November 1887; Ledger Book of James Fairbairn (RH Mss Afr. s 226).

4 Four seals are known to have been made for Lobengula. Of these only two belong to the period after 1882; of these two only the one mentioned here is known to have been used for documents. Ivon Fry claimed that his father had made it for Lobengula. See E.E. Burke, "Lobengula's Seals," in *Africana Notes and News*, 11 (1955), pp.339-44.

5 Papers of Thomas Leask (National Archives LE 2/2/16,17); Diary of George Westbeech (WE 1/2/1), p.57; Political Papers of J.S. Moffat, Moffat to R.W. Thompson, 11 September 1888; Diary of B. ("Matabele") Wilson (WI 6/2/1), 3 July 1888; Tabler, *Pioneers of Rhodesia*, s.v. Fairbairn; Wallis, *Diaries of Thomas Leask*, pp.1-11; Thompson Papers, Leask to Rudd, 30 November 1888 (Queen's, pp.229-231).

6 Political Papers of J.S. Moffat, Moffat to Leask, 1 August 1888.

7 CO 879/29/358, no. 33, encl. 2; RH Mss Afr. s 73, pp.22, 38. Henry was a brother of George Pauling, the railway builder, also associated with d'Erlanger. Henry was believed to represent the Caisse des Mines, but this was denied by the manager (CO 879/30/369, nos. 50, 66, pp.142, 173-5). Henry Pauling returned to England with two options for d'Erlanger, this one for the Disputed Territory, and another for a deep level proposition on the Rand; d'Erlanger chose the former. (E.B. d'Erlanger, *History of the Construction and Finance of the Rhodesian Transport System*, p.6.)

8 Frank Johnson in his memoirs (*Great Days*, pp.87-9) gives an account of the origin of the Exploring Company which is somewhat confused and difficult to interpret. By this account the Company was originally the Exploring Syndicate, entirely financed (as Maund was said to have been employed) by the Cape Town group, the Northern Goldfields Exploration Company. By some financial sleight-of-hand the syndicate was filched from its original owners by Gifford and Cawston; therefore the shares in the Chartered Company and Central Search which were allocated to the Exploring Company should by rights have belonged to Johnson and his associates in Cape Town. Some of Johnson's "facts"—e.g. that Maund had got a concession from Lobengula—are mistaken, and his explanation of how "we had been badly tricked" is not coherent. The important fact is that Johnson for the rest of his life nursed a bitter grudge against Gifford and Cawston. He may be right in attributing this to

their acquisition of the Exploring Syndicate, but see below, ch.4, for an alternative explanation.

9 RH Mss Afr. S 73, pp.22, 38; CO 879/29/358, nos. 20, 22.

10 RH Mss Afr. S 73, pp.40-1; 45; CO 417/27/2107, p.242, and 2695, pp.319-21.

11 J.G. Lockhart and C.M. Woodhouse, *Rhodes*, ch. 7; Basil Williams, *Cecil Rhodes*, pp.92-105.

12 RH Mss Afr. S 73, p.44; Reminiscences of Ivon Fry (FR 2/2/1); Dawson Papers (DA 1/1/1), Heany to Dawson, 16 March 1888. There is a mystery about Fry's grievance. On 1 July 1889 Cawston gave the Colonial Office an account of the amalgamation, and among the united interests he mentions Fry, which must mean Ivon Fry (CO 879/30/372, no. 105). On 8 January 1889 Rudd wrote to Maguire and Thompson that he had "lent young Fry some money and have started him here," i.e., on the Rand. (Thompson Papers; Queen's, p.240.)

13 J.I. Rademeyer, *Die Land Noord van die Limpopo*, pp.65-7; Political Papers of J.S. Moffat, notebook, 24 August 1888, and also 24 July 1888, Moffat to Shippard, quoting Helm, 12 July 1888; CO 879/30/369, no. 41, encl., which gives a version very slightly different from that in Moffat's notebook; C5918, no. 18, encl., p.103.

14 CO 879/29/358, no. 33, encl. 4, 5, 6; no. 34, encl. 1; Rademeyer, *Limpopo*, p.64.

15 CO 879/30/369, no. 40, encl., pp.59-131; no. 9, encl., pp.16-18; no. 88, encl., pp.203-10; Rademeyer, *Limpopo*, pp.67-74; CO 879/30/372, no. 37, encl., pp.27-32 (Joubert's report on Grobler's death). Correspondence with Kruger on this matter continued for a long time (e.g. CO 417/29, 30, *passim*), ending with a British pension to Grobler's widow. The affray almost certainly took place north of 22° S., and so outside the protectorate. (Paul Maylam, "The Significance of the Disputed Territory in Bechuanaland, 1887-1893" [M.A. research paper, Queen's University], pp.27-30, 81.)

16 Rademeyer, *Limpopo*, p.70; CO 879/29/358, no. 1, encl., pp.2-11; Political Papers of J.S. Moffat, Moffat to Shippard, 24 August 1888 (official and private letters); Lobengula Papers (LO 1/1/1), Lobengula to E. Clark, 17 May 1888; CO 879/30/369, no. 77, encl., p.184; "H.M.G.J.," Notes on Chiefs Gampu and Sikhombo, in *Native Affairs Department Annual (NADA)*, 1925, p.13.

17 Political Papers of J.S. Moffat, Moffat to Shippard, 24 August 1888; LMS Papers, (LO 6/1/5), Helm to LMS, 15 September 1888. Ralph Williams reported Grobler's aggressive plans from Pretoria on 12 October 1888 (CO 879/30/369, no. 44, encl., pp.138-9.)

18 The standard statement of this view is G.S. Preller, *Die Grobler Moord*.

19 RH Mss Afr. S 73, p.23.

20 RH Mss Afr. T 5, f. 440.

21 Lockhart and Woodhouse, *Rhodes*, pp.141-2; N. Rouillard, ed., *Matabele Thompson, an Autobiography*, pp.92-6; Hiller in Fripp and Hiller, *Gold and the Gospel*, pp.150-1, 154.

22 CO 879/30/372, nos. 1, 2.

23 Hiller in Fripp and Hiller, *Gold and the Gospel*, pp.158, 177 (for the whole journey, pp.155-81); Political Papers of J.S. Moffat, Newton to Moffat, 25 August 1888; RH Mss Afr. S 73, p.45.

24 Hiller in Fripp and Hiller, *Gold and the Gospel*, pp.180-1; Rouillard, *Thompson*, p.101.

25 CO 879/30/369, no. 64, encl., pp.155, 158; Diary of Matabele Wilson, 3 October 1888; Fripp in Fripp and Hiller, *Gold and the Gospel*, pp.25, 28-9. In 1883 the "wizard" (Pasipamire the medium of Chaminuka), who was showing signs of disobedience and of wealth, was brought to Bulawayo and executed. An impi then destroyed Chitungwiza and its people.

26 Fripp in Fripp and Hiller, *Gold and the Gospel*, p.19; Political Papers of J.S. Moffat, Moffat to Helm, 15 May 1888.

27 LMS Papers (LO 6/1/5), Helm to LMS, 15 September 1888.

28 RH Mss Afr. s 73, pp.41-4.

29 LMS Papers (LO 6/1/5), Helm to LMS, 11 October 1888; CO 879/30/369, no. 64, encl. A, p.164.

30 Fripp in Fripp and Hiller, *Gold and the Gospel*, pp.90-1; Hiller in ibid., p.191; Diary of Matabele Wilson, 5 October 1888; LMS Papers (LO 6/1/5), Helm to LMS, 11 October 1888.

31 CO 879/30/369, no. 64, encl., pp.153-7. The Impande or Impandine regiment, mentioned in this report, does not figure in any of the lists that have been compiled.

32 CO 879/30/369, no. 65, encl., pp.169-72.

33 RH Mss Afr. t 5, ff. 442-5.

34 RH Mss Afr. s 73, p.23; Political Papers of J.S. Moffat, Moffat to Shippard, 21 September 1888; LMS Papers (LO 6/1/5), Helm to LMS, 11 October 1888; Hiller in Fripp and Hiller, *Gold and the Gospel*, pp.181-2; Thompson Papers, Diary, 24 November 1888 (Queen's, p.19).

35 Newton Papers (National Archives NE/1/1/10), Maguire to Newton, 27 October 1888; RH Mss Afr. s. 73, pp.43, 45; Thompson Papers, Rudd to Thompson and Maguire, 1 November 1888 (Queen's, p.204).

36 Wallis, *Diaries of Thomas Leask*, p.iii; Thompson Papers, Rudd to Rhodes, 1 December 1888 (Queen's pp.222-31). According to Rudd, Leask had also another motive for negotiating. Fairbairn and Phillips were heavily in his debt (Phillips alone to the tune of £3,000), and Leask "practically supported them." By selling the concession to Rhodes he hoped to be "relieved" of them. When Leask and Phillips came out as fellow passengers about 1861 it was Leask who was penniless and Phillips who set him up in business; hence Leask's moral obligation. Leask had asked Fairbairn and Phillips to go back to the king and try to get better terms; this would be another reason for their silence in October.

37 CO 879/30/369, no. 65, encl., p.170.

38 Diary of Matabele Wilson (WI 6/2/1), 15 October 1888.

39 Hiller in Fripp and Hiller, *Gold and the Gospel*, p.206.

40 CO 879/30/360, no. 64, encl. F,K,L, pp.167-9; no. 66, encl., pp.173-5; no. 105, encl., pp.235-8; Wood's Journal (WO 1/2), 17 November 1888. Knutsford doubted the legality of the proceedings against Wood (CO 879/30/369, no. 122).

41 CO 879/30/369, nos. 31, 35, pp.49-50.

42 CO 879/30/369, no. 69, pp.176-7.

43 Fripp in Fripp and Hiller, *Gold and the Gospel*, p.22; C.L. Norris Newman, *Matabeleland and How We Got It*, p.159.

44 CO 417/18/23521, p.349.

45 Hiller in Fripp and Hiller, *Gold and the Gospel*, pp.202-3. The fear of a Boer inva-

sion is a theme running through the whole of the records of discussions with Lobengula.

46 C4643, no. 34, encl., p.117.

47 CO 879/30/369, no. 65, encl., p.172.

48 LMS Papers (LO 6/1/5), Helm to LMS, 29 March 1889; CO 879/30/369, no. 89, encl., p.210.

49 Hiller in Fripp and Hiller, *Gold and the Gospel*, pp.201-2; Diary of Matabele Wilson, 13 March 1889; Rouillard, *Thompson*, p.131. Lotshe was certainly the chief advocate of the concession; Sikhombo probably supported him but was afraid to speak out in his defence; the evidence about Makwekwe is conflicting. See Foster Windram oral interviews (WI 8/1/1), Siatcha, p.12; Mvutu and Posela, p.4; Mcupela, pp.3-7; Miscellaneous (J.P. Richardson), p.3; (WI 8/1/2) Ntabeni Khumalo, p.20.

50 The document can be found in various collections; a convenient one is Hiller in Fripp and Hiller, *Gold and the Gospel*, pp.219-20.

51 CO 879/39/459, no. 38; Rouillard, *Thompson*, pp.94-5; Thompson Papers, Rudd to Thompson, 9 October 1888 and 20 January 1889, and notarial instrument of 7 January 1890 (Queen's, pp.198-9, 245, 308-10). Thompson was offered the alternative of a quarter-share without paying expenses, but he eventually chose the half-share. This was put into legal form on 7 January 1890, by which time Thompson's half took the form of 5,390 Central Search shares and 13,791 shares in the BSA Co. In addition, Rudd paid £500 into Thompson's bank account and helped him further with some speculations in the share market. See Thompson Papers, as above. For the role of the Gold Fields Company in the operation, see below, ch. 8.

52 Hiller in Fripp and Hiller, *Gold and the Gospel*, pp.203-17; Rouillard, *Thompson*, pp.134-5; Thompson Papers, Rudd to Thompson and Maguire, 23 November 1888 (Queen's, pp.213-14).

53 Thompson Papers, Rudd to Thompson and Maguire, 23 November 1888 (Queen's, pp.214-13); Rouillard, *Thompson*, pp.134-5.

54 *Cape Times* and *Cape Argus*, 24 November 1888 (reproduced in CO 879/30/369, no. 75, encl., pp.179-83); Thompson Papers, Rudd to Thompson and Maguire, 23 November 1888 (Queen's, pp.213-14).

55 Thompson Papers, Rudd to Rhodes, 1 December 1888 (Queen's, p.222).

56 CO879/30/369, nos. 70 and 89, pp.178, 210-12; Diary of Matabele Wilson, 1 November 1888; CO 417/24/24623, p.295.

57 CO 879/30/369, no. 106, encl., pp.239-40.

58 CO 879/30/369, no. 96, encl., p.217; Rouillard, *Thompson*, p.130.

59 Diary of Matabele Wilson, 12 March 1889.

60 RH Mss Afr. s 73, pp.58-74.

61 Maund Papers, B25.

62 RH Mss Afr. s 73, pp.64-6.

63 Diary of Matabele Wilson, 25 November 1888. The date is wrongly entered as 1890. The king's promise to Maund is recorded, with Helm, Tainton and Colenbrander as witnesses, in Maund Papers, 2a.

64 Political Papers of J.S. Moffat, Moffat to Shippard, 6 August 1889; RH Mss Afr. s 73, pp.67, 69-70; CO 879/30/372, no. 122, encl., p.119. See below, ch. 4. I have assumed that Bosumwane and Bhozongwane (variously spelt) were the same person.

65 CO 879/30/369, no. 147, encl. 3a, pp.278-9; RH Mss Afr. s 73, p.62; cf. *The Times*, 1 November 1926, and Lobengula Papers (LO 1/1/1) for a slightly different version.

66 For Colenbrander's life, see B.H. Kemp, "J.W. Colenbrander as Military and Diplomatic Agent in Zululand, Swaziland and Matabeleland, 1879-1896" (thesis, University of Natal). I am also indebted to Dr J.C. Colenbrander, of Pietermaritzburg, for biographical notes of his father.

67 RH Mss Afr. s 73, p.67; LMS Papers (LO 6/1/5), Helm to LMS, 29 March 1889. The published notice and the original are in the collection of Dawson papers included in the Hole Papers (HO 1/3/1). The original is in Phillips's handwriting, bears the seal but not Lobengula's signature, and is signed by Phillips, Reilly, and Usher as witnesses and Tainton as interpretor.

68 The indabas extended over four days; according to Thompson, for 7, 5, 10½ and 5 hours respectively. Thompson Papers, letter to his wife, 15 March 1889 (Queen's, p.187).

69 Dawson papers included in Hole Papers (HO 1/3/1), memorandum by Dawson of the meeting to consider the Rudd Concession; Diary of Matabele Wilson, 10-15 March 1889; LMS Papers (LO 6/1/5), Elliott to LMS, 27 March 1889, and Helm to LMS, 29 March 1889.

70. LMS Papers (LO 6/1/5), Elliott to LMS, 27 March 1889 and Helm to LMS, 29 March 1889.

71 Political Papers of J.S. Moffat, Moffat to Shippard, 1 May 1889; CO 879/30/369, no. 113, p.244; no. 119, encl., p.250; Thompson Papers, Diary, 1 February 1889 (Queen's, pp.86-7).

72 Rouillard, *Thompson*, pp.153-4, 217; CO 417/32/17624, pp.437-47; 18485, pp.745-62; CO 417/33/18867, pp.42-57. In a letter of 4 February 1889 from Rudd to Thompson and Maguire (in Thompson Papers, Queen's, p.250) two names have been erased except for the inevitable initials, but they are not difficult to guess: "We have been very anxious about the guns because the thing is now quite public. S——— has behaved like a brick and sent them thro Bechuanaland and is now at Sechele's or thereabouts and will send for K——— personally and make matters right with him." This operation was at least one reason why Lord Gifford, unlike some of his associates, was "not a downright worshipper of Rhodes. I think the last Cape Papers show clearly that the way the arms were got through to Lobengula does not redound to the credit of anyone, certainly not the authorities. 'A big job.'" (RH Mss Afr. s 73, p.122.)

73 Diary of Matabele Wilson, 14 March to 13 April 1889. Rouillard, *Thompson*, pp.141-2, 147, 163-9. Here I have followed Wilson's diary, which is contemporary and precise. Thompson's Autobiography is strangely confused about these events, e.g. about the arrival of the rifles, Jameson's movements, and Maguire's departure, which Thompson does not associate with Jameson's. See Ian Colvin, *Life of Jameson*, vol. 1, p.99. It is hard to believe that Jameson left Bulawayo on the 12th, as he passed the border post on that day. He could not have been in (or beyond) Bulawayo much more than a week. Thompson's diary (or what survives of it) is no help, as it peters out at the time of the indabas in March, reviving briefly in July. If he indeed ceased to write it then, some later parts of the Autobiography would have depended too much on a fading memory.

74 Thompson Papers, Rudd to Maguire and Thompson, 4 February 1889 (Queen's, pp.248-9).

75 Dawson papers included in Hole Papers (HO 1/3/1) for original draft of the letter; Dawson Papers (DA 1/1/1), Edwards to Dawson, 27 March 1889; C5918, no. 101, p.201, the letter as sent (which in Fairbairn's covering letter is wrongly dated 23 April 1889); Political Papers of J.S. Moffat, Lobengula to Knutsford, 26 April 1889.

76 Political Papers of J.S. Moffat, Harris to Knutsford, 12 May 1889; Rouillard, *Thompson*, p.140. Neither Thompson's letter nor any reference to it can be found in the Colonial Office files.

77 Hole Papers (HO 1/3/4), Hole to Maund, 25 November 1927.

78 Diary of Matabele Wilson, 15 March 1889 and 23 May 1889.

79 LMS Papers (LO 6/1/5), Elliott to LMS, 27 March 1889, Helm to LMS, 29 March 1889; Political Papers of J.S. Moffat, Colenbrander to Harris, 10 February 1891; Diary of Matabele Wilson, 13 March 1889; "H.M.G.J.," Notes on Chiefs Gampu and Sikhombo, in *NADA*, 1925, p.18.

80 R. Summers, "The Military Doctrine of the Matabele," in *NADA*, 1955, p.9: Political Papers of J.S. Moffat, Renny-Tailyour to Forbes, 5 July 1889.

81 Political Papers of J.S. Moffat, Renny-Tailyour to Forbes, 5 July 1889, and Moffat to Shippard, 13 June 1889; Diary of Matabele Wilson, 11 June 1889.

82 Diary of Matabele Wilson, 2-18 May 1889.

83 John Lee was a bigamist of a different kind from the others: he had two *white* wives and families, all living in the same house. (Thompson Papers, Diary, 10 December 1888; Queen's, p.41.)

84 Political Papers of J.S. Moffat, Moffat to Shippard, 13 June and 10 July 1889. Moffat repeats the rumour of the ultimatum, but is "not quite certain" of it. CO 879/30/372, no. 121, encl., pp.117-18, and no. 122, encl., p.119.

85 Rudd Papers (RU 2/1-4), Rhodes to Rudd, 26 December 1888 (this letter was not published in *Gold and the Gospel*); Dawson Papers (DA 1/1/1), Edwards to Dawson, 27 February 1889; Diary of Matabele Wilson, 11 March 1889.

86 Diary of Matabele Wilson, 24 February, 3 June, 26 July, 19 August 1889 and 9 August 1890; Rouillard, *Thompson*, p.137; Thompson Papers, Rudd to Maguire, 11 April 1889, and enclosures; Maguire to Thompson, 14 June 1889 (Queen's, pp.276-81, 292-7).

87 Political Papers of J.S. Moffat, Renny-Tailyour to Forbes, 5 July 1889, and Renny-Tailyour to Lippert, 1 August 1889.

88 Political Papers of J.S. Moffat, Moffat to Shippard, 1 August 1889; Diary of Matabele Wilson, 1 August 1889; *Cape Argus* weekly, 26 June 1889.

CHAPTER 3

Company Promotion and the Charter

While Lobengula was holding both the white adventurers and his own agitated subjects at bay, their fate was being decided elsewhere. The movements of Maund and his companions provide a thread which gives at least the appearance of cohesion to these complicated decisions.

The Colonial Office heard of the deputation, its objects, and its progress, from two sources. Maund himself reported by telegraph to his superiors in London; Gifford and Cawston, always careful to keep on the right side of the authorities, passed on the information to Knutsford. At the same time messages went from Moffat, at Shoshong, through Shippard to Robinson, who likewise reported to Knutsford. According to Maund, the envoys were instructed to disavow the Rudd Concession. To the Colonial Office there was nothing alarming in that; but Maund had added that he would not communicate with Moffat or Robinson. On that point the officials were naturally sensitive, and it was in reaction to the threat to by-pass the regular channels that Knutsford cabled to Robinson "that deputation cannot be received."[1]

Maund was, of course, right in believing that Robinson, Shippard, and Moffat were committed to Rhodes's schemes, though Moffat had qualms about his involvement and was not so much a partisan of Rhodes as an opponent of his rivals—of Maund above all. After what had happened to Wood, Francis, Chapman, and others, it was natural for Maund to suspect that the envoys might be stopped in Bechuanaland and turned back. From Shoshong therefore the party left the Missionaries' Road and travelled through Pretoria on their way to the railhead at Kimberley. A plausible excuse was provided for this departure: water was scarce on the road, the rains were late, the temperature rose above 100° every day, and the envoys were old men, easily fatigued by the hardships of the journey. Nobody was deceived by this reasoning; the Transvaal route was associated in the minds of officials and chiefs alike with threats to the peace.[2]

At Kimberley there was an encounter which Maund in his old age recollected thus:

> Rhodes knew I probably was [the] bearer of documents from the King which might be of material importance to him. Dr. Jameson came across to the club

and asked me [to] come and see Rhodes. Scenting trouble, I went and found Rhodes lying on his bed (a favourite thinking and scheming place of his), and Jameson sitting on edge of bed in a small room of quite a small house just close to the club.

After friendly greetings Rhodes asked quite a lot of questions about the route I had followed down from Matabeleland—through the Transvaal. Why? Had I seen Um Paul? Why not through Bechuanaland—What did I think of the country? Were the Traders stories of gold true? Had I seen his party Maguire and Thompson?—and like a lady's postscript, Did I know his and Rudd's Concession for all Loben's Mineral Rights was a solid certainty signed and sealed and now in the hands of the Government and nothing in shape of documents could thwart it now—To all and much more I answered simply and in the most friendly manner as I had a genuine liking and admiration for both the man and his methods up till that moment.[3]

While noting that Maund's accounts of his own affairs must always be accepted with reserve, we may now follow the party to Cape Town. Rhodes threatened to have the envoys stopped there.[4] As Knutsford had already put his foot down, and Robinson was a Rhodes partisan, the dice would seem at this point to have been heavily loaded against the deputation.

Though Robinson could not prevent the travellers from going to England—the day of exit permits had not yet dawned, and Lobengula was paying the expenses—both the Colonial Office and the Foreign Office had made it clear

The deputation.
Clockwise from left: Mshete, Maund, Babayane, Colenbrander

that the envoys would not be officially received in London unless their mission had the high commissioner's approval. He was not likely to give that approval if, as he had been informed, their object was to oppose the Rudd Concession; and in response to his threat to avoid the regular channels, Maund had been told by his principals to consult the high commissioner.[5]

To discover the truth of the matter, Bower, the imperial secretary, with Newton as a witness, interviewed Maund, and Robinson interviewed the whole deputation twice. As a check on Colenbrander, he provided himself with an independent interpreter. For several reasons, however, the truth was not easy to discover. Maund as usual held his cards close to his chest. Mshete and Babayane were under orders to deliver a message in England, but not to divulge it to anyone along the way. Furthermore, Maund's purpose, though not the envoys', underwent a radical change while he was in Cape Town.

Gifford and Cawston, at an early stage of their South African operations, had approached the Colonial Office with a view to getting official support, and if possible a charter, for their company. Rhodes had done the same. The reply in both cases had included the point that the government could not favour one company that was in competition with others. To Gifford it might appear that the imperial authorities on the spot had not been observing this principle very scrupulously, but the Colonial Office continued to proclaim it. In December, Sir Robert Herbert had pointed out its obvious implication: if Gifford and Cawston wanted government support, let them first come to an agreement with Rhodes.[6]

"If you can't beat 'em, join 'em" was a maxim that commended itself to both parties. One side held the concession and had the support of Robinson and his subordinates; the other had the ear of Lobengula, the hope of a concession in the Mazoe valley, an actual concession in Bechuanaland, and more influence than Rhodes could command in the City of London and also in Westminster. Maund accordingly, when he reached Cape Town, received a cable from his principals "to propose to Mr. Rhodes that we should work together for the objects we both had in view." Rhodes, an experienced player at this game, "replied immediately, consenting to the proposed amalgamation, and offering to come to England to settle details."[7]

Maund, who a few weeks earlier had been writing triumphantly that the envoys would repudiate the Rudd Concession, was now put in an ambivalent position. He left Bower with the impression "that the natives accompanying Mr. Maund are prepared to make some statement in regard to concessions, in addition to the ostensible message respecting the Portuguese encroachments; and that this statement is being held back pending the negotiations for amalgamation, but that if Mr. Rudd or his supporters, whoever they may be, do not accede to the terms of the Bechuanaland Exploration Company, then the messages which are now held back will be brought forward."

This was a reasonable interpretation of Maund's own behaviour, but was mistaken when applied to Babayane and Mshete. They knew nothing about the financiers' negotiations. In obedience to the king's orders, at the first interview they politely but firmly refused to tell their message to Robinson. He accordingly "refused them the road." At the next meeting they were more amenable. They admitted that they were sent "to see if there is a Queen," to bring back a report on England, and to acquire a short-horned bull to improve the king's stock. That was all. Nothing about concessions could be extracted from them; nor did Maund now have anything to say on the subject.[8]

Robinson seems to have assumed that because Maund was now potentially on Rhodes's side, the deputation as a whole had ceased to be a threat to the concession. He agreed to recommend to Knutsford that they be received. This was a point gained, but the travellers, who had already missed one mail steamer, were impatient to be on their way. Without waiting for Knutsford's reply, they embarked in the *Moor* and sailed from Cape Town on 6 February 1889.

The next day Robinson received Knutsford's cable: "Her Majesty the Queen is going abroad, and I could not anyhow advise Her Majesty to receive messengers, which would be indication of disposition undertake protection of Lo Bengula . . ."[9] The logic of this statement is obscure, but the decision was apparently firm. The nervous envoys travelling across the great water were blissfully ignorant of Knutsford's cable, and of the minutes then being written on the files: "They cannot of course have an interview with the Queen, but they might be enabled somehow to see her." They must not be received or recognized: "of course in any case will not see the Queen—though they might be shown Windsor."[10]

Knutsford and Robinson, on the other hand, were unaware that the deputation was being befriended on board by a fellow passenger, Lady Frederick Cavendish, whose standing at court might enable her to remove some of the obstacles which the officials had erected. Luckily for her plans, Lord Lothian, who was a member of the government, came on board at Madeira. In the few days left before Southampton she enlisted his interest and support. Though a few difficulties had still to be resolved, the envoys and Colenbrander were duly received by the queen at Windsor on 2 March. "They seemed quite pleased," she wrote in her journal, "and, when I asked them whether they minded the cold, they answered I could make the weather cold or hot!" Knutsford reported that "the two chiefs were profoundly impressed and gratified by their reception."

On the previous day they had had their first interview (to be followed by two more) with Knutsford. Like Robinson, he had provided himself with an independent interpreter—none other than Selous, who had been another passenger in the *Moor*. As a matter of course they were also entertained—to breakfast—by the Aborigines Protection Society; among the many distinguished guests were Rider Haggard and his concessionaire brother, Alfred.

They were shown the Zoo, the Bank of England, Westminster Abbey, and St. Paul's; they spoke to each other on the telephone, steamed around Portsmouth harbour in a launch, and were taken to the first big field-day of the year at Aldershot. The purpose of all this was very obvious; as Maguire expressed it later to Thompson, "there seems to be an idea among both Kafirs and white men that Loben, when he hears from his messengers that he is not strong enough for the white people, will trek. There is I think always a possibility of this, and we should be prepared to buy all his rights from him if he shows the least sign of making a move."

No such result followed. To Babayane and Mshete the whole purpose of the visit was to carry out Lobengula's instructions, which they had done when they had seen the queen and given her the message. If they had missed the *Moor* in Cape Town they would not have seen her. A few days after the interview she left for a quiet holiday at Biarritz and a brief visit to Spain, returning to England early in April. The dates are important for another reason: though Knutsford's reply, in the queen's name, to the envoys' oral message was dated 26 March, it must have been composed, and given her approval, before she left.[11]

On 6 March, as the queen was leaving England, Rhodes sailed from Cape Town.[12] The Colonial Office knew at that time that an amalgamation of his and the Gifford-Cawston interests was in prospect, and that Herbert's terms for government support would in that case be met. The Office had as yet, however, by no means resolved to give its support to an enterprise based on the Rudd Concession, whether amalgamated or not. It was unhappy about the rifles and ammunition, unimpressed by the argument that they were less dangerous than assegais, and perturbed by Alfred Haggard's complaint that Maguire had turned him back at the border. "We must soon make up our minds," Fairfield wrote, "whether we are to allow all these concession mongers to cut each other's throats or not. If the principals could be put in the front of the fight it would be a solution of the question that would not be without its compensations." A few days later he suggested a policy for the government: to take no sides in concession matters, but to reserve the right, if it should ever assume greater responsibility for those territories, to examine all concessions and either ratify them or not.[13]

The news of the Rudd Concession and the rumour of a charter for an amalgamated company had stimulated organized opposition in the form of a South African Committee, which brought together a number of members of both Houses of Parliament and representatives of several missionary societies. Among them were Joseph Chamberlain (chairman), Sir Thomas Fowell-Buxton, Albert Grey, the aged third Earl Grey, Evelyn Ashley (former parliamentary under-secretary for the colonies), Sir John Colomb, Wardlaw Thompson (London Missionary Society), John Walton (Wesleyan Missionary Society), and—present at the meetings, though not listed as a member—John Mackenzie. The principles which drew these and other members together were concern for the Africans, whose interests they believed to be threatened by colonists and capitalists, and advocacy of direct imperial as opposed to colonial control of British Bechuanaland, the protectorate, and the sphere of influence.

Mackenzie had been at work, since the end of 1885, arousing the British public in support of these causes, and most specifically in favour of his pet nostrum, the separation of the high commissionership from the governorship of the Cape. He addressed meetings, wrote articles, published his two-volume apologia, and interviewed statesmen. The members of the South African Committee were only a few of the influential men he had enlisted; among the others were Sir Henry Barkly (former high commissioner), Sir Charles Mills (agent-general of the Cape in London), and, of course, his old friend Sir Charles Warren.[14]

The Rudd Concession was a handy weapon for members of the committee to use in their sparring with the government. When Cawston, on 18 May 1888, had approached Knutsford for support of his schemes in Matabeleland, the colonial secretary had replied that "Her Majesty's Government could give no countenance to any concession or agreement unless it were concluded with the knowledge of and approved by the High Commissioner." The words could be read in the Blue Book. On 20 December 1888 Sir John Colomb in the House of Commons asked some questions about the Rudd Concession, and Sir John Gorst replied: "As we have at present no protectorate in Matabeleland, we have no right to interfere with any grant or concession which Lo Bengula may choose to make." The inconsistency hardly needed underlining, but the committee rubbed it in: "There is no apparent difference between the cases of the two applicants, except that the former is an Englishman without any influential support behind him, while the latter is a Cape colonist, who is believed to have received very influential support in the commercial part of his undertaking from persons in authority at the Cape."[15]

At about the time when Knutsford was drafting his reply to Lobengula he granted an interview to this formidable committee, which met again on 4 March to consider its results. From Mackenzie's point of view they were not entirely satisfactory: "Considerable progress has been made, but it needs great firmness on our part to prevent the Colonial Office from swinging us all around—Chamberlain and all."

Similar trepidation was felt on the other side. "Mr. Mackenzie," Fairfield noted two months later, "has a power of creating and directing 'public opinion' greater than any other man of his calibre in this country." This was what Herbert meant, in part, when he wrote seven months later that the reply to Lobengula had been "written at a time when the obstacles to granting a charter seemed insurmountable and when there was a strong feeling against recognizing the concession granted by Lobengula to Rudd and Co."[16]

The reply in question was Knutsford's answer, by the queen's direction, to the oral message delivered to her by Mshete and Babayane. It read as follows:[17]

I, Lord Knutsford, one of Her Majesty's Principal Secretaries of State, am commanded by the Queen to give the following reply to the message delivered by Umsheti and Babaan.

The Queen has heard the words of Lo Bengula. She was glad to receive these messengers and to learn the message which they have brought.

They say that Lo Bengula is much troubled by white men, who come into his country and ask to dig gold, and that he begs for advice and help.

Lo Bengula is the ruler of his country, and the Queen does not interfere in the government of that country, but as Lo Bengula desires her advice, Her Majesty is ready to give it, and having, therefore, consulted Her Principal Secretary of State holding the Seals of the Colonial Department, now replies as follows:

In the first place, the Queen wishes Lo Bengula to understand distinctly that Englishmen who have gone out to Matabeleland to ask leave to dig for stones have not gone with the Queen's authority, and that he should not believe any statements made by them or any of them to that effect.

The Queen advises Lo Bengula not to grant hastily concessions of land, or leave to dig, but to consider all applications very carefully.

It is not wise to put too much power into the hands of the men who come first, and to exclude other deserving men. A King gives a stranger an ox, not his whole herd of cattle, otherwise what would other strangers arriving have to eat?

Umsheti and Babaan say that Lo Bengula asks that the Queen will send him someone from herself. To this request the Queen is advised that Her Majesty may be pleased to accede. But they cannot say whether Lo Bengula wishes to have an Imperial officer to reside with him permanently, or only to have an officer sent out on a temporary mission, nor do Umsheti and Babaan state what provision Lo Bengula would be prepared to make for the expenses and maintenance of such an officer.

Upon this and any other matters Lo Bengula should write, and should send his letters to the High Commissioner at the Cape, who will send them direct to the Queen. The High Commissioner is the Queen's officer, and she places full trust in him, and Lo Bengula should also trust him. Those who advise Lo Bengula otherwise deceive him.

The Queen sends Lo Bengula a picture of herself to remind him of this message, and that he may be assured that the Queen wishes him peace and order in his country.

The Queen thanks Lo Bengula for the kindness which, following the example of his father, he has shown to many Englishmen visiting and living in Matabeleland.

This message has been interpreted to Umsheti and Babaan in my presence, and I have signed it in their presence, and affixed the seal of the Colonial Office.

Colonial Office   26th March, 1889.

(signed) Knutsford.

This was the reply to the oral message delivered by the envoys. That message had been recorded in the Colonial Office thus:

Lo Bengula desires to know if there is a Queen. Some of the people who come into this land tell him that there is a Queen, some of them tell him there is not. Lo Bengula can only find out the truth by sending eyes to see whether there is a Queen.

The Indunas are his eyes. Lo Bengula desires, if there is a Queen, to ask her to advise and help him, as he is much troubled by white men who come into his country and ask to dig gold. There is no one with him upon whom he can trust, and he asks that the Queen will send someone from Herself.

If the version of the message which Moffat and Carnegie learned from Bo-sumwane and Mlugulu was correct, the last two sentences of the Colonial Office version were unauthorized additions to it. When Moffat, reading Knuts-ford's reply to Lobengula, came to the passage about a request for the queen to send a representative, Mshete "very decidedly objected," saying "that word did not begin with us; it came from the Queen, and not from us." Lobengula agreed: "I have not asked the Queen to send anyone to me."[18]

How, then, did Knutsford come to be misinformed about the content of the message?

It will be remembered that there was also another message, a written one, of which Maund was the bearer. The burden of it was a complaint about Portu-guese encroachment. The answer to this was kept separate from the answer to the envoys, and was sent through the high commissioner. The written message ended with the words "to be protected against my enemies." On the day be-fore that letter had been put into its final form, Maund had written a first draft of it. The draft, torn down the middle and pasted together again, was handed in to Knutsford together with the authorized letter. The draft contained two passages following the end of the letter that was dispatched. The first—"and an adviser whom I can consult about white men's affairs. I wish a man from the Queen not one sent to the petty chiefs down below"—was crossed out, Maund explained, "because the usual difficulty cropped up as to what 'protection' and a protectorate meant." The sentence "I mean by this to be protected against my enemies" appears in fact, in a slightly different form, as a substitute for the deleted words. The final passage in the draft was not crossed out, though it did not appear in the authorized letter: "I give my promise not to give away my country, or any part of it, or to enter into negotiations with any party, until Mr. Maund who has been to me before, brings back the Queen's answer with my men."[19]

Why did Maund give Knutsford this torn document? Partly, it may be as-sumed, because the last sentence, not appearing in the real letter, was flattering to himself. But the passage deleted by the king's order, yet handed to Knutsford, still legible, contains the very words which the envoys said "did not begin with us." They began with Maund, and were perhaps also conveyed to Knutsford orally in some way, becoming confused in the record with the actual words of the envoys. Maund's purpose in this chicanery is transparent: he wanted to be "the man from the Queen," and was determined to convey that request to Knutsford, whatever Lobengula might say.

In comparison with the ox-and-herd letter, which was a direct invitation to

Lobengula to repudiate the Rudd Concession, the reply to his written message might seem innocuous. It took the form of a letter to Robinson: "Her Majesty's Government desire that the following answer should be made to Lo Bengula in reply to the letter in Mr. Maund's handwriting, and sealed with the elephant seal . . . I request that you will take the necessary steps to have the answer conveyed to Lo Bengula . . . That the Queen's advisers cannot suppose that the Portuguese Government intend to claim and give away any land that does not belong to Portugal, but that the declaration made last year that Lo Bengula's Country south of the Zambesi is within the sphere of British influence, will prevent the Portuguese from taking any of that country, which, after proper inquiry, may be found to belong to Lo Bengula. That it will be Lo Bengula's duty to refrain from taking any hostile or unfriendly action against the Portuguese . . ."

When the time came to make up the next Blue Book, the Foreign Office decided to exclude this letter from it, because it revealed that Lobengula's letter was in Maund's handwriting, spoke of Lobengula's territorial claims as requiring confirmation, and told him not to take hostile or unfriendly action. "All these," wrote Sir Percy Anderson, "are, we think, dangerous weapons to put in the hands of such cunning controversialists as the Portuguese." The omission from the Blue Book—Lobengula's letter had, of course, to be omitted too—had the curious result that the written message was ignored by historians, including Marshall Hole, until Maund published it in a letter to *The Times* on 4 November 1926.[20]

Though the ox-and-herd letter was not signed until 26 March, and its contents were not known outside the Colonial Office (except to the deputation and to the acting high commissioner) until it was read and translated to Lobengula in August, the essence of its message was revealed to the House of Commons in March. On the 11th, Chamberlain asked a question about the Rudd Concession, referring to "the disadvantages and dangers to the peace of the country of such a monopoly." Would the government refuse to recognize it? The Baron de Worms replied that the government had hitherto abstained from interfering in such matters, and that Lobengula "has not, until lately, asked for advice . . . In the meantime I may state that Her Majesty's Government do not approve of that term in the concession referred to which provides for the supply of arms and ammunition, and they would advise Lo Bengula to have the term altered." If a protectorate were declared, at his request, over his country, the government would discountenance any concession containing such terms. Four days later, in reply to another question, de Worms let the cat out of the bag: Lobengula would be "recommended not to grant concessions without careful consideration and advice, and not to give to any individual a monopoly of enterprize in his country."[21]

In addition to Knutsford's, Maund was the bearer of another letter to Lobengula, which Rhodes afterwards called "similar one only stronger from the

Aborigines Protection Society." The main purpose of this was to apprise the king of the society's existence, and of its work in helping "distant races of men . . . to obtain justice at the hands of our fellow-countrymen." Since it was the task of the society "to oppose the actions of our fellow-countrymen when they do wrong," its advice would be likely to carry weight with Lobengula; and its advice, on the subject of granting concessions, was to be "wary and firm in re- sisting proposals that will not bring good to you and your people."[22]

The envoys and Colenbrander, but not Maund, left England on 29 March. As Maund was detained for a further week by other business, they were to wait for him at Madeira and join his ship there. The other business[23] concerned the amalgamation: Rhodes had just arrived in London, and had gone to work immediately to unite the Gifford-Cawston interests with his own, that is to say with the group that owned the Rudd Concession. The owners, so far, were the Gold Fields Company, Rhodes, Rudd, and Alfred Beit. By a "conditional memorandum of arrangement" on 28 March, the Exploring Company was given a quarter share in the concession as a whole, but a half share in respect of operations in the Mazoe and Shashi-Motloutsi areas.[24] This was the first and the most important step towards the general amalgamation which the Colonial Office had made a condition of its support, and of the possible grant of a char- ter.

It was the most important step because it united the only groups holding large capital investments, substantial concessions, and political influence. There were, however, many other groups and individuals with claims of a sort and power of a negative kind; these had to be "squared" if they were to refrain from mischief. Some of the small men had been squared, as we have seen, be- fore Rhodes left the Cape; others received in the course of the year enough money, scrip, or promises to take the steam out of their opposition. Most of the remainder were in England themselves or were represented by legal firms in London. They included all the interests, active, dormant, or merely hope- ful, on the Tati; the Austral Africa Company, whose agent, Alfred Haggard, had been turned back by Maguire; Sir John Swinburne, whose claims were not confined to the Tati; Erlanger and Company, holding the Wood Concession— granted by Lobengula for the disputed territory, and so guaranteed to arouse the Bechuanaland Exploration Company, holding the same concession from Kgama, to furious indignation; the Matabeleland Company, associated with Swinburne, claiming to have bought the Baines concession; a still more insub- stantial body called the Matabele Komalo Syndicate, claiming not an actual concession but the promise of one; Eduard Lippert, represented in Matabele- land by Renny-Tailyour, Boyle, and Reilly—"coquetting" with Rhodes, but still independent; and Louis P. Bowler, an Englishman resident in the Tran- svaal, who claimed a concession in Mashonaland, eastward from the Um- vukwes, granted by the chief Mcheza in May 1888.[25]

Before dealing with any of these, the principal negotiators spent nearly two months elaborating their own "conditional memorandum of arrangement." The fruit of the discussions was the formation, on 23 May, of the Central Search Association, to which, a week later, the ownership of the Rudd Concession was transferred. Any mineral rights obtained thereafter in Lobengula's dominions by any of the original members, or by any of them jointly with any other party, whether in or outside this circle, were to belong to Central Search absolutely. The capital was fixed at £120,000 in one pound shares; of these, 92,400 would belong to the original parties, who would procure subscriptions in cash at par for the remaining 27,600. The sum of £120,000 was not supposed to bear any relation to the value of the asset. It was chosen merely as a convenient basis for allotting the shares in the concession to the various owners.

On 1 July Cawston, in a letter to Sir Robert Herbert, gave a brief and misleading history of the amalgamation, including a list of the interests which had been united. United into what? Not (unless prospectively) into the British South Africa Company, which had not yet been formed. If the reference was to Central Search, it was misleading again, because the list included at least one group, "Baron Erlanger's syndicate," which, according to the same letter, remained outside the amalgamation: "We have agreed to give them a portion of the profits resulting from the minerals in the 'disputed territory' without calling upon them to contribute towards the expenses of the Company." The Bechuanaland Exploration Company was not at this stage, like its alter ego the Exploring Company, involved, ostensibly because it was important that Kgama and Lobengula be handled by two distinct sets of people. There may have been another reason: this company was Gifford's favourite project, and Gifford wanted to preserve his little empire intact. Cawston's ambiguity (to use no stronger word), however, was a chicken that would come home to roost in due course.

The Austral Africa Exploration Company had to be appeased, weak as its claims were. It assigned 6,000 of its shares to Central Search and received 2,400 Central Search shares in return. It was to be given also exclusive charge of the minerals in an area of 400 square miles, to be selected by Austral Africa in agreement with Central Search. Alfred Haggard accordingly arrived in South Africa at the end of September and did some travelling between Cape Town, Kimberley, and Shoshong. He saw Rhodes several times, wrote to him several times, but the question of the 400 square miles was always met with a blank refusal, and a warning that if Haggard tried to go to Matabeleland Rhodes would have him turned back. Haggard learned the game the hard way: Austral Africa, Rhodes pointed out, was now controlled by the British South Africa Company and would be given shares in that company in lieu of the separate concession which was refused.

Cawston had assembled organic unions and promises of various kinds into one story of "amalgamation." The men in the Colonial Office were afterwards puzzled: wasn't Erlanger amalgamated with the others? Cawston, moreover,

Rhodes and Jameson at Groote Schuur, 1891

114 Rhodes and Rhodesia

had said that "all those who were considered to have rights in Matabeleland up to the present time are united in one Company." Herbert had failed to notice that "were considered" did not mean the same as "claimed." The claimants were heard from in due course.[26]

The greatest damage to the amalgamated interests was done, however, by one of their own men—Maund. While it is easy to understand his hostility to the Rudd Concession up to the time of his arrival in Cape Town with the envoys, his conduct after Rhodes's acceptance of the amalgamation proposal is a puzzle which cannot be solved by direct evidence.

In 1926, when Marshall Hole had published *The Making of Rhodesia*, Maund wrote indignantly to him in justification of his own role in the story. "Lord Knutsford's foolish letter," he said, "I had nothing to do with except to tell Rhodes what it contained." The implication was that he told Rhodes this in his rooms at the Westminster Palace Hotel, where the financiers were gathered to make their agreement two days after the date of the letter. At this meeting, Maund wrote, "Lord Gifford, Rhodes, Beit and I think Rudd, Cawston, my brother Oakley and myself were present. I went by direction straight from the meeting to inform Lord Knutsford of the amalgamation and to ask him that this clause [not giving the whole herd to the first comer] might be altered or eliminated . . . I returned and told the meeting that Lord Knutsford said 'that the letter had already received Her Majesty's approval, and could not, therefore, be altered'." In another version, Rhodes "personally tried his level best to get it changed and failed because the Queen was at Cannes."[27]

The idea that a group of financiers would send Maund to the Colonial Office to tell Knutsford how to word an official letter from the queen is so preposterous that one is tempted simply to accept the verdict of Moffat and Shippard, that Maund was a stranger to the truth; more charitably, one might say that by 1926 his memory of the events of 1889 had become confused. Rhodes, in October 1889, is likely to have had a clearer recollection of what had happened in March. "You remember," he wrote to Cawston, "how he [Maund] hid in that room of mine and said there was no such message in the Queen's letter. If he had told the truth we could then have remedied the evil but he deliberately denied there being any such expression." The matter was so much on Rhodes's mind that he came back to it a few lines later: "You better read this to his brother who will remember his brother's gratuitous lie to me in the Westminster Palace Hotel, when he said there was no such expression in the Queen's letter."

Rhodes must have asked Maund whether the letter contained some such message as the under-secretary had anticipated when replying to a question in the House of Commons on 15 March. We may be sure that Maund was mistaken in saying that he told Rhodes the truth about this. Rhodes unluckily could not try to "remedy the evil" until this late date, becaue he had been on the high seas.

There is another puzzle. If Maund had been loyal to his associates he would have warned them of the danger. It may be, as Rhodes thought, that "his one idea is to start fresh and parcel out the country in a number of minor concessions in each of which he will of course have a private share." Or it may be that the destruction of the Rudd Concession was only a secondary consideration, the main object being the queen's sending "someone from herself" to Matabeleland. That was the point that Maund had successfully put across in spite of Lobengula's orders to the contrary. It had been a constant theme in all his communications. When the representative came to be chosen, who should it be but the man with unique influence over Lobengula?[28]

It appears, then, that for the moment the financiers were unaware of the time-bomb that Knutsford had planted under their scheme. They had two preoccupations that held most of their attention: the financial arrangements, culminating initially in the formation of the Central Search Association on 23 May, and the quest for official support in the form of a royal charter.

The second object was pursued without waiting for the specific realization of the first. The directors of the Exploring Company were granted an interview by Knutsford on 17 April; arising out of that, Gifford wrote formally to him on the 30th:

> . . . The objects of this company will be fourfold:—
> 1. To extend northwards the railway and telegraph systems in the direction of the Zambesi.
> 2. To encourage emigration and colonisation.
> 3. To promote trade and commerce.
> 4. To develop and work mineral and other concessions under the management of one powerful organization, thereby obviating conflicts and complications between the various interests that have been acquired within those regions and securing to the Native Chiefs and their subjects the rights reserved to them under the several concessions.

I am authorised by the gentlemen who are willing to form this association to state that they are prepared to proceed at once with the construction of the first section of the railway and the extension of the telegraph system from Mafeking, its present terminus, to Shoshong and that for this purpose a sum of £700,000 has already been privately subscribed.

Having regard to the heavy responsibilities which are proposed to be undertaken by the association, and which cannot be considered as likely to be remunerative for some time; and whereas a proper recognition by Her Majesty's Government is necessary to the due fulfilment of the objects above-mentioned, we propose to petition for a charter on the above lines, and we ask for an assurance that such rights and interests as have been legally acquired in these territories by those who have joined in this association shall be recognised by and receive the sanction and moral support of Her Majesty's Government.

By this amalgamation of all interests under one common control, this association as a chartered company with a representative Board of Directors of the highest possible standing in London, with a local board in South Africa of the most influential character, having the support of Her Majesty's Government and of public opinion at home, and the confidence and sympathy of the inhabitants of South Africa, will be able peacefully and with the consent of the native races to open up, develope, and colonise the territories to the north of British Bechuanaland with the best results both for British trade and Commerce and for the interests of the native races.

On the same day a letter issued from the London office of the Gold Fields of South Africa, signed by Rhodes, Beit, and Thomas Rudd, supporting Gifford's proposal.[29]

This was not the first time that Gifford had broached the question of a charter. He had been angling for official support since the previous May, and in December, according to Cawston's account, Knutsford had made the "suggestion" that the competing interests ought first to amalgamate. Perhaps it was this hint that encouraged Gifford to write to Sir Robert Herbert on 3 January 1889, envisaging a union of the Exploring Company with the Bechuanaland Exploration Company. This time he wanted to know how the government would react to a request for a charter. The reply was noncommittal—"not . . . without full consideration of its effects," not without the high commissioner's recommendation, and so on—but the comments made in the privacy of the Colonial Office were even less encouraging.[30]

The chartered company as an instrument of empire had quite recently reappeared on the scene. Of the great seventeenth-century prototypes the Hudson's Bay Company survived, but had lost its administrative powers. The East India Company, already on its deathbed, had been given the *coup de grâce* by the Mutiny. After all that had been said about John Company one would not have expected to see its like again, at least in the nineteenth century. The new companies were, indeed, unlike the old in some respects, but they followed them in others—the royal charter and the exercise of governmental functions. By 1889 there were three examples to hand: the British North Borneo Company (1881), Sir George Goldie's Royal Niger Company (1886), and the Imperial British East Africa Company (1888). Both Gifford and Rhodes had these examples in mind.[31]

There was nothing to prevent them from forming companies under the ordinary joint stock acts and with these doing anything they chose in foreign parts, if the local authorities there allowed them; the African Lakes Company in Malawi was a precedent for that course. A chartered company, on the other hand, could be bound to act in relation to native tribes, foreign powers, and commercial competitors as instructed by the government. While this kind of control might be a safeguard against wars, oppressions, and difficulties with foreigners, the British government would be under a greater obligation to intervene in any of those circumstances than it would if the company were a purely private business.

The Colonial Office might weigh the pros and cons of the question, but would have in the end to defer to the Foreign Office in a matter so far-reaching and fraught with so many diplomatic dangers and possibilities as this. Even on the diplomatic side, however, there was a division of function between the departments. Because of the special role in South Africa of the high commissioner, and because of the elusive "suzerainty," British relations with the South African Republic were handled by the Colonial Office. So, *a fortiori*, were relations with Lobengula and Kgama. The Foreign Office on the other hand dealt with the European powers, and in 1889 its chief preoccupations were Germany and Portugal. It happened that this division almost coincided with a geographical one: the attention of the Colonial Office was drawn mainly to the regions south, that of the Foreign Office to those north, of the Zambezi. As British occupation of various territories developed from the activities of consuls in Mozambique and Zanzibar, the Foreign Office for a number of years was in the business of colonial government, while the Colonial Office was in charge of the purely diplomatic relations with Pretoria.

The gradual conversion of Her Majesty's government to the policy of supporting the amalgamated financiers, and conferring a royal charter on this company, can best be interpreted by relating the stages of the conversion to the impact of the impressions being received by the two departments respectively.

In the early stages the Colonial Office handled the problem by itself. If a single theme can be detected in the comments of officials and secretary of state through the first three months of 1889, it is an anxiety to avoid new expenses and responsibilities. The refusal to support the financiers, though not the anxiety, was modified only by a gradual realization that they would go into Matabeleland anyway, and that the Office faced a choice of evils. The realization dawned sooner on the minds of the secretary of state and the permanent under-secretary than on their junior colleagues.

Fairfield, as might be expected, was hostile to the Rudd Concession, charter, official recognition, and involvement of any kind up to the moment when he was overruled; he never committed a recantation to paper. At the beginning of the year his comment on Gifford's application set the tone: "This is a mere piece of financing. Something is to be got which will look well enough to invite fools to subscribe to. Such a Chartered Company could never really pay. It would simply sow the seeds of a heap of political trouble, and then the promoters would shuffle out of it and leave us to take up the work of preserving the peace, and settling the difficulties . . . Lord Gifford and Mr. Cawston evidently find that their existing schemes are likely to come to little—hence this restlessness and change of proposal." It was not bad prophecy, though Herbert pointed out that, with such large capitalists involved, shortage of money could not be at the bottom of it.[32]

At the beginning of May, when the definite enquiry from these capitalists reached the Office, Fairfield's reaction was still negative. Public opinion (given

Mackenzie's unique power of manipulating it) would not support the venture. The company would be swept away, "if not protected by our police," once payable gold was found in the country. All the poor and discontented gold-seekers of the Transvaal would move in. Bramston, too, continued to oppose a charter, though he was reconciled to the inevitable: an ordinary joint stock company would serve as well as a chartered one.[33]

This had been Knutsford's view also, at first. It was fortified by a dispatch from Robinson, received at the beginning of March, pointing out that neither Lobengula nor Kgama was "at present in the least disposed to part with their sovereign rights, and the discussion of any proposal based upon the acquisition by a commercial company of a sovereignty over the territories of those Chiefs might, if it became public at the present time, jeopardise our relations with them."

Knutsford's minute on this dispatch[34] was written on 5 March, the eve of the queen's departure from England; she must by then have given her approval to the controversial letter to Lobengula. The minute also followed by a day or two the interview between the minister and the South African Committee, on which Mackenzie had commented that "it needs great firmness on our part to prevent the Colonial Office from swinging us all around."

Which side, one may well ask, was Knutsford now on? He had composed the ox-and-herd letter, he had expressed his opposition to a charter, though not strongly, and even to any offical recognition of the financiers' operations.[35] On the other hand, he had advised Lobengula to trust the high commissioner, who, whatever he might think of a charter, was a whole-hearted supporter of Rhodes and the Rudd Concession; and, in Mackenzie's opinion, he had tried to "swing us all around." Perhaps, in his interview with the committee, he had assumed the role of devil's advocate, and in the process had half convinced himself.

This was the more natural in that opposition to the Rudd Concession did not imply agreement with the committee's views. Knutsford and his officials wanted above all to avoid involvement, responsibility and expense; the committee, inspired by Mackenzie, wanted the government to incur all those—through annexation and direct imperial rule. In arguing against that policy Knutsford would find himself backing into the corner occupied by Rhodes and his associates.

However that might be, on 26 March the secretary of state signed the letter to Lobengula and handed it to the deputation with due form and ceremony. He was therefore still prepared at that date to destroy the foundation on which the proposed charter was to rest. There is no contemporary record of what the permanent under-secretary thought of this letter, but it can be inferred that he would not have written such a letter himself. It was Herbert who had held out hopes to Gifford in December, if the competing interests were united. It was Herbert who on 5 March struck the discordant note, precisely because the amalgamation was now in prospect: he "would require the competing concession-claimers to amalgamate and form a strong Company to be controlled as regards sale of arms and spirits, etc. by a Charter and an official Director. And this Company should pay the costs of the Resident who would be their 'Governor'. Khama-land to be under said Company."[36]

The decisive word which absolutely convinced Herbert, and swung Knutsford into line with him, came from Robinson. Written on 18 March, it reached London on 10 April. Robinson had read in the papers a report of the Baron de Worms's reply to the question in Parliament on the 15th. This provoked him to a defence of the monopoly. Admitting that it had its disadvantages, he made the telling point that "Swaziland presents a striking example of the evils resulting from an opposite course." In Matabeleland the only alternative to the proposed monopoly was a free-for-all: "Lo Bengula would be unable to govern or control such incomers except by a massacre. They would be unable to govern themselves; a British Protectorate would be ineffectual, as we should have no jurisdiction except by annexation; and Her Majesty's Government, as in Swaziland, would have before them the choice of letting the country fall into the hands of the South African Republic or of annexing it to the Empire. The latter course would assuredly entail on British taxpayers for some time at all events an annual expenditure of not less than a quarter of a million sterling."

While, apart from money considerations, he would favour outright annexation, he had observed that previous annexations had been followed by "a perpetual wrangle with the Treasury." The example of British Bechuanaland was to the point. That colony, "after nearly four years of Imperial rule, as regards its prisons, hospitals, schools, public buildings, roads and the civil servants generally, is a forcible illustration of the effect of attempting to administer a Crown Colony—if I may be permitted to use the expression—'on the cheap'."[37]

These arguments were unanswerable. Exactly a week after the arrival of Robinson's dispatch, the representatives of the Bechuanaland Exploration Company were received by Knutsford at an interview, which must have given them some encouragement; the letters of 30 April arose out of it. Herbert's comment on those letters shows that he was now convinced that a charter was necessary in order to control a company which, having "already subscribed £700,000, may do immense good or harm in South Africa." He thought that much would depend "upon the personnel of the Board of Directors, and upon the provisions to be made for securing the rights and interests of Europeans and Natives"; to which Knutsford added, "Nor can the attitude of Lo Bengula in respect of the concession be left out of consideration." Herbert's minute ended with a suggestion that this correspondence should be sent to the Foreign Office, and that Lord Salisbury should be asked whether it might not be as well to include in the Company's sphere such territory north of the Zambezi as it might be important to control.[38]

The decision-makers of the Colonial Office, Knutsford and Herbert, are thus shown to have been won over to the idea of a charter by the beginning of May, and probably two or three weeks earlier. The persuasiveness of Gifford and Cawston may have contributed to this result, but the cause must really be found in the logic of the circumstances, and it was Robinson who revealed that logic convincingly to his employers. There is no evidence that Rhodes had any direct influence on the decision, though he had an indirect influence through Robinson, and through Gifford and Cawston because he was cooperating with them.

On 16 May Bramston, for the Colonial Office, wrote to the Foreign Office, enclosing the correspondence of 30 April and announcing that Lord Knutsford had consented "to consider this scheme in more detail." The reasons given were the importance of having the operations of such a company "directly subject to control by Her Majesty's Government," and the increasing expense to the government of the present administration in the protectorate. Herbert's idea of including territory north of the Zambezi was submitted for Salisbury's consideration. On 27 May Sir Villiers Lister replied that Salisbury agreed that the proposal deserved "attentive consideration." He did not agree, however, that territory north of the Zambezi should be placed under the Company in the first instance. The charter "should reserve to Her Majesty's Government the power of permitting the company to add other districts by simple license."[39]

The motives which led Salisbury to agree to the charter in principle—which was what this letter amounted to—were not entirely the same as Knutsford's or Herbert's. He was even less enthusiastic than they about imperial expansion merely for the sake of glory, but he happened to be in charge of the British Empire at the apogee of its power. His duty was to maintain that power in face of the increasing competition of other nations. He did not start the "scramble," but if Africa was being partitioned Salisbury would not allow his country to fall behind in the race, or the balance of power to be tilted against it by the expansion of others. He was prepared to go to some lengths to prevent other powers from precluding British advances into regions to which they, the other powers, had no indefeasible claim. In 1889 it was the Portuguese who presented the chief threat of this kind, and Salisbury's diplomacy was largely directed to meeting that threat.

Secondly, the principal area of this confrontation lay north of the Zambezi, where the Portuguese were trying to realize their dream of a transcontinental belt from Angola to Mozambique, but where the British had actual interests and settlements. These were mainly Scottish: the missions of the Scottish churches, and in support of them the African Lakes Company, in the Shiré Highlands and on the western shore of Lake Malawi. The career of Livingstone had given that country, as well as the region west of it (soon to become Northern Rhodesia), a special place in Scottish hearts; but the Portuguese claimed them.[40]

Salisbury wanted to extend the British sphere of influence, pegged out south of the Zambezi by the Moffat treaty, into those regions to the north, but was hampered by the tight-fistedness of the Treasury ("a Department," Sir Harry Johnston once called it, "without bowels of compassion or a throb of imperial feeling"). Casting about in 1889 for a means to do this, he chose Harry Johnston, then a young man of thirty in the consular service, and with considerable African experience behind him. Johnston spent a week-end at Hatfield in distinguished company, was given Salisbury's ideas, and encouraged to write an article for *The Times* ("Great Britain's Policy in Africa," by "an African Explorer") in the hope of arousing public opinion. In November he was appointed consul at Mozambique, nominally, but with the actual task of securing for Britain the countries of the interior in which Salisbury was interested. In March 1889—we note the coincidence in time with the heart-searchings in the Colonial Office—when he was ready to leave for Africa, Salisbury imposed another task upon him. He sent this young man on a special mission to Lisbon, to get, if he could, Portuguese agreement to a demarcation of boundaries.

Johnston may have been chosen for his diplomatic skill, as well as his command of the Portuguese language. He did get the Portuguese to give up their transcontinental belt, but part of the price was the Shiré Highlands, to be left on their side of the border. Salisbury rejected the agreement. He was not prepared to abandon the British subjects already established there. The news of the proposal provoked an uproar in Scotland, and the royal and parliamentary burghs as well as 11,000 ministers and elders of the churches petitioned against it.

Salisbury seemed pleased to have his hand strengthened in this way, but the demarcation was still to seek. The case against Portuguese claims in the interior was that they were not supported by actual occupation and control; but, outside the handful of mission stations and trading posts, there was no British occupation or control either. To make good his claims Salisbury would have at the least to get numerous treaties with chiefs, and a more substantial British presence would have to follow; but the most that could be got out of the Treasury was Johnston's pay and some money for treaty-making within the narrow limits of Malawi.

The way out of the difficulty was provided by Rhodes. As will be seen presently, he offered on behalf of the company-to-be to bear the initial expense of treaty-making and occupation as far north as Salisbury cared to go, and as a down-payment gave Johnston a cheque for £2,000. This would enable Johnston to extend his operations well to the west of Lake Malawi. Early in May he was in Salisbury's office again, explaining how the way had been made straight. The prime minister did not yet know much about Rhodes—"Rather a Pro-Boer M.P. in South Africa, I fancy?"—but was reassured when Rothschild guaranteed him as "good for a million or more." The immediate effect of his intervention was to make possible the treaty-making work ultimately entrusted to Alfred Sharpe. In the longer term, the hope of effective British occupation north of the Zambezi could now be entertained. It could not be effective, however, without a corresponding occupation of the line of communication from the south, and this would be ensured by the plan submitted to Salisbury by Knutsford.[41]

Salisbury, like Knutsford and Robinson and, for that matter, Mackenzie and the South African Committee, would have preferred direct imperial administration of all those vast territories. Like Knutsford and Robinson, however, but unlike Mackenzie, he knew that it was politically impossible because of the expense. He could not risk with his chancellor of the exchequer, Goschen, the storm that had been provoked by the departure of the previous chancellor, Lord Randolph Churchill. The logic of the situation brought Salisbury, by a slightly different route from Knutsford, to the conclusion that a chartered company was the only practicable solution to his problem. For Salisbury the usefulness of the company lay, for the present, south of the Zambezi. To the north its financial help would be welcome, but relations with the Portuguese and the Germans made it necessary for the Foreign Office to keep those regions, for a time, in its own hands.[42]

If these were the positive reasons for agreeing to the charter, the removal of the negative factors in the other scale must also have had some effect, though it is difficult to measure. The chief negative factor was public and parliamentary opinion, as influenced and directed by Mackenzie and the South African Committee; a secondary one was the antipathy, felt in varying degrees in official and political circles, to Rhodes, who was widely regarded as a colonial adventurer, an "Africander," and possibly even an enemy of the imperial connection. Mackenzie's book had contributed notably to this picture.

From the records of the financiers, as distinct from those of the government, one gets the impression that everything depended on personal contacts, timely introductions, words whispered into the right ears, and a judicious distribution of the future shares. It is most improbable that the decisions of Salisbury and Knutsford were arrived at on this basis. On the other hand, it is true that, when almost convinced by the logic of the circumstances, they were held back by fear of public opinion and of questions in Parliament. It is therefore significant that Mackenzie met his match in the manipulation of these forces.

The weakness of his case lay in the fact that he wanted the impossible. He argued for British control of the interior as opposed to colonial, company, or foreign control. Direct imperial administration being ruled out for financial reasons, the other alternatives remained. Every argument that Mackenzie had used could then be turned to the advantage of company rule. "In brief, as Mackenzie afterwards pointed out, his own years of hard labour in educating the British public regarding South Africa had prepared the way for the Chartered Company."[43]

In the period between late March and early May 1889, when the government was making up its mind and the financiers were organizing their business, Rhodes was at work also, making friends of his former opponents and of influential people who now met him for the first time. He had a peculiar talent for doing this; in addition, the man and his time were well matched. There were many imperial dreamers; Rhodes had the means, and was willing to use them, to make the dreams come true.

The best documented, and among the most useful, of his new contacts were those with Harry Johnston and W.T. Stead. Two years earlier Rhodes had conceived an admiration for Stead, editor of the *Pall Mall Gazette*, because of his courage in exposing "the maiden tribute of modern Babylon." He had tried in vain to visit him in gaol. On 4 April 1889, Stead went somewhat unwillingly to lunch with Sir Charles Mills, the agent-general for the Cape Colony, who had invited him to meet Rhodes. After a three-hour tête-à-tête Stead wrote ecstatically to his wife, "Mr. Rhodes is my man!"—and Stead had been a supporter of Mackenzie.[44]

Johnston, an old Africa hand, knew of Rhodes but had never met him. In view of the trust placed in Johnston by Salisbury, the other financiers thought it advisable for Rhodes to meet him. While Rhodes and Beit were in Paris in April, no doubt because of Beit's connection with Jules Porges and Company (though this aspect of the trip is not mentioned in the correspondence), Ricarde-Seaver, who was one of the party, wrote to Cawston:

> I thought it necessary, in the general interest, to confide in him [Rhodes] as far as I might consistently with my promise to Verschoyle, all we know about the mission of a certain little explorer now in Portugal [i.e., Johnston]—and knowing as you do the scope of his action as to territories north of the Zambezi, and his good will towards Verschoyle, do you not think it would be wise to consult him and get his views before we present any demand for the Charter?
>
> The results of his mission to Lisbon *may* very materially modify the views of our Foreign Office, and I am convinced that his aid and advice on the subject of the Charter would be of great value and moreover I think he might prove of great use in *influencing* Lord S. to consider our prayer favourably. He will soon be here—nay, may be now in London—and I would suggest you should see Verschoyle *at once* and work thro' him in this direction. I know we can count on Verschoyle and you may rely on his doing his utmost to serve us.

Three days later Ricarde-Seaver wrote again: "I have a letter from Verschoyle. He has written to Lisbon and will have news soon. I have told Rhodes *all* I could tell him without breach of confidence to Verschoyle. He is delighted with the idea, and wants to meet V. and J. (if possible) on his return to London and says he will find the money to send him (V.) out to write a book and get us some good footing on the North of Zambesi."[45]

History has not accorded to the Rev. John Verschoyle the vital role which seems to be assigned to him in this correspondence. He was the assistant editor of the *Fortnightly Review*, doing far more work for it (according to Johnston) than Frank Harris, the editor. He was also curate of a church in Marylebone, though "of such broad theology that all the strait Christian doctrines seemed to have slipped through the meshes of his mind." Perhaps it was for that reason that "he worked desperately hard as an Imperialist." Johnston had known him for some years, and on his return from Lisbon was invited by him, "about the end of April or the beginning of May," to meet Rhodes at dinner. The other guests, including Frank Harris and Walter Pater, were only of peripheral interest to Johnston and Rhodes, who talked business until the host apologetically turned them out after midnight. The discussion was continued at Rhodes's hotel until breakfast time.

Johnston thought he had found a fellow spirit in Rhodes. Johnston, too, was an imperial dreamer. It was he, not Rhodes, who first conjured up the Cape-to-Cairo vision. At this moment he was about to leave on an empire-building expedition to Africa. So Rhodes's money was given to him, not to Verschoyle to write a book. We have seen that Johnston was able to present Rhodes in a favourable light to Salisbury. About what Verschoyle was doing behind the scenes the records are silent.[46]

Among the converts Rhodes won to his ideas at this time was Flora Shaw, the colonial expert on the staff of *The Times*. (Her future husband Frederick Lugard reacted differently, because Rhodes had held out a prospect of employing him in Nyasaland, and then "dropped the scheme and left England without seeing him again, or even telling him that he was leaving.") For the purpose of influencing public opinion, *The Times*, the *Pall Mall Gazette*, and the *Fortnightly Review* were no mean conquests. Rhodes is said also to have enlisted the Baroness Burdett-Coutts, who in turn presented him to the prince of Wales; and A.L. Bruce (son-in-law of Livingstone, nephew by marriage of J.S. Moffat), a useful link in Scotland with the missions and the African Lakes Company.

That company was approached in the middle of April with a proposal for "association with the Charter Company." The amalgamated financiers "agreed subject to the approval of Her Majesty's Government, to unite their [the African Lakes Company's] interests with the Chartered Company, and to spend a sum of not less than £9,000 a year on administration and police in those districts. In case Her Majesty's Government does not feel prepared at the present time in include in the Charter the country north of the Zambesi, we shall act in this matter as they desire, and will be willing by private subscription to assist the Lakes Company and the Scotch missions pending the settlement of the boundary question with Portugal and the ultimate extension of the Charter."

The British consul in Zanzibar, Colonel (later Sir Charles) Euan-Smith, was opportunely in England for his health at this time; the financiers were in frequent contact with him, and made shares in various companies available to him. Like Johnston, he carried weight with Salisbury. Lord Rothschild had become a business associate of Rhodes at the time of the De Beers amalgamation, and was a large shareholder in the Bechuanaland Exploration Company. He was useful now, not only financially but because of his influence in political as well as business circles; he happened also to be the father-in-law of Lord Rosebery. In comparison with all these, Parnell and his Irish Nationalist party were of little account, but it was as well that their voices and votes would not be directed against the charter in the House of Commons. Rhodes offered to give the party £10,000 on the excuse of ensuring that the Home Rule bill would provide for Irish representation at Westminster, and so set a pattern for imperial federation; but he needed the votes too.[47]

Whatever weight may be attached to these personal influences, it is clear that the government had agreed in principle to a charter by the end of May. Further than that it could not go until the details of the charter had been worked out. The extent of its commitment was revealed when Lobengula's letter of 23 April, repudiating the concession, reached the Colonial Office on 18 June. The officials made no comment whatever on this file; they merely drafted a letter to the acting high commissioner asking him to inform Lobengula that the letter had been received and that the queen thanked him for it. It would have been unwelcome to them, not only because the policy of 26 March had now been abandoned, but also because it had not been sent through the regular channel. Rutherfoord Harris, from Bulawayo, warned the Office of the irregularity. Though the extinguisher which Thompson claimed to have sent does not appear in the records, the resourceful Rhodes was at hand to provide another. He got Maguire (also, now, in London) to write a letter based on his expert knowledge of the situation: "Those acquainted with Matabeleland, as a rule, attach little importance to any document stated to be signed by Lobengula which is not witnessed by one of the missionaries whom the Chief regards as his most independent advisers." Other similar statements purporting to be signed by Lobengula "have subsequently been proved not to have been signed by him" (no examples were given to illustrate this statement); the rifles had now been taken to one of his kraals (Maguire omitted to say that they were still in the custody of Rhodes's agents); and the king had regularly accepted his £100 every month.[48]

In Maguire's letter to Thompson about the matter there was none of this jaunty confidence. He wanted Thompson to collect evidence from the old hands themselves, or better still from Lobengula, that his letter had been written under a "misapprehension" and could be disregarded. What he meant by misapprehension was that Fairbairn, Phillips, and Usher had "concocted" the letter before they had been "squared." If, on the other hand, the deed had been committed after the squaring, pressure should be put on them by withholding their money until they gave "practical proof of good will such as getting the Chief to withdraw his letter."[49]

Rhodes was backed in London by an ally even more useful than Maguire: Sir Hercules Robinson, whose term of office ended with his departure from Cape Town on 1 May. A few days earlier, at a banquet in his honour, he had said that there was "now no permanent place in South Africa for Imperial control on a large scale . . . the idea of the permanent presence of the Imperial Factor in the interior, of a South African India in the Kalahari, is simply an absurdity."[50] This was painful reading to Salisbury and his colleagues, and confirmed the wisdom of their decision, at the beginning of the year, not to renew or extend Robinson's appointment. Once he was back in England, however, the Colonial Office treated him as a kind of oracle to be consulted on every difficult South African question.

Even so, the road to "Runnymede" (Rhodes's code word for the signing of the charter) was full of pitfalls. The most important of these, though from the records one would gather that it was passed over with scarcely a bump, was the question of the company's directorate. Much would depend, as Herbert had said at an early stage, on the personnel of the board of directors. There was never any possibility of conferring a royal charter on a band of mere "colonial adventurers." Though that label could not be attached to Gifford or Cawston, even they lacked the kind of eminence that was required.

In the search for directors Rhodes's talent for winning friends was put to effective use, both directly and through the friends already won. The proposed chairman was Lord Balfour of Burleigh, who had just served a year as lord in waiting to the queen and was about to become parliamentary under-secretary to the Board of Trade. After careful enquiry into the characters and financial standing of the men involved he accepted, but later withdrew on the ground that his political position made it inadvisable for him to preside over the company. In his place the financiers were able to get the duke of Abercorn, who was socially even more eminent and was not disqualified politically. At Euan-Smith's suggestion—evidence, again, of the wisdom of enlisting in the enterprise such well-connected men as the consul in Zanzibar—the next director to be approached, and who accepted, was the earl of Fife, a member of the South African Committee.[51] On 27 July he married the Princess Louise, daughter of the prince of Wales, and was then raised to the dukedom.

"With his sure instinct for conciliating opponents," as Basil Williams says, "Rhodes then approached Albert Grey," the future fourth Earl Grey, prominent member of the South African Committee, friend of Mackenzie, and opponent of the Rudd Concession. After some hesitation, and in spite of Chamberlain's advice to the contrary, Grey too accepted a directorship, and very soon became Rhodes's devoted ally. Because of his great reputation for probity, Grey, the perfect gentle knight, "the paladin of his generation," was the greatest catch of all. It may even be said that Grey's love was the best testimonial in Rhodes's dossier, weighing heavily against much that was unsavoury in it. Though the two dukes had been given the freedom to nominate the rest of the board, there could hardly be any doubt who the other directors were to be; they were Gifford, Cawston, Rhodes, and Beit.[52] A year or so later one more was added, Horace Townsend-Farquhar, but for the moment we are concerned only with the original seven.

The company was constructed from the top downwards; the directors were chosen, but there was as yet no company, capital, shareholders, premises, or staff. The government thought it undesirable for the company to be formed under the joint stock acts in anticipation of the charter, but the provisional directorate was the body to start the proceedings by petitioning the queen. It did this on 13 July, reciting its aims and making its requests as previously agreed upon in discussion with the Colonial Office. The board was then required to submit a draft charter, which on 23 July was laid before the Queen-in-Council, and referred by council to a committee.[53]

While the charter was pending, the directors and their associates faced the problem of raising the capital. For a company which in the event did not declare a dividend during its first thirty-three years, the procuring of what Rhodes called the sinews of war was curiously easy. The problem was not how to find the money; it was how to confine the privilege of shareholding to people who could be relied upon to support the aims of the promoters.

On 5 October Rhodes, writing from Kimberley where he was likely to be a few weeks out of date in his information from London, understood the capital so far subscribed to be approximately £200,000, made up as follows: De Beers, £80,000; Friends, £20,000; Gold Fields, £30,000; Beit and Company, £40,000; Exploring Company, £30,000. Allowing for some uncertainty about the identity of the "friends," it will be seen that the subscribers so far, with the important exception of De Beers, were virtually identical with the members of Central Search, and that the bulk of the capital had been put up by Rhodes's own companies. When the trust deed of De Beers Consolidated had been drawn up the previous year he had thought of that company as his imperial instrument; so, in a sense, it became, but indirectly and no longer exclusively. Rhodes, however, thought that "with our objects £200,000 is absurd"; he wanted a capital of a million, not all paid up, but all available at call. He suggested that another £800,000 be issued, paid up only to the extent of 2s.6d. in the pound, and offered to the original subscribers *pro rata*. The original shares had been in two categories, some fully paid and some at three shillings in the pound.

As the charter negotiations approached their successful conclusion, the capital was increased more or less in accordance with Rhodes's wishes. When it became necessary to bring new participants into the business, the total was increased by the number of shares allotted to them. Rhodes somewhat grudgingly agreed to 75,000 for the Exploring Company; "I rather did it," he told Cawston, "to please you." Other additions were made for different reasons. Rhodes demanded at least 20,000 "for colonial people of political position who will help us as against the Transvaal"; by December it appeared that

34,000 shares had been distributed in this way. Another 50,000 (at most) were used to "square" various concession-claimants in South Africa.

Each of the directors was allowed to take up 3,000 shares; Gifford apparently had not been told of this provision, had asked for only 1,500, and wrote plaintively to Cawston on the subject. As will be seen, that wrong was soon put right. All of the directors were solicitous for their "friends," as they are called in Rhodes's list. In various cases both directors and "friends" were allowed to hold shares in their own names, but in trust for others.

Apart from the 50,000 shares used to buy off the concession-claimants, none of the capital was "water," all shares being either fully paid or partly paid—three shillings in the pound—with the rest available at call. No prospectus was issued. The shares were not opened to public subscription, and they were not transferable for two years from the date of the charter. The duke of Abercorn, soon after that date, was "beginning to think that we should offer some shares to the public," but Beit was against it. So, after some hesitation, was Cawston. It would have given too many people the right to attend the meetings.

A few months after the granting of the charter, Cawston summed up the financial position for Sir Charles Dilke. Of the million one-pound shares, 750,000 had then been subscribed in cash, either fully or partly paid, 50,000 had been used for "squaring," and the rest were still "in reserve."[54] Those who took up these last 200,000 were, however, included in the list of "original shareholders" which the company was later required to produce. A selection of some names from the list, with the number of shares held by each, reveals various interesting facts. The names are arranged here in alphabetical order, except for the two groups of coupled names at the end:[55]

Abercorn, duke of/9,000	Euan-Smith, C.B./2,000
African Lakes Company/850	Exploring Company/75,000
Barnato, Barney/30,000	Farquhar, H.B.T./8,000
Beit, Alfred/34,100	Fife, duke of/8,000
Borrow, H.J./3,000	Gifford, Lord/10,300
Boyle, F./3,000	Goldfields of South Africa/97,505
Bruce, A.L./4,570	Goold-Adams, Major H./900
Burnett, A.E./1,575	Grey, Albert/9,000
Buxton, Sir T. Fowell/500	Haggard, Alfred/5,375
Cawston, George/3,236	Haggard, H. Rider/720
Colenbrander, J./500	Harris, F. Rutherfoord/3,250
Colquhoun, A.R./4,500	Hawksley, B.F./1,500
Currie, Sir Donald/5,000	Heany, Maurice/3,000
De Beers Consolidated Mines/211,000	Hofmeyr, T.J./3,000
De Villiers, Sir J.H./750	Jameson, L.S./4,500
De Waal, D.C./2,500	Johnson, F.W.F./3,825
Dilke, Sir Charles/1,200	Leask, Thomas/2,250
Doyle, Denis/1,500	Lippert, E.A./7,100
Eckstein, H.L./6,000	Maguire, R./18,695

Matabeleland Company/45,000
Maund, E.A./1,500
Maund, J.O./3,000
Metcalfe, Sir Charles/1,820
Mills, Sir Charles/350
Moffat, H.U./50
Renny-Tailyour, E.R./3,700
Rhodes, C.J./45,212
Robinson, Sir H./2,100
Rothschild, Lord/10,000
Rudd, C.D./17,897

Sapte, Major H.L./100
Seear, J./5,000
Stevenson, J./5,268
Thompson, F.R./12,291
Tiarks, H.F./3,340
Willoughby, Sir J.C./1,000
Zwilgmeyer, G. and
Smart, H.A./5,000
Beit, A. and Cawston, G./6,475
Rhodes, C.J. and Beit, A./11,100

Something is lost in the arrangement—which was originally "in order of entry in share ledger"—and in the selection, but without these changes the list is unmanageable. Even in its abridged form we can see that some of the financiers' high-minded critics, like Sir T. Fowell Buxton (though their motive may have been only to have access to information) were willing to touch pitch. J.S. Moffat is represented by his young son, H.U., the future premier. Frank Johnson, for all his venom, owned more shares than his enemy George Cawston. Major Sapte, who was to play his part in preventing the Company from seizing Beira, was a small shareholder, and Sir Hercules Robinson (no longer high commissioner) quite a substantial one. Colenbrander and Willoughby, who were to acquire large stakes in Rhodesia, had relatively small holdings in the Company. Outsiders and rivals like Lippert, Renny-Tailyour, and above all the Matabeleland Company had used their nuisance value to good effect.

But the main significance of the list is the dominant position of the promoters themselves, and with that the relative positions of the two principal groups. Figures are only approximate, because of the way interests were interlocked, and because of the large number of small, and not so small, shareholders who were in effect clients of the big ones. Even without looking at those ramifications we can see that Rhodes, Beit, Rudd, their associates, and the companies they dominated subscribed not much less than half the total capital—certainly as much as £460,000. On the other hand, Gifford, Cawston, their agents and associates, and their Exploring Company, counted for not much over £105,000. Though a study of all the shareholders might cause this picture to be modified, it could not greatly change the relative strengths of the Rhodes and the Cawston groups. Of course the amalgamation was supposed to wipe out the distinction and all that remained was the fact that the Company was dominated by its promoters; nevertheless these figures have some bearing on the role Rhodes was to play in the Company's affairs.

Long before the capital of the company-to-be was thus provided for, the principal subscribers had earmarked some of it in advance, and also guaranteed other sums, for certain special purposes: the railway, the telegraph, and the expense of maintaining a resident at Lobengula's court.

The extension of the railway northwards from Kimberley was of course a basic requirement of the whole grand scheme, but it had awkward political implications. The first section, up to the border between Griqualand West and British Bechuanaland, would lie within the Cape Colony and could only be built by, or with the consent of, the colonial government. That government was subject to pressure by the Afrikaner Bond, which in turn was sensitive to the feelings of the republics. Kruger wanted to keep the colonial railways away from his country until the non-British line from Lourenço Marques was completed. If the Cape railways were to advance at all he preferred that they should run through the Free State. So did the government of that state, though many of its burghers would rather have kept their republic undefiled by an invention which would in time destroy the profitable business of ox-wagon transport-riding. Under these pressures an agreement had been made to extend the Cape midland line from Colesberg to Bloemfontein, but for the present no further.

The financiers interested in the north required a railway which would not enter the republics at all, but would run like the Missionaries' Road along their western borders. Such a line would attract traffic from the neighbouring regions inside the republics. For that reason, and because it would bring nearer the danger of a future extension into his territory, Kruger was against it and the Bond was against it. The antipathy of the Bond and of other Cape Colonists was increased by reports of utterances in England indicating that British Bechuanaland might not for some time be given to the Cape—for the reasons regularly expounded by John Mackenzie.[56]

Because of this opposition the Bechuanaland Exploration Company (and later the Exploring Company which became responsible for this part of the enterprise) found the going rough when it tried to negotiate a contract for railway construction. The negotiation involved the Cape Colony and British Bechuanaland, with the possibility of later including the protectorate as well. The rewards demanded lay entirely, for the present, in British Bechuanaland: large grants of land; mineral rights; a tax on land adjacent to the line, to be paid to the company; rights of irrigation; the right to lay out European townships; and similar powers, when the time came, in the protectorate. Robinson objected to some of these terms, and so did the Cape government, as the prospective heir to the Bechuanaland estate.

The proposed deal was therefore never concluded, but without waiting for its conclusion the promoters of the chartered company guaranteed the sum of £500,000 for railway construction from Kimberley to Vryburg as well as £200,000 for the development of the land. This money was distinct from the capital to be raised for the company itself, and was the bait dangled by Gifford in his approach to the Colonial Office on 30 April. For the time being, indeed, it was not money at all but merely a guarantee that the money would be found. In addition to this, Rhodes offered the government £30,000 for the extension

Beira-Mashonaland railway, platelaying

of the telegraph line from Mafeking to Shoshong and £4,000 for the maintenance of a resident with Lobengula. These sums, however, were on behalf of the future company and were to be taken from the capital about to be raised.

In spite of the close links between the Exploring Company and the Chartered Company, the former put up a fight to get the railway contract for itself. To meet the objections of the Cape government to the original proposals it agreed to accept a larger land grant in exchange for the other types of concession. The railway was Gifford's special interest; perhaps his not being a "worshipper of Rhodes" had something to do with his failure to carry it through. Rhodes, too, acting for the charter (though he was a director of the Exploring Company as well), was in a better position than Gifford to negotiate with the Cape government, which held the whip hand. The outcome, in January 1890, was an agreement between the government and the British South Africa Company by which the latter was to build the railway to Vryburg and the former had the right to take it over when built, on terms that were defined. The company's reward, on the other hand, lay in British Bechuanaland and was for the British government to give: 6,000 square miles of land in respect of the line to Vryburg, and another 6,000 if it were extended to Mafeking.[57]

In the meantime steps had been taken to extend the telegraph line, a much cheaper operation. As early as 17 June, when the government was barely conscious of having agreed to the principle of the charter, Rhodes was reaching for his cheque-book and offering to pay the promised sum at once. It could not, of course, be accepted, though the government "entertained" the offer with the same favour as it gave to the charter itself. Late in August, after Rhodes had left England, the Colonial Office thought the time had come to think about accepting the money. Even so it was not until October that Gifford was so informed and that the promised sum was paid to the crown agents for the colonies.[58]

This simple negotiation was thus delayed because there was many a slip between the decision in principle to grant a charter and the affixing to the actual document of the queen's sign manual and the Great Seal of the Realm. One reason for the delay was the careful scrutiny and amendment of the draft document by several departments on grounds of high policy, but this process would not have taken four months. What did take all that time was meeting the objections of business rivals who claimed that the charter would infringe the rights arising out of concessions they claimed to hold. Unless they withdrew their objections, they had the right to be heard by the Privy Council before the charter business could proceed.

Many of the objections were based on real or imaginary claims in the Tati district. Lobengula excluded that district from the Rudd Concession, but that was not enough to satisfy the Tati interests. They were silenced by an amendment to the charter, specifically excluding the district from the company's sphere. Others were bought off in various ways; the most obstinate objector, Sir John Swinburne, was the greatest single cause of the long delay.[59]

On 29 October 1889—one year, all but a day, after the Rudd Concession—the Royal Charter was signed and sealed and the British South Africa Company came into existence. The charter was based on those of the similar companies of the same decade. It differed from them, and also from the draft submitted by Gifford, mainly in the scope of the control assigned to the secretary of state and the high commissioner. A great deal of thought had been given to the first clause, which defined the area of the company's operations and which had not appeared in Gifford's draft. Whereas Salisbury had at first wanted the company's sphere to lie, for the time being, south of the Zambezi, he soon decided against expressing that limitation in writing. For purposes of negotiating with foreign powers it was better that the sphere should remain elastic: he did "not want it to dot the i's too much." The northern limits were therefore not defined.[60]

Nor were the western limits, an omission to which the German ambassador quickly drew Salisbury's attention; Salisbury pointed out that the Anglo-German border was protected by the article which obliged the Company to observe the provisions of treaties. In other directions different precautions were needed. "North of Bechuanaland" was explained by Gifford to mean "north of the Protectorate." Rhodes confirmed this and gave the reason: the Company must stay out of the protectorate at present, "otherwise they would be strongly opposed by the Rev. John Mackenzie and his followers." Fairfield was appalled; if this were agreed to, the imperial government would continue to be responsible for the expense of the protectorate and of keeping open the Company's line of communication.[61] The protectorate was therefore included in the company's area, but on the understanding that it would at first be excluded in practice. "West of the Portuguese Dominions" was acceptable in principle though its meaning on the map had still to be defined. So was "west of the South African Republic," but Rhodes feared that Kruger would take advantage of the implication that the north was open for him. The first clause therefore defined "the principal field of the operations" of the Company as "the region of South Africa lying immediately to the north of British Bechuanaland, and to the north and west of the South African Republic, and to the west of the Portuguese Dominions."

The most important clauses, of the gravest import for the future, were those which seemed to confer governmental powers on the Company. The corresponding clauses in the North Borneo and Royal Niger charters put an imperial stamp on powers which the companies were already exercising. The British South Africa Company did not exist until it received its charter, and its promoters at that date had not acquired, by concession or treaty, governmental powers of any kind. That Rhodes's aim was to found a colony was well known. The only source from which the Company could acquire land and the right to colonize and govern it was Lobengula, or other legitimate rulers in its immense sphere of operations.

These facts had not been overlooked. The Crown did not confer on the Company any powers which were not the Crown's to bestow; it gave official approval to the exercise of powers which would be derived from other sources, but which could not normally be exercised by private citizens. Thus, by Article 3:

> The Company is hereby further authorised and empowered, subject to the approval of one of Our Principal Secretaries of State . . . from time to time, to acquire by any concession agreement grant or treaty, all or any rights, interests, authorities, jurisdictions, and powers of any kind or nature whatever, including powers necessary for the purposes of government, and the preservation of public order . . . and to hold, use, and exercise such territories, lands, property, rights, interests, authorities, jurisdictions and powers . . .

These were, for the time being, castles in the air. The only powers that could be used immediately were those derived from "divers concessions and agreements which have been made by certain of the chiefs and tribes inhabiting the said region." The most important of these, the Rudd Concession, gave mining rights only; and while it certainly belonged to "the Petitioners," it did not belong to the Company which was now authorized to exercise the rights derived from it. The concession continued to belong to Central Search, which made an agreement with the Chartered Company as follows. The Company was to bear all the expense of development but was to divide the profits equally with Central Search; roughly speaking, until the Company had spent £800,000 on development the gross profits, thereafter the net profits, would be so divided. As the Chartered Company was controlled at the beginning almost wholly by members of Central Search, the agreement was easy to make; the losers would be the outsiders admitted to the wider group but not to the narrower, and—more importantly perhaps—the creditors of the Company if it went bankrupt.

Incredible as it may seem, this fact was not known to the Colonial Office until long after the grant of the charter; the officials assumed that the Company owned the concession. The first article of the draft charter submitted by the petitioners included the words "is hereby authorised and empowered to hold and retain *either on its own account or on behalf of others* the full benefit of the several concessions" etc.; the concessions were qualified by the clause "*ceded to or vested in or that may be ceded to or vested in the Company.*" When this article was amended in the Colonial Office the italicized words were omitted without comment—perhaps as being cumbersome, redundant, or unintelligible. The petitioners' solicitor Hawksley likewise made no comment on the omission; least said, he seems to have thought, soonest mended.[62]

Her Majesty's government, when it learned the truth, was not amused. Knutsford had failed to demand from the interested parties a copy of this curious agreement. After the change of government in 1892 his successor, Ripon, did so. Sydney Olivier then wrote for the Colonial Office a memorandum on the origin and operations of the Company. "Her Majesty's Government," he stated flatly, "were misled." What was called the Company had turned out to be two companies. If the Chartered Company's resources were exhausted, as appeared in October 1892 to be the case, and if it were liquidated, the chief asset would escape the liquidators. Sir Robert Herbert was quoted as saying that "no persons connected with Her Majesty's Government had any idea that such a scheme was in contemplation when the charter was being considered and settled. It it had been disclosed the charter would certainly have been refused. It may even be a question whether the announcement of it now does not render it necessary to consider whether the charter should be revoked." Bramston commented that paragraph 2 of the petition for the charter was "a deliberate *suggestio falsi* if not a *suppressio veri.*" The temptation to revoke the charter was, however, resisted for the very reason that had caused it to be granted: the imperial government was not willing to bear the expense of administering the new territory.[63]

In the autumn of 1889 these revelations still lay several years ahead. For the moment the authorities were much more interested in other questions. The charter went on to specify in some detail the powers of the Company in the hypothetical case that it acquired such powers from those who had the right to confer them. They included powers appropriate to a government: to establish or authorize banking and other companies; to make and maintain roads, railways, telegraphs, harbours, and other works; to grant lands, either absolutely, or by way of mortgage or otherwise; to settle such lands, and to aid and promote immigration; to make ordinances for the preservation of peace and order, and to establish and maintain a force of police.

Other powers were appropriate to any business corporation: to issue shares of different descriptions; to borrow and to lend money; to acquire, hold, or charter steam vessels and other vessels; to carry on mining and other industries, and to make concessions for the same purposes; to improve, develop, clear, plant, irrigate, and cultivate lands; to carry on any lawful commerce, trade, or business.

Any of these powers might be abused, and abuse of the political or administrative powers could embarrass and involve the imperial government. The safeguard against abuse, and even against any act or policy whatever of which the government disapproved, was the power reserved to the secretary of state.

Following the precedents of the other companies, and no doubt also the hints received informally, the promoters included a number of powers for the secretary of state in their draft charter. New concessions or treaties had to be ratified by him and the Company was bound to carry out its own obligations under such concessions; if the secretary of state objected to any dealings of the Company with a foreign power, to any act of the Company that conflicted with an adverse claim (i.e., by a rival concessionnaire), or to any of its proceedings in relation to the inhabitants of its territory in respect of slavery, religion, jurisdiction, or any other matter, the Company was bound to carry out the suggestions of the secretary of state duly signified. Any system of patent or copyright would be subject to his approval. He was the final arbitrator in disputes between the Company and native chiefs or tribes.

To these restrictions the Colonial Office in amending the draft added others. While the draft had required the company to send copies of its concessions to the secretary of state, the revised charter demanded not only his ratification of those instruments, but also his specific approval, absolutely or on conditions, of each of the powers conferred before the Company could exercise it. Ordinances for the preservation of peace had not been mentioned in the draft; they were provided for in the revised version, but subject to approval by the secretary of state. Another new clause required the Company to furnish him annually with accounts of its budget, revenue, and expenditure on its administrative (though not its commercial) side, and with any other accounts, reports, or information he demanded.

The draft had not mentioned the high commissioner. In the final version the officers of the Company were invited to communicate freely with him, and "any other Our officers who may be stationed within any of the territories aforesaid, and shall pay due regard to any requirements, suggestions or requests which the said High Commissioner or other officers shall make to them or any of them, and the Company shall be bound to enforce the observance of this article."

The Company was of course made subject to, and required to perform (the promoters had neglected to include this in their draft) all obligations "undertaken by Ourselves under any treaty . . . between Ourselves and any other State or Power whether already made or hereafter to be made." The Company had to be and remain British in character and domicile, the head office to be in Great Britain and the directors, other than the original directors named in the charter, to be British subjects, unless the secretary of state permitted otherwise. (The loophole was provided because Alfred Beit was a German.)

The Company was required to abolish, as far as it could, the slave trade, and to put down the sale of liquor to Africans. There was to be no interference by the Company or its officers, as such, with the religion of the inhabitants, except in the interests of humanity. In the administration of justice, due regard must be paid to the customs and laws of the people involved.

Within one year, unless the secretary of state granted an extension (which he did), the Company was to draw up a deed of settlement defining its organization and financial structure. While it was permitted to carry on business operations of almost any kind, it was specifically forbidden to establish a monopoly, except in railways, telegraphs, banking, and the monopolies conferred by patent and copyright. (This was the most obvious difference between the new and the old chartered companies.)

The original seven directors were named in the charter. Three of them—the two dukes and Albert Grey—were to be irremovable except by death, resignation, or incapacity. The charter could be revoked at any time if the Queen-in-Council should decide that the Company had "substantially failed to observe and conform to the provisions of this Our Charter." Even without this condition, the political or administrative provisions of the charter could be revoked or amended after twenty-five years, and at ten-year intervals thereafter. The queen could at any time annex the territory occupied by the Company to the crown, or declare a protectorate over it.

The charter reflected, in varying degrees, the pressures that had been applied to the Colonial Office during the year—by the promoters, the aggrieved rivals, the Foreign Office, the Treasury, Mackenzie and his friends. It was certainly a way of building an empire "on the cheap"; it did not cost the Treasury at the time, and did not threaten to cost it in the near future, a single penny. Some precautions seemed to have been taken to enable the secretary of state for the colonies to protect native tribes and chiefs from injustice, rapacity, and undue interference, to prevent the Company from involving the empire in foreign complications, and to defend the interests of commercial rivals. The objection to saddling a new imperial domain forever with the government of a business corporation had been met by providing for periodical revision or revocation.

The sequel would show whether the precautions were sufficient. In the meantime the charter was open to a kind of criticism which was difficult to formulate then, is difficult now, but can be justified by hindsight. The elaborate provisions for ordinances, police, railways, land settlement, and the rest were much more prominent than the qualification which meant "first catch your hare." The reader of the charter would have no doubt that it was a program of imperial expansion. He would not gather that the sole foundation of the structure was a batch of purely mining concessions, of which the most important had been repudiated by the grantor. By its provisions, by the complicity of the government, and by the eminence of some of its promoters, the charter generated a psychological climate in which it was easier and more natural for the imperial authorities to support than to frustrate the Company's advance into its domain.

What other course could have been followed? One of the theoretical alternatives—direct imperial control by either annexation or protectorate—was politically impossible for financial reasons. But for this obstacle Salisbury would certainly have chosen it. On the other hand, the British government could have taken Fairfield's advice from the time of the Moffat treaty onwards, refused to be involved in any way, and allowed the South African Republic, Portugal, and Germany to contest the prize. In that case most of Zimbabwe would have fallen to the Transvalers, which was what both Mackenzie and Rhodes in their different ways had been inciting the public in Britain and the Cape Colony to prevent. Once the sphere of influence had been accepted the flag was, psychologically speaking, nailed to the mast. The government could have left it at that, refused to grant a charter, and sat back while the capitalists went to work on their own with a joint stock company. By choosing this course it would probably have had the worst of both worlds: the Company's frictions with Africans, foreign powers, and commercial rivals would have forced the imperial authorities to intervene, while they would have had no means of preventing the friction by controlling the Company.[64] Could the charter have been further delayed? Could its terms have been more restrictive? Comparison with, for example, the East India Company shows that they could, without involving the imperial government in expense. But in 1889 the politicians and officials seemed to think that the charter as it stood would prevent the company from usurping any authority to which it had no right.

Why it failed to do so will appear in the sequel. The government, presumably through indifference to any aim except imperial expansion on the cheap, had failed to retain in its own hands the appointment of officials. The omission was only partly rectified after the rebellion, and the consequences of leaving this power to the Company will be disastrously apparent in what follows. It will be seen also that one of the chief reasons for the weakness of the Colonial Office in this situation was the factor of distance, which had often been the great obstacle to imperial centralization. The secretary of state was far from the scene of action; Rhodes was near. The Company had its agents in Matabeleland; the Colonial Office had none except, on a temporary basis, Moffat.

After the departure of Jameson and, later, Harris, Thompson was Rhodes's only agent at Lobengula's kraal. He was not so much an agent as a target for the hostility that had been worked up against the Rudd Concession. Moffat, though regarded with suspicion because of his association with Bechuanaland as well as his support of Rudd and Rhodes, had to be treated with some respect, the more so because he was the bearer of welcome news. On 5 May he reported to Shippard that he had given the king the secretary of state's message, sent through the high commissioner, in reply to the letter about Portuguese claims and encroachments. The king received it without comment. A few days later Moffat was able to tell him the queen's oral reply to the envoys' message, and also the text of that message as recorded in England. Even this, with its unauthorized addition, failed to provoke any response from him: he "proposed that the matter should stand over until the return of the messengers. This plainly shows that I have not recovered his confidence and that he has not yet made up his mind who of the various claimants is the Government envoy."[65]

On 5 August Mshete, Babayane, Maund, and Colenbrander returned at last to Umvutshwa. The next day Moffat was summoned to interpret Knutsford's letter to the king in the presence of the two envoys. As all except Mshete understood Tswana, Moffat translated the letter into that language; an interpreter translating from Tswana into Ndebele for Mshete's benefit was the only other person present. If something was lost in the translation it was not the essence of Knutsford's message. Lobengula understood the words about a king giving a stranger an ox, not his whole herd, very clearly. The references to his supposed request for an officer to be sent by the queen were clear enough after double translation to provoke Mshete's protest, already mentioned.

Apart from the misunderstanding on this point, Knutsford's letter gave great satisfaction to Lobengula and in due course, when it was more widely publicized, to the indunas. It called for a reply, which the king dictated on 10 August and which Moffat signed as a witness; there could be no pretence that this one was "faked" or "concocted." Nor was there any attempt to avoid the proper official channels. The letter was addressed to Shippard, to be sent by him through the acting high commissioner to the queen:

Sir,
I wish to tell you that Umsheti and Babyane have arrived with Maund. I am thankful for the Queen's word. I have heard Her Majesty's message. The messengers have spoken as my mouth. They have been very well treated.

The white people are troubling me much about gold. If the Queen hears that I have given away the whole country, it is not so. I have no one in my country who knows how to write. I do not understand where the dispute is, because I have no knowledge of writing.

The Portuguese say that Mashonaland is theirs, but it is not so. It is all Umziligazi's country. I hear now that it belongs to the Portuguese.

With regard to Her Majesty's offer to send me an envoy or resident, I thank her Majesty, but I do not need an officer to be sent. I will ask for one when I am pressed for want of one.

I thank the Queen for the word which my messengers give me by mouth, that the Queen says I am not to let anyone dig for gold in my country, except to dig for me as my servants.

I greet Her Majesty cordially.

It was now the queen's turn to say, of the last paragraph, that "that word did not begin with me." It was Mshete who insisted on this part of the message, while Babayane "held back." The two envoys disagreed on many points. According to Babayane, Mshete had "been telling lies to the Chief. But that his time to speak will come and then the Chief will hear all about England." Moffat was sure that Mshete's message referred to in the last paragraph was a mistake, but he was not in a position to correct it. The envoys had come from the queen whereas he had not. Thompson too "called upon Collenbrander [sic] to deny this and he remained mum." Moffat's explanation—that Mshete had "been on the carouse nearly all the time since he arrived, and Kaffir beer does not clear men's heads"—was not adequate. There had been some failure of communication on this point, as there had been in the delivery of Lobengula's message.

This was less serious than the failure of communication that now followed. The king's letter of 10 August was addressed to Shippard, and could not have taken more than three weeks to reach him. As he did not forward it to Cape Town until 14 October, it reached London on 18 November, twenty days after the charter had been signed and sealed. Maund's report of his arrival, written three days earlier, had been delivered on 23 September. Shippard had once again proved a faithful ally of Rhodes. There is no knowing what the Privy Council would have done about the charter if this letter had been in its hands in time.[66]

For some unexplained reason the letter from the Aborigines Protection Society was held back for several weeks. Moffat reported on 26 August:

> On Thursday Mr. Maund took in to the Chief a letter by the Aborigines Protection Society. I was requested by the Chief to read it to him in the presence of the other white men on the spot. The advice given by the Society is not—or at least is construed as not—favourable to the granting of concessions. A long discussion took place, a large number of indunas being present; and next morning a still larger meeting was called, and the letter from the Secretary of State for the Colonies was again read, especially that sentence relating to monopolies; and a determined onset was made on Mr. Thompson as representing the Rudd Concession; but there was an evident feeling, which is hardening into a determination on the part of both the Chief and of the people, to repudiate all concessions. Unshete [sic] repeated his false injurious statement that he was told by the Queen to warn the Chief against granting any concessions, and to allow

people to work for him as his servants. I was much disappointed that Colenbrander did not contradict him on the spot, instead of half chiming in with him. I have spoken to Mr. Maund about this since, and both he and Colenbrander defend the course that the latter took in temporising. They say that to have contradicted Umshete publicly would have been to discredit all his testimony. Better this than that such a lie should be allowed to pass . . .

Worse than all, poor little Lotje, who has been the consistent advocate of friendly relations with white men and has been in favour of these concessions, is once more the object of spite, and it is feared that he will be made a scapegoat of, old grudges being brought up against him, and his death is deliberately proposed.[67]

Ever since the first "determined onset" on Thompson in March, the king had suspected or pretended to suspect that the copy of the concession, on which the conflicting arguments were based, differed from the original. He wanted the original sent back, perhaps to confute the critics, perhaps—as Thompson frankly told Rhodes—for the purpose of tearing it up. In spite of this risk Thompson begged Rhodes to send it, "as it would be a matter of life and death to me." Rhodes reluctantly agreed, telling Thompson in effect not to hand it up "until the knife is at your throat." It was sent through official channels from Robinson to Moffat, Robinson assuring Knutsford on 25 April that he did this only "as non-compliance with the request might involve the personal safety of English gentlemen now in Matabeleland." The knife not yet being actually at his throat, Thompson buried the document in a pumpkin gourd with a little seed corn, so that in the event of his death the growing corn would reveal its position to his Zulu servant Charlie.[68]

There it remained during the winter months, while the envoys returned, the letters were read to the king and indunas, and Thompson and Lotshe were threatened. On 10 September the tragic denouement came. The death sentence on Lotshe was passed and carried out at once, followed by the executions of all his family.[69] Thompson happened to be at Hope Fountain that day. Driving back in a four-horse cart, he met a boy who gave him a note from his brother Backhouse, then at Umvutshwa, telling him of the executions. Next he encountered an emissary of Lobengula's who appears to have been spying on his movements. Soon a band of young warriors appeared, and it is possible that from someone he received a hint that "the killing was not yet over." Thompson unfastened one of the horses, rode it bareback as far as Dawson's, where he borrowed a saddle and bridle, and rode off, ostensibly to Helm's to tell him the news. The driver of the cart brought it to Wilson with a message from Thompson to the same effect. But Thompson was riding for the border. After some grim experiences of desert travel he reached Shoshong, and thence Mafeking. The concession was still reposing darkly in its buried gourd.

In a few days it was realized that Thompson had fled. "Au! Au!" said Lobengula, "just as Maguire did." He need not be accused of cowardice. The omens were bad enough, he had once witnessed the murder of his father, and he had more than done his duty to Rhodes. By his agreement with Rudd in October, before the concession was obtained, he had undertaken to remain in Matabeleland for four months at most. In February he had been induced to stay by the promise that "the Concession a/c will send up his wife and family with every comfort and build him a house near the Helms or elsewhere if he wished," but that was the last he heard of that proposal. Just before Lotshe's death, Thompson had written to his wife from Hope Fountain: "I am now worrying about you. I know life is too short to be parted for the time we have. Rhodes is supposed to be here at the end of this month. If not I must really come away, I cannot possibly stand it. I have strained nerve after nerve to remain until now I am getting desperate. I feel as if I could run clean away."[70]

Rhodes would have none of it. Not only must the original concession be shown to the king—and who could do it but Thompson?—but it must be recognized and all opposition withdrawn. Thompson must go back. Jameson was already at Mafeking, accompanied by two Natalians who had entered Rhodes's service, Denis Doyle and Major Thomas Maxwell. So from Mafeking, almost from the threshold of his home, wife, and children, Thompson retraced his steps with Jameson's party.

They reached Umvutshwa on 17 October. The concession was duly unearthed, and translated to the king by the newcomer Doyle. Thompson busied himself again with the remaining white opponents, of whom only the waverer Tainton now made difficulties. His solatium had been £25 a month, but he complained that it was not enough, or alternatively that he had never received it and did not want it. When the concession was read, however, to the whole gathering of white men, they found no fault with it at all. Lobengula, smiling and rubbing his hand across his mouth, looked round at them—the Ushers and Fairbairns and Dawsons. "Tomoson has rubbed fat on your mouths," he said. "All you white men are liars. Tomoson, you have lied the least."

Lobengula, who had held the precious document in his hands, returned it to Moffat, to the latter's immense relief. Though it was now supposed to remain in his custody, he "yielded to Dr. Jameson's earnest importunity and gave it to him, to take away with him, and accepted in its place a notarial copy."[71]

The king had repudiated it twice, he had reason to think that the queen and Knutsford disapproved of it, but it would be some time before he could expect to hear the British government's response to his latest letter. In the meantime he still refused to accept the rifles, which remained in the custody of Wilson and then of Cooper-Chadwick. At one time Wilson had thought that he ought at all costs, even by blowing them and the ammunition up and himself with them, to keep them out of the hands of the Ndebele. Maund once suggested that the king ought to arm his indunas with them as a means of keeping the young hotheads in check. There had been a rumour among the local white men that the sights of the rifles were defective. One of the characters in this drama wrote to Rhodes suggesting that the spiral springs should be removed from the blocks—a suggestion which Jameson at once rejected.[72]

The death sentence on Lotshe, in which the king concurred reluctantly, was a sign of the strength of anti-European feeling among his subjects. There could be no doubt of its strength. Early in December what Helm called the Ngamhlope Division[73] came to the king ostensibly to perform a dance, actually for a more serious purpose:

> One of the principal men of the country came out in front of the rest and called out loudly that all the Europeans should leave the country. All, he said, every one, John Moffat also. Then came responses from the main body, Yes, that is what we all say, let them clear, let them inspan their wagons at once. On their way to their scherms that night they used most insulting language to all the white men they saw or whose wagons they passed. The second day they were again abusive. But the third day they were quite quiet. The Chief had most probably given them a good lecture.[74]

Even without Lotshe to advise him, Lobengula knew that the danger did not come from the Europeans now in the country; it would be increased, not removed, by expelling them. Neither he nor any of his people knew of the negotiations of the previous months between the financiers and the government in London, the charter which resulted, or the nature of the threat which the charter presented. The curtain was lifted only a little by Moffat, who wrote on 13 November:

> I had an opportunity yesterday, whilst informing the Chief that the Charter had been signed by Her Majesty, of entering at some length into topics connected with it.
> It would be neither desirable nor easy to give him a detailed translation of the text of the Charter throughout. A native cannot understand the prominence given to certain contingencies which may never arise, but for which provision has to be made.
> I have, however, placed clearly before the chief the salient points, viz., that Her Majesty's Government has granted the Charter; that the charter confers upon the Company the power of maintaining its own rights, with the concurrence of the Chief; and that no other Europeans, except those working under the Chartered Company, will be recognized by the Government. This was about as much as I could get him to take in at once on the general subject.[75]

Moffat was right to fear the consequences of giving Lobengula a detailed translation; but "the contingencies might never arise."

Lobengula might well be puzzled even by Moffat's brief report on this "general subject." The queen, who in her last letter had advised him not to give the whole herd to the first comer, had now done herself what she had told him not to do. The chartered financiers and the men in the Colonial Office were well aware of the inconsistency. Another letter would have to be written to the king.

The letter originated, in substance and in detail, in the office of the Chartered Company.[76] The duke of Abercorn sent the suggested text to Knutsford, who was duly "commanded by Her Majesty to send this further message to Lo Bengula":

> . . . Since the visit of Lo Bengula's Envoys, the Queen has made the fullest inquiries into the particular circumstances of Matabeleland, and understands the trouble caused to Lo Bengula by different parties of white men coming to his country to look for gold; but wherever gold is, or wherever it is reported to be, there it is impossible for him to exclude white men, and, therefore, the wisest and safest course for him to adopt, and that which will give least trouble to himself and his tribe, is to agree, not with one or two white men separately, but with one approved body of white men, who will consult Lo Bengula's wishes and arrange where white people are to dig, and who will be responsible to the Chief for any annoyance or trouble caused to himself or his people . . .

Recovering his breath after this laboured sentence, the composer of the letter descended from the general to the particular: "The Queen, therefore, approves of the concession made by Lo Bengula to some white men, who were represented in his country by Messrs. Rudd, Maguire and Thompson." After careful enquiry the queen was able to assure Lobengula of the reliability of these men, with whom indeed "some of the Queen's highest and most trusted subjects" were now associated; she approved Lobengula's wisdom in "carrying out his agreement with these persons." As he was understood to dislike settling disputes among white men, and was ignorant of their laws and customs, he "would be wise to entrust to that body of white men, of whom Mr. Thompson is now the principal representative in Matabeleland, the duty of deciding disputes and keeping the peace among white persons in his country." This was merely a helpful suggestion, not an order: "this must be as Lo Bengula likes, as he is the King of the country, and no one can exercise jurisdiction in it without his permission." Finally, since the king wanted a representative of the queen to reside with him—his denial of this report being overlooked—he was now informed that Mr. Moffat was the man.[77]

The letter was dated 15 November 1889. Knutsford must have felt some embarrassment in signing it, and the Chartered Company some anxiety about how it would be received. To ensure the best possible reception, the letter was taken to Matabeleland by a party of five officers and men of the Royal Horse Guards, who were presented to Lobengula on 29 January 1890. Dressed in full regimentals, they made a glittering show. The king was favourably impressed and spent some time examining their accoutrements. The letter, however, which was read to the king by Moffat and translated by Doyle, had undergone a few modifications since it had left London. Moffat had received from Shippard an advance copy, which he had time to digest before the arrival of the guardsmen. In conversation with Jameson, and partly with the prior approval of Loch and Knutsford, who were informed, it was decided that "Rhodes" should be substituted for "some white men"; that Jameson instead of Thompson should be named as the principal representative, Thompson being now out of favour; that some expressions should be softened, the question of jurisdiction played down and the reference to the queen's representative omitted.[78]

Lobengula was not deceived. When the guardsmen left he told them "that the Queen's letter had been dictated by Rhodes and that she, the Queen, must not write any more letters like that one to him again." His formal reply on 15 February went straight to the point: "The Chief Lo Bengula has received the Queen's letter. He has heard the words contained in it. As he understands the words brought by Babyane and Umshete, there is a difference in the words that have come to-day." He had not sent his envoys to talk about Rhodes. He had "not yet reported that he has been annoyed by the white men. He is still listening to the words brought by Umshete and Babyane and thinking about them." Moffat thought the letter "very disappointing in its tone." Shippard felt "assured that in the main the reply is not unsatisfactory," that it confirmed "the expediency of steadily persevering in the policy of conciliation which we have hitherto pursued with Lo Bengula and his people." He underlined the expediency of this policy by adding the information, gathered from Jameson and the guardsmen, that "the fighting strength of the Matabele has been underestimated, and that it cannot be reckoned at less than from 15,000 to 20,000 men."[79]

Though Moffat had thought it unwise to read to Lobengula the passage in the queen's letter referring to himself as her resident envoy in Matabeleland, he had in fact assumed that position at the beginning of 1890. The Colonial Office had agreed to the Company's offer to bear the expense of such an appointment. Moffat had agreed to accept it. With an increase of salary, a travelling allowance, and provision for a private secretary, he was transferred from the Bechuanaland service to become officially what he already was informally, the queen's resident at the court of Lobengula.[80] He knew that the post was no bed of roses; he did not know quite how thorny it would prove to be.

Lobengula, for his part, did not know when he received the queen's letter that preparations for a major invasion of his country were already well advanced. The preparations were conditioned, and partly determined, by some events to which we must now revert.

NOTES CHAPTER 3

1 CO 879/30/369, no.130, encl., p.264; CO 417/36/347, p.181; RH Mss Afr. S 73, p.76.

2 RH Mss Afr. S 73, p.80; CO 879/30/369, no.147, encl., p.277.

3 Maund Papers, B94.

4 J.G. Lockhart and C.M. Woodhouse, *Rhodes*, pp.149-50.

5 RH Mss Afr. s 73, pp.77, 83.

6 C5524, no.16, p.23; CO 879/30/372, nos.2 and 3, p.2, and 105, pp.98-9; RH Mss Afr. s 73, p.104; RH Mss Afr. t 5, f.440.

7 RH Mss Afr. s 73, p.104; CO 879/30/369, no.146, encl., p.275, and 372/105, p.98. Rudd had "wired to Rhodes . . . and strongly advised him to settle with both Maund and Haggard." (Thompson Papers, Rudd to Thompson and Maguire, 28 January 1889; Queen's, p.247.)

8 CO 879/30/369, no.153, encl.1, 2, pp. 286-91.

9 CO 879/30/369, no.127a, p.257, and 132, p.265.

10 CO 417/28/2453, pp.20-1, and 3184, pp.180-2.

11 CO 879/30/372, no.19, pp.10-11; CO 417/28/4220, p.75; *Letters of Queen Victoria*, third series, vol. I, pp.477, 486; Maund Papers, B93; Lady Frederick Cavendish, "Five Months in South Africa," in *The Living Age*, Boston, vol.185, pp.294-6 (taken from *Murray's Magazine*); E.P. Mathers, *Zambesia: England's Eldorado in Africa*, pp.148-55; Thompson Papers, Maguire to Thompson, from Mafeking, 8 May 1889 (Queen's, pp.287-8).

12 *Cape Argus*, 6 March 1889 (passenger list).

13 CO 417/24/750, p.524, and 1216, pp.615-18.

14 CO 879/30/372, no.61, encl., pp.54-63; W.D. Mackenzie, *John Mackenzie, South Africa Missionary and Statesman*, ch.15, 16; Anthony J. Dachs, ed., *Papers of John Mackenzie*, pp.149-54.

15 C5524, no.16, p. 23; CO 879/30/372, no.61, encl., pp.54-60; Hansard Parl. Deb., 51-2 Vic., vol. XI, col.879-80.

16 Mackenzie, *Mackenzie*, p.432; CO 417/36/6080, pp.324-5, and 37/8773, pp.412-15.

17 CO 879/30/372, no.32, encl., pp.24-5.

18 CO 879/30/372, no.19, encl., p.11; Political Papers of J.S. Moffat, Moffat to Shippard, 6 August 1889.

19 CO 417/38/4306, p.501; CO 879/30/372, no.122, encl., p.119.

20 CO 879/30/372, no.32, p.24; CO 417/36/6080, p.324a; letter to *The Times* is in Lobengula Papers (LO 1/1/1) and in Hole Papers (HO 1/2/1), where the original and the published version are compared. The differences are slight.

21 Hansard Parl. Deb., 52-3 Vic., 1889, vol. I, cols.1401, 1795-6.

22 H. Marshall Hole, *The Making of Rhodesia*, p.84; Mathers, *Zambesia*, pp.155-6.

23 CO 417/36/6080, p.325. Maund's besetting sin was committed again even on this occasion. Gifford wrote to Cawston on 26 March: "I was a little astonished to-day to learn that E.A. Maund was going to see Rhodes to-morrow evening. What should be done is that myself and yourself should discuss all points with Rhodes; certainly not Maund." RH Mss Afr. s 73, p.93.

24 CO 879/30/459, no.38.

25 For these claims, see CO 417/28, pp.362-85; 29, pp.477-84; 30, p.199; 36, pp.427-32; 37, pp.95, 105-81, 408-11; 38, pp.52-3, 69-72, 400-24.

26 CO 879/30/372, no.105; 39/459, no.38; RH Mss Afr. s 73, p.105; Rhodes Papers, Charters, 3A/1, no.3; CO 417/38/22225, p.69; 69/1569, pp.513-18.

27 Maund Papers, B120, B25.

28 RH Mss Afr. t 5, ff. 524-9. In July 1888 Gifford had broached to Knutsford the ques-

tion of a resident with Lobengula, and had suggested Maund for the post. (CO 537/124B/716.)

29 CO 879/30/372, no.66, pp.65-6.

30 CO 879/30/372, nos.3, 4, pp.2, 3; no.105, p.98; RH Mss Afr. s 73, p.104. Knutsford's "suggestion" may have been oral; there is no official record of it.

31 For the three companies, see, e.g., K.G. Tregonning, *Under Chartered Company Rule: North Borneo, 1881-1946*; John E. Flint, *Sir George Goldie and the Making of Nigeria*; John S. Galbraith, *Mackinnon and East Africa, 1878-1895: A Study in the New Imperialism*. Galbraith's classic work on the BSA Company, *Crown and Charter: The Early Years of the British South Africa Company*, appeared after most of this book had been written; it is appropriate at this point to apologize for not having made more use of it or reference to it.

32 CO 417/28/4221, pp.79-81.

33 CO 417/37/8773, pp.412-13.

34 CO 879/30/372, no.7, pp.4-5; CO 417/28/4232, pp.124-5.

35 CO 417/38/245, p.217.

36 CO 417/28/4221, p.81; RH Mss Afr. s 73, p.222 (Cawston to Rhodes, 6 November 1889, *re* Herbert: "He disapproved entirely of the cattle letter").

37 CO 879/30/372, no.44, p.36.

38 CO 417/37/8773, pp.414-15.

39 CO 879/30/372, nos.76, p.71 and 83, p.77.

40 Lady Gwendolen Cecil, *Life of Robert, Marquess of Salisbury*, vol. IV, ch.8, 9.

41 Ibid., vol. IV, pp.242-3; Foreign Office Confidential Print 6178, no.142, and 6482, no.274; Sir Harry Johnston, *The Story of My Life*, pp.201-5, 210, 214-16, 220-2; E. Axelson, *Portugal and the Scramble for Africa*, pp.195-200; Roland Oliver, *Sir Harry Johnston and the Scramble for Africa*, pp.140-4.

42 Cecil, *Salisbury*, vol. IV, pp.242-3; Lockhart and Woodhouse, *Rhodes*, p.165; CO 879/30/372, no.83, p.77; CO 417/36/10772, p.348, and 13372, pp.385-9a.

43 Mackenzie, *Mackenzie*, p.433.

44 Frederic Whyte, *The Life of W.T. Stead*, vol. I, pp.269-78; Lockhart and Woodhouse, *Rhodes*, pp.110, 162.

45 RH Mss Afr. s 73, p.99 (21 April 1889) and p.100 (24 April 1889).

46 Foreign Office Confidential Print 6482, no.274; Johnston, *Story of my Life*, pp.217-21. Johnston acknowledged his debt to Edwin Arnold for the "Cape to Cairo" idea (Leo Weinthal, ed., *The Story of the Cape to Cairo Railway and River Route*, vol. I, p.69). On Verschoyle's activities there is a tantalizing statement in a letter of his to Cawston, undated but probably written in December 1889: "That I did not cease to do all that lay in my power for the Charter (even after I thought you and Beit would do little for me) will be plain to you, if you enquire what I was doing the day preceding and following its appearance." (RH Mss Afr. s 73, p.283.)

47 CO 879/30/372, no.105, pp.98-100; RH Mss Afr. s 73, pp.73, 97, 143-4, 182-3, 221, 256-7; Lockhart and Woodhouse, *Rhodes*, pp.163, 167-8; Nancy Rouillard, ed., *The Autobiography of Matabele Thompson*, p.172. Examples of propaganda in the *Fortnightly Review* are articles by F.I. Ricarde-Seaver and Sir Charles Metcalfe on 1 March 1889, Selous on 1 May 1889 and Flora Shaw on 1 November 1889. The shares

of the Bechuanaland Exploration Co. were widely spread. Leopold de Rothschild and Harry Mosenthal, each with 3,500, were the biggest holders; Lord Gifford, with 100, was one of the smallest. There were many shareholders in Paris, some of them later connected with the Mozambique Company. (CO 417/21/11562, pp.56-8). Rhodes's offer of £10,000 to the Irish Nationalist party is well known. Evidence that it was actually paid is, however, lacking. From Conor Cruise O'Brien, *Parnell and his Party, 1880-1896*, pp.266-7, notes, it appears that a payment of £5,000 ("source unknown") *may* have been an instalment from Rhodes.

48 CO 417/38/12074, pp.201-6; 13697, pp.287-9; 12442, pp.642-6.

49 Thompson Papers, Maguire to Thompson, 24 June 1889 (Queen's pp.298-300).

50 CO 879/31/380, p.4.

51 CO 879/30/372, no.105, pp.99-100.

52 Basil Williams, *Cecil Rhodes*, pp.135-6; Mackenzie, *Mackenzie*, p.435; Galbraith, *Crown and Charter*, pp.113-17.

53 CO 417/37/14024, pp.77-94; 38/14996, pp.297-301.

54 RH Mss Afr. s 73, pp.203-6, 211, 227, 242, 247-8, 276-8, 280.

55 British South Africa Company, List of Original Shareholders, tabled in the House of Commons on 28 December 1893; now in the House of Lords Record Office. I owe this reference, and a copy of the list, to Paul Maylam.

56 Jean van der Poel, *Railway and Customs Policies in South Africa, 1885-1910*, pp.28-31, 37-43; J.P. Vanstone, "Sir John Gordon Sprigg, a Political Biography" (PH.D. thesis, Queen's University), pp.257-96.

57 CO 417/27/2469, pp.339-88; 28/4225, pp.111-17 and 5689, pp.389-425; 32/14438, pp.147-53 and 14912, pp.180-4; 33/21278, pp.427-34; 37/14288, pp.459-62, 22185, pp.622-34, 24086, pp.684-9 and 24728, p. 701; 38/11069, pp.625-33, 12068, pp.638-41 and 14990, pp.681-4; RH Mss Afr. s 73, pp.106, 198-202, 223-5, 241, 246.

58 CO 879/30/372, nos.94, p.86, 104, p.98, 147, p.146 and 148, p.146; CO 417/32/18090, p.598; 38/11069, pp.625-33 and 12068, pp.638-41.

59 CO 417/37, correspondence with Council Office on pp.77-181; also 20097, pp.230-5; 38/18168, pp.400-24, 18425, pp.425-32, 17783, pp.475-7. Swinburne's concession was later acquired by the BSA Company at the price of £5,000 to Swinburne and 5,000 shares to the Matabeleland Company, in which the concession had been vested; the relevant deeds were dated 14 December 1889 and 4 June 1890 (CO 417/52/15971, pp.645-50).

60 CO 417/36/10772, p.348, 13372, pp.385-9a, 16241, pp.422-4, 17271, pp.435-7; 37/10340, p.418, 12433, pp.435-8, 14186, pp.439-58. Successive drafts and proposed amendments of the charter are appended to 37/15024, pp.77-94; 38/14996, pp.297-301, 16191, pp.314-32, 16236, pp.333-51, 16285, pp.352-69, 17155, pp.381-92. The charter in its final form, deed of settlement, and other public papers in RH Mss Afr. s 71.

61 CO 417/36/13372, pp.385-9a; Salisbury Papers, Hatzfeldt to Salisbury, 25 August 1889 (A/64/127), and Salisbury to Hatzfeldt, 26 August 1889 (A/64/81).

62 Compare the texts in CO 417/37, p.82 and 38, p.339; Fairfield's comment in 69, pp.513-18. In the later versions the passage quoted (without the italicized words) was transferred to Article 2. "Heads of Agreement" between the Company and Central Search are in CO 879/39/459, no.38.

63 CO 879/37/439, Olivier's memorandum, pp.9-11; CO 417/88/366, p.11. But see also Bramston's comment on the Company's 1891 report in CO 417/72/24524. He learned from the report about the United Concessions Company, and thought of asking the BSA Company to explain the relationship. Knutsford evidently did not do so.

64 But see CO 417/88/366, p.8n, which suggests that it would probably not have been lawful for British subjects to exercise coercive jurisdiction anywhere without special leave of the Crown.

65 CO 417/32/16688, pp.224-41; CO 879/30/372, no.122, encl., pp.118-9.

66 CO 879/30/372, no.170, encl., pp.169-70; LMS Papers, Helm to LMS, 20 December 1889; Thompson Papers, Thompson to Rhodes, 27 August 1889 (Queen's, p.357). According to Rutherfoord Harris (ibid., Queen's, p.351), Maund on the journey up to Bulawayo was not on speaking terms with Colenbrander or the envoys. This is credible, though the source is suspect. In February 1891 Labouchere asked in the House of Commons, among other awkward questions, whether Lobengula had not repudiated the Rudd Concession, and whether the rifles were still in possession of the Company. Sir John Gorst replied that while Lobengula had written, "if the Queen hears that I have given away the whole country, it is not so," the Company did not claim that he had done this; and that his not yet having accepted the rifles did not constitute a repudiation of the concession (CO 417/69/3645, pp.12-15).

67 Political Papers of J.S. Moffat, Moffat to Shippard, 26 August 1889.

68 Rouillard, *Thompson*, pp.140-1; CO 879/30/372, no.78, p.72.

69 Maund did not agree with the general opinion that Lotshe was thrown to the wolves because he had been the leading advocate of friendship with the whites: "The King interrogated by me told me absolutely that Lochi's death was in no way to be attributed to the white men; that his offences had dated from some ten years back, and I shrewdly suspect that his principal crime was that of being too rich, as many thousand head of cattle were added to the King's herds after his death." (Maund Papers, 832.) This explanation was almost certainly wrong. Lobengula was reluctant to kill Lotshe, but gave way to the strong and sustained pressure of public opinion, the ground of which was certainly Lotshe's advocacy of friendship with the whites. See Foster Windram Oral Interviews (WI 8/1/1), Siatcha, p.12; Mvutu and Posela, p.4; Ncupela, pp.3-7; Miscellaneous, p.3 (J.P. Richardson); and WI 8/1/2, Ntabeni Khumalo, p.20.

70 Thompson Papers, Rudd to Thompson and Maguire, 10 February 1889 (Queen's, p.255); Thompson to his wife, 12 September 1889 (Queen's, p.192). This letter is dated 12 September, two days after the killing, but it was written from Hope Fountain and obviously, from the contents, before that event. Thompson probably mistook the date.

71 Hole Papers (HO 1/3/1), copy of letter, Thompson to Rhodes, 18 September 1889; Diary of Matabele Wilson (WI 6/2/1), 11 September, 13 September and 17 October 1889; Diary of Thomas Maxwell (MA 1/2), entries from 29 September to 24 October 1889; Rouillard, *Thompson*, pp.178-86; Political Papers of J.S. Moffat, Moffat to Shippard, 27 December 1889. The first two of these items of contemporary evidence, one from Thompson himself, show that the account in the Autobiography is unreliable; e.g., Thompson did not witness the execution.

72 Hole Papers (HO 1/3/1), copy of letter, Jameson to Rhodes, 14 October 1889, with

summary of letter making the suggestion. As this is not the original and bears no signature, I forbear to mention the name of the putative author. For the preceding points, Diary of Matabele Wilson (WI 6/2/1), 22 August 1889, 25 October 1889, 2 February 1890, and Diary of Thomas Maxwell (MA 1/2), 30 October 1889.

73 If Julian Cobbing ("Evolution of Ndebele Amabutho," *Journal of African History*, xv, 4 [1974]) is right, the Mhlope "Division" was not an actual formation but a nostalgic memory. But Helm uses the term for the soldiers described in the passage.

74 LMS Papers (LO 6/1/4), Helm to LMS, 20 December 1889.

75 CO 879/30/372, no.218, encl., pp.208-9. The puzzle is: How could Moffat know, on 12 November, that the charter had been signed by the queen on 29 October, and also know the details of the document? The details could have been sent to him months before, as they were sent to Thompson (Thompson Papers, Maguire to Thompson, 26 July 1889; Queen's, p.302). The news of the signing could have reached the end of the telegraph line at Mafeking by 30 October. But from there to Bulawayo it could not have been taken in less than 18 days (see above, ch.2).

76 CO 879/30/372, no.153, pp.151-2. Though it may seem odd for the Colonial Office to act thus as a mouthpiece for the Company, the situation had changed radically since Maund had claimed to dictate an amendment to Knutsford's letter; the charter and the eminent directors made the difference.

77 Ibid., no.166, pp.165-6.

78 Ibid., nos.200, p.193; 204, p.195; 212a, p.204; CO 879/32/392, no.77, encl., p.100; Political Papers of J.S. Moffat, Jameson to Harris, 17 January 1890.

79 CO 879/32/392, no.98 and encl., pp.121-2; Diary of Matabele Wilson, 15 February 1890.

80 CO 879/32/392, nos.15, 67, 105, 106, 128, 131, 138, 177, 259.

CHAPTER 4

The Pioneers and Their Rivals

It will be remembered that Frank Johnson in 1887 had prospected as far as the Mazoe, and had tried vainly to get a concession for that area from Lobengula. He convinced his associates, as he had convinced himself, that of all the regions he had seen the Mazoe valley was the richest in gold. This conviction remained while the Northern Gold Fields Exploration Company busied itself with Kgama's concession, which was taken over by the Bechuanaland Exploration Company. The members of the former company sent Johnson to Lisbon, where in August 1888 he obtained a Mazoe valley concession from the Mozambique Company. It is probable that Maund, when composing for Lobengula the letter he was to take to the queen, knew something of this move of Johnson's. The purpose of the letter was to assert Lobengula's claim, against the Portuguese, to the Mazoe valley, and it was there that Maund hoped to get a concession. How much Lobengula knew of what was afoot is another question. It would have been easy to persuade him to define his boundaries without bringing Johnson into view at all, especially as Portuguese expeditions were frequently being reported from Mashonaland.

About the end of January 1889 Selous arrived in Cape Town after his memorable adventures north of the Zambezi. On his way through Bechuanaland he met Johnson, who enlisted him in the service of the Cape Town group. It must have been at this time that the group (which there were "grounds for identifying" with the members of the Northern Gold Fields Exploration Company) took the name of the Selous Exploration Syndicate. Its plan was to send Selous, who knew the country, to take possession of its Mazoe claim. As this could not be done safely until later in the year, Selous went to England in February—by the same ship, it will be remembered, as Maund and the envoys.

Selous appears to have approached Gifford, on behalf of his principals, with a proposal that the Bechuanaland Exploration Company should take over the Mazoe Concession as it had taken over Kgama's. Gifford refused, on two grounds. First, Maund held out the prospect of a concession of the same area from Lobengula. Second, and much more important, Gifford was on the point of amalgamating his interests with those of Rhodes, which included the whole of the Mazoe valley—provided that it could be shown to belong to Lobengula. To recognize Portuguese sovereignty there would spoil the chances of a much bigger operation. The syndicate would therefore have to play a lone hand in opposition to the mammoth interests now being merged in England.

While in England Selous wrote an article for the *Fortnightly Review*, extolling the wonders of "Mashunaland and the Mashunas . . . the fairest and perhaps also the richest country in all South Africa." It had, moreover, been devastated by invaders, and "remains to the present day an utterly deserted country, roamed over at will by herds of elands and other antelopes." All this was what the assistant editor wanted to hear, and to publish. But Selous was mindful of the interests of his syndicate. The deserted country had inhabitants, and "there are numerous tribes of Mashunas who are in no wise subject to Lobengula. They pay him no tribute . . . " These sentences were published, but Selous had written others even more damaging to the amalgamated financiers' case. Verschoyle wrote to Cawston: "I have, not without difficulty, got rid of the pages of dangerous matter in S's article . . . He is still sore about the omissions I have insisted on making." The article, even in bowdlerized form, was read with consternation by Verschoyle's friends.[1]

When Selous reached Cape Town again there was another discouragement: the Portuguese government had cancelled the concession. Still undaunted, the syndicate tried another approach. It sent Selous round by the Zambezi and Tete to get the Mazoe concession from the local chiefs. He did so. In September 1889 the Korekore Chief Negomo having refused, Selous persuaded two of his headmen, Mapondera and Temaringa, to grant the desired mining concession, and to sign a paper stating that they were entirely independent and had never paid tribute, directly or indirectly, to the Portuguese.

The claim of Negomo—though his headmen were not entitled to make it—to be independent both of Portugal and of Lobengula was a good one, but the syndicate had weakened its case by shifting its ground. To get the concession it had recognized the sovereignty, successively, of Lobengula, Portugal, and the local chiefs. The syndicate's hopes were raised by the fact that this concession was granted before the signing of the charter; the charter provided for the recognition of all legitimate existing claims.

When Selous returned to Cape Town in December, the syndicate offered to sell its concession to Rhodes. There are two mutually contradictory accounts of what followed.[2] According to several members of the syndicate, Rhodes agreed to take over the concession and to allot to its owners 100 square miles in Mashonaland, "the Charter to work it on halves." These terms being rejected, Rhodes defeated the syndicate by taking Selous and Johnson into his own service. As these two owned a bare majority of the shares, he tried to round off the operation neatly by buying those shares. Selous sold, but Johnson "loyally" refused to do so. Thus the syndicate remained, to bombard the Colonial Office with complaints. Though its case was good, Knutsford had chosen his side and steadily refused to reopen the question.

Rhodes told the duke of Abercorn quite a different story. He had neither recognized the concession nor offered to buy it; he told Selous that "it was not worth the paper it was written on." He also convinced Selous that the assertion that the Korekore chiefs were independent of Lobengula would play into the hands of the Portuguese. Merely as compensation for his trouble, and without reference to the concession, Rhodes paid Selous £2,000; in plainer language, he bribed him to come over. He paid lesser sums to Selous's companions on the journey, and his offer to the syndicate, which was rejected, was 100 *claims*. Johnson, as will be seen, entered into a different kind of relation to Rhodes, without defecting from the syndicate. In both cases the change required a re-writing of history after the manner of a new edition of the Soviet Encyclopedia. The reader of *Travel and Adventure in South-East Africa* would never guess what lay behind the Selous expedition to the Mazoe. Johnson, in *Great Days*, attributes his hatred of Gifford and Cawston to the manner in which the Exploring Company acquired a rich (and nonexistent) concession supposed to have been obtained by Maund. It may be that the real reason was Gifford's dealing with the Selous Exploration Syndicate, of which Johnson was the prime mover.[3]

The bribe to Selous was open to various interpretations, and the two sides naturally interpreted it differently. Whichever of these accounts was nearer the truth, the important and incontrovertible facts were that Selous and Johnson, the chief members of the syndicate, entered Rhodes's service, and that the imperial government refused to recognize the concession.

The Rudd Concession, the charter, and the Company were always intended by Rhodes to be the means to a political, not primarily an economic, end: occupation, settlement, the founding of a colony. It was clear to all who could read that the means did not in themselves serve this purpose. Unless Lobengula granted further concessions, the Company would have no right to land or to powers of government.

On the other hand Rhodes was in a hurry—"so little done, so much to do"; and there was good reason to believe that if the Company failed to occupy Mashonaland in 1890, the Boers or the Portuguese would do so. Mashonaland was the immediate objective. Not only did it possess the "Northern Gold Fields" of Mauch and Baines, the riches of which had grown in the telling; it was asserted by Selous, Mackenzie, and others to be an agricultural paradise, the best region in all southern Africa, and much of it was believed to have been conveniently depopulated by the Ndebele.

The road to Mashonaland ran through Bulawayo, and no one supposed that the Ndebele would allow a column of settlers to march up it in peace. An alternative route, up the Zambezi, was ruled out after Selous had tried it. In any case the Portuguese were rival claimants to Mashonaland; they would not look favourably on an expedition that would deprive them of what they regarded as their own. These difficulties led almost inevitably to the conclusion that the mask of friendship for Lobengula would have to be discarded.

The first to put into words the unspoken thoughts of many seems to have been Maund. On 30 October 1889 he called on Jameson in Bulawayo and read him a letter that he, Maund, had written to Rhodes: "It was suggesting the invasion of the country about May: to employ 500 Boers, giving farms as compensation and to form a police of 1,500 men to protect the diggers. Soon as spot has been [ap]pointed wherein to commence operations two invading columns to enter country by way of Tuli and one by the main road, native contingents to be used in conjunction." Two days later Jameson wrote to Rutherfoord Harris: "I have spoken freely to Helm and Carnegie, and they with Moffat are convinced that Rhodes is right in his decision that we will never be able to work peaceably alongside the natives, and that the sooner the brush is over the better. There is a general idea here that if this advance is not made in the coming winter, the Boer filibusters will make it then, and that will be an additional incubus."[4]

At the time of these letters and discussions Selous was at Tete on his way back from the Mazoe. He also, on the basis of his own sources of information, was convinced that the time for a British advance was running out; "now or never is the time to act," as he wrote to his principals in Cape Town.[5] He struck the note of urgency again in a long letter to *The Times*, published on 6 January 1890.

Rhodes hardly needed this kind of advice. He was determined to take possession of Mashonaland in the coming season, to plant colonists—not merely miners—in it, and to forestall both Boers and Portuguese. The obstacles he faced were Lobengula and the Colonial Office. In the last months of 1889 he intended to remove the former by force, and he decided to entrust the job to Frank Johnson.

In September Harris had written to Johnson urging him to come to Kimberley and assuring him that Rhodes recognized "the desirability of enlisting all good men and true under the flag."[6] Johnson was not easy to enlist; because of his animus against Gifford and Cawston, who were directors of the BSA Company, he refused absolutely to be employed by the Company. The way out of this difficulty was to use him as a contractor instead of an employee. On 7 December Johnson and Heany signed a contract or agreement with Rhodes (who signed "for the British South Africa Coy."), by which they undertook "to raise in South Africa an auxiliary European Force of about 500 men for service under the British South Africa Company for a period of six months or longer if required." They undertook "with the aforesaid auxiliary force to carry by sudden assaults all the principal strongholds of the Matabele nation and generally to so break up the power of the Amandebele as to render their raids on surrounding tribes impossible, to effect the emancipation of all their slaves and further, to reduce the country to such a condition as to enable the prospecting, mining and commercial staff of the British South Africa Company to conduct their operations in Matabeleland in peace and safety." Johnson proposed either to kill Lobengula or, preferably, to take him hostage. All the expense of raising and maintaining the auxiliary force was to be borne by the Company; but if the assault was successful the contractors would receive £150,000 and 50,000 morgen of land. Some of the other details were identical with the provisions of the later (and effective) contract. It is a curious point, for instance, that this one was to be in force until 30 September 1890. No lawyer was employed in drawing it up. Rutherfoord Harris was the only witness.[7]

The sudden assault was, of course, not made; but the circumstances of its cancellation are shrouded in mystery and contradiction. By Johnson's account, Heany in his cups blurted out the story to Hepburn at Shoshong; Hepburn wrote to Shippard, who travelled post-haste to see the high commissioner in Cape Town; Loch summoned Rhodes, who professed ignorance and cast all the blame on Johnson; Johnson loyally took it upon himself, explaining that he wanted "to get his own back" on Lobengula for his treatment in 1887, and, no doubt, to settle the fate of the disputed territory. Some details of this account are, however, at variance with known facts. According to contemporary evidence, Moffat received a "wild and excited" letter from Hepburn about the end of January, with news of some aggressive scheme. In this version, Rhodes attributed the rumour to Kgama's warlike intentions, of which it had once been intended to make use, but a change in Lobengula's attitude had "rendered any further action unnecessary." As the aggressive scheme had been abandoned several weeks earlier, this version of the story is inadequate too. The two versions could be partly reconciled if Shippard's informant had not been Hepburn, and if Hepburn, hearing the rumour late in January, was unaware that other plans had then been made.[8] The plan, its secrecy, and its cancellation as soon as Loch heard of it, throw a vivid light on Rhodes's disregard, even contempt, for the "imperial factor."

When Selous met Rhodes in Kimberley he suggested that the Pioneers should march to Mashonaland by a route which avoided the Ndebele towns— the route which was ultimately adopted. At that time Rhodes, busy with his contract with Johnson, was not amenable to the suggestion. He became amenable when the "sudden assault" plan had to be abandoned because of its premature revelation to Loch. In the meantime the intention to march in through Bulawayo, though not of course the details of the Johnson contract, had been published in the English press. Reading this, John Mackenzie put aside his antipathy to the Company and wrote to Knutsford, warning him of the consequences of using the proposed route, and suggesting an alternative which was virtually the same as Selous's proposal.[9]

Rhodes having been won over to this plan, and Selous and Johnson having been persuaded to work for Rhodes, a new contract was drawn up and signed in Cape Town on the first day of 1890. Again it was a contract between Rhodes, acting for the Company, and Johnson. Selous agreed to act as guide to the column. It was now hoped, and Selous expected, that the march to Mashonaland would be peaceful. The party of Europeans would therefore not be primarily an army, though it would have to be able to defend itself. It would be essentially a band of settlers, the nucleus of the colony of Rhodes's dreams. Johnson contracted to recruit this band, to cut a good wagon road ("not inferior to that of the present trade route south of Palapye") along the chosen route to Mount Hampden (the objective suggested by Selous), to build a fort at that place, and to hold and occupy a defined district. The road was to be completed by 15 July, or the contractor would be fined £100 for every day after that until the completion; but the fine would be remitted if the delay was caused by any orders issued by the Company, or—an interesting phrase—"by reason of any act of God or the Company's enemies."

The Company would provide, on loan, arms, ammunition, and other military equipment; all other expense was to be borne by the contractor. Every European member of the expedition was to receive, as soon as the Company was in a position to grant it, 1,500 morgen of land. Each would be entitled also to fifteen mining claims. The contractor would be paid £87,500 (which he hoped would leave him a fair margin of profit), 40,000 morgen of land and twenty mining claims. The whole operation was to be completed by 30 September.[10]

The peaceful march, unlike the sudden assault, required Lobengula's consent. Jameson had been in Matabeleland continuously, but for two brief intervals, since 17 October, representing Rhodes and the Company. Even before the Selous-Mackenzie plan was adopted, Jameson's task was to smooth the way with Lobengula as far as possible. Early in December he got the king's permission for digging to commence on the Ramakwabane, that is to say on the Bulawayo side of the Tati concession. Operations in that area, on the old Missionaries' Road from the south, were no great innovation and the request met with little opposition from the king. Jameson did not expect gold to be found there. His tactics were to report failure in that region and then to ask for another place—meaning Mashonaland.[11]

On 31 January, when the queen's letter and the glittering guardsmen were still fresh in Lobengula's mind, Jameson approached him again, telling him that no gold had been found in the southwest.

> Then we said we did not now wish to come any further for fear of interfering with him and his kraals. He answered, "Yes, look for another place," to which we replied, "Where, King?" As usual he said, "Oh, you know." We then pointed to the north-east and asked to be allowed to go there. He said "Yes." Then we told him how we wanted to go in, and brought out the map, explaining the road you [Harris] and Selous suggested from the extreme south-east corner of his country. We also asked [him] to allow us to hire his men to take out trees and stumps to make a road for the waggons to pass along. He answered "Yes, you can go there. Go and see the place and then come to me for the men to take out the stumps for the road when you know where you are going to dig."[12]

A fortnight later Jameson left for the south with this important, though oral and unattested, permission.[13] Denis Doyle was left at Bulawayo to represent the Company.

Rhodes, as usual, had anticipated Jameson's successful diplomacy. Lobengula, in giving permission in December to prospect in the direction of the Tati, had agreed that if that area proved barren he would give another. This vague promise was thought to justify not only the final contract with Johnson, but also an official conference with the high commissioner, which was held at Government House, Cape Town, on 10 January. It was attended by Sir Francis de Winton (special commissioner for settling the affairs of Swaziland), Sir Sidney Shippard, Sir Frederick Carrington (commanding the Bechuanaland Border Police), Rhodes, and Selous. Rhodes expounded to Sir Henry Loch his plan of operations. At a date to be fixed, Selous was to be ready to cross the Shashi "with some 80 waggons, accompanied by 125 miners (white) and about 150 (black) men for clearing and making a road for waggons; these, with the men for the waggons, would represent altogether a body of between 400 and 500; besides these a certain number of mounted police to act as scouts." It was suggested that Sir Frederick Carrington would protect the column at the beginning of its march with 200 of his police and 250 of the Company's police. The former would remain in the protectorate, the latter would advance with the column; after crossing the Shashi they would be entirely under the command of their own officers. The route to be followed from the Shashi to Mount Hampden was laid down approximately.

The high commissioner approved of these arrangements and made certain conditions. When the preparations were complete, Rhodes was to report to him; he would receive reports also from Shippard, and through him from Carrington and Moffat. In the light of these he would decide whether to give permission for the column to advance. The conversation was recorded in a note of which Rhodes, Moffat, and Knutsford received copies.[14]

It is hard to explain the mental processes of some of these men. In spite of evidence to the contrary, it was still officially supposed by Knutsford, Moffat, and even Loch, that the sole purpose of the operation was to exploit the mining concessions: to take "the requisite steps for securing the concessions which have been granted . . . by Lo Bengula." While Carrington was begging for more policemen for his force, and proposing to establish a new police camp nearer to Matabeleland, Loch was insisting that this camp be south of the Motloutsi, and not in either the disputed territory or the Tati district. The movement of police into those areas would "justify Lo Bengula in the belief that the object of the Company, supported as it is by Her Majesty's Government, was for the purpose of acquiring possession of land instead of working the mineral concessions."[15] Knutsford agreed; the presence of police in the disputed territory might be regarded by Lobengula as a step towards annexation on behalf of Kgama. Nor did he think that the "general permission given by Lo Bengula to work the concession" could justify the proposed invasion of Mashonaland. Herbert thought that the Company, instead of trying to "win the race," should wait until Lobengula called upon it to help him against the Boers.

Perhaps Knutsford and Loch, if not Moffat, were using the device made notorious by Chamberlain in connection with his foreknowledge of the Jameson Raid: keeping their "official" knowledge and their private information in separate mental compartments. The evidence of Rhodes's intentions was available, yet they remained officially ignorant of it.

At the Government House conference Rhodes had been careful to refer to his pioneers as "miners." Yet it was an open secret that they were intended for much larger purposes. Fairfield had been shocked by Sir John Kirk's speaking to him of "its being a matter of course that we had granted the charter with a view to driving the Matabeles out of the country across the Zambesi and settling the whole country with 'volunteers' whose services were to be paid for by free land grants (like the freebooters of Goshen and the New Republic). Of course this is quite contrary to the provisions and spirit of the Charter."[16]

Fairfield's next shock was administered by the report of the conference in Cape Town. "The cat," he noted, "is being now let out of Mr. Rhodes's bag, and proves a very ferocious animal indeed." He did not believe that the duke of Abercorn or the other London directors would approve of the scheme reported from Cape Town. It could "hardly fail to involve us in a war with Lo Bengula, and is therefore objectionable on that account." It would risk the lives of Moffat and the other Europeans in the country. In another of his minutes he reported an objection from the War Office: according to General Brackenbury, it would be "perfectly impossible" to send an expedition up through the protectorate, yet this was what Rhodes's scheme might lead to. Fairfield seems to have sensed, though, that he was fighting a losing battle. His remark that "I fear that the people in South Africa are getting out of hand" carried the overtone of sad resignation to which he was now growing accustomed.

Moffat was hardly less perturbed than Knutsford on receiving his copy of the memorandum from Cape Town. His chief objection was to the presence of the police. Against whom were they to protect the column? Not, he thought, against the Boers or the Portuguese, "and surely not from the Matabele, to whom this would seem nothing but a menace, uncalled for, and likely to bring on the catastrophe of a collision." His advice had been asked about whether the Europeans with wives and children—i.e., the missionaries—should withdraw from the country before the column advanced. This proposal shocked him too: "the very fact of their withdrawing would add fuel to the flame." There was some irony in his belief "that Dr. Jameson and Mr. Doyle are both with me in their views";[17] a few months earlier Jameson had supposed that Moffat was with *him* in thinking that "the sooner the brush is over the better."

Rhodes had, however, one important ally in his adventure: Kgama. About the end of December, before the new plan had been substituted for the old, Heany had told him that the company intended to put a stop to the Ndebele raids, and that there was no hope of doing this peaceably. Kgama wrote to Shippard expressing his approval: "The murders you English know to-day are the murders I have known every day since I first heard the name Matabele." He quoted examples, and went on to the rhetorical question: "The murders of the Mashona and Makalaka tribes, who can count them?" If the Company would now put an end to this menace, it could rely on Kgama's full military support.[18]

In taking Kgama so far into his confidence—whatever the truth about his talking to Hepburn—Heany was speaking out of turn. The new plan had been approved by Loch before he heard of Kgama's views; no conflict was now expected. Even Loch had been a little rash in giving provisional approval to the new plan. At that time the only permission Lobengula had given to the Company was to dig on the Ramakwabane, with a vague reference to other places if that one proved unfruitful. On 14 February therefore Knutsford, with the full support of his officials, cabled to Loch that Her Majesty's government, as at present advised, could not "sanction movement in force in Matabeleland or Mashonaland which is not specifically sanctioned by Lo Bengula."[19]

On the same day Jameson left Bulawayo with what he chose to regard as the specific sanction Knutsford required. If the king had meant what Jameson reported him to have said, it is certain that his permission referred to a small party of diggers, not to an invading army; and if he had given any permission at all, he soon repented of it. On 17 March Selous, impatient to begin his road-making, arrived in Bulawayo in Sam Edwards's wagon. His recent journey into Mashonaland from the east, which had received wide publicity, could hardly have been unknown to Lobengula, and touched the king on a sensitive spot. Selous had come to make specific arrangements, but he found that the king's attitude had changed since Jameson's departure. He now denied having given permission for the new road, insisting that the only way to Mashonaland was the old route through Bulawayo. "If the road is good for you it is good for the Boers. You have this road that is already made." He complained that he had always to deal with subordinates instead of with Rhodes himself. "Let Rhodes come, let Selous go for him to-morrow." There was much more talk, but the king was inflexible; he refused the road. "He has not yet learned," Doyle reported, "to trust us fully and is afraid that our object in making the road is with some ulterior motive which he cannot guess."[20]

Selous returned to Kimberley with this unwelcome news. Rhodes could not, at that moment, leave his headquarters, but Jameson again stepped into the breach. He reached Bulawayo on 29 April, and the next day had a long interview with the king. Now, for the first time, Lobengula was told of the Pioneer Column.

"He looked pretty grave and hummed a tune to himself during the recital, as much as to say 'What damned impudence!' Then asked minutely after the police—what they were going to do, what we were going to do, etc., etc.; that we talked well and our words were many, but that this was not what we asked for at the meeting at Bulawayo [on 31 January]." Jameson conceded this, with much talk about the queen not allowing her subjects to be taken all those extra hundreds of miles to Mashonaland without protection. "Next grunt, with 'Before it was only Rhodes; now it is always the Queen and Rhodes'."

Three days later there was another interview, which has been variously reported. Doyle interpreted; Jameson said he was going to Rhodes to tell him that Lobengula had refused the road. There may have been some words about impis and fighting. Lobengula replied, "No, I have not refused you the road, but let Rhodes come." On that they shook hands, and Jameson left at once for the south. He was not destined to meet the king again.[21]

To treat this as Lobengula's "specific sanction" would be stretching a point and would not make convincing reading in London. As so often before, however, the resistance of the Colonial Office was overcome by a factor that interested the Foreign Office: this time the Transvaal Boers.

Rumours of proposed treks over the Limpopo from the Transvaal had been flying about almost continuously since the days of Grobler's mission. They acquired some substance on the first day of 1890, when Louis P. Bowler issued a prospectus in the Transvaal, inviting farmers to join the "Great North Trek" to the country stretching eastward from the Umvukwes, where he claimed to have got a concession from the independent chief Mcheza. Bowler was a British subject resident in the Transvaal. Like Selous, Johnson, and others he was broad-minded about flags and sovereignty. When the Privy Council had the proposed charter on its agenda, Bowler's was one of the protests submitted against the monopoly based on the Rudd Concession. He had written on this subject directly to Lord Salisbury as early as July 1889, and kept up a correspondence with Williams, the British agent in Pretoria. The burden of all this was that Mcheza was independent of Lobengula; Bowler, as a British subject, wanted the British government to recognize his concession.

Independent Shona chiefs were a diplomatic liability; if they were acknowledged to be independent of the Ndebele, they would be claimed by the Portuguese. The British government therefore having spurned his appeal, Bowler looked for other support. His scheme was to entice land-hungry Transvaal burgers with the offer of 930 farms, each of 3,000 morgen (the traditional area of a Boer farm) on easy terms. His prospectus provided for a form of government, for the laying out of towns and other requisites of colonization. It provided also for the recognition of any European government that was found to be established in the concession area. The Portuguese consul-general in Pretoria lost no time in pointing out that it belonged to His Most Faithful Majesty, who would gladly welcome immigrants who acknowledged this fact.

Ralph Williams reported the prospectus and Bowler's correspondence to

Loch, warning him to take the threat seriously. However visionary and impracticable it might seem, equally small beginnings had led to large consequences in Stellaland, Goshen, the New Republic, and Swaziland, and might do so in this case. Williams informed Bowler that the territory he claimed lay within the British sphere of influence.

Selous, in a letter to the *Diamond Fields Advertiser*, asserted that neither Bowler nor his supposed Portuguese agent had been in Mcheza's country in 1887 or 1888, when the concession was said to have been obtained. Selous had himself been in the neighbourhood in those years. The old hand "Elephant" Phillips added his testimony that Bowler, who had been to Bulawayo when Phillips was there, had not gone beyond that place.

It is fortunately unnecessary to sift the arguments of so many interested parties to discover the truth of the matter. The Bowler trek was "emphatically disapproved" by Kruger's government in a public notice on 15 February; the reasons given were the danger of bloodshed and—the real reason—"important matters about which this Government is in correspondence with the British Government."

The important matter was Swaziland, which Kruger coveted as a step towards the seaport of his hopes. Unlike Joubert, Kruger was not an expansionist. He badly wanted a seaport, but had little interest in territorial aggrandisement as such. He was prepared to cooperate with the British in the north if they would pay his price in the east. Sir Francis de Winton, who had been sent from England to deal with the problem, strongly supported a deal of this kind; so did James Sivewright, the Cape politician, who discussed the proposal with Kruger in Pretoria. Kruger suggested a "summit conference" at Blignaut's Pont on the Cape-Transvaal border, where he and Loch could arrive at an agreement.

In the meantime Selous had been on a visit to the northern Transvaal to gather information about the country through which he was to lead the Pioneer Column. What he got was some more important information, about another Boer trek, quite distinct from Bowler's. This one was being organized in the Soutpansberg by Jan du Preez and "Klein" Barend Vorster. It was to consist of some 1,500 to 2,000 Boers, mostly Transvalers who wanted to escape from the Englishmen who had been crowding into the republic since the gold discoveries, but including other recruits from as far away as Paarl. Their objective was *southern* Mashonaland or Banyailand. Selous believed that this was the real threat, and that the Bowler trek was a mere blind to distract attention from it. He reported also that the leaders of this trek were prepared to acknowledge Portuguese sovereignty, and that the Portuguese consul-general was encouraging them.[22]

On 12 March Kruger, Loch, Rhodes, and their staffs met at Blignaut's Pont, where Loch drove a hard bargain. Kruger's prohibition of the Bowler trek was not a bargaining counter; Loch had insisted on it as a condition precedent to the conference. The existing condominium in Swaziland was continued; the Transvaal could have the territory only at the price of entering the Customs Union already formed between the Cape and the Free State, a price which the Volksraad refused to pay.

The Swaziland Convention blocked the loophole in the London Convention by forbidding Transvaal expansion to the north, and required the republic to use its influence to support the authority of the Chartered Company in its sphere. Kruger had indeed forbidden the Bowler trek, but took no cognizance of the plans of du Preez and Vorster. If they emulated the "freebooters" of Stellaland and Goshen, and tried to cross the border as private individuals, what "influence" would Kruger exert over them? The British government did not wait for the Blignaut's Pont conference to raise or answer this question. On 7 March the Foreign Office wrote to the Colonial Office that, while decisions depended on the outcome of the conference, Lord Salisbury observed "that it would be dangerous to withhold much longer from the High Commissioner authority to sanction the advance of the Company's armed police force into Mashonaland." Knutsford accordingly cabled to Loch: "You have authority to exercise discretion as to advance of the British South Africa Company into Mashonaland. Would be important to obtain from Lo Bengula promise to afford assistance to British South Africa Company if necessary, against trekkers from South African Republic."[23]

The emphasis had changed since Herbert had expected Lobengula to ask for assistance from the Company. The new emphasis was more realistic; whether Lobengula would actually fight for the Company was another question. At their final meeting he said to Jameson, " 'I think you are keeping the Boers out to make room for yourselves.' I replied that was exactly what we would do, which seemed to astonish him, and brought forth the usual grunt."[24] Candour was one of Jameson's more engaging qualities. Lobengula showed his usual perspicacity; what he did not realize was that the decision "to keep the Boers out" would take effect because it had been made, not by Jameson or Rhodes, but by the British prime minister.

It was now the first week of May, and the Pioneers were already assembling. Johnson had been recruiting them ever since the plans had been drawn up in January. He was not given a free hand, as Rhodes insisted that the influential families of the Colony, and all sections of South Africa, should be represented. He explained the policy to Johnson in this way: "Do you know what will happen to you? You will probably be massacred by the Matabele, or at least we shall one day hear that you have been surrounded and cut off! And who will rescue you, do you think? I will tell you—the Imperial Factor. And who do you think will bring pressure to bear on the Imperial Factor and stir them to save you? *The influential fathers of your young men!*" That was cunning, but it was not the whole story. Just as Rhodes had taken care that Chartered shares should be widely distributed in South Africa, so he wanted the human investment in his venture to ensure widespread political support. He advised John-son not to recruit in Cape Town or Kimberley as he could rely on those towns anyway.

So, with the help of local notables in various places, Johnson sorted out the applicants. Rhodes's principles of vote-catching and "influential fathers" re-sulted in the inclusion of such men as F. Schermbrucker (whose father was to become a minister in Rhodes's cabinet), Robert Coryndon (the future colonial governor), a son of Sir John Brand (late president of the Orange Free State), and Lionel Cripps, well connected in England. As family connections did not in themselves guarantee success in battle, Johnson regarded military experi-ence as an important qualification. Where that was lacking, athletic prowess was accepted as a substitute.

An important recruit not obviously qualified in these respects was William Harvey Brown, an American zoologist visiting parts of the African coast to collect specimens for the Smithsonian Institution. When his ship, uss *Pensacola*, reached Cape Town, he heard of Johnson's recruiting campaign, got leave from his employers, and enlisted with the Pioneers. We shall be meeting "Curio" Brown again.

Care had been taken to include a wide variety of trades and professions in the corps. "It comprised clergymen, doctors, lawyers (in those days, in my ig-norance, I thought them a necessity to civilised society), farmers, miners, sail-ors, builders, tailors, butchers, etc.—in a word, the complete nucleus of a self-contained civil population." Johnson was mistaken there: there were, for good and obvious reasons, no women in the column. This was no folk-migration such as have made the sagas of the South African and the American plains. It was a military formation with civil potentialities. Its strength and its weakness lay in that fact.[25]

From various directions, the chosen Pioneers converged on Mafeking, where attestation papers were signed and the men formed into three troops, A and B troops of mounted infantry, C troop of artillery. The whole body was placed under military discipline, a process which led to endless wrangling with the Colonial Office. As the force was under the Company, not the Crown, the officials were puzzled by the rumour that Loch had "commissioned" the offi-cers. Loch's protest that he had only approved arrangements made by the Company did nothing to remove the doubt. The company could not "commis-sion" officers; surely it could do no more than "appoint" them in the same manner as clerks? How, then, could discipline be maintained? Part of the problem was solved by placing the company's *police* under Carrington's com-mand until they passed out of the protectorate; beyond that border the laws had, as yet, no effect.[26] The discipline of the Pioneer Column itself was a sepa-rate question; it was a temporary problem, and, as we shall see, the rickety command structure held together long enough to serve its purpose.

Johnson, with the rank (whatever its validity) of major, commanded the Pioneer Column. As an old quartermaster-sergeant in Warren's expedition, he did an efficient job in issuing supplies: brown corduroy tunics and trousers, "digger" hats, rifles, revolvers, Maxim, Gatling, and Nordenfeldt guns, a searchlight with dynamo and steam-engine mounted in a wagon, salted horses, 2,000 oxen, 117 wagons, and food supplies for the duration of the march. In addition to captains and lieutenants in each troop, there were an adjutant, intelligence, transport, and medical officers, and chaplains of commissioned rank.

When the column moved out of its advanced base on the Motloutsi the total strength on the payroll, officers and men, was 186. Attached to it also were nineteen civilians. Most of these were prospectors, perhaps the only men in the party whose entry was really authorized by Lobengula; one of them was Allan Wilson. Among them also were Archibald Colquhoun, late of the Indian Civil Service, whom Rhodes had chosen as the head of the future civil administration of Mashonaland, and Jameson, who appeared to be altogether supernumerary but who (unknown to the others) carried Rhodes's power of attorney.[27]

According to the arrangement approved by the high commissioner, the Pioneers were to be accompanied by a body of the Company's police, for which the charter had made provision. The recruiting of this force had gone on parallel with the recruiting of the Pioneers. Though the threat of a Boer expedition had caused their numbers to be raised from 250 to 500, there was no lack of recruits. Many came from all ranks of society, attracted by the aura of romance which enveloped the operation. Few had had any military experience. To command this force, and to be in supreme command of the combined body of Pioneers and police during the march, Maj. E.G. Pennefather was seconded from the 6th Inniskilling Dragoons and given the rank of lieutenant-colonel.[28]

In addition to the Pioneers, the civilians, and the police, the party included African labourers and servants to do the jobs assigned to them by South African custom. Lobengula had at first offered to supply these. As he became less cooperative the risk was taken of using 350 Ngwato labourers, under the command of Kgama's brother Rraditladi, not only in their own country but all the way to the Lundi. Another class, including Griqua, Zulu, and Sotho (in short, British subjects) supplied the cooks, drivers, and other skilled workers.

The distribution of authority in the column was complicated and delicate. Pennefather was in supreme command of the combined body of police and Pioneers on the march, inasmuch as it was a military formation. Johnson on the other hand, in addition to commanding, as major, the three Pioneer troops, was responsible in terms of a business contract for getting them to their destination in a specified time. Selous, with the title of intelligence officer, was responsible for choosing the route and cutting it through the bush. Colquhoun had no authority during the march. Nor in the ordinary course had Jameson, but he held Rhodes's power of attorney to be used in the case of dispute among the others. It was fortunate for the column that he did not have to use it; the intrusion of one more civilian factor into a regular chain of military command might have compounded the difficulties.

As it was, though harmony was preserved, there were jealousies beneath the surface. Johnson's jealousy of Selous was still evident when he wrote his memoirs fifty years later; he treats Selous as a mere nuisance who had to be given some job to keep him out of mischief. There was a small grain of truth in this; Rhodes had enlisted Selous, given him a solatium of £2,000 and appointed him to guide the column, partly to prevent him from publishing more articles asserting that the Shona were independent.[29] Nevertheless there were solid reasons for making Selous the guide. He had had many years of experience in the interior, including most of Mashonaland; the twenty-three-year-old Frank Johnson was a novice in comparison. Selous had been one of the select company at the Government House conference; Johnson had not. The deference paid to Selous on the march stands out in all the contemporary accounts; Johnson was not seen in the same light.

Few men were able to make an enemy of Selous; not even Pennefather, whom he found considerate and obliging. The officer commanding made a different impression on others: "a tall, slight man, small headed and featured, irascible, petulant and disliked by his officers."[30]

Two conditions had to be met before the column could begin its march from the Motloutsi: Selous had to make a road and the high commissioner had to give the signal. The first part of the route ran across the disputed territory, hitherto preserved inviolate by orders from London. As there could be no advance without crossing it, Selous examined the terrain during May, was given instructions by Pennefather and Jameson, and with the help of twenty Ngwato labourers had a wagon track made from the Motloutsi to the Shashi (or Tuli) by 10 June.

Since the middle of May Maj.-Gen. Paul Methuen, deputy adjutant-general of the Cape Command, had been at the police camp on the Motloutsi, about twenty-five miles west of the Pioneer camp. Methuen spent some weeks there, observing the operations. Towards the end of June he reviewed the Pioneers, who went through their wagon and skirmish drill to his satisfaction. The high commissioner had imposed on Methuen the responsibility of deciding whether the two forces were in a state of readiness; and, if they were, of authorizing the advance. This having been done, the forward movement over the Motloutsi began on 27 June: the Pioneers and A Troop of the police, followed a few days later by B and C Troops, leaving D and E in camp with the BB Police. The main force reached the Shashi or Tuli on 1 July and began immediately to build Fort Tuli on the right or west bank. The disputed territory had been crossed; beyond the river lay, indisputably, Matabeleland.[31]

The next six weeks were to test the nerves and the resolve both of Lobengula and of the invaders to the limit. The tension was even greater among the Europeans still in Matabeleland. The missionaries were faced with an almost impossible choice, as someone whose name has been suppressed appears to have told Lobengula that "when the Missionaries clear out of your country you may expect war, but not before." It was, as Wilson wrote, "a mean and dastardly thing to do," but as the tension increased the missionaries had no other option open. They and their families were all out by the middle of June.[32]

There was no such way of escape for Lobengula. He and some of his older indunas knew, as they had known all along, that while it would be easy to wipe out the few Europeans in his country—and even the little column now invading it—the price of that victory would be a bigger and irresistible invasion. Remember Cetshwayo. The mass of his people thought otherwise. The king had now to perform his balancing act under much greater difficulty than before.

Late in May, when the young men were begging for the order to attack,[33] his reply was that they "would have the white men soon," but must be patient; they must go home, take their cattle to the white men and buy powder and lead, make all the preparations for war, but stay quiet until they received the order. Instructions of this kind were issued from time to time until the Pioneers were more or less safely at their destination.[34]

Another tactic was to vent anger on particular scapegoats. At the critical stage in June and July the scapegoat was Denis Doyle, who had interpreted for Jameson and had left for the south on 9 May. A month later Rhodes instructed him to return; Maxwell was losing his nerve and Doyle was to return to Bulawayo and remain there until the column was out of danger. On reaching the Tati, however, Doyle received information which decided him, rightly, to turn back. He had become the scapegoat.

> From what I can gather it came about in this way:—Lobengula asked Maxwell some days after I left who gave the Road to Mashonaland. Maxwell replied You King gave it to Doyle. The King, cornered in front of his people said "No, that is a lie, Doyle is a liar. Jameson could not understand and Doyle told him what he pleased. I only gave Grobelaar's Road not the Road into Mashonaland. Rhodes thinks he is doing what I wish and thinks I gave the Road whereas Doyle is the Liar. He gave the Road without my knowing it."

Doyle realized that his return to Bulawayo would enable the whole question to be reopened. What was more, "a messenger came in from one of the King's trusted men [with a message] which was as follows:—'Doyle don't come in the King will catch you and hold you.' I am inclined to think the King was instrumental in sending that message so as to prevent me coming on and having an Indaba on it."

Messages—preferably to distant addresses—were Lobengula's chief instruments at this crisis for checking the ardour of the regiments. About the middle of June a party of six Ndebele headmen with their attendants arrived at the

Tati with a message to be delivered to Pennefather: "Have I killed any white man that a white impi is collecting on my border? Why cannot we live together without war?" As this message passed down the line to Cape Town it was taken by all as a sign that Lobengula did not want to fight.[35]

The high commissioner had by then sent, through Moffat, a message to the king, informing him that he, Loch, had given permission for the column to advance into Mashonaland, "and I wish you to know that these people come as your friends." At the end of June, Moffat not yet having returned to Bulawayo, Lobengula dispatched a message to Loch. Sam Edwards refused to handle it before Moffat arrived, but Lippert's agents, Renny-Tailyour and Boyle, offered their services. It was arranged that Boyle should go straight to Cape Town, while Renny-Tailyour went by way of Natal, to get from Sir Theophilus Shepstone an introduction to Loch. As if this were not in itself a sufficient guarantee of long delay, Denis Doyle prolonged it further by arranging at Palapye that "when Boyle and the envoys get here, they will find that there is *no room* in the Post-cart and they will have to travel by ox-wagon." Boyle, Renny-Tailyour, and the envoys—one of whom was Mshete—therefore had their interviews with Loch between 27 July and 5 August. The substance of their message was that Rhodes's men were going all over the country for gold. "The Chief is troubled. He is being eaten up by Mr. Rhodes." Moffat was Rhodes's man. Lobengula wanted another man to represent the queen, one direct from England. Loch sent reassuring messages to the king, though insisting that Moffat was his official representative; but the envoys did not reach Bulawayo until 7 September. This operation had given Lobengula a breathing space of more than two months.[36]

During that time, however, it had been necessary to send messages to the column itself. On 30 June one was written for the king by Sam Edwards and directed to the police camp on the Motloutsi: "Why are so many warriors at Macloutsie? Has the king committed any fault, or has any white man been killed, or have the white men lost anything that they are looking for?" A fortnight later another was written by Maxwell and taken to Jameson (with the column, and now ten miles beyond the Lundi River) by Colenbrander, Cooper-Chadwick, and four headmen:

> I gave permission to dig for gold in the Country near "Sam's." From whom did the Doctor hear the King give [*sic*] permission to dig in Mashonaland? How is it that the Doctor agreed at Bulawayo to dig only in a place pointed out by the King? And now he wants to dig where the King objects, and will not allow. Does the Doctor want to "phasela" (invade) the King's Country and "Imba n'ga mantla" (dig by force)? The Doctor says the King showed the road at Imganemeni [*sic*]. The King asks whether the Doctor understood the King's language. And on that day did the Doctor understand the King's word.

This time, at any rate, it was easy to understand the king's word; this was not the language of menace or ultimatum. (Jameson most ungratefully called it one of the king's "shuffling answers.") Nor did the method of delivery suggest urgency. Colenbrander was told to take the letter to Fort Tuli, from which—as the king knew perfectly well—the column had departed more than a month before. It was beyond the Lundi when the letter was delivered.

Colenbrander appears also to have conveyed, orally, a command for the column to turn back. Jameson having no official position, a reply was written by Pennefather: he was a soldier obeying the queen's orders, and would not turn back except at her order, nor stop until he reached the highveld. Back at Fort Tuli, Colenbrander gave the reply to the headmen to take to the king; he himself—again on Lobengula's instructions—went down to Kimberley to repeat the message to Rhodes. When Pennefather's reply was read to Lobengula on 20 August, he took it calmly, and was "very pleased to know Johan [Colenbrander] has gone to Mr. Rhodes with his message as it gives him an opportunity for delay." Public interest was concentrated on beer-drinking, and, as Moffat reported, "apparently business left to slide."[37]

This result had not been achieved easily. If the king's argument with two or three great indunas in the goat kraal on 15 July ("He was being importuned to let them have at least one slap at the pioneers and he was urging objections") was overheard by a white man, many more such meetings must have been held out of earshot of reporters. As invaders themselves, the Ndebele had some idea of what the small white impi struggling through the bush portended. Though the fiction about "digging" was kept up, they were not deceived. Nor were they taken in by the assurances from Loch, Moffat, and others that the column's military strength had been provided as a defence against the Boers.

There is some evidence that the battle-lust of the king's army and people was inspired by the fear, not so much of losing the Shona raiding grounds and being outflanked on the east, as of being attacked in the Ndebele heartland itself. On 20 August Maxwell wrote: "Several of the Majakes . . . have asked me 'Why don't you leave the country? You are sure to be killed when the Impi gets to Bulawayo!' I have always told them they will not see an Impi at Bulawayo, and they now tell me I have spoken truly." The Pioneer column was at all times shadowed by a small Ndebele patrol of two or three hundred men, relieved and replaced at intervals, and sending regular reports to the king. He always received the reports "coolly"; they showed that the column was giving the Ndebele kraals a wide berth, as had been promised.

Moffat, asked to explain why Pennefather had said that he would not stop until he reached the highveld, "replied it was better for the health of the men and the cattle: King replied 'No that is not it: they know they will be better able to fight there.' " Lobengula, knowing this too, appears to have been almost as anxious as the Pioneers themselves for them to reach the high and open country.[38]

The route chosen by Selous, afterwards called the Selous Road and still faintly visible today, described an arc from Fort Tuli to the proposed destination at Mount Hampden, the concave side towards Bulawayo. The column would thus keep well away from the Ndebele towns and posts. For about 170 miles the way ran through the lowveld of the Limpopo valley, in bush that was always dense, mostly stunted, but in parts thick with mopani, and with the antediluvian shapes of the baobabs standing out here and there. The tributaries of the Limpopo, and farther on of the Sabi, ran transversely across the route. The tasks of the column were to cut a road for the wagons through the bush, to get them across the river beds (at that season the obstacle was sand rather than water), and to defend itself against the Ndebele if attacked in country so unfavourable to European methods of fighting.

The advance from Fort Tuli began on 6 July. The way had to be cut through the bush, the road-makers defended if attacked, and warning of attack to be given by scouting parties ahead, at the rear and on the flanks. The first few days revealed the impossibility of forming, at short notice, a laager out of a train of wagons extending for more than two miles; thereafter the wagons advanced in two parallel columns. Though two roads had now to be cut, the hardest engineering feat was not the road-making but getting the wagons across the rivers. This was achieved. Every night a square laager was formed, the searchlight played on the surrounding bush and explosive charges were laid in position outside the laager and detonated from time to time.[39] The sweating troopers did not know that, during this early stage of their march, Rhodes had become prime minister of the Cape Colony.

On 28 July the Nuanetsi was crossed. A small party of Ndebele—no doubt detached from the watching patrol—appeared in the camp. Ellerton Fry re-

The laager near Lundi River, 1890

169 The Pioneers and Their Rivals

marked to Dr. Brett that they were a fine lot of "Boys." "One of them, who probably understood the meaning of the word Boy as used by South Africans, turned on us. He said they were not Boys but Matabele. It was splendid, we both could not but admire him."

On the evening of 1 August the main body reached the Lundi, where there was a halt for five days, while Selous with two white and two black scouts reconnoitred the country ahead. This was believed to be the critical moment of the march. The jumbled hill-ranges to the north marked the edge of the Mashonaland plateau, but between the Lundi and the edge of the escarpment lay fifty miles of rough country, where if at all Lobengula must wipe out the invaders. Moreover, it was not known whether a way practicable for the wagons would be found through those hills.

On the second day of his reconnaissance Selous scanned the country from the top of Zamamba hill, and spied what might be a pass up the main range. Crossing the Tokwe, where a ford suitable for the column was found, Selous and his companions were well up the pass by the next evening. With high hopes he rode on in the dusk, finally climbing a hill to get a wider view: "My feelings may be better imagined than described when I say that I saw stretched out before me, as far as the eye could reach, a wide expanse of open grassy country, and knew that I was looking over the south-western portion of the high plateau of Mashunaland . . . A weight of responsibility, that had at times become almost unbearable, fell from my shoulders, and I breathed a deep sigh of relief." The patrol was back at the Lundi on 5 August with the good news. The next day the column resumed its advance.[40]

That evening at midnight, Colenbrander rode in with Lobengula's "shuffling answer," which gave a new urgency to the march. After this the force was in almost hourly expectation of attack, though the king's letter hardly justified the fear.

At the Lundi Rraditlandi and his men turned back, possibly because they feared that when the river rose they would be cut off from home if they were beyond it. In any case they had ventured much further into the lion's den than was prudent for Kgama's subjects. One party of them, however, had hardly set out when it returned to the camp in panic, reporting the presence of 2,000 Ndebele in the neighbourhood. Extra precautions were taken, the scouts made a wide sweep to the west, fires were seen, but no Ndebele.

Colquhoun's secretary Harrison suggested that the pass discovered by Selous be named Providential Pass. The march to it was made in an atmosphere of tension, but there was no attack. On 14 August the column debouched on to the plateau. A few miles further on it halted: this, according to the original plan, was to be the site of another fort. During the halt of a few days Sir John Willoughby and C Troop of the police arrived with a train of supply wagons and the mail from the south; a rugby match was played; and there were visits to Great Zimbabwe, about which various ill-founded opinions were expressed. The amateur archeologists were, however, less interested in the history of the place than in searching for its hidden gold. None was found.

Leaving C troop of the police to hold and garrison Fort Victoria, the rest of the force resumed its march on 19 August. Now the danger of attack had receded, if not altogether disappeared. In the relatively open savannah country the column had little to fear from the Ndebele army. As they rode on, feeling relaxed now, the Pioneers thought of the farms that could be carved out of this promised land. Some thought only of mining. One Irishman planned a lucrative business in cattle-raiding beyond the Zambezi. More immediately there was the excitement of the chase, which some managed to combine with their patrol duties. After a fortnight of this the column halted again, on 3 September, on the watershed between the headwaters of the Sabi and of the Ngezi. There a third fort—Charter—was built, and A Troop of the police left to garrison it.

At this point Colquhoun, accompanied by Selous, Jameson, and a small escort, left the column. According to instructions he was to visit the Chief Mutasa, get a concession of mineral and other rights from him, get if possible the right of communication with the seaboard, and report on the best route for a railway to it. The Company, in other words, was now braced for a direct confrontation with the Portuguese. We shall return to the story of this expedition later.

The prospectors attached to the column likewise hived off at Fort Charter, to the envious indignation of the attested men who had to stay in the ranks until formally demobilized. Beyond the Umfuli some engineers were detached to survey farms between that river and the Hunyani. Again the men in the ranks were indignant because this was inferior bushy country and they had understood they were to select their farms wherever they pleased. There were other people who might have felt even more indignant, but who for the moment knew nothing of the danger lurking in a theodolite.

On 10 September the column crossed the Hunyani. The next day Pennefather, Sir John Willoughby, and Ted Burnett rode ahead to choose the next, and final, stopping place. E.E. Burke has identified their route: "in modern terms the party rode that day from the Hunyani to the Seven Miles Hotel, up the Makabusi, across the centre of Salisbury and perhaps through Alexandra Park and Mount Pleasant to the area of the Marlborough Race Track; then across to Glenara and back along the edge of the escarpment overlooking the Mazoe valley and then to the Causeway area, perhaps by Pomona, and Alexandra Park again. This is a distance of 40 miles." Pennefather explained: "Finding that the water supply in the Gwibi valley and at the edge of the plateau was not sufficient for what might eventually be the seat of government, with a considerable population, I returned to the valley of the Makobisi and selected the site where the camp now is." On the morning of 12 September the column camped on the plain below the Kopje.[41] The following items appeared in the orders for the day:

1. It is notified for general information that the Column, having arrived at its destination, will halt.
2. The name of this place will be Fort Salisbury.

On the next morning at 10 a.m. the column paraded, in full dress, before a flagstaff which the naval men had cut from the straightest tree they could find. The Union Jack was hoisted by Lieutenant Tyndale-Biscoe, the two seven-pounders fired a 21-gun salute, and prayer was offered by Canon Balfour, the police chaplain. In a loyal gesture which had, however, no legal effect, the lands included in the Rudd Concession were annexed to the British Empire. After three cheers for the queen the men dispersed.

Work was begun at once on the fort, situated on what would later be Cecil Square. The mail was dispatched to the south. On the last day of the month, the fort being completed and Johnson's contract fulfilled, the Pioneer Column was disbanded and returned to civilian life.

It had marched, ridden, and hacked its way some 360 miles from Fort Tuli without loss of life. That was due directly to Lobengula, but indirectly also to Kgama, to the efficient armament of the column, to the patient diplomacy of the representatives in Bulawayo, and to the police still poised on the Motloutsi, on Lobengula's other flank. The safe passage need not detract from the courage of the men, who were never sure, till they were over Providential Pass, that they would not be annihilated. Indeed, they were not sure yet, and many were destined to fall to the stabbing assegai within the next seven years. For the time being, though, the column had eliminated one of the alternatives in Fairfield's Delphic pessimistic prophecy: "I think we had better say nothing, and let them all go quietly over Niagara in their own way. It may be a success—or it may not."[42]

September 1890 is of course a turning point in Zimbabwean, which now became Rhodesian, history. White men had been moving about the country for decades. A few missionaries and traders had settled on an almost permanent basis. But the arrival of the Pioneers had a very different implication: conquest, occupation, an alien society and government to be superimposed on the indigenous, white on black.

Before this process can be described, two old themes must be followed to their provisional conclusions: the Matabeleland concession-hunters and the Boer trekkers. In spite of Rudd, the charter, and the occupation, both these groups continued their operations, to some extent in collusion with each other.

Through all these events it had been clear that the Rudd Concession suffered from a serious weakness, in that it granted nothing but mining rights. Although the grantees were authorized to turn back all persons seeking "land, metals, minerals or mining rights," the temptation to others to seek concessions of anything not specifically granted to Rudd was overwhelming. Some of those tempted were men of small substance, including of course a few unreconciled "old hands" in Matabeleland, but to the Company these were only a petty nuisance. Of a different order were Eduard Lippert and Oscar Dettelbach, German-Jewish financiers of Johannesburg. Lippert, well known as an early holder of Kruger's dynamite monopoly, was also a cousin of Alfred Beit, Rhodes's close associate, but this fact did not determine his concession-politics.

We have seen that Lippert, represented by Renny-Tailyour, Boyle, and others, had been in the game from the beginning. He also stayed in it to what may be called the end. Dettelbach came later; his representative was Ernst Hassforther, who had been in and out of Matabeleland since 1886, but was described by Mrs. Lippert as "a horrible liar and not worthy of attention." This was the judgment of an ally; Hassforther's enemies were even less charitable. Though the Lippert and Dettelbach parties were distinct, they worked in close conjunction. Dettelbach's objective was a trade monopoly, Lippert's was land. Both had the advantage, in dealing with Lobengula, that the king needed some leverage to use against the all-powerful Company, and these men could offer to supply it.

Hassforther was in Bulawayo in October and November 1890, on mysterious business. That he was working for Lippert as well as Dettelbach is shown by a letter he received from the former: "The Charter Co. probably got wind of your intention for Mr. Eckstein came to me saying he had been instructed to ask me if I had sent an expedition to Mashonaland and I naturally denied it . . . When you get the concession for minerals from the King please do not fail to hint that it was given you some time ago! Also have it witnessed by as many reliable white men as possible."

No mineral concession was obtained; Lobengula was too astute a diplomatist for that. What was obtained on 18 November was the sole right of trading, of collecting natural gums, cotton, and rubber, and of building roads. As the price of the concession was £50 a year, Lobengula's purpose in giving it could only have been to divide his enemies. In addition to the concession, the king dictated a letter to the kaiser, asking him to arbitrate between himself and the Chartered Company. The old Bulawayo principle of keeping secrets was carried to a curious length. Hassforther, Mshete, Karl Khumalo, and John Makhunga brought a document to Fairbairn, keeper of the Elephant Seal, asking him to affix the seal to the document but *not to read it*. It thus remained uncertain whether the paper contained "the King's words." Khumalo and Makhunga were two adventurers from the south, the former the son of one of Mzilikazi's officers who had betrayed his master to Shaka at the battle in 1822. They worked closely with the Lippert and Dettelbach parties. They and Hassforther exploited Lobengula's fears of the Rudd Concession to the full, culti-vating in the king's mind the suspicion that he had sold his birthright for a mess of pottage. Instead of the £100 a month and the "rotten English rifles," they said, he should have had half the mining profits. Hassforther appears to have suggested that he would bring other rifles and money from Germany, so that the king could return all that had been paid or given by the Company, and so effectively cancel the concession. Late in November Hassforther set out for Germany, accompanied by John Makhunga.[43]

Moffat took all this very seriously. His warnings passed through Cape Town and London to the ambassador in Berlin. Perhaps they were effective; perhaps they were unnecessary. The German officials seem to have taken Hassforther's measure as easily as Marie Lippert did, and with the ink hardly dry on the He-ligoland treaty they would not in any case have been willing to enroach on the British sphere. Hassforther returned in July 1891, in a chastened mood, but with a load of goods for the king.

By this time many things had happened to complicate the situation; Dettel-bach's supposed concession had become a small part of a large whole. First, there was Lippert, whose operations were much more dangerous to the Com-pany than Dettelbach's. We have seen Lippert's agents—chiefly Renny-Tail-your, Boyle and Reilly, but Colenbrander had originally been one of them—at work in Bulawayo from an early date. In July 1889 it had been reported that they were "coquetting" with Rhodes on the Rand, but were to be careful not to change sides at Bulawayo too obviously.[44] The course of this coquetting did not, however, run smooth. By the time the Pioneers were on the march the Lippert party was doing all it could to frustrate their enterprise. Thus on 17 July it was Boyle and Reilly who "had the King's stamp over at their place for nearly two hours"; it was Boyle who then took the king's envoys direct to Cape Town to complain to Loch, while Renny-Tailyour travelled via Natal. Reilly stayed behind, and read to the king an extract from the *Diamond Fields Advertiser* which assured nervous settlers that Lobengula was doing all he could to help the Company in Mashonaland. This was true, but to publish it in Bulawayo was a neat way of shattering the king's careful diplomacy. The news of these doings reached Loch in a telegram from Moffat while the interviews with the delegation were in progress. The high commissioner accordingly warned Renny-Tailyour and Boyle that if they continued to stir up trouble they would not be allowed to enter Matabeleland. When they did return in September Moffat reported that they were "all going to be good boys in fu-ture."

Only up to a point. On 22 April 1891 the "good boys" got something which they claimed was the concession they were after, and of which a copy after-wards reached Loch. The story of this concession can be pieced together from subsequent statements by Acutt and Lippert. Renny-Tailyour "represented to the King that, while the Charter Company had merely obtained a gold concession, they were taking the land also. Mr. Tailyour undertook to go and contest the matter with the Company, and the Chief said that on his return from doing so, he would give him a concession. Mr. Tailyour wanted a sort of general power of attorney, and said he could not draw it up properly here, but would put it into proper form when he got to Johannesburg." He therefore equipped himself with two pieces of paper. One remained a blank sheet, except that it bore the date, elephant stamp, Mshete's mark, and the signatures of Renny-Tailyour, Acutt, and Reilly. The other was supposed to contain, in layman's language, the details that were to be transferred to the first "in proper form."

Either the contents of the second paper were written by Renny-Tailyour and not shown to his colleagues or to the king, or what was transposed to the signed and sealed paper in Johannesburg was very different from what the second paper had contained when it left Bulawayo. Lippert, who professed a kind of childlike innocence in such legal matters, consulted Advocate J.W. Leonard (a well-known figure in Uitlander history), who "then put the concession into the form it now bears." When a copy of it reached Moffat from Loch, the former showed it to Acutt, who said "it contains a great deal more than what was specified on that occasion." Leonard, as we shall see, got his reward.[45]

The concession, in the form it assumed in Johannesburg, gave Renny-Tailyour, who transferred it to Lippert, the sole right to grant land titles in Lobengula's dominions. Whether or not Lippert had any misgivings about the strength of his precious document, his policy was to assume a confident and aggressive air. In playing against Rhodes one had to have good cards—or a good poker face. If Lippert did not yet hold a respectable concession, he was at any rate playing cunningly. The Company's greatest weakness was its inability to grant land. If Lippert could acquire the right to do this, he could hold the Company to ransom. That was the most he could do, for the British government would not allow a rival authority into the Company's sphere, and Germany after 1890 would not interfere there. The possibility that the Boers, or the Boers and Portuguese in combination, might drive the Company out still existed in theory in April 1891, but it is impossible to believe that Lippert took this prospect seriously. His curious mixture of reliance on the "Home" government, appeals to Boer prowess, and vilification of Rhodes was therefore directed to the single end of raising his price to the Company.

The second complicating factor was the so-called Adendorff trek. Even after the successful march of the Pioneer Column, the threat of a Boer incursion from the south remained one of the chief anxieties of Rhodes, Loch, and the Foreign Office. Lippert therefore exploited the trek movement for his own purposes.

It will be remembered that Bowler's proposed trek had been forbidden by Kruger as a necessary preliminary to the conference at Blignaut's Pont. Bowler is next heard of at Quelimane, trying to get to his concession by way of the Zambezi, but he was too late: the Pioneers got there first. The other trek observed by Selous, under the leadership of Jan du Preez and Klein Barend Vorster, was less easily disposed of. The trekkers who had gathered in the Soutpansberg disbanded for a time, but this was a prorogation rather than a dissolution. About the end of July 1890, some of the leaders—including du Preez, Louis Adendorff, and Piet Mayer—crossed the Limpopo, reached the neighbourhood of the Pioneer Column (of which they said they had a good view from a koppie), visited Chivi, from whom they claimed to get a concession, and were back in the Soutpansberg late in August.

According to Sir Frederick Carrington's informant this concession-hunting journey was undertaken on the orders of Kruger's government. The truth of this is hard to determine, but there were some curious coincidences. When the Volksraad ratified the Swaziland Convention on 7 August, it went on to request the annexation to the republic of two areas, one in Bechuanaland and the other in the north. The latter, stretching from the Limpopo to 21°S. and from 29°E. to the Portuguese border, bore a strong resemblance to the supposed Adendorff concession, except that in his generosity Chivi extended his grant northwards to the Zambezi. There was a resemblance also to an earlier supposed concession on which the original trek scheme was based. As the Swaziland Convention, effective on 7 August, forbade Transvaal expansion northwards, the date 5 August on Adendorff's concession was curiously convenient. When the Volksraad passed its resolution it could not have known of the concession. The pieces of the puzzle fit together too neatly.

In September the high commissioner received an official request from the Transvaal government to make these annexations. Loch at first had some doubts about the claim in Bechuanaland, but in the end decided against it. He had no doubt that the other request must be refused, since the area in question was specifically included in the territory assigned to the BSA Company by charter. After some dilatory correspondence between Loch, the Colonial Office, and the Foreign Office, the high commissioner replied to the president on 2 April 1891, that "no proposal, therefore, for the cession of any portion of this territory can be considered or discussed."[46]

The answer had probably been foreseen. The trek leaders went ahead with their scheme on the assumption that they would form an independent Republic of the North, for which the South African Republic would have no responsibility: Stellaland and Goshen over again. The trekkers were to cross the Limpopo on 1 June, and on the following day to proclaim their republic, with a constitution based on those of the Transvaal and the Free State. The justification of their proceedings, as published in the Transvaal papers, is interesting:

> 1. That we regard the act of the Imperial British Government in granting exclusive right in the interior to the said Chartered Company as an unwarrantable usurpation of authority, and as an act at variance with the national and constitutional rights of the various Governments and people of South Africa.

2. That the said Chartered Company, therefore, in pretending to exercise the exclusive authority, is acting in direct conflict with the rights of the South African peoples without possessing legal or other justification for so doing.
3. That the responsibility of all bloodshed or other evils that may follow from these illegal and unconstitutional usurpations rests, therefore, with those who have permitted or perpetrated the same.
4. That the right of directing the policy and destinies of the South African Continent rests solely with the South African people, and that all interference with or usurpation of that right is illegal and unconstitutional, and in contempt of the natural liberties of the South African people.

The judgment of this statement hinges, of course, on the meaning of the word *people*. Even, however, on the narrow assumptions of the authors of this document, the argument had some defects. Two of the governments referred to, with the support of the elected representatives of their "people," opposed this trek, and the head of one of them was Rhodes. When Kruger, too, joined the opposition and issued a proclamation forbidding the trek, nothing was left of the legal and constitutional arguments, whatever Natural Law might have to say.

The claim to have obtained a concession from the "Banyai" chief Chivi rested on uncertain evidence. A document was brought back, bearing the crosses of Chivi (or "Sebasha"), "Mozobe," and eighteen indunas; but the only witnesses to these marks were three of the concession-hunters themselves (D.J. Brummer, H.L. Brummer and C.G. Nel), and a literate but otherwise unknown African, Micha Makhatho. In addition to the concession Chivi and the indunas put their marks to an elaborate proclamation, in Dutch, denouncing the invasion of their country by "Roads" and the "Garsten" (Chartered) Company. Some evidence was given at a meeting of the Afrikaner Bond at Paarl to the effect that Adendorff and his companions had not been in Chivi's neighbourhood in early August; the defenders of the concession could do no better than suggest that there might be a mistake in the date, and in any case the date arouses suspicion. If these objections were removed, an insuperable one would remain: Chivi was tributary to Lobengula. No; the source of the movement was neither a document nor any other legal right, but the old *trekgees*, the need to leave the crowded Transvaal for spacious farms out of sight of their neighbours' smoke, with a little "shooting of *rooineks*" thrown in to attract the young.

On 13 April a proclamation by the high commissioner warned against any attempt to set up an independent government in the British sphere. Loch appealed also to Kruger, who tried at first to deny all responsibility on the ground that most (this was an exaggeration) of the trekkers would come from the Cape Colony. When Loch pointed out that, whatever their origin, they must inevitably launch their movement from a Transvaal base, Kruger on 25

April issued his proclamation forbidding the trek. (His essential motive was the fear of losing Swaziland). In May the Volksraad confirmed this proclamation, and provided a punishment of a year's imprisonment with hard labour, or a fine of £500, for infringing it. The power of president and Volksraad to enforce it was, however, the more doubtful because of the strong national emotions involved. The "people" whose rights were invoked were the Afrikaners in general and the citizens of the republics in particular. The trekkers were to take a printing press with them and to issue an official newspaper, not in Dutch but in Afrikaans. The *Transvaal Observer* and, of course, *Di Patriot* of Paarl were lyrical about the country to be occupied and about the expansion of Afrikanerdom. There was talk of five thousand trekkers, who would have made the combined forces of Pennefather, Colquhoun, and Carrington, and perhaps even of Lobengula, look small indeed.[47]

Loch considered it vital to put a damper on this movement before the would-be trekkers had sold their farms, after which there could be no looking back. He wanted reinforcements for the Bechuanaland Border Police, and if possible some imperial units to be sent north. He believed also that there was collusion between Boers and Portuguese, which would not have been surprising. The alarm was at its height during April 1891, a critical month in the relations between the Company and the Portuguese, as will be described in the next chapter.

There was a Portuguese concession to T. Kleinenberg and H. van Reenan, who planned to settle about 150 Boers from the northern Transvaal in the disputed region of Manica; the plan fell through when the 1891 Anglo-Portuguese Convention put the area in question on the British side of the line. The high commissioner was more perturbed by information from two officials in Zululand, who had received it during March from various local Boer farmers. Portugal was said to have invited two thousand Boers to take up land in Manica, or, by another account, in Mashonaland. Each was to bring two rifles, but ammunition would be supplied. Each would receive two farms of 8,000 (by the other account, 6,000) acres. The settlers were to help the Portuguese against all external enemies and against all Africans in their territories who would not submit to Portuguese authority.

This scheme, whether the report was true, false or exaggerated, was quite separate from that of Louis Adendorff and his associates, but the new threat gave additional plausibility to Loch's demand for a warship to be sent to Beira. For defence against Adendorff Loch wanted troops, a demand to which the Treasury was never quick to respond. The Colonial Office naturally cast the responsibility on the Company: let it use its own police. On 17 April Rhodes accordingly instructed Pennefather to station fifty men of that force, and to build a redoubt, at each of the drifts of the Limpopo leading from the Transvaal into the Company's territory. When the trekkers attempted to cross, each was to be required to give a written undertaking to obey the Company's

laws and regulations. Those who gave this were to be conducted by civil officers to locations where they might settle; those who refused were to be turned
back.

The high commissioner issued more detailed instructions to Sir Frederick
Carrington, who had overall command of the Company's forces as well as of
his own Bechuanaland Border Police. An increase of forty in the strength of
the latter was authorized. A battalion of the East Yorkshires was sent to Mafeking to relieve the police in the Crown Colony. The general instructions
given by Rhodes were repeated in more detail, and a special problem was
faced: what to do if trekkers in large numbers signed the document. In principle they should be admitted, but if they were in great strength they might later
feel free to repudiate their promise. The solution would be to admit small
numbers at a time, and to settle them close to the various mining communities
in Mashonaland. This would reduce the military danger and increase the economic advantage of their presence.

It may be that a large migration across the Limpopo would have taken place
but for the measures taken by Loch and Kruger to stop it. In the circumstances
of 1891 such a trek would have conformed to the rules of Afrikaner history.
Consistently with those rules, the movement was weakly coordinated. Innumerable reports of little independent parties moving from here and there probably had some foundation in fact. Kruger's proclamation, the Volksraad's law,
Kruger's personal intervention with some of the leaders, and the measures
taken by the high commissioner and the Company were probably the factors
that took the steam out of the movement. Jacobus De Wet, the British agent
in Pretoria, out of an exiguous budget was able to employ a few informers who
gave him due warning of the movement that did occur.[48]

Small as it was, Lippert intended to make use of it. On 15 May he had written to the Company's secretary in Cape Town, suggesting a meeting. Negotiations had dragged on unsuccessfully. The Company could not afford at that
time to pay Lippert's price, and Rhodes affected to regard the concession as
worthless. Lippert therefore turned on the heat. F.J. Dormer, editor of the Johannesburg *Star*, informed Rhodes that Lippert would not sell for less than
£250,000. Next, if Rhodes did not give a favourable answer within ten days,
Lippert would publish his concession in full-page advertisements "in all leading papers"; the rush to get farms under the scheme might then all but sweep
the Company away. On 22 May Dormer sent more news about "what these
devils are up to": the plan was to give the Banyailand trekkers land titles under the Lippert Concession. If, then, they were resisted by the company's forces, there would be an appeal to "the English courts," which would uphold the
concession and the trekkers' titles.

No Great Trek occurred. The old leaders had for various reasons dropped
out; most of their followers, many of whom were Free Staters, went home or
were given land in the Soutpansberg. The party of 112 that tried to cross the

Limpopo at the Main Drift on 24 June 1891 was led by Col. Ignatius Ferreira, a penniless (according to De Wet, insolvent) old veteran of the Zulu War. Ferreira, who with a few companions did cross the river, ran into the Company's police, Jameson, and soon afterwards a party of Bechuanaland Border Police under Goold-Adams.

Jameson crossed to the south bank and held a palaver with the trekkers. A few accepted his terms and the rest dispersed. Ferreira was arrested. He then gave up a letter written to him a few days before by Lippert. The gist of this was that, pending ratification by the British government, of which he had no doubt, he intended to go ahead and issue land titles,

> and shall shortly issue titles to 500 farms in Mashonaland. For the first 500 farms I have fixed the price at £5 for 3000 morgen and £2 per annum: for the next 500 farms the price will, of course be raised. I propose to deposit the money in the hands of trustees in the Bank, to be returned to the owners of the farms if, within 12 months, I have either not obtained recognition of their rights by the English government, or the Charter Company, or if they have not taken forcible possession of the farms.

Lippert expected on these terms to get 500 farmers from the Free State to go in at once, with thousands more to follow. He denounced the recent proclamation by the high commissioner as

> a breach of faith, in so far that Mr. Beit promised me that while he was negotiating with me respecting the recognition of the Concession, nothing should be done prejudicially to me; but Rhodes, with his usual unscrupulousness, took no notice thereof, and I believe that Mr. Beit is very much ashamed of what Rhodes has done. My reports from Buluwayo are not very peaceable. I hear that Lo Bengula is very much annoyed at the constant stream of people coming into the country, and I should not wonder if he could not restrain his people any longer. Of course that would be the opportunity for the Boers of this country, because with all the Police and British Regiments that Rhodes can send up, it is, after all, only the Boers who can deal with the Matabele.

In conclusion, the time had "not yet come to appoint Ferreira Administrator."[49]

Almost everything about this letter suggests that it was intended to fall into Jameson's hands. The key words are "obtained recognition by . . . the Charter Company." We shall see what a rich reward that recognition brought to Lippert. By contrast, the idea that this dealer in quarter-millions would court a financial and military war for the sake (in the first phase) of £2,500 down and £1,000 a year is rather a weak joke, even though his debts were becoming unmanageable in 1891.[50] The point would have been lost on the bankrupt Colonel Ferreira, but not on Jameson. That only the Boers could deal with the Matabele, and the reference to taking forcible possession, were matters weighing heavily on the minds of Jameson and others when Lippert wrote his letter, though they had lost their terror by the time Ferreira and the letter were in Jameson's hands.

Recognition of the concession by the British government would have been one of the points that Jameson took seriously. Loch and Moffat were already concerned about the validity of the document. In a month or two Loch would be writing that the signatures on it appeared to be genuine and that the company ought to buy it, for some of the terms "provide for a land settlement, which is so much desired." Moffat would reply that the signatures were all those of Renny-Tailyour's employees, except that of Mshete "who nevertheless may justly be included in the same category." Moffat was waiting for an opportunity to read the document to Lobengula, because he was satisfied "that the Chief had no idea of the powers that he was granting to Tailyour."[51] Yet Lobengula had actually repudiated the Rudd Concession, and what a great tree had already grown from that seed!

The time had "not yet come to appoint Ferreira Administrator." One can hear Lippert chuckling to himself as he added this gratuitous parting shot for the benefit of prospective Administrator Jameson. On the other hand it is difficult to understand why Ferreira, who had evidently been in touch with Lippert before, should need to receive these detailed plans and comments in a letter written to him as he was on the point of going, as it were, into battle. In any case, as a letter to Ferreira, it served no purpose; as bait for Jameson and Rhodes, it worked.

Lobengula's—or should we say J.W. Leonard's?—concession to Renny-Tailyour gave

> the sole and exclusive right and privilege for the full term of one hundred years, to lay out, grant, or lease, for such periods as he may think fit, farms, townships, building plots, and grazing areas, to impose and levy rents, licenses and taxes; to get in, collect, and receive the same, to give and grant certificates in my name for the occupation of any farms [etc.]; to establish and to grant licenses for the establishment of banks; to issue bank-notes; to establish a mint . . .

The price of the concession was £1,000 down and £500 a year.[52] If it were valid, and recognized by the secretary of state, the Chartered Company would be in trouble.

The immediate reactions of the high commissioner and the Company to the captured letter were what could be expected: Renny-Tailyour was arrested at Tati and Hassforther, returning from Germany, at Tuli. To complicate matters, Lobengula too had reacted to the developing conflict between Rhodes, Lippert, and the trekkers. He had dictated a letter, written by Helm, to Hans Lee (the pro-Boer frontiersman of Mangwe), asking him to come to Bulawayo and act as his adviser. Many questions were put to Lee, some in the letter but most of them orally by the indunas who conveyed it. Were two opposite parties coming into the country, and would this "lose him his own"? Would not the occupation of Mashonaland by the Company encroach on him, Lobengula? Did the Boers want to come into the country? If so, the indunas were to welcome them. If they met with opposition he would send assistance. Why were the Company's people trying to prevent the king's "brothers the Boers" from coming in?

The messengers found Lee in the company of Nicholson (presumably R.G., a leader of the Pioneers) and Captain Tye. Lee, who was trimming his politics to the new realities of power, revealed all the messages to the Company's men, and returned an answer which Tye dictated. Lobengula, who was extending his policy of playing Lippert against Rhodes to include the Boers also, therefore missed the mark with this shot. The Company and Loch, however, had been firing rather wildly too. By what right had Renny-Tailyour and Hassforther been arrested? The high commissioner's proclamation of 30 June would have given him the necessary powers, but it did not take effect till 2 August, some days after the arrests. Renny-Tailyour had therefore been arrested under a warrant from Kgama; but this could have no legal effect at Tati, where the arrest was made.

Hassforther was given the opportunity of signing his submission to the Company. On Dettelbach's orders he refused to do so, but was then allowed to cross into the Transvaal. Renny-Tailyour, like some of his predecessors in custody in Bechuanaland, escaped, reached the Transvaal, and wrote a protest which the Colonial Office, if not Loch, took seriously. Henry Labouchere, the Radical MP and journalist, whose antipathies sometimes betrayed him into curious alliances, took up the Lippert cause in Parliament and in his paper, *Truth*.[53]

However dubious the Renny-Tailyour concession of 22 April may have been (Lobengula in his customary way now denied to Moffat that he had granted it, but the full story of the "blank cheque" was not yet known), Rhodes understood that his talent for amalgamation must now be used. Beit had persuaded his cousin to delay the threatened publication, but had warned Rhodes that he must either negotiate or fight. Accordingly Rhodes told Loch that he had given Rudd the authority to negotiate with Lippert. Loch, who had had an interview with Renny-Tailyour and had decided that he had been "misjudged," now gave permission for Lippert, his agents, and Hassforther to enter Matabeleland on condition of signing the declaration not to disturb the peace. Lobengula, who had been threatening Moffat, was quickly reconciled to him. The Colonial Office thought it a good thing for Rhodes to come to terms with his rivals, but advised that the terms should include an undertaking by Renny-Tailyour and Hassforther not to lay charges against imperial officers for illegal arrest. As there was no sign of their intention to do so, this advice was disregarded, for fear of putting ideas into their heads. Lippert's gunboat diplomacy thus brought results; out of the strong came forth sweetness.

On 12 September 1891, Lippert and Rudd signed a contract, by which the latter agreed to take over the concession on condition that Lippert went to Bulawayo, had it confirmed in really "proper form" by Lobengula, and gave proof that the king had actually accepted the down payment. Rhodes and Lippert "shook hands . . . and said we wished to be again good friends." The agreement was ratified by the Matabele Syndicate, the relation of which to Lippert is not clear. The members of the syndicate considered that they shared in the concession in some way; yet the later, authentic concession was granted to Lippert alone. The ambiguity would have unpleasant consequences in due course.[54]

On 29 September Lippert and his young wife set out from Pretoria for Bulawayo; a lively account of the expedition is preserved in Marie's letters. She was appalled by the procrastinating ways of the Ndebele court, but there was no help for it. The history of all concessions and negotiations had to be gone over again at length. On the other hand Lippert had to conceal from the king all evidence of his collusion with Rhodes. Lobengula's sole reason for giving, or confirming, so dangerous a concession was to thwart the Company, to throw the affairs of the white invaders into a disarray which would slow down their operations and win precious time for him. Moffat knew the truth, but to his intense disgust was under instructions from Loch to join in the game and keep his knowledge to himself.

On 17 November the concession (this time to Lippert, not to Renny-Tailyour) was signed and sealed. The witnesses were not only Renny-Tailyour and Reilly but also Fairbairn (an outsider) and, instead of Mshete, a "servant" whose name is given as James Umkisa. Lippert had managed to omit a provision of the earlier concession about defending the king's rights against the BSA Company. Banking and currency were dropped too. Otherwise the words of the former document were repeated; the grant was to cover "all such territories as now are, or may hereafter be occupied by, or be under the sphere of operations of the British South Africa Company." Tainton and Acutt were the interpreters. Lippert certified that those present at the discussion were: the king, the Regent Mhlaba, the indunas Mlagela, Gampu, Mjana and Luthuli; Moffat, Renny-Tailyour, Lippert, Tainton, Reilly, Acutt, and the servant James Umkisa. Moffat certified "that this document is a full and exact expression of the wishes of the Chief Lo Bengula." He refrained from adding, as he must have been sorely tempted to do, "as at present informed."

The happy party travelled down to Vryburg, and from there to Cape Town by train, without incident. On Christmas Eve Rudd and Lippert signed the agreement envisaged three months before. Rudd acquired the concession, which he made over to the BSA Company on 11 February 1892. Lippert received £5,000 in cash, 30,000 paid up shares in the Chartered Company, 20,000 United Concessions shares,[55] and £1,630 for his recent travelling expenses: not a bad price, though very different from £250,000. These were the terms provisionally agreed on before his journey. A few days before leaving he had written to Beit, explaining the terms and adding that he would be able to keep only a little more than half the shares and money for himself; the rest would go in the discharge of various obligations. In evidence given in 1897 he said of the shares "but naturally I had to cede them [i.e., all of them] to other persons." A quarter went to Renny-Tailyour, who had done the spade-work and was the original grantee of the first concession. The rest went to "the various other persons who had helped me." Prominent among these were J.W. Leonard and Leo Weinthal. In the latter case "the payment was for services rendered in his paper." Weinthal was a friend of Kruger and editor of the pro-government Pretoria *Press*, and the services would have been in connection with the dynamite monopoly, of which Lippert was the most famous holder.

If these statements are true they make a sad story: nothing to show for all those efforts! Nothing, that is, unless the net result was to clear Lippert of debt, or of some of his debts. Yet the statements do not ring quite true. By "ceding" did he not mean, in part, selling? After the provisional agreement with Rudd, Marie had written: "as soon as we get the Chartered shares—so I preach—sell them at once, for we must not identify ourselves with this gang of speculators." There is the further question of Lippert's relations with his associates in the Matabele Syndicate. Renny-Tailyour appears to be accounted for, but he was a paid agent ("from February 1891 I paid all of Tailyour's costs"); on the other hand Lippert gathered in a letter from Acutt "that Renny-Tailyour had not dealt with me in good faith." The syndicate came to the conclusion that Lippert had not dealt with it in good faith either. In 1893 it started legal proceedings against him. In 1897, since Lippert could not leave Germany because of his wife's illness, his evidence was taken down by the Dutch commissioner in Hamburg. Though he must have been on oath, he could take even more liberties with his poor memory than other sworn witnesses were doing at the same time, on the subject of the Jameson Raid, in Westminster. Lippert, moreover, having set himself up comfortably "in our newly-established home" near Hamburg, Hohenbuchen, seems to have been in easy circumstances until the collapse of the mark after World War I. He had not done too badly.

The BSA Company had done better. It had acquired not the land, but the right to confer title to land on Lobengula's behalf. On 5 March 1892 the secretary of state cabled his approval of the Lippert Concession and of its transfer by Rudd to the Company.[56]

NOTES CHAPTER 4

1 *Fortnightly Review*, vol.45 (n.s.), pp.661-76 (1 May 1889); RH Mss Afr. S 73, p.258.
2 T.O. Ranger, "The Rewriting of African History during the Scramble: the Matabele Dominance in Mashonaland," in *African Social Research* (4 December 1967),

p.273; F.C. Selous, *Travel and Adventure in South-East Africa*, ch.14-16; Frank Johnson, *Great Days*, pp.85-9; Dawson Papers (DA 1/1/1), Heany to Dawson, 17 July 1889; CO 879/32/392, no.118, p.133, no.141a, p.173, and nos.51, 66, 70, 74, 75, 102, 110, 117, 137, 142, 147a, 159, 182.

3 One piece of evidence which does not easily fit this interpretation is provided by a letter of Rutherfoord Harris, 25 July 1889, to Thompson (Thompson Papers, Queen's, p.340). According to Harris, Maund "quarreled with Johnstone [*sic*] here and Johnstone cabled to Lord Gifford, who sent Maund a frightful damning cable." No dates are given for these events, so they could have occurred before the rift between Johnson and Gifford. Harris, however, is an unreliable witness.

4 Diary of Thomas Maxwell (MA 1/2), 30 October 1889; Political Papers of J.S. Moffat, Jameson to Harris, 1 November 1889.

5 Selous, *Travel and Adventure*, pp.310-11, 313-25.

6 Johnson Papers (JO 3/1/1), Harris to Johnson, 7 September 1889.

7 The agreement is in the Johnson Papers (JO 3/1/1), and is referred to in the suppressed chapter of Johnson, *Great Days* (see next note).

8 Johnson's account is in the original chapter v of his *Great Days*, the relevant part of which was excised before publication and is in the National Archives in typescript. The book was published in 1940; it was thought inadvisable at that time to reveal anything so discreditable to the British record (information from Mr. V.W. Hiller). For the second version, CO 879/32/392, no.84, pp.110-11. Jameson told Moffat that the rumour had reached Hepburn in a letter from one of the Company officials—who appears to have been Harris (Political Papers of J.S. Moffat, Moffat to Shippard, 4 February 1890).

9 J.G. Lockhart and C.M. Woodhouse, *Rhodes*, p.179; Basil Williams, *Cecil Rhodes*, pp.145-6; W.D. Mackenzie, *John Mackenzie, South African Missionary and Statesman*, pp.440-1. I have not been able to find the contemporary evidence of Selous's meeting with Rhodes.

10 The text is in Appendix E of Johnson, *Great Days*, pp.326-332.

11 Diary of Thomas Maxwell, 8 December 1889.

12 Political Papers of J.S. Moffat, Jameson to Harris, 31 January 1890; CO 879/32/392, no.82, pp.107-8.

13 Diary of Matabele Wilson (WI 6/2/1), 14 February 1890.

14 CO 879/32/392, no.11, pp.27-8; CO 417/39/2387, pp.143-5; Political Papers of J.S. Moffat, under date 14 January 1890.

15 Political Papers of J.S. Moffat, 14 January 1890; CO 879/32/392, no.22 and encl., pp.47-50.

16 CO 417/39/2642, pp.238-40, 2594, pp.292-308 and 2643, pp.316-17. Fairfield's minute on 2594 is really his reaction to 2387 (report of Government House Conference).

17 CO 879/32/392, no.132, p.147.

18 Ibid., no.23, pp.50-3.

19 Ibid., no.26, p.54; CO 417/39/2387, pp. 143-5, for the origins of this decision.

20 Papers of Thomas Maxwell (MA 1/2, i.e., the Diary, in which copies of correspondence were entered), Doyle to Harris, 17 March 1890 (wrongly dated 1889).

21 Political Papers of J.S. Moffat, Jameson to Harris, 30 April 1890 and 5 May 1890; Diary of Thomas Maxwell, 3 May 1890; Ian Colvin, *The Life of Jameson*, vol. 1,

pp.131-2, quoting Seymour Fort, *Dr. Jameson*, pp.94-5. There is another version of the meeting, told by Jameson to Howard Pim in November 1891, and recorded by the latter in 1926. According to this Lobengula had asked angrily, "Who told Selous he could make that road?" The next day Jameson and Doyle committed the sacrilege of entering the goat kraal while the king was sacrificing. Jameson went up to him and said "The King told *me I* might make that road. Did the King lie?" After a silence Lobengula said, "the King never lies" and Jameson replied, "I thank the King," and left. (RH Mss Afr. s 8.)

22 CO 417/36/16769, pp.427-32; 38/692, pp.74-81; 39/2588, pp.241-5; 2589, p.246; 2641, pp.312-15; 4300, p.434; 4302, p.466; 4569, pp.518-24; 2968, pp.525-8; 51/4854, pp.110-21; CO 879/32/392, nos.20, pp.38-46; 21, p.47; 27, p.55; 39, p.67; 42, pp.68-9; 54, pp.78-9; 56, pp.80-2; 57, pp.82-3; 60, pp.84-5; 61, pp.86-8; 62, pp.88-90; 71, pp.94-5; 81, p.104. For the later development of this trek plan see below.

23 879/32/392, no.58, p.83; no.64, p.90; D.W. Kruger, *Paul Kruger*, vol. II, pp.128-30; Williams, *Rhodes*, p.147.

24 Political Papers of J.S. Moffat, 30 April 1890, Jameson to Harris.

25 Johnson, *Great Days*, ch. VII, especially pp.111, 115-121; Adrian Darter, *The Pioneers of Mashonaland*, ch. III-VI; W.H. Brown, *On the South African Frontier*, ch. IV-VI.

26 CO 417/40/7454, pp.5-34; 60/12967, pp.426-32. See below, ch.8.

27 Johnson, *Great Days*, pp.124-6, and ch. VIII; Brown, *South African Frontier*, pp.66-7, 71; Darter, *Pioneers of Mashonaland*, pp.198-213. This last is the best nominal roll of the Pioneers. Darter lists 187 attested men. The National Archives have a document (in PI 2/5) in which Mr. V.W. Hiller, in 1944, made some corrections to this and other copies of the roll; the corrections involve the spelling of surnames, initials, regimental numbers, and the addition of three names to the list of civilians.

28 A.G. Leonard, *How We Made Rhodesia*, p.26; A.S. Hickman, *Men Who Made Rhodesia*, pp.20-24.

29 Johnson, *Great Days*, pp.121-4, 131-2; CO 879/32/392, no.141a, p.173.

30 Leonard, *Rhodesia*, p.28; Darter, *Pioneers of Mashonaland*, p.64.

31 Selous, *Travel and Adventure*, pp.363-8; Johnson, *Great Days*, p.134; Political Papers of J.S. Moffat, Bower to Moffat, 6 June 1890; Brown, *South African Frontier*, pp.73-6; Leonard, *Rhodesia*, pp.37-8. Colvin, *Jameson* (vol. I, p.140), gives a curious speech by Methuen at the inspection, but no reference for it. The Colonial Office was worried, on the score of expense, by Loch's proposal to send Methuen to inspect the column. Permission was given because Fairfield noted that sending any more telegrams would be too expensive: the last two had cost £28.15.0, and Methuen's extra expenses for the inspection would be only £30! (CO 417/41/7249, pp.341-5.)

32 Political Papers of J.S. Moffat, Jameson to Harris, 5 May 1890; Moffat to Shippard, 20 June 1890; Diary of Thomas Maxwell (MA 1/2), Jameson to Maxwell, 11 May 1890; Diary of Matabele Wilson (WI 6/2/1), 21 May 1890; LMS Papers (LO 6/1/5), Elliot to LMS, 12 June 1890.

33 This information came to Maxwell from Reilly, who identified the young men as the "Igapu" regiment. Unless the reference is to the so-called iGapha division, it cannot be identified.

34 LMS Papers (LO 6/1/5), Elliot to LMS, 12 June 1890; Political Papers of J.S. Moffat, Shippard to Loch, 21 June 1890; Diary of Thomas Maxwell (MA 1/2) 24 May 1890; Maxwell to Elliot, 15 July 1890; Maxwell to Jameson, 20 August 1890; 22 October 1890.

35 Political Papers of J.S. Moffat, Rhodes to Doyle, 9 June 1890; Shippard to Loch and Doyle to Harris, 18 June 1890; Doyle to Harris, 7 July 1890; Moffat to Loch, 28 July 1890; Diary of Thomas Maxwell, 9 May 1890.

36 Political Papers of J.S. Moffat, Loch to Moffat, 12 June 1890; Doyle to Harris, 7 July 1890; Loch to Lobengula, 29 July and 4 August 1890; papers relating to interviews, etc., 29 July to 5 August 1890; Diary of Thomas Maxwell, 9 September 1890.

37 Political Papers of J.S. Moffat, Lobengula to Jameson, 13 July 1890; Harris to Bower, 14 July 1890; notebook, 19 August 1890; Diary of Thomas Maxwell, Maxwell to Jameson, 22 July and 28 August 1890.

38 Political Papers of J.S. Moffat, Moffat to Loch, 15 July 1890; Moffat to Shippard, 5 August and 6 August 1890; Moffat to Harris, 19 August 1890; Diary of Thomas Maxwell, Maxwell to Jameson, 20 August 1890.

39 Brown, *South African Frontier*, pp.79-85; Darter, *Pioneers of Mashonaland*, pp.67-70; Selous, *Travel and Adventure*, pp.369-74; Johnson, *Great Days*, pp.136-8.

40 CO 879/32/392, no.307, encl., pp.331-3; Reminiscences of Ellerton Fry (FR 1/4/1); Selous, *Travel and Adventure*, pp.374-7.

41 Following the prevailing usage, I have retained the Dutch spelling for Salisbury's Kopje, while using the Afrikaans *koppie* for the common noun. For the last part of the column's trek, and for the selection of the site of Salisbury, see E.E. Burke, "Fort Victoria to Fort Salisbury, the Latter Part of the Journey of the Pioneer Column in 1890," in *Rhodesiana*, no.28, pp.1-15. Johnson, *Great Days*, pp.140-53, claims to have chosen the site himself. Burke, charitably, rejects the claim only on the ground that Johnson was writing (nearly fifty years) later.

42 Brown, *South African Frontier*, pp.92-112; Selous, *Travel and Adventure*, 377-82; Darter, *Pioneers of Mashonaland*, pp.83-107; CO 417/41/7473, p.70; Colvin, *Jameson*, vol. I, p.144. It will be appropriate, after this point, to use for the white colony the name Rhodesia, which would soon be in common use and would become official. *Zimbabwe* will be retained where the reference is not specifically to the colonial period.

43 Political Papers of J.S. Moffat, S.G. Slade to Moffat, 2 September 1890; Moffat to Harris, 12 November 1890; Moffat to Loch, 24 November 1890; Colenbrander to Harris, 30 December 1890; Lobengula to Loch, 20 August 1891. Diary of Thomas Maxwell (MA 1/2), Lippert to Hassforther, 29 October 1890; Moffat to Harris, 12 November, 20 November 1890; Colenbrander to Harris, 25 November 1890; 28 December 1890; 17 March 1891; Biographical notes by Miss Monckton Jones, at the beginning of her transcription of the diary, s.v. Hassforther. CO 879/33/403, no.83 and encl., pp.94-5; no.105, encl., pp.113-14; no.130, encl., pp.126-8; no.202, encl., p.162; CO 417/59/12976, pp.199-226; Eric Rosenthal, trans., *The Matabele Travel Letters of Marie Lippert, 1891*, p.29.

44 See above, ch.2, last pages.

45 Political Papers of J.S. Moffat, Fairbairn to Doyle, 17 July 1890; papers relating to interviews at Government House, 29 July to 5 August 1890; Moffat to Loch, 4 Sep-

tember 1891; Archives of Rand Mines, Lippert file, under dates May-September, 1891 (evidence given by Lippert in Hamburg in 1897). I owe the references to this file to my colleague Alan Jeeves.

46 CO 879/32/392, no.217, encl., p.237; no.232, p.257; no.322 and encl., pp.345-6, no.333, encl., pp.378-9; CO 879/33/403, no.339, encl., p.284; J.I. Rademeyer, *Die Land Noord van die Limpopo*, pp.138-41.

47 CO 879/33/403, no.226, p.212; no.272a, encl., pp.222-30; no.297, encl., p.245; no.298, encl., pp.247-51, no.389, encl., pp.329-30; CO 879/36/426, no.14, encl., pp.16-22; no.84, encl., pp.120-1; *Cape Times*, 20 May 1891 (cutting in CO 417/58/11593, pp.433-5); Rademeyer, *Limpopo*, pp.138-41. Dr. D.N. Beach in *The Rising in South-Western Mashonaland, 1896-7*, pp.166-72, shows that the real Chivi had no dealings at that time with either Jameson or the Adendorff party. Both negotiated with (different) pseudo-"Chibis" who were, however, pretenders to the title. See also D.N. Beach, *The Adendorff Trek in Shona History* (Henderson paper no. 14), pp.12-19 (and in *South African Historical Journal*, III (1971), pp.42-8).

48 CO 879/33/403, no.217, p.188; no.317, encl., p.265; no.340a, encl., p.285; no.393, encl., p.333; CO Confidential Print, African (South) 414 (not included in microfilm series CO 879), nos.153, 154; Rademeyer, *Limpopo*, pp.136-7.

49 CO 414, nos.38, 65, encl., 153, encl. (see previous note); CO 417/59/12638, p.118; Political Papers of J.S. Moffat, Lippert to Ferreira, 16 June 1891; H. Marshall Hole, *The Making of Rhodesia*, pp.269-75 (based partly on his own contemporary notes); Rademeyer, *Limpopo*, p.151. For Loch's proclamation, see below, ch.8.

50 As appears from Lippert file in Archives of Rand Mines.

51 Political Papers of J.S. Moffat, Loch to Moffat, 4 August 1891; Moffat to Loch, 28 August 1891.

52 CO 414 (see note 46, above), no.11.

53 CO 417/60/14604, pp.404-7; 61/16095, pp.533-58; 62/17455, pp.40, 134, 159. The files include a characteristic official worry: the cost of feeding Renny-Tailyour and Hassforther while under arrest had been £9.16.2 (CO 417/66, p.203).

54 CO 417/59, p.380; 62, p.362; 64, pp.185, 264-7; 64/19603, pp.337-54; 19632, pp.378-84; 65, pp.2ff.; CO 879/36/426, no.22, encl.1, pp.27-9; Archives of Rand Mines, Lippert file, under date 12 September 1891.

55 For the United Concessions Co., the successor of the Central Search Association, see below, ch.8.

56 Political Papers of J.S. Moffat, Loch to Moffat, 12 September 1891; Moffat to Loch, 7 October 1891; Moffat to Rhodes, 9 October 1891; CO 879/36/426, no.9, encl., pp.9-10; no.22, encl.2, pp.29-30; no.51, encl., p.68; no.55, p.69; Archives of Rand Mines, Lippert file, under dates February-September 1891, 11 September 1891, 25 September 1891; Rosenthal, *Lippert*, pp.iii-v, 3.

CHAPTER 5

The Company, the Foreign Office, and Portugal

The thrust of the British South Africa Company into Mashonaland, though only indirectly an act of the imperial government, was a crucial step for Britain in the "scramble" for Africa. On its success depended the possibility of further advances to the north, and of the expansion of the British at the expense of other empires.

It has been said in an earlier chapter, and it is worth repeating, that there was no chance at all in the late nineteenth century of the Central African chiefdoms' retaining their independence. They could not stand (even in combination, of which there was no question) against either the British or the Boers. Whether they could have been overwhelmed by the Portuguese is much more doubtful. The Portuguese, however, were concerned less with effective conquest and exploitation than with nominal sovereignty, which if recognized by other European powers might be turned to good account later, at leisure.

The fate of the indigenous peoples and their countries therefore depended on the will, rather than the ability, of the interested powers to conquer them. In the British case it was Rhodes and his associates who had the will, as we have seen, in abundance. The *trekgees* of the Boers, diffused through a restless population, could be contained only by the most formidable pressures on the trekkers themselves and on the old president. Whichever of these invaders "won the race"—in the event, the British—had then to contend with the third competitor, Portugal. Unlike the Boers, the two finalists were world empires with complex interests and responsibilities. Their conflict over African land could not be decided by skirmishes among the hills of Manica, as the last word lay with the authorities in London and Lisbon, who had to take wider and longer views than the local swashbucklers. Thus it came about that the division of territory between Britain and Portugal, south of the Zambezi and elsewhere, did not exactly reflect the balance of military power on the spot.

When the race for African territory began, the writ of Portugal did not run over all the territory which was afterwards acknowledged by treaty to be hers; still less over the area she *claimed*, as for instance in the *mapa côr de rosa* of 1886. In the seventies Portuguese occupation of the east coast was confined to a few enclaves. Mozambique itself was an island; in 1884 "the Governor-General complained that even from the windows of his palace on the island of Moçambique he looked out over territories which were absolutely beyond Portuguese jurisdiction." The authority of the governor of Ibo (another island) was hardly more extensive. At Quelimane, the port of entry to the Zambezi, there were in 1874 a garrison of eighty-four and a customs revenue of about £800 for the year. Sofala, on the mainland, was abandoned as too exposed. Its fort was in disrepair and the governor and garrison were on the island of Chiloane; in 1875 there was not a single Portuguese resident, mulatto, or literate African in the district.

The other coastal stations were Inhambane, where the Portuguese did control an area some seventy miles by fifteen, and Lourenço Marques, which gave few signs yet of its future importance. It had a population of a few hundred (including ninety-three European Portuguese), all being either officials or traders. Up the Zambezi there were precarious toe-holds at Sena (four inhabitants, one of them a soldier) and Tete, with a garrison of 118. None of the officers there was white, and most of the men, there as in other garrisons, were *degredados*, criminals sentenced to this kind of transportation.

Though the vast estates called *prazos da coroa* had been abolished by decree in 1832, they continued to be held by such ruffians as António Vicente da Cruz ("Bonga"—the wild cat) and Manoel António de Sousa ("Gouveia"). The former massacred or scattered four expeditions sent to arrest him, the governor of Tete being one of the casualties. The best the authorities could do was to set a thief to catch a thief, using Gouveia against the others.[1]

After nearly four centuries of occupation this was not much to show, but before 1880 the decay hardly seemed to matter. Portugal had been left in peace to dream of her past grandeur. The sudden advance of more active nations into tropical Africa shook the Portuguese out of their inactivity, if not out of their dream. In 1885 the Warren expedition made it clear that the prophecy of Dr. Lacerda nearly a century before was being fulfilled: a British advance northwards from the Cape was threatening to insert a patch of red between Angola and Mozambique. At the same time the Germans were appearing to the north, on the coast leased from the Sultan of Zanzibar. In the previous year Portugal had been frustrated on the Congo. Out of this dispute had come the Berlin West African Conference of 1884-5, which made the rules for the "scramble."

The rules, for what they were worth, suited Portugal well. "The whole idea of laying down rules for effective occupation," according to S.E. Crowe, "was . . . not only German but anti-British in origin." Making title to any part of the interior dependent on effective occupation, whatever its effect on others, would have been disastrous for Portugal. The British argued for such a regulation, but were overruled. The requirement, amounting anyway to little more than a pious hope, applied only to the coast: "The signatory powers of the present act recognise the obligation to ensure the establishment of authority in regions occupied by them on the coasts of the African continent, sufficient to protect existing rights, and, as the case may be, freedom of trade and of transit under the conditions agreed upon." Not only were claims to the "hinterland" not subject even to this obligation; protectorates, as distinct from annexations, were not subject to it either, even on the coast. This point was carried by the British representative, Lord Selborne, in spite of opposition in the Foreign and Colonial Offices and in the cabinet itself.

There was another obligation: a power which henceforth took possession of "a tract of land on the coasts of the African continent outside its present possessions," or declared a protectorate there, had to notify the other signatory powers. No need, then, for Portugal to notify anyone; she had claimed the coast from Delagoa Bay to Cape Delgado for centuries. No need of "effective occupation" in the interior; the Berlin Act did not apply there.[2] It could be argued that Portugal had not "established authority" along the whole of the coastline claimed, but the new rules did not apply to old claims.

The occupation of African territory was, however, only slightly influenced by the Berlin Act. Portugal could claim regions in the interior without effectively controlling them, and so could everyone else. Nevertheless, in that jungle possession was nine points of the law; actual occupation was a difficult card to beat. Not quite such a good card was a treaty with an African chief, which was useful to the stronger party but liable when played by the weaker to be treated as a worthless piece of paper. The trump card was a treaty between the imperial powers themselves, defining a boundary and barring either side from occupation or concession-hunting on the wrong side of it.

When the Pioneer Column set out from Fort Tuli to occupy Mashonaland there was no treaty between Britain and Portugal demarcating their respective spheres. The spheres, indeed, as defined by proclamations and decrees on either side, overlapped. Rhodes might send his Pioneers to Fort Salisbury, but when they got there they were, by Portuguese reckoning, in His Most Faithful Majesty's district of Zumbo. The conflict involved more than the future eastern frontier of Southern Rhodesia. Portuguese claims on both sides of the Zambezi were extensive, including a continuous transcontinental belt linking Mozambique with Angola. They were based not on occupation but on historical (or what Salisbury called "archeological") grounds.[3] Harry Johnston, on the other hand, dreamed of a British transcontinental belt "from Cape to Cairo," a dream (without even an archeological basis) which Rhodes appropriated and did his best to realize. The two powers were on a collision course.

The issue was not decided by the actions of Rhodes, Johnston, and their Portuguese counterparts. It was decided, in the context of those actions, by the governments of London and Lisbon, and above all by Lord Salisbury himself. Prime minister and foreign secretary from 1886 to 1892, he was as we have seen determined that, in the partition of Africa, Britain's share should be commensurate with her position in the world. Being also a master of the diplomatic art, he understood the limits which it imposed on the aggrandizement of a great power.

The Portuguese realized, even before 1885, that archeological arguments were not enough. They would have to be strengthened by establishing a presence in areas that were, or might be, disputed. There had been no Portuguese presence in those areas since, at least, the conquests of Soshangane earlier in the century. Soshangane had died in October 1858, and the succession had been disputed by his sons Mawewe and Mzila. Mawewe, who succeeded initially, moved his headquarters from the middle Sabi valley to a place nearer to Delagoa Bay. Then he was driven into exile by his brother, who returned to the old neighbourhood on the Sabi. Mzila's thirty thousand Zulu-trained warriors were the scourge of eastern, as the Ndebele were of western, Mashonaland. They were also the great obstacle to the Portuguese in their attempt to revive old claims to the interior. Mzila was Lobengula's father-in-law. The Sabi was the recognized boundary between them.

To some of the disputed areas Portuguese claims were, if weak against the native inhabitants and chiefs, at least as good as those of any rival European country. Successive governments and ministers, however, instead of using the diplomatic skills and setting themselves the targets appropriate to a weak state, conducted the business in the manner of a great power, thus incurring national humiliation when a stronger power chose to call their bluff. They made the mistake, too, of offending foreign states or their subjects for the sake of small gains, thus weakening Portugal's position later when greater issues were at stake. In 1886-7 a claim to Tunghi Bay, on the southern side of Cape Delgado (at the northern extremity of Mozambique) was successfully asserted; but in the course of the operation some British Indian traders had their possessions destroyed by bombardment. Reference to this matter kept cropping up in later negotiations. In June 1889 a Portuguese decree rescinded the contract with Edward McMurdo to build the railway from Lourenço Marques to the Transvaal frontier. Though some of the reasons for this act were sound, an injustice was committed. McMurdo was an American and most of the capital in his venture was British. When Portugal was in difficulties and looked to the United States for support, the American response was cool and included a reference to the McMurdo contract.[4]

These were minor items in the Anglo-Portuguese dispute. The major areas of conflict were Mashonaland and Malawi.

Malawi became a field of British missionary work as a result of Livingstone's "Expedition to the Zambezi and its Tributaries" in 1858-63. During those years the (Anglican) Universities Mission to Central Africa had gone to the Shiré Highlands and withdrawn again, moving its base to Zanzibar. In 1886 it reached back to Lake Malawi, establishing its mission on Likoma Island. In the meantime the life and death of Livingstone had inspired his Scottish countrymen to continue his work by sending two missions to the same region: the Church of Scotland mission at Blantyre (named after Livingstone's birthplace) in 1876, and that of the Free Church of Scotland, Livingstonia, located at first on Cape Maclear, in 1875. In 1881 the latter moved to Bandawe further up the lake.

The missionaries, having come to a turbulent country with no stable government, felt obliged to assume the functions of government themselves. Some of those at Blantyre were unfit for this responsibility. Injustices were committed, cruel punishments inflicted and executions carried out. The scandal led to reform, but not before the missionary communities had been exposed to the danger of attack by the surrounding tribes. They suffered from a lack not only of government but of trade. To save the missionaries from becoming traders also, a group of Glasgow business men in 1878 formed the Livingstonia Central Africa Company, later called the African Lakes Company, which soon had two steamboats on the Zambezi and one on Lake Malawi. The Free Church mission also had one, the *Ilala*, on the lake.

Clearly, then, the British were ahead of the Portuguese in those regions; but these could only be reached by way of the Zambezi and Shiré, through Portuguese territory. Lord Salisbury persistently claimed that the Zambezi was an international waterway, open freely to the commerce of all nations. On this point international lawyers were divided. Some rejected the claim altogether; others held that it depended on whether or not the whole course of the river was under Portuguese sovereignty. If so, it was a Portuguese river; if not, an international waterway. The weight of opinion was against this view, but the weight of superior armed force supported it. In any case, before 1889, seagoing vessels could not enter the Zambezi. Goods had to be unloaded and carried overland to boats in the river channel, and no one could pretend that this did not mean crossing Portuguese territory. Britain had, therefore, no free access to the "Nyasa settlements," and for a time based her policy on that fact.

As a result of the troubles at the Blantyre mission, a British consul was appointed in that region in 1881. The only force at his disposal was moral (Salisbury called it "bluster"), but his presence on the scene was important. He kept his superiors informed, and merely by being in such a spot acted as a kind of trip-wire in his own person.

The peaceful operations of missionaries and traders were threatened from various quarters, of which two were most relevant to the crisis that followed. The first and the more persistent threat was from the so-called "Makololo" in the Shiré valley. When Livingstone left those parts in 1864 a number of his Kololo porters remained there and set themselves up as chiefs over the local Nyanja population. They could hardly have survived in that region without developing military habits. The Scottish missionaries, the African Lakes Company, and individuals associated with these often had unpleasant encounters with some of them when passing up or down the Shiré. The Portuguese, busy consolidating their position in the immediate neighbourhood, were destined to have similar experiences.

The Ruo at its junction with the Shiré was accepted on all sides as the southern boundary of the Kololo chieftainships. The Portuguese, before the 1880s, had exercised no authority on the Shiré above its junction with the Zambezi. At that point they had a customs house, where the African Lakes Company could collect the rebate on goods in transit, it being understood that these passed out of Portuguese jurisdiction as soon as they went up the Shiré. In 1884, however, in reaction to an attempt to impose taxation and the arrest of Chief Vingwe for protesting against it, his tribe and others went on a rampage which cost some lives and much loss of property, threatened Quelimane itself, and among other things destroyed the customs house on the Shiré. The Portuguese bore this loss complacently. As it had carried the implication of a frontier towards the interior, they never replaced it, though pressed by the British government to do so.

Murders by the Kololo were obvious excuses, to say the least, for Portuguese interference north of the Ruo to restore order. In 1886 the governor-general himself mounted an expedition for this purpose, only to find that the murderers had already been disposed of by a rival chief. Then, for a time, the spotlight moved to the northern end of Lake Malawi.[5]

The African Lakes Company had a station at Karonga, from which the Stevenson Road led to the southern end of Lake Tanganyika. An Arab slave-trading community under the self-styled "Sultan" Mlozi established itself in stockaded villages athwart the Stevenson Road, about twelve miles from Karonga. In July 1887 the Arabs killed two neighbouring chiefs, and began a war which soon involved the Company. For some years the fighting was indecisive. It was notable for the arrival on the scene in May 1888 of an officer on sick leave, Capt. Frederick Lugard, whose African career began at Karonga.[6]

It also had more immediate consequences. The little force of the African Lakes Company was unable to defeat Mlozi without artillery. The Portuguese were reluctant to let this through, on the ostensible ground that it might fall into the hands of rebellious tribes along the Zambezi. This was a genuine danger, but they were aware also of the danger of arming their European rivals. On the other hand, the peril of a little band of defenders of the faith, standing at bay against Arab slave-traders, and deprived by the Portuguese of adequate means of defence, was just the thing to arouse passions in Britain and especially in Scotland. Repeated protests from the British government persuaded the Portuguese cabinet to give way on this question, in spite of counter-demonstrations by its own people.

Problems of this kind would never be solved until a boundary was agreed upon. We have seen that Johnston, sent by Salisbury on a special mission to Lisbon in March 1889, reached an agreement with Barros Gomes by which Portugal abandoned the transcontinental belt, but was given the region east of the Shiré. Whether the Côrtes would have ratified this (the constitution required such ratification of treaties) is doubtful, but the question did not arise as the agreement was rejected by Salisbury. The officials of the Foreign Office would have conceded the Shiré highlands, and even the transcontinental belt. Opposition to the first claim came from Scottish interests associated with the missions; to the second, from empire-builders such as Johnston and Rhodes. Salisbury chose to associate himself with the views of both groups. He refused to hand over the Nyasa settlements to Portugal.

The obvious alternative to doing so, namely taking them under British protection, had not been adopted because they were inaccessible except across Portuguese territory. At this very time, however, D.J. Rankin "discovered" the Chinde mouth of the Zambezi, already known to the Portuguese. This was a channel which could be entered from the sea. On Salisbury's interpretation of the law, Britain now had independent access to Malawi.

The British government's concern for the Nyasa settlements had been intensified by the war between the African Lakes Company and Mlozi and by the disturbances in the Shiré valley. The evidence of British ambitions in those and other disputed areas provoked Portugal to a supreme effort to establish her claims before it was too late. A large party under Antonio Maria Cardoso, including 1,200 armed men, reached the southeastern corner of Lake Malawi at the end of 1888. Although Cardoso did not succeed in all his objects, he obtained the submission, by treaty, of many chiefs. Before this success had been reported, a relief expedition under Serpa Pinto had been sent to support Cardoso. Information about these moves was obtained by the British minister in Lisbon, G.G. Petre, from a spy. This was the information which prompted Salisbury to send Johnston to Lisbon to reach a territorial agreement.[7]

While Johnston was trying to do so, Serpa Pinto arrived on the Zambezi. Although his expedition purported to be "scientific," his 731 armed men seemed to imply more serious business. By the middle of August 1889, when the expedition was stalled on the Shiré because the Kololo chiefs refused to allow it to pass, Johnston—newly appointed consul at Mozambique—arrived at the same point on a "tour of his consular district." At the same moment Buchanan, the British acting consul in the region, took it upon himself to proclaim that the Shiré highlands and the Kololo country, north of the Ruo, were under British protection. He had persuaded a number of chiefs to sign treaties, but the proclamation covered others, also, who had not.

There followed a bizarre competition between Serpa Pinto and Johnston to hoist flags and get crosses made on treaties. As Johnston had made great professions of friendship for the Portuguese, and travelled in the interior with letters of recommendation from Mozambique, his sudden appearance in the role of an enemy naturally aroused furious indignation in Lisbon. Johnston, however, had to rely on the old weapon, "bluster"; Serpa Pinto commanded a respectable little army. The resistance of the Kololo to this army, encouraged by the British on the spot, invited reprisals. By November Serpa Pinto had reached the Ruo. In crossing it he entered not only the territory of the Kololo chiefs, but the sphere of Buchanan's proclamation and of avowed British interest. He had thrown down a gage, and nobody should have been surprised that Salisbury took it up.[8]

This Malawi affair, which might seem remote from the concerns of Mashonaland, had a very direct relation to them. It was the immediate cause of an Anglo-Portuguese confrontation which led by successive steps to the demarcation of the Chartered Company's boundaries. There were, however, subsidiary causes also. Portugal had been trying to stake claims south as well as north of the Zambezi, and this was the area in which Rhodes and his associates were at first most directly interested.

The access of the Portuguese to the territory that was to become Southern Rhodesia was from two directions: from the Zambezi, up its tributaries; and directly from points on the coast such as Inhambane. The difficulty about the latter route was that it ran through the lands of the great king of Gazaland, Mzila; and, after his death in October 1884, of his successor Ngungunyane. Mzila, and also Ngungunyane at first, were far from acknowledging any dependence on Portugal, and acted as absolutely independent sovereigns. Their capital was at Mossurize, not far from Mount Selinda on what became the Portuguese side of the boundary. Though the subjection of Gazaland was a major Portuguese concern, it was at first only of subsidiary interest to Rhodes, whose attention was concentrated on Mashonaland itself, its eastern marches, and a possible extension further eastwards to the coast. As it became apparent that Ngungunyane's influence reached into those areas, Gazaland became the focus of Rhodes's attention also.

Much of the new Portuguese activity south of the Zambezi was both prompted and carried out by Capt. J.C. Paiva de Andrade, a man of energy and determination who combined imperial patriotism with company promotion in much the same fashion as some contemporary Englishmen. His first company was given by the government a vast mining concession in 1878. No mining resulted, but Paiva, in trying to occupy his concession, penetrated new territory. It was thus that he became, in 1881, the first white man to enter Manicaland in sixty years. His next venture, the Anglo-French Ophir Company, was given a mining monopoly of a large area, different from the previous one, by a decree of February 1884. Most of the capital raised was British, but it was not enough to fulfil the condition laid down by the decree. Nevertheless the government, in June 1884, proclaimed a new administrative district for the area involved, Manica, the capital of which was in due course to be Macequece, the ancient Vila de Manica. As the western boundaries were to be the Mazoe and the Sabi, Mashonaland was being preempted with a vengeance.

Paiva's vision, and his travels, extended well into the interior. In 1887 he crossed northeastern Mashonaland. Early in 1889 he was strengthening the Portuguese hold on Manica. He advanced into Makoni's country, where he hoisted the flag, and planned a further advance to the Mazoe and the Hunyani.

By the middle of the year another expedition, under Vitor Cordon, was advancing south from Zumbo on the Zambezi, obtaining professions of allegiance from chiefs as it went; at its farthest point, the junction of the Sanyati and the Umfuli, Cordon built a stockade. In the meantime, in the middle of 1888, Paiva had floated the Mozambique Company, of which more later. During 1889 Paiva, Cordon, and others obtained, in exchange for guns, treaties of submission from chiefs over the greater part of Mashonaland; this activity was continued in 1890, up to the very moment when the Pioneers arrived. On 7 November 1889 the achievements to that date were officially recognized by the proclamation of still another district, Zumbo. Its boundaries south of the Zambezi extended Portuguese territory from the existing limits of the Manica district westward to the Umfuli, along its whole length, and the Sanyati, from the Umfuli junction to the Zambezi. In the light of recent Portuguese activities these boundaries were not unreasonable; indeed, chiefs as far to the southwest as the Lundi were claimed for Portugal.[9] But there were also the activities of Hartley, Baines, and Selous to be considered. The British South Africa Company was now a week old and eager to begin operations in its "sphere." The news of the proclamation of 7 November was followed quickly by the report that Serpa Pinto had crossed the Ruo. The Chartered Company, by acquiring shares as a first step towards the absorption of the African Lakes Company, was now directly interested in the Ruo as well as the Umfuli. The Portuguese "encroachments" thus provoked an agitation in Britain in which "philanthropy plus five per cent" (or "Gold and the Gospel") were jointly involved.

Salisbury submitted willingly to their pressure. Buchanan's proclamation and treaties and Johnston's treaties had come to be regarded by the Foreign Office as having established a British interest which could not be abandoned. South of the Zambezi, the Moffat treaty and the Rudd Concession were held to have established a British claim (as against other European powers) to Lobengula's "dominions," uncertain though their extent might be. The news of Portuguese advances, reaching Salisbury in exaggerated form from the various consuls and from Rhodes, provoked him in December to demand an assurance from Portugal that she would not interfere with the Nyasa settlements, the Kololo chiefs, Lobengula's territory, or any other territory declared to be under British protection.

During the last weeks of 1889 and the first of 1890 the confrontation approached rapidly. Arrangements were made for the withdrawal of the British minister from Lisbon. Naval units were concentrated at Gibraltar and in neighbouring waters. The press reported rumours of a projected seizure of Lourenço Marques and other places. Though Barros Gomes gave the assurance that Serpa Pinto's expedition had returned to the coast, this was contradicted by news from the consul at Mozambique. Salisbury therefore required Petre to demand that the Portuguese government order the withdrawal of its forces from the Shiré, the Kololo country and Mashonaland; a copy of the telegraphic order to be shown to Petre. If this demand were not acceded to by 10 p.m. on 11 January, diplomatic relations would be broken off.

The Portuguese government could only comply. Its appeal to the chancelleries of Europe had brought no response; "all, more or less, had washed their hands like Pilate." The outburst of popular fury which followed the news of the ultimatum was not a passing tantrum; the memory of the event has rankled in Portugal to the present day.[10] The ultimatum, however, was only an insult; the injury was to follow when the boundaries were settled. Salisbury was in no hurry to settle them, partly because he wished first to reach an agreement with Germany on African questions. This was done in the so-called Heligoland treaty, signed on 1 July 1890.[11]

Thus negotiations for an Anglo-Portuguese treaty began only on 6 July, the very day on which the Pioneer Column began its march from Fort Tuli. They were completed, and the treaty signed, on 20 August. The Pioneer Column had moved on from Fort Victoria the previous day; a fortnight later, the Manica party separated from the main column for its visit to Mutasa. It knew nothing of the treaty. Its instructions had been issued before the negotiations had begun, but at a time when they were in prospect.[12] Rhodes wanted to stake out all possible claims before a treaty could restrain him.

Mutasa's country, however, was a very different matter from Lobengula's. In the diplomatic exchanges of the preceding years the bone of contention, south of the Zambezi, had been Mashonaland; the key question was whether or not it was subject to Lobengula. That king had no doubt of the answer. When Cordon was reported to be at the Umfuli-Sanyati junction, Lobengula wrote to ask him "by what authority you are doing this in country that belongs to me. I am your friend, Lo Bengula." In northeastern Mashonaland there was room for argument about the extent of Lobengula's sway. What was not open to argument was the fact that Lobengula accepted the Sabi as his eastern limit, though his impis very seldom ranged as far as that. The Sabi divided his empire from that of Ngungunyane. Mutasa was a vassal of Ngungunyane, and his country, which Colquhoun and Selous were instructed to acquire, lay to the east of the Sabi. It was included by the Portuguese in their district of Manica. The Company's sphere, according to the charter, lay "west of the Portuguese Dominions"; if that phrase begged the question, it still cast its shadow over some of Colquhoun's operations.

These facts were clear to the Foreign Office, if their gravity did not weigh much with Rhodes. On the other hand the British negotiators were well aware of what was happening in Africa while they were talking; the Pioneers were advancing and Portuguese officials arrested the river steamer *James Stevenson* on the Shiré. The Chartered Company opposed the very idea of negotiating. The British terms, therefore, became stiffer as the talks went on. The Portuguese minister in London, Barjona de Freitas, raised many objections, but he signed the treaty because he realized that the terms were more favourable than Portugal could expect if there were further delay.

The territorial provisions can be visualized by comparing them with those which ultimately prevailed. In the north, Angola was to extend to the upper course of the Zambezi, thus embracing half of Barotseland. On the other hand most of the bulge between the Shiré and Zumbo was denied to Portugal: the line ran from the Shiré-Ruo junction to a point on the Zambezi half-way between Tete and the Cabora Bassa rapids. Zumbo itself, with a zone ten miles in radius round it, was conceded, and westwards from Zumbo Portugal was given the right to construct lines of communication in a twenty-mile belt along the north bank of the Zambezi to link Mozambique with Angola. South of the Zambezi the Portuguese sphere included what was later retained, but also, approximately, the later districts of Melsetter, Umtali, the southern half of Makoni, and part of Inyanga. Thus the Sabi, over much of its course, was recognized as the boundary. The treaty included many articles dealing with trade and navigation, and one peculiarly offensive to the Portuguese: they could not dispose of any of their territory south of the Zambezi without the consent of Great Britain. They undertook to build a railway from the mouth of the Pungwe to the British boundary.[13]

Rhodes was appalled: "cannot too strongly urge upon you," he cabled to the directors, "you must abandon the agreement." He had read the terms "with great surprise, and with the utmost disappointment." His instructions to his minions had been: "Cable at once Home Board they must at once inform Foreign Office that having now seen Treaty I strongly object to it and hope they will take this opportunity to drop whole matter." In the Colonial Office Graham commented that "Mr. Rhodes should be Prime Minister and Foreign Secretary of Great Britain as well as Premier of S. Africa! [sic]." The duke of Abercorn, who often looked down from his pedestal with ingenuous but pained surprise at the doings of his inferiors, wondered how Rhodes expected the Company to dictate foreign policy to the prime minister. Nevertheless he spoke to Salisbury in defence of Rhodes's objections and suggested that if the Portuguese raised any difficulties the best course might be "to let the matter drop." Albert Grey, the company's conscience, thought that the simplest way to get rid of the Portuguese altogether would be to ratify the agreement. Another Transvaal would then grow up east of the boundary, and the new Uitlanders would drive the Portuguese into the sea. As this would involve a grave loss of national honour to Britain, the best course for all concerned would be to abandon the treaty. Cawston seems to have been an odd man out among the directors. He thought the terms the best that could be got without going to war, but suggested an interesting addition: a right of access to the coast similar to the line of communication along the Zambezi that was offered to Portugal.

War with Portugal, which Sir Philip Currie at the Foreign Office, like Cawston, thought inadmissible, did not worry Rhodes. Salisbury however, who submitted to vulgar pressure only when it suited him, was not to be dictated to. The treaty was signed on 20 August without regard to the protests; but it still required ratification by the Portuguese Côrtes. It was not ratified. The Portuguese public was even more upset than Rhodes and his fellow directors. The Côrtes met; the government was forced to resign; though Salisbury agreed to some minor modifications, the session ended on 15 October with the treaty still unratified. Salisbury having warned that Great Britain would not be bound by the treaty if the Côrtes failed to approve it in that session, it lapsed.[14]

Rhodes's delight with this outcome would have been enough, if there had not been even more serious indications, to warn both governments of the danger of a free-for-all in the disputed regions. It was in the highest interests of both Britain and Portugal that further negotiations be conducted in an atmosphere of détente. Their solution was a *modus vivendi*, a standstill agreement, signed on 14 November, effective immediately and to last for six months. By this, the boundaries of the lapsed treaty were to be observed in practice, though without prejudice to the claims of either side for their future modification. Portugal conceded free navigation of the Zambezi, the Shiré, and the Pungwe, and passage on the land routes where the rivers were not navigable, and between the Pungwe and the British sphere. The BSA Company had asked for another provision: freedom of either side to acquire concessions in the territory of the other. This was neither permitted nor forbidden by the agreement, which forbade only the making of "treaties," the exercise of a protectorate, and "acts of sovereignty" beyond the provisional boundary.

As the British government did not consider the treaty of 20 August to have lapsed until the prorogation of the Côrtes, there was a month—15 October to 14 November—during which there was no legal obstacle to filibustering. Though he hardly needed the advice, Rhodes seized upon some expressions of Salisbury's—*beati possidentes* and "take all you can get and ask me afterwards"—and gave instructions in that spirit. Unfortunately for his schemes, his agents did most of their "taking" either before or after the open season.[15]

The operation began when Colquhoun, Selous, Jameson, and others left the Pioneer Column at Fort Charter. Jameson, having fallen from his horse and broken some ribs, had to be carried back in a litter to Fort Charter and on to Fort Salisbury. The others went on their way, not knowing that a treaty, signed a few days before, had set a limit to their operations at the Sabi; nor that the treaty had not yet been ratified; nor that the British government regarded it as being nevertheless provisionally in force. On 13 September Colquhoun and his companions arrived at Mutasa's kraal, perched on a high granite koppie some twenty-five miles north of Umtali.

At the interview the next day, Colquhoun's first task was to find out whether Mutasa was bound by treaty to the Portuguese. He hotly denied having signed any treaty with them, while admitting that he had given them some rights to dig for gold. If he lied, they could "cut off his right hand." The way was therefore thought to be open for a treaty with the Company. This was duly signed and witnessed on 14 September. It gave the Company exclusive rights in Mutasa's territory, not only of prospecting and mining, of every kind of industry and trade and banking, but also to construct and operate public works, "including railways, tramways, docks, harbours, roads, bridges, piers, wharves, canals, reservoirs, waterworks, embankments, viaducts, irrigation, reclamation, improvements, sewage, drainage, sanitary, water, gas, electric, or any other mode of light, telephonic, telegraphic, power supply, and all other works and conveniences of general or public utility." (One wonders at the interpreter's skill in translating this into the Manyika language.) Further, Mutasa undertook "not to enter into any treaty or alliance with any other person, Company, or State, or to grant any concessions of land without the consent of the Company in writing, it being understood that this Covenant shall be considered in the light of a treaty or alliance between the said nation and the Government of Her Britannic Majesty Queen Victoria." The concessions to the Company applied not only throughout Mutasa'a present territory, but also to any future extensions thereof; and considerable extensions would be necessary before the Company could make use of its right to build docks, harbours and piers. In return for all this the Company would pay Mutasa £100 per annum (or the equivalent in trading goods, among which rifles, powder, and caps were specified), appoint a British resident "with a suitable retinue and a suite of British subjects," and maintain Mutasa in his chieftainship and defend him against attack.[16]

Mutasa accepted the treaty either because he valued this last provision (the enemy in view was the terrible prazo-holder and *capitão mor*, Manoel António da Sousa, or Gouveia), or else because on 14 September Colquhoun's party was the most powerful force immediately in sight.[17] As soon as that party moved away to a camp on the Umtali river, Mutasa had second thoughts. He sent messengers to the Baron de Rezende, representative of the Mozambique Company at Macequece, complaining that he had been forced to sign the treaty.

Colquhoun sent Selous and two companions to the same place. They were of course received very coldly by Rezende, who complained of the invasion of Portuguese territory by armed force, pointed out that Mutasa, as a vassal of Ngungunyane, was not entitled to sign treaties, and sent a deputation back to Colquhoun with a written protest to the same effect. Colquhoun rejected Rezende's claims and arguments, and departed for Fort Salisbury, leaving a single policeman to represent the Company at Mutasa's.

It was soon reported that an armed force, under the formidable leadership of Paiva de Andrade and Gouveia, was on the way to that chief's kraal. Mutasa, never able to choose between the Devil and the deep sea, appealed to Colquhoun, who sent several small detachments under Capt. P.W. Forbes and

Lieut. Eustace Fiennes, to oppose the Portuguese. On 3 November Forbes sent Lieut. M.D. Graham to Macequece with a threatening message: get out of the Company's territory or be forced out. Paiva, sure of the justice of the Portuguese claim and of his vast military superiority over Forbes's puny detachment, told Graham that the letter was too absurd to answer. " 'As to force, if I chose with one sweep of my hand I could wipe you all out of Mashonaland.' Poor old boy he little foresaw the future." Mutasa's hereditary enemy, Makoni, asked Gouveia to lend him some troops, with whose help he would soon dispose of Mutasa. This offer was not accepted, but on 8 November Gouveia with 200 armed followers established himself in Mutasa's kraal. Graham delivered a message to him too, "and all the answer I got was that no 'Inglese' would turn him out." He was soon joined by Paiva, Rezende, the French engineer de Llamby, and another hundred armed men. With the belated arrival of Fiennes, Hoste, Tyndale-Biscoe, and a small detachment, the Company's strength had risen to about fifty.

On 15 November Paiva held an indaba at the kraal, to which the prospectors in the neighbourhood had been summoned. The Portuguese flag was hoisted. No sooner was the ceremony over than a sudden commotion marked the execution of Forbes's plan. All the Portuguese officers were arrested, while their scattered followers were fleeing or being disarmed. Paiva and Gouveia were taken under escort to Fort Salisbury and thence, on parole, to Cape Town. It was noted in the Colonial Office that the Company had no power to make such arrests, even in Lobengula's territory, not to mention Manica.[18]

At Semelale, a few miles west of Fort Tuli, the party met Jameson on his way up. A.G. Leonard of the police, who was there too, made the prisoners the subject of one of his little character-sketches.

> D'Andrade is a colonel in the Portuguese service, and a very nice fellow, Mundell tells me; and he certainly struck me as such when introduced to him later on. He is very swarthy and slight, and, in appearance, not unlike a dark-skinned dancing master. He is naturally very indignant with the fact of his having been made a prisoner in what he considers is Portuguese territory, by mere filibusters, acting on the orders of an able adventurer without receiving the countenance of the British government. Working himself up into a pitch of intense excitement, he informed me, in good English, that he knew Mr. Gladstone, and that he has great influence at the European courts, which he intends exerting to his utmost . . . What a horrid nuisance excitability of temperament must be, either individually or nationally; and here was a man who, on the mere memory of what had happened, and in anticipation of the rumpus he is contemplating, converts himself into an insensate fury on a hot day, and at the risk of bursting a blood-vessel . . .
>
> Gouveia, who is a general and a marquis in the Portuguese service, was dressed in a striped sleeping-suit of various colours, and appeared to be rather a retiring, mild-mannered, old half-caste gentleman . . . This man is a notorious slave-dealer

and villain, and virtually ruler of the whole of Manica, but you would not think so by his looks, which evidently belie him.[19]

The dancing master and the mild old gentleman went on to Cape Town, where they were honourably treated; on the last day of the year Paiva sailed in the mailship, changing at Madeira for Lisbon. At each point, interviewed by the press, he repeated the excited denunciation reported by Leonard. Meanwhile Forbes, leaving a garrison of six men at Mutasa's, rode over with the rest of his force to Macequece, where he released Rezende and de Llamby, and then hurried on for the purpose of taking the rest of the country down to the coast. He obtained, from several chiefs in the vital strip between the Pungwe and the Buzi, mining concessions which included the right the build a railway. He intended also to destroy Gouveia's headquarters while the going was good, but before he could do that, or complete his concession-hunting to the coast, he was recalled by Colquhoun on the reluctant instructions of Rhodes. The high commissioner had given orders for the observance of the *modus vivendi*.[20]

Rhodes, in truth, desired desperately to possess his "road to the sea." Economically, though not politically, Mashonaland needed this even more than Burgers and Kruger had done. It cost £45 a ton to bring goods overland from Cape Town to Salisbury; Frank Johnson was prepared to do it, via Beira, for £11. Hence the instruction to Colquhoun to go to Mutasa's; Jameson's letter sent after him, urging territorial acquisitions "to the coast if possible"; the treaty of 14 September and the outrage of 15 November; Forbes's new concessions and his attempt to reach the sea; and more attempts to follow.[21]

Colquhoun's treaty with Mutasa had been obtained when the ratification of the Anglo-Portuguese treaty was still pending; on the British government's own assumptions it was therefore null and void. Against this clear principle the Company's counter-arguments could not prevail: that Colquhoun was unaware of the treaty, or that Mutasa had never made any agreement with Portugal. On the other hand Salisbury was impressed by the fact that the Company, and various prospectors who were willing to submit to it, were established in Mutasa's country, and that the Portuguese were not. In the following months, when the Company was repeatedly ordered to observe the *modus vivendi*, its occupation of the country down to what ultimately became the border was tacitly and sometimes openly permitted.

The rights and wrongs of Forbes's coup are a little harder to judge. He carried it out on the day after the signing of the *modus vivendi*; his ignorance of this did not make the coup any more legitimate. But Forbes was only reacting to Gouveia's arrival at Mutasa's with an armed force, which had occurred on 8 November. The validity of Forbes's action therefore depended partly on the validity of the treaty of 14 September. While that treaty ought to have been of no effect, Salisbury's ambivalence towards it precluded him from treating the coup as a clear breach of the *modus vivendi*. Then the Company put some more weights in the scale: Portuguese flags had been hoisted by Makoni, Mangwende, Nemakonde, and I'sanga (a chief living west of Fort Charter), which could be taken as evidence that the *modus vivendi* was being disregarded by the Portuguese themselves. In the end, as will be seen, these juridical subtleties were of little account. Salisbury allowed the fact of possession to weigh heavily where he thought it appropriate, as at Mutasa's and in Malawi, but not elsewhere, as at Macequece, which the Company continued to occupy after Forbes's raid. But this is to anticipate.[22]

It emerged from the Manica incidents that the absence of a prior Portuguese treaty with Mutasa was not a sufficient proof of his independence. Portugal's claim was based on the vassalage of Mutasa to Ngungunyane. The question to be settled was whether that king was subject to Portugal. If he was not, the field was open; if he was, his dependence included that of Mutasa. All independent observers agreed that Mutasa was a vassal of Ngungunyane and paid tribute to him. The BSA Company denied this, but the extreme importance it attached to bringing Ngungunyane under its sway revealed its doubts.

The question of Ngungunyane's independence is difficult to decide. At almost all points the evidence from British and that from Portuguese sources conflict. One reason for the conflict is that the king trimmed his policy to the exigencies of the moment. Another was the usual one that Africans and Europeans placed different interpretations on the same document. Yet it is possible on the conflicting evidence to say that, in his own estimation, Ngungunyane in 1890 was an independent sovereign; that to the Portuguese he was a subject or client of doubtful loyalty; and that his effective status could only be decided by superior force.

From time to time Portuguese deputations visited him, as they had visited his father, at Mossurize. An important one was sent by the governor-general in June 1885, ostensibly to congratulate Ngungunyane on his accession. It succeeded in raising the Portuguese flag at his kraal. He was unwilling to sign the treaty presented to him, but he sent two envoys to Lisbon, where in October they did homage on his behalf to His Most Faithful Majesty. They also took back a treaty, which Ngungunyane after much hesitation accepted on 20 May 1886. He became a Portuguese colonel, with uniform, received a thousand *milreis* (in the money of the time, about $1,000 or £200) a year; flew the Portuguese flag and received a resident; undertook to refrain from aggression against Portuguese territory, and to deliver to Portuguese justice wrongdoers who were not his own subjects (whereas his subjects committing offences in Portuguese territory would be tried there), to give free transit across his territory to Portuguese subjects, to protect schools and missions, and to permit mining by Paiva's company. His boundaries were defined, and he was not to consent to the dominion of any nation other than the Portuguese over his territory.

This treaty was at least as authentic as those obtained from Lobengula by Moffat and Rudd, not to mention Grobler. The advantages to the European power were greater than in those, and the price cheaper than that of the Rudd Concession. There were, however, resemblances in the sequel. Ngungunyane had second thoughts. He did not formally denounce the treaty to the Portuguese, but on three occasions he denied its existence to the British vice-consul in Lourenço Marques, and he refused to observe some of its terms. He would allow no mining in Manica, and he waged war beyond the defined boundaries, to reassert his authority over subjects whom the treaty had removed from it. But times were changing. In September 1886 his army, invading the Inhambane district, was defeated and expelled by the Portuguese. At the end of the previous year a Portuguese punitive expedition had subjected Rupire and Massaua, districts which extended across the later Rhodesian border into Mtoko, which were then claimed by Ngungunyane, but which the treaty consequently denied to him. He was offended by these actions, but also chastened; he reaffirmed his loyalty to Portugal.

According to the treaty, his northern boundary ran along the Pungwe; the boundary he claimed was the Zambezi. The change in the fortunes of war began to convince him that this was no longer attainable. He now permitted mining in Manica, where early in 1887 some thirty prospectors were at work; two years later he agreed to the establishment of a Portuguese residency in Mashonaland. (This one does not appear to have been established.) He could not, however, tolerate insubordination in his vassal Mutasa. In May 1888 Mutasa invited the Portuguese to appoint a resident at his kraal. This was not done, but Ngungunyane assembled an impi—which apparently did not carry out its mission—to bring Mutasa to heel.[23]

In the winter of 1889 Ngungunyane, partly because he saw that his pretensions in the north were doomed to disappointment, but mainly because of the need to deal with Portugal's Chopi allies,[24] moved his capital. In a vast movement, beside which the treks of Boers or of Ndebele were small affairs, king and tribe moved to a spot about eighty miles north of the Limpopo mouth, brushing aside the previous inhabitants.

This event provided some evidence of Ngungunyane's independence. According to an account of it in a Lisbon paper, *O Tempo*, on 11 June 1890, the king on this trek had passed through "the most populous region of the Crown Lands" with 50,000 men, together with women and children, and had "pilfered and destroyed everything." He had attacked and defeated several chiefs, including Bingoana, "the most powerful chieftain in the Crown Lands," whose Portuguese flag he had captured. In the face of these events the Portuguese governor had remained inactive. This was not a new situation. When an American missionary party had departed for Ngungunyane's in 1888, the governor of Sofala had "informed us that he would in no way be responsible for our lives."

In February 1887 Ngungunyane sent a friendly embassy to the governor of Natal, and in the winter of 1890 another to the British vice-consul in Lourenço Marques, both of which flatly denied that their king was in any way subject to Portugal: "his country belongs solely to himself." He had never promised any white men to give them his lands. The Portuguese had always paid him a yearly tribute to be allowed to occupy part of his country on the seaboard—an interesting view of the thousand *milreis* of the 1886 treaty. On 11 July 1890 his messengers proclaimed his independence publicly in Lourenço Marques. He had also admitted to the vice-consul and others that he knew that white men were spreading their rule over the whole of Africa, and asserted that when his turn came he would prefer to be ruled by the British.[25]

Whether this assertion was sincere or not, it had a double value to the BSA Company. If Ngungunyane was independent of the Portuguese, so was Mutasa; and if Ngungunyane was prepared to accept British protection, the way was open for the Company to exploit the whole of Gazaland, including the coast.

Rhodes had not waited for the latest revelations of Ngungunyane's independence to take advantage of it. He had sent a Colonial doctor, Aurel Schulz, to Gazaland at the same time as Johnson was leading the Pioneers to Mount Hampden. Schulz claimed to have got from Ngungunyane, on 4 October, a concession not unlike Rudd's, except that it was given orally and not in writing: exclusive mineral and commercial rights in the kingdom, in return for a thousand rifles, 20,000 rounds of ammunition, and £500 a year.

The delivery of the rifles would be still more difficult than in the former case. The only possible route was up the Limpopo, whose estuary was controlled not by Sir Sidney Shippard but by the Portuguese. The problem was tackled by the company's cloak-and-dagger man, Rutherfoord Harris, who chartered a small steamer, the *Countess of Carnarvon*, under the command of an old salt, Captain Buckingham. Captain Pawley was responsible for the cargo and its delivery. The ship went up the Limpopo and the arms were unloaded. A Portuguese official then appeared and demanded *the payment of customs duty*. When Pawley had given a personal bond for £2,000 the official allowed the goods to be taken to Ngungunyane.

Pawley's encounter with the official took place on 21 February 1891, by which time the *Countess of Carnarvon* was slipping down the river again and back to Durban for repairs, fuel, and provisions. On 2 March three ragged and emaciated white men with their carriers arrived at Ngungunyane's after a grim overland journey of nearly seven weeks from Fort Salisbury: they were Jameson, Denis Doyle, and G.B.D. Moodie. The timing was fortunate and not entirely accidental. In the presence of many Portuguese as well as of Jameson's and Pawley's parties, Ngungunyane affirmed his loyalty to Portugal. But Jameson swung him round by assuring him, in writing, that the rifles were a present to him from Queen Victoria. Ngungunyane put his mark to a treaty confirming the concession of 4 October and placing himself under British protection.

The *Countess of Carnarvon* had returned to her berth on the river, but when Jameson reached the ship he found a Portuguese gunboat moored alongside her. Before he was arrested he managed to dispatch his treaty overland to Lourenço Marques, where he recovered it later. The Portuguese seized the *Countess of Carnarvon*, took it to Lourenço Marques, and professed to retain it as a guarantee that the £2,000 duty would be paid.

Though his biographer calls this treaty with Ngungunyane the most notable of all his achievements, Jameson had overreached himself. The Company put great emphasis on the concession supposedly obtained by Dr. Schulz. Its subsequent assertion that the treaty with Jameson was the only one to which Ngungunyane had ever put his mark was a sufficient proof that no written document had been obtained by Schulz. Jameson's assurance that the rifles were a gift from the queen increases the doubt, as there is no record of Ngungunyane's having asked where, then, were the rifles promised by the Company? It is hard to understand how Rhodes could have expected a concession of which there was no written evidence to be taken seriously. If the date—4 October—was fictitious, it was ill chosen. At that date the Anglo-Portuguese treaty was not considered to have lapsed. When Jameson got his written document, the *modus vivendi* was in force. The Foreign Office therefore considered both to be worthless on the ground of the dates alone, without the need to examine any of the other evidence. The case was not helped by the revelation of the agents in the business that "the Company told them to avoid 'any *public* breach' of the *modus vivendi*, which by implication authorized a 'secret breach'." The Company was also reprimanded for making free with the queen's name and for offering a protectorate, which only the Crown could do at any time, but which was forbidden at this time by the *modus vivendi*.

There was equal clumsiness on the Portuguese side. The official who found the arms unloaded on the Limpopo bank and accepted a bond for £2,000 thought he had served his country well by getting the importers to recognize Portuguese sovereignty by paying duty. His superiors thought otherwise. Pawley gave the bond, though under protest. Once the duty, or a bond for it, was paid and accepted, how could Portugal afterwards object to the landing of the goods? When the *Countess of Carnarvon* entered the Limpopo the second time, followed by a Portuguese gunboat, and was seized, she was in ballast and had no cargo to unload. The governor of Lourenço Marques made the lame excuse that the ship was being held as a guarantee of the payment of the bond, yet at the same time asserted (wrongly it appears) that his officers had taken possession of the arms and ammunition, in which case customs duty would not be relevant. He was right in saying that the officer on the Limpopo had exceeded his powers, but that was Portugal's problem, not Britain's.[26]

Rhodes repeatedly stigmatized Portuguese claims—almost all of them—as "absurd" and "ridiculous." One of his methods of impressing this point on the imperial authorities was to call racial prejudice to his aid. The captured Gouveia, passing through Kimberley, was found to be "a common black man." "Mr. Rhodes feels sure," Rutherfoord Harris wrote to Bower, the imperial secretary in Cape Town, "His Excellency will recognize the absurdity of an occupation headed by a Native dressed in European clothes." We learn from the same source that J.J. Almeida, who was a pure Portuguese and the most effective defender of his country's interests in Gazaland, was another "black man."

None of this chicanery helped the Company's cause, but it illustrates the length to which Rhodes would go to secure his road to the sea. It will be remembered that after the Manica incident in the middle of November 1890, Forbes had taken a step in that direction by securing treaties from certain chiefs between the Buzi and the Pungwe rivers. Consistently with this achievement, the Company informed the Colonial Office in January that Ngungunyane was collecting tribute as far north as the Buzi, but not beyond. Most of the country between the Buzi and the Pungwe was known as Quiteve. Yet a few weeks after the previous communication a telegram from Kimberley reported, on the evidence of Forbes, that "in the Kiteve district . . . Portugal is powerless to confer rights of way, Gungunhana has full power." In the event, Salisbury would not recognize either Jameson's treaty or Forbes's.[27]

What mattered most to the Company was to secure Manica and a route from it to the coast. The importance of this had been realized from the beginning of Rhodes's plans for the march of the Pioneers, which is why Johnson included a collapsible boat in his impedimenta. As soon as he had fulfilled his contract he prepared to make a journey to the sea. His syndicate in Cape Town was instructed to charter a small steamer, the *Lady Wood*, which was to cruise up and down the coast until it located him. There was not much doubt about the point he would make for: the mouth of the Pungwe. The advantages of this estuary were discovered early in 1885—nearly four centuries after the arrival of the Portuguese on the coast—by Paiva de Andrade and H.C. Lima, the governor of Manica. There the somewhat amphibious port of Beira arose as the gateway to Paiva's field of enterprise.

Hearing of Johnson's plan, Jameson insisted on accompanying him. "His best friend," Johnson wrote of Jameson, "could not pretend that Providence had intended him for life on the open veld." His limited experience on the Missionaries' Road and in the highly organized and provisioned Pioneer Column was an inadequate training for the journeys that followed. In addition, he suffered from haemorrhoids and, at this time, from broken ribs still in plaster. Nevertheless he joined Johnson, the Zulu interpreter Jack, and a young Colonial farmer and left Fort Salisbury on 5 October. As the wagon could not be got across the eastern mountains, the boat and stores were taken on by porters. All went reasonably well until the party reached the village of Sarmento on the Pungwe. There Jameson sat in a hut in the evening, writing his diary by the light of a candle. Johnson happened to knock the candle over, with the result that not only the hut but the entire village, with almost all the party's stores, clothing, and possessions, went up in flames. The boat remained. The four men managed, under fearful hardships, to get it to the mouth of the Pungwe, there to be blown out to sea at night and to find themselves, in the dark, up against the hull of the *Lady Wood*. The captain had intended to give up the search that day, but had by chance had to lie at anchor for one more night.[28]

In no time Jameson was back in Cape Town, up to Kimberley, and on his way back to Mashonaland. He had passed by Mutasa's before Forbes's coup, but at Semelale, as has been mentioned, he met the escorted prisoners. Reaching Fort Salisbury on Christmas day, he waited only three days before setting out on his next expedition, which took him to Ngungunyane's kraal and the *Countess of Carnarvon*.

Johnson and Jameson's journey to Beira was the BSA Company's introduction to its coveted route to the sea. It was followed by the Manica incident, Forbes's treaty-making down that same route, and the various efforts to bring Gazaland into the Company's sphere. The *modus vivendi* and the cold reception of these adventures by the Foreign Office gave little hope that the Company would soon be building harbours, jetties, and piers. But Rhodes had not yet exhausted his resources or ingenuity. There were still two loopholes available. The *modus vivendi* guaranteed free navigation of the Pungwe and use of the land route from the head of navigation to Mashonaland; and the *modus vivendi* would expire on 14 May 1891, after which, presumably, might would be right.

The need to use the Beira route to Mashonaland, whether or not the Company owned and controlled it, was desperate. The summer of 1890-1 was unusually wet. The flooded rivers were impassable; supplies could not reach Mashonaland by the Selous Road. The obvious solution was to get them in from Beira. It was not quite so obvious that this should be done by 240 armed men, which was what Rhodes planned to do. News of this scheme leaked out in time for Loch, on orders from London, to hold back most of the armed force. He tried also, through the vice-consul at Lourenço Marques, to stop the rest of the party until arrangements could be made with the Portuguese; this message could not be delivered. So the party which was taken to Beira by the Union Company's ship *Norseman* consisted of only five Europeans and ninety-one unarmed African labourers, for the purpose of surveying and making a road to the interior. The formality of asking the Portuguese authorities for permission to do this was omitted. Most of the arrangements were handled by the syndicate of Johnson, Heany, and Borrow. It was Johnson who issued written instructions to the captain of the paddle-steamer *Agnes* and who provided also the steam launch *Shark* and a string of lighters. Cargo from the *Norseman* was to be loaded into the lighters and towed up the Pungwe by the *Agnes*, and from the head of navigation taken overland by a road which was still to be made. Included in the luggage was a stage-coach to ply on the future road.

All this was straightforward business enterprise, provided for by the *modus vivendi* itself—except for the road-building without Portuguese permission. Another element in the plan was of a different order. The man chosen to command the operation was Sir John Willoughby, late staff officer of the Company's police and destined for some strange adventures afterwards: the kind of man most unlikely to obey the orders of the Portuguese. A.G. Leonard, one of his police officers, described him as "that fidget on wheels . . . a mixture of nonchalance, presumption and speculation." To objections that the Portuguese might shoot him, Rhodes is said to have replied with the light-hearted assurance that "they will only hit him in the leg." The instructions given to the captain of the *Agnes*, and taken over by Willoughby, included the payment of customs duty, an interview with the local governor reporting the intention to proceed up the river, and: "at daylight on the day succeeding that on which you interviewed the Governor of Beira, you will leave that port and proceed *very carefully* up the Pungwe"—whether the Governor permitted this or not. "From sunrise to sundown you will, *under all circumstances*, fly the English ensign." If fired on, he was to return to Durban.

The intention was clear: the Portuguese were to be given the choice of abdicating their control of the Pungwe or of firing on the British flag. On reading the instructions, the high commissioner pointed out that private enterprise had no right to usurp a function of Her Majesty's government, which alone could decide what to do if Portugal failed to observe the *modus vivendi*. If, therefore, the governor refused permission for the *Agnes* to go up the Pungwe, the captain was to ask for this refusal in writing, and after receiving it to go back the way he had come. If no written refusal were received within twenty-four hours, this could be taken as evidence of consent. The modified order was received by the captain of the *Agnes* in a telegram from Johnson, without any intimation that it came from the high commissioner.[29]

Willoughby claimed to have carried out the original orders to the letter, by which he meant that he asserted what he took to be his rights under the *modus vivendi*, but refused to obey orders from the governor which he thought inconsistent with those rights. From the beginning, the governor—who turned out to be J.J. Machado, governor-general of Mozambique, come to Beira for the occasion—refused to allow the party to ascend the Pungwe. Willoughby insisted that it had the right to do so. He offered to pay customs duty. This was not accepted, since the passage of the cargo was forbidden. Nevertheless, on 15 April the convoy began to move up the river, red ensign flying. After warnings, a blank shot was fired at the *Agnes* by the corvette *Tamega*. As the blank was to be followed by shell, Willoughby then gave up. The Portuguese impounded the *Agnes* and *Shark* and detained their crews, allowing the rest of the party to depart in the *Norseman*.

Machado had not handled the affair with the requisite skill and aplomb. His reasons for refusing permission changed as the crisis developed. First, the river was not open (a breach of the *modus vivendi*), because a state of siege had been proclaimed. Then it was not, and would not be, open to the BSA Company specifically. Then foreign ships on the river must fly the Portuguese flag. Then the convoy was fired on, and the ships impounded, because duty had not been paid. (It had in fact been offered but not accepted.) The final explanation was that the troops up the river were so incensed against the British that there would be bloodshed if the convoy proceeded. There was ill-feeling at Beira also: various British subjects complained, with or without justice, of offensive treatment there.

Machado had good reason to turn the convoy back. That the expedition was not, as he had expected, a small army, was due only to the prompt action of Sir Henry Loch. It was not due to any change in Rhodes's intentions. Jameson had got his treaty from Ngungunyane a month before. A few months before that, Forbes would have marched into Beira but for Loch's order. The Company had "occupied" Macequece and was still there; this was the specific ground of Machado's discrimination against it. Repeated orders from the Foreign Office to relinquish Macequece were disobeyed on the excuse that there were only four men there, whose function was to protect the property of the Mozambique Company until the Portuguese could take charge of it. Willoughby's expedition merely confirmed the just suspicion that Rhodes was determined to get Beira and its hinterland by one means or another.

Machado saw through all this, but he did not see quite far enough. Among the items impounded—though in this case restored the next day—was a bag of Her Majesty's mail. This, and the firing on the British flag, were exactly what Rhodes wanted: "an insult and outrage that the Government of Portugal would have to answer for to the Government of England." The shot from the *Tamega* continued to reverberate across the world until the arrival at Beira of HMS *Magicienne* and two gunboats indicated the success of Rhodes's trick.[30]

It was a much more limited success than he had intended. If the public in Cape Town and in England were roused to excitement by the "insult and outrage," the Portuguese public felt even more insulted and outraged. Volunteers, including large numbers of students, had for some time been enrolling in Portugal and in Lourenço Marques in an expeditionary force to uphold the national honour, and the outrage of 15 April gave the movement a new fillip. This in itself was not unwelcome to Rhodes; from his point of view, the more "incidents" the better. The Portuguese government, on the other hand, saw the matter in the same light as Rhodes. Whereas it had been hoping for better terms than in 1890, it now became more tractable. It would save what it could before its bargaining position was undermined by more incidents. This was the Company's actual reward for Willoughby's patriotic bravado. It got the reward because Salisbury wanted a treaty with Portugal on his own terms.

Those terms were not Rhodes's. Salisbury would exclude Portugal from areas to which her claims were "archeological." That description did not, in his opinion, cover any part of the Mozambique coast. It did not apply to Macequece. Rhodes was mistaken in thinking that a little crude swashbuckling could throw Salisbury off balance.

So he prepared to play his next card. The *modus vivendi* would expire on 14 May. Surely, after that, Salisbury would agree that *beati possidentes*? In fact, when it expired, the agreement was extended for another month, and for some time the Foreign Office had been sending out warnings that no action must be taken after 14 May on the assumption that the *modus vivendi* was no longer in effect.

As Loch's order for the evacuation of Macequece would take five or six weeks to reach the place by the overland route, the Portuguese government allowed him to send an officer up from Beira with the instructions. Loch sent his military secretary, Major Sapte. The Company had, however, withdrawn its last protector of Portuguese goods from Macequece long before Sapte could get there. In the course of March and April the Portuguese volunteers, and other troops, had been arriving at Beira in batches. It was also reliably reported that an army of 10,000 Africans was being assembled near Sena. The objective of all these forces was Macequece; and, perhaps, points further west. Captain Heyman with his sixty troopers at the camp on the Umtali river looked like having a difficult passage to the coast when D-day, 14 May, dawned.

The Portuguese were well aware that Heyman would be tempted to advance at that time. Their forces were moving into the interior for defensive as well as offensive purposes. As they approached Macequece, Heyman withdrew his last man from the place. Maj. Caldas Xavier, accompanied by J.J. Ferreira, governor of Manica, and some 250 troops, occupied it. Heyman took up a position on a hill overlooking Macequece, waiting for the day. Once again the Portuguese made a mistake. Xavier anticipated Heyman's move by attacking him on the 11th. The attack was repulsed with some Portuguese, but no British, losses; during the night Xavier evacuated Macequece; the next day Heyman occupied it.

The Portuguese really had a case: though the evidence suggests that they had been tactically the aggressors, Heyman had no right to be in the neighbourhood of Macequece. Yet Xavier ought to have known that his attack would loom larger at the conference table than the question of Heyman's precise position. His mistake would have been redeemed by victory; it was compounded by defeat. Heyman had been attacked, his enemy was repulsed, the original *modus vivendi* expired, and the road to the sea was open before him.[31]

Heyman's force was only an advance guard. Behind him were Pennefather and Selous, who followed the retreating Portuguese for some distance, but gave up the pursuit when it appeared that a substantial force could not be supplied through such difficult country. News that the Portuguese were in difficulties then inspired another pursuit, by seventeen troopers under the command of Lieutenant Fiennes. A mile outside Chimoio this party met Bishop Knight-

Bruce on his way up and heard the unwelcome news that Major Sapte, with in-structions from the high commissioner, was not far behind. Sapte duly ap-peared, too late to prevent the fight at Macequece but in time to forestall an-other at Chimoio. The disconsolate Fiennes had to return to Umtali.[32] Rhodes is reported to have administered a mild rebuke to him: "Why didn't you put Sapte in irons and say he was drunk?" As Lockhart and Woodhouse rightly re-mark, "Jameson would have done it."

While the Company's attempts to seize Portuguese territory were frustrated by the Foreign Office, its right to use the Beira route to Mashonaland, spelt out clearly in the diplomatic document, was enforced. Three British warships off Beira and the Portuguese government's anxiety about the terms of a new treaty quickly disposed of most of the obstacles erected on 15 April. The men in Lisbon, like those in London, took a wider view than their agents in Africa. Orders were given to allow foreign ships, under their own flags, up the Pungwe as far as Mponda's. There was no more difficulty about paying the three per cent duty on goods in transit, nor any objection to travellers carrying arms for their own defence. Road-building in Portuguese territory was still dependent on permission from the authorities, but they were not likely to be obstructive. The firm of Frank Johnson and Company resumed its efforts to make a line of communication, and Sir John Willoughby and his labourers reappeared at Beira.[33]

So far, the BSA Company has figured in this story of Anglo-Portuguese rela-tions only as a lawless body of freebooters, continually trying to present the diplomatic negotiators with a fait accompli. Sometimes it appears to have been encouraged, at other times restrained, by the Foreign Office. Behind the scenes, however, the company was at the same time operating on a different plane, where politics mingled with business. On the Portuguese side, too, there was a company, also interested in both politics and business. By a decree of 20 December 1888, Paiva de Andrade's Mozambique Company was given a concession of the basins of the Pungwe and the Buzi and the territory between them. Half the capital was Portuguese, half French, but the Portuguese part figures obscurely in the records. The French financier Bartissol was so large an investor that "la Compagnie," it was said, "c'est lui."

The Mozambique Company farmed out mining rights to subconcessionaires, many of whom were British. Other prospectors derived their rights from the BSA Company, and—the international boundary being undecided—concessions by the two companies tended to overlap in the same area. When the governments reached agreement on the frontier, what would be the posi-tion of either company, and its subconcessionaires, in the area that fell on the wrong side of the line? Anxious as Rhodes, Cawston, Bartissol, and the rest were for a political settlement in their own respective interests, they never lost sight of the financial aspect of the problem. Negotiations were therefore opened, towards the end of 1890, between the two companies.

213 The Company and Portugal

At that time Bartissol was angling for a charter, in the BSA style, from the Portuguese government. The charter was to be given to a newly formed company, much larger than the old: capital, £800,000. The old Mozambique Company would form an important part of the combination, but where was the rest of the money to come from? The BSA Company could supply it.[34] If Portugal objected, the decencies could be preserved by an indirect investment through a French company. Cawston, who conducted the negotiations with Bartissol through Alfred Tiano, his Paris agent, hoped that the new Mozambique Company would become a subsidiary of the BSA Company. The latter would acquire the substance and Portugal would be left with the shadow.

In December, when the new charter was drawn up, the Portuguese government blighted these hopes by forbidding the BSA Company to hold a majority of the shares. A few weeks later it took a harder line: the BSA Company was to have no interest in the new company in any shape or form. Negotiations continued, but only on the question of the respective rights of the two companies when the boundary came to be fixed. Each was to be confined to its own side of the border, but was to be compensated for losses by receiving a percentage of the profits on mines in the disputed areas; or alternatively by receiving, as sub-concessions, claims in the other company's territory. Argument about these details was still going on when the two governments at last agreed on the frontiers; it continued thereafter, while the line was being demarcated on the ground. By that time the dispute over mining rights was overshadowed by the question of the railway from the coast, to which we shall return.

These negotiations were related, both as causes and as effects, to the events in Manica, Quiteve, and Beira. Forbes's actions in November may have influenced Bartissol in his willingness to try to retrieve in the boardroom what was lost on the battlefield, though Cawston afterwards offered a different explanation: Bartissol used the fact of negotiation with the BSA Company as bait to attract capital from other sources. On the other hand Forbes's actions certainly made Bartissol's Portuguese associates less willing than ever to give any points away. It may have been developments in Gazaland that turned the Portuguese government against allowing any association between the companies. The refusal of the BSA Company to accept Bartissol's terms produced from the latter a violent reaction on 10 March. Since the Portuguese troops were still on the coast and apparently unwilling to move, he and his company would take matters into their own hands. They would march into the interior, even before the expiry of the *modus vivendi*, easily "exterminate" the BSA Company's 300 men, "et nous reprendrons possession de ce qu'on nous a volé"—in particular, the Umtali valley. The Mozambique Company was not itself able to mount such an operation, but this language seems to have some bearing on the Portuguese attack on Heyman two months later.

The BSA Company's disappointment at the failure of the negotiations was shared by the Foreign Office, which had hoped that the companies would prepare the way and simplify the task of the governments. A note by Cawston on 9 March shows that the Foreign Office, or at least Sir Philip Currie, had at that time an even closer sympathy with the Company: "Sir Philip Currie says it is no use going on negotiating with the Mozambique Company. All we have to do is to sit still and do nothing, the modus vivendi is running out." This advice was not needed. The contrary advice given later, not to assume that it would run out, was disregarded. The clash at Macequece on 11 May, and the events that followed, would not have happened if the negotiations between Cawston and Bartissol had been successful. They could not, however, have succeeded without a surrender which neither side was willing to make.[35]

The governments had therefore to solve their problem without help from the companies. On the contrary, the views of the directors of the BSA Company were summed up in a cable from Rhodes: "decidedly prefer no settlement . . . if there is no settlement we shall acquire everything." After the various appeals to arms, the incursions in the direction of Beira and the appearance of British warships on the scene, the Portuguese government came reluctantly to a similar conclusion. The Portuguese public did not. The repeated yielding to British demands had aroused in it a resentment which, following the Brazilian example, was taking the form of republicanism. The governments of Vienna, Rome, Madrid, and Stockholm, not to mention Queen Victoria herself, were alarmed by the threat to the "monarchical principle." Salisbury had reason to think that the danger had been exaggerated, and wrote that the Portuguese were "making the most of their weaknesses. They should be made to feel that if they do attempt to show their temper by upsetting their king, the only result will be the loss of their whole Colonial Empire, and their probable absorption by Spain." He did not allow this threat to count for very much in the negotiations but he was too good a diplomatist to push his advantage to the utmost.[36]

His forbearance eased the passage for the Portuguese government. Living in what Salisbury called "a fool's paradise," it had put forward proposals to modify the 1890 agreement in its own favour. It was soon convinced that time was not on its side. On 28 May Salisbury and L.P. de Soveral, the Portuguese chargé d'affaires in London, signed a draft convention, which was then approved by the Côrtes and signed by King Carlos on 11 June.

The convention fixed the boundaries as they have since remained, except for that of Angola, which took many years to settle. As can be seen by a comparison with the treaty of 1890, the BSA Company profited from its forceful proceedings on the eastern border of Southern Rhodesia, though not nearly as much as it had hoped. That boundary was advanced to a line to be demarcated on the spot, but to be kept within the limits marked by the meridians 32° 30' and 33° E. North of the Zambezi Portugal was compensated with the enlarged salient in the Zumbo-Shiré sector. The whole of Barotseland was to be in the British sphere, but as the boundary of that kingdom was disputed the line would be decided by arbitration. The zone along the north bank of the Zambezi, in which by the previous treaty Portugal was to have transit rights, disappeared.

Other provisions, not in the treaty, were arranged by an exchange of notes. The use of this method was a concession to the Portuguese, who had objected to some of the 1890 terms on grounds of punctilio rather than of substance. Now the lease of a small area at the Chinde mouth to persons named by the British government was made less offensive by being omitted from the treaty itself. The notes also provided for the construction of a road from the coast to the frontier, for the rates to be levied on the future railway, and for the passage of the troops of either power across the territory of the other.[37]

From the date of this convention the boundaries, where they had been defined—as in Manicaland, though not in Barotseland—were secure against filibusterers or conquistadores on either side. The BSA Company had failed to get a road to the sea under its own flag, but was assured of communications through Portuguese territory. On the other hand, it was still possible for private individuals and companies to hold concessions on either side of the boundary, subject to confirmation by the recognized authorities of each territory; hence a battle of the concessions in Manicaland with curious resemblances to what had happened in Bulawayo.

The fate of the African Portuguese Syndicate may not be important in the large context of history, but its contest with the British South Africa Company had important results. It is impossible to give a confident judgment on the rights and wrongs of this case, mainly because of Mutasa's habitual perjury. Each side therefore submitted evidence, complete with affidavits and signatures, which flatly contradicted that of the other. It appears that on 3 November 1888 George Wise got from Mutasa a concession of mining, cultivating, and trading rights in return for two hundred cotton blankets a year. As the document was "lost," another was substituted for it one year later. At this stage Mutasa demanded woollen instead of cotton blankets, and at the same time Wise made over the concession to the African Portuguese Syndicate, represented by Reuben Beningfield. Because of the change from cotton to wool, the blankets could not be produced at that time, but in December 1890 Herbert Taylor, representing the syndicate, was approaching Mutasa's with a load of woollen blankets to pay two years' rent. It was not a good moment for calling in question the BSA Company's recent but precarious achievements in that area. By order of Denis Doyle, Taylor was arrested. He managed to deliver the blankets and to get a receipt for them. Released, he returned to Durban by way of Salisbury and Kimberley. He demanded compensation from Colquhoun and from Rutherfoord Harris in turn, but did not get any.

Taylor reached Mutasa's again at the end of 1891, and remained for some time. The Company had no longer to fear for its frontier with the Portuguese, but the syndicate presented a different kind of danger. It held, or claimed to hold, a concession for *land*, and the Company and its settlers were already occupying the land. According to the syndicate, Mutasa represented to Taylor in January 1892 that the Company had burnt six of his villages, destroyed the stock and crops, and driven out the inhabitants; the names of the village headmen were given. In June two "minor headmen" of Mutasa were reported to have arrived in Durban to lay the complaints before Beningfield. Mutasa "only recognized him, he having granted him the concession on which the native kraals [i.e., those that were burnt] were." The kraals were supposed to have been burnt by the police because some of their inhabitants, pressed into service as labourers, had absconded and returned home.

Rhodes flatly denied the charge. Loch was not convinced by the denial but wanted independent evidence. Arrangements were made to obtain this. In September, according to the syndicate, L. Rice Hamilton paid Mutasa the rent for 1892. About the same time Mutasa was said to have sent messengers to the Company's representative at Umtali to complain that the Company was trespassing on the syndicate's concession. The messengers were arrested, but released when Taylor's colleague Logan protested.

The syndicate's claims alarmed not only the Company but also the white inhabitants of Umtali and its neighbourhood who occupied land by leave of the Company. They held a public meeting, at which both Jameson and Taylor were present, to demand some security of title. Jameson reassured them. The Beningfield concession, he said, had lapsed long ago through nonpayment of rent; "they all knew the way Mr. Rhodes had of smoothing the fellows off with a few shares, which no doubt they were working for, and would in all probability get a few." The Company claimed that Mutasa had told Colquhoun of the Beningfield concession, and of its having lapsed, at the time of their agreement in September 1890. He had regarded Taylor's blankets not as rent but as a present.

Two more or less independent witnesses tried to sort this tangle out. Sir Charles Metcalfe, the railway engineer, reported that Mutasa would have nothing to do with Taylor or Logan. They had escaped by night across the border, had a rendezvous on the Portuguese side with the chief's son, and persuaded him to go with them to Durban. As they were said to have been "tampering" with a chief in Portuguese territory, the local commandant went down to Beira to arrest them, but Colonel Machado decided that there was not enough evidence to justify an arrest.

In November 1892 Maj. J.J. Leverson, RE, representing the Foreign Office (he was the chief British boundary commissioner under the convention), made an investigation at Mutasa's kraal. As the chief was said to be very ill, he could not be seen, but Leverson interviewed his son and three of his headmen. These conveyed Leverson's questions to the chief and reported back. It appeared that the three (not two) men who had accompanied Hamilton to Durban were not envoys, but porters to carry his baggage. They had no instructions to lay complaints before anyone. Some huts had been destroyed "some two years ago," but there had been nothing to complain of since then.

(In parenthesis, this is Mutasa's version of Leverson's visit: the chief had heard unofficially that an imperial officer had been sent to make an enquiry, but Mutasa had never seen him; he did not apply to Mutasa for information, nor ask to see the burnt kraals.)

The Company, in the person of Captain Heyman, held its own enquiry at Mutasa's kraal. Heyman interviewed the chief in the presence of his indunas and people. There was now a question of Mutasa's having sent envoys to Cape Town. He denied this, and asked the Company to expel Taylor from the country.

(Mutasa's version as relayed through the syndicate: "Not long since Captain Heyman . . . came to my kraal with a body of police and produced a paper which he first tried to induce, and then ordered, me to sign, the purport of the paper being that I was to acknowledge the White Chief at Salisbury, which I understood to mean the Chief Official of the Company. I refused to sign this paper, and after threatening me he took it away." As Heyman's report was written in March, and Mutasa's complaint made in November, the complaint might refer to a later visit by Heyman.)

Among Mutasa's statements in a petition to Ripon through the syndicate was a denial that he had ever given a concession to the Chartered Company. This gave the bewildered secretary of state a cue: "Lord Ripon is bound further to observe that he is unable to give credence to any statement purporting to proceed from Umtassa, or his son, or his headmen . . . The sweeping statement in paragraph 8 of the petition that Umtassa had given no concession of any kind to the British South Africa Company is sufficient of itself to discredit the whole of this document as an expression of Umtassa's views. It is beyond doubt that on the 14th September 1890 a treaty was concluded in open council between Umtassa and Mr. Colquhoun, as representing the British South Africa Company."[38]

The syndicate may well have been discouraged by the hostility of Ripon and of Loch, but it was not silenced. It was to be heard from again as the years passed and the circumstances changed. At this point it is necessary only to remark that the Manyika people were unfortunate in their chief. Caught between the aggressions of the Chartered Company, the syndicate, and the Portuguese, Mutasa had no more statesmanlike policy than to befriend each to his face and then denounce him as soon as his back was turned. Not having the military power of a Lobengula or Ngungunyane he needed friends, but this was not the way to win them.

Little need be said of other concession-hunters in the region. F.J. Colquhoun (no relation of the administrator) addressed himself to Ngungunyane, who gave him a generous grant. The area in question, however, lay not only within the British sphere but west of the Sabi, and so outside Ngungunyane's kingdom, even on his own most ambitious reckoning. The secretary of state had no difficulty in rejecting it.[39]

The weakness of the Wise-Beningfield concession, if it was weak, had other implications. It was rejected because Mutasa's word could not be believed; but the Company's claim also depended on Mutasa's word. To the syndicate he denied having granted anything to the Company, to the Company he denied having granted anything to the syndicate, or to the Portuguese. Among otherwise valid concessions, the earliest in time ought to prevail. The Company might induce Mutasa to echo its assertions; but who could tell what inconvenient evidence might come to light at any time? What made the question important and urgent was that the African Portuguese Syndicate claimed a right to land. The Company and its settlers were occupying some of that land, and, as will be seen, more was earmarked for a new trek now being organized.

The acquisition of the Lippert Concession gave the Company land rights, of a sort, in Lobengula's dominions; but they extended only to the Sabi. East of that river the Company could claim what Mutasa had conceded in September 1890—but land was not included in that concession.

To solve this problem Rhodes took a leaf out of Lippert's book. Two days before Lippert had his concession confirmed by Lobengula, Denis Doyle got Ngungunyane to put his mark to a concession which gave the company "sole and absolute power and control over all waste and unoccupied lands situated in my territory." The Company received the power to graze cattle and cultivate land, to grant titles, sign leases, receive rents, cut and remove timber, and otherwise use the land, all in return for an annual payment of £300. Ngungunyane was evidently taking a leaf out of another book—Lobengula's: this grant might make the same sort of trouble for the Mozambique Company and the Portuguese government as Lippert's was intended to make for Rhodes. The circumstances, however, were quite different. Doyle had no plan to sell the concession to the Portuguese. On the contrary, this was a final gamble by Rhodes on the chance that the Anglo-Portuguese Convention could still be undermined.

Neither the Salisbury government nor its successor (Gladstone's) was prepared to play that kind of game. There were, however, two aspects of the concession (as also, now, of the Schulz-Jameson mineral concession) that the British authorities would not reject out of hand. In so far as it was a mere business deal, it might be valid if the Portuguese would confirm it. Secondly, some of the territory claimed by Ngungunyane lay on the British side of the boundary; in respect of this, the secretary of state might well accept the concession.

The problem was resolved after a three-cornered correspondence between the Foreign and Colonial Offices and the Company. Rhodes made the reasonable point that he could not pay Ngungunyane as much for a part of each concession as for the whole. No change could be made in the terms without the agreement of Ngungunyane himself, and as he was then preparing to make war on the Portuguese he was not likely to agree to changes which would frustrate his essential purpose in making the grant. Rosebery, at the Foreign Office, was reluctant to approve either concession; Ngungunyane had little understanding of the BSA Company and its objects, and might become difficult when he saw his concessions being put into effect in the British sphere. He was powerful, and had close relations with Lobengula. Thus the company might run into trouble from which the imperial government would have to rescue it.

Loch countered this argument with the analogy of German South-West Africa. The boundary of that territory, a mere meridian, cut through tribes; the Germans allowed concessions from those tribes to take effect on their own side of the line. What converted Rosebery, however, was not this, but the news that the Portuguese themselves had granted a concession over most of Ngungunyane's territory without consulting that king. There could hardly therefore be any objection to confirming his concessions to the Company in respect of territory in the British sphere. The Company agreed to pay Ngungunyane the whole of his rent, provisionally and pending a Portuguese decision on rights within their sphere. On 9 February 1893, Ripon returned the Doyle concession to the company with his *nihil obstat* on it.[40]

NOTES CHAPTER 5

1 E. Axelson, *Portugal and the Scramble for Africa, 1875-1891*, pp.1-12, 167. For the prazos, see Allen F. Isaacman, *The Africanization of a European Institution: The Zambesi Prazos, 1750-1902*. Portuguese writers have considered that these wars—especially against Bonga, but also against Vingwe and others (see below)—were what prevented Portugal from making the link from coast to coast while it was still possible; see A. Baião, H. Cidade and M. Murias, eds., *Historia da Expansão Portuguesa no Mundo*, vol. III, p.396. The *mapa côr de rosa*, which was appended to the Portuguese-German treaty of 30 December 1886, is reproduced in ibid., opposite p.352. The map included in the Portuguese sphere all of the future territory of the BSA Co. except (in modern terms) northern Malawi and the northeasternmost part of Zambia. The above treaty is in E. Hertslet, *The Map of Africa by Treaty*, vol. II, pp.705-6; the map (green instead of pink) faces p.706.
2 S.E. Crowe, *The Berlin West African Conference, 1884-5*, pp.178-90.
3 CO 417/50, p.11.
4 Axelson, *Portugal and the Scramble*, pp.110-16, 222; Jean van der Poel, *Railway and Customs Policies in South Africa, 1885-1910*, pp.19-23, 27-31, 39-40, 43-4.
5 A.J. Hanna, *The Beginnings of Nyasaland and North-Eastern Rhodesia, 1859-95*, ch. I, secs. 2, 3; Axelson, *Portugal and the Scramble*, pp.166, 168-9. Livingstone had applied the name Nyasa to Lake Malawi; that name, and the corresponding name of the country (Nyasaland), remained until 1964.
6 Apart from a brief experience in the Sudan.
7 Hanna, *Beginnings of Nyasaland*, ch. I, sec. 4; Axelson, *Portugal and the Scramble*,

ch. IX, and pp.202-4; D.J. Rankin in *Fortnightly Review*, vol.47 (N.S.), pp.149-63. To Petre, the Portuguese government played down the importance of Cardoso's expedition, and would not tell him where it was going (Salisbury Papers, A/81/60).

8 Hanna, *Beginnings of Nyasaland*, ch. II; Axelson, *Portugal and the Scramble*, pp.205-13; J.P. Oliveira Martins, *Portugal em Africa: A Questão Colonial—o Conflicto Anglo-Portuguez*, pp.42-6; J.J. Teixeira Botelho, *Historia Militar e Politica dos Portugueses em Moçambique, de 1833 aos Nossos Dias*, pp.339-50.

9 Axelson, *Portugal and the Scramble*, ch. VII; CO 879/30/372, no. 192, encl., pp.187-8. See the "memorandum on the rights of Portugal in the territories to the south of the Zambesi," submitted to the British government by Barjona de Freitas, in Foreign Office Confidential Print 179/279, no.57, pp.32-5; and D.N. Beach, "The Rising in South-Western Mashonaland, 1896-7" (PH.D. thesis, University of London, 1971), pp.175-95. In this it is argued (p.195) that the Portuguese treaties and the guns given for them convinced Lobengula that he had lost Mashonaland, and therefore had nothing further to lose by allowing the Pioneers into it.

10 R.J. Hammond, *Portugal and Africa, 1815-1910*, p.128, and ch. IV generally; Axelson, *Portugal and the Scramble*, pp.223-30; Martins, *Portugal em Africa*, p.49. (This book, a collection of press articles written during the events and appearing in book form in 1891, conveys vividly the violence of the emotions felt at the time.) Botelho, *Portugueses em Moçambique*, pp.364-9; Baião *et al., Expansão Portuguesa*, vol. III, pp.347-9. In England the Company's allies in the press had helped to work up anti-Portuguese feeling—e.g. an article in the *Fortnightly Review* on 1 January 1890; the article was anonymous, but RH Mss Afr. s 73, p.286 shows that it was by Verschoyle, and that "the Govt. are most anxious for the vigorous support of public opinion in England and that they look to the very article I sent you to stir up the press on all sides."

11 Lady Gwendolen Cecil, *The Life of Robert, Marquis of Salisbury*, vol. IV, p.300; Hertslet, *Map of Africa*, vol. III, pp.899-906.

12 I.e. on 13 May 1890. See CO 879/32/392, no.198, encl., para 4, p.225.

13 Baião *et al., Expansão Portuguesa*, vol. III, pp.349-51; Axelson, *Portugal and the Scramble*, pp.242-4, and ch. XII generally; Botelho, *Portugueses em Moçambique*, pp.372-4; for text of treaty, CO 879/32/392, pp.389-93.

14 RH Mss Afr. s 74, pp.155-6, 166-8, 201-3, 220-1, 227, 240, 242; CO 879/32/392, no.324 encl., p.368; CO 417/51/18840, p.545; Axelson, *Portugal and the Scramble*, pp.260, 268.

15 CO 879/32/392, p.385; Axelson, *Portugal and the Scramble*, pp.270-1; Ian Colvin, *Life of Jameson*, vol. I, p.203. A. Baião *et al., Expansão Portuguesa*, vol. III, p.351. The Company's attitude to the *modus vivendi* appears in a letter from Abercorn to Cawston: "We must now work on quietly and hold our own in South Africa and make the occupation of Manica by Portugal at the end of six months an impossibility." (RH Mss Afr. s 74, p.312.)

16 P.R. Warhurst, *Anglo-Portuguese Relations in South-Central Africa, 1890—1900*, p.20. It was pointed out in the Colonial Office that the monopoly of trade was in breach of the charter (CO 417/48/24839, pp.96-106). J. de Azevedo Coutinho, in *O Combate de Macequece*, pt. II, p.35, maintains that Mutasa had "submitted to the Portuguese government in 1874 or 1875," and had "renewed his vassalage in that

year." He was then "invested" at Sena with his chieftainship and received a flag. According to Coutinho the record of the vassalage and the investiture existed in the Sena archives in 1891. All this is difficult to reconcile with the Portuguese insistence on the vassalage of Mutasa to Ngungunyane. E.g. (Botelho, *Portugueses em Moçambique*, p.377), "Gungunhane being our vassal, there could be no doubt as to Mutassa." This author, however, (p.376) sees no inconsistency between Mutassa's vassalage to Ngungunyane and his direct "submission to the Portuguese government." Douglas L. Wheeler, "Gungunyane the Negotiator: a Study in African Diplomacy," *Journal of African History*, IX, 4 (1968), pp.585-7, supports the view that Mutasa was at least *de facto* independent of Ngungunyane. This view is modified by H.H.K. Bhila, "Manyika's Relationship with the Portuguese and the Gaza-Nguni from 1832 to 1890," *Rhodesian History*, VII (1976), pp.36-7.

17 CO 879/36/426, no.23, pp.31-2; A.R. Colquhoun, *Matabeleland: The War, and our Position in South Africa*, p.55.

18 CO 879/33/403, no.48, encl. 1 and 3, pp.53-5; no.68, encl., pp.76-83; CO 417/51/24157, pp.621 ff.; Papers of Lieut. M.D. Graham (GR 6/1/1), Graham to his mother, 21 November 1890; Warhurst, *Anglo-Portuguese Relations*, pp.27-30; Axelson, *Portugal and the Scramble*, p.267; Botelho, *Portugueses em Moçambique*, pp.377-9.

19 A.G. Leonard, *How We Made Rhodesia*, pp.150-1.

20 CO 879/33/403, no.53, encl. 1 and 2, pp.58-9; no.56, encl., pp.60-1; no.74, encl., p.87; no.78, encl.1, p.88; *Cape Argus*, 31 December 1890; *The Times*, 20 January 1891.

21 CO 879/33/403, no.31, encl.2, p.21; Baron E.B. d'Erlanger, *History of the Construction and Finance of the Rhodesian Transport System*, p.11; A.R. Colquhoun, *Dan to Beersheba, Work and Travel in Four Continents*, pp.379-80; Colvin, *Jameson*, vol. I, p.173. According to Jameson the overland cost was £72 per ton; Johnson reckoned £60. The Beira Railway Co., however, whose estimate was £45, would have been inclined to put it as high as possible.

22 CO 879/33/403, no.9, p.4; no.32, p.21; no.49, p.56; no.53, encl.2, p.59; no.72, encl., p.85; no.78, encl.1, p.88; RH Mss Afr. s 75, p.11. The Portuguese themselves drew a distinction between Macequece, in the retention of which they thought national honour was involved because of previous occupation, and the area west of the modern boundary, where apparently it was not. See Salisbury Papers, Soveral to Salisbury, 22 December 1890 (A/81/70) and Petre to Salisbury, 8 February 1891 (A/81/68).

23 Axelson, *Portugal and the Scramble*, pp.125-35; CO 879/33/403, no.164, encl., p.147; Botelho, *Portugueses em Moçambique*, pp.423-4. The Portuguese attack was what made the old chief Mtoko ("nearly if not quite one hundred years old") willing to sign a treaty with the BSA Company, represented by Selous, on 6 January 1891. (Colquhoun, *Matabeleland*, pp.70-5). Alan K. Smith, "The Peoples of Southern Mozambique: an Historical Survey," *Journal of African History*, XIV, 4 (1973), pp.565-80, shows that the Portuguese hold on the Inhambane district was based on an alliance with the local Chopi and Tonga population, ethnically distinct from the Tsonga who formed the bulk of the Gaza Kings' subjects. For the complexities of the 1885-6 treaty, see G. Liesegang, "Aspects of Gaza Nguni History, 1821-1897," *Rhodesian History*, VI (1975), pp.10-11.

24 Douglas L. Wheeler, "Gungunyane," p.587.

25 co 879/32/392, no.209, encl., p.231; no.210, encl., pp.232-3; no.214, encl., pp.235-6; no.241, encl., p.267; no.245, encl., p.270; no.265, encl., pp.285-8; co 879/33/403, no.148, encl., pp.137-40; no.269a and encls., pp.213-8; Axelson, *Portugal and the Scramble*, pp.135-6.

26 co 879/33/403, no.1, p.1; no.31, encl., p.18; no.134, encl., p.131; no.143, encl., p.134; no.173, encl., pp.151-2; no.203, encls. 2 and 5, pp.169-70; no.206, encl., pp.175-8; no.215, p.187; no.283, encl., pp.234-5; no.311, p.261; no.315, p.264; Marshall Hole Papers (HO 1/3/4), letter from Capt. Buckingham to Rutherfoord Harris; Colvin, *Jameson*, p.181; co 417/55/6561, pp.723-4.

27 co 879/33/403, no.68, encl., p.81; no.72, encl., p.85; no.74, encl., p.87; Axelson, *Portugal and the Scramble*, p.281.

28 Frank Johnson, *Great Days*, pp.164, 166, 193; Colvin, *Jameson*, vol. I, ch. XII; Axelson, *Portugal and the Scramble*, p.124; co 879/33/403, no.31, encl.2 (pp.19-21). The only sources for this story and its semi-miraculous conclusion are the adventurers themselves.

29 co 879/33/403, no.182, encl.1 and 2, p.155; no.170, p.149; no.204, encls., (pp.171-4; no.224, p.190; Leonard, *Rhodesia*, pp.236-7; Colvin, *Jameson*, vol. I, p.185. It is not clear whether the 240 (or 250?) armed men existed in reality or only in rumour. In reply to orders from London, Loch merely says that "they will be held back"; there is no other solid evidence of their existence. Note that on 11 April the Colonial Office heard by telegram that supplies had reached Fort Salisbury via Matabeleland. (co 879/33/403, no.185, p.156.)

30 co 879/33/403, nos.180, 181, p.154; no.245, encl., p.203; no.341, encl., p.287; no.345, encls., pp.290-8; no.347, encl., pp.299-300. On 10 April the Portuguese consul in Cape Town told Loch (no.180) that the party would not be allowed to pass until Macequece had been evacuated.

31 co 879/33/403, no.186, p.156; no.191, pp.157-8; no.240, pp.200-1; no.275, p.231; no.284, p.235; no.289, p.237; no.300, p.254; no.360, encl., p.308; no.361, encl., p.309; no.380, p.326; no.425, encl., pp.360-2; co 417/59/12977, pp.227-41; 12979, pp.297-302; 60/14050, pp.149-53; 14053, pp.258-62; 61/15559, pp.444-58; 62/17173, pp.80-3; Botelho, *Portugueses em Moçambique*, pp.381-9. It is not necessary to go into the controversies about this battle—Heyman's position, which side was tactically the aggressor, etc.—since Heyman was clearly the aggressor strategically. The importance attached to the battle by the Portuguese is suggested by the two slim volumes on *O Combate de Macequece* by João de Azevedo Coutinho. Published forty-four years after the event, it surveys the whole history of South Africa, including Portuguese achievements since Bartolomeu Dias, to culminate in the climax of the battle of Macequece. For the battle itself, pt. II, pp.59-69. It is a curious coincidence that the Company was fighting, at almost the same moment, the Portuguese under J.J. Ferreira and the Boers under Ignatius Ferreira. The Afrikaner family was, of course, of Portuguese origin in the male line.

32 Sapte's account is in co 417/61/16097, pp.591-664. Sapte says nothing of any argument with Fiennes; merely that the detachment accompanied him as he went on his way to Macequece. It was evidently Knight-Bruce who broke the bad news to Fiennes, viz. that Sapte was following and would turn him back (61/16484, p.706).

33 co 879/33/403, no.259 and encl., p.208; no.282, p.233.

34 How the BSA Company was to raise this money was not explained.

35 The negotiations are covered at great length in RH Mss Afr. s 75, pp.1-236; see especially pp.228-31 (from a Foreign Office Confidential Print), and pp.226, 236 for quotations in the above passage.

36 Salisbury Papers, Petre to Salisbury, 31 December 1890 (A/81/67); W.E. Goschen to Salisbury, 10 September 1891 (A/81/69); Salisbury to Petre, 24 December 1890 (A/81/75); the Queen to Salisbury, 4 November 1890 (A/45/97); Axelson, *Portugal and the Scramble*, pp.233-4.

37 Salisbury Papers, Salisbury to Petre, 24 December 1890 (A/81/75); Axelson, *Portugal and the Scramble*, pp.276-7, 289-97; Botelho, *Portugueses em Moçambique*, pp.391-8; for text of conventions, C6370. Martins (*Portugal em Africa*, pp.125-6) regarded the lease of the Chinde mouth to Britain as analogous to the cession of Bombay to England in 1661. It was nothing at the time, but see what it became and what grew from it! For a more recent Portuguese account of the "incidents" and of the Convention, see Baião *et al.*, *Expansão Portuguesa*, vol. III, pp.351-8.

38 CO 879/36/426, no.219, encl., pp.259-60; 37/441, no.46, pp.50-1; no.80, p.75; no.113, pp.114-15; 39/454, no.72a, pp.87-8; no.136a, pp.140-7; 40/461, no.35a and encl., pp.58-73; no.122, pp.204-5.

39 CO 879/36/426, no.78, encl., pp.110-12; no.91, p.125; no.109, encl., pp.152-3; no.133, pp.175-6; no.188, p.232; no.192, p.236; no.203, p.248; no.215 and encl., pp.254-5.

40 CO 879/36/426, no.42, p.45; no.68, encls., pp.88-9; no.99, p.133; no.113, pp.154-5; no.132, p.175; no.192, p.236; no.230, p.272; no.232 and encl., pp.273-4; no.256, encl., pp.295-6; no.269, p.305; 37/441, no.7, pp.5-6; no.37, p.42; no.45, p.50; no.57, pp.63-5; no.79, p.74. For a fuller treatment of many of the topics in this chapter see Doris Baker, "The British South Africa Company versus the Portuguese in Manicaland and Gazaland, 1889-1892" (M.A. thesis, Queen's University). Specifically, for the Doyle Concession and its background, including the visit to England of envoys sent by Ngungunyane, pp.158-73; for the African Portuguese Syndicate, pp.174-82.

CHAPTER 6

Jameson's War, I: The Incidents and the Intrigue

Though the safe arrival of the Pioneer Column at Fort Salisbury was due mainly to the steady nerve of Lobengula and his skilful handling of his people, the king could have had no illusions about the meaning of the event. The advancing white tide, which had engulfed so many great chiefs and tribes, was now lapping round his borders. What could he do?

The immediate implications of his policy are clear: his purpose was to win time and postpone the evil day. What he intended to do when that day came is less clear. Perhaps to lead a great trek across the Zambezi; but the evidence about this is conflicting. Colenbrander, for instance, said that it was "a popular fallacy about the Matabele being in readiness to cross the Zambesi and make for fresh pastures."[1] They would not willingly have made for any pastures where tsetse fly would kill their cattle. Yet circumstantial evidence suggested at various times that the northward trek was at least an option that Lobengula wanted to keep open. If that was his intention, the prospect darkened when on 27 June 1890, F.E. Lochner obtained for the Chartered Company from Lewanika—by less than straightforward means—an exclusive mineral and commercial concession over Barotseland. The white wave was not actually breaking on Lobengula's northern border, but the storm warning was out.

The threat to the Ndebele came from the Company; the Company had enemies, and the king looked among them for allies. There was the queen, who had advised him not to give the whole herd to the first comer. Though the advice had been withdrawn in the letter brought by the guardsmen, that letter, said Lobengula, "had been dictated by Rhodes"; he continued to refer to the earlier one as if it had expressed the queen's real opinion.

The queen was represented by Loch, and Loch by Moffat. No help was expected from the assistant commissioner. In spite of the close bond between their fathers, the king distrusted Moffat from the beginning because of his association with Kgama. The distrust was intensified by Moffat's support (reluctant though it was becoming) of Rhodes and the Company. Moffat was not the queen's man, said Lobengula, but *umfana ka Rhodes*, Rhodes's boy. When Mshete and his white companions returned, early in September 1890, from their interview with Loch in Cape Town, Moffat was "haled before a judge, to wit, Lobengula," for sending the telegram which had made their visit unprofitable. Three months later, because he still refused to countenance the theory that the Rudd Concession had never been granted, Moffat reported that he had "never known the chief so sullen and discourteous." When Hassforther was arrested in Bechuanaland in the winter of 1891, his associates Karl Khumalo and John Makhunga came on and told the king that Moffat was behind it. Moffat was ordered to go and fetch Hassforther and Renny-Tailyour. He prepared to leave the country permanently, but this storm blew over.[2]

Moffat, however, was still the queen's representative, and could not always be treated so badly. To push matters to a breakdown of diplomatic relations would be to invite the very trouble that the king was determined to avoid. The better course was to be civil to Moffat but to go past him to Loch.

In October 1890 the high commissioner, accompanied by Rhodes, travelled through Bechuanaland as far as the Motloutsi, and had a mind to go on to Bulawayo. Both Colenbrander and Matabele Wilson, however, who encountered the official party on the road, advised against a visit to Lobengula. The Ndebele appeared then to be settling down to an acceptance of the new situation in Mashonaland. The appearance of Loch, and still more of Rhodes, would cause all the old issues to be reopened. The advice was taken, Loch using the excuse that Lobengula had failed to send the appropriate embassy to the border to receive him. The king was deeply offended:

> Why did you turn back at Macloutsie with Rhodes? I have been asking Rhodes to come and see me for the last two years. What was told to you that you returned without coming to see me? . . . I would have been glad to have met you and have spoken to you as to the lies which have been told by Rhodes and Doyle to see whether you believed or denied them. In any case we could have talked the matter over. When I heard that you had returned from Macloutsie I thought it was owing to Doyle's lies, and that you were satisfied he spoke the truth.

There was no help from the high commissioner.[3]

If the queen persisted in recognizing the company—presumably because she was badly advised—there were white men well known to Lobengula who needed less persuasion to serve his purpose: the representatives of Lippert and Dettelbach. The king heard that the Company was surveying Mashonaland into farms, for which there could be no pretence that he had given permission. His letter to Loch, just quoted, had something to say about this also: "I have heard that my Country is being cut up and given out. Why should this be done without my consent? . . . Did not the Queen say in her letter by Maund that I should not give all my Herd of Cattle to one man? Have I given all my Herd to the people now in Mashonaland? Who has got the Herd to kill today?"

Thus the way was prepared for the Lippert and Dettelbach concessions. Lobengula probably thought of the former, at any rate, as a master stroke, but the weapon broke in his hands. When the Rudd-Lippert negotiations were completed, and Moffat was ordered to conceal the fact from the king, he obeyed only because he thought it "a contest of knavery on both sides." Nevertheless he opened his mind to Rhodes: "I feel bound to tell you that I look on the whole plan as detestable, whether viewed in the light of policy or morality. When Loben finds all this out, as he is bound to do sooner or later, what faith will he have in you?" The deception was kept up while the concession was being confirmed, but in May 1892 it fell to Moffat to break the news of the fusion to the king. "He evidently did not like the idea at all, and could not understand how it could have been brought about, so possessed is he with the conviction that these interests are entirely irreconcilable." Yet Moffat adds that "he seemed jovial enough, so the announcement I had made did not act as a thunderclap at all events." In the sequel, Lobengula displayed no further interest in what was actually a serious diplomatic defeat; he had other anxieties.

The concession won by Hassforther, but afterwards reduced to a mere licence to import arms and ammunition, gave no concern to the Company or Loch and little comfort to Lobengula. Hassforther was "a man of no consequence," and he kept bad company. His associate Karl Khumalo (or Mvulana) was not commended to the king by his father's record as a traitor to Mzilikazi. By May 1892 Moffat could report that he (Khumalo) "has fallen on evil times, and is within a measurable distance of being knocked on the head himself." In one way or another the German adventurers had ceased to count.[4]

There remained the Boers. To the English Lobengula regularly expressed his abhorrence of the Boers. When Moffat told him of the measures to deal with the threatened Adendorff trek, "he made some remarks of general satisfaction, except on one point: he was sorry that you were letting any Boers come over the Limpopo at all, even under written engagement." Yet at that very moment his indunas were on their way to the Limpopo with a letter to Hans Lee and friendly messages for the king's "brothers the Boers."[5] Which side was he on? When he said that he feared the Boers more than the British he probably spoke the truth, because he was always conscious of two facts: the Boers were near, and the British far; and the Boers had beaten the British at Majuba.[6] They had also, several times, beaten the Ndebele, which the British had not yet done. These very facts suggested the wisdom of insuring against another Majuba in the north, but Lobengula now discovered, as we have seen, that the time for such manoeuvres was past. Hans Lee's reply was dictated by Captain Tye of the police, the Adendorff trek was repulsed, and Ferreira arrested. None of the diplomatic tricks worked.

The staving off of the catastrophe thus depended on the king's control of his subjects and his direct relations with the new authorities in Mashonaland. His subjects, especially the younger ones, were restive. Regiments came up to Bulawayo to plead for permission to "make a breakfast" of the white men. In February 1891 it was, as usual, the Imbizo and Insuka regiments that made the request through their "spokesman" Makwekwe: the king should "think well over the whites' invasion into his country and . . . allow them to go and exterminate the whites." The king, who "knew best," told them that "he would never attack the whites, for see what overtook Cetewayo." This argument was reinforced by another: "The white men did not wish to fight him or otherwise Johan [Colenbrander] and others would not come in with their wives: and he would not mind if the white men occupied the country all round him as long as they left him unmolested here in his own Territory." It may be that the king thought that raiding the Shona was no longer feasible after the Portuguese had provided them with guns in 1889, and the English had occupied the country in 1890; but most of his subjects seem to have thought otherwise. To the ears of a predatory nation this was strange language.[7]

Three months after Makwekwe's plea, Moffat, while travelling through the country, met a detachment of the Imbizo regiment, "and they behaved with the greatest insolence to me personally, shaking their clubs and cursing me . . . I hear that the Mbizo have lately been acting in the same manner to other white men, and that they are longing for a collision."[8]

If the regiments were not to get out of hand they had to be kept occupied, if not in military operations then at least in preparation for them. By the end of 1890 it had become difficult to send impis in any direction without running into the white man. All things considered, however, there was most to be said for the northwest. The Barotse were traditional enemies, the Lochner concession had not yet been acted upon, it was desirable to find out what the Company was up to in that region, and perhaps the policy of keeping the Batoka plateau empty and available was becoming increasingly relevant.

On 29 April 1891 an impi was accordingly dispatched in that direction. Though there was general eagerness to take part, no crack regiments were allowed to join the expedition, which was composed of *amahole* only. Perhaps it was thought that the hard core of the army might at any moment be needed nearer home. More probably, Lobengula did not at this time want a serious clash with Lewanika, the Company's new protégé, which the battle-hardened *abezansi* might have provoked. The impi was said to have strict instructions not to interfere with any white men. Result: some three months later it returned with no fanfare and, as far as anyone could observe, no large booty. Moffat put it down as a failure.[9] If its real purpose was reconnaissance it may have been a success.

In 1892 the troops were kept busy in a different way. About the end of March Lobengula set out for the northeast with about two thousand men. Colenbrander specified, in the king's party, five regiments—Imbizo, Bulawayo, Hlambalaji, Ingubo, and Intemba. He speculated on the king's purpose:

to prevent the extension of prospectors from Mashonaland westwards, or he may mean it as a blind for his own nation and make them believe that he has done and is doing all he can to prevent the white man spreading over his country—or he has taken it into his head to be personally at the Insuka regiment's quarters, perhaps with the idea of punishing them, for the latter have been misbehaving and are very disobedient.

Later, having followed the expedition, Colenbrander reverted to the second of these possible motives, namely "that the King has intentionally come for this outing, and will make it do instead of the usual winter war-path for the nation, as it keeps the tribe very busy going to and fro for food, etc."

Camping on the Gwelo river, Lobengula proceeded to place four regiments (from north to south: Umcijo, Ihlati, Amaveni, and the "disobedient" Insuka), at fifteen to thirty-mile intervals, as a kind of border defence.[10]

A fortnight before Colenbrander's second report, Captain Lendy with two policemen had reached Lobengula's encampment on a reconnaissance patrol from Salisbury. The purpose of the patrol was to discover the king's position and intention, but it was disguised as a border inspection to ensure that no white men strayed into Matabeleland. After crossing the Que Que river and reaching the first Ndebele kraals, Lendy reported his presence and asked to be taken to Lobengula.

> April 16th. Started at daybreak and rode straight to the King's camp, about 12 miles away. On entering the camp, the Natives naturally all turned out and passed sundry remarks about the white soldiers and what they wanted. The several Indunas, however, protected us from molestation and we were conducted to the King's Kraal, situated in the centre of some 10 or so other kraals, occupied by, I should say, some 1,500 to 2,000 of his followers. The King then asked me my business, and I repeated what I had told Quasa Quasa, adding that, having heard of his close vicinity, I thought he would not have liked me to have ridden away without seeing him. From what followed, I drew the conclusion that he was friendly disposed, and that I must not give him cause to suspect my presence in the country to be for any other reason than what I had said. During the interview the King was surrounded by some of his principal Indunas. The King gave us meat and beer and we were dismissed for that day.

On the following days the good relations were maintained. The king "expressed himself as well pleased"; "he behaved in the most friendly manner possible, repeatedly requesting me to drink beer out of his own cup, and shaking hands on each occasion." Presents were exchanged, including a sporting rifle for the king's son. "When we were not actually in the King's presence we were living in the midst of his men, and on no single occasion were we subject to ill-treatment or insult." Lobengula did not appear to be losing his grip.[11]

The appearance may have been deceptive. A few weeks later there was a great "smelling out" in Bulawayo, as a result of which the hereditary regent, Mhlaba, was strangled on 5 June and his brother Sidlodlo shot the next day. The Imbizo regiment was then turned loose to kill the wives and children of the two men, to capture their cattle and slaves, and even to stone their dogs to death. The excuse for these proceedings was that the men had inherited from

229 Jameson's War, I

their father Mncumbate a powerful medicine, which being passed on from fathers to children could be got rid of only by destroying the whole family. By means of this they "drugged the Queens, and raped them afterwards (of course the Queens are never to blame)." Having some forewarning, "poor old Umhlaba had his town shifted from the neighbourhood of the Queens, but all for no good."

Moffat's nephew, Robert Vavasseur, camped on the Khami river near Mhlaba's kraal, was a close observer of some of the events. While the trial was proceeding in Bulawayo, two of Mhlaba's sons were sitting with their father. When the sentence was pronounced on the father, the sons jumped up and made a dash for safety. One was caught as he tried to scale a fence, but the other, Ntenende, got away—in the circumstances an almost incredible escape. Late that night he reached the family kraal "and told the people to scoot," which they did; a few who foolishly returned later were killed. The butchery extended far beyond Mhlaba's family. It was said to have included three or four of the king's brothers. The Imbizo regiment was given its fill of blood. But Mhlaba's son and brother, Ntenende and Mnyenyezi, having escaped from the country, lived to fight another day—and not on Lobengula's side.[12]

It is hardly necessary to argue that these murders were not committed solely, or at all, to protect the virtue of the queens. "Smellings out" invariably resulted in charges of witchcraft, which, almost invariably, were a mere cover for reasons of state. One such reason, which may be mentioned simply as background, is that in 1870 Mhlaba had been one of the envoys sent to Natal to find and identify Nkulumane. They had not found him, but may have been suspected of gathering more information than it was good for loyal subjects to know. Yet at that time and for twenty-two years afterwards Mhlaba had been a strong supporter of Lobengula. It is hard to believe that the massacre of 1892 was merely the king's delayed reaction to a suspicion aroused in 1870, but two Ndebele witnesses have offered a plausible connection between the succession crisis and the killing. Lobengula was said to have complained that Mhlaba (and/or his father before him) had not given him, Lobengula, "full power." His wife Xwaijilile had not borne him a son, and he suffered from gout. Mhlaba admitted that he had (on instructions from Mncumbate) withheld "full power" from Lobengula, because Nkulumane might at any time return. The king associated this offence with Mncumbate's effort to find Nkulumane; so the regent family was punished for treason. The great victim of 1889, Lotshe, had narrowly missed being one of the envoys to Natal in 1870, and had commanded a disastrous expedition in 1885. The reason for Lotshe's execution, however, was clearly that he was the chief advocate of concessions to the white men, and of friendly relations with them. Mhlaba's political position is less clear. He was never reported as taking a strong stand in controversial matters, but as the most eminent subject in the land he would naturally have belonged to the class of "older men" who were always said to support the king in his resistance to the "hawks." Circumstantial evidence points in the same direction. At the end of 1890, when Lobengula proposed to send Major Maxwell and Mshete with a message to Loch, Maxwell wrote: "Let him do so, but send one high man also, *Mhlaba*." Colenbrander, reporting the judicial murder, said that "the best man in the country, and I should say the most harmless, was smelt out by these devils." A white man and company representative would have had his reasons for making this assessment. Mhlaba was probably known to the young firebrands as a key member of the peace party.[13]

Soon after the killings the king's policy took what proved to be a fatal turn towards confrontation with the whites. If this is the right explanation, Lobengula's grip was not as firm as it had seemed. He was forced to throw victims to the wolves, and the event could have had a wonderful effect on the political opinions of the surviving indunas.

What followed was a series of forcible interventions in Mashonaland. Since the arrival of the Pioneer Column there had been only one such irruption, and that in an area where there were very few whites. In November 1891 the Chief Nemakonde (Lomagundi), whose district still bears his name, was visited by some of Lobengula's men. They wanted to know why he had taken presents from the English and the Portuguese, shown the English where to dig for gold, and given them guides to lead them to the Zambezi—all this in Lobengula's country, and without asking for his permission. Nemakonde's failure in 1891 to pay his usual annual tribute was another offence, which had drawn attention to his disloyalty. The chief wanted to delay his reply till the next morning, but in the morning the Ndebele patrol shot him and three of his indunas. This was merely Ndebele "law and order" in the old style, but Jameson thought it inappropriate in the new circumstances. To his remonstrance Lobengula replied: "I sent a lot of my men to go and tell Lomogunda to ask you and the white people why you were there and what you were doing. He sent word back to me that he refused to deliver my message and that he was not my dog or (ghole) slave. That is why I sent some men in to go and kill him. Lomogunda belongs to me. Does the country belong to Lomogunda?"[14]

That was the key question. The country belonged to Lobengula. If it had not, the Rudd Concession would have had no force in it. Lobengula had given to Rudd the mineral rights, and to Lippert the right to lay out, grant, and lease farms and townships *on behalf of the king*. Neither concession had given away the land itself or the sovereignty over it. Lobengula could not admit that his authority over his Shona subjects had been in the least affected either by the concessions or by the occupation. The killing of Nemakonde drew attention to this fact.

As far as northern Mashonaland was concerned, this was not only the first such disciplinary action after the arrival of the Pioneers but also the last. The king had made his point. Other killings were left to the Company, though not without occasional protests from him. His policy being to keep the peace as far as possible, his usual practice was to assert his rights in more peaceful ways. A few days after the Pioneers had reached Fort Salisbury he sent James Dawson there to mark out some mining claims for him. Colquhoun was not asked for these; he was merely to be informed what claims the king had decided to reserve for himself: "I hereby instruct him [Dawson] to proceed with my servant Indabambi to mark out several pieces of ground, both reef and alluvial, including the reefs on the Umfuli and Zimbo Rivers, which were prospected by Dawson in 1876, and also a certain extent of alluvial ground on the Mazoe and its tributaries." Colquhoun, protesting to Dawson that he could not acknowledge the king's right to reserve claims for himself, nevertheless "offered" him forty claims on the Lower Umfuli (reef) and two on the Mazoe (alluvial). The Company was "anxious to meet the chief's wishes."

While Lobengula tried to intervene in Mashonaland as a capitalist, many of his subjects began to go there as workers. In February 1891 Moffat reported that they were going in considerable numbers, but that most, if not all, of them were *amahole*—the servile class, of Shona origin. By November the acting administrator in Salisbury was writing favourably of these "Matabeles" and wanting more to come. A year earlier, Moffat was said to have expected that "this nation [would] be absorbed from natives going to work in Mashonaland and finding themselves better off with the white men than under the present King's régime." Moffat was not the only one who saw the matter in this light. Those who wanted to be "better off with the white men" were even more attracted by Johannesburg than by Mashonaland, and in September 1891 Lobengula was receiving complaints from his subjects about the departure of their "boys" in that direction. The country, it was said, was being drained of young men—meaning, of course, men of the labouring class.[15]

Peace could be bought at too high a price. The men of the regiments could not give up either their raiding grounds or their servants; the king could not permit a restriction of his sovereignty. For his policy in these circumstances there was a precedent—of a kind, and not quite analogous—on his southwestern border. Kgama, he had said, was only a slave of Mzilikazi and had no country. Thus there was no southwestern border; the king's writ must run in Palapye as it did in Bulawayo. For practical purposes, however, the British protectorate made a boundary necessary, and the Motloutsi had long been accepted by Lobengula as the dividing line. As Kgama insisted on the Shashi, even that was recognized in so far as the Disputed Territory was allowed to remain a no-man's-land.

An eastern border came into existence in the same fashion. The initiative was taken by Colquhoun, who within a few months of the occupation was instructing prospectors not to go south of the Umsweswe river, "to avert chance of collision or complications." The question was inseparable from another, namely the nature and basis of the Company's authority in the occupied area, which was a constant preoccupation of the high commissioner and the Colonial

Office. In the middle of 1891 Loch addressed some questions about this to Moffat, who replied at first that the boundary ought not to be defined. A few days later, after a conversation with Lobengula, he changed his mind: there should be a clear boundary between Matabeleland and Mashonaland.

In an ambiguous way, the king agreed. If he protested against the movement of prospectors too far to the west (e.g., in October 1891 to the Que Que), some kind of border was implied. In November 1891 he appeared to place it at the Umfuli. At the same time Jameson was reprimanding men who had gone west of the Lundi. A year later he appears to have fixed the line, to the west of Fort Victoria, at the Shashe, from which it followed the flow of the water into the Tokwe and from that into the Lundi. Further north the boundary in Jameson's mind was a line from the Shashe to the Umniati where the gap between them was narrowest, and then the Umniati for the rest of its course. The Umfuli, with mining operations on both banks, would not do; but there had been an advance from the earlier limit of the Umsweswe. Such was Jameson's "border agreed upon between the king and myself."[16] The king's "agreement" to this seems to have been of the same order as his "giving the road" in 1890; Jameson had a way of stretching the meaning of the king's words.

Whatever its basis, the border stopped short of the country actually occupied by the Ndebele. The Shona population extended well to the west of the Shashe and Tokwe. When Lendy visited Lobengula's encampment in April 1892 he had crossed the Que Que before reaching the first Ndebele kraals. To Lobengula and his army this fact had only a limited relevance. Foreign intrusion into the heartland was certainly more offensive than the occupation of mere raiding grounds. Prospectors, traders, and others who wandered too far west were given rough treatment by Ndebele patrols, as well as reprimand from Salisbury. No white man was interfered with east of Jameson's line; nor, apart from the punishment of Nemakonde, any black man. But in thus exercising restraint, Lobengula was only recognizing the boundary *de facto*; he had not abated his claim to Mashonaland one jot. Does the country belong to Lomogunda?

Even if this disagreement in principle had been composed, there remained an even more difficult conflict of jurisdiction. When the road and, from the beginning of 1892, the telegraph line from Fort Victoria to Tuli and the south crossed the Tokwe, they crossed the "border" into what by Jameson's admission was Matabeleland. The safety of the route was vital to the Company and its settlers, but who was to ensure it? In principle, Lobengula; by the law of self-preservation, the Company. Disagreement about this was to be a factor in the coming trouble.

It is surely significant that the king's policy of keeping his forces west of the border and forbidding them to interfere with white men was abandoned soon after the great smelling-out of June 1892. That event and the change of policy appear to have a common cause: pressure on Lobengula by his warriors, which had reached the point where he had, if only for his own safety, to throw some sops to them.

The first sign of the change came in August. An impi passed through the camp of the Mashonaland Agency, between Fort Victoria and the border, probably in that month. The Shona workers at the camp were terrified, though not actually molested, but there appears to have been a raid on their homes, when women and children were killed. Parties from the same or another impi were reported elsewhere in the Victoria district. Their purpose—"collecting such tribute as was due to Lobengula prior to the white occupation of the Country"—was ominous. The collecting of all such arrears would be a large and widespread operation. A few days after this report two hundred Ndebele stopped a traveller, Mr. Hill, on the road from Tuli twelve miles north of the Nuanetsi and took his rifles from him. A few weeks later the post cart was robbed between Victoria and Charter, but it could not be proved that the culprits were Ndebele. A month later still, a transport rider was ill-treated and robbed of all his goods on the road between the Lundi and the Nuanetsi.[17]

These incidents were pin-pricks without serious consequences. In December 1892 a complication was introduced, not by the Ndebele but by some of their Kalaka tributaries. The telegraph wire running across the country, and offering so much material for personal adornment, tempted them irresistibly. Near the Lundi river a length of it was cut and removed. The officer sent to investigate was told by the people of the neighbouring kraals that the wire-cutters were a party of Ndebele under two indunas who were named. Jameson took this news so seriously that he not only wrote to Lobengula about it, but had the letter conveyed by Captain Lendy and an escort. Lobengula was asked to make an enquiry; if the report was correct, "I would ask you to inflict the most severe punishment on these men." Most of Jameson's letter was a lecture on the importance of Lobengula's keeping his men on his side of the border (not that it had been crossed in this instance) and avoiding the chance of a collision.

While Lendy was still in Bulawayo, however, he received a message from Jameson to say that the people at the scene of the wire-cutting had admitted that they, and not the Ndebele, had done it. The king was pleased, and stressed the point to Lendy: his people were always being falsely accused of depredations which were actually committed by "the Amaholis." Lendy replied that "we shall on future occasions endeavour to catch and severely punish offenders ourselves."

A "future occasion" was indeed at hand. About 1 May 1893 the wire was cut again; five hundred yards of it disappeared without trace. The offending kraal was found to be that of a petty chief called Khokhomere, who was given the alternatives of surrendering the culprits or paying a fine in cattle. He paid the fine, but omitted to mention that the cattle belonged to Lobengula. Reporting the event to his immediate overlord Chitawudze, he complained that the Company's officers had seized the cattle although told that they were the king's.

Chitawudze reported to Bulawayo accordingly, and, as Colenbrander wrote to Jameson, there was now "the devil to pay." Lobengula wrote hotly: "Why should you seize my cattle—did I cut your wires? . . . I also wish you to know that my people begged and prayed of me to be allowed to go and fetch the cattle, but I would not allow it and prefer settling these matters amicably." Jameson lost no time in sending the cattle to Tuli, for Lobengula's men to collect them there.[18]

The telegraph wire incidents were provocations—though unintentional—by Jameson; the next provocation came, or appeared to come, from the king. The original offenders indeed were Shona from the neighbourhood of Fort Victoria, who stole cattle from other Shona who were Ndebele tributaries. These retaliated against Chief Bere, but the latter was protected by the Company's police. Thus a complaint reached Lobengula, who sent a small party of some seventy men to chastise the offenders. Some men of Bere's kraal were killed, and some women, children, and cattle carried off; but the mission was only partly accomplished. Lendy rode out, came up with the raiders, learned of their instructions and purpose, and expressed himself satisfied. He gave the induna in charge a letter to the king, warning him in polite language to watch his step.[19]

So far, each provocative incident had been accepted meekly, or explained away, or neutralized by compensation and apology. Now the limit of compromise had been reached; the next incident would light a fuse destined to burn all the way to Bulawayo. Lobengula gave the provocation and his enemies launched the war. It would be unprofitable to try to apportion the blame between the two sets of invaders, the men of the stabbing spear and the men of the machine-gun. The important question to answer is a different one: who, on the company's side, made the decision for war, when, and why? More specifically: was the decision made by Jameson, Rhodes, or the directors in London? Was it made before or after the "Victoria incident" now to be described? Above all, was it based on local Mashonaland considerations, or on the financial difficulties and needs of the Company?[20]

Stafford Glass has shown convincingly that up to the middle of July 1893 Jameson—as administrator, the supreme authority in Mashonaland—was determined to remain at peace with Lobengula. While insisting that the "border" be respected by both sides, he responded to each successive provocation by what the settler press called "a timorous remonstrance." Looking at the contrast between this and the firm hand with which the Shona were held down, the same press complained of the Company's "present policy of bullying the weak and cringing to the powerful." Jameson seems to have thought that he had no choice. The Company could not afford a war at that time. Even on 9 July, when the big impi was on the rampage round Fort Victoria, Jameson urged Lendy to seek a peaceful solution. Though fighting might in the end be necessary, "from a financial point of view it would throw the country back till God knows when."[21]

The case is not altered by the evidence that the idea of an inevitable "show-down" with Lobengula had long been entertained in Company and settler circles. The abortive plan of a "sudden assault" on the Ndebele continued to be talked about after the peaceful invasion had succeeded. Within the first few months of the occupation of Mashonaland Maxwell, in Bulawayo, reported on several occasions that Lobengula's days appeared to be numbered: "they intend snuffing him out next winter." According to Matabele Wilson, "Moffat and I are of the same opinion that nothing will ever be done in Matabeleland until the people are put down." By June 1891 Moffat had slightly modified this view:

> I am sorry to see an evident disintegration, a lapse of discipline as well as character. Even in such matters as personal cleanliness the people have woefully degenerated. These things make it more possible that a collision may take place, the more turbulent spirits getting out of control; but they will also tell in favour of our people, who will thus have a disorganized rabble to deal with, more half hearted and disorganized every year. The possibility of a Matabele attack must not be entirely dismissed, though there is nothing at present actually pointing towards it.

By November Moffat's assessment was different again: "the longer a row with the Matabele is staved off, the better it will be for us. I go further than this, and say that there is no need for a row and that, if it comes, it will probably be provoked by ourselves."[22]

When these words were written, Jameson had recently become administrator. His views, like Moffat's, had changed. As the years passed without serious trouble he came to believe in peaceful coexistence with the Ndebele, at least in the immediate future. The reduction of the Company's police force, in 1892, from 700 to 40 is perhaps the strongest evidence of this belief. Settlers enrolled in a "burgher force," the only remaining line of defence, were not then thought capable of conquering Matabeleland. What changed Jameson's mind back to that conquest was the "Victoria incident."

The origin and the course of this event are difficult to trace, for the usual reasons: the black and the white witnesses disagree at many points; the white evidence was recorded at the time, or soon afterwards; some black evidence was recorded then too, but by white men; some in 1937-40 by R. Foster Windram, who was himself completely objective—but he was recording old men's memories, which are notoriously subject to the ravages of time.

Out of this confusion some facts emerge. There was a second cattle-rustling incident. Some of the Shona living on the white side of the so-called boundary stole cattle from the other side; these had been in the care of *amahole* herdsmen, but belonged to the Ndebele of the Enxa regiment. On the death of the commander of that regiment his son, Mgandane Dlodlo, had been passed over for the command because of his youth, but it was he who complained to the king about the theft of the cattle. What is not certain, but was asserted many years later by several Ndebele, is that the theft of the cattle was a "put-up job"—the whites persuading the *amahole* herdsmen to drive them across the border so as to provoke an attack by Lobengula. There are several reasons for rejecting this story.

The theft, however, could not be overlooked. Failure to punish the thieves and recover the cattle would mean a collapse of law and order such as no undefeated people could tolerate. Yet the decision to act was a hard one for Lobengula to make. For three days, Matabele Wilson reported, the matter was debated in a great indaba: "once or twice I noticed that the king was sitting inside the wagon, with his head in his hands, and his elbows resting on the wagon box, looking somewhat anxious." As Colenbrander summarized the decision, the force sent in June to punish Bere and his people for the theft of cattle "did not quite succeed. The King has therefore decided to send a *large* force to punish 'Bere' or 'Bele' *and others* for their misdeeds (and I fancy he will go for the recent wire-cutters also)." The danger in this course was the greater in that the impi was ordered not to bring back any slaves, but "to sweep them off the face of the earth," as the king's father of blessed memory would have done. This information was given to Wilson and Fairbairn by Lobengula's brother Mlagela.

The theft had been reported by Mgandane, whose regiment had owned the cattle. But the impi now dispatched was under the command of an older induna, Manyewu Ndiweni. It consisted of three regiments—Mhlahlandlela (his own), Enxa (Mgandane's), and Insuka—and parts of eight others, together with about a thousand *amahole* who were picked up along the way. Thus Mgandane had many reasons to be resentful; he was an angry young man.

According to several witnesses, the expedition now sent was "not a raid" but a mere police operation to recover stolen goods. If the distinction was drawn by the king it was not accepted by Mgandane, who wore in his headgear the white ostrich feathers that were the badge of the raider.

Lobengula tried desperately to have the best of both worlds. He agreed to the dispatch of the impi (whatever its mission might be called) and appointed Manyewu and not Mgandane to command it, but was equally resolved to keep the peace with the whites. On 28 June he dictated to Dawson a letter to be sent to Lendy at Fort Victoria:

> Sir,—an impi is at present leaving this neighbourhood for the purpose of punishing some of Lo Bengula's people who have lately raided some of his own cattle. The impi in its progress will probably come across some white men, who are asked to understand that it has nothing whatever to do with them. They are likewise asked not to oppose the impi in its progress. Also, if the people who have committed the offence

have taken refuge among the white men they are asked to give them up for punishment.—Written at Lo Bengula's request by J.W. Dawson.

The next day, 29 June, Colenbrander took down three letters at the king's dictation—to Moffat at Palapye, to Jameson at Fort Salisbury, and another to Lendy. These three were taken by runners to Palapye, whence those for Jameson and Lendy were to be forwarded by telegraph. All the letters conveyed the same message: the quarrel was not with the whites, they would not be harmed, but they must not interfere with the impi and must not shelter its intended victims.

The letter written by Dawson was given to "a boy that used to work for the whites called B'shulungu (a Matabele) to take to Victoria." So Wilson reported, and he was in a position to see what happened; but all the old men giving evidence in 1937 stated that the letter was given to the two indunas, and it seems at first to have been in the possession of Mgandane. The "boy" may have been a servant in attendance on one of the leaders. Again, there is general agreement that at some point Manyewu took the letter from Mgandane in order to deliver it more quickly; Manyewu was riding a horse. There is no doubt that the king had given the most emphatic orders that the letter was to be delivered before any punitive operations were begun. Manyewu, probably deliberately, disobeyed this order. None of Lobengula's letters served its purpose; they all arrived after the attack.[23]

On 9 July Charles Vigers, the mining commissioner, and Lieutenant Weir of the police were riding about three miles from Fort Victoria. There they met a mob of frightened Shona who announced that the Ndebele impi was approaching. The two white men soon got impressive confirmation of this news: the sight of some 3,500 warriors advancing on Fort Victoria. By the time the two riders got back to the township two hundred of the attackers were already in it, near the hospital, while others, close to the church, had killed the clergyman's house-boy. At three o'clock the clergyman, while conducting Sunday School, found the "church and parsonage surrounded by an impi of Matabele, who were on all sides massacring the Mashonas without mercy, simply out of thirst for blood."

Lendy reported at once, by telegraph, to Jameson in Salisbury. On the following day, the 10th, the various messages from Lobengula were received. Lendy went out with a patrol to find the induna who was said to be bringing a letter. At the same time this induna, Manyewu himself, came into the township with twelve men to deliver it. All Ndebele witnesses agree that Manyewu was responsible for withholding the letter and turning the recovery operation into a murderous raid. Moreover he compounded this offence, when challenged by the whites, by casting the blame on Mgandane. In the absence of Lendy, Vigers read the letter, and was thus faced with the demand to hand over the Shona refugees to their executioners. He seems to have wired to Jameson for instructions, and received the reply: "You can give up nothing. On Lendy's arrival the induna can lay his complaint against [sic—before?] him as a magistrate."

Vigers had thus to detain Manyewu and his men until Lendy returned. Among other ways of passing the time he thought of showing the visitors the guns of the fort. While inspecting the guns they were able to look into the fort, where they saw something more interesting: the huddled mass of Shona men, women, and children who had taken shelter there. When Lendy arrived at four o'clock Manyewu demanded that these refugees be handed over to him. He would not, he said, kill them in the river and pollute the water, but would have them dispatched in the bush. The impi would then retire and bother the white men no more.

Even without Jameson's telegram to Vigers, Lendy could hardly have complied with the demand. It was not that he was squeamish. His own record, as we shall see, was somewhat bloodstained. But failure to protect the Shona from their former masters and butchers would have dried up the source of labour in Mashonaland absolutely and at once. Even Lendy would have understood, also, that giving up the refugees to execution would have damaged the Company's reputation in England seriously, if not fatally. His reply to Manyewu was, therefore: "If you have any charge to make against these people, I will hear it as a magistrate, and if I find your charges correct I will hand them over to you to be dealt with; but you must point out to me the men you charge. I will not give up the women and children, as they have not committed any crimes." Manyewu was astonished. The king had handed wrongdoers over to the Company for punishment; why should not the Company reciprocate? He did not specify any wrongdoers who had been handed over; perhaps he was referring merely to Lobengula's tolerance of the Company's activities in Mashonaland. He departed in anger.[24]

After the initial irruption the impi left the white men's village alone. Its attention was concentrated on the kraals and farms of the surrounding countryside. Pillars of smoke by day and of fire by night signalled the destruction being visited on the so-called cattle-thieves. The inhabitants fled to the granite fastnesses that were their traditional refuge, but many failed to reach safety in time. In one case a girl was left sitting on a rock to distract the assailants while others made their escape. Labourers on farms and mines fled with the rest, but some were caught and dispatched before the eyes of their employers.

The horrified observers of these events may have exaggerated the extent of the killing. Four hundred people were said to have been killed, and the roads to be strewn with their corpses. The evidence about this, and about the destruction of white men's farms, is conflicting. It cannot be disputed, however, that there was a general destruction of Shona kraals, whose inhabitants lost all that they possessed; that there was a good deal of bloodshed; and that the work of mines and farms ceased. The black invaders had offered the white ones a challenge which they could not overlook.

Yet Jameson, in his peaceful quarters at Fort Salisbury, still thought that the dispute could be settled amicably. The opening sentence of his telegram to Cape Town on 10 July set the tone for his messages for the next week: "Exaggerated reports about Matabele near Victoria sure to reach Colony; so that you may contradict, give you full text." The "text" that followed was the message just received from Lobengula, showing that the whites had nothing to fear. Then Jameson gave, in full, his own reply to the king. The gist of this was that while the white men "had nothing to do with his punishing his own Maholis," the Ndebele "are not allowed to cross the border agreed upon between us." Jameson had heard that the border had indeed been crossed, kraals burnt, people killed, and cattle belonging to the white men or the government taken. Those cattle must be returned and the impi must retire across the border at once, or else it would be forced to do so. Jameson did not expect to resort to force. "The Victoria people naturally have got the jumps," he reported to Rutherfoord Harris; Lendy was told to get rid of the impi "without any collision, which I feel sure he can do."

As soon as the news of the attack reached Cape Town, the high commissioner began to bombard Lobengula with telegrams. He thought the king would take more notice of him than of the Company's men. Loch's messages were expressed in language which, among civilized powers, is not used until the resources of diplomacy are almost exhausted:

> These acts on the part of your people cannot be permitted to continue; they will bring upon you the punishment that befell Cetewayo and his people. I wish to control the anger of the white people, but when aroused in just indignation I shall find it difficult to restrain them, nor shall I say to them "stop" unless you at once withdraw your impis and punish the indunas who have brought this trouble on you and your people . . . Dr. Jameson . . . sent forward only a mere handful of white men who charged and scattered your impi like chaff is blown before the wind, and chased them for miles, killing more than double their own number. Be warned in time.

This is to anticipate—we have not yet come to the scattering of the impi like chaff before the wind—but the important point is the menacing language in which all Loch's messages after 9 July were expressed.

Lobengula was surprised. He had expected the white men to be sensitive to threats to their own lives or property, and had taken pains to avoid threatening them. In his realistic moments he knew too, that "the whites will say that I am cruel to my subjects." Yet he seems to have persuaded himself that they would not make a serious issue of this. "I have received your message," he wrote to Moffat on 6 July, "and am pleased to be able to inform you that I had the induna (who I consider a very trustworthy man) closeted with me for two full days, drumming into his head to be very careful not to molest any white men or take their property . . . or should . . . the natives who I sent to punish seek protection from them, to go himself to the white people and ask them to give them up." Later he referred to the wire-cutting: "I am well aware that it is a serious matter cutting and carrying away the telegraph wire, as it is the white man's mouth, but I have no doubt you will hear more of this." No doubt, because his impi was at that moment "going for the recent wire-cutters."

To Jameson's remonstrance the king replied humbly and almost penitently:

> You are quite right, your people would probably get exasperated at the behaviour of some of my young men, and trouble would come of it . . . I hope, however, that my Indunas will have restored to you the captured cattle ere this. I am also very glad indeed that you asked Captain Lendy to order my people back. I acknowledge that I was wrong in sending my impi so close to the white people, but it was nevertheless necessary that I should punish these Maholies for cattle stealing and other offences.

He had not yet heard that Lendy had refused to give up the refugees in the fort. Those "maholis" belonged to the king ("Are the Amaholis then yours?"); there would be trouble when it was known that Lendy was appropriating the king's property. Moreover, when the white men struck back, as they were about to do, their motive was to stop the killing, even more than to recover lost property which Lobengula would have restored anyway. All his letters emphasized the orders to Manyewu to leave the whites alone, but to go to them in person to ask for the surrender of refugees. The obvious deduction is the king's belief that the whites would make no difficulty about this. Here was his great miscalculation.[25]

After a few days of the grim news from Fort Victoria, Jameson had to go there to see for himself. On 13 July he left Salisbury on horseback. A few miles out of Victoria he transferred to Philip Bourchier Wrey's mule cart, and for the rest of the way was regaled with first-hand stories of the recent events. As they approached the village Jameson got the evidence for himself. He arrived at Fort Victoria on the 17th.

A small patrol was immediately sent out to convey a message to Manyewu: he and his colleague Mgandane were to come in the next day for an indaba with the administrator. By mid-morning on the 18th, there being no sign of them, Jameson sent off one of his confident telegrams to Loch: "The Indunas have failed to appear: probably frightened." He would send out a mounted party, the impi would retreat, and "it will only be a local matter." Hardly had the telegram gone when a formidable Ndebele party was seen approaching. With some difficulty they were persuaded to lay down their arms. Manyewu, Mgandane, and some fifty warriors then came up to the gate of the fort and squatted on the ground, facing Jameson seated in his chair. The walls of the fort were crowded with white men, straining to hear every word of the discussion.

"Doctela," though still apparently determined on amicable diplomacy with Lobengula, took a stern line with the men in front of him: "What do you mean by coming here and doing what you have done?" They came by the king's command, said Manyewu. After some more talk Jameson gave his decision: the impi must depart for the "border" within an hour, or would be driven out by force. What did an hour mean? There was some pointing to different positions of the sun. To the question, where was the border?, Jameson's brusque answer was "Tell him he knows."

It was during this discussion that Manyewu pointed out Mgandane (with the white ostrich feathers) as the man responsible for the killing and for withholding the letter. Mgandane is said to have been truculent and insolent, which in the circumstances would not be surprising. When asked by Jameson whether his young men had got out of hand, Manyewu replied that they had. The administrator accordingly told Manyewu to depart with the men who obeyed him; for the rest, "leave your young men to me and I will deal with them."

The indaba broke up about 12.30. The white men went to lunch; Manyewu returned to Makohori's kraal, some ten miles north of the village, to prepare to withdraw the impi; Mgandane, muttering, "We will be driven across," or words to that effect, moved off with other plans in mind.[26] The reminiscences of Hobasi Khumalo notwithstanding, we can be sure that Mgandane was not killed as he was leaving the indaba.

The irruption of 9 July had caused the whole white population of the district to move into the village, where a laager was formed against the wall of the fort. About four hundred white men had assembled there, and were formed into two units, the Victoria Rangers and the Victoria Burghers. All were well armed. The limiting factor was the shortage of horses, of which there were only about fifty fit for service.[27]

Lendy, under instructions from Jameson, recruited a party of about forty— as many as could be mounted—which fell in after lunch and rode away about 2.30. "I don't want them to think this is merely a threat," Jameson told Lendy; "they have had a week of threats already, with very bad results. Ride off in the direction they have gone, towards Magomoli's kraal. If you find they are not moving off, drive them as you heard me tell Manyow I would, and if they resist and attack you, shoot them."

There is no record that either Jameson or Lendy had Mgandane particularly in mind, but the Ndebele witnesses agree that the patrol intended to "get" him. Their accounts differ widely over such details as time and distance, and there are important and irreconcilable differences between them and the official report on the circumstances of the encounter. According to the latter, the result of an enquiry in 1894, the advance guard of the patrol, under Sergeant Kennelly, sighted a party of fifty to eighty Ndebele three or four miles from the fort. These were Mgandane and his followers, carrying loads of grain and driving cattle before them. Instead of submitting to Jameson's order they had raided Mazaviri's kraal (west of Fort Victoria) and were now carrying off their loot—not towards the "border" but in a *northeasterly* direction. One of the advance guard rode back to Lendy with this news. Lendy replied with the order, which was taken to the advance guard, "commence firing." Kennelly fired a shot in the air, after which the firing became general. The Ndebele did not shoot back, but ran. Some of them—probably about nine, including Mgandane himself—were killed. Lendy's patrol went forward to Makombe's kraal, then being besieged by another Ndebele party, which was driven off. ("Come out," they had shouted to the Shona villagers, "we want to kill you.") The patrol then broke off the action and returned to Fort Victoria.

Most of these details are consistent with the evidence given by Ndebele survivors in 1937-40, at any rate at the points where those witnesses were agreed. But there are important exceptions. According to this evidence, the patrol was at first not shooting to kill. (Siyatsha: "They shot wide of them." Ginyilitshe: "The Europeans were firing in the air.") When they saw Mgandane, who was recognized by his ostrich feathers, "they talked to him in a language he did not understand. He was sitting down when they came up, and they told him to stand up, and they shot him in the pit of the stomach or the heart [the witness indicated the position described] when he stood up." Though this account has variants—as for instance that Mgandane was not sitting but walking—there is universal agreement that Mgandane was the specific victim they were looking for and that he was shot deliberately. There is agreement also that either one or two others were shot, making a total of two or three, not nine. There is no doubt that after his death, Mgandane's headring was removed and that his genitals and possibly other parts of his body were cut off.

This last operation would have a meaning in the context of African—e.g., Shona—custom, but none whatever in a European context. Though the Ndebele witnesses were sure that it had been done by the Europeans, it is likely that their Shona allies were the culprits, and also that it was the Shona who raised the death toll above the two or three that Lendy's patrol certainly accounted for. Mpagama testified that "only two people were killed by the white people; but a lot of people were killed by the Mashonas. The Mashonas waited for them in a narrow defile in the hills, and they shot them as they passed through."

After this exploit the patrol returned to Fort Victoria, and Lendy reported to Jameson "that on the edge of the commonage he had come across about 300 of the Matabele, with Umgandan amongst them; that Sergeant Fitzgerald had been fired upon, but had not been hit; that he then ordered his men to charge and then fire; that about thirty natives were killed; and that he had then ordered the retire, as it was getting towards sundown."[28]

One may speculate on Lendy's reasons for telling so many lies. There is no need to speculate on the consequences. Because Lendy's version of the event was believed by Jameson, Loch, and the Colonial Office, his action was approved. If it had been known that Lendy's order to fire had been unprovoked, the official reaction would have been different, as Graham's minute shows: "After the 'Ngomo atrocities', when Captain Lendy killed 23 Mashonas, it was thought here that the Company should get rid of such a fire-eater . . . If happily this affair has no serious consequences, it will not be thanks to Captain Lendy, who will sooner or later raise indignation in this country over more Mashona atrocities, or excite Lobengula's 'young men' to an attack in force." Add to this the doubts in the Colonial Office about the supposed "border," on which Jameson's whole case depended, and it appears that the official scales could very easily have been tipped against him and Lendy. "I have never seen anything in our correspondence," Sydney Olivier noted, "of the nature of an undertaking on Lo Ben's part to keep within any line." His colleagues agreed. If there was no border and no abdication of sovereignty, the impis had the same right (such as it was) to massacre in Fort Victoria as in Bulawayo.[29]

The time was past, however, for juridical subtleties. When the sun set on 18 July Jameson had experienced, apparently in a few hours, a complete change of heart. No doubt new thoughts had been gestating in his mind under the influence of his impressions of the last twenty-four hours: smoking ruins, blood, abandoned farms and mines, the bellicose spirit of the whites. At a public meeting on the 15th the demand had been made: "Dr. Jameson must settle the Matabele question at once, now and forever." The impressions of the indaba may have contributed. Lendy's mendacious report would have contributed more. It showed not only that force had had to be used because diplomacy had failed, but also that a small party of *settlers* had easily routed what was believed to be an enemy force six times its size. War with Lobengula could thus be seen in a new light. If these considerations were not enough, another would have weighed as heavily: when Lobengula heard what had happened, he might unleash his regiments without leaving the initiative to Jameson.

These thoughts seem all to have been brought into focus as Lendy made his report. Ivon Fry, whose reminiscences written many years later are unreliable, nevertheless conveys the spirit of the change correctly. Fry was one of Lendy's patrol:

> Then we went back to Fort Victoria. When we reached the town, the walls of the Fort were still crowded with people. Jameson came out and Lendy rode forward and said "Doctor, you told me if I struck I was to strike hard; and I think I have accounted for 300! [sic]" Jameson then turned round to the people on the walls and said: "I hereby declare war on the Matabele!"

Hans Sauer, who was one of the bystanders, supplements this story. Jameson asked him to go to some "Dutchmen" in the village and ask them how many men they thought would be needed to fight the Ndebele. Sauer returned to say that they had all agreed on the figure of one thousand. Jameson at once said, "I'll do it."[30]

The initiative was Jameson's, but the power of decision lay elsewhere. For the whole of that evening of 18 July the administrator sat in the telegraph office conducting a "conversation" with Rhodes and Loch. While no record of the telegrams survives, three witnesses have left evidence of what they were about. They were about the necessity of war. At one point Rhodes sent his famous message, "Read Luke XIV, 31." The telegraph clerk having produced a Bible, Jameson read: "Or what king, going to make war against another king, sitteth not down first, and consulteth whether he be able with ten thousand to meet him that cometh against him with twenty thousand?" On the basis of the "Dutchmen's" advice Jameson could give the assurance that numbers were not a problem. What about money? Rhodes argued that war was impossible because the Company had none left, and his own ready money had all been spent on the telegraph line. Jameson would have none of this: "You have got to get the money. By this time tomorrow night you have got to tell me that you have got the money."

By the next morning—and Forbes in Salisbury was so informed by telegraph—the administrator had even decided on his plan of campaign, which with very little modification was the plan afterwards acted upon. Mounted columns under Forbes, Lendy, and Raaff were to start from Salisbury, Victoria, and Tuli respectively, and converge on Bulawayo. If, after this time, Jameson's resolve had weakened, it would have been brought back to the sticking point by the settlers. At public meetings and in private, in speeches and letters to the press, all over Mashonaland the demand was the same: "the absolute necessity of an immediate settlement of this question." Either the Ndebele must be put down, it was said, or the settlers would have to leave the country.

It was easier to demand war than to wage it. With the whole white community influenced by war fever, there would be no difficulty in recruiting the men. But, as Hans Sauer insisted, all experience of African warfare showed that against such an enemy the white troops, to be sure of success, had to be mounted. As there were only a hundred horses available in Mashonaland, a large number would have to be sent up from the south. Loch pointed out that this operation would take at least two months.[31] Rhodes had to find the money. Not least, in terms of Article 10 of the charter, there could be no offensive movement without the secretary of state's permission.

It may be said, therefore, that by the morning of 19 July Jameson had decided to fight, but that he had not yet converted any of the ultimate decision-makers to his policy. In the two months and more that it took to collect the horses this conversion had to be effected. It was certainly helped by the very process of preparation. As so often in history, *para bellum* was a vicious circle: preparation for war made war more likely, and the more likely it became the greater and more urgent the preparations that were needed.

After making his decision Jameson lost no time. He sent Capt. P.J. Raaff, resident magistrate at Tuli, to the Transvaal, not only to buy a thousand horses

245 Jameson's War, I

(of which Loch was informed) but also to recruit 250 men (of which Loch was not informed). The two volunteer units at Fort Victoria, afterwards merged into one under the name of the Victoria Rangers, had already been organized; Lendy having refused the command, it was given to Allan Wilson. Forbes, at Fort Salisbury, had no difficulty in raising his own force of 250 men and equipping them from the Company's stock of supplies. Raaff, unlike the others, had no local settler population to draw upon; hence his recruiting campaign. Unfortunately for the secrecy of this operation, the recruits (whom the officials in London called "Raaff's riff-raff") seemed to forget that they were not yet in enemy country. As the state secretary informed Loch, "a troop of persons in the service of the Chartered Company are trekking through the Republic and . . . are stealing and robbing along the road." Kruger's proclamation stopping the recruitment came too late. The riff-raff were then well on their way to Tuli, which they reached on 23 September.

Jameson was there, waiting for them. After satisfying himself that they would soon be ready for action he hurried back to Fort Charter, to which place Forbes's column had advanced to await the arrival of the horses. Some, but still not enough, having been sent up by Raaff, Forbes commandeered all the horses that could be found in private possession. Having thus found the Salisbury Column ready to march, Jameson turned back to Fort Victoria. When he arrived there on 2 October, the Company's forces were ready for the fray.[32] They had not been ready earlier; nor would it be easy to use them later. While the columns were mobilized the economy of Mashonaland, such as it was, was paralysed. Neither the Company nor the settlers could afford to sustain that condition for long. The moment had arrived when Jameson needed from the high commissioner the permission to advance. How he managed to extract that permission at precisely the right moment is the question that must now be answered.

The most puzzling role in this affair is Loch's. Throughout the months of preparation he was, in the somewhat naive words of the Colonial Office, "doing all in his power, with Lord Ripon's strong support, to avert further hostilities." There is no doubt about Ripon, but Loch's efforts to preserve the peace were equivocal. He repeatedly urged Lobengula to withdraw his impis from the neighbourhood of the white men, and as late as 1 October assured him that "if there are no impis out I shall not allow the white people to attack you." His messages to Jameson were consistent with those to Lobengula. If there were no impis "actually in dangerous proximity to white settlements, no aggressive movement is to take place" (24 September). Jameson could send out scouting parties which "should not go beyond a distance to be prescribed by you, within which area, if there are no impis, it would be safe for miners and others to return to their usual avocations without danger of sudden attack. Under such circumstances all necessity for aggressive operations would be obviated" (26 September). In the first of these messages the prohibition was balanced by a conditional permission: if the impis were found to be in dangerous proximity, Loch would "decide whether the Company should be left to exercise its own discretion as to the best means of securing the safety of the lives and property of the people."[33] There was nothing aggressive about that; but from these and other injunctions Jameson drew the obvious conclusion that a threat from the impis was all that was needed to get the green light from Loch.

If war should come—and after 18 July this was at the least a serious possibility—the high commissioner would be responsible for the defence of Bechuanaland. It was no more than his duty to make provision for that defence, though to do so would mean increasing the tension instead of reducing it. He hastened to bring the Bechuanaland Border Police up to strength, and then twice to increase that strength, dragging consent from a slightly puzzled secretary of state. Of the force thus enlarged to 524 about half were, by the beginning of October, at the border camp on the Motloutsi. Loch proposed also "under certain eventualities" to present "some of Khama's men" with ammunition and horses, at a cost probably not exceeding £4,000. Having been assured that these were needed "for defence, not offence," and "that it is not contemplated that they are to be used by Khama acting on the offensive against Lobengula," Ripon assented even to that. Kgama was sounded on the possibility of providing a force of a thousand men if the need arose. He did not refuse, though he thought war both unnecessary and inadvisable.[34]

In making these arrangements, which he claimed were purely defensive and precautionary, Loch was moving into a position where he might be predisposed to abet rather than to thwart Jameson's aggressive schemes. The sequel would show something of what was in his mind. It was not that he himself wanted the war; it was that, thinking it probable, he was determined to assert the supremacy of the imperial power over the company in waging and above all in concluding it. As he might one day have to allow the Company's columns to enter Matabeleland, he must be sure that the little force under Goold-Adams would be ready to rush in and get to Bulawayo first. Jameson must not succeed too quickly; nor must he run the risk of defeat, for which Loch, like Sir Bartle Frere before him, would be blamed. Both contingencies were provided against by forbidding the columns to move until the high commissioner, satisfied that "preparations were sufficiently advanced, so that humanly speaking, success would be assured," gave the word. Nor must war be precipitated too soon by demanding, as Jameson proposed to do, compensation from Lobengula.

As the Colonial Office could see, hear, and act only through Loch, his views and intentions were in the end decisive. Nevertheless the Office had its own opinions, which were less favourable than Loch's to the Company's proceedings. It is true that the Victoria incident had damaged Lobengula's case there as elsewhere. Graham remarked that he had "never believed that the permanent occupation of Mashonaland could be effected without a trial of strength between the white man and the Matabele." Olivier, while looking for the cheapest way of stopping Lobengula's raids, insisted that he had a *right* to raid in Mashonaland: "whatever view the Coy may take, the Govt. cannot take the view that he has no such right, having ousted Portugal on the ground that he has." Meade's opinion was exactly what Jameson's and Rhodes's had been before July: "the longer the evil day is put off the better, and the stronger will be the Company to deal with it."

The factor which weighed most heavily in Downing Street against war was, as usual, the cost. In giving permission to equip Kgama's men Ripon relied on Loch "not to spend more than is absolutely necessary." On the additions to the strength of the police, "it is presumed that you have made arrangements with regard to batches of recruits so as to be able to reduce strength again as soon as practicable, and will limit expenditure by every possible means." The Treasury was assured that "there is no practical question of the forces of the Crown joining with those of the Company in offensive operations against the Matabele." Ripon therefore announced on 26 August that

> under existing circumstances I should certainly prohibit any offensive movement in the interests of British South Africa Company no less than in those of the Empire at large. It is therefore important that British South Africa Company should not by menacing Lobengula commit themselves to any course of action which I might afterwards have to reverse. Their duty under existing circumstances must be limited to defending their occupied territory, and Her Majesty's Government cannot support them in any aggressive action. Any line of action tending to implicate Imperial Government without their consent in quarrels of the Company with Lobengula would be strongly condemned here, and would be fatal to their interests as a Company.

While this statement left loopholes through which Jameson would drive his mule-cart in due course, the tenor of all Ripon's messages shows that he meant this one (including as it did a veiled threat to revoke the charter) to be a strong discouragement to aggression.[35]

Jameson was not discouraged. Raaff's recruitment of men and horses was far advanced. Rhodes, having been told that "You have got to get the money," raised £50,000 by selling some of his own Chartered shares. That was not much to finance a war, but arrangements had been made for the volunteers to be remunerated not in cash but in loot. The terms were agreed upon between Jameson and Allan Wilson on 14 August in what came to be called the Victoria Agreement. With some additions this became the Attestation Roll of the Victoria Column, signed by its members and by Jameson on 3 October. The terms applied, however, not only to that column but to the whole invading force.

By this agreement, every member of the force was to be rewarded with a farm of 3,000 morgen in Matabeleland, fifteen mining claims on reef, and five alluvial claims. The marking out of these by the claimants was not to begin until the authorities considered the country sufficiently peaceful, "and a week's clear notification will be given to that effect." The claimants would then have four months in which to make their choice, after which no claims would be valid "with the exception of the rights belonging to members of the force killed, invalided or dying on service." The government had the right to purchase farms from the holders at £3 per morgen with compensation for improvements. Occupation of the farm by the holder was not required, but a quitrent of ten shillings a year would be charged. Finally, the "loot" (the captured cattle) was to be divided, "one half to the B.S.A. Co. and the remainder to officers and men in equal shares."[36]

The document could not be kept secret, and in the hands of Labouchere it became a heavy missile to hurl at the company. Naturally so, since it was nothing less than a contract for robbery under arms. The spoliation of an enemy by the individual combatants had long ceased to be a legitimate war aim in Europe. The Victoria Agreement accordingly shocked sensitive consciences there. Two or three generations later the condemnation would be all but universal.

While endorsing the condemnation according to the best standards even of that age, we may qualify it a little by reference to the context of the event. The principles of the Victoria Agreement were not new in southern Africa, or peculiar to the BSA Company; they were merely antiquated. A hundred years of warfare on the eastern border of the Cape Colony, between white colonists and Xhosa tribesmen, had recently ended. At every stage of that conflict the fruits of victory had been land and cattle: the colonists had adopted the war ethic of Africa. Only in the last few years had governors and secretaries of state made difficulties about wars of spoliation. When Sir Bartle Frere had proposed to get Boer recruits for the Zulu War, it was on "the ordinary commando terms—promise of cattle looted and of farms carved out of conquered territory." When, on the other hand, the Cape government waged war against the Sotho in 1880, without being allowed to offer the lands of Basutoland as the reward of military service, the colonists failed to volunteer.

Secondly, the agreement only gave the Ndebele a dose of their own medicine. How had they acquired the lands (and to a large extent the cattle) of which they were now to be robbed? By robbing their predecessors with even more violence and less restraint. Nevertheless, though the Victoria Agreement brought out the volunteers, it was in a tradition now discredited, at least in England. In choosing to conform to the old African custom Jameson's men committed themselves to the proposition that might is right, and to all the consequences of that commitment that the future might hold.[37]

For the present it was the Ndebele who had most to fear from a trial of strength. Lobengula knew this; most of his subjects did not. Up to this time he had steered skilfully between the opposite dangers from his own people and from the Europeans, but his problem then had been how to hold his regiments back. Now that the aggression was to come from the other side the old game could no longer be played.

The king's tragedy can be read in his letters to Loch, Jameson, Moffat, and the queen. Immediately after the Victoria incident, reprimands arrived from Jameson and from Loch. Lobengula received them with astonishing humility, and wrote his apologetic replies.[38] The soft answer might turn away wrath, but it had no effect on Lendy's patrol or on the partial failure of Manyewu's mission.

A week or so after the events of 18 July, messengers from the impi reached Bulawayo with the news, though without the corroborative detail that would be brought by the impi itself. The king's tone changed, and there is no reason to suppose that his anger was not genuine. In a telegram to Rutherfoord Harris he complained about Lendy's refusal to give up the *amahole* and their cattle, and of his turning his "cannon" on to the impi.

> Let my cattle be delivered to my people peacefully. I wish you to let me know *at once*. I thought you came to dig gold, but it seems that you have come not only to dig the gold but to rob me of my people and country as well; remember that you are like a child playing with edged tools. Tell Captain Lendy he is like some of my own young men; he has no holes in his ears, and cannot or will not hear.

On the same day, 27 July, another angry message was sent to Moffat. The emphasis in this was on punishing the wire-cutters. Lobengula had been asked by Jameson to punish his own subjects, yet when he tried to do so his impi was fired on: "so what have you got to say now?"

About the beginning of August the impi returned to Bulawayo. Manyewu's version of the events seems to have been no nearer the truth than Lendy's; the main distortion was that the deputation to Jameson was fired on after having been disarmed. This embellishment was hardly needed to fill the king's cup of bitterness to overflowing. He taunted his soldiers with cowardice for running away when attacked. Their reply was: "We had your orders, King, not to touch the white people, or otherwise we would have had a different tale to tell, and the King would have had no cause to complain." Lobengula was so incensed that he forgot, for the moment, his need to treat the high commissioner diplomatically:

> I shall return no cattle or compensate anyone for either cattle captured by my impi or damage done to property until such time that Mr. Rhodes first returns to me all the captives, their wives and children, cattle, goats, and sheep which were given protection to by the Victoria people, and had I known at the time when I despatched my impi in the direction of Victoria what I know now I would have ordered them to cap-

ture and loot all they could lay their hands on belonging to the white [*sic*] to compensate myself for the people and their property which was withheld from me.

This was fighting talk indeed, and in tune with the mood of the people. At this moment, 2 August, Colenbrander reported that "the whole country is up in arms and anxious for the fray" and that "the Amajaka are clamouring for war." According to Kgama's spies (who did not penetrate to Bulawayo) the immediate reaction to Manyewu's report was a decision to fight the whites at once. Then this decision was reversed and the day of reckoning postponed, ostensibly for a good military reason.[39]

The reason was the absence, in Barotseland, of an impi of 6,000 men. This formidable army had left Bulawayo about 11 June, several weeks before Manyewu set out in the other direction. Like previous Barotse expeditions, this one is hard to explain with any confidence. Towards the end of the previous year a Ndebele force, clashing with the Barotse near the Zambezi-Kafue junction, had lost one man killed and three taken prisoner. Lewanika kept the prisoners for some months, and on 4 January 1893 sent them home with some professions of his friendship for Lobengula. What had prevented him from sending them before was an outbreak of smallpox, which became another ingredient in this witches' brew.

Instead of responding in kind to these approaches, Lobengula sent forth the great impi whose acts were thus described by Lewanika: "They scoured Batokaland for three months, destroying property and killing many of my people in the most revolting manner. Women were ripped open and impaled, men and children were made targets of and roasted alive like meat. Nothing, not a dog, escaped where they passed. No one knows how far they might have gone had not small-pox broken out among them." The victims had neither stolen Lobengula's cattle nor cut Jameson's telegraph wire. The expedition might be further evidence of the supposed plan to keep the Batoka plateau available for a possible Ndebele migration. It could just as well have been no more than a means of satisfying the warriors' bloodlust without provoking Jameson.

Lewanika's "three months" was an exaggeration. On the day Manyewu's impi returned to Bulawayo, at the beginning of August, runners were dispatched to call the other impi home; and it would have crossed the Zambezi on the outward march early in July at the soonest. The evidence about its return is conflicting. At some point on the homeward journey the impi—or perhaps only a part of it—was ordered to stop and remain in quarantine. About the middle of September it was reported that the men had been released from quarantine and had gone home. On the 22nd Dawson reported from Bulawayo that "the people who belong to the impi are dying daily, but so far as we have heard no others have caught the infection; the admitted deaths amount to a great many hundreds." The return of the impi, instead of strengthening Lobengula's army, threatened to weaken it.[40]

It is probable, however—almost certain—that the king, in securing the postponement of an attack because of the absence of this impi, had no intention of launching one even if it had returned in good health. It is true that he was inflexible in his demand for the *amahole* and their cattle that the white men had protected. It may have been ominous that from the end of 1892 he had been changing his mind about the Company's thousand rifles, which till then he had refused to touch. The last of them were handed over by Fairbairn and Matabele Wilson in June 1893, for the use of the two impis. In case the king's acceptance of them should be interpreted as confirmation of the Rudd Concession—which of course it was—he made a contrary gesture on 13 August by refusing to accept the monthly payment by the Company for its two concessions. By that time the remaining Europeans were being insulted and threatened by the amajaha; these were still held back by awe of the king, but his stock of influence was being used up. To his relief, the whites—Matabele Wilson, missionaries, Colenbranders—were leaving the country. Only Dawson, Fairbairn, and Usher remained.[41]

Nevertheless, Lobengula wanted peace. As his spies brought in the evidence of preparations at the Company's assembling points and at Motloutsi, he sensed the danger and the impending doom. His messages convey the feeling:

(To Moffat, early in August): I want to know from you, son of Umshete, why don't you speak, why do you keep quiet, what great wrong have I done?

(To Loch, late in August): Your letter has come; I do not know the things you speak of. Your people have been telling you lies. I ask you, what was the reason why your people quarreled with mine; my people were sent to get my cattle which the Mashonas stole; what did they do that your people should fight with them? If they had been sent to fight, they would have fought.

(To the queen, 19 August): When the impi reached Mashonaland they found my cattle mixed with the Europeans', where they were killed. In the meeting they had, they told my people that the white men had bought the country and the people who live in it. Your Majesty, what I want to know from you is if people can be bought at any price. I have no more cattle left . . . When the meeting was held my impi was told to leave their arms coming into camp. Their disarming was a clever trick to attack them armless. Further, they stated that I do not allow them (Europeans) to enter my kraal with arms; neither do I. Your Majesty, allow me to ask by disarming whom did I mislead first and then kill?

Even in translation, the tone is unmistakable.[42]

These and other messages give credibility to the opinions of white observers able to judge Lobengula at close quarters: "The King himself does not wish for war, so he says; on the other hand, he also intimates that his is not the only hut that will burn" (Colenbrander, 2 August). "Mr Rees . . . is of opinion that personally the Chief is anxious for peace, and he showed his friendliness by sending a man with Mr Rees as far as Tati. Mr Rees gathered from conversation that he was doubtful about controlling his own people; he evaded any direct promise of protection to persons remaining in the country" (Moffat, 21 August; Rees had left Bulawayo on 1 August). "From all I hear our Government intend to force Loben to fight. Most of the whites I have seen from Bulawayo say that the King does not want to fight; but Tainton, whom I have seen to-day, declares that the King will not give up any cattle his people took" (W.F. Kirby, general manager at Tati, 18 August). "Crewe reports King will certainly not fight unless forced and all depends on action of our Government" (Kirby, Tati, 4 September).

P.D. Crewe, the last witness quoted, had made several unsuccessful attempts to leave Bulawayo. When he did get away on 20 August it was as the conductor of an embassy to the high commissioner and, if possible, the queen. The ambassador was the experienced envoy and traveller Mshete. His companions, apart from Crewe, were John Makhunga, the literate immigrant from the Cape Colony who was an associate of Karl Khumalo, and a Zulu named James. They were the bearers of the letter to the queen which has been quoted, and which was written by Makhunga. Lobengula, tired of complaining that his messages were not answered, was trying to make himself heard.[43]

To say that he was not heard because of Jameson's intrigues is probably an oversimplification. The killings at Fort Victoria had stopped all white men's ears—not only Jameson's and Colenbrander's but Loch's, Moffat's, and the missionaries'—against Lobengula's pleas. The composition of the embassy was unfortunate too. Mshete had not only been one of the envoys who went with Maund in 1889, but had been the one to give an extra twist to the ox-and-herd letter when he returned, to the great annoyance of Moffat as well as the Company men. John Makhunga had been one of Hassforther's coterie.[44] James was a newcomer, but, said Moffat, "anything but an upright man." Colenbrander reported that Mshete was "an infernal liar" and that none of the four was to be trusted. He "fancied" that the sending of the embassy was "to gain time." The simpler, and the true, explanation is that Lobengula wanted not to delay Jameson's attack but to avert it altogether.

The mission failed. After being delayed on the way by dysentery Mshete and his companions arrived in Cape Town on 23 September. Their letter, which Mshete had hoped to take to the queen himself, was forwarded by mail. Loch, having discovered that the envoys had no authority to treat, and that the "Matabele will not accept a boundary, and will not undertake to give up raiding the Mashonas," reported that "with such fundamental divergence of view there is very little hope of successful negotiations." The date of Loch's cable was 5 October; the time for negotiations was past.[45]

This was the moment when both the Company's and the imperial forces were at last ready to march. Knowing that Loch would not allow him to begin the attack unless he could show that the Mashonaland settlement was in immediate danger from the Ndebele, Jameson made it his business to show that it was. Large impis were reported to be "collecting to the north-west of Salisbury and vicinity of Victoria." Loch relayed this information to London on 21 September, coupled with reports that Lobengula was said to be anxious for peace, that he feared invasion, and that his movements could be intended for defence, not aggression. Nevertheless, the Company had at great expense assembled and equipped its force, and would want to bring matters to a conclusion, "for they can neither stand protracted expense nor lengthened uncertainty." After this came a shot at the bull's eye: "Do not see, unless Her Majesty's Government are prepared to assist the Company with men and money, and to accept all the responsibilities that now attach [to] the Company, how Her Majesty's Government can exercise the right of interfering with the Company's freedom of action." Loch therefore proposed, first, to find out whether the impis were "actually in dangerous proximity to the white settlements." If they were, but not otherwise, he wanted to be free to decide whether to allow the company to "exercise their own discretion as to the best means of securing the safety of the people and property for which [they] . . . are responsible."[46]

This was a poser for Ripon. For some weeks he and his officials had been reading Loch's dispatches with growing anxiety. They comforted themselves with the thought that the preparations were intended merely "to have a wholesome effect on Loben"—that is to say that Loch was bluffing. What they feared was that Lobengula, under pressure from his subjects, might "break out"; if the idea of an unprovoked aggression by Jameson (which would have to be authorized by Loch) crossed their minds, they did not commit it to paper. Ripon seized upon those parts of the cable with specific implications and used them in his reply: if Lobengula would withdraw the impis from, and undertake not to raid in, districts to be specified, he should be assured that he would not be attacked. But the other contingency had to be provided for: "I recognise necessity in certain eventualities of prompt action. Therefore, if you consider that time will not permit of reference home, you have the authority you request to be exercised on the conditions you propose."

The permission was given reluctantly, because it was realised that "Sir H. Loch will go on as long as we let him." The spirit in which it was given did not alter the fact that control had now passed practically, though not theoretically, out of Ripon's hands. Events followed in an almost preordained sequence.[47]

The course of these events shows that Jameson was determined to have his war by fair means or foul and that Lobengula would go to great lengths to avert it. Loch's mind cannot be read so easily. On 26 September, when Jameson was on his way back from Tuli to Fort Victoria, Loch pointed out to him that "all our information respecting movements of impis has hitherto been derived from the Makalaka and other natives, whose natural apprehensions, as well as a desire to see the Matabele destroyed by the white men, may lead them to exaggerate the hostile intentions of Lobengula." He therefore advised that small parties should be sent forward to investigate, not "strong patrols

254 Rhodes and Rhodesia

which would probably confirm Lobengula in his fears that invasion is intended." It was easy for Jameson to reply that small parties would not do; to allay the fears of his people the border must be thoroughly patrolled. On 28 September Loch authorized the strong patrols, but told Jameson to avoid a collision.

If the high commissioner believed Jameson's alarmist reports, his replies were justified; the question is whether he did believe them. We have just seen that on 26 September he had his doubts. We shall now look at evidence which ought to have confirmed these doubts.

On 13 August Colenbrander and his wife left Bulawayo for Palapye. They had intended to go on to Cape Town, but Rhodes insisted that Colenbrander remain at Palapye. In view of what followed, Stafford Glass has argued plausibly that Rhodes must have given him further instructions, which Colenbrander then carried out. The instructions would have been to work up a "war scare" on Lobengula's southern border.

He did so by a very simple method. Having "heard" that impis were advancing, he rode out on 16 September to see for himself. Along the way he informed every inhabitant he met that the *white* impis were coming. The trick worked: a black impi moved down to Mangwe in response to the scare. On the 23rd Colenbrander was able to send alarming news to Cape Town. It was all Jameson and Rhodes could have wished for, but it was not the last word on the subject.[48]

In the next few days Loch received a series of telegrams from Moffat (at Palapye). One of these relayed a message from Lobengula with a covering letter from Dawson, who was "firmly of opinion that Lobengula does not want to fight and that he will not do so unless actually forced to it in self-defence . . . I cannot see where the probability of hostilities occurring becomes apparent, unless, of course, the third factor, i.e. the Company, is so powerful as to have its own way in case they wish to see the thing out." Then: "Khama hears through Makalaka that general feeling in Matabele is not to fight unless attacked; his own opinion is that small-pox will prevent any early movement, but that the real crisis will be the dance in January or February." On the 28th: "Khama tells me that he has a boy in this morning from Tati who states that the impi has come no further than Mangwe, and that the alarm has been caused by a white man on horseback, who was met by some natives on the other side of Tati and said that two white impis were on their way up." On 3 October Moffat had received a letter from Kirby which was "a distinct indictment of Colenbrander as the originator of the alarm on both sides."[49]

One would have thought that at this point Loch would be treating the reports of impis massing on the borders with extreme scepticism, if not total disbelief. If there were no impis on the borders his scepticism would then have extended to the "border incidents" of which he was now informed. When Jameson arrived at Fort Victoria on 2 October he was told by Capt. the Hon.

C.J. White, in charge of a patrol stationed at the Shashe river border, that two men of his patrol had been fired on while investigating the report of an impi eight miles beyond the border. They had also seen tracks which they interpreted as those of six to seven thousand men. The date of these events was not given, but is assumed to have been about 30 September. On 3 October Loch relayed this news to Moffat, who replied the same day that both he and Kgama were most sceptical about the impi of 6,000. Kgama's scouts reported no Ndebele, except spies, south of Mangwe, and found the people tending their gardens. Usher reported from Bulawayo that all the people "of any standing wish for peace with the whites."

However this might be, Goold-Adams telegraphed on 5 October that a patrol of his had been fired on "by, as far as they could gather, about 30 Matabele." He made light of the incident. He could not hear of any large body of Ndebele, and supposed "this was only a party pushing forward to see what we were doing." Whatever its purpose it had, by this account, fired on the queen's own forces. Loch had his *casus belli*.[50]

Jameson had hoped that the first incident would be enough to get him his marching orders, but was disappointed. Loch's response was merely to allow another patrol, "supported by a strong force at some little distance," to persuade the indunas to withdraw their impi. If they refused to withdraw, Jameson might act at his discretion. This was followed by another telegram, asking for more scouting parties and more information. Jameson duly supplied it: Brabant had taken a scouting party along the headwaters of the Tokwe and the Lundi; both he and White were satisfied that an enemy force of seven to eight thousand was massed in three bodies. On 5 October, on the basis of the information then available, which did not yet include Goold-Adams's report of the second border incident, Loch wired to Jameson: "Whatever your plans are with regard to the advance of the columns from Fort Charter and Fort Victoria, they had better now be carried out."

The eagerly expected message had not been sent in response to the first border incident; nor to the second, the news of which arrived later in the day. What then had decided Loch? On 3 October he had asked Goold-Adams whether, with the force at his disposal, he could get to Bulawayo before the rains set in, and with what force he could hold it through the wet season. Goold-Adams replied that with his present force, "starting almost immediately," he could reach it by 1 December; 250 men of the police could hold it. The next day was spent in clarifying arrangements for the discipline and the marching route of the Tuli column; by the morning of 5 October, therefore, Goold-Adams was ready to move, and Loch gave *Jameson* permission to do so.[51]

He could not yet give permission to Goold-Adams, because the imperial forces had not yet been attacked. Ripon had repeatedly insisted that the Company must fight its own battles; the forces of the Crown would fight only if at-

Salisbury. Above, 1890. Below, about 1898, from Kopje; Pioneer Street in foreground

257 Jameson's War, I

tacked. Within a few hours of the message to Jameson the news of such an attack was provided, and Goold-Adams could march too.

Loch's moves are intelligible on the assumption that, while preferring peace, he knew that it would be hard to hold Jameson back and was determined if war came that the Crown should beat the Company to Bulawayo.[52] In the final weeks this determination so dominated his thinking as to push the peaceful option into the background. His holding Jameson back with suggestions of scouting parties and patrols was therefore not a last desperate attempt to avert hostilities but a delaying action to give Goold-Adams time. Jameson's position was no more critical on 5 October than on the 3rd; but Goold-Adams's preparations were completed in the interval.

While in that state of mind it was easy for Loch to ignore the possibility that the border incidents were faked. He probably allowed himself to believe the reports of them. The evidence that they had never occurred, and that no impis were anywhere near the border, would however not be long in coming. It was circumstantial but convincing.

There is the suspicious circumstance that a border clash at about this time was foretold by both Jameson and Harris. The reports of the incidents were extraordinarily vague. In the second case, one of the members of the patrol is said to have written that they had fired volleys at rocks in the river bed, and that the report to Goold-Adams had no other foundation than this.[53] More suspicious still is the incredible opportuneness of the event. No clash occurred until the day, almost the hour, when the columns had been inspected and were ready to march. Finally, the Ndebele impis were not where they had been reported to be.

There is some evidence that a few spies, scouts, and reconnaissance patrols were hovering on the borders. Wherever they were, they were men under orders; discipline had not broken down. It is unlikely that a reconnaissance patrol would have precipitated the destruction of the kingdom by firing random shots at a few troopers. It is certain that Lobengula would not have permitted them to do so. Nor would such shots have come from an impi; this was not the Ndebele way of opening a battle. The weightiest argument, however, is the fact that there were no impis anywhere near the places where the incidents were said to have occurred.

The proof is found in the history of the campaign. The Salisbury column crossed the supposed border, the Umniati river, on 9 October. On the 14th a party looking for cattle (as supplies for the column) made contact with an enemy patrol, also rounding up cattle; this seems to have been a detachment of the Insuka regiment. On the 16th the Salisbury and Victoria columns met at Iron Mine Hill; on the 22nd the invaders came into the proximity of a large Ndebele force, for the first time, in the Somabula forest. That force included the Insuka regiment, which had been in its kraal two days earlier, but had abandoned it and withdrawn to the west on the approach of the column. It may be significant that on the 18th it was the advance guard of the *Victoria* column (the source of the story of the first border incident) that spied what were probably about a hundred frightened Shona on a hill and supposed them to be 4,000 Ndebele.

The southern column left the Motloutsi on 11 October and encountered no opposition until it was attacked by Gampu's force on the Singwesi river on 2 November. As for reconnaissance, it was not until 12 October that Lobengula heard that the kingdom was being invaded; whereupon indunas began to arrive in Bulawayo, "apparently for the purpose of devising some plan of action in the present crisis." This report was from Dawson, who had been at that place throughout the critical time. If the nation had been put on a war footing several weeks earlier Dawson could hardly have been ignorant of the fact. So far was this from being the case that measures had to be hastily improvised several days after Forbes, Wilson, and Goold-Adams had crossed the border. Lobengula had not mobilized because he had "been repeatedly told by white men that we never fight without giving our enemy warning. I hope," Dawson added, "one of the best traditions of our race is not going to be violated in this case."[54]

The news that it was being violated reached Lobengula about the same time as a message from Loch, dated 1 October, which rang strangely in the king's ears: "If there are no impis out I shall not allow the white people to attack you . . . Be wise, keep your impis away from the white people and send some of your Chief Indunas to talk over matters with me, so that there may be peace." Lobengula's reply was that of a tired and disillusioned man: "What impi of mine have your people seen and where do they come from? I know nothing of them. Why should I send more men; I have already sent Mshete . . . "

If Lobengula had been the warmonger of Jameson's imagination he might have left it at that and attended to the defence of his realm. Instead, he decided even at that late hour to "send more men." The men chosen were eminent: Ingubogubo, the king's brother; Ingubo, Gampu's brother; and Mantusi. Dawson, one of the three white men still in Bulawayo, was sent with them as their liaison and guarantor with the white authorities. They took with them a letter from Lobengula to Loch, which should be quoted in full:

> I am tired of hearing the lies which come to me every day, how many of your people have my people killed; you say my people have fired on yours twice. How many are dead? Are your people stones that bullets do not kill them; you hear what your people say, send two men of yours to me and I will give them what assistance I can, to find out who were the people who have done this shooting, your people must want something from me—why don't you catch the people who fire upon you, either at Victoria or Macloutsie; when these reports are made to you, why don't you ask how many of your men are killed? This is not right, they say the things which may lead to what their hearts wish for; I have no people out on my border, my people are sick and stay at their homes; when you have made up your mind to do a thing, it is not right to

blame it on my people. You send me no answer to all the letters I send you. I do not understand this. 15th October. [Postscript, 16 October] I hear again that your people have taken more of my cattle, this is now four times my cattle have been taken; my people whom [sic] you say fired on my people, how many cattle have they taken.

The postscript was written immediately before the departure of the bearers. On the evening of the 18th they arrived at the Tati, a few hours after Goold-Adams, who was already there, had been joined by the main body of his column.[55]

Dawson was surprised to see the soldiers at Tati; he was conducting a diplomatic mission and had not heard of any declaration of war. Being tired and thirsty, he went off to get a drink of water, leaving his companions in charge of the Tati Company's foreman. He made the mistake of omitting to tell anyone who they were and the purpose of their journey. Before he had occasion to do so, the manager Kirby had sent for Goold-Adams, who ordered the three Ndebele to be disarmed and marched over to his camp as prisoners. He intended to interview them the next morning to find out their business.

The envoys were, naturally, dumbfounded and alarmed. Mantusi suddenly seized a bayonet from a trooper and wounded two men before he was shot. Ingubo tried to make a dash for safety, but was mortally wounded with a blow from a rifle butt. Ingubogubo, too shocked to speak, submitted to being bound. When Dawson, who had been told that "something serious had happened," arrived and gave his belated explanation, the hurried writing of self-exculpating reports began. The shame of the killing did not, however, prevent it from being repeated. On the same day the two regular post-boys, with a companion, reached Tati from Bulawayo. They too were promptly arrested. The next day one of them, followed by the other two, tried to escape. Shots were fired, and all were wounded, two of them mortally. Dawson and Ingubogubo then continued on their way to Palapye.

These events are explained partly by misunderstanding, and by the fact that Ndebele on peaceful business ran unwittingly into a military force that was already at war with their people and sensitive about matters of security. Yet there is little doubt that if the victims had been white—say, Germans in 1914—there would have been no misunderstanding and they would not have been shot. Glass's comment is to the point: "perhaps the readiness to pull the trigger was not due entirely to the military needs of the moment but may be attributed to the nineteenth century colonial mentality." Poor Dawson was made the scapegoat; yet his conduct of the envoys, and his previous reports, could have helped to avert war if the authorities had been willing to listen. They listened rather to Jameson, who said, "Dawson's information, living at Bulawayo with the King, is of no value—the King being a master of deceit and his word utterly unreliable."[56] The mission of the envoys would have been in vain even if nothing "serious" had happened at Tati; they died because they met an invading army well inside their country. The war had begun.

NOTES CHAPTER 6

1 A.G. Leonard, *How We Made Rhodesia*, p.56.
2 Diary of Thomas Maxwell, 9 September 1890, 21 November 1890, 25 December 1890; Political Papers of J.S. Moffat, Moffat to Harris, 15 December 1890; Moffat to Loch, 13 August 1891; Lobengula to Loch, 14 August 1891; Moffat to Loch, 16 August and 17 August 1891.
3 Political Papers of J.S. Moffat, note by J.P.R. Wallis, 24 September 1890; Lobengula to Loch, 1 January 1891; Diary of Thomas Maxwell, 30 December 1890; Diary of Matabele Wilson, 27 September 1890.
4 Political Papers of J.S. Moffat, Lobengula to Loch, 1 January 1891; Moffat to Loch, 7 October 1891; Moffat to Loch, 24 May 1892; Moffat to Loch, 27 May 1892; Diary of Thomas Maxwell, 20 December 1890.
5 See above, ch.4.
6 Political Papers of J.S. Moffat, Moffat to Loch, 13 June 1891.
7 Diary of Thomas Maxwell, Colenbrander to Harris, 10 February 1891; D.N. Beach, "The Rising in South-Western Mashonaland, 1896-7" (thesis, University of London), p.195.
8 Political Papers of J.S. Moffat, Moffat to Loch, 24 May 1892.
9 Ibid., Colenbrander to Harris, 29 April 1891; Moffat to Shippard, 14 May 1891; Moffat to Loch, 10 August 1891.
10 CO 417/77/9804, pp.341-2 (dated Bulawayo, 30 March 1892); CO 879/36/426, no.182, encl., p.227. Of the regiments placed on the border Colenbrander estimates the strength of the first three at 1400-1600, but gives no estimate for Insuka. Thus the total was probably about 2000. For the spellings of regimental names I have followed R. Summers and C.W. Pagden, *The Warriors*.
11 CO 879/36/426, no.183, encl., pp.228-30. Foster Windram oral interviews (WI 8/1/1), Ginyalitsha, p.32; (WI 8/1/2) Ntabeni Kumalo, pp.33-4, 44, 78-9. According to this witness the meeting took place "at the junction of the Somabula River and the Gwelo River, beyond Somabula siding." (With reference to this collection, see above, ch. 1, n.32.)
12 CO 879/36/426, no.233, encl.1 and 2, pp.275-6; *Native Affairs Department Annual* (*NADA*) 1923, p.31. Vavasseur calls Mhlaba's son Khami, which was the name of his place of residence. In the light of all subsequent evidence he must be identified with Ntenende.
13 CO 879/36/426, no.233, encl.1, p.275; Diary of Thomas Maxwell, 12 December 1890; Foster Windram (WI 8/1/1), Ginyalitsha, p.7; (WI 8/1/2) Ntabeni Kumalo, p.15.
14 Political Papers of J.S. Moffat, Colenbrander to Jameson, enclosing message for Lobengula, 15 January 1892; Stafford Glass, *The Matabele War*, pp.48-9.
15 Political Papers of J.S. Moffat, 18 September 1890 (letters of Lobengula); Colquhoun to Dawson, 1 November 1890; Moffat to Harris, 17 February 1891, and other letters at this time; Moffat to Jameson, 9 September 1891; Diary of Thomas Max-

well, 26 October 1890; Papers of W.F. Usher, f. 27-8, A.H.F. Duncan to Lobengula, 10 November 1891.

16 Political Papers of J.S. Moffat, Moffat to Loch, 11 July, 17 July and 4 October 1891; CO 417/99/15222, Minute by Sydney Olivier; Glass, *Matabele War*, pp.31-6, 156-8, and map at p.295; CO 879/39/454, no.42, encl.6, p.40.

17 Glass, *Matabele War*, pp.33-4, 52-6.

18 Lobengula Papers, Jameson to Lobengula, 23 December 1892; CO 879/37/441, no.116, encl.2, pp.116-17; CO 879/39/454, no.2, pp.1-3; Beach, "Rising in South-Western Mashonaland," pp.232-7; Glass, *Matabele War*, pp.60-5. In most of the sources Khokhomera and Chitawudze are called "Gomalla" and "Setoutsie" respectively. Because of a series of mischances, Lobengula never received the cattle that were sent to Tuli (see Glass, *Matabele War*, p.65 n.25).

19 Glass, *Matabele War*, pp.66-7, D.N. Beach, "The Shona and Ndebele Power" (Henderson Seminar Paper 26), p.21 (or published version, "Ndebele Raiders and Shona Power," *Journal of African History*, xv, 4 [1974], pp.649-50); The *Rhodesia Herald* of 1 July reports this raid very calmly in one paragraph.

20 An answer to this question will be attempted in chapter 8.

21 Glass, *Matabele War*, pp.54, 86 and ch.3.

22 Political Papers of J.S. Moffat, Moffat to Loch, 13 June 1891, Moffat to Surmon, 9 November 1891; Diary of Thomas Maxwell, 9 November and 28 December 1890; Diary of Matabele Wilson, 21 September 1890.

23 CO 879/39/454, no.27, encl., p.18; Diary of Matabele Wilson, June 1893 (pp.311-13); Glass, *Matabele War*, pp.70-1, 102; Summers and Pagden, *Warriors*, p.105; Foster Windram (WI 8/1/1), Hobasi Kumalo, p.6; Siatcha, pp.14-15; Ginyalitsha, p.12; Mvutu and Posela, pp.5-6; Mpagama, pp.1-2; (WI 8/1/2) Ntabeni Kumalo, pp.21-2.

24 C7555, Report of F.J. Newton, 1894, on Victoria incident, p.4, and pp.4-12, passim; Glass, *Matabele War*, pp.72-5; Ian Colvin, *The Life of Jameson*, vol. I, pp.247-51; Beach, "Rising in South-Western Mashonaland," pp.236-7.

25 CO 879/39/454, no.17, encl., pp.10-11; no.27, encl., p.18; no.33, encl.2, pp.23-4; encl.14, p.27; no.34, encl.5, p.32; no.35, encl., p.33; no.36, encl.8, pp.34-5.

26 CO 879/39/454, no.26, encl.13, p.17; C7555, pp.5-6; Glass, *Matabele War*, pp.87-8, 90; Colvin, *Jameson*, vol. I, pp.250-2, 254; Beach, "Rising in South-Western Mashonaland," pp.236-7; Foster Windram (WI 8/1/1), Siatcha, p.15; (WI 8/1/2) Ntabeni Kumalo, p.22. On his journey to Fort Victoria, first on horseback and then by mule-cart, Jameson was suffering badly from haemorrhoids.

27 Colvin, *Jameson*, vol. I, p.253. As a result of the economies of 1892, there were only seven policemen in Fort Victoria.

28 C7555, pp.4-12 (Newton's report) and the evidence which is appended; Glass, *Matabele War*, pp.106, 112, 113, 118; Foster Windram (WI 8/1/1), Siatcha, p.16; Ginyalitsha, p.13; Mvutu and Posela, p.6; (WI 8/1/2) Ntabeni Kumalo, p.23.

29 CO 417/97/13012 and 99/15522, minutes by Graham and Olivier respectively.

30 Glass, *Matabele War*, p.94; Reminiscences of Ivon Fry, p.30; Colvin, *Jameson*, vol. I, pp.258-9. Meetings at which action was demanded were held at various places. The Salisbury meeting was presided over by E.A. Maund, the former would-be officer of Lobengula's government. See *Rhodesia Herald*, 22 and 29 July 1893, for this and for the Victoria incident generally.

31 CO 879/39/454, no.33, encl.21, p.30; no.61, encl.12, pp.66-9; Glass, *Matabele War*, pp.98-100, 122-3, 144; Colvin, *Jameson*, vol. I, pp.259-60.

32 Glass, *Matabele War*, pp.144-9; Colvin, *Jameson*, vol. I, pp.260-5; CO 879/39/454, no.77, encl.1, p.94.

33 CO 879/39/454, no.59, p.62; no.108, encl.27, pp.128-9 and encl.36, p.131; no.137, encl.20, p.154.

34 CO 879/39/454, no.39, p.36; no.48, p.46; no.49, p.47; no.57, p.61; no.137, encl.12, p.152; CO 417/100/15182 (minutes); Glass, *Matabele War*, pp.137-40.

35 CO 879/39/454, no.33, encl.21, p.30; no.42, encl.8, pp.40-1; no.43, p.44; no.45, p.45; no.49, p.47; no.59, p.62; no.64, pp.74-5; CO 417/99/15804 (minutes).

36 National Archives B 4/2/4. This document is a *copy* of the "agreement" (of August 14) but the *original* (bearing the signatures of the Victoria volunteers) of the "attestation roll" of 3 October. Colvin, *Jameson*, vol. I, p.261. For an important commentary on the Victoria Agreement see P. Stigger, "Volunteers and the Profit Motive in the Anglo-Ndebele War, 1893," in *Rhodesian History*, II (1971), pp.11-23. It is there argued that what the volunteers wanted was money; that they were attracted by the rewards offered not in themselves but as saleable commodities; and that of the three commodities the cattle were the most marketable and therefore the most desired.

37 Glass, *Matabele War*, p.150. When Labouchere gave notice of a question in the House of Commons about the Victoria Agreement, the directors were asked by the Colonial Office for information. The reply, on 27 November, was that they were "without advices of the terms upon which the Company's Police Force now engaged in the military operations in Matabeleland was enrolled." (CO 879/39/459, no.89, p.89.)

38 See above, p.241.

39 CO 879/39/454, no.42, encl.1, p.38, encl.3, p.39, encl.9, p.41; no.56, encl.14, p.56, encl.18, p.57, encl.23, p.59; no.66, encl.3, p.81; no.136, encl., p.140.

40 CO 879/39/454, no.34, encl.1, p.31; no.48, p.46; no.56, encl.25, p.60; no.66, encl.9, p.84; no.67, p.85; no.73, encl.12, p.91; no.78, encl.4, p.96, no.137, encl.22, p.155; Papers of W.F. Usher, ff. 33-5, Lewanika to Lobengula, 4 January 1893; CO 879/75/686, no.26, encl.5. The Ndebele knew and practised a form of inoculation against small-pox, which must have reduced the number of deaths from this epidemic. See Foster Windram oral interviews (WI 8/1/1), evidence of Siatcha, p.21, and cf. Eugenia W. Herbert, "Smallpox Inoculation in Africa," *Journal of African History*, XVI, 4 (1975), pp.539-76.

41 CO 879/39/454, no.66, encl.3, p.81; Political Papers of J.S. Moffat, Colenbrander to Harris, 30 December 1892; Diary of Matabele Wilson, June 1893; Reminiscences of P.D. Crewe. Wilson showed Jameson, in Fort Victoria, a telegram that he wanted to send (via Palapye, taken from there by runners) to his friends in Bulawayo "that we were coming in, and for them to clear out." Jameson would not allow this, but smilingly assented when Wilson reduced the message to the single word "Get."

42 CO 879/39/454, no.56, encl.20, p.58; no.90, encl.9, p.108; no.136, encl., p.140. Dates of the messages cannot be given precisely, as the dates on them are those of the telegraphic dispatch from Palapye.

43 CO 879/39/454, no.56, encl.18, p.57; no.61, encl.10, p.66; no.66, encl.1, pp.79-80; no.73, encl.5, p.89, and encl.8, p.90 which gives the date of Crewe's departure as 21 August; no.78, encl.5, p.99; Reminiscences of P.D. Crewe.

44 See above, ch.4 and 5.

45 CO 879/39/454, no.73, encl.5, p.89, and encl.10, p.90; no.81, p.102; no.136, p.139.

46 Ripon's consent to this suggestion was followed by Loch's message, in the same words, to Jameson (see above, p.247).

47 CO 879/39/454, no.67, p.85; no.70, p.86; CO 417/100/15182 (minutes).

48 CO 879/39/454, no.33, encl.11, p.26; no.108, encl.24, p.128, and encl.36, p.131; no.137, encl.16, p.153; Glass, *Matabele War*, pp.166-9; CO 417/103/20030.

49 CO 879/39/454, no.108, encl.29, 30, 33, 34, pp.129-30; no.137, encl.1, p.147, and encl.37, pp.160-1. In a letter of 21 March 1894 Colenbrander repudiated the charge, but in such general terms as to be unconvincing. (CO 879/40/461, no.178, p.266.)

50 CO 879/39/454, no.137, encl.26, p.156, encl. 29, p.157, encl.31 and 33, p.158, encl.37, pp.160-1; W.A. Wills and L.T. Collingridge, *The Downfall of Lobengula*, p.193; Glass, *Matabele War*, p.173. The officials in London expressed puzzlement and scepticism over the reports of the border incidents (CO 417/101A/17998, 102/17649 and 102/18728, minutes), and thought the second was far from being a *casus belli* for Loch. "I have my suspicions that the firing on our men was a 'put up job' on the part of some of the underlings of the Charter Group." (Fairfield.) Olivier regarded the reports of Colenbrander's activities as damning evidence (CO 417/102/18728 minutes), but Loch believed the second incident to be evidence of Lobengula's intention to advance to Tati (CO 879/39/459, no.24, p.13).

51 CO 879/39/454, no.137, encl.27, pp.156-7, encl.30, p.157, encl.36, pp.159-60; no.138, encl.3 and 4, p.162; CO 879,39/459, no.25, encl.9, p.17 and 10, p.18; Glass, *Matabele War*, pp.174-6. The emphasis in Loch's telegram to Jameson was on the importance of trying by peaceful means to persuade the (nonexistent) impis to retire.

52 Fairfield agreed that Goold-Adams's getting to Bulawayo first would "give us an advantage, as against the Company, in negotiating a final settlement." (CO 417/102/17649, minutes.)

53 Glass, *Matabele War*, p.181, quoting article by Walter Howard.

54 CO 879/39/454, no.137, encl.22, p.155; CO 879/39/459, no.48, encl.2, p.60; Wills and Collingridge, *Downfall of Lobengula*, pp.85, 89-93, 98, 102, 110, 215, 219.

55 CO 879/39/454, no.137, encl.20, p.154; CO 879/39/459, no.48, encl.2, p.60; no.64, encl.4, p.69.

56 CO 879/39/454, no.137, encl.2, p.148; CO 879/39/459, no.64, encl.6, p.70; CO 879/40/461, no.39a, encl., pp.78-84 (Major Sawyer's report of his enquiry into the incident); Glass, *Matabele War*, pp.201-5; for first reactions of Colonial Office, CO 417/103/19498. Sydney Olivier commented: "Whether or no Lobengula is 'a master of lies and deceit', as Dr. Jameson describes him, he is certainly a master of the art of sending messages which make the case against him look very queer." (CO 417/102/19162, Olivier's minute.)

CHAPTER 7

Jameson's War, II: The Victory of the Maxim Gun

We have been looking at the reasons for the war; now we come to the reasons for the defeat, which are easier to establish. The Ndebele, however, were not the only defeated party in this campaign; it was a three-cornered fight in which there was a second loser—Loch, and with him the imperial power.

The plan of campaign had been clear to Jameson, and was made explicit, as far back as 19 July. The plan used in October was essentially the same: the Salisbury and Victoria columns invading from the east, Goold-Adams from the south. Where in this scheme was the place for Raaff's "riff-raff" at Fort Tuli? It could serve no useful purpose operating independently of the neighbouring Bechuanaland Border Police. On 2 October, therefore, Loch asked Goold-Adams if he would care to take any of the Tuli men under his command. The reply, the same day, was that he would be glad to have them all. Jameson heartily concurred in this arrangement. As soon as the news of the second "border incident" reached him, Loch asked Jameson to place Raaff's column under Goold-Adams's command, and asked Moffat to approach Kgama for the thousand men previously arranged for. On 7 October Goold-Adams was allowed, at his discretion, to advance with this force as far as Tati and the Monarch mine.

In his messages to Goold-Adams Loch had never struck either an urgent or a belligerent note. Satisfied with the undertaking that the column could get to Bulawayo by 1 December, he was concerned less to urge it on than to save it from rash action and possible disaster. Jameson was working to a different time-table, and was no less determined than Loch to win the race. He therefore ordered Raaf not to move from Tuli until a week after the start of the Salisbury and Victoria columns. Raaff, now under the command of Goold-Adams, was placed in an impossible position. He disobeyed the order from his new superior to leave Tuli on 9 October. Loch's furious reaction to this disobedience betrayed an anxiety which he had generally managed to conceal. The Tuli column did set out the next day to join the BBP at Motloutsi camp, which the combined force left on the 11th. On the Shashi river they were joined by Kgama with 130 mounted and 1,760 unmounted men, of whom half had Martini-Henry rifles. Officers and men of the BBP numbered 225, of the Tuli column the same number, and together they had 406 horses, two seven-pounder guns, five Maxims, and the appropriate supply train. By the 18th they were all at Tati.

The next day—the deaths of envoys and post-boys notwithstanding—the column moved on by two routes, and on the 23rd was united again on the Ramakwabane river. That river, which is today the frontier between Zimbabwe and Botswana, was then a boundary of a different sort. It was the eastern limit of the Tati concession, which in theory was still a part of Lobengula's kingdom. In practice, though, it was no less a "border" than that on the Mashonaland side, of which Jameson made so much. Goold-Adams, who had now gone a little way beyond the Monarch mine, was hesitant to go further without specific instructions. Loch began impatiently to urge him on, but in the absence of a telegraph line and even of heliograph stations the messages took many days to reach him. So Goold-Adams waited five days on the Ramakwabane, then advanced a short distance to the Singwesi with a part of his force, and was still there at the beginning of November.

Fairfield's assessment of Goold-Adams was that he was "a very ordinary Irish infantry officer, good enough at police work"; his advance to Bulawayo gives substance to that judgment. Loch had himself to blame too: up to this moment his telegrams had emphasized caution rather than speed. He seems to have assumed that his man, like Rhodes's man, would "take the bit between his teeth." By moving swiftly, Goold-Adams might have taken Bulawayo. The slightest delay, not to mention a delay of ten days in the Ramakwabane-Singwesi area, enabled Jameson to get there first. Rhodes could have spared himself the trouble of writing angrily to London that he had not asked for Goold-Adams and did not want Goold-Adams. He strongly repudiated "our interfering in the question, and the whole press and public of South Africa are crying out at our 'Criminal Imperialism' in doing so." They need not have worried either.[1]

In retrospect Jameson's victory seemed easy, a "walkover," but it might not have been so. The Ndebele proved much harder to defeat in 1896 than in 1893, though they appeared to have many advantages in the war which they did not have in the rebellion.

Perhaps, then, Lobengula was not an asset in 1893. He foresaw defeat and he tried to stave it off by diplomacy. This effort was not only vain but also a delusion. He trusted to what the white men had told him, that "we never fight without giving our enemy warning"; in vain. The invaders were well inside the country before he began to organize the defence, and then his army was riddled with smallpox: "my people are sick and stay at their homes." Only a part (perhaps half) of the great Ndebele army was ever brought into action against the invaders, and then not until they were dangerously near their objective. Lobengula held his people back too long.

This is not to say that by acting sooner he could have avoided defeat: remember Cetshwayo. He might, however, have made things so hot for Jameson's force that Loch's dream and the Treasury's nightmare would have come true—more Imperial forces would have been needed, and Loch would have been in a position to dictate the postwar settlement. As it was, the columns from Mashonaland won the war.

Until they reached the Somabula forest their advance was a matter of mere marching. Foraging parties occasionally ran into trouble, and there were some casualties on both sides, but there was no battle. The Salisbury and Victoria columns, united at Iron Mine Hill (or Sigala) on 16 October, came under the command of Forbes. Jameson's rôle was a little less supernumerary than in 1890, since he was now administrator, but as a civilian he stood outside the chain of command. Sir John Willoughby was with the column primarily as Jameson's military adviser. For all his famous victories on the eastern border, Forbes was the wrong man to command such a force. Burnham, the American scout, said of him that "he had all the pluck of a bull-dog and just about as much judgment." What was more to the point was the report of Norris Newman: "All seemed agreed that Major Forbes showed himself fidgety, bad-tempered, abusive in his language, and utterly lacking tact and courtesy, jealous of advice or interference, and forgetful of the fact that most of the men under him were pure volunteers, of equal social status, of greater age and experience, and with large commercial and financial interests in the country." He was said, too, by his dictatorial conduct to have "alienated all his best friends."

Whether Allan Wilson could have been called one of these is doubtful, but it clearly needed all Jameson's tact and bonhomie to keep the peace between Wilson and Forbes, as well as between Lendy and Forbes. No doubt the force was a difficult one to command, every man in it either being, or thinking that he ought to be, an officer; but this merely made it all the more important to have a tactful commander.[2]

Forbes nevertheless led his column successfully to Bulawayo. One of the factors in his success was, almost incredibly, that his intelligence service was better than Lobengula's. Such men as Matabele Wilson, Robert Vavasseur, and the American scouts Burnham and Ingram played useful parts in this service, but there can be no doubt that the key men were the survivors of the Mhlaba family massacre, Mnyenyezi and Ntenende. Thirsting for revenge, uncle and nephew put their knowledge of country and people at the disposal of the column. It was probably they who warned Forbes of the danger in crossing the Somabula forest, at that time a dense forest narrowing down to a point south of Gwelo. It was with this in mind that the column steered well to the south of the old Hunters' Road, keeping near to the watershed (and to the later road and railway route), so as to cross the forest where it was narrow. This was done in great anxiety—a track for the wagons having to be cut—on

First Street, Fort Victoria, 1893

the morning of 22 October. "To make things worse," Forbes thought at the time, "a fog came on." He should have been glad of its protective covering, for an enemy force was in fact waiting for the column in that forest.

That it missed its prey may have been due partly to the fog, but a more important reason was that the ambushers did not know where or when the column had entered the forest; they were waiting for it in the wrong place. As this was in their own country, inhabited by their own people, the failure to keep precise track of the column's movements is remarkable.

Again, on the day of the Bembesi battle, it was Mnyenyezi who warned Forbes to keep clear of the bush where the élite regiments were waiting to pounce on the column. Keeping to open country was of course the obvious policy for a force depending on fire-power, but it was a counsel of perfection which had to be disregarded except where danger was imminent. Jameson was in too great a hurry to afford anything but the direct route. Moreover, Forbes underestimated the danger: at the Shangani he formed the laager in the bush, though there was open country two or three miles further on. Forbes' argument that a halt was called because "we expected some trouble in getting the waggons across the river" is unconvincing. The operation was complete by 4.30 p.m.; another hour would have sufficed to get clear of the bush and hills.

The column fought two pitched battles on its way to Bulawayo. The first, called the Shangani by the whites and Bonko by the Ndebele, was at this ill-chosen site.

The combined Salisbury and Victoria columns consisted of something over 650 white volunteers, 155 "Colonial natives" who acted as wagon drivers, *voorlopers*, and cooks, and about 900 Shona camp followers. These, who made themselves useful "in bushing the laagers, making kraals for the cattle, and driving captured cattle," joined the expedition mainly in the hope of recovering their stolen women, children, and cattle. There were thirty-nine wagons, a Gardner, a Nordenfelt, a Hotchkiss (captured at Macequece), two seven-pounder guns, and finally—the newest thing in military hardware—five Maxim machine-guns.[3]

After the crossing of the Shangani on the afternoon of 24 October the wagons were formed into two laagers joined by a bush fence, with horses and most of the cattle within the enclosure. As the Shona camp followers were not on cordial terms with one another, one party of them made a *skerm* of its own about 600 yards northeast of the laager. The men had with them some of their women and children who had just been recovered.

The Ndebele commander on this front was Mtshane Khumalo, a cousin of the king. The regiments at his disposal on 25 October cannot be specified with much certainty, as the evidence is conflicting. Insuka was certainly there; Induba, Ihlati, Isiziba, and Amaveni almost certainly; Inqobo probably. They were joined later in the battle by the older men of Enxa, Ujinga, and Inzwananzi. Forbes and Sir John Willoughby thought between five and six thousand Ndebele were engaged; Summers and Pagden think 3,500 nearer the mark. Many of them carried the Rudd Concession rifles and ammunition as well as their traditional arms.

Mtshane's plan was to rush the laager when the moon was at its zenith about 10.30 p.m. This was to be a silent attack with cold steel and no firing. The bush would have covered the approach, up to a point. Could that attack have succeeded? Probably not, because the pickets could have given the alarm in time for the machine guns to be brought into action. Nevertheless it would have been for the invaders a worse ordeal than they faced in the event.

At 8 p.m. three signal rockets were sent up, in the vain hope that patrols from the southern column might see them. There is no suggestion that they were intended to alarm the enemy, but that, according to reports from the white side, was their chief effect. The white man was seen by witchcraft to knock the stars out of the sky and bring them down. Presumably he could bring the moon down too. At about 10 p.m. the night attack was called off.

It was the custom of the column to stand to at 4 a.m., which was regarded as the favourite Ndebele time to attack. (The whites had no experience of this. Did the information come from Mnyenyezi?) On this morning of 25 October Mtshane's army was preparing to do just that. A few minutes earlier, however, two of the Shona pickets went successively into the bush to relieve themselves.

As neither came back, a third went to investigate. Before the waiting *ijaha* could strike him down he was able to fire a shot, which gave the alarm and precipitated the attack at 3.55 a.m.

Those who were approaching from the northeast, instead of having a clear path to the laager, found the Shona *skerm* in their way. To rush upon this, stabbing indiscriminately, was familiar work, but the despised *amahole* gave a good account of themselves. Most of them succeeded in getting into the laager, as did the pickets, but some of the Shona who were guarding cattle panicked, and in fleeing to the laager ran across the line of fire. The machine guns were firing blindly into the darkness, killing friend and foe without distinction. After half an hour of this the attack was called off.

The shot fired by the picket—or, by Forbes's account, the unexpected discovery of the Shona *skerm*—had brought the attackers' rifles into play and so spoiled Mtshane's plan. As in the abortive plan for the previous evening, so now, the intention was to rush the laager with the stabbing spear, under cover of darkness. Lobengula's order had been to attack the column on the move and not in laager. Having failed to catch it in the forest, Mtshane took the chance of attacking the laager because it was in a vulnerable position.

At daylight the attack was renewed. Watching the hillside to the southeast through his field-glasses, Forbes noticed two or three hundred men walking quietly down towards the laager. They had no shields, and were taken to be "some of our natives who had escaped into the bush at the first alarm . . . They advanced down the slope in a most casual way, without hurrying or attempting to take cover, and I allowed no firing at them. When they got to the bottom of the slope they suddenly sat down and commenced to fire at us." Far from being "our natives," these were the Insuka regiment which had left its shields behind the hill, and had made its unhurried advance down the slope, precisely in order to create this deception.

Bravery was not enough to neutralize the fire from two or three Maxims and two hundred rifles; Insuka was forced to retire with less dignity than it had advanced. Some units attempting to reform on a ridge west of the laager were dispersed by shell-fire. Mounted patrols went out to see whether the attackers had retired; one of them, under Heany, narrowly escaped being surrounded and cut off by the newly arrived regiments. The Ndebele then withdrew in good order. It was all over in four hours.

It had been the first battle between Ndebele and white men since Potgieter's day, but in his day there had been neither machine-guns, rifled barrels, nor breech-loading mechanisms. The Ndebele now faced machine-gun fire for the first time and found it too much for them. The rockets had played upon their superstition. So, possibly, had the artillery. If their enemies' explanation can be believed, the Ndebele thought that, when a shell burst, numbers of little white men came out of it and began firing with their rifles; the Ndebele who had firearms therefore directed a concentrated fire at the place of the explosion. They used their new rifles in more conventional ways also, but fired too high: they thought that the higher the sights were raised the more effective the shooting would be. For the moment, the old argument that the Ndebele were "no good with rifles" seemed to have something in it.

The attackers are thought to have suffered five or six hundred casualties; the defenders, sixty-one, mostly among the camp followers (and mostly shot by their own side)—only one white man and one "Colonial native" had been killed, six whites wounded. The implications of this imbalance, and of the column's ability to move on its way by 3 p.m. on the day of the battle, were not lost on either side. "The column was unstoppable by any Matabele means, or so it appeared." There had been no lack of the old spirit: Insuka sauntering down the hill; one warrior firing away in spite of five wounds and a broken leg; one induna with both legs broken, deserted by his retreating troops, hanging himself—perhaps to avoid surviving defeat; an old "ringkop" falling on his assegai, presumably for the same reason. All in vain; about 900 men, believed by some to be the Amaveni regiment (though by other accounts Amaveni fought again), now opted out of the war and retired to a flat-topped hill on the border of Mashonaland.[4]

The column marched on. For six days there was no big fight, though several small ones. The retreating army was unable to slow down the column's advance, but it nearly succeeded in cutting off several of the patrols which reconnoitred ahead and on the flanks and burned all the kraals within reach. One scout, Capt. Gwynyth Williams, was killed. On 31 October a laager was made in a good position and in expectation of attack by large Ndebele forces that could be observed. Artillery fire scattered these and, Forbes believed, prevented an attack that night. If he was right about this, the battle was opportunely delayed. By the next day the retreating units were reinforced by the crack regiments of the Bulawayo reserve: Imbizo, Ingubo (the king's bodyguard), and, probably, Bulawayo under the command of Makwekwe.

These proud soldiers, hearing from Insuka and other regiments the frightening story of the Bonko fight, were full of contempt: Imbizo and Ingubo would undertake the job, they would not have to fight, they would merely walk through the laager, killing the older men and bringing the others back as slaves. They marched out of Bulawayo on the 31st, spent the night at Intaba yezinduna, and were in the line the next morning. The column, too, was marching that morning. On the advice of Mnyenyezi it steered to the south of the thorn bush round the source of the Bembesi river and at 11.50 a.m. laagered on the southern side of the watershed, 500 yards from the edge of the bush.

As usual the Salisbury and Victoria laagers were separate, and joined by bush fences to make an enclosure for the cattle and to provide for communica-

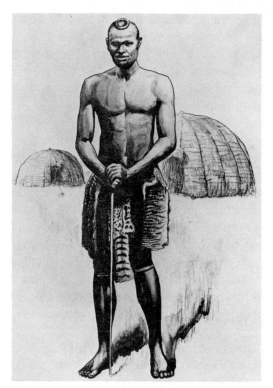

Mhlaba

The battle of Egodade (Bembesi), 1893

272 Rhodes and Rhodesia

tion. Immediate attack was evidently not expected: the bush fences were not completed, and the cattle and horses were sent down to the stream, 1,200 yards to the south, to drink.

One of the mysteries about the battle of Egodade (called the Bembesi by white historians) is why it was fought at all, in defiance of Lobengula's orders. Among these were, first, that the column should be attacked on the move, never when in laager; and second, that the decisive attack should be made when it was crossing the Umguza river (there was only one practicable crossing on the route to Bulawayo), and when half of it was across.

Forbes believed that his enemy mounted a classical attack with frontal assault by the chest and enveloping movements by the horns. This would have shown premeditated disobedience to the king's order by the commander of the army. It would also have shown his incompetence, as the movements of chest and horns were not coordinated: the left horn lagged far behind the chest on its right, and the right horn was never deployed at all.

Summers and Pagden have worked out an ingenious and convincing hypothesis to explain these facts. The Bulawayo regiment under Makwekwe's command went out with the rest of the reserve. When these units joined the retreating army Makwekwe, being senior to Mtshane, assumed the supreme command. Though Makwekwe was an able officer, and though he had come out with the king's crack regiments, neither he nor they had had the sobering experience of Bonko. They had, however, heaped jeers and insults on the men who had had that experience, so that some mutual antipathy had been stirred up among the several regiments and commanders.

The crack regiments—Imbizo and Ingubo—were in the position which would have been the chest if the classical formation had been adopted. According to this inspired guess, the induna of Imbizo took in the essence of the situation at a glance: the two laagers were not effectively connected, and the horses were widely separated from their riders. The decision to attack the Salisbury laager (the nearer of the two) was, then, made and carried out at once at this regimental level. Ingubo, on Imbizo's right, joined the movement so quickly that its induna failed to notice and to use some dead ground which would have been invaluable to his men. The supreme commander—Makwekwe, on this hypothesis—was taken completely by surprise when he saw the movement. After a delay he ordered up the units on the left flank, but forgot about the right until too late. Those men on the right, veterans of the Bonko fight, were smarting under the insults of the people from "general hindquarters" who now boasted of walking through the laager. Very well, they would stay where they were until they had positive orders to move.

The regiments that had been at the Shangani would not have charged so boldly into the Maxim's mouth. Imbizo and Ingubo charged three times. The movement, being unplanned, was badly coordinated. Suddenly someone in the laager shouted "Look, the bush is full of the b——s," and they were described as advancing "more in the shape of a lot of locusts than anything else." The disorder may have blunted the charge, but it would have been hopeless gallantry in any case. The machine-guns mowed them down in lines. Imbizo, on the left, was in a position to be enfiladed by one of the Victoria Maxims. "I doubt if any European troops," Sir John Willoughby wrote, "could have withstood for such a long time as they had the terrific and well directed fire brought to bear on them." The journalist Vere Stent thought that "the facing of the maxims by the Ingubo regiment at a distance of a hundred and ten yards was, perhaps, one of the most magnificent displays of physical courage that Africa has ever seen." Imbizo, out of a strength of 700, was reckoned to have suffered 500 casualties that day. The Light Brigade at Balaclava lost 247 killed and wounded out of 673.[5]

Amid the inferno some of the warriors noticed the dead ground and made use of it to creep closer. One was seen to emerge from the bush, run the gauntlet of all the machine-guns and take cover behind anthills and stumps as he edged forward, firing all the time until he was killed. As the charges were broken the survivors fell back "in a sulky sort of way, not hurrying or taking cover, but walking quietly back until they were out of sight." From the cover of the bush these remnants, as well as the units that had not been closely engaged, kept up a long-range fire. Patrols, covered by artillery, then forced them to retreat.

It was not the old-fashioned unequal contest between fire-arm and spear. The Ndebele, altogether about 6,000 strong at Egodade, carried and used nearly three times as many rifles as the whites. Being untrained, they handled them ineffectively; but what defeated them was the machine-gun—*isigwagwa* they called it. These battles were very nearly the first in which the Maxim was used, and perhaps the first in which its potential was fairly tested. Again it helped to account for the vast difference in casualties between the two sides. The attackers lost perhaps 800; the defenders, three killed (including the picket Thompson who failed to mount his horse in time) and seven wounded. The carnage lasted not much more than an hour, and it decided the fate of Lobengula's kingdom. The "headstrong and unruly" regiments had always wanted to wash their spears in the blood of the white men. They were given their chance at last, and if their vain boastings were now silenced they more than redeemed their honour by their unforgettable valour. As one of them, mortally wounded, was carried into the laager he looked round at the defenders and laughed: "Fancy the Imbizo being beaten by a lot of boys!"

A great victory for Forbes—but it came within an inch of being a disaster. As soon as the action began a trumpet call ordered the guards to bring the animals back to the laagers. At the height of the battle, about 1.25, the horses began to arrive, but the agitation of the grooms or the noise of the guns suddenly caused them to stampede. They galloped straight towards the regiments (Ihlati and Isiziba) on the right of the charging Ingubo. They, of course, ought to have lain low and quiet and allowed the horses to continue on their wild career. Without them Forbes's men would have been, if not helpless, certainly immobile. Without the mounted patrols which kept the enemy well away from the column on the march it would have been vulnerable whenever it moved. Without the oxen—if they had been lost too—it could not have moved at all.

Ihlati and Isiziba, lacking both orders and inspiration, fired on the horses, causing them to wheel to the left and then away to the south. Luckily for the men in the laagers, a few of them had not sent their horses to water. A party was, therefore, able to ride out and, though at one point under heavy fire, bring the horses in. Makwekwe, with too much on his mind, had not been quick enough to seize this opportunity and give the appropriate order to the regiments on his right.[6]

The column was now within twenty miles of Bulawayo, and the way lay open and undefended.

When Forbes sent up his rockets on the evening of 24 October, hoping that the southern column would see them, Goold-Adams was in fact about 150 miles away, dallying at the Ramakwabane river before moving on a few miles to the Singwesi. While the other column was locked in battle on 1 November, Goold-Adams with a part of his force was at the Singwesi and had not yet encountered the enemy.

The enemy were some of the regiments known collectively as the iGapha division,[7] under the command of Gampu. Either because he did not trust Gampu or because he correctly assessed the priorities, Lobengula had given very few firearms to these units. This fact is not likely to have any bearing on Gampu's failure to attack for almost a month after the so-called second border incident; but the failure to attack during that time is almost enough proof that the incident was faked.

Goold-Adams was hampered by the shortage of water for his large force. This still being the problem when he reached the Singwesi, he decided to call up the remainder of his own column and the whole of Kgama's force, which had stopped down the road, and get the fight over as soon as possible. The Ndebele were reported to be in force on his immediate front. Goold-Adams laagered in the best position he could find close to water, and on 1 November Kgama with his army joined him. The same evening the rear party was reported to be three miles away, but unable to go further because of the lack of water for the oxen. The oxen were sent on without the wagons to water at the Singwesi. The next morning they returned and the rear party began to move forward. Gampu was able to throw six or seven hundred men of the Nyama-yendhlovu and Amabugudwana regiments against this wagon train in motion, something Mtshane had never succeeded in doing to the other column. Yet even under these favourable conditions nothing more was achieved than the destruction of the rearmost wagon and the capture of its oxen. The corporal and driver in charge were killed. Selous, who rushed to the scene, was wounded; but a mounted patrol was able to escort the rest of the train safely to the laager, the attackers following through the bush. When they were 150 yards from the laager the Maxims opened fire and the attack petered out.

One might have expected Gampu to do better than that. Having been in the king's bad books more than once, he may have been half-hearted in the fight; his indunas, indeed, accused him of treachery. However that may be, there is little doubt that the news of Bonko and of Egodade demoralized both Gampu and his regiments. After the fight at the Singwesi (or Manyala) and the news of Egodade, they withdrew to the northwest. This was as well for Goold-Adams, for on 5 November Kgama, whose men had begun to catch small-pox, insisted on taking his army home. Small-pox was the excuse, but there were other reasons. The men were needed at home: the Ngwato economy, like the company's in Mashonaland, could not survive prolonged campaigning. And how this campaign was prolonged! Kgama could stand only just so much lethargy, and the limit had been reached. By deserting when more enemy resistance was still expected, Kgama blotted his copy-book; it was only the next day that messengers from Jameson confirmed the rumour that the Ndebele had been defeated and Bulawayo occupied. Goold-Adams could relax. "Travelling by easy steps," he reached that place on the 15th.[8]

Forbes's column had moved forward on the 2nd. The next day the scouts Burnham, Ingram, and Posselt were sent forward to spy out the situation in Bulawayo. While they were on their way a great explosion could be heard, and a column of smoke showed that the town had been put to the torch. It was the remains of the king's stock of ammunition that had blown up.

Captain Borrow and twenty men were hurried forward to occupy the place that evening. It had been abandoned by the entire population and the king had given orders for its destruction. Borrow's party did, however, find two men in the old white men's camp: Fairbairn and Usher, sitting on the roof of the store playing poker. Lobengula had protected them as long as he was there, but in the chaos of defeat they feared for their lives. Forbes's "galloper," Tanner, following the scouts, reached Bulawayo after dark. The fires still burning illumined the place, but as he rode into the great courtyard, *umdanga*, where every year thousands of warriors had stamped in unison in the Big Dance, the only sign of life now was "hundreds of Kaffir dogs running about. It must have been a very eerie sensation."

The next day, 4 November, the column made its triumphal entry. Goold-Adams was still sixty miles away. Much was made of his great contribution to victory by forcing Lobengula to divide his forces, but the importance of this must not be exaggerated. The southern front was left to Gampu and his so-called "division," whose loyalty and therefore utility were in doubt. Of the 4,000 men of that division, at most 700 were actively engaged against the invaders. Subtracting from the rest of the army the regiments that had been on the Barotse expedition, about 8,500 men should have been available against

Forbes's column. In fact, fewer than 7,000 were so used, since the force at Egodade, estimated at 6,000, included most of those who had fought at Bonko. It cannot therefore be assumed that, without the diversion caused by Goold-Adams, a much bigger number would have fought against Forbes. Moreover, even with no southern column in sight, the mere presence of Kgama and of the imperial power in that direction would have made it necessary to guard the southern approaches. Rhodes was aware of the implications of this. Speaking to the victorious troops, in Bulawayo, he said that "if the Imperial Government interfered the consequences would be very unpleasant indeed." At which Stent overhead an officer mutter, "My God, they will—for us."

The fall of Bulawayo did not end the war. Lobengula had left Umvutshwa with his household after the defeat of his army at Bonko, moving away to the north. At Shiloh he heard the news of Egodade, and the remnants of defeated regiments began to join him as he continued on his way. These and the great indunas, and the women and children and the cattle, seemed at last to be trying to carry out the plan so often mooted before—a Great Trek across the Zambezi. The route followed—north to the Shangani, then down that river—was the only way to the Zambezi that was free of tsetse. Most of the whites were unaware that the bulk of the Ndebele army was still intact and in place.

It is possible that this migration, often mooted as it had been, was not the course Lobengula would have preferred. Matabele Wilson, who had left Bulawayo for Mashonaland at the beginning of July and who was to be the chief guide of the columns in October, gave Jameson and Forbes various pieces of advice. His greatest fear was that the Ndebele would fall back into the Matopos, in which case "we were doomed." To avert this doom, Wilson, with Jameson's reluctant consent, concocted a message to Lobengula that the whites would advance in four columns with the intention of surrounding him in the Matopos. The message was taken back by the "boys" who had come with Wilson from Bulawayo. He did not claim that this message had any influence on the king's decision, but did assert that "he went North against the wishes of most of his chiefs and people, which was a blessing to us." The course of events in 1896 suggests that there may be something in this theory, though there is no evidence to confirm it.[9]

As long as the king was at large the Ndebele were unlikely to submit to the conquerors. Jameson therefore sent him a letter, conveyed by three plucky "Colonial boys," appealing to him to surrender, and giving him two days after the return of the messengers in which to do so. The leader of this little band was Jan Grootboom, of whom more will be heard in this story. The messengers brought a reply written by another "Colonial boy," John Jacobs, who was with the king: he had received Jameson's letter, "and so I will come." Evidence was soon at hand that he had resumed his northward trek immediately after dictating his reply. It was therefore decided to send a mixed party, made up of elements of the Salisbury, Victoria, and Tuli columns and of the BBP, to pursue and catch Lobengula. Forbes was placed in command of this.[10]

The task was performed in two stages. On 14 November the force set out from Bulawayo, going by way of Shiloh and Inyati. By the 19th it was on the Bubi. Though there was information that the king was not far ahead, the expedition then turned back. At Shiloh it met Captain Napier bringing supplies and reinforcements. Almost half the force was sent back to Bulawayo when the remainder went north from Shiloh on 25 November, in the tracks of Lobengula's wagons. Three days later Forbes further reduced his strength by dismissing all his dismounted men and his remaining wagons, which these men escorted back. With 158 mounted men, two Maxims, and pack horses carrying rations for ten days, Forbes reached the Shangani on 3 December.

Though the high drama was still to come, there is controversy enough about this approach march. The first things to strike an impartial reader of the narrative are the disharmony and indiscipline of the force. The Salisbury and the Victoria men had been through the whole campaign together, but in a spirit of rivalry and mutual criticism. On the other hand, they shared a somewhat patronising attitude to the people of the southern column, who had had no useful experience of this kind of warfare. A good commander could have composed these differences, but Forbes had already "alienated all his best friends" and was fidgety, bad-tempered, and all the other things that Norris Newman reported. Forbes's own account is full of scathing references to Raaff, who was in command of the combined Tuli and BBP men. Though he writes of Allan Wilson (who commanded the Victoria section) with approval, it is hard to avoid the conclusion that in this case the account was influenced by subsequent events: *de mortuis nil nisi bonum*. The conflict of wills in the movements of 3-4 December suggests something less than harmony. So do the arrangements for the departure from Shiloh on 25 November. Napier having brought wagons for the use of the patrol, Forbes felt obliged to take some of them, though intending to send them back on the first excuse. He therefore included a hundred dismounted men in the party with the deliberate purpose of sending them back with the wagons. These men were all from the Victoria column.

Forbes's grievance against Raaff was that he was continually harping on the danger of the mission, insisting on caution, and infecting the men with his fears. There is an implication that the task might have been accomplished but for the delay so caused. When the Bubi was reached on the first advance, "there was great dissatisfaction in the force about going further"—because of Raaff's demoralizing influence. The volunteers (though not the BBP who were professionals) were then consulted. The Victoria men were for going on, most of the Salisbury and almost all the Tuli men for going back. Thus the retreat to Shiloh was inevitable. It would be difficult to accuse Raaff of personal cowardice. A few days later he halted his men and went forward alone to investigate some shelters that might have been full of Ndebele. Raaff's concern was for the safety of the men and for the success of the mission, and it was justified by the event.

Forbes claimed, in retrospect, that as they approached the Shangani he and Wilson fully expected to be attacked by two or three thousand men, but that "we had seen in our two fights . . . that the natives could not stand against the Maxims." Not only was this confidence unjustified, but as thus expressed it was an understatement of Forbes's real opinion. On the original advance from Bulawayo the force carried rations for *three days*. Though these were eked out by looted cattle, it is not surprising that there was "great dissatisfaction." This, and the reduced strength and fire-power of the party on the second advance, suggest that Forbes expected to capture Lobengula merely by a quick dash to overtake him.

The demoralization of the defeated Ndebele, though great, was not as complete as Forbes believed. What was left of the regiments decimated at the Shangani or broken at the Bembesi joined the king in his retreat. The fresher regiments of Gampu's division fell into the line too, but soon dropped out again. It may be that there was even more mutual recrimination on the defeated than on the victorious side. Lobengula, too, jettisoned ballast. The pursuers passed two of his wagons, abandoned and burnt beside the track, and then his Bath chair, in which he had been pulled by sixteen men. On 3 December he and his party left their camp south of the Shangani to cross the river, a few hours before the pursuers entered the camp and found the fires still burning.

Lobengula had with him a considerable remnant of his army and some of the indunas who had been prominent in peace and war, including Makwekwe, Mtshane, Manyewu, and Gampu. These were joined later by Ingubogubo, the king's brother, who had survived the "killing of the indunas" at the Tati and had now made his way back.[11] It is reasonable to suppose that it was on their advice, or with their concurrence, that the king composed the message which Mtshane was ordered to dispatch: "Take this and go back. I am conquered." "This" was a bag of gold sovereigns, reported later to have been a thousand. Mtshane entrusted the message and the bag to two messengers, Sihuluhulu and Begani, who were to give both to the white impi. They recrossed the Shangani, intending to approach the impi from the front, but by miscalculation found themselves in its rear. There they encountered two stragglers, almost certainly two batmen who were in the habit of lagging behind, Daniel and Wilson. Being afraid to push through the column to find its "induna" they delivered the message and the money to the batmen, who undertook to pass them on to the right quarter. The temptation was too great. For the sake of the gold they concealed the message too. Nothing was known of it until rumours from the Ndebele side reached Bulawayo more than a month later.[12]

Near the Shangani and in the recently deserted camp two young boys were captured, one being a son of Makwekwe and the other a slave-boy. The former gave misleading, and the latter correct, information. Though the mission of Sihuluhulu was not mentioned, Forbes was told that the king had sent his son Mnyamande (Nyamanda) to Bulawayo with a message of surrender to Jameson. He learned, on the other hand, that a force of about 3,000 had been sent back to attack the column in the bush. They had not done so (possibly because they discovered the Maxims, which they had supposed the column not to have), but were expected to launch their attack during the coming night, 3 December. Forbes formed a so-called laager (without wagons) in an open space near the river. It was as well: the remains of Insuka, Ihlati, and Isiziba, under the command of Manondwane, were in the offing with the king's orders to attack.

The tracks of the king's wagons led away down the left bank of the river. Forbes did not know that they crossed the river not far away. He was taking precautions against attack by the impi supposedly of 3,000, "the majority of whom," however, he "knew to be of very little use from a fighting point of view." According to his information the king had no more than a hundred men with him—a gross underestimate. In the light of these beliefs Forbes intended "to take fifty men and a galloping Maxim on the next morning and make one rush for the King."

Before doing this he needed fuller information. He therefore ordered Allan Wilson to take "his twelve best horses and push on along the spoor as fast as he could to see which way it went, returning by dark, this was about five o'clock, and there was about one-and-a-half hour's more daylight, I said to him that if he went fast he would be able to do five or six miles out and back." It was not expected that in following the trail he would have to cross the river. Wilson went out with seven officers and twelve men. Forbes then sent the American scouts Burnham and Ingram after them to join the patrol.

When the king's trail crossed the river the patrol followed it. After some miles it led to a series of *skerms* and hide-outs in the bush, in which the occupants were preparing their evening meal. These were men of the Babambeni regiment with their families. Wilson seems to have thought that he could achieve his object without firing a shot. The patrol rode through the Ndebele encampments calling out "to the Ubabambeni in kitchen kaffir, 'Hikona dubula, Ubabambeni [don't shoot]'. Then the Mbambambeni didn't shoot." Reaching the king's remaining wagon, they tried the standard greeting, "Sakabona, Lobengula! Sakabona, Lobengula!" They lifted the flap of the wagon-tent, found no one there, but took away a quantity of ammunition.

It may have been at this point that they captured a man named Siluwane, but afterwards "released him, telling him he had better go back to his people and not come any more, saying You can go and stay now. The matter is finished now. We only want Lobengula now. And that man turned round the other way and ran fast and found Magwegwe and told him and warned him."

At about 6.30 p.m., which was sundown, Wilson decided that soft words would not do. He "called a halt and consulted us. It was decided by all to make a dash and try to catch the King. The howling, shouting, scurring [sic] as we dashed through the scherms occupied by the King's guard and their families . . . must be left to one's imagination." Again the prey eluded them, and the patrol moved away a short distance to camp for the night. No fires were lit—an elementary precaution—and Wilson may have hoped that the king would return to his wagon under cover of darkness; so at least the Ndebele believed. Lobengula however had abandoned the wagon and, with Makwekwe, "taken to horses."

When the startled Babambeni and Ingwekwe (the other regiment involved) realised how small Wilson's party was, they ceased their howling and moved to surround it. The move was stopped by rain, which had now started to fall heavily, accompanied by thunder. The patrol was therefore not attacked during the night. During this respite certain dispositions were made. Two men whose horses were unfit were sent back across the river. In addition Captain Napier and two other men, moving separately, made their way back to Forbes with a message. This included a report of the events and situation and also (according to Napier, who committed it to his diary at the time) a request: "to ask him to be here very early in the morning, with the rest of the column and the Maxim guns."

As Wilson was under orders to return to camp by nightfall, the change of plan was an act of disobedience which, for the moment, puts the responsibility for what followed squarely on his shoulders. The unfortunate relations of Forbes with his subordinates were a factor too: a different commander might have been obeyed. Forbes, however, subsequently took over the full responsibility by approving of Wilson's decision. The decision and the approval are easy to understand. Wilson had the prey almost within his grasp. Three of his men had got lost in the bush, he could not return without them, and they were not found by Burnham until after the message to Forbes had been sent. On this point the blame is hard to apportion. Napier, who was the intermediary between the two officers at the critical moment, wrote in his diary: "Whatever may befall this action, no blame can ever be attached to a single individual."

According to Forbes, Napier (who arrived about 11 o'clock) considered that the column would have to join Wilson by 4 a.m. if it were to attack the king at daylight. Forbes rightly refused to commit his force to such a night march across the flank of an impi of 3,000 which was believed to be, and part of which was, in the adjacent bush waiting to attack.[13] He had, then, three options: to recall Wilson, whose patrol now consisted of seventeen men and was much more manoeuvrable than the whole column; to send him limited reinforcements, or to leave him to fend for himself. He refused to recall Wilson because "I had absolute confidence in his judgment and he had decided to wait there, he knew as well as I did how important it was that the King should be caught and he knew, which I did not, the exact state of affairs about the King. If I recalled him I undid all that we had been striving for so long." He refused also to leave the small patrol to its own devices. Raaff begged him not to deplete the column: "We are too small as we are." So Forbes compromised. He decided to send Capt. H.J. Borrow (fellow adventurer over the years, and now business partner, of Johnson and Heany) with twenty men, but, in deference to Raaff's remonstrance, no Maxim, to support Wilson.[14] This was the main decision for which Forbes has been blamed. He got the worst of both worlds, and merely fattened the patrol for the slaughter.

Borrow left the camp soon after midnight. One of Napier's fellow messengers went back to show him the way. Two of the men, getting lost, rejoined the column. The rest of Borrow's patrol reached Wilson without incident.

At first light an attempt was made to carry out the plan of the previous evening—to rush the king's wagon and capture him. The Ndebele are said to have been forewarned by Mtshane, the induna who had commanded at Bonko: "I know the white men . . . and I know they will be here very early in the morning so get up and get ready." The attackers were beaten back without having reached the wagon. Wilson withdrew his men and fell back slowly along the track towards the river. Soon after this Burnham, his fellow American scout Ingram, and W.L. Gooding of Borrow's party were making their way back to Forbes. By Burnham's account, Wilson had asked him whether he thought he could get through to Forbes, presumably to urge him on. Burnham said he would try. He and his companions ran the gauntlet of a shower of bullets from a large party of Ndebele who were closing in on the patrol from the south (the river) side, but succeeded in getting away and reaching the river, which they found to be in flood. After following it upstream for a mile and a half they managed to swim their horses across. So far Burnham; in Marshall Hole's papers, however, there is some correspondence tending to show that the three scouts were not sent back by Wilson, but ran away. Hole's theory is that they were out scouting, saw the patrol surrounded, and made a dash for it.

However this may be, Burnham, Ingram, and Gooding were the last white men to see Wilson's party alive. Immediately after shaking off their attackers "they heard Major Wilson's party come to them, and heavy firing began." The rest of the story comes from Ndebele who were there, but whose accounts do not all agree. Mhlahlo of the Insuka regiment remembered it thus:

> We surrounded them and started to fight. They got off their horses and fired at us over them. All the horses were killed, and then the white men, those of them that were left, lay down behind the dead horses, and fired at us. After many of the white men were killed, the few that were left, all of whom were wounded, lay on their backs, and held their rifles between their feet, and fired. After a little, the firing stopped, and we knew the cartridges were finished. We then rushed up and assegaied the remainder, who covered their eyes with their hands. We lost many more than the number of white men, for they were men indeed, and fought us for many hours.

According to others of their admiring enemies, some were seen at the end to be writing hasty notes. Several witnesses agree that at one stage the white men stood up and sang—the national anthem? "Nearer, my God, to Thee"? The song was not identified.[16] Those who covered their faces with their hands were said also to have prayed. When not many were left, one called out in Fanakalo, "Hikona qeda zonke, Matabele" [Don't finish us all], but it was a hopeless cry. As the Martini-Henry ammunition gave out the survivors began to use their revolvers, and there is some evidence that some used their last rounds to shoot themselves.

Mhlahlo said that the last white men were assegaied; if so their fate was exceptional, because the Ndebele were using firearms throughout the fight. But here is another version, from Ntabeni Khumalo: "There was one of the white men who never took shelter. He stood there all the time with a little stick in his hand. All the others were dead, and we thought that he ought to be taken prisoner; but a young majaha could not resist the temptation and shot him." If Ntabeni's memory can be relied upon, this can only have been Wilson himself. One skeleton was afterwards found ten yards from the rest, but was not identified; the other thirty-three were huddled together.

The fight had begun at daybreak. Though the Ndebele were not then familiar with clocks, they could in later years translate their impressions into clock time. Mhlahlo thought "it was all over when the sun was there (indicating about 10 o'clock)." Siyatsha thought eleven; Ginyilitshe said that the end could not have come before one or two o'clock, and that "the people who had died in the morning had already blown up before the battle was over." Which, if any of them, was right? The answer depends essentially on how much ammunition Wilson's men had taken from Lobengula's wagon the night before, and no one knows how much they took. Apart from that supplement, each man had no more than a hundred rounds for his rifle and twenty for the revolver. The fighting was not continuous. The first encounter was followed almost at once by the attack of the other impi on Forbes, south of the river. Those opposing Wilson, thinking that Forbes had arrived to support him, broke off the action and scattered; then the mistake was realised and the attack resumed. By all accounts the interval was short, but it must have been during that break that Wilson withdrew along the track and that the scouts left the patrol. Colenbrander, who was riding behind Forbes as the column moved out of camp at daybreak, heard "terrific firing" across the river and called to Forbes, "They cannot keep that up long, Sir, with their stock of ammunition." Nor did they, if we can trust the reports of the men on the south bank.

So died Wilson's patrol. These were brave men and the enemies who killed them—themselves "connoisseurs of bravery"—were impressed. It is not unfair to say that the gallantry of this band was less than that of Imbizo and Ingubo at Egodade; those regiments charged to their deaths by their free decision, whereas Wilson's men had no option but to sell their lives as dearly as they could. Yet the honours were now better balanced. Each side won its greatest glory in defeat.

One factor that cannot be blamed is the flooded river. It is a wonder that it had not risen before. Forbes's column had struggled through heavy rain and mud all the way, but the Shangani at the place of the action was easily fordable during the night of 3-4 December. Floods higher up brought it down in spate early on the 4th, so that Burnham and his companions were the first of the various messengers to have difficulty in crossing. Wilson knew nothing of this when he asked Burnham (if he did ask him) to go back. A few minutes later the patrol was surrounded, and could not after that have got to the river. Forbes on the other hand could not then cross the river to Wilson's side, because he was otherwise engaged. We may safely assume that by the time he was again free to attempt a crossing, it would have been too late. The flooding of the Shangani made no difference to the outcome, though it prevented Forbes from going to the scene and learning the truth.

Forbes had begun to break up his camp at daylight with the intention of going to the assistance of the patrol. "Just as we were ready to move we heard heavy firing across the river where the King was, it lasted several minutes, and then ceased." Before he could learn the meaning of this his column itself came under fire as it moved down an open space between the bush and the river. Manondwane's impi[17] was firing from the shelter of the bush. After some brisk shooting and casualties on both sides, each party withdrew and the action was broken off.

If the loss of Wilson's patrol had not convinced Forbes that he underestimated his enemy, the experiences on the return march up the Shangani ought to have done so. He had arranged to have a relief column meet him on the Shangani where the Hunters' Road crossed it. The march up the river bank began on the morning of the 5th, and it was not till the evening of the 14th that the relief column was met twenty-two miles out of Inyati. For most of the distance the king's rearguard harassed the column. Rations were almost exhausted. Cattle were captured, but often driven off again by the Ndebele during an attack. Horses had to be abandoned every day. On the 10th, after a surprise attack, the column had to escape by a ruse. Some horses and much equipment were left to deceive the enemy, while the column slipped away in silence at 10 p.m., the Maxims now being carried by relays of six men each.

From first to last Forbes had underrated his enemy. The doomed patrol lasted as long as its ammunition: one hundred rifle rounds per man, plus twenty for the revolver, and what they could take from Lobengula's wagon. Forbes calculated that on the return march he had enough ammunition for one "big fight," but after that he would have to laager and wait for supplies to reach him. On leaving Shiloh the men carried rations for ten days; they had to subsist for twenty before meeting the relief column. All was done on the assumption that a small, lightly encumbered party could make a "quick dash" for the king; on the assumption, therefore, that the king would be weakly defended. The assumption was wrong. A well-equipped force, however, though it would not have run into a glorious disaster, might never have caught up to Lobengula at all.

A confused report was blurted out to Jameson by Ingram, whose nerves were overstrained after a dangerous ride from the Shangani. The relief column at Inyati included not only Jameson and Sir John Willoughby but Major Sawyer, Loch's military secretary, and Rhodes himself—a sure indication of the concern felt about the fate of the patrol.

There was another indication. A Court of Inquiry—Goold-Adams, Willoughby, and H.M. Heyman—was set up to investigate the story of the Shangani patrol. It did so, but by Loch's decision neither the evidence given nor any conclusions to be drawn from it by the court or by the general officer commanding were allowed to be published. Raaff, who fell ill after returning to Bulawayo, died before he had finished telling his story.[18]

Thus Lobengula was spared the humiliation of being brought back in triumph to Bulawayo. It was to protect the king that the battles on the Shangani had been fought; he was riding on to the north, with a faithful remnant of followers, while the regiments at the river were holding back his pursuers. Before he left he made a last bitter speech:

> You have said that it is me that is killing you: now here are your masters coming. You disobeyed my orders, and now you have put me in this bad fix. You want me to be caught by the white men. But the white men will never catch me. I will throw myself over a height. Now you will find what real trouble is. You will have to pull and shove wagons; but under me you never did this kind of thing . . . All my property will be taken by the white people. You can take my cattle back; but the white people will have them . . . Now you be joyful because here are your future rulers . . . The white people are coming now. I didn't want to fight with them . . . Oh, I am remembering the words of Lotsche . . .

He protested that not he, but they, had been responsible for the many killings with which people charged him, and he identified one scapegoat: "Bhozongwane, you were the man who caused so many people to be killed by telling lies about them." After the speech he mounted his horse and rode away "with a body of people whose hearts wanted to go with him and who followed him."

The king and a small party went down the Shangani till they came to Pashu's country, east of Wankie and some thirty miles south of the Zambezi. A larger party followed a different route, so as not to betray the king's trail to the enemy. The story is taken up by Siyatsha, who was a boy of about sixteen at the time and was with the larger party:

> We joined the King and his people in Pashu's country at a place now [1943] called Mlindi. I cannot remember what this locality was called before the events I am

now relating took place. The King was camped with his Counsellors and we camped some distance away. A few days later there came word by one Baza that the King's impis had surrendered. I overheard the King speak to Magwegwe. He said "Do you remember your words?" Magwegwe replied "Yes, King." The King said again to him "what were those words?" The reply came "When you die so shall I." As soon as those words had been said the King took a small bottle and drank some of the contents. Magwegwe picked the bottle up and did likewise. After about three or four hours the King and Magwegwe, *Ilunda le Nkosi* (meaning the mouthpiece of the King) died.

Makwekwe was buried near by.

The king's body was wrapped in the skin of a black ox and carried on a stretcher by a party of principal mourners. The body was in a sitting position. It was taken some distance and buried in a cave, together with many of the dead king's possessions.

"A King is always buried in a cave," Siyatsha said, "but not a commoner."[19] He was a king, and more: "he was a gentleman in his way," said Moffat, "and was foully sinned against by Jameson and his gang."[20]

The king was dead, but the statements made in this chapter, and by other historians, that the Ndebele were defeated in 1893 have been challenged by Julian Cobbing in *The Ndebele under the Khumalos*. He has argued "that the Ndebele were by no means decisively defeated in 1893, that their political leadership, although temporarily shaken, remained intact, that the Ndebele 'military system' (largely misunderstood, especially by the Company) was not broken up, and even that the full extent of Company spoliation during 1894 and 1895 has not been brought out."[21] It follows that the fighting that broke out in 1896 was not a "rebellion" or a new war, but merely a resumption of the original conflict, temporarily suspended.

The fact of continuity in political leadership and military organization is, I think, Cobbing's important contribution at this point. Whether or not the Ndebele were defeated in 1893 is largely a question of semantics. The Company robbed them of land and cattle, and imposed on them a system of forced labour, punishments not tolerated by an undefeated people. Yet their potential for resuming the fight was left intact. The Company and its men discovered that truth in 1896.

NOTES CHAPTER 7

1 CO 879/39/454, no.137, encl.36, p.159; no.138, encl.2, p.162; 39/459, no.25, encl.11, 13, 14, pp.18-19, encl.31, pp.24-5; 40/461, no.14, pp.14-16; CO 417/64/19251, pp.251-8; 103/19543, minutes; W.A. Wills and L.T. Collingridge, *The Downfall of Lobengula*, p.197; Stafford Glass, *The Matabele War*, pp.196-7 and 209-10.
2 C.L. Norris Newman, *Matabeleland and How We Got It*, pp.187-8; Oliver Ransford, *Bulawayo, Historic Battleground of Rhodesia*, p.54; Neville Jones, *Rhodesian*

Genesis, p.82; Ian Colvin, *Life of Jameson*, vol. I, p.274. Frank Johnson (in *Great Days*, pp.220-4), asserts that both he and Jameson assumed that he, Johnson, was to command the combined columns. Jameson refused to allow them to take wagons. As Johnson insisted on having wagons, he was not given the command, and was told to leave the country; his presence there would have discouraged the men from following Forbes. Forbes took command, and got the wagons after all. I have not found confirmation of this story in any other source.

3 Wills and Collingridge, *Downfall of Lobengula*, pp.101-5, 110; R. Summers and C.W. Pagden, *Warriors*, p.30; C.H.W. Donovan, *With Wilson in Matabeleland*, pp. 246-7; Glass, *Matabele War*, p.192; Colvin, *Jameson*, vol. I, p.272; Diary of Matabele Wilson, p.324.

4 Wills and Collingridge, *Downfall of Lobengula*, pp.105-12; Summers and Pagden, *Warriors*, pp.114-17; Donovan, *Wilson in Matabeleland*, pp.239-43; Jones, *Rhodesian Genesis*, pp.85-7; CO 879/39/459, no.141, encl., pp.153-5; CO 879/40/461, no.15, encl.1, pp.17-20.

5 A.W. Kinglake, *The Invasion of the Crimea*, vol. II, p.578. The American, Burnham, made the comparison with Pickett's charge at Gettysburg, but that was on quite a different scale: 6,000 casualties out of 15,000 (*Oxford Companion to American History*, s. v. Pickett's Charge.) Almost all the information on which this account of the war is based came directly or indirectly from sources connected with the Company. Julian Cobbing has argued that these sources gave a greatly exaggerated estimate of Ndebele losses in the war; e.g. that according to the missionary Helm the total losses of Imbizo, Inqobo and Insuka in its whole course were only about 130 ("The Ndebele under the Khumalos," p.367, n.7). I prefer, for the present, to leave the accounts of the two battles as they stand, but with the postscript that all the estimates must be accepted with some reserve.

6 For Egodade, Wills and Collingridge, *Downfall of Lobengula*, pp.120-5; Summers and Pagden, *Warriors*, pp.118-25; Ransford, *Bulawayo*, pp.54-8; C.H.W. Donovan, *Wilson in Matabeleland*, pp.265-7; CO 879/40/461, no.15, encl.2, pp.20-3; Foster Windram oral interviews (WI 8/1/1), Siatcha, pp.16-17; Ginyalitsha, p.16; (WI 8/1/2) Ntabeni Kumalo, p.24.

7 See above, ch.1; these regiments did not form a "division."

8 Wills and Collingridge, *Downfall of Lobengula*, pp.218-21; CO 879/40/461, no.14, encl.1, pp.14-16; no.54, encl.1, pp.118-19; no.65, encl.1, p.138. Kgama's men received the "Queen's shilling"—£1,100 altogether. (CO 879/40/461, no.133, p.209 and no.146, p.226.)

9 Wills and Collingridge, *Downfall of Lobengula*, pp.109-10, 126-30; Reminiscences of P.D. Crewe; Diary of Matabele Wilson, August 1893. A small force of BBP was all that was needed in the Matopos (CO 879/40/461, no.77, pp.150-1; no.161, p.252). Ntabeni gave evidence that has a bearing on Wilson's story: ". . . the indunas said to him: 'You go to Ematojeni (in the Matoppos) and hide there.' And Lobengula replied: 'Is that the place that you have already told the white people they will find me at?' And he refused to go there." (Foster Windram, WI 8/1/2, Ntabeni Kumalo, pp.26-7.) According to Fairbairn and Usher, as reported to Goold-Adams, the king left Umvutshwa on 23 October, i.e., before the Bonko battle. (CO 879/39/459, no.145, encl.7, p.161.) Vere Stent, *A Personal Record of Some Incidents in the Life of Cecil Rhodes*, p.7.

10 CO 879/39/459, no.131, encl., pp.141-2. Sources for the story of the Shangani Patrol which follows are: Wills and Collingridge, *Downfall of Lobengula*, ch.10, 11, 12; William Napier, Diary of the Shangani Patrol (Misc. NA 4/1/1); H. Marshall Hole, *The Making of Rhodesia*, pp.318-25; Statement by Mhlahlo (Misc. MH 1/1/1); Reminiscences of Gambo (Gampu) recorded by C.L. Carbutt (Misc. GA 2/1/1); Summers and Pagden, *Warriors*, pp.127-30; Glass, *Matabele War*, pp.226-33; Jones, *Rhodesian Genesis*, pp.94-104; CO 879/40/461, no.49, encl., pp.104-7; F.R. Burnham, *Scouting on Two Continents*, ch. XVI-XVIII; Foster Windram oral interviews, WI 8/1/1 and 8/1/2, interviews with Siatcha, Ginyalitsha, and Ntabeni.

11 CO 879/40/461, no.48, encl.2, p.103.

12 The troopers Daniel and Wilson were later tried and sentenced to fourteen years' imprisonment. Irregularities in the trial led to a review of the case, and their release in 1896. In the meantime they had been temporarily released because the Salisbury gaol was needed for other purposes during the rebellion. (Glass, *Matabele War*, ch. XX; and cf. below, ch. 12.)

13 Capt. Coventry estimated the number, when they attacked the next morning, at 200. (CO 879/40/461, no.44, p.105.)

14 Wills and Collingridge, *Downfall of Lobengula*, p.162.

15 Marshall Hole papers, HO 1/3/4(i); Burnham, *Scouting on Two Continents*, pp.184-8. Some of the Ndebele thought, mistakenly, that one of the scouts returning from the patrol was "Johan" (Colenbrander). He was with Forbes.

16 According to M.D.W. Jeffreys (Johannesburg *Star* weekly, 8 August 1970, p.14) the consensus of opinion a few years after the event was that the men sang "Nearer, my God, to Thee." Wills and Collingridge, *Downfall of Lobengula*, p.168; statement by Mhlahlo (Misc. MH 1/1/1).

17 Gampu (in Misc. GA 2/1/1) afterwards claimed that he was in command. At the time of this fight, care had to be taken to prevent the loss of the cattle which were Forbes's commissariat. The man who did this was Jan Grootboom, for whom see below, ch.11.

18 Wills and Collingridge, *Downfall of Lobengula*, ch. XII; Glass, *Matabele War*, pp.230-2.

19 Foster Windram oral interviews (WI 8/1/1), Siatcha, p.21; Ginyalitsha, p.21; Mvutu and Posela, p.7; (WI 8/1/2), Ntabeni Kumalo, pp.26-7; *Rhodesiana*, 23, article by C.K. Cooke, pp. 3-53 (generally), and pp.14-16 (specifically). This article is the definitive one on Lobengula's death and burial and on the discovery of his grave by an official party in 1943. In his final speech Lobengula spoke as if his subjects had wanted to be ruled by the whites rather than by him. This implication will seem incredible, but was later stated as a fact by several Ndebele witnesses; e.g. Ncupela (Foster Windram WI 8/1/1, p.4): the indunas "plotted secretly to kill [Lotshe] . . . That was a way of getting Lotje out of the way. Then Lobengula could be conquered by the Europeans, if he fought them at all . . . Yes, that is so. They would rather be ruled by the white people." The king's last speech as given in the text has been put together from the various statements in WI 8/1/1-2.

20 R.U. Moffat, *John Smith Moffat*, p.346.

21 Cobbing, "Ndebele under the Khumalos," pp.366-7.

CHAPTER 8

Bricks without Straw

THE COMPANY'S FINANCES

Jameson had won his war; but was it his war? We have not quite disposed of that question. So far, the evidence has all pointed to the conclusion that the war originated in Jameson's mind under the impact of the Victoria "incident." There is, however, quite a different theory which has been widely accepted: that the war was provoked by the Company in order to avert a financial catastrophe. It was a tempting explanation at the time to anyone at all familiar with the Company's methods, especially as the beneficial effects of a conquest of Matabeleland had been canvassed years before the event—by the *Financial News*, for instance, on 9 January 1891.

Thus, when the news of the "second border incident" reached London, Fairfield reacted in his usual fashion:

> I have my suspicions that the firing on our men was a "put up job" on the part of some of the underlings of the Charter Group. It was the general opinion, as I was told 2 days before the occurrence, that such firing would send up the shares and help the Bulls out of their difficulties; and as a matter of fact it had this effect. [Marginal note by Olivier: "I heard this also, and the shares went up *before* we heard of the firing!"]

Does this mean that the real purpose of the war was to boost "Chartereds" on the stock exchange?[1]

The circumstantial evidence tends to support this theory, the direct evidence to refute it. Jameson on 18 July was reacting to the situation before his eyes, not play-acting in order to disguise the fact that he was obeying orders from London. Rhodes, the same evening, meant what he said when he insisted that there was no money for a war. The directors in London responded to the news from Fort Victoria with doubt and anxiety, modified in varying degrees by their confidence in the men on the spot. On 15 July 1893, Maguire wrote to Rhodes that "this bother with Lobengula is a nuisance just when we are pressing for a hut tax but it has not excited much attention and so far nothing has been said." On 1 September, when the war preparations were well in hand, Albert Grey wrote to Rhodes:

I gather that it is your intention to find some way round the Govt. Prohibition and settle the Matabele question this September once and for all. The recent Mails from the Cape and your short but confident cables show us that you think you can do it and without running undue risk. We are in the darkness, at least I am as to your plans, but I have the fullest confidence in the wisdom of any move which you and Jameson may agree in thinking the right one, and if you decide upon a forward Policy I shall be satisfied that you have sufficient resources within your reach to make your forward course the right and prudent one. So I can only say, do whatever you think right. We will support you whatever the issue, but keep us as fully informed as you can for our guidance with the Govt. and the Public . . . Old Ld. Grey [who though a negrophilist thought the Ndebele should be taught a lesson] shares the nervousness of Military Men as to the dangers which surround an advance by a small body of men into a difficult and bush country.

It is clear that the forward policy did not originate in St. Swithin's Lane.[2]

That is not quite the whole story, however. Jameson's policy could not have been supported by the directors without the concurrence of Rhodes. Rhodes, whose immediate reaction was negative, came round to Jameson's view. The circumstantial evidence (which is all there is) suggests that the financial needs of the Company may have been a large factor in his conversion.

It is difficult for various reasons to put together a coherent story of financial operations which Rhodes with unconscious euphemism called "combining the commercial with the imaginative." The *Economist* commented with restraint that "in this instance, at all events, the imaginative element has been uppermost, so far as the proprietors are concerned, though the commercial element has not been absent, in the dealings of some of those behind the scenes." It referred to "the curious financial methods which are adopted by the group of companies of which Mr. Rhodes is the paramount chief, and they are not of a kind which would be tolerated in ordinary joint-stock undertakings." The Chartered Company and its imperial venture were in fact a gamble against long odds. With an aura of Monte Carlo hanging over the operation one cannot expect to explain it by simple logic.

If there is any peg on which to hang the varied manipulations it is the parasitical relation of the Central Search Association to the Chartered Company. It will be remembered that the former, constituted in May 1889 by the amalgamation of rival interests, owned the Rudd Concession. The leading members of the association were also the promoters of the Chartered Company. Before the charter brought the latter company into existence these promoters drew up certian "Heads of Terms for Working Agreement" between the association and the company-to-be. A "curious financial method" indeed: one of the parties to it did not yet exist, but the negotiators on the two sides were the same people. Though the "Working Agreement" was submitted to the Colonial Office, on paper, in 1893, the document naturally bore no signatures and was in no sense an agreement between two parties. It was a declaration of intent, addressed to themselves, by the promoters. Hawksley was close enough to the truth when he admitted that there was no agreement "in writing." The content was as remarkable as the form: the BSA Company was to bear all the responsibility and expense and the association was to receive half the profits.

In July 1890 Central Search wound itself up and transferred its assets to a successor, the United Concessions Company. The ostensible reason for the change was that several companies, through agreements with members of Central Search, had an interest in the association without formal membership. They wanted scrip; a public company (which the association was not) would provide it and tidy up the irregularities. The capital of Central Search was "deemed" to consist of 120,000 one-pound shares (subsequently increased to 121,000), but this was an arbitrary sum used merely for the purpose of apportioning shares in the asset among the owners; it was said to have no relation to the real value of that asset. The United Concessions Company, on the other hand, was capitalized at £4,000,000—quite a big jump from £121,000. In view of what followed, it is reasonable to suppose that the most important reason for substituting the new company for the old was the need for this more "realistic" valuation. It was "understood," Sydney Olivier wrote, that the figure chosen was the result of this calculation: the capital of the Chartered Company was one million pounds, and the shares at that time stood at £4—book value therefore £4,000,000. United Concessions would own half the profits, so that its capital should be equal to that of the BSA Company.

In devising the "Working Agreement" the promoters so far overreached themselves as to include a sixth clause providing that, after the Company gave up its administrative responsibilities, it would have to give Central Search *seventy* per cent of the profits. This outrageous clause became one of the reasons for making a change in the agreement.

"Whereas the insertion of Clause 6 in the draft Working Agreement was not authorized by the Chartered Company and was an error; and whereas" the Rudd Concession authorized its holders to exclude rivals from Lobengula's dominions, "it is expedient that the Chartered Company should acquire the Lobengula Concession." In August 1890, therefore, the newborn United Concessions Company, the Exploring Company, and the BSA Company made an agreement which it was hoped would remove some of the inconveniences of the old one with Central Search. Now the Chartered Company was to acquire the Rudd Concession, together with certain assets of the Exploring Company. The price was to be a million shares (925,000 to United Concessions, 75,000 to Exploring), newly created for the purpose. So the capital of the BSA Company would be doubled without significantly affecting the distribution of profits: the inner group would still get its half share, but under a more respectable guise. Thus the metamorphosis of Central Search into United Concessions made sense: it would have been difficult to convince anyone that a million pounds (or four million) was a fair price for an asset carrying a price-tag of £121,000.

By this acquisition the Chartered Company, however, was expected to gain also. Its gain would be in the credit-worthiness badly needed for the purpose of borrowing. The three companies (BSA, UC, and Exploring) were to hold shareholders' meetings to ratify the agreement before the end of 1890.[3]

In October 1890 Chartered shares were at last made available to the public, which had the privilege of buying them at a premium of nearly 300 per cent. The moment chosen was a good one: the Pioneers had just arrived safely at their destination and everything seemed possible; but such moments were not destined to recur. Driving up the shares on the market ("helping the Bulls out of their difficulties") was an absolute necessity if large sums were to be borrowed at reasonable rates,[4] but in the years to come this was achieved, when at all, by the members of the inner circle's buying from one another.

The agreement of August was not, after all, ratified before the end of 1890. The Chartered Company did not hold a shareholders' meeting. On 25 November it made an agreement with the other companies to postpone the deadline for a year. The reason given to the Colonial Office three years later for the postponement was that circumstances had arisen and were "likely to continue for a considerable time rendering it inexpedient to convene extraordinary general meetings of the members of the Concessions Company the Exploring Company and the Chartered Company respectively for the purpose of such sanction." The only conceivable reason for its being "inexpedient" then and "for a considerable time" to convene meetings was that they were not expected to give "such sanction." The fear was not soon removed: as the new deadline approached it was further postponed to 1892 and then again to 1893.

The postponements would be easier to explain if it were not that the first, at least, was decided almost by the spin of a coin:

> Beit, Cawston, C.D. Rudd and Maguire have had many discussions as to the expediency, or otherwise, of deferring the amalgamation scheme, and we have felt it very difficult to determine which is the better course; there are so many points pro and con. On the whole I think in recommending a postponement the right policy has been adopted . . . the postponement gets rid of the necessity for a meeting of shareholders of the B.S.A. Coy. for the present.

Yet as late as 3 October Beit was expecting the meeting to be held on 10 November, and thought "we will carry the fusion all right." In 1891 and 1892 ordinary general meetings of the Company were held, but at these it was possible to divert attention from a difficult question as it would not have been at an extraordinary general meeting called for the specific purpose of settling that question. At the meeting in December 1891 the directors confronted the shareholders for the first time. On the credit side of the books they could show capital, but not income; on the debit side it could be seen that the capital was being rapidly sunk in the great enterprise. On the whole, however, Grey thought the meeting "a decided success." It is true that "there was a growl against the half profits arrangement with the owners of the Rudd Concession— but it did not amount to much. I wish we had that arrangement which you made for us [the acquisition of the Concession] *formally*, as it is virtually, settled. We shall find the want of it when the time comes for issuing debentures."[5]

At the second annual general meeting, on 29 November, 1892, every trick of rhetoric and juggling with figures was used to make the best impression. Rhodes himself was there to make a heart-warming speech. "The Directors," Olivier commented, "avoided any disagreeable questions by Rhodes' stoking up of the enthusiasm of the meeting: which infected all the morning papers, and knocked the P.M.G. [*Pall Mall Gazette*] incoherent." There was no question of profit or dividends, but the Mashonaland enterprise was proudly proclaimed to be "self-supporting." As Fairfield noted, the figures had been made to balance by omitting from the debit side items which added up to £135,600—as well as others on which there was no information.[6]

The time was approaching when the shareholders would demand the "commercial" as well as the "imaginative." The directors were haunted by the fear of this; occasionally they clutched at straws which they hoped might save them, such as the acquisition of the Lippert Concession. In June 1891 Beit had a bout of optimism: "We have lately educated the public up to the half share business and paved the way for the fusion of the United Concession with the Charter." This was a flash in the pan; the deadline was again postponed. In August 1892 Maguire was writing to Rhodes, "I fear there will be great difficulties with the second million," and another postponement followed.

That was in November, shortly before the "enthusiastic" meeting. The next agreement, on 31 July 1893, provided for a future debenture issue by the BSA Company, and bound United Concessions to subscribe (or to procure subscriptions for) £185,000 of this issue, and likewise the Exploring Company to procure £15,000. These obligations would be effective only when the "principal agreement"—the doubling of the capital and the transfer of the Rudd Concession—had been sanctioned and confirmed. The arrangement by which the BSA Company was to give Exploring 2,000 of its Bechuanaland Railway shares (as will be explained presently) was also a part of this agreement of July 1893.[7]

As we shall see, the Company all this time was drifting towards the rocks. It needed money desperately, and could get it only by borrowing. Some of the questions prompted by this combination of circumstances are: was the Company's ability to borrow held to depend on the carrying through of the "amalgamation," and, if so, why? If so, again, why was no attempt made to carry it through for more than three years? Lastly, how was the conquest of Matabeleland expected to facilitate the "amalgamation," or was it intended to save the Company in some more direct way?

The answer to the first question is probably that, while the deal with United

293 Bricks without Straw

Concessions was not regarded as essential and urgent in the euphoric atmosphere of 1890 (obviously it was not), or even in the grimmer times of 1891 and 1892, it had come to be so regarded in 1893, when alternative ways of raising the Company's credit had failed to produce any effect. On 12 October 1893, Hawksley wrote to Cawston that "Rhodes wants the amalgamation put thro' in order to raise the £200,000." That was the sum provided for in the agreement of 31 July.

The question whether or not to face the shareholders with this proposal was, as we saw, difficult to answer in 1890, but it was answered in the negative then and in the following two years. The reason for holding back was fear of an opposition party, at the heart of which were A.O. Ochs, F.A. Gillam, and their associates in the Matabeleland Company, who claimed to own the Baines Concession. To buy off their threatened opposition to the charter in 1889 they were given 5,000 shares and the right (still withheld from the general public) to buy other shares. It was apparently only after this deal that Ochs formed the Matabeleland Company, whose sole capital was the 5,000 Chartered shares. Others who had been similarly rewarded for calling off their opposition—such as Alfred Haggard of the Austral Africa Company—became, like the Ochs group, cuckoos in the Chartered nest. They acquired information which they passed on to Henry Labouchere for use in his campaign against the Company in *Truth* and in the House of Commons.

The objection of all these was not to the substitution of a new profit-sharing agreement for the old, but to the original agreement itself and to the sleight-of-hand by which it was introduced. This was what the "growling" at the first annual general meeting was about; this was one of the "disagreeable questions" avoided at the 1892 meeting by "stoking up enthusiasm." There was an element of blackmail in the opposition: in 1891 Beit wrote that "Ochs people are still disagreeable, but they have not the slightest right to claim anything in a new issue, as they wish to make their shareholders believe." By 1893, having apparently realised this, they were seeking from the Chancery Division an injunction restraining the BSA Company from paying half of its profits to United Concessions, and claiming not unreasonably that no agreement to this effect actually existed. The case was lost in Chancery and on appeal, because as successive judges pointed out the remedy lay with the plaintiffs' fellow-shareholders. At the extraordinary general meeting in November 1893, the plaintiffs had their say, but were so vastly outvoted that the chairman declared the resolution to be passed unanimously.[8]

This result makes one wonder why the directors had been afraid to bring the matter to a decision in previous years. It is possible that they overestimated the danger. They were certainly hoping, as every mail arrived, for news of vast gold discoveries which would dissipate opposition to anything they proposed. In the meantime, as no such news came, the critical condition of the Company drove cautious investors to unload their shares. It is possible, though there is no positive statement of it, that the directors were hoping that Ochs and the other harsh critics would sell out altogether, and so cease to trouble the shareholders' meetings. In June 1891 the Matabeleland Company was reported to have sold about 15,000 Chartered shares; but it did not eliminate itself entirely.

The main difference between 1893 and earlier years was that hope had had time to fade and alternative methods of salvation to be exhausted. At first it was not too difficult to borrow from the obvious sources, such as De Beers, but these were short term loans which had to be repaid. The directors themselves sold shares and lent to the Company, partly it may be assumed out of the proceeds of these sales. The balance of seventeen shillings on the partly paid-up shares could of course be called, and even when it was not it could figure as an asset in the books; but all this was still inadequate.[9]

In December 1891 Farquhar wrote to Rhodes: "We understand that the De Beers Co., will settle for the £35,000 due at the end of the month—we have to pay £30,000 in Feb., £30,000 March and hear that another £30,000 is on the way so that what with sundries quite half the £200,000 remaining, when *all* calls are paid, is *gone* . . . We are . . . *on our last legs*. Our shares are at $^{15}/_{16}$ @ £1—and *few* buyers." The position continued to deteriorate. In January 1892 "the last £75,000 to De Beers and the £35,000 due to Beit and yourself [Rhodes] was a terrible blow . . . Our expenses and responsibilities maturing amount in all to £215,000—and our *calls* and cash to £217,000." At the end of 1892, a few weeks after the meeting at which Rhodes "stoked up enthusiasm," Cawston was explaining that though the board had agreed to pay £500 to Joseph Thomson for his hazardous treaty-making work north of the Zambezi, the Company was not now in a position to pay this sum. It would do so when the funds allowed; in the meantime, if Thomson was in need, Cawston personally would advance something to him. Six months later there was anxiety to pay Hawksley, the Company's solicitor, his fees, for which he had been waiting a long time. Throughout 1892 there had been talk of "panic," of "dealing with each bill as it comes," and of pressure from the Standard Bank.[10]

The accounts laid before the shareholders at their first meeting in December 1891, and covering the period from the charter (29 October 1889) to 31 March 1891, would have been enough to frighten anyone whose judgment was not distorted by "the imaginative." What were called "general expenses" for that period amount to £402,050, nearly half the total capital of the Company. These items included office expenses, administration, the police, the Pioneer Column (meaning essentially the payment to Frank Johnson and the military equipment provided by the Company), and the construction, maintenance, and working of the telegraph line. Most of this expenditure had been incurred in less than a year. Then there was the cost of the various concessions and the expeditions to get them, *including £21,391 for the Rudd Concession.* (The BSA Company, though not owning it, had the privilege of paying for it.) A shareholder, A.A. Baumann, MP, complained in *The Times* that "1. The directors have spent all the shareholders' money. 2. Not a penny of that money has been spent on the main business of the Company—namely, mining operations." Though Hawksley's reply was disingenuous, he did have a point: the Company was building an empire. Making allowance for further expenditure up to the date of the report (December 1891), Fairfield calculated that at that date the Company's remaining resources would barely cover one more year's expenditure. The situation at the end of 1892 showed that he had been right.[11]

These financial difficulties were due primarily to the fact that the Company was a government and, what is more, a pioneer government building a state from the foundations. Other companies had managed to do this and still make money, but they governed countries in which a flourishing trade existed. The BSA Company was involved in what Rhodes had wanted at all costs to avoid— the "government of a shell." His great imperial operation was built on a hope, the hope that another—even a better—Witwatersrand lay somewhere among those granite koppies and msasa trees. Where else, it was widely argued, had the wealth of King Solomon and the Queen of Sheba come from?[12] The Company, itself busy with greater matters, did not propose to exploit the minerals directly. Others were to do that, and to allot to the Chartered Company half the shares in each company formed—an amount which, if it had been levied in the Transvaal, would have so enriched Kruger as to change the course of history.

It soon appeared, however, that Mashonaland might not be another Transvaal. If there was really very little wealth buried under its soil, the whole house house of cards would be in danger of collapsing. Thus the directors sat in St. Swithin's Lane, metaphorically biting their nails in impatience for the news that never came. "The Directors are extremely anxious about gold news," Maguire wrote to Rhodes in July 1891; "any tangible news would have an excellent effect."[13] *Tangible* was a well-chosen adjective.

Instead, what they got was bad news, and it came with all the authority of Lord Randolph Churchill. Lord Randolph, with an elegantly equipped party, reached Salisbury about the middle of August 1891 and left on 20 October. His observations were published serially as letters in the *Daily Graphic* and afterwards in book form as *Men, Mines and Animals in South Africa*. He distributed praise and blame fairly. The settler population in Salisbury was praised for its energy, and the place itself "had a thriving, rising, healthy appearance." The firm of Johnson, Heany and Borrow got very high marks. The police, fortifications, roads, and soil got low marks. All this could have been shrugged off by the directors; what mattered was the mines. Lord Randolph made many enquiries. He found miners busy everywhere and in some places good reefs had indeed been found on the surface, but all petered out at a shallow depth.

"What is to be done with this country?" he asked. Agriculture on a large scale, except to feed a large mining population, "would be a wild and ruinous enterprise. The climate seems to be altogether adverse to colonization and settlement by small emigrants . . . it occurs to me that there must be upon this great continent some awful curse, some withering blight, and that to delude and to mock at the explorer, the gold-hunter, the merchant, the speculator, and even at ministers and monarchs, is its dark fortune and its desperate fate."[14]

These Churchillian periods cut the Chartered men to the quick. "Randolph's letters saying '*No gold*' etc. etc.," Farquhar wrote in December 1891, "have played the devil with the market." The next month he was telling Rhodes that because of Randolph it would be impossible to borrow £200,000 at 6 or 7 per cent; he urged Rhodes to come home and "smash Randolph with the public." What Lord Randolph was publishing was bad enough, but it became known that the views he expressed in private letters—no doubt to influential people—were worse: that "B.S.A. Co. funds have all been expended and no gold has been found." There is no reason to suppose that Lord Randolph had gone to Mashonaland with anything but an open mind, though his brother, the duke of Marlborough, as a director of the Mozambique Company, had interests conflicting with those of Rhodes.[15]

The pessimistic view was confirmed by some of the people in Mashonaland, who could not be accused of superficial knowledge. On 15 April 1891, Arthur Pattisson, a Pioneer who was also correspondent of the *Daily News*, wrote to his brother in England about the woes of the Pioneers, who thought they had been defrauded of their free rations (specifically by Johnson and Company, who received the supplies from the Company), whose personal luggage had not yet been sent after them (they had been allowed only forty lb. each on the march up), who were weak and emaciated, and so forth. Four days after writing the letter Pattisson died of dysentery and malaria. Such events were attributed to the unavoidable parsimony of the Company; they were heard about in the City of London.[16]

Soon after this Major Maxwell, after serving the Company through fourteen dangerous months in Bulawayo, arrived at the Colonial Office looking for a job in the imperial service. The reason: he had no confidence in the future of the Company, and wished to be in some other employment long enough to qualify for an adequate pension. He reported that much gold had been found, but of a low grade. "As to agricultural settlement he regards it as out of the question." Maxwell's reports to his present employers had been frank enough to get him into bad odour with them, but his views must have been known to a much wider circle than the directors.

As there was no immediate prospect of profit, the survival of the Company and its enterprise even into 1893 depended on large-scale borrowing. A debenture issue had to be secured by credible assets, but what assets did this company have? The Rudd Concession—whose value was becoming doubtful anyway—did not belong to it. The Lippert Concession did, but if Lord Randolph and Maxwell were right about agriculture, that would be worthless. The capital itself had almost all been drained away. Something "tangible" was urgently needed. In the short run, lenders might be found if the price of shares pointed to confidence shown by the investing public, but that confidence was not shown. After a time even the inside operations of the "bulls" failed to do the trick. Rhodes might "stoke up enthusiasm" on 29 November 1892, among his hearers, but the enthusiasm did not help "Chartereds." On the contrary, the shares dropped three shillings after the meeting, and then another five shillings—perhaps, Olivier thought, because speculators thought this was "the last lift they can look for and the moment was come to unload."[17]

Among Rhodes's "curious financial methods" was the use of one of his enterprises to shore up another. Rhodes, wearing one hat, came to the rescue of Rhodes in another of his hats. His first company had been De Beers, and it had taken an all-night sitting with Barney Barnato to get that diamond magnate to agree to a trust deed enabling De Beers to build a territorial as well as a financial empire. De Beers and the Gold Fields had in due course become the main foundation stones of the Chartered Company. Those founding corporations had, however, other shareholders besides Rhodes and men of his way of thinking, and their obstruction was persistent. When Rhodes thought he could use De Beers to bail out the tottering Chartered Company he ran into the kindly but firm opposition of his friend and admirer Lord Rothschild. In June 1891 Rothschild was thinking that De Beers should not "hold so speculative a security" as Chartered shares. In January 1892, when the Company was looking everywhere for means of salvation, Rothschild blandly informed Rhodes that "You will have to obtain [money] from other sources than the cash reserve of the De Beers Company." He went on to explain that though the articles of association might leave a loophole (they had been intended by Rhodes to be one huge loophole), people nowadays were disposed to construe such articles more severely. If it were known that De Beers had lent money to the Chartered Company, "some shareholders" might agitate, procure an injunction to prevent it, and even turn out the present directors and elect others. Perhaps Rhodes could guess who "some" of those shareholders might be.[18]

As we have seen, De Beers had indeed lent considerable sums to the BSA Company, and the need to pay some of these back was the reason for much of the agonizing by the directors at the moment when they were getting this unwelcome warning. Nevertheless, Rothschild did not have his way; De Beers would come to the rescue again and again.

There was another company, the Gold Fields of South Africa Company, that Rhodes hoped to use in the same way, but which proved to be less pliable than De Beers. Gold Fields had been launched in February 1887. Its investments in mining properties on the Rand were unfortunate—they were not only exclusively outcrop properties, which all the early mines were, but they turned out to be low grade. During 1888 the directors sold many of these properties

298 Rhodes and Rhodesia

and invested the money in De Beers. The managing director, C.D. Rudd, then agreed to lead the team that was to get the concession from Lobengula, an operation which from his point of view was meant chiefly to revive the sinking fortunes of the Gold Fields Company. The directors in England thought, and so informed the shareholders, that the concession was to be the exclusive property of their company. They were to be disillusioned in stages. First, the concession when obtained was made over to "The Gold Fields Company, Cecil John Rhodes and the said Charles Dunell Rudd," that is to say to the company and its two managing directors. By the time Rhodes had amalgamated these interests with others into the Central Search Association, the Gold Fields Company's share of the concession had become only 8½ units out of 30, or 25,500 out of the 90,000 fully paid shares. Gold Fields also obtained 97,505 of the million shares of the BSA Company. The shareholders of Gold Fields were persuaded to increase their capital from £250,000 to £370,000, using the additional funds to develop the "Matabele Concession." Then they learned that the new one pound shares were to be offered to them at £3. They angrily rejected that proposal, and at the same time voted to sell the shares which the Company held in De Beers. This, however, was apparently not done.

All this had happened by the end of 1889, and it was to have a permanent effect on the relationship of the company to Rhodes and his other enterprises. Rhodes was furious with the shareholders ("a more ungrateful crew I have never come across"), decided not to attend their meetings, and in fact never did so. In 1891, when both Gold Fields and the BSA Company seemed to be on their last legs, the former distributed a dividend in the form of Chartered share certificates instead of cash; there was another growl from the "ungrateful crew," who also failed to take up most of the new share issue of that year.[19]

In the meantime, in 1890, United Concessions had taken the place of Central Search. Though United Concessions was capitalized at £4,000,000, for the reason explained by Sydney Olivier, only £1,306,000 of this was taken up in the first instance. The members of Central Search were entitled to participate in the new company *pro rata*, and most of them did more or less that. The Gold Fields Company, however, did not figure as such in the new group at all. Though the company's accountant, F. Lowrey, wrote that "this Company has received 336,200 shares on account" in United Concessions, the list of shareholders on 21 November 1890, attributes no shares to the Gold Fields Company, but 336,200 to Thomas Rudd and Henry D. Boyle, who were respectively its chairman and secretary.

While there is no record of the reason for this arrangement, it was surely related in some way to the feud between Rhodes and the Gold Fields shareholders. According to its Memorandum of Association, the first object of the new company was to take over the Central Search Association "as a going concern," and "with a view thereto to enter into an agreement with that Association and its Liquidators" in terms of a draft already drawn up; and "to carry the same into effect with or without modification." Further, according to the Articles of Association, "the shares shall be under the control of the Directors, who may allot or otherwise dispose of the same to such persons and on such terms and conditions . . . as the Directors think fit." These arrangements might well serve to consign an ungrateful crew to its proper place. In any case there is no mystery about their practical effect. Those shareholders had a legal interest in the Chartered Company. They had no legal (though they may have had an equitable) interest in United Concessions. As for De Beers, which was by far the biggest shareholder in the BSA Company, it was never involved in either United Concessions or Central Search.

In 1892 the fortunes of Gold Fields changed. It was beginning to be known, or believed, that the great wealth of the Witwatersrand lay in the deep level mines. The Gold Fields Company was able to amalgamate with three small companies which owned deep level properties but did not have enough capital to work them. Thus was born the Consolidated Gold Fields of South Africa, which three years later could show an annual profit of over two million pounds. This giant did acquire a small holding in United Concessions, but the old Gold Fields heritage in that company, now swollen to 840,400 shares out of a little over three million, was still registered in the joint names of Thomas Rudd and Henry D. Boyle.[20]

Thus the proposal to double the capital of the Chartered Company and "acquire the Rudd Concession" affected the interested parties in different ways. All the interests were really determined by what lay under the ground of Mashonaland. If the promoters' hopes of golden riches were realised, it would be necessary for the BSA Company to acquire the Rudd Concession, though there might reasonably be "growling" about the price, and about the trickery which withheld the concession from the Company in the first place. If, on the other hand, there was no gold in Mashonaland, the Rudd Concession was worthless, and in acquiring it for a million new shares the Company would be merely watering its capital. Those who had an interest in the Chartered Company but not in United Concessions would naturally oppose the amalgamation.

Though few men, if any, suspected that the Chartered Company would have no profits to divide during its first thirty-three years, Lord Randolph was not the only observer to believe that the mineral wealth of Mashonaland belonged to the category of the "imaginative." There were many besides Ochs who hoped for a legal injunction against the prospective profit-sharing with United Concessions; or, when that attempt had failed, for a vote of shareholders to the same effect. Among those who entertained these hopes the "ungrateful crew" of Gold Fields would have been prominent.

It is not surprising then that the Chartered men feared the shareholders, though not the directors, of that enterprise. When the extraordinary general meeting of the BSA Company to ratify the amalgamation was at last decided upon, "after a full and anxious discussion the *10th. November* was fixed for the meeting, but absolute secrecy was enjoined that nothing may come out until we send out the notices. It is important to have all proxies, and the Gold Fields meeting [presumably an *ordinary* annual general meeting] must go off before it is known."[21] For some reason the date of the Chartered meeting was changed to 20 November, and that meeting, at any rate, turned out to be much better disposed than could have been hoped. But there is no record of a meeting, ordinary or extraordinary, of the Consolidated Gold Fields in the latter part of 1893. The important decisions were understandably made by the directors on their own responsibility.

Before we arrive at the decisions made by those directors and others, resulting in the long-delayed amalgamation and all the consequences that resulted from it, we have to deal at some length with a related question—the railways. In the various approaches of the capitalists to the imperial government for support and for a charter, a railway to the interior was the first item on the list of inducements offered. The bait which was dangled before the government in the final stages was a guarantee of £700,000 by the principal promoters— £500,000 for the railway and the rest for "development." This was arranged, like some other important matters, before the Chartered Company existed; it was therefore not that Company, but its most important members, who were bound to build a railway from Kimberley to Vryburg. Gifford intended that the job should be done by, and the benefit accrue to, the Exploring Company. When Rhodes negotiated a railway agreement with the Cape government on behalf of *the BSA Company*, Gifford uttered a cry of anguish ("his breach of good faith should be *publicly* shown up"), but all that he could, at that stage, salvage from the wreck was 25 per cent of the concessions which the Chartered Company might get from the imperial government for building the line.[22]

Rhodes's first agreement with the Cape government was made on 29 October 1889, the day the charter was granted; like Napoleon, he could not on this occasion be accused of having lost a quarter of an hour. A slight delay was allowed for Sir Gordon Sprigg, the Cape premier, to make a speech about it on 1 November; construction of the earthworks out of Kimberley began on 2 November. The agreement provided for the building of the line to Vryburg. It was a gamble, because the Company had to pay for this part of the operation, while trusting to the success of the next negotiations to provide a way of getting its money back. The Cape government eased the task of construction by putting its powers of expropriation, and some of the technical and purchasing facilities of the Cape Government Railways, at the Company's disposal.

The success of the gamble was assured by the two agreements which Rhodes, on behalf of the BSA Company, signed on 23 January 1890. The first was with the high commissioner in his capacity as governor of British Bechuanaland. This provided for that part of the line which lay beyond the Cape border, in consideration of which the Crown Colony would hand over to the Company 6,000 square miles of land. Another 6,000 square miles would be given if the

Company chose to continue the line to Mafeking. The other prerequisites which had been demanded, in the earlier negotiations, by the Exploring Company, had been dropped in deference to the views of the Cape ministers, but that Company, as we have seen, would now get a quarter of the Chartered Company's receipts (if any!) from the sale of the land.[23]

The second agreement was with Sprigg, representing the Cape government. As anticipated, that government undertook to raise a loan and to advance the money to the Company on the same terms as the government itself obtained— inevitably much more favourable terms than the Company could get on the market.[24] With this money the Company would build the line to Vryburg. The line itself and the first 6,000 square miles of land would be mortgaged to the Cape government as security for the loan. At any time up to 30 June 1891, the government could exercise the right to buy the line with the money already advanced; in that case it would take also two-thirds of the proceeds of the first land grant, and the Company would then be obliged to continue the line to Mafeking.

In July 1890 Rhodes succeeded Sprigg as prime minister, and could then assume the congenial rôle of one negotiator with two hats. By August the Cape Parliament had passed an act empowering the government to carry out the terms of the agreement of 23 January. Net balance at end of operation: railway completed to Vryburg at no cost to the BSA Company or its promoters; the latter had discharged their obligation to the imperial government; the Cape government owned and operated the line to Vryburg but was saddled with the debt to pay for it, against which it could set its two-thirds share of the first land grant; the BSA Company now had (actually or in prospect) 8,000 square miles of land but was obliged to build the next section of the line. The first section, however, had proved that to build a railway you did not have to spend your own money.[25]

Those square miles of land loomed large in all the bargaining. They were the first "tangible" asset the Company possessed. They were supposed to bring in a profit from the sale of farms, into which the land would be surveyed, and from the minerals, the reservation of which to the Crown was, with a minor exception, waived. The surveyor-general of British Bechuanaland estimated the value of the 12,000 square miles at £362,856, or a little under a shilling an acre. As the land lay in the district of Kuruman, with an extension into northwestern Vryburg, this estimate could be questioned. Knutsford noted that the lands were "practically a part of the desert," and in the hands of the government were "likely to remain wholly valueless . . . for a long series of years." They yielded no minerals. They did, however, serve as valuable counters in the game of company-promotion. A clause in the agreement of August 1890 (the original agreement for the doubling of the capital and the buying out of the United Concessions Company) increased the share of the Exploring Company from a quarter to three-quarters of the profits from the land grants.[26]

The Vryburg line, already owned by the Cape Government Railways, was opened for traffic in December 1890. More than two years then passed without a sod being turned for the next section. The reader of the directors' private correspondence is not surprised, but the Company's failure to act seemed strange to those who believed the puffs given out at the annual general meetings. It is true that Rhodes and the other Company men were now more interested in the Beira railway, on which the fate of Mashonaland seemed to hang. Dealings with the Portuguese in 1890 and 1891 showed, however, that a line from the south was a necessary reinsurance against renewed obstruction from the east.

It happened that an extension from Vryburg would be of even more immediate benefit to the finances of the protectorate than to the colonization of Mashonaland. It was calculated that a railway to Palapye would save the protectorate at least £20,000 a year—on the conveyance of mails, government stores, and personnel; on the police, because with greater mobility the force could be reduced; and because of the increase of revenue resulting from the development promoted by the railway. Loch therefore became a keen advocate of an extension not only to Mafeking but beyond, and of the use of imperial resources to promote it.

It was at first assumed that the BSA Company would build the line to Mafeking under its existing obligation, and that an extension beyond that point would require an imperial guarantee of £25,000 a year for five years. The Treasury would not look at this proposal until the line to Mafeking was actually opened. Then Loch and Rhodes together hatched a different scheme, on Loch's initiative.

It was to merge the old obligation (Vryburg-Mafeking) in a new and larger one to build the line from Vryburg at least to Gaborone, but on new conditions. The money would be made to stretch further by using a narrow gauge. A new company would be formed to take over the railway project and also the land grants attached to it. When the line reached Gaborone the railway company would receive an annual subsidy of £15,000 a year for ten years, two-thirds from the Bechuanaland (in effect, the imperial) government and the rest from the BSA and Tati companies. When the line reached Palapye the subsidy would be doubled. The £20,000 a year from the imperial treasury was justified by the savings the railway would ensure.[27]

The Cape Colony expected to benefit by the trade and the railway traffic to be drawn to it, but as an interested party it objected to the proposed break of gauge at Vryburg. On 28 July 1891, the House of Assembly passed a resolution accordingly, and Rhodes afterwards gave an assurance that the South African standard gauge of 3 ft. 6 in. would be maintained. Loch still thought in terms of a "light" railway of cheap construction, which would be enough if speeds were limited to ten or twelve miles an hour. The negotiations dragged on, but there was still no sign of any activity by contractors. Sprigg, though said to have no sense of humour, brought this matter before the House of Assembly on 5 July 1892—Rhodes's birthday. His motion deprecating the Company's failure to fulfil its obligation was debated at length and drew some excuses from Rhodes, but the penury of the great Company was not one of them.[28]

Rothschild's financial puritanism had not prevailed at the De Beers board. That company was registered, and its meetings were held, in Kimberley, which was virtually a company town. Rhodes, the boss, was on his home ground there and could have his way as he could not count on doing with companies whose headquarters were in England. Accordingly, when the annual meeting of the BSA Company in November 1892 was told of the decision to issue debentures for £500,000, the Colonial office noted that these were mostly to cover loans already received, largely from De Beers. By an agreement of 7 December that company was committed to take up Chartered 6 per cent debentures to the amount of £212,000. At the end of that financial year, on 30 June 1893, it held £133,000 worth. Without these advances the BSA Company would presumably have gone out of business, but in addition to its routine expenditure it had now to find a way of building the railway extension from Vryburg. Though this was to be done by a subsidiary company, the responsibility still rested with the parent organization.

By May 1893 the plans for the railway company had matured. It will be remembered that the Exploring Company had acquired a three-quarter interest in the concessions obtained in respect of the railway, which now stood at 8,000 square miles of semi-desert. As it was intended to endow the railway company with the whole of the land grant, the Exploring Company was now to have its share of the land commuted for a one-third interest in the railway company, together with a grant from the Chartered Company of 600,000 acres in Mashonaland. Another one-third interest was to be given to De Beers in part payment for its loans. Accordingly, on 23 May 1893, the Bechuanaland Railway Company was formed, with a nominal capital of £6,000. The ownership was divided equally between the BSA Company, the Exploring Company, and De Beers, and the whole of the land grant was vested in the railway company. Of that, 2,000 square miles were "tangible," what remained of the grant in respect of the railway to Vryburg. The other 6,000 square miles would be received when the line reached Mafeking. The subsidies would not begin to be paid until it had reached Gaborone.[29]

The railway could not of course be built with that kind of capital; the real money would come from debentures, of which the railway company issued £300,000 in the first instance, and these were taken up by the Chartered Company in terms of an agreement of 4 August 1893. This, it will be recalled, was a fortnight or so after Jameson had been telling Rhodes "you have got to find the money" (for the war). By another agreement, the Cape Government Railways undertook to maintain and operate the line to Mafeking, for one year, in return for a payment of £11,000 by the railway company. The work on this section was begun on 10 May 1893 (before the railway company was formed) and the line was opened to Mafeking on 3 October 1894.[30] It was only then that the railway company became entitled to the final 6,000 square miles—but this is to anticipate; we are concerned with the months before the war.

At the time when the decision for war was being made, the BSA Company had not actually taken up the railway debentures, but it faced the prospect of having to do so. The money had been obtained by its own debenture issue, or loans in anticipation of that issue. This operation, however—borrowing from Peter to pay Paul—was not regarded as one of Rhodes's "curious financial methods," because the railway company was considered a sound proposition. The rivalry between competitors for the right to build it, the eagerness with which De Beers and the Exploring Company took up their one-third shares, and the wistfulness of the Chartered Company's directors about not being able to float and operate it unhampered by "agreements," all point to confidence in its profits, even if some might not think much of its 8,000 square miles of land.[31] While the Chartered debentures might be regarded by conservative investors as "speculative," the railway debentures held by the Chartered Company were not so regarded. They were considered a "tangible" asset, though hardly a source of income, since what came in from Paul had to be handed over to Peter. Thus, between July and September 1893, the BSA Company committed itself to a sound railway operation, but by using borrowed money. The operation could not in the short run provide the Company with a credit balance, and the imperial subsidy lay far in the future—at Gaborone.

The Company had all along been much more interested in the railway from Beira, for the obvious reason that it would provide the shortest and cheapest route to Mashonaland. It might even be the decisive factor in the survival or collapse of the colonizing venture, whatever might be the prospects for the Company's finances in general. Rhodes's filibustering having failed to force Salisbury's hand, the Anglo-Portuguese Convention of June 1891 left the territory east of Umtali, but also the obligation to build a railway, to Portugal. The concession to build it had already been given by that government to the Mozambique Company.

The attempt of the BSA Company to get control of the Mozambique Company had been frustrated by the outraged Portuguese government, but for many reasons the Chartered men were determined to have the railway for themselves. If its operation was in other hands the Mashonaland enterprise could be held to ransom at any time. The railway itself would be a good tangible asset. But the Portuguese government (until the British government intervened) was adamant—the BSA Company was to have no part in it, even by the roundabout means of a French holding company in which Bartissol seemed to acquiesce.

On 12 September 1891, the Mozambique Company concluded a contract with H.T. Van Laun, who was given the right and obligation to construct and run the railway on terms specified. The most important provision was one which bestowed on Van Laun's company the proceeds of the 3 per cent transit duty to be charged on goods going through Beira to Mashonaland. Out of these proceeds Van Laun would pay 6 per cent interest on the money he raised for the railway. The Mozambique Company also gave the contractor the land needed for the line, for docks and wharves, and alternate blocks along the route, amounting in all to about 10,000 acres per mile of railway.[32]

In floating a company to operate this concession Van Laun had the support of a group of British investment trusts and other companies, and of the British directors of the Mozambique Company. The duke of Marlborough and his American brother-in-law guaranteed Van Laun to these investors.[33] The company could have been formed without the participation or approval of the BSA Company. That it in fact provided for a very large participation by that Company, in spite of Portuguese opposition, may have been due partly to the terms of the Anglo-Portuguese Convention. It was for the British government to say whether the Portuguese obligation to build a railway had been discharged. Sir Philip Currie of the Foreign Office made a point of establishing friendly relations between Van Laun and the Chartered directors. On 7 November 1891, Farquhar and Maguire, for the Chartered Company, signed with Van Laun an agreement the details of which are not in the records, but which probably foreshadowed the arrangements made in the following year. It seems to have been been left to Van Laun to bring the Portuguese into line. Sir Philip Currie said that if necessary the minister in Lisbon would be asked to apply pressure, but that it was better where possible to work through one channel, in this case Van Laun. What inducements were held out to Van Laun, and what he offered to the Portuguese government, are not recorded.[34]

The outcome was the incorporation of the Beira Railway Company on 12 July 1892. This was done in terms of the British Company Acts of that time, which allowed for a "company limited by guarantee": if it went bankrupt, each of its members was liable for its debts to the amount of *one pound* and no more. The original subscribers were a handful of men, great and small, from the Chartered Company's office, and the railway company, like the Bechuanaland Railway Company, had its offices at 19 St. Swithin's Lane, the address of the BSA Company. These facts, however, do not reflect the real situation quite accurately. The Company had 600,000 shares, to which no specified value was attached because nobody bought them (this was one of the features of a company limited by guarantee). The money was raised by the issue of debentures—£250,000 in the first issue. For every pound subscribed to this the buyer would receive, as well as the debenture, one share. It will be noticed that at this rate not even half of the shares would be accounted for, nor was it intended that they should be. Room had to be left for later debenture issues. Above all, the voting power must not be left to chance. The Mozambique Company was allotted 295,000 shares. The other 305,000 (a majority) might be subscribed by anyone, but would all be held in trust for the investors by the BSA Company, which would thus control the majority of votes without needing to subscribe a penny. Nevertheless, it did subscribe no less than £110,000 to the debenture issue. How could it do this when it had no money? The Baron E.B. d'Erlanger wrote that the Paulings, the railway contractors, "came to see my father and me in London to ask on behalf of Rhodes and themselves to help with the financing of the Beira Railway Company and the contract to construct the track, which they had obtained. We agreed to do so." He does not mention any direct investment by his bank in the company, and it must be assumed that its role was to find the money for the suppliants. Pauling and Company took up £43,500 of the debentures, paid for no doubt in the same way, and the rest was subscribed by the public. The interest on the debentures was funded for three years, and in fact no interest was paid in cash until 1900.

The distribution of voting power did not, however, determine the the choice of the six directors. Two of these were always to be nominated by the Mozambique Company, two by the Chartered Company, and two by Van Laun. This would look good to the Portuguese, but in matters requiring a vote at a shareholders' meeting the BSA Company was in a commanding position. It was able to place its own engineer, Sir Charles Metcalfe, alongside Sir George Bruce, already appointed by the other interests.[35]

To have got even this degree of control of the railway without having to pay for it, except with borrowed money, may have been astute business, but it added nothing to the tangible assets of the BSA Company. The effect on the Company's finances was indirect: the completion of the railway would reduce the cost of administering Mashonaland. Thus the Beira and the Bechuanaland railways were both useful props to the Company. By 1893 neither may have cost it a direct capital outlay, though both had involved large borrowing operations; neither of them, on the other hand, had become an asset that could help the Company out of its difficulties.

We now return to those difficulties, which in the period from July to October 1893 were formidable. The expenses of administration still greatly exceeded the revenue, though the gap could be made to seem narrower by the methods Fairfield pointed out in 1892. The Company controlled, in varying degrees, the two railway companies, but the interest it received on the railway debentures would be wholly committed to the payment of its own creditors. In the Beira case, indeed, no interest was to be received before 1900, whereas d'Erlanger would need to be paid his interest from the beginning. The Company could not possibly have received enough from those sources to cover its obligations to the holders of its own £500,000 debentures. Some receipts were coming in from the telegraph line, but otherwise nothing substantial can be found on the credit side. As information about the Company's debts has to be culled from many sources, it is probable that the balance was more adverse than even these figures suggest.

In the second half of 1893 the Company, to survive, had to borrow again on a massive scale. It did so, and survived. The key questions we have to answer are, whether or how far this borrowing was made possible by (i) the war, and (ii) the acquisition of the Rudd Concession and the doubling of the capital; and whether (ii) was facilitated by (i)—the question we posed at the beginning.

The financial operations which saved the Company were almost all carried out in December 1893 and January 1894. On 18 December an Interim Report of the Chartered directors announced a new issue of £750,000 six per cent debentures, the interest to be guaranteed jointly by De Beers, Consolidated Gold Fields, and Rhodes. The next day the United Concessions Company held a meeting to wind itself up according to plan. It will be remembered that the plan dated back to the agreement of the previous July among the companies. It involved not only the distribution among the members of the 925,000 new Chartered shares, but also the distribution among them, *pro rata*, of an obligation to "procure subscriptions" for £185,000 of the new Chartered debentures. The Exploring Company was similarly responsible for £15,000, and the remaining £550,000 had to be raised from a gullible public—or from "friends."

The most helpful, or gullible, friends were the shareholders of De Beers. On 18 January 1894, the annual meeting of that company was held in Kimberley. Rhodes, in the chair, "stoked up enthusiasm" by defending some of the company's measures which had, not unnaturally, invited criticism. De Beers had lent £100,000 to the BSA Company for the Mafeking railway, and another sum of "about £150,000" for unspecified purposes, both loans being covered by the new six per cent debentures. More of the same debentures were to be acquired at the rate of £3,500 a month for the coming year. All this was from a company which had had no share in United Concessions. It was under no obligation arising from the agreement of July 1893, but was, of course, bound by that of December 1892. Finally, as a special boon, the De Beers shareholders had been given Chartered shares in lieu of cash dividends.[36]

Though Rhodes assigned no precise date to any of these operations, it is clear that the taking up of debentures had followed the decisions announced a month before. The £100,000 for the railway had probably been advanced earlier. It was on 4 August that the BSA Company agreed to take up the whole £300,000 debenture issue of the Bechuanaland Railway Company. As it had parted with a third of the shares to De Beers and another third to Exploring, it is likely that it parted with the debentures in the same proportion. The remaining Chartered share of those debentures would thus have been £100,000, which it would have paid for by borrowing that sum from De Beers. De Beers accordingly received £100,000 of Chartered debentures, when they were issued in December, to cover that loan. Finally, on the appearance of a million new Chartered shares (virtually "water"), which were cluttering the safes in various offices, it seemed good business to give some of them to the De Beers shareholders, with much blowing of trumpets, in lieu of cash. That there was something slightly irregular about all this is suggested by Rhodes's far-fetched argument to defend it. De Beers had been saving money by using wood instead of coal as fuel, and the railway would give access to new sources of wood! If, however, the £100,000 De Beers loan had been advanced as early as August, which seems almost certain, it had not been justified either by the war or by the amalgamation. Like other cases of similar assistance, it must be explained simply by Rhodes's influence over De Beers.

Now we turn to Consolidated Gold Fields, which company on 15 January 1894, announced a 5½ per cent debenture issue of £600,000. This was to be secured by the whole of the company's assets, but as additional security it placed in the hands of trustees its stocks, to the value of one million pounds, in De Beers and five Rand mining companies. The issue was over-subscribed on the first day. The only thing that was not explained in the prospectus was what the money was wanted for. The *Economist* thought that the main purpose must be to buy Chartered debentures, which the former shareholders in United Concessions were obliged to do. The *Economist*, however, had overlooked an important point: it was not Consolidated Gold Fields, but its chairman and secretary, that incurred the obligation. If, though incurred by them, it was discharged by their company, there would have been strong reasons for the directors to carry through the operation without consulting their shareholders.[37]

One of the significant facts in all these operations was the refusal to consult the shareholders of the various companies, except, necessarily, those of the Chartered Company on 20 November and of De Beers on 18 January. Though De Beers and Consolidated Gold Fields were large shareholders in the BSA Company, they would have been represented at its meeting by their directors. The BSA Company's extraordinary general meeting had been carefully planned to take place, and even to be announced, after the Gold Fields meeting was over. There was, however, no Gold Fields meeting. Though it is difficult to prove a negative, an examination of *The Times*, the *Economist*, the chief South African newspapers, and the Gold Fields collection in the Rhodes Papers, through the period from October to January, produces no reference to any meeting of Consolidated Gold Fields. It is reasonable to assume therefore that the directors decided that discretion was the better part of valour. In November they produced a report and accounts for the year ending 30 June 1893, but said nothing then about a projected debenture issue. That issue was announced in January—but to the world at large, not to a meeting where questions could be asked and votes taken.

The directors of the Exploring Company (and who would they be but Rhodes, Beit, Cawston, and Oakley Maund?) on 19 December issued their report for the year ending 30 June 1893. This, too, was published to the world in general; the directors had deferred the annual general meeting until after the meeting of the BSA Company, so that the report of the latter would be available. But there was no ordinary annual general meeting of the BSA Company. And no meeting of the Exploring Company.[38]

This is all circumstantial evidence. Such as it is, it points to the conclusion that Rhodes and his friends were using De Beers, Gold Fields, and Exploring to bail out the Chartered Company. They feared hostile reactions from the shareholders, so avoided meeting them, except for those of De Beers who met in Kimberley. There Rhodes, on his home ground, successfully used the arts of the demagogue to subdue opposition. But none of this was attempted until the war was won, Bulawayo occupied, and the "amalgamation" deal confirmed.

These achievements, taken together, appear then to have been the necessary basis for the debenture issue of £750,000 which saved the Company from collapse. After November the directors took the risks both of the debentures' not being taken up and of shareholders' revolts in the other companies. They had not dared to take those risks earlier. As it was, they scraped through by means of secrecy, deception, and a heavy dose of "the imaginative." This is not to say that the gamble would not have come off at an earlier date. It shows only that the directors did not believe it would, which is the relevant point.

The debenture issue was necessarily preceded by the doubling of the capital and the acquisition of the Rudd Concession. The directors evidently believed that the conquest of Matabeleland would tip the balance, at the extraordinary general meeting, in favour of that operation. The decision to hold the meeting, a decision from which they had drawn back fearfully year after year since 1890, was made early in October, when the columns had begun to move. The date they chose for the meeting was a month ahead, when, as they would have known, Jameson would either have won the war or got into such trouble that the responsibility would have passed out of the directors' hands. It is a fairly safe guess that, once the war began, they seized upon it as giving them the long-awaited chance of carrying through the "amalgamation." On the other hand it is certain, and no guess, that the directors in London had not planned the war for that or for any other purpose.

The debentures were issued not in the hour of victory but weeks after its novelty had worn off. They were issued as a direct consequence of the "amalgamation" and of the arrangements made among the various companies in connection with it. So it would seem that at every stage it was that operation, and not the war itself, that was expected to strengthen the Company and its credit with the investors. The chief investors, or lenders, were the companies "of which Mr. Rhodes was the paramount chief." It was an inside job.

Perhaps it was for this reason that the fluctuations of "Charters" on the market fail almost completely to reflect the benefits which either the war or the capital operation was supposed to confer.[39] The shares reached their peak for 1893 about the beginning of May (buyers 48s.). They then dropped sharply to 28s. 6d., rose slowly to 36s., declined again steadily through July until news of the Victoria incident caused them to drop to 21s. As August and September brought "disquieting news" the price plummeted to 16s. on 28 August, and, after a slight recovery, down again to 17s. on 13 September. The outbreak of war pushed them up to 25s. on 6 October, but they declined again until the news of victory at the beginning of November caused a sharp rise to 27s. It was temporary; for the rest of the year and through most of January the shares remained within the range 21s. 6d. to 23s. They never, in 1893, got back to the prices that had prevailed before the Victoria incident. The sub-editor of the Johannesburg *Star* was wide of the mark when he headed the financial column on 2 November "Bull-away-o!" As for the extraordinary general meeting of 20 November and the debenture announcement on 18 December, they had no effect whatever.

It can be said that the successful outcome of the war was, indirectly, a cause of the successful issue of debentures. The London directors, who took advantage of the war for this purpose, had not planned it. Jameson planned it, for reasons to be found in the local situation. But Rhodes? It was Rhodes who, on second thoughts, supported Jameson and got the support of the London board. At that time the desperate financial situation of the Company was weighing on his mind. Did he then foresee the whole sequence of events—war, amalgamation, debentures? He must have hoped for that sequence, and he wanted Matabeleland anyway ("all red—that's my dream"). But he must also have known how easily the war could have led to disaster. In spite of that he threw his weight on to Jameson's side. From the financial point of view his decision was a gamble—to stake all on one throw. If he lost, the Company collapsed; but if nothing were done it would collapse anyway. Rhodes, the financial gambler, and Jameson, the (amateur) military gambler, won; but the victory betrayed them into another, analogous, but disastrous, gamble two years later.

Some historians have tried to see in Rhodes a typical or stereotyped capitalist, motivated essentially by the desire for gain or profit. The evidence does not support that interpretation. If there is such a person as a typical capitalist so motivated, he is presumably one who regards the gain as an end in itself, who collects dollars as an Indian brave collects scalps. Rhodes did not conform to that type. If he had done, he would not have sat up all night arguing with Barney Barnato, who when his resistance was worn down had to agree that De Beers Consolidated would be able to raise an army and govern provinces, not merely to make money. At every stage Rhodes was using the lure of trade or gold or adventure as a means to drawing people into his territorial, not merely financial, empire. The means varied but the end remained the same.

This would not by itself explain why Rhodes was a gambler, but these two facets of his mind were related. The success of the imperial venture, of Rhodesia—the country which was unofficially known by his name even in 1892—was much more important to him than the financial operations that were meant to ensure that success. In 1896 he would show that he valued his colonial creation more than his life; in 1893 he gambled with the life of the Company when a mere capitalist would have preferred caution. Caution would not have saved the Company at that stage, but from a purely capitalist point of view it was not worth saving.

If the house of cards had collapsed, the railway companies would have collapsed with it. To the capitalist mind of that day, when railways were a favourite investment everywhere, those two ramshackle lines looked like promising ventures. They figured prominently in the Chartered balance sheet. But it would be misleading to treat them mainly from the point of view of finance. Railways and telegraphs were two basic elements of the infrastructure by which the whole Mashonaland enterprise was supported. Even if the Company and its colonists had vanished, these instruments of nineteenth century technology were the means by which the peoples of the interior could be exposed to the modernizing influences of the outside world. But the Company and colonists did not vanish; their survival and their development of a viable economy and society were made possible by these instruments.

The telegraph line was easier and cheaper to construct than the railway, more profitable to operate, and relatively free of political complications. When Rhodes advanced the money for it in 1889 he did so on behalf of the future Chartered Company, which was happy to assume the responsibility as soon as it was formed. There was no question of a subsidiary company, debentures, or "curious financial methods" for the telegraph. It was a paying proposition and was made to bulk very large in the directors' first report.

Connecting with the Cape and British Bechuanaland system at Mafeking, it was pushed northwards with reasonable speed, reaching Ramoutsa on 14 June 1890, and the Palla camp of the BBP, at the Notwani-Limpopo junction, on 20 August. There were difficulties with some of the Tswana chiefs; Lentswe barely tolerated the line across his country, and objected strongly to the opening of a station at Motshodi. Nevertheless the subjects of each chief were recruited for the construction across his country. The whole work was supervised by Sir James Sivewright, who was in and out of Rhodes's cabinet while the telegraph line marched on, and the service was operated by telegraphists lent by the Cape government. Work was held up during the rainy season of 1890—1, but by November 1891 Rhodes was able to send a telegram from Fort Victoria, and on 16 February 1892, the line reached Salisbury. Its vital importance for the Mashonaland enterprise will have been clear enough from this narrative.[40]

The railway was not pushed northwards with anything like the same speed. Reaching Mafeking at the end of 1894, it had got no further when, a year later, Jameson's raid made its shattering impact on the Company, its territories, and its railway.[41] The chief reason for this was that all available resources were directed to the much more important Beira railway.

The company for that line having been formed, as we have seen, in July 1892, George Pauling's firm got to work soon afterwards on the construction.

The limited resources were applied only to the absolutely necessary section of the route, from the head of navigation on the Pungwe—Fontesvilla—to a point supposedly beyond the fly-belt, seventy-five miles inland. The line was of two-foot gauge—"like a toy railway," Pauling afterwards wrote. Narrow and short as it was, it levied a toll on its builders which puts it in a class by itself for southern Africa. Pauling reckoned that in each of the years 1892 and 1893 the climate killed sixty per cent of the white employees, including incidentally all of the teetotallers (so he said, but Pauling was prejudiced in this matter). "At one time practically every white employee on the job was suffering from fever, and then I fervently wished that I had never heard of the Beira railway. In one fortnight we lost six white men, including my bookkeeper." Pauling did not record the deaths of black men, but d'Erlanger adds, "and a very much larger number of his native workers."

In the rainy season of 1892-3 it was no longer possible to distinguish the banks of the Pungwe: "nearly all the country was under water." The tug *Agnes*, which seems to have been destined to untoward adventures on the Pungwe, strayed seven miles from that river before the flood subsided and left it high and dry. There it remained for three years until it could be floated on another flood. When there was dry land, it swarmed with all the game from the Ark; good shots like Harry Pauling, George's cousin, were able to supply the labourers with meat from this source. In spite of dangers from disease, flood, heat, and wild beasts, the first section of the line was finished in October 1893, just as Lobengula, far to the west, was going down in defeat.

Those seventy-five miles of fly-belt were the vital section. Pauling was able to advertise in Umtali that "a passenger train will leave the 75 mile station every Wednesday at 6.30 a.m. connecting with the mail steamer at Fontesvil-la." Early in 1894, however, Pauling made a contract to continue the line to Chimoio, and that section was completed in 1896. Further extensions of this railway, as of the Bechuanaland line, will appear in this story in their contexts.[42]

THE GOVERNMENT

If one of the Company's remarkable achievements was to spend money without having it, another was to exercise political and administrative powers to which it had no title. On the slenderest of foundations, if it can be called a foundation at all, a state was erected. By what sleight-of-hand did this state establish itself and function in Mashonaland, superseding not only the Shona paramounts who for most purposes had been at least the *de facto* rulers before, but also Lobengula, whose claim to sovereignty was recognized by the Company itself? Did the country belong to Lobengula? Or to "Doctela"?

The charter, it will be remembered, did not confer any governmental powers on the Company. It allowed the Company and its officers to exercise such powers as Lobengula and other legitimate chiefs might concede to them. The attempt to obtain powers from Lobengula had therefore to be made, and it was regarded as important. The Pioneers had hardly reached their destination when Moffat received a request from Rhodes to ask Lobengula's permission for the Company to exercise jurisdiction over the Europeans in Mashonaland. Moffat decided to present the request as coming from the government, not Rhodes, and as applying only to the area actually occupied by the Company. Even thus modified, the request fell on deaf ears, as can be understood from Lobengula's letter to Loch on the first day of 1891: "Mr Moffat has asked me to give Mr Rhodes power to punish those who do wrong in Mashonaland. They ask for this now, but they went into my country without doing so. Why do they now come and ask. When did we speak on this matter?"

As was to be expected, Jameson surmounted such an obstacle with ease. The technique, as explained to Rutherfoord Harris on 21 November 1890, closely resembled the method of "getting the road" for the Pioneers:

> When I was in Matabeleland as the representative of the British South Africa Company in October 1889, and after our prospectors were actually at work in the country north of the Tati Concession, King Lobengula, when applied to on some matters in connection with the white men in Matabeleland, replied, "No, go to those people" (referring to myself and the employes of the British South Africa Company). "I am Chief of the Black people, but I have made them chief over the whites." This I then considered as giving us absolute authority over all whites in his dominions. Mr. Moffat, the Assistant Commissioner, was at the time with us at the King's Kraal in Matabeleland. In view of Lobengula's well-known aversion to signing documents, this will be taken as sufficient evidence to satisfy Clauses 3 and 4 of the Charter dealing with the Civil Administration of the country.

The Colonial Office did not at first take it as sufficient evidence, even when Lobengula's pegging out mining claims was added to clinch the argument.[43]

The Office was more susceptible, however, to an argument of a different kind from a different quarter. Loch, even in 1890, was keen to impose imperial authority in some form on the Company's sphere. He proposed that Her Majesty's government "assume" jurisdiction and then confer it on the Company. Fairfield, whose first reaction to the proposal was to prefer grants from the Shona chiefs, changed his mind when Hawksley pointed out that negotiations for such grants would be resented by Lobengula. He came round to the view that Elizabethan precedents would justify the assumption of jurisdiction by the Crown. Knutsford, however, at this time, the end of 1890, would not agree.

Loch returned to the charge in February 1891, with a bolder proposal. He wanted the existing Bechuanaland Protectorate and also the sphere of influence annexed to the Crown, and British Bechuanaland handed over to the Cape Colony. His argument was financial; he showed how the Treasury would benefit. Though this proposal brought no response, Providence then intervened, using as instruments the Adendorff trekkers. How could they be stopped if neither the British Crown nor the Company possessed legitimate jurisdiction in the sphere of influence? At the least, a protectorate must be declared over that territory. As in the previous year, when a threatened Boer trek quickly removed all scruples about the Pioneer Column, so now the Colonial and Foreign Offices agreed that authority sufficient to stop the Adendorff trek must at all costs be assumed.[44]

This necessity opened up some difficult juridical questions. It was agreed, on one hand, that annexation would give the Crown and its agents full legislative, judicial, and executive power over the territory, and on the other that a mere sphere of influence did not in itself confer any power at all. Between these extremes lay the protectorate, a concept whose meaning seemed to change from hour to hour under the eyes of the beholder. There was also the power over British subjects provided by the Foreign Jurisdiction Act of 1890 (the latest of such acts), which could be exercised in any foreign territory whose ruler permitted it by "treaty, capitulation, grant, usage, sufferance and other lawful means."

Jurisdiction over British subjects could be acquired by any of these means; over the native inhabitants of the territory, only by the deliberate concession of the local ruler, or else by annexation. The Adendorff trekkers, however, belonged to neither of these categories but were "subjects of a foreign power." They could not be brought under British Jurisdiction in terms of the Foreign Jurisdiction Act without their own consent or that of their government. Nor was it believed in 1891 that a protectorate would in itself subject foreigners to it; but in a protectorate the subjects of powers that were parties to the General Acts of the Berlin and Brussels conferences would come under the jurisdiction of the protecting power. The South African Republic, however, was not a party to those acts.[45]

The assumption of jurisdiction carried responsibilities with it; with the power to punish went the duty to protect; a foreign government could hold the protecting power responsible for the safety of its subjects and of their property, and this could be an expensive duty to perform. Hence the reluctance of the British government to assume such powers except where absolutely necessary. In the case of this sphere of influence it had hoped that the Foreign Jurisdiction Act would be sufficient, and that it was applicable on the grounds (*pace* Jameson) of Lobengula's "sufferance." But this was seen to be inadequate when the law officers gave the opinion that without a protectorate there would be no jurisdiction over foreigners. On 9 May 1891, therefore, on the excuse that the queen by treaty, sufferance, etc. possessed jurisdiction there, an order-in-council proclaimed a protectorate over the country within the boundaries of the future Southern Rhodesia. As late as 18 April Knutsford was insisting to Loch that "it is of great importance that Lobengula's consent should, if possible, be obtained to such measures as we may deem necessary for the government of the whites," but as the need was pressing the consent was dispensed with.

While the Adendorff trekkers were the immediate reason for this order-in-council and for its urgency at that time, there were other reasons why it could not have been long delayed. The most pressing of these was the need to maintain discipline in the Company's police. There had been doubt about the authority to discipline even the Bechuanaland Border Police when they were in the protectorate. Hence the earlier order-in-council of 30 June 1890, which gave Loch, as governor of British Bechuanaland, power to give effect by proclamation to Her Majesty's jurisdiction in the protectorate. The order was not sent to Loch until 17 July, after delays for consultation with the law officers and the Foreign Office, and he was then told to use it at present for one purpose only. That purpose was expressed in his two proclamations in September, applying the provisions of the Cape Mounted Riflemen Act, 1878, to the BBP and to the Company's police in the Crown Colony and the protectorate. Those proclamations, and the attachment of the latter force to the former while in Bechuanaland, solved the immediate problem. It will be noticed that the jurisdiction so proclaimed was over British subjects only, namely the two police forces.

The problem reappeared as soon as the Company's men entered Lobengula's dominions. While the queen by prerogative had the power to discipline her armed forces when outside the realm, the Company could not draw on this source of authority for its own purposes. Though its police officers and those of the Pioneers used titles of rank, they held no real commissions. As for the Company's own authority to impose discipline, "it will be necessary for them to enforce discipline by an Ordinance enacted by the Company with the approval of the Secretary of State, and based upon some grant of authority from Lo Bengula so to legislate."

The Company therefore, in November 1890, submitted for the approval of the Colonial Office a draft ordinance for the control of the police. Admitting that it had no written authority from Lobengula to make or enforce such legislation, it proposed to act on the oral permission described by Jameson. Though Fairfield thought "we need not boggle at that," W.P. Schreiner had given the opinion that the ordinance would be *ultra vires* without a specific concession from Lobengula. The Colonial Office therefore submitted it to the law officers. Before they could report, which they were ready to do in February 1891, the police question had been overshadowed by the general problem of jurisdiction. It was laid aside, to be taken up again after the order-in-council of 9 May had provided a different foundation for the legal edifice.[46]

Almost a year had then passed during which the Company's power to control its police was, at the least, doubtful. The Colonial Office feared that one of Rhodes's numerous enemies would pass on this useful information to the troopers in the bush, but in this matter, too, the Company's luck held.

316 Rhodes and Rhodesia

It was not only in respect of the police that the Company's government functioned for at least eight months before the order-in-council gave it a kind of leg to stand on. From the moment the Pioneers were disbanded on 1 October the powers of government, in all its aspects, had to be exercised over them.

Applications for licences and for mining rights had to be dealt with; disputes had to be settled; mining commissioners appointed; regulations for the proper control of the settlers prepared; roads constructed to the different parts of the country where mining operations were taken in hand; a postal system inaugurated; townships laid out; sanitary and municipal regulations framed; and measures taken generally for the settlement of the country and for raising revenue requisite to meet the expenses of government.

Lobengula might well ask, "when did we speak on this matter?"

He could not deny having spoken about mining. The Company had foreseen that the Pioneers would lose no time in staking out claims. In June 1890 it had therefore submitted to the Colonial Office a proposed "proclamation" under the title "Mining Laws." The inevitable objection arose: the Company had no power to legislate. Perhaps the Rudd Concession implied, at least, the power to make mining regulations. Fairfield, in ignorance of the real ownership of that concession, thought that the Company might assume the power on the basis of that implication. It assumed the power all right, but without trying to stand on such treacherous legal ground. A "Memorandum of terms and conditions upon which persons are permitted to prospect for minerals and metals in Mashonaland," signed by Rutherfoord Harris, was published in the Cape papers on 24 October. The essential points of the earlier draft proclamation were in it, notably the provision that the Chartered Company claimed half the vendor's scrip in every mining company floated. Up in Fort Salisbury, Colquhoun was appointing acting mining commissioners and claim inspectors to administer this "law" and to keep the registers of claims.

The postal service, too, had been planned well in advance; in July the Company had submitted to the Colonial Office its designs for postage and revenue stamps. By October Salisbury was linked to the imperial posts in Bechuanaland by relays of the Company's police along the Selous Road. The claim that the mails took twenty-three days from Cape Town to Salisbury may have been a little optimistic—reports from Salisbury were published in the *Cape Argus* about a month after dispatch—but even the longer period was creditable to mule cart and mounted policeman. These, however, were dry season statistics. When the rivers rose in flood all communication with the south was cut off.

The posts were not politically important; the land was. The Pioneers had been promised farms, though the Company had no rights whatsoever in the land until it acquired the Lippert Concession. It is true that in the wild optimism of 1890 mining seemed much more attractive than agriculture. Nevertheless Maguire told Fairfield that "every fellah" liked to think he had a farm

317 Bricks without Straw

marked out for him. Every fellah could therefore mark one out for himself, though his title would be provisional and not confirmed until the Company acquired the right. A small team of surveyors was employed, but was at first fully occupied on mining claims. The Company, however, had no qualms about making land grants before it got the Lippert Concession, as a dispute over a farm right between A.L. Tomes and John Howe showed. "I have heard," Lobengula wrote, "that my Country is being cut up and given out. Why should this be done without my consent?"[47]

The man directly in charge of all these operations was A.R. Colquhoun, sent up with the Pioneers to be "Administrator" of Mashonaland. The Company could call him what it liked, but the imperial authorities would not recognize this title, call him "His Honour," or otherwise give him the same status as, say, Sir Sidney Shippard. In spite of his slightly irregular proceedings in Burma, which led to the termination of his services there, Colquhoun was, however, too much of a stickler for legal and political propriety to suit the jolly buccaneers whom he was supposed to rule but was really serving. One of his first acts was to forbid Johnson and Jameson to go on their hair-raising trip to the east coast. When they went nevertheless, Colquhoun sent a policeman after them to arrest them and bring them back. Jameson's comment when told of the administrator's command was "Damn the fellow! I got him his job."[48]

The order-in-council of 9 May 1891 brought a kind of legality into what had been absolutely illegal and unauthorized proceedings. To what extent and by what means the illegal proceedings were now made legal is, for several reasons, hard to say. There were differences of opinion at the time among the authorities on the subject, there have been differences since, and the law about it had a chameleon-like capacity to adapt itself to the facts as they unfolded.

Up to the early months of 1891, the British government was anxious to have as little responsibility as possible in its new sphere of operations; and of course the Crown had none. The Company's attempts at legislation came to nothing—"Mining laws" were transformed into an advertisement in the press.

The threat posed by the Adendorff trekkers threw a different light on the situation. It was now necessary to have, in the Company's sphere, courts with valid jurisdiction, especially over foreign subjects, and to have a watertight case against any new Stellalands and Goshens. "The chief reason for passing the Order-in-Council of 9th May," Sir Robert Herbert wrote a few weeks later, "was the necessity of having some jurisdiction to which we could refer foreigners and others in support of our claim to control the country under the protection of the Queen."

It was this order-in-council that first declared the country to be under the queen's protection. The step was taken because the law officers advised that without it a mere application of the Foreign Jurisdiction Act, 1890 (which the Colonial Office would have preferred) would not give jurisdiction over foreigners. The protectorate conferred this jurisdiction—but not over people such as Transvalers whose governments were not parties to the Berlin and Brussels acts. A case could be made out, even without the protectorate, for jurisdiction over British subjects in Mashonaland. It would be based not so much on Lobengula's remark to Jameson as on his passive acceptance of the fait accompli, which could reasonably be called "sufferance." Combined with the two General Acts and the declaration of a protectorate, this sufferance was probably enough to justify the main inference drawn from it—jurisdiction over whites (though not really all whites) in Mashonaland.

There was, however, another implication which that sufferance was, by tortuous reasoning, made to provide—jurisdiction over the native inhabitants. The process was not really reasoning; it was cutting the Gordian knot with a sword. Lobengula's remark had been: "I am Chief of the Black people, but I have made them chief over the whites." He had "suffered" the company to rule the whites in Mashonaland, but not, as many incidents showed, the blacks: "Lomogunda belongs to me." Jurisdiction over the blacks was not conferred by Lobengula, the protectorate, the General Acts, or the Foreign Jurisdiction Act.

The order-in-council ought not to have conferred it either, because it professed to be merely declaratory: "the High Commissioner may on Her Majesty's behalf exercise all powers and jurisdiction which Her Majesty, at any time before or after the date of this Order, had or may have within the limits of this Order." No new powers were conferred by it on the Crown, except those which followed necessarily from the declaration of a protectorate.

But no one goes so far as he who knows not whither he is going. It was impossible to draw a line of colour or nationality through the judicial process. Blacks and whites would have cases against each other. If there were a division of authority between Lobengula and the British it would have to be territorial, not racial: British jurisdiction would have to apply to all persons in Mashonaland. Lobengula's writ should run on one side of Jameson's supposed "border" and Colquhoun's on the other. But that was an arrangement which the order-in-council could not make, because the rights derived from the Moffat treaty, the Rudd Concession, and now potentially the Lippert Concession all depended on the recognition of Lobengula's sovereignty in Mashonaland as well. The queen, the high commissioner, and the Company had specifically and on many occasions recognized that sovereignty.

So there was nothing for it but usurpation on the big scale. The order-in-council (its declaratory character being forgotten, or misapplied) prescribed that the high commissioner might by proclamation

> provide for the administration of justice, the raising of revenue, and generally for the peace, order and good government of all persons within the limits of this Order, including the prohibition and punishment of acts tending to disturb the public peace.

The High Commissioner in issuing such proclamations shall respect any native laws or customs by which the civil relations of Chiefs, tribes or populations under Her Majesty's protection are now regulated, except so far as the same may be incompatible with the due exercise of Her Majesty's power and jurisdiction.

In subsequent dispatches both the Company and Loch were told to confine their legislative and judicial attentions, as far as possible, to the Europeans, because of the doubt about their authority over the Africans; but these instructions did not cancel the words "all persons within the limits of this Order." Respecting (within limits) the laws and customs of the chiefs and tribes was a far cry from having no jurisdiction over them.

The reasoning by which Fairfield and his colleagues, and Knutsford himself, justified this usurpation was pitifully weak and betrayed their lack of confidence in their case. Much was made of the Berlin and Brussels acts, which as we have seen did not cover the case. Fairfield observed that the practice, in native territories under British control, of deriving jurisdiction from grants by their rulers was "usual, but not universal." To provide therefore for the contingency of such grants not being obtainable, the Colonial Office had inserted into the charter Article 10, which was not in the draft submitted by the promoters. This article read: "The Company shall to the best of its ability preserve peace and order in such ways and manners as it shall consider necessary, and may with that object make ordinances (to be approved by Our Secretary of State), and may establish and maintain a force of police." Fairfield's desperate recourse to Article 10 was the first time that Loch, or probably anyone else, learned that it was supposed to confer power and not merely capacity. Its application had always been understood to depend on the grant of the power by Lobengula. Two years later Fairfield confessed as much: "as they [the Company] had rushed into Mashonaland without any such powers and seemed totally unable to acquire them, we decided to treat them as having legislative powers for certain ordinary purposes in virtue of a few words which had crept into Clause 10 of the Charter, but which we had theretofore ignored."

There was, of course, a simple method by which the Crown could have acquired all the necessary powers, and more—annexation; but annexation would have placed the power, and the responsibility, squarely on the shoulders of the government. That was not wanted. The arguments against imperial involvement, which prevailed when the charter was granted, still held good. The Company was to exercise the powers, but it would have to receive from the Crown any which had not accrued to it from other sources. The Crown wanted to possess the power but not to use it, to delegate it but also to hold it in reserve for international emergencies; to have—shameful thought!—power without responsibility. Because of its anxiety to avoid responsibility it failed to acquire the power by any means which would stand up to legal scrutiny.

The charter and Lobengula had not, between them, provided all the powers needed. The Company had (by Jameson's reasoning, by sufferance, or whatever it was) received some judicial power from Lobengula, but had not received from the Crown the right to exercise it; it had received legislative capacity from the Crown but not legislative power from Lobengula. The Colonial Office made the pretence of correcting the latter omission by falling back on Article 10; to deal with the former the order-in-council gave the high commissioner the power to appoint "Deputy Commissioners, or Resident Commissioners, or Assistant-Commissioners, or Judges, Magistrates and other officers," and to "define from time to time the districts within which such officers shall respectively discharge their functions." In addition, the courts of British Bechuanaland were to have the same jurisdiction, civil and criminal, original and appellate, within the limits of the order as they had in the Crown Colony itself.[49]

The order did not spell out Knutsford's intention. The reader could be pardoned for assuming that it conferred all powers of government on the high commissioner and withdrew them from the Company. Loch, making that assumption, issued on 10 June a proclamation which did everything that the order in-council permitted him to do, and more. He imposed a complete administrative and judicial system both on the Bechuanaland Protectorate and on the Company's sphere beyond it: resident commissioners, subordinate officials, inspectors of police, marriage officers, magistrates; control of immigration, liquor, arms and ammunition, trading licences, land titles, coinage, weights and measures—all on the high commissioner's authority. The law to be administered by the courts was, "as nearly as the circumstances of the country will permit . . . the same as the law for the time being in force in the Colony of the Cape of Good Hope," except that no Cape Act passed after the date of the proclamation would apply to the territory. On the ground that the Company's right to legislate was doubtful, Loch assumed that power too. The Company's administration was not legitimized; it was superseded.

The clerks in Downing Street were appalled. The proclamation, as far as it related to Mashonaland, was "contrary to every declaration which Her Majesty's Govt. has made during the last seven or eight weeks—except as regards erecting courts and appointing judicial officers." It courted the danger that he who called the tune would have to pay the piper, and the Treasury was resolved not to do that. It also involved the Crown in a risky speculative venture—perhaps deliberately, in order to save the Mashonaland operation when the Company collapsed—and this involvement was what the imperial government had all along taken great pains to avoid.[50]

Knutsford had intended the order-in-council ostensibly to clarify, though actually to increase, the powers of the Crown; but he intended these powers to be used by the Crown only in exceptional cases. Normally, they would be delegated to agents, in particular the Chartered Company, which was even to make the judicial appointments. But Loch had issued his proclamation and his face had to be saved. He was therefore told that the parts of the proclamation dealing with courts and magistrates could stand, but none of the rest. When other arrangements had been made he would have to make another proclamation, cancelling the offending parts of the first on the ground that they were no longer necessary. Even subsequent appointments and changes in the judicial sphere were to be left to the Company.

Before Loch could be stopped in his headlong career he had compounded his offence. The proclamation of 10 June had created offices; another, on 27 June, nominated people to fill them and defined the boundaries of their jurisdictions. Sir Sidney Shippard, who was administrator of the Crown Colony, was made resident commissioner of the Bechuanaland Protectorate. This was appropriate, and the Colonial Office had no objection, though Fairfield thought Shippard "a peculiarly intractable and wrong-headed officer." Fairfield also thought it dangerous to include the disputed territory, as well as the Tati district, in Shippard's jurisdiction, as the boundary dispute seemed thereby to be decided in favour of Kgama; but in this Fairfield was overridden by his superiors. That Colquhoun should be made temporary resident commissioner in the Company's sphere was emphatically not acceptable to the Office; he could be given the strictly judicial title of chief magistrate, but the imperial authorities must have nothing to do with his other functions. Magisterial districts and the officers for them could be accepted: Tye at Fort Tuli, Chaplin at Fort Victoria, Colquhoun at Fort Salisbury, Forbes at Hartley Hill, and Heyman at Umtali. Strictly, though, these appointments were the Company's business and did not require imperial approval.

If he had not been stopped, Loch in his zeal would have enacted the Company's mining regulations (still floating about in some legislative limbo) by another proclamation. "Sir Henry Loch," Fairfield minuted, "like the British infantry, never knows when he is beaten." He was told to leave such things alone. It was true that the order-in-council purported to give legislative power to the high commissioner, but, Knutsford explained, it was *a*, not *the*, right to legislate. It was to be used only in special circumstances. Normally the Company would legislate by ordinance. Its ordinances and appointments would be *confirmed* by the high commissioner, to remove doubts of their validity.[51]

In fact the doubts would not be removed by this procedure. Nothing had occurred in 1891 to confer either on the Company or on the Crown any legislative power which they did not have in 1890, when they clearly had none. An order-in-council was not an instrument by which the Crown could acquire power it did not have before. Even if it had acquired such power, which the changing character of protectorates would provide a few years hence, it would accrue to the Company only through specific delegation by the Crown, and there was no such delegation. In default of it a mere "confirmation" by the high commissioner would not do.

Even on the judicial side, where there was a case for some of the Crown's claim to jurisdiction, that claim had not been made watertight. It must not be supposed that in 1891 the rights of chiefs such as Lobengula counted for nothing in international law. Though there were some jurists who regarded the lands of "uncivilized" or "savage" peoples as *territorium nullius*, open to the first civilized comer, the weight of learned opinion was against them. Agreements with such chiefs were binding. As for British law, that is what the courts say it is. The Foreign Jurisdiction Act, 1890, included a clause which applied the doctrine of "act of state" to the assumption of jurisdiction in foreign territory by a British court. If the court doubted its power to deal with cases in such territory it could apply to a secretary of state for a ruling. His decision on the scope of its jurisdiction was final, and binding on the court. Had such a question been put and answered within the two or three years following May 1891, the assumption of jurisdiction by the Crown (if not by the Company) in the Company's sphere might have been validated in British law. But it was not put. In later years, when the question had become academic, both the Company and the Judicial Committee of the Privy Council recognized that the assumption of powers up to 1893 was, at least in part, an illegal usurpation. The difference after May 1891 was that the Colonial Office now connived at the offence.[52]

The Company, having been given the signal to legislate, on 1 July produced Ordinance No. 1 for Knutsford's approval. This provided at last for the discipline of the Company's police. By the end of the month the directors had submitted Nos. 2 and 3, which dealt respectively with the trading and delivery of firearms and with coinage and weights and measures.[53] After some slight amendments Knutsford approved of these. Loch then issued the proclamation dictated to him by his superiors, cancelling as being no longer necessary all except the judicial provisions of his proclamations of 10 and 27 June.

The sudden intrusion of the imperial power into the Company's work of government, and its precipitate withdrawal a few weeks later, were consistent with its policy over the previous two or three years. Its bursts of energetic interference were always responses to threats from colonial competitors—Boer, Portuguese, or German. Just as surely, the cessation of the threat was followed by a shaking off of imperial responsibility. The alarm about the Adendorff trek was at its height when the order-in-council of 9 May and the proclamation of 10 June were being prepared. The attempted crossing of the Limpopo and the arrest of Ferreira occurred on 24 June. Knutsford's abandonment of all responsibility to the Company followed immediately. So great was the anxiety to avoid being involved that the secretary of state and his officials, including the high commissioner, now neglected most of the supervising and controlling functions over the Company which even the charter had imposed on them. They did look, even at the draft stage, at the ordinances which the directors submitted to them, but there were only three of these in 1891 and none in 1892.

The Company proposed at least two more: one to enact the mining regulations which were already, without legislative sanction, in force; the other to introduce a general code of laws. This last, which Bramston called a "verbose and ill-drawn document," had been submitted to the Colonial Office in January. In July, now that the Office had made up its mind that the Company must legislate by ordinance, this and the mining regulations were put into that form. As some details needed amendment, and Rhodes had to be consulted, nothing more was heard of these proposals for a long time.[54] Fairfield believed that the reason for the legislative inactivity was that Hawksley, on whom the Company depended to draft its ordinances, had too much to do. The Colonial Office even offered to sanction an ordinance giving the administrator the power to make regulations, but, probably for the same reason, the Company failed to draw it up.

The administration at Fort Salisbury seems to have borne the lack of good legal foundations with the same unconcern as it bore its material privations. The administrator made do with a mud hut without glass widow-panes. When Marshall Hole arrived in 1891 to take up his job as assistant to Rutherfoord Harris (then secretary in the administration) he looked for the "rent-free Government Quarters" he had been promised. Harris pointed out to him a suitable piece of veld on which to build his hut, "a clump of trees where I could cut the requisite poles, and a pit where the right kind of mud could be procured."

Even under the relatively sophisticated conditions of 1895, George Pauling carried out administrative duties in the spirit which had been characteristic from the beginning. A deputation came to see him in his capacity as postmaster-general: no mail had arrived for six weeks. As the fault did not lie with that department, he advised them to come back the next day to see the commissioner of public works, who was the same George Pauling as the postmaster-general. In the meantime he proposed on adjournment to the Avenue Hotel, across the road, for some "liquid refreshment," and "we parted very good friends." At the next interview the commissioner of public works disclaimed responsibility and passed the complaint to the minister of mines—also George Pauling. There was the same adjournment to the hotel and the same parting in a convivial spirit. The next day he managed to stave off the crisis a little longer, in the hope—which was fulfilled—that the mail would arrive before their next meeting.

That, however, was under a later regime. Colquhoun did his best to observe the administrative proprieties, but circumstances were against him. For most of his time there was no legal basis for anything he did or needed to do ("Damn the fellow!"). What was more, his political basis was weak. As he himself clearly understood, the real authority in Mashonaland was Jameson, with his power of attorney from Rhodes. The only reason for making Colquhoun, and not Jameson, administrator, was to free Jameson from the daily chores of government so that he could deal with the big questions—the East

Coast route, Gazaland, the Portuguese, the Boers, Lobengula. These matters (as we have seen) kept Jameson almost constantly on the move, so that he spent more time out of Mashonaland than in it during Colquhoun's tenure. Nevertheless, Colquhoun was only a stop-gap. His retirement a year after the occupation came a little earlier, perhaps, than originally intended, and he himself was able to explain it on grounds of health—he could not face another rainy season in the country. The real reasons for his removal by the Company are suggested by a comparison between his government and his successor's; they were also anticipated as early as February by Thomas Maxwell when he referred to the departure of Colquhoun's secretary Harrison: "It would appear Harrison has been removed owing to his being *the strong man in Mashonaland*, and that Colquhoun is *slow and very straight* therefore it will be expedient to remove him. Jameson will do this in time."[55]

Colquhoun resigned in August; on 18 September Jameson was appointed chief magistrate (by the high commissioner) and administrator (by the Company). One of his first duties was to go to Umtali to meet Rhodes, who arrived there in October on his first visit to the country. During his visit it was well understood that he, and not Jameson, was the real fountain of authority—as Jameson had been when Colquhoun was administrator, though the cases are not otherwise analogous. Complaints were brought to Rhodes, and there was much to complain about. Rhodes tried "the imaginative" on the settlers as he did on the share-holders, and got from a hard-bitten Scot the rejoinder that "I would have ye know, Mr Rhodes, that we didna come here for posterity." On the whole, in comparison with the dream, Rhodes found the reality disappointing, but as usual adversity strengthened his resolution. Out of his discussions with Jameson came administrative and financial reform.

We have seen why it was urgently necessary to reduce expenditure. By far the largest item of expenditure in Mashonaland was the Company's police, which cost about £150,000 a year. Jameson's idea of a policeman's lot (in his spare time "driving post-carts, carrying chains for surveyors, or doing clerical work in the administrative offices") was different from the notions held by the seconded imperial officers who commanded the force. Moreover, such was the sense of security among the whites of Mashonaland that nobody supposed a police force of 650 to be necessary for defence; nobody, that is, except the Colonial Office. To disarm criticism from that quarter, Jameson combined the reduction of the police force from 650 to 40 with the enrolment of a body of volunteers called the Mashonaland Horse. Though this was "at first little more than a paper regiment" whose parades were neglected by those who were neither officers nor NCO's, its formation gave a respectable reason for the drastic reduction of the police. The reduction was carried out by the end of 1891; in 1892 the expenses of the police and volunteer department were about £25,000, out of a total administrative budget of £70,000.[56]

In that year the Company passed no ordinances, yet law was being enforced.

The courts could hardly limit themselves to the three topics on which there had been regular legislation in 1891. The gap was filled by Jameson in his characteristic way. Without benefit of the abortive enabling ordinance, "Regulations" were drawn up, announced in the local press, and treated as having all the force of law. A few of these were reported by the Company to the Colonial Office, which solemnly observed that they ought to be in the form of ordinances passed by the directors and approved by the secretary of state. Nothing was done to give effect to such observations.

In January 1892, for instance, the gap left by the disbanded police and only partly filled by the Volunteers was further plugged by a Burgher Force in the manner of the Cape Colony, whose laws after all now applied to Mashonaland. All males between the ages of eighteen and fifty were liable under this system to be called up; obviously *white* males were meant, but the regulations did not say so. Again following the Cape example, the office of field cornet was created. These amateur office-holders had to keep the registers of burghers, as well as perform other duties enumerated in twenty-four articles. They arrested criminals, held inquests, looked after stray children, dealt with diseased animals, and guarded against stock thefts. It was typical of the system that the Burgher Force was created by Articles 7 to 13 of a document headed "Instructions for Field Cornets."

For the rest, Jameson did not even trouble the Colonial Office to look at his "regulations." Sometimes he treated as an ordinance what was actually only a draft note approved by the secretary of state. He even "amended" such a nonexistent ordinance by regulation. Some of these measures imposed taxation, such as licence fees and the rates of local sanitary boards, and some included penal sanctions. Yet the Colonial Office, as if paralysed with fear and shock after Loch's attempt at active imperialism, turned a blind eye to all these proceedings. Not even the fear of Labouchere could drive it to interfere with the Company.

The law was interpreted and enforced as informally as it was made, which is not surprising when "half a dozen young officers, with no more experience of judicial practice than they had acquired in the orderly-room, suddenly found themselves appointed Resident Magistrates." The most that could be done to ensure a little regularity was to appoint Alfred Caldecott, an able Kimberley attorney, nominally as public prosecutor, actually also as mentor to the orderly-room magistrates. In that close-knit society (Robert Coryndon, for instance, destined to a distinguished career in the Colonial Service, but then clerk to the administrator, was Caldecott's nephew) the public prosecutor was liable to be placed in an ambiguous position. He once very ably prosecuted a number of men for playing baccarat in a gambling den; the laughter in court was due to the generally known fact that the public prosecutor had been there himself, but happened to have left before the police arrived. When an Indian accused another Indian of fraud, before the chief magistrate himself, and it be-

Pioneer Street, Salisbury. Above, 1891. Below, about 1900

327 Bricks without Straw

came apparent that the charge was trumped-up and vindictive, Jameson sentenced the *accuser* to ten lashes, and some of his witnesses to five each.

In March 1892 the magistrates were appointed marriage officers. Fairfield was worried about this, for the usual reason that the Company had no authority in matrimonial matters. He would have been still more worried if he had foreseen the cases of Marshall Hole unwittingly marrying an old Boer to his seventeen-year-old niece, or of the Hon. Harry White marrying a number of couples before he had been commissioned as a marriage officer.

These little matters could be put right (the incestuous marriage, unhappily, only by the husband's death in the rebellion), but there were other judicial questions that had to be taken more seriously. The most important were trials on capital charges and the execution of capital sentences. As might be expected, a murder of white by black was thought by this small and insecure white society to require exemplary punishment; a murder of black by white was treated more lightly. The drunken bar-keeper of Umtali who was irritated by the noise of drums and fired a shot into the darkness, killing an African, was, of course, guilty of manslaughter and not murder. Jameson's sentence—a £50 fine, of which the accused paid £25 in cash and gave an IOU for the rest—was, however, significantly lenient.[57]

When an African was brought to court on a murder charge he had a good chance of a fair trial: no capital sentence could be carried out without the sanction of the high commissioner, who insisted on knowing all the details of the case, and the Colonial Office itself was watching over his shoulder. The British government, too, had set its face against trial by jury, which would have meant a white jury. So the Chief Chirumziba, arrested as an accomplice in the murder of the Frenchman J.F.V. Guérolt, was released when no witnesses could be brought to give evidence against him and the murderers themselves could not be found; and this although some of the dead man's possessions were found in the chief's own hut.[58] A Zulu known to history only as "Jim" was less fortunate. The evidence that he had murdered a white man, woman, and child, and mortally wounded the husband of the woman, seems incontrovertible. Jameson and five assessors tried the case and condemned Jim to death. As an excited crowd in Salisbury wanted to lynch the prisoner, and was only dissuaded by Jameson with a plea not to do anything to avert the expected boom, the administrator begged the high commissioner to confirm the death sentence by telegram without waiting for the full report. Loch refused to oblige, treating Jameson to a little lecture on the legal proprieties. When these had been complied with the execution was carried out.[59] As we shall see, however, the failure of Africans to obtain justice was not mainly a fault of the courts; it was due to the administration's habit of settling disputes out of court, by military means.

From the death penalty to a hut tax might seem an anticlimax, until one considers that there were few candidates for the gallows but many occupiers of huts. As Loch noted, the hut tax was a source of revenue utilized by all South African governments. As the Company estimated its expenditure in Mashonaland for the year 1892 at £70,000, and its revenue at £15,000, it inevitably turned its attention to this means of bridging the gap. A draft ordinance was drawn up in 1892 and a long correspondence between the Company, the Colonial Office, and the high commissioner followed. Schreiner, the Cape attorney-general, gave the opinion that a hut tax could be levied only on Crown land or land that had been alienated by the Crown to private owners; the land occupied by the people of Mashonaland was their own, did not belong and had never belonged to the Crown, and could not therefore be taxed. Fairfield thought this argument "purely fantastic." He could not see, if the Company could pass ordinances on other subjects, as the secretary of state had allowed it to do, why it should not legislate about hut tax.

In this matter, however, the legal were outweighed by the political considerations. Whatever the law might be, the levying by the Company of a tax from people whom Lobengula claimed as his tributaries was sure to cause trouble. Loch suggested that the tax be imposed only to the east of the 30th meridian (roughly the line Hartley-Selukwe-Shabani-Beit Bridge), or alternatively east of the telegraph line. These were interesting variants of Jameson's "border," but such a restriction would not solve the problem. Lobengula claimed as far as the Sabi. The argument was still proceeding when the rise of Charterds on the stock exchange gave Fairfield the kind of opening he relished: "the price of the Company's shares in the market would seem to show that it is in good credit in the city of London, and must, therefore, have the means of carrying on its administration for the present." (And in an aside on his minute paper: " 'Rigged', no doubt, but they can't say that.") Then came the war, to make all the arguments irrelevant.[60]

THE MATABELELAND ORDER-IN-COUNCIL

The invasion of Matabeleland was the very thing to bring the imperial government down from its Olympic detachment to impose a controlling hand on the Company again. When the dust had settled, however, the control was seen to be less extensive and direct than the high commissioner, if not the secretary of state, had intended.

In the early stages of the fighting it was assumed that Lobengula, after being defeated, would surrender, and that terms of peace would be arranged with him. On 10 October Ripon told Loch that "any arrangements with regard to the future between Lobengula and the British South Africa Company may involve questions of general policy affecting many interests in South Africa, and must therefore be submitted to Her Majesty's Government under Article 7 of the Charter for their sanction." In his reply the following day Loch proposed that "all negotiations with Lobengula, and the policy respecting the future administration of that country, should be arranged by the High Commissioner, subject to the approval of Her Majesty's Government." A few days later, Loch asked some specific questions, one of which drew the reply that all negotiations were to be conducted by him alone, and that he was so to inform the Company.

These proposals, and the shocked protests which they drew from Rhodes and the Company, became irrelevant; there were no negotiations with Lobengula. The future of Matabeleland, however, had still to be settled. Loch of course took every opportunity of pushing his policy of direct imperial administration; he argued this in a dispatch of 18 October. By 12 November, however, he could no longer delude himself: "the great success of the Chartered Company now renders it in my opinion impossible to adopt the recommendations contained in my secret despatch of 18th October." Those recommendations had already been rejected in London, on two grounds. The first was the expense of direct administration, the reason which had been decisive in the granting of the charter and in subsequent refusals to revoke it. The second reason for holding to this course was adduced by Fairfield on 6 November: "to adopt the contrary policy would probably lose us South Africa." These considerations gave the secretary of state the courage to stand up to attacks from the opposite side. Fairfield noted in the same minute that "Mr Labouchere will attack our laager on Friday next." The attack was repulsed.[61]

The reference to South Africa was not baseless speculation. Loch had just cabled the contents of a memorandum he had received from Sir Gordon Sprigg (in the absence of Rhodes in the north) on behalf of his cabinet colleagues. The ministers expressed their "unanimous and firm conviction that . . . it is of the highest importance that the British South Africa Company should . . . exercise, subject to the approval of Her Majesty's Imperial Government, a free hand in the measures to be adopted, with a view to that satisfactory settlement which your Ministers have every reason to hope will follow from the action of the Company . . . Ministers desire to add that there can be no doubt that a very strong and widespread opinion exists . . . in this Colony and South Africa, in favour of the views expressed in this Minute." Though Loch reproved the ministers for presuming to advise him, in his capacity as high commissioner, on matters beyond their competence, he passed on the message and it was clearly understood in London.[62]

When, therefore, as the war was petering out, specific proposals for the future of Matabeleland were required, it was Loch, in consultation with Rhodes, who made them. During January and February 1894 drafts, arguments, and proposed amendments passed back and forth between Loch, Rhodes, the Colonial Office, the individuals in the office (who disagreed on many points) and a committee of the cabinet. The terms emerging from these arguments became an "Agreement" between the government and the Chartered Company, signed on the queen's birthday. With little substantial change this became the Matabeleland Order-in-Council of 18 July 1894.[63]

In spite of its name, it was to apply to the whole territory soon to be known as Southern Rhodesia. Although the intention to put an end to the irregularities of the past was plain in every clause, legal doubts were not altogether removed even now. Legislative power was being assumed over foreign territory—which to the purists Matabeleland still was. Had the power been duly conferred by the foreign ruler? No; he had been eliminated and was no longer able to confer it. Had the power been acquired, then, by conquest? Conquest implied annexation, and annexation was being shunned like the plague. Moreover, the victory and its fruits—whatever they were—belonged to the Company, a body of private persons. The Chartered Company could not acquire any portion of sovereignty by conquest; it could conquer only on behalf of the Crown, but in this case the Crown rejected the gift. The legal knot would be unravelled by the Privy Council in 1918, but in the meantime it remained firmly tied, to worry the scrupulous and the legal-minded.

One of these was Bramston, to whom Fairfield replied, "I do not see that the agreement substantially extends or claims to extend the character of the powers which have been in exercise in Mashonaland since 1891. It only extends the area of the exercise of the power." If Fairfield was referring only to the juridical status of British authority in Lobengula's country, and not to the details of the agreement, he had a point; but, as we have seen, the juridical position was confused under the order-in-council of 1891, and it was still so under that of 1894.[64]

These subtleties had little practical importance at the time. The Crown presumed again to possess powers in Matabeleland which it could, in part, exercise directly, and in part confer on the Company. It was intended, as before, that the Company should govern and the high commissioner and secretary of state merely guard against what they might regard as abuses. The growth of the Company's colony in Mashonaland, however, and its extension into Matabeleland, made necessary a more elaborate system of government than had existed before. The irregularities under the old system had shown the need for tighter controls.

In its general outline the measure was little changed between the first draft and the last. The office and title of administrator were now recognized; his tenure was for three years and could be renewed. No one denied the need to substitute a qualified judge for the old, very amateur chief magistrate, nor the need to provide the administrator with a Council. The Council was to consist of the judge and three other persons, the heads of executive departments; the latter would hold their appointments as councillors for six years. Fairfield had a "rooted objection" to the judge's participating in executive acts, but on this the cabinet committee overruled him—the example of the Crown colonies was to be followed.[65] The administrator was to consult the Council, unless this were impossible in an emergency, in which case he had to lay his decisions before it at the first opportunity. He could disregard a majority vote of the council, but would have then, if required by a dissenting member, to submit his reasons in writing to the board of directors. These could "reverse any action of the Administrator whether taken with, or without, or against, the advice of the Council." It was agreed that the Administrator-in-Council should have some legislative authority, but the precise scope of this was a subject of argument. No fines or taxes were to be levied except under legislative authority.

All salaries were to be paid by the Company. Those of the administrator and the judge were to be determined by the directors with the approval of the secretary of state, and could not then be altered without the consent of the latter. The territory was to be divided into districts under magistrates, from whose courts appeals would lie to the judge.[66] The law and the procedure were to be, in so far as they were applicable, those of the Cape Colony. This had been the principle of Loch's proclamation three years before, but Roman-Dutch law was now established in the territory by direct authority of the Crown. The judge (or "High Court of Matabeleland") was given complete jurisdiction over all persons and causes, but from his court an appeal would lie—as soon as the Cape Parliament had so resolved—to the Supreme Court of the Cape Colony. In civil cases between Africans, "native law" was to apply, with the usual proviso that it was "not repugnant to natural justice or morality," or to any order-in-council, proclamation, or ordinance. The Court might "obtain the assistance of one or two native assessors to advise it upon native law and customs," though the decision in the case would be that of the judge or magistrate alone. All the drafts provided that "Natives shall not be subject to any exceptional legislation save as regards liquor, arms and ammunition," but there was a great deal of argument about further exceptions to be added to this list.

So far the plain sailing; now for the controversies, which are the significant part of this business. The most important arguments concerned, of course, the rights of Africans and the ways of safeguarding them. There was some dispute also about the respective roles of the board of directors, the high commissioner, and the secretary of state. Finally there was the technical question of omitting provisions that were already covered by the charter or by previous orders-in-council. It was not always clear whether they were so covered or not, but the tendency of the officials, when in doubt, was to omit. To repeat an existing injunction would be to weaken its force by calling its efficacy in doubt.

Where Loch allotted powers to himself, to the administrator or to the secretary of state, Rhodes usually inserted the words "in consultation with the Board of Directors," and the Colonial Office almost always struck them out. The intention was not to weaken the Company but to strengthen the "men on the spot" by avoiding unnecessary reference to England. Rhodes's suggestion (as against Loch) that the administrator, judge, councillors, and magistrates should be appointed by the directors, with the approval of the secretary of state, was accepted by the Colonial Office and the cabinet.[67] They accepted also Rhodes's proposal that all except the judge could be removed by the directors (in the case of the administrator and the magistrates, with the secretary of state's approval), but added clauses enabling the secretary of state himself to remove the administrator and magistrates. Only the secretary of state could remove the judge; the high commissioner could "suspend" judge or magistrates, and the secretary of state could either confirm or reverse such a decision.

In view of some recent events, this meticulous attention to the powers of appointment and removal was wise. Recent events, which were also perhaps coming events casting their shadow before, inspired a clause which after many revisions forbade the armed forces of the Company to operate outside the territory defined in the order without the permission of Her Majesty's government. (Rhodes wanted this clause omitted, but this request was refused.) Another interesting check was added at the cabinet level: the high commissioner might, under the powers conferred by the order-in-council of 1891, appoint a "Deputy High Commissioner" or other officer to "reside temporarily" in the territory. In an excess of generosity the government agreed to pay this official out of its own money.

There was a good deal of argument about the legislative power. Curiously enough, no word was said in the Colonial Office about the scandal of Jameson's "regulations," although it was recalled that the Office had offered to approve an ordinance by the directors giving the administrator that power. Rhodes, too, had often asked the directors to confer legislative power on the administrator, or alternatively on himself. The need for the man on the spot to possess it was obvious. What was in doubt was the relation between his laws and those of his various superiors.

The system ultimately agreed upon was complicated. The directors, as before, could pass ordinances; the order-in-council made no change in that respect. The administrator, with the concurrence of at least two members of the Council, could pass regulations, which would take effect when approved by the high commissioner and published in an official gazette (for the time being, that of the Cape Colony). At any time within a year a secretary of state could disallow a regulation. A regulation or an ordinance could, with the previous consent of the high commissioner, amend or repeal a proclamation; even without such consent a regulation could suspend the operation of an ordinance. An ordinance, on the other hand—this was the word for legislation by the directors—could repeal or amend a regulation. Neither ordinance nor regulation could alter an order-in-council or, except with the high commissioner's assent, a proclamation. Either an ordinance or a regulation could empower municipal authorities to levy rates and pass by-laws.

It was originally proposed that "no member of the civil service shall have

333 Bricks without Straw

any interest, either direct or indirect, in the commercial undertakings or shares of the British South Africa Company, nor in any mines within the said territories.'' Loch thought the restriction should apply only to a few senior officers, and that a high commissioner's proclamation could provide the list of these. In a letter to Rhodes, Sir Thomas Scanlen pointed out that no such restriction had ever applied in the Cape Colony, and suggested that it should be limited to judicial officers. Fairfield drew attention to the peculiarity of the case: the directors themselves "had an interest," so that the governing body was in a quite different position from that of an ordinary government. If they chose to allow their servants to have a similar interest there could be no objection. This view prevailed, and the order-in-council made no reference to the matter.

Not surprisingly, some eyebrows were raised in London by the proposed "customs clause." This was an old story. The fiscal heretics of the colonies were always hatching schemes for preferential tariffs and the guardians of free trade orthodoxy in Britain had the duty of quashing them. That the company or its local representatives might impose a customs tariff was fair enough, but the suggestion that the duties should never be higher than those in the existing South African Customs Union looked a little suspicious. The suspicion was confirmed when Rhodes proposed an alteration: the limitation should refer only to English [sic] goods, and the produce of the Cape Colony should be free of duty. The original limitation was allowed to remain, but the preferences for "English" and Cape products were struck out.

These controversies, though of some interest, are completely overshadowed in importance by the sparring—essentially between Rhodes and the whole body of officialdom—over "native rights." Rhodes did not like the prohibition of racially discriminatory legislation, and produced the plausible argument that "everything of this nature must in any case be dealt with by an Ordinance which requires the approval of his Excellency the High Commissioner." The Colonial Office retained the clause because it was very important "from the point of view of public opinion here," and went on to "propose words that will meet Rhodes's objection." Thus to the original exceptions of liquor, arms, ammunition, and hut tax, was added "any matter which the High Commissioner, with the assent of the Secretary of State, may by Proclamation define." As in other cases, the Colonial Office believed that the controlling hands of those two officers provided all the safeguard that could be desired against abuse.[68]

If Rhodes had not blotted his copy-book within eighteen months of this order there is no knowing how his persuasive powers would have been brought to bear upon Loch and Ripon. As it was, no harm was done by this clause; but the provisions in respect of land, since they were intended to be, and were, carried out at once, were a much more serious matter. They were among the chief causes of the rebellions.

It was clear from the beginning that victors and vanquished would be sharing Matabeleland, and that without imperial intervention of some kind the victors might grab it all. Someone would have to ensure that the Ndebele were not altogether driven off their land.[69] Loch set the ball rolling by proposing to establish a Land Court of three persons—the judge and one nominee each of the secretary of state and the directors. The court would "assign land sufficient and suitable for the personal and individual agricultural and grazing requirements of the natives now inhabiting the country, wherever application is made for European settlement within near proximity to the lands occupied by the natives."

Rhodes proposed two changes in this wording. The change from "now inhabiting" to "who shall now inhabit" looks like a distinction without a difference, but its significance appeared as the discussion went on. It was meant to emphasize the point that the land allotted was to be sufficient for the present population but not for its future increase. This change was accepted deliberately by both Loch and his superiors in London; the legal draftsman who composed the final document reverted to "natives inhabiting Matabeleland," but the words were understood as Rhodes intended. The intention was made clear when Loch, in accepting Rhodes's amendment of another clause, commented that "as it stands, it would make the Company liable to find free land for the natives as they increase in numbers, and I feel sure this is not meant." The paragraph which Loch and Rhodes here agreed to strike out would have bound the Land Court to find "an additional and sufficient portion of land" whenever the portion allotted was shown to be insufficient or unsuitable. The changes were accepted in London without comment. Loch's words seem to imply that the land to be allotted was "free," a gracious gift by the Company, so that future generations could have no claim to it.

Even more serious was Rhodes's insertion, after the words "assign land," of "in Matabeleland." Loch objected that "that might be taken to exclude the operation of this clause to [sic] the whole of Mashonaland," which was of course exactly what Rhodes intended. Fairfield's opinion decided the issue: an extension to Mashonaland "would be long and costly; Mashonaland has had no serious land difficulties, and the public interest is centred in Matabeleland." The decision was made in the light of Loch's statement that "probably two-thirds of the territory under the administration of the Company is either wholly uninhabited or at great distance from any possible European settlement." An attempt to survey it all would entail not only great expense but also delay.[70]

It was not intended that the tribesmen should own the mineral wealth under the land—any more than the white settlers did. If therefore the Company needed any land for "mineral development" the court could order the African occupiers to give it up and to accept an "equivalent extent" of land elsewhere. If any of their land were needed for sites of townships, railways, or other public works, the court could order them to give it up. In its place they were to receive, according to the original draft, land "of equal value" elsewhere. Rhodes objected that these words might imply that the mineral value of the land was included. His amendment—"of equal arable or grazing value"—was thought to open the door, as the original version would have done, to interminable litigation; the operative words became "just and liberal compensation in land elsewhere . . . so far as possible, equally suited for their requirements in all respects as the land from which they are ordered to remove." There was no objection by anyone to the principle that "the land allotted to natives shall include a fair and equitable portion of springs and of grazing and arable land." Nor could anyone question the justice of Bramston's comment, "something should be said about cattle." This took the form of a sentence ordering the Land Commission to direct the administrator to deliver to the Ndebele "cattle sufficient for their needs."[71]

Rhodes objected, from the beginning, to the plan of assigning these duties to a court; he wanted a commission. Loch agreed, most of the officials agreed, and the Land Court duly became the Land Commission, with the same personnel as had been proposed for the court. The reason given in the Colonial Office for the preference was that the decisions of a commission would be subject to approval or revision, whereas those of a court would be final; and "we must retain . . . control of the native settlement in our own hands."[72] Curious, then, that Rhodes had the same preference; but he had great confidence in his influence over the high commissioner. It was agreed, also at Rhodes's suggestion, that after the commission had completed its original work—which amounted to demarcating reserves—it should be disbanded and its continuing tasks performed by the judge alone. Here Rhodes was thinking of the expense, even more perhaps than the greater ease of overawing one man than three.

There was no argument about the useful provision that the commission could appoint a subordinate district land court, in any district, to advise it.

Rhodes's record as an advocate of "equal rights for every civilized man south of the Zambezi" is not convincing; these interventions in the making of the Matabeleland Order-in-Council help to show why. Yet it would be too simple to classify him as a racist in the narrow sense. He was for keeping the Matabeleland reserves within what he regarded as proper bounds, but it never occured to him to prevent an African from owning land—if he had the means to acquire it—outside the reserves. On this point the Colonial Office could not in any case have yielded an inch: "Natives shall have the right to acquire and hold landed property." The original draft, however, went on to say that they could not alienate, mortgage, or in any way encumber the same without the permission of the Land Court. Rhodes objected to this: "if any of them show intelligence or capacity to acquire property of their own, they certainly should not be debarred from doing so; but then I think they should be treated as ordinary citizens." This rings true. Rhodes's *bête noire* was the "loafer." Most Africans he would have thought were loafers; but good luck to any who overcame the sin of sloth.

The Colonial Office saw the point, but maintained its own: alienation or encumbrance of property by an African was to be possible only before a magistrate, who had to satisfy himself that the terms were fair and that the seller understood them.[73]

Clause 25 may have seemed a small matter at the time: "In case of a revolt against the Company, or other misconduct committed by a native chief or tribe, the Administrator and Council may impose a reasonable fine upon the offender. The Administrator shall forthwith report every such case to the High Commissioner, who may remit the fine in whole or in part . . . "

Such were the main provisions of the order-in-council which became in a sense the starting-point of Rhodesian constitutional development. Before its successor was issued, four years later, the Jameson Raid and the rebellions had provided interesting glosses on many of its clauses and on many of the arguments which influenced the text.

NOTES CHAPTER 8

1 CO 879/36/426, no.26, encl., p.37; CO 417/102/17649, minutes.

2 Rhodes Papers, Charters, 3B, no.214c, Maguire to Rhodes, 15 July 1893, and no.217, Grey to Rhodes, 1 September 1893.

3 CO 879/37/439, p.10; 39/459, no.38, pp.42-54; *The Economist*, 3 December 1892, pp.1519-11; *The Times*, 17 November 1893, p.14, and 18 November 1893, p.8; RH Mss Afr. s 73, p.205. It is interesting that Rhodes's secretary Currey cabled to Cawston (no date, but Currey refers to this cable in a letter of 13 October 1890): "Rhodes strongly opposed to working agreement. Amalgamation must go through." (RH Mss Afr. s 74, p.243).

4 E.g., "If Lippert and Co. were to throw their shares on the market we should have no price *at all*—and this is most important for in this event how are we to borrow another shilling?" (Rhodes Papers, Charters 3A/2, no.199, Farquhar to Rhodes, 10 December 1891). For the sale of the shares to the public, see *The Economist*, 3 December 1892.

5 CO 879/39/459, no.38, p.49; Rhodes Papers, Charters 3A/1, no.70, Hawksley to Rhodes, 21 November 1890; 3A/2, no.199a, Grey to Rhodes, 25 December 1891; CO 417/72/24524, pp.214-36.

6 CO 417/88/23165, pp.381-422 (for this note by Fairfield, p.384). Cf. Maguire to Rhodes, 23 July 1891, in Rhodes Papers, Charters, 3A/2, no.182: ". . . before you can get much more on any but ruinous terms it will be necessary to shew that the country is on the way to becoming self-supporting."

7 Rhodes Papers, Charters, 3A/2, no.173a, Beit to Rhodes, 23 June 1891; 3B, no.208, Maguire to Rhodes, 6 August 1892; CO 879/39/459, no.38, pp.53-4.

8 Rhodes Papers, Charters 3A/1, no.4, BSA Co. to Matabeleland Co, 3 July 1890; no.6, Hollams to Rhodes, 11 July 1890; no.30, encl. 18 July 1890; no.37, Cawston to Rhodes, 5 September 1890; 3A/2, no.173a, Beit to Rhodes, 23 June 1891; RH Mss Afr. s73, p.211; CO 417/52/15971, pp.645-50; 69/1569, pp.513-8; *The Times*, 17 No-

vember 1893, p.14, 18 November 1893, p.8, 21 November 1893, p.8, 9 December 1893, p.12.

9 Rhodes Papers, Charters 3A/2, no.173a, Beit to Rhodes, 23 June 1891. The directors appear to have ruled (the deed of settlement did not prescribe this, but gave the board the power to refuse to register a transfer) that before any share was transferred it had to be fully paid up. See RH Mss Afr. s 76, pp.127, 156-7. There are various other passages having the same implication.

10 Rhodes Papers, Charters 3A/2, no.199, Farquhar to Rhodes, 10 December 1891; no.201b, same to same, 20 January 1892; 3B, no.213, Maguire to Rhodes, 10 June 1893, RH Mss Afr. s 76, pp.48, 110-12; CO 417/88/23165, p.383.

11 CO 417/72/24524, p.229 (the accounts are on pp.20-1 of the Report); 88/366, p.14 (cutting from *The Times* of 26 December 1891.)

12 Bartissol's opinion of the gold of Mashonaland: "le Transvaal n'est rien à côté de cela." (Tiano's letter of 2 November 1890 in RH Mss Afr. s 75, p.7).

13 Rhodes Papers, Charters 3A/2, no. 182, Maguire to Rhodes, 23 July 1891.

14 Lord Randolph Churchill, *Men, Mines and Animals in South Africa*, pp.175, 195-209, 273, 296-7, and generally the whole of chapters 15 and 17.

15 Perhaps the duke's association with the Mozambique Company was not totally unconnected with the fact that his first wife, who divorced him for adultery, was a sister of the duke of Abercorn.

16 Rhodes Papers, Charters 3A/2, no.199, Farquhar to Rhodes, 10 December 1891; 3B, no.201b, same to same, 20 January 1892; RH Mss Afr. s 76, p.73, coded telegraph Cawston (London) to Rudd (Cape Town); *The Times*, 2 October 1891, duke of Marlborough's letter (cf. CO 417/64/19247, p.219); CO 417/69/12940, pp.694-5.

17 CO 417/72/14068, pp.166-72; 88/23165, p.381.

18 Rhodes Papers, Charters, 3A/2, no.172a, Maguire to Rhodes, 12 June 1891; 3B, no.201a, Rothschild to Rhodes, 15 January 1892; no.201b, Farquhar to Rhodes, 20 January 1892.

19 A.P. Cartwright, *Gold Paved the Way*, pp.46-54; Consolidated Gold Fields of South Africa, *The Gold Fields*, pp.20-30.

20 Rhodes Papers, Gold Fields, 10/1, 1890-4, no.8, Lowrey to Currey, 20 October 1890; Public Record Office, BT31 4815/31926 x/K2372 (United Concessions Company); specifically, Memorandum, 3(1), Articles 5, and lists of shareholders. See also Rhodes Papers, Finance, no.14, Beit to Rhodes, 22 January 1891. According to this letter the possession of Central Search shares "entitled" the holder to United Concession shares *pro rata*—in the first instance ten for one. It appears also that the claim to U.C. shares, based on holding 3 out of 30 units in Central Search, by Leask, Fairbairn, and Phillips, was divided between Gold Fields, Rhodes, Rudd, and Beit. The reason for this transfer is not given, but the authority to make it may also account for the transfer of the Gold Fields shares to Thomas Rudd and Boyle.

21 RH Mss Afr. s 76, p.265, Hawksley to Cawston, 12 October 1893.

22 RH Mss Afr. s 73, pp.137, 198, 224-5, 246; CO 897/30/372, no. 199, pp.190-1; and see above, ch. 3.

23 Cape of Good Hope, *Votes and Proceedings of House of Assembly*, 1890, Appendix I, vol. I, A6-'90, pp.3-5; CO 879/30/372, nos. 213, 214, 217, 219, 221, 225, 229, on pp.204-222 (see especially the last of these items); 32/392, no.26, pp.60-6, no.141,

encl. 1, p.168; no.172, pp.207-8; co 417/33/21278, pp.427-34; and see above, ch.3, as for preceding note.

24 Even in the raising of this government loan there was an element of deception. Sir Charles Mills, the Cape agent in London, wrote to Sprigg that he hoped "the question of the Kimberley Extension Loan will not be raised. If it should be, it may be as well not to speak of borrowing the money temporarily for other purposes . . . I think it would be better simply to say that the money will be devoted to the purpose for which it was raised, . . . the purchase of the Kimberley Extension from the South African Company. That indeed is the pith of your instructions?" (Mills to Sprigg, 26 December 1889, in Sprigg papers, 230, Ms.10.001. I owe this reference to J.P. Vanstone.)

25 co 879/32/392, no.36, pp.60-6, and no.164, pp.197-200; *Cape Argus*, 4 and 5 August 1890, for Northern Railways Bill. Surely there must have been one debit item—the interest on the loan? But this is never referred to.

26 co 879/32/392, no.131a, pp.145-6 (and map opposite p.143); no.141a, encl., p.172; no.164, pp.197-8; Rhodes Papers, Charters, 3A/1, no.43, encl. For the agreement of August, 1890, see above, pp.5-6.

27 co 879/36/426, no.51, pp.73-9; no.87, pp.122-3; nos. 103, 104, pp.148-9; nos.154, 162, 163, 167 on pp.200-7; no.195, pp.237-8; no.217, pp.255-6; 37/441, nos.18, 23, 24, 33, 41, 42, on pp.28-49 (of them no.23 is the most informative, no.42 gives the Company's terms); co 417/69/22018, pp.356 ff.; 74/5059, pp.396-450; Paul Maylam, *Rhodes, the Tswana and the British: Colonialism, Collaboration and Conflict in the Bechuanaland Protectorate, 1885-99*, pp.69-70. For some earlier plans for the railway see Rhodes Papers, Charters, 3A/1, nos.49 and 58.

28 Rhodes had foreseen this trouble. A year earlier he had written to Cawston, "we shall have to begin construction before next session of Cape Parliament." (RH Mss Afr. s 75, pp.282-3.)

29 co 879/36/426, no.195, p.237; *Cape Hansard*, 1892, pp.115-36; co 417/88/23165, minutes on pp.381-6; 24096, pp.526-33; Leo Weinthal, ed., *The Story of the Cape to Cairo Railway and River Route*, vol. I, pp.649-50; *The Times*, 20 December 1893, p.3; *Cape Argus*, 19 January 1894, Johannesburg *Star*, 20 January 1894, and *Standard and Diggers' News*, 19 and 20 January 1894, for report of De Beers meeting; Maylam, *Rhodes, the Tswana and the British*, p.94, n.133. Part of the claim of the Exploring Company was based on its having done almost £6,000 worth of survey work for the railway. Some of these transactions were formalized in the agreement of July 1893. Giving De Beers a one-third interest in part repayment of a loan implies that that repayment was not made in cash; i.e., that 2,000 vendor's shares were given to De Beers without any corresponding expenditure of cash by the Chartered Company. The rest of the nominal capital of the Railway Company was presumably of the same order.

30 The Directors' Report for 1892-4, p.4 (microfilmed in collection co 468/1).

31 Rhodes Papers, Charters, 3B, no.256, Harris to Rhodes, 15 August 1895. E.g., "From Palapye the line is *our own* and we can make a profit on promotion and construction which we can't do now." What was expected immediately was profit on operation of the line.

32 RH Mss Afr. s 73, pp.1-9; s 75, series of letters on pp.288-90, 292-303; co 417/88/24094, pp.560-81.

33 The companies referred to were: The London and New York Investment Corporation, the English and Scottish Mercantile Investment Trust, the Union Debentures
Company, the Trustees, Executors and Securities Insurance Corporation, and the
South American and Mexican Company. (RH Mss Afr. s 75, p.284.) There may be
some doubt about the importance of their participation: early in 1894 the last two
were in trouble, and the last was actually in the hands of a liquidator. (*The Times*,
company reports, 16 January, 1 February, 21 February, 22 February and 26 February 1894.)

34 RH Mss Afr. s 75, series of letters on pp.288-90, 292-303, 312-13.

35 CO 417/88/24094, pp.560-81; Weinthal, *Cape to Cairo Railway*, vol. I, pp.641-3;
Baron E.B. d'Erlanger, *The History of the Construction and Finance of the Rhodesian Transport System*, pp.10-12; Henry C. Burdett, *Burdett's Official Intelligence
for 1893*, pp.600-1.

36 Newspaper references as in n.25. See above, p.293, for the agreement of July, 1893.

37 *The Times*, 16 January 1894; *Economist*, 20 January 1894; Johannesburg *Star*, 20
January 1894. For every hundred United Concessions shares the holder got 23 BSA
Co. shares. For every 23 of these £4.12.5 had to be invested in debentures. Consolidated Gold Fields was said to have got about 200,000 of the new BSA shares, so
would have had to buy about £40,000 worth of debentures. (*The Times*, 20 January
1894, p.3.) This report, too, overlooked the role of the chairman and the secretary.

38 Johannesburg *Star*, 18 November 1893; *Standard and Diggers' News*, 13 November
1893; *The Times*, 20 December 1893; CO 417/88/24096, p.532. Gifford had retired
from this board.

39 The share prices are found in *The Times* in the column headed "The Money Market," not in the Stock Exchange report. Each day's paper refers of course to the
prices of the previous day.

40 CO 417/43/13212, pp.294-5; 45/17654, p.345; CO 468/1 (Directors' Report for 1889-92,
p.4); CO 879/32/392, no.300, pp.325-7.

41 Pauling says that the work on the line from Mafeking began at the end of 1895
(George Pauling, *The Chronicles of a Contractor*, p.158); there was no sign of the
tracks at the time of the raid.

42 Pauling, *Chronicles of a Contractor*, pp.132-3, and illustration facing p.129; d'Erlanger, *Rhodesian Transport System*, p.12. New debentures were issued for the extension of the line, and again financed by d'Erlanger. According to d'Erlanger, the arrangements were made in "the latter part of 1893"; Pauling says the spring of 1894.

43 The Political Papers of J.S. Moffat, Moffat to Shippard, 13 October 1890; Colenbrander to Harris, 19 November 1890; Jameson to Harris, 21 November 1890; Colquhoun to Moffat, 24 November 1890; Lobengula to Loch, 1 January 1891; CO
417/72/497, pp.435-8.

44 CO 417/47/24191, pp.251 ff.; CO 879/33/403, no.80, pp.91-3; no.177, p.153.

45 CO 417/69/8790, p.138; Claire Palley, *The Constitutional History and Law of Southern Rhodesia, 1888-1965*, p.63. The whole question of the Crown's powers in a protectorate, of the Foreign Jurisdiction Act, etc., is dealt with in Part I, ch.4 of this
book. For texts of the General Acts, Sir E. Hertslet, *The Map of Africa by Treaty*,
vol. II, pp.468-518.

46 CO 417/52/2221, pp.663-71, and 24932, pp.680-96; 60/12967, pp.426-32; 61/13232,
pp.4-10; 69/3579, pp.100-14 (for the original submission of the draft ordinance in

March 1890, cf. CO 417/42/7053, pp.509-26); CO 879/32/392, no.243, pp.268-9; 33/403, no.177, p.153; no.214, p.186; no.220, p.189; no.248, p.204; no.252, p.205; 34/410 (memorandum on powers in protectorates); Palley, *Constitutional History*, p.89.

47 CO 417/43/13557, pp.415-26; 51/13422, pp.425-9; 16852, pp.508-22; 61/15051, pp.289-308; 62/17869, pp.345-57; Political Papers of J.S. Moffat, Lobengula to Loch, 1 January 1891, and Moffat to Shippard, 16 May 1891; CO 468/1 (Directors' Report for 1889-92, p.7); *Cape Argus*, 24 October 1890 and 12 December 1890 (after the notice on 24 October the memorandum was run as an advertisement for some time); National Archives of Rhodesia, *Guide to the Public Records*, pp.179, 183-4, 190.

48 CO 417/47/24195, pp.290-5; Colvin, *Life of Jameson*, vol. 1, p.15.

49 CO 417/60/14616, pp.514-16; 69/9715, pp. 52-71; 7848, pp.115-32; 8790, pp.133-8; 107/20368, minutes; 95/9805, Fairfield's minute; Palley, *Constitutional History*, p.101; M.E. Lindley, *The Acquisition and Government of Backward Territory in International Law*, pp.144, 355-7; Hertslet, *Map of Africa*, vol. II, pp.468-518; the text of the charter is available in various places, e.g., RH Mss Afr. s 71.

50 CO 417/59/11892, pp.343-8; 60/13784, pp.42, 48-9; 69/9715, pp.55-6. See Sec. 19 of the proclamation for the introduction of Cape law.

51 CO 417/59/11892, pp.343-8; 60/12195, pp.3-7; 13784, pp.42-53; 12633, pp.114-24; 12778, pp.167-71; 14616, pp.488-529; 14617, pp.550-60; 64/19251, pp.251-8; Colonial Office Print 414, no.128 (not included in the microfilm series 879).

52 Palley, *Constitutional History*, pp.67-71, 94-7; Lindley, *Backward Territory*, chapters 3, 4, 5, 19.

53 I.e., the chief items which gave offence in Loch's proclamation. It was the Colonial Office which ordered the Company to draw up these ordinances. CO 417/72/13221, pp.158-65; 15356, pp.180-7; Palley, *Constitutional History*, pp.98, 102.

54 CO 417/72/13250, pp.507-10; 13257, pp.511-12; 112/2262, pp.155-6; Palley, *Constitutional History*, pp.100-3.

55 A.R. Colquhoun, *Dan to Beersheba: Work and Travel in Four Continents*, pp.288-9, 295; Pauling, *Chronicles of a Contractor*, pp.145-7; H. Marshall Hole, *Old Rhodesian Days*, pp.22-3 (*Note*: attached to a copy of this, HO 1/6/1, in the National Archives of Zimbabwe is a "key to the aliases" used in the book); Diary of Thomas Maxwell, 22 February 1891.

56 CO 879/36/426, no.84, encl.2, p.121; no.266, p.303; Hole, *Old Rhodesian Days*, p.32; H. Marshall Hole, *The Making of Rhodesia*, p.283; Colvin, *Jameson*, vol. 1, p.216. Colin Harding in *Frontier Patrols*, p.27, says the police were reduced to 150; but in this instance the Company report for 1889-92, p.5 (CO 468/1), which says 40, should be reliable.

57 CO 417/75/6004, p.241; Hole, *Old Rhodesian Days*, pp.31, 66-9; Colvin, *Jameson*, vol. 1, p.232; Palley, *Constitutional History*, pp.103-6. For examples of Colonial Office attitudes, CO 879/36/426, no.95, pp.130-1; no.153, p.199; no.160, p.202.

58 There was a lot of correspondence about this. See CO 879/36/426, nos. 57, 83, 93, 101, 128, 140, 158, 208, respectively on pp. 70-1, 119-20, 127-9, 134-7, 167-8, 185-6, 201, 260-2. For the Guérolt case, see below, ch. 10.

59 CO 417/93/6273; Hole, *Old Rhodesian Days*, p.70. Only one white man ever suffered the death penalty in our period (see ibid., p.31).

60 co 879/36/426, no.266, p.303; 37/441, no.109, p.113; no.117, pp.117-20; no.122, pp.123-4; co 417/95/9805, minutes.

61 co 879/39/454, nos.93, 95, p.115; no.116, p.133; no.128, p.136; no.130, p.137; 459, no.1, p.1; no.21, pp.8-10; no.38a, p.55; no.47, p.60; co 417/102/18831a, minutes.

62 co 879/39/459, no.30, p.30.

63 Fairfield thought that the best remedy would be a supplementary charter; but "the Home Office would charge some frightful sum in fees for this," and an order-in-council would cost nothing (co 417/112/2262, p.156). The successive drafts of the agreement (order-in-council), with comments and alterations, can be found in co 417/112/2262, pp.154-226; 113/3570; 116/6887; co 879/40/461, no.40, pp.85-92; no.55, pp.119-23; no.82, pp.166-9; no.160a, pp.247-52; no.192, pp.280-2; no.195, pp.283-8 (this is the text of the "Agreement"); no.221, pp.325-6; no.265, pp.375-82 (the text of the order-in-council).

64 co 417/121/10833, minutes by Bramston, Fairfield, Ripon.

65 co 417/113,3570, Fairfield's minute. Fairfield thought that the composition of the Council might be made elastic, "so as to provide hereafter for an unofficial minority—if Mr Rhodes and the Company will agree." (co 417/112/2262, p.156.)

66 There was an apparent inconsistency in the reference to the judge. In relation to the Council he was mentioned in the singular; when it came to "the High Court of Matabeleland" provision was made for any number of judges. In fact there was only one at first.

67 The head of the police was included in the group in most of the drafts, but was omitted from the final text.

68 co 417/112/2262, pp.166-7, 176, 210-11.

69 For the successive versions of the clauses dealing with land, see co 417/112/2262, pp.180-8, 203-5, 215-17, and 113/3570, 116/6887.

70 co 417/112/2262, pp.180-1.

71 Ibid. Anyone removing "natives from any kraal or from any land assigned to them," without an order by the Commission, or except in execution of the process of a competent court, was liable to imprisonment up to two years, a fine up to £100, or both. For the cattle question, see below, ch. 10.

72 co 417/112/2262, pp.158-9.

73 Ibid., pp.184-5.

CHAPTER 9

The White Society, 1890-1896

This is the story of the birth of a colony. In the strictest sense a colony consists of colonists, and there have been a few places in the world where colonists have planted themselves in a land empty of inhabitants, or nearly so. It is notorious that in Rhodesia this was very far from being the case. A community of white immigrants was superimposed on a vastly bigger indigenous black community.

That this arrangement produced acute tensions and problems in later times hardly needs to be said. We are concerned now with its origins. The old black tribal societies developed under the impact of strange new forces. A new white colonial society grew in their midst. The old and the new remained forever separate, though becoming economically and in other ways interdependent. Was this pattern inevitable?

We look first at the immigrant society. Between the arrival of the Pioneers at Fort Salisbury in September 1890 and the outbreak of the rebellion in March 1896 a white Rhodesian community emerged and took on a shape that would still be recognizable three generations later. Some of the factors that gave the community its distinctive character can be identified. For example: the provenance of the immigrants—by nationality, country of origin, and class; the heavy preponderance of males among those immigrants; the circumstances of their entry into Mashonaland and Matabeleland respectively; the expectation and intention that the basis of the colony's economy would be gold mining; the inaccessibility of the country in the early years—whether measured by miles, by time, by expense, or by the marked and unmarked graves that lay beside the roads to the Promised Land; government by a Company; alcohol; malaria. An important factor is the community's date of birth: immigrants who came from South Africa, Britain, or elsewhere in the early 1890s brought with them cultural goods of a particular vintage. The difference between this cultural equipment and that of the native inhabitants at the time is the basic reason for the separation between the societies; but white immigrants of that date brought with them, also, attitudes and theories about race which ensured that the separation would be maintained.

For an explanation of early White Rhodesia, the problem of communication

343 The White Society

is as good a starting point as any. The problem has been evident at every stage of this story. The base from which the British, whether missionaries, traders, soldiers, or the Chartered Company, approached Rhodesia was the railhead of the Cape system. By December 1890 that railhead was at Vryburg; four years later it had moved on to Mafeking. From either point the journey to Salisbury or even to Bulawayo was formidable. Under the conditions of 1890 the mails took nearly a month from Salisbury to Vryburg—before the rains came; parties travelling by ox-wagon took from two to four months. Two years later "Bezuidenhout's Royal Mail Carts" advertised a twelve-day schedule between Salisbury and Tuli; they connected at the latter place with Zeederberg's coaches plying to Pretoria: "through passage in 18 days." After the conquest of Matabeleland, the railhead having by then advanced to Mafeking, coaches followed the route through Bulawayo. Time from Mafeking to Salisbury, 12½ days; fare, £37. The coach route from Pretoria was cheaper and quicker: 8½ days in 1893.

The public was informed that "parties not pressed for time, who have much baggage, will find it considerably cheaper to travel by ox-waggon." Most parties of immigrants did so. There were hazards—water shortage, lions, snakes, the overturning of wagons, sticking fast in drifts, the loss of oxen, malaria in its season—but there were compensating pleasures, and these difficulties could be overcome by the pluck and grit of the frontier.

No amount of pluck could reduce the cost of transporting goods. There was no standard rate for this. The customers bargained with the transport riders. In 1894 the Company suggested that the following would "give some idea" of the range of charges for carting 100 lb: Mafeking to Bulawayo, 12s. 6d. to 17s. 6d.; Bulawayo to Salisbury, 13s. 6d. to 20s. This would mean, from Mafeking to Salisbury, between £26 and £37.10.0 a ton. In 1892 goods transported from Cape Town to Salisbury, including the railage to Vryburg, had been said to cost £45 a ton, and to take three months.[1]

These statistics explain the importance of what was called the East Coast Route. Before the building and opening of the narrow gauge railway in 1893, transport from the head of navigation at Fontesvilla had to be by human porterage; the fly saw to that. The cost of this operation can never be stated precisely. Not only did the porters bargain for beads, cloth, and similar articles, the cost of which varied with the types in fashion, but they were liable at any time to drop their loads and decamp. So long as the East Coast Route depended on porters it was uncompetitive.

When the rains began these figures became irrelevant. The rainfall was very heavy in the first season after the occupation. W.H. Brown gives it as fifty inches at Fort Salisbury between 10 October and 15 March; Lionel Cripps put it at sixty-three inches. By December the rivers across the Selous Road had become impassable and all communication was halted. A little garbled news got through by being shouted across the flooded Lundi. "Colonel Pennefather is delayed at Fort Tuli" became "died at Fort Tuli." After his possessions had been sold the ghost walked into Salisbury and demanded them back.[2]

This was a small matter. The big matter was the exhaustion of the food supply. This had been foreseen by Colquhoun, but Colquhoun was regarded by the Company adventurers as a mere stodgy civil servant. They neither did what he asked nor even replied to his urgent letters. The person mainly responsible for this neglect was undoubtedly Rutherfoord Harris. He had got the job he badly wanted—secretary of the Company in South Africa—but was already showing the incompetence which his role in the Jameson Raid would reveal more dramatically. Jameson's judgment of his fellow practitioner was correct: "a muddling ass—on the surface a genius, but under the crust as thick as they are made."

The contract for the supply of food to the Pioneers had been given to the Bechuanaland Trading Association, a small Chartered Company subsidiary, but it was unable to fulfil the contract adequately or in time. Colquhoun had foreseen this, but the "muddling ass" Harris refused to allow any other source to be used. His muddling was compounded by that of Major Tye, in command at Fort Tuli, who allowed perishables to be stacked in the open, and supplies generally to accumulate, till they were inedible and, once the rivers had risen, could not have been forwarded anyway. Result: by the end of 1890 the Pioneers were trying to survive on "Kaffir corn" porridge and pumpkins traded from the Shona. Even those could not be relied upon for long, because there was a shortage of trade goods too, and the supply of locally grown food dwindled as the old stock was used up and there were months to wait before the next harvest.

After food, raiment. The Pioneers, like modern air passengers, had been allowed to take with them only forty pounds of luggage for each man; the rest was to be sent after them. It was not sent before the rains stopped transport. Men's boots disintegrated, there were no replacements, and they were down to their bare feet. The police were in like case: all the boots in their quartermaster's store were size eleven. As there were no changes of clothes and not much protection from the rain, men wore wet clothes and were more prone to fever. There was hardly any reading matter: one man memorized all the hymns in the hymn book and another did all the exercises in a school arithmetic book. Harris and Tye must not be blamed for everything; the Pioneers' luggage was Frank Johnson's responsibility.

When supplies did get through to Salisbury, flour was sold at £12 for a 100 lb. bag; tinned butter at 12s. a lb.; sugar at 7s.6d. a lb.; condensed milk at 12s. to 15s. a tin, and jam at 8s. to 16s. a tin. A loaf of bread (of which "I had two mouthfuls and it was finished!") cost 2s. These were famine prices and have no long term relevance, but the famine itself and the other hardships of that terrible season had lasting psychological effects. The rain broke through the flimsy roofs of the grass huts in steady trickles. Very large rats came in out of the rain to seek the shelter of the huts, such as it was. They, too, were short of food and had voracious appetites. They nibbled at a sleeping man's toes or hair. One later victim of their attentions had to have his badly mauled thumb amputated—which put more trivial offences, such as chewing a Bible or making off with a set of false teeth, in perspective. The rats in turn attracted the snakes. Mosquitoes swarmed and became a major nuisance. That they were something more serious than a nuisance was not yet understood, but malaria struck hard.[3]

Among those to reach Salisbury by wagon during 1891 was Richard Moffat, who on his journey was passed "by some swell outfits [including that of Lord Randolph Churchill] and also by some very funny ones . . . One trolly took up a billiard table. Two men pushed a wheelbarrow, while another couple had a whisky case on perambulator wheels, drawn by a donkey." Other sights were less funny, but more significant of the hard realities of the frontier:

> At the Lundi there were over forty graves and between that river and the Tokwe we counted forty more victims of fever and dysentery. Somewhere along the road we saw a very sick man who had been picked up by a passing wagon. He had also been with a party and they, not wishing to have the trouble of burying him, had thrown him out by the roadside to be eaten by the hyenas. He was vowing vengeance and swore that when he caught up to his companions he would shoot the lot. I never heard the sequel.

The police, having to be out in all weathers, experienced the rainy season more fully than the civilians. Lieut. M.D. Graham, travelling from Umtali to Salisbury in January, was stuck in a bog for five days. He reported also that a man crossing the Tokwe had had his foot bitten off by a crocodile. He managed to reach Fort Victoria. A trooper there, who was supposed to have some surgical knowledge, amputed the leg with the troop's meat saw. The patient died.

The East Coast Route surpassed the Selous Road, not for impassable rivers, but for lions, fever, mountains, and troubles with porters. Rose Blennerhassett and her companions were the first white women to walk that way. Their porters deserted and they had to leave most of their luggage to be fetched later; Rose's own luggage was never seen again. They arrived at the police camp, Umtali, with one of the women running a temperature of 105°. "Here and there we met unfortunate young fellows who had had the fever; had tried to reach Fort Salisbury; but, alas! had been obliged to turn back, and were then on their way down to the coast, ill and half ruined."[4]

The difficulties of transportation explain the high prices of imported goods. The neglect of agriculture, which will be another topic for this chapter, was the main reason for the high cost of local produce. In October and November 1892—the end of the dry season, when imported stocks though not local produce would have been at their most plentiful—some market prices in Salisbury may be compared with those in Kimberley:

Item	Salisbury	Kimberley
Flour per 100 lb.	75s. to 85s.	10s.6d. to 10s.9d.
Fresh butter per lb.	5s. to 6s.	1s. to 1s.9d.
Potatoes per lb.	10d. to 1s.4d.	Between 1½d. and 2d.
(in February 1893)	4d.to 6d.	
Bacon per lb.	2s.3d. to 2s.6d.	5d. to 6d.

There was a slight compensation in the price of venison (the only meat listed in the market reports), which was sold at from 4d. to 6d. a pound. On the other hand, paraffin, which was the domestic electricity of that age, was 10s. to 10s.6d. a gallon; galvanized iron 2s.1d. to 2s.3d. a foot; and, what perhaps worried the Pioneers more than all this, whisky from £3 to £3.5s.0d. for a case of a dozen quart bottles.

These dry statistics are in some ways more important than the gruesome experiences of travellers; they were among the basic facts of the Rhodesian economy. When to these we add the prohibitive expense, if not impossibility, of transporting heavy mining machinery all that way by ox-wagon, the imperative need of railway connections is easy to see. Frank Johnson had realised this even before setting out with the Pioneers; he had hoped, however, to open up the East Coast Route immediately with a road, coaches, and wagons. This was what Willoughby's filibustering on the Pungwe was about. Johnson having not allowed for the fly, his coach was soon abandoned at the roadside, his oxen dead, and his business £25,000 the worse for having tried the experiment. The Beira Railway Company was duly formed, and by October 1893 the narrow-gauge railway had been completed from Fontesvilla to the seventy-five-mile post.

By that time it was realised that "the fly" did not end there; the line would have to be continued to Chimoio at 118 miles from Fontesvilla. The Beira Railway Company issued £250,000 of 6 per cent debentures at a heavy discount, £43,500 of these being taken up by Pauling's company, the constructors; the money being provided by Erlangers. The line was accordingly extended, and reached Chimoio on 25 November 1894. There was no further construction beyond that point, or beyond Mafeking, before the rebellion.[5]

The rebellion showed that slow and difficult transport was a military as well as an economic liability. For this the Company might find a slight compensation in its postal and telegraphic communications. From the beginning, even while the Pioneers were on the march, the conveyance of mails was undertaken by the police. Relay stations were placed at roughly fifty-mile intervals along the Tuli-Salisbury road. As the service was performed on horseback, and not many horses were "salted," the losses were heavy. Horses died of horse-sickness or were mauled by lions. The rider might spend the night in a tree, be laid up by fever or eaten by a crocodile; the mail bag might be lost, or ruined by water. These hazards ceased for a time when the rains stopped communication. Early in 1892 the Company began to operate a mail cart service between Salisbury and Umtali, to connect with the Portuguese system, and between Salisbury and Tuli, connecting with Bechuanaland. The police were then relieved of their postal duties.

In August 1892 the Company's Post Office came into existence. Stamps, which had been printed in 1890, were released for postal use, and by agreement with neighbouring countries became valid beyond the borders of Mashonaland. Contractors such as Bezuidenhout and Zeederberg carried the mails by cart or coach, and a letter from Salisbury could then reach Cape Town in ten days.

From most points of view the telegraph line, which reached Salisbury in February 1892, was more important than the fast conveyance of mails. Though the service was often interrupted, as by the several thefts of wire preceding Jameson's War, it usually functioned. In time of danger it was possible to summon help instantly by telegraph, and it was possible for the high commissioner to keep a close watch on Rhodesian affairs. From the Company's point of view this was no advantage, but by the same means Rhodes and Jameson could "converse" with each other. Mashonaland was expensive and difficult to get to, but it was not isolated.

One of the expenses, as we have seen, was the cost of whisky. When a deputation complained to Rhodes in 1891 of the cost of food, he retorted that their real grievance was the cost of liquor. Rhodes did not think this funny. The sale of liquor in Mashonaland had at first been prohibited. The vicomte de la Panouse, who was offering bottles of whisky at £5, was forbidden by Colquhoun to sell them. The news that he had a stock in his Tatagura camp having reached Salisbury, an irrepressible demand for it arose in connection with the celebration of St. Patrick's Day, 1891. After the sufferings of the rainy season Colquhoun had not the heart to resist the demand. On that St. Patrick's Day, Rhodesia became, in a different sense, "wet."[6]

Dr. James Johnston was a hostile observer, but his assertion that in 1892 seventy out of a hundred wagons on the road to Salisbury carried each an average of two thousand bottles of intoxicating liquor was probably close to the mark. When C.E. Finlason arrived in Salisbury in November 1891, "nine out of the ten men who shook hands with me asked if I had brought any liquor up." Finlason described the alcoholic drought of the 1890-1 summer, and concluded that "the inhabitants got such a thirst then that subsequent attempts to meet the demand failed for many months."

That and many other things could account for the demand: the cheapness of life in fever country ("let us eat, drink and be merry"); the myth that alcohol warded off malaria ("My stomick won't hold quy-nyne, but it sucks up whisky like a sponge. Give me a bottle of whisky a day and I'll defy the fever"); boredom; and the masculinity of the population. We shall return to this. In some societies, at least, there seems to be a negative correlation between the consumption of alcohol and the presence of women. In Matabeleland, for all the same reasons, the "old hands" had shown the same fondness for the bottle.

Given the demand, the supply is easily explained. E.F. Knight, on his way to the coast, "met several trains of coolies bound for Umtali from the railway terminus, laden for the most part with cases of beer and whisky." These were the commodities that gave the biggest return for their weight; it was as simple as that. The supply having grown to meet the demand, the Rhodesian white community acquired a trait that it would take years to modify. Rose Blennerhassett, while "deploring the fact that two thirds of the population [of Umtali] were at that time almost always drunk," thought that it would be "extremely unfair to judge them too harshly." Nature exacted her price from them. A patient in the Umtali hospital, brought in unconscious after a drinking bout, died "after a succession of the most terrible epileptiform attacks." It was found that he owed £50, of which £39 was for whisky. At Christmas 1891 the white population of Umtali, having passed through "the good-natured stage of drunkenness," got to the quarrelsome one. The resident magistrate ordered the civil commissioner to be arrested. The civil commissioner suspended the magistrate from his functions and the magistrate suspended the civil commissioner. By midnight all the police had been arrested. "Next day all was forgotten and forgiven." Next year a new magistrate put curbs on the drinking. According to Rose Blennerhassett, "perhaps for a week at a time not a case of drunkenness would occur, and in proportion to the decrease of drink, so did the fever diminish, without, however, entirely dying out." Public opinion would not easily have accepted that doctrine.[7]

Malaria was rampant chiefly because its cause was still unknown. In March 1891 the Pioneers celebrated the end of the rains with aquatic sports in the Makabusi, and "the malarial mosquitos took advantage of the presence of spectators and competitors to such a degree that the hospital tents and huts were completely filled with patients, while others were unable to find accommodation." Throughout that summer the tents and huts had been accommodating thirty patients, mostly malarial. Dr. Rand, the medical officer of the police, administered a mixture of quinine, Epsom salts, and other components which came to be known as "Rand's kicker." It was believed to be effective, but Rand knew no more than anyone else about the cause of the disease. His reproof to a trooper who had a relapse was: "I suppose you have been eating tomatoes and pumpkins, you fool, although I told you not to do so."

Dr. Thompson, of the American Mission at Mount Selinda, was nearer the mark when he pointed to the wrong siting of farmhouses. Most of the trekkers who settled the Melsetter district between 1893 and 1895 built their houses near water—as anyone from the Free State might be expected to do. Partly for that reason, the Gazaland trekkers were decimated by fever, as exemplified by the case of the Mynhardt family in March 1895. The father died on a Saturday morning, the eldest daughter a few hours later, and the mother on Monday. At the same time other deaths were reported from all over the district: Herselmans, van Rooyens, Marks, Moodies . . . twenty-two altogether in that season.

All the letters and reminiscences have this monotonous woeful theme of fever running through them. For many it was an excuse to take to the bottle; for some, a reason to leave the country; for all, debilitating and a serious waste of man-hours. Even without malaria the new colony would have needed medical services, but malaria emphasized the need and drew a response.

Three medical men who had gone up with the Pioneers were distributed between Salisbury, Hartley Hills, and Umtali. In addition, Salisbury had Dr. Rand, who became a controversial public figure. It was he who insisted on reasonable sanitary regulations and their enforcement. There was no hospital, but as the patients began to arrive the Roman Catholic chaplain, Father Hartmann, offered his three huts for the purpose. Now there were huts, patients, and doctors, but no nurses. Dominican Sisters had indeed offered their services, but had been held back at Motloutsi when the Pioneers went in. At that stage no women were allowed into the danger zone. At last in July 1891 Mother Patrick and her four companions arrived in Salisbury, and were installed in the unfinished huts that were to be the hospital. These were soon superseded by more substantial structures, and these, in 1894-5, by a real brick building. Dr. Rand moved into private practice.

All the records testify to the great impact on the frontier community not only of the Sisters' ministrations, but of their personalities. In due course they were followed by others of their order, so that a hospital could be staffed at Fort Victoria in January 1893. After the conquest of Matabeleland a hospital was planned for Bulawayo as a memorial to Allan Wilson and his patrol. This was a solid and even pretentious building, capable of taking sixty patients. Again it was the Dominican Sisters who provided the nursing staff when the hospital opened in July 1895. Umtali owed its hospital to the Anglican church and Bishop Knight-Bruce, who recruited a team of nurses that arrived there in 1891. Again there was the progression from crude hut to bigger huts to a building known as the Bishop's Palace, which became the hospital when Knight-Bruce was forced by ill health to return to England. Thus the "white man's medicine" reached Zimbabwe, one result of the invasion that by any standard was wholly good.[8]

Medicine was one item of the cultural equipment which the invaders brought into the country, and which was so alien to the ancient ways that it set its possessors apart from the old inhabitants. A cursory view of some of this equipment will show how wide was the gulf between the cultures and how profound the change which the newcomers imposed on the country.

The characteristic institution of civilization is the city. Though *city* is the wrong word for those mere blemishes in the Zimbabwean bush that were known as townships, the potentiality of the city was there. The township was the framework for the culture.

The beginnings of Salisbury illustrate the point. For many years it was an ugly, untidy blot on the landscape, in comparison with, say, Lobengula's Bulawayo. Lobengula's town, however, was incapable of becoming anything other than it was; Salisbury was an embryo whose full development was invisible but latent.

When the Pioneers were disbanded at the end of September 1890 they had very little equipment with which to work. There was a severe shortage of tools of all sorts, even of axes and pickaxes, in a community most of whose construction depended on the chopping down of trees and the digging of holes in hard ground. Nevertheless, with great difficulty, huts of poles, mud and grass were built in the indigenous style. The authorities having omitted to design a town plan, the huts could be planted anywhere. The fort, police camp, and other official quarters grew up at the spot where the flag had been hoisted—Cecil Square. Most private citizens preferred the foot of the Kopje, where Pioneer Street took shape about a mile from the cluster of official quarters known as the Causeway. Kopje and Causeway were separated not only by a black marsh which was difficult to cross but also by politics: the Kopje men were agin' the government.

Colquhoun determined to impose form on the chaos. His nephew Tom Ross, who was also a captain in the U.S. Army, had been invited to join the Pioneer Column, but had come too late for that. When he arrived he was given the task of making a town plan. Colquhoun would have liked to buy out the Kopje residents and develop the whole town from the Causeway. The opposition being too strong, Ross had to design a town in two parts. The streets below the Kopje had to conform to the existing irregularity but on the Causeway side Ross laid them out in the rectangular pattern which he knew in America. He would have given numbers to both streets and avenues, but Dr. Rand prevailed on him "to name some of our thoroughfares [the avenues] after blazers of the African trail"—including the duke of Fife! Thus were rectangles imposed on a land which from the first human occupation had known only circular designs.

Many of the "streets" existed only in theory, until some rows of trees were planted to show where they were on the ground; but the plan ensured that, with time and maturity, the ideal would become real. For a short time this consummation was in doubt, as Jameson and others entertained the idea of moving Salisbury to another site. Failure to find a better one, together with the protests of vested interests, caused that scheme to be abandoned by November 1891. The next year Harry Sawerthal, town surveyor, filled in part of the gap in Ross's plan by laying out some streets in the swamp area. This had partly dried up after the lighter rains of 1891 and 1892. The physical rift in the town began to heal.

After Ross's survey, the town now being divided into "stands," the Company began to sell them at £25 apiece; the first townsmen had got their land for nothing. By August 1891, when there were "about 400 buildings in camp," the owners of stands, with huts on them, were asking £30 to £40. In September, when it was uncertain whether the town would remain on its old site, prices were ranging from £10 to £38.

Marshall Hole, who arrived in Salisbury at that time, wrote that

> it would have been easy . . . to pass within a hundred yards of the place itself without noticing it. The surrounding country was clothed with a dense growth of coarse grass five feet or more in height. From this emerged a low tree-covered hill—the "Kopje"—at the foot of which were a couple of score of thatched huts hardly differing from those of the native kraals we had seen on the road. This was the "business" quarter of the township. A mile or so away were other groups of huts, in some of which Dr. Jameson and his new staff lived, messed and carried on the work of "Government." The Police quarters looked like cow-sheds, and were arranged round an earth-work— the Fort—above which flew the Union Jack charged with the Company's badge of a golden lion. Scattered here and there were canvas tents, waggons protected by buck-sails, and the framework of more huts in course of erection.

It is not surprising that, when Rhodes caught his first glimpse of Salisbury in October 1891, disappointment was written on his face. It was shared by other early visitors who have left their impressions.

They were comparing the place with older urban communities. A different judgment is possible if Mashonaland before 1890 is used as the standard of comparison. Within three years of the occupation Salisbury could boast of hotels, specialized tradesmen, churches of various denominations, schools, a library of sorts, theatrical performances, organized British sports, a hospital and medical services, a weekly newspaper, local government on a partly elective basis, political controversy in the British manner, solid brick buildings, a bank, a cash economy—and a shortage of cash. Apart from trade in certain commodities by barter, all of these things were new and alien to the Shona world.

A good deal of enterprise and ingenuity were needed to bring some of them into existence. At the start a baker went into business, using an ant-heap as his oven. A butcher donned his apron and offered the public the meat of game which he shot himself. A barrister and an accountant formed a partnership which did good business in a community where syndicates and companies were being formed in some numbers. General dealers, sellers of tobacco and aerated waters, agents, attorneys, and auctioneers hung out their signs. There were the doctors and a solitary dentist. One astute businessman installed a billiard-table—presumably the one Richard Moffat had seen going up—and had customers in spite of the slant of the table and the bias of the balls.

Possibly the most lucrative business—if only the "good-fors" could be turned into hard cash—would have been driven by the hotels, the bottle stores, and the wholesale liquor dealers. Hotels were opened with the minimum of equipment. Finlason saw one consisting of "an ancient weather-worn marquee, with an extra canvas roof, which flapped drearily at every gust, like the sail of a deserted ship. Outside was the alluring intimation: 'Cleanliness and civility a speciality. Single meals 2s. 6d.' " The Mashonaland Hotel, on the site of the Parliament House of later times, was the venue of the St. Patrick's Day dinner of 1891. Before long that hotel went bankrupt, because the "good-fors" were no good, but other hotels and bars met the public need.[9]

The most enterprising business in Mashonaland was the firm of Johnson, Heany and Borrow. Early in 1891, with the help of Rhodes's money, this became Frank Johnson and Company. Johnson had made a handsome profit out of his contract. When the Pioneer Column was disbanded its civil equipment remained the contractor's property. Acquiring a piece of land on the further slope of the Kopje, the partners set up there an establishment called the Ranche, where all the surplus stores were collected and offered for sale. Johnson had taken the precaution of bringing £5,000 in gold with him, so that he was immediately able, as few others were, to buy the only commodities the Pioneers had to sell—their farm and claim rights. He offered £100 for either. He could hire out wagons to those eager to get to the gold reefs, and sell various items of equipment. When he had disposed of the surplus stores he found that he had made a profit of £20,000 out of the contract. In addition he had been promised twenty claims and 40,000 morgen of land.

As even these assets were not enough for the development Johnson was expected to do, Rhodes arranged for the formation of the company. Rhodes gave Johnson £100,000 in fully paid up shares as the value of the partners' assets and tried to get the Gold Fields company to invest an equal amount.[10] Johnson's company thus became the most active concern in the country, with a finger in every pie—mining, trade, land, and transport. Even the carping Lord Randolph Churchill was full of praise for this firm: "whatever they have done has been well done." He described the Ranche with its "large storehouses, stables, and sheds for cattle, a workshop and a smithy," a dwelling house mainly of brick, and the beginning of a promising garden, the only one in Salisbury; and referred to the firm's other establishments at Hartley Hills and Umtali.

Lord Randolph did not notice some enterprising brothers, the Meikles, who were doing business at Fort Victoria and bringing up more stocks from the south; their firm was to become more conspicuous, and to last much longer, than Johnson's. The arrival of white women in greater numbers induced the men to take more care of their appearance. To meet the demand by both sexes for better clothing, Store Brothers of Johannesburg, in May 1893, dispatched James Lamb and his wife to open a branch in Salisbury. Their shop boasted of the first plate glass window in the town, and Mrs. Lamb brought with her the

353 The White Society

first gramophone and one of the first sewing machines. Their child, born in August 1893, received the first birth certificate in the country.

By that time the life of Salisbury had expanded in many directions. The first race meeting had been held on the queen's birthday, 1891; the Mashonaland Turf Club had since laid out a racecourse next to the Ranche, and races had been run there. Cricket and rugby were being played in an organized way. The dining-rooms of the Masonic and Hatfield hotels in Pioneer Street (both opened early in 1892) had been used as theatres by the Musical and Dramatic Society—for concerts, and, at Christmas 1892, for a performance of *Ticket O'-Leave Man*, with men necessarily playing the women's parts. The Hatfield Hotel acquired a piano, with the help of which Salisbury's first ball was held on 12 August 1892—waltzes, Gay Gordons, quadrilles, Lancers, and Schottische—though there were only seven ladies to go round. The previous month the Standard Bank of South Africa had opened a branch, using two of the four rooms of the new burned-brick administration building (Jameson lived in a third and the country was governed from the fourth). In May 1893 the Salisbury Club opened its doors.

There had been more fundamental developments also. The Pioneers brought with them their religion; chaplains had been attached to the column. Of these the Roman Catholic Father Hartmann was, in the opinion of his Anglican confrère Canon Balfour, "without doubt the best man, and to my mind the nicest man, in the place." His congregation of forty Catholics was the most visible manifestation of Christianity in Salisbury. Canon Balfour, whose talents did not lie in the direction of ministering to frontiersmen, had no more than six communicants on the first Easter day. By the efforts of a few devout laymen an Anglican church of sorts (wattle and daub) was built and furnished. In September 1892 Archdeacon Upcher arrived in Salisbury to take the place of Canon Balfour. Upcher not only made himself very popular, but put much-needed life into his church. He appealed at once for funds for a brick building; as he preached, the roof of the mud church began to disintegrate. The money was collected and the new Church of All Saints, predecessor of the Cathedral, was dedicated in January 1893.

In the church we have one of the few institutions of the immigrant society that were not set up primarily to benefit the immigrants, or to enlarge the barrier separating them from their black neighbours. These clergy, as we shall see, were concerned as much with blacks as with whites. Yet, in the nature of the case, the demand for their services came more urgently from established Christians than from resistant heathen.

Other churches followed. In September 1891 the Methodist ministers Owen Watkins and Isaac Shimmin reached Salisbury, shortly before Rhodes himself. This was their good fortune, as Rhodes was able to brush aside the bureaucratic objections of Harris and give them three farms, one of which was Epworth where their principal mission station was founded, and five town stands near the Kopje. This denomination began to worship, like the others, in the usual mud hut, but soon graduated to a brick church. A few weeks after Watkins and Shimmin came the Salvation Army, led by Major Pascoe with his wife and two daughters, who were probably the first white children in Salisbury. The Army, too, soon acquired its own premises, though most of its evangelization, to the sound of drum, brass and tambourine, was done in the open air. "As religious workers," says Marshall Hole, "they made little headway, for the white population was not of the class to which the revivalist meetings of the Army were likely to appeal, and the problem of converting the natives was too big for two or three individuals, however enthusiastic, to tackle." Major Pascoe, who was a builder by trade, soon gave up his commission and became a builder again, to the great benefit of the material development of Salisbury.

The work of the Anglican Church in Rhodesia had begun with the journey of G.W.H. Knight-Bruce, bishop of Bloemfontein, to Mashonaland in 1888. Canon Balfour, who for a time was the only Anglican priest in the country, urged the importance of a bishopric for it. In February 1891 the Provincial Synod concurred, and created the diocese of Mashonaland, including Matabeleland and parts of Bechuanaland and Mozambique. The bishopric was offered to Knight-Bruce, who accepted it in June when he had reached Umtali. In 1894, his health being undermined, he had to return to England; William Gaul succeeded as bishop in 1895. Gaul was the right man for the job. His informality, infinite compassion, pugilistic skill (in spite of his small stature), moral and physical courage, and energetic devotion to his duties were to make their mark not only on his own church but on Rhodesia generally.

Knight-Bruce had brought the nurses to Umtali and made the beginnings of a hospital. The Dominican Sisters brought the nursing profession to Salisbury, Fort Victoria, and Bulawayo. The churches also, as might be expected, were the founders of the first schools. Though the Dominicans went to Salisbury to nurse, they were really a teaching order. Sister Yolanda, who was a later recruit to their number and was a trained teacher, became the first to practise that profession with white children in Rhodesia. On 8 September 1892 Father Hartmann "laid" the foundation pole of a school hut. "Each Sr. gave some medal or picture she prized to put under the pole—nothing was acceptable but what would prove a sacrifice." By the end of the year there were twenty children in the school. At the beginning of 1894, as a result of the efforts of Archdeacon Upcher, All Saints' School opened with eight pupils. The teacher, H.C. Rankillor, had brought desks, books, and equipment with him from Pretoria. This school, being too small to be economic, was closed by Bishop Gaul in 1895.

The Pioneer Column had included four Jews, and others of their faith arrived in the succeeding years; but Hebrew congregations were not established until August 1894 in Bulawayo, and June 1895 in Salisbury. Rhodes, who had many Jewish friends and associates, was said to have exclaimed in 1891 that "my country is all right if the Jews come"; but in the early years it would be difficult to point to a distinctive Jewish contribution to the life of the country.[11]

The Christians were not only more numerous; their churches provided the organization which supported such amenities as hospitals, schools, and H.C. Rankillor's books. Those were not the only books. As early as July 1891 Sergent-Major Bodle had opened a circulating library of 400 volumes. Some of the inhabitants may have borrowed, too, from the Rev. Isaac Shimmin, who had his own library of the same size.[12]

The opening of Bodle's library came hard on the heels of another cultural advance, the launching of *The Mashonaland Herald and Zambesian Times*. The Argus Company of South Africa had obtained from Rhodes a promise that no facilities for publishing in Mashonaland would be given to any other company. As a first step, W.E. Fairbridge was sent to Salisbury as a correspondent. After a discussion with friends he prepared at once to produce a weekly newspaper, which made its first appearance under this pretentious title on 27 June 1891. Fairbridge wrote it all, news, articles, and advertisements, on waxed paper with a cyclostyle pen. The copies were run off with home-made ink, the qualify and legibility of which varied from one issue to another. The editor then rode round the "camp" delivering the copies to his patrons, "whose subscriptions—such as were paid at all—took the form of a packet of candles or a tin of marmalade—in one instance, he told me, an old spade." Fairbridge bravely kept his paper going in this form until 8 September 1892, when preparations for a printed paper were in hand.

After some delay the new paper, *The Rhodesia Herald*, appeared on 29 October in respectable type and format. Fairbridge thought it necessary to justify the use of the name *Rhodesia*. He had not invented it. The word had been used, on and off, at least since the beginning of 1891, and was by no means universally popular. Some years later the *Herald* attributed the invention of the name "to a clever radical journalist on the *Pall Mall Gazette*."[13]

All this remarkable progress was halted by the mobilization preceding Jameson's War. The Salisbury Column was cheered on its way to Fort Charter and the triumphs and tragedies ahead of it. When the veterans returned they were received in the manner of bigger cities: with a triumphal arch, bunting-lined "streets" and cheering "crowds"—but it was noticed that of those who had marched out a few months before, only a quarter returned. Some had been killed—there were eighteen Salisbury men on the Shangani Patrol—but the majority had "transferred their interests to Bulawayo." Salisbury was eclipsed.

A combination of factors brought prosperity back towards the end of 1894. The unhealthy boom on the Witwatersrand spilled over into Rhodesia; capital flowed in. The Matabeleland Order-in-Council provided for an increase in the official establishment: this was when Joseph Vintcent arrived as judge, George Pauling as commissioner of public works, and Col. Frank Rhodes as acting administrator in Jameson's absence. More public buildings went up, and E.A. Maund, now resident in Salisbury, built the Market Hall.

The years 1894 and 1895 saw the building of the new hospital; the development of the Reading and Recreational Club into the Salisbury Public Library, with its own building paid for by debenture shares; a lawn tennis club; the arrival from England of a pack of foxhounds (the quarry in Rhodesia was mainly jackal and duiker); a Chamber of Commerce and a Chamber of Mines; and a second newspaper, the *Nugget*, which violently attacked the *Herald*. The sale of urban stands by the Company was resumed, 451 stands in Salisbury realising nearly £32,000.

There was another element in the revival of Salisbury's fortunes—the military element. Rhodes and Jameson gave much attention to the organizing of the Rhodesia Horse Volunteers, including the Mashonaland Regiment of that force which was based in Salisbury. Arms and equipment flowed in. The local people were a little mystified and wanted to know in which direction Jameson would "throw his assegai." They were given no hint.

By that time Salisbury had its experienced local politicians. In July 1891 a Sanitary Board for Salisbury had been created without legal authority—the usual administrative procedure at that time. Later in the year, as a result of Rhodes's visit, it became a short-lived Board of Management, and by the beginning of 1892 a Sanitary Board again: three elected members and two nominated by the administrator. Its functions were "to maintain and regulate streets and traffic; to deal with obstructions, noises, filth, disease and concerns of health, the pollution of water, native locations and all matters affecting the health, safety and rights of the inhabitants." Its revenue came from a ten shilling rate, which was difficult to collect—the more so because, like all the board's activities, it was illegal. There was no ordinance approved by the directors. Jameson made do with "Regulations" and "Government Notices."

The board had plenty to do and its meetings were extensively reported in the *Herald*. They were not always concerned with merely municipal affairs; the board was the obvious representative body to address the authorities on wider political questions, such as unemployment among white artisans. Vigorous protests and demands were made to Jameson, Albert Grey, and Rhodes. And in 1895, by the Towns Management Ordinance, the Sanitary Boards and their powers were belatedly given a respectable legal basis.[14]

That is the story of the founding and the growth, through five and a half years, not only of a town but of a culture planted in alien soil. The story is repeated on a much smaller scale at Fort Victoria and Umtali, and on a bigger scale in Bulawayo.

Fort Victoria had its beginnings when the Pioneer Column emerged from Providential Pass and put down its first garrison on the highveld. The mud fort was not a great defensive work—"a trench and breastwork," wrote Dr. James Johnston, "that would be no formidable barrier to the advance of a company of schoolboys, not to speak of a charge of Zulus." There were a few stores and houses, and the police garrison. Selous had chosen the site unwisely—it was too far from water. In 1892 the decision was made to move the place about five miles to the north. Streets were laid out, stands surveyed and sold (the first sale was in July), and a new fort built, the fort which figures in the "incident" of the following year. A hospital was begun, Dominican Sisters came down from Salisbury to staff it and James Brett, one of the three doctors of the Pioneer Column, was in attendance. The move from the old town site was made in September 1892, and the hospital opened in the following January. By that time Fort Victoria, like Salisbury, had its Sanitary Board; it had a hotel famed in its day, the Thatched House; and even a Chess and Draughts Club.

E.F. Knight, visiting the town in 1894, thought it

a far more prettily situated place than the seat of government . . . It is a smart, pretty little township of neat red brick houses with verandahs, and gardens of homely English flowers. Even the fort, hurriedly raised at the time of the Matabele scare, is almost picturesque. The mud houses, of which there are still many, deep-eaved with thatched roofs, have a comfortable old-world air; and when the avenues of blue gum trees are fully grown this will look even more charming and cheerful a place than it does now.

Knight had to admit, however, that "Victoria was very quiet when I was there; there had been an exodus of two-thirds of the inhabitants to booming Matabeleland; most of the houses were shut up, and there were scarcely more than one hundred white men left."

If the opening up of Matabeleland was a setback to Salisbury, it was almost a death blow to Fort Victoria. The reason was not merely the supposedly superior prospects of the new territory; it was that Fort Victoria ceased to lie on the line of communication. Traffic from the south now flowed through Bulawayo to Salisbury; the Selous Road began to be obliterated by grass; Fort Victoria became a backwater.[15]

Umtali was moved not once but twice. It began as the police camp (with fort) which was the base for the Gilbertian campaigns of 1890 and 1891. This camp was about a mile from the site of St. Augustine's Mission. It looked like becoming the nucleus of a town when to a broken-down "Reading Room" (equipped with a few old tattered newspapers) was added a small group of huts to serve as a hospital. The three nursing sisters recruited by Bishop Knight-Bruce arrived, after an adventurous walk from the coast, in July 1891. The bishop had intended the hospital to be a part of the mission complex he was planning, and for the first few years it depended entirely on the resources and personnel he could raise, apart from some gifts by Rhodes and others.

By a curious oversight, the Company had neglected to proclaim Umtali as a township. When enterprising prospectors discovered gold within the camp, and proceeded to peg the area for mining, it became necessary to move Umtali to another place. As the fort was commanded by higher hills within gunshot, there were military reasons also for moving. The new site, to which the move was made in December 1891, was six or seven miles to the west of the old. The nurses were provided with new hospital huts and a town was planned. As there was to be yet another move, this was what is now called Old Umtali; at the time it was New Umtali.

During 1892 and the following three years Old Umtali grew and the familiar institutions developed in it. In addition to the magistrate, the civil commissioner, the police and other official personnel, the hospital with doctor and nurses, and a gaol which at first had no door (at night a prisoner's thumbs were tied behind his back), there were by 1895 three hotels and four stores. In October 1894 the Bishop's "Palace" became the hospital. The Anglican church and parish had been founded in 1892. The old Reading Room was succeeded by a public library. In May 1895 the Umtali Musical and Dramatic Club produced the first opera in Rhodesia, *Trial by Jury*. The sports club used the main street as its racecourse.[16]

In November 1893, when Forbes's column was camped outside the smoking remains of Lobengula's town, Jameson gave immediate attention to the founding of a new town at that place. It might have been built on the ruins of the old, had not a prospector announced the discovery of a gold reef at the spot. Nevertheless, Rhodes, who arrived at the beginning of December, insisted that the new town should be as near as possible to the old, and should bear the same name, Bulawayo.

The victorious troopers had set up their shacks and shanties in and around what had been the "white men's camp" of the Dawsons, Fairbairns, and other old hands—"Grass Town" or "Shanty Town" as it came to be called. The haphazard development of the Kopje area of Salisbury being fresh in Jameson's mind, he made it clear from the beginning that Grass Town would have no permanence. He and Rhodes and Willoughby rode about the surrounding country day after day, until they had decided on a site about three miles south of the old king's kraal. Patrick Fletcher, a trooper in the column whose talent had been spotted by Rhodes and Jameson, was ordered to plan the town and survey it on the ground. Working under occasionally conflicting and even absurd suggestions or orders from Willoughby and Jameson, Fletcher made his plan, and very soon had it surveyed. Much ingenuity had to be used: the defeated enemy's assegai-heads, for instance, were used as pegs.

Fletcher conceived what has remained Bulawayo's most distinguishing feature, the belt of parkland on either side of the Matjesumhlope stream, with a rectangular grid to the west for the business section (it became largely residential too), and another to the east which has never had any more imaginative name than "Suburbs." The streets and avenues were respectively 120 and 90 Cape feet wide: Rhodes had been disappointed by the narrowness of the Salisbury streets, but there seems to be no evidence to support the traditional ex-

359 The White Society

planation that he wanted a full span of oxen to be able to turn in a Bulawayo street. Fletcher provided for a large Market Square at what he intended to be the centre of the town, but when more streets were added on the western side the centre moved away from the square. In Bulawayo it was the streets that had names and the avenues numbers.

On 24 March 1894 the first sale of stands by auction was held. The upset price was £30, the highest price paid £160. Oliver Ransford describes the sequel:

> On 1 June 1894 Dr Jameson officially declared the new town open. Nothing is more typical of Jameson's informal ways than the manner in which he made the historical declaration. He first posed a little stiffly with a small crowd for a photograph in front of the temporary bar which the enterprising "Tottie" Hay had already opened at the incompleted Maxim Hotel on Fife Street opposite Market Square. Then he mounted a box, and came to the point very quickly: "It is my job," he said "to declare the town open, gentlemen. I don't think we want any talk about it. I make the declaration now. There is plenty of whisky and soda inside, so come in."[17]

The Sanitary Board had been elected and appointed three weeks earlier, and two cyclostyled newspapers had been in circulation for two months before the town was founded.

These facts were prophetic of the speed of Bulawayo's development. In March 1895, when it was nine months old, its white population was 1,537, as against 493 in Salisbury after four and a half years. Two months after Jameson's unconventional "proclamation" there was another sale of stands in Bulawayo, from which the Company realized £36,530; one stand went for £900. By that date £50,000 had been "laid out in building." On 12 October the *Buluwayo Chronicle* made its appearance in print, carrying more than sixty advertisements for businesses of various kinds—auctioneers, hotels, butcheries, general merchants, "Painters, Paperhangers, Signwriters and Gilders," bakeries, solicitors, a "Civil Mining Engineer and Architect," photographers, receiving and forwarding agents, "Coachbuilders, Blacksmiths and Farriers," chemists, builders and contractors, an aerated water factory, a stationer and bookseller, livery stables, surveyors, agents of various kinds, and of course the big trading and mining companies, including the Rhodesia Printing and Publishing Company (the Rhodesian associate of the Argus Company), which published this paper. Amid all this feverish activity the editor proudly pointed out that "twelve months ago, the scanty British forces destined to effect the conquest of the Matabele . . . had barely crossed the threshold of the hostile territory."

From the beginning Bulawayo had something of a wild western flavour. Even in the days of "Grass Town" the keynote was struck by a trooper, one of "Raaf's riff-raff," who had been "imprisoned" in a bell-tent. On the day of the

Easter sports he made his way from the prison to the Canteen, where he drank his fill; then to the armoury, where he picked up a Maxim gun; then to the races, where he fired a succession of bursts at the competitors. Luckily he was aiming high, a few feet over the heads of the riders, who are said to have dismounted in record time. On another occasion it took all of Jameson's skill to foil an attempt at lynching by an enraged mob—but this had happened in Salisbury too. Yet there was a marked difference in atmosphere between the two places. The presence of officialdom in Salisbury was one factor. A greater one was the knowledge that the subsoil of Mashonaland was not, after all, made of gold, as against the still confident hope that Matabeleland was the true El Dorado.

Prospectors and miners came and went. Some who were lucky came into town to "blow" their gains on a wild spree. Confidence in the future of the place was unbounded. In 1895 one of the stands (original upset price £30) changed hands for £5,000, and by then the buildings of the town were valued at £394,000. In all directions the development was quicker and on a bigger scale than in Salisbury: amateur dramatics, golf club, turf club, Bulawayo Club, cricket, hospital, Chamber of Commerce, Standard Bank, stock exchange, churches and synagogue, waterworks company (with the prospect of electricity), the telegraph line (connecting Bulawayo with the world by July 1894), newspapers, concerts, roller skating rink, fancy dress ball.

Though Lobengula's kraal had been rejected as the place for the new Bulawayo, Rhodes insisted—reef or no reef—on having a cottage for himself on the site of the king's house, next to the "indaba tree" where he used to sit in judgment. The *Buluwayo Sketch* caught the symbolism of this in the caption of a cartoon: *le roi est mort, vive le roi!* To which it added, with partial accuracy: "Then—Idleness; Now—Industry." There were many contrasts between Then and Now, among them this one: at the beginning of 1893, the Big Dance; two and a half years later, the noisy transactions of a stock exchange. An old Ndebele town had to be moved every so often because it had no sanitary arrangements. The Sanitary Board of the new Bulawayo displayed great energy in compelling the standholders to dig pit latrines and to dispose properly of their rubbish.

Rhodes had visited the place soon after the entry of Forbes's column. When he came again in September 1894 he was able to occupy his cottage. Obviously the simple *rondavel* was inadequate as an expression of regal symbolism; Rhodes now ordered a real Government House, modelled partly on his own Groote Schuur, to be built next to the cottage. This work was undertaken at once.[18]

The building of Bulawayo was followed by that of the next Matabeleland township, Gwelo;[19] but there is no need to elaborate on that. Enough urban history has been told to make the point. The social and cultural institutions of the British colonial world were planted in townships scattered about Rhodesia.

The immigrants must needs live like Englishmen, as nearly as frontier conditions would allow, and they would see to it that those conditions would soon be transformed. As Rhodes had said, however, it is no good having big ideas unless you have the cash to carry them out. The colonial culture had to have an economic foundation.

It was not provided by the towns. The money spent in the shops and hotels had to come from somewhere; an economy could not be based on the taking in of one another's washing. The intention, of course, was to base the economy on gold mining.

It is difficult now to recapture the optimism of the early 1890s in this regard. Bartissol had expressed the general mood when he said that "à côté de cela le Transvaal n'est rien." The whole chartered operation was undertaken in the belief that a greater Witwatersrand lay under the soil of Mashonaland. When this hope faded, all eyes turned to Matabeleland. The shareholders of the Company expected some day to receive a dividend; gold would provide it. The Pioneers, and after them the Volunteers of the Victoria and Salisbury Columns, hoped for quick fortunes—from gold.

In spite of the fuss that he made about it, gold was not Rhodes's primary interest; it was a means to an end. Rhodes, like the Company shareholders, wanted all the money he could lay his hands on. But he wanted it for the purpose of building a territorial, not essentially a financial empire. The man who heaved a sigh of relief when the bad news he got at the end of 1896 turned out to be only that his house (Groote Schuur) had burned to the ground was not motivated like an ordinary shareholder. Everything in his career confirms the view that his ultimate purposes were political. For Rhodesia, his primary interest lay in colonization and farming, building a country; mining wealth would both pay for the operation and attract into it the colonists who would inevitably be concerned with the "commercial" rather than with the "imaginative."

As the Pioneers and the police marched into Mashonaland in 1890, every man had visions of the riches he would win from the fifteen mining claims, each 150 by 400 feet, which he could peg wherever he chose. There were also a few civilians with the column, and hard on its heels came other fortune-seekers; anyone, provided that he made his application in person in Mashonaland, was allowed to peg ten claims. The only conditions imposed were a shilling for the prospecting licence and the obligation to sink a thirty-foot shaft within four months.

When the Pioneers were disbanded at the end of September there was a rush for the goldfields, and some grumbling that prospectors representing Frank Johnson, groups of officers, and others had stolen a march on the men who had till then been under military discipline. Some made for the Mazoe or for Lomagundi, but the favourite field was the Umfuli. Frank Johnson and his associates, who of course knew Hartley Hills of old, were well to the fore in that area. W.H. Brown borrowed a wagon from them for his own purpose of collecting specimens for the Smithsonian Institution; in return he was to take provisions to Hartley Hills for Johnson's prospectors who were already working there. "Great excitement," Brown reported, prevailed at Hartley Hills. "Scarcely had I arrived when Pioneers came to me, almost breathless, with the query: 'Have you pegged yet? You had better look sharp and peg your ground, or you will lose your chance for a fortune.' "

H.S.M. Montague was one of a party of seven who lost no time in hiring a wagon and making for the same destination, but too late: "we found we had been forestalled by other prospectors and the whole country was pegged with claims." Adrian Darter and his partners enlisted the services of a chief's son, who led them to Hartley Hills by a short cut. They found the area "bristling with pegs and our bullocks could not help knocking down some of them." A regular greeting among these optimists was "See you in Chicago in '93" (at the Exhibition).

Prospecting in Mashonaland needed no skill. It was realized from the beginning that "the ancients," whoever they might be, had unerringly located all the reefs. Prospecting was thus reduced to finding "ancient workings," to which one could be guided by any of the local inhabitants for a small reward. An ancient mine having been found, the Pioneer got to work on it with the crudest instruments. A spade head and an axe head might be got, at least by the early shoppers, from the Company; the handles and a windlass were provided by msasa trees; buckets and rope were made from eland's hide. A small iron mortar might be used for crushing quartz, and the panning could be done in the local stream.[20]

In the light of the results, there is pathos in the excitement and the optimism. A policeman wrote:

> Stories of the richness of the gold up at Mount Hampden and in the Manica Country are constantly reaching us, so our hopes are at "high pressure", for, as you may have heard, every man in the service of the BSA Company is entitled to 10 gold claims, besides which 50 claims per troop have been given to us by Mr. Cecil Rhodes. I have heard of many offers for the "police gold rights," varying from £200 to £650; but I know of only two cases in which such offers have been accepted.

Most of the surviving accounts strike the same note:

> The men who have secured claims on the old workings in the districts referred to seem to be very sanguine and jubilant . . . Some samples taken from the vicinity of an old working are marvellously rich in visible gold . . . C. was in a couple of days ago, very secretive, and evidently has found what he wants . . . The virgin quartz sent up by the bucket is magnificent stuff. One can scarcely take up a piece that has not several coarse blotches of visible on it. The pannings indicate more ounces to the ton than would be credited if stated . . . Mr Webster has brought down with him a large number of very rich specimens of quartz from the Birthday, Natal and Huntly reefs. Most of

363 The White Society

these literally sparkle with gold, and if they are to be taken as an illustration of the general richness of Victoria district, then there [*sic*] wealth must indeed be beyond the dreams of avarice.

This Mr. Webster and his partners, Dunlop and Campbell, evidently preferred a bird in the hand: they sold two-thirds of their interest in the Birthday reef to the Mashonaland Agency for £3,000.[21]

In the official literature the optimistic note was, of course, struck loud and continually. The Company's report for 1894-5 gives a "Tabular Statement of Mining Properties," 112 of them, which purports to be a complete list of reefs. Next to each there is an assessment of "prospector's pannings." The range of assessments is limited to "good" and "very good."

Nevertheless, a different opinion was sometimes expressed, and not only by such unbelievers as Lord Randolph Churchill. E.F. Knight, whose observations cover the first half of 1894, was generally a favourable reporter. He had no doubt of the extent of the auriferous reefs or "the marvellous richness of the surface quartz" in Matabeleland. Experts told him that they knew of no other country in which there was so much visible gold. But he kept coming back to the uncertainty about the depth of the reefs. He thought that Mashonaland had proved itself, yet had to admit that it had "passed through a long period of depression," because of the general stoppage during the war and then the rush to Matabeleland. The over-statements and strident propaganda of the Company and other interested parties really revealed the same gnawing uncertainty.

No man could peg more than ten—or, if a Pioneer, fifteen—claims, but the claims were negotiable. It was a curious system: a limitation imposed on the prospector but not on the company promoter. In many cases groups of individual claim holders formed syndicates and pooled their claims. In others, individuals were bought out by companies. These developments had been foreseen; they had happened before in Kimberley. The Chartered Company had therefore promulgated "Mining Regulations" which, as we have seen, derived their legislative authority solely from their appearance as an advertisement in the press. They included the provision that the BSA Company must have a half-share in every mining company formed; in other words, half its nominal capital was to be "water" for the benefit of the government. This rule, like many others, seems to have been enforced in a haphazard and irregular way; as one writer expressed it, "each case is treated on its merits." Lord Grey claimed that the Chartered Company seldom had more than a quarter interest in a subsidiary company.

The process of amalgamation and absorption began early and advanced rapidly. Frank Johnson's company began buying claim rights for £100 each from the moment the Pioneers were disbanded. Sir John Willoughby and other promoters were doing the same. The sellers, being without cash, often had no option. Many of them left the country; some, says Darter, "found employment with Johnson and Co."

By 1895 the registrar of claims could list ten mining companies, with a total nominal capital of £1,210,000, in which the BSA Company had a "share interest." There were another 187 companies and syndicates of whose formation the Chartered Company had been informed, "and in the various Mining interests of which, so far as they are within the Company's territories, this Company has a share." These 197 companies owned all the mines which were named as the "principal properties" or "more important properties" in the mining commissioners' reports. Among the companies a few stand out as the big enterprises: the Mashonaland Agency, the Exploring Company (general manager, E.A. Maund), and the companies revolving round Sir John Willoughby, Robert Williams, and Frank Johnson.[22]

These concentrations made more efficient methods possible. Frank Johnson boasts that his company was the first to bring a three-stamp mill into Mashonaland, for use on one of its Mazoe mines. This was followed by a five-stamp mill for a mine at Hartley Hills. During 1892 many more such mills were imported and installed. By the beginning of 1894, however, the Mazoe, the Umfuli, and Mashonaland generally—mines, farms, and towns—were comparatively neglected. There had been a rush to the new El Dorado in Matabeleland. A year later the reports of the mining commissioners reflected little or no work for some time (Mazoe), neglect of the district since the war (Umfuli), or much pegging and development but still no returns (Salisbury). Matabeleland was then going through the same cycle—several years of prospecting, "development," and wildly optimistic reports, without any actual production of gold.

Early in 1895 the registrar of claims gave a summary of the gold production of the country to date. The total for the four and a half years was 4,400 ounces, less than the Witwatersrand was then producing *per day*. Moreover, 3,000 of those ounces came from the Victoria and 1,000 from the Umfuli mining district, both of which had been in the doldrums since the middle of 1893. Neither Bulawayo, Gwelo, nor Salisbury had produced anything so far.[23]

Before those reports were made, Rhodes had taken the important step of bringing John Hays Hammond, the great American mining engineer then working on the Rand for the Consolidated Gold Fields of South Africa, to assess the mineral prospects of Matabeleland. Lord Randolph, too, had brought American experts, who had given damning reports; perhaps Hammond would be able to counteract their effect.

The party, which included Hammond, Rhodes, Jameson, Sir John Willoughby, Maurice Gifford, Robert Williams, and several other mining experts, began its journey in September 1894. Among the subjects discussed round their camp fires in Matabeleland were the unrest in Johannesburg and the possibility of an Uitlander rising there. Out of this fact, which Hammond in his autobiography admits, arose the myth—which he convincingly denies—that the discussion of these matters was really the main purpose of the expedition. This is to misunderstand the Rhodesian situation and the mind of Rhodes. The most serious question on his mind at that moment was the geology of Matabeleland. Hammond was there to do a professional job.

On his return to Johannesburg he submitted his report to Rhodes. It was "a complete but naturally conservative report on the mines of the country." He pointed out that the reefs "belonged to the class of ore deposits known as true fissure veins, and that veins of this character are universally noted for their persistence in depth; but I called attention to the fact that this attribute does not imply the occurrence of pay shoots or bodies of commercial value in their veins." He warned investors to be careful in their choice of properties to invest in, and companies to prove the value of their reefs before incurring heavy expenditures for their development. Subject to these conditions he "confidently commended the country to the attention of mining capitalists."

Both the warnings and the moderate optimism were justified in the event. Rhodes defended Hammond and the report, and was careful not to distort its meaning, but Jameson and others were less scrupulous. "To judge from the remarks of the various mining promoters," says Hammond, "I must have visited every mine and claim in Rhodesia and reported glowingly on them all." Their wilful blindness was natural. If there were no fabulous gold reefs, what was left of the great dream?[24]

A good deal of money must have been sunk in the mining venture: stamp batteries, the transport of which was very expensive; wages and salaries; the buying out of claimholders. The return had been less than a day's output from the Rand. This was no basis for a solvent economy.

There remained farming. To Rhodes this was not a mere *pis aller*. Colonization of the land—the settling of immigrants who would strike roots and acquire a "stake in the country"—was his primary purpose. Mining was important because it was expected to finance the colonizing operation as well as to satisfy the hungry shareholders; but Rhodes wanted, above all, families of settlers on the land. In that hope, too, he was to be disappointed during his lifetime.

Though some of the causes of this failure were beyond Rhodes's control, many were not. In this, as in everything else, the Company's methods were irregular. They were also short-sighted. Every Pioneer and policeman was promised 1,500 morgen of land.[25] Neither this promise nor the conditions attached to it can be found in any document.[26] When Rhodes arrived in Salisbury in October 1891 an angry deputation waited upon him, complaining that Jameson insisted on occupation as a condition of the land grants. How could they occupy their farms when they were looking for gold? This took Rhodes by surprise, because he knew nothing about the grants or the conditions. Who had promised the Pioneers farms? Johnson had. Johnson was summoned, and admitted the fact. "Who authorised you to do that?" Rhodes asked. "You did, of course," said Johnson. By a little twisting and adaptation Rhodes then arranged that occupation would not be insisted on for the Pioneers, though it would be required in all other cases.

At that time, more than a year after the arrival of the column, the Company still had no legal right to grant land. Johnson had had to explain this to the Pioneers when he disbanded them. No matter; in May 1891 a form of "licence" was devised to serve as a title-deed until the omission could be rectified. It was rectified by acquiring the Lippert Concession. Then, in April 1892, two kinds of title deed were issued, one for the Pioneers and another for the rest. "Bona fide and beneficial occupation" was required of the latter, but not of the former. Otherwise the conditions were the same: an annual quitrent to the Company, subsequently fixed at £3 per 1,500 morgen; the reservation to the Company of all mineral rights and of the rights of entry and expropriation for public purposes; the cost of survey and all legal costs to be borne by the grantee. The normal grant was 1,500 morgen. Some were bigger, but the Company "reserved the right" not to give any grant of more than 3,000 morgen.

This was a strange reservation, and, one would have thought, unnecessary. Surely the Company was under no obligation to make any land grant whatever (except to the Pioneers and the police), and therefore, *a fortiori*, a grant of over 3,000 morgen? In fact the interest of this stipulation lies in the irregularity it implies. On that first trip, late in 1891, Rhodes had with him the Bond politician D.C. de Waal. As they drove up from Umtali to Salisbury de Waal stopped his cart, to look admiringly at the adjacent country: this was where he and his friend Venter would like to have farms. "Mr. Rhodes then requested Mr. Duncan, the Surveyor-General of Mashonaland, who was with us just then, to measure out two farms there, one for Mr. Venter and one for myself." The votes of the de Waals and the Venters were vital to Rhodes in Cape politics, but this was a very small favour.

There was the question of encroaching on lands belonging to the original inhabitants. Colquhoun tried to prevent this by confining the pegging of farms to the belt between the Hunyani and the Umfuli, said to be very thinly populated; Jameson removed this restriction. At first there was to be no pegging within six miles of Fort Salisbury. When Rutherfoord Harris arrived he pulled in the boundary of the commonage to three miles, thus giving later comers an advantage denied to the first arrivals. "Native villages and gardens" (a very restricted definition of Shona lands) were still in principle secured against appropriation. It was for this reason that the civil commissioner of Victoria in 1893 told George Grey not to peg the land he had chosen, but not all officials were so scrupulous.

Though almost all energies were at first directed to finding the fabulous gold reef that would make a man rich "beyond the dreams of avarice," the land was not forgotten. As Maguire had said, "every fellah" liked to think that he owned a farm. So, as opportunity offered, men looked about for the land they wanted and marked its approximate position with their pegs. When C.E. Finlason accompanied some of them down the road to Umtali late in 1891, he found that they "were always on the look out for the beacons with their names thereon. Not one of them knew within fifty miles where his farm was, for the land had not then been surveyed." As Pioneers, these men could be absentees and their title was protected against all comers. All others were required to occupy, failing which a later comer could peg, and take, the same farm.

Farm rights, like mining claims, were negotiable. Why buy a farm right when you could get one for nothing? Because an individual, in normal cases, could have only one farm of 1,500 morgen. The buyers were companies, which could in this way assemble large estates. According to W.H. Brown, by the end of 1891 more than half of the Pioneer farm rights, together with the exemption from occupation, had passed into the hands of "commercial syndicates." Brown's theory was that the exemption was granted precisely because it was in the interest of the companies that acquired the rights.

As usual in the affairs of the BSA Company, its practice, its records, and the impressions made on observers are hard to reconcile. In June 1892 Percy Inskipp sent Rutherfoord Harris a list of all the farms granted in Mashonaland up to that time. Apart from Johnson's company, H.C. Moore, the Laurencedale settlement, Moodie for his Melsetter scheme, the missionaries and churches (granted farms for mission purposes), Rhodes, and a few corporate bodies that received one, or at the most two, farms each, the grantees listed were all individuals—340 of them. Of these, eleven got two farms each, two got very small grants, and each of the remaining 327 one standard farm of 1,500 morgen. There is no mention of any other company. Willoughby's name is missing. De Waal is registered for two farms, but Venter is not on the list.

As the country had not been surveyed, the farms could not be properly identified. In some cases no location was attempted, but most farms were given this sort of identification: "13 miles from Salisbury on Manica Road," "30 miles from Salisbury, W. of Fourie's block," "On Makabusi, left of road to Charter," or even nothing better than "near Fort Charter." The list did not distinguish between Pioneers and others, but Inskipp thought this unnecessary; the board had a list of the Pioneers, so would be able to decide which grants were, and which were not, subject to the occupation clause. Nor was there any attempt to discover whether a grantee had in fact occupied his farm. Many would not do so, and an unspecified number of grants would then revert to the Company. We can only conclude that the Pioneer farms rights to which Brown referred had already been bought by companies when Inskipp made his list, but that the transactions had not come under official notice.[27]

Brown's hypothesis that the exemption from occupation was granted with a view to these transactions is unnecessary. Jameson, Harris, and the rest, who made "regulations" without authority to do so, broke them whenever they were inconvenient. The rules were meant for, and intermittently enforced against, the small fry. There was no question of requiring occupation by the big companies and magnates to whom favours were lavishly distributed. The case of Frank Johnson was not in the irregular category. He was entitled by his contract to 40,000 morgen, and he got them; they were among the varied assets of his company. H.C. Moore, the American concession-hunter who had caused much trouble and anxiety to the Chartered financiers, had to be bought out: he got 22,678 morgen. But that "fidget on wheels," Sir John Willoughby, was the lord of no fewer than 110,441 morgen in Mashonaland, with more in Matabeleland still to come. The land granted up to February 1893, excluding "outspan farms," amounted to 973,688 morgen, or which 173,119 morgen had gone to these three gentlemen alone.

There were other lucky grantees too. Jameson was so generous to his friends, especially what Sir William Milton afterwards called the "Honourable and military element," that the supply of land was in danger of running out. By April 1893 Rhodes had made the decision that no more free grants would be made, except (of course) in special circumstances. Henceforth the Company would sell the land at 1s.6d. a morgen. Milton, surveying the scene a few years later, was appalled "that Jameson has given nearly the whole country away to the Willoughbys, Whites and others of that class so that there is absolutely no land left which is of any value for settlement of immigrants by Government . . . I think Jameson must have been off his head for some time before the raid."[28]

Milton was writing in 1896, when the abuses had been magnified by their extension, with even less restraint, to Matabeleland. There the Volunteers, in terms of the Victoria Agreement, were entitled each to 3,000 morgen, free of occupation. At high speed they pegged the very area—central Matabeleland—which had been, and still was, the Ndebele heartland. There was no question here of avoiding "native villages and gardens." *Vae victis!* We shall return to that, but for the present note that on 25 April 1894 (the Volunteers having done their pegging), Matabeleland was thrown open to settlement. There, too, the land was to be sold, but for 3s. a morgen. The conditions were then more precisely defined. Occupation, where it was required, was to begin within five months of the grant; it was to be continued by the grantee in person or by someone else approved by the administrator; after three years of continuous occupation and the erection of buildings worth at least £200 the requirement would be waived.

Occupation of what? Of every 3,000 morgen by one grantee? In 1895 Alfred da Fonseca, a Cape Town schoolboy, cut his classes, called on the prime minister (sending in a note marked "Urgent"), told Rhodes of his desire to go to Rhodesia, and was given a kindly reception. When he explained that he wanted to farm, not to mine, the prime minister became enthusiastic. A plan to cross local donkeys with Spanish jackasses was discussed. Shortly afterwards Alfred descended from the coach in Bulawayo with a grant of 33,000 acres (say

15,000 morgen) twenty miles out of the town. Such examples make a farce of the solemnly promulgated rules and regulations.

In its experience of having land concentrated in the hands of speculators and absentees, Rhodesia was not unique or even unusual among colonies. One consequence was invariably a sparse population (of colonists) on the land, concentration of people in the towns, but also a slower development of the colony than might have been possible under other conditions. In the long run this may have been the consequence in Rhodesia also; but for the short run it is difficult to make a confident judgment.

Farms were claimed, located, granted, and surveyed, but few of them were farmed. "Farming," says Marshall Hole, "at first meant only cutting down trees and selling the wood, or cultivating a small patch of mealies." When W.H. ("Curio") Brown was asked what he *raised* on his farm, his reply was that his "energies were mainly directed toward *razing* timber, which, when sent to Salisbury, brought remunerative returns." Even in 1894 E.F. Knight reported that "most of the so-called farmers are merely prospectors and store-keepers, who have done next to no work on their land."

That little arable farming was done is not surprising. Because of the difficulty and expense of transportation, the farmer could not compete on distant markets. At the end of 1891 Finlason reported empty wagons going down the Selous Road almost every day. The farms within a short radius of the townships had an accessible market for vegetables, milk, eggs, and forage, but in this trade the white farmers faced severe competition. The townsmen bought "vegetables from the Coolies, grain from the Mashonas." This was in fact the indispensable, universal source of basic food. Townsmen, prospectors, traders, transport riders, and "farmers" all depended essentially on "trading with the Kaffirs" for mealies, millet, pumpkins, even eggs and milk, throughout and beyond the decade of the nineties. It was cheaper to buy mealies from the Shona than to grow them.

For the first year after the occupation there was no European farming worth mentioning in Mashonaland. By the end of the rains in 1894 judgment could be passed on what little there was.

A few miles east of Salisbury there was a group of "ten adjacent farms, representing an area of about 40,000 acres, all occupied and with portions cultivated." This situation, according to J.A. Edmonds of Glen Lorne (one of the ten) was "unique" in the country. Most of those farmers had completed their dams, and were ready to produce both summer and winter crops when the increase of population warranted the outlay. Fruit trees had been planted. Tobacco grew well. Yet all of that was merely prospective: the only market as yet was for vegetables. One of the most "go-ahead" farmers, Walter Tapsell (presumably one of the ten neighbours—his farm was fourteen miles east of Salisbury) at the end of 1893 had nearly finished an irrigation furrow 10,000 feet long, was about to bring 500 acres under cultivation and had then ploughed half of that area. He had fifty pigs and had chosen a site for a flour mill.[29]

Robert Vavasseur, J.S. Moffat's nephew, whom we saw on the Khami River at the time of the judicial murder of Mhlaba, acquired a farm near Fort Charter which he called Stonybroke. In June 1893 he wrote to a friend in England describing his farm and his life. His nearest white neighbour, Potgieter, was ten miles away. Immediately to the south was Colenbrander's farm (not occupied). Vavasseur was busy building a two-roomed wattle-and-daub hut.

> Very comfortable huts they are when well made. I have a big kraal for my cattle and other livestock, and have been breaking up the ground and my ploughs too down by my fountain, or spring, where I am making a "garden" for irrigation . . . I like the life though my experience might have been greater with advantage. I have been here just a month and have been ploughing and making irrigation ditches nearly the whole time. I hope to finish my ploughing for the present this week, and to finish the house next, and then to go in to Salisbury our capital to sell some cattle. I am hopeful of making a good thing out of it if only I can tide over the first year or two.

A month later the Victoria incident forced Vavasseur to leave his farm and take refuge in Fort Victoria. He went into Matabeleland with the Victoria Column and was thus able to peg another farm there, but he later returned to Stonybroke to pick up the threads he had been rudely forced to drop.

The lack of markets was not the only, and probably not the chief, reason for the sluggishness of agriculture. A more important reason was the character of the immigrants. Most were adventurous young men seeking their fortunes; at any rate seeking adventure. Real colonization required a different motivation, and it required women. There were no women among the Pioneers. Even in 1895 most of the whites in the country were bachelors (as Vavasseur and Tapsell were) or grass widowers.[30]

The significant contrast with all these is provided by the *trekkers*. Bowler, Adendorff, and others had tried to organize "treks" to take possession of tracts of Rhodesian land. These were treks in the Afrikaner tradition—father, mother, children, sons-in-law, daughters-in-law, flocks, herds, half-tented wagons, even a few servants, moving slowly up the continent rather in the spirit of Abraham. Rhodes had stopped those who had tried to "jump his claim," but once the Company's position was established he welcomed all who agreed to submit to it. Treks, not in defiance of the Company but under its aegis, were accordingly organized, notably in the Orange Free State.

The first to organize one with Rhodes's approval and blessing was G.B. Dunbar Moodie. He belonged to a well-known family with wide ramifications. Three Moodie brothers, from Melsetter in Orkney, had landed in Cape Town in 1817, three years ahead of the main body of British settlers. The descendants of two of the brothers had spread over South Africa. Some had settled in the Free State. Dunbar, who was born in Natal in 1861, became a mine manager for the Sabi-Ophir Gold Mining Company in Manica. He was at Mutasa's kraal when Forbes carried out the coup of arresting Paiva de Andrade and Gouveia, and was able to give the company men useful local information. Consequently, when Jameson and Doyle made their epic march to Ngungunyane's kraal early in 1891, Dunbar Moodie was the third member of the trio. These associations cost him his job with the Sabi-Ophir Company, but he had his reward: Jameson offered him seven farms on the usual conditions, including occupation. He would have to bring in settlers to occupy them.

Moodie wanted farms in the country he knew, the mountainous district where the Anglo-Portuguese boundary was about to be surveyed. Jameson wanted settlers in that area in order to stake a claim to it before the Portuguese could do so, and to act as a barrier to Portuguese expansion or infiltration. So Moodie negotiated with Jameson, then with Rhodes, then with his kinsman Thomas, an older man who farmed in the Bethlehem district of the Free State. The outcome was a trek of sixty-eight people, including women and children, in seventeen wagons, under the leadership of Thomas Moodie. They left Bethlehem in May 1892.

Dunbar did not accompany them. He went by sea to Beira, looked over the land again, and rode on to meet the trekkers. He found them at Tuli. When they reached Fort Victoria dissensions caused the party to break up. Many professed to be surprised when told that their destination was Gazaland. They were told by the local people that they would never cross the Sabi, because of the quicksands, and that even if they did they would all die of fever in that malarial country. Groups then broke away and moved up the road to Salisbury; some of these stopped in the Charter district, where Enkeldoorn became the centre of a settlement to which some later trekkers were drawn. (Their neighbour Vavasseur called some of them "low class Boers from the Transvaal border who have settled all over the district.") Thomas and Dunbar, with a remnant of the original party, struck out eastword from Fort Victoria across an almost uncharted wilderness of bush, crossed the Sabi, climbed what they called the Driespanberg because each wagon required three spans of oxen to pull it up, were attacked by bees and (in their ignorance) by mosquitoes, went down with fever, and for a time were too sick to move. So in January 1893, well into the rainy season, they arrived on the mountain slopes that Dunbar had chosen for them. Fourteen men, four women, and three children constituted the party.

The dissensions, the secessions, and the failures detract only slightly from the significance of this migration. The Moodie trek, disasters and all, was quickly followed by others, largely from the Free State: the Moolman and Webster families in 1893; the Edenburg, Martin, Du Plessis, Mynhardt, and Utrecht treks in 1894; the Kruger, Bekker, Henry, and Steyn parties in 1895. All went to the eastern mountains where the Moodie trek had shown the way.

Many of these pioneers, as we saw, were ignorant of the necessary precautions and built their houses near water instead of on breezy hilltops. Malaria and blackwater then took their heavy toll: Thomas Moodie died in 1894, Dunbar in 1897, and many others within the first few years of the settlement. The leaders had wasted no time in pegging and registering the farms, though it had to be done in the heavy rain of the first summer. They also pegged a township which, as Thomas had wished from the first, was called Melsetter. The chronicler of the treks innocently reports that "for the site they used the kraal and property of a native chief, Chipinga, but re-christened it 'Melsetter.'" Later immigrants, however, extended the settled area so much further north that there were soon complaints that the township was inconveniently placed, as well as unhealthy. In the face of bitter complaints from a minority, the township and official quarters were at the beginning of 1896 moved some seventy miles to the north. To add insult to injury, the new site took the name of Melsetter and the old one, consecrated by so much Moodie blood and tears, reverted to the old name Chipinga.

What made these Melsetter treks so important was, of course, the presence of women. Many of the immigrants came in families, which in spite of suffering, death, and disaster dug themselves in and appropriated the land. This was not only because they were Afrikaners with long roots in the African soil. The importance of the female element stands out in the contrast with the van der Byl trek.

P.L. van der Byl had had his own plan to develop the whole of Rhodesia, but was discountenanced by the imperial government and forestalled by Rhodes. He came in, however, under the new regime in a more modest capacity. Even before the Moodie trek van der Byl led twenty-five young Cape Colonists to the promised land and settled them near Marandellas on the estate which he called Laurencedale. They got malaria and their leader died. This was no worse a fate than the Melsetter parties had suffered, but at Laurencedale there were no women. In the absence of those ties the settlement dissolved. Population figures underline the contrast: at the end of March 1895 there were about 300 whites settled—almost all on farms—in the Melsetter district, and many of the pioneer trekkers were still to come. In the magistracy of Salisbury, which then meant the whole of Northern Mashonaland, the rural white population was 233, and many of those were miners. This population was grouped in districts, in only one of which the figures were broken down into adults (28) and children (72). That district was Charter, to which many of the trekkers intended for Gazaland had been diverted.[31]

These figures might have been different if Mashonaland generally had been settled by frontier-hardened families as Melsetter was. But this factor must not be exaggerated. Bachelors such as Tapsell and Vavasseur were working hard on the land. Vavasseur, in the letter quoted, gave a hint of another explanation: he was going to Salisbury to sell cattle. At a distance from markets and cheap transport, stock and not crops gave the best hope of making farming pay; but whites in Mashonaland in 1893 had few cattle.

Jameson's War changed that. Matabeleland was, and was known to be, good ranching country. The Victoria Agreement promised the Volunteers not only land, but "loot"—the enemy's cattle (half to the Company, half to the members of the force). The loot operation has naturally left very few traces in the records. The Colonial Office tried to protect the defeated Ndebele in the possession of their cattle, but could not deny to the Company, as the new government, the right to take over whatever had belonged to Lobengula in his royal capacity. The difference between Western and Bantu ideas on ownership and possession enabled Jameson and his men to throw out a smokescreen of confusion, behind which they tried to establish a title to all the cattle in Matabeleland. For two years after the fall of Bulawayo parties were scouring the country to round up cattle, others were surrendered by the Ndebele as they gave in their submission, the "loot kraals" filled up, and the bulk of the loot was left in charge of its original possessors as a fund to be drawn on by the authorities at their pleasure.[32]

It was almost two years before the cattle had been counted. During that time great numbers had been seized by the whites, the Shona, and cattle-rustlers and traders from the south, as well as by the Company itself. No statistics are available before the completion of the count about October 1895, by which time more than half of the stock (at the most conservative estimate) had been disposed of. After December 1895 the number made available to white farmers was 32,870; before that date it can hardly have been less than 50,000. In the absence of information, contemporaries relied on rumour. During the winter of 1894 it became known that the Company had given up its right to a half share, and that the whole of the loot, amounting it was thought to 30,000, would be divided among the volunteers. Some of them complained that the Company was cheating them by offering this number, instead of "at least 50,000," which they seem to have thought was the total in Ndebele possession. Those who were far from Bulawayo complained too that they were being kept in the dark about the handling of the business. It was being conducted by a "Loot Committee," which should have represented the holders of "loot rights," but was actually appointed by Jameson.

"Loot rights," like farm and claim rights, were negotiable. Very many of the fighters of 1893, like the Pioneers of 1890, sold their rights. Many of the buyers were companies, such as those of Willoughby and Williams, and the Bechuanaland Exploration Company. It was not till July 1894 that the Loot Committee began to dispose of what it had collected. Every holder of a loot right was then offered £25 worth of cattle, on condition that they were not sold in Matabeleland or Mashonaland until all the loot had been disposed of. In addition, each holder was awarded a £10 "dividend," to be followed by other dividends as the sales proceeded. On 2 August the first sale was held in Bulawayo by the

Loot Committee. Five thousand cattle were sold; cows fetched £2.10.0, oxen and calves "in proportion." Thereafter, sales were held regularly on Saturdays. In May, when the prospects were uncertain, a "loot right" could be bought for £6.10.0 or £7; by August it was £18 and difficult to get at that.[33]

Before the reader assumes that there was anything regular or systematic about this disposal of the loot, let him ponder an advertisement in the *Rhodesia Herald* (Salisbury) on 13 April 1894, more than three months before the sales in Bulawayo began; M. Savile and Company, Auctioneers, announced a "Great Sale of Matabele Cattle: 2000 Cattle will shortly be in from Matabeleland, and will be sold by public auction without reserve."

Apart from the questions of morality and of policy to which the spoliation of the Ndebele gives rise (we shall return to these), there were queer features in the distribution of the loot; there was not even honour among thieves. The Company had claimed a half share, but waived the claim. The cattle were then to be equally divided among the holders of "rights"; some were so divided, but others were sold by auction and the holders of rights were awarded successive dividends, without any public accounting of the transactions. Most of the "loot certificates" seem to have been presented not by men who had fought in the campaigns but by the agents of the Willoughbys and others who had bought them out.

One small example may throw some light on the proceedings. A well-known but retired coach conductor, Alexander Gibson, travelled up from the Transvaal, bought loot rights, and "arranged with the Loot Committee to redeem all the certificates, taking stock as payment. An agreement was signed, and Alexander was to pick his beasts. The price was not to exceed twenty-five shillings a head, and he was not to take less than five hundred head of cattle." No auction, and half the price that cows fetched on the sales! Once again each case was being "treated on its merits." For Gibson it was not the stroke of fortune that he had expected. Back in the Transvaal he got into trouble with the customs authorities for cattle smuggling, and lost them all.[34]

The "loot" did not give quite the shot in the arm to the white farming community that might have been expected. The Bulawayo correspondent of the *Rhodesia Herald* pointed to one reason: the "rights" had fallen into "comparatively few hands." This did not mean merely that a few companies had bought loot certificates entitling them to the proceeds of auctions. It meant also that Jameson ("off his head for some time before the raid") had diverted loot to his "Honourable and military" friends. Of the 32,870 head taken by the Company "to be distributed among farmers" in the final allocation at the end of 1895, 8,850 were allotted to Sir John Willoughby by name.

This would account for an uneven distribution among the white farmers and companies, but it ought not to have affected the total number. Yet by March 1895 the number of cattle reported on white farms in Matabeleland was 8,108; by the end of August, 15,000. Of those earmarked for white farmers at the end of the year, over 9,000 were for Mashonaland. Even if all of Willoughby's remained in Matabeleland, the total for that province would have risen only to about 38,000. Nearly 20,000 more had been used as "police rations," a useful economy for the Company but a curious commentary on its waiving its right to a share of the loot. The number taken by the Company from the Ndebele was variously estimated at between 80,000 and 200,000. Some had gone to Mashonaland, but where were the rest?

Wherever they were, those in European ownership in Matabeleland were certainly in "few hands." The white population on farms in the province in March 1895 was 250—fewer than in Melsetter. These people (the figures would include some women and children) were occupying 150 farms, but the number of farms, each of 3,000 morgen, pegged at that date was 1,070. It is true that the Volunteers of the late war were not required to occupy their farms, but that was not the main reason for the absentee ownership. "Farm rights" under the Victoria Agreement, like those of the Pioneers, like "loot rights" and mining claims, had been bought on a large scale by the handful of companies that had come to dominate the wealth (or potential wealth) of the country.

As a result of all these factors the white population on farms in the whole of Rhodesia in March 1895, as far as can be deduced from unsatisfactory statistics, was about 700, out of a total white population of some 5,000; and nearly half of that farming population was in Melsetter.[35] It is clear that at that date farming, like mining, still lived mainly on hope. White Rhodesia, considered in isolation, did not yet have an economic leg to stand on. What supported it was on one hand the investment and other remittances coming from outside, and on the other hand Black Rhodesia.

Rhodesian history, like South African history, must be read in the light of the alternative courses which lay open to its makers at the beginning. The kinds of society which in theory could have evolved in Rhodesia were these. First, a black society as in West Africa, with no white intruders; the preceding chapters have shown why there was no chance of that. Second, a white society such as colonists established in Australasia and most of North America, pushing the original inhabitants aside. Third, the kind that developed in Brazil, where white (and in that case black) immigrants amalgamated with the aboriginal population. Each of these kinds of society was viable in the long term. South Africa and Rhodesia did not evolve in any of these ways. They developed societies in which white and black became interdependent economically—parts of a single economy—while the whites maintained a rigid social barrier against the blacks and excluded them both from the white society and from the citadel of power. Of all the courses open, this was the only one sure to lead sooner or later to a revolutionary explosion. Having shown that the whites could not have been excluded from Rhodesia, we have now to ask, first, why they did not adopt an Australasian system in which the white community was economically self-contained; and second, if that alternative was excluded, why not a Brazilian system in which the races fused?

Why not a self-contained white society? For Rhodesia, the answer lies mainly in the South African background. The choice had been made long ago in the old Cape Colony—in 1658, when the first slaves were landed, or at the latest, according to Professor Eric Walker, in 1717, when the decision was made in Holland not to encourage further white settlement. By the nineteenth century the association of "Kaffir work" with social degradation was deeply ingrained in white South African minds. Even a short sojourn anywhere south of the Limpopo was enough to convert the newly arrived Englishman to the same way of thinking. In any case, if we may judge by those British immigrants whom we know anything about, most who came from "Home" were of the class who had domestic servants and were accustomed to relegate dirty and unskilled work to the lower classes.

The dirty work had to be done; there was no white class that would do it for a wage; the whites were not prepared to do it for themselves. There remained the Shona, but the Shona had no wish to work for wages. Their refusal might then have forced the whites to roll up their sleeves and "do" for themselves. But there were several reasons why it did not work out that way.

Take the case of domestic servants. Obviously no Shona villager in 1891 or 1892 could have presided over a white kitchen without provoking the exasperated owner to violence. The citizens of Salisbury solved the problem by bringing in African servants from neighbouring territories where they had had long experience of that kind of work. "Shangaans," the subjects of Ngungunyane, "who had long been accustomed to work for slothful Portuguese employers," were the favourites, but most tribes south of the Limpopo—all lumped together under the title of "Cape boys" or "Colonial natives"—were represented. From this source too were recruited the wagon drivers, camp cooks, and others requiring skills that could not be found locally. Within a few years, under pressures which will be discussed in the next chapter, the Shona began to enter the labour market, including domestic service. It must have been an interesting experience for them; certainly the simplest and most direct means of acculturation to the strange ways of the immigrants.

The economy, however, could presumably have functioned without this kind of assistance. It could not have functioned without African labour on farm and mine.

The precedent had been set on the mines of Kimberley and the Witwatersrand: the high wage necessary to attract the skilled (white immigrant) miners was economically possible only on condition that unskilled labour was paid the lowest wage sufficient to attract the available black labour. The companies and syndicates that mined in Rhodesia followed the precedent. In 1895 European miners were paid from £20 to £25 a month, of which they had to spend from £5 to £8 on their food. African miners, if Shangaans, who were "usually considered the best boys for mining," received about 25s. a month with food (which cost £1); "other natives," 10s. with food. No European would work for this wage; but a mine that paid its unskilled workers at the lowest rate any European would accept (£10 a month) would be forced out of business. Even worse: the *Buluwayo Chronicle* complained that "we hear that as much as three pounds a month is being paid to boys in some districts. This wage . . . will practically shut down the works belonging to the smaller class of syndicates, and individuals will not be able to proceed with their development at all." Yet "we cannot do without the native." The dilemma was brought to Rhodesia in the wagons of the Pioneers.

The dependence on African labour is illustrated by an anecdote of Hyatt's. The Geelong mine was forced to close for lack of that labour. Hyatt's point is that he, as a labour agent, had recently offered the mine a supply of workers, which had been refused. The closing down was fraudulent (something to do with "Bears," he thought), but the relevant point here is the excuse that was used.

The farmer's need was the same. It was never suggested (as it was in East Africa a few years later, but without the desired result) that family farms of 160 or 640 acres on the Canadian model might be appropriate for Rhodesia. A farm of 3,000 morgen had been the traditional Afrikaner birthright for nearly two centuries. It could not be worked without the help of cheap labour; nor could the farm half that size which was the rule in Mashonaland. Robert Vavasseur will serve as an example again. He was not building his house, ploughing, or making irrigation ditches with his own hands: "Once established there I can work out from it provided we can get labour and sinews of war in sufficiency . . . I can't get enough boys to work, that is my main difficulty . . . It's a very tiring life with countless petty worries occasioned by the contrary behaviour of the cheerful 'boy' or Kafir on whom one depends for labour." It was a precarious dependence. As the *Buluwayo Chronicle* ruefully concluded, "there still remains the hard fact that the native does not like labour in any shape or form, and will not lose any sweat from his brow if he can avoid it." There was only one solution: "sooner or later the natives will have to be forced to work."[36]

There could be no self-contained white community. That leaves us with the question why, in an economy in which blacks and whites had interdependent functions, a rigid colour bar prevented the fusion of societies and cultures.

The immigrants' ideas on this subject were brought with them from their countries of origin and further developed under the impact of Rhodesian experiences. What, then, were their countries of origin?

There was no systematic census in the nineties. The most useful analysis comes from a local census of the township of Bulawayo at the beginning of March 1895. Though it might not be a representative cross-section, at least the total of 1,537 was nearly a third of the white population of the whole country. For what it is worth, it gives the most important national groups as:

United Kingdom 1,017
"Colonials" 299
U.S.A. 33
Germans 108
Others 79

The "Colonials" appear to include people from all parts of South Africa; but, as the adherents of the Dutch Reformed Church numbered only 86, most of the Colonials were probably of British stock.

The proportion of Colonials, and also of Afrikaners, was very much higher in Melsetter, Fort Victoria, and some other districts. We can make no more than an informed guess for the whole country; that would be that a substantial majority of the white population was of United Kingdom birth, but that the South Africans were more strongly represented than the 20 per cent in the figures for Bulawayo. In many cases, too, men of British birth had spent some years in various parts of South Africa before moving to Rhodesia. The South African background was certainly a stronger influence than would be indicated by the number of South African born, whatever that figure might be.[37]

It is tempting to attribute many aspects of race relations and of white racial attitudes in Rhodesia to this background. Patterns of thought and behaviour in the context of race had been evolving in South Africa for two and a half centuries before the white settlement of Rhodesia. That they were brought to Rhodesia by people of South African origin can be demonstrated *ad nauseam*.

We saw J.G. Wood confiding to his diary the idea of herding the whole "native population" into Bechuanaland (not a well-thought out scheme, but it conveys the idea). When it was suggested to Dunbar Moodie that he should not appropriate land occupied by Africans, he laughed. He did not laugh when he heard it rumoured that white settlers in Melsetter had been marrying native women. He protested: "The very thought of intermarrying or having any such connection with coloured people is most repugnant to *White* people, especially the Boers." Most people in Melsetter, he said, "are married, and have families, and are most respectable people in every sense." The politician de Waal, seeing a party of "young, tall, strong Matabele, with beautifully shaped bodies" on their way to the Rand goldfields, thought, "What excellent labourers these men would make for the white man! If Kafirs only knew the advantages of serving under white masters, they would gain more civilisation in one year than they do from missionaries in fifty." And so on.

Yet it is wrong to suppose that such notions were peculiar to South Africa and could reach Rhodesia only from that source. The second half of the nineteenth century was "the golden age of racism" in Britain and, more generally,

379 The White Society

in Northern Europe and its colonial offshoots; it was no coincidence that this was also the golden age of imperialism.

The notions of race that became general in Britain in that age were propagated by scientists of repute. Long before the publication of *The Origin of Species*, the biblical account of the creation of man began to be called in question by thinkers who could not believe that the "higher" and the "lower" races had a common ancestry. (Their doubts were shared by Mzilikazi, who refused to believe that Ndebele and San were both descended from Adam.) Thus arose the theory of "polygenesis," in opposition to the "monogenesis" implied by the biblical story; noble races like the Anglo-Saxon could be freed from the stigma of having disreputable relations. The different races were different species and had been separately created. The infant science of anthropology came to the aid of the polygenists by measuring skulls and by various means demonstrating the innate inferiority of the lesser breeds. For a time Darwin and the biblical fundamentalists were strangely associated in common opposition to polygenesis; but it came to be understood that Evolution left room for vast racial divergences. The popular debasement of Darwinism into "the survival of the fittest" at last provided a respectable rationalization for the subjection, exploitation or even extermination of alien races, as might be convenient.[38]

The history of the contact of Britons and Africans in the late nineteenth century is a gloss on these doctrines. The Englishman in Africa, whether missionary, official, explorer, or hunter, was always conscious of a racial superiority which had to be sustained by conscious effort. No insolence, disobedience, or even familiarity from the inferior race could be tolerated.[39] Selous, a public school Englishman, sums up the result:

> Kind and considerate though any European may be under ordinary circumstances to the savages amongst whom he happens to be living, yet deep down in his heart, whether he be a miner or a missionary, is the conviction that the black man belongs to a lower type of humanity than the white; and if this is a mistaken conviction, ask the negrophilist who professes to think so, whether he would give his daughter in marriage to a negro, and if not, why not?[40]

These familiar ideas were not the monopoly of South Africans.

Whatever their source, ideas of racial superiority, social segregation and a society organized on a colour-caste system were evident in Rhodesia from the beginning of white settlement. Before they took definite shape, however, Rhodesian society passed through a phase that left a special imprint on the country's racial pattern. This was the phase of masculinity.

There were no women in the Pioneer Column, and for years to come women were heavily outnumbered by men in the white population. In the middle of 1891 "four or five hundred sun-burnt young men, clad for the most part in flannel shirts, weather-beaten corduroy breeches and broad-brimmed slouch hats . . . constituted the population of Fort Salisbury. There was said to be a white woman somewhere in the camp, but she must have remained in *purdah*, for we never saw her." At that time there were no white women in Fort Victoria. A year later in Umtali, when society had evolved to the point of "dances got up by the men for the pleasure of the ladies," the ratio of the sexes on the dance floor was 100:8. All the travellers who recorded their impressions in the nineties commented on this phenomenon.

Census figures or estimates confirm the impression. On 1 March 1895 there were 1,232 white male and 164 white female adults in Bulawayo. The figures for Salisbury in November were 507 and 88. The disproportion was less in districts settled by trekker families, but greater out on the mining frontier. Even in the towns it was, from one point of view, greater than the figures suggest. These concentrations of men were powerful magnets to women of the oldest profession, to whom we find many references in spite of the Victorian reticence which must have censored much of the evidence. When Melina Rorke arrived in Bulawayo in 1894 she was "the only eligible white woman in the town"; though the statement is her own it was close to the truth. Many of the "adult white females" of the statistics were, to say the least, ineligible as wives for the "sun-burnt young men."[41]

The logic of this situation emerges with euclidean simplicity: the needs of the young men were met by African women. When we pass from the general to the specific, however, the simplicity turns to complexity.

In the old days of Lobengula's Bulawayo the African concubine or harem was the regular and recognized appurtenance of almost every white Matabele-lander. The girls were brazen and importunate too. Matabele Thompson describes a "Scotch unsophisticated girl about 18 years old and as green as one comes across," who

> was telling us of two young Kafir girls having been to their waggon and got up and sat on the front box. She ordered these girls off and they turned round and called her proud, saying that they were allowed to get on the white men's waggons and to sleep on their beds too. She in her ignorant way asked all if it was true. You can imagine how the bulk of the white men felt. It is the fact what the Kafir girls said and nearly every white man here has two or three girls in their waggons with them.

All accounts of precolonial Matabeleland tell the same story. H. Vaughan-Williams had scarcely crossed the border in 1889 when he was subjected to the attentions of the all-but-naked girls. "Two or three intombis, as the maids were called, turned up and tried to get into bed with us. One of them attempted to creep in under my kaross." They tried to make themselves irresistible by wearing round their necks little bags of scent which were described as smelling like a mixture of human excrement and rotten flesh. Vaughan-Williams was told "that they would offer themselves to any white man for two yards of eelembo, as blue cloth was called."

Lobengula saw no harm in this, as long as the girls were unmarried. "He said that their bodies belonged to them and they could do as they liked with them, but when married their bodies belonged to their husbands." Fornication across the racial line was indeed a subject of much jocularity, teasing, and leg-pulling at Lobengula's court. Vaughan-Williams tells a story, which is confirmed by two other witnesses, of Mollie Colenbrander's going to the king to complain "of the conduct of the white men in Matabeleland with the native girls. Lobengula looked at her and replied: 'Do you think you would be sufficient for all the white men in the country?' "[42]

The change of regime at the end of 1893 seems to have made no difference. So many Ndebele women—more accurately, women in Matabeleland— "offered themselves voluntarily to the white men" that the abuse of their power by white officials and policemen for purposes of sexual gratification is hard to explain. That this happened, and was a minor cause of the rebellion, will appear in the course of the narrative.

That it happened in Mashonaland is less surprising. The Shona had had too many experiences of Ndebele raids, one of the purposes of which was to capture women, not to be sensitive to this threat. Finlason, visiting a Shona village, found that "it was impossible to get near the women, for on our approach they fled, shrieking in terror, to their huts." A police trooper said dispiritedly that "they run like buck." Writing of Mashonaland in the late nineties, Hyatt said that "it is by no means easy—in fact it is often impossible—for a white man to get possession of a native girl." H.C. Thomson, a judicious and unprejudiced observer, thought that the keeping of African concubines by white men was almost unknown in Salisbury and Umtali. It occurred chiefly in remote places, and even then the women were not Shona. The white man "generally gets a woman from Zumbo in Portuguese territory, paying about £5 for her, and she almost always has a happier lot with her white owner than she would have in her own kraal." The moral principles of the Shona women were reinforced by the belief that if they lived with white men they would beget snakes.

In these circumstances the reports of "some of the police formerly stationed there making a practice of assaulting and raping any native woman they found in the veld alone," and that whites "had killed some of Mangwende's people and outraged the women" are the more credible. In the present context we are concerned, however, not with outrage but with intimacy.

The intimacy of white men with black women was not matched by similar relations between white women and black men. In these relationships the man is in the superior role and the woman remains attached to the offspring. The children belong to the mother's social group; the man may go his way and put the regrettable incident behind him—as some of the highly respected white characters in this history did. These are some of the reasons why the whites, believing themselves to be superior, found the irregular unions of white men— for a time and on certain conditions—tolerable, whereas the idea of such behaviour in white women sent them into paroxysms of rage and murderous passion.

The blacks, though bitterly antagonized by the sexual outrages of white policemen and others, were not driven to frenzy by the voluntary relations of their women with white men. They had never been taught that they belonged to a superior race. Given the technological advantages of the whites the theory would have been unconvincing anyway. And there were other reasons. The whites—Anglo-Saxon and Afrikaner—still carried about with them the heavy incubus of the Puritan ethic; the blacks, Ndebele and Shona, had no such heritage. The whites too, especially those of British middle-class background, were influenced by the Victorian ideal of womanhood. Sir Harry Johnston conjured up a picture of "a modest girl . . . shielded with such jealous care from contact with anything coarse or impure" coming among African women who would "talk glibly to her of matters that the most depraved of her sex in her own country would hesitate to mention."[43]

The difference between the case of the man and the case of the woman in these interracial intimacies warns us that the profligacy of the frontier, or whatever it should be called, was not destined to lead to a fusion of the races.

When white women arrived in Rhodesia to marry the "sun-burnt young men," or to join their husbands, they at once attacked this profligacy with the whole armoury of Victorian taboos. They would have done so if the temptresses had been white. That they were black gave the reaction extra force because, first, of the prevalent ideas of racial difference, and, second, of the power structure which made black women particularly vulnerable and so exposed white men to stronger temptation.

Melina Rorke, writing of Kimberley, where too there had long been a preponderance of males in the white population, described the "amorous advances" of African women to "every white man, whether married or single."

The subject, of course, was never openly discussed; "but white wives and mothers were careful never to employ Kaffir women. With bland faces and knowing eyes they ignored the presence of black women in the houses of bachelors, or even of men whose wives were away from Kimberley, but when a white man so far forgot himself as to marry a Kaffir girl the public rose in its wrath and blotted him out of the social picture." It is a succinct explanation: the pranks of young men and the future composition of society are quite different questions. No alien genes were to be admitted to the society, especially not genes which, according to the prevailing theory, were stamped with perpetual inferiority.

Like the ladies of Kimberley, the Hyatt brothers in the Rhodesian bush erected a barrier against temptation: "no native woman was ever allowed in our camp, unless she came to trade, accompanied by her own menkind." Negative evidence suggests that the white housewives of Rhodesia followed the same example and employed, with very rare exceptions, only male servants.

Sexual relations across the colour line were not necessarily, however, promiscuous or casual. In the early years there is no record in Rhodesia of an interracial marriage by Christian rites or European law, though a few couples so married did come up from the south. But marriages by African custom were not unknown, and appear in various cases to have been stable. Among the white men whose black consorts can be called wives were officials of the Company such as A.D. Campbell, W.L. Armstrong, M.E. Weale, and Henry Short. In connection with the rebellion we shall hear of three white storekeepers near Inyati, all of whom "had native wives." In speculating on the might-have-beens we are brought back again to the white women. Had they never entered the country, the result of the mixed unions would have been racial amalgamation. Once the white women had come in significant numbers the boom was lowered, and the mixed couples and their offspring were left on the wrong side of it.[44]

This polarization was helped by the cultural gulf which in the 1890s very nearly coincided with the distinction of race. The great question for the future was what would happen to race relations when the cultural gulf had shrunk (to a very narrow slit in the case of many individuals) while the racial gulf had not.

In the nineties the omens were not good. It quickly became an article of faith among the whites that education "spoiled the native." Hyatt's opinions on this question are representative:

> The product of these ancestors . . . is to be made into a civilised man—by Education! If it were not so pitiful, it would be delightfully Gilbertian . . . The only use to which I ever knew an African native put his knowledge of reading and writing was the forging of white men's names, usually with a view to obtaining liquor . . . No white man would risk having [an educated native] in his house; they were generally regarded as a gang of thieves and forgers, and were kept at arm's length by the whole white community.[45]

So that theft and forgery were the only occupations open to them. If the white community had its way, the process of narrowing the cultural gulf would not be allowed to begin.

Their attitude, however deplorable, must be judged with some compassion. We may well believe that there was fire behind all that smoke. The "educated natives" in question had not drunk deep at the Pierian spring. The process of transition is always painful, and the whites were witnessing some fellowmen who were in a state of cultural shock. It is hard to be tolerant of thieves and forgers, and many "mission boys" may have fallen into those occupations. Most of them were "Cape boys," too, who in the old Colony had had free access to liquor, thanks to the politics of the vine-growing Bondsmen. In Rhodesia they were forbidden European liquor, so resorted to forgery to get it. The Europeans, who knew something about thirst, might have been more sympathetic.

Yet it would be wrong to give too much emphasis to cultural shock, transition, or inadequacy. Those whites were unable to adjust their traditional notions of a racially stratified society to changes in the premisses on which the notions were supposed to be based. This was the essence of their tragedy.

NOTES CHAPTER 9

1 *Rhodesia Herald*, 29 October 1892 and following issues; co 468/1, BSA Co. Report for 1892-4, pp.6-7; R.C. Smith, *Rhodesia: A Postal History*, pp.8, 9, 42. For freight charges, see above, ch.v, pp.203, 222 n.21.

2 W.H. Brown, *On the South African Frontier*, p.159; Neville Jones, *Rhodesian Genesis*, p.53; Papers of Lieut. M.D. Graham (GR 6/1/1), 18 February 1891; H. Marshall Hole, *Old Rhodesian Days*, pp.10-11 (cf. ch.8, above, n.52).

3 Thompson Papers, Harris to Thompson, 10 July 1889 (Queen's, p.329); Ian Colvin, *Life of Jameson*, vol. 1, p.229; G.H. Tanser, *A Scantling of Time*, pp.21-2, 41-3, 49, 51-2, 60; Jones, *Rhodesian Genesis*, pp.40-1; Diary of Matabele Wilson (WI 6/2/1), beginning of 1891.

4 Reminiscences of Richard Moffat (MO 4/1/1); R. Blennerhassett and L. Sleeman, *Adventures in Mashonaland*, pp.136-9, 143, 183-4.

5 *Rhodesia Herald*, 29 October 1892; 16 and 30 November 1894; *Cape Argus*, 1 and 21 November 1892; E.F. Knight, *Rhodesia of To-Day*, p.118; Frank Johnson, *Great Days*, p.200; Baron E.B. d'Erlanger, *History of the Construction and Finance of the Rhodesian Transport System*, p.12; George Pauling, *The Chronicles of a Contractor*, p.133. For Beira Railway, see above, ch.8.

6 Smith, *Rhodesia: A Postal History*, pp.13-14, 39-43, 89-93, 310 349; D.C. de Waal, *With Rhodes in Mashonaland*, p.229; Tanser, *Scantling of Time*, pp.53-4.

7 James Johnston, *Reality versus Romance in South Central Africa*, p.248; C.E. Finlason, *A Nobody in Mashonaland*, pp.175-7; Knight, *Rhodesia of Today*, p.118; Blennerhassett and Sleeman, *Adventures in Mashonaland*, pp.172-3, 183, 213, 231-2.

8 M. Gelfand, *Mother Patrick and her Nursing Sisters*, pp. 66-8, 70-3, 81-8, 125-7, 161-2, 194-5; Blennerhassett and Sleeman, *Adventures in Mashonaland*, the whole, but especially ch.5-8; Tanser, *Scantling of Time*, pp.49-52, 62-3, 99; Hole, *Old Rhodesian Days*, p.12; Brown, *South African Frontier*, p.160; Jones, *Rhodesian Genesis*, p.53; S.P. Olivier, *Many Treks Made Rhodesia*, pp.109-15; Jeannie M. Boggie, *First Steps in Civilizing Rhodesia*, pp.111, 114-16.

9 Tanser, *Scantling of Time*, pp.34-5, 53-4, 74, 80-3, 123; Hole, *Old Rhodesian Days*, pp.22-4; Finlason, *Mashonaland*, pp.164-8; Jones, *Rhodesian Genesis*, p.39; Johnson, *Great Days*, p.207; Lord Randolph Churchill, *Men, Mines and Animals in South Africa*, pp.281-90; *Mashonaland Herald*, 28 August 1891; co 468/1, BSA Co. Report for 1894-5, pp.58-60.

10 The shareholders were shy: they took up only £53,000 worth. (A.P. Cartwright, *Gold Paved the Way*, p.58.)

11 Barry A. Kosmin, "A Comparative Historical Population Study: The Development of Southern Rhodesian Jewry, 1890-1936" (Henderson Seminar Paper No.17), pp.1-2.

12 Tanser, *Scantling of Time*, pp.38-40, 66, 77-9, 83, 84, 95, 102-4, 116-17, 123-4, 146-7; Churchill, *Men, Mines and Animals*, pp.281-90; Jones, *Rhodesian Genesis*, pp.66-7; Boggie, *Civilizing Rhodesia*, pp.53-7, 65, 194-7; Hole, *Old Rhodesian Days*, pp.27, 75; Gelfand, *Mother Patrick*, p.84; Cecil Lewis and G.E. Edwards, *Historical Records of the Church of the Province of South Africa*, pp.714-19; C.T.C. Taylor, *A History of Rhodesian Entertainment, 1890-1930*, pp.16-19, 23-4; J.A. Henry and H.A. Siepmann, *The First Hundred Years of the Standard Bank*, pp.120-1; *Mashonaland Herald*, 25 July 1891; *Rhodesia Herald*, 14 January 1893 (at which date Bodle's Library had a thousand volumes). The pioneer journey of Bishop Knight-Bruce is recorded in Constance E. Fripp and V.W. Hillier, *Gold and the Gospel in Mashonaland, 1888*.

13 Tanser, *Scantling of Time*, pp.38, 65-8; Hole, *Old Rhodesian Days*, pp.27-8; Finlason, *Mashonaland*, pp.170-3; *Rhodesia Herald*, 29 October 1892, 26 April 1895.

14 Tanser, *Scantling of Time*, pp.91-2, 94, 119-22, 125, 128-9, 131-2, 136-7, 140-3; Claire Palley, *The Constitutional History and Law of Southern Rhodesia, 1888-1965*, pp.105, 121 n.4.

15 Johnston, *South Central Africa*, p.257; Gelfand, *Mother Patrick*, pp.84, 125-7, 136-60; Jones, *Rhodesian Genesis*, p.66; *Rhodesia of Today*, pp.96-7; *Mashonaland Herald*, 27 August 1892.

16 Gelfand, *Mother Patrick*, pp.70-3; 194-5; Jones, *Rhodesian Genesis*, pp.63-4; Finlason, *Mashonaland*, pp.224-6; Taylor, *Rhodesian Entertainment*, pp.20-1; Boggie, *Civilizing Rhodesia*, pp.111, 114-16; Blennerhassett and Sleeman, *Adventures in Mashonaland*, ch.5-8; Lewis and Edwards, *Church of the Province of South Africa*, pp.716-17.

17 Oliver Ransford, *Bulawayo, Historic Battleground of Rhodesia*, pp.67-8 (for the preceding description, pp.61-8); Knight, *Rhodesia of Today*, p.46.

18 Ransford, *Bulawayo*, pp.68, 71-7 (and between pages 36 and 37 for an illustration of the cartoon); Knight, *Rhodesia of Today*, p.47; CO 468/1, BSA Co Report for 1894-5, pp.64, 71; Boggie, *Civilizing Rhodesia*, p.222; *Buluwayo Chronicle*, 12 October 1894. The *Chronicle* used this spelling at first, but changed to *Bulawayo* on 7 March 1896. The two cyclostyled papers were called *The Matabele Times and Mining Journal* and *The Matabeleland News and Mining Record*.

19 Knight, *Rhodesia of Today*, pp.33-4, gave this early description of Gwelo: "When I passed through it the township consisted of one mud, thatched hut—the post-office and hotel combined, but since then a number of stands have been purchased from the Company, and building is rapidly progressing."

20 Brown, *South African Frontier*, pp.119-20, 122, 141-2; Jones, *Rhodesian Genesis*, pp.38, 47; Hole, *Old Rhodesian Days*, pp.37-8; Adrian Darter, *The Pioneers of Mashonaland*, pp.108, 112.

21 E.P. Mathers, *Zambesia: England's Eldorado in Africa*, pp.376-8; *Rhodesia Herald*, 29 October 1892 and 19 November 1892. Though anyone could peg, claims had a sale value because (a) late comers thought that the wealth lay in the ground already pegged, and (b) companies and syndicates tried to accumulate claims.

22 CO 468/1, BSA Co. Report for 1894-5, pp.47.-9, 51-60; Knight, *Rhodesia of Today*, pp.67, 80, 91-106; Darter, *Pioneers of Mashonaland*, p.109.

23 CO 468/1, BSA Co. Report for 1895-5, pp.43-6, 50; *Rhodesia Herald*, Mining Reports, passim; Johnson, *Great Days*, p.209; Hole, *Old Rhodesian Days*, pp.97-8; Knight, *Rhodesia of Today*, p.36. There was no secret about the difference in yield between Rhodesia and the Rand: the *Buluwayo Chronicle*, 14 December 1895, gave the Rand output for the month of November, 1895, as 195,218 oz.

24 John Hays Hammond, *Autobiography of John Hays Hammond*, vol. I, pp.277-80, 288-90.

25 1 morgen = 2.11654 acres or 0.85655 hectare.

26 The promise was indeed incorporated in Johnson's contract with the company; by Clause 17 the Company bound itself to obtain, as soon as it was in a position to do so, 1,500 morgen for each member of the contractor's force. But the contractor agreed not to give this promise in writing to any of the members—to have done so, when the Company had no right to the land, would have invited trouble. By Clause 18 the grantee was required to reside on his grant. Thus the Pioneers had no written promise of land, but were given the promise orally by Johnson. Hence the altercation described in the following sentences. (Johnson, *Great Days*, p.330, Appendix E.)

27 BSA Co. Papers, LO 5/2/21, pp.236-47. This speculation is supported by other documents, e.g. LO 5/2/22, pp.283-4. For de Waal and his farm, see de Waal, *Rhodes in Mashonaland*, p.216.

28 BSA Co. Papers, LO 5/2/8, pp.333-5; LO 5/2/18, pp.12-16; LO 5/2/19, pp.144-5; LO 5/2/25, pp.352-6; LO 5/2/26, p.210; LO 5/2/37, pp.252-4; R.H. Palmer, "The Making and Implementation of Land Policy in Rhodesia, 1890-1936" (Ph.D. thesis, University of London), p.56; R.H. Palmer, "Aspects of Rhodesian Land Policy, 1890-1936" (Central Africa Historical Association Local Series 22), pp.9-10; Brown, *South African Frontier*, pp.120, 168, 174-5; Jones, *Rhodesian Genesis*, pp.54-5; Tanser, *Scantling of Time*, pp.74-5; Finlason, *Mashonaland*, p.192; de Waal, *Rhodes in Mashonaland*, p.216; *Mashonaland Herald*, 10 October 1891; T.O. Ranger, *Revolt in Southern Rhodesia, 1896-7*, p.104.

29 Knight, *Rhodesia of Today*, pp.39, 47-8; Hole, *Old Rhodesian Days*, p.74; Brown, *South African Frontier*, p.305; Finlason, *Mashonaland*, p.182; Melina Rorke, *Melina Rorke: Her Amazing Experiences in the Stormy Nineties of South Africa's Story*, pp.160-1; Boggie, *Civilizing Rhodesia*, pp.188-93; *Rhodesia Herald*, 22 December 1893, 2 February 1894, 4 May 1894.

30 RH Mss Afr. s 4, ff. 135, 138, 143.

31 Jeannie M. Boggie, *Experiences of Rhodesia's Pioneer Women*, pp.133-6, 148-53, and ch.3, 4, generally; Olivier, *Many Treks*, pp.27-8, 52, 108, 114 and ch.3-11, passim; Shirley Sinclair, *The Story of Melsetter*, pp.27-8; de Waal, *Rhodes in Mashonaland*, pp.253-4; CO 468/1, BSA Co. Report for 1894-5, pp.64, 85. For P.L. van der Byl see above, ch.2.

32 For this operation as it affected the Ndebele see below, ch.10.

33 *Rhodesia Herald*, 23 February 1894, 13 April 1894, and 3, 17, 31 August 1894.

34 H. Klein, *Stage Coach Dust*, pp.166-7.

35 CO 468/1, BSA Co. Report for 1894-5, pp.64, 67-8, 71, 73, 77, 80, 85; *Rhodesia Herald*, 7 September 1894; CO 879/47/517, no.423 and encls., p.465.

36 CO 468/1, BSA Co. Report for 1894-5, pp.63, 66, 91-2; RH Mss Afr. s 4, ff. 135, 143; S.P. Hyatt, *Diary of a Soldier of Fortune*, p.120; Hole, *Old Rhodesian Days*, pp.46, 51; *Buluwayo Chronicle*, 1 February 1895, 5 April 1895, 21 June 1895.

37 *Buluwayo Chronicle*, 8 March 1895; CO 468/1, BSA Co. Report for 1894-5, p.78.

38 P.G. Reynolds, "Imperial-Racial Thought in Mid-Victorian England, 1857-69" (MA thesis, Queen's University), ch.1; Philip D. Curtin, " 'Scientific' Racism and the British Theory of Empire," *Journal of the Historical Society of Nigeria*, 2 (1960), p.42 (quoted by Reynolds, "Imperial Racial Thought," p.2); Palmer, "Aspects of Rhodesian Land Policy," p.9; BSA Co. Papers, LO 5/2/39, pp.35-8; de Waal, *Rhodes in Mashonaland*, p.105.

39 H.A.C. Cairns, *Prelude to Imperialism: British Reactions to Central African Society, 1840-90*, passim, especially ch.2.

40 F.C. Selous, *Sunshine and Storm in Rhodesia*, pp.30-1.

41 Hole, *Old Rhodesian Days*, p.22; Boggie, *Rhodesia's Pioneer Women*, pp.74, 115; Rorke, *Melina Rorke*, p.149; S.P. Hyatt, *Off the Main Track*, pp.15, 128-31; CO 468/1, BSA Co. Report for 1894-5, p.71; Report for 1897-8, p.249.

42 Thompson Papers, Diary, 6 March 1889 (Queen's, p.133); H. Vaughan-Williams, *A Visit to Lobengula in 1889*, pp.87, 97, 100-1; Foster Windram oral interviews (WI 8/1/1), Miscellaneous, evidence of H.G. Huntley and J.P. Richardson.

43 "British Missions and Missionaries in Africa," *Nineteenth Century*, November 1887, p.718, quoted in Cairns, *Prelude to Imperialism*, pp.60-1; Ranger, *Revolt in Southern Rhodesia*, pp.67, 83; Finlason, *Mashonaland*, pp.189, 320; de Waal, *Rhodes in Mashonaland*, pp.243, 271-2; Hyatt, *Off the Main Track*, p.73; H.C. Thomson, *Rhodesia and its Government*, pp.76-7.

44 Rorke, *Melina Rorke*, pp.47-8; Hyatt, *Off the Main Track*, p.70; Boggie, *Civilizing Rhodesia*, pp.169-80; D.N. Beach, "The Rising in South-Western Mashonaland," pp.201, 350-1; and see below, ch.11.

45 Hyatt, *Off the Main Track*, pp.25-6; and cf. the same author's *The Old Transport Road*, p.32.

CHAPTER 10

The Black Experience, 1890-1896

The Ndebele were a nation in arms; the Shona, in spite of their feuds and tribal wars, struck all observers as a peaceful and industrious people. The Company and its settlers "occupied" Mashonaland; they conquered Matabeleland. These differences go far to explain the different impacts of the white presence on the two provinces.

Even by 1896 many of the Shona had had little or no contact with Europeans. They were hardly inconvenienced by the building of "towns"; we remember Marshall Hole's quip that one could have passed within a hundred yards of Salisbury without noticing it. Very little space was occupied by the miners, busy on their reef or alluvial claims. The taking of land by farmers would have been a different matter, but for reasons which were noted in the last chapter very little land had been taken from the Shona in fact, whatever dispossessions there may have been on paper. "Every fellah" liked to rejoice in the ownership of 1,500 morgen, but none of those who travelled to Umtali with C.E. Finlason late in 1891 knew within fifty miles where his farm was. Two and a half years later the group of ten farms east of Salisbury, each with "portions" cultivated, was said to be unique in the country.[1] With no access to markets, and with the dream of golden riches not yet faded, the settlers were too busy on their mining claims to bother about farming. And from 1894 they were deserting even those for the supposedly fabulous riches of Matabeleland. Except for the almost invisible surveyor's pegs, the land was left to its original owners.

It is therefore unnecessary, in this early period, to debate the question whether or not the whites and the Shona had different preferences in types of soil. As the whites as yet cultivated hardly any soil, the Shona could cultivate where they pleased. They were not being pushed off their land.

To this generalization there was of course one conspicuous exception, though it was not strictly in Mashonaland: the district of Melsetter. There were more settlers on the land there than in the whole of northern Mashonaland; they were all real farmers and had families; they were mainly Afrikaners from the republics—*vaBunu* to the Shona—and respect for the property rights of "Kaffirs" was not in their tradition. They parcelled out most of the district in complete disregard of such rights.

The Ndau of Melsetter were the exception. In general, the old Shona way of life went on without fundamental change. Classic descriptions of it were written by W.H. Brown, as for instance of one of Mashayamombe's villages early in 1892. His account of a hut shows both the continuity with the past and Brown's own powers of observation:

> The roof was thatched with grass on top of a framework made of long slender poles placed closely side by side, and reaching from the top of the wall of the hut upward and inward, until all converged at a point directly over the centre of the floor, the entire framework being bound firmly together with bark. The roof really resembled a great conical basket turned upside down, so that its apex pointed skyward, while the large open rim rested over the top of the wall of the hut. The thatch was made of long grass, placed with its tops downward, extending in layers from the highest point down to about two feet beyond the wall. The thatching was so skilfully done that not a drop of water could enter during a hard rainstorm. The floor was made of pot-clay obtained from large ant-heaps, and it had been beaten down smooth and hard; in fact, it was so hard that the destructive white ants could not penetrate from below.[2]

And so on to the sleeping and eating arrangements, the supper menu, the firelight and the smoke, the garments, ornaments, utensils, storage bins, marriage customs, manners, and conversation.

More significant for our purpose are Brown's impressions as he approached the village: " . . . the path wound through fields of mealies, Kafir corn, rukwaza (a sort of millet), sweet potatoes, pumpkins, peanuts, and then across rice-beds in the marshes . . . Small boys were driving homeward herds of little Mashona goats and cattle which they had been minding during the day in the meadows between the fields of grain." This was in the immediate neighbourhood of Hartley Hills, one of the Pioneers' favourite mining areas.[3] Most parts of the country were in even less danger of disturbance.

In 1896 there was said to be "practically no permanent white population" in Lomagundi—though the outbreak of the rebellion did reveal the presence of a few Europeans. One of the dramas of the rebellion would involve some whites in the Mazoe valley, but farmers had hardly disturbed that district either. In October 1892 the *Rhodesia Herald* wrote of the valley: "The hillsides in many places have been cultivated almost to the summit by the natives . . . Here and there are a few farmhouses, or, rather, farm huts, of one or two of the Pioneers, who have chosen stock farming . . . A couple of Kafir villages are in sight on the banks of the stream leading to the gorge, which from end to end is fringed with gardens, now well in progress."[4] It is true that this was reported in 1892, but by 1896 there were fewer, not more, whites in Mashonaland. Always with the exceptions of Melsetter, of the mini-Melsetter round Enkeldoorn, and of some spots near Salisbury, the Shona were not disturbed in the possession of their land.

Matabeleland was different. The reason was not merely the Victoria Agreement. By that agreement every volunteer was entitled to his 3,000 morgen, and he could peg the farm wherever he liked. He invariably did so in the area with the best soil and climate, the highveld within a sixty-mile radius of Bulawayo. That was exactly the area that had appealed to the Ndebele and had been their "heartland." The 1,070 farms pegged by 1895 covered an area of over 10,000 square miles, identical with the region settled by the Ndebele. "Before many weeks had passed," Alexander Boggie wrote of the end of the war, "the country for sixty miles and more around Bulawayo was located as farms."[5]

This did not mean, however, that white farmers were immediately superimposed on the inhabitants. The volunteers, and those who bought their rights, could be absentee owners. As was shown in the last chapter, by March 1895 only 150 of those farms were occupied. Many of the others had been absorbed into the estates of the big companies and syndicates. The change of ownership did not in itself mean the displacement of most of the Ndebele, but there were other factors which, in combination with the pegging, placed them in a very different situation from their neighbours in Mashonaland.

The most obvious was the war itself. The Ndebele were not displaced by a stealthy, creeping "occupation." They were dealt a blow which sent women and children with a few possessions, as well as defeated regiments, fleeing to the northeast, the northwest, or the Matopos. When the fighting was over they drifted back, commonly to find their villages (always, if they were military towns) destroyed. It is unlikely that there was any volunteer who did not know within fifty miles where his farm was. Though they might become absentees, they were swarming over Matabeleland as soon as they were demobilized, every farm-pegger for himself and the Devil take the hindmost. This was at the very time when the Ndebele were returning to their former homes. They were quickly informed that they were now living on white men's farms. An official of the Native Affairs Department wrote later that the word *amaplazi* (farms, from the Afrikaans *plase*) "stands, it may be said, for almost all that is most distasteful in our rule. Almost it stands for helotage and servitude to a chance-made master."[6]

The fact of dispossession, even if it did not result at once in physical expulsion, was enough to arouse bitter resentment. In most cases there was no physical expulsion. Many of the farmers in occupation regarded the "resident natives" as a valuable reservoir of labour. Absentee owners, and especially the companies, saw them in the same light. But there were exceptions. "Several white farmers," the *Buluwayo Chronicle* reported in August 1895, did not like to have natives residing on their farms. Though they might be a source of labour, they were not accustomed to working "year in and year out." They did not pay rent, or compensate the farmer adequately for using his land. Many farmers therefore would rather have their land to themselves, and get labourers from elsewhere through the native commissioners. The *Chronicle* in an understatement said that it was "rather awkward for the natives who settle on a farm and after being there three or four months are told by the farmer to quit, and the same treatment may follow them in the next three or four places they settle." The constant moving not only made them discontented, but made it impossible for them to grow their own food; and not only their own, but food for sale to the whites, who depended on them for it.[7]

These points were set forth by the *Chronicle* in support of its complaint that nothing had been done to implement the recommendations of the Land Commission of 1894. That commission had demarcated two "native reserves." Why were people not moving into them?

In most of South Africa, and even to an extent in Mashonaland after this time, it was usual to define as reserves areas that were actually occupied by Africans. Matabeleland was peculiar in that the two reserves of 1894 were specifically the parts of the country that were *not* so occupied. The paradox is worth a little examination.

The Matabeleland Order-in-Council of 18 July 1894 provided for a Land Commission that was "to assign land sufficient and suitable for the personal and individual agricultural and grazing requirements of the natives" of Matabeleland. The commission consisted of the judge (Joseph Vintcent), Capt. C.F. Lindsell representing the imperial government, and Capt. H.M. Heyman representing the Company. It held its first meeting in Bulawayo on 15 September. Long before that date the commissioners would have known that the Company had "made many grants of land to Europeans in portions of the country where the natives formerly resided, and are in many cases still residing." This point established, they looked (on a map made by Stanford for George Cawston) for the nearest unallotted areas, and found them on the Shangani, where Wilson's patrol had died, and on the Gwaai to the northwest. On the very day of the first meeting Lindsell wired to Bower in Cape Town that he and Vintcent were going to inspect those areas. All that they saw of the first was a section of the south bank of the Shangani and a route back from that river to Lake Alice, across a terrain which they, on their own sketch map, described as "covered with dense forest." They did not go to the Gwaai at all.

Back in Bulawayo, and joined now by Heyman, they called in witnesses. It is very obvious that the commissioners did not listen to these with open minds. They had decided where the reserves were to be before they had either heard or seen any evidence. The evidence of each witness, as reported, consisted of a series of statements about the conditions in various places. Such statements could have been made only in reply to a corresponding series of questions. Unlike the published proceedings of most commissions of enquiry, this one omits the questions, but it is not unlikely that many of them were leading questions. The commissioners knew the answers that they wanted, and they believed they had got them.

Though African custom and etiquette notoriously require, in answer to a question, the reply which the questioner is believed to want, the commission deceived itself in thinking that this is what it got from the witnesses. Readers of its report need not be deceived.

The names of the witnesses carry weight. Among them were such distinguished indunas as Mtshane, Ingubogubo, Somabhulana, and Mazwe, three of whom would take up arms eighteen months later because of what had been done or not done in 1894. Another witness was Colenbrander. From all of them the commission heard what it wanted to hear. The indunas said that Lobengula's intention before Forbes pursued him had been to settle with his people on the Shangani. (Sir Richard Martin afterwards pointed out that this might have been his intention, but only because he had no other option.) The evidence could be made to confirm the wisdom of Lobengula's choice. "The Shangani district is splendid for cattle" (Ingubogubo). "The country on the Shangani, below the Drift, where the King crossed, is good for agriculture, there being lots of garden ground" (Mtshane). As for the Gwaai, afterwards shown to be almost desert, Mazwe testified that "we can always get water, there is plenty of it. The country to the north of the Manzaniana, and to the south-west of the junction of the Gway and Kami Rivers, is well-watered . . . The country to the west of the Gway is a beautiful cattle country, and was the King's principal cattle run." And so on.

There were other pieces of evidence, however, which it would be charitable to think the commissioners did not notice or understand. In many cases the lavish praise was bestowed on portions of a river, or on other areas, which were *not* included by the commissioners in the reserves. Thus Mtshane: "The country round the Gwampa and Bubi river is good for agriculture; the Bubi river is, in my opinion, the better of the two. The Gwampa is feverish, but it is good for cattle." (The Gwampa became the southern boundary of the reserve but the Bubi was excluded from it.) Mtshane again: "The Karna is a very feverish country . . . The ground between the Karna and Shangani on the upper part of the two streams [which was included in the reserve] is thickly wooded, sandy, and not good for agriculture." These opinions were confirmed by Ingubogubo: "The country between the Shangani and Karna Rivers that I know is sandy and heavily timbered . . . In winter [it] is good for cattle, but not in summer, because the grass becomes very rank and the cattle can't eat it. The Karna and Pupu districts [which were included in the reserve] are not good for agriculture." There were many more such statements which in some way escaped the commissioners' notice. It may have been a little easier for them to be misled by what the witnesses said about the Gwaai. Yet Stanford on his map had written across a part of the future Gwaai reserve: "Dangerous to cross with cattle (Oct. to Dec.) owing to a poisonous lily."[8] Though the map was full of inaccuracies the commissioners could hardly plead them as an excuse, as they seem not to have noticed any of them. So they placed the Shangani and Gwaai reserves on the map: 3,500 and 3,000 square miles respectively.

That the defeated Ndebele had fled in those directions might almost suggest that they had chosen the reserves themselves. But some had concentrated in the Matopos, and there was no question of making a reserve there. "It would be most inadvisable," said Colenbrander, "to mark off a location in these hills. They are natural strongholds, and offer many opportunities for hiding stolen cattle; besides, . . . private farms have been pegged off."

So we are brought back to the basic reason for choosing feverish or drought-stricken areas for reserves. Colenbrander stated that "there are many Matabele and Maholies on farms which have been pegged off by whites. These people are there with the consent, as far as I know, of the owners and are now hoeing the ground." Somabhulana's evidence supported this: "My people are scattered all over the country; some live on white men's ground, and are ploughing. I am living on a white man's farm." Jameson afterwards explained: "Most of them I permitted, for this year [1894] at all events, to remain in their former localities, a few moving to localities selected by themselves removed away from the high roads and present gold workings. All this I have explained to them is temporary . . . All the chiefs seem perfectly satisfied and very friendly." The commissioners got the same impression: "the natives occupying the farms are contented, and have expressed no desire to move elsewhere." That is to say, they had no desire to leave the land on which they had always lived. That they were "contented" that the whites had taken possession of it is another question.[9]

In any case none of them moved into the reserves. After the rebellion in Matabeleland was over, the deputy commissioner, Sir Richard Martin, was asked to report on the "suitability" of those reserves. He pointed out many of the discrepancies between evidence and conclusion which have been shown here, and quoted other evidence, which he collected, of the fever in one case and the drought in the other. His discoveries were made three years too late.[10]

The Land Commission had been ordered to report on cattle as well as on land. Though it took evidence on the subject, it recommended that "the distribution of cattle for the needs of the natives . . . be left in abeyance for some period." Before any reasonable distribution could be made, officials would have to report from each district on the numbers of natives and of cattle. As the report was written in October 1894, its advice on this subject, too, amounted to locking the stable door after the horse—or the cow—had gone.

In the nature of the case it is harder now, and was harder at the time, to discover the truth about the cattle than the truth about the land. The statistics vary widely from one source to another; the actions of the Company and its agents differed widely from the policies and regulations which it proclaimed, and, it is to be feared, from some of the reports which its agents afterwards gave of the actions.

The Victoria Agreement had made no nice distinctions among the cattle of the Ndebele: all cattle captured would be "loot." The fighting had hardly ceased when newspapers in England reported that the victors were seizing cattle from the vanquished. Ripon, the secretary of state, protested. Back came the reply, through Loch: the cattle seized were Lobengula's; seizing them was the best way to prove to the Ndebele that they were defeated.

This point was debated for years, though the evidence of the indunas before the Land Commission was unequivocal. Mtshane: "the bulk of the cattle were King's. Very few people had private cattle." Ingubogubo: "most of the cattle in the country were King's cattle." Every witness agreed to this. They were unanimous on all the essential points. The king's cattle were apportioned among the military towns and villages for herding, and the people had the use of the milk. "There were some natives who had private cattle, but it was dangerous to have too many as it meant 'smelling out'." A private owner in the king's time might have had ten head; Mtshane, a very eminent man, had not more than 100; Ingubogubo had about 200. Many individuals had none.

They were asked how to distinguish the royal from the private cattle, and all agreed that it would now be impossible to distinguish them even though "each military kraal had a special mark for the King's cattle." By the time the commission met there had been so much wrongful appropriation by all parties that the confusion had become impenetrable.

As with land, so however with cattle, the Company men had not waited for the commission's report before acting. The seizures that began during the war were indiscriminate. After the war all appropriations were described as "King's cattle." Jameson gave the assurance, however, that in all cases where Ndebele had submitted they were allowed to keep sufficient cattle for their requirements. Ripon was not satisfied but wanted detailed information of the numbers. It would be two years before details were available, and the difficulty in understanding what happened is due partly to the fact that the statistics of December 1895 do not explain the situation of December 1893.[11]

In the confusion following the war there appears to have been what Martin afterwards called a "wholesale seizure of cattle." Detailed evidence is difficult to come by, but the process can be illustrated by the case of the Tati Concession. This area was specifically, by the charter, excluded from the BSA Company's sphere, but it belonged to Lobengula and its people were his subjects. Therefore, the Company reasoned, their cattle were the king's and were part of the loot. After the war no less a person than Herbert Taylor, the future chief native commissioner, entered the concession and proceeded to brand cattle with the Company's brand.[12] As he had stepped outside his own bailiwick there was in this case someone to report the event and to tell Taylor to desist— Charles Vigers, the Tati Concession Company's general manager. Taylor went away, but Thomas, another native commissioner, came. He proved to Viger's satisfaction that the branded cattle had in fact been the king's, but it then appeared that the Company intended to take the unbranded cattle as well. A long correspondence followed. To take one instance: Sabina, a Kalaka chief in the Concession, was ordered to send all the king's cattle in his charge to Mang-we. He sent about thirty, but was afterwards made to surrender others, and by the beginning of 1895 was complaining that he had no cattle left. At the end of that year Company officials were still seizing cattle in the Tati district.[13]

The operation took a long time. On 1 April 1895 Goold-Adams arrived in Bulawayo and found that Gampu, the last induna to surrender, had just come in, bringing a thousand of the king's cattle. All through the previous year the process had been going on. The Ndebele, Loch wrote, "drive in the King's cat-tle, and in other instances state where the King's cattle are herding, and when asked what cattle they themselves possess, they at once point out the distinc-tion, and state the number of cattle they have of their own and at their kraals."

Strange, then, that at the very time this was happening the indunas were tell-ing the Land Commission that it was impossible to distinguish the two catego-ries. The Company claimed, most of the time, that while the distinction was sharp in principle it was impossible to make in practice. Its policy therefore was to treat *all* the cattle as the king's, to claim ownership of all, but to con-cede that when both the information and the cattle had been collected "suffi-cient" would be returned to the Ndebele for their needs. The Land Commis-sion approved of this policy as the only practicable one. Martin afterwards pointed out that it would have been easier to distinguish the king's cattle from the rest than to discover what each individual was entitled to.[14]

The Company appears to have acquired the cattle in three ways. First, pa-trols went out and "seized" cattle, always described as the king's, and brought them in to the "loot kraals." Second, the people themselves, as described above in Loch's dispatch, brought in what they admitted were the king's. As the numbers in the loot kraals became unmanageable, the people who thus came in were told to take the cattle back and care for them on behalf of the Company, as they formerly had on the king's behalf. Third, when the counting was done, no distinction was made between this last category and the cattle claimed as private property. As all were enumerated together, all were equally at the Company's disposal. The constant harping on the distinction between the king's and private cattle seems to have had no other purpose—in which it did not entirely succeed—than to confuse the secretary of state.

It would have been better to omit this hypocrisy. The Company argued as if the distinction were the same as would be drawn in Western legal systems. A conqueror takes over the property of the defeated government, but not the property of the citizens. Ndebele ideas of ownership were different. Private ownership of cattle was very important for certain purposes, most of all for the payment of *lobola* which gave legal effect to marriage. But in other ways the differences might be blurred. No man could slaughter a beast of the king's without his permission, but, Mtshane told the Land Commission, "it was most unusual for us to slaughter our own cattle . . . We used to get our meat from the King . . . Occasionally the King would give a few cattle for us to slaughter, but not often. The staple food was grain and milk. We would sometimes kill a goat or a sheep." As for milk, it could be taken either from one's own or from the royal cows. The Company afterwards pretended that it had in this matter merely taken Lobengula's place, but that was absurd. Could the Company personify the nation or propitiate its ancestors?

Leaving the king's herds in charge of their former custodians was, in another way, a fraudulent substitute for the old system. It was never intended or admitted to be anything but a temporary expedient. Drafts were made on this stock to keep the loot kraals full or to make various irregular distributions. The native commissioners appointed towards the end of 1894, as a result of the Land Commission's report, were ordered to summon meetings of headmen in their districts and to explain to them that the cattle were to be held by the people in trust for the Company; that the people were to have the milk; that permission could be given to anyone to sell a beast in order to buy grain, clothing or food, and to headmen to slaughter cattle for their own use. The native commissioners were also to send in to the government fifty cattle a month from each district. These seem to have been taken without regard to the fact that the Ndebele "still considered some of the cattle claimed by the Company but left in their charge as their own property, and the result of these cattle-collecting visits of the Native police must have kept them in a continual state of dread and uncertainty. They never knew when the next drain would be made on the herd in their possession, nor how soon they might be deprived of those cattle that they considered their own."

The Company, however, was not the only despoiler. As the Ndebele power collapsed, cattle-rustlers of all descriptions moved in. The term is inappropriate for the Shona allies, who merely seized the opportunity to recover what the Ndebele had taken from them over the years, but they would have been no more discriminating than the Company in what they took. Moreover the *amahole* in Matabeleland itself, who before the war possessed few if any cattle, now took all they could, and in many cases made off to Mashonaland with them.

The white volunteers, observing that "if this thieving continued it would mean so much less for the members of the column," preferred not to wait for the Company's "loot certificates." Some of them wired to Rhodes and got his permission to seize what they could, giving half to the Company. At one kraal, where the "King's cattle" turned out to be "one very old bull and one older cow," while some 300 head were privately owned, the raiding party refused to be deceived but seized the lot, so that "these natives were disposed to be rather nasty." At another kraal this party collected "some 1500 head," seventy-two for each man.

Other cattle-rustlers and "unscrupulous traders" came up from the south. Their ploy was the plausible story that the government intended to confiscate all the cattle; this was enough to induce the owners or guardians to sell at low prices while the going was good. It must have been easy to get these cattle into the Transvaal, though police were patrolling the Limpopo to prevent it. As late as January 1895 the magistrate at Tati reported that he had stopped over 300 looted Ndebele cattle which were being driven through the bush; he thought that many others must have been taken through undetected. Some of Gampu's people had been reported, in August 1894, to be selling cattle in the Tati district.

During 1895 the native commissioners were counting the people and the cattle, and by October their returns were in. They had counted all the cattle in the possession, or custody, of the people at that time; that is to say all that were left after the seizures by the Company, the volunteers, the Shona allies, and the *amahole*, and the sales to the "unscrupulous traders," the Tati people and various privileged individuals. The total came to 74,600, of which 40,930 were earmarked for Ndebele private owners "as their absolute property," 700 were set aside as police rations, and 32,970 were to be retained by the Company for distribution as "loot." No such precise figures exist for the operations which took place before this counting. Grey told Martin that "the Company had possessed themselves of about 80,000 head of cattle previous to the rebellion, but Mr. Carnegie asserts that some 200,000 head had been taken previous to the distribution in December 1895." Though Carnegie could not swear to that number, he was sure that enough had been taken to give the Ndebele the impression that they would lose all in the end. Early in 1894 Rhodes gave a "rough estimate" of 200,000 cattle in the country, and reckoned that from 20,000 to 30,000 of these belonged to private owners.

On the Company's own admission, these figures mean that it had taken possession of nearly 50,000 head before the counting began, and that some 75,000 more had disappeared. We may be sure that the figures are conservative. Carnegie's could be nearer the mark.

In December 1895, after the proposals had been explained to a meeting of some two hundred indunas and headmen, who declared themselves satisfied, the distribution of the 40,930 to the Ndebele was undertaken by the native commissioners. The distribution was "almost complete" when the rinderpest struck. The Company managed to make the worst even of this operation. The cattle distributed were branded and registered, which made the people suspect that they were destined to be taken back.[15]

In the meantime steps had been taken to stop the leaks and to legalize the whole process. At the beginning of 1895 the Administrative Council drew up its "Sale and Disposal of Stock Regulations," by which no person might acquire stock "from any native" without written permission from a magistrate. As the high commissioner was advised that such regulations discriminated between races, they could not take effect until the secretary of state authorized them on 21 February. They cannot have been very effective.

On 15 June 1895 Robinson issued a proclamation giving effect to the Land

Commission's proposals. The Shangani and Gwaai reserves were proclaimed. As for the cattle, the ownership of "all such cattle as were in Matabeleland on or before the 31st of December, 1893, and the offspring of such cattle . . . now in the possession of any native resident in Matabeleland" was vested in the Company.

In 1897 Sir Richard Martin made his report on the causes of the rebellion. Some of his remarks on the cattle question have been quoted. He thought that "a fatal mistake" had been made in treating all cattle as the king's and taking them all for the Company. He was sure that the operation had caused "universal discontent" even if it was "perhaps concealed." Then, whatever might be said of the fairness of the distribution undertaken in December 1895, the authorities by maintaining their Sale and Disposal Regulations *after* the distribution aroused distrust in their intentions.

That the confiscation of cattle from the Ndebele was one of the causes of the rebellion is a truism. What is less often realised is that they were confiscated from the Shona too.

After the war the Shona had fallen upon the Ndebele herds to recoup the losses they had suffered in many raids, and *amahole* had crossed into Mashonaland with what stock they were able to seize. The high commissioner's proclamation in June 1895 vested the ownership of all cattle that had been in Matabeleland at the end of 1893 in the Company. Therefore many of the cattle which the Company, in law if not in equity, owned were in Mashonaland. The Sale and Disposal of Stock Regulations did not mention boundaries; they applied to the whole of the Company's territory. The Shona were no more allowed than the Ndebele to sell stock. On the excuse that cattle must have been stolen from Matabeleland the police could seize them in the other province as well.[16]

In one of his letters to C.E.J. Webb, Robert Vavasseur asked for some questions to be put in the House of Commons (by "some respectable M.P. not Labby"). Among them was this: "Is it not the fact that all the cattle sheep and goats which the Mashuna at some kraals in the Charter district possessed before the Matabele war have been taken by the BSA Co.'s police? . . . It is a fact that the BSA Police have taken all the stock belonging to the natives in this district, which they owned before the war, and that not in payment of hut tax but in a simple raid conducted by men who could not speak the language."[17]

Not in payment of hut tax . . .

The impecunious Company had been thirsting for this tax for a long time. As nothing in the concessions authorized it, it could not be imposed without imperial authority. About the time of the Victoria incident Maguire wrote to Rhodes that "this bother with Lobengula is a nuisance just when we are pressing for a hut tax." When the smoke had blown away the ordinance drafted in 1893 was brought out and pressed again on the Colonial Office, which decided in June 1894 to approve it. The Company claimed that the conquest of Matabeleland implied the conquest of its dependency Mashonaland. The Crown could not admit that the fruits of conquest could accrue to private persons; but the practical objection to taxing the Shona—the offence to Lobengula—had been removed.

The hut tax was a standard device in colonial Africa. Its rationale was that every wife in a polygynous marriage had her own hut, that the number of a man's wives, and therefore huts, gave a rough indication of his wealth and status, that huts were easily visible and countable, and that to tax each hut was to tax its owner in proportion to his wealth. Though this reasoning was an over-simplification, the objection to the tax arose not from the principle of assessment but from the very fact of taxation by an alien power, and for purposes which the taxpayers ("without representation") rejected. In some colonies, such as Basutoland, the tax was willingly paid. Hut taxes had been imposed, for instance, in Natal, Zululand, and Bechuanaland. The Company now drafted an ordinance based on the last two of these precedents.

There were too many precedents for the Colonial Office to object to the tax in principle. A few minor amendments were made, permission to impose the tax was provided by the Matabeleland Order-in-Council of 18 July 1894, the Company's ordinance was issued on 27 July, and took effect in September. By this law every male African was to pay a tax of ten shillings a year for each hut occupied by him, by one of his wives, or by "any woman of the kraal of any such native" during any part of the year. The tax was to be paid in sterling coin, but where this was impossible grain or stock, valued at the prices prevailing in the nearest market, could be accepted. The ordinance would not apply to Matabeleland until the recommendations of the Land Commission had been made and implemented. The first payment (for half a year only) would fall due in Mashonaland on 1 October 1894.[18]

The tax was meant, as in the other colonies that imposed it, to serve two purposes. Of course it was supposed to help to pay for the Company's administrative expenses, but it had also another and not less important purpose. People living in a subsistence economy had no money. To obtain money for the tax they might sell grain or stock (or in the first instance pay the tax directly in these commodities), but they would naturally be unwilling to deplete their supplies of these beyond a certain point. Then the only alternative would be to go out and work for wages. The hut tax was the classic instrument for producing a supply of labour.

So pressing were these needs that the acting administrator, Duncan, did not even wait for the order-in-council or the ordinance before putting the collecting machinery into operation in March. The Colonial Office took note, and required a clause in the ordinance providing that anything paid before the collection became legal was to be credited to the taxpayer.

The process of tax-collection, it is hardly necessary to say, was of the *ad-hoc*, hand-to-mouth, filibustering type characteristic of the Company's proceedings. When the collection began illegally in March 1894 the collectors were whatever agents were available in each locality—mounted police, mining commissioners, field-cornets, or, in default of these, farmers empowered to collect "on a share basis." The taxpayers resisted the operation in every way they could. Some of the collectors were little better than bandits, making as much profit as possible out of the job.

By the time the tax had been made legal it had become obvious that the collection would have to be regularized. During the second half of 1894 the essential steps were taken: J.S. Brabant, interpreter at Fort Victoria, Shona linguist, and "rough diamond," was appointed native commissioner with a staff of hut tax collectors under him; the collectors were soon called native commissioners and Brabant chief native commissioner. The commissioners at their discretion collected staffs of African policemen who were called "messengers," provided with whatever arms their employer could find, and paid ten shillings a month and rations. "Wiri" Edwards dressed his in second-hand red infantry tunics. In 1895 these messengers were reinforced by fifty Ndebele from the new police of the other province. The "Native Department" had come into existence.[19]

Its tone was set by its chief. When the Budjga of the Mtoko district forcefully resisted the first collectors, Brabant organized an expedition of white police and Shona "friendlies" to bring them to heel. Four of the local commissioner's messengers, dressed in cricket blazers and second-hand boots, came out to meet the force. Brabant, who was enraged "to see a raw native wearing boots," had these men and the rest of the African staff flogged for their failure to bring in the tax. Chief Gurupira was then sent for and upbraided.

> One of the counsellors said something to which Brabant evidently took exception and on continuing to be insolent Brabant took a jambok out of a police boy's hand and struck him with it. Immediately Guripira and his counsellors made a dash for liberty but most of them were stopped. MaGuripira then opened a box he had brought with him and displayed a helmet and breastplate of brass together with a sword and belt and sabretash; this he offered to Brabant as a peace-offering, but Brabant spurned it with his foot and called upon everybody to go raiding the country . . . He explained to Guripira that he could either go in person or send his counsellors to tell his people that we were going to burn and shoot everything we saw until he sent to stop us and ask for mercy, but that before we would cease he would have to fill the valley with cattle for us to pick from for hut tax and that he was also to furnish us with 200 of his picked men to go and work in the mines . . . We then proceeded down the valley in search of something to destroy. The police boys and messengers and camp followers scattered over the hills and burnt down all the kraals they came across until the whole atmosphere was dense with smoke of burning rapoko and other corn and grass . . . We returned to camp to find the valley literally full of cattle, all lowing and bellowing.

The tax was collected in cattle and goats, Gurupira had also to pay a fine in cattle, and 500 men were taken away to work in the mines.[20]

Though tax collection was in most cases less violent than in Mtoko, there was more of this kind than was good for the peace of the country, as the astonished whites were soon to discover. The tax could be paid in money, cattle, or other movable property, or labour. The official figures do not make the distinction, but it is likely that in the early years payment was usually in cattle or goats. Labour was exacted too, either for private employers or for work on the roads, but it is impossible to find statistics of this form of payment.

Vavasseur accused the Company of seizing cattle in the Charter district "not in payment of hut tax but in a simple raid." Simple raids had been conducted in Mashonaland ever since the end of the war, to take the cattle that the Shona were accused of "stealing" from Matabeleland, where all had become the Company's property. To the Shona the distinction between a simple raid and a tax-collection must have seemed a fine one. For tax-collection alone, D.N. Beach gives the figures for the Tuli, Victoria, and Charter districts from August 1894 to December 1895: 3,903 cattle and 5,655 sheep and goats collected. These numbers represented about a third of the cattle and a quarter of the sheep and goats owned: capital levies of about 24 per cent and 18 per cent per annum respectively. The total depletion of the stock would not be in the interest of the treasury any more than of the taxpayer. When, therefore, H.M. Taberer succeeded Brabant as chief native commissioner, Mashonaland, in November 1895, one of his first circulars (No. 10) instructed his officials to avoid taking any more cattle in payment. "If possible you are requested to make a point of instilling into the minds of the Natives the idea that the Government are not anxious to take their cattle as payment for hut tax, but that it would be for the good of the Natives themselves and of their districts that they should earn by labour the money with which to pay their tax."[21]

The tax was not collected in Matabeleland; the rebellion broke out before the conditions required in that province by the ordinance had been realised. Ndebele cattle were seized on a different excuse. But the indirect object of the tax, to provide a supply of labour, was attained in Matabeleland, and for that matter in Mashonaland too, by more direct means.

In our survey of the white community we saw why it was dependent on black labour. Some of that labour was imported from Mozambique or the south—Shangaans, "Zambezi boys," "Cape boys," and "Colonial natives." But there would never be enough of those to supply the mass of unskilled labour for mines and farms. It would have to be supplied by the local population. We have seen too that one segment of that population, the *amahole* or servile element in Matabeleland, did provide some labour for Mashonaland, as well as Kimberley and the Rand, from the beginning. Many of them were willing to change masters, but the independent peasants of Mashonaland, not to mention the proud Ndebele warriors, were another question. Their slight contact with the material culture of the West might create a demand for a few European artifacts, as indeed it had been doing for many years before 1890, but not so great a demand as to make a man willing to work full-time for long periods to gratify it. The hut tax provided a stimulus that was harder to evade.

Before it was introduced, individual employers applied their own pressures, negotiating with neighbouring chiefs, offering inducements or threatening force. "The whole gamut of persuasion and compulsion was run, with varying degrees of success." Many people in Umtali, the magistrate reported, went out to the villages pretending to be officials, brought in a supply of "boys," and when their month was drawing to an end ill-treated them so that they ran away without waiting for their wages. Duncan, the acting administrator, told Heyman that the refusal of employers to pay the wages due was one of the reasons for the difficulty in getting labour; consequently "I cannot consent to your firing upon any kraal for the purpose of getting labourers." In March 1893 a headman at Amanda's kraal (Mazoe) replied to a demand for "boys" that "his men were not going to work for white men and that if Police came he would fire on them." Police came, arrested the headman, fined him six goats and three cattle, and gave him fifty lashes in the presence of his people.

The assumption by native commissioners of the duty of recruiting labour did not end the abuses. "I have sent word to most of the Chiefs in the lower part of the district to send boys for mine work, and expect a regular supply about the middle of February," the native commissioner, Victoria, wrote in October 1895. Three months later the mining commissioner, Lomagundi, reported that "a practice obtains in the Native Department of sending Native Constables to collect boys to work, unaccompanied by the Native Commissioner or an assistant, and power so placed in the hands of Native Constables is very liable to be abused, and this is just what is taking place if the reports which reach me indirectly are true." About the same time a similar practice was reported to have prevailed in Melsetter.[22]

This was on the eve of the rebellion. In the midst of the fighting Sir Richard Martin began the investigation which was to result in his report on the causes. One of the questions he asked every magistrate and native commissioner was, "did there exist in your district, previous to the outbreak, any practice [of] exacting compulsory labour from Natives?"

Martin concluded from the replies that there was "not sufficient evidence to show that compulsory labour was in force in Mashonaland." It was a very cautious conclusion to draw from the evidence before him. Four magistrates denied the charge. Of the six native commissioners who replied, one admitted it, one was equivocal and others put the emphasis on the desire to earn money to pay tax. The most emphatic *no* came from Mtoko, the district from which Brabant took 500 men after burning and shooting everything in sight. A few of the other answers—and one must remember that the respondents were Company officials, trying to put its administration in the best light—certainly throw light of some kind on the process:

> No practice exacting compulsory labour exists in this district. Natives have been asked to turn out and work for the Company for pay. They were never forced to obey but considered it their duty to do so. It was generally done through the Chiefs to whom the advantages of working and securing money with which to pay the hut-tax were represented by the Native Commissioner. Natives in the mines were obtained occasionally in the same way.
>
> (Resident Magistrate, Victoria)

> Compulsory labour did exist in my district to a certain extent, but was done through the Chiefs the labour was obtained from. I have not supplied any mines with labour from my district. I have supplied public work and private persons with labour.
>
> (Native Commissioner, Charter — the only affirmative reply)

> Whenever I have been under the necessity of collecting Natives for labour I have never used force, but have induced the Natives to go to labour by telling them that they would require money to pay their hut tax. I have found this argument always sufficient to induce them to go to work.
>
> (Native Commissioner, Melsetter)

The picture of men coming forward willingly to work for the tax money emerges in all districts.

The last respondent, however, omitted a very important part of the evidence. In Melsetter, where the trekkers had made a point of appropriating the lands that were most densely populated, the normal source of labour was (as in the republics, and after 1893 in Matabeleland) the labour tenants. In the eyes of the farmers their status was approximately that of medieval serfs. The farmer had the first call on their labour; they were not to work elsewhere without his permission; their children must not go to the mission school; even the son of a tenant, who had engaged himself to a missionary before the farmer had arrived in the district, must be brought back to the farm. When the head of the mission complained, he was told by the arch-slaveholder D.G.B. Moodie not to make a nuisance of himself. The first native commissioner of the district, Newnham, who told the Africans that they need not work for their landlords unless paid, and the magistrate Heugh who supported him, became so unpopular with the farmers that the government transferred them to other posts.

As the tax itself was universally resented—the reports from the districts make that clear—the willingness to work for it was no more than a decision to submit quietly to the inevitable. As the native commissioner, Marandellas, put it, "they certainly did not like supplying labour. They preferred remaining at their kraals doing nothing." This was the impression almost always made by people in a pre-industrial stage on those who had inherited a part, at least, of the puritan ethic. We may conclude that in Mashonaland labour was obtained by pressure on chiefs, the threat of force, bullying by "messengers," occasionally actual assault and murder, always the pressure of the tax-collectors; yet Martin thought that in comparison with Matabeleland the methods were not oppressive enough to be mentioned in his report.

The attitudes of the people directly affected, both to the recruiting and to the working experience, have left little direct evidence. It is significant that both the press-gang methods and the ill-treatment of labourers, often designed to make them abscond before pay day, were condemned by the authorities on the ground that they made labour difficult to obtain or to keep. Similarly the refusal to surrender victims to the Ndebele raiders at Fort Victoria was due partly to the reasoning that if the Shona were not protected they would refuse to come out to work. The desertion of labourers was one of the problems dealt with by the police. Thus there was in the system a voluntary element of sorts.[23]

"Curio" Brown illustrates a Shona custom—that when two parties met on a path their greetings included a detailed report by the leader of each on everything that had happened to him during the day—with an anecdote full of convincing detail. One such narrator, after explaining that he and his friend were going to Salisbury to trade some fowls and meal for beads to give to their sweethearts, described a meeting with two white men camped near the Hunyani,

> One named Blough and the other called Mondavana. We squatted down by their fire and Mondavana said, "Do you Kafirs want work?" We said, "Yese, Baas." Mondavana said, "How much money do you want?" Umtanitchani said, "One month, one pound." Mondavana said, "All right, I will give you a pound a month, and you can begin work now if you like." Then we said, "No, Baas, we can't work, because we are going to see our mother, who is dying, and who has sent for us to come at once and give her some beer." Then both the white men said, "Damity nogud bludylie; maninge lazy bloodyfulu; hamba wena, vootsache damity niggers." Mondavana threw stones at us and Blough got the long ox-whip and chased us down to the river, where we dodged him in the bushes.[24]

The sense of humour was the narrator's as well as Brown's.

There was less scope for humour in the Matabeleland labour situation. As we have seen, most of the people remained on their old land while the white man's farms were superimposed on them.

"From these," Grey reported, "the owners drew the labour they required, agreements being made fixing the period of engagement and the wages to be paid." We have seen also that some farmers preferred to expel the inhabitants and "get labourers through the native commissioners"; the mines, not having areas of inhabited land attached to them, had to do this too.

In Matabeleland the answers to Martin's enquiry amounted to a frank admission that compulsory labour had been exacted. The direct agents of com-

405 The Black Experience

pulsion were the indunas and headmen; the agents for compelling *them* were the "Native Police." From the replies to Martin we cull some revealing sentences:

> The Chief was simply informed that he was expected to supply a certain number of boys, at the same time being assured that they would each receive a monthly wage (never less than 10s., food and lodging), and that they would be well treated. A large number of Natives were thus induced to come into work, many coming quite voluntarily . . . Previous to the outbreak a practice exacting compulsory labour did exist. Natives were compelled to work, for a period of two months, for companies or for private persons. This had, I consider, a beneficial effect upon the Natives generally in this district, as it brought them into contact with civilisation . . . Previous to the outbreak the practice of exacting compulsory labour . . . did exist, inasmuch as the young men were compelled to work a period of three months in a year; of course working to the Native was lowering, and if they could possibly get out of it they did, that is why we had to use the means we did . . . I called upon Indunas to supply labour. In the event of their failing to supply same, and upon stating to me that they had no control over their people and could not manage them, and further asking me to act for myself, then I sent Native police to collect labour . . . Compulsion of a more direct nature was then used upon the young and idle men . . . The effect upon the Natives, physically, morally, and financially, was decidedly good, but they, nevertheless, evaded the work whenever possible.

Grey, in a speech in Bulawayo, said that he thought the treatment of labourers by prospectors and others was one of the greatest causes of rebellion, if not the greatest; Martin put the blame less on "this practice of obtaining labour" than on the "manner in which it was carried out." Even the government's insistence on the registration of every labour contract was of little if any benefit to the worker, because, according to one witness, the system was used to prevent a man from "hiring himself out privately." The prohibition cannot however have affected the dealings of a white farmer with the inhabitants of his farm.

Every respondent to Martin's question gave ten shillings a month, food and lodging as the standard rate of pay. But there were several indications that "when the boys remained, their wages were doubled or even trebled, and that on the whole they were fairly treated. Possibly had the wages in the first instance been fixed at a higher rate, they would have been more content to stay, knowing that voluntary labour was being paid at a so much more advanced rate." This example was from Gwelo, and from Lesapi (Rusape), where there was said to be no compulsion, the explanation given was "our offering high wages."

The degree of bitterness aroused by forced labour, or even the kind of "willing" labour described by these officials, depended on some subjective factors also. When labour was demanded of the *abezansi* aristocrats they had an easy solution: to send some of their *amahole* "dogs." When these returned, their wages were sometimes appropriated by their former masters, who refused to work themselves. As "this condition of semi-slavery could not be tolerated by a civilised Government . . . the young men of the Abezansi were called upon to work for two months in the year. This they refused to do . . . In some cases the Native police had to call out some of the young men to work."[25] It ought to have been possible for the whites, who fully shared this attitude of the *abezansi* to doing what they regarded as degrading work, to understand the humiliation they were inflicting. But when it led to murder they were surprised.

There were certainly labourers—it is impossible to say what proportion of the work force—whose relations with their employers were good. Though the evidence of the employers could not itself be conclusive, the fact that some servants remained in the same employment for several years must carry weight, as must the loyalty of many to their employers when the confrontation came in 1896. They may even have been numerous, but that is unlikely. The resort to force was too common.

Whether labour relations were good or bad, they included a component that the social historian cannot overlook: *Fanagalo*[26] or "Kitchen Kaffir." This was, and is, a crude means of communication which is a "language" only in the sense that it can be used to convey some elementary meanings. It has a limited vocabulary, which has been analysed as 70 per cent Nguni, almost entirely of the Zulu form of Nguni; 24 per cent English and 6 per cent Afrikaans. It has no grammar, the words being strung together in something like the English word-order (as the speaker pleases) but without any of the concords, inflexions, or other forms characteristic of the Bantu languages. White employers and black employees generally use this jargon as their *lingua franca* today. Historically, the interesting fact is that it appeared in Mashonaland at the very beginning of the occupation.

D.T. Cole has shown that it must have originated in Natal about 1860; whether it was the Indians who created it as a means of communication with the Zulus, or Europeans who evolved it slightly earlier, is uncertain. From Natal it was taken to the Diamond Fields, and one is tempted to guess that one of those who took it was Rhodes himself. As the black workers of Kimberley spoke many languages, and those of the Witwatersrand, the next habitat of Fanagalo, still more, the *lingua franca* became indispensable in those polyglot communities. Kimberley in turn became the railhead, fitting-out and starting point for movements to the north. Many of the colonizers of Rhodesia were associated in some way with De Beers. Whether or not these facts help to explain it, "Kitchen Kaffir" is recorded in Mashonaland all through the nineties: "Here, piccanin, boss up! Hamba bona lo skoff—kokeele?" "Ya, missis, kokeele." We heard more of it in the monologue quoted by "Curio" Brown. Though his book was published in 1899, he puts the remark "Panu skellum meninge" (which he translates very loosely as "a bad place for lions") in the context of the rainy season of 1890-1, and there is no reason to suppose that he did not hear it then. There is a further mystery. Though the basic vocabulary was Zulu, and the language of the Ndebele was essentially Zulu, there are no early references to Fanagalo in Matabeleland; it was used in Mashonaland, where the indigenous language was not Nguni at all.[27]

Labour for the white "boss" was a grievous burden, but Martin had a point when he emphasized the method of recruitment. In Matabeleland the force was applied by the "Native Police"; of all the grievances aired at the indabas at the end of the rebellion, the Native Police were the first and the worst.

In the Company's report for 1894-5 Col. Frank Rhodes "furnished the following interesting report on the newly formed Native Police Force." The force of 150 NCOs and men (plus fifty more who were sent to Mashonaland), organized in May 1895, and armed with Martini-Henry rifles, consisted entirely of Ndebele. "A great many," said Frank Rhodes, of the Imbizo and Insuka regiments joined the force. He rightly described these as "crack regiments," but seems not to have understood the implications of the fact. Insuka had borne the brunt of the battle of Bonko; Imbizo had charged the Maxims at Egodade. Insuka was a young regiment, just due to marry when the war came in 1893. These men were not looking for soft jobs when they joined the police. They would have opportunities to practise their military skills, first against their own countrymen and then against the white conquerors. And to improve the skills: "The majority are becoming fair shots," Frank Rhodes complacently observed.[28]

When he was writing his report the victims of the new police were still the Ndebele themselves. About a year later, at the first indaba in the Matopos, Somabhulana recounted the exploits of these police and of their employers. He told of the native commissioner who interrupted a wedding procession and exercised the *droit de seigneur* on the bride, though she was the daughter of a chief. He told of an occasion when he himself visited Bulawayo, accompanied by a retinue appropriate to a man of his rank, and waited all day to pay his respects to the magistrate, H.M. Heyman. In the evening he mentioned that his people were hungry,

> and when the white men visited me it was my custom to kill that they might eat. The answer from the Chief Magistrate, my father [Rhodes], was that the town was full of stray dogs; dog to dog; we might kill those and eat them if we could catch them. So I left Bulawayo that night, my father; and when I next tried to visit the Chief Magistrate it was with my impis behind me . . .

Vere Stent summarized the next part of the speech:

> He spoke of the brutality of the Zulu police, who ravished their daughters, and insulted their young men, who tweaked the beards of their chieftains and made lewd jokes with the elder women of the Great House, who abused the law they were expected to uphold, who respected none but the Native Commissioners and officers of

police, who collected taxes at the point of their assegais, and ground the people in tyranny and oppression.

Stent probably embellished Somabhulana's words with glosses of his own: the police were not Zulus; they were collecting "loot," not taxes; they carried rifles as well as assegais. Somabhulana returned to this point when Rhodes raised the question of the killing of white women and children: "Who commenced the killing of women? Did not your tax-collectors, collecting the Company's cattle, shoot four women in cold blood when there was peace, because the women would not tell them where the cattle were hidden?" Rhodes had never heard of this incident, but Colenbrander had, and he vouched for its truth.[29]

A large part of the "Native Police force" went over, in 1896, to the side of the rebels, but that belated repentance evidently failed to compensate for the misdeeds of the preceding ten months.

Though fifty of those Ndebele police were drafted to Mashonaland, neither they nor the locally recruited "messengers" figured as prominently among the grievances of the Shona as they did in Matabeleland. The Shona had had a longer experience of the operations of the *white* police before the "Native Department" was set up, and before the imperial authorities had begun to check the Jamesonian style of government. Some incidents in 1892 will illustrate the experience.

On 22 January in that year J.F.V. Guérolt, a prospector of French origin and American citizenship, was murdered near Hwata's hill in the Mazoe district. The motive was not discovered; it may have been robbery or, as Lobengula suggested, Guérolt may have been an adulterer. Several well-known characters were involved in the drama that followed. The party sent to investigate the crime was led by Capt. M.D. Graham, whom we last saw operating on the Manica border. It included R.C. Nesbitt, destined to fame and a vc for his part in the Mazoe patrol, and Capt. C.F. Lendy, whose exploits have been less widely appreciated. Information was obtained from the local field cornet, the vicomte de la Panouse. The body was found. The kraal nearest the scene was deserted, but one man was captured on the hill. This prisoner gave the information that the local chief's name was "Chirumziba, and that the latter had instigated his two sons to commit the murder and that he, Chirumziba, was present when the murder was committed." Further investigation led to a small kraal where Chirumziba was captured. Guérolt's coat, trousers, and clasp knife were found in one of his huts. So far this was a straightforward police operation, except that in the capture of the chief one of his men was shot "while trying to escape."

Chirumziba's kraal was burnt. The trail led to another deserted kraal, which was burnt also. It was then decided to "take action against the chief Golodaima," because three of his people had been with Guérolt when he was murdered, there were "reasonable grounds of suspicion" against one of them, there had been cases of intimidation against white men, and, anyway, these people were notorious thieves. The kraal was accordingly attacked; six of its inhabitants were killed and three wounded, and "an enormous quantity of stolen property" was found in the huts. Some ammunition belonging to the patrol having been stolen, the kraal nearest to the scene of that crime was burnt too. "The punishment they received," Graham concluded in his report was "in no way in excess of what they deserved."

The incident typifies the Company's style in the early years. It was not a case of mere unjustified aggression. A murder had been committed, a suspect arrested, and there was circumstantial evidence against him. There would have been a case against Golodaima and some of his people for theft. But instead of proceeding regularly against the suspects the authorities struck out wildly, killing and burning merely because there were "strong reasons to suppose," or "other evidence in support," or "reasonable grounds of suspicion," none of which grounds were specified. The Company was very mildly rebuked for its indiscriminate destruction; the high commissioner was more perturbed by the continued detention of Chirumziba without trial.[30]

The forms of law might have been better observed if the Company, the police, and the settlers had not been so thin on the ground. The shooting and burning were not the reaction merely to one murder. "There were numerous complaints," Jameson wrote, "of the impertinent and threatening attitude of the natives . . . but no distinct charge which could be dealt with, until the murder of Guerold." More of the background was later filled in by C.M. Rolker, the Company's chief mining expert, who said that "a not disguised independence and recklessness on the part of the natives was felt by us at the beginning of the rainy season [of 1891-2]. It showed itself in an unwillingness or in a flat refusal of local chiefs to furnish men for labour, or aid in getting labour. Also in a marked reluctance to trade for food and fodder." Even Jameson's patience with Lobengula was interpreted as the white man's fear of the black: "then the independence gradually changed in instances to impertinence and insolence and it culminated in the Mazoe in the killing of Guerold . . . I have heard it frequently expressed that unless the subdued animosity of some of the natives was promptly checked it would become dangerous for prospectors to travel about alone, which, of course, would check developing the country."[31] The demonstration of power had been necessary to conceal the real weakness of the whites. Their security depended on the awe they inspired in the blacks.

The Guérolt case was followed by the so-called "Ngomo affair," in which several historical threads are woven together. James Bennett was a policeman in charge of the Company's trading station near Mangwende's. Discharged from the police at the end of 1891, he formed a partnership with Llewelyn Meredith, first in farming, and then at the old trading station which they reopened as a private venture. That Bennett afterwards cheated his partner may be relevant to the affair. About the beginning of March 1892, Bennett took some trade goods to the kraal of Gomwe (always called Ngomo or Gomo in the contemporary accounts) and erected a small enclosure from which to trade. He would not allow anyone to enter the enclosure, but Gomwe's son entered all the same. After he had done this several times in the teeth of Bennett's protests, Bennett pushed him out. Gomwe, enraged, called on his people to kill the white man; but the ex-policeman laid about him, drove off his assailants, and got away. He went to Salisbury to complain to Jameson.

The people of the area, and Gomwe in particular, had for some time impressed the authorities with their "impertinence" and "insolence." They had recently murdered a Coloured wagon-driver, but the murderer had not been traced. "Travellers and traders on the Manica Road one and all quoted the natives as speaking in a contemptuous way of the white man's authority 'That they only talked, and did nothing', no doubt alluding to the before [mentioned] unpunished murder."

Jameson dispatched a patrol under the command of Lendy. Having picked up an interpreter on the way, Lendy quite properly went to Paramount Chief Mangwende to ask for his assistance in arresting Gomwe, his subject; the intention was to bring Gomwe to Salisbury for trial. "Maguende said that he was unable to do so; that he was afraid of the Chief Gomo, who was too strong for him, and that if I wanted him I must take him myself; that Gomo would fight, and that he, Maguende, did not wish to interfere, but to let the white men settle the matter with Gomo themselves."

Lendy had stumbled unwittingly into a politically delicate situation. As Shona chieftainships did not normally pass from father to son, but circulated in the family, the scope for dynastic disputes was very great. About 1869 the Mangwende title had been assumed, with the proper Rozvi investiture, by Hundungu, to the exclusion of his elder brother Zinyemba. Civil war followed, in which Zinyemba's forces, led by his son Gomwe, were defeated by Hundungu's, led by his son Mungate. Gomwe retired to the hill-top where Bennett later found him. In 1878 Hundungu was succeeded by Katerere, who died in 1879. After a short interregnum, Hundungu's eldest son Mungate succeeded in 1880, to the exclusion of Katerere's two sons Chirodza and Chibanda. Chirodza however had taken charge during the interregnum and made himself very popular. The danger to the reigning Mangwende caused him to have Chirodza put to death, thus compounding the bitterness of the original dynastic quarrel.

Mungate was the Mangwende who refused to deal with Gomwe but told Lendy to do so himself. Mungate was a man who loved peace and quiet, which he would probably have ceased to enjoy if he had broken the uneasy truce that had followed the usurpation, the civil war, and the murder. Gomwe, however, had perforce to swallow his pride and, in the face of Lendy's patrol, to ask the paramount chief to help him against the white man. Mangwende would not allow Gomwe into his kraal, and told him—as he had told Lendy—to fight his own battles. We may well believe Lendy's report that after Gomwe's death "Maguende expressed himself as delighted with what had been done."

Having failed to get Mangwende's help, Lendy sent a message to Gomwe, giving him until sundown to give himself up. As he failed to appear, Lendy returned to Salisbury for reinforcements. Equipped with these, with Maxims, and with a 7-pounder, Lendy appeared before Gomwe's kraal at daybreak on 17 March.

> Day had fully dawned before the natives became aware of our presence, and, catching sight of some of the mounted men, one man in the kraal, presumably Gomo himself, shouted to the others to come on and kill the white man. A well-directed shot from the 7-pounder was the signal for the firing, which was pretty general on both sides for some minutes; the shooting of the natives, however, was very erratic, and they made but a very short stand, the shells from the 7-pounder bursting in amongst the huts thoroughly demoralising them, all who were able escaping, the remainder taking refuge amongst the caves in the rocks. After sounding the "cease firing," I counted 21 killed, among them being the Chief, Gomo, himself. I captured 47 head of cattle and several goats.

Lendy was sure that "a wholesome lesson" had been given to all the chiefs in the district.

Jameson had dealt with Gomwe as Lobengula had dealt with many uppish and independent chiefs before. "Gomo belongs to me," the Doctor might have said; "does the Country belong to Gomo?" But Lendy had made a serious mistake in including W.E. Fairbridge, the editor of the Salisbury paper, in his party. His report of the incident reached the press in England almost at once, as Lendy's report would never have done. Even the first telegraphic news to the high commissioner brought forth the mild rebuke that "the punishment inflicted . . . appears utterly disproportionate to the original offence." When the full report was received in London, it "would, in Lord Knutsford's opinion, have justified much stronger terms of remonstrance than were used by the High Commissioner . . . Proceedings of this character are likely to do incalculable injury to the British South Africa Company in public estimation in this country."[32]

The injury that was immediately relevant was done not in British but in Shona public estimation. One more item had been added to the bill that the rebels would present four years later. The effect of the injury cannot however be measured in such simple terms. Mangwende had been "delighted." Lendy's operation happened to fit into a pattern of tribal and dynastic politics, in terms of which his injury to one party was a blessing to the other. And the case of Gomwe did not stand alone.

A few days before Gomwe's assault on Bennett a minor chief near Fort Victoria, Mugabe, raided a neighbouring chief, who appealed to the Company for

Chief Chipfunhu Mugabe and his Indunas at Great Zimbabwe, 1891

protection. Chaplin, the local magistrate, and a few men "were sent to assist the raided Chief, and give Moghabi a lesson. Chaplin now reports Moghabi resisted, so his kraal was burnt, and Moghabi killed." The news of this event was sent to Lobengula, who was then doing his border inspection on the Gwelo. He did not like it. "What does it matter if the Mashonas fight amongst themselves? It is bad if you mix yourself up with such matters, why don't you leave the natives to settle their own disputes."

Nevertheless the officials were "mixing themselves up" with yet another dispute a few months later. When the newly installed Chief Gutu complained to Fort Victoria about some interference and cattle-stealing by whites, the officials who went out to investigate "were seized and assaulted by rival claimants to Goto's chieftainship." A Maxim was duly brought out, one of the opposition party was killed, and the district settled down.[33]

All these events happened in the first half of 1892, when Jameson was still appeasing Lobengula, and so justifying the settlers' charge of "bullying the weak and cringing to the powerful." But they reveal also an important aspect of the Shona world at that time: the attention of the Shona was still focused on their domestic politics. Mangwende and Gutu were far more concerned with

413 The Black Experience

threats from dynastic rivals and tribal oppositions than about hypothetical dangers from the handful of whites in the country. The same could be said of many other paramounts and their supporters. For others, again, the Ndebele were the danger. The whites were generally looked upon as possible allies to be used in domestic disputes, and they were often so used. Thus Mangwende could rejoice when Lendy had solved one of his problems for him. Even in the midst of the rebellion, as we shall see, the installation of a new Rozvi Mambo was an event probably unconnected with the war; the people responsible for it were a mixture of rebels and neutrals.

It was still assumed that the Europeans, like others of their kind before 1890, were birds of passage who would soon be gone. It was in 1892 that a visit to a Shona kraal gave W.H. Brown the cue for his description of its life and customs. "My hostesses," he wrote, "were very talkative, and asked many questions." They led up to the key question, "what the white men intended to do with the gold they were digging, and how soon they would have enough of it and all return to Diamond (Kimberley)." Jameson's War gave them an answer. Though there was a drift of Europeans away from the country of Brown's "hostesses," the implications of the conquest of Matabeleland were clear. The conquest was quickly followed by the hut tax and the loss of cattle. Police raids and above all the conscription of labour began to appear as permanent impositions. Many *amahole* returned from their bondage bringing their military habits to Mashonaland. A new restlessness came over the people, preparing the minds of many for the war propaganda that would soon circulate among them. Of many, but not of all; the old feuds between and within chiefdoms would ensure that when some rose in arms against the whites, others would join their enemies.[34]

Feuds were not the only reason for this. Some were on the white side because they were Christians. All that has been said here of the black community has shown it to be suffering from a variety of oppressions, but the impact of Europe on Africa was bound to have another aspect. The chief representatives of it were the missionaries.

African nationalists have with good reason accused the Christian missionaries in general of being agents of their governments in conquest and subjugation. We have seen that those of Inyati and Hope Fountain longed for the overthrow of Lobengula and his regime. We have seen also their reason: while the regime survived they could make no converts. It would be misreading the minds of almost all of them to suppose that any other aim was more important to them than conversion. If the regime supported their work they supported it—as in the case of Kgama. If it put obstacles in the way of evangelization they wanted it removed—as in the case of Lobengula.

The LMS, which was said to have seventeen "adherents" in Matabeleland in 1890, was not the only society to have suffered frustration in that country. The Jesuits had been there in the eighties, founding a station at Pandamatenga in

1880 but abandoning it in 1885. In June 1887 Father Peter Prestage, having been given permission by Lobengula to teach, began his work at Empandeni, some twenty miles south of Plumtree. By the beginning of the next year there was a school with an average attendance of sixty. Two other priests joined Father Prestage, but in October had to report that there had still been no baptisms; "we teach daily, but our scholars are few and come very irregularly." Further frustrations led to the abandonment of Empandeni in November 1889. It was not till December 1895 that Father Prestage reopened it.[35]

Jameson's War, which was fought in Matabeleland, destroyed not only the principal obstacle to the work of Christian missions there, but the missions themselves. Hope Fountain and Inyati were in ruins; Empandeni had been abandoned long before. After the war all was begun again. When a new church was built at Inyati in 1895, Africans gave £11.11s. towards the cost, "the first collection ever made in our native church in Matabeleland." In the same year the LMS began a third station, at Dombadema, northwest of Plumtree. It had little to report before the rebellion. Nor had the Seventh Day Adventists' station at Solusi (thirty-three miles west of Bulawayo), first occupied likewise in 1895. The men at Hope Fountain were still unable "to speak of any new converts," but the LMS had reason to hope that it would soon "begin to see the fruit of the many years' labour in this land." The report for 1895 may, however, have betrayed something of the cultural gap between missionaries and their charges in its premature rejoicing: "For the first time the natives are having a taste of real freedom. They are free to wear European clothing instead of skins, free to work and to hold the proceeds of their labour, free to attend Christian worship and to send their children to school."

In contrast to Lobengula's regime, the Shona chiefdoms in this matter as in others offered variety. It is true that the impression made on the Shona, before the rebellion, by all the Christian missions together was as slight as the impression made on the bush by the embryonic townships. The Africans received into the Methodist Church by 1893 numbered five, the first Roman Catholic baptism, apart from one on a deathbed, was administered on Holy Saturday, 1895, and the first Dutch Reformed baptism at Morgenster (founded 1891) in 1896; but this is not a matter to be measured by arithmetic.[36] The seed was small but a great tree would grow from it. It was the missionaries, too, and they alone, that brought to these Africans literacy, western education generally, and western medicine. Even the feeble beginnings of all these and of Christianity are an important counterpart to the deeds of tax collectors, cattle collectors, native commissioners, white and black police, Graham, Lendy—and Jameson.

When the rebellion began in Mashonaland in June 1896, missions were at work in many parts of the country: Anglican, Roman Catholic, Methodist, Dutch Reformed, Seventh Day Adventist, and American. The American Board of Commissioners for Foreign Missions, which entered Rhodesia from Mozambique, concentrated on the Melsetter district. Four missionaries, with

415 The Black Experience

several Zulu helpers, began the station at Mount Selinda in 1893; twenty miles to the west, Chikore was founded in 1894. Rhodes offered the usual 1,500 morgen farm for each missionary family. The Dutch Reformed field was Fort Victoria; A.A. Louw founded the great Morgenster mission in that district in 1891. These two districts, and the missions in them, were little touched by the rebellion, though the Morgenster people were compelled to take refuge, for a time, in Fort Victoria.

The other churches were in a different case. The Anglican story begins with the journey of Bishop Knight-Bruce in 1888. Having no intention of poaching on LMS ground, he moved on from Bulawayo and travelled over much of Mashonaland. When he returned in 1891 it was by the east coast route. Thus he entered the Company's territory at Umtali—the oldest of its three sites— and decided to make that the centre of his church's activities. When the town moved away the mission founded there, later called St. Augustine's, remained on the land originally granted by Jameson. More land was granted in the new town (Old Umtali), and a church as well as a hospital arose there; but this church was essentially for the whites. The "mission farm at Penhalonga" had not developed much by the time of the rebellion, when messages were sent out to the catechists to take refuge there.

The Anglicans from the beginning depended largely, for mission work, on what Livingstone called "native agency." Knight-Bruce when he arrived in 1891 brought, apart from one or two doubtful starters, two African catechists: Bernard Mizeki, a waif from Gazaland who had found his way to Cape Town and eventually to Zonnebloem College, and Frank Ziqubu, a Zulu from Piet-ermaritzburg. The bishop moved on from Umtali without delay, and as he went he planted these catechists, Bernard at Mangwende's and Frank at Ma-koni's. Mangwende gave the church, for Bernard's station, some stone build-ings that had been occupied by Gouveia during his stay at the place.

By February 1892 there were five African catechists and three Europeans working in Shona villages. A church was built by Africans at Chidamba's, fifteen miles north of Salisbury, and two more in other villages by the lay mis-sionary Frank Edwards, who had walked most of the way up from Cape Town, and before the end of 1892 had taught in seventy villages. In 1895 the first Afri-can priest, Hezekiah Mtobi, a Mfengu from Grahamstown, reached the new diocese. He was stationed at Mutasa's.

The quick proliferation of Anglican mission stations resulted in, and was fa-cilitated by, land grants to match. Whereas the Ndebele monarchs had in more than thirty years given the LMS ground for only two stations, the Anglicans came in under the Company's regime and were presented with the standard 1,500 morgen farms wherever they chose to work. Knight-Bruce thought that "in all about twenty-five tracts were selected." The appropriation troubled his conscience. He thought that white intruders, even if missionaries, had no right to take any "land which the natives of this country actually inhabit." Though he sought comfort in the old argument, which had been used to justify invasion and colonization, that "the Mashona only occupy a very small part of the country, and land which they have never occupied may with justice be said not to belong to them," he offered also a much better justification:

> With the exception of one or two cases, it was not intended that these tracts of land should be appropriated as farms for our mission. There was no other way under the land system of the British South Africa Company by which any rights could be obtained than by formally applying for rights to map out so many "farms"; but we intended them practically as native reserves, so that if the natives were ever crowded out of their lands they might have some place near at hand where they could grow their crops and keep their few cattle. So nearly every one of our "mission-farms" is touching, or almost touching, the chief's village.[37]

The other missions in Mashonaland benefited in the same way. As early as December 1890 the Jesuits were granted what amounted to four standard farms at Chishawasha, twelve miles east of Salisbury. After a false start in 1891 the fathers put up their main building, 110 feet long, in 1893, and began their work. Attempts to open new stations at Mtoko's and in the Umtali district failed, and for the time being all the work of this mission was concentrated at Chishawasha.[38]

The Wesleyan Missionary Society received two farms in 1891, one at Epworth on the southeastern outskirts of Salisbury and the other at Hartleyton in Lomagundi. Two more stations were opened in 1892: Nengubo, southwest of Marandellas, and Kwenda, in Gambiza's country southwest of Mount Wedza. The mission work was begun by Isaac Shimmin, who arrived in Salisbury in 1891 primarily to minister to the European Methodists, but (his companion Owen Watkins having returned to the Transvaal) he was joined in 1893 by G.H. Eva, in 1894 by John White, and in 1895 by G.W. Stanlake. Like the Anglicans, the Methodists used "native agency," and had eight African catechists in the field by 1893.[39]

The important question is the impact of all this activity on the Shona.

The Christian gospel is not easily received by minds that have had no preparation for it. Isaac Shimmin's experience was typical: "Men, women and children listened eagerly to the strange Gospel, but the simple truths of the Bible were utterly beyond them. I had clever interpreters, and as clearly as I could I told them the 'old, old story' of redemption, but even this was above their grasp; I spoke of sin, repentance and forgiveness; they only smiled and looked puzzled."[40] When the Jesuits baptized their third convert at Chishawasha in December 1895, the boy's mother was in despair, threw herself on the ground, said she would drown herself, and begged her son to "come back." He persevered and she did not drown herself, but the incident starkly reveals the human drama near the centre of every conversion, as well as the gulf dividing Christian from pagan. Seen from the pagan side, the magical powers of the

417 The Black Experience

strangers would seem to bode ill. When the building at Chishawasha was going up in the latter part of 1893 the rains were due, but did not come. The people drew the obvious inference: the fathers were praying for dry weather until they had finished the thatching. The popular anger was slightly appeased, but the suspicion confirmed, when the rains fell on the day the thatching was completed.[41]

Several chiefs and headmen having been persuaded to move their villages on to the Chishawasha property, the fathers had material for conversion close at hand. The headmen were gathered together in January 1894 and told that a school would be opened and that they must send their sons to it. The order provoked "shuffling" and objection. Some boys came, and soon adapted themselves, but the attendance was inadequate. At the end of the year the formidable native commissioner, J.S. Brabant, was called in to tell the people the conditions on which they could live on the farm: listen to the missionaries and send their children to school. The children were sent.

In 1895 (there were now eight kraals on the property) Father Biehler summed up the position. Nothing could be done with the adults, but he had twenty boys in the school and was instructing them with some success. He could not allow them to come to Mass or Benediction, but conducted a special service for them on Sundays. At this they said prayers, received instruction, and learned to sing the Rosary. At the sound of the Angelus bell they always knelt and said three Hail Marys. Their day was made up of prayer, religious instruction, elementary teaching, singing, drill, and manual work.[42]

The Anglican H.R. Burgin travelled from Fort Victoria to Melsetter to establish a mission, which was removed as soon as the inadvertent trespassing on the American Society's ground was realised. Burgin however reported that at every point on his journey he was well received and intently listened to. This may have been no more than ordinary African courtesy; missionaries were occasionally too gullible in reporting that a chief was "*longing* to be taught," or begged "that teachers might be sent at once, so that he might see a change before he died." Makoni, after all, professed that he was "in earnest," only to turn and rend the missionaries soon afterwards.[43]

Most of the ground may have been stony; many of the seeds were choked with thorns; but the outcome showed that some at least had fallen on good soil. Knight-Bruce's Zulu catechist Frank Ziqubu is described as more a farmer than a teacher, but his colleague Bernard Mizeki was an apostle:

> Teachers and evangelists of other denominations had now reached Mashonaland, and Bernard visited the Methodists at Nenguwo and the Seventh Day Adventists at Tsungwezi. He gained the friendship of neighbouring chiefs and headmen, who received him courteously, and he arranged for the building of mission huts. Often Mangwende would send for him, and the elderly chief and the young catechist would sit in the sun, talking of the cities in the south, of the Mashona people before the white

man came, of the African peoples of Zululand, Pondoland, Kaffraria, and Bernard's native Mozambique, of the great God Almighty, who was the father of all men, whether they were black or white. Zandiparira, Mangwende's head wife, was attracted to Bernard and his teaching very early. She was one of the first to attend the mission services regularly . . . "Wherever he went at Mahopo," said the aged Chinemha, fourth wife of the old Chief, "he was followed by a pack of laughing children." They would cling to the cassock which Bishop Knight-Bruce had given Bernard, and which he sometimes wore with Father Puller's copper cross hanging from its belt.[44]

Bernard's mission was to last barely five years; his death would bring to light some evidence of his ministry.

However small the missionary achievement before 1896 might seem, historical perspective requires it to be recorded alongside the secular operations of the white invaders, and not only because of the fruit it was destined to bear. Some aspects of mission work won approval from the authorities. After a visit to Chishawasha in January 1895 Frank Rhodes wrote that it was "quite one of the best pieces of work that I have seen in South Africa"—but that was because of the order, discipline, and industry. It was different when the missionary played John the Baptist to the Company's (or the settler's) Herod. Almost from the beginning the standard of conscience raised by the missionaries in Mashonaland became an affront to Company official and settler alike. "Who will rid me of this turbulent priest?" is a theme running through the whole Rhodesian story. The Methodists were among the first to earn the hostility by reporting the misbehaviour of white men, especially their violence to Africans. George Eva had drawn attention to the misdeeds of one settler, who received no more punishment than a warning from the magistrate. The next Methodist missionary to arrive in Mashonaland, in 1894, was John White, one of the great saints of the mission field. White, new to the country, happened to enter a store at the same time as the reprimanded settler, who noticed his clerical dress. "These damned parsons ought to be kicked out of the country," he shouted. "Here is one of them, and I have a damned good mind to take it out of *him*." White stood his ground: "I have heard big words from the like of you before; but they are nothing more than wind." The reply drew sympathy; the laughter of the company in the store decided the aggressor to leave with no more hostile action than a parting oath. During the rebellion, however, White published in England some evidence of its causes; the publication made him for a time a marked man in White Rhodesia.[45] The fact that Christian converts refused to support the rebellion did not suffice to reconcile the beleaguered whites to the "damned parsons." But this is to anticipate.

The offence of the parsons was to unsettle the supposedly immutable—and divinely ordained—pattern of white racial superiority and the exclusion of blacks from the normal benefits of justice. And the parsons were not the only offenders. We saw in the last chapter that there was a particular prejudice against "educated natives"—tangible evidence that the pattern was not immutable—and that many of these were "Colonial natives." (Immigrants can be "natives" in southern African usage.)

These immigrants, like the real "natives," were the victims of discrimination, which was the more galling because they thought of themselves as a part of the white immigrant, rather than of the indigenous, society. The government itself regarded the "Cape boys" with such suspicion that it issued regulations to prevent them from practising deceptions on the simple aborigines of the country. Evidence supporting either that imputation or the charge of general thievery and forgery is hard to find. The numbers involved could not have been great. In October 1896 there were 345 "Colonial natives" in Mashonaland, almost all in the Salisbury district. Their importance lay in what they had acquired of European civilization and in the antipathy which that achievement aroused in the whites.

The missionaries themselves were not blameless. Nancy Jones, a black American girl at the Melsetter mission, provoked among the white missionaries all the standard white prejudices by failing to "keep to her place," by functioning as if free of any sense of inferiority, and by so befriending a Zulu girl at the mission as to add another element of confusion to the stratification by colour. She was driven to resign and leave.[46]

There was yet another small but distinct group in the population, the Asians, that failed to conform to the "savage" stereotype and was accordingly resented and penalized. This community consisted entirely of "passenger Indians," emigrants from India who had paid their own fares. Unlike most colonies that received immigrants from that source, Rhodesia took no indentured labourers from India. The passenger Indians were of what might be called (in Western terms) middle-class origin. In later years the Indians in Rhodesia, Hindu and Muslim, were almost all Gujarati-speakers from the Bombay Presidency. At the beginning there was probably an admixture of other ethnic groups. They were all able to enter the Company's territory because of imperial opposition to discrimination against British subjects: they were deflected to Rhodesia by the obstacles then being set up by the self-governing colonies and republics to the south.

Their possession of an ancient civilization did not protect them from the full blast of white prejudice. As in other parts of Africa, the principal root of anti-Indian feeling was commercial rivalry. Indian traders by frugal living could undercut their white competitors. Though we may raise a sour smile at Hyatt's use of the myth that the Indian lived on "the smell of an oily rag," it must be observed that protection against the competition of cheap labour is a respectable objective in most places and times.

The antipathy did not end, and probably did not entirely originate in the haggling of the market-place. Early in 1895, when the Salisbury Chamber of Commerce began a campaign against Indian traders, the *Buluwayo Chronicle*

420 Rhodes and Rhodesia

gave its hearty support. The "Arabs," it said (this was what Muslim Indians were commonly called), "pander to all the lower passions of the natives, if it will tend to the acquisition of money"; they never miss a chance of illicit trade; they send their money out of the country; their habits are insanitary. The following October the *Chronicle* admitted that some Indians were good citizens, but it supported the Bulawayo Chamber of Commerce in its opposition to the grant of a trading licence to an "Arab." At the same time the chamber forwarded, with approval, to one of the local printing offices a complaint from the Rhodesia Typographical Society that the firm was employing a coloured compositor. It was suggested "that the objection petitioned against be removed."

The Indians were not numerous. In November 1897 there were only forty-three, of both sexes and all ages, in Salisbury. It was in February 1894 that people in that town were said to "buy vegetables from the Coolies." In December 1892, by the admission of the *Rhodesia Herald*, their number was insignificant; but on the principle that a stitch in time saves nine the paper then called for a halt to "the slow but steady invasion of the insidious Asiatic."[47]

Thus the evidence all points to one conclusion: that the white community, as it consolidated itself, offered an almost inflexible opposition to racial mixture between whites and others; and an all but unanimous, if slightly less violent, opposition to the competition of people of colour, whatever their attainments, in trade and employment. The indigenous population, having supposedly no power, could be treated as part of the natural, but not human, resources of the country. Anthropological science was believed to have relegated it to this role. The actual military weakness of the whites only intensified their arrogance. If they had been planning to cause an explosion they could not have worked more effectively.

NOTES CHAPTER 10

1 See above, ch.9.
2 W.H. Brown, *On the South African Frontier*, pp.198-203, and ch. v generally.
3 Ibid., p.191.
4 J.A. Edwards, "The Lomagundi District, a Historical Sketch," *Rhodesiana*, 7, p.11; *Rhodesia Herald*, 29 October 1892.
5 Alexander Boggie, *From Ox-Wagon to Railway*, p.26.
6 Quoted by T.O. Ranger, *Revolt in Southern Rhodesia, 1896-7*, p.103.
7 *Buluwayo Chronicle*, 9 August 1895.
8 co 879/42/484, no.19, p.24; no.68 and encl., pp.97-107.
9 co 879/40/461, no.160, encl.3, p.247.
10 co 879/47/517, no.513 and encls., pp.550-6 (comments written by Martin on 24 May 1897 and not included in his report).
11 co 879/39/459, no.113, p.124, no.118, p.135, no.136, p.151, no.140, p.153, no.146, pp.163-4; 42/484, no.68, encl., pp.103-5.

12 co 879/47/517, no.23 and encls., pp.22 ff. The future Sir Herbert Taylor, chief native commissioner, was the former agent of the African Portuguese Syndicate, who was a thorn in the side of his future employers. See above, ch. 5.

13 co 879/42/484, no.124, encl. 1, p.146; 44/498, no.174, pp.168-9.

14 co 879/40/461, no.47, p.99; 47/517, no.416, encl., p.432. According to Jameson the last induna to surrender was not Gampu but Manyewu, the Victoria incident man: co 879/40/461, no.284, encl., p.400. Julian Cobbing has pointed out that (a) the distinction between privately owned and other cattle was clear, was indicated by earmarks, and that without it *lobola* could not be paid, *lobola* cattle being taken exclusively from private herds; (b) the king had his own *private* herds, while most of the cattle called the king's were in reality communal, under the control ultimately of the king but immediately of the indunas, and were more or less permanently "farmed out" for herding; and (c) the "ultimately successful attempt to abolish communal cattle ownership undermined perhaps even more than the loss of the kingship the social and political cohesion of the Ndebele state. ("The Ndebele under the Khumalos," pp.157-69; for the quotation, p.169.)

15 co 879/40/461, no.50, encl.1, p.107, no.160a, p.250, no.300 and encls., pp.432-3; 42/484, no.68, pp.102-7, no.152 and encls., pp.176-7; 47/517, no.179, p.161, no.350, encl., p.355, no.416, encl., pp.432, 437, no.423, encl., pp.465-6; D.N. Beach, "The Rising in South-Western Mashonaland, 1896-7", pp.274-5; Ranger, *Revolt in Southern Rhodesia*, pp.109-10, quoting John Meikle. co 879/47/517, no.416, encloses Martin's Report. See at p.437 Grey's estimate of the total number of cattle in Matabeleland at the end of the war as 130,000. See above, ch.9, for the loot question as it affected the whites. For a fuller, and different, analysis of the loot question see Elizabeth S. Hemker, "The Role of J.W. Colenbrander in the Occupation and Conquest of Rhodesia, 1893-6," (M.A. thesis, Queen's University), ch. III.

16 co 879/42/484, no. 139, encls., pp.164-7; 44/498, no.2, pp.1-7; 47/517, no.416, encl., p.432.

17 RH Mss Afr. s. 4, pp.146-7, (letter of 22 September 1895); the same letter in co 879/47/517, no.88, encls., pp.72-4.

18 Rhodes Papers, Charters, 38, no.38, p.214c; co 879/40/461, no.270, encl., pp.386 ff.; co 417/136/11911, pp.276-94. For background of the hut tax, see above, ch.8.

19 J.J. Taylor, "The Origins of the Native Department in Southern Rhodesia, 1890-8" (Henderson Seminar Paper no.7), pp.8-12; co 468/1, BSA Co. Report for 1894-5, p.77; Ranger, *Revolt in Southern Rhodesia*, pp.73-4. For the origin of the Field-Cornets see above, ch.8.

20 Reminiscences of M.E. Weale (WE 3/2/5), quoted by Ranger, *Revolt in Southern Rhodesia*, pp.75-6; co 879/47/517, no.439, p.478; and see below, ch.12, p.513.

21 D.N. Beach, "The Politics of Collaboration, South Mashonaland, 1896-7," (Henderson Seminar Paper no. 9), p. 19 (and generally, pp. 17-19); co 87947/517, no.416, encl., pp.442-3.

22 Beach, "Politics of Collaboration," p.18; Taylor, "Origins of the Native Department," pp.7, 10; Ranger, *Revolt in Southern Rhodesia*, pp.58, 67, 78-9.

23 co 879/47/517, no.416, encl., pp.429, 440-4; J.K. Rennie, "Christianity, Colonialism and the Origins of Nationalism among the Ndau of Southern Rhodesia, 1890-1935" (thesis, Northwestern University), pp.184-5.

24 Brown, *South African Frontier*, pp.210-11.

25 CO 879/47/517, no.416, pp.430, 437, 440-8.

26 Literally "like this"; major stress on the first and minor stress on the last syllable.

27 More accurately, I have not found any references in Matabeleland. The use of Fanakalo by Allan Wilson's patrol (see above, ch.7, pp.279, 281) might seem to belie
this statement, but note that (a) the speakers had come from Mashonaland, and the
Nguni words would have been intelligible to the Ndebele even if they had never
heard Fanakalo; and (b) the evidence was given by the survivors many years later,
when they would have become familiar with the patois. See D.T. Cole, "Fanagalo
and the Bantu Languages in South Africa," *African Studies*, XII, 1 (March 1953),
pp.1-9; letter by Patrick Duncan in ibid., XIII, 1, p.45; Strachey Chambers, *The
Rhodesians* (1900), p.66; Brown, *South African Frontier*, p.147.

28 CO 468/1, BSA Co. Report for 1894-5, p.18; R. Summers and C.W. Pagden, *The
Warriors*, p.147.

29 Vere Stent, *A Personal Record of Some Incidents in the Life of Cecil Rhodes*, pp.40-
2, 46.

30 CO 879/36/426, no.101, encls., pp.135-7; no.128, encls., pp.167-8; no.208, pp.250-2.

31 CO 879/36/426, no.144, Annexure, p.189; no.218, encl. 1, p.257.

32 Jean Farrant, *Mashonaland Martyr: Bernard Mizeki and the Pioneer Church*,
pp.107, 127, 150-2; A.S. Hickman, *Men Who Made Rhodesia*, p.250; David Chanaiwa, "A History of the Nhowe before 1900," pp.141-3; CO 879/36/426, no.131, encl.2,
p.174; no.136, encl., p.179; no.143, p.188; no.218, encl. 1, pp.256-7. Mungate continued to steer clear of trouble and to reign until 1924.

33 CO 879/36/426, no.72, encl., p.108; no.171, encl., p.212; Beach, "Politics of Collaboration," p.13. The Dutch Reformed mission at Morgenster had recently been
founded in Mugabe's country, and barely escaped involvement in the operation
against him (A.A. Louw, *Andrew Louw van Morgenster*, pp.120-7).

34 Beach, "Rising in South-Western Mashonaland," pp.274-5, 403-8; Brown, *South
African Frontier*, p.201. For the Mambo installation see below, ch.12.

35 N.M.B. Bhebe, "Christian Missions in Matabeleland, 1859-1923," (thesis, University of London), p.198; *Zambesi Mission Record*, vol. II, pp.114-19, 235 ff., 277 ff.,
316-19, 353-7. For a general survey of the missions, see Edwin W. Smith, *The Way
of the White Fields in Rhodesia*.

36 Richard Lovett, *The History of the London Missionary Society, 1795-1895*, vol. I,
p.631; Smith, *Way of the White Fields*, ch. III; Bhebe, "Christian Missions in Matabeleland," p.221; G.G. Findlay and W.W. Holdsworth, *The History of the Wesleyan
Methodist Missionary Society*, vol. IV, p.384; *Zambesi Mission Record*, vol. III,
pp.116-17, 156-9; Louw, *Andrew Louw*, p.178.

37 Smith, *Way of the White Fields*, pp.52-71; Farrant, *Mashonaland Martyr*, pp.82,
102-4, 110, 116-26; Cecil Lewis and G.E. Edwards, *Historical Records of the Church
of the Province of South Africa*, pp.715-17, 720; G.W.H. Knight-Bruce, *Memories
of Mashonaland*, pp.98-9; Louw, *Andrew Louw*, ch. VIII. The thorough examination
of the American mission in Melsetter by Rennie, "Nationalism among the Ndau,"
shows very little impact before 1902—another important piece of negative evidence.

38 *Zambesi Mission Record*, vol. II, pp.476-7, 594-7, 636-7; vol. III, pp.36-9, 77-9.

39 Findlay and Holdsworth, *Wesleyan Methodist Missionary Society*, vol. IV, pp.382-4.

40 Ibid., p.384.
41 *Zambesi Mission Record*, vol. III, pp.78, 159.
42 Ibid., pp.116-19.
43 Knight-Bruce, *Memories of Mashonaland*, pp.102, 104-6, 171-2.
44 Farrant, *Mashonaland Martyr*, pp.118-19, 121. (Cf. Knight-Bruce, *Memories of Mashonaland*, p.171).
45 *Zambesi Mission Record*, vol. I, p.9; C.F. Andrews, *John White of Mashonaland*, pp.38-9.
46 CO 468/1, BSA Co. Report for 1897-8, p.7, and "Report on the Native Disturbances," p.122; Rennie, "Nationalism among the Ndau," pp.295-8.
47 F. and L.O. Dotson, *The Indian Minority of Zambia, Rhodesia and Malawi*, pp.27-42; S.P. Hyatt, *Off the Main Track*, p.58; *Buluwayo Chronicle*, 8 February and 12 October 1895; *Rhodesia Herald*, 17 December 1892, 2 February 1894; CO 468/1, BSA Co. Report for 1897-8, p.249.

The Rebellion, I: Umvukela[1]

In March 1896 the match was put to this combustible material. The signal had been given by the Jameson Raid and its failure.

The raid was, of course, not a cause of the rebellion, perhaps not even a *conditio sine qua non*, but it provided an opportunity. The connection between the two events is a reminder that, in other ways also, the raid had a Rhodesian dimension. The success of Jameson's gamble in 1893 was a factor in his disastrous adventure two years later. The raiders were largely Rhodesian police, their leader was the administrator, his part of the plot was hatched in Bulawayo, the whole operation was a Company affair, and its worst effects, in the short run, were felt by the Rhodesians, white and black.

Rhodes and Jameson wanted a military force on the Transvaal border, poised for invasion when the expected revolution broke out in Johannesburg. A precedent for this plan had been set by Loch during a previous Anglo-Transvaal crisis in 1894. Loch had intended to put imperial troops on the border; Rhodes and Jameson had their own private army in mind—the Company's police. The chief instigator of this part of the scheme was almost certainly Jameson. "You may say what you like," Edmund Garrett reports his saying about his plans on the stoep of Government House, Bulawayo, "but Clive would have done it."[2]

The 1,500 men proposed for the invading force would have to be found. The Company would have to control the launching pad, for Chartered police were not allowed to operate in an imperial protectorate. The second problem was easier to solve than the first. Indeed, the manoeuvre to bring the whole or a part of the protectorate under the Company's administration was conducted with a plausibility and finesse that were conspicuously absent from the rest of the operation.

The idea of transferring the administration of the protectorate from the Crown to the Company was not new in 1895: the charter itself had defined the Company's sphere as lying "north of British Bechuanaland." It was Rhodes who had proposed to exclude the protectorate, for fear of "the Rev. John Mackenzie and his followers"; it was the Colonial Office that insisted on its inclusion. There was merely an understanding that, for the present, the Company would keep out of it. The Colonial Office likewise hoped that the colony of British Bechuanaland would be annexed to the Cape. There had been various political objections to this step in the years following 1885, but by 1895 they were thought to have been removed. When Chamberlain took over the Colonial Office in the middle of that year the stage was set for negotiations.

The imperial motive was, as usual, economy. The Cape wanted the crown colony for reasons of sentiment and "manifest destiny," for reasons connected with the railway, and because the white colonists there were "kith and kin." The objections of some of the chiefs were treated by Sir Hercules Robinson as "unfounded" and were later withdrawn, though there was talk of "vacillation." The imperial government insisted on making the reserves inalienable without the consent of the secretary of state. The Cape ministers (then headed, of course, by Rhodes himself) reluctantly agreed to this. On 15 November 1895 British Bechuanaland became a part of the Cape Colony.[3]

The protectorate was a harder nut to crack. The Company's proclaimed object was at first quite modest. The extension of the railway beyond Mafeking had become urgent (it was indeed overdue), and the Company needed the land over which it was to run. Ripon had provided for this in a dispatch to Loch in December 1892. So on 21 August 1895 the Company told Chamberlain that it wanted a strip extending to a mile on either side of the line, together with twenty square miles at Gaborone, the provisional terminus, where a township was to be built. In asking for this the directors in London, except Beit and Maguire (Rhodes's alternate on the board), were sincere: they wanted land for the railway. These two, who were in Rhodes's confidence, would have known that the twenty square miles were needed for military purposes.

Gaborone was on the border, and about 170 miles in a straight line from Johannesburg. As the immediate objective of the railway it was a natural site for a township. Many people and stores would be gathered there. Some of the local people were opposed to the building of the railway. A construction camp was liable to be disorderly. Police would therefore be needed, but Rhodes, knowing the reluctance of the imperial government to spend money, and wishing to be helpful, proposed that the place might be policed by the Company.

The idea did not catch on at once. Robinson objected to the confusion of jurisdictions, but thought that the difficulty might be overcome by placing Gaborone and the railway strip under the administration of the Company. Chamberlain would do all he could to get the necessary land from the chiefs, but "as at present advised" (on 30 August) did not want in the protectorate any body of armed men not under the exclusive control of the Crown.[4]

From these unpromising beginnings the negotiations developed rapidly in the direction desired by Rhodes. He did not get all that he wanted. The rumour that the Company was going to take over the protectorate led to protests, petitions, and finally the journey of Chiefs Kgama, Sebele, and Bathoen to London. They wanted to remain under the protection of the Great Queen, not to be abandoned to the mercies of the Company. The reason, repeated in all the petitions and interviews, was simple, and was simply expressed in the petition of the Kwena: "We do not wish to be protected simply from those who would make war upon us but from those who would divide our country up into allotments."

While these three chiefs were in London, Shippard took Rhodes's brother Frank to negotiate with two others, Ikaning and Montshiwa. The latter's headquarters were at Mafeking, but some of his land, and all of Ikaning's, lay in the protectorate. The new line would run for the first hundred miles through their territories. Under pressure from Shippard both chiefs agreed to the transfer of the administration of these territories to the Company. There was another important transaction. Montshiwa's nephew Silas Molema took the party out to his farm Mabeti, at a place called Pitsani Potlugo, and agreed to sell it to the Company "for a seat of magistracy." Frank Rhodes accepted. The transfer of the administration of these lands to the Company was proclaimed in the Cape Government Gazette of 18 October. The same issue announced the appointment of Jameson as resident commissioner of this little territory and of the Hon. Robert White as magistrate. The "seat of magistracy," Pitsani, was then substituted for Gaborone, in the plan of the conspirators, as the base for the invasion.[5]

Before proclaiming the transfer of Ikaning's and Montshiwa's territories, Robinson had suggested delaying this act if it would be possible, instead, to hand over the whole protectorate to the Company. The delay would have been a long one, the need to begin "railway construction" (read "military preparations") was urgent, and the smaller transaction had to be completed on 18 October. At the same time the three chiefs in London were fighting their rearguard action, which had some immediate success. In so far as their pleading took time and delayed decisions, it led in the long run to complete success.

As bidden by Chamberlain, the chiefs listened to the proposals of the Company men, but "we do not like their words." They may not have listened to the proposals with open minds, because they had previously reported from their own country that "we hear the words of the Makalaka and Matabele, who live under the Company, and we see that these people do not like their rulers." The Company would have done well to take this report to heart. Chamberlain was forced to concede something to the chiefs. The agreement which he reported on 7 November provided for the demarcation of reserves for each of the tribes they represented, Ngwaketse, Kwena, and Ngwato. The reserves were to continue to be administered by the high commissioner and his representatives. The rest of the protectorate would pass under the control of the Company. As if to justify the fears which had caused the delay, the Company's secretary reported, after the terms were known, that "the directors are greatly disappointed that such large areas are proposed to be allotted to the three chiefs for native reserves."

The decision had been made in London; it had still to be carried out in Bechuanaland. On 21 December Robinson cabled to Chamberlain, reporting that Rhodes thought the time had come for a proclamation putting the transfer into effect. Eight days later, before permission for the proclamation had been received, Jameson "took the bit between his teeth" and invaded the South African Republic without the excuse of a revolution in Johannesburg. When the Company next raised the question it was told that, in view of "recent events," the matter must stand over for the present. Though no firm decision was made immediately, the protectorate was never given to the Company. The administration of Montshiwa's and Ikaning's lands was retransferred to the Crown. One of the few positive achievements of the raid was to save the Tswana from the Company.[6]

Though the transfer of even a small area turned out to be temporary, it sufficed for the purposes of the plot. But Jameson needed men, as well as the ground for them to use. There were to be 1,500 men, or by other accounts 1,200. The final cryptic telegram to Johannesburg reported that "the contractor has started on the earthworks with 700 boys"; in fact he had 511. He was overconfident in trying the invasion with the smaller number, but equally so in supposing that he could assemble 1,500 at Pitsani.

The invading column had to be entirely under the control of Jameson, acting for Rhodes. The only force answering to that description, at the time when the plot was being hatched, was the Rhodesia Mounted Police, successor to the "British South Africa Company's Police" which had accompanied the Pioneers in 1890. The strength of this force had been drastically reduced in 1892—from 650 to 40—to help the finances of the tottering Company. At some date soon after the reduction the small force was given the name of Mashonaland Mounted Police. After Jameson's War 150 of Forbes's volunteers were recruited to form the Matabeleland Mounted Police, the name "Rhodesia" being introduced in 1895 to cover the two regiments.[7]

These were to be the core of the invading army at Pitsani. In September twenty-six of the Mounted Police left Salisbury, but without fuss, and the local public had no clue to what was afoot. On 20 October, two days after the transfer of the jumping-off ground to the Company, the first contingent rode out of Bulawayo. When all were assembled there were about 250 of them in the camp, and only sixty-three policemen left in all of Rhodesia. Jameson could not have based his plans entirely on this source of manpower.

After setting up the camp at Pitsani he went to Cape Town, where with the help of J.A. Stevens he enlisted about a hundred recruits for the Mounted Police. In this way the total number at Pitsani, including officers, who rode out on D-day had been raised to 372. These were still too few, and most of them were mere boys without military experience.[8]

From the beginning of the conspiracy Rhodes and Jameson had their eyes on another source from which they could add not only to the numbers but to the quality of their force. While the Crown Colony and the protectorate were imperial responsibilities they were patrolled by the Bechuanaland Border Police. The transfer of the Crown Colony to the Cape and of a length of railway strip along the border to the Company would greatly reduce the tasks of these police. It was proposed to reduce their numbers to two hundred. When the transfer was extended to include the whole of the protectorate, except for the three reserves, it was decided to disband the BBP altogether. The Company would police its railway strip—which for the section immediately in view meant the Transvaal border—and its other acquisitions. All that was thought necessary for the three reserves was a force of sixty "native police" under a few ex-BBP officers. Some of the old unit were expected to, and did, join the Cape Police, which became responsible for British Bechuanaland. The rest were invited by the Company to enlist in its force.

This aspect of the change in Bechuanaland was given a high priority by Rhodes and Jameson. As they needed to incorporate the new element into their police as early as possible, their increasingly urgent demands for the transfer of the administration were prompted not only, or perhaps even mainly, by the desire to set up the camp at Pitsani. In the event, as we have seen, the transfer of the bulk of the protectorate was never carried out. The disbandment of the BBP, however, was—in anticipation of the transfer, and only at the last minute. All except one troop, which could not arrive in time, were assembled at Mafeking. In the course of December the officers and men made their choices. Over a hundred were taken into the Cape service. Not many more—122 officers and men—joined the Rhodesia Mounted Police; this was barely half the number Jameson had counted on. These were the men who rode out of Mafeking on the night of 29 December and united with the Pitsani column at Malmani. They were of a much higher military quality than the Rhodesian contingent. At the end of the year the remnant of the BBP was discharged.

Thus the police who came down from Rhodesia, the recruits gathered in the Cape Colony, and the officers and men of the BBP who transferred to the Rhodesian force, together with a staff of seventeen officers, made up the 511 who rode over the border. Though Jameson was disappointed by the response he got from the BBP, the best possible response would have given him only about another hundred. The plan called for a much larger number. Provision had indeed been made for a large addition from yet another source.[9]

On 19 April 1895 the *Buluwayo Chronicle* announced that a volunteer corps was to be raised. A few weeks later a meeting was held at the Charter Hotel, Bulawayo, to organize the Matabeleland Regiment of the Rhodesia Horse Volunteers. There were to be parades every Saturday, shooting competitions, and other excitements. The *Chronicle* thought that, while there was no practical need for anything so warlike, it would be good entertainment: "The natives will love to see a big military show." At the same time the Mashonaland Regiment was being organized in Salisbury. Lieut.-Col. the Hon. H.F. White, who was in command of the Rhodesia Mounted Police, also commanded the Mashonaland Regiment of the Volunteers. Lieut.-Col. H.M. Heyman, of Macequece fame, who was O.C. the Matabeleland Regiment, was also civil commissioner and resident magistrate of Bulawayo. In December, White being at Pitsani and Heyman in Johannesburg, the Volunteer regiments were commanded by William Napier and J.A. Spreckley. Before leaving for Pitsani Sir John Willoughby gave instructions to these officers to call out the Rhodesia Horse when they received the word from Jameson. Ten supply depots were set up between Bulawayo and Pitsani to provide for the Volunteers on their march to the south. One of the last messages sent by Jameson before he cut the wires on 29 December was the signal to Napier and Spreckley to bring the Rhodesia Horse down to the scene of action. As the two regiments eventually mustered about a thousand men, they would have brought Jameson's numbers up to the original figure of 1,500.[10]

Consider the implications of this fact. Jameson's 372 men at Pitsani were a subject of speculation and rumour. The excuse of protecting the railway builders from resentful tribesmen quickly wore thin, especially as the tribesmen were quiet and not a sod had been turned. Another thousand at Pitsani would very soon have precipitated decisions, republican and imperial, unfavourable to the conspirators. This was so obvious that there is no evidence at any stage that Jameson intended to have the Volunteers with him at the start of his invasion. If he did not, the Johannesburg plotters were cruelly deceived in thinking that there would be 1,500, or even 1,200, men on the border.

The evidence shows that during the final months of 1895, whatever may have been the idea earlier, Jameson wanted the Volunteers to move only *after* the invasion from Pitsani. As the police had taken six weeks on the journey from Bulawayo to Pitsani, the Volunteers according to this plan would have a role to play only if the invasion precipitated a major civil war in the Transvaal. Jameson did not expect this. The summoning of the Volunteers in these circumstances was of a piece with Jameson's prophecy that "anyone could take the Transvaal with half-a-dozen revolvers."[11]

Think, though, of the position in Rhodesia if Jameson's order to Napier and Spreckley had been obeyed. As it was, the administrator had denuded the country of all but a handful of its police. All that remained for defense was the Rhodesia Horse Volunteers. What might have happened if they, too, had departed will appear from what follows.

Jameson and his boys surrendered to the Boers at Doornkop at 9.15 a.m. on 2 January. As soon as the news of the invasion had reached Cape Town the high commissioner had repudiated it, ordered Jameson to return, and forbidden British subjects to assist him. Chamberlain likewise lost no time in repudiating the raid. Both Chamberlain and Robinson, as we now know, were accessories before the fact, but neither they nor Rhodes nor anyone else had foreseen a raid unsupported by Johannesburg. Chamberlain and Robinson recognized a lost cause when they saw one. Chamberlain ordered the directors to forbid Napier and Spreckley to move, but Rhodes, in a brief lucid moment, had already done this. The directors saw their duty and dismissed Jameson from his administratorship, which he was now in any case unable to exercise. The secretary of state gave his approval to this decision on 5 January. Rhodes was obliged to resign as prime minister; his retirement took effect on the 12th, and on the 15th he left for England.

He had not resigned his seat in Parliament (that was a question for his constituents), nor any of his directorships. His career as a private businessman was his own affair, but one of his directorships—that of the Chartered Company—was really a public charge. Moreover, the Company itself had been besmirched by Jameson's action, questions were raised about the charter, and Rhodes was prepared to resign from the board if this would help the Company to weather the storm. He and Beit placed their resignations in the hands of their fellow directors, but these were reluctant to accept them. Discussion between the board, the two delinquents, and the Colonial Office dragged on.

One reason for delaying the decision was the rebellion. Rhodes, whose visit to England had been short, had arrived in Rhodesia, where the embattled settlers appeared to think that their survival depended largely on his leadership. It was assumed that his resignation from the board would entail his removal from the Rhodesian scene, at least as a principal actor, and the rumour of resignation produced a cry of anguish and a spate of indignant editorials. The directors feared the consequences of Rhodes's removal in these circumstances. They also shirked the responsibility, repeatedly asking Chamberlain to make the decision. Chamberlain shirked it too, and one wonders whether the blackmail of the missing telegrams, which enabled Rhodes to keep Chamberlain in line after the Enquiry in 1897, was not here casting its shadow before. Rhodes himself was reached by telegraph in the laager at Gwelo, whence he sent his melodramatic message: "Let resignation wait. We fight Matabele again tomorrow." Eventually Chamberlain advised that the resignation of Rhodes and Beit from the board, and of Rutherfoord Harris as secretary, should be accepted. This was done on 26 June.[12]

That the resignation in itself made little difference to Rhodes's role in Rhodesia will soon appear. But there were also other and more effective changes. Jameson's action had made it necessary for the imperial government to put such curbs on the Company and its officers as would prevent embarrassments of that kind, not to say possible disasters, in the future.

The essential change was the appointment of an imperial officer as commandant-general of all armed forces in Mashonaland, Matabeleland, and Bechuanaland. The Company was not to have any armed force at its disposal, though it would have to pay for the force in its territory. The same officer was to be deputy commissioner for Rhodesia. In that capacity he would have a seat, but not a vote, on the Administrative Council, and would be kept informed of all decisions by the administration. In this second capacity he was an imperial watchdog, responsible to the high commissioner. The officer appointed, on 12 March 1896, was Sir Richard Martin, a retired colonel of Dragoons, "a handsome, courteous officer of the old school," according to Marshall Hole. Whistling Dick, Hole says the Rhodesians called him, "in allusion to his principal occupation while in Rhodesia." It was not Martin's fault that he had too little to do; when he sailed from England on 4 April events had already made his instructions out of date.[13]

The new administrator who was to take Jameson's place had departed a fortnight earlier. He was Albert Grey, the life director, who in 1894 had succeeded his uncle in the earldom. He, too, landed in a situation which had not been foreseen when he was given the job—or even when he left England. The news of the rebellion greeted him on his arrival in Cape Town.

There was an urgent task which could not wait for these officers. Major (later Field Marshal) Herbert Plumer (assistant military secretary to the high commissioner) was sent to Bulawayo, not only to convey Robinson's warning against further Jamesonian adventures, but to take possession of all arms and ammunition belonging to the Company. When he had done this he handed the armoury over to Capt. J.S. Nicholson of the 7th Hussars, the only imperial officer then in Bulawayo. Heavy responsibilities fell upon Nicholson until the arrival of Martin.

It was not only the imperial authorities that made reassessments and new plans as a result of the raid. The Ndebele made theirs too.

Their mood of resentment and rebellion was accounted for in the last chapter. To the factors described there, contemporaries and historians have added, as final incentives to revolt, the three natural disasters of drought, locusts, and rinderpest. These were factors in the explosion, but their importance must not be exaggerated. The locusts had appeared in 1890, the very year of the occupation, and had reappeared in each subsequent year. It was only in the summer of 1895-6 that they swarmed, becoming the "great black clouds sweeping up from the horizon, blotting out the sun," described by Melina Rorke. The drought had begun after Jameson's War, and since then, according to Matabele Wilson, the rainfall had dwindled to about half the normal amount. The coincidence in time of these calamities with the arrival of the white men was unfortunate.

But Selous was certainly right in treating these as very minor factors in the rebellion. The drought did not affect all areas equally, and it happened that the districts in which the revolt began—Umzingwane, Filabusi, Insiza—had had good rains in the season then ending. They had also been little damaged by the locusts, and "the rinderpest had not yet approached this part of Matabeleland." It had not taken hold in the crucial district of Belingwe even by the middle of June.[14]

The rinderpest was described as "a specific malignant and highly contagious fever characterized by acute inflammation of the mucous surfaces," affecting cattle and some kinds of wild animals. The fever, inflammation, and nasal discharge were usually followed quickly by death. From an endemic centre in Somalia the disease broke out in 1889, reaching Uganda in 1890 and (the future) Zambia in 1892. The Zambezi appears to have kept it at bay for a few years, but early in 1896 there were reports of its having spread south of the river. On 7 March the *Buluwayo Chronicle* reported that information had come to hand "within the last few days" that the disease had reached Matabeleland. Many cattle had died in Shiloh and around Inyati, and a whole herd had been "swept off" at Intaba yezinduna.

Meetings of agitated farmers followed. Officials tried to stop the contagion by the wholesale destruction of healthy as well as diseased animals. The Cape and other governments closed their frontiers, but most of the precautions were ineffectual. Once the disease had reached Matabeleland it was in a region of ranches, roads, and regular communications, through which it spread like a veld fire. From Bulawayo southwards it moved on at a speed of twenty miles a day, littering the countryside with carcases and bringing ox-wagon transport to a stop. Late in 1897 the game on Rhodes's Groote Schuur estate outside Cape Town were dying. By then it was estimated that, south of the Zambezi, 2,500,000 cattle had perished in this visitation.

The Ndebele, smarting under the loss of most of their cattle by confiscation, now suffered two more blows: the death of most of the remainder from rinderpest, and the death by government order of many of those that survived the disease. This alone might have been almost enough to drive a proud people—especially a cattle-loving people—to rebellion. But, as we have seen, there had been more than enough provocation before these events. The decisions had been made. Rinderpest and cattle-killing served only (and not even in all cases) as final spurs to action.[15]

What had turned massive discontent into specific plans for revolt had been the defeat of Jameson. In Bulawayo the white community got the news of the raid, from its beginning to its inglorious end, quickly if not always accurately. Jameson's telegram to Napier and Spreckley, ordering them to bring the Volunteers to his assistance, was published in a special edition of the *Chronicle* on the very evening that "the contractor started on the earthworks." The news turned Bulawayo "into a seething mass of excited people, breaking the Sunday evening calm by patriotic songs and fervid speeches . . . No sooner were the sheets out than the Club was a scene of great excitement, which spread all over the town."[16] The excitement, fed by the wildest rumours, continued during the following days. The news that the high commissioner had repudiated Jameson was received with disbelief, as it was taken for granted that the latter would not have moved "without the orders of the Imperial Government or Mr. Rhodes."

On 3 January the order forbidding the movement of the Volunteers reached

Bulawayo and added to the frustration and dismay. The same afternoon another special edition of the *Chronicle* announced the surrender of Jameson and his boys. This time the town exploded in anger, directed at the cowards in Johannesburg who had let Rhodesia's hero down.

The news reached Salisbury in a different way. During the whole period of the raid Salisbury was out of touch with the world because the telegraph line had broken down. It was repaired on 3 January. Marshall Hole describes a jolly New Year dinner party which was interrupted in mid-course by a messenger who brought in an envelope from the telegraph office. The company settled back to hear Judge Vintcent, the acting administrator, read what they expected to be routine news. What they heard was a series of telegrams telling the story of the raid from beginning to end. "Good Heavens! Jameson, Willoughby, White—all our police officers, prisoners, at the mercy of Kruger! Then a garbled casualty list . . . Deeply and bitterly we cursed the treachery of the Committee at Johannesburg . . . Our dinner party was forgotten. Most of us broke away at once to seek further news at the Club or the Newspaper Office." In Salisbury as in Bulawayo the anxiety was for the bereaved, and for the poor prisoners at the mercy of the Boers. That Rhodesia had been denuded of its police seems hardly to have occurred to anyone.[17]

It had occurred to the Ndebele. Selous, who had returned with his wife from England as manager of a vast estate, belonging to Willoughby's company, at Essexvale, found himself a near neighbour of Mlugulu. This was the old "head dance doctor," the highest ritual authority in the Ndebele nation. In happier circumstances the secular leadership after Lobengula's death would have been assumed by the hereditary regent Mhlaba. But in 1892 Mhlaba and his family had been judicially murdered, the survivors had taken their revenge by guiding Forbes's column in 1893, and there was no regent. Nor had a successor to Lobengula been formally recognized. His son Nyamanda was before the rebellion, and again at the end of it, the generally accepted heir. But evidence on this point is lacking for the period immediately after the outbreak. Contemporary officials believed, or asserted, that the older indunas preferred Lobengula's brother Mfezela. Even if this idea was unfounded, there is no doubt that the cleavages in the nation revealed in 1868-70 were even wider in 1894-6, and may have made unity behind a new king harder to achieve. The death of Lobengula, like the death of his father, had to be followed by a long interregnum because of the customs of succession and inheritance; the interregnum, especially in the absence of a regent, gave scope for the development of factions. In these circumstances, there being for the moment neither king nor regent, a heavy responsibility had to be assumed by Mlugulu.[18]

He and Selous seemed to be the best of friends. They met often and discussed the questions of the day. Mlugulu was "always most courteous and polite in his bearing," and "by us he was always treated with the consideration due to one who had held a high position and been a man of importance in Lo

Bengula's time." Mlugulu wanted Selous to look after some of his cattle and run them with his own, or else buy them, to save them from seizure by the Company. Selous could not do this, but from the moment Mlugulu heard the news of Jameson's surrender he dropped the matter. Instead, he persisted in questioning Selous closely about the details of the raid. Selous believed that it was at that time that Mlugulu made the final decision to rebel.

If we can believe what Matabele Wilson later recollected, the plans must have been far advanced by then. "About the end of November 1893," he wrote—he should of course have written 1895—he and Usher were looking for old workings on the fringes of the Matopos. After noticing some suspicious signs they paid a visit to Lekuni, the late king's brother.

> When we arrived at Lekuni's kraal we went into his hut and had a talk with him, and to help to make him talk, we brought out a bottle of whiskey from our wallets and gave him some. We told him what we had seen and asked him what it meant? and if he knew anything about it. After talking a long time Lekuni told us there was a big meeting of chiefs in the hills and that they wanted to kill the white men in the country . . . Next day I went into town, saw the Acting Administrator and told him exactly what I had seen and heard. He said "For God's sake Wilson do not tell anyone in town what you are telling me, or you will create a panic." . . . Of course I did not.

According to other accounts it was Usher who gave the warning, and there were still others whose reports fell on deaf ears.[19]

At such meetings as these the indunas evolved their plans. But the settlers and officials of the time believed that the responsibility for the rebellion was shared by the oracular priests of Mwari. The Europeans assumed that the Ndebele (originally Sotho) word for the high god, Mlimo, was the exact equivalent of Mwari. Selous expressed the general opinion when he wrote: "I believe, however, that the Umlimo was made use of for the purposes of the present rebellion by Umlugulu, and other members of the late King's family." The leading historian of the rebellion, T.O. Ranger, argued cogently that the Mwari priesthood fomented rebellion for reasons of its own, cooperating with the Ndebele secular authorities in a "marriage of convenience."

Here we tread on treacherous ground. Outside observers have been reporting on the cult of Mwari for the last hundred years. They have described it as functioning in a varying number of caves in the Matopos, and also, in earlier times, outside that area. It was generally believed to be a Rozvi religion, and to have once had its principal centre at Great Zimbabwe; perhaps even to have dated from long before the Rozvi era. In later times, at any rate, each of the cult caves in the Matopos had a staff of priests or officials. Their most obvious function was oracular. To each cave there came, from places far and near, deputations of "messengers," representing the chiefs who appointed them, with offerings and requests to the high god Mwari. An officer, called by some writers the Ear, received them and passed on the requests. The oracle in the cave uttered his prophecies and commands, which were passed back to the messengers by another officer, the Mouth. A third officer, the Eye, was the priests' source of information, which might be quite comprehensive, as the succession of messengers from every part of a wide region contributed to it. The subjects of the messengers' requests and the priests' oracles could be either matters concerning the public weal, such as famine, drought, or pestilence, or more private and personal problems.

Some confusion has been caused by the fact that the name *Mwari* has been generally used among the Shona as the name of God, and has been so used in their translations by many Christian missionaries. But the oracular cult in the Matopos is a more specific matter.[20]

Julian Cobbing has given well-documented reasons for rejecting the theory that the Mwari priests played any major part in either hatching or directing the revolt. Among the reasons are: that the "shrines" and their officers were not of Rozvi origin, but were brought to the Matopos in the middle of the nineteenth century by Venda from the northern Transvaal; that they could not therefore have stirred anyone up by appealing to memories of Rozvi power; that they were still less able to influence the Ndebele, who regarded the cult with, at best, amused tolerance; that the principal Matopo shrines were inactive in 1896, their "priests" being in exile, or having been killed by Lobengula; that the southern Shona chiefdoms which either remained neutral or supported the whites in the rebellion were precisely those which were most strongly influenced by the cult.

The argument, which demolishes assumptions held by virtually all previous historians, is persuasive as well as bold; but its author does not "imagine . . . that it will end the debate." There may be some room left for the Mwari cult after all.

One of the strongholds of the Ndebele rebels was the Intaba zikaMambo, the hills where the Rozvi monarchy had made one of its last stands. According to Ranger, a new Mwari shrine was set up there after 1893 by Mkwati, a Leya who had been a prisoner of war or slave, but developed some oracular talent, served an apprenticeship as a *nyusa* or messenger of Mwari, and finally assumed the role of priest or presiding officer in a new shrine. Cobbing asserts that Mkwati did not go to the Mambo hills until after the rebellion had broken out, and then did so because it was the nearest place of safety to his home.[21]

There is no doubt that the network of caves in those hills provided a refuge for a large number of women and children, as well as storage space for immense quantities of loot, during the fighting. But the caves were well suited also to the utterance of oracles, and Mkwati uttered them.

Zenkele and Ndebambi were there during my interview with the M'Limo, but Umkwati had disappeared, and we did not see him again until the interview was over . . . Umkwati has always been known as a child of the M'Limo, but the people now say he is the M'Limo, as he is never seen when the M'Limo is speaking, but only appears when the M'Limo is off. The M'Limo has one wife, an old woman, and three children. Umkwati is the father of these children. He sleeps in the same hut as the woman, and besides, the woman could not be impregnate by an invisible spirit.

This statement, the acting chief native commissioner, H.M. Jackson wrote, "discloses the imposture practised by Mkwati, who personates the M'Limo."

The wife referred to was the mysterious Tenkela, who was regarded as Mwari's wife, or as his mother. Another of Mkwati's wives was a daughter of Uwini, the Rozvi chief who led the rebellion in the Gwelo district. Mkwati thus had intimate links with both the secular source of the rebellion and the supposed religious source. But it may well be that Mkwati's influence, over both the origin and the course of the rebellion, has been exaggerated.

The cult of Mwari may have been of recent and Venda origin, and have influenced only a limited area. But there was an older, more deeply rooted and universal religion among the Shona, the cult of the spirit-mediums. There is no argument about the importance of this as a factor in the rebellion of the Shona, and its influence can be traced in the earlier rebellion also.

The spirits in question were those of ancestors—ancestors of the private citizen, of the chief, and (in the north) of the Munhumutapa himself; yet this was not ancestor-worship. The Portuguese were near the mark in saying that the Shona called upon the *Midzimu* (spirits) "as we the saints," but the analogy must not be carried too far. The spirit was thought to have its normal earthly abode in a lion, but from time to time it took possession of a human being, who went into a trance and became the vehicle for the spirit's utterances.

The presence of the spirits and his dependence upon them were fundamental elements in the Shona's thought. They were graded in a hierarchy corresponding to the social arrangements of this world. The spirits of his own ancestors (specifically, his parents and grandparents) were concerned with the welfare of their family; they were the ones to be consulted about family problems such as sickness. Through the medium it could be learned what sacrifice would be acceptable to the family spirit (*mudzimu*); when he was suitably appeased the sickness would depart.

When the problem was a collective one such as drought or famine, one must look to the tribal *mhondoro*, the spirit of one of the chief's ancestors, especially of the founder of the tribe, who was concerned with those public matters but not with the petty affairs of the individual. In extreme cases, when the times were out of joint and the whole country was suffering from disaster, it was necessary to go higher still, to the spirit of the mythical Chaminuka, perhaps a dimly remembered ancestor of one of the early dynasties. At intervals a rarely privileged medium would be possessed by Chaminuka himself, and would give directions for the salvation of the whole land and people.[22]

There is evidence, even in the rebellion in Matabeleland, not only of some

437 The Rebellion, I

religious influence but of a syncretism of the two cults, as in the case of the fifteen-year-old boy Malimba.

> I have heard . . . that Malimba was possessed of the 'Umlimo, and soon afterwards, one evening he threw himself on the ground and rolled about proclaiming to us (the impi) that the M'Limo had entered into him. He gave us messages from the M'Limo. We credited these messages and believed him to be inspired by the M'Limo. He spoke in a voice quite different to his ordinary voice. On several occasions he gave us messages from the M'Limo, and on each occasion concluded his remarks with the M'Limo's valedictory utterance, "Sengi tantabala, baze kulo" in the Seswina [Shona] language meaning "I am going to sleep, go home."

The linguistic point is significant: both the boy and his hearers were Ndebele.[23]

Another character whose role is not quite clear is Siminya, or Siginyam-atshe, a man of considerable reputation in the supernatural arts, who ranked as a "child of Mwari." He became Mkwati's representative and mouthpiece with the army in the field.

One of the four shrines counted by Ranger, but not dealt with specifically by Cobbing, was Mkombo, sometimes called Mangwe. It was in the latter district, and so classified by Schoffeleers among those "outside Matopos." Its presiding officer was Jubane Hlabangana. It is a fact that the people south and west of the Matopos, which is supposed to have been the area of this shrine's influence, opposed the rebellion and supported the government; hence the theory that their course was decided by Jubane, who took a neutral line when the other oracular centres supported the rebellion. If the theory is wrong in re-spect of the other centres it does not follow that it was wrong in Jubane's case. But the "loyal" people whom he is thought to have influenced happened also to be under the leadership of Gampu, who controlled the so-called "iGapha division" and the local Kalanga population. Gampu's influence was thrown on to the government side, and it is impossible to say whether Jubane was leading the opinion of that section or merely expressing it.

However this may be, there is so much evidence that the rebellion was hatched and directed by secular leaders that little room is left for any primary role by the Mwari shrines. As Cobbing has shown, the Shona who rose with the Ndebele in March were precisely those who had been subject to the Nde-bele state. The Shona of the Belingwe district, at least those north of the Me-hingwe river, rose as one man at the beginning of the rebellion; their neigh-bours to the south and east did not stir for another three months. (The former had a Ndebele regiment stationed in their midst.) The rising in Gwelo was led by Uwini, who, whatever his Rozvi origins, was the representative of Ndebele authority there.

The military and civil apparatus of the Ndebele state had not been destroyed in 1893, and it was within this apparatus that the rising was plotted. Mlugulu

438 Rhodes and Rhodesia

had a priestly function, specifically in connection with the *Inxwala* ceremony, the Big Dance, so that the Europeans always called him a "dance doctor"; but he belonged to the royal family and had no connection with the Mwari cult. There is some uncertainty whether, in March 1896, he was supporting Nyamanda as Lobengula's successor. It is certain that the leading figure among the younger indunas, who appears in the records as Mpotshwana or Mposhwana, though there is some doubt whether that was his real name, was a supporter of Nyamanda and an associate of Mkwati and Siginyamatshe.

When Bulawayo was almost surrounded, one gap was left in the circle—the road to the south through Mangwe. The Europeans at the time believed that this resulted from a decision by "the Mlimo" to tempt them to escape from the country. Ranger gives the neutral stance of Jubane as the reason; Cobbing the "treachery" of Gampu. Either way, the result was decisive; the beleaguered Europeans could hardly have survived if the road had been closed.[24]

The whites benefited not only from the neutrality of some sections of the population, but from the active support of others. Older ethnic groups were intermixed with the *abezansi* and *abenhla*, and the history of the country had left many scores to pay off. The role of the "friendlies" in the war will appear later. An incident that deserves to be remembered, especially in association with Rhodes's indabas that ended the rebellion, is the action of the Jesuit missionary Father Prestage within a couple of weeks of the outbreak. He "left his mission station near Mangwe last week, with only one attendant, bravely to go into the Motoppo Hills, and endeavour to alienate many chiefs known to him from taking the rebel side, arrived in town, bringing with him 18 representatives of the leading 10 indunas, representing some 600 people, who were desirous of being protected by us, and granted special protection passes." By the middle of April such passes had been given to 125 headmen in the Bulawayo district, representing about 600 men, and a further 1,200 had been issued for servants.[25]

Nevertheless, the bulk of the Ndebele rebelled. Their regimental organization had not been dismantled after 1893, most of the firearms used in that war had been buried and not surrendered, and military habits had not had time to atrophy. To say that the "regimental" organization had not been dismantled is really to say that the civil and political structure—chieftaincies, villages, official hierarchy—remained intact; military units and command were interwoven with these. Cobbing has examined eighteen case-histories of the genealogies of "great indunas," the "chiefs" who loom large in the story and whose power over their chieftaincies (*izigaba*) was hereditary. The continuity of this power in their families is traced. Of the eighteen representatives of these families in 1896, fourteen led their people into the rebellion and the other four (though not in all cases their followers) supported the government. This study is perhaps the most convincing evidence that the Ndebele system of mobilization and command survived the war of 1893 and was ready to function whenever called upon. Moreover, most of the *izigaba* south and southeast of Bulawayo had not even fought in 1893.[26]

The history of the bloody deeds then about to be done in Rhodesia would be false if it did not emphasize their moral and emotional aspects. On both sides there were cruelty and hatred. If it was the blacks that were cruel first, and the whites that retaliated, it was the whites who had robbed the blacks of their country in the first place. It has been said that the grass grows quickly over the battlefield, but over the scaffold never; nor does it easily cover the remains of women and children murdered in cold blood. Terrible things that were done on both sides entered into the folk-memories of both, and became factors in their later history.

The war of the Ndebele, and later of the Shona, against the white invaders and rulers was from their point of view the great national struggle to recover freedom and independence. It differed from most such revolts in the nature of the enemy. What stood between the old race and the repossession of its country was not merely a political machine or an army of occupation. It was rather an alien economic and cultural network represented by the inhabitants of half-a-dozen small towns, by prospectors, miners, and farmers, with their increasing attachment to their new land and property, their racial exclusiveness, and their cohesion as a group. So long as they remained in position they would increasingly control the country, take the land and cattle, compel the inhabitants to labour, and reduce them to servitude and dependence.

These invaders could not be gently shouldered aside and made to mind their own business. They could not be absorbed, as others had been, into the existing society and culture. The only way they could be prevented from taking over the country and everything in it was to remove them all entirely. If they could be wiped out, it seemed to the plotters of revolt, the *status quo ante* would be restored and the problem solved.

The rebels did not achieve either their immediate or their ultimate object. Their ultimate object could not have been achieved anyway. They did not know that even the penny-pinching men in the Colonial Office had always taken for granted that a catastrophe to the Rhodesian settlers would have to be followed by imperial retribution, whatever the cost. But now, as in 1893, there was a great difference between defeat by the local whites and defeat by the imperial forces. In 1893 the Company won the war almost unaided, and came near to dictating the peace. Now, if the rebellion was to be crushed anyway, very much would depend on who did the crushing.

The remote origin of the rebels' plan was said to have been the instructions which Lobengula, just before his death, had sent to Mlugulu by the induna Mazwe. When the opportunity came the former was to revive the Big Dance and all the rites of the kingdom. The capture of Jameson having provided the opportunity, and a partial eclipse of the moon on 28 February the divine signal, Mlugulu and a number of leading indunas planned to hold the dance on the border of the Filabusi mining district at the full moon on 29 March. The rites would be restored and the new king (Nyamanda, though there has been some argument about whether he was universally supported at this time) inaugurated. Doubts about what was intended have never been resolved, because the *Inxwala* was not held. Various eager patriots acted too soon and the plans went awry. According to the official report of Duncan and Norris Newman it was a quarrel between "certain natives and some of the native police" in Filabusi about a woman that caused the shooting to begin prematurely.[27]

If the revolt was to begin with a massacre, the price of white hatred, vengeance, and stiffened resolution had to be paid, but there might have been a compensating gain if the Company and the settlers had been eliminated as factors in the peace settlement. The failure to achieve this was a disaster for the rebels.

They failed because of their divisions, because some of them acted prematurely, but also because of a strategic mistake which might still have been made even if there had been unity. The most elementary principle of strategy, as of tactics, is to concentrate at the decisive point. The decisive point in Matabeleland was Bulawayo. If the Ndebele had overwhelmed the town before it had prepared its defences, the isolated whites in the rest of the country could have been mopped up at leisure. Selous believed that an attack would have succeeded: "if 2000 of them, or even a smaller number, had made a night attack upon the town before the laager had been formed, I think it more than probable that the entire white population would have been massacred."[28]

Instead, the rebel plan was to murder the isolated whites first, and then concentrate on the big kill. If this strategy were to have any chance of success, it would depend on secrecy and speed. "Celerity," said Napoleon, "is better than artillery," but the rebels took a long time to concentrate for the attack on Bulawayo. There was some secrecy in the opening moves, but most of its advantage was lost because those moves were not synchronized.

The elements of surprise and of horror are made vivid, and perhaps some evidence of the "oracular" factor too is provided, by the simple account of Nganganyoni, who lived near Inyati:

> We had the news from the Matopos that Mlimo was going to help us, so we just decided among ourselves that there were white people over there and we had better go there. We had no grievance against these people. We killed them merely because they were white people. We were going to kill all the white people because we had the news that the Mlimo was going to help us. These white people had a store built of brick with a thatched roof . . . The three white men lived in the three huts, and all three had native wives . . . We got in the store and asked for limbo [cloth] . . . While we were still talking to Wani [the storekeeper] and he was looking at the limbo hanging up and pointing to different pieces and asking us which piece we wanted . . . I caught hold of Wani and we both fell down, and while we were on the floor Kafuli struck him with an

axe behind the head as we were struggling on the floor. The one blow killed him . . . When Matekenya and Ngonye reached Mandisi [another of the white men, who was reaping in the field] he did not know they were coming to kill him, because he knew them . . . When they got to him, he greeted them and told them that as they had come they had better help him with the reaping. They walked near him and then they hit him once and Ngonye then chopped his neck with an axe.

The third white man was in bed, "very, very ill," so that dispatching him was no problem.[29]

Other early victims were taken equally by surprise. The Cunningham family—parents, six children, and grandfather—lived on a farm near the Insiza river. On Monday, 23 March, while the grandfather was lying on a couch reading a newspaper and the rest were having their midday meal—unaware of any trouble brewing in the country—a party of Ndebele suddenly burst into the house and bludgeoned them to death. One of the daughters, aged about seven, escaped to the river, survived a few days, and was then found by a party of Ndebele women. One of these held the girl down with one hand, and with the other smashed her head with a stone. A few hours after the first murders a party similarly armed with knobkerries and battle-axes approached the huts of Thomas Maddocks and two other miners at the Nellie Reef, a few miles from the Cunninghams' farm. They put the white men off their guard by saying that they were looking for work. In the next instant, to the shout of "Shaya!" (strike), Maddocks was felled, but one of his companions was able to enter his hut, reach his revolver and kill one of the assailants. He and the other miner, both wounded, managed to make their way to Harry Cumming's store, about three miles away. Some twenty others had collected there; the murder of the Cunninghams had given the alarm.

The next morning a party led by Mfezela himself, believed by some to be a claimant to the throne, entered the store of E.C. Edkins at Filabusi, killing the storekeeper, three other white men, two African servants ("colonial natives"), and the Indian cook. Near by was the office of the native commissioner, Arthur Bentley. He was stabbed from behind while sitting at his desk writing a letter. In the same neighbourhood, at or near the Celtic mine, two white miners were killed, and a "colonial native" was left for dead (his mouth slit open from ear to ear for good measure). But he recovered and was able to give evidence against the assailants.

In this manner some two hundred whites (if those listed as missing are included) were dispatched at lonely mines, farms, native commissioners' offices and trading stores, or at the roadside, in the bush, or in the river bed as they were trying to escape. With them perished many of their black servants, and other Africans and Indians, but these are not listed either by name or even collectively in the official records of the murders. The omission has a profound significance.[30]

The whites, however, were not in a mood of judicial detachment. Many of the murders were gruesome, many of the bodies mutilated, and some of the victims were women and children. Selous spoke for all his countrymen:

> With others I went down to the scene of the massacre of the Fourie family early in the morning and found the remains of four people—a woman and three children, the body of Mr. Fourie and those of three of the children being missing. The murders had evidently been committed with knob-kerries and axes, as the skulls of all these poor people had been very much shattered. The remains had been much pulled about by dogs or jackals, but the long fair hair of the young Dutch girls was still intact, and it is needless to say that these blood-stained tresses awoke the most bitter wrath in the hearts of all who looked upon them, Englishmen and Dutchmen alike vowing a pitiless vengeance against the whole Matabele race.

Three months after the outbreak, Captain Laing and his column halted at the Cunningham farm and found the remains of that family. "It has not been the lot of many," Laing wrote, "to behold a more melancholy, heartrending, and revolting spectacle . . . The slight glance I had at Cunningham's was too much for me . . . A very slight glance at the faces of the men around the grave, whilst the service was being read, would have convinced the most casual observer that mercy would be the last thing the rebels might expect to get from them."[31]

If all human feeling could be stifled, what would seem to be most significant about the murders was that they were not, as a cunningly devised plan would have ensured, simultaneous. Each murder served as a warning to other intended victims, so that if a couple of hundred whites in lonely places were killed, many more had time to escape to safety. Above all, Bulawayo was warned.

If Mlugulu's plan had been carried out, the Big Dance would have been held at the full moon on 29 March, a king would have been installed, and there would have been unity of command.[32] This event would presumably have been the signal for the massacre of the isolated whites, everywhere at the same time. It is not clear why the plan to revive the *Inxwala* was abandoned, though dissensions among the leaders could have had something to do with it. Even if there was to be no dance or coronation, it would have been sensible to keep the day of the full moon as the day for the outbreak. Instead, Mfezela— supposed by some to be a claimant to the royal succession—led a killing party on the 24th, and other murders had been committed the day before that. When Nganganyoni and his friends got "news" from the Mlimo, and then "just decided among themselves" to kill the local white men, the implication is that no precise date had been given to them.

So Harry Cumming, at whose store refugees gathered after the murders on the 23rd, was in Bulawayo with the news by the next morning. Arthur Cumming (no relation to Harry) got to town the day after that, reporting the Filabusi murders. The news then flashed along the telegraph lines.

Belingwe was not on a telegraph line, but early on the 26th the native commissioner, S. Jackson, received a note from his colleague H.P. Fynn at Insiza, telling him of the murders and advising him "to see Captain Laing and get all the prospectors and miners to concentrate at the Belingwe Store until we can get further news." Messages were sent out at once to all the whites known to be in the neighbourhood, so that "about thirty Europeans, a few Colonial natives and a number of Zambesi natives employed on the mines concentrated at the Consolidated-Belingwe Development Company's headquarters. Captain Laing took command, and everything was done to place the camp in a proper state of defence." This laager was successfully held through the rebellion, and no Europeans were killed in the Belingwe district.[33]

Gwelo, being on the telegraph line, heard the first tentative reports on the 25th. The local families—all eight of them—at once made preparations to go into laager, and sent "warnings to the miners and prospectors all round the Gwelo district to come in at once, . . . and from then till a week after, the wagons, light traps, scotch carts and indeed every kind of conveyance in the District came pouring in." Within a few days the telegraph wires on all sides were cut (a sign of increased sophistication since 1893), and Gwelo was then so short of ammunition that it could not have withstood an attack for more than a quarter of an hour. It was not attacked. Gwelo, like Belingwe, held out to the end.[34]

They could not have held out if Bulawayo had fallen. The outcome of the struggle depended on Bulawayo, which as Selous said could have been overwhelmed in the first few days. As soon as the first reports came in, the immediate concern in the town was for the safety of the whites who might still be alive in the countryside. For two or three weeks patrols were going out to rescue any that could be saved. The first, led by Maurice Gifford (brother of Lord Gifford), left on the evening of the 25th for Harry Cumming's store. Gifford had one day in which to strengthen the defences there before a determined attack was made, before daylight on the 28th, by an impi of about 300 under the induna Msindazi. The defenders barely succeeded in warding off the attack, and in getting back to Bulawayo after a three days' march.

After the killings described by Nganganyoni, the remaining Europeans at Inyati (except the missionary Rees and his family, who had been allowed to depart unmolested) tried to escape. In a five-hour fight all except one white miner and his African companion were killed. The patrol on its way to save them had itself to be reinforced before it could get back, fighting a sharp skirmish on the way. The first Victoria Cross of the campaign was won on this patrol.

Still less successful, and much more severely mauled, was the Gwanda patrol under Captains Brand and van Niekerk. They led a force of a hundred men, with a Maxim gun, to rescue the white population of Gwanda. As that population was on its way to safety in the Tuli laager before the patrol arrived, Brand had to return with nothing accomplished. In the course of the journey he handed over the command to the more experienced van Niekerk. As they went back up the road, smoke signals on the hills gave them some warning of what was to come. The induna Babayane, sometime envoy to England, was now in the Matopos organizing an impi of over a thousand men to destroy the patrol. The running fight on 10 April was grim for both sides, but the patrol got through, with a loss of eight killed and twenty wounded.

By that time Bulawayo had enough to do to defend itself, without trying to save the stragglers. Indeed, this had been the case from the beginning, and the absence of the competent leaders—Napier, Spreckley, Maurice Gifford, Macfarlane, George Grey, Selous, van Niekerk—with many indispensable men on rescue operations had been a sore point with the townspeople.[35]

The first reports of murders, on 24 March, had been received calmly, as isolated incidents, though the authorities began to take precautions. When further news came in on the 25th the mood changed. The danger was compounded by the restraints which the imperial government had imposed after the Jameson Raid. Captain Nicholson, in charge of the Bulawayo armoury, could not issue arms or ammunition without the high commissioner's permission. This was asked for on the 24th, but Robinson delayed his reply. When it came it was permission to issue arms, and one hundred rounds each, to a maximum of one hundred volunteers. A greater number would cause too much excitement in the Transvaal, especially as Rhodes had now arrived in Rhodesia. Robinson's sights were still set on Kruger and the raid, but on the 25th Nicholson opened the armoury on his own responsibility, and Robinson, now better informed, approved.[36]

The false alarm of an attack gave Bulawayo its brief moment of panic:

> The Government store was besieged by a clamouring and excited crowd of citizens, eager above everything to obtain possession of a rifle, and, if needs be, die fighting. After what seemed an eternity of waiting, the window of the building was thrown up, and rifles handed out as fast as possible. Then the clamour and confusion was increased tenfold. Men fought their way up to the source of supply, clambering on to each other's shoulders, grabbing and snatching the coveted weapons, some struggling in vain for a place, others more fortunate getting away with two rifles, and so under the moonlight the distribution of arms went on until the last of the supply had been given out.

Many who received rifles were handling them for the first time in their lives. They would have had short shrift if the Ndebele had marshalled their regiments for an attack that day.

In the meantime "a mass of people streamed through the streets seeking safety or clattered into town on vehicles of every description."

445 The Rebellion, I

The scene when the false alarm was given was a weird one. The figures hurrying in the bright moonlight towards the Court-house, the cries of women—altho' be it said to their credit these were few and far between, the majority of the ladies taking things admirably—the tinkling bells of the oxen, the crowing of the fowls, and the howls of the dogs, who, with all the marvellous instinct of dumb animals, seemed to know something unusual was happening, all these combined to make the scene one which will live in the memory of everyone present.[37]

But the rebels, after all, were not ready to attack, and their delay gave the defenders time to organize. The surveyor-general, Andrew Duncan, who was acting administrator of Matabeleland, under pressure from the public appointed a Council of War. It consisted of eight officers, including such well-known figures as General Digby Willoughby (chief of staff), Selous, Norris Newman, Macfarlane, and Nicholson, and for some weeks was the effective authority in the beleaguered town.

Apart from a handful of police, the only defence Jameson had left in Rhodesia (and he had intended to withdraw even that) was the two regiments of the Rhodesia Horse Volunteers, commanded respectively by Napier and Spreckley. The Matabeleland Regiment, whose members found themselves in various laagers, could no longer function as a unit. The Council of War therefore dissolved it, and in its place formed, for Bulawayo, a unit of regularly enlisted and paid men, the Bulawayo Field Force—five troops plus artillery—under the command of Spreckley. In addition to this there were the "Afrikander Corps," commanded by W.H. van Rensburg, George Grey's company of scouts, and a corps of over a hundred "Colonial natives," forty of them armed with rifles, raised, armed, mounted, and commanded by Colenbrander. Napier, with the rank of colonel, was put in command of all the forces in Matabeleland.

It was easier to enlist men than to arm and mount them. There were about 800 men in Bulawayo available for service, but only some 400 rifles and 100 serviceable horses. Ammunition for small arms was plentiful, the number of horses was raised within a month to nearly 450 by commandeering, and the armourers got to work on old and defective weapons. At the beginning there was in Bulawayo only one Maxim in good order; there were seven other guns of various kinds, but some were short of ammunition and the seven-pounder was immovable, its carriage having been eaten by white ants. Such was the equipment for the patrols which the Council of War sent out in the first three weeks.[38]

And for the defence of the town. No time was lost, however, in constructing the passive defence works. The building of a laager on the Market Square was begun on 26 March. The Market Building formed a kind of keep in the middle of the bailey. The laager consisted of a double row of wagons arranged in a square, chained together and sandbagged. Outside this there were three barbed wire fences and a belt, thirty yards wide, of broken glass. There were at first several gateways; later only one. A well was dug inside the laager to en-

446 Rhodes and Rhodesia

Market Square, Bulawayo. The laager, 1896

Umtali, from racecourse, about 1900

447 The Rebellion, I

sure a water supply. Strongpoints were established in other parts of the town. A watchtower, a searchlight, and minefields added to its defensive strength. When the work was complete Selous thought it was probably the strongest laager ever constructed in South Africa, and that "the whole Matabele nation, I think, would never have taken it by assault."[39]

The rebels had missed their chance. It is easier, however, to point to their weaknesses in organization, coordination, and timing than to suggest how these defects could have been remedied. Even if there had been perfect unity of command, the plans could not have been revealed in advance to more than a small number of leaders without the risk of their leaking to the enemy. So the plans, such as they were, were made known only to a few, not apparently very systematically chosen, and in various forms and to various degrees. How this necessary restriction affected the operations is shown by the role of the Native Police.

In the light of what was said about these in the last chapter, one would have expected them to be the first victims of the rebellion. Such collaborators with the regime have usually been prime targets in a revolution, and these collaborators had been widely singled out as a special grievance. And in a very limited way they were—or rather one of them was—the first victim.

On the night of Friday, 20 March, a group of Ndebele under the induna Mzobo approached a party of police who were camped near the Mzingwane river. They kept taunting the police; one of them crept round stealthily with his assegai but was detected; there was a scuffle in which the man with the assegai, but also two boys who carried blankets for the police, were shot. The assailants then moved off to a neighbouring kraal belonging to a nephew of Lobengula, roused him and went on with him to yet another kraal, where they were challenged by a policeman, whom they shot.

This was in fact the first act of the rebellion, but when the news reached Bulawayo there were few who suspected that it was more than an isolated incident. The important points about it were, first, that Mzobo was unable to restrain his patriotic zeal any longer, though D-day (if there was one) was still more than a week ahead; and second, that the police acted throughout as loyal servants of the government.

More light is thrown on their conduct by other examples. When Fynn at Insiza sent the news of the first murders to Belingwe, and so enabled Laing to organize the defence there, the message was carried by one of the Native Police. That policeman, however, "never returned to his duty, but . . . went over to the rebels with his rifle and bandolier full of cartridges." In the meantime Laing had sent out messages in all directions warning Europeans to come into laager. These messages were faithfully carried by *his* Native Police. The next day, as Jackson reports, "two strange natives" passed through the camp. The demeanour of the police immediately changed. They deserted to the rebels, after being frustrated in their design to murder Jackson, Laing, and others.

Thus many of the whites were saved because the Native Police had not been told in time that the rebellion had begun. Once they were told they deserted in large numbers, taking with them not only rifles and ammunition but the musketry training which made the marksmanship of 1896 much better than that of 1893.[40]

It is hard to say whether the conduct of Gampu was decided by this lack of coordination in the outbreak of the revolt. He had never been a very enthusiastic defender of the old order, and his relationship with Lobengula had been ambivalent. It is possible that he expected the killing to begin at the full moon. However that may be, when the news of the murders came through several days earlier, Gampu happened to be in Bulawayo. He was detained there, and never joined the rebellion. Most of his followers likewise "sat still."

Not quite still. Gampu's "head induna" Mazwe had his kraal some miles off the Figtree road. On 4 May the kraal was attacked by a small impi under Mayeza, and most of the women, children, and stock carried off. One of Mazwe's men, however, named Hobasi after the "Oubaas" Hartley, rallied others from neighbouring villages, pursued the impi, killed eleven men, and recovered the captives. Thus Gampu kept a considerable region in the south and west on the government side. As he had a long record of opposition to Lobengula, it is unlikely that he would have acted differently, even if he had not been caught in Bulawayo, or influenced by the oracle of Mkombo.[41]

The defection of most of the Native Police was a great gain for the rebels, but it would have been greater if it had not been delayed by ignorance of what was happening. Within a few days, too, the rebel forces were well supplied with firearms, dug up from the hiding places of 1893; but the initial murders were by knobkerrie and axe. The recovery of the firearms took time.

Gathering the regiments before Bulawayo took time too. They were divided geographically. Mlugulu and his allies formed a distinct group based in and near the Matopos. It was they who had nearly destroyed the Gwanda patrol. After that fight their main impi of about 2,000 lay across the Tuli road some twenty-five miles south of Bulawayo. Babayane and Dliso, of the same faction, with 800 men were further to the northwest, on the Khami river.

A larger force of about 4,000 men, the main army facing the Europeans in the first phase of the war, formed a great arc round the north and northeast of Bulawayo. Nyamanda, the royal heir, was with this force. There must have been some unity of command on that front; Nyamanda himself does not appear in the role of a fighting general; there is some evidence that Mtini, induna of the Inqobo regiment, played that part, though perhaps only as the first among equals. Ranger has claimed some kind of leadership, religious rather than military, for Mkwati, whose resort to the Mambo hills has been variously explained. The military commander was accompanied in the earlier battles by the "child of Mwari," Siginyamatshe, in the combined role of spiritual guide and comforter, information officer, and political commissar.[42]

Thus, by the middle of April, the opposing forces were in position. There were no more isolated whites for the rebels to murder or for the patrols to rescue. In the second phase of the war, now opening, the object of each side was military victory over the armed forces of the other. In the event, neither side could achieve this unaided. The issue would depend on help from outside.

The stalemate was revealed by operations in the second half of April. The immediate danger to Bulawayo came from the rebels on the northern side, who occupied the north bank of the Umguza river. Their front extended for many miles, and at one point was within five miles of the town. On 12 April one of their raiding parties came within a mile and a half of the Memorial Hospital. Unless this impi of 4,000 were driven off, it could attack Bulawayo, almost without warning, at any time. In fact Mtini appears to have had no intention of doing this. He hoped that in a series of battles and skirmishes the limited force of the whites would be so reduced as to make the town defenceless.[43]

The defenders provided the battles. Parties of various sizes sallied forth to the Umguza on 16, 19, 20, 22, and 25 April. The first four of these sallies were unsuccessful in that the Ndebele held their ground, though suffering losses. The fifth was a victory. The rebel force broke and was pursued for some distance by mounted men.[44]

Some reasons for the failures on both sides can be identified. The immense numerical superiority of the Ndebele, which (as they had firearms and used them better than in 1893) might seem to guarantee their success, was compensated by the whites' advantage in horses and machine-guns. At the critical stage of the fight at Colenbrander's farm on 25 April it was the Maxim that in an hour of hot fighting kept the rebels at bay. On 19 April the whites faced near disaster when the Maxim jammed. They were close to disaster again on 10 April when Bissett, in command, failed to bring the Maxim and the Hotchkiss into action at the decisive moment.

As in all previous South African wars, mounted men had an immeasurable advantage over impis on foot, in that they could choose their point of attack, fire their volleys, and retire before the "horns" could close round them. The advantage was less in 1896 than it had been in the past, because the enemy, though on foot, was using firearms; but the importance of the horse was obvious in all those encounters on the Umguza. Each time the attackers were in serious difficulty they withdrew safely. The sufferers were those who, because they were wounded or their horses had been killed, could not ride. Yet it is possible to give the horses too much of the credit. Some of the successes in those skirmishes were scored by the "Cape Boys" or "Colonial Kafirs," who fought on foot. Thus Selous describes part of the action on 22 April:

> As the kafirs [Ndebele] were in possession of some ridges just in front of us as well, I was asked to advance with the Colonial Boys from the centre, and endeavour

to chase them across the river . . . The boys came on capitally, led by their officers, who were all mounted, and we soon drove all the Matabele in this part of the field through the Umguza, and following them up at once, pursued them for about a mile over some stony ridges covered with scrubby bush . . . A number of the Matabele had built little fortifications of loose stones near the bank of the river, from behind the shelter of which they fired on us; but the warlike Amakosa and Zulus charged them most gallantly, and engaging them hand to hand drove them out of their shelters into the river, and killed many of them in the water.

The party Selous was describing consisted of a hundred men.[45]

The mounted whites numbered 110. That they could score such successes against an army of 4,000 was due mainly to the fact that the latter could usually not concentrate at short notice. In each encounter it was only a small part of the Ndebele force that was engaged. This explains also why the successes of the whites, such as they were, were short-lived. As soon as the rebels began to converge on the point of attack, the attackers were forced to withdraw. On 20 April, when Napier with his 230 whites and 100 local African levies (armed only with assegais) reached Colenbrander's farm, he found 3,000 rebels prepared to resist his crossing of the river. He retreated at once. On 25 April a battle was fought on the same site, the rebels were beaten and driven away, but the victory was temporary; the Ndebele could not be prevented from returning to their old position.

Yet there are some grounds for regarding that fight as an important turning-point in the war. The victory restored the failing morale of the besieged and seriously damaged the morale of the besiegers. That morale derived much of its strength from superstitious or religious factors. On 19 April, the day the Maxim jammed, the whites under Macfarlane were in serious danger until a spring hare crossed the path in front of the Ndebele pursuers—who then ceased their pursuit because of the unpropitious omen.

The role of superstition in these fights has been questioned, partly because much of the evidence for it comes from Company sources, and partly perhaps because it seems discreditable to the Ndebele. But the chief evidence does come from statements made later by Ndebele deponents; and recourse to superstition has been common to many forces putting up what seemed to be a hopeless resistance—from the Xhosa cattle killing to the Angel of Mons. Thus the "news from the Mlimo" was said to include more important matters than spring hares, such as that if the white man crossed the Umguza they would be struck blind, or (in another version) that their horses would drop dead and their bullets would turn to water. These certainties were vouched for by Siginyamatshe, the spiritual and political commissar of Mtini's army. The army was constantly reminded of his presence and his authority by blasts on his kudu horn, by which he signalled an attack or taunted the retreating enemy. When, therefore, the enemy crossed the Umguza with impunity on 25 April, the rebels' hearts failed them for a time, and some serious damage was done to Siginyamatshe's authority.

The rebels could not take Bulawayo, but they could not be driven away either. For a month after the last fight at Colenbrander's farm all was quiet on the northern front.

Bulawayo, like many another town that could not be taken by assault, would have fallen if it had been starved out. It was indeed almost surrounded by the rebel impis—but not quite: the road to Mangwe and the south remained open. The people of the besieged town were puzzled as well as grateful. They concluded that the road had been left open by the rebels to tempt the whites to escape from Matabeleland. The true explanation is the influence of Gampu, with or without encouragement from the local Mwari shrine.

The road was not entirely safe; it ran too close to the Matopos, the base of the southern party of rebels. Small forts were therefore built at intervals along it, largely by Selous. In ordinary circumstances supplies could thus have been brought into Bulawayo in large quantities. The rinderpest, however, which reached Matabeleland almost at the moment of the outbreak, nearly destroyed the system of ox-drawn transport. Mules had to be substituted for oxen. A mule wagon could carry only about a third of an ox-wagon's freight load, mainly because it had to take fodder for the mules as well, whereas oxen grazed on the veld. During the first critical month supplies reached Bulawayo in a trickle, but they were enough.[46]

It was not only supplies that were needed, but reinforcements. This question was of course being considered from the moment of the outbreak, and decisions had been made, but they were very difficult decisions. The intervention of imperial troops in the fighting would mean a corresponding imperial intervention in the subsequent settlement. Though the British Government had the legal right to that intervention anyway, troops or no troops, the suppression of the rebellion by Company and settlers alone would inhibit the imperial factor when the terms of peace were being decided. The war of 1893 had shown that. Yet the price of refusing imperial help might be disaster. The price of accepting it was not merely imperial dictation of the peace settlement. It was a price measured in money, for the Company would be expected to pay for any imperial troops that were provided. If it were allowed to raise any for itself it would of course pay for those too. No wonder the decision to accept the imperial troops gave Grey a sleepless night.

Grey, the new administrator, was not yet in Rhodesia. He landed in Cape Town on 7 April, having sailed from England before the beginning of the rebellion, and had immediately to assume responsibility; but before his arrival some decisions had been made by others. Duncan, the Company's representative in Bulawayo, had asked Col. David Harris in Kimberley to raise 500 volunteers for the relief of Matabeleland. Harris (no relation of Rutherfoord) was a De Beers man and commander of volunteers in Kimberley. Robinson, however, quickly stopped this Company scheme. Five hundred volunteers might indeed be raised, but they must be under the command of imperial officers. Pending the arrival of Sir Richard Martin, who it was then assumed would command all forces in the Company's service, the man in charge would be the same Major (promoted Lieutenant-Colonel) Plumer who had been to Bulawayo to take over the armoury. Plumer, who was assisted by other imperial officers, went to Mafeking to supervise the enrolment.

There was no lack of volunteers. In accepting them, priority was given to the old police who had ridden with Jameson and were now at a loose end, some in England and some in South Africa. Those who had returned to England were now sent back in small batches by different ships—in order to avoid alarming Kruger. They and their colleagues who had remained in South Africa found their way to Mafeking and joined up. There were about 220 of them, and it had been decided that this number would be additional to, not included in, the original strength of 500. All this had been arranged, and partly carried out, before Grey's ship reached Table Bay.[47]

The sensitivity to Kruger's feelings was natural and necessary. The first batch of Jameson's raiders had left England well before the outbreak in Rhodesia, the rumour of "troops from England" reached Kruger's ears, and he was alarmed. Duncan, in his first panic, had suggested that reinforcements should be sent to him through the Transvaal, a suggestion which was brushed aside by his superiors as "absurd." Kruger may have enjoyed the irony of offering Transvaal burghers to help against the Ndebele rebels, but the offer was made to discourage the dispatch of troops from England. It was declined with thanks.

As the danger in Matabeleland increased, the high commissioner was bombarded with demands for more reinforcements; as the danger from rebels appeared to recede and the spectre of bankruptcy loomed larger, the Company men withdrew the demands. The net result of the oscillation was that the high commissioner authorized two additions to the force being raised by Plumer.

The first arose from Duncan's request for "a force of 500 Cape Colonial boys as scouts and to fight with Col. Plumer's force of 720 men"—a request that seems to have originated with Martin before he left England. After several modifications, including a plan to recruit in Basutoland, which was thought unwise by both the resident commissioner there and the president of the Free State, this corps became the 200 "Cape Boys" recruited in Johannesburg by Major Robertson. They were mostly mineworkers, included Cape Coloured men as well as Africans, and were attached to Plumer's Matabeleland Relief Force. They were armed with rifles and bayonets, but had no scabbards, so that their bayonets were fixed at all times. The cold steel gave them a frightening appearance, but, as will be seen, was not the only reason the enemy had to fear them.[48]

The other reinforcement was a response to a cry from Grey on 12 April for

500 more white troops in addition to the force being raised by Plumer. Robinson pointed out several objections to increasing the number of volunteers in this way, including the difficulty in finding horses for them; he suggested, instead, sending 300 cavalry and 200 mounted infantry drawn from the imperial garrison in Natal. The change was proposed almost casually, but it was fundamental. Grey had asked for volunteers; he accepted the regulars reluctantly, and spent a sleepless night after doing so, even though the regulars would be "a cheaper and better force, and one that is immediately available." Even before Grey (who had reached Mafeking) telegraphed his acceptance, Chamberlain had seen the directors in London and been assured that they would pay for the imperial troops.

The messages back and forth between Grey, Duncan, Robinson, and Chamberlain on 12, 13, and 14 April show that Grey's anxiety in accepting the regulars was not caused by the expense. That was a perpetual source of anxiety, but the expense would have been no less if the additional troops had been more volunteers. Grey's worry was about the participation of the imperial factor in the war and, consequently, the peace. Volunteers recruited in Kimberley or Mafeking were not imperial troops. Plumer, who raised them, described his own position as that of·"an Imperial Officer appointed by the High Commissioner in Connection with the forces of the British South Africa Company," though it was understood that Sir Richard Martin was to be in supreme command when he arrived.

The decision to employ imperial forces changed all that. Chamberlain cabled on 17 April: "As Imperial troops are being employed, War Office insist on command being entrusted to military officer on full pay and approved by them. I am sorry for Martin's disappointment but he will doubtless recognise impossibility of divided command." The officer selected was Maj.-Gen. Sir Frederick Carrington, former commander of the BBP and veteran of many South African wars. Martin, who would be only a part-time commandant-general, did not meet the War Office's requirement. The division of authority between him and Carrington was subtly and flexibly defined.

The imperial force was, in the end, not composed exactly as had at first been planned. Lieut.-Col. E.A.H. Alderson was summoned from Ireland to command a composite force of mounted infantry culled from various units at Aldershot. These reached Cape Town on 19 May and were detained there for a month. The rebellion in Mashonaland having broken out, Alderson and a part of his force were sent round to Beira, where they were later joined by a detachment of the West Riding Regiment from Natal. Alderson took the responsibility also of removing from another ship some troops on their way to Mauritius. The combined force was moved up to Umtali and fought in Mashonaland. The remaining units from Natal—7th Hussars and some mounted infantry—which were the imperial force originally accepted by Grey, were sent to Mafeking. On 20 June their movement up to Motloutsi was authorized. Though they later went on to Bulawayo, they were essentially a reserve, which in the end was hardly needed. The imperial forces, as distinct from officers, played no significant part in the fighting in Matabeleland.

Plumer's column did. Not the least of Plumer's achievements was to move it up through drought-stricken country to Bulawayo without ox-drawn transport. The column moved in small detachments, the first leaving Mafeking on 12 April and the last on 1 May. In addition to the white volunteers and the "Cape Boys" the column included a party of 240 Ngwato and others raised in Kgama's country. Most of these, however, were found to be useless in action, and were soon disbanded and sent home.[49]

They were not the only people travelling southwards. There are records of a coward or two, such as the young "member of a famous English family" who "was too frightened to sleep in the men's laager" but was put into the women's and children's quarters. After several frantic attempts he succeeded in getting down to Mafeking. Perhaps some of the other emigrants were really white feather men too, though putting a bolder face on it. At any rate the south-bound coaches were full, and by late April the *Chronicle* was deploring the departure of so many people, "including many ladies," for the south. At the end of August a similar flight began from Salisbury. The reason was not only, perhaps not even mainly, cowardice. The economy of Rhodesia had almost ground to a halt. The departure of everyone who was not taking an active part in the war, or its support behind the lines, was actually an advantage to the authorities, who would have had to feed them.

Bulawayo could do without mouths, but it needed hands, and there was one other quarter from which they came—Salisbury. The news of the murders having been received there on 25 March, a detachment of ten men of the Rhodesia Horse Volunteers, under Captain Gibbs, with two Maxims, 50 spare rifles, and much ammunition, set out "at a couple of hours' notice." They reached Gwelo on the 29th. Captain Gibbs took command there and enlisted a force of "284 volunteers, 52 burghers and 180 natives," which patrolled the Gwelo district and established forts at various places. The main relief force from Salisbury, 150 men of the Rhodesia Horse under their own officer Lieut.-Col. Robert Beal, did not get away till 6 April because of what the rinderpest had done to the transport. They took with them "ample supplies" for the Gwelo laager. And they took Cecil Rhodes.[50]

Rhodes had returned from his flying visit to England by the East Coast route, landing at Beira and avoiding Cape Town. A Parliamentary committee in Cape Town was investigating the raid, and censured Rhodes, who was still a member of that Parliament, for absenting himself. If he had got involved in that enquiry he would not have reached Rhodesia for a long time. So he made his way up from Beira, had an attack of fever, and was still ill when he reached Salisbury. Disregarding his health he went with Beal's force to Gwelo. With half of his life's work in ruins, and rebels threatening the other half, Rhodes was now at the beginning of his "finest hour." It was from the Gwelo laager that he sent his cocky telegram, "Let resignation wait." It was there too that he conferred upon himself (causing what Chamberlain in an understatement called "comment and misunderstanding" in London) the rank of full colonel. He did this to end the bickering between the officers of two columns, neither of whom would serve under the other, but both willingly under Rhodes, as he informed Chamberlain: "For Secretary of State for Colonies. Tell him there is no colonel more unhappy than I am; obliged to take position to smooth over individual jealousies as to rank between the various officers. The result is I have to go out into the field and be fired at by the horrid Matabeles with their beastly elephant guns, which make a fearful row. It is a new and most unpleasant sensation."

On 14 May, the very day of this characteristic message, Martin arrived in Bulawayo and took command. On 3 June Carrington arrived and took over the military part of Martin's functions. A fellow passenger in the coach with Carrington was Lieut.-Col. Robert Baden-Powell, his chief of staff, whose favourite and most successful occupation in the campaign was to be scouting. A few days before these officers, Beal's column from Salisbury, Napier's column that had gone out to meet it, and Rhodes, had reached Bulawayo. Plumer himself had come in Martin's coach, and most of his column was there by the end of May. All of these arrived barely in time for what was to prove a decisive battle.[51]

Within two days of Carrington's assumption of command, columns under Plumer and Macfarlane moved out to the northwest and north, but failed to engage the enemy. On the evening of 5 June Burnham, the American scout, and Sir Charles Metcalfe, the railway engineer, went out looking for Beal's camp. What they thought were its lights were found to be the fires of the main rebel army, from which they had a narrow escape.

The rebel leader in the north, whether Mkwati or one of the regular military commanders, had indeed managed to put his army together again after the defeat of 25 April, to restore its morale, and to revive the belief that the whites would be struck blind if they crossed the Umguza. There was now a force of between 1,000 and 1,200 along the river, elite troops picked from eight regiments. Carrington could not send anything like that number against it immediately, as Plumer and Macfarlane had taken most of the men out in other directions. A third column, under Spreckley, was due to go out on the 6th, and did so, but now for a bigger operation than it had expected. Spreckley had 150 mounted men, including some of the Salisbury column and such unattached officers as Baden-Powell; "one hundred men from the Native Contingent, under Captain Colenbrander, followed soon after at a quick march, and came up with the main body at the Welsh Harp Hotel."

The column crossed the Umguza at various points and deployed, while still in what was dead ground to the rebels: "we were hidden from the Kafirs by the slope of rising ground behind which they had retreated, but when this was crested they were seen in the bush little more than a hundred yards in front of the foremost horsemen." The attackers were puzzled to notice that, while they were crossing the stream, their enemies were moving about calmly and without excitement. They learned afterwards that this self-confidence arose from the belief that the Mlimo was about to dispose of the whites by drowning—"he would cause the stream to open and swallow up every man of us." (This was another variant of the theme; it could have been blindness, or bullets turning to water.)

But something had gone wrong with the M'limo's machinery, and we crossed the stream without any contretemps. So, as we got nearer to the swarm of black heads among the grass and bushes, their rifles began to pop and their bullets to flit past with a weird little "phit," "phit," or a jet of dust and a shrill "wh-e-e-w" where they ricocheted off the ground. Some of our men, accustomed to mounted infantry work, were now for jumping off to return the fire, but the order was given: "No; make a cavalry fight of it. Forward! Gallop!"

It was not a real cavalry fight; those mounted infantry had no swords, let alone sabres or lances. Nor was it the famous "cold steel" of the British soldier's bayonet. But the effect was that of a cavalry charge. The rebels broke, fled, and were pursued for four or five miles. Many hid in the grass and used their rifles against the horsemen. One shot at Baden-Powell from a tree. But their position was hopeless. They lost at least fifteen indunas and two hundred men. There are good grounds for thinking that a factor in this defeat, as in the less decisive one on 25 April, was superstition. In spite of the earlier fiasco, the rebels persisted in believing in a miracle and in basing their tactics on that belief. The Mlimo had, wisely, forbidden his devotees to retain any of the loot they took; all had to be brought to him. When this order was disobeyed, as it frequently was, he had his explanation for the failure of his prophecies. The magic had failed before, but it might still work next time. Confidence had thus been restored by 6 June, so that when the horsemen rode through the Umguza "without any contretemps" the rebel morale cracked. They were not in the state of mind in which to stand up to a cavalry charge.[52]

This time the prestige of the priestly elements was irreparably destroyed. Siginyamatshe and his horn had no more authority. Some of the Ndebele, and many more of the Karanga elements, fell back on the stronghold of Intaba zikaMambo, where Mkwati still exercised some kind of leadership. More Ndebele went south to join the Mlugulu faction in its impregnable fastness of the Matopos. The direct threat to Bulawayo had been removed. The crucial battle which led to this result had been fought by a local column of Bulawayo whites and their black allies.

The Ndebele rebels were now forced on to the defensive. Their hope of taking Bulawayo and recovering their country by assault was gone. The main

Ndebele force in the Matopos might hope to wear its enemy down in a war of attrition, and that was the kind of war that Carrington intended to wage. But the campaign in the Matopos opened on 23 June with a tragicomedy.

It was generally assumed among the whites that Mwari, or the Mlimo, and his priests were the chief instigators of the rebellion, though their (the whites') knowledge of this religious organization was vague. It seems to have been assumed by many that there was only one cult centre, and there was some confusion of the deity with his human agents. Some information came to the ears of Bonner W. Armstrong, native commissioner, Mangwe, who was told of a cave where sacrifices were offered. He reported this to the authorities in Bulawayo. According to Burnham, it was he who was first approached by Armstrong, and they went together to Grey. They proposed to go to the cave and by killing the Mlimo to remove the cause of the rebellion. Grey gave his permission. Carrington insisted that he was not ordering them to go on this desperate mission, but accepting their voluntary service. They should capture the Mlimo if possible, kill him if necessary.

So there followed an adventure worthy of Burnham's wild western background. He and Armstrong made their way stealthily, through wild country, to the cave. In spite of the presence of a large number of Ndebele, they slipped into it unobserved and hid in the shadows. Ahead of the worshippers a solitary figure approached the cave, "pausing at certain points along his ascent to make cabalistic signs and utter prayers." When he entered, Burnham put a bullet under his heart. The two white men then had a furious ride and a running fight for two hours, "until we were nearly exhausted, but the savages abandoned the chase after we had crossed the Shashani river." The deed was highly commended in Bulawayo, where it was hoped that "the killing of the Mlimo" might quickly end the war. Each of the actors was presented by the board of the Chartered Company with a gold watch.

Almost immediately sceptics expressed doubts about the story; Burnham's dramatic imagination was well known. Eventually, by Rhodes's order, Judge Watermeyer of the High Court made an enquiry and handed in a report. Though the report was soon withdrawn from public access and withheld from the archives, it had been read by Marshall Hole, who reported the true story:

Carrington considered it desirable to remove the alleged Mlimo, and detailed the scout Burnham, an American, who had shown initiative and capacity in the Matabele War of 1893, to accompany Armstrong to the spot. The two men proceeded forthwith to Mangwe, and set out for the cave in company with a native confederate called Kutji (who shortly afterwards died). On arriving at the cave Kutji pointed out a native named Dshobani in the fields. Armstrong sent for him and ordered him to walk towards the cave. When at the mouth of the cave he was shot deliberately from behind. The party then returned to Mangwe, where Armstrong called the principal natives of the district together; informed them that he had killed the Mlimo and told them to spread the news through the country.

Thus died Jubane Hlabangana, whose influence, whatever it amounted to, had been used to discourage the rebellion, and who may have been a factor in keeping the Mangwe road open. If his priestly power had been as great as some have supposed, his death might well have provoked the people of his region to join in the rebellion.

Armstrong, who was in the bad books of the authorities for other reasons also, returned his watch and was later dismissed from the service. Burnham kept his watch and departed for the Klondike. There was a third scout—Robert Baden-Powell—who was to have joined in the adventure but was prevented by "all the extra work in the office due to the Mashonaland outbreak." He was disappointed, but as Ransford rightly says he "was fortunate; it is doubtful whether even his reputation would have survived the killing of a man who at best was just about the only African ally the white man had in Matabeleland, and at worst the victim of a faked story and a cold-blooded assassination."[53]

The whites were lucky; southwestern Matabeleland did not rise. The rebels were now concentrated in two groups, the larger in the Matopo Hills and the smaller in the even wilder (but smaller) Intaba zikaMambo. Their morale and unity had been boosted on 25 June by the formal "election" of Nyamanda as King.[54] On the other hand the whites had been reinforced both in numbers and in professional military leadership. Carrington planned the systematic destruction of the rebel forces.

He began with the northern impi, and was able to send against it a much more formidable body than the whites had yet put together in this war: 750 whites, mounted and dismounted, 200 "Cape Boys," Maxims and seven-pounder mountain guns. Plumer, in command, reached the western edge of the hills in the small hours of 5 July—Rhodes's birthday. Rhodes accompanied the column. ("One man drew out ahead," wrote Vere Stent of the attack on one koppie, "in spite of warnings and expostulations. I spurred to see. It was Rhodes himself, riding unarmed, switch in hand, leading the hunt.")

Plumer attacked the stronghold by launching a clockwise hook round it, the horsemen on the outer perimeter and the footmen further in, where they ran into the Ndebele defences head-on. At the same time Major Kershaw, with a smaller force which made less headway than Plumer's, struck across the chord of the arc toward the same objective. Everywhere it was a bloody fight, often at close quarters.

After six hours of this, Plumer called off the fight at noon, and began to fall back at 2.30 p.m. He had lost eighteen men killed and fourteen wounded; it is not clear whether these figures included the "Cape boys." He estimated the rebels' losses at about a hundred, but their losses were not in fighting strength only. The five or six hundred women and children who had taken refuge in the caves had to be abandoned. The loot collected there now fell into Plumer's hands, and that loot included a thousand cattle and two thousand sheep and goats, Mkwati's commissariat.

Mkwati, however, had not been present at the battle. He, the military commander Mtini, other indunas, members of Lobengula's family and other associates of Mkwati had left the previous day for the Somabula forest. Siginyamatshe stayed behind with the rest of the force, but apparently intended to follow the others the next day. Plumer's attack prevented this, and perhaps the removal of women, children, and property. Siginyamatshe survived the battle, fled south to the Matopos, and lost touch with Mkwati. The latter, with those who had followed him the day before and others who escaped after the battle, moved off to take part in the Shona rebellion. Others of the survivors went south to the Matopos; still others tried the old plan of a trek to the north. Plumer was denied the decisive victory which the capture of some of these leaders would have given him.[55]

In Matabeleland one centre of rebellion remained—the Matopos, which Carrington optimistically planned to reduce. There is no doubt that this could not have been done even by a much larger force than Carrington had at his disposal. The Matopo hills, covering an area of some fifty miles by thirty, are a jumble of granite rocks, deep clefts, caves, and tangled bush which Weston Jarvis reported to be "just about the most difficult country in the world—worse than Afghanistan or Chitral."

Nevertheless Carrington had several cracks at it. The major attacks were on 20 July and 5 August. The reader of Baden-Powell's account might conclude that both were successful, in that the enemy was chased out of one rocky fastness after another. The victories, however, were bought at the cost of more casualties for the attackers than for the defenders; and when the fight was over Plumer, like the noble duke of York, marched his men down again and the rebels returned to their former positions.

They occupied three positions. The westernmost, held by Mabiza and Hole, was to the west and the south of the site of Rhodes's grave. The eastern impi, reaching down to the point on the Tuli road where the Gwanda patrol had been mauled on 10 April, comprised the units commanded by Nyanda, Sikhombo, and Mlugulu. The men under Babayane and Dliso occupied the middle position, on Nkantola hill. Carrington and his staff were accurately informed of these facts by scouts, notably Baden-Powell himself, whose boundless enthusiasm for that kind of work is the keynote of his book on the campaign.

The attack on 20 July consisted of two operations. Plumer, with 800 whites, two corps of "Cape Boys" under Robertson and Colenbrander, and 200 Ndebele "friendlies," was based opposite Nkantola; a few days later Baden-Powell built Fort Usher near the spot. The supporting party of 170 whites, 300 "friendlies," and three guns moved out of Figtree and on the evening of 19 July camped below Inungu hill. This force was commanded by Capt. D. Tyrie

Laing, the same who had successfully defended Belingwe from the beginning of the rebellion. He had also led some successful offensive operations, notably against Selemba and Senda, in that district. By his coolness and courage he now succeeded in extricating his men from dangers to which his rashness had exposed them. Their camp of the 19th was commanded by the surrounding heights, but they had the luck not to be attacked that night.

On the morning of the 20th, Plumer's column attacked. Babayane was driven back. That result having been achieved, Plumer fell back to his starting point. According to a prisoner, the rebel losses had been heavy: "large number of their best men killed, including five chiefs and Nuntwani, their general, severely wounded in leg." Further to the west the roles were reversed. It was not Laing, but Mabiza and Hole that took the initiative, with the help of Dliso who moved over to assist them. They launched a furious attack on the laager from the north, getting to within forty yards of the defenders before being checked by rifle fire. If the attack had gone according to plan, the main onslaught would then have been made from the south. This plan went awry partly through bad timing, partly because more time was wasted in butchering the "friendlies," and partly because of Laing's skill.

Capt. Laing was here, there and everywhere encouraging the men with quiet remarks such as "Steady boys," "Give it to them," "Don't waste your ammunition." . . . Whilst I was sitting up against the wagon I couldn't help admiring old Laing. He was bringing up the 7-pounder into action and to bring the gun round smartly he manned the wheel himself, sighted the gun and then remarked "Now then boys give them Hell." Bang went the seven Pounder and he remarked "Good shot."

Laing had more to do than to keep cool. Several times he prevented a rout by pushing men back into the fight, threatening to shoot any who hid under the wagons, or rallying the "friendlies" to make a successful rush. It was a near thing; the rebels had good reason to be confident—"their leaders shouted out that they were getting the best of it and they again started on us with renewed vigour."

The attack was beaten off, at the cost of four whites and twenty-eight blacks killed, and ten whites and eighteen blacks wounded. The rebels had lost about a hundred men, but they still hoped to annihilate Laing's force. They would have done so if he had not suspected treachery in his guides, abandoned the attempt to reach Nkantola, and turned about to fall back on Carrington's base at Fort Usher. He thus avoided an ambush, survived further dangers, and on the night of the 21st was met by Baden-Powell and a party sent to guide him in.[56]

Nothing had been achieved by either side, unless it were a little strengthening of the rebels' morale.

One more great attack was tried, on 5 August. This was an attack on the eastern end of the rebel line. In preparation for it, Plumer's force was marched round from Fort Usher to the Tuli road. To cover the main attack, Captain Beresford with 138 men and two guns was sent to occupy a koppie commanding the line of advance. Far from commanding or covering anything, this force was almost surrounded by 3,000 Ndebele. It was saved by some heroic actions, in one of which Lieut. Hubert Hervey was mortally wounded. In the attack on the main stronghold Major Kershaw, among others, was killed. One of the rebel marksmen, who had taken up position on a boulder, was knocked off it by the recoil of his weapon every time he fired.

Again the attack achieved nothing. Positions were occupied, but could not be held. Four days later, Plumer was able to take a patrol through the strongholds attacked on the 5th, and now deserted, but he could not occupy them. Over the camp dinners Rhodes used at this time to calculate "how long it would take at this rate of loss for Carrington's force to be entirely exterminated. As may be imagined, these calculations were not appreciated by the military gentlemen." Carrington decided that nothing effective could be done before the rains, but that he would ask for 2,500 more white troops, one or two thousand carriers, engineers for blasting operations, and more mountain guns, to take the Matopos in the dry season of 1897. Because all these, as well as the forces already in the field, had to be paid for by the Company, not the imperial government, Carrington was asking for the moon.[57]

For this reason the campaign in Matabeleland was now in fact almost over. Nobody knew it on 5 August, but this is a good point from which to look back at certain aspects of the fighting.

The first edition of Olive Schreiner's *Trooper Peter Halket of Mashonaland* had a famous, or notorious, frontispiece: a photograph of three Africans hanging from a tree, and seven whites and one African standing in the background, contemplating their work with satisfaction. The victims were rebels "caught red-handed, looting and burning property" by Mazwe's "friendlies" and sent into Bulawayo on 10 April by Josana. Selous was present at their trial, and was satisfied that justice was done; he does not say by what law the death penalty was imposed for looting and burning. The tree still survives as "the hanging tree" in a Bulawayo street. For the most part, however, it was only spies that were executed. The *Bulawayo Chronicle* has a few casual references: "During the afternoon another Matabele spy was executed . . . A Spy was captured in Gwelo, tried and shot, and one was also shot in town a few days ago . . . Two or three Matabele spies were arrested in town during last evening and to-day . . . Some spies were caught by the friendlies and brought into town."

Though their usual fate was to be shot rather than hanged, they were not executed out of hand. On 8 April "four Kaffirs" were captured under suspicious circumstances and tried by court martial. They were found to be servants, and were accordingly discharged. It is hard to pass a confident judgment on these proceedings. Death is the invariable fate of spies caught in wartime. The only mitigation one can ask for is a fair trial. As far as one can judge from brief reports, the trial was often fair enough; the accused sometimes confessed to being a spy; occasionally one against whom there was strong evidence was nevertheless discharged. One can only guess that, because of the prevailing passions and of the language difficulty, justice may often have miscarried.[58]

There is also the question of law, as distinct from justice. We have seen before that the anomalous political status of the Company's territories had left such amenities as military discipline in a kind of limbo. The question of spies was referred by the high commissioner to a legal expert, the future Sir Malcolm Searle, at the beginning of the rebellion. In Searle's opinion, a suspected spy could be tried by a military court if he was accompanying the force—the force whose court was to try him. If he was not accompanying the force but was captured, there was no way to try him except by a civil court. This opinion was relayed to Duncan in Bulawayo on 8 April. The examples just given show that no notice was taken of it.

After spies, prisoners. Both problems arose on the white side only. The rebels took no prisoners and had no need of courts martial, as the killing of all whites (and all hostile blacks) who fell into their hands was the essence of the rebellion. A certain reluctance among the whites to take prisoners, except for the purpose of getting information, was natural, but was countered by official policy. H. Adams-Acton of the Matabeleland Relief Force wrote of a prisoner whom Plumer wanted to release but the men determined to kill—by taking him out at night and cutting his throat. "Afterwards," in Adams-Acton's experience, "when a prisoner was brought in he was always publicly shot in the evening."[59] Carrington issued an order on 18 June: "General Officer Commanding desires it to be distinctly understood by all ranks under command of him that, during the continuance of hostile operations against the rebels, clemency is to be shown to wounded. Women and children are not to be injured, and prisoners are to be taken whenever possible."

The need for such orders and for their enforcement is illustrated by Frank Sykes:

> The ferocity exhibited on several occasions by the captors towards their victims was anything but an edifying spectacle. A revolting instance occurred on the line of march, and excited feelings of disgust in those who witnessed it. A rebel had been taken prisoner, and was handed over to a trooper to be escorted into camp. His hands being secured behind his back, a rope was fastened round his neck, one end of which was held by his mounted guard. Without any apparent reason, and with no other motive than sheer brutality, the trooper started off at a gallop. The unfortunate captive kept up for some distance, until the pace was purposely made too hot for him, when from sheer exhaustion he fell forward and was dragged at full length along the rough ground until his body, acting as a brake, caused the rider to pull up.

This case was not brought to Plumer's attention. Other cruelties and irregularities were reported to him, to Carrington, Martin or Grey, and so to Cape

Town and London. As Searle had advised that spies (and this included all prisoners against whom charges were laid) could be tried only by civil courts, and as there was only one judge—Vintcent—in Rhodesia, the first remedy to hand was to appoint an additional judge. It was decided that he was to have no special status but to be an ordinary judge of the High Court. Lieut.-Gen. Goodenough, the acting high commissioner, recommended the Cape advocate J.P.F. Watermeyer for the post. Chamberlain approved.[60]

In the meantime there were prisoners whose disposal could not wait for Watermeyer's arrival. At the beginning of the rebellion the operations of illegal "courts martial" could be overlooked. Not so in August, when awkward facts began to come to light. It appeared that in May Captain Gibbs, commanding on the Shangani where he was building a fort at Makalaka Kop, captured a woman and child who were watching the proceedings. No doubt this could be called spying; the chief fact they learned was the weakness of Gibbs's force. For this reason they could not be released. Men could not be spared to take them to Gwelo. A "Board of Officers" examined the woman and condemned her to death, and Gibbs confirmed the sentence. She was shot, and because of a "misunderstanding" the child was shot too. When Carrington heard of this he had Gibbs arrested.

In September Baden-Powell took command of a small force that had been attacking the stronghold of Uwini, our old acquaintance the rebel leader in the Gwelo district. There had been fierce fighting, there was a prospect of heavier losses, but in a desperate encounter Uwini had been wounded and captured in the depths of a cave. Baden-Powell, who had not received the high commissioner's order to the contrary, had Uwini tried by field general court martial. He was condemned and shot the same day, 13 September. Rosmead ordered Carrington to put Baden-Powell under open arrest.

In due course the cases of Gibbs and Baden-Powell were investigated by courts of enquiry. In both cases the decisions were ambivalent. Rosmead, in his report to Chamberlain, pointed out that the woman shot on Gibbs's authority had not been informed of the charge against her, or of the sentence, and had not been "given a proper opportunity of defending herself"; and that "the proceedings generally were irregular to an extent that amounted to a parody of justice." He thought that the officers concerned should be severely reprimanded, but in view of the military circumstances he was "not prepared to state that a crime had been committed." Carrington, on the basis of the evidence before the court, had likewise acquitted Gibbs of anything more serious than "a grave error of judgment." In the opinion of the War Office, Gibbs's conduct was "regrettable but not censurable."

Baden-Powell's offence was found to be even less censurable, because Uwini was an "arch-ringleader," and at the time of his execution the government excepted all ringleaders from the amnesty it had offered to the rebels.

They were, however, to be tried by a civil court. A court martial, in British military law, was empowered to try a prisoner accused of such a violation of the customs of war as would carry, on conviction, the death penalty. In Rosmead's opinion rebellion was not such a violation, and Baden-Powell's proceedings were illegal. But they too were condoned on the ground of military expediency. *Inter arma silent leges*.[61]

The victims of these "parodies of justice" were prisoners captured during operations. A different problem was presented by rebels who "opted out" of the rebellion, surrendered voluntarily—commonly with their families—and for whom provision would have to be made. Once the tide of war had turned it could be expected that surrenders of this kind would become more frequent. The war would be shortened by encouraging them. These considerations led Goodenough, the acting high commissioner, to propose an amnesty proclamation, which after much correspondence and amendment was published in the Cape *Government Gazette* on 6 July.

The proclamation represented the imperial authorities' method—which was soon to conflict with Rhodes's method—of ending the rebellion. It applied to seven specified districts of Matabeleland. Rebels were invited to surrender themselves and their arms by 10 August. After that date all who were found bearing arms, or assisting others who were bearing arms, against the government would be liable to arrest and trial as rebels, and on conviction to be sentenced to "death or lesser punishment." Those who surrendered before the deadline would be exempt from prosecution, but from this amnesty were excluded the "ringleaders" whose names appeared in the schedule (thirty-eight of them), those who had committed murder ("wilful killing . . . otherwise than in actual warfare"), and Native Police who had "committed offences against the laws relating to the police force." The deadline was later extended to 25 September, the list of ringleaders amended, and Martin given leave to pardon ringleaders, but not murderers, at his discretion.

When rebels surrendered, what was to be done with them? Discussion of this question, between Goodenough, Grey, and Martin, had begun before the end of June. It was no longer pretended by anyone that the Gwaai and Shangani reserves were the answer. The Ndebele would have to feed themselves; they could do this only on good land; the good land was already in the hands of white owners. An inescapable logic led to the settlement of the surrendered rebels, whether as labour tenants or as share-croppers, on private (white) and company land. Lord Grey made arrangements with George Grey, manager of the Buluwayo Syndicate (and of Grey's Scouts), for the settlement of many; the syndicate was attracted by the idea of a reservoir of labour. Others were placed on some of Rhodes's farms. The contractors building the Bechuanaland railway were asked if they could offer employment. The problem was not serious in August. Even by the proclaimed deadline in late September, the surrenders in Matabeleland amounted only to 621 men, 703 women, 1,140 children, 79 guns, and 903 assegais. But long before that date Rhodes had in effect taken the matter out of imperial hands.[62]

In Rhodesia as in the Cape Colony Rhodes was a private citizen with no official position. His intervention, however, was on behalf of the Company, and the Company's moral right (it had no independent legal right) to negotiate and offer terms depended on the role of its forces and its money in the war.

The question about the money is easily answered: the whole expense was borne by the Company. What about the expenditure of blood? In the fighting in Matabeleland there were imperial officers but, until late in the war, no imperial troops. The men under the supreme command of Carrington and the immediate command of Plumer, Baden-Powell, Laing, and others were Rhodesian settlers, Rhodesian ex-policemen, or volunteers from the other colonies. Alderson's column was an imperial force, but by the time it reached Rhodesia its services were needed in Mashonaland and it played no part in putting down the older rebellion. The imperial officers were important, but were few in number, and even they were paid by the Company. When Beal's force and others were sent from Bulawayo to the aid of Salisbury, the detachments of the 7th Hussars and Mounted Infantry from Natal, which had been held back at Mafeking, were sent on to Motloutsi, to be within reach of Matabeleland in case they were needed. About the middle of July some 200 men from these units moved up to Bulawayo. They did not take part in the battles in the Matopos, but carried out mopping-up patrols in August and later. They had been used essentially as reserves. By November there were 428 of them in addition to special troops, but they had played only a minor part in the fighting in Matabeleland. That, however, is not the last word on the distribution of military honours.[63]

After the taking of Intaba zikaMambo Plumer addressed the troops, complimenting them on their success, and "singled out Major Robertson's Cape Boys as worthy of special mention for the prominent part they had taken in the fight." The compliment was deserved. They had been in the van in the seizure of the principal hill. As Capt. W.J. Boggie described it,

> Immediately my men ceased firing, I heard the charging cheer, and saw the Cape Boys with their orange-coloured puggarees and swarthy faces clear the intervening space with leaps and bounds, and in a briefer space than it takes to tell, they throw [sic] themselves upon the Matabele . . . The intrepid Matabele warriors met the rush with superb bravery, while the Cape Boys dashed forward with reckless indifference to the storm of bullets, assegais and battle-axes which they encountered.

It was the same story on the Umguza on 22 April. It was the same in the attack on Babayane's stronghold on 20 July. Though on that occasion the "friendlies" lost their heads and became "a useless rabble," they had succeeded while cooperating with Colenbrander's "Boys" in driving the enemy out of the kraal. At one of the crises of the battle it was Robertson's "Boys" who were called upon, and their attack "succeeded at all points." They knew how to use the bayonets that were never removed from their rifles. In the fight on 5 August the same corps provided a succession of volunteers for the suicidal task of passing in front of the caves to draw the simultaneous fire of all the rebels inside. As soon as one of these heroes fell, riddled with bullets, his companions rushed into the cave and bayoneted the enemy before they had time to reload. The "Cape Boys" and the "friendlies" together played the leading parts in Laing's operations in June, as for instance against Belingwe mountain and Senda's kraal.

The examples can be multiplied. They do not detract from the gallantry of the white troops, but they deserve particular attention because, though the two corps of Cape Boys played decisive parts in the fighting, their memory has been almost obliterated from the record. Their losses were never included in the casualty lists.[64]

One individual stands out of that anonymous mass—not one of Robertson's or Colenbrander's "Boys" but an individual scout, Jan Grootboom. He had come to Rhodesia as a wagon driver for C.D. Helm, had lived at Hope Fountain for many years, and had played a brave and daring part on several occasions in Jameson's War. He was probably, though this is not certain, a Mfengu (Fingo) by origin, but he could speak siNdebele fluently, and with his chin shaven, and his hair plaited in the *dhlodhlo* or headring, could pass among the Ndebele unnoticed. He was not only an incredibly brave, but a highly skilled scout, worthy to associate with the great white scout whom he admired and called Colonel Baking Powder. Many an operation was preceded by one of Jan's reconnaissances. He penetrated into the rebel lines, moved among the camp fires, overheard conversations, noted the strengths and dispositions of the impis and the lie of the land. He had various hairbreadth escapes, in situations from which no white scout could have escaped.

One of these was on the Tuli road when he was trying to overtake Brand's Gwanda patrol. He eventually reached it, came back with it, and took part in the fight on 10 April. The success of Plumer's attack on Intaba zikaMambo owed much to Jan's report of "the exact disposition of the rebel impis, together with other valuable information." In late July and early August, before the battles in the Matopos, he was scouting in association with Baden-Powell.[65]

Not all "Cape Boys" fought on the white side; some brought their skills to the service of the rebel cause. The chapter may end with Karl Khumalo, whom we met long ago as a courtier of Lobengula and a rather devious character. At the outbreak of the rebellion he happened to be in Bulawayo. In some irregular fashion he was caught—there is no evidence of any trial—and handed over to two troopers who were told to take him out and shoot him. By one account, they were to shoot him only if he attempted (which they said he did) to escape, but where he was to go if he did not escape is not explained. At any rate they shot him. One bullet struck his forehead and apparently came out at the back of his head. After the troopers had left, the corpse "got up and walked off in the other direction." As Baden-Powell explains it, "the bullet which struck him on the head was not strong enough for his skull, and merely glanced round under his scalp without breaking the bone, and came out through the skin at the back, giving the appearance of a shot clean through his head." More fortunate than Rasputin, he escaped to the Matopos, survived to be pensioned by Rhodes with a farm, and lived for fifteen more years.[66]

NOTES CHAPTER II

1 The Ndebele word for the rebellion.
2 F.E. Garrett, *The Story of an African Crisis*, pp.28-9.
3 CO 879/43/491 (memorandum of the incorporation of British Bechuanaland); CO 879/43/495, no.40, p.45; Albert Grey papers, no.72, Rhodes to Grey in February 1895 (giving reasons for transfer of the Crown Colony to the Cape and the protectorate to the charter—e.g., the Company's mineral rights, the Company's and the Cape's land claims, the railway; Rhodes himself suggests that H.M. government should mark out reserves before transferring the territories).
4 CO 879/37/441, no.42, pp.44-9; 44/498, no.38, p.46, no.49, p.56, no.51, p.57; H. Marshall Hole, *The Jameson Raid*, pp.67-8.
5 CO 879/44/498, no.31, p.43, no.121, encl.1, pp.123-6, no.136, encl., pp.138-9; P.R. Maylam, *Rhodes, the Tswana and the British: Colonialism, Collaboration and Conflict in the Bechuanaland Protectorate, 1885-99*, p.164, no.28. The substitution was made because Gaborone fell within the land grant, which the Company had recognized, by Sebele to Riesle and Nicholls.
6 CO 879/44/498, no.88, p.94, no.123, p.128, no.128, pp.131-2, no.129, pp.132-4, no.153, p.155, no.203, pp.196-7, no.217, p.226; 47/517, no.16, p.17.
7 Hole, *Jameson Raid*, p.95 and Appendix II: J.P. Fitzpatrick, *The Transvaal from Within*, p.123; A.S. Hickman, *The Men Who Made Rhodesia*, p.49.
8 Hole, *Jameson Raid*, pp.80, 95 and Appendix II; Hickman, *Men Who Made Rhodesia*, p.52; CO 879/47/517, no.423, encl., p.466. Of the policemen Jameson left behind, only five were in Matabeleland—two of them being in hospital with broken legs.
9 CO 879/44/498, no.178 and encls., pp.172-8; Hole, *Jameson Raid*, pp.102-3, 159 and Appendix II.
10 *Buluwayo Chronicle*, 19 April, 10 May, 28 June, and 12 July 1895; Hole, *Jameson Raid*, pp.105-7; Ian Colvin, *The Life of Jameson*, vol. II, p.54.
11 RH Mss Afr. s. 8.
12 CO 537/130/174, pp.438-57 (minutes): CO 417/197/571, pp.14-18; RH Mss Afr. s 77, ff. 148-67; CO 879/47/517, nos.127, 128, p.114, no.130, p.115, no.136, p.122, no.175, p.159, no.176, p.160, no.182, p.163.
13 CO 879/47/517, no.58, p.50, no.63, p.53, no.119, p.107; H. Marshall Hole, *Old Rhodesian Days*, p.104. Kruger's reaction was thought important: he had no objection to Martin's appointment.

14 Herbert Plumer, *An Irregular Corps in Matabeleland*, pp.2, 8; Melina Rorke, *Melina Rorke: Her Amazing Experiences in the Stormy Nineties of South Africa's Story*, p.198; F.C. Selous, *Sunshine and Storm in Rhodesia*, pp.11, 51-2; D. Tyrie Laing, *The Matabele Rebellion, 1896: With the Belingwe Field Force*, p.243.

15 C. van Onselen, "Reactions to Rinderpest in Southern Africa," *Journal of African History*, XIII, 3 (1972), p.473; W.H. Brown, *On the South African Frontier*, p.320; *Bulawayo Chronicle*, 7 March and 28 March 1896; *Standard Encyclopedia of Southern Africa*, vol. X p.302. Eric Rosenthal, *Encyclopedia of Southern Africa*, s.v. Rinderpest, gives an estimate of 4½ million cattle dead. The estimates are rough and the smaller may be for a smaller area.

16 *Buluwayo Chronicle*, 4 January 1896.

17 Hole, *Old Rhodesian Days*, pp.102-3.

18 Julian Cobbing, "The Ndebele under the Khumalos," pp.262, 281-4, 417-20.

19 T.O. Ranger, *Revolt in Southern Rhodesia*, pp.138-9; Selous, *Sunshine and Storm*, p.12; Matabele Wilson Papers (WI 6/2), Supplementary Notes to Diary (written in 1942—hence the confusion of date); Frank W. Sykes, *With Plumer in Matabeleland*, pp.13-14; CO 879/47/520, no.3, encl.2, p.8. Lekuni was "loyal" in the rebellion. (Hans Sauer, *Ex Africa*, p.309.) Of the three priestly brothers, Nungu had formerly been called "head doctor". I assume that he had died before 1896, but have not found a reference to his death. The third brother, Bosumwane or Bhozongwane, was denounced by Lobengula before his (Lobengula's) death. All agree that after that event Mlugulu was the spiritual leader.

20 Ranger, *Revolt in Southern Rhodesia*, pp.142-55; M.L. Daneel, *The God of the Matopo Hills: An Essay on the Mwari Cult in Rhodesia*; J.M. Schoffeleers, "An Organizational Model of the Mwari Shrines" (unpublished paper); G. Fortune, "Who was Mwari?" *Rhodesian History*, IV (1973), pp.1-20; T.O. Ranger, "The Meaning of Mwari," *Rhodesian History*, V (1974), pp.5-17; J. Blake Thompson and Roger Summers, "Mlimo and Mwari: Notes on a Native Religion in Southern Rhodesia," in *Native Affairs Department Annual (NADA)*, 1956, pp.53-8; W.J. van der Merwe, "The Shona Idea of God," in *NADA*, 1957, pp.39-63; Selous, *Sunshine and Storm*, pp.16-17. For the difference between Mwari and Mlimo, see Cobbing, "Ndebele under the Kumalos," pp.220-1.

21 Julian Cobbing, "The Absent Priesthood: Another look at the Rhodesian risings of 1869-7," *Journal of African History*, XVIII, 1 (1977), pp.61-84.

22 For this subject see M. Gelfand, *Shona Ritual, With Special Reference to the Chaminuka Cult, Shona Religion, With Special Reference to the Makorekove*, and *Medicine and Magic of the Mashona*; Charles Bullock, *The Mashona*; D.P. Abraham, "The Roles of 'Chaminuka' and the Mhondoro Cults in Shona Political History," in *The Zambesian Past*; and articles in *NADA* as follows: A. Burbridge, SJ, "In Spirit-Bound Rhodesia" (1924, pp.17-29); H.C. Hugo, "The Spirit World of the Mashona" (1925, pp.14-17); F.W.T. Posselt, "Chaminuka the Wizard" (1926, pp.35-7); E.R. Morkel, "The *Mondoro* or Ancestral Spirit of the Wabuja" (1930, pp.11-14); Macharanowada, "*Mudzimu, Shabe, Ngozi* and other Spirits" (1932, pp.7-10); N.G., "Magango Hutari" (1933, pp.29-31); E.R. Morkel, "Spiritualism amongst the Wabudya" (1933, pp.106-16); M. Gelfand, "The Religion of the Mashona" (1956, pp.27-31). For the Portuguese reference, D.P. Abraham in *The Zambesian Past*, p.37.

23 CO 879/47/520, no.326, encl.1, pp.481-2, evidence of Malima and of Umsimbo.
24 Cobbing, "Absent Priesthood," pp.63-72; D.N. Beach, "The Rising in South-Western Mashonaland, 1896-7," pp.124-5, 307, 315; Ranger, *Revolt in Southern Rhodesia*, pp.148, 153, 156, 175-7; Schoffeleers, "Mwari Shrines," Appendix, s.v. Mangwe.
25 CO 879/47/520, no.122, encl.12, p.151; *Bulawayo Chronicle*, 18 April 1896.
26 Cobbing, "Ndebele under the Khumalos," pp.64-81, 382-3, and ch. III, passim.
27 CO 879/47/520, no.111, encl.1, p.107; R. Summers and C.W. Pagden, *The Warriors*, pp.137-8; *Bulawayo Chronicle*, 29 February 1896 (the first item under "Local and General"); "Reminiscences of the 1896 Rebellion, by S.J.," in *NADA*, 1927, pp.61-4. Most writers about these events have for some reason given the wrong date for the full moon (e.g., Ranger, *Revolt in Southern Rhodesia*, p.138, "at full moon on the night of March 26th"); according to the almanacs the date of that full moon was 29 March (e.g., *Whitaker's Almanack*, 1896, p.21).
28 Selous, *Sunshine and Storm*, pp.90-1.
29 Foster Windram oral interview (WI 8/1/3), evidence of Nganganyoni, pp.3-5.
30 CO 879/47/520, no.111, encl.1, pp.106-10, the official report of the events of the first ten days; Selous, *Sunshine and Storm*, pp.33-6, 38, 263-9; Laing, *Matabele Rebellion*, p.251; Roger Howman, "Orlando Baragwanath," *Rhodesiana*, 28, pp.41-3.
31 Selous, *Sunshine and Storm*, p.209; Laing, *Matabele Rebellion*, pp.251-3.
32 Howman, "Orlando Baragwanath," p.45, n.32; Oliver Ransford, *Bulawayo, Historic Battleground of Rhodesia*, p.81; and see above, n.27, for date of full moon.
33 Howman, "Orlando Baragwanath," pp.41-3, "S.J." in *NADA*, 1927, pp.61, 64; Laing, *Matabele Rebellion*, pp.15 ff., 61-4.
34 Mrs. A. Hurrell, "The Gwelo Laager 1896," *Rhodesiana*, 22 pp.6-10.
35 Ransford, *Bulawayo*, pp.87, 92-4; Selous, *Sunshine and Storm*, pp.38-42, 117-26.
36 CO 879/47/520, no.1, pp.1-2, no.1a, p.2, no.72, encls., pp.30-3; Ransford, *Bulawayo*, p.87.
37 *Rhodesia Weekly Review*, 28 March 1896, p.8; Ransford, *Bulawayo*, p.88; Sykes, *Plumer in Matabeleland*, p.16.
38 *Rhodesia Weekly Review*, 28 March 1896, and *Bulawayo Chronicle*, same date, in both cases under "BSA Co. Gazette", Notice no.2, dated 25 March; *Bulawayo Chronicle*, 4 April 1896, under "BSA Co. Gazette", Notice no.2; CO 879/47/520, no.9, p.6, no.111, encl.1, pp.108-9, no.117, encl.2, p.128; Ransford, *Bulawayo*, pp.84, 88; Selous, *Sunshine and Storm*, pp.54-5; Plumer, *Irregular Corps*, pp.2-4. George Grey was a third cousin of the administrator, and brother of the future foreign secretary.
39 CO 879/47/520, no.117, encl.3, p.130, encl.26, p.137. Most of the inhabitants repaired to the laager only at night, but many of the women and children remained there in daytime also. The population of Bulawayo was reported on 24 April as: white men, 1,466; white women, 328; white children, 460; "Native servants and families," 1,683; "Natives looking for work," 24; "Cape Boys," enrolled in the forces, 168; Indian men, 60, women, 8, children, 5. Ransford, *Bulawayo*, pp.89-90, 95; Selous, *Sunshine and Storm*, p.90; Sykes, *Plumer in Matabeleland*, pp.20-2.
40 Selous, *Sunshine and Storm*, 19-22, 136; Laing, *Matabele Rebellion*, pp.26, 31-3; 'S.J.", *NADA*, 1927, pp.61-2.

41 CO 879/47/520, no.137, encl. 1, pp.181-2; Selous, *Sunshine and Storm*, pp.181-4.

42 For Cobbing's account of the Ndebele leadership at this point, see Cobbing, "Ndebele under the Khumalos," pp.388-93.

43 Ranger, *Revolt in Southern Rhodesia*, p.175; Ransford, *Bulawayo*, p.96.

44 For the April battles: CO 879/47/520, no.122, encl. 1, p.144, 19 and 20 April; no.133, encl. 1, pp.166-7, 22 and 25 April, no.137, encl.14, pp.184-5, 25 April; CO 468/1, BSA Co. Report on the Native Disturbances, p.33, 22 April; pp.35-7, 25 April.

45 CO 468/1, Report on the Native Disturbances, p.33; Selous, *Sunshine and Storm*, pp.157-8. The local "friendlies" took no part in this fight. According to Ransford, (*Bulawayo*, pp.98-9), Selous had only sixty men.

46 Ransford, *Bulawayo*, pp.94-5, 97, 98, 101; Ranger, *Revolt in Southern Rhodesia*, p.148; R. Baden-Powell, *The Matabele Campaign*, p.32; Plumer, *Irregular Corps*, pp.40-2; CO 879/47/520, no. 279a, p.374, no.294, encl.23, pp.423-4.

47 CO 879/47/517, no.80, p.67, no.86, p.71, no.223, p.204; 520, no.16, p.8, no.21, p.10, no.24, p.11, no.72, encl.45, p.43, no.89, encl.8, p.57, encl.10, p.58, encl.11, p.58, encl.21, pp.60-1, encl.53, p.66, encl.55, p.66; Plumer, *Irregular Corps*, ch. II; *Cape Argus*, 8 April 1896.

48 CO 879/45/505, no.259, p.274, no.262, p.282; 47/520, no.28, p.13, no.30, p.13, no.42, p.18, no.46, p.19, no.88, pp.50-2, no.104, encl.16, p.84, encl.47, p.90, encl.53, p.91, encl.63, p.94, encl.81, pp.97-8, encl.88, p.98, no.117, encl.23, p.136, no.122, encl.6, p.162, encl.7, p.162; Sykes, *Plumer in Matabeleland*, pp.83-6; Plumer, *Irregular Corps*, p.53.

49 CO 879/47/517, no.118, p.105; 520, no.46, p.19; no.51, p.21; no.56, p.23; no.60, p.25; no.70, p.29; no.90, encl. 1, p.68; no.104, encl.27, p.86, encls.63 and 64, p.94, encl.65, p.95, encls.90 and 91, p.99, encls.94 and 95, p.100, encls.98 and 99, p.101; no.151, p.191; no.166, p.202; no.181, p.208; no.190, p.211; no.211, encl.10, p.229; no.244, encl. 21, p.307; no.261, encl.4, p.342; Ranger, *Revolt in Southern Rhodesia*, p.170; Plumer, *Irregular Corps*, pp.54, 89-90, 98; E.A.H. Alderson, *With the Mounted Infantry and the Mashonaland Field Force, 1896*, ch. II, III.

50 CO 879/45/505, no.259, p.274, no.262, p.282; CO 468/1, Report on the Native Disturbances, Schedule G, p.38; Sauer, *Ex Africa*, p.298; *Bulawayo Chronicle*, 22 and 25 April 1896; *Rhodesia Herald*, 2 September 1896.

51 CO 879/47/520, no.108, p.104, no.114, p.123; J.G. Lockhart and C.M. Woodhouse, *Rhodes*, pp.346-7; *Bulawayo Chronicle*, May-June, passim. Martin assumed command on the 15th, the day after his arrival.

52 CO 879/47/520, no.219, encl. 1, p.243; *Bulawayo Chronicle*, 10 June 1896; Baden-Powell, *Matabele Campaign*, pp.53-4, 57, 63; Selous, *Sunshine and Storm*, p.223; Ranger, *Revolt in Southern Rhodesia*, p.181; Ransford, *Bulawayo*, p.106; Foster Windram oral interviews (WI 8/1/1), evidence of Nganganyoni, pp.5-6.

53 CO 879/47/520, no.219, encl.8, p.247, encl.41, p.258; F.R. Burnham, *Scouting on Two Continents*, ch. XXIII, and especially pp.256, 258; Ransford, *Bulawayo*, pp.108-12; Baden-Powell, *Matabele Campaign*, pp.80-2; H. Marshall Hole Papers, HO 1/3/4. Ransford was of course wide of the mark in calling Hlabangana "just about the only ally."

54 Cobbing, "Ndebele under the Khumalos," pp.417-20.

55 CO 879/47/520, no.280, encl. 1, pp.378-87; Plumer, *Irregular Corps*, pp.125-39; Sykes, *Plumer in Matabeleland*, 130-55; Vere Stent, *A Personal Record of Some In-*

cidents in the Life of C.J. Rhodes, pp.12-26; Ranger, *Revolt in Southern Rhodesia*, pp.232-3; *Bulawayo Chronicle*, 18 July 1896.

56 CO 879/47/520, no.220, p.263, no.221, p.264, no.326, encl.1, p.479; Plumer, *Irregular Corps*, ch. VIII; Baden-Powell, *Matabele Campaign*, ch. VI; Sykes, *Plumer in Matabeleland*, pp.167-75; Laing, *Matabele Rebellion*, pp.218-21, 230-7, 284-97; Ransford, *Bulawayo*, pp.116-22; C.H. Halkett, "With Laing in the Matopos," *Rhodesiana*, 24, pp.6-7.

57 CO 879/47/520. no.326, encl.1, p.485, no.354, encl.7, p.543; Plumer, *Irregular Corps*, ch. IX; Baden-Powell, *Matabeleland Campaign*, ch. VIII, and specifically pp.212-13; Sykes, *Plumer in Matabeleland*, pp.192-201; Sauer, *Ex Africa* p.308; Ransford, *Bulawayo*, pp.123-5; Ranger, *Revolt in Southern Rhodesia*, p.237.

58 CO 879/47/520, no.117, encl.12, p.147, no.219, encl.61, p.263; *Bulawayo Chronicle*, 11 April, 25 April, 2 May, and 16 May 1896; Laing, *Matabele Rebellion*, pp.46-7, 69-70, 77-8; Selous, *Sunshine and Storm*, pp.136-7; Ransford, *Bulawayo*, fig.48 (following p.130).

59 H. Adams-Acton Diary (AC 1), 1 May 1896.

60 CO 879/47/520, no.104, encl.18, p.85, no.144, p.189, no.154, pp.192-4, no.216, p.232, no.238, p.291, no.301, pp.431-4; Sykes, *Plumer in Matabeleland*, pp.98-9. Goodenough was then acting high commissioner because Robinson was on leave in England.

61 CO 879/47/520, no.314 and encl., pp.448-9, no.331, p.498, no.335, p.499, no.342, pp.501-3, no.388, pp.590-9, no.389, encl.8, p.608, no.434, p.730, no.436, p.738— for the whole report, pp.738-52; Baden-Powell, *Matabele Campaign*, pp.286-99. Sir Hercules Robinson had returned from his leave in England as Baron Rosmead.

62 CO 879/47/520, no. 235, encl.7, pp.271-2; no.258, encls.1, 2, 4, 6, 8, pp.316-20; no.270, encls. 1, 3, 4, pp.350-3; no.279, encl., p.373; no.292, pp.406-7; no.293, encls. 3, 4, 6, pp.408-9; no.303, encl. 13, p.440; no.316, encls. 9, 10, p.454, no.372, encl.22, p.583.

63 CO 879/47/520, nos.147, 148, p.190; no.211, encl.10, p.229, no.393, p.612; Baden-Powell, *Matabele Campaign*, p.256; Hickman, *Men Who Made Rhodesia*, p.68.

64 Laing, *Matabele Rebellion*, pp.218-21, 230-7; Sykes, *Plumer in Matabeleland*, pp.155, 163, 171-2; Sauer, *Ex Africa*, p.311.

65 Gwenda Newton, "The Go-Between—John Grootboom", *Rhodesiana*, 29, pp.68-76; Baden-Powell, *Matabele Campaign*, pp.171-2, and passim; Sykes, *Plumer in Matabeleland*, pp.138, 263-9; Plumer, *Irregular Corps*, pp.132-3.

66 Stent, *Personal Record*, pp.57-9; Baden-Powell, *Matabele Campaign*, pp.258-9; Biographical Notes by Miss Monkton Jones, prefixed to her transcription of Thomas Maxwell's Diary (MA 1), s.v. Kumalo, Karl. Baden-Powell says Khumalo was "tried and sentenced to be shot." Stent says that "he does not appear to have been tried by any court martial." I have found no evidence of a trial. J.G. McDonald's version, in *Rhodes: A Life*, pp.274-8, differs from the others in almost every detail. It ought to be compared with the other accounts, but I believe the others to be more reliable for the statements I have made in the text.

CHAPTER 12

The Rebellion, II: Chimurenga

MASHONALAND, 1896

The traditional division of the upheaval of 1896 into "the Matabele Rebellion" and "the Mashona Rebellion" is roughly, but not entirely, accurate. Among those who rose in revolt in March were many who, though they belonged geographically to Matabeleland, were ethnically Shona. It was only in June that Mashonaland launched its own revolt, the *Chimurenga*.

We have seen that the Shona had their own grievances, not entirely the same as those of the Ndebele. What they did not have was a centralized monarchy, or an effective tradition of one, or anything comparable to the Ndebele military system. In the days when they were raided by their predatory neighbours they had, of course, fought back, and with increasing effect as they acquired Portuguese guns. Before the Company got round to suppressing the custom they had had little wars among themselves. But it was above all the lack of a central, unifying power that put them at a disadvantage.

Two kinds of weakness were apparent in 1896. When a paramount chief joined the rebellion his traditional enemy, the neighbouring paramount, in several cases took the other side merely for reasons of intertribal politics. Secondly, the weak system of succession encouraged a pretender to further his own interests by taking the opposite side from the paramount in office.

In spite of this, once the fighting began each paramount chief seems to have been able to draw upon a latent reserve of loyalty in his subjects. In 1897 the native commissioner, Salisbury, in his report to the chief native commissioner, emphasized the point: "It is absolutely useless to expect the smaller chiefs to give in before the paramounts no matter how anxious they may be for peace; if the paramounts held no power before the rebellion they certainly have a great influence now." The suppression of the rebellion involved a campaign against each of the paramounts in revolt.[1]

Disunity is the most obvious factor in the failure of the Shona rebellion, but there was also a certain amount of cooperation that has to be explained. Once the first blows had been struck, the revolt spread through parts of Mashonaland like a veld fire. In the absence of any common political authority, was there any other central directing factor that accounts for this? The answer was found by contemporaries, and later by T.O. Ranger, in the Mwari shrines and particularly in the upstart leader Mkwati. As in the Ndebele, so also in the Shona case, this influence has been denied by Julian Cobbing.

The most convincing reason for accepting Cobbing's view is that, in general, the parts of Mashonaland that rebelled were those least influenced by the cult, while those most closely connected with it were either neutral or on the white side.[2]

The influence of the *mhondoro* or spirit medium cult is another question. But here we are concerned with a pantheon of spirits without anything like a directing mind behind them. The divisions among the people were matched by divisions among the spirits, and it is not always easy to decide on which side the prevailing advice originated. In the early days of the Ndebele rising, before the Shona had stirred, Paramount Chief Chivi (Chibi) held a meeting, at which one of his subchiefs argued for revolt. The spirit of the tribal founder Chikanga, however, through his medium, strongly opposed this motion. The spirit, like Chivi himself, may have had good political reasons for taking that side, but one is reminded of the case of Hlabangana and the Mkombo shrine in the Matopos.

D.N. Beach has explained both the rising and the disunity of the Shona in political, not religious, terms. He has shown how the internal politics of the chiefdoms, their mutual relations, and their relations with the Ndebele and with the whites can account for their division into rebels, neutrals and collaborators. His evidence shows too that, with few exceptions, the relations of a chiefdom with the Ndebele before and in Jameson's War set the precedent for its course in 1896. Those who had accepted subjection to the Ndebele before 1893 fought for them in that year and rebelled in 1896; those who had resisted the Ndebele before were either neutrals or collaborators both in 1893 and in 1896. The explanation both of this continuity and of the exceptions to it is found in Shona politics within and among the chiefdoms.[3]

A case which illustrates all of these factors is that of Chirumanzu (Chilimanzi). On the death of a chief of this title, not long before the arrival of the Pioneer Column, he was succeeded according to custom by his brother, who received the necessary Rozvi installation. But it happened that the former chief's son, known as Chinyama, was a favourite of Lobengula. With the king's help he was able to drive his uncle out and usurp the chieftainship: patrilineal succession seemed right and proper to the Ndebele. This Chirumanzu was thus a client of Lobengula's, and there was some fear in official circles of what he would do in the war of 1893. He appears however to have been a realist, and his realism may have been encouraged by the marriage of his daughter to the local native commissioner, M.E. Weale. Far from supporting his overlord and benefactor Lobengula in the war, Chirumanzu (who "thought that the Europeans would win") sent a force composed of his best men to fight on the Company's side.

Thus Chirumanzu burnt his boats; a Ndebele victory in 1893 would have been fatal to him. So would it in 1896, and he was accordingly found totally committed to the white side in the rebellion. More or less similar reasons, as well as the influence of the spirits, explain the commitment of Chivi to the same side. The chief holding the Gutu title was defended in it against rival claimants by both Lobengula and the Company; after 1893 by the Company only. Thus there was a great belt, running roughly through Chilimanzi, Victoria, Chibi, and Ndanga, that was either neutral or actively anti-rebel. This served as a kind of fire-break; it was impracticable for those east of the belt to rebel, whatever their feelings might have been, because they were cut off from contact with the main rebel forces. This would have been one reason why the Ndau of Melsetter "sat still," though they had more solid grievances than anyone else in the country. Their land had been taken from them, and not many others under the Mashonaland jurisdiction could yet complain of that.[4]

Their northern neighbour Mutasa sat still too, mainly one may guess because of his hereditary enmity to the rebel Makoni. Mutasa refused an invitation, or bribe, to send a force against Makoni, but he advertised his loyalty by paying his tax on 26 June; working both sides of the street was a habit with him. The Njanja chiefs in the Charter district had old disputes with Mutekedza and Maromo, so collaborated when these rebelled. There was a belt of neutrals also in the far north, though in that case it is supposed that the Tonga and Korekore remained quiet because the white invasion had not yet affected them.[5]

The remaining paramounts rose in revolt. The leader among them, the first to act and the last to be subdued, was Mashayamombe, whose seat lay twelve miles up the Umfuli from Hartley Hills. Like most of the Shona in close contact with the whites, this great paramount chief and his people had much to complain about. Against a background of general grievances a particular incident seems to have given the final push to Mashayamombe: his nephew Muzhuzhu having thrashed the wife of one of Native Commissioner Moony's messengers, Moony flogged Muzhuzhu.

Great conflicts are often precipitated, but they are never caused, by trivial incidents. The causes of the Shona revolt are of course to be found in the Shona experiences under the Company and the settlers. But there is a further question about the timing and the details of this outbreak. Ranger's view that Mkwati, from his stronghold of Intaba zikaMambo, played a part in pushing Mashayamombe into action is doubted by Cobbing, but it is based on evidence given at the trials after the rebellion. According to that evidence Mkwati had sent Tshiwa, a Rozvi "child of Mwari," to summon envoys of Mashayamombe to Intaba zikaMambo. It was understood—or pretended—that the purpose of this journey was to get some powerful medicine that would kill the locusts. The spirit medium Kaguvi, unwilling to pay Mashayamombe the cow that was demanded for a share of the medicine, sent his own emissaries independently on the same errand. Bonda, a Rozvi headman from Charter, was another who responded to the summons.

The instructions which all these received had nothing directly to do with locusts. They were told that Mkwati "was a god and could kill all the whites and was doing so at that time in Matabeleland, and that Kargubi would be given the same powers, as he Umquarti had, and was to start killing the whites in Mashonaland."[6]

This advice or instruction was not a bolt from a blue sky. There had been earlier discussions at Mashayamombe's, at which it had been decided that fires on the hills would be the signal for revolt. The question to which an answer can only be guessed is why Mashayamombe planned his revolt, and Mkwati sent his instructions and his medicine, in June and not three months earlier. When the Shona—or some of them—rose, the tide had in fact turned in Matabeleland, though that fact was not yet obvious. If the Shona and the Ndebele had risen at the same time the revolt would have been vastly more formidable than it was. One partial answer to the question is that Mkwati's influence was used to stir up Mashayamombe and others because the Ndebele rebels, forced on to the defensive, had a desperate need to "open a second front." The other answer is that the Shona rebels, far from wanting to help the Ndebele out of their difficulties, were under the impression in June that the whites in Matabeleland were being defeated. This, then, was the moment to strike, the more so because the absence of many white fighting men from Mashonaland provided an opportunity, as Jameson's folly had to the Ndebele. On this view the Shona who eventually rebelled did not do so earlier because they wanted first to assess their chances in the light of the Ndebele experience.

As the rising in Mashonaland was so little coordinated, these two theories are not mutually exclusive. When the messengers who had been to Mkwati returned to Mashayamombe's, a Ndebele regiment accompanied them. They at any rate would have been concerned about a "second front." So we come back to the native commissioner, Moony, who had flogged Muzhuzhu. Moony was accordingly pursued and killed. Some Indian traders near the Umfuli were murdered on 14 June. Parties went out in several directions on similar errands, for example to kill two miners at the Beatrice. Kaguvi sent messages wherever his spiritual influence extended. Bonda returned to his home district, Charter, with the same message. Signal fires began to burn.

Not far from Mashayamombe's, up the Umfuli, was Chitungwiza, the kraal where the "wizard" Pasipamire, the medium of Chaminuka, had flourished until Lobengula had wiped him out in 1883. One who escaped from that massacre was Pasipamire's brother Gumporeshumba, who fled to the Shawasha country beyond Salisbury. He was a member of the Chivero chiefly family, which had been dominant in the Hartley area until superseded by that of Mashayamombe. During his exile Gumporeshumba developed the kind of spiritual power that had possessed his brother, and became a medium himself. He was a medium not of Chaminuka but, like his grandfather before him, of Kaguvi, and he was thereafter generally known by this name. (The original Kaguvi had lived apparently in the late seventeenth century.) When the times were again propitious, the new Kaguvi moved back to his old country and settled at a kraal to the north of Mashayamombe's. Thus the *mhondoro* and the great paramount were neighbours. They had their disputes, as over the payment of the cow, but cooperated in the great matter of "killing all the white men." Kaguvi's influence, however, seems to have been confined to the two areas in which he had lived, on the Umfuli and in the Shawasha country. As for the Chaminuka cult, whose centre (Chitungwiza) was near Beatrice, in the territory of the petty Chief Rwizi, its weight was probably thrown *against* the rebellion; Rwizi himself remained at least neutral.[7]

When Kaguvi was on trial in 1897 he said to the court, "I want Nehanda, Goronga and Wamponga brought in. They started the rebellion." Wamponga was another name for Tenkela, the wife or mother of Mwari—in her human manifestation the wife of Mkwati. Goronga was the great spirit medium of Lomagundi. Nehanda, the most powerful of all after Kaguvi, was the female medium dominant in the Mazoe district. As the original Nehanda was believed to have been the wife of the original Kaguvi, the collaboration of their respective mediums in 1896, and the acceptance by Nehanda of Kaguvi's supremacy, were natural. There is no doubt about the influence of these spirit mediums on the rising in Mashonaland. The decision to rebel may have been essentially political. But Kaguvi, Nehanda, and their like did much to keep a divided and rather unmilitary people in the field long after any realistic hope of success had vanished.[8]

Neither these influences nor their power nor the fighting capacity or will of the Shona were understood by the whites. They assumed that the Shona were happy and grateful for what they had been given—peace, security, and work. The first reports of murders were therefore received incredulously, and their implications rejected. Thus the *Rhodesia Herald* on 17 June: "We do not see sufficient evidence in the murders and the attitude of the natives to conclude that anything like a general, or even a partial, rising is contemplated." And the *Bulawayo Chronicle* three days later:

> The rebellion, if such it be, has been started in a similar manner to the one in Matabeleland by the massacring of isolated parties, and unless checked at the beginning will assume large dimensions. However, we do not anticipate an insurrection of anything like the magnitude it is here, as the Mashonas are notorious cowards, and have not the quantity of arms and ammunition which the Matabele had secreted . . . and they have not a large native police force to help them as was the case here.

As late as 3 July Grey (from the relative security of Bulawayo) wrote to Chamberlain that "those who know Mashonaland well are not uneasy—they are unanimous in the belief that the rising will not prove formidable."[9]

The secret had been well kept and the first murders, in widely separated places, caught most of the victims by surprise. The tone of the *Rhodesia Herald* of 17 June was calm, though the paper reported the murder of the two white men at the Beatrice mine, thirty miles south of Salisbury, on the 15th, other murders in Lomagundi, and rumours from several directions. The next issue, on 24 June, was a record of horror: the traders van Rooyen and Fourie killed about fifteen miles out on the Hartley road; "poor Stunt's murder a little further out"; Keeley and Wills, of a police patrol investigating a murder in Lomagundi, butchered; the bodies of the Norton family, "all terribly mutilated," identified; two successive parties (the Mazoe Patrol) sent out to try to save the people at the Alice mine. "Towards evening hopes were dashed to the ground on the appearance of Mr. Arnott, accompanied by Mr. Hendriks, who was badly shot in the mouth," with a pessimistic report of the party returning from Mazoe. "Later Messrs. A.D. Campbell and Stevens came in with further bad news. The natives from Ballyhooley northwards were in full revolt."

At 10 o'clock [on the evening of 20 June] a wagon and horsemen were heard approaching laager, and scarcely had the sentries challenged when it became known that by some miracle the Alice party and the relieving patrols had, after being given up as lost, actually turned up in camp. Loud and prolonged cheering burst forth from the garrison as the men and women were assisted into laager . . . Later in the evening still, Mrs. Orton, with whom came in Messrs. Manning, Brown, and Reid, arrived. The escape of this party was nothing short of miraculous, Mrs. Orton and her party having abandoned their cart in full view of the natives, and made their way over the veldt.

The story of the Mazoe patrol was told, and the stories of deaths, battles, and rescues in all directions. Of the Hartley patrol: "The whole country is up. The contingent encountered at least 2,000 natives yesterday. One volley numbered at least 150 shots." From Marandellas:

On Tuesday afternoon [23 June] Messrs. G. Lamb, Count de la Panouse, Hudson, Haig, Finch, Davidson and Miss Carter came into town in a cart, the party having been attacked this side of Marandellas and fired at all the way to Ballyhooley. The natives were in force at places, and came as close as 30 yards to them keeping up a stinging fire. How the party escaped is a mystery. They passed on the road dead and horribly mutilated bodies of J. Weyers, his wife, girl and baby. They picked up a Cape boy badly wounded. At one spot they were so thickly surrounded and hard pressed that the little party gave up hope and Miss Carter is said to have borrowed a revolver to save herself from death by the assegai. The Count and his companions showed lots of pluck and endurance and these qualities doubtless saved the day.

478 Rhodes and Rhodesia

There was a long list of the killed and the missing. There was also political news: a public meeting attended by over two hundred men, vigorous criticism of the government "for the want of protective measures taken as regards the people of the district," the election of a Defence Committee, and the building of a laager based on the gaol, the strongest building in the town. The prisoners were released (among them the two troopers who had appropriated Lobengula's bags of gold in 1893) without fear of their attempting to escape, and their accommodation turned over to "the ladies."[10]

Of these items of news, two were destined to prominent places in the canon of white Rhodesian history: the Mazoe patrol and the murder of the Nortons. Norton had been farming for a year or two near the Hunyani Poort, had been on a short visit to England, and had recently returned with his wife, baby, the nurse-companion Miss Fairweather, and Talbot, a young farm pupil. There were also two white assistants, Alexander and Gravenor, on the farm. On the morning of 17 June Norton found that all his servants and labourers had disappeared. He sent Talbot to Salisbury on a bicycle to report this, while Alexander went out to brand some calves and Norton himself went to the nearby kraal of Chief Nyamwenda, the source of most of his labour, to seek information. That was the situation when the rebels broke into the house. The two women and Gravenor defended themselves with revolvers and brought down four of the assailants, but inevitably they and the baby were killed, as was Alexander out with the calves. As for Norton, he had in Marshall Hole's words "walked straight into a death trap, and was mercifully spared the knowledge of what took place at the farm in his absence." A police patrol the following night discovered the bodies, exept Norton's which was found some weeks later.[11]

Inspector R.C. Nesbitt, who commanded that patrol, was soon given a more difficult assignment. Twenty-seven miles north of Salisbury, at the poort which later became the site of the dam, were the offices of the native commissioner, Mazoe, and the mining commissioner, together with a few huts and a store; nearby, the Alice mine, and about a mile beyond that the telegraph office. Various prospectors were working in the area. This was the country of Chief Hwata, of the dynasty whose adventures a generation earlier were mentioned in chapter 1. The chief and his people were drawn into the rebellion by Mhasvi, a policeman who, on hearing the first reports from Hartley, went out from Salisbury to raise the Mazoe valley. As this was also the bailiwick of the spirit medium Nehanda, Mhasvi's task was easy.

Because of the telegraph office, the mine manager, J.W. Salthouse, could be informed as early as the 16th of the murders at the Beatrice mine, and on the 17th he was advised to warn all Europeans in the area. Of the prospectors only one, Darling, had time to reach the mine manager's house. The native commissioner, Pollard, out on tour, was captured and brought before Nehanda, who personally gave the order for him to be killed. ("I heard Nianda say to

Wata 'Kill Pollard but take him some way off to the river or he will stink', so they took him off . . . Wata said, 'Nianda sent me.' Then he took his axe and chopped him behind the head.")

About eight miles to the south was a Salvation Army farm, run by Mr. and Mrs. Cass, with whom Mrs. Dickenson, wife of the mining commissioner, was then staying. She, her husband, and the Casses were able to reach the Alice mine. As the whole party planned to walk to Salisbury, the authorities there sent a wagonette to bring in the three women (Mrs. Salthouse and the two mentioned). The wagonette was brought by J.L. Blakiston, an "unsuccessful kind of intellectual" who had failed to make good anywhere. He had somewhat reluctantly accepted a job in the telegraph company, but did not like Rhodesia or its people and was a misfit on the frontier. With him now were the driver Hendrik (a "Cape Boy") and H.D. Zimmermann of the Rhodesia Horse Volunteers.

These people and a few others who had gathered at the mine set out for Salisbury on the morning of the 18th, soon after the arrival of Blakiston. Some of the men walked ahead, the wagonette followed an hour later, and four more men delayed while some telegrams were sent off. The advance party walked into an ambush. Some of them, riding behind in a cart with the baggage, looked ahead and saw "a number of natives striking something on the ground with knobkerries." They ran back, stopped the wagonette, which returned to the mine with mules at full gallop, the rear party turned about, and all repaired to the rough laager which had been constructed when the first warning was received.

There was no food in the laager and only one keg of water, the heat of the sun was reflected from the rocks, and the rebels had surrounded the place. The only hope of survival was help from Salisbury, but Salisbury believed the party to be now well on its way to town. The telegraph office was a mile from the laager, and the way to it was covered by the enemy. The local telegraph operator, Routledge, was naturally reluctant to make the trip. "After some delay, Blakiston said to Routledge: 'Will you go, if I go with you?' He said he would, so off they started." Even with the covering fire from the laager, it is surprising that they reached the telegraph office alive. The message was sent, though cut short by enemy fire. According to Marshall Hole it was: "We are surrounded, Dickenson, Cass, Faull killed. For God's sake—". The *Rhodesia Herald* learned from the operator in Salisbury that Blakiston had "added the simple word 'Goodbye.' "

The story is taken up by the prospector Darling:

> I was guarding on my right, and was too busy to look around, when Mrs. Cass said: "There they come from the telegraph office, one on horseback and one on foot . . . Oh, they are firing on them—the horse is shot—he is down—no, he's not, he's up again—the man is shot; they're down—no, the man is up, he's running, he's running

hard. Oh, he's down, he's dead, he's dead!'' All this time I could not turn my head, but was banging away on my right. I asked about the other man. "He's running toward the bush," she replied, "and they are firing at him." He disappeared and some more shots were heard, and we knew that he was killed.

The sacrifice was not in vain. In response to the telegram a rescue party of Lieut. Judson, of the Rhodesia Horse Volunteers, and six men was sent out. Later, as it was realised that this party was not strong enough, Inspector Nesbitt and a detachment of twelve followed. Each had to fight most of the way. Both parties reached Mazoe. Then the rescuers and the rescued had to get to Salisbury.

Salthouse fixed sheets of iron on the sides and back of the wagonette, in which the women were to travel. The bullet marks on the iron afterwards showed that the passengers would not have survived without it. Apart from the three women, the party consisted of thirty men and eighteen horses. Six horses drew the wagonette, twelve mounted men rode in advance, in the rear and on the flanks, and the remaining men walked beside the wagonette. The route, up the Tatagura valley by the "Old Mazoe Road" which runs between the later main road and the railway, was a track lined by tall grass. It was also, on 20 June 1896, lined by rebels who used the grass as cover. "Mr. Salthouse and other eye-witnesses state that the natives had horses and many good marksmen and guns, and they heard the voices of Matabele among them." (Darling, during the siege at the mine, heard a sentry on a rock call out, "asking why they, the Mashonas, had left him, a Matabele, without tobacco, and ordered them to send some up at once.").

According to a rebel account,

> Mhasvi and his party saw the new and fresh party arriving from Salisbury and go into the laager. He knew the party had come to get all those in the laager. He quickly left the mountain and went to wait at a place called Chomu Koreka, which means a place of death, when one is forced to be at that place during a fight. "Chomu koreka" is a place where there is a swamp to the east, a small stream and a bushy hill to the west, whilst the main road ran parallel to the stream close to the bushy hill . . . It was not long before the coach, which was carrying the few women and men, arrived at this dangerous place, and Mhasvi and his men were upon it. They fired upon the coach as it passed this place, killing men and several of the horses that were pulling the coach, but somehow the coach, although under such heavy fire, managed to pass through, making its way to Salisbury.

Judson, in his instructions to his patrol, had spoken of a "valley of death." The spot Mhasvi described was the Tatagura drift.

When the white party reached it, two troopers were killed. For fourteen miles after that the fighting was continuous, the attackers, hidden by the grass, coming in places to within ten yards of the road. Pascoe (the Salvation Army major turned builder) volunteered to ride on top of the wagonette as a look-out man; he was able to direct the fire of those on the ground, and miraculously came through the ordeal unhurt. Three of the advance guard were killed; the remaining two, cut off from the main party whom they thought unlikely to have survived, went on—one of them badly wounded in the face—and staggered into Salisbury as the *Herald* reported. The main body arrived a few hours later. Only Nesbitt got the VC for this operation; perhaps it should be regarded as a collective award.

This story took its place beside that of the Shangani patrol in the folk-memory of the white Rhodesians. The story included, but perhaps under-emphasized, the gallant actions of the two "Cape Boys"—Hendrik, the driver of the wagonette, and George, the Salthouses' cook. When Judson's party arrived and was seen to be inadequate, and it was not known that Nesbitt was on his way, a message had to be sent to Salisbury asking for stronger reinforcements. The telegraph office was now out of the question. Hendrik then (with a reward of £100 dangled before him) set out for Salisbury alone by night, riding the best available horse. He fell in with Nesbitt's party and returned with it, but if necessary he would have tried to go the whole way. Salthouse, in his own report, paid tribute to Hendrik for deliberately risking his life on two or three occasions, and the *Herald* trusted "that the boy will get his £100, and also be kept in mind in the future." During the fight at the laager, rebel marksmen occupied some huts which enabled them to fire at the laager from cover. Before dawn George, the cook, went out alone, set fire to two of the huts and brought back some food from the house. The two shared the dangers of the whites on the journey to safety. Their role, like that of all the black allies of the whites, deserves attention.[12]

Among the black victims was one whose death was little noticed by the white or the black public at the time, but shone forth with a particular brilliance afterwards. On the night of 17 June Bernard Mizeki, the evangelist placed at Mangwende's by Bishop Knight-Bruce, heard the voices of some of his young proteges who could not sleep. He went out to quieten them, and as he looked up at the hills the signal fires were being lit. They meant trouble, of which there had been warnings and forebodings for some days. Bernard's wife and others had begged him to leave, but many calls of duty, including the plight of an old man who had no one else to care for him, kept him at his post. His death had been determined upon by Mangwende's son Muchemwa, the relentless foe of the whites and all their works, and by the local *nganga* whose influence was threatened by Christianity. In the small hours of the 18th Ziute and Saridjgo, members of the chief's family, entered the hut, dragged Bernard out and stabbed him, amid the frantic struggles of his wife to save him. A great fear came upon many of the people because at the moment of Bernard's death the place was enveloped in a blinding light, and there was a noise "like many wings of great birds." Bernard earned an honourable place among Anglican martyrs; if his church had been in the Roman obedience he might in due course have been canonized.[13]

One more drama should be mentioned. On the evening of the 20th, the day the Mazoe patrol fought its way to Salisbury, two riders left Headlands for Marandellas. They were W. Edwards, native commissioner at Marandellas, and Kenneth Jakins, a transport rider. The main purpose of the journey was to save, or else destroy, certain stores at Marandellas. The reinforcements from Natal had passed that way, wagonloads of supplies followed them, but at that point the oxen succumbed to rinderpest. Many wagons full of supplies were stranded at Marandellas, waiting for mules to take them on. The most important item in these loads was 38,000 rounds of Martini-Henry ammunition.

Two nights before, the signal fires had been burning on the hills. Some of the messengers attached to Edwards's office at Marandellas had then decamped, taking their families and their rifles. Others of the messengers took the opposite side. One, Jan, was later entrusted by Edwards with a rifle, went out to warn a white farmer, Green, and escorted him into Marandellas under fire. Jan was afterwards killed fighting against the rebels. Another, Mabiza, ran down the Headlands road and met Edwards and Jakins coming up. He told them of the position at Marandellas—messengers absconded and store surrounded. By 10.30 p.m. Edwards, Jakins, and Mabiza reached the store and were able to get into it. The small party of whites there had sandbagged the building and brought in all the precious ammunition. There were also six mule wagons there, arrived on the 19th to take the stores away, but unable to leave again.

During the night three of these wagons were loaded. The party to go with them comprised nine white men (including Green who had just been brought in by Jan), the inevitable white woman, Mrs. van der Spuy, with baby, and an unspecified number of "Colonial wagon drivers," loyal messengers and other blacks. Mrs. van der Spuy was protected on her wagon by bags of flour—and cases of ammunition.

As the sun rose on the 21st the convoy started down the road to Headlands. Luckily for the party, the rebels had expected it to go the opposite way, and were waiting for it on the Salisbury road. Before they could correct their mistake the wagons had got a sufficient start. Edwards and his party would never have been able to shoot it out the whole way in the manner of the Mazoe patrol. It was a race, with some brief shooting at one point where the pursuers tried to head the wagons off by taking a short cut. People, wagons, and ammunition got safely to Headlands, and thence (with those who had made a laager there) to Umtali.[14]

More of the isolated people would have been saved if they had attended to the warnings they received. Jan had brought Green in. Another messenger had been sent to James White, who replied on the evening of the 19th: "Thanks for the warning, but there is no sign of any trouble here. If you hear of anything more, let me know. Captain Bremner is here and is going into Marandellas early to-morrow." The next day White and Bremner were dead. White, bleeding to death but still alive, had been rescued by the Methodist evangelist Molimile Molele, but both he and White were later effectively dispatched. The party of the vicomte de la Panouse, making for Salisbury from Marandellas, found Harry Graham at his store, trying to build "a sort of rough defence." He refused the invitation to join the party, and was killed shortly afterwards. D.E. Moony, native commissioner, Hartley, was told by one of his spies, three weeks before the outbreak, what to expect, but reported that "I attach no importance whatever to the above." We have seen what happened to him.

We last saw Robert Vavasseur returning, after serving in the Victoria column in 1893, to his farm Stonybroke near Fort Charter. His interests after that can be followed in his letters to his friend C.C.J. Webb at Oxford. His last letter to his parents was dated 9 May 1896. "In it he *expressed no* fears, simply saying he had *thought* of joining the Gwelo column, *but could not leave his cattle*. And for them he has sacrificed his precious life!" He must have refused again to leave his cattle when the rebellion erupted on his own doorstep. His murder, about 18 June, was arranged by the local chief Mushava on the orders of Mashayamombe and Kaguvi.[15]

The failure of communications was another reason why many victims were caught off guard. The telegraph lines connected only a few places, and the rebels soon cut them; Salisbury was out of telegraphic communication after 26 June. Where there was no telegraph, and runners could not get through, people remained in ignorance of what was happening—except, if they survived long enough, in their own neighbourhood. Two men came into Salisbury on 21 June, one riding a bicycle, "without having seen a single native, and without any knowledge of the rising." The men who defended themselves in a laager at Hartley Hills were not relieved until 22 July; it was only then that they learned that the rising was not a purely local one.[16]

The month ending about that date was described by one who experienced it in Salisbury as a nightmare. The whole population (of all races) spent every night in the laager. At first the rule applied only to women and children, exceptions being made for three women, who slept at the hospital under guard. As they were the wives of the acting administrator of Mashonaland (Judge Vintcent) and of two members of the Defence Committee, the granting of the privilege did not help to endear the authorities to the population. A false alarm on 19 June ended the discrimination, as all who were outside the laager got themselves into it—Dutch farmers bringing their wagons, Indian gardeners their vegetables—as quickly as they could.

The second week of this "nightmare" was almost as full of sudden deaths, daring rescues, miraculous escapes, and bloody fights as the first. It had been a week of nightmare for the handful of men at the Ayrshire mine in the Lomagundi district. On the 21st a "Zambesi boy" reached the mine, his arms tightly bound. He had been captured but had escaped. A temporary laager was formed and a warning was sent (too late) to the camp of the native commissioner, Meynhard. Then the ten whites and twenty blacks set out for Salisbury. They were ambushed, had to hide in a river bed, travelled in various directions to try to elude their pursuers, but time and again found that their tracks had been followed and that they were surrounded. At 5.30 p.m. on the 27th, twelve miles out of Salisbury, they were met by a patrol and brought in—five whites and the "boy." The other whites had been killed and the carriers apparently lost during the escapes through the bush. "Mr. Hawkins says no praise is too strong for the Zambesi boy, who was with them. He saved their lives time after time by his scouting, guidance and in procuring them roots and water, whereas, if he had chosen, he could have got through to Salisbury much more safely by deserting the white men."[17]

The first week of July was reported as "comparatively quiet," but the danger to Salisbury had hardly receded. Its capacity for defence in men and horses was limited, it was out of touch with the rest of the country, and no defeat had been inflicted on the rebels. As from Bulawayo three months earlier, so now from Salisbury, patrols were sent out to warn and to rescue isolated whites. But whereas the civilians of Bulawayo had complained that the town was being denuded of defenders by this practice, those of Salisbury had to complain that the Defence Committee wanted to use its whole force to defend the laager, abandoning the outsiders to their fate. Nevertheless, under pressure from the public, patrols were sent. The Mazoe patrol has been described. Marshall Hole, in his official report on the rebellion in Mashonaland, lists thirty-seven patrols from Salisbury between 17 June and 23 July.

Some were for purposes of rescue. Most were offensive. Though no Shona army concentrated for an attack on Salisbury, as the Ndebele had threatened Bulawayo, the small forces of individual chiefs were active everywhere, even to within two or three miles of the town. The most that the handful of defenders could do in the fighting line was to drive these enemies a little further away. They could also begin, in a small way, what was to be the policy on a bigger scale when the defenders had been reinforced: they could destroy the kraals, the food supplies in them, and the crops on which the rebels were dependent. Better still, they could bring the food and the stock into town.

Thus, in early July, we read of Captain Taylor taking thirty mounted whites and 140 Zulus to Chirumba's kraal, which was deserted but full of food supplies, which were brought away; this and seven other kraals were burnt. A patrol of ten whites and sixty Zulus collected grain from Beza's kraal. Forty whites (half of them mounted) and 100 Zulus, with a Maxim and wagons, went to Briscoe's farm and brought back forage, mealies, and some household effects. They had been attacked by from four to five hundred rebels, whom they repulsed, killing between thirty and forty, with no loss on their own side. A patrol under Major Hoste—sent out from Beal's column, not from Salisbury—had been to Merema's kraal and had been attacked. It had killed fifteen rebels, burnt sixteen kraals, and captured stock.

These operations may have helped slightly to blunt the rebel offensive, but they hardly brought the end of the rebellion any nearer. Luckily for Salisbury, Jameson had not been able to lure its Rhodesia Horse Volunteers after him to Pitsani and Doornkop; nor had the mistake been made of sending them all to Bulawayo in its hour of need. Beal had marched off then with 150, but some sixty had been kept back—to their own disgust—in case they should be needed nearer home. These, with the handful of police (Mashonaland Regiment, Rhodesia Mounted Police) who had not gone with Jameson, were the core of Salisbury's defence. To these were added about 250 civilians who in terms of the "burger law" were liable for compulsory service. About thirty or forty horses were all that could be mustered. Privately owned firearms were commandeered; even so the number available in the town was only "not less than 250 effective guns of all sorts." There were about 250 women and children to be defended. As the laager (with the rest of the town) was commanded by the Kopje, a garrison had to be placed there and connected with the laager by telephone.[18]

With these meagre resources Salisbury had to defend itself, rescue isolated parties and launch local offensives. No time had been lost, however, in calling for help. While the telegraph wires were still intact the news of the Mashonaland rising had been flashed to Bulawayo and to the world. Judge Vintcent obtained permission from Lord Grey to intercept the "Natal Troop," about seventy volunteers with 120 horses and two Maxims, who were then at Charter on their way from Beira to Bulawayo, and to engage them in Mashonaland instead.

As a matter of course, the "Salisbury Column" which Beal had taken down by slow stages to Gwelo and Bulawayo had now to return. It left Bulawayo on 21 June. In addition, 100 men under Major Watts and about seventy of Grey's Scouts (these commanded by Capt. the Hon. Charles White) left Bulawayo for Salisbury. Then there was the imperial force under Col. Alderson, which moved up from Beira to Umtali in the course of July. This, too, was now diverted from the old war to the new.

White (one of the three brothers, another of whom was then in Wormwood Scrubs for his part in the Jameson Raid) brought his scouts into Salisbury on 16 July, and Beal's column arrived on the 17th. Both had seen much fighting along the way. Their arrival ended the month of "nightmare." On 19 June Vintcent had imposed martial law on Salisbury; it was rescinded on 23 July. The next day the inhabitants were given permission to sleep out of the laager. The sick were removed to the hospital, which was given a guard of twenty-five at night. At the same time the Salisbury Field Force was disbanded and the civilians could resume their normal vocations if circumstances permitted. As in

Bulawayo, so here, the intention was to enrol many of these men in a new full-time force. The conditions offered, including the obligation to serve anywhere and under any commander, having failed to attract, were then modified. A hundred signed on for three months only, merely to defend Salisbury with picket and guard.[19]

One of the earliest patrols sent out had tried but failed to reach Hartley Hills. The arrival of the reinforcements made another attempt possible. White led a force consisting of his own scouts (65), the Natal Troop (75), the Salisbury Field Force, not yet disbanded (60), artillery (10), and 40 Zulus, which left Salisbury on 19 July. Near the Hunyani there was a fight. A troop of the Salisbury men, dismounted, and the Zulus captured a ridge in the face of enemy concealed in the long grass. Further on another ridge was seized just before the rebels could reach it. This enabled the whole column to get past a danger point and to camp beyond it. That night the rebels fired a volley into the camp "by way of a good-night, and men replying by derisive cheers." After more fighting the Hartley Hills laager was reached and the occupants—ignorant till then of what was happening in the country—brought away. A rebel attempt to trap the column failed. The kraal which Kaguvi had made his headquarters was attacked, but the *mhondoro* himself escaped. This place was the great depot for the loot which Kaguvi ordered to be brought to him. The victors found much of the property of the Nortons and of Pollard, great quantities of arms and ammunition and stock, and brought away all they could. The column reached Salisbury on the 28th.

In the meantime Beal's column had moved out to the Jesuits' farm, Chishawasha, to set up a defended post for the sake of the large quantity of grain stored at the mission. On the way the column, which included the unit of "Cape boys" known as the Black Watch, had some sharp fighting on the hills. To the troops, the sight of the destruction wrought at the mission station was "saddening and maddening," but the Jesuits now returned and began to build again. This force was to get into a bigger fight when it left Chishawasha a couple of weeks later.

Before this—on 19 July—the advance guard of Alderson's column had at last reached Umtali. The imperial factor was about to intervene.[20]

As the little parties scattered over the country had made their way to safety, or been rescued, or massacred, the white population of Mashonaland with its black allies had been confined to the laagers of Salisbury, Charter, Enkeldoorn, Victoria, and Umtali. Of these only the first three were in rebel country, but of those three Salisbury was the key to the whole campaign, and the survival of Salisbury depended on the supplies that could reach it.

This was a war of attrition; success or failure on either side depended more upon supplies and lines of communication than on any other factor. The supplies of the rebels were decentralized. There were stocks of grain in every village and, as the villages were abandoned, in the caves. Rebels looted stores and drove the cattle from white farms. The animals were harder than the grain to defend. They were driven from point to point as the enemy approached, but not many could be taken into the caves. The government forces not only eked out their own supplies by capturing stock and seizing supplies of grain wherever they went, but counted on wearing down the rebels by destroying all supplies that could not be taken away.

The capture of stock and grain from the rebel villages helped Salisbury a little, but was no substitute for the supplies normally imported. Alderson had been expected to bring great quantities with him, but it was all he could do to organize a two months' supply for his own force. Even so, when that reached Salisbury half of it had to be turned over to the local population, with unfortunate results for the military operations. Salisbury was short, but the small laagers at Charter and Enkeldoorn were reduced to severe siege conditions.

The campaign on the government side can be largely explained by logistics. Supplies, both civil and military, had to go to Salisbury via Beira and Umtali. They could not go until Alderson had opened the route, which he had done by about the second week of August. At that time Robert Beal, who had brought his column back to Salisbury from Matabeleland, was made responsible for the line of communication between Beira and Umtali, and on 25 August H. Wilson Fox, quartermaster of Beal's column, was placed in charge of transport and supply. His task was to get to Salisbury six months' supplies for 2,000 people. This was done, but the statistics of the operation show what the absence of a railway between Chimoio and Salisbury meant. As almost all the oxen were dead, mules had to be brought from the Cape by sea, and then from Fontesvilla to Chimoio on the narrow-gauge railway, which could not carry more than thirty animals (some accounts raise the number to forty or fifty) a day. Five hundred mules reached Beira on 5 September. Beal arranged for the wagons and the gear to be collected at Chimoio, and the wagons packed, before the mules were entrained. As they reached Chimoio they could therefore start on their journey at once. Carriers were employed, in addition to the wagons, to take loads to Umtali. The round trip from Chimoio to Umtali and back took a mule-wagon, on the average, thirteen days and an ox-wagon nineteen; from Umtali to Salisbury and back, twenty-four and thirty-two days respectively. An incomplete list gives the number of wagons available for the route as forty-nine.

There were a few "salted" oxen, but even some of those were accidentally poisoned. Some of the supplies had to be taken to Charter and Enkeldoorn, and some of the transport had to be withdrawn from this service for use on military forays. For all these reasons the main convoy did not reach Salisbury until the second week of October. If there had been a railway, supplies would have begun to roll into Salisbury, and in larger quantities, in the wake of Alderson—two months earlier. And that is on the assumption that the rising could have got off the ground at all. Again, on the same assumption, more imperial troops would probably have been used in operations. Their number was limited not only by the Company's finances, but by the facilities for supplying them. This note is struck again and again in the discussions between administrator and high commissioner.[21]

Eleven years earlier there had been a rebellion on the Canadian prairies. Because the building of the Canadian Pacific Railway was then nearly finished, it was possible to get 3,000 troops from eastern Canada to the theatre of war in two weeks from the first clash at Duck Lake, and to supply them, and the rebellion was quickly suppressed. That would certainly have been the outcome in Rhodesia if either of the railways—from Mafeking or from Beira—had been complete by the beginning of 1896. Operations would have been much more effective even if the ox-wagons had been rolling, but the rinderpest prevented that. The whites could be thankful for two facilities: the railway from Fontesvilla (and, by October, from Beira) to Chimoio, and above all that the Mangwe road had been kept open by Gampu, with or without the help of Hlabangana before Burnham murdered him.

Difficulties of supply, therefore, hampered both sides; but they did not determine the strategy or tactics of either side. The Shona rebels, even more than the Ndebele in this war, were the prisoners of their own history. It has been pointed out[22] that the Ndebele, up to the war of 1893, had never evolved a theory of defensive warfare. They seem to have assumed that victory must always

Arrival of first train in Bulawayo, 4 November 1897

489 The Rebellion II

go to the attackers, meaning themselves. The Shona on the other hand had usually had to fight defensively. There was no case in this war where they, like a Ndebele impi, advanced openly to attack. Their attacks took the form of ambushes, of firing upon an approaching enemy from cover. Their fighting tactics, said "Curio" Brown, "were of a character differing widely from those of the Matabeles. From thickets, from kopjes, from ant-heaps, and from caves in the rocks all about us, volleys of slugs began to pour forth from muzzle-loading guns, the tremendous reports of which sounded quite like a genuine battle. Fortunately for us, our adversaries were not good marksmen." As they had taken to the typical granite koppies of their country for defence against the Ndebele, so they took to them now in a kind of offensive. They had expelled the whites from all except five spots on the map, and the whites could not return until they had winkled all the rebels out of their rocks and caves. And the rebels were not all such bad marksmen, or as ill armed, as those Brown described. They used mounted scouts.[23]

These facts determined the strategy on the government side. There could be no concentration for a decisive battle. Each rebel paramount had to be attacked separately. In some cases there was difficulty even in locating the enemy. At the beginning of August patrols came into Salisbury without having found a single rebel. "Vanished?" asked a headline in the *Herald*, though everyone knew that a defenceless party would find rebels soon enough. Everyone knew also that Salisbury did not have the resources to deal with any important enemy force.

So by this time—the end of July—Salisbury's hopes were concentrated on Alderson's column, all of which had reached Umtali from the coast. Its arrival, like that of Beal's column in Salisbury, made possible the return of the civilian defenders to their ordinary business, and Alderson organized a new force of 132 volunteers which joined his column. On 28 July the whole of Alderson's force, accompanied by "a number of private gentlemen and merchants who had been detained at Umtali owing to the unsafe condition of the road," moved out in the direction of Salisbury. The primary task of the column was to reopen communication between Salisbury and Umtali and the coast. Hostile forces on or near the road had to be driven off and made harmless. As some formidable rebels lived along the route, defeating them would contribute largely to the suppression of the rebellion.

The most formidable, and one of the leading rebel chiefs of all Mashonaland, was Makoni. Alderson duly attacked his kraal on 3 August. There was a fierce fight, about sixty rebels were killed for a loss of three killed and four wounded on the attacking side, most of the inhabitants retreated into the caves, the kraal was burnt, and the column continued on its way. As Makoni could dispose of about 4,000 fighting men, Alderson had not achieved very much. He did establish forts or garrisoned posts at a few points along the road, and a few days later his column met that of Major Watts coming from the opposite direction. This was one of the reinforcements that had been sent from Bulawayo. Instead of following Beal into Salisbury it had been diverted from Charter direct to Marandellas, where a fort had been built and garrisoned. Another was now established at Headlands, and the forces moved on to Salisbury and Umtali respectively. The route, patrolled by the Umtali Volunteers, could now be considered open, and the column had repaired the telegraph line also.

This accession of strength made possible patrolling on a bigger scale. In all directions kraals were attacked and burnt, but in every case their inhabitants retired into caves. No important rebel chief surrendered. Alderson's intention after reaching Salisbury had been to attack the most important of all, Mashayamombe, but lack of supplies prevented him from doing this until 5 October. In the meantime Major Jenner, with a part of Alderson's force, had fought his way through various kraals in Marandellas and Charter until he came to that of Mutekedza, the principal chief of the district. On 15 and 16 September, with a large force which included 1,100 "friendlies" from Victoria, he attacked this kraal and destroyed it. The rebels retired to their caves, but after an hour's heavy fighting Mutekedza surrendered on condition that his life be spared. Most of his people escaped. A few days earlier Simbanuta's people, who had likewise retreated into their caves when attacked, had been less fortunate. The attackers had ended the operation by dynamiting the caves, a solution to the problem that was now becoming standard.[24]

Alderson's attack on Mashayamombe was intended to be the culmination of the campaign. Though the arrival of supplies, and the expected arrival of more, enabled him to set out from Salisbury on 5 October, what he was able to take was only two weeks' rations. Jenner's column having joined Alderson's, the combined force ravaged the Hartley Hills district, burnt kraals and blew up caves, but then, with supplies running short, had to leave the task half done. It was not realised that the great medium Kaguvi, after the destruction of his kraal on 26 July, had moved his headquarters to a cave on Kaguvi Hill (already so named, from the earlier Kaguvi mediums), on the south bank of the Umfuli facing Mashayamombe's stronghold. The chief, too, retired to a cave, and when the column marched away neither he nor Kaguvi had been killed or captured; the battle honours went to the rebels. If a fort could have been built and a garrison left to tie them down it would have been a different story, but Alderson did not have enough men for that. In his own words,

We might, at a pinch, have spared the men (though we had Lomagundi's, Mapondera's, and other districts to visit before the rains), and other difficulties on the way, such as terms of service (for the garrison must come from the local forces), medical arrangements, clothing, etc., etc., might have been overcome. The real stopper was the old question—supply. We ourselves could not provision the fort, and we knew that Salisbury, even if we sent back there, was equally powerless in this respect.[25]

491 The Rebellion II

By October both sides knew that the rains would soon put an end to the campaign for some months. The rebels would be able to sow, and perhaps reap; their remaining stock would be safe and villages could be rebuilt. Hence Alderson's hasty campaigning in October and November. The rebels frustrated him in two ways. They fled—and those in the northern districts, Mazoe and Lomagundi, on which Alderson was concentrating, had not far to flee before they were in "the fly" and safe from the mounted infantry. Alternatively they expressed a willingness to surrender, while being careful never actually to give up their arms.

The diplomacy of Chidamba and some other Mazoe chiefs on 21 September illustrates the method. Having offered to surrender, they had a rendezvous at the Golden Stairs on that day with Vintcent, Scanlen, Marshall Hole, Alderson, and others. As an earnest of their good faith they surrendered Mazwe ("much to his disgust"), a former policeman who had rebelled. They undertook to give up their arms the next day. None were given up, on the excuse that "their young men would not come in because they thought we had killed Mazwe and they wanted first to see him alive." Mazwe was brought back under escort to be exhibited. The next night he was kept in the Mazoe fort, an earthen breastwork surrounded by a six-foot ditch and barbed wire entanglements. The prisoner was handcuffed and tied by a cord to one of the guard. In the morning, nevertheless, he was found to have escaped. The imperial troops who had thus lost their prey were roundly abused by the white Rhodesians— "but as the majority of people imagined, in spite of one of the guard being tried by court martial afterwards, that we had not been able to resist the temptation of taking Mazwe out quietly and shooting him, we got off with less than we should otherwise have done."

The war having been resumed, several days were spent in attacking a fastness in the "Granite" or Iron Mask Range, at the heart of which was Chidamba's kraal. More important, it included Nehanda's cave. The attackers knew of her importance and were very anxious to capture her, but she escaped before the place was taken.

If the imperials incurred ridicule for letting Mazwe escape on 24 September, and the popular hope that they had really shot him was unfounded, they had perhaps learned caution from the case of Makoni three weeks earlier.[26]

In outline, the story is as follows. On 19 August the local native commissioner, A.R. Ross, heard that Makoni wished to surrender on condition that his life were spared. Ross told him that if he came in his life would be spared and that he would have a fair trial. Conversations went on for ten days, without result. In the meantime Alderson had ordered Major Watts, who was commanding the line of communication troops from Umtali, to concentrate as many of those troops as could be spared at Fort Haynes, near Makoni's, to be ready to accept the surrender. This was done, and, Makoni having ignored several ultimatums, the force advanced on his kraal on 30 August. During the next few days Watts, through Ross, called five times on Makoni to surrender, promising that his life would be spared—though he would have to face a trial and its consequences.

During those days Makoni and his people kept up an intermittent and sometimes heavy fire from their caves, and made some sorties, while Watts's force tried to block all escape routes. From the 30th onwards dynamite was used on various caves, and at various times some men and many women and children came out and gave themselves up; others succeeded in getting away. On the night of 2-3 September there was a determined attempt by the rebels to escape from the caves, and by the troops to prevent the escape. Makoni approached one of the cave mouths, guarded by Lieut. Fichat of the Umtali Artillery Volunteers, and announced that he would be coming out "after some little while," but then retired further into the cave. When he later came near the entrance again, followed by a man holding a candle, Fichat went towards him and caught him by the hand. This was at about 2 a.m. At that moment heavy firing at the other end of the cave showed that an attempt was being made to break out at that side, and Makoni tried to pull away from Fichat. The latter stated in evidence:

> I immediately pulled my revolver out of my right tunic pocket, and held it to his head and told him, another attempt like that and I would blow his brains out. I told the man holding the candle behind Makoni that if he blew the light out I would shoot Makoni and loose my revolver amongst the remainder of them. I then said to Makoni, "Come along;" he sat down and wanted to talk in the caves . . . I pulled him out, and he again sat down. I had the revolver at his head all this time, and holding him. I took him alone . . . and handed him over personally to Major Watts.

The following afternoon at 3.30 Watts assembled a field general court martial of five officers (two of them imperial) to try Makoni. He was assigned a solicitor for his defence, but as the charge was armed rebellion the verdict could hardly be in doubt: guilty. Sentence: death.

The reason for conducting the trial on the spot, instead of sending the prisoner to Salisbury or Umtali for trial, was that Watts could not spare the men for an escort. The line of communication was dangerously denuded as it was. A brother of Makoni's, who had remained "loyal," was present with two hundred of his armed followers. They appeared dangerously excited, and Ross assured Watts that if Makoni were taken away an attempt at rescue was almost certain. The same reason explains what follows. Watts sent telegrams to the high commissioner, to Baden-Powell as chief staff officer in Bulawayo, and to Alderson, asking for confirmation of the sentence. As the nearest open telegraph office was at Umtali, which it took a runner two days to reach, Watts soon thought better of that plan, and without waiting for replies took the responsibility of confirming the sentence himself.

Accordingly, at noon on 4 September, Makoni was shot inside his own kraal in the presence of the troops. Before his death he handed over his two small sons, who were present, to Colin Harding, commander of the firing party. He died with the dignity becoming a great chief.

As soon as the high commissioner heard of the event he ordered Watts, like Baden-Powell, to be placed under open arrest. A court of enquiry met in Salisbury on 18 September. On the basis of the evidence presented to it Rosmead came to the usual conclusion: the court martial had been illegal, but Watts had acted in good faith, in the belief that the military situation made his action necessary. He, Rosmead, did not intend to proceed further in the case.[27]

The historian may proceed a little further. The Latin maxim about *suprema lex* may apply. The military circumstances may have forced Watts's hand. A civil court, if Makoni had been brought before it, might have handed down the same sentence; there is no doubt that Makoni had instigated not only rebellion but murder. Yet his death cannot be brushed under the carpet as easily as some of his enemies thought it could.

The court martial, like those set up by Gibbs and Baden-Powell, was illegal. The fact that only the civil courts could try for rebellion was well known, or ought to have been: it had been proclaimed by the high commissioner, and the additional judge had been appointed specifically for this reason. Moreover, Clause 25 of the order-in-council of 1894 had provided that "in case of a revolt against the Company, or other misconduct committed by a native chief or tribe, the Administrator and Council may impose a reasonable fine upon the offender." It had provided also that the high commissioner could "remit the fine in whole or in part."[28] It should therefore have been foreseen that if Makoni surrendered he would have to be escorted to some seat of civil jurisdiction. An arrangement to receive his surrender—and that is what the concentration of troops at Fort Haynes was—should not have been made without provision for that necessary consequence.

That Makoni should be tried at all was a decision arrived at before Watts's move from Umtali, and after much argument. Makoni had offered to surrender if his life were spared. The Company men—Vintcent, Duncan, Scanlen, and Grey (the last after some hesitation)—wanted to accept his surrender on those terms. Alderson and Carrington agreed with them because the only alternative was to starve Makoni and his people out, for which Alderson had not the time or the resources. It was the imperial officials, Martin and Goodenough, that objected. They insisted that the surrender and trial of all guilty of murder was an indispensable condition. Goodenough thought that accepting Makoni's terms would be a bad precedent, and even wanted to insist on unconditional surrender. Martin and Goodenough agreed to "stretch a point" and offer terms, provided that all who were guilty of murder were given up for trial. The final proposal, to which Goodenough agreed, was that Makoni should be told that "if he desires to surrender, he and his people must come in and lay down their arms, and that he and his principal men will undergo a fair and full trial before a court of law, and that his own life and the lives of his people will be spared, unless he or they have been directly concerned in any murder."

It was on this basis that the native commissioner, Ross, and later Watts, had repeatedly told Makoni that his life would be spared if he surrendered. The offer was not unconditional, and Makoni knew as well as everyone else that at the meeting of chiefs on 9 June, at which he had laid plans for the rebellion, one of the specific orders he had sent out was for the murder of Ross. His unwillingness to surrender can thus be understood.

In the end, did he surrender? Watts was emphatic in his answer: Makoni "was captured, did not surrender." But, as Fichat's testimony shows, it would have taken a medieval schoolman to solve that semantic problem. If he was captured, the terms offered fell away. In that case Makoni was a prisoner, and as such could be tried on various charges—but only by a civil court. The dispatch of troops to Fort Haynes, but not in sufficient numbers to provide an escort, was bound to end in lawless action. Yet it is likely that lawful proceedings would equally have resulted in the chief's execution.

The amnesty proclamation had not been extended to Mashonaland. Even if it had, Makoni would have been one of those excluded from the amnesty. But by the date of his execution it was beginning to appear, from events in Matabeleland, that the proclamation might be superseded by other arrangements.[29]

MATABELELAND: THE INDABAS

Military deadlock had been reached in Matabeleland by August, when Rhodes stepped in to resolve it in his own way. How is this, his "finest hour," to be judged? Vere Stent, who had good opportunities for observation, saw the indabas germinating in Rhodes's mind after the battle of Intaba zika-Mambo. The death of eighteen white soldiers—the "Cape boys" who lost their lives are not mentioned—weighed on his mind. As was his custom in such cases, he sat apart, silent and pensive. It may be that, like one of Stephen Leacock's characters, he was thinking not only of the bloodshed but of the Company's balance sheet and the price of Chartereds. There would have been nothing discreditable in that; war is waged with sinews as well as with blood. Whatever the reasoning, it led to the conclusion that this war must be ended as quickly as possible.

The soldiers had to be allowed some useless bloodletting in the Matopos before they could be induced to think of peace, but even while the battles were being fought Rhodes was at work on the alternative. Hans Sauer, who had returned from imprisonment in Pretoria for his part in the abortive Johannesburg revolt, was sent to interview Likuni (also spelt Lekuni), one of Lobengula's brothers. This was the chief from whom Matabele Wilson and Usher had got warning of the coming rebellion. He was asked to go, or to send some of his men, into the Matopos to make contact with the rebels. He absolutely refused. He and his people, having remained loyal to the government, would get very short shrift at the rebels' hands. At Sauer's suggestion, Rhodes turned to Colenbrander, who provided two of his "Boys" for the job. Having been given instructions and the promise of a reward, they were sent into the hills, but were never seen again.

Then came the day when Carrington, who knew nothing of these overtures, moved his camp eastward towards the Tuli road. Rhodes and Sauer got his permission to establish a separate little camp for themselves; this made their secret operations easier. They were ready to try again, this time with two prisoners of war, when the battle of 5 August had a sobering and, from the peacemakers' point of view, beneficial effect on the soldiers. By that time, too, Carrington had got wind of what Rhodes was up to. He was prepared, as he would not have been before, to tolerate the next move.

Before that move was made, a patrol went into the hills to capture a large quantity of grain that was reported to be stored in some caves. Rhodes and Sauer accompanied the patrol. The grain having been secured, it was then learned that there were chickens in a deserted kraal at the northern point of Sikhombo's mountain. On the way to this the patrol ran into Jan Grootboom and ten "Cape Boys" on the same errand. Together they entered the kraal and rounded up the chickens. During the operation "an old native lady emerged from a hut and attacked Rhodes in voluble Zulu, calling him a stealer of hens and other uncomplimentary names." She proved to be one of the widows of Mzilikazi.

That was a royal quarry indeed. Narrowly escaping a small impi that was running towards them, the patrol got down to the camp with its prisoner, Grootboom and his men covering the retreat with rifle fire. The royal lady was the mother of Nyanda, one of the rebel leaders in the hills. Negotiating with her took time. For two days she would say nothing, but contented herself with spitting every time she saw one of her captors. In the end she gave up this behaviour and was prepared to listen. She was given simple instructions. The rebel leaders were to be told to show the white flag if they wanted peace. Equipped with a large piece of white calico, the old lady set off. For about a week, no more was heard of her or of the result of her message.

During that week Jan Grootboom and James Makhunga went into the hills three or four times, for twenty-four hours at a time. They succeeded in speaking to some of the indunas, African fashion, by shouting from one hill-top to another. The distance was gradually reduced until the two scouts and two rebel leaders met face to face. Though the scouts were not Ndebele, and had less to fear from the rebels than people like Likuni, their encounter surely took even more courage than Rhodes was about to summon up. The message they brought from their final meeting was that the white flag would soon be displayed, and a day or two later it was seen flying from the appointed tree.

As so often in the past, it was the older indunas who now wanted peace, and the younger leaders and warriors who wanted to fight on. The strongest argument for peace was the same on the rebel as on the white side: supply. Stores of grain had been accumulated in the Matopos, from which they were distributed in various directions as needed. Laing discovered a large stock of it in grass bags, sealed with clay, in dense bush in the Insiza district. It had been put there recently, and Laing's column also at several points crossed the line of communication between that spot and the Matopos. He called it the "grain track," and as he went westward he noticed it "still keeping straight for the Matopos." But he had captured the grain, and what he now saw on the track was evidence that a large party of men, women and children, cattle and sheep, had just passed along it in the westward direction. The traffic had originally been outward from the Matopos; now the people were moving towards the hills and the grain had been lost. The capture of rebel food supplies, here as in Mashonaland, was a regular task of the patrols.[30]

There was still food in the hills, but there were more mouths to feed. And how would the stocks be replenished? That depended on the next crop, but most of the crop had to be grown on the plains, not among the rocks and impenetrable thickets of the Matopos, and the sowing season was at hand. This is the kind of problem that responsible leaders face, but that ardent young soldiers tend to brush aside. In this case the responsible leaders had not only to keep their young men in hand, but also to find out what the price of peace would be. They were not in a mood for peace at any price. So it came about that the leaders gathered for a parley. As soon as the white flag was seen, Grootboom and Makunga set out again. In the early afternoon of 21 August they returned to camp with the fateful message. The chiefs were ready to meet Rhodes at a place they designated, well up in the hills. He might bring, at the most, three other white men with him.

Rhodes ordered the horses at once, but he was not quite a free agent. For a quarter of an hour he was seen pacing up and down with Carrington. If the general had objections, they must have been overcome. If he had suggestions, they were at least listened to. Rhodes had invited Sauer and Colenbrander to go with him. That Grootboom and Makunga should go was a matter of course, but the chiefs' stipulation applied only to the number of whites. As the party was setting out, Sauer suggested adding a fourth white man: Vere Stent, the young correspondent of the *Cape Times*. Of course he leapt at the chance. There were imperial officers who leapt at it too, and Rhodes agreed to take them, but Grootboom put his foot down. If there were more than four white men treachery would be suspected, and in that case he, Jan, would not go. The imperial officers seem to have blamed Sauer for excluding them, and never to have forgiven him.

Rhodes asked his companions if they thought the adventure dangerous. Stent and Sauer both claim to have pointed to the fate of Piet Retief. Stent later described the scene:

It was a lovely winter's day, the sun just beginning to western; comfortably hot; the grasses, bronze and golden, swaying in the slight wind; the hills ahead of us blurred in the quivering mirage of early afternoon. We talked very little. Must I confess it?—we were all a little nervous. Perhaps we all thought of Piet Retief. We had entered the hills and were nearing a narrow canyon, where a rough track, commanded by a towering bluff upon one side, was bordered by a deep wooded valley on the other. The track debouched into a tiny basin, rimmed by kopjes and floored by fallow. In the centre of the fallow lay some tree stumps and the remnants of a big ant heap.

It was the appointed place. Though there was some comfort in the thought that it was a piece of open ground, the comfort was an illusion. The bluff which they had passed was already filling up with rebels.

Hans Sauer had some sort of a patent American repeating pistol with him. He suddenly said, quite thoughtfully, "By the way, how does this thing work?" and slipped his hand into his pocket. We were all pretty jumpy, and it seemed to me quite undesirable that Sauer should "monkey" with an American gun at that moment. I said, "For goodness' sake let that thing alone." I always admired the way in which he rounded on me. "Steady," he said, "don't show any signs of nervousness." My indignation nearly choked me.

As the party halted there was a moment's hesitation. Colenbrander said quietly to Sauer, in Afrikaans, "Don't let Rhodes dismount." Rhodes overheard the remark, and overruled it: "Dismount," he said, "dismount of course. It will give them confidence. They are nervous too." They tied the horses and, Rhodes leading the way, sat down on the remains of the ant-heap. Soon they could descry in the distance the huge white flag on a stick, and black figures gathering round it. Led by James Makhunga, who had gone to escort them and who carried the white flag, the procession wound down, halted before the ant-heap, and piled arms.

The leader and spokesman was Somabhulana. There were present about forty important indunas and officers, and a crowd of their juniors who appeared to be mat-bearers and other servants. Among the leaders were Mlugulu, Sikhombo, Babayane, Dliso, Nyanda, Malevu, and Gunu, every one of them excluded by name, in the proclamation, from the benefits of amnesty. For the moment they left the speaking to Somabhulana.

Rhodes, prompted by Colenbrander, gave them the greeting of peace: "*Amehlo amhlophe*"—the eyes are white. In reply there was a chorus of "*Amehlo amhlophe, nkosi yenyamazana*." At Rhodes's invitation Somabhulana then rose to speak. Like Stephen before his martyrdom, though the cir-

The first indaba, August 1896

cumstances and the outcome were quite different, the old chief recited the history of the Ndebele nation from the first days of Mzilikazi. The early chapters were innocuous. As the narrator got to 1893, the death of the envoys at the Tati, the theft of Lobengula's gold by the troopers, the death of the king and the confiscation of cattle, the atmosphere warmed up. "We are no dogs!" Somabhulana exclaimed, "the Children of the Stars can never be dogs." A restless stirring; exclamations of approval from the crowd.

> The moment was inflammable. The least indiscretion might precipitate a massacre. I realised this perhaps more clearly than anyone else. To my right, about two yards away, was a gentleman with an exceedingly useful-looking battle-axe. He had no business to bring it . . . As, however, the excitement waned I made up my mind that if a rush took place I would try and settle with the owner of the battle-axe first.

Rhodes spoke, through Colenbrander who was interpreting: "By whom and how were they made dogs?"

This gave Somabhulana the opening for his final thrust. He gave his recital of the tyrannies of native commissioners and abuses of power by Native Police. After Rhodes had replied that there would be no more Native Police, and this remark had been greeted with applause, another induna asked about Colonel X, a universally hated official; one of the crowd interjected, "Let him keep a canteen on the Transvaal side of the river; that's about what he's fit for." Rho-

499 The Rebellion II

des was not to be drawn into a dispute about Colonel X, but he did think that Somabhulana was having things too much his own way. The tables must be turned.

After more protestations of peace, and assurances by Rhodes that he would not go away and leave them without meeting their requests and remedying their grievances, he came to the point: why had they murdered women and children? Colenbrander at first refused to translate the question, but did so when Rhodes displayed anger.

Somabhulana replied with the question, "Who commenced the killing of women?" and told the story of the four women who were shot by the cattle-collectors.

> Dead silence. It was getting on towards evening. The winter wind rustled through the scant scrub, and a dust devil whirled across the fallow. It was another tense moment. The natives, especially the younger men, upon the outside of the demi-lune, cast ugly and malignant glances at us. I can't swear I didn't look back to see how near our horses were. Somabulana stared straight in front of him, with all the appearance of a cross-examining lawyer who has put an unanswerable question to a hostile witness.

Rhodes had never heard of the incident. Colenbrander, whose intimate association with the Ndebele gave him special sources of information, had. In an undertone, he told Rhodes that it was true, but advised him to drop the subject. This may have been the most dangerous moment in the whole indaba. The slightest sign that Rhodes was going to defend the tax-collectors could have made his hearers abandon hope of redress; then the killing could have started. Rhodes seemed as if he might be about to argue; Colenbrander, in a firm and commanding tone, repeated his original advice: "I should drop the subject."

"Well," said Rhodes, "all that is over. And now you have come to make peace." The tension subsided. The sun was setting. Somabhulana stood up and the conference was at an end. The affirmations were repeated—the eyes are white. Go well.

Suddenly there was a commotion. Stent and Colenbrander remembered that it was at the *end* of the conference that Dingane had ordered the death of Piet Retief's party. Rhodes, who was unarmed, in that instant feared that one of the others might draw his revolver. "It's all right," he called out, "they only want tobacco." Tobacco had been the unobtainable commodity in the Matopos. The indunas were dying for a smoke, and when Sauer produced a tobacco bag there was a rush towards him. Detente again; Rhodes and his party rode slowly down through the defile and reached camp about twilight. "By jove," Sauer said to Stent, "you *were* nervous." "Sauer," Stent replied, "if you had been half as nervous as I, you wouldn't have gone at all."

The least nervous of the party, or so it seemed to the others, had been Rhodes; and after him, Grootboom. By Stent's account, it was when the rebel party was seen approaching the ant-heap that Rhodes said, "This is one of those moments in life that make it worth living!" In Sauer's version, this was said as they were riding away at the end. Perhaps Rhodes said it on both occasions. The repetition would have been in character, and the remark was worth repeating. This, rather than any of the moments of triumph in politics or finance, was the high point of Rhodes's life. He risked that life to save the work to which he had devoted it; in 1893, for the same purpose, he had only gambled with other men's lives.

No doubt gambling was in the air, but some of the actors in the drama could now see the prospect of a very safe speculation. After a dinner to celebrate the day's work, Stent and Sauer, accompanied by an escort of troopers under Capt. Cardigan, rode through the moonless night—and some dangerous places—to Sauer's house in Bulawayo. They got there at 3 a.m.; while the others slept, Stent sat up writing his report for the *Cape Times*, the scoop of his journalistic life. When the telegraph office opened at nine, Stent and Sauer were on the doorstep. Even before the dispatch to the *Cape Times*, some urgent cables had to be sent to stockbrokers in London. These speculators had a unique opportunity to buy Chartereds before the rush. But Stent afterwards wrote a sad postscript to the operation: "We made little money out of our shares. We held on too long!"[31]

That business having been disposed of, an airy note from Rhodes to Grey ("the war is over as far as this part is concerned") was delivered. Grey informed Martin, who received the news ungraciously.

Martin, Carrington, Goodenough, and Chamberlain were acutely embarrassed by the indaba. Rhodes and his companions were all private citizens, yet here was Rhodes assuming the role of a high contracting party. There is no record of what Carrington said to Rhodes before the ride into the hills on 21 August, but his attempts to seize the initiative and take control had begun at least on the 13th, when he wired to Goodenough: "Have ordered temporary cessation patrols [in the Matopos], and sent a prisoner, Inyanda's mother, into hills, to explain terms of surrender to that Chief. Colenbrander and Rhodes go out to-morrow to further this." The depreciation of Rhodes and his actions could hardly have been more explicit. Further reports were in the same tone. On the 18th, the delicately managed approach of Grootboom and Makunga to some rebel spokesmen was reported by Carrington in these terms: "Have opened communications through prisoners and Cape Boys with rebels at Nyanda's." The staff diary avoided the difficulty by using the passive voice: "The mother of Inyanda . . . was yesterday sent back." All those moves must of course have been authorized by Carrington, but the initiative was clearly Rhodes's; it was Rhodes whom the rebel leaders were prepared to meet, and Rhodes who was ready to go, unarmed, to meet them.

The drama of 21 August gave the lie to Carrington's pretensions, but Grey tried to smooth things over: "I, after consultation with, and with the approval of, General Carrington, asked Mr. Rhodes, who is looked upon by the natives with the greatest respect as the big white Chief and the conqueror of their country, to try and open negotiations with them with the view of bringing the rebellion to an end." Grey was of course prejudiced in Rhodes's favour. A different bias was shown by G.A. Witt of the Colenbrander Matabeleland Development Company, who wrote to the secretary of the BSA Company asserting that the success of the indabas had been due entirely to Colenbrander, and complaining of the Company's stinginess in rewarding him. Colenbrander was indeed not only the indispensable interpreter, but the adviser who several times saved Rhodes from making a fatal mistake.[32]

The question that now agitated the imperial officers, however, all the way from Carrington's camp to London, was less the origin of the negotiation than its substance. What terms had been offered and accepted? Martin's telegram to Cape Town on the 22nd was wishful thinking: "The exact result of conference is at present unknown, but it is believed to amount to what is practically an unconditional surrender on part of rebels." There had been no such thing. Rhodes had promised to disband the Native Police, and had given other, less explicit, promises of reforms. Martin and his superiors were more concerned about the question of amnesty. Ten months later Rhodes revealed that he had guaranteed the security of the indunas who were at the meeting, on condition that they had not ordered any specific murder. None would be punished for a *general* order to murder whites. Yet on 27 August Martin received a message from Rhodes (indirectly, through Grey and Lawley) that he "had given no undertaking or promise to the Chiefs of any kind." The rebels, for their part, had promised nothing more than that "it is peace" and "the eyes are white."

Further meetings would have to follow, and it was at those that Martin intended, and was virtually ordered by Goodenough, to take control. "The Queen's word," Goodenough said, "can only be pledged by the Queen's officers." Behind Goodenough was Chamberlain, who had no objection to Rhodes's conducting the negotiations, so long as he was acting under instructions from Grey, with Martin's concurrence. Chamberlain suggested playing for time until Robinson, in his new guise as Lord Rosmead, arrived in Cape Town, where he was due in a few days. But the delay was prevented by the indunas themselves, who were gathering again. This time they asked to see Martin, who, they had heard, was the queen's special representative.[33]

Grey panicked. On the 22nd, when he had cabled to the directors that "war is over," he had added a postscript: "VERY PRIVATE AND CONFIDENTIAL. Fear Deputy Commissioner and Acting High Commissioner may insist on unwise interference by requiring capital punishment [to be] inflicted on proscribed Native Chiefs, would suggest that Secretary of State for Colonies telegraphs instructions to them [to] leave settlement in my hands . . . " On the 27th, with the second indaba coming up, Grey cabled at 3.30 p.m.: "VERY URGENT.

PRIVATE AND CONFIDENTIAL . . . It is absolutely necessary negotiations should be left . . . in Mr. C.J. Rhodes's hands. Position most critical; any interferences now by Deputy Commissioner will prove fatal to success . . . " On the 28th, at 12.05 p.m.: "Goodenough has instructed Martin to proceed to Matopos Hills and insist upon Native Chiefs surrendering for trial before a certain date, which means in minds of Natives they will all be hung . . . I must protest against this step in strongest manner."

The Colonial Office kept reassuring Grey; nevertheless Martin rode out to the camp on 28 August with a heavily armed escort of twenty or thirty mounted police. Colenbrander and Grootboom at once objected to the escort, but Martin thought it absolutely necessary for the support of his dignity: no escort, no conference. Rhodes was heard to call out in his falsetto voice, "All right, all right! Let him stop away. Let him stop away. He'll be out of it; he'll be out of it *again*." The conference proceeded without Martin.

This time the meeting-place was at a large tree beneath Usher's kop, about a mile southeast of Fort Usher. Rhodes took a larger party than on the first occasion; it included Plumer, Sir Charles Metcalfe, H.J. Taylor, J.G. McDonald, and two women—Mrs. Colenbrander and her sister. Mollie Colenbrander was justly renowned for her courage, but this adventure was surely the greatest example of it.

The rebel party was larger too, and it included what Stent called "a very sinister and mutinous element." The young warriors were present in some strength; they swarmed down to the meeting place "in a very excited and apparently far from friendly mood." The two white women were made to stay on their horses, though if it had come to shooting the horses could not have saved them. Rhodes looked round at his companions and complained that "you're all stuffed full of revolvers like partridges," and the burst of laughter at the absurd simile broke the tension. Rhodes then walked away from his own party and sat down among the indunas, "seeming," Stent wrote, "to speak for them."

This indaba was a severe test of Rhodes's tact, diplomatic flair, or whatever it was that he displayed in his folksy, superficially crude way. He found himself confronting Karl Khumalo, miraculously restored to life. Khumalo at once went over to the attack. A man saved from death only by the toughness of his skull, who moreover—by his own account—had had nothing to do with the rebellion, had been living quietly in Bulawayo, and was shot merely because he was an "educated native," had a strong case. His statements could not be tested, Rhodes merely promised him a free pardon, and Khumalo "thanked him for nothing."

In an increasingly tense atmosphere, Stent recalled,

> a young chief, who might best be described as insolent to the elders of his own tribe, and particularly so to the white men, put a pertinent question: "Where are

we to live, when it is over?" he said. "The white man claims all the land." Rhodes replied at once: "We will give you settlement. We will set apart locations for you; we will give you land." The young chief shouted angrily: "You will give us land in our own country! That's good of you!" The retort was difficult to counter, and there was silence, while the elder chiefs endeavoured to soothe the tumult which was arising. The young man spoke again: "Where will you give us land?" he said. "Well," said Mr Rhodes, "you seem very fond of the Matopos. We will give you land there." There was laughter at this, for the natives are quick to appreciate a counter-thrust in debate.

Rhodes told the young man to put down his rifle. He refused, on the ground that it was only when he carried his rifle that the white men would listen to him. The tension increased alarmingly, but Capt. the Hon. J.G. Beresford, the officer who had commanded the forlorn hope on 5 August, had chosen this time to stretch out on the grass and go to sleep. "Colenbrander kicked him sharply on the shin: 'Don't go to sleep,' he said in his quiet undertone, which always suggested calm alertness, readiness for any emergency; 'don't go to sleep; you may want to be very wide awake in a minute or two.' 'Eh-what?' said Beresford, as he sat up, 'going to be a scrap?' "

The discussion seemed to have reached a deadlock, when the young men, led this time by the sophisticated Khumalo, complained of the absence of Martin. Why was he not present? Rhodes at once exploited this opening. They wanted to see Martin, but Martin would not come without his police, and the police would have rifles. Nevertheless Rhodes would tell him that they wanted to see him. On that doubtful note the indaba ended. No one distributed tobacco this time. But Rhodes had been a little more specific in his promises and his demands. The rebels could return to their kraals and start planting; all arms must be given up; all murderers would, on proof of the crime, be punished. Nothing was said about the future of the indunas as such.[34]

Martin's comments and objections are revealing. "The negotiations," he wired to Rosmead, "appear to have been rather of a conciliatory than dictating character, and, though this policy may appear expedient to the government of the country for the time being, it can have only one effect on the native mind, namely, to exaggerate their strength and our weakness." He complained that the attitude of the chiefs was one of self-defence, not of submission, and objected to Rhodes's going into the Matopos at all: according to African custom, the lesser chief should be made to come to the greater, not the other way round. He was entirely opposed to the manner in which the negotiations were being carried on, as inconsistent with the terms of the proclamation. The chiefs should be told in unmistakable language the conditions on which they must surrender. None of the principal chiefs in the Matopos should escape trial. The hills should be cleared of natives and the troops should march through them as a sign of victory. Peace on Rhodes's lines would be unsatisfactory and not permanent.

Rosmead might well have replied with the question, "Going to be a scrap?" In very tactful language, and relying on Grey's opinion, Rosmead's answer to Martin amounted to a hint on those lines. Peace must be made quickly. Murderers must be punished. Martin and Grey between them must settle the terms, and they must be committed to writing to prevent misunderstanding.

In two dramatic indabas the ice had been broken and there had been professions of peace, but no terms had yet been accepted. In the opinion of the imperial authorities they had not even been officially offered. They had to be offered by Grey and Martin together.[35]

The possibility of a meeting of the indunas with these officers had been opened up in the concluding moments of the second indaba. Before it could take place the rebel leaders, who still suspected a trap, required many assurances. They were afraid to go into Plumer's camp, but agreed to go to the camp of Grey and Rhodes. When both camps were moved further west there was more alarm and suspicion. After getting a guaranteed safe-conduct from Martin the indunas arrived on 9 September at the appointed place, not far from the site of the second indaba, near Fort Usher. The rebels were represented by Sikhombo, Dliso, Mhluganiswa, Babayane, Sikhota, Nyanda, and about thirty others. The principal members of the white party were Grey, Martin, Rhodes, Colenbrander, Taylor (chief native commissioner), Martin's secretary Longe, the missionary Carnegie (who interpreted for Martin), and Capt. Beresford. Martin was escorted by an imposing posse of twelve lancers under a noncommissioned officer.

The proceedings were opened by Grey, who explained the high commissioner's terms: the rebels must come out of the hills and return to their lands to plant the next crop; they must surrender their arms; white men's property still in their possession must be returned; murderers, though not "those who killed white men in open fights," would be punished.

It was then Martin's turn to speak, and he struck a jarring note:

> How a man like Babyaan, who has been to England and has been allowed to see the Queen, can have been induced to take part in this rebellion, I cannot conceive, nor can the Queen. He must have known war was so hopeless, and that the Queen would not allow the rebels to go unpunished . . . Mr Rhodes told them the other day that there would be no more native police, and I now confirm that from the Queen's Government. A great deal was said about native police when they met Mr Rhodes. This is not the time for them to air their grievances. The native police raised in the country before I came were their own people . . . These very police they complain of assisted them in killing the Queen's own people, and even now they are on their side.

As the speeches were succeeded by discussion, Martin contributed to that, and always in the same hectoring tone.

It very soon appeared that the rebels' basic objection was to the surrender of arms. "Before there was no mention of arms," said Babayane; "is that the sore point now?" Grey replied gently but firmly to this, and Martin issued another *diktat*. Once again the tension was relieved by Rhodes:

> I say few words. We might talk for hours. The Queen has forgiven you. If I were you, Sikombo, I would mount my horse and ride out to my place to-morrow and start my women hoeing. I can say no more . . . What is troubling me is, that you wait so long that the Queen's man says: "Oh! they want to fight again." I was not afraid to come and see you . . . Now, come out from the hills; come and help me.

"All will come," said Sikhombo. "No man forgets his stomach." The meeting ended with a plea from the indunas for time.[36]

It could not yet be said that the terms had been accepted. Martin was thoroughly dissatisfied. He complained that "the Chiefs did not salute, and at times showed a decidedly independent air, and spoke as though they had as much right to demand the withdrawal of the troops, which they complained were in their gardens, as we had to call upon them to lay down their arms." He was taken aback by the brazen statement that they had laid down their arms in 1893, and had none now to surrender. A more credible excuse came from the statement of one young chief to Colenbrander, "that if they had to give up their arms they might just as well die like dogs at once."

Perhaps Martin's ideas of peace and victory were too European, or at least based too exclusively on the relations among centralized states. He was dissatisfied on 9 September because a clear-cut agreement, binding on and submitted to by all, had eluded him. The war could not be ended in that way. Each induna, indeed virtually every warrior, had to make his own decision to surrender. They had been doing so at least since July, and during the period of the indabas they were coming in in greater numbers, but throughout the discussions there was a refrain that "the young men are afraid to come out of the hills." They had reason to be afraid. Grey reported on 18 September that "some men with passes returning to their homes from the hills were killed by the troops at Malsenwana, and that a drunken trooper returning from Buluwayo to Plumer's camp fired on some friendlies at a kraal within five miles of Malunwana, the town." By 12 October, after three indabas and within a day of the fourth, the surrenders in Matabeleland totaled 2,354 men, 2,892 women, 4,144 children, 329 guns, 3,275 assegais and 150 rounds of ammunition. Martin was not very happy with these statistics.

From the day of the first indaba Rhodes had been insisting that the war was over, and Martin had been protesting that it was not. Rhodes's view was more or less confirmed by the weekly staff diaries forwarded to Cape Town. After the middle of August the fighting in Matabeleland had continued, apart from a few trivial skirmishes, only in the Matopos, briefly on the Gwaai, and on the eastern marches—Belingwe and Gwelo—which were not ethnically Ndebele. When it died down in the Matopos it could be said that the Ndebele had stopped fighting. But it could not be said that they had laid down their arms. Martin's argument was that there could be no secure peace until the rebels had been effectively disarmed.[37]

He had a point, but had overlooked two things. No man, as Sikhombo had said, forgets his stomach, and the rebels needed peace for that reason. If that was a temporary need, which would not prevent the war from flaring up again after the next harvest, there was a second factor which should have given Martin, as it gave Grey, confidence: the railway from Mafeking was being pushed rapidly forward. Once it reached Bulawayo, as Grey said, "the Queen will be able to throw as many troops as she likes at a moment's notice into the country."

The remark was made at the fourth and last indaba on 13 October. The enumeration of these affairs is misleading. Throughout this period Rhodes had been encamped at various places on the edge of the hills, and rebel indunas had come down to talk to him.

Day by day they would come down in twos and threes to his camp at the foot of the hills, and squatting down under the shade of the "Indaba Tree," would smoke the pipe of peace with the white men. So pleasant were these visits made for them, that after a while the hospitality of the camp was noised abroad, with the result that the place was besieged with chiefs, who came by the score from far and near to express their submission, and carry away such gifts as the great white induna might think fit to bestow upon them . . . Now and then Mr Rhodes, accompanied by one or two of the party, would ride in amongst the hills, and his fearless bearing probably had a greater moral effect on the native mind than anything else he could have done or said.

It was on one of those rides, accompanied on that occasion by Grey, that Rhodes stumbled upon the great granite dome of Malindidzimu. Having climbed to the top and surveyed the expanse of the Matopos from it, he said to Grey "I call this one of the world's views." He later referred to it as "a view of the world"; the name was popularly corrupted to "World's View"; but it was on this original visit that he decided to be buried there, and to bring the remains of Allan Wilson and the Shangani patrol to be buried there too.

Peace was achieved as much by those informal meetings as by the full-dress indabas, but a fourth and last indaba was needed to tie up the loose ends. The leading whites and the leading rebels were joined this time by the principal chiefs—Gampu, Faku, Mtshane—who had remained loyal to the government. They met on 13 October at Rhodes's latest camp, at the junction of the Maleme and Manzambomvo streams.[38]

This time not even Martin could complain that the rebel indunas were not submissive. There was even, or appears to the modern reader to have been, something unreal about their submissiveness. What was in their minds? No doubt, above all, the military facts. As professional soldiers they would have understood that they could no longer hope to break out of the Matopos. Carrington was busy closing the hills in with a ring of forts. Grey's remark about the advance of the railway—made with the engineer, Sir Charles Metcalfe, standing beside him—would have been appreciated too. Inside the ring the rebels could have fought on, but their supplies were running out and could not be sufficiently replenished. (They would not have understood that their starvation would have been partly compensated by the ruin of the Company.) Perhaps there was some significance in the conversation between Babayane and Dliso, overheard early in the negotiations by Colenbrander, when they spent the night near his wagon: "Babayana was of opinion that it was as well they did not have to negotiate with the General [Carrington]. He looked too fierce. 'Yes, Babayana,' Dhliso answered, 'he'll kill us all, I can assure you, if we give him the opportunity.' "

Perhaps for these reasons, and partly as a result of the many informal talks with Rhodes, the indunas were firmly resolved on peace. Grey began the indaba with a speech, in which he not only pointed out the hopelessness of further resistance, but appealed to them not even to have "a wish in your hearts to change the government, and therefore we are willing to listen to your grievances and to consider them, and if we find them well proved, to remove them."

The principal grievance of the indunas now was that they had no authority or power; the young men laughed at them. This would be remedied. The loyal indunas would immediately receive government appointments and monthly salaries, and their authority would be upheld. They, and the rebel leaders who had submitted, would be given horses. These leaders too, when they had shown that they could be trusted, would get appointments, salaries, and support. They still complained, though of one thing: "We have no leader, and it is impossible for a nation to live without a leader . . . We want someone to whom we can go, before we go to Mr Rhodes, to whom we can report our troubles." When they were told that the administrator was the man, they expressed great satisfaction. Though the chorus of praise and thanks was led by Faku, one of the "loyal" chiefs, he was strongly seconded by Somabhulana, and the meeting ended with an assurance by "the Chiefs"—no names mentioned—"that they would lick the ground he [Grey] was standing on."

This and the fulsome expressions of satisfaction came strangely from men who had launched and conducted a war of independence based on genocide. Only six years earlier Ellerton Fry had heard the proud boast that "they were not boys but Matabele." What were they now? They may have been playing for time, dreaming of a better day to come; they could hardly have resolved to descend to the level of "boys." Yet as military aristocrats, who had always owed their position to superior force, they could not escape the logic of that position; so for the present, at least, they accepted defeat. During Grey's speech Sikhombo crossed over to Gampu and tood snuff with him; the division in the nation was to be healed.[39]

There had been division, or at least sharp differences of opinion, among the victors also. On one side Martin and Carrington had been insisting that the war was not over, the rebels had not submitted, and a strong imperial force as well as police would be needed to hold Matabeleland through the coming rainy season. On the other, Grey and Rhodes had insisted on the need to economize, and had therefore persuaded themselves that "the eyes were white." In his correspondence with the high commissioner, and with Martin, Grey never referred to the Company's shaky finances. The argument was always "that it daily becomes more and more evident that distress among the natives is greater and more widespread than was at first supposed, and it is clear that the resources of the Government will be taxed to the utmost to keep the people from starvation." And, by the same token, that "the natives have been so severely punished by war and their physical exhaustion owing to disease, and scarcity of food is so great, that all fear of a renewed rising on a combined and dangerous scale may be dismissed."

These words are quoted from Grey's "statement of views" addressed to Martin on 12 October, the day before the last indaba. The same statement includes the terms that Grey was about to offer to the indunas. Grey went on to draw the conclusion that "unless it can be shown that such absolute necessity actually does exist, the 400 Imperial cavalry should not remain in Matabeleland, but upon the successful termination of the patrol upon which they are now engaged, should forthwith proceed to the south." The indaba having strengthened his case, Grey in the next few days sent a succession of telegrams to the Company's office in Cape Town, asking for pressure on the imperial authorities to remove their troops from Matabeleland and from Mafeking (where some were kept at the Company's expense) and to sell the horses if they could not be got out of the country: "as we have no longer any need for their services I must refuse to be held responsible for any further charges on account of their maintenance."[40]

MASHONALAND: THE SECOND PHASE

In arguing for the withdrawal of troops from Matabeleland on the ground that all danger was over, Grey had a strong case. The case for a withdrawal from Mashonaland was much weaker, but it was pressed for other reasons. There the imperial forces were engaged in wild-goose chases, wholly unproductive because the villagers fled before the advancing columns, well into November. At the end of October the rains began. On 13 November it was "very heavy wind, rain, hail and thunder storm," and it was clear that there could not be much more fighting.

Though it was absurd to pretend that the rebellion in Mashonaland was over by 23 November, when Carrington so informed Martin, Grey, and Rosmead, a conspiracy to make that claim was not surprising. The imperial officers wanted the credit for a victory, and wanted to get out before the rains; Grey wanted them out to save expense. So Grey and Rhodes endorsed Carrington's opinion. Carrington, with Baden-Powell and the rest of his staff, had moved from Bulawayo to Salisbury, where they arrived on 19 November, and they had seen no rebels on the road. It was from Salisbury that Carrington announced that the fighting was over in Mashonaland. The withdrawal of the troops was arranged without delay.

Grey's persistence had already borne fruit in Matabeleland. Plumer's men (not that they were imperial troops) had enlisted for the duration of the war; on 20 October Carrington recommended their disbandment. With them he coupled Robertson's "Cape Boys," time-expired. Rosmead having agreed, all the troops except some two hundred of the 7th Hussars left Matabeleland during November. The departure of the Mashonaland contingent followed quickly. In December the troops in Salisbury were paraded, inspected, and marched off to Umtali. Last of all Alderson himself left on 11 December, and his Mashonaland Field Force ceased to exist. By the 19th Carrington, Baden-Powell, Rhodes, Metcalfe, and other important actors in the drama were aboard ss *Pongola*, steering out to sea between the mudbanks of the Pungwe estuary.[41]

This narrative has shown that in Mashonaland, if not in the other province, the imperial forces had played an indispensable part. The most obvious example of their role is the line of communication, which was cleared by Alderson, but which the local forces had been unable to open. As the survival of the laagers and the white population beyond October depended on new food supplies, and as those could come only by the Beira-Umtali route, it is unnecessary to say more. But the services of the imperial officers and troops were not limited to the line of communication. If Alderson's and Jenner's attacks had left Makoni, Mashayamombe, and other chiefs bloody but unbowed, they had inflicted great losses in food supply, and some in men, which contributed to later successes.

It was in the interest of the Company, and in the long run of the white settlers, to depreciate this contribution. Carrington wrote confidentially to Rosmead on 4 January 1897, complaining of the misrepresentations of "interested individuals, including the officials of the Company, both in Rhodesia and in England." These, he said, "have, probably with a view to reassuring the share-market, systematically endeavoured to make the least of the dangerous aspect of the rebellion, and, possibly from fear of the Imperial Government obtaining too strong a claim upon the country, they have steadily opposed the bringing in of Imperial troops, and have belittled or ignored the work done by those troops when brought in."

Carrington thought that "the local forces, although possessed of individual courage, hardihood, and aptitude for veld life, were difficult to work with. They were very independent, would not willingly do fort duty, long patrols, or unpleasantly dangerous work. Their discipline, reconnaissance, and shooting were poor." For these reasons he thought that the quickening of the operations so as to "bring them to a successful conclusion before the setting in of the rains" had been due entirely to the arrival of the imperial forces. (Here the "misrepresentation" was Carrington's—the "successful conclusion," in Mashonaland, was still to seek). But even in Matabeleland the imperial officers, if not troops, had he thought played an indispensable part. It was the organization by them of the "commissariat, transport, ordnance, and medical departments . . . which enabled the troops to keep the field."

The letter ended with some quotations, in which the offending words were italicized by Carrington:

> Lord Grey to the Directors, October 16, 1896: "I do not think the remarkable character of the feat which the *Company has performed* in carrying on a war for six months, 587 miles away from the railhead, and keeping in a state of efficiency a fighting force of 3,000 men and 3,000 animals, and storing in addition supplies to feed 40,000 natives for three months, has been properly appreciated by the British public." Notice to shareholders from the Secretary, Herbert Canning, on October 17, 1896: " . . . the heavy and largely increased expenditure incurred in connexion with the rebellion in Rhodesia, but which, the Directors are glad to say, is now *practically over, thanks to the bravery and energy displayed by the settlers in Rhodesia*, and to the splendid services, voluntarily rendered, at great personal risk, by Mr. Rhodes."

Circumstances, as will be seen, conspired to confirm the Company, and above all the white Rhodesians, in these opinions.[42]

Of course there was no intention, when withdrawing the imperial forces, to denude Rhodesia of defenders, in the Jameson manner. The first line of defence was to be a new police force, whose recruitment, strength, and conditions of service had concerned both the imperial authorities and the Company from the moment that Kruger's commandos had disposed of the old force. The discussion of these questions, interrupted at the outbreak of the rebellion, was resumed as the fighting died down. The proposal to withdraw troops always included as a corollary the recruitment of police.

Though some of the old force—from the handful that had not gone with Jameson, and from Jameson's men who had returned and joined the various relief columns—enlisted in the new, and though the new force for a short time retained the pre-rebellion name of Rhodesia Mounted Police, it was in every respect a new organization. It was under the command of Sir Richard Martin, in his capacity as commandant-general (which was, when the appointment was made, his primary role). The commandant-general was to be "exclusively responsible to His Excellency the High Commissioner," and the officers "exclusively responsible to the Commandant-General"; the Company paid for the force but had no power over it. To make assurance doubly sure it was proposed at first that no member of the force should have any pecuniary or property interest in the Company, in its territory, or anywhere in South Africa.

This rule was in the end relaxed: it applied only to officers, and only to the Company's sphere—Rhodesia and Bechuanaland. Chamberlain objected to the force's old name, either because "the name 'Rhodesia' has never been formally recognised by the Imperial Government" or because in the original plan the police were to function in Bechuanaland too. He "would be inclined to adopt some such name as 'The British South Africa Police'." Rosmead reminded Chamberlain that he had already given another name to the unit in the protectorate, so that the new one would be used in Rhodesia only. In this way the title that was to last many years, even after Rhodesia had severed all relations with Britain, was adopted. It appears to have been used officially for the first time in Rhodesia on 12 December 1896.

In Matabeleland the recruitment and organization of the new police were synchronized with the disbandment of the military forces, so that as many experienced soldiers as possible could be enlisted. Thus a first step was taken when the Bulawayo Field Force was disbanded on 4 July. Captain Nicholson was able to recruit 180 of the 400-odd disbanded for a three-month period "on the old lines of the Matabeleland Mounted Police." By October, when all but two hundred troops, which formed a garrison for Bulawayo, were withdrawn from Matabeleland, the police strength authorized for that province was 600.

A similar establishment—580 white and 100 native police—was provided for Mashonaland. The latter were "Zulus, Shangaans and Zambesi boys" who were already in the Company's service. (In Matabeleland there could, in virtue of Rhodes's promise at the first indaba, be no native police.) When Capt. the Hon. F. de Moleyns took command of the new force in Mashonaland in December, it consisted of 200 white BSA Police—all raw recruits just arrived from England—50 Mounted Infantry from Alderson's column, permitted by the War Office to transfer to the police, 120 "Native Contingent," and 400 Volunteers. These last were colonials who on the dissolution of the various local forces had signed on for short terms of full-time service; they were used with rare exceptions only as town garrisons. De Moleyns had no more than 370 men, black and white, for offensive operations.[43]

They were not intended for offensive operations. They were intended to keep order in a country already pacified. Carrington had proclaimed the rebellion at an end. The *Rhodesia Herald*, in the early weeks of 1897, filled its few pages with peace-time trivialities; police patrols were reported but not emphasized.

The authorities, however, were not deceived. In a coded telegram at the beginning of the year Grey told Rhodes that unless something were done to impress the Shona (who naturally "attribute our inaction to impotence") with the Company's power, there would be a renewal of trouble, and probably on a larger scale than before, after the rains. Friendly chiefs, including the new "loyal" Makoni, had warned that the rebels were only waiting to gather their crops before fighting again. The spirit of resistance was typified by the petty

512 Rhodes and Rhodesia

chief Nyamwenda, who had been responsible for the Norton murders at the beginning of the rebellion. His stronghold on the Hunyani was visited by a patrol in the middle of December. To the question whether he intended to live at peace with the white men, he replied that if they would pay hut tax to him he would allow them to live in Salisbury. On 15 January Paramount Chief Svosve (Marandellas district) spoke even more confidently: "I have nothing to talk to the white man about . . . What do you want to return for? Are you leaving anything behind you? Go away and remain away. I wish to have nothing to do with you white men. Go and live in Chimoio and I will send boys to work for you there if you want them."

Because of Svosve's influence the native commissioner, Marandellas, reported that there were no "friendlies" in his district. To his north there was another rebel paramount, Mangwende, who had been joined by two of the former Makoni's sons; together they had a force of 700. Between that area and Salisbury there were some powerful rebels—Kunzwi, Chikwakwa, Mashanganyika; nearer still to the capital, and south of it, Seki; an important rebel area to the north in Mazoe; and the toughest centre of all on the Umfuli, where Mashayamombe boasted of three victories and, near by, Kaguvi had taken up headquarters in the cave associated with his spirit.

These were strong forces, but they occupied a limited area. Other areas had been effectively subdued in 1896. It is not easy, however, to explain this localization of the rebellion in 1897. Ranger finds the main cause, as contemporaries did, in the influence of the spirit mediums Kaguvi and Nehanda. Nehanda's power was confined to the Mazoe district, and Beach has shown that Kaguvi's was really effective only in the two areas he had lived in, Hartley (north of Mashayamombe's) and Chishawasha. Though he had been closely associated with Mashayamombe, he quarrelled with him in the end, but the paramount fought on as hard as before. As for Svosve, Grey pointed out that he had never been "visited by our force." Perhaps this fact, Mashayamombe's successful resistance in the past, and the influence of the mediums may together account for most of the continued resistance in 1897.[44]

De Moleyns did not wait for good weather to begin operations, but to say that he had 370 men for the purpose would be misleading. The 120 men of the Native Contingent were "undisciplined and unreliable," and the 200 English recruits were not only untrained but often sick. The fever they had contracted on the way up from Beira resulted in a sick list of between 25 and 50 per cent, and on some patrols in low-lying country even 60 or 70 percent, until May.

In these circumstances the rebels might well "laugh at the idea of paying hut tax or giving up any of their guns." De Moleyns at first could do no more than harry a few kraals without daring to risk his force too far. An attempt to surprise Kaguvi on 11 January failed, so no attack was made. Kaguvi slipped away to the east, was pursued, and though many women and children of his party were captured, the *mhondoro* himself escaped. Kraals belonging to Seki,

513 The Rebellion II

Svosve, and Makombe were destroyed. A fort facing Chikwakwa's stronghold was built and manned, and on 16 February the stronghold was occupied. An attack on Mashanganyika's failed, but in the Mazoe district four kraals and from sixty to seventy wagonloads of grain were captured.

These blows, whatever they may have done to sap the strength of the rebels, did not weaken their will or cause any surrenders. In this deadlock, as at earlier stages of the fighting, both sides needed reinforcement. It has been suggested that the "revival" of the Rozvi imperial title in December, when Mudzinganyama Jiri Mteveri assumed the Mamboship at the invitation of "an impressive delegation," was a move to give the Shona rebellion a focus and direction. This may have been the intention of some of the movers in the matter, but it is more likely that the event was essentially independent of the rebellion. The succession to the Mamboship had in fact continued unbroken since the disasters early in the century; some of the men who installed the new Mambo were rebels, but others were not; and the installation took place in the Ndanga-Bikita area, which was not in rebellion and was separated from the rebels by a belt of neutrals and collaborators.

The whites could not expect any great accessions to their own strength till the dry season, but in the meantime they looked for more allies. They judged rightly in looking to Chief Gurupira of Mtoko in the Budjga country. In 1889 this house had been exceptional in refusing to deal with the Portuguese. Selous on the other hand had made a treaty with it. These people nursed a grudge against their Shona neighbours for acting against them as forceful tax-collectors, and an even older grudge for a defeat inflicted on them by Mangwende and Nyandoro in a dispute over Gouveia and his guns in 1889. The local native commissioner, W.L. Armstrong, had married into the tribe. Accordingly a small force of twenty white and twenty black BSA Police under Colin Harding, accompanied by Armstrong and by Grey's private secretary Hubert Howard, left Salisbury for Mtoko on 4 March. They were fired on the whole way, but reached Gurupira's safely. The chief raised a force of 500 of his subjects and the combined party moved off towards Salisbury. They were attacked at a pass in Kunzwi's country. Three hundred of the new allies then deserted, but the other two hundred with their chief stood by the police patrol. Fifty miles from Salisbury the party halted, Howard went on to ask for help, and was too ill to return with the reinforcements, but these arrived in time to save the patrol. Attacks were made on various kraals and finally on the granite peak Shangwe where a large number of rebels had congregated. The hill was invested, shortage of water drove the defenders to risk death by descending the precipitous east side, where many fell, and the hill was captured.

During this operation Gurupira was killed. He and those of his men who had not deserted "did most excellent work during the siege, which [de Moleyns] could not have attempted without their help." Armstrong with a small police escort led the Mtoko men back to their own country. On the way, according to his message, they "turned on him," because they blamed him for the death of their chief. He managed to reach Umtali alive.

Before that event the rebels suffered their first important setback. On 11 April a patrol of volunteers (Umtali Rifles) and 200 Shangaans under Major Browne attacked Svosve's stronghold without success. But another fifty mounted infantry, recruited for the police from their regiments in the Cape Colony, having joined Browne, the stronghold was captured on 25 April, and Svosve himself taken prisoner.[45]

As the rains abated, and communications improved, reinforcements began to arrive. The fifty mounted infantry were followed in May by 180 police recruits from England and the Cape; about a fifth of these had seen service before. Forty Zulus arrived to join the Native Contingent. With this help it was possible to attack Mashanganyika, who with his people retired into caves. In a week's operations all the caves were destroyed with great loss to the occupants, and the force under Major Gosling moved to Kunzwi's stronghold on 19 June. That and a neighbouring fortified koppie, but not the chief, were captured after two days' hard fighting. Major Gosling thought, "from the amount of grain stored away, and the quantity of pigs, goats, etc., in the stronghold . . . that Kunzi was confident of repulsing the whites, and had made ample preparations for a long stay; this opinion was confirmed by the determined resistance offered, the engagement being the most severe the police have as yet taken part in."

At this point—on 25 June—the resources of Matabeleland began to move to the assistance of the other province. Those resources included the only imperial force remaining in Rhodesia, two squadrons of the 7th Hussars. Now these, with fifty BSA Police, forty "Cape Boys," a 12½-pounder gun and a Maxim left Bulawayo in two columns. For some time the War Office had been agitating to withdraw the Hussars (they were inactive and had become virtually a dismounted unit, which was a waste of trained cavalrymen), but had agreed to let them remain and to take part in the attack on Mashayamombe. Their departure caused protests in Bulawayo.

This time no chances were to be taken in suppressing the greatest secular leader of the rebellion. The fort which Alderson had been unable to build or man in October had now been built and manned close to the paramount's kraal and named Fort Martin. This was the work of Inspector Nesbitt, VC, the hero of the Mazoe patrol. Nesbitt commanded a garrison of thirty white and thirty black police, with one 7-pounder. De Moleyns marched to the spot with 180 white and 140 black police, three 7-pounders and two Maxims. A junction was made with the two columns from Bulawayo, and Sir Richard Martin at last assumed the command of a field operation. The attack was launched on 24 July. The kraal was captured in the first rush and the inhabitants retreated into their caves. The usual tactic was adopted: 130 men with a Maxim maintained a cordon, night and day, to prevent escape. The paramount's reply to a summons to surrender was to tell the white men to go to hell. Escapes were attempted, and in the early hours of 25 July Mashayamombe himself, trying to move from one cave to another, was shot. The next day the caves were destroyed. The rebel losses had been heavy, and 100 men and 320 women and children were captured by the attackers. Among the killed was Bonda, who had played an important part at the beginning of the rising.

Kaguvi, as we saw, had left this dangerous neighbourhood after de Moleyns's abortive attack in January; he had gone to his old haunts near Chikwakwa's kraal. Mkwati, who had taken refuge with Mashayamombe after his defeat, had likewise departed early in January. After joining Gwayabana, the last Ndebele leader to continue resistance in the Gwelo district, he moved to Mazoe. The rebellion was now confined to that district. Whatever may have been the motivations of the great paramounts who were now dead or in captivity, the significant fact about the continued hostility after July is that Kaguvi, Nehanda, and Mkwati were concentrated in Mazoe. White officials and colonists and black allies were agreed in their conviction that the death or capture of the "witch-doctors," and nothing else, would end the war.[46]

No time was lost, after the attack on Mashayamombe, in pursuing the "witch-doctors." After an all-night march a strong column entered Kaguvi's kraal at daybreak on 15 August, only to find it recently deserted. The column went on through the district, meeting with no resistance, seeing few people, and finding even the strongly fortified granite koppies abandoned. On 20 October de Moleyns wrote his report of the year's operations, and ended with the comment that "prospectors are now . . . out in many parts of the country, and though a certain amount of mutual distrust still exists I do not think any further trouble is to be feared." He was right, but the drama was not quite over. Mkwati, who also had narrowly escaped on 15 August, made his way northwards into the Korekore country. A month or two later the people there, having heard that he was "causing trouble," killed him. To guard against the resurrection of so powerful a wizard "they cut him up in pieces while he was still alive with choppers." Kaguvi was attacked again early in October, and again escaped, though most of the women of his party were captured. He took sanctuary further north in Sipolilo's country, but even he no longer had any illusions about the situation. He surrendered to Native Commissioner Kenny on 27 October. "Kukubi, the Mischievous," said the editor of the *Rhodesia Herald* in his next issue, "is now safe in gaol, an incident which may be said to finally close the era of the Mashona rebellion."

Though Nehanda was not captured until December, the rebellion was indeed over. For two generations the BSA Police would boast that they had never since 1897 had to fire a shot in anger. Peace and security prevailed everywhere. But beneath the calm surface there was something that was not peace. White women and children had been hacked to pieces, black women and children had been blown up in caves with dynamite. The hangman and the firing squad had disposed of religious leaders and great chiefs. The Shona people had fought (brutal though it was) a brave fight to recover their country from the invaders. The effort exhausted them for a long time. The victors faced the task of reconstructing and uniting a land divided by a river of blood.[47]

NOTES CHAPTER 12

1 D.N. Beach, "The Politics of Collaboration, South Mashonaland 1896-7" (Henderson Seminar Paper no.9); T.O. Ranger, *Revolt in Southern Rhodesia, 1896-7*, pp. 196-7, 199.

2 Julian Cobbing, "The Absent Priesthood: Another Look at the Rhodesian Risings of 1896-7," *Journal of African History*, XVIII, 1, pp.76-9; Ranger, *Revolt in Southern Rhodesia*, pp.200-2.

3 D.N. Beach, "The Rising in South-Western Mashonaland, 1896-7," pp.306, 320-4, 331, 345, 388-9. There was also a class of exceptions among the great chiefdoms of north central Mashonaland. These had been hostile to the Ndebele, but took the lead in the rebellion; they were the great sufferers from the white occupation.

4 Ibid., pp.299-300, 380-2; Beach, "Politics of Collaboration," passim. J.K. Rennie, in "Christianity, Colonialism and the Origins of Nationalism among the Ndau of Southern Rhodesia, 1890-1935," p.538, suggests four reasons why the Ndau stayed out of the rebellion: isolation (religious and political as well as geographical), fear of Ngungunyane (who had only just been defeated by the Portuguese), the absence of rinderpest, and the refusal of the white authorities in Melsetter to heed the warning they were getting from the west. Because they took no precautions, the Ndau were not provoked. No doubt the first two of these reasons were the important ones.

5 Beach, "Rising in South-Western Mashonaland," pp.380-2; *Rhodesia Herald*, 1 July 1896 (for Mutasa's tax); J.C. Barnes, "The 1896 Rebellion in Manicaland," *Rhodesiana*, 34, pp.1-8.

6 D.N. Beach, "Kaguvi and Fort Mhondoro," *Rhodesiana*, 27, pp. 35-7; Ranger, *Revolt in Southern Rhodesia*, pp. 202, 218. The personal name of this Mashayamombe was Chinengundu.

7 Beach, "Kaguvi and Fort Mhondoro," pp.31-4, 37-8; "Rising in South-Western Mashonaland," pp.346, 359, 364-7; Ranger, *Revolt in Southern Rhodesia*, pp.203, 216, 220.

8 Ranger, *Revolt in Southern Rhodesia*, pp.209-10, 212, 219 n.1; Beach, "Kaguvi and Fort Mhondoro," p.33.

9 *Rhodesia Herald*, 17 June 1896; *Bulawayo Chronicle*, 20 June 1896; Chamberlain Papers, JC 10/6/1/4.

10. *Rhodesia Herald*, 24 June 1896. See also 29 July 1896 for more about Lamb's party: at Bromley "we were shown a boy, severely wounded, who had managed to crawl to the homestead to warn Mr. Graham . . . This boy had had a hand-to-hand conflict with the rebels in his flight from Rand's farm."

11. A.S. Hickman, "Norton District in the Mashona Rebellion," *Rhodesiana*, 3, pp.14-28; H. Marshall Hole, *Old Rhodesian Days*, pp.107-9; *Rhodesia Herald*, 11 August 1897 (note the date).

12. *Rhodesia Herald*, 24 June and 8 July 1896; W.H. Brown, *On the South African Frontier*, pp.354-5; Hugh Pollett, "The Mazoe Patrol," *Rhodesiana*, 2, pp.29-38; R.C. Howland, "The Mazoe Patrol," *Rhodesiana*, 8, pp.17-19, 29; E.E. Burke, "Mazoe and the Mashona Rebellion," *Rhodesiana*, 25, p.4; Hole, *Old Rhodesian Days*, p.115; L.H. Gann, *A History of Southern Rhodesia*, p.136; Ranger, *Revolt in Southern Rhodesia*, p.209. Marshall Hole wrote the official account: the Company's Report on the Native Disturbances (CO 468/1), p.64; as this was written before most of the evidence was collected it is unreliable (see Beach, "Kaguvi and Fort Mhondoro", p.37 n.41). My identification of this "Mr Pascoe" with the Salvation Army man (see ch.9) is speculative, but probable.

13 Jean Farrant, *Mashonaland Martyr: Bernard Mizeki and the Pioneer Church*, pp.207-17; and cf. above, ch.10.

14 W. Edwards, "Memories of the '96 Rebellion," in *Native Affairs Department Annual (NADA)*, 1923, pp.20-7.

15 Ibid., p.23, CO 468/1 (Report on the Native Disturbances), p.65; G.G. Findlay and W.W. Holdsworth, *The History of the Wesleyan Methodist Missionary Society*, vol. IV, p.386 (Molele, when his wife tried to dissuade him from the suicidal mission, said, "I am a Christian teacher, and I must do what is right at all costs"); Beach, "Rising in South-Western Mashonaland," p.376; *Bulawayo Chronicle*, 2 September 1896; Ranger, *Revolt in Southern Rhodesia*, p.202; RH Mss Afr. s 4 (Vavasseur), ff. 153-4.

16 CO 468/1, Report on the Native Disturbances, p.61; *Rhodesia Herald*, 29 July 1896.

17 G.H. Tanser, *A Scantling of Time*, pp.158-9; *Rhodesia Herald*, 1 July and 29 July 1896; CO 468/1, Report on the Native Disturbances, p.101; J.A. Edwards, "The Lomagundi District, a Historical Sketch," *Rhodesiana*, 7, pp.11-14.

18 CO 468/1, Report on the Native Disturbances, p.57; *Rhodesia Herald*, 8 July 1896; Hole, *Old Rhodesian Days*, pp.106, 110; Tanser, *Scantling of Time*, p.158.

19 CO 468/1, Report on the Native Disturbances, pp.55, 58, 69; *Rhodesia Herald*, 29 July 1896; CO 879/47/520, no.261, encl., p.330; and see above, ch.11.

20 Hickman, "Norton District," pp.23-4; CO 468/1, Report on the Native Disturbances, pp.71, 103; Beach, "Kaguvi and Fort Mhondoro," pp.39-40; *Rhodesia Herald*, 5 August 1896.

21 CO 468/1, Report on the Native Disturbances, pp.72, 112-15; CO 879/47/520, no.244, encl.17, pp.306-7, no.298, encl., p.429; E.A.H. Alderson, *With the Mounted Infantry and the Mashonaland Field Force, 1896*, pp. 35-6.

22 R. Summers, "The Military Doctrine of the Matabele," *NADA*, 1955, pp.7-15.

23 Brown, *South African Frontier*, pp.366-7; *Rhodesia Herald*, 8 July 1896.

24 CO 468/1, Report on the Native Disturbances, pp.71-3, 112; CO 879/47/520, no.395, pp.614-15, no.427, p.715; Alderson, *Mashonaland Field Force*, ch. V, IX, and specifically pp.65, 100-2, 106; *Rhodesia Herald*, 23 September 1896. From these sources the following points may be added: one of the reasons for the disbandment of the "burghers" was that they were discontented and not likely to serve much longer; the Salisbury-Bulawayo telegraph line was repaired on 5 August, though there were frequent temporary breaks after that date; the personal name of the Makoni was Mutota Cirimaunga. Mutekedza had at first supported the government, and then went over to the rebellion; his people were divided and his object at each stage was prob-

ably to support the winning side. (Beach, "Rising in South-Western Mashonaland," pp.378-9.)

25 CO 879/47/520, no.361, encl.1, p.553, no.402, encl.4, pp.640-1; Alderson, *Mashonaland Field Force*, p.209; Beach, "Kaguvi and Fort Mhondro," pp.40-1. For the whole history of the Mashonaland operations see CO 879/47/520, no.443, encl., pp.757-90, which is Carrington's report on the history of the rebellion (his summary is on pp. 758-65); Appendix III, pp.765-70, Alderson's report on operations in Mashonaland. For the Hartley operation, Alderson, *Mashonaland Field Force*, ch. XII.

26 Alderson, *Mashonaland Field Force*, pp.163, 179-80.

27 CO 879/47/520, no.427, pp.712-22; Alderson, *Mashonaland Field Force*, pp.131-4; Colin Harding, *Frontier Patrols*, p.95. Lord Rosmead was Sir Hercules Robinson, returned from leave with a peerage.

28 CO 879/45/512, p.4.

29 CO 879/47/520, no.144, pp.188-9, no.316, encls., pp.451-4, no.427, encl. E 1, p.719. D.P. Abraham (see his article, "The Principality of Maungwe: Its History and Traditions," *NADA*, 1951, p.76) was told by Mariyeni that three Africans, of whom he was one, went forward to Makoni in the cave and said that his life would be spared if he surrendered, which he then did; but this evidence was not produced at the court martial.

30 D. Tyrie Laing, *The Matabele Rebellion, 1896: With the Belingwe Field Force*, pp.248-9, 268; CO 879/47/520, no.303, encl.2, p.437 (in this Carrington reported a patrol which went to Nyamandhlovu and brought back 72,000 lb. of grain, all that could be carried, and destroyed the rest). J.G. McDonald in *Rhodes: A Life*, gives an account of the origin and course of the indabas which differs widely from the other accounts. Though McDonald was on the spot, he seems to have relied on a treacherous memory when writing his book thirty years later—e.g., he says that the party going to the first indaba set off early in the morning. At some points, however, he agrees with at least one of the other sources. He says that Grootboom went into the hills with *two* African companions (p.249). Cf. CO 879/47/520, no.343, encl. 1, p.507, according to which Grootboom went with "two friendlies, two prisoners and two Cape Boys," and met about a thousand rebels, among whom were Sikhombo and Nyanda. For Vere Stent's idea of the origin of Rhodes's peace plan, see *A Personal Record of Some Incidents in the Life of Cecil Rhodes*, pp.20-1.

31 The chief authorities for the indaba are Stent, *Personal Record* (based on his press report at the time) and Hans Sauer, *Ex Africa*. For the reason given in the last note I have, in general, rejected J.G. McDonald's version. For the above account see Stent, pp.31-3, 39, 41-2, 47, 49, 51-5, and Sauer, pp.305-25; CO 879/47/520, no.278, pp.373. The differences between Stent's and Sauer's accounts are minor. For points mentioned in Somabhulana's speech, see above, ch.10. "Nkosi yenyamazana" = "King of the animals," i.e., mighty hunter.

32 CO 879/47/520, no.303, encl.17, p.441, no.317, encl.7, p.464, no.326, encl.2, p.486, no.327, encl.1, p.491; Rhodes Papers, Charters, Home Board, no.2, Canning to Rhodes, 15 May 1897.

33 CO879/47/520, no.278a, p.373, nos.288, 289a, pp.404-5, no.317, encl.17, p.466, no.327, encl.7, p.493; Ranger, *Revolt in Southern Rhodesia*, p.246.

34 CO 879/47/520, no.297, pp.427-9, no.344, encl.3, p.520, encl.5, p.521; CO 537/130,

no.18269, pp.460-1, no.18169, pp.463-5; Stent, *Personal Record*, pp.56-60; Eric A. Nobbs, *Guide to the Matopos*, p.51.

35 CO 879/47/520, no.344 and encls., pp.518-26, and specifically encl.4, pp.520-1.

36 CO 879/47/520, no.372, encl.2, pp.574-7.

37 Ibid., p.575; CO 879/47/520, no.362, encl.3, p.558, no.402, encl.2, p.640. "Malsenwana" and "Malunwana" are obviously the same place, one of the spellings being a misprint for the other. I am not able to identify it. Staff Diaries are in 520, beginning at pp.456, 475, 483, 505, 536, 551, 570, 601, 618, 636, 650, 667.

38 Frank W. Sykes, *With Plumer in Matabeleland*, pp.233-4; Nobbs, *Guide to the Matopos*, p.53; McDonald, *Rhodes*, p.279.

39 Sykes, *Plumer in Matabeleland*, pp.235-6; CO 879/47/520, no.419, encl.1, Appendix B, pp.692-3.

40 CO 879/47/520, no.396, encl.27, p.632, no.402, encl.16, p.644. Though Grey and Martin were both in Bulawayo, they sometimes expressed their views to each other on paper, for the record.

41 CO 879/47/520, no.393, p.612, no.396, encl.27, pp.631-2, no.400, pp.634-5, no.401, p.635, no.402, encl.1, p.636, encl.16, p.644, no.404, p.645, no.407, encl.5, p.658, encl.11, p.659, encl.15, p.660, no.411, encl.10, p.678, no.435, pp.734-5, no.437, encl.3, p.753; Alderson, *Mashonaland Field Force*, pp.245, 252-5; R. Baden-Powell, *The Matabele Campaign*, pp.492-3; Herbert Plumer, *An Irregular Corps in Matabeleland*, pp.201-2.

42 CO 879/47/520, no.445, pp.792-3.

43 CO 879/47/517 no.33 p.31 (and the whole volume passim) no.233 encl. p.215, no.253, p.240, no.307, encl., p.288, no.323, p.315, no.340, p.340, no.343 and encls., pp.342-9; 520, no.390, p.611, no.417, p.683, no.435, pp.734, 736, 737, no.443, p.759; A.S. Hickman, *Men Who Made Rhodesia*, p.72.

44 Rhodes Papers, Administrators, no.1; Ranger, *Revolt in Southern Rhodesia*, pp.287-8; CO 879/53/559, no.1, encl.2, pp.4-10 (report by de Moleyns of operations from December 1896 to October 20, 1897); CO 468/1, Report on the Native Disturbances, pp.76-9 (summary of operations by Percy Inskipp).

45 CO 879/47/517, no.439, p.478; CO 879/53/559, no.1, encl.2, pp.5, 7, 10; CO 468/1, Report on the Native Disturbances, p.76; Beach, "Rising in South-Western Mashonaland," pp.122, 350-1, 389-91, 403-8; W. Edwards, "The Wanoe," *NADA*, 1926, pp.16-17. De Moleyns was bitterly criticized by Hubert Howard for his extreme caution. (Ranger, *Revolt in Southern Rhodesia*, p.293.) Among the items of loot recovered at Seki's was the communion plate from the cathedral in Salisbury. A postscript to Armstrong's Mtoko adventure: Colin Harding on 21 September found the people there "very well disposed and anxious to help in every way" (559, no.1, encl.2, p.10).

46 CO 879/53/559, no.1, encl.2, pp.8, 9; CO 417/231, no.9315, pp.178-9, no.10308 pp.192-4; Beach, "Rising in South-Western Mashonaland," pp.343, 413; Ranger, *Revolt in Southern Rhodesia*, pp.300-2; *Rhodesia Herald*, 26 May, 30 June, 28 July, and 4 August 1897.

47 CO 879/53/559, no.1, encl.2, p.10; Ranger, *Revolt in Southern Rhodesia*, pp.306-10; *Rhodesia Herald*, 3 November 1897.

CHAPTER 13

The Fate
of the Vanquished

Peace had returned to Matabeleland a year before the rebellion in Mashonaland ended in a whimper. It was important, too, for the sequel, that the fighting in the two provinces had terminated in quite different fashions. In Mashonaland the rebellion was suppressed piecemeal, by dynamiting cave after cave, killing or capturing chief after chief. There were no negotiations with the Shona as a group, no indabas, no terms of peace. But the rebellion of the Ndebele had been ended by indabas and agreements.

One misunderstanding about those agreements, namely whether the official amnesty proclamation had been modified by Rhodes's promises in the Matopos, was cleared up during June and July 1897 by correspondence between Grey, Martin, Rhodes, Herbert Taylor, and the new high commissioner, Sir Alfred Milner. They agreed in the end that persons who had instigated specific murders, as well as the actual perpetrators, were excluded from the amnesty; those whose complicity was "vague and indirect" were not to be prosecuted. Arrests having been made, a series of trials before Judge Vintcent and assessors began in Bulawayo. By December Milner could report twenty-five prosecutions for murder in Matabeleland, all but one of the crimes having been committed in the latter part of March 1896. One of the accused had been acquitted. In another case the conviction was quashed because the "murdered" man had turned up "safe and well." After a careful study of the cases by his legal adviser Malcolm Searle, who found the trials to have been fair and the evidence incontrovertible, Milner confirmed the death sentences of the others.[1]

The trials in Mashonaland began in February 1898. By July Milner had reported fifty death sentences submitted to him from Salisbury. Of these he confirmed thirty, quashed one, and commuted nineteen to prison sentences of from five to twenty years. The reason for the commutations was either the youth of the accused or the comparative insignificance of his role in the crime. Milner then expressed the hope that the series of trials might now end and the book of the rebellion be closed. This was accordingly to be done after the next sessions—which resulted in twelve death sentences, three of which Milner confirmed—except for cases of "ringleaders or of notorious criminals, guilty of acts of peculiar atrocity." Among the condemned, both executed on 27 April 1898, were the Kaguvi medium, Gomporeshumba, and Nehanda. Nehanda was dragged screaming and kicking to the scaffold. Kaguvi, after resisting for a long time, yielded to the entreaties of Father Richartz on the day of execution, and was received into the Roman Catholic Church. He was baptized with the name of the good thief, Dismas, and died quietly and with dignity.[2]

Between them the machine-gun, dynamite, and the noose had crushed the revolt and the spirit of the rebels. The Shona were stunned and demoralized. Many, though not all, were also disillusioned and ready to abandon the spiritual and secular leadership that had brought them to disaster. In August 1898 the *Rhodesia Herald* thought that though the Shona did not love the white man they were generally submissive; the Korekore, however, a good deal less so than the others. The Korekore, who had not been involved in the rebellion, were reported to be proposing another attempt to drive out the whites. Their southern neighbours were said to have sarcastically wished them luck.

Taberer, the chief native commissioner, found no exceptions: "his thorough investigation into the state of the districts leaves no room to doubt the perfectly pacific attitude of the Mashonas. Neither did Mr. Taberer find any materially different attitude on the part of the tribes beyond Mount Darwin"—the Korekore. Taberer was exaggerating slightly; not quite all the Shona were "pacific." Muchemwa, for instance, the man behind the murder of Bernard Mizeki, led an attack on Matunike's village in November 1898, in which two women were killed. But Muchemwa then became a fugitive in Mozambique, where he remained for some years. He surrendered to the Rhodesian authorities in 1903 and was placed under close surveillance.[3] It would be not far from the truth to say that the Shona suffered more from the war, and the Ndebele, as will be seen, more from the peace. By March 1898 peace had long been restored to Matabeleland. Patrols through the Matopos at that time reported the people to be "very friendly and satisfied" and that "the general demeanour of the natives was decidedly peaceful and respectful." It is hard to believe that the spirit of '96 had been exorcised as completely as that. But the Ndebele had learned the lesson that, whatever might be the best way to restore the dignity, freedom, and independence of the nation, the way tried in 1896 was certainly the wrong one.

In February 1898 W.E. Thomas, acting chief native commissioner, with his wife and small son, visited his old district, Bulalima. Gampu and his people gave them a great welcome. These people had of course been "loyal" in the rebellion, but there was also a sprinkling of ex-rebels in the crowd. Rumours of a new rising had come from Bulawayo, probably from servants who overheard the talk of their employers. So Gampu,

> turning to the natives, said, "—If we hear of any man who talks of rebellion in this district, we will wring his neck for him." Mbambeleli, who was one of the royal indunas, and a rebel in the late outbreak, stood out in front of the rest, and in a

very impressive manner swore allegiance to the Government. This action was quite voluntary on Mbambeleli's part. He said he had been fooled once, but would not be again. He was an old man . . . [but, calling a man out of the crowd, said] "here is my eldest son; if anything happened he would fight to the death for the Government." Others, addressing the Commissioner, said they felt it a little bit hard that more had been made of the rebels than of themselves. This, added to the taunts of the rebel faction, who called them "white men's dogs," appeared to rankle in their minds.

During the proceedings young Master Thomas walked over and sat among the indunas. At one point he made Gampu laugh in the middle of a serious oration by tickling his feet.[4]

Good humour, however, did nothing to solve the problems which had provoked the rising and which remained when it was over. In Matabeleland the central problem was land, since the whites had taken it all. In Mashonaland this was not a pressing issue in 1898, any more than it had been in 1895. As late as 1904 the Methodist missionary John White went on a circuit from Epworth (on the outskirts of Salisbury) and in the course of a ride of 250 miles encountered only "two *bona fide* farmers."

In Matabeleland everything turned on the question of land. In 1904 Gampu and Sikhombo gave evidence to the Lagden Commission. Gampu and his people were on a reserve; Sikhombo and his were on private land and seemed to have no alternative: "it appears that all the land is occupied by farmers; there is nobody but farmers."[5]

This question had been weighing on the minds of the Ndebele in 1896, when they were fighting, and it was still disturbing them when they met Rhodes in the Matopos. Where were they to live, now that the white men had taken all the land? Martin, in his report, pointed out the inadequacy of the Gwaai and Shangani reserves. Grey acknowledged that more land for reserves would have to be found. Nobody, however, thought of reserves as the ideal or the ultimate solution of the problem. Grey, the colonists, and the imperial officers all agreed that the best place for the Ndebele was on the farms of the white men, for whom they would then provide a supply of labour. As those farms were the former lands of the Ndebele, they too preferred to live on them, though they could have dispensed with the new owners.

The intention therefore was to extend to Rhodesia the system of "private locations," as they were called in the Cape Colony. This was done by the proclamation of 14 October 1896. The following year Milner expressed the hope "that the number of natives who may be provided with land under that Proclamation will be large and constantly increasing, for it seems to me that this method of settlement is more promising for the development of the country and the maintenance of peace, as well as for the progress and well-being of the natives themselves, than the reserve system."

In another context Milner made a useful analysis of the distribution of the African population:

Sikhombo

524 Rhodes and Rhodesia

Natives may at present be found residing (1) within the boundaries of a municipality or township (2) on lands granted to settlers, either (a) with the consent of the owners, under the provisions of the Proclamation of October 14, 1896, or (b) with the consent of the owners, but without the adoption of the arrangement provided for by the said Proclamation; or (c) without the consent of the owners, the latter not having occupied or exercising any actual control over lands; (3) on lands to which the Company has not yet granted title, but which are not native reserves or intended to be made into native reserves; (4) on lands set apart or intended to be set apart as native reserves.

The appearance of the fourth category at the end and almost in the guise of a residue reflected the wish of the authorities, and, at first anyway, the fact. "Our policy," the acting administrator, W.H. Milton, wrote to Milner, "is where possible to get them to live on private farms and come to working arrangements with the proprietors."

Nevertheless more reserves had to be provided, if only to silence the critics in Britain who now knew about the Gwaai and the Shangani. Milton, in the same letter, expressed the purpose: "The object of the Reserves is precisely as described by you viz. that there may be land under the control of Government and not alienable without consent of Impl. authority sufficient to provide for natives who are not willing to live in locations on the property or enter into the permanent service of settlers."

The difficulty in Matabeleland in 1897, as it had been in 1894, was where to find land that had not been alienated. The difficulty in Mashonaland—where there were now to be reserves too—was that the survey had been much less complete in that province than in Matabeleland, while the destruction of pegs and beacons had been much greater. Whatever the difficulties, the task of demarcation was begun soon after the appearance of Martin's report. The spadework was done, district by district, by the native commissioners. For Matabeleland the proposals were submitted to Milton by the acting chief native commissioner on 24 July 1897. Milner insisted that the reserves be "both suitable in quality and adequate in extent," and also that the present proposals, whatever they might be, should not be final but subject to future alteration. Not enough was yet known either about the land itself or about the population to make a final decision. And if the hope that more and more Africans would choose to settle on European farms, at the price of doing some work for wages, were realised, the reserves would gradually be phased out. Milner expected this: "the reserve system," he wrote, "is essentially a transitional one."

The old Gwaai and Shangani reserves amounted to 4,224,000 acres. The new proposals increased the area by a mere 29 per cent, to 5,445,000 acres. Milner was satisfied with the new areas, because though smaller in extent they were much better known than the old reserves and nearer to the centres of white settlement; he had no doubt of their suitability. Perhaps his confidence was largely based on the descriptions in the acting chief native commissioner's report: "very suitable," "splendid ground," "absolutely the best and most suitable sort of ground and veld for native location." But then the description "some of the finest land in Rhodesia, and coveted by Dutchmen now in Matabeleland" referred to the Gwaai.

One of the criteria of suitability was defined by Milton: "we are endeavouring to move them out of Kopjes or other difficult and defensible strongholds, and put them onto the flat where they are easily manageable." The report of 24 July had included 60,000 acres in the Matopos; this suggestion was allowed to stand by Milton (in spite of his "endeavours") but was deleted by Chamberlain. So was Sauerdale, which was a block of farms bought by Rhodes from Sauer's company, and had been included in the list by mistake. Even then, some of the proposed reserves were on privately owned land which the government hired from the owners.[6]

The excision of Sauerdale (81,000 acres) and the 60,000 acres in the Matopos reduced the Matabeleland total, which was divided among the districts as follows (the figure in brackets being the number of reserves in the district):

District		Acres
Mangwe	(4)	216,000
Bulalima	(2)	2,424,000 (one being the Gwaai)
Bulawayo	(2)	36,000
Mzingwane	(1)	6,000
Bubi	(4)	1,982,000 (one being the Shangani)
Gwelo	(1)	120,000
Insiza and Belingwe	(2)	290,000
Belingwe and Tuli	(1)	180,000
Mawabeni	(1)	60,000
		5,314,000

All the proposed areas were already occupied by Africans, who would not have to move if they wished to live in reserves; there was no intention by the government, however, to compel anyone to move, though a private landowner had the right to do this.[7]

When Chamberlain had approved of the proposals, as amended by him, Milner assured Milton that the Administrative Council, without further reference to the high commissioner, could establish the new reserves by regulation. It was not, however, until 5 November 1902, that the Executive Council—there was now a new constitution—approved of the proposals, and then only with what the 1915 Commission called "very considerable changes." The significance of the arrangements is best illustrated by statistics showing the distribution of the African population of Matabeleland in 1905:

	Square miles	Population
Native Reserves	12,114	55,106
Farms unalienated	47,508	47,505
Private farms (1,167), with agreements under proclamation of 14/10/1896 —60,727	11,163	80,750
Without agreements—20,023		
Special tenure: Fingo location		1,291
Town locations	50	836
European premises		8,683
	70,853	194,171[8]

The demarcation in Mashonaland was begun later and was even more unsystematic than what had been done in the other province. As each native commissioner followed principles of his own devising, the pattern varied from one district to the next. The only principle suggested by the central authorities was an average acreage per family. In Matabeleland this was supposed to be nine acres of arable (after the example of Glen Grey in the Cape Colony), but in the absence of information about land and population no exact result could be obtained. In Mashonaland there does not seem to have been even this kind of principle, but when the job was done each family had between fifteen and twenty acres of arable. The larger area was justified by the rocky nature of the country. Because the proposals were made by the native commissioners, district boundaries became the boundaries of reserves, though they seldom corresponded with tribal boundaries.

One official would mark out a separate reserve for every petty clan, so that his district would be "covered with small patches of reserves sandwiched between European farms." Another would make almost the whole district a reserve—Mrewa was an example—because there happened to be no European settlement. Another, in a district where much land had been alienated, established hardly any reserves. The patchwork, such as it was, was approved by the Executive Council on 27 October 1902.[9]

All the arrangements for the Ndebele, though imposed on them by the authority of the victors, were accompanied by consultations and explanations. Thus the indabas in the Matopos were followed by another in Bulawayo on 5-8 January 1897. A large and representative gathering of indunas was addressed by Lawley, the acting administrator, Taylor, the chief native commissioner, and Colenbrander. The white public also pressed into the Stock Exchange building to watch the proceedings. The officials explained the system of administration in outline: districts, native commissioners, indunas and sub-indunas, with a clear chain of command and responsibility. The districts were defined, and most of the indunas and sub-indunas named; these were to be paid from £3 to £5 a month, and from £1 to £3 a month, respectively. Most of the appointments were received with approval, but in some cases the announcement of a name provoked discussion and protest. In those cases the officials agreed to postpone the appointments until the people could agree upon names to suggest to the government.

Some of the indunas were given horses. It was announced that an induna who was disloyal or incompetent would be removed from office. The audience was reminded that arms had to be surrendered and suspected murderers given up. The people were assured that they would not be disturbed in their occupation of land, now under white ownership, where they had planted their crops, but warned that this guarantee would not last beyond the present season.

On 24 June 1897, there was another indaba, addressed this time by Lawley and Rhodes. The indunas had been invited to share in the celebration of the queen's Diamond Jubilee. The queen, they were told, had begun to reign before Mzilikazi came to Matabeleland, which was now the newest province of her empire. If this fact was what the indunas were expected to celebrate, their joy in the occasion would not have been unmixed. They had some complaints to lay before their new masters. The custom of *lobola*, for instance, had fallen into disuse, because for various reasons there were no longer any cattle for the young men to pay for their brides. There was a universal desire to restore the custom, but how were the cattle to be acquired? Both Lawley and Rhodes exploited this opening: "the best thing for them," said Rhodes, "is to teach their young men to go out and work." There were complaints about land tenure. Dliso, who had been given ground on Rhodes's farm, was not allowed to dig his own garden. Rhodes promised to see about that.

It was the presence of Rhodes that gave this encounter its otherwise inexplicable air of contentment and satisfaction. There was not much for those 150 indunas to be happy about. But this description rings true:

> The changes of manner too as he put the different answers were remarkable, there was a touch of masterfulness when he said, "Tell Somabulana (who was absent) that he had better come and see me." But coming to speak to the indunas individually Mr. Rhodes' manner underwent a startling change, it assumed a boyish exuberance and aspect of pleasure, which was immensely gratifying to the indunas personally known to him, and though the remarks might be the same, still, there was a suggestion conveyed to each of the circumstances under which they had last met, which indicated an extraordinarily capable memory.

Rhodes was at his best in the paternal role. So the indaba, against all reason, was punctuated in the classical manner by "chorus of indunas: 'Nkos! Nkos!' " or, to vary the monotony, "Yebo! Yebo!"[10]

Rhodes himself was one of the white landowners on whose estates the Ndebele had now to live. He had bought a block of farms, Sauerdale, on the northern edge of the Matopos, and there set himself up as a landlord of Ndebele tenants. On Sunday, 4 July 1897, he was host to a constantly growing crowd of black visitors—about 500 by midday—as well as of whites whose clicking cameras recorded the scene. For the blacks a flock of 200 sheep had been collected; when two officials gave the signal, the young men fell upon the sheep "and the mutton began to disappear rapidly." Gifts of blankets and tobacco were handed out. By Monday morning, Rhodes's birthday, 1,200 Ndebele, including many of the leading indunas, had gathered at the farm. The purpose was not merely social; Rhodes settled some people on his land, listened to grievances, and held out hope of redress.[11]

What Rhodes could not do was to confiscate the Victoria Agreement farms and give them back to their original owners. On 24 November 1898, a number of indunas met at Mtshane's kraal in the Matopos. Mtshane had summoned the meeting in response to the invitation of a white man who called himself an attorney and whom Mtshane supposed to represent the government. The meeting was to ascertain the grievances of the people, and to lay before them the "Native Regulations" which were about to be promulgated. The grievances in question concerned land.

The news of this event produced an apoplectic reaction from the *Bulawayo Chronicle*. White renegades allied themselves "with such natives as Karl Kumalu and Umlugulu, whom we hope the Government will speedily send out of the country." On 12 December the offending indunas were addressed at Government House by Lawley and others. Mtshane, who had been a "loyal" induna in 1896, explained the origin and character of the meeting he had summoned. To no avail—he was told that the district native commissioner was his only channel of communication with the government; for his offence he was at once deprived of his office and salary. Others who had been at the meeting were asked to step forward; each was to lose one month's salary. After that they were allowed to state their grievances. Mlugulu, who now as before the rebellion was in effect the acting head of the Ndebele nation, said that the indunas wished to send a deputation to the queen. This was not allowed; he was told that the queen had appointed a resident commissioner, Sir Marshall Clarke, who would hear any complaints they wished to address to her.[12]

A new note of bureaucratic rigidity had been struck; it would not have been heard in the old jolly days when "each case was treated on its merits." The change was far-reaching, and it followed from the intrusion upon the scene of Chamberlain and Milner and their representatives, and of the lessons they had learned from the events of 1896-7.

Prominent among the causes of those events had been the grievances of forced labour and the "native police," the latter being used to procure the former. These abuses could not be reformed in isolation. Because of their ramifications the subjects were included in a comprehensive measure entitled "Native Regulations" which was submitted to Milner in October 1897, and tossed back and forth between Salisbury, Cape Town, and London for many months.

It was gazetted on 29 November 1898, immediately after the order-in-council which was, in part, its legal foundation.[13]

The regulations were intended to bring order and system into the very unsystematic Native Department, but in the circumstances of 1898 the change meant an assumption of legal and regular power by a government that had been exercising it, though irregularly, only by right of the Maxim gun. Instead of Lendy patrols to instil obedience there would now be courts enforcing laws.

The hierarchy was clearly defined. Below the Administrator-in-Council stood the secretary for native affairs, head of the Native Department and "principal executive officer of the Administrator in Council in regard to native affairs." Below him were the two chief native commissioners of Mashonaland and Matabeleland. The country was to be divided into districts and sub-districts "for the purpose of native administration"; over each district there was to be a native commissioner, who might have assistant native commissioners to help him. All this was mere tidying up of the irregularities inherited from Jameson. Much of it was in effect long before the formal promulgation, as we noticed at the indaba of January 1897.

The powers given to these authorities were the measure of the rebels' defeat. The Administrator-in-Council appointed all chiefs and, with the approval of the high commissioner, could depose them. By the same authority a chief and his family could be removed from one reserve or piece of vacant land to another, a tribe could be divided or several tribes amalgamated. The native commissioner was given the power, "subject to the approval of the Administrator-in-Council, of assigning lands for huts, gardens and grazing grounds for each kraal on vacant land or reserves in his district, and no new huts shall be built or gardens cultivated without his consent and approval of the position selected . . . He shall, from time to time, and subject to the approval of the Chief Native Commissioner, fix the number of huts which shall compose any kraal. He shall be responsible for the proper registration of huts within his district, and for the collection of hut tax when due." The sting was in the tail; it is the last item that explains this officer's concern with huts.

The essential meaning of all this is that the white authorities had taken over the power formerly belonging to the chiefs, who were now to "hold office during pleasure and contingent upon good behaviour and general fitness" and to "receive such pay and allowance as shall be fixed from time to time." The chief was transformed, in European if not in African eyes, into a minor civil servant. He became responsible to his white superiors for maintaining order, preventing or in the last resort reporting crimes, reporting "suspicious disappearances," deaths, and outbreaks of disease, and giving publicity to government orders and notices, in his tribal district. He was to aid the police in arresting offenders, and besides other more general functions was to submit the names of suitable men to be nominated by the secretary for native affairs as district headmen. These were to perform for the chief the sort of duties that he performed for his superiors: reporting and notifying in both directions, keeping order, arresting criminals (they were to "rank as constables within their sub-districts"), and checking on the movements of strangers.

All these provisions, though subversive of the old order, passed from administrator to high commissioner to secretary of state and back again with scarcely a comment. There were other proposals that fared differently.

One of the consequences of the Company's penury had been a scarcity of qualified (or even unqualified) magistrates. The time and trouble involved in bringing an offender to a distant court was one of the reasons for the scandalous proceedings of police patrols. It was therefore proposed to confer some judicial authority on native commissioners, at least in areas far from a seat of magistracy. The chief difficulty about this, which caused the original proposal to be modified, was the shortage of officials to whom such powers could be entrusted. Milner's suggestion was to reduce the number of native commissioners, increase the number of assistants, and give judicial powers only to some of the former. So it was provided that a native commissioner "may, where such a course may seem desirable, and subject to the approval of the High Commissioner, be appointed a special justice of the peace." One so appointed would have all the powers of a special justice of the peace in the Cape Colony, as well as the powers under the Masters and Servants acts which in the Cape had been given to resident magistrates only. Milner thought that these were the judicial powers it was most important that native commissioners should have, "so as to give them power to try the class of cases most likely to arise, i.e., cases of desertion of servants, of injury to a master's property by wilful breach of duty, neglect, or drunkenness, etc., etc."—the cases which in the past had most commonly been handled by the aggrieved party with his sjambok. The practical alternative to giving these powers to native commissioners, Milner thought, was that the white settlers would "take the law into their own hands in such matters, which is just what it is so necessary to prevent." He failed, probably by an oversight, to mention cases in which the aggrieved party was the servant. But the native commissioner would have such cases to try. Further, if he had the necessary legal qualifications, he might be appointed magistrate or assistant magistrate for his district.[14]

It was in connection with these regulations that Milner listed the categories of Africans according to place of residence. In his view, the native commissioner's authority should not be the same for all categories. That is why that officer's control of huts and gardens was limited to "each kraal *on vacant land or reserves*." These were Milner's categories 2c, 3, and 4; in towns and on occupied private land there were local authorities and landowners to exercise such powers.

The duties of native commissioners and their subordinates included some that implied the help of policemen. In Mashonaland before and during the rebellion the first native commissioners had created their own little police forces of what were called "Messengers." Some of these had joined the rebels, but many had stood by their employers. These had of course been armed during the fighting, and were still armed. It was now proposed to form them, still carrying firearms, into a more regular police force to assist the native commissioners in preserving order and arresting malefactors. The messengers would not be natives of the country—in the light of the rebellion, that would be unthinkable—but Zulus or other "Colonial boys." Since they would for that reason be unlikely to know all that was going on in the villages, they were to be assisted by unarmed men belonging to the locality. These were at first called "detectives," a term which Milner changed to "Assistant Messengers"; their essential duty was to keep their ears to the ground.

Chamberlain rejected all of this, on the ground that armed police under the unsupervised orders of native commissioners were too far from the eyes of the imperial authorities. The armed police would have to be drawn from the "native contingent" of the BSA Police, which was under the command of the commandant-general, an imperial officer. The assistant messengers therefore disappeared, the messengers became what their name implied, and detachments of the "native contingent" could be stationed at each native commissioner's camp.[15]

There remains the most controversial point, which to the authors of the measure in Rhodesia may well have been its principal feature. The original fourth clause of Part I read, in part: "The Administrator in Council has power to call upon Chiefs, District Headmen, and all other natives to supply men for the defence of the territory, and for the suppression of disorder and rebellion within its borders, and for public works at fair wages." They would certainly have liked to add something about work for private employers, but were afraid of what might be said about this "at home." Milner, too, kept his eye on Downing Street, but was prepared to try his powers of persuasion. In case Chamberlain should use his veto, and to enable the rest of the regulations to go through without delay, Milner removed the words about *corvée* from clause 4, and included them in a separate clause 4a, which was to apply only to the reserves. The chiefs in those areas only could be required

> to furnish annually a certain contingent of adult male labourers for Public Works, provided always that a sufficient number of natives shall always be left on the land occupied by the natives to secure proper cultivation of such land and the safety of the crops, and that no man shall be called upon to serve for a longer period than three months in any one year under this Regulation. If not required for Public Works, the labourers so called up may be employed in the service of private persons, for purposes and under conditions approved by the Administrator, but in either case they shall receive fair wages at the current rate for native labour.

Chamberlain rejected this *in toto*; nor would he allow any part of it to creep back into the original clause 4.

Milton argued that, though reserves were unavoidable, they would in the nature of the case, being havens for won't-works, become "pauper-warrens." Milner pointed out that the development of the country would be held back unless the people in the reserves could be made to work. He even claimed that "the native tribes . . . might fairly be expected to give some *quid pro quo* for the lands thus assigned to them," forgetting that the lands belonged to the native tribes in the first place.[16]

This excuse was a rationalization. No doubt the "development of the country" was so important in itself, to all Europeans having any responsibility for it, that it seemed to justify the use of the stick where the carrot was not effective. But the motives of Milner, Milton, and even the white colonists themselves, were really more complicated than that.

The basic fact of race relations in Rhodesia was the dependence of the whites on black labour, a fact which was examined in an earlier chapter. The unwillingness of Africans to offer their labour was seen as a threat to the survival of the white community and its economy. This was one reason for the monotonous denunciations by the whites of the black race and all its members, but it was not the only reason. Before the rebellion ideas of white superiority, derived from the pseudo-scientific notions of the time, had been universal among the Europeans. After the rebellion these ideas took on a blood-red tinge. And there was a third factor, the force of the "work ethic" as an element in the European moral code.

Thus the *Rhodesia Herald*, after deploring the folly of the missionaries in instilling "false notions of equality" into the Africans, ridiculed the "howls of execration from the hypocrites of Exeter Hall," but substituted some of its own. In Rhodesia

> we are fully alive to the pernicious influence of Exeter Hall . . . We have a worse class of native to deal with than can be found throughout the whole length and breadth of South Africa. They are cowardly, cruel, treacherous and without an atom of gratitude in their nature. The Matabele are not much better. The vice of cowardice, however, cannot with equal truth be attributed to them . . . The natives are children in everything but vice and therefore ought to be treated accordingly. We should treat them with firmness but justice, always impressing upon them the wholesome fact that they are our inferiors, morally, socially, and mentally, and can never hope to be otherwise. If we try to do that which has been attempted in the past, viz.: to civilize them in as many years as it has taken centuries to civilize us, we shall not only ignominiously fail but hand this vexed question down to posterity, far more involved and complicated than we found it.

Four months later the *Herald* could add a few more adjectives: "They are nothing but a horde of cunning, treacherous, cowardly, idle thieves."[17]

At the end of 1898 Hans Sauer was electioneering. Putting all the weight of his medical education and scientific studies behind his words, he told the voters that it had been proved beyond doubt by great men of science—Darwin, T.H. Huxley, *et al.*—that

> the African negro was not the white man's equal in mental capacity, in sentiment, or in any of the finer feelings of the human race. It had been proved that the average African native had three ounces of brain less than the average European, therefore his brain capacity could not be equal to that of the European. That being so, he might say shortly that he believed and he thought it was the proper policy for the white man in Africa to govern the native by a benevolent despotism. He should be treated as a child. He should be governed justly, but with a rod of iron (applause).

Neither Sauer nor anyone in the audience drew the logical inference that privilege should be based on cranial capacity rather than on skin colour.[18]

White racial attitudes had thus many roots. Physical fear, the fear of numbers, racial doctrines, and the sense of cultural distance would have been enough to produce a pattern of racial exclusiveness and superiority even without economics. But the form which that pattern in fact took was decisively influenced by white dependence on black labour.

The colonists could hardly help themselves. The complementary roles of black labour and white supervision, partly a heritage from the days of slavery, were locked into the society and economy of southern Africa so firmly that a self-sufficient white community in Rhodesia, doing its own work, was inconceivable. Not quite; the idea indeed was conceived, as when the *Rhodesia Herald* yearned for white settlement in the Australian or Canadian fashion, or when "Curio" Brown startled the Lagden Commission by saying that it would be better if the Africans refused absolutely to work—"if they did not work at all we would have them out of the way, and have a white race in the country"; but this was mere day-dreaming. The black worker was indispensable, in Rhodesia as in the rest of the subcontinent. The blacks of the older colonies and states, however, had long been accustomed to wage labour and the cash economy; those of Rhodesia had not.[19]

To the frustrations of white employers short of labour was added a more respectable motive, the imperatives of the "work ethic." To the heirs of the Puritan and Industrial Revolutions idleness was a sin, and a peculiarly offensive and infuriating one. So to the denunciations of mineowners and farmers were added those of the missionaries:

> No one will contend for a moment that a crowd of idle loafers, whether white or black, is as useful to the community as a company of industrious labourers. But in this country we have thousands of savages living in sloth, and who are thus ready for all kinds of mischief, and yet we, who know that to them the discipline of work for a few months in the year would be of the highest moral benefit, are helpless to influence them in the right direction without risking a charge of patronising slavery. (The Rev. Isaac Shimmin, Chairman and General Superintendent of the Wesleyan Missions.) In

my opinion the natives of this country . . . are but grown up children. Unfortunately, they do not possess the innocence of children, but . . . are given to many vices, conspicuous among them being their strong inclination to idleness, strengthened by long habit . . . Consequently, men in authority . . . ought . . . to do all they can to make them acquire habits of work and industry. As this cannot be obtained by mere moral persuasion, authority must necessarily be used. (The Rev. Father A.M. Daignault, SJ)

The missionaries, like the colonists, seem to have defined "idleness" in a special way: it meant not working for white employers. Not a voice was raised to suggest that an African active in his own concerns might not be idle. On the contrary, it was repeatedly stated that the tribesmen would not "work" because they had enough land to provide them with a living. The *Rhodesia Herald* thought that Shona and Ndebele alike were growing "fat, rich and happy," but could not demonstrate that the riches took the form of manna falling from heaven.[20]

This fallacy being universally accepted, a plausible case could be built on it. As a writer to the *Bulawayo Chronicle* put it, if a white man does not work he starves. Yet the black man need not work because the Company feeds him (this was during the lean year after the rebellion). There were references to Adam and the sweat of his brow. Week after week the newspapers hammered at the theme. No one doubted that "making the native work" was the key to the country's future; but how could it be done? There was the hut tax, a device respectable enough to get past the watchdogs in London, but the assumption that working for wages was the only way to earn the tax money was not always correct. The whites depended on the blacks not only for wage labour but also very largely for food supplies. When the harvest was good and the animals breeding well, tax money could be earned in the market. Moreover, even the labour that was available tended to be seasonal: it was offered shortly before the tax was due, and at times when work on the land was slack.

The restoration of *lobola* might help, by creating the need to buy cattle. But the colonists had lost faith in such palliatives. "Could our natives," wrote the *Rhodesia Herald*, "by any arts of persuasion, be induced to work for us, then to compel them to do so would decidedly be wrong. Persuasion has hitherto utterly failed, and, therefore, compulsion becomes an imperative duty." The difficulty was that the local authorities refused to apply the obvious remedy because they were "too afraid of the terrible bogies raised by the disordered brains of certain fanatics at Home." The attacks of those fanatics never failed to stir up the Rhodesians: "We have heard this piffle before, and, like Free Trade, the abolition of slavery is a doubtful blessing." Having thus let the cat out of the bag, the editor, frightened by his own temerity, incongruously added, "but we have no intention of compelling the natives to work."[21]

Of course they had the intention. They even gave the local authorities credit for having it too, but

The fear of Exeter Hall hampers them, and they have not the courage to put the matter straight to the Imperial Government. Surely the Colonial Office has learnt some lessons in the last half century. It was Exeter Hall and its representatives that drove the Boers away in the Great Trek of 1836, and the same sinister influence seems destined to mar the growing fortunes of Rhodesia. We owe the Transvaal Republic to that influence; are we to owe an independent Rhodesia to the same cause?

Though the drama of UDI was thus foreshadowed, all the pleas and arguments fell on deaf ears in London. The white Rhodesians might be nostalgic and unrepentant, but the British government had learned the lessons of the rebellion. Aware also of the "fanatics" in the House of Commons, Chamberlain would not dare to face the House with Milner's proposed labour clause. "Oh for 4A," Milton sighed in a letter to the high commissioner.[22]

Compulsion being forbidden, the employers had to devise other methods. The employers in question were essentially the mineowners. Farmers could draw on "resident labour"; even where they could not, farm work was the most familiar and the least unattractive to "boys" in search of money. Even on the mines there was little difficulty about labour on the surface; it was the underground workers that were hard, often impossible, to get.

"Shangaans" were held to be the best men for underground work. In the middle of 1897 the Bulawayo Chamber of Mines sent two men to Gazaland on a recruiting expedition. They had some success. Other recruiting trips were made to the remoter parts of Rhodesia, and occasionally brought back a few workers. But the Chamber of Mines worked under a handicap, "because the chiefs knew the agents it sent were not sent with government authority." The agents, moreover, were commonly unemployed whites who took on this job as a last resort.

The two Chambers of Mines were thus driven into the business of recruiting in a more serious way. The Salisbury chamber appointed a committee to operate a Native Labour Bureau and to build and run a compound to receive the labourers. The agents sent out were Africans, the bureau received a capitation fee for each worker from the employer who took him, and in due course it was able to pay its way. It had the blessing of the chief native commissioner, and some government financial support at first, but otherwise was a purely private institution. It began operations on 12 July 1898, but for the first few months could not keep pace with the demand for labour. In the eight months ending in March 1899 the bureau recruited 2,891 workers; in the corresponding months of 1899-1900, 4,691. At the same time, because of the war, economic activity had slackened, so that the supply of labour more or less met the demand. The bureau considered that for underground work the mining industry could "not depend to any great extent on the labour supplies of this country"; Shangaans were preferred, and though the Shona were "useful merely as surface boys . . . it is needless to say much about this tribe as mine labourers."

The Matabeleland Native Labour Bureau, on the other hand, thought that recruiting was most successful from "the Mashona and Makalaka castes. Where agents have had to work amongst a population leavened with the pure bred Matabele, the success has not been so great." This bureau depended, as the other did not, on government support. The Bulawayo chamber insisted on this from the moment the scheme was proposed. Probably for this reason— Lawley, with an eye on the "fanatics at Home," was reluctant to have anything to do with the business—the Matabeleland bureau did not begin to function until July 1899. From that date to the end of March 1900 it recruited 10,787 workers. The bureau received a very small capitation fee from the employer; for the rest its expenses were shared by the government and the chamber. In spite of the efforts of the two bureaux the labour supply, before the war, usually fell short of the demand. For lack of it mines—such as the Glendarra in October 1898, and the Bonsor and the Dunraven in August 1899—had to shut down. And whenever the rains indicated the beginning of the planting season, or other duties in the home village called, there were desertions from the mines.[23]

These problems had prompted Rhodes, in cooperation with F.R. ("Matabele") Thompson and Walter Stanford, secretary for native affairs in the Cape Colony, in April 1898 to hatch a more imaginative scheme: to settle 10,000 Mfengu ("Fingos") from the Transkei on three new reserves to be created in Rhodesia, to provide labour for the mines. Each family was to have a site for a house, grazing rights, and ten acres of garden. As far as possible the principles of Rhodes's own Glen Grey Act were to be applied. The *Bulawayo Chronicle*, which at first objected to the scheme on the ground that the Mfengu were no better mineworkers than the local variety, had second thoughts. The white man held South Africa, said the *Chronicle*, because of the divisions and mutual hatreds among the blacks. The Mfengu had always been loyal to the whites. Introducing such "an orderly and industrious colony of men of their own colour" would provide a good example to the Ndebele. It would arouse in them a desire to possess "European adjuncts of civilization," a desire which they could satisfy only by going out to work.

The enthusiasm was premature. Only one of the three "Fingo locations"— the Bembesi—was surveyed and settled. In December 1898 the local native commissioner reported that "there were only about six young men at the Fingo location; of these three have gone to Selukwe to work and two are employed as messengers." More came in the following years, so that by 1904 about 300 families—a thousand individuals altogether—had settled in the location. Each family had its ten acres of arable and grazing rights over the whole reserve, which comprised five standard farms or 15,000 morgen. Each plotholder had to go out to work (for anybody) for at least three months a year. After he had worked for thirty-six months the obligation ceased and he obtained freehold title. No rent was charged during the labour tenancy. The terms were attractive.

537 The Fate of the Vanquished

A few Ndebele had applied to join the scheme and had been accepted, and Mfengu in the Cape were continuing to apply. Yet this was a far cry from the ten thousand expected at the beginning, and Lawley reported in 1900 that the Mfengu had no inclination to work, and that none had sought employment on the mines.[24]

The mines continued to be short of underground workers until the war, which forced many mines to close and so reduced the demand. The general reluctance to work underground was attributed to unfamiliarity—the taste for it took some acquiring; to dynamite, which similarly was a discouragement to the novice; and to the working conditions, which in the early years the owners did nothing to alleviate. A miner might come to the surface at midnight on a winter's night and have to walk a quarter of a mile to his hut, without a shirt or a blanket. There were many deaths on the mines, especially from pneumonia, but the companies appear not to have informed the bereaved families. The miner just failed to return and his fate was unknown.

Nevertheless the flow of labour to the mines increased. For the year 1899-1900 the chief labour agent, Matabeleland, estimated that "fully 40,000 boys" had been employed as mine labourers; 15,000 of these had been recruited by the Labour Bureau and other agencies, and the rest had sought work on their own initiative. Most of them had worked for three-month periods. The figure for Mashonaland was 39,000; this was for all kinds of labour, "the bulk of these," however, "being registered to mines for periods varying from one to four months, and in some cases six months." In 1904, when mining was still in the doldrums, it was said that "in normal times"—i.e., before the war—the mines employed about 25,000 workers every day. That figure can be reconciled with the 70,000 or so employed for periods of one to six months in the year.

Wages on the mines varied widely. The official report for Matabeleland in 1900 gave a range of 25s. to 60s. a month (or 10d. to 2s. a day) with rations, and "the native is entitled to receive his pay (irrespective of illness or other causes) on the fifth Saturday after his arrival at the mine, and upon each succeeding fifth Saturday." The same report shows that in Gwelo the rate for miners was £5 for "Colonial or Zulu boys" and £1 for "Mashonas." Umtali paid the same, with an intermediate rate of 30s. for Shangaans. After the war the average rate in Mashonaland was from 36s. to 38s., not for a calendar month but for thirty days actually worked.[25]

Labour on white farms was very different from labour on the mines, both as an experience for the labourers and as a problem for the employers. When the Lagden Commission visited Rhodesia in 1904 many of the characters familiar to us in this story appeared before it as witnesses. Where their evidence was based on experiences extending back to 1890, or nearly as far, it can be used in the present context. From that evidence a picture of black labour on white farms emerges.

In both provinces farm labour was of two types, "resident" and "volunteer." The volunteers were men who left their homes in search of wages and offered their services on farms as others did at the mines. They built their own huts in a "compound" and were purely wage labourers. The others were the labour tenants, settled on the farm—which might have been their own land in the first place—with their families, cultivating their gardens and running their stock, and giving some labour in return. There were of course still other tenants who paid rent but gave no labour.

There are no precise statistics of these classes. H.J. Taylor, who was in the best position to know about Matabeleland, asserted that there were many "volunteer labourers" on the farms. Col. William Napier had "quite a few" on his farm. W.H. ("Curio") Brown, generalizing about Mashonaland, stated that "considerably more than 50 per cent of our labour" came from north of the Zambezi; but this information for 1904 cannot be projected back to an earlier date, and Brown did not positively state, though it was very likely, that the strangers from the north were volunteers.

These were isolated comments. Almost everything that was said to the Commission about Africans on European farms related to tenants with families, paying either rent or labour. We have seen that most of the Ndebele were resident on the conquerors' farms. In 1904 the black population of Mashonaland was distributed thus: on farms, 64,000; on "reserves or vacant land," 310,830; and a "floating population in the towns and mining centres" of 7,000. Although those on the farms were a small minority, they could have provided more than enough labour for the handful of farmers in Mashonaland.[26]

African tenancy on European farms, a common arrangement in Natal, the republics, and the Eastern Province of the Cape, arose in Rhodesia as a result of Jameson's War and of the rebellions. As rebels began to surrender in Matabeleland provision had to be made for their accommodation on farms; hence Robinson's proclamation of October 14, 1896. This legalized in Rhodesia what in the Cape were called "Private Locations." The Cape law would apply when the landowner established not fewer than seven heads of families on his farm. They were to cultivate "grain and other crops" (after all, this was where the white men's food came from); they were secured against removal for the first two years; the landowner had a claim to the labour of any who would work for wages; he might (though he was not obliged to) enter into agreements with residents on his property to work for him for wages; such agreements required the approval of the chief native commissioner and were for a maximum of one year. Neither labour nor rent could be demanded for one year after the establishment of the location. Though there was no compulsion to enter into a labour contract, it was generally done because of the protection it gave to both parties. From the date of the proclamation to the sessions of the Lagden Commission in 1904, Chief Native Commissioner Taylor had had no complaint from either landlord or tenant. The agreement could be terminated by either side on one year's notice. There was no legal limit to the number of tenants, nor did the landlord limit the area the tenant might cultivate for himself.

The terms of the agreement were not uniform. Where the tenant gave no labour he usually paid a rent of £1 per hut, or per adult male in the family. Most tenants, according to H.J. Taylor, preferred to pay rent; but there were farmers such as Col. William Napier who had only labour tenants on their estates. The usual requirement was three months' labour a year, but the period could be flexible. Napier might call his men out for two, four, or five months, according to his needs, though his average was about three; and "when I am free of him, I give him a note saying he can go and labour for as many months as I do not require him." The contract was made, not with each adult male separately, but with the "head of the kraal," a man who might have a number of married sons, or several families, under him. Napier called only on the younger men to work, never on the older—that would be *"infra dig."*

In most cases the labour tenant was paid a wage while doing his labour service, the same wage as would be paid to a "volunteer" labourer. Most farm wages fell within the range 10s.—£1 a month, with rations. Col. Raleigh Grey (Mashonaland) gave his scale as 5s.—£1, and said that "you could get plenty for 10s." Grey's company owned much land and had many tenants on it; they paid no rent but gave their labour "when required." On one of its estates there were between 80 and 100 able-bodied male residents; at any one time between 30 and 40 of them were at work, and all worked at some time. Col. P.D. Crewe owned 18,000 acres in Matabeleland. The 200 "resident boys" gave on an average four months' labour a year. For this they were not paid if they worked on the farm—in this case herding cattle—but they were paid if they worked "off the farm"; Crewe did not explain how he employed them off the farm. E.A. Hull (Matabeleland) required three months' labour a year from tenants, and paid them for it; but at "pressing times" such as harvesting extra work might be demanded of them.[27]

Every European farm had, therefore, its "compounds," kraals, or groups of huts in which various categories of labourers, with or without families, lived. Though they were now subjected to conditions very different from those of the old days of independence, something of the old village structure and life was preserved. After the day's work, and far into the night, the rhythmic sounds of chant and drum from the compound told the white family in its farmhouse that the heart of old Africa was still beating; but the records of the time say nothing of any inferences that were drawn from this knowledge.

None of these witnesses of 1904 had any difficulty in obtaining labour. As Hull explained, there was no problem for an employer who knew "how to treat them properly." Those who had difficulty, said Crewe, were the farmers who "do not understand how to work the boys." This is a mere truism in all labour relations, but it must be remembered in the context of the loud denunciations of the "idle and lazy natives."

The denunciations quoted earlier were made in 1897 and 1898; the evidence to the Lagden Commission was given in 1904. Though human nature could not have been radically transformed in that short interval, the lapse of time had made some difference. E.A. Hull had come to Rhodesia in 1897; in 1904 he said that "the natives were more inclined to go out to work now" than then, because their wants had increased.

That increase of wants was an historical fact at least as important as the better documented and more dramatic events described in this book. It was encouraged by pressure on the Africans from several directions. The white traders and importers had a primary interest in it. Employers in general depended on it as an inducement to the labour force. Missionaries and teachers fostered it for its own sake. George Wilder, American missionary in Melsetter, reported that his mission school taught students to make bricks and lay them straight, because "we believe it is necessary for any man, if he is going to be at all educated, to live in a permanent, upright house, with a chimney in it." He was supported even by some of the local whites. One of the Melsetter farmers told him that "if they [the Africans] remain with us, they must either be enslaved or educated and civilised; one of those two things."

The white man's artifacts were not the only things that could be bought for money. The ravages of war and pestilence could be repaired by buying beasts. C.D. Helm reported in 1904 that people who had lost all in 1894-6 now owned large herds; in 1902 they had 55,155 cattle. But, according to Helm, the same people now bought clothes also. So great was the demand for money among the Ndebele by 1904 that the supply of labour had outstripped the demand: there were not enough jobs.[28]

Some of the jobs were in the towns. When Africans moved into them, the local authorities arranged to house them in "locations" in the traditional South African manner. The ordinance which established Sanitary Boards, the first local authorities (No. 2 of 1894), empowered the boards "to provide for, establish, regulate and control native locations." This crude accommodation was provided, but no African was compelled to live in it; that refinement came later. The vast majority of black urban workers lived not in the locations but on their employers' premises; in Matabeleland, as we have seen in the figures for 1905, 8,683 as against 836. The locations were dormitories where there was very little life in the daytime.

The taste for European goods would have been acquired most easily by those who worked in the towns, and most of all by domestic servants. That occupation, however, came to be monopolized by "alien natives." The first white householders had set the pattern by preferring "Colonial boys" and others who were familiar with European domestic arrangements. Then the incumbents used their influence in favour of their friends. Marshall Hole said that domestic service was "coming to be monopolized by aliens—East Coast boys, Somalis, Zambezi Natives." The official wage statistics for 1900 show, however, that "Mashona" servants in Salisbury were paid 15s. a month (but Shangaans 30s. and "Colonial or Zulu boys" £3).

In any case it is clear that by the turn of the century the institution of wage labour, on mine and farm and in town, had been firmly established. Money circulated among the indigenous population and was increasingly desired. A large proportion of the population would have been so affected. The number of Africans in the country in 1898-9 was officially estimated as: Mashonaland, 269,521; Matabeleland, 144,257; total, 413,778. In that year, and in 1904, as in earlier years, women remained almost entirely outside the labour market. Marshall Hole said in 1904 that the one or two female servants commonly employed by a native commissioner were the exception. Thus we are concerned only with adult males. Even if these figures were a gross underestimate (we have seen a much higher figure for Mashonaland in 1904), a comparison with the various labour statistics shows that few Africans can have been left altogether outside the new economic system. The tenants on farms provided "resident" and the people of the reserves (as well as the tenants in their spare time) "volunteer" labour.[29]

Of all the consequences of the white conquest, apart from the loss of land and independence, it was no doubt wage labour and the market economy that affected the greatest number of people. There were however other consequences which, though less extensive, may have been more profound in their influence. The most important of these was the work of the missionaries.

It has become a commonplace of African nationalist historiography that Christian missionaries were agents of European imperialism, working to undermine indigenous institutions and to "soften up" the population for the imperial take-over.[30] In the Rhodesian case there is much truth in this interpretation so far as it is applied to the missionaries' motives and intentions. Lobengula's power, and to a less extent that of the Shona paramounts, were obstacles to conversion. The missionaries of that day, almost all of them, tended to include most of European culture in their definition of Christianity. Thus no progress could be made until the old regimes were overthrown. But this theory is much less defensible as an explanation, or partial explanation, of the white conquest of Rhodesia. Whatever the missionaries' motives, their influence on African individuals and society before the conquest was minimal. The Moffat treaty, the Rudd Concession, the charter, the march of the Pioneer Column, and Jameson's War would all have occurred with little modification if the only advance agents of imperialism had been secular. In 1896 the Christians took no part in the rebellion, but they were too few to affect the outcome. It was the military defeat of the Ndebele and the Shona that paved the way for missionary influence, not the other way round. The cross followed the flag.

Nothing succeeds like success. In 1896-7 the African gods let their people down, but the white man's God was invincible. The blood of the martyrs is the seed of the church, and the rebellion had made Christian martyrs. That was not all. It was among the missionaries that the defeated people found compassion, encouragement and help in their hunger and despair. "The Jesuit Fathers," writes Lawrence Vambe of the time when they returned to Chishawasha, "assumed a role which made even the most anti-white and anti-missionary feel ashamed of the unhappy fate they had originally designed for this religious community." No wonder, then, that by July 1897, in the last days of the rebellion, there had been 474 baptisms in the Jesuit mission. In 1895 there were only three. By 1906 there had been 1,200, but that date falls outside our period.[31]

While the impressive growth of the churches belongs to the years after 1902, the upward turn in their fortunes is clearly visible immediately after the rebellion. The Seventh Day Adventists at Solusi made their first converts among the starving children who gathered there in 1896-7. The LMS, which had had its first meagre successes after the fall of Lobengula, could count 600 adherents at Inyati and Hope Fountain in 1900-1, though only twelve full members of the church. In 1901 the same society could report that the villagers round Centenary, near Figtree, had "started to hold weekly prayer-meetings, where they prayed for the success of the Gospel throughout the country." They had begun to feel the burden of their sins and to search for the truth.[32]

The Methodists had their martyr, Molimile Molele, who was buried with James White, the man he had tried to save, at Nengubo. There, in 1898, the missionary John White founded an institution (later called Waddilove) for the training of evangelists and teachers. Chief Chiremba and his people, who at the outbreak of the rebellion fled from Epworth into Salisbury, returned to Epworth and rebuilt their village; in 1900 the chief and his family were baptized. The Wesleyan society had in 1895 been granted a farm west of Bulawayo, but its work there was stifled at birth. In 1897 the farm, Tegwani, was marked out and a mission station established by G.W. Stanlake. The station was promptly visited by Gampu, who asked Stanlake to set up another station near his home. Gampu said that he himself would never change, but he wanted his son Sibindi to be well educated. The Methodists lost no time in getting to work among the Mfengu settled on the Bembesi. They had an advantage there: many of the Mfengu were already Methodists, products of the missions in the Cape Colony. But their success was short-lived—the Mfengu Methodists broke away and formed a separatist church.[33]

In 1904 C.D. Helm summed up some of the results of this evangelization, as far as he could judge them from his own experience. In Lobengula's time there had been hardly a chaste girl in the country; though the level of chastity was still very low, it was high among the Christians. He thought that there was now far more honesty, and less stealing, among the Ndebele. He had a high opinion of Ndebele energy, industry, and capacity for learning. After the rebellion the LMS had been much more successful than before in its schools. Formerly, pupils had attended for short periods and then left. Now they stayed the course. One illustration of the resulting advance in education was that in 1902 the LMS had published a thousand copies of the Ndebele New Testament, and that all had been sold.

By that time there was some support among the white laity for the policy of educating Africans. John Kerr, a merchant, disagreed with the view that "education spoilt the native," pointing out that "a little learning," dangerous as it might be, was a necessary step on the way up. E.A. Hull, a farmer, qualified his opinions by making distinctions. Among the Ndebele, he said, "breeding" made all the difference. The *abezansi*

> will learn anything, from driving teams to working machinery, and the more responsibility you put on them the better they are. Others you find exactly the reverse, and as soon as you put them in a responsible position they abuse it immediately . . . I have boys who have remained with me for seven years, all the time I have been in the country, and who are absolutely capable men to-day, though they were perfectly raw when I started with them.

Wilder, the missionary from Melsetter, was no less enthusiastic about the industry and the learning capacity of his people. Among other things they operated a sawmill at his mission.

So the Africans, by the turn of the century, were earning good marks from the purveyors of European and Christian values and skills. What marks did the purveyors earn from the Africans?

This question is harder to answer, because the Africans were discreet and still, for the most part, unable to record their opinions in writing. Gampu, when asked by the Lagden commissioners "are you happy?", replied with discretion: "We have not got used to the ways of the white men altogether." Why was education desired? Because "we would then understand the white man and his laws better." Sikhombo, asked to choose between enlightenment and progress and a return to the old ways, was more positive: "No man would like to be kept down, and be only the size of a rabbit, when he might be made into a big man. We would like to progress."

But Sikhombo's answer to another question gave a brief glimpse of the wide, deep gulf that still divided Ndebele from European values. He was asked how the African way of life had changed as a result of the defeat.

> "At the present time we are freer than we used to be. We go where we like. A man can go to Selukwe, for instance, or anywhere he wants to. Before, if a man left this country and went to Bechuanaland it was reported that he had run away."
> "Is that a change that is agreeable to the people?"
> "No; they did not like it under their own rule, and they do not think it is right now. Under their old rule they did not like the people to be allowed to wander about just as they liked, and they do not like it now."[34]

544 Rhodes and Rhodesia

That was an old officer of a military despotism speaking; the opinion he expressed was not necessarily shared by the Shona, but it is revealing. Sikhombo probably did not know that there were whites who shared his opinion, and were already demanding that freedom of movement—for blacks—should be curtailed.

NOTES CHAPTER 13

1 co 879/52/552, no.61 and encls., pp.64-70; 53/559, no.10 and encl., pp.21-3. For the trials of the murderers of the Cunninghams and the Fouries, *Bulawayo Chronicle*, 19 August 1897. It was assumed that the man whose case was quashed had probably murdered a different victim.

2 co 879/53/559, no.184 and encl., pp.219-20, no.303 and encl., pp.323-3, no.419 and encl., pp.442-3; T.O. Ranger, *Revolt in Southern Rhodesia*, pp.309-10, quoting *Zambesi Mission Record*, vol. I, no.2 (November 1898).

3 Lawrence Vambe, *An Ill-Fated People*, pp.142-5; David Chanaiwa, "A History of the Nhowe before 1900" (thesis, University of California), p. 258; *Rhodesia Herald*, 1 August, 13 August, and 7 September 1898.

4 *Bulawayo Chronicle*, 18 February and 4 March 1898.

5 Intercolonial Native Affairs Commission, 1903-5 (the Lagden Commission), Evidence, vol. IV, p.94 (Q 35211 and 36094). The commission visited Rhodesia in 1904.

6 co 879/53/559, no.32 and encls., pp.59-66; no.190, encl. 2, p.233; Milner papers, Milton to Milner, 5 February 1898; Claire Palley, *The Constitutional History and Law of Southern Rhodesia, 1888-1965*, pp.142-3, 178-9.

7 co 879/53/559, no.32, encl., pp.63-4.

8 co 879/53/559, no.188, encl., pp.227-8; 86/763, no.289, p.386; British Sessional Paper (Bluebook) Cd 8674, no.4, pp.8-9.

9 British Sessional Paper Cd 8674, pp.7-9. I have not been able to find a tabulation of the Mashonaland reserves in the material available to me up to 1905.

10 *Bulawayo Chronicle*, 9 January and 26 June 1897. The words in the last quotation mean *chief* and *yes* respectively.

11 Ibid., 10 July 1897 and 4 February 1898. Rhodes bought Sauerdale from the Sauerdale Estates Co., which then wound itself up. Hans Sauer was the chairman of that company.

12 Ibid., 17 December 1898.

13 For the "Native Regulations" discussed in the following pages, see co 879/52/552, no.165, and encls., pp.178-89, and co 879/53/559, especially no.190, pp.231-43 and no.285, pp.321-4.

14 co 879/52/552, no.165, pp.179-80.

15 co 879/53/559, no.20, p.49 and no.190, encl.3, p.237.

16 co 879/52/552, no.165, pp.181-2.

17 *Rhodesia Herald*, 2 December 1896 and 21 April 1897. Exeter Hall, which for generations was the bogey of white southern Africans, was not an institution designed to persecute them. It was an ordinary public meeting-place on the north side of the Strand, opened in 1831. It was used, e.g., by the Sacred Harmonic Society for the performance of oratorios, but was also let to various missionary societies for their

"May meetings." In 1880 the lease was purchased by the YMCA, the building was re-modelled, partly rebuilt, and reopened in 1881. It was used by the YMCA, but the Great Hall and the Lower Hall were let to other bodies, e.g., the missionary socie-ties, for their meetings. See Henry B. Wheatley, *London Past and Present*, vol. II, p.26.

18 *Bulawayo Chronicle*, 24 December 1898. Sauer might have reflected that Mzilikazi had a small skull, but overcame the handicap very successfully.

19 *Rhodesia Herald*, 12 January 1898; Lagden Commission Evidence, vol. IV, p.106 (Q 35365).

20 Lagden Commission Evidence, vol. IV, p.156 (Q 36022-3); CO 879/53/559, no.19 and encls., pp. 46-8; *Rhodesia Herald*, 17 August 1898.

21 *Rhodesia Herald*, 21 April 1897; *Bulawayo Chronicle*, 3 December 1897, 24 Sep-tember, and 1 October 1898.

22 *Bulawayo Chronicle*, 1 April 1898; CO 879/53/559, no.20, p.49.

23 *Bulawayo Chronicle*, 22 July 1897, 8 April 1898, 13 May, 22 July, and 5 August 1899; *Rhodesia Herald*, 10 May, 6 September, and 26 October 1898; CO 468/3, BSA Co. Report for 1898-1900, pp.13, 160, 252-3.

24 CO 468/3, BSA Co. Report for 1898-1900, p.28; *Rhodesia Herald*, 18 April 1898; *Bulawayo Chronicle*, 22 April 1898 and 22 January 1899; Lagden Commission Evi-dence, vol. IV, pp.145 (Q 35770-92), 151 (Q 35905-12), 153 (Q 35958), 154 (Q 35970).

25 Lagden Commission Evidence, vol. IV, pp.54 (Q 34687-91), 68 (Q 34876), 176 (Q 36313), 182 (Q 36371), 210 (Q 36752-54), 232 (Q 37050); CO 468/3, BSA Co. Report for 1898-1900, pp.149, 156, 160.

26 Lagden Commission Evidence, vol. IV, pp.41-2 (Q 34445-6), 154 (Q 35962-3).

27 Ibid., pp.66-9, (Q 34854, 34882-6, 34907-9), 113 (Q 35427), 142-4 (Q 35725, 35728-9, 35733-8, 35755-61), 153-4 (Q 35949-52, 35966), 164-8 (Q 36151-60, 36170-2, 36206, 36232-3), 191 (Q 36491-510) 225 (Q 36935-8); CO 879/47/517, no.295 and encl., pp.273-5.

28 Lagden Commission Evidence, vol. IV, pp.1 (Q 33986), 5 (Q 34012), 171 (Q 36275), 173 (Q 36284), 192 (Q 35518-20), 225-6 (Q 36935-8, 36949-54, 36063-7); British Ses-sional Paper Cd 8674, no.4, p.9.

29 CO 3/1, p.64, Ordinance 2 of 1894, Sect.23(m); CO 468/3, BSA Co. Report for 1898-1900, pp.13, 315; Lagden Commission Evidence, vol. IV, pp.56 (Q 34721), 188-9 (Q 36440, 36467); *Bulawayo Chronicle*, 23 July 1898.

30 See above, ch.10 (for missions generally).

31 *Zambesi Mission Record*, vol. I, p.7; vol. III, pp.156-9; Vambe, *Ill-Fated People*, p.143.

32 N.M.B. Bhebe, "Christian Missions in Matabeleland, 1859-1923" (paper, Univer-sity of London), pp.221, 298; Centenary must not be confused with the better-known place of that name in northern Mashonaland.

33 C.F. Andrews, *John White of Mashonaland*, ch. VIII; G.G. Findlay and W.W. Holdsworth, *History of the Wesleyan Methodist Missionary Society*, vol. IV, pp.387-90; Bhebe, "Christian Missions in Matabeleland," p.251; Lagden Commission Evi-dence, vol. IV, p.90 (Q 35154); and see above, ch.12, p.542. The ashes of John White, too, were buried at Waddilove.

34 Lagden Commission Evidence, vol. IV, pp.2 (Q 36110-4), 161 (Q 36106-14), 171-4 (Q 36275, 36281, 36290), 226-7 (Q 36968).

CHAPTER 14

White Politics

The "Native Regulations" of 1898 were one aspect of a general reform precipitated by the Jameson Raid and then delayed, but also influenced, by the rebellion. The first instalment of that reform had been the disarmament of the Company and the appointment of Sir Richard Martin.

Further reforms involved both the constitution of the Company and the government of its territories. The Select Committee of the House of Commons, appointed on 29 January 1897 to enquire into the responsibilities for the raid, had been asked also "to Report what Alterations are desirable in the Government of the Territories under the Control of the Company." As it did not attempt to do so, the government proceeded without it.[1]

The changes were effected by two measures: the Southern Rhodesia Order-in-Council, gazetted on 25 November 1898; and the Supplementary Charter of the Company, signed and sealed on 8 June 1900. The delay over the charter was caused by long correspondence between the Company and the Colonial Office, protests by the directors, meetings of the board, and extraordinary general meetings of the shareholders. Yet the two measures were really complementary and interdependent. The directors would have preferred to have no supplementary charter, and to have some of its clauses hidden among the technicalities of the order-in-council, but there were two good reasons why this course could not be followed.

In the first place, the original charter conferred on the directors certain powers which were now to be taken away. As the charter was to run for twenty-five years, the Crown could not unilaterally alter its terms before 1914. It could revoke the charter if the Company had failed to observe those terms, and there was no lack of evidence of that. But revoking the charter would mean an imperial take-over of Rhodesia, which at every point the government had been determined to avoid. What was more, so long as Joseph Chamberlain was secretary of state for the colonies, his dealings with the Company were restrained by the knowledge that it possessed the compromising "missing telegrams" which had been withheld from the "Committee of No Enquiry." Nevertheless the threat of revocation was the means by which the directors were made receptive to alternative proposals.

Secondly, the order-in-council was issued by virtue of the powers conferred on the Crown by the Foreign Jurisdiction Act, so could not apply within the queen's dominions; but the Company was domiciled in London. So it was necessary to alter the principal charter by means of a supplement agreed upon between the two parties.

Chamberlain had broached the question to Sir Robert Herbert in June 1897. He pointed out that the system of quasi-official directors (originally Abercorn, Fife, and Grey) had broken down and "even been made ridiculous," and that the clauses of the charter "which might have prevented mischief have been ignored or incompletely observed." Following the example of Pitt's handling of the East India Company in 1784, Chamberlain proposed to create a Board of Control to supervise the Chartered Company in all its operations; but this would have involved the expense of a new department of government, and its abandonment was due presumably to objections by the Treasury.

There could be no Board of Control, but the Supplementary Charter gave to the secretary of state and his subordinates most of the powers that Chamberlain had designed for his Board. It also, however, and this was no paradox, took one power away. The original Article 29, which provided for the appointment of life directors, was repealed; all directors were to be elected by the shareholders. On the other hand the new charter repealed so much of the original Article 10 as enabled the directors to legislate by ordinance. The order-in-council had already done this, but with doubtful legality, so the doubt was removed. The new measure forbade the Company to "establish or maintain any force of military police." This of course had been forbidden after the raid, but again with doubtful legality, since the principal charter expressly permitted such a force. That doubt too was removed.

Then came the provisions that upset the directors. As the Company had always held its cards too close to its chest, it was now required to forward to the secretary of state, within eight days of their passing, all resolutions, orders, and minutes; the secretary of state could annul any of them of which he disapproved. Any person authorized by the secretary of state was to have access to all the documents of the Company at all times. Finally any director, officer or servant of the Company who failed to comply with any requirement made by the secretary of state, in terms of the principal or the supplementary charter, was to be dismissed by the Company when the secretary of state so directed. This last was what the directors referred to as the "penal clause." They found it very offensive.[2]

The only weakness in these reforms was that they came about ten years too late.

The directors who suffered this humiliation were not all the same men as had been so carefully picked in 1889. After the raid Rhodes, Beit, Farquhar, and the duke of Fife had left the board; the first two, as we have seen, somewhat involuntarily. At this point there were only four directors. At the special board meeting on 2 May 1896, the demand for the resignation of Rhodes and

548 Rhodes and Rhodesia

Beit had been moved by Cawston. In February 1897 a correspondent whose name is not given reported to the latter what he had heard from "a very rich" and well-informed South African: that after the Enquiry Rhodes intended "to kick Cawston out . . . Everyone knows that Cawston did all the work with the Government at the beginning but Rhodes will never recognise this and he will never forgive him for having disapproved of Rhodes remaining a director."

Cawston resigned from the board in 1898. At first he would give no reasons. When he did, he said nothing about a stab in the back. He referred to the Committee of Enquiry, which had censured the board for not sufficiently controlling Rhodes. Cawston had had no chance to reply to this charge. Though Rhodes was no longer managing director in South Africa, his influence was undiminished. Cawston refused to remain in a position where he was exposed to the possibility of censure by a committee of the House of Commons.

So Cawston went; but Rhodes came back. Time and the indabas had washed some of his sins away. Sir Sidney Shippard (who had got the guns through, and held up Lobengula's letter), Rochfort Maguire (who had formerly been Rhodes's alternate on the board) and Lyttelton Gell completed the roster. Only Abercorn, Grey, and Gifford represented unbroken continuity with the past.[3]

Grey remained on the board, but he ceased to represent it in Rhodesia. He went to England on leave in July 1897. Six months earlier he had told Rhodes that, much as he would like to remain in Rhodesia, because of "other calls" he would not be able to do so. He vacillated about this for a time, but resigned while on leave. On Grey's suggestion Milner—another new man on the scene, high commissioner since May—appointed W.H. Milton, a Cape civil servant, as acting administrator. In November 1896, Grey then having his hands full in Salisbury, the Hon. Arthur Lawley had been sent to Matabeleland as acting deputy administrator; this post was made permanent when Grey left. In one way and another the raid was a factor in many of these changes.[4]

That was not the end of its consequences. Among them can be included some of the boundaries of Southern Rhodesia.

The Company's territory was not confined by the Zambezi. The difference between its claims north and those south of the river was originally that they had been based on different concessions; later, on conquest to the south but not to the north. Lobengula, however, as the letter he sent by Maund showed, claimed some territory north of the Zambezi. The Company might have argued that it succeeded to that claim, but in fact it based its case there on the concessions by Lewanika and those acquired by Alfred Sharpe and Joseph Thomson, patchy as they were.

In practice the boundaries in the north depended less on concessions than on negotiations with Portugal, Germany, and the Congo Free State. For this reason the Foreign Office had taken a special interest in the area, with which the Colonial Office did not directly concern itself. The British Central Africa Protectorate—Nyasaland, Malawi—was, for the same reason, a Foreign Office protectorate. Of the Company's territories, what came to be called North-Eastern Rhodesia was inaccessible from the south; hence the arrangement by which it was administered, if at all, by Sir Harry Johnston from Zomba, in return for a subsidy. After wrangling and recrimination, this arrangement came to an end on 30 June 1895. Rhodes then appointed Major Forbes as administrator there. Forbes administered from Zomba, where he went as Johnston's guest, until ill health forced him to resign in 1897.

The Foreign Office was more interested, now, in the North-West, because of the unsettled border with Angola. The Company had done nothing whatever to administer that area. To remedy the defect the Foreign Office submitted to the Colonial Office, on 24 December 1895, a draft order-in-council extending the provisions of the 1894 (Matabeleland) order to "the parts of South Africa bounded by the Portuguese possessions, the British Central Africa Protectorate, the territories of the German East Africa Company, lake Tanganyika." This would have introduced an administration: "the effect of the draft Order will be simply to add the northern territory to the southern, so that the northern will be under the general government of the Administrator, and judicially under the High Court of Matabeleland." And consequently, it might have been added, under Roman-Dutch law, and Cape statute law as far as applicable. But it will be noted that this proposal was sent to the Colonial Office only five days before Jameson crossed the border.

The two secretaries of state soon agreed to "postpone" ("pigeon-hole" would have expressed their intention) this draft order. They could not withhold Northern Rhodesia from the Company, as they withheld "the balance of the Bechuanaland Protectorate," because it had already been recognized as Company territory; but the draft order would be going too far. The raid had led to the appointment of an imperial officer to command the Company's police. It would not be practicable for Martin to control police north of the Zambezi also; communication was too difficult. Police north of the river should be commanded by a separate officer. As Sir Percy Anderson wrote from the Foreign Office,

> The conditions of the two territories are, moreover, widely different. In the northern territory there are at present but few whites . . . the natives are peaceful, except where they are in contact with the disturbed parts of the Nyasa district. A police force under Imperial control would have for its chief duty to prevent complications with the British Central Africa Protectorate, and with the neighbouring territories under the influence of Germany, Portugal and the Congo State. It would thus appear that the main control must be exercised for the present by this department, which administers the Central Africa Protectorate, and has to deal with questions affecting the foreign powers alluded to.

So the draft order remained in its pigeon-hole, and Zambia, like Botswana, owes its independence today largely to Jameson.[5]

The Foreign Office therefore appointed an administrator for the North-West. The man chosen was Hubert Hervey, who became involved in the fighting in Matabeleland before he could take up the job. He was mortally wounded in the Matopos, and as he lay dying murmured to Rhodes that he might soon be annexing parts of Jupiter to the British Empire. The next choice of the Foreign Office, on the recommendation of the Company, was Robert Coryndon, who had been one of the Pioneers of 1890, and was destined to a distinguished career in the Colonial Service. He went to Barotseland in June 1897.

There was still nothing that could be called administration north of the Zambezi. In 1898, when the new order-in-council for the south was pending, the Company proposed to the Foreign Office that it (the Company, with the secretary of state's approval) should appoint two deputy administrators in the north; two, because of the lack of means of communication between the two sides of the territory. The northeastern man was to be subordinate to the administrator of Mashonaland, the northwestern to the administrator of Matabeleland. In general, except for these subordinations, the Foreign Office found these suggestions acceptable.

For various reasons, including negotiations with Lewanika, nothing was regularized during that year. In April 1899 Milner explained to Chamberlain that the high commissioner still had "no authority whatever over anyone who is across the river. Neither has the Company any well-defined authority." He was not concerned with the North-East, as imperial supervision over that would have to be exercised from Zomba, but he welcomed the prospect of an order-in-council for the North-West. The government of that area rested on a different basis from the government south of the river, where two wars followed by two orders-in-council had given all powers to the Crown and the Company. North of the Zambezi the Company, in terms of its charter, possessed only such powers as were conferred by Lewanika and recognized by the secretary of state.

There were other reasons too why

it seems to me undesirable to give the Legislative Council of Southern Rhodesia any power to legislate for any portion of North Rhodesia. This is of importance, with a view to the future. The Zambesi is the natural northern boundary of what will some day be self-governing British South Africa. Beyond that river, we come to a tropical country, which will never, in my opinion, hold a sufficient white population to be a self-governing State. It must be regarded as a dependency, and governed on the principles which we apply to other tropical dependencies. But, if so, then it ought ultimately to be an Imperial and not a Colonial dependency. Company rule is, of necessity, transitional. In Southern Rhodesia it will, in time, give way to self-government. In Northern Rhodesia it may continue longer, but, if so, it should be under Imperial control, and the way should be left open to the establishment, when the Company disappears as an administrative factor, of government by Imperial officers, and not by Colonial officers.[6]

Two measures were accordingly drafted and discussed during 1899, the Barotseland-North-Western Rhodesia and the North-Eastern Rhodesia Order-in-Council, the latter not taking effect until 1900. Each territory was now to have an administrator, but while that officer in the North-East was appointed by the Company with the approval of the secretary of state, his western colleague was appointed by the high commissioner on the Company's recommendation. All ultimate power ih North-Western Rhodesia was given to the high commissioner. English common law, not Roman-Dutch law, was introduced into both northern territories. In the long run these arrangements and the factors of climate and communication proved effective restraints on the expansion of "Colonial" powers and institutions across the Zambezi.[7]

In this way, and by these stages, Southern Rhodesia came to be limited to the north by the Zambezi. There was never any question about the Limpopo as the southern boundary. The border on the east had been fixed in principle by the Anglo-Portuguese Convention of 1891, but it was only in 1898 that the last beacon was placed on the ground. The demarcation in some places cut through farms, and in others left farms granted by the BSA Company entirely on the Portuguese side of the line.[8]

The western boundary, however, like so much else, was affected by the Jameson Raid. The 1894 order-in-council had made the Company's territory border on Kgama's; subsequently, in November 1895, Kgama's "reserve" had been more narrowly defined, as part of the compromise between the Company's demand for the whole protectorate and the defence put up by the chiefs in England. There was now therefore a large area between Kgama's new boundary and the Chobe, and the Company claimed it. The Colonial Office argued that the Company's claim to that area could not be based on the 1894 order, which by "Kgama's territory" meant the territory as understood at that date. It could be based only on the proposal to transfer the whole of the protectorate, outside the reserves, to the Company's administration, and that proposal had been aborted by the raid: "the Company evidently fail to recognise that it is entirely owing to the action of their own officers that the compensating advantages which would have been theirs under the general settlement have not accrued to them." So the Pandamatenga road became the western boundary. This question generated more heat in the framing of the order-in-council of 1898 than all the most crucial constitutional questions together.[9]

One of these questions was fundamental. British colonists had never been slow in demanding control of their own affairs, and those of Rhodesia were no exception. We have seen them protesting and demanding from the beginning; the rebellion, however, gave a new urgency and a sharper edge to the protests.

Throughout the troubles the press maintained a continuous attack on the government, its policies, and its incompetence. The opinions of the readers were commonly more immoderate than those of the editors.

Within a few weeks of the outbreak the *Rhodesia Herald* summarized its causes: "it is simply the Government's own policy, stretching over many years past, which has unluckily brought about the situation." By "the Government" was meant, first, the local authorities (Lord Grey "has yet to do something to earn respect"), and, second, the directors in London. Rhodes himself was seldom attacked. His mistakes, like those of a monarch, were always attributed to bad advice: "Keenly and unswervingly as we look forward to the time when this country shall be a dependency in name only, to the time when the Government here shall be by the people for the people through the people of this territory, we all gladly concede this importance to the position of Mr Rhodes, and, failing him, will accept a period under the Crown direct." (*People*, as always, had a special meaning in Rhodesia.) Without Rhodes "the Company would appear to possess neither a vestige of intelligence nor life." Failing rule by the Crown, and if the alternative were the Company without Rhodes, the Rhodesians would form a republic. But the *Herald* took comfort: Rhodes would not retire from the Rhodesian scene.

The unifying theme running through all the complaints was the suspicion, even conviction, that the aforesaid "people" were merely pawns in a bigger game, pawns that the players would not hesitate to sacrifice. Looking back from July 1896 one now had second thoughts about the raid. It had shown "even the dullest settler that Rhodesia has never been regarded as an end in itself, but merely as a means to altogether different ends." So bitter was the feeling that even the name of "the Founder of our country" slipped into the charge sheet: "We are asking ourselves whether we are not in precisely the same position as the American colonies, and whether Mr Rhodes and his capitalistic and official allies are not merely a new version of the crushing oligarchy that blundered and bullied under the sceptre of George the Third." The grievances were specific, but for the moment we are concerned only with the general, and that was the demand for popular representation in the legislature.[10]

It was not only in the press that the demand was made. In October 1896, when Rhodes was expected back after his adventures in Matabeleland, a public meeting was held in Salisbury to arrange to present a united front to the uncrowned king when he arrived. The meeting was called by the Chambers of Mines and of Commerce, the Sanitary Board, and the Agricultural Society—a group as representative as could be found. The meeting, which was reported at great length, made the usual demands and supported them with a telling argument. Jameson had ridden into the Transvaal to help the Uitlanders to get their just rights. Surely then the Company could do no less for Mashonaland?

Rhodes came, was interviewed, and as usual defused the mine that seemed about to explode under him. The deputation was mollified, if not entirely convinced, by his replies. Most of the argument was about the railway, but in regard to

> legislative affairs, Mr Rhodes said he was cordially for the propositions in connection with having an elective system in the Council . . . They must look to the future, and that future would be a change from the present to a semi-responsible body; that was to say, certain elective members in the Council, and finally complete self-government. They could not expect to have a majority of votes in the Council until they were prepared to pay the expenditures . . . Two members for Mashonaland and Matabeleland was, he thought, a very fair proportion.

He meant two for each province; Rhodes was weak in English.[11]

Constitutional reform could not be expected before the rebellion had been suppressed, but the case was not allowed to go by default. On 15 June 1897 about five hundred people attended a meeting in Bulawayo; the chairmen of the Chambers of Mines and of Commerce and members of the Sanitary Board were on the platform, and a Mr. Scott moved a resolution which had been widely canvassed beforehand. The time had come, so the resolution ran, for the "inhabitants" of Rhodesia to assert their right to a voice in the government of the country, and for legislation to be "initiated in a legislative body sitting in the country." The demand was made, not in a spirit of antagonism to the Company, but because the time had come for a change, and the change would have to be in the direction of popular representation. One reason

> why Rhodesians were entitled to a voice was that Rhodesia was essentially theirs by right of conquest. If ever that was true of a land in the history of the world it was true of both Matabeleland and Mashonaland. Many of the people had laid down their lives or had been murdered in its acquisition and retention, and if anything in the world entitled a large body of men to have a voice in the government of a country, it was that they had fought for it and their friends and relations had died in its defence.

(Again it was the "people.") In case anyone should argue that the time was not ripe, there were references to the area and the population, and to the fact that representative government was given to Natal when its white population was only 8,000. The resolution was passed.[12]

A similar resolution was passed—unanimously—by a meeting in Salisbury the following day. The resolutions were two-pronged: the Council to have an elected element, and (with reference to the power then enjoyed by the directors) all legislation to be initiated within the country. On the same day as the Salisbury meeting the directors replied to an invitation by Chamberlain to submit proposals for changes in the administration of Rhodesia. Their reply included the points conceded by Rhodes to the deputation in Salisbury: two elected members for Mashonaland, two for Matabeleland, and a majority of official nominees. These proposals had now been accepted by all parties and were not further discussed.

Rhodes, in conceding the point to the deputation, had not merely succumbed to popular pressure. He intended Rhodesia to be an important, even the key, member of the South African federation for which he was working. Therefore, as he explained to Milner, it was "destined to pass through the usual stages of colonial evolution, leading . . . to the colony with responsible government, and the sooner it passes through them the better." He had also a more immediate motive, which Milner explained to Lord Selborne:

> Things are working up for a fine row in Rhodesia between the BSA Company and Martin . . . Rhodes is going for [a representative element in the Council] "hot and strong," avowedly with the object of strengthening his own position in any differences with the Imperial Govt. They may bully the Company, he says frankly, but they won't dare to bully a representative Council. At the same time it is quite obvious, that this representative Council will simply be Rhodes, even more completely than the Company is.

Though there was no difficulty about the representative Council, there was a great deal of argument about other points. The draft order-in-council was revised six times before the final text was gazetted in London, Cape Town, and Salisbury on 25 November.[13]

The basis of the document was the Matabeleland Order-in-Council of 1894; the early drafts were merely prints of that order with some old passages struck out and new ones inserted in italics. The provision of the earlier order for a Land Commission was of course omitted now. So was the old complicated hierarchy of legislative powers, since these were now to have a single focus. They were concentrated in the Legislative Council, as the executive powers were in an Executive Council, succeeding in their different spheres the old Administrative Council.

The appointment of Lawley as a deputy in Bulawayo had pointed the way to at least an executive separation of the two provinces. This was a Company matter to which the Crown was indifferent. The order permitted the Company to have as many administrators as it liked, provided that one was designated senior administrator. The term of office was normally to be three years; rules of succession in case of vacancies were laid down; for the rest, the office was governed by the terms of the 1894 order. Under the new dispensation Lawley became administrator of Matabeleland and Milton of Mashonaland, with the senior rank.

The office of deputy commissioner and commandant-general had been envisaged (the civilian part of it) by the 1894 order, but not created until after the raid. The new order changed the first title to resident commissioner and by implication separated the civil from the military office. The resident commissioner, as before, was to be paid by his imperial employers, was to inform the high

commissioner of all matters of importance, including everything relevant to ordinances and appointments submitted for the latter's approval, and had the
right to be supplied by the administrator with any information he requested.
He was also incorporated into the new system by being made a member of
both the Executive and the Legislative Councils, in each case with a voice but
without a vote.

The resident commissionership was a very important office, the indispensable instrument of imperial control, but it was no longer held by Sir Richard
Martin. At the end of 1897 he, like Grey, went home on leave. While he was in
Cape Town Milner wrote to Selborne: "I think, as I dare say you know, that if
he now retires with honour it will make Rhodesian questions easier to deal
with, and I fancy with a little pushing he would not be unwilling to leave Rhodesia. But of course if it is decided to send him back *I can work with him* all
right, though I should prefer a less tactless agent."

In March 1898 Martin duly sent in his resignation, and the Company in a
kind parting letter offered him a thousand guineas as a small token of its es-
teem. (For some reason, perhaps a clerical error, the cheque actually sent was
for a thousand *pounds*.) Since his departure from Rhodesia Col. P.T. Rivett-
Carnac had been acting in his place. In August Chamberlain offered the post,
provisionally at first, until the order-in-council took effect, to Sir Marshall
Clarke. The choice was a measure of the importance attached to the job;
Clarke had had a long and creditable administrative career which included
such offices as commissioner of police of the Cape Colony, and resident commissioner successively of Basutoland and Zululand. At the same time the
office of commandant-general was given to that well-tried officer, Capt. J.S.
Nicholson.[14]

The Native Department was another innovation since the order of 1894, and
was provided for by the new order. It was doubly authorized, because its organization was defined also in the "Native Regulations," put into effect by a
proclamation which was gazetted four days after the order-in-council. The provisions of the order for the appointment, removal, and salaries of magistrates
were to apply also to the secretary for native affairs, the chief native commissioners, and the native commissioners. The clauses of the 1894 order forbidding racial discrimination (except in certain cases), protecting Africans on
their land, and providing for their compensation if removed, remained unchanged. Another clause taken over unchanged from the old order to the new
was 88. After all that had happened it was decided to leave this as it stood: "In
case of a revolt against the Company, or other misconduct committed by a native chief or tribe, the Administrator-in-Executive-Council may impose a reasonable fine upon the offender" and the high commissioner could remit this in
whole or in part. The Company and the secretary of state must have been confident that there would be no more rebellions.

There were a few changes in the judicial system. The right of appeal to the

Supreme Court of the Cape Colony, provisional in 1894, was made definite now. The salaries of magistrates, like those of the judges, were fixed and could not be changed without the consent of the high commissioner.

The "Rhodes Customs Clause" was changed a little. In 1894 there was a clause providing that the duties imposed in Rhodesia should never be higher than those levied at that time by the South African Customs Union. Rhodes had wanted this restriction to apply only to British goods, and he had wanted South African products to be admitted free of duty. The Colonial Office had refused to sanction such heresies. In Article 47 of the 1898 Order Rhodes, with the (at first reluctant) help of his fellow-heretic Chamberlain, was able to achieve a little more. This time the Rhodesian government was prevented from imposing higher duties than those (now lower than in 1894) of the Customs Union on imports from "Her Majesty's dominions or Protectorates." We shall see what use was made of this.[15]

But all these matters were overshadowed by the creation of a partly representative Legislative Council. There were to be two elected members from each province, as promised. It was also clearly understood that the Company, which bore the financial responsibility, must nominate a majority of the Council. It was therefore to consist of the administrator, or senior administrator, who presided; the other administrator(s); the resident commissioner, who could not vote; five members nominated by the Company, and four elected. The life of the Council was three years, unless it were earlier dissolved, and the order included many of the other provisions usual in the constitution of legislatures. On the other hand the vital questions of the qualifications for the franchise and for election, of changes in constituencies and the number of elected members, and of the mechanics of elections, were left to the high commissioner to decide by proclamation.

The Rhodesian "people" had demanded also that all legislation be initiated within the country. This demand was met in that the old power of the Board of Directors to legislate by ordinance was abolished. Legislation was to be by ordinances passed by the Legislative Council, submitted to the high commissioner together with reports by the resident commissioner, and assented to by the former. If the high commissioner assented, he was to send the ordinance to the secretary of state, who within one year could dissallow it, either on his own initiative or at the request of the directors. The latter no longer had any direct veto, but the restriction of their power was formal rather than real. The administrators were their men, as were the five nominated members; as we shall see, the opposition of four elected members could do nothing against this monolith.

The Company, bearing the ultimate financial responsibility, quite rightly insisted that no money measure could be proposed in the Council except by the administrator, acting on the instructions of the directors.

As before, the high commissioner could legislate by proclamation, but an ordinance could repeal or amend a proclamation. The Crown could legislate by order-in-council, which could *not* be overridden by an ordinance. In case of conflict between them the ordinance would be void to the extent of the repugnancy. Thus the demand that all legislation be initiated in the country had not been entirely met; but the colonists had never proposed to abolish the legislative power of the Crown.[16]

The advent of popular representation was keenly anticipated, and the great questions of the day debated in the press and on the platform. The focus of the anti-government campaign during 1896, 1897, and 1898 had indeed been the demand for elected representatives, but it was the need to remedy specific grievances that gave force to that demand. There was the question of favouritism:

> the best tracts of land, the most extraordinary and impolitic concessions were flung as freehold and unconditionally at the heads of the highest bidders, or at groups thought to be influential at Court. Within three years [the best districts] had passed into the hands of financial groups, few of whose chiefs deserve the name of Rhodesians, and whose influence has been of the most disastrous character towards the *bona fide* settlers . . . Unlike the Willoughbys, the Beits, and other great lights of the Kafir circus, . . . the genuine residents of the country have not made even competences during the five years that have now gone.

The beneficiaries of the abuses being the "speculators" and "wire-pullers," there was naturally "widespread surprise" in Mashonaland when the names of the men accompanying Rhodes at the first indaba were published.

> Probably there are no two men in the entire community in their capacity as settlers who have less claim on the political confidence and respect of Rhodesians than Mr Colenbrander and Dr Sauer. That of Mr Stent being added to the peacemakers merely tends to make what is unsatisfactory ridiculous . . . We invariably see some notorious local speculator, company promoter or parasite bracketed with the official representatives of the Chartered Company.

(Stent's sin was to have reported some atrocities during Jameson's War.)

The *Herald* feared that Rhodes was looking at Mashonaland "through the glasses which Dr Jameson was wont to do, judging the entire public by the thin but constant stream of self-seekers and axe-grinders that visited . . . the old red building on Jameson Avenue."[17]

The Colonial Office at the time, like the historian afterwards, wanted statistics on the lavish grants to the axe-grinders and parasites. The answer it got from the Conpany was this:

> Since the occupation of Mashonaland and the conquest of Matabeleland, the Company has made grants of land on such terms from time to time as appeared

558 Rhodes and Rhodesia

most calculated to further the development of the country and benefit the Company. No "system" of making grants has been adopted, and it would be impossible, except at great labour and cost producing little result, to prepare a statement of grants made during the last eight years.

Some impression can be obtained from scattered sources. In April 1892 the Company undertook to grant to Sir John Willoughby 600,000 acres in Mashonaland on condition that he raised £40,000 for its development before selecting the land, and spent £30,000 on developing it within three years. By the following February he had taken up somewhat less than half that area. But to him that hath shall be given: we have seen him being presented with 8,850 loot cattle after Jameson's War. In August 1897 the Colenbrander Matabeleland Development Company bought Edmondson's Mashona Company. When the transfer was completed, Colenbrander's company would own 1,790 mining claims, 175,000 acres of "choice farm land," 27 town sites in Bulawayo, Salisbury, Umtali and Victoria, and a "working balance" of about £65,000, besides buildings, mills, etc. Its share capital was £279,520. Altogether, of 15,762,364 acres alienated by 1899, 9,276,222 acres were in the hands of companies.[18]

The grievance was not merely that favours were given to "parasites" and cronies. It was thought that Mashonaland itself was being sacrificed for the benefit of other communities. The evidence for this was found in the failure to advance the railway from Beira at more than a snail's pace. During the rebellion the very existence of the Mashonaland settlement was jeopardized by the absence of railway communication beyond Chimoio. Yet at the same time the line from Mafeking to Bulawayo was being pushed forward with all speed. It was easy to read a sinister meaning into the contrast. The extension of the Mafeking line was in the interest of the Cape Colony; a line from Beira to Salisbury would undermine that interest. Rhodes was anxious to return to Cape politics. Perhaps the Bulawayo line was part of an agreement between him and the British government to improve the position of both in the Cape Colony and at the same time to use Matabeleland in some strategic plan against the Transvaal. These were the bitter suspicions in September 1896, a time when nerves in Mashonaland were frayed.

Salisbury had its railway by the time the Legislative Council met, but that was not the end of the railway grievance. And there were others, not confined to Mashonaland: land titles, mining regulations ("that fifty per cent"), the official personnel, the "Asiatic menace," the shortage of labour, and others. They were all thrown into relief by the first election campaign.

As soon as the Southern Rhodesia Order-in-Council had been gazetted, the acting high commissioner, Major-General Cox, issued a proclamation defining the constituencies (the two provinces), the franchise, and all the minutiae of the electoral system. In almost every detail the proclamation followed the electoral law of the Cape Colony at that time, including the important amend-

559 White Politics

ments of 1887 and 1892. This meant that the law made no distinction of race: as in the Cape, the voter had to be a male British subject over twenty-one, to own or occupy premises worth £75 (or alternatively to receive a salary or wages of not less than £50 a year), and to be able to sign his name and write his address and occupation. As in the Cape since 1887, a share in tribally or communally owned property did not qualify (this change had been made in the old colony to remove most Africans from the roll without mentioning race). But the circumstances of Rhodesia led to two modifications of the Cape law. Ownership of a block of reef claims or of an alluvial claim was accepted as an alternative to the other property qualifications. Rhodes was anxious, too, not to discriminate against immigrants from the republics who were not British subjects. As the Company had as yet no power to naturalize, the alternative was offered of an oath of allegiance and of intention to reside permanently in the country. As in other constitutions, criminals and people of unsound mind were disfranchised. As in the Cape since 1892, voting was to be by secret ballot. Each voter had two votes, but could not give more than one to one candidate.[19]

The order-in-council and the proclamation precipitated the first election campaign. There were of course no organized parties, but some of the functions of parties were discharged by other bodies. In Bulawayo the Chambers of Mines and of Commerce agreed that each of these interests would put up a candidate and would support the candidate of the other. A gathering of mining men on 15 December unanimously chose Hans Sauer. According to the *Bulawayo Chronicle* it was "well known" that Commerce was likely to choose Charles Vigers (whom we met earlier at Fort Victoria and in the Tati district) but this was merely the editor's opinion, and wish, and was mistaken.

On 23 December Sauer and Vigers addressed a meeting in Bulawayo, with the mayor, C.T. Holland, in the chair. Sauer, who was received with "mingled greetings," set the tone for the whole campaign. He attacked the mining law, though admitting that it had its good points (it allowed the claim-holders to follow the reef underground). The Company's 50 per cent should be reduced, and there should be no favouritism. (No one in the audience said, "Who's talking?") Landowners must be given title, the Company had not kept faith with the Pioneers in this matter, and the survey regulations were "iniquitous." He wanted to keep Rhodesia out of the Customs Union so long as it was not self-governing. He gave his little scientific lecture, already quoted, on the congenital inferiority of the African, who "should be governed justly, but with a rod of iron (applause)." He wanted the Pondoland Act, by which anybody instigating natives to make trouble could be kept in gaol without trial. He wanted the hut tax of 10s. increased: that would make them work (applause). He was not a rabid opponent of the BSA Company, which in many ways was more amenable to pressure than the Colonial Office, and he admired Rhodes: "he was the greatest living British statesman of the day (applause). There was no other Englishman living who had done so much for his flag and country as Mr Rhodes. (A voice: and for himself). He took exception to that statement because Mr Rhodes had never made a single farthing out of his imperial schemes." Finally, Sauer was in favour of trial by jury.

Most of the campaign issues were there. Sauer's speech was well received and a vote of confidence in him was passed by a large majority. There was no such majority for Vigers, who was received with "mingled cheers and groans." He had much to say about himself, and in justification of his "standing for this great town and great country (laughter and interruptions)." When a vote of confidence in Vigers was put to the meeting the majority seemed to the *Chronicle* reporter to be negative, but the chairman declared the motion carried, "amidst loud booing, whistling, and a varied assortment of calls and howls." Vigers got the message; he withdrew his candidature early in the new year.

Nomination day was 25 March 1899. In the meantime there had been many more meetings, and sustained interest and excitement, in Bulawayo and elsewhere in Matabeleland. On some questions there was virtual unanimity among the candidates and the appropriate applause from the audiences: "the native must be made to work"; increase in the hut tax; "no law was severe enough for Asiatics. (A voice: British subjects were white, black, yellow, and tan. Mr. Lewis: Well, you're a good judge. Laughter)"; there must be no favouritism or nepotism by the Company; the Company's 50 per cent share in mining must be reduced; Rhodesia must stay out of the Customs Union; there must be trial by jury.

The question on which the voters were most clearly divided was the land question. E.St.M. Hutchinson attacked Sauer as the biggest monopolist in the country, and used Sauer's Township (on what were then the northern outskirts of Bulawayo) to illustrate his point. Sauer rebutted the charge: that land had been given by the Company to the "old hands" Fairbairn, Dawson, and Usher "for services rendered"; two of them had sold their shares to Sauer's company. Most of the candidates attacked the big landholders generally and impersonally. The locking up of land prevented settlement; Sam Lewis said that there were only 10,000 "people" in the country, where there could be 150,000. But this sort of charge cut the speculators and parasites to the quick. C.T. Holland, the mayor of Bulawayo and himself a candidate, represented a big company which he said would let land to settlers on reasonable terms. Walter Forbes, manager of White's Consolidated, hastened to tell the *Chronicle* of the terms offered to settlers by his firm. It was selling 1,500 morgen farms in the Makoni district for £150 each, 10 per cent of the price to be paid on selection, another 15 per cent within six months, and the rest in instalments over one or two years.

Some candidates felt strongly about the need to restrain absconding debtors and to tighten the insolvency law; there were naturally many voters who were unenthusiastic about these proposals. Sam Lewis, who called himself the candidate of the working man, and was treated by the others with a kind of patronising tolerance, had a scheme for light railways to all the mining areas. It would have required a contribution of £5,000,000 from the imperial government.[20]

The candidates nominated for Matabeleland on 25 March were Holland, Hutchinson, Lewis, and Sauer. On election day, 17 April 1899, the votes were distributed thus: Sauer, 1,187; Hutchinson, 1,007; Holland, 797; Lewis, 668. The first two were declared elected. The result was evidently determined as much by personalities as by issues, but did not confirm the *Rhodesia Herald*'s opinion of Sauer. Of the voters, 1,716 were polled in Bulawayo and 595 in the rest of the province.[21]

The campaign in Mashonaland differed in some respects from the one in Matabeleland. It may be said to have opened on 19 November, almost a week before the order-in-council was gazetted, with a meeting of the Farmers' Association in Salisbury. Two prospective candidates for the election addressed the meeting: W.E. Fairbridge, editor of the *Herald*, and C.T. Roberts, a mining man. Both concentrated, as was natural in the circumstances, on the land question, and specifically on the "locking up" of the land by the big companies. A graduated land tax was suggested as a means of unlocking it; this was to be aimed at the big companies and so graduated as to spare the small men. The crowd of three hundred at the meeting was thought to be a record for Salisbury. Both Fairbridge and Roberts offered themselves in response to numerously signed requisitions.

The voters had begun to requisition candidates long before the details of the new constitution were known. As early as August the people of Umtali were trying to recruit Jameson, but by the end of December his committee dissolved, Jameson having refused to stand. (In view of the abuses that the electorate wanted to see removed, it would have been interesting to watch Jameson as an elected member in opposition to the Company's establishment.) Martinus Jacobus Martin, a Melsetter farmer, then agreed to stand "in the farming interests." It is noteworthy that this Afrikaner, speaking to a largely Afrikaner audience, made it clear that he thought Jameson would be the best candidate: "having a very high opinion of the administrative qualities of the Doctor, he was confident that the mining, commercial and farming interest could not be trusted to a better man." He had himself been a member of the Jameson committee. If it were not true that Jameson had withdrawn, he, Martin, would stand down. He expressed his own views, which were chiefly "about large tracts of lands owned by syndicates," and about secure titles for bona fide farmers.

Before any of the meetings the *Herald* had tabulated what it regarded as the issues, general and provincial, major and minor. The major questions of concern to the whole country were: "Mining Ordinances and Regulations; Land

Ordinances and Regulations; Native control and adequate Police; Constitutional details; Finance (Customs and taxation); State aid or initiative towards industries (mining and agricultural); Internal railway system; Public works, roads, telegraphs, etc." The minor questions were partly mere riders to the major; so were some of the questions labelled "provincial," but at the head of the provincial lists came "Beira Railway rates" and "Cape Government and B. Co. Railway rates" respectively. The railway question was much more prominent in Mashonaland than in the other province.

Personal rivalries were rather sharper too. An important factor was the candidacy of Fairbridge, who as editor and founder of the *Rhodesia Herald* ought to have been the strongest single influence on the Mashonaland election. The *Herald* threw all its weight behind the Fairbridge-Roberts team. While it regarded the Melsetter farmer Martin as a satisfactory candidate in himself, it opposed his entering the lists because he would endanger the chances of one or both of its own favourites.

The centre of the opposition was the *Herald*'s rival paper, the weekly *Rhodesian Times*, and its founder van Praagh who had declared his intention to "smash" Fairbridge. It accused Fairbridge of frightening capital away from the country by his critical reporting, and at the same time of being a tool of the Chartered Company because, among other reasons, his press held the contract to publish the Government Gazette. In retaliation, Fairbridge asserted that if he "were not standing in certain people's way to make money unjustly and at the expense of this State and the investors in its valuable mines, he would not be deemed worth while such extraordinary onslaughts."

The *Rhodesian Times* gave its support to Col. Raleigh Grey, who entered the lists late because he had been on a visit to England. Grey, a former member of the BBP, a Jameson Raider, a second cousin of the late administrator, and now manager of the United Rhodesia Goldfields Company, faced the electors for the first time on 16 March. It would be hard to find anything in his views to distinguish him from other candidates. He was for breaking up large estates, for restocking the country (importing cattle), developing the mines (conditions for this were better than in the Transvaal; "this country . . . had a very fair chance of becoming one of the most productive in the world"); for reducing railway rates, increasing the police, and keeping Asiatics out; and "as to the natives it was admitted on every hand that they did not do enough work."

Much of Grey's speech was a defence against attacks that had been made on himself and his company. He pointed out several times that he did not have his own newspaper, so that his achievements had not received much publicity. In reporting the meeting, the *Herald* did not omit to say that when the chairman mentioned the name of Mr Fairbridge he was interrupted by "a perfect storm of applause," nor that Grey, at the end of his speech, "resumed his seat amidst some applause." The heckling was reported (" 'rot' and other signs of dissent") and, in particular, the voting on the motion of confidence. There were at least 250 people present. On a show of hands there were about thirty in favour—even, giving him the benefit of the doubt, perhaps forty—and the chairman declared the motion carried without asking for the *nays*. A vote of thanks to the chairman "was scarcely heard in the confusion of the audience making its rapid exit."

That this was partisan reporting soon became evident. The Fairbridge-Roberts team did not stay the course, because Roberts decided for business reasons to withdraw his name. The committee that had backed him immediately substituted W.P. Grimmer, an attorney who had supported Roberts and Fairbridge. He presented himself at the meeting on 25 March at which Roberts's withdrawal was announced. As a candidate drafted at short notice he had little to say about the issues, but he did strike one new note: he was not an anti-Company or an anti-Rhodes man; he thought that on the whole the colonists had been treated more generously by the Company than they would have been by the government of any other country.

That meeting was held on nomination day; the candidates nominated were Fairbridge, Grey, Grimmer, and Martin. On 17 April the voting was: Grey, 583; Grimmer, 522; Fairbridge, 499; Martin, 322. Thus the *Herald*'s reports had been misleading; the silent majority thought otherwise. Grey and Grimmer joined Sauer and Hutchinson as the people's representatives. Whether or not these legislators represented the "people," they certainly represented the speculators in land.[22]

The nominated members were the judge, Joseph Vintcent, and the four members of the Executive Council: Sir Thomas Scanlen, legal adviser; J.M. Orpen, surveyor-general; Townshend Griffin, commissioner of mines and public works; and H.H. Castens, then acting public prosecutor but subsequently chief secretary. The Legislative Council included also Milton, who presided, the other administrator Lawley, and Sir Marshall Clarke, who had no vote. At 11 a.m. on 15 May the Council was formally constituted, in the converted dining room of the Cecil Hotel; the inaugural ceremony at noon was attended by a large number of the public.[23]

The session would be a stormy one. All the problems that had long agitated the electorate now came before the Council, but few were solved to the satisfaction of the elected members or their constituents.

One problem which the Council did nothing to solve, though it had caused more altercation than any other, was the railway problem. The bitterness with which this had been discussed was due partly to the rivalry between Salisbury and Bulawayo. Salisbury was the capital, but Jameson's War had drained it of people and business; Bulawayo became a much larger and more prosperous town. Bulawayo was served by a railway from the south, which reached it in November 1897; Salisbury by a railway from Beira, which reached it in May 1899. The two lines were built over very different kinds of terrain and were financed in different ways. They differed in their relationships to Rhodes and the BSA Company.

It was natural that Salisbury should give a sinister interpretation to the difference in speed of construction. The first steps in the extension of the Bechuanaland Railway beyond Mafeking were being taken at the time of the Jameson Raid, though the troopers were not really gathered at Pitsani to protect the earthworks. On 7 May 1897 Major Panzera, protectorate government engineer, signed a certificate that the ninety-two miles of track from Mafeking to Gaborone were completed. The company had thus earned its subsidy, the first half-yearly instalment of which was paid on 7 November. The government was exacting in its requirements; the line was actually in operation far beyond Gaborone in May.

It was pushed on rapidly, often at the rate of a mile a day. It was avowedly a "pioneer" line, of light construction, running across river beds (not usually a great hazard in the protectorate); bridges, better track, and other improvements would come later. When Milner went up it for the inauguration his train covered the hundred miles before Francistown in eleven hours. For all that, it was a technological revolution. The *Bulawayo Chronicle* reported progress in every issue. On 23 January 1897, the "end of rails" was at 236 miles 40 chains from Vryburg (about 140 miles from Mafeking); on 13 February Palapye siding was reached, a fact that was not officially acknowledged until 1 July. Day by day the track was pushed on, and behind the railhead station buildings and other structures went up.

The economic consequences were important. The fall in transport costs and therefore of retail prices in Bulawayo was "unexpectedly sudden." On 27 February the *Chronicle* speculated that there might at that moment be wagons on the way up which loaded goods in December at Gaborone, at a charge of 110s. per 100 lb., and others which loaded at Mahalapye in February, at a charge of 40s. per 100 lb. Provisions then being sold by auction on the Market Square, from wagons arriving, were in many cases 50 per cent cheaper than they had been a month before. But would the influx of people not outrun supplies?

On 19 October a reporter went out to the railhead, then only half a mile from what was to be the terminus, and saw a construction train draw up at a siding.[24]

Plans had been made for the ceremonial opening by the high commissioner. Invitations had been sent to almost everyone of any distinction in South Africa, or connected in any way with the Chartered Company. Few accepted, but there was a fair sprinkling of notables from the colonies and the republics.

The ceremonial opening was on 4 November, four years to the day since Forbes's column had entered the smoking ruins of Lobengula's town. Milner, who had arrived the day before, was driven "a little way up the line, where the De Beers car and an engine came to fetch me. We steamed into the station to open the railway. An address was presented and I made a short speech . . . Big

565 White Politics

Beira railway, east of Umtali

Chief Mutasa
(Chifamba Usiku)

public banquet at 7.30. Lawley spoke very well. There were 400 people present, and it was a really wonderful turn out for a city just springing up in the wilderness." One of the visitors, who spoke at a later banquet, was H.M. Stanley, at the end of his career; Milner did not mention him in the diary.[25]

In the meantime the other railway was advancing so slowly that the movement was almost invisible from the offices of the *Rhodesia Herald*. In the circumstances of July 1896 it was natural for the *Herald* to write that "we no longer ask, but demand, the rapid construction of the Beira line to Salisbury." For the rest of that year the complaints about the railway, or lack of it, were frequent and outspoken.

Early in September the Chamber of Mines drew up a petition to the administrator. The extension from Chimoio, said the chamber, was begun in April, yet the earthworks had only reached Macequece (40 miles); bridges, culverts, and cuttings had not even been begun. The authorities had promised that the line would reach Umtali in May 1897—65 miles in thirteen months! And this was at a time when the Bechuanaland railway was advancing a mile a day. Capital for the railway had been offered but refused, in order to preserve the monopoly of George Pauling, who was also commissioner of mines and public works. The rates on the Beira railway were "usurious" and the handling of mails, held up at Umtali, "a disgrace."

Grey, who was in Bulawayo, went out to the Matopos to consult Rhodes about the petition. The effective answer to it came from Rhodes himself when he reached Salisbury in November and met the deputation representing the public meeting of the previous month. The present narrow-gauge trains, he said, could carry only twenty-five tons, and the maximum number of trains was three a day: total seventy-five tons. At this rate it was impossible to extend the line more quickly, but he promised that it would reach Salisbury by May 1898. If October 1897 was insisted on, no one would tender. He reassured them about the rates. Fairbridge was not satisfied with Rhodes's answer; with more sidings and more rolling stock, he said, the tonnage could easily be increased.[26]

The construction was not accelerated; it was slowed down. By November 1897 the trains were running only to Macequece; the tracks were laid to within six miles of the future Umtali station and the earthworks complete to the station. The railway however was not brought to Umtali; Umtali was brought to the railway. Pauling had seen that it would be financially impossible to build the line to the Umtali of 1896; the gradients would be steep and there would have to be, among other things, a tunnel under the Christmas Pass. He met Rhodes and showed him the problem on the spot. Rhodes summoned a public meeting and invited Pauling to speak. The result was an agreed decision to move the town for the second time. Pauling chose the site, a replica of the old town was laid out, new sites were given in exchange for old, and compensation paid. During 1897 Umtali moved. The first train steamed into it on 11 February 1898.

In the meantime traffic had been assisted by the removal of a bottleneck. The narrow-gauge line had originally started from Fontesvilla on the Pungwe. Between that point and Beira transportation was by boat on the river. But the Pungwe had shifting sandbanks; floods, as we have seen, sometimes deposited vessels miles across the flats; and transshipment at Fontesvilla was a slow business. The railway had to be continued down to Beira. This was undertaken by a new company, the Beira Junction Railway Company, which completed the line in October 1896, and the Pungwe bridge the following month.

Yet another body, the Mashonaland Railway Company, was set up in April 1897 to continue the line from Umtali to Salisbury. This company was spared the difficult terrain which had plagued the engineers and the financiers of the Beira-Umtali section, as also the restrictions arising out of agreements with Portugal; but at the insistence of the Mashonaland colonists, with the acquiescence of Rhodes, it was compelled to build to the standard South African gauge of 3'6". The first train reached Salisbury on 1 May 1899; the line was ceremonially inaugurated on the 23rd, eight days after the opening of the Legislative Council and one year after the date promised by Rhodes.

One job remained to be done. The flow of traffic was still severely limited by the low capacity of the narrow-gauge railway and by the change of gauge at Umtali. Money was found to enable the Beira companies to convert their lines to the broader gauge. The conversion was finished on 1 August 1900, from which date through trains ran between Beira and Salisbury.[27]

Behind this catalogue of developments lay the economic and political facts which explain their meaning.

The Bechuanaland railway ran through a British protectorate, which was why the imperial government agreed to subsidize it to the tune of £10,000 a year when the line reached Gaborone and double that sum when it had reached Palapye. The agreement was modified by another on 3 August 1894, providing that the railway company was to pay the imperial government 12½ per cent of its profits. By contrast, the Beira railway got no imperial support; it ran through Portuguese territory.

The Bechuanaland Railway Company was financed almost entirely by debentures, of which £1,300,000 had been issued by July 1897. A meeting of debenture-holders then agreed to the issue of another £700,000. The proposal was to use the entire line to Bulawayo as security for the whole two million, not to divide the line and its security at Palapye, up to which the existing debentures applied. There were no objections. At that time the net profits were £4,000 a month, which, even after interest on the debentures had been paid, was not a very big return on the investment. But it was not a loss, and it was not a significant figure; the line had barely reached Motshodi, and the real profits could hardly be expected until it was through to Bulawayo. The net earnings of the company for the year following the completion to Bulawayo were £98,160.13.5, an amount which Chamberlain however still found unimpressive.[28]

The finances of the Beira Railway Company were of a very different order. It had been created, as the reader will remember, by a very "curious financial method," the company "limited by guarantee"; the voting power, the ownership of shares, and the debentures (which alone, as in the other company's case, provided the cash) were distributed in different ways. The contractor was Pauling and Company, the firm formed by George and his brother Harry in September 1894; George being then about to take up several portfolios in the Rhodesian government, the chairmanship of the company was given to E.B. d'Erlanger, the young son of the banker. The original working capital of the railway company, with which 75 miles of track were built, had been provided by £250,000 in Series A six per cent debentures. In 1894 another £250,000 at the same rate, Series B, formed the capital for the next section of the line, from 75 to 118 miles. Most of these debenture certificates were given to Paulings to pay for the construction; but as Paulings needed cash, not paper, the certificates "were subsequently, though not without difficulty, placed for their account by Erlangers at the price of £60 per cent." That was the measure of the credit-worthiness of the company. When the £600,000 of Series C were created in April 1896, to finance the rest of the line to Umtali, they were taken up at a price of 65 by Paulings and the Chartered Company. The receipts of this railway company were "totally inadequate" to pay the interest on its debentures, which helps to explain its dilatory construction and its inability to finance the extension down to Beira. Yet, like the Chartered Company itself, it survived.

The Beira Junction Railway Company was created by what E.B. d'Erlanger called "the craziest piece of finance with which I have ever been associated."

First, the Beira Railway Company gave the contract for building the Beira-Fontesvilla line to the London and Paris Exploitation Company, which was controlled by Erlangers, Paulings, "and other interests." This company in turn promoted a limited liability company, the Beira Junction, to which it transferred the concession. The capital of this consisted of £62,500 in five-shilling shares and £250,000 in six per cent debentures. The ordinary shares were all given to the London and Paris Exploitation Company in consideration of the concession, as were also most of the debentures. The latter company entered into a contract, which included the transfer of a large block of shares, with Paulings to build the railway.

The reader will have noticed that up to this point many pieces of paper had been passed back and forth, but no money. The Exploitation Company, however, did pay Paulings £100,000 in cash, in addition to the shares. Then, "with the greatest difficulty our firm [Erlangers] was able to place £196,100 of the Beira Junction Railway Company debentures privately at 52 per cent of their face value with a substantial bonus in shares." The gullible public, however, "readily absorbed the shares at their par value, or even higher!" It may be assumed that it would not have done so if Rhodes, in answer to the protests of deputations, had publicly explained these financial details.

E.B. d'Erlanger concludes succinctly: "if the 168 miles of the Beira Railway to Umtali could not then carry the burden of a debt of approximately £6,500 a mile at 6 per cent, neither could the 35 miles of the Beira Junction Railway stand the weight of £7,000 a mile at the same rate of interest." The essential reason for the high cost of construction was the difficult nature of the country. These were the stubborn facts against which the demands and protests of Salisbury beat in vain.[29]

The Mashonaland Railway Company was an easier and a sounder business, but its birth was accompanied by the same juggling with pieces of paper that we have seen in the other cases. The share capital consisted of 450,000 one-pound shares, all owned by the Chartered Company as vendor's shares. The money, as usual, came from debentures, of which an issue of £1,150,000 at five per cent was credited to the Chartered Company, likewise without its paying for them. The railway company was to operate the line, but the Chartered Company had the responsibility for building it. It discharged this in the usual way by giving the contract to Paulings, who received the above-mentioned debentures and just under half the shares. The debentures were then, at a price of 90, unloaded upon the public, who paid for the railway; they were over-subscribed.

The Mashonaland Railway Company, being in good odour, was therefore able to go to the help of its poor brothers. In April 1899 it issued a further £900,000 debentures to the public and £50,000 to the Chartered Company. Some of this money was used for building bridges and stations on the Rhodesian section, but most of it was lent, on terms favourable to the lender, to the

569 White Politics

two Beira Companies to convert their line to the standard gauge. They could not have raised it themselves.[30]

The contrast between the two railway systems was visibly expressed in their rates. What the *Rhodesia Herald* called the "almost prohibitive tariffs" for goods between Beira and Umtali is exemplified by a general rate of £11 per short ton, £6 per short ton on flour, meal and grain, and £7 for a horse or mule. Even this was deceptive. In some cases the company insisted on translating weight into cubic measurement, so that Fairbridge was able to say that the real average tariff was £20 a ton. The first-class single passenger fare was £6. When the line had been completed to Salisbury the general rate from Beira to Salisbury (374 miles) was between £13 and £16 a ton, approximately the same as the rate from Cape Town to Bulawayo. In the opposite direction, Salisbury to Beira, half rates were charged, not so much to subsidize exports as because there were so few that the down trains were almost empty.[31]

There was a good economic reason why the tariff on the Bechuanaland line should be lower: it was built—585 miles from Vryburg to Bulawayo—at a cost of £2,900 per mile, less than half the cost of the other railway. The tariffs for most goods between Cape Town and Bulawayo (1,360 miles) ranged between £13 and £17 a ton. But there was also a special rate of £3.3.0 per ton for South African produce. This was a purely political factor, to which we shall return presently. There was nothing comparable on the Beira line, which had the further handicap of poor harbour facilities at Beira. Ships anchored in the roadstead there and unloaded into lighters. Shipping charges from Europe were higher to Beira than to Cape ports. Mainly for these reasons the Cape got the lion's share of the traffic. For the first three quarters of 1898 imports into Rhodesia through Beira were valued at £148,735; via Bechuanaland, at £410,813.[32]

The gap between the two systems, between Bulawayo and Salisbury, was an economic liability even before the outbreak of the war in October 1899, when the Boers cut the line south of Mafeking and so reversed the fortunes of the two towns. The closing of the gap was intended to be a part of a larger scheme, no less than the great Rhodes fantasy of a Cape to Cairo railway. As the imperial government would not help, mining companies in Rhodesia were persuaded to buy debentures in return for promised rebates on the railway tariff for their machinery. A line would be built from Bulawayo, through Gwelo, as far as the Globe and Phoenix mine (Que Que). The main line would veer north from Gwelo across the Mafungabusi plateau (where coal had been found), across the Zambezi, and over the Company's territory to Lake Tanganyika. In May 1899 Rhodes addressed the shareholders in the Cannon Street Hotel, "stoked up enthusiasm," and launched a scheme to raise £4,250,000 for the Bechuanaland Railway Company in debentures, the interest on which was to be guaranteed by the Chartered Company. It was the right moment; as E.B. d'Erlanger put it, "the success of the Rand had driven the gold fever to the boiling point," and Chartered shares stood at 72s. 6d. The first train had arrived in Salisbury. The *Bulawayo Chronicle* thought the speech "historic."[33]

The Bechuanaland Railway Company, in view of these proposed extensions, changed its name on 1 June 1899 to Rhodesia Railways, Ltd. On 30 May, in the presence of a large crowd of prominent people, the first sod of the Bulawayo-Gwelo section was turned. About fifty miles of earthworks had been completed when the war stopped construction by cutting off supplies from the south.

As is the way with railways, however, the economic factors in the construction and the rating policies of these lines were complicated by politics. The Beira railway was the outcome of a diplomatic and military struggle with Portugal, and continued to be an important influence on Anglo-Portuguese relations; but these need not concern us, as there was no important overt change in those relations for the rest of our period.

The politics of the Bechuanaland railway are a different matter. When the building of the line from Vryburg to Mafeking was begun, the company had made an agreement by which the Cape Government Railways were to operate the line in return for a fixed payment. When the railway was continued through the protectorate this agreement was superseded by another, which was signed on 28 May 1897, by Sir James Sivewright, for the Cape Government Railways, and Rhodes, as managing director of the Bechuanaland Railway Company. The Cape railways were to work and maintain the whole line from Vryburg to Bulawayo, in return for defined rates of hire for engines and rolling stock, and a proportion *pro rata* of overhead costs. Each railway administration could fix the tariffs over its own line, and the rates for through traffic would be the sum of these. That was quite straightforward, but there was an important rider to it: "no higher rate shall be charged on the lines belonging to [the Bechuanaland Railway Company] for the conveyance of Cape Colonial produce than are, for the time being, charged for the conveyance of the same on the lines of the Cape Government Railways." This was, or could be, equivalent to a preferential Rhodesian customs tariff in favour of Cape produce. It must be remembered that Rhodes was at that time hoping to recover a position in Cape politics, the Sprigg government was still in office, and Sivewright had been a minister in Rhodes's first cabinet.[34]

When the Legislative Council met in May 1899, there was little it could do about railway matters, though Chambers of Commerce and others were continuing to protest against the rates on the Beira line. The government did, however, introduce a bill to empower it, without reference to the Council, to execute any railway contracts it (that is to say the Chartered Company) might conclude in the future. All four elected members opposed the bill, but were outvoted.[35]

Nevertheless there was little fuss about this, because it was understood that the Council had little power over railways. The mammoth debate, and the violent popular opposition to the government, were about a closely related question, the customs tariff. The relation between these questions was close because both the customs tariff and the railway tariff were elements in the prices at which imported goods were sold in Rhodesia, and because they could be manipulated in relation to each other.

The customs question itself was a part of a larger question, the South African Customs Union. The original parties to it were the Cape and the Free State; Basutoland and the Bechuanaland Protectorate had joined later, and in 1898 a reluctant Natal came in, exacting as her price the reduction of the general *ad valorem* duty to 7½ per cent. Kruger firmly kept his republic out. The Customs Union was indeed a Rhodes scheme. Taking as his model the late German *Zollverein*, he built an economic as a step to a political union.[36]

Every candidate in the 1899 election wanted Rhodesia to stay out of the Customs Union. The country's only exports were minerals, and of what was consumed by the white population—strictly, the population that was in the market economy—a large proportion was imported. As there had to be taxation, there was general agreement that duties should be imposed on luxuries; for the rest, the fewer duties the better. The Rhodesian cost of living was high enough as it was.

When the government introduced its customs bill in June, the reaction of the elected members and of their constituents was bitter: "the iron has entered the soul of the people," wrote the *Bulawayo Chronicle*; "we asked for bread and we are given stones." What they were given was a tariff virtually identical with that of the Customs Union, except that the free list was longer. The general *ad valorem* rate of 7½ per cent, the rate of 20 per cent on an assortment including blankets, coats, carriages, and carts, and the special rates—18s.9d. a hundredweight on jams and confectioneries, 15s. a gallon on spirits, 4s. a pound on cigarettes, and so on—were identical in the Customs Union and the Rhodesian tariffs. Moreover, no duties were charged in Rhodesia on any products of countries in the Customs Union. Duties on goods in the special class were retroactive, that is to say imposed on articles already in the country, if in excess of the regularly imported quantities.[37]

The order-in-council had forbidden Rhodesia to impose higher duties on *British* goods than those levied by the Customs Union. The Customs Union tariff made no distinctions among countries of origin; nor therefore, for practical though not legal reasons, did the Rhodesian tariff, always with the South African exception. But Rhodesia pushed its tariff to the maximum permitted.

The helpless minority in the Council, the press, Chambers of Mines and of Commerce, and mass meetings in Salisbury, Bulawayo, and elsewhere exploded in anger. A meeting in Salisbury on 20 June, which resolved to circulate throughout the country a petition to the high commissioner asking him to withhold his assent from the customs bill, "finally broke up amid loud cheering and a tremendous demonstration to the elected members of the Council and the Mayor."

The objections were embodied in the petitions to Milner, who summarized them in his reply, sent through Milton. The first objection was to the virtual inclusion of Rhodesia in the Customs Union. Next, to the free admission of South African products, which was unfair to British exporters and also to Rhodesia, "since a legitimate source of revenue would be lost." Incipient local industries would be stifled. The views of the people had been disregarded. The newspapers added more points. The free admission of South African products, combined with the preferential railway rates, turned Rhodesia into an almost closed market for the Cape Colony. And of course there was objection to the taxation of existing stocks.

Milner disposed of most of these arguments. There had been a time-lag in Rhodesia—presumably because of the need for the high commissioner's assent—between the introduction of the bill and the date when the collection could begin. Traders therefore "took advantage of the notice thus given to them to introduce stocks far in excess of their ordinary requirements," and if those stocks could not have been taxed the revenue would have been greatly reduced. The argument about the popular will was brushed aside on the ground that all colonies at the same stage of development had been in a similar position.

The most difficult pill to swallow had been the free admission of South African, as opposed to the taxation of British, imports. This might perhaps have been avoided if the Rhodesian government could have set up all the machinery of a customs department at short notice. As it could not, it made an agreement with the Cape government to collect the duties at the ports. (This was the regular arrangement within the Customs Union; the collecting government kept 15 per cent and passed on the rest.) But the Cape also stipulated, as a necessary condition, that products of the Customs Union be admitted free. Hence the clause which caused most of the argument.

Some at least of the protests were against customs duties *per se*. If this seems an irresponsible attitude, it must be remembered that none had hitherto been imposed in Rhodesia. The *Chronicle*, while not going as far as that, was unfortunate in its choice of an example to illustrate the rise in the cost of living: a whisky and soda would now cost 1s. 6d. instead of a shilling.

Milner refused to withhold his assent; the ordinance came into force on 1 August. The Bulawayo Chamber of Commerce, supported by all the other chambers, then decided to contest the ordinance in the High Court. They lost the case. The Cape government duly collected the duties on Rhodesian imports coming through its ports; Bulawayo, Tuli, and Umtali were made ports of entry to Rhodesia; duties were collected on the large stocks of liquor and tobacco that had recently come in.[38]

These well-laid plans, however, went agley. Duties were collected at the

Cape for some two and a half months, at the end of which Boer commandos cut the communications between the colony and Rhodesia. Thereafter the only customs duties were collected at Umtali—except for the retroactive ones, which accounted for about half of the total for the eight months from August 1899 to March 1900. The preferences (railway and customs) to the Cape Colony became, for the time being, meaningless. The great fight put up by the Rhodesian Hampdens and Pyms had become almost irrelevant.

The fight put up by their official opponents had not. They had counted on £60,000 in customs duties for the eight months of the financial year that remained after 1 August; they got £40,591. Even the larger sum would have been a small contribution to the total expenditure of £694,099 for the year 1899-1900. The revenue for the year was £325,180, of which £77,220 was "Native Revenue," essentially hut tax. The government had budgeted for £40,000 in receipts from land sales; it got about £10,000. The deficit of £363,919 was of course made up out of the funds of the Company. In 1898-9 it had had to meet a deficit of £500,145. These figures explain, among other things, the fascination of the hut tax and the imposition of the customs ordinance in the teeth of raucous opposition.[39]

The Company could not afford such payments. When we last looked at its affairs, about the time of Jameson's War, we found them in a state of near-insolvency. Since then there had been some unusual expenses, including about £2,267,000 for suppressing the rebellion.[40] How did an almost bankrupt company manage this? In 1897 the Committee of Enquiry had demanded a statement of accounts for the preceding years. This should have been unnecessary, as the charter required the Company to furnish the secretary of state with the figures as a matter of course. Chamberlain asked for them on four occasions, and what he got called forth such comments as these in the Colonial Office in February 1898:

> These figures, while including some items which are not intelligible to me as they stand, are obviously incomplete, as other items are not included in them which are of the nature of general expenditure, notably "Suspense Account being cost of Police equipment, stores, etc.," £91,000, which reappears in the accounts of the next year still unsettled and is presumably connected with the raid . . . These figures take no account of Rhodesia Defence expenditure . . . Some of the balance sheet is mere guesswork, e.g. "By shares in Companies the value of which cannot at present be estimated"—*the estimate given however is not added in* . . . I cannot understand what the difficulty can be in furnishing such returns. Presumably there is none, but the Co. fear that if published the obvious deficits would frighten the public, whereas as long as the administration accounts are muddled up with a lot of other figures more or less hypothetical nobody will notice . . . The "summary of expenditure" 1 April '97—31 Jan. '98 is really the most miserable exhibition, and I wonder they had the face to send it in.

Though Fred Graham thought the returns more intelligible than some that he had seen, the comments of his colleagues were not unfair.

Several officials tried to make sense of the accounts. Let us take Graham's version: "it may be gathered that the annual cost of local administration (including Northern Rhodesia but excluding the Police and the telegraph construction) was about £158,000 for '95-6 and about £168,000 for '96-7 and will probably have been £178,000 for '97-8." As the police would now cost about £200,000, the annual expenditure would be not far short of £400,000. The largest source of revenue in 1895-6 was called "Land Fund" (£211,000), which Graham rightly "took to mean sales of land"; that is to say, the Company was paying current bills out of capital. Deducting that source, he found that local revenue would yield no more than £200,000 a year. He did not include 1896-7 in his calculations, as "of course that year was a very bad one." But these figures, on both sides of the balance sheet were "local" only; they took no account of

> the cost of the London and Capetown offices [or of] interest and sinking fund on the Debenture Debt which in the Balance Sheets is so mixed up with capital expenditure that it is impossible to calculate it. But assuming that the Company will have to issue another quarter million of Debentures bringing the total up to £1,500,000, the charge will be at least £100,000, which added to the local deficit makes £300,000 a year. Where is this to come from? So far as I can see the only thing they have to look to is their half share in the minerals. The nominal value of this share is about £1,000,000 and the mines will therefore have to pay 30% to meet the annual deficit, before any dividend can be paid to the Company's shareholders. It is quite clear that the stability of the BSA Co. depends entirely on the minerals being a gigantic success.

That was a forlorn hope, but the Company had saved itself before by ingenuity, resourcefulness and "curious financial methods," and would do so again.[41]

At the very moment when the officials were writing their comments on the accounts—February 1898—the Company was putting forward its next ingenious proposal: "in view of the large expenditure and the heavy financial responsibilities of the Company in connection with the administration of Southern Rhodesia, all future administrative expenditure not met by revenue, as also a fair proportion of past expenditure of the same nature should, in justice to the Shareholders, be regarded as a first charge upon the country, and eventually be constituted a public debt."

Graham's comment was that "this proposal is, like most of those emanating from Mr Rhodes, plausible but sketchy." It was very plausible. The Company was incurring great debts in the public interest, debts arising out of its operations as a government, quite distinct in nature from its operations as a commercial business. Why should the administrative debt not be removed from the Company's books and become a public debt, thus to be taken over in due course by the self-governing colony—or the Crown? This was the very question at issue twenty years later when the government was in fact about to be taken away from the Company.

The hawk-eyed officials, however, were not to be deceived.

> The position of Rhodesia is peculiar . . . First of all, the policy of the Company has all along been to conceal deficits on administration and to lump everything together. In the second place, they have already parted with a great portion of the assets of the country, the land is sold or granted away, the minerals are being worked on the half profit system and may realise the dreams of avarice, but it is not clear whether the Company mean to treat these profits as commercial receipts apart from revenue applied to administrative purposes . . . The approval of the Secretary of State is, I imagine, invited, so that, if the Company went to smash and the Imperial government took over Rhodesia, the public debt would have to be taken over as such by the Imperial government . . . Such approval would be treated as an indirect guarantee of the public debt, and would be so represented to the Company's shareholders . . . and debenture holders.[42]

The superficially attractive idea of distinguishing the administrative from the commercial accounts was in fact an illusion.

It was an illusion with reference to the past, but need not be so in the future. Henceforth there would be a budget presented to the Legislative Council; the items included in that budget might reasonably be treated as administrative. Attempts to confuse the public in the ways noted by the Colonial Office would have to be made under the unfriendly eyes of elected members. So they were not made. The deficit stood out in its stark reality.

But we must not be too hard on the Company. Milner, after opening the railway to Bulawayo, jolted across the country by mule-cart to Gwelo, Fort Victoria, Salisbury, and Umtali, and thence across the border to the other railhead. (Some wag whom he met on the journey asked him whether he did not think the Rhodesian roads were very good; adding, while Milner fumbled for an answer, "of course, seeing they have not been made.") Back in Cape Town, he wrote his report. Apart from the "Native Administration," of which he was critical—and the roads!—he found much to praise. Making allowance for the fact that the Company and its settlers had been in one province for only seven years, and in the other for four, and that for most of those years their efforts had been hampered by war, droughts, locusts and rinderpest, he thought that

> in view of all these drawbacks it is simply astonishing to see how much has been done to establish a regular government. Rhodesia has a complete system of administration, departmentally organised, such as you might expect to find in an old settled country . . . The expenditure for administrative purposes exceeds £600,000 a year . . . The fact that the Chartered Company spends this enormous sum upon the machinery of government seems to me to dispose absolutely of the charge that it is running Rhodesia as a mere commercial concern . . . The expenditure on government is only part of the colossal effort which is being made . . . The towns in Rhodesia, few in num-

ber, and still of inconsiderable size, are nevertheless marvellous products, considering how short a time they have existed at all. They are not mere rough mining camps, but civilised communities with a beginning of civic life, and, considering their extreme youth, quite a number of public institutions. The streets are well laid out.

And more in the same strain, including the fact that the Company had, without argument or delay, compensated the victims of the rebellion—those on the government's side of course—for their losses. It paid £360,500 under this head.[43]

Milner was writing at the end of 1897. Two years later he could have given a still better catalogue of achievements. One of the enactments of the Legislative Council in 1899 was an Education Ordinance, under which schools conforming to certain requirements were subsidized by the government. The essential requirements were: a sufficient number of pupils; the teaching of basic subjects; the teaching and the admissions to be undenominational; the school to be inspected by an inspector who was appointed under the ordinance; the inspector to approve of the qualifications of the teachers. Under these conditions the government paid half the salaries and half the cost of the "school requisites." It would also advance loans for the building of new schools in future. The inspector in his report explained that the schools were not undenominational but omni-denominational: the first half hour of every day was set apart for religious instruction by the clergy of all denominations, the pupils being channeled to the appropriate rooms according to their affiliations.

Almost all the existing schools had been built and were maintained by religious bodies, but most of the (in practice) white schools adapted themselves to the government's requirements for the sake of the subsidies. The ordinance did not classify the schools in racial terms—this would have required the secretary of state's permission—but it made special provision for "Native mission schools," and there was no question of interfering with the existing segregation. The mission schools were to receive subsidies of ten shillings a pupil, to a maximum of £50, provided that there were at least fifty pupils and that they received industrial training for at least two hours a day. In fact none of them was subsidized during the year 1899-1900. Of the white schools, eight were aided. There was one school (St. Cyril's, Bulawayo) that catered for both white and Cape Coloured pupils (only one white in 1899). Five unaided white schools existed, and the incomplete statistics show twenty-five mission schools.

The white schools were small affairs: a total of twenty-two teachers (only five certificated) and 339 pupils of both sexes. Their programs were arranged by Standards in accordance with the system in the Cape Colony. Only five of the eight schools went beyond Standard IV.[44]

This was a small beginning, but it was an important step in the organization of an educational system. The quality of the teaching is harder to assess. In 1898 Rhodes had asked E.B. Sargant, formerly of the British civil service and

577 White Politics

soon to be the organizer of schools in the concentration camps and the conquered republics, to report on education in Rhodesia. It was Sargant who proposed that the existing schools should be subsidized rather than a public system be set up *de novo*, and that religion should be taught by the different clergy to their respective pupils in the same school. The ordinance of 1899 was the result of his report. Sargant also, writing privately to Rhodes, gave some frank opinions of what he had seen. The Roman Catholic schools got high marks. He had the greatest admiration for Father Barthélemy, the Jesuit in charge of the Grammar School (St. George's) in Bulawayo. (He "is no ordinary Jesuit. I learn that during the war he buried a Wesleyan according to Wesleyan rites, and in other ways showed that he recognized the necessity of obliterating church distinctions in time of need."). Sargant had discussed the Anglican schools with the bishop, and the chief impression he had got was one of religious exclusiveness and a dog-in-the-manger attitude. The Dutch Reformed school in Bulawayo catered to children of the "transport-rider type," and Sargant ranked it high in terms of sacrifice by the teacher (a *predikant*) and of service to the poor.

> Mr. Groenewald is at once master of the school, minister of the church, and missioner to the Kaffirs, work for which our own [Anglican] church has an ecclesiastical organization of six parishes. His perseverence and cheerfulness are reflected in the faces of the children, but of course the instruction given is very slight. Imagine what it is to keep six separate classes at work in the same room (a juggler twirling his six plates is nothing to it), with bad desks, broken slates—I saw one in use not bigger than the palm of my hand—and other school material just as inadequate.[45]

Where schools belonging to churches were not available, they could be built and run by municipalities. Municipal institutions with all the ordinary functions had been introduced in 1897 in succession to the old Sanitary Boards. They had much to report by 1899 on sanitation, drainage, street paving and lighting, parks, poor relief, municipal support for public libraries and hospitals, and, as we have seen, on Native Locations. Electric light had been introduced into the towns.

Another municipal function, assumed in 1898, was the partial control of municipal police. After the rebellion the reorganized police, now called the British South Africa Police, were, like their predecessors, a paramilitary force, armed, mounted, capable of regular military operations, and therefore under the command of an imperial officer. That kind of force being inappropriate for the ordinary police work of a "bobby on his beat," an unmounted and unarmed constabulary, still under the commandant-general, was separated from the main police force for work in the towns. There was no reason why this unmilitary body should be controlled by the imperial officer, so in 1898 it was placed, for disciplinary purposes, under the respective local magistrates. The municipalities paid part of the cost and were consulted by the magistrates in the running of the forces. The constabulary numbered no more than 156—officers and men, black and white—and policed the towns of Salisbury, Umtali, Victoria, Bulawayo, and Gwelo.[46]

In July 1899, when political passions were at their hottest, the Bulawayo Chamber of Commerce found time to debate the important but uncontroversial question of Standard Time. There was as yet no uniformity in this matter. Bulawayo, the railway to the south, and telegraph offices throughout the country used Cape mean time, one and a half hours ahead of Greenwich; the Beira and the Mashonaland railways used Beira time, two and a quarter hours ahead of Greenwich; Salisbury and other Mashonaland towns kept their watches, "for business purposes," at two hours in advance of Greenwich. The chamber recommended that this last practice, based on 30° east longitude, be adopted for the whole country. The government did this in its own offices on 1 August 1899; the furthest it would go towards general enforcement was to say that this standard was "recommended for adoption by business men and private individuals."

Among the other civilized amenities introduced at this time was the telephone. The first lines linked police camps and their outlying forts; we heard of this during the rebellion. The first public telephone exchange was installed in Salisbury in August 1898, for thirty-seven subscribers. By 1900 there were exchanges in Salisbury, Bulawayo and Umtali, with a total of 235 subscribers, government, business and domestic.

One of the most important reforms was effected by the Civil Service Regulations introduced in 1898. These created a regular organized civil service, with rules governing appointment, promotion, dismissal, transfers, hours of work, conduct, leave of absence, pensions, and, for those holding magisterial office, law examinations (those of the Cape Colony). More than any other reform, this one marked the end of the happy-go-lucky Jamesonian regime.[47]

In the large perspective of history all these developments could become quite as important as the racial confrontations of the time, not to mention the parish pump politics of the white community.

But we must return to those. The customs bill had been the greatest generator of heat and polemics in the first session of the Legislative Council. By contrast the juries bill (for criminal cases) had an easy passage. For some time the press had been agitating for that great bulwark of the Englishman's freedom, trial by jury. It was thought necessary to dispose of the objection that there were not enough qualified people in Rhodesia to form the juries. Nowhere in the controversy was the real objection raised: that the juries would in fact be white, and would be biased against a black offender and in favour of a white one. Where the accused was of one race and the victim of the other that bias was inevitable.

When the bill came before the Council the elected members found that it made no distinction of race. They proposed an amendment to ensure that jurymen would be Europeans. Hutchinson took a very serious view of this matter, on general principles. This, he said, was the first measure they had debated in which white and black were treated as equal; a stand must be made. The officials defeated the amendment, thus making their own stand for a principle; but in practice the argument hardly mattered, since only qualified voters were eligible as jurymen.[48]

In spite of the prominence of mining questions in the election campaign, the first session produced no legislation on this subject. The comprehensive ordinance of 1895, with its amendments of 1898, remained in force. The absence of legislation gives a distorted reflection of the public concern. The press in 1899, as in previous years, gave a very large part of its space to detailed reports of mining operations. That Rhodesia would become one of the richest mining countries in the world was a universal assumption continually expounded in the press and from the platform. Hutchinson, for example, in an election speech, said that he was "satisfied that this country was one of the largest gold-bearing countries the world had yet seen." It was largely this hope that gave the lilliputian white community (estimated at 13,365 in 1900) the pretensions of a great nation in embryo. All other questions revolved round the mines. If Mashonaland suffered from lack of a railway, it was because the mines were held back for lack of machinery. If agriculture was not developed, it was because it was waiting for the mines to provide it with a market. The learned sub-editor of the *Rhodesia Herald* summed up the position in a headline: *Aut Output Aut Nihil*.

The output was not impressive, though more so than it had been before the rebellion. Whereas the total gold production from the occupation to July 1898 was only 6,470 oz., there was a dramatic increase thereafter: from August 1898 to May 1899, 52,214 oz.; for the years 1899-1900 (under war conditions), 55,071 oz.; and in 1900-1 (communication with the south being restored), 106,567 oz.[49]

The improvement was needed. Rhodesia lived largely on imports, the quantities of which, however, it is impossible to discover before the application of the Customs Ordinance in 1899. The Cape Colony gave returns of goods entering its own ports and destined for Rhodesia, and there were returns of imports through Umtali; these figures together amounted to £721,497 in 1898 and £615,097 in 1899, but do not include imports of South African origin. In the next few years the statistics become clearer. The values of the imports in the returns "represented the cost at the places where goods were purchased by importers. From enquiries made it has been ascertained that the average cost of importation, including agency, insurance, freight, harbour charges, railage, etc., but exclusive of Customs duty, amounts to 73 per cent of the invoice values given above." This percentage being added, the value of the imports on arrival in Rhodesia, but before payment of customs, was approximately: 1900-1, £2,100,000; 1901-2, £2,500,000. The real value in 1899 cannot have been much less.

What exports could be sent in return? In a deadpan understatement Milton wrote in his report that "the principal item in the export list is Gold," valued thus: 1900-1, £383,277; 1901-2, £640,588. As the production figures show, the value of this export would have been much less before 1900. No figures are given for the value of other exports, but in 1901-2 there were sent down the line from Bulawayo sixty-one tons of skins, hides, horns and ivory, and 545 tons of agricultural produce. "The most noteworthy item," wrote Milton, was "Agricultural produce, consisting chiefly of hay from farms around Bulawayo for which there is a good demand in Kimberley. This industry is capable of considerable expansion, the area of grass land within easy reach of the railway being very large." The adverse balance of trade was as big in its own way as the administrative deficit.[50]

Not many years later the Company, having sadly admitted to itself that Rhodesia was not one of the great gold-bearing countries, decided that its proper economic basis must after all be farming. By that time the chaos left by Jameson in the titles to land had been reduced to some kind of order. The reduction was made in the years after the rebellion, and in face of violent protests.

There was a general demand by farmers and by the great landowning companies for secure titles. In 1899 many or most had not yet got them, because of what Sauer in an election speech called "the iniquitous survey regulations." This meant the regulations of 1897, against which the Matabeleland Landowners' and Farmers' Association protested in a petition to Chamberlain. The other grievance of the farmers was the "occupation clause."

The Company's case for the Land Survey Regulations of 1897, and subsequent amendments, was clearly put by J.M. Orpen in his Surveyor-General's Report for 1897-8. The Company had granted to the Pioneers, to the Volunteers of 1893, and others, not farms but farm rights, physically represented by "certificates of right." The holder of such a certificate looked for the land he fancied and marked it with pegs in the ground. How could he know that it measured 1,500 or 3,000 morgen? How could he know that it did not overlap someone else's claim? To strengthen his own he then commonly employed a surveyor to mark out his boundaries. This was a private arrangement which took no account of conflicting claims.

The Rhodesian government consulted Dr. David Gill, astronomer royal in Cape Town, who explained that the only way to avert chaos was to make a geodetic survey of the whole country, and to fit the boundaries of farms into the triangulation so provided. The Rhodesian administration accordingly began that survey, and in consultation with Gill, the surveyor-general of the Cape Colony, and Milner drew up the Land Survey Regulations of 1897. These provided for the announcement from time to time in the *Gazette* of areas, each entrusted to a single government surveyor, whose boundary lines would supersede previously claimed boundaries if they were illegal or overlapping, and would provide surveyed farms where there had been no survey. Announcements of such areas, inviting all claimants to submit evidence of their claims, appeared regularly in the *Gazette*.

Land included urban land. In the townships there could be no question of a title without survey. Streets and stands were always professionally marked out. Landowners on the outskirts of the towns were making a good business of subdividing their farms into small agricultural lots or into suburban townships; these too had necessarily to be surveyed. Orpen could report that in the six months from October 1897 to March 1898 the number of such suburban lots surveyed was 1,176; of titles issued for urban "stands and freehold plots," 399. But in the same period only fifteen titles were granted for *farms*, apart from twenty-four to volunteers who fought in the rebellion.

The difficulty about the farms was not the survey. Much of Matabeleland had been surveyed, yet few farmers had applied for titles. This was because they objected to the "occupation clause." In 1894, after the "Victoria Agreement" farms had been pegged, the rest of the land was made available to purchasers on several conditions, one of which was bona fide occupation. Orpen reported in 1898 that "few farms have been sold under these conditions."

The government and the popular representatives fought over these questions when the land bill was before the Legislative Council in June 1899. The government, which is to say the Company, would have had an easier task if it had not been burdened with the heritage of Jameson's and Rhodes's slapdash methods.

The people's representatives wanted to get rid of, and the government wanted to retain, the occupation clause wherever possible.

> Dr. Sauer: At the meeting I have referred to Mr Rhodes emphatically protested that the Company never would impose the occupation clause into any grant where it was not specifically mentioned.

> Captain Lawley: My recollection is that Mr Rhodes on that occasion said that it was not intended to impose occupation conditions upon such grants as had been exempted from occupation, which is a very different thing.

A correspondent of the *Bulawayo Chronicle* doubted whether in any country occupation was made a condition of land that was purchased, as distinct from free grants. If land that had been purchased was forfeited to the government, and the government afterwards sold it again, that would be robbery.

Occupation was not required under the Victoria Agreement, or under the agreement with the Pioneers of 1890. But, with the usual loophole for special cases, it was required, and redefined, in all other cases. It was of course no bar to genuine settlers on the land. It was a serious obstacle to speculators in land, and the great fuss over this question is one more indication that in Rhodesia, as in other pioneer countries, land speculation was one of the colonists' main interests. "The occupation clause of the Land Act," said the *Chronicle*, "has rendered land valueless."

There was argument also over the government's insistence that "selection" meant selection with the consent of the administrator. This was not mentioned in the Victoria Agreement. Sauer would have less objection to it if it did not affect farms under that agreement, but he said that "the experience of Bulawayo was that invariably the Administrator did not approve of the ground selected, and the Company became possessed of information at the expense of the locator." Lawley quoted the Survey Regulations of 1894 to show that the consent of the administrator to the selection had been required since that date. Nevertheless, as Hutchinson said in a speech in Bulawayo, "Every man, with a few exceptions, holding land, did so still under a certificate of right, and in that certificate were generally those words, 'Provided that his farm shall have been located.'" Under the new law this would mean "with the approval of the Administrator"—who could refuse to approve after a man had been on his farm for years.

At one point in the debate on this bill three elected members—all except Raleigh Grey—walked out in protest. The excitement was exceeded only by that over the customs bill. The landowners, or land claimants, were defending in some cases genuine farms that they feared could be taken from them on some pretext; in others, speculative ventures on which they had counted to profit. The Company, at its wits' end for money, was trying to recover some of the land carelessly given away. The land was its best remaining asset. Sold to bona fide occupiers, it would increase the revenue both directly and, through general development of the economy, indirectly.

Milner's prophecy that "this representative Council will simply be Rhodes, even more completely than the Company is" was now, however, proved correct. The official majority had steam-rollered the bill through, but the unofficials evidently won the ear of Rhodes. On the ground that the bill omitted a clause which had been in the draft approved by him, and which provided for the payment of £5 per thousand morgen as an alternative to occupation, Rhodes decided that the bill must be disallowed. Milton, who had gone to England after the session, cabled to Rhodes, in the hope that he was not too late, pleading that failure to pass the bill would be "very serious"; to no avail. The land bill was dropped.[51]

Almost every vote in that session had been decided by the seven official against the four unofficial members. The unofficials made proposals of their own, such as Sauer's to petition the imperial government to "abrogate the franchise at present extended to natives." (The franchise was indeed colour-blind, but it is almost certain that in 1899 no black Rhodesian was on the roll. In 1904 there were forty-two black voters, but all were "Colonial Natives.") It was Sauer, too, who complained—not in the Council, but to the Chamber of Mines—that the blacks did not pay their fair share of taxation. He calculated that the whites were taxed at an average of £38 a head, whereas "each adult male native" contributed no more than five shillings. He adduced an argument which must be recorded: "When it is borne in mind that the entire cost of the police is necessitated by the native population, the proportion of the cost of government paid by them is ridiculous." In the Council Hutchinson had moved, with Sauer as his seconder, that all jurymen be white. But every motion by the elected members was defeated, as every motion by the government was carried, 7-4.

The *Chronicle* expressed the general opinion:

> We doubt if any Council has managed to raise more enmity in a given time than has been accomplished by the Government nominees in the present parliament. The reason, too, is obvious; they have not the interests of the country at heart, but only the benefit that can accrue to the Chartered Company . . . The whole country is up in arms, and the brute majority persists in forcing the measures down the throats of the people.

Sauer, addressing a meeting of five or six hundred in Bulawayo, said he thought that the sole reason for introducing the constitution had been to enable the government to impose taxation, justifying it by saying that the Legislative Council included elected representatives. But this was a farce. The nominees had always voted solidly; never once had any of them voted with the popular representatives. In no instance had the representatives been given enough notice to enable them to communicate with Bulawayo by letter; sometimes not even by telegram. He spoke of taxation without representation— because what they had could not be called representation. He spoke of the Boston Tea Party.[52]

The patriots seem to have taken no account of the fact that in the past year their country's revenue had fallen short of the expenditure by half a million pounds, that the Company had covered the deficit, and that he who wants to call the tune must pay the piper. But the patriotic oratory was important. This little white community of some 13,000 people had its epic, its heroes and honoured dead, and now also its struggle for political liberty.

It was a pity that the great debate should be tarnished by the persistence of a personal vendetta. At the end of the session Fairbridge petitioned the High Court to annul Raleigh Grey's election on the ground of "bribery, treating, undue influence and corrupt and illegal practices before, during and after the election." Grey immediately resigned, explaining that he had made investigations and found that in a few instances his supporters had been overzealous, and too generous in their "hospitality." He placed himself in the hands of the electors. Fairbridge brought the question to court by claiming costs, but the judge dismissed the case. Fairbridge in turn then resigned from the Town Council and the Mayoralty. Grey stood for the vacancy in the Legislative Council and was returned unopposed.[53]

The session was over. The passions appeared to have subsided; the *Bulawayo Chronicle* complained that the constitutional agitation was "flickering out." But to say that was to misinterpret the evidence. Political interest had only been diverted, temporarily, from domestic to external affairs.

Even as the "people" were shaking the country with their agitations, the press was giving an increasing amount of space to another matter. The high commissioner was in conference with Kruger at Bloemfontein; the obstinate old president denied the Uitlanders their just rights. Kruger made an offer, but Chamberlain accused him of dribbling out reforms like water from a sponge. As the weeks passed, news of "The Crisis" crowded other items, even the Dreyfus affair, out of the papers.

By September the question was no longer whether, but when.

The *Goth* with the Manchester Regiment reached Durban and disembarked the soldiers on Wednesday morning . . . Prominent people, fearing commandeering, are secretly leaving Harrismith for Natal . . . Many women and children are leaving Bloemfontein for the Colony, as it is considered a foregone conclusion that the Free State will decide to assist the Transvaal . . . Official quarters are abandoning hope of a peaceful settlement . . . The second battalion of the Gordons and the remainder of the 19th Hussars have sailed from Bombay . . . Eight hundred and thirty of the Irish Fusiliers sailed from Alexandria on Saturday for Natal.

On 3 October the *Herald* reported news from the Transvaal under the headline: Commandos of Guns for the Border: Pretoria in a Fever of Excitement: the Commandant-General takes the Field.

Every issue of the papers reported troop movements, and the readers were informed of the exact strength, composition, and disposition of the British forces in South Africa. It must have been with a sense of relief that they read the British government's reply to Kruger's ultimatum: "the conditions demanded by the Government of the South African Republic are such as Her Majesty's Government deem it impossible to discuss."

From 5 p.m. on 11 October 1899, a state of war existed between the British Empire and the Boer republics.[54]

NOTES CHAPTER 14

1 Elizabeth Pakenham, *Jameson's Raid*, p.262. The committee, appointed in 1896, had automatically dissolved at the end of that session; it was reappointed in 1897.

2 CO 417/253/19081, pp.495-505; Chamberlain papers, JC 10/8/1/17, Chamberlain to Sir Robert Herbert, 10 June 1897; CO 879/54/562a (the text of the Supplementary Charter).

3 RH Mss Afr. S 77, pp.148-51, 194, 261, 264, 269-70; CO 468/1, BSA Co. Report 1897-8, and CO 468/3, Co. Report 1898-1900 (lists of directors at the beginning of the reports, the same in both cases). The obituary notices of the duke of Fife and of Lord Farquhar in *The Times* (30 January 1912 and 31 August 1923) omit all reference to their associations with the Company. The Farquhar notice also glosses over (virtu-

ally denies) his financial delinquency, for which see Lord Beaverbrook, *The Decline and Fall of Lloyd George*, pp.203-4.

4 Rhodes Papers, Administrators, no.3, Grey to Rhodes, 11 January 1897; Grey Papers, Grey to Rhodes, 12 April 1897; CO 879/53/559, no.39, p.47; no.81 and encl., p.91.

5 CO 879/47/517, no.1 and encl., pp.1-2; no.92a, pp.75-6; no.117 and encl., pp.103-5; no.218a and encl., pp.196-8; no.221a and encl., pp.200-1; A.J. Hanna, *The Beginnings of Nyasaland and North-Eastern Rhodesia, 1859-95*, pp.245-64.

6 CO 879/53/559, no.172 and encl., pp.211-13; 57/574, no.114, pp.202-4; H. Marshall Hole, *The Making of Rhodesia*, pp.223-4.

7 CO 879/57/574, no.169 and encl., pp.260-1; no.172, pp.263-4; no.191, p.286; no.192, pp.287-8; no.305, pp.519-21. The last is the text of the order-in-council.

8 CO 879/52/552, no.82, p.91; no.91, p.99; no.103, p.106; no.122, p.133; no.140, p.141; no.143, p.142; CO 417/253, p.696.

9 CO 879/53/559, no.294, pp.328-9; CO 417/253/13576, pp.327-8.

10 *Rhodesia Herald*, 8 July, 29 July, and 16 September 1896.

11 Ibid., 28 October and 11 November 1896.

12 *Bulawayo Chronicle*, 19 June 1897.

13 CO 879/47/517, no.503, p.539; 52/552, no.15, pp.17-20; no.78, pp.86-8; Cecil Headlam, ed., *The Milner Papers*, vol. I, pp.110-11.

14 CO 879/53/559, nos.322, 324, 326, 327, pp.351-3; no.334, p.357; no.342, p.368; no.394, encl., pp.415-6, specifically Art.12; no.418, p.442; CO 417/253, p.191; 253/20302, pp.570-1; 253/23085, pp.585-7 (in which the Treasury could not resist the temptation to suggest that after five years the Company might be asked to take over the expense; the Company protested, and the Colonial Office did not pursue the suggestion); the Milner papers (unpublished), Milner to Selborne, 29 December 1897. The *Bulawayo Chronicle* (10 December 1898) regretted the implication that Rhodesia was to be split up, but rejoiced in the practical consequences of the executive division; the officials in Salisbury were "too provincial," the distances were great, and the single Legislative Council would hold the country together.

15 CO 879/53/559, no.394, pp.420-5; no.477 and encl.1, pp.486-9.

16 CO 879/53/559, no.394, pp.416-19; CO 417/253/2896, pp.42-8, 9975, pp.294-5.

17 *Rhodesia Herald*, 29 July, 2 September, and 16 September 1896.

18 CO 879/53/559, no.60, p.93; CO 468/3, BSA Co. Report, 1898-1900, pp.175-6; BSA Co. Out Letters, LO/3/1/7, pp.147-8; *Rhodesia Herald*, 25 August 1897. The Company's profession of ignorance throws a curious light on the list of grantees in June 1892— and vice versa.

19 *Rhodesia Herald*, 16 September 1896; CO 455/1, BSA Co. Government Gazette, 29 November and 2 December 1898. An order-in-council of 7 March 1899 enabled the Southern Rhodesian government to naturalize aliens (CO 417/253, pp.564, 622, and CO 879/53/559, nos.349, 356, 362, 404, 411, 413, 414, 424, 429, 435, 450, 469, 482).

20 *Bulawayo Chronicle*, 24 December and 31 December 1898, 7, 14 and 21 January, 4 and 18 March, 15 and 29 April 1899.

21 CO 455/1, BSA Co. Government Gazette, 4 May 1899; *Bulawayo Chronicle*, 29 April 1899.

22 *Rhodesia Herald*, 16 August, 9 November, and 28 December 1898; 12, 21, 25 and 28 March 1899; CO 455/1, BSA Co. Government Gazette, 28 April 1899.

23 CO 455/1, BSA Co. Government Gazette, 10 May 1899; *Bulawayo Chronicle*, 20 May 1899; CO 879/53/559, no.468, pp.484-5, no.472, pp.484-5; 57/574, no.144, p.243; G.H. Tanser, *A Scantling of Time*, p.210.

24 *Bulawayo Chronicle*, the whole period of the railway construction, and specifically 16 and 20 January, 20 and 27 February, 27 March, 1 May and 21 October 1897; Milner papers (unpublished) Diary, 2-3 November 1897; CO 879/52/552, no.47, p.51.

25 Milner papers (unpublished), Diary, 4 November 1897.

26 *Rhodesia Herald*, 29 July, 9 September and 11 November 1896.

27 *Rhodesia Herald*, 25 November 1896, 17 November 1897, 16 February 1898, 5 and 24 May 1899; George Pauling, *Chronicles of a Contractor*, pp.156-7; E.B. d'Erlanger, *The History of the Construction and Finance of the Rhodesian Transport System*, p.14.

28 CO 879/52/552, no.4 and encls., pp.8-9; no.41, pp.47-8; no.43, p.49; no.56, p.60; no.94, p.101; no.97, p.102; no.104, p.107; no.112, p.115; British Sessional Papers, 1894 LVII, 277; d'Erlanger, *Rhodesian Transport System*, pp.21-2; *Bulawayo Chronicle*, 19 August 1897; CO 879/57/574, no.36, p.62. The imperial subsidy was complemented by one of half the amount from the Chartered Company and the Tati Company.

29 d'Erlanger, *Rhodesian Transport System*, pp.12-14, 20; Pauling, *Chronicles of a Contractor*, p.142.

30 d'Erlanger, *Rhodesian Transport System*, p.15; E.B. d'Erlanger in Leo Weinthal, ed., *The Story of the Cape to Cairo Rail and River Route*, vol. 1, p.647; *Rhodesia Herald*, 2 May 1899.

31 CO 468/3, BSA Co. Report, 1898-1900, Appendix, p.286; *Rhodesia Herald*, 9 March 1898, 16 May, and 17 May 1899.

32 CO 468/1, BSA Co. Report, 1897-8, pp.336-9, 349; CO 468/3, Report, 1898-1900, Appendix, pp.281-2; CO 879/53/559, no.304, encl.4, p.336. The figures for imports via Bechuanaland would have come from the Cape Customs Department, so comprised only imports from overseas.

33 CO 468/1, BSA Co. Report, 1897-8, pp.402-3; d'Erlanger, *Rhodesian Transport System*, p.23; *Bulawayo Chronicle*, 6 May 1899; CO 879/57/574, no.27, p.35; no.36, pp.61-3; no.98, p.170; no.105, p.189; no.126, pp.231-2; no.145, pp.243-4. Chamberlain had advised the Treasury that H. M. government should not support the railway extension by loan, guarantee, or otherwise, unless the Cape Colony bore its share. Rhodes was unwilling, for political reasons, to involve the Cape government.

34 CO 879/52/552, no.39, encl., pp.32-3; *Bulawayo Chronicle*, 3 June 1899.

35 *Rhodesia Herald*, 10 June 1899.

36 Jean van der Poel, *Railway and Customs Policies in South Africa, 1885-1910*, pp.101-2.

37 Cape of Good Hope, Appendix 1, vol. II, to *Votes and Proceedings of Parliament*, 1898, G. 81/'98, pp.413 ff.; CO 455/2, BSA Co. Government Gazette, 4 August 1899; CO 468/3, BSA Co. Report, 1898-1900, Appendix, p.179; *Bulawayo Chronicle*, 17 June 1899.

38 CO 468/3, BSA Co. Report, 1898-1900, pp.137-9; *Bulawayo Chronicle*, 24 June, 5 and 12 August, and 9 September 1899.

39 CO 468/3, BSA Co. Report, 1898-1900, pp.13-14, 57-8.

40 This was the expenditure only to 31 March 1897.

41 co 417/253/3093, pp.52-69 (minutes are on pp.52-7).

42 co 417/253/3878, pp.83-8.

43 co 879/53/559, no.6, p.28; co 468/1, BSA Co. Report, 1896-7, p.37; *Rhodesia Herald*, 1 December 1897. On 4 August 1899, H. Wilson Fox calculated that the Company's cash reserves amounted to £634,481, and investments and loans to £1,317,733. The anticipated expenditure up to March 1900, plus various obligations in connection with railways, would result in a cash deficit then of £7,519. These figures were given to show how difficult it would be to convert the existing 6 per cent debentures to 4 per cent. (Rhodes Papers, Charters, Home Board, no.25, Fox to Maguire.)

44 co 468/3, BSA Co. Report, 1898-1900, pp.336-46, and Appendix, pp.228-31.

45 Rhodes Papers, Administrators, nos.18, 38 Encl.

46 co 468/3, BSA Co. Report, 1898-1900, pp.286, 297-8, 307 and Appendix, pp.221-7; co 455/2, BSA Co. Government Gazette, 21 July 1899, Government Notice no.160; co 879/53/559, no.4 and encls., pp.18-20; no.196, pp.249-52; no.428, p.448; 57/574, no.53 and encl., pp.111-12, the proclamation of 31 December 1898; *Bulawayo Chronicle*, 8 July 1899.

47 R.C. Smith, *Rhodesia: A Postal; History*, pp.150-2; *Bulawayo Chronicle*, 17 December 1898. The Civil Service Regulations (Government Notice no.6 of 1898) are given in the Company Reports; e.g. for 1898-1900, Appendix, pp.14-25 (co 468/3).

48 *Bulawayo Chronicle*, 17 December 1898, 10 June 1899; co 455/2, BSA Co. Government Gazette, 21 July 1899, Ordinance 4, Art.6.

49 co 468/1, BSA Co. Report, 1897-8, p.203; 468/3, Report, 1898-1900, pp.56, 251; *Rhodesia Herald*, 19 August 1896; *Bulawayo Chronicle*, 31 December 1898. For comparison, the gold output of the Witwatersrand for the month of February 1899 was 404,335 oz. (*Bulawayo Chronicle*, 11 March 1899).

50 co 468/3, BSA Co. Report, 1898-1900, pp.183-4; Report, 1900-2, pp.23-4.

51 co 468/1, BSA Co. Report, 1897-8, pp.74-87, 124-8; *Bulawayo Chronicle*, 23 July and 24 December 1898; 17 June 1899 (note that the land bill never became an act); 24 June 1899; 1 July 1899 (letter by J. Cameron); *Rhodesia Herald*, 15 June 1899 (the reference was to a meeting in Bulawayo in 1897); Rhodes Papers, Charters, Home Board, no.29. The Volunteers who fought in 1896-7 were offered farms north of the Gwaai Reserve, provided that they owned no other land in Rhodesia. For specimens of different kinds of title deeds, see H. Bertin, *Land Titles in Southern Rhodesia* (1912), especially pp.14-42.

52 Intercolonial Native Affairs Commission, 1903-5, Minutes of Evidence, vol. IV, p.150 (Q 35886-8), p.153 (Q 35954); *Bulawayo Chronicle*, 17 June, 1 July, and 12 August 1899.

53 Bulawayo Chronicle, 22 July 1899; *Rhodesia Herald*, 4, 16, and 22 August 1899; Tanser, *Scantling of Time*, pp.217-18.

54 *Rhodesia Herald*, 26 and 27 September, 3 and 12 October 1899; Headlam, *Milner Papers*, vol. I, p.558.

CHAPTER 15

War and Peace

The role of Rhodesia in the Anglo-Boer War was peripheral. It was never invaded. No battle was fought on its soil. But the war came nearer to destroying what Rhodes and the Company had built in the last decade than these facts might suggest, and its effects on the country were varied and far-reaching.

The most important reason for the war's destructive effect at long range was the cutting of one of the lines of rail and the throttling of the other. The Southern Rhodesian economy was peculiarly dependent on imports. Secondly, the black population, or much of it, was smarting under its recent defeat and punishment, and there were Afrikaners in the country whose kith and kin were at war with the British. Any of these latent dangers could become mortal if things went wrong—or continued to do so, for they certainly did go wrong at the beginning—on the battlefields to the south. Hence the vital importance to Rhodesia of the military operations, even in distant theatres.

As the war approached, many of the British military—not to mention the civil—authorities appear to have had little more understanding of what they were up against than Jameson, four years earlier, with his notion of half-a-dozen revolvers. In May, Lieut.-Col. J.S. Nicholson, commandant-general in Rhodesia, devised a plan by which, if war came, 1,400 men based on Tuli would invade the Transvaal, capture Pietersburg, cut the railway south of it and "exercise what was described to be a very decisive influence on the general campaign." The document was "dated prior to the Bloemfontein Conference," so presumably some time in May. From the high commissioner's office it reached the desk of Sir William Butler, General Officer Commanding. His comment is to the point:

> One reading of the scheme sufficed to show its imbecile nature, but that was not its chief fault. Once countenance such a proposal at a place some fifteen hundred miles distant from Cape Town, and with officers and men not in the least degree under my command, or answerable in any way to me, and the danger of having the Jameson fiasco repeated with graver results was evident. I put the paper aside as a thing too silly for official language to deal with calmly.[1]

But Sir William was to have his fill of "silly things" in the next few months.

The War Office at least assessed the situation in the north more realistically; its plans for Rhodesia were defensive. If the country were attacked, its defence would depend primarily on the police, and secondly on the Southern Rhodesia Volunteers, so named on 5 October when the units in the two provinces were given a common title. All were under the command of the imperial Commandant-General J.S. Nicholson, according to the system that emerged after the rebellions. In the belief that these forces were inadequate, the War Office in July sent some twenty officers on "special service" to see to the defence of Rhodesia.

This was before the last Anglo-Transvaal negotiations had broken down, and it was the kind of provocative act that Butler was anxious to avoid. As he was powerless to prevent other far more provocative acts, we may allow that the situation required a precaution of this kind. In view of their experiences in 1896-7 the choice of Baden-Powell as commander of this band of officers, and of Plumer as second in command, is not surprising. The task imposed on Baden-Powell was to raise two regiments of mounted infantry, to organize the defence of Rhodesia and Bechuanaland if war should break out, and to keep the enemy forces occupied, as far as possible, on those fronts.

The officers arrived in Bulawayo in August, and began recruiting at once. Each regiment was 450 strong, and included a large number of Cape Colonists, mainly from the Eastern Province, as well as Rhodesians. The officers had just two months in which to train these forces before hostilities began. Baden-Powell decided for various reasons, not all good, that the key point for him to defend was Mafeking. He would use one of his two units, called the Protectorate Regiment, for that defence. The initial difficulty about this was that Mafeking was in the Cape Colony, and that neither the Cape Government nor Sir William Butler would allow defensive preparations there; their object was to reduce, not increase, the existing tension. Baden-Powell therefore took his regiment down to Ramathlabama, seventeen miles north of the town, and over the border in the protectorate.

Just at that time Butler, unable to resist Milner's aggressive policy, resigned his command. His successor, Sir Frederick Forestier-Walker, was of Milner's persuasion. The obstacle being thus removed, Baden-Powell was able in September to move his force down to Mafeking. There he had under his command not only the Protectorate Regiment, but the first division of the BSA Police, some Cape police, and some local volunteers.

As soon as the war began Baden-Powell and his men were besieged in Mafeking. Though he regularly sent and received messages through the Boer lines, he was not in a position to exercise the overall command that had been conferred on him. Plumer therefore, with the other new unit which was called the Rhodesia Regiment, had to act independently and take charge of all operations north of Mafeking.[2]

The chain of command had become confused. In terms of the order-in-council of 1898, Nicholson as commandant-general was responsible to the high commissioner for all armed forces in Rhodesia and the protectorate. The War Office had now given the same responsibility to Baden-Powell, who in practice had delegated it to Plumer. When, as we shall see, still another force appeared on the scene under the command of that old Rhodesian hand Sir Frederick Carrington, it became necessary to amend the order-in-council so as to subordinate all to the commander-in-chief, Lord Roberts, instead of to Milner; and Carrington superseded the others in the local command. But none of this was very important. In practice each officer did his own job without getting in the way of the others.

In Nicholson's plan Tuli had been the base—a new Pitsani—for the invasion of the Transvaal. Baden-Powell designed it as the forward base for the defence of Bulawayo. On the day war was declared, the police detachment stationed there was joined by Plumer with his Rhodesia Regiment. Four squadrons of the regiment were deployed along the Limpopo from Rhodes Drift to the Shashi junction. For the time being the defence of the railway down to Mafeking was left to Nicholson.[3]

By comparison with what was happening elsewhere, the operations on those fronts were trivial. Their interest lies in their potentialities which never materialized.

The Boers, fearing an invasion from the north, placed the Waterberg and Soutpansberg Commandos, under Assistant Commandant-General F.A. Grobler, on that front. His task was to forestall invasion by destroying the railway line opposite him and by raiding right up to Bulawayo. Grobler and his subordinate, Assistant-General H.C. van Rensburg, being timid and unenterprising officers, the task was not carried out. Plumer on the other hand was under orders to act on the defensive, protect the border, amd not invade the Transvaal without a specific order. He never received that order. His opponents had their orders, but failed to carry them out. The fighting in that sector therefore amounted to no more than a few weeks of skirmishing on or near the Limpopo.

The skirmishing included one fight—it can hardly be called a battle—when a small convoy of wagons, bringing supplies to Plumer's outposts, halted on 2 November at Bryce's Store, about six miles north of Rhodes Drift. Van Rensburg's burghers, supported by Maxims and artillery, crossed the Limpopo, overwhelmed the escort at the store, captured some prisoners, and took possession of the supplies. They then attacked a small detachment of the Rhodesia Regiment under Lieut.-Col. J.A. Spreckley. There was a great slaughter of horses by the Boer artillery, but Spreckley's men were able to withdraw to Tuli on foot, abandoning all equipment except their rifles.

Bryce's Store was in the protectorate, but was the point at which the fighting came nearest to Rhodesian territory. After a little more patrolling and desultory shooting, the Boer force on 26 November fell back on Pietersburg. Its contribution to the war had been no more than an insignificant side-show.[4]

The operations "down the line," as they were headlined in the *Bulawayo Chronicle*, were of a different order of importance. The very first action of the war had been the successful Boer attack on the armoured train at Kraaipan, south of Mafeking. That town was then surrounded, and was besieged for seven months by forces under the command first of Cronje, and then of Assistant-General J.P. Snyman. While the ring was closing round Mafeking, burghers of the Marico and Rustenburg Commandos began the destruction of the railway to the north.

For more than eighty miles the line north of Mafeking ran close to the Transvaal border, so was wide open to attack. Reports reached Bulawayo, day after day, of heavy firing, of the arrest of gangers and the looting of their cottages, of the destruction of stations and bridges, at point after point up the line: Pitsani, Lobatsi, Ootsi, Crocodile Pools, Gaborone.

Nicholson had arranged for the conversion of engines and trucks, in the Bulawayo railway workshops, into armoured trains, of which there were eventually six. At the first news of the Boer advance on the railway he ordered all trains then running southwards, and all engines and rolling stock north of Mafeking, to be withdrawn towards Bulawayo.

The armoured trains then began their probing. On 17 October the line as far as Ootsi was reported to be intact. The next day there was a hot exchange of fire between the train and the Boer troops south of Crocodile Pools.[5] The trains, however, had soon to withdraw from that place (now called Notwani), from Gaborone and, on 27 October, from Mochudi (now called Pilane, the station for the town of Motshodi). On the 31st it was found that a culvert about two miles north of that station had been destroyed. It was the furthest point reached by the Boers; by 8 November the armoured trains were back at Mochudi. Between that point and Crocodile Pools a succession of advances and retreats continued for two months. It was in that neighbourhood that the railway and the Transvaal frontier converged, which is one of the reasons for the Boers' poor performance to the north and their tenacity to the south of it.

Their failure to capture, derail, or destroy any of the armoured trains is remarkable. Such trains were found to be death-traps at Kraaipan, on 13 October, and at Chieveley (where Churchill was captured) on 15 November. The train could of course be halted by destroying the line ahead of it and then, when it was stopped by the obstruction, behind it. Attempts to do this on the Bechuanaland line always failed because the teams on the trains had enough fire-power to hold the enemy off while the train retreated or the track was repaired. They seem always to have had timely warning of the approach of artillery. The trains were equipped with Maxims, were themselves impervious to small-arms fire, and were well camouflaged with green paint and boughs of trees. One Boer patrol rode towards one of the trains, in motion, to within 300 yards without seeing it. On the other hand the Boers were too slow. Snyman delayed responding to the first urgent call for help against an armoured train, because it came on a Sunday.

In December, as it gradually became clear that the Soutpansberg and Waterberg Commandos had withdrawn from the Limpopo, Plumer found himself free to move his force over to the railway line at Palapye, and to take the offensive against the enemy who had been faced until then by the armoured trains alone. Plumer's men were taken by rail to Mochudi, whence they advanced to Gaborone, which was reached on 14 January without opposition. It had been occupied by the Boers since 24 October.[6]

The next advance was slower; it took until 25 February to dislodge the enemy from his strong position on a ridge at Crocodile Pools. During that time the bridge over the Metsimasuane River had to be rebuilt under fire from Boer guns which had the range perfectly. All the guns available to Plumer, such as they were, were brought into use, the bridge was finished and the Boers fell back. By 1 March Plumer had reached Lobatsi. It is no discredit to him, with his small force and inadequate artillery, to say that he owed his success mainly to events elsewhere. On 15 February Kimberley had been relieved. On the 27th Cronje with the main Boer army surrendered at Paardeberg, and Ladysmith was relieved the next day. The forces that had been opposing Plumer now had higher priorities.

The continued siege and, if possible, capture of Mafeking was still high on the list. On the other side, the relief of Mafeking was Plumer's objective as he advanced down the line; he intended at least to cooperate from the north with forces coming up from the south for the same purpose. But, though he had a thousand men, his lack of guns prevented him from tackling a besieging army well provided with artillery. His final move towards Mafeking had to await reinforcements from the north.[7]

The siege and relief of Mafeking are a well-known story which will not be told again here, but some of the long-range effects of the siege have appeared in the preceding pages. The destruction of the railway, to prevent relief from the north, was one of the besiegers' objects. The repair of the railway and Plumer's advance down it were means to the opposite end, the relief of the town. The railway was a kind of jugular vein, if not of Rhodesia then at least of Matabeleland. The importance to that province of freeing it from the Boer grasp will be explained presently. The value to the Boers of the capture of Mafeking cannot be assessed as accurately or certainly, but one can point to the probabilities.

It was universally assumed by the Rhodesians that the fall of Makeking would be followed by an advance of Snyman's army up the line to Bulawayo. Whether it would have been would have depended partly on when the fall occurred. Strategically, the possession of Rhodesia by the Boers would have had little if any effect on the decisive operations of the war. As a bargaining counter it might have been a useful weight in the scale, already weighed down by the Cape government, the pro-Boers in Britain, the pressure of foreign governments, and other influences, in favour of a negotiated peace. Even as a bargaining counter it would not have been worth any great effort or sacrifice to obtain. But it might have been obtained without great effort—if Mafeking had fallen and Snyman's army had been set free for the job.

The defence of Rhodesia required, in the first place, men. The number available locally was small, and many of those available there were needed, and used, in more distant fields. This was especially true in Mashonaland, which was in less immediate danger than Matabeleland from the enemy. Recruits for the Rhodesia Regiment were drawn chiefly from the latter province. The Southern Rhodesia Volunteers were intended for home defence; most of the 250 SRV men who left the country to enlist in the Cape and Natal were from Mashonaland, where home defence seemed a tame prospect. The strength of the force during the critical months of 1899-1900 was therefore reported as: Mashonaland, 256; Matabeleland, 906. Most of these, however (150 and 800 respectively) were subsequently called out for active service.[8]

The objection to something like a general mobilization in 1899-1900, as in 1893 and 1896-7, was that it would bring the business of the country to a halt. But beggars could not be choosers. Of the two new regiments that were supposed to defend the country, one was shut up in Mafeking and the other having difficulty in holding on to its base at Tuli. Many of the police, also, were at those places; and still the armoured trains had to be manned and points in the protectorate garrisoned. So by the second week of the war Nicholson was sending sixteen BSAP and eighty-five SRV to Palapye, and Lawley (administrator of Matabeleland) was calling out 400 of the SRV in Bulawayo for a few weeks' training. On 27 November, for reasons which will be mentioned presently, all the Volunteers remaining in Matabeleland were called out for active service. By Christmas 584 of them, including seventy-five railway men, were serving in the protectorate.

Nicholson had had no alternative, but this arrangement upset the Colonial and War Offices for financial reasons. Plumer's Rhodesia Regiment had been at Tuli and on the Limpopo during those first two months. The Volunteers, in terms of regulations laid down in 1898, were paid ten shillings a day—twice the rate of imperial troops (and, for that matter, of the Canadian and Australian Volunteers). Why should not the Rhodesia Regiment—an imperial unit, in spite of its colonial recruitment—be sent to the protectorate, and the company use the expensive Volunteers to defend its own territory?[9]

The exchange was made, though for other reasons. Plumer had by then moved away from his Tuli base to the railway. Grobler's Commandos had retired and the Limpopo was in flood. Plumer and Nicholson agreed to send 100 more SRV as reinforcements to the protectorate (they left Bulawayo on 14 December), and to bring the rest home for disbandment (the first 150 reached Bulawayo on 15 December). In the meantime a "Reserve Force," numbering 200 by the beginning of December, was organized in Bulawayo to take the place of the "somewhat useless" Town Guard that had been raised by the Town Council. Even this Reserve had to be drawn on for the protectorate, but the squadron so used was brought back and disbanded in the middle of January.

By that time Plumer had taken his regiment over to the railway, moved down to Gaborone, and taken over from Nicholson the direct responsibility for defending the line. Plumer now wanted reinforcements for his regiment, but raising recruits for the duration was harder than drawing on the SRV or the Reserve for short-term assignments. In the middle of February the resident commissioner reported that Salisbury was having difficulty in raising 150 men for Plumer, and there was equal difficulty in Bulawayo. Most who were able and willing to enlist had done so, either directly into Colonial units or by transfer later from the SRV. Altogether some 12½ per cent of the total white population of the country was on active service.[10]

Milton, Lawley, Clarke, and Nicholson agreed in demanding imperial aid for the defence of Rhodesia, and in assessing the danger to the country in the last weeks of 1899 as grave. On 19 November Nicholson reported information coming from a spy at van Rooyen's farm and from other sources among the "Mangwe Dutch": on 3 December the Boers would attack Bulawayo, drawing support from their fellow-Afrikaners along the way; Plumer and Kgama would be attacked at the same time. This was false information, or at least false prophecy; the Boer force fell back from the Limpopo on 26 November. But its effect was decisive: on 25 November martial law was proclaimed in the districts south of Bulawayo, and a detachment of BSAP left for Plumtree to disarm the potential rebels; on the 27th the SRV were called out for active service, and more of them sent after the police; others went down the line to garrison Palapye and Motshodi. The Volunteers included a troop of cyclists, organized by Lieut. Charles Duly. They served as dispatch riders, earning some distinction for their work in the protectorate and later in the Transvaal.[11]

The "Mangwe Dutch" were disarmed—of twenty firearms and a thousand rounds of ammunition, and no incriminating documents were found. Lawley was able to name the "Dutchmen" who were to guide the invading force, but martial law and disarmament forestalled them. Martial law was then extended to the districts of Belingwe, Victoria, and Chibi, and many Afrikaner families were reported to be trekking out of the southern districts towards Salisbury. No doubt their motive was to avoid involvement as much as to have the protection of the courts. One of Nicholson's "agents" had reported from Mangwe by 8 December that because of the forces sent to that district the Boer plan of invasion had been abandoned.

The invasion scare may have had no solid foundation at all, but it was based at least on the boastings of the Greefs, van Rooyens, and other "Mangwe Dutch." They had been boasting too soon; the retirement of Grobler's force on 26 November made the idea of an invasion in December absurd. At the end of the year the War Office gave the Colonial Office the evidence that Rhodesia was in no immediate danger. But a week later the directors of the Company reported their latest information: the original Boer plan had been to invade the protectorate and Rhodesia in strength after the fall of Mafeking; the successful resistance of the town had so far prevented this; but when the tide turned against the republics the Boers would trek north and occupy Rhodesia. Its reconquest would be difficult. Reinforcements were needed now before it was too late.[12]

The Company undertook to organize a force if it were provided with officers and with guns. The nucleus of this force was intended, at first, to be a thousand Rhodesians. Nicholson at once objected: reinforcements for Plumer were the first priority, and these were proving very difficult to get. Though the Volunteers who were still serving with Plumer were given the choice of joining his regiment (at the imperial rate of pay) or of taking their discharge, and though most chose to join, Plumer would still need all the recruits that could be raised in the country. The Company then suggested that some of the BSAP could be included in the new contingent; which drew from the Colonial Office the comment that "the Company propose to get W.O. to pay for some of their police force!" There could be no Rhodesians in the contingent; the truth was that the bottom of the manpower barrel had been scraped.

When the War Office agreed, in January, to the principle of reinforcing Rhodesia, it stipulated that there was to be no recruitment from sources that could be used for the other theatres of the war. It was willing to invite the Imperial Yeomanry Committee to raise a thousand men, but there could be no others from Great Britain. A Company scheme to "make it known" in Canada that volunteers might present themselves in Cape Town came to nothing. The bright idea of recruiting in the United States was very promptly vetoed. In the end the War Office had to relent, and to include nearly two thousand Australians and New Zealanders in the force. At the last moment C Battery, Royal Canadian Artillery, was attached also. Sir Frederick Carrington was appointed to command not only the new contingent, but all the troops in Rhodesia; Nicholson became second in command of the police only. Thus was formed the Rhodesia Field Force, one of the minor fiascos of the war.[13]

In April, when the first detachments of the RFF were landing in Beira, the risk was taken of denuding Rhodesia of all remaining policemen who wished to go on active service; very few men under arms then remained in the country. But Carrington and his five thousand were on the way, and the Company hoped to kill several birds with that stone: "[the troops] are not only absolutely essential safety Rhodesia but will materially benefit country during inevitable period depression . . . Board of Directors also think prompt and successful measures on the part of Company will greatly improve its position with Imperial Government and bring credit to Administration and Officers." On which a Colonial Office comment by J.F. Perry was: "I will not say that it lets the cat out of the bag, but it gives a glimpse of the end of her tail."[14]

The danger to Rhodesia of being virtually unarmed was made much more serious by the breakdown or partial breakdown of the lines of communication.

We have had several occasions to note how close the precarious Rhodesian economy came to collapse when anything went wrong. Its survival depended on the working together of various factors, of which the two lines of railway were among the most important. Of these, the line from the south was cut by the Boers on the second day of the war. The economy of Matabeleland had depended on that line. From the day through traffic ceased, all imports into that province had to come through Beira and Salisbury. For Mashonaland that was the normal route, but the additional demands not only of Matabeleland but of the armed forces, including Plumer's and afterwards Carrington's, overloaded it.

The increased expense of supplying the army was an imperial matter. But the civilians in Bulawayo, by February 1900, were paying twice as much for most imported goods as they had been paying in September, and the *Chronicle* reported that "a certain article" (unspecified) which formerly cost 13s 6d. was now selling at 32s 6d. This, however, could be regarded as a hazard of war. Civilians must expect to tighten their belts. And the government helped them by accumulating stocks, and using the threat to open its stores to the public as a means of preventing profiteering. Basic foodstuffs had been stockpiled in Bulawayo during the last months of peace, and orders for imports continued to be placed in good time. The government by 20 January had bought seventy spans of transport oxen, and planned to buy more, to make sure of keeping Bulawayo supplied.[15]

The chief direct effect of the high cost of food on Matabeleland was its effect on the mines. As unskilled labour was paid in food as well as in money, many small mines were forced to close down. Unemployed whites, "chiefly of the miner and contractor class," drifted into Bulawayo. They were evidently not suitable material for the army, as Lawley and Nicholson could only suggest to Plumer that he "employ" some of them on his line of communication. The government provided relief works—brickmaking, and the building and repairing of roads, at five shillings a day—for the "genuinely unemployed." Yet, by 18 January, 130 men were eating the free lunches paid for by a public fund.[16]

By that time the government had been told that unless communications with the south were soon restored, all the mines in Matabeleland would have to close down. As this would have meant pulling the rug from under the Company's whole operation in that province, it had to be prevented. The government undertook to import, through Beira, the supplies needed by the Matabeleland mines and to deliver them by ox-wagon at Gwelo; this was done at a loss to the government of about £5 a ton. It was not easy to do: in January the narrow gauge line near Beira was under water for a distance of sixty miles, in some places to a depth of three or four feet.

When the supplies needed were, even in the widest sense, military, it was difficult to deliver them at all. At the beginning of January two consignments of supplies, including a million rounds of small arms ammunition, passed through Beira and reached Rhodesia safely. When a further shipment of half a million rounds was landed, the local authorities held it up and told the British consul that the first consignment had been allowed through by mistake.[17]

If Portugal had declared herself neutral in the war she would have had no option in the matter: military supplies could not have been allowed to go through to either belligerent. The British government had foreseen that contingency, in relation particularly to coaling facilities for the Royal Navy at Lourenço Marques. In spite of the secret clauses of the Anglo-German treaty of 1898, providing for the possible partition of the Portuguese colonies by the two powers, the approach of the Anglo-Boer War made it necessary for Britain to come to an agreement with Portugal. A treaty, which would have become public because of the necessity of ratification by the Côrtes, was fortunately not needed. It was enough merely to dig out of the Archives, and to reaffirm, the Anglo-Portuguese treaties of 1642, by which Portugal undertook not to declare neutrality in any of England's wars, and of 1661, by which England was bound to defend all the possessions of the Crown of Portugal against all enemies. These existing obligations were merely restated, with a few glosses, in the Anglo-Portuguese Secret Declaration of 14 October 1899.

Moreover, there was Article xiv of the Convention of 1891, as follows: "In the interests of both Powers, Portugal agrees to grant absolute freedom of passage between the British sphere of influence and Pungwe Bay for all merchandize of every description, and to give the necessary facilities for the improvement of the means of communication." Between them, the Convention and the Secret Declaration bound Portugal to practise a kind of nonbelligerence favourable to the British.[18]

It had to be practised with discretion if the Transvalers were not to be given an excuse to march on Lourenço Marques. Hence Sir Robert Herbert's minute on the passage of the first million rounds through Beira: "if these stores were sent through *openly* the Portuguese authorities will have been obliged to veto similar proceedings." They did. Not only ammunition, but railway building materials were detained as "contraband of war." It was because of the obstruction at Beira that Plumer had to make do with the ten field guns and twenty-eight machine guns, of all types, that were in Rhodesia at the beginning. The Lisbon government was, however, prepared to turn a blind eye, as long as such consignments were not sent too frequently, and Milner said he would try to "limit the number of occasions."

On 17 March Milner relayed a message from Sir Marshall Clarke in Salisbury:

Following received from Consul at Beira yesterday. Begins. Local authorities forbid passage of draught mules, waggons and carts, flour and cargoes of *Catalonia* and *Pondo*. Ends. This appears to me direct breach of promise given by Portuguese Govt. to H.M. Govt. and contrary to provision of secret treaty. Needless to point out that if decision is not reversed proposed military preparations in Rhodesia would become impossible and that country would be at the mercy of a Boer trek in force which is not an improbable contingency a couple of months hence. I have reason to suspect that the action of the Portuguese Governor at Beira is due to instructions from the Gov. Gen. at Lorenzo Marques who appears to have pro-Boer leanings. I think direct and stringent orders should be sent from Lisbon to Beira.

H.W. Just in the Colonial Office minuted that "the Portuguese Govt. have been told that unless the difficulty be removed without further delay the matter will become very serious."[19]

Six days after Just wrote his minute Roberts entered Bloemfontein; the turn of the tide made it less necessary for the Portuguese to consider Boer, and more necessary to consider British, susceptibilities.

Plans for the dispatch of the Rhodesia Field Force to Beira were then well advanced. The local governor's objection to wagons, mules, and flour suggests that it would have been difficult to get an army of five thousand through his port when the fortunes of the republics were still in the ascendant. The changed circumstances made him less obstructive. The Lisbon authorities having given permission, the RFF began disembarking on 11 April, and the process continued until 23 May. There was no hitch there, but there were other difficulties that could not be removed by diplomacy or goodwill.

Some parts of the operation were efficiently handled. "Doel" Zeederberg suspended his regular coaching business to place his whole organization at Carrington's disposal. Relays of mules were stationed along the road from Marandellas, where the troops detrained, to Bulawayo. The Canadian artillery and some Queenslanders were moved up the line quickly and, with Carrington himself, were officially welcomed at Marandellas on 27 April by the administrator, the resident commissioner, and other dignitaries. By 7 May they were in Bulawayo, and a week later had joined Plumer just in time for the final battle for Mafeking.[20]

The rest of the job was mismanaged. By 6 June, of a force of 5,229 men, only 367 had passed through Bulawayo, 384 were at that place, 2,939 were along the way between Beira and Bulawayo, and 1,539 were still in Beira. Half of the Yeomanry, having camped all these weeks in the malarial coastal belt, were sick.

This failure could have been foreseen. The narrow gauge line was being converted to the standard gauge. The change was completed from Umtali to Bamboo Creek, sixty miles from Beira, on 5 April 1900. As the conversion proceeded, the engines and rolling stock originally used on the Salisbury-Umtali line had to serve the longer stretch from Salisbury to Bamboo Creek, whereas the narrow gauge equipment, originally used between Beira and Umtali, now operated only on the sixty-mile section from Bamboo Creek to Beira. War conditions had prevented the delivery of more standard gauge engines and rolling stock until May, when the first new engines were landed. Therefore the narrow gauge trains delivered men and horses at Bamboo Creek faster than the other trains could remove them. The men succumbed to malaria and the horses died of horse-sickness.

As the Mashonaland engines were not suited to the steep gradients below Umtali, the shortage was compounded: the train reaching Umtali on 24 May had taken fifty-four hours to cover the 144 miles from Bamboo Creek. The numbers of men and horses reaching Marandellas at that time were respectively fifty-four and ninety-one per day. As postscripts to this pitiful operation it should be mentioned, first, that the Company had great hopes of recruiting settlers by offering farms to the members of the Field Force. The hopes were dashed: the Yeomanry lost interest because of their experience of fever at Bamboo Creek, and the Australians because horse-sickness was a "fatal objection." Secondly, sending 5,000 mounted infantry to Rhodesia, with a long stop at Bamboo Creek on the way, was a curious mistake to make. The War Office in December had warned that Rhodesia (let alone Bamboo Creek) was a country "peculiarly fatal to the health of horses." Final result: when the RFF was at last clear of Mozambique, it was sent down to chase raiders in the Cape Colony.[21]

The failure of the railways was matched by the obstruction of the posts and telegraphs. On the afternoon of 12 October the telegraph line from Mafeking to Bulawayo failed; after communication had been restored several times the line finally went dead at 5.50 a.m. on the 13th. Bulawayo was cut off from the world beyond Mafeking. Matabeleland as well as Mashonaland thus depended for communication on the telegraph line—which was often interrupted—to Beira. But Beira itself was a dead end; the cable running down the east coast touched only at Zanzibar, Mozambique, Lourenço Marques, and Durban.

Arrangements were therefore immediately made with the governor of Beira, who placed his tug *Ophir* at the disposal of the Rhodesian government. It left Beira on 14 October, carrying telegrams to Lourenço Marques, whence they were sent on by wire. The tug waited thirty-six hours to receive telegraphic replies with which it returned to Beira. The British and Rhodesian authorities then hired a vessel, the *Undine*, to ply between Beira and Lourenço Marques carrying both telegrams and mail. When this little ship broke down in February another, the *Formosa*, was obtained to take its place.

As a result of the breakdown of direct communication, the Rhodesian press and public received their news of the war more than a week late. Sometimes they were without news, though well supplied with rumours, for a fortnight. Buller's first disaster, for instance, happened on 15 December; on the 23rd the *Bulawayo Chronicle* could only report the rumour of a reverse "near Colenso." Official reports to Milner and to the High Command, and orders from them to Salisbury and Bulawayo, were similarly delayed. On 11 February Milner's latest information from Rhodesia was dated 27 January, which as he said was "altogether too long."[22]

The need to communicate through Beira had other consequences too. Milner had to reprove Nicholson for sending a telegram *en clair*, and to remind him that all his messages were read by the enemy. Civil and military authorities were especially sensitive about news of the Rhodesian Field Force and its movements (pathetically, as there was very little movement, and what there was could be observed in Mozambique) and about the flow of supplies. Lawley, from Bulawayo, urged in this connection that "the greatest care should be used and only those who are quite beyond suspicion should in any way be connected with it . . . All merchants here employ Dutchmen and nothing is safe. This town is full up with Dutch spies, and Dutch have an agent at Customs House. There are also several people buying up everything they can by way of provisions and shipping them to Delagoa Bay."

The government reacted to this situation by declaring martial law over the whole of Southern Rhodesia. Thus armed, it imposed a censorship on all telegrams, and on all mail for points in Mozambique, though not on mail for further destinations. Travel to points outside Rhodesia was made subject to permit.[23]

Two days after these drastic steps had been taken Mafeking was relieved.

During the seven months since the outbreak of war the Rhodesian civil and military authorities had feared a Boer invasion not only as a directly hostile action but also as a detonator of domestic rebellion.

Among the 13,000 whites in the country about a thousand were assumed to be Afrikaners. There was believed to be evidence that those in the southwest, at least, would rise and join an invading Boer army. Others were certainly spying for the republics. There were also Africans, whose resistance had been bloodily suppressed less than three years before the beginning of the new war. Would they seize this opportunity to rise again? Worst of all, would Boers and Africans make common cause against the British?

The short answer is that serious trouble could have been expected if the run of Boer victories had continued, and had included an invasion of Rhodesia; but both Afrikaners and Africans showed great fear of being found on the losing side.

Some of the Afrikaners, placing loyalty to kith and kin above such craven calculations, rode off to join the republican forces. The magistrates' reports counted fifty-three, of whom nine either gave up the attempt or were arrested on the way. Frederik Greef, having tried to disarm a guard at a railway bridge, was forbidden to return to his farm for ten days, and a few other suspected characters got similar treatment.[24]

When the tide of war turned in March, republican sympathies were safely stored away. The Dutch Reformed Church in Bulawayo joined in the rejoicings at the relief of Mafeking, after which a number of its members, led by the Rev. J.S. Groenewald, signed an address of loyalty to the queen, expressing also their hearty appreciation of the "protection and extended liberties" they enjoyed under the Company's rule. Among the signatories was W.H.J. van Rensburg, who had commanded the "Africander Corps" in 1896. These sentiments were not necessarily insincere. At the beginning of 1901, when Milton was alarmed because the Afrikaners at Enkeldoorn had been buying horses, Sir Marshall Clarke believed that the Rhodesian "Boers" did not want to fight on either side. But he admitted that they would give trouble if the country were invaded, or if the British met with a serious reverse in the south.

Though there might seem something anomalous about the collaboration of Boer and African against the British, the necessities of war make strange bedfellows. On 25 October 1899 a settler in Salisbury wrote to his father in England that "the Dutch traders have not been idle: they have been at work up North for months selling arms and ammunition. *Lee Metford* mind you!" This, under the eyes of a government that needed every rifle and cartridge that it could get, would have been surprising though not impossible. But the rumour is significant. Was there really a serious chance that the Africans would seize this opportunity to avenge their recent defeat?[25]

Everyone was aware of the possibility. As soon as the war began, native commissioners, administrators, and Sir Marshall Clarke himself summoned and addressed indabas all over the country. The causes of the war and the expected nature of the operations were explained, not—it need hardly be said—in a way that would satisfy an objective historian. The government wished to give its version of the events before other versions had time to circulate. It wanted to assure the Africans that they had nothing to fear, that they would be protected and could pursue their peaceful occupations as usual, and that they would not be called upon to fight.

The reception of this news varied. A few leaders who had fought on the government side in 1896-7 offered to do so again, but the offer was declined. There was an unwritten understanding between the belligerents that this was a white man's war and that neither side must seek or use African combatant support in it. Most who expressed opinions at the indabas were glad that they would not be called upon. Some ingratiated themselves with the authorities. Sikhombo expressed astonishment that the Boers had had dared to fight the queen, for "if a man tries to catch the sun, surely he will burn his fingers." Most, when asked if they had anything to say, remained silent. Kunzwi, at the Salisbury indaba, made the comment that "we are only goats and are being herded by the Government."

The young man who wrote to his father about the Dutch traders selling Lee Metfords was on surer ground when he said that "the Natives are leaving the mines here wholesale: we are 600 natives short at Glendarra where our mine is, and have had to almost stop work." Major Johnson, he said, feared that the motive for the desertion was not so much to till the lands as "to watch events." The early events of the war would have encouraged anyone who was plotting revolt. On 18 March Milton wired to Milner that "reports of native attitude [are] rather more unfavourable since my last telegram." But the potential rebels made no move at that time, and the tide had already turned.

Alarming reports from native commissioners were always shown to be unfounded or greatly exaggerated. Yet, in reading the reports, one senses that the Africans generally were "watching events," keeping their own counsel and keeping their options open. Any who gave evidence of a hostile attitude were dealt with under martial law, where that applied: four Africans were arrested on suspicion and "detained for a long period" in Bulawayo gaol. The unfortunate Karl Khumalo fell foul of the authorities again and was clapped into Fort Usher.[26]

The fear that Africans would collaborate with Boers worried the authorities rather more in the protectorate than in Rhodesia. In one way this is surprising. Africans in the protectorate had never been conquered or bloodily suppressed. Most of them owed their relative independence—meaning specifically freedom from annexation by the Transvaal—to British protection, and framed their policy accordingly. Kgama in particular never wavered in his support of the British side, even in the disastrous weeks of December. His offer to contribute troops was, for the usual reason, not accepted.

Lentswe however, during the early weeks of the war, sat on the fence. This was partly because a section of his people had been left, by the successive delimitations, on the Transvaal side of the frontier. A more important reason, in the eyes of the British authorities, was the presence of a Dutch Reformed mission in his town of Motshodi. According to Nicholson's information, the missionaries had from the beginning counteracted the advice of the assistant commissioner, W.H. Surmon, and of the British officers. The members of the mission were accordingly arrested and at very short notice removed to Bulawayo, except for one, Knobel, who as a suspected spy was lodged in Palapye gaol. The evidence against him does not appear; he was later allowed to join his friends in Bulawayo. They were well treated, and allowed to go anywhere they pleased except back to Motshodi.

If the missionaries had indeed tried to get Lentswe to support the Boer cause, their efforts failed. Boer attacks on Kgatla villages and tribesmen, old grudges such as the thrashing of Lentswe's father by Paul Kruger, and a shrewd calculation of the military prospects may all have played a part in the decision to support the British side.

Lieut.-Col. G.L. Holdsworth, Nicholson's chief of staff, who early in November took command of the SRV and the BSAP in the protectorate, decided to attack a Boer laager at Sekwani, or Derdepoort, just inside the republic and some forty miles east of Motshodi. This was believed to be the base from which the forces at Crocodile Pools and other points on the railway were supplied. Assistant Commissioner Surmon remained at Motshodi. His young colleague Jules Ellenberger accompanied, as interpreter, Holdsworth's force of eighty-five SRV and police. Though Surmon informed Holdsworth, in writing, that he objected to Lentswe's men being employed over the border, these men became involved. Holdsworth had asked them to remain on the protectorate side as a defence in case his force was pursued by the Boers on its return, and also to provide him with guides. Because of misunderstandings, the lack of discipline among the Kgatla, and various mistakes, which there is no space to examine here, Holdsworth called off his attack and retired, leaving the Kgatla to wreak some havoc among the Boer troops and civilians. A white woman was shot in bed and seventeen women and children taken prisoner. Holdsworth returned these under escort to the Boer side. Excuses and explanations were written, but the "massacre of Derdepoort" on 26 November became a subject of bitter recrimination by Afrikaner contemporaries and historians. Though Holdsworth's troops were mostly Rhodesians, no blame can be attached to them. But African combatants had after all fought on the British and not the Boer side.[27]

There was indeed one African enemy that the Rhodesian forces were fighting at this time, but if there was any link between this fight and the Anglo-Boer War it was a very tenuous one. The Korekore headman, Mapondera, whose claim to independence of Lobengula and of the Portuguese we noted at an earlier date, asserted his independence also against the Company in 1894. That was when the hut tax and the Native Department began to make themselves felt. An attempt to arrest Mapondera at that time failed. He withdrew from his old country and was not heard of again until 1900, when he returned to northern Lomagundi. According to Taberer he had "a following of some 30 or 40 men, composed of wanted murderers, criminals, and scoundrels from all parts of the country." This description may have been accurate, as these men preyed on their neighbours, seizing women, children and cattle, and killing or wounding various men. It was to arrest those responsible for one of these shootings that Capt. C.D.L. Monro left Sipolilo's, about thirty-five miles south of Mapondera's, with a police patrol on 7 June 1900. Two days later the party was shot at, found itself in a trap, and retreated. A month later Lieut.-Col. John Flint returned to the attack, but this time the police were supported by the 65th Coy. Imperial Yeomanry, whose slow journey to the front was interrupted by this little service. Mapondera was taken by surprise, his party broken up after suffering more casualties, and some captured wives and children rescued. One of Mapondera's former victims, Navuri, with his whole kraal, came out with Flint in the hope of settling near Sinoia.

Though Mapondera may have been the criminal that the authorities said he was, there was another side to his activities. When he attacked another police patrol in February 1901, he had 120 followers. When Capt. C.H. Gilson retaliated on 3 March, Mapondera's force numbered 600, and they were well armed. Though they lost at least forty-one killed in that fight, and were driven off, they were not effectively defeated. The Mashonaland Native Police retired without orders and forty-five carriers deserted. Mapondera was not captured. In July he and his allies raided Chief Valeta, killed eight men and carried off a number of women. The numbers of chiefs and sub-chiefs in the north and northeast who were freely, not under pressure, rallying to Mapondera was growing. Those who refused to do so were being called "white men's neph-ews." The reason for all this was the hut tax, which these rebels were refusing to pay.

But they were fighting a losing battle. In January 1902, after spies had re-ported Mapondera's whereabouts, Gilson went after him again, but failed to surprise him. By the following September he was reported to have taken ref-uge with a chief in Mozambique, and the Portuguese agreed to give him up if they caught him. They did not catch him that year.[28]

Mapondera was not representative of any large body of Africans. Most sub-mitted to the government without any apparent reluctance. When the Great Queen died in January 1901 there was another round of indabas at which the accession of Edward VII was announced. Mlugulu, of all people, at the meeting in the Matopos said that when they heard the news of the queen's death "they did not know how they could continue to exist." All the indunas held up their right hands and swore allegiance to the new king, while a Union Jack was un-furled. Sikhombo hoped that under the king's rule the beer, the cattle, the crops, and the rain would return to them.[29]

But this was not 1896; the Company's enemy this time was not the African but the republican Afrikaner. The consequences of this fact can be measured only in an impressionistic way, but the measurement is convincing. While it is true that the fury of the British South Africans against the republics, their ide-als and their supporters was unleashed in the Cape Colony as well as in Rhode-sia, the long-term effects were different in the two cases. In the Cape the Afri-kaners formed some two-thirds of the electorate, and those who had actively supported the republican cause were enough to tip the balance in a general election. In the course of years British sentiments therefore came to be muted in public. Not so in Rhodesia, where the "Dutch" were a small minority, and English the only official language.

The surrender of Cronje and the fall of Bloemfontein were followed by a se-ries of meetings all over the Cape and in parts of Natal, organized by the "Conciliation Committee." Resolutions were passed at all the meetings con-demning the "unjust war" and insisting that the peace terms should include the continued independence of the republics. These proceedings provoked counter-resolutions, demanding the annexation of the republics, passed at other meetins, summoned by "Vigilance Committees" throughout the Cape and Natal. Most of these meetings were held on 3 April 1900. They were not always composed as one might expect. At the meeting at Paarl a few days earlier half of the audience of 2,000 was Coloured, and most of the whites were "Dutch Africanders."[30]

The Cape Town meeting at noon on 3 April gives a sufficient idea of the feelings expressed. Twenty thousand people crowded into Greenmarket Square in ninety-degree heat. As the *Cape Argus* put it, the resolutions were brief and simple and the speeches would be equally so; no purple rhetoric was wanted. The mayor was in the chair and all the leading public figures of the pro-war persuasion on the platform. Sprigg moved the resolution. When someone shouted that he should put his hat on he replied that he did not need a hat while he was protected by this flag—the Union Jack floating above him. Few people could hear his speech, but when the resolution was put a trumpet sounded, and the square became a sea of waving handkerchiefs and hats. All verses of the national anthem were sung; after ringing cheers the crowd ended the proceedings—they were all over in a quarter of an hour—with "Rule, Britannia."[31]

Rhodesia was not afraid of "purple rhetoric." On 5 May twelve hundred people gathered at the Grand Hotel, Bulawayo, to express their "entire concurrence with and approval of the refusal of Her Majesty's Ministers to allow the South African Republic and the Orange Free State to retain their independence," a resolution which, as Hutchinson the chairman put it, would "strengthen the hands of Her Majesty's Ministers in abolishing for ever that hotbed of corruption and extortion, the Transvaal Republic." It was arranged that the motion should be moved and seconded by "an Englishman and a Dutchman," C.T. Holland and W.H.J. van Rensburg, the same who had commanded the "Africander" Corps in 1896.

Commandant van Rensburg, who "met with an enthusiastic reception," preferred to speak in Dutch, but agreed to begin his speech in English. He was "proud to stand there that evening as a Dutch-born Africander of the Cape Colony and a loyal subject to Her Majesty the Queen (cheers)." He referred to his natural difficulty in supporting a motion of this kind, but explained that "when he thought of what had happened from the time he was quite a youth until that evening, he said it was necessary and quite time it should be done (applause)."

The sins of the republics were recited at great length, and contrasted with the glory of the empire, loyalty to the queen, and "Bravo B.-P." The Grand Hotel was of course aglow with bunting, and, significantly, "in the centre the splendid Stars and Stripes blazed in company with a huge Union Jack." Americans had been prominent in the white population from the beginning; the sentiments engendered by the Spanish-American War were still strong; in 1901 the Rhodesian papers would carry almost as many black borders for the assassination of McKinley as for the death of the queen. Thus there was a touch of the pan-Anglo-Saxon in the emotions; but they were above all British and im-

Market Square, Bulawayo. Above, 1894. Below, about 1900

607 War and Peace

perial. After the singing of the national anthem at the opening of the meeting the whole crowd cheered. The speakers mounted the platform to the strains of "Soldiers of the Queen." The resolution was carried unanimously. In the belief that there must have been some dissentient, "there were cries of 'chuck him out,' but there was no one to chuck out"; then, "Rule, Britannia," "God Bless the Prince of Wales," and the national anthem again, "followed by a volley of cheers." A week later the same resolutions were passed unanimously at a meeting in Salisbury.[32]

These displays of imperial patriotism were rehearsals for what was to follow within a few days. The besiegers of Mafeking were at last driven off by a combined operation under Col. Bryan Mahon, bringing a flying column from the south, and Plumer, with his now enlarged force from the north. On 17 May these troops entered the town.

The reaction to this event in London, and indeed throughout the empire, is well known. But, for reasons that have been explained in this chapter, there was no other place under the Union Jack, except Mafeking itself, to which it meant as much as to Bulawayo. It seemed to mean an awakening from a bad dream; and at the awakening the dream was found after all not to be the reality.

On Saturday morning, 19 May, the *Chronicle* published the news in a special edition. Official confirmation had been preceded by rumour, and bets had been laid. But it was not till the notice was posted outside the *Chronicle* office at 10 o'clock that the bunting began to go up all over the town. Bulawayo's Market Square was not Piccadilly Circus, and the great news did not provoke anything like the mad "mafficking" in London. But if the celebrations were more orderly they were no less pregnant with meaning than the wild rejoicings elsewhere.

Those rejoicings were a sign of sickness in the empire; it had passed its apogee and, unperceived by contemporaries, had begun to decline. The mood of Mafeking Day would pass. For Rhodesia, in a sense, the mood did not pass.

In 1900 the queen's birthday and Ascension Day happened to coincide, and Bulawayo combined its Mafeking celebrations with both. The town was *en fête* from 9.30 a.m. to midnight. First, a military parade on the Market Square. Then, immediately after the parade, the official service of thanksgiving: "Praise the Lord, ye Heavens, adore Him"; the collect for Ascension Day; "Now thank we all our God," and three verses of the national anthem. The crowd of three thousand was then addressed by Judge Vintcent, in the chair; by the administrator, Lawley ("such a speech as has never been heard here before"), and by the mayor. They moved three resolutions, of congratulations to the mayor and people of Mafeking; of congratulations to Baden-Powell and his brave men; and thirdly to open a fund for the presentation of a memento to Baden-Powell.

Whole pages of the newspaper reporting these events were filled with an uninhibited sentimental patriotism that would sound unfamiliar to later generations; but perhaps less unfamiliar in Rhodesia than elsewhere:

> The people are moved beyond expression by the gallant defence of Mafeking, they recognise in it a tribute to the tenacity, the energy, the power of our race, and as if to give tangible form to the unity of the Empire, there were gathered together representatives of almost every nation or colony over which Her Most Gracious Majesty holds sway . . . It was a scene that no Bulawayan who took part in it can or ever should forget. There was something more than mere talking in the congregation, there was as it were an electricity, a pride of Empire, a belief in the Anglo-Saxon destiny, a belief that Britain has a God-given right to civilise the waste places of the earth.

The speeches about the glory of the empire and the brave defence of Mafeking were punctuated by "tremendous cheering."

> Cannon to right of them,
> Cannon to left of them,
> Cannon in front of them
>   Volleyed and thundered.

Mafeking's name "shall endure so long as records last of British pluck and British chivalry." In sombre contrast were the references to "the corrupt Pretoria gang." And "I am not here today," said Lawley, "to ask the why and the wherefore of actions by the Government of the Cape Colony" (hisses).[33]

In some respects the rejoicings were premature. No one suspected that the war would last another two years. Although a notice at the Post Office on 31 May informed the public that mails for the Cape, Natal, and overseas would now be sent via Mafeking, and the first passenger train for Cape Town left Bulawayo on 15 June, the movement of both passengers and goods by rail was severely restricted by military priorities. Passengers from the south could not travel to Bulawayo without permits which were sparingly given. Movement the opposite way was not discouraged; the *Chronicle* complained of an "exodus" from Bulawayo. As for imported goods, Milton reported that for a time only the barest necessities were allowed through. The restriction was maintained until the peace.[34]

After Mafeking the war moved into the Transvaal, and then turned into guerrilla war waged all over South Africa. Some of the Rhodesian forces, and Carrington's, were drawn into those operations. In August J.A. Spreckley, who commanded both E squadron of the Rhodesia Regiment and the whole corps of SR Volunteers, was killed at Hammanskraal. By the end of 1900 the Rhodesia Regiment had been disbanded and the Volunteers, except for those who enlisted in other units, had come home. The war was expected to end soon, but in its new guerrilla form it offered special scope for the talents of

609 War and Peace

such as Colenbrander, who in January 1901 was authorized to raise and command Kitchener's Fighting Scouts.

Though some Rhodesians continued to fight in this later phase of the war, the military aspect is of minor importance in the Rhodesian history of those years. The continued hostilities helped, however, to fan the flames that had burned so brightly at the relief of Mafeking. The same note of imperial patriotism continued to be struck, if less stridently, throughout the last two years of the war. The Cape government—a "hotbed of disloyalty"—was not spared. Pleas for moderation and magnanimity by such as Merriman became, when reported in Rhodesia, "ravings." Demands were made that English be the sole medium of instruction in the schools of the former republics, and the only official language throughout South Africa. Rhodes's original vision of his new country as an appanage of his old one, a field for Cape expansion and exploitation, had become blurred even before 1899—the raid had something to do with that—but it was the war that dissolved it.[35]

We have seen, however, that the war also dissolved some of the Rhodesian economy, thereby weakening the country's capacity as an independent unit among the South African colonies. After the relief of Mafeking the centre of interest in Rhodesia therefore shifted from the military operations to the restoration and development of the economy.

The basis of the economy was gold. Though the government saved the hard-pressed Matabeleland mines by delivering supplies to them at less than cost price, the mining industry continued to be restricted in both provinces by the military demands on the railways. It was restricted still more by the shortage of labour, which obsessed the public, press, and politicians almost to the point of overshadowing the war still raging in the south.

The evidence about the shortage of labour is conflicting, but it is safe to assume that the occasional general statements from official sources that the supply was adequate were mostly whistling in the dark. This is not true in relation to farm labour, though where the labour was "resident" there was always the difficulty that the heavy demand by the landowner came at the same seasons as the need of the labourers to attend to their own lands. But white farmers who "knew how to handle labour" were never short. The problem was in the mines, whose relative importance is shown by the figures for African employment in Matabeleland in March 1902: employed in mines, 8,137; in all other occupations, including farms, domestic service, railways and government, 6,197.

The work of the mines was not seasonal; labourers who worked for one month and then departed, having earned the money for their hut tax, were no solution to the problem. Sir John Willoughby complained that if the Bonsor mine took on 800 "boys," after a month there would be only two to three hundred left; and the Bonsor needed 600 continuously. Because these could not be had, the mine had by January 1901 been closed for eighteen months. While a mine was attempting to operate, expensive white labour had to be kept on whether it was being used or not.

The problem had become acute early in 1901 because various mines were then passing from the development to the crushing stage. "Development" might possibly be carried on with interruptions, but it was not economic to start a stamp battery unless it could be continuously supplied with ore. Willoughby's anxiety at this time was due to the fact that the Bonsor and Dunraven mines, belonging to his company, would be able to start crushing if they had the labour. Others had already started: the Selukwe, which for a time had been running at half strength because of shortage of labour, was again using all its forty stamps by September 1900; the Globe and Phoenix began crushing in August, and for some time after that was producing nearly half the gold mined in the country. At the time when this crushing began the Rhodesia (Bulawayo) Chamber of Mines estimated the need of African labour in the Matabeleland mines at 20,000, whereas the number actually employed was 3,500.[36]

In these circumstances extraordinary measures were taken to obtain labourers. For various reasons they were sought abroad. The domestic supply was thought to have been tapped to its maximum extent; labourers who worked near their homes preferred short contracts; most of the local labour was regarded as inefficient. The employers preferred Shangaans from Mozambique, who had long been the main constituent of the labour force on the mines. It was reported in 1902 that of 7,500 labourers "on certain mines on which careful statistics were kept, less than 700 were aboriginal natives of Southern Rhodesia."

The manager of the Labour Board in Salisbury accordingly went to Lourenço Marques and in September 1900 was reported to have engaged 2,000 men. Then the Portuguese forbade the emigration of labourers. The BSA Company turned to the British government for help, but was told that this was not the time for the Foreign Office to put pressure on Portugal; the Company could itself negotiate in Lourenço Marques. The minister in Lisbon did make enquiries, and was told that the Lourenço Marques district was itself short of labour; that the French wanted labour for Madagascar, and that their demand could not be resisted if a precedent were set for Rhodesia; and—how Senhor Arroyo must have chuckled as he added this parting shot!—that the Côrtes would not "be prepared to sanction the almost wholesale removal of the native population, the more as by so doing it would inevitably be considered here [in Portugal] as a sort of revival of the Slave Trade under cover of paid labour."[37]

In this impasse Milton, in consultation with Rhodes, decided in November 1900 to look further afield. He sent two agents to recruit men from British Somaliland, Abyssinia, and the Aden Protectorate. The first batch rioted on arrival at Beira, which is not surprising if, as was reported, the stokers on the ship had amused themselves on the voyage by telling the recruits that they would work underground in chains and would be enslaved for life. With the help of the Beira police the riot was suppressed and the party sent on its way. These men had been recruited specifically for two employers, the Surprise Mine and the Roads Department in Matabeleland. The statistics of the operation given by Milton in October 1901 reveal something of the arithmetic of labour recruiting: left Aden, 411; reached Beira, 385; left Beira, 349; reached Marandellas and Salisbury, 267; sent on from those points, 200 (156 to the Surprise Mine and 44 to the Road Party); wastage en route, over 50 per cent. After all that the judgment of the employers was that the Somalis were "useless," though the rest were good. One reason for the "uselessness" of the Somalis was that they had been promised that they were not to work underground, and the government held the mine to this promise.[38]

Other sources were tapped—Ngamiland, the Transkei, Northern Rhodesia; two officers of the Globe and Phoenix Mine travelled over seven hundred miles north of the Zambezi and brought back six hundred recruits, "a splendid type," on a six months' contract. The government sent no less an agent than Marshall Hole to Aden, but still the demand was not met.

As early as May 1900 Major Frank Johnson in an address to the Salisbury Chamber of Mines proposed the importation of Chinese coolies. In Rhodesia, as later in the Transvaal, this proposal was the beginning of a violent controversy. In the Rhodesian case, however, it had no sequel. The white Rhodesian "public" gave vent to its racial antipathies. Some of the mining interests pointed out that "if the gold mining industry is embarrassed and impeded there is likely to be very little 'public' to have an opinion." The British authorities insisted on safeguards against abuses. The Legislative Council passed an immigration ordinance in 1901, and, on Milner's insistence, an amending ordinance in 1902. The administrator was prevented by this from bringing the original ordinance into effect without the consent of the high commissioner. The consent was never given; no Chinese coolies ever came.[39]

The chief reason for this anticlimax is that on 18 December 1901, a *modus vivendi* was signed in Lourenço Marques. It concerned Mozambique labour for the Rand, and Rand traffic on the Delagoa Bay line. But the bitter cries of the BSA Company had been loud enough to ensure the insertion of "and Rhodesia" in Article 1, dealing with labour. Rhodesia, like the Transvaal, would pay the governor-general of Mozambique 13s. for each labourer recruited, and would do everything possible to discourage clandestine recruitment. The governor-general had the right to prescribe the route by which labourers must go and return. And the Rhodesian mines got their Shangaans.[40]

Thus the mining industry, and with it the whole Rhodesian economy of which it was the basis, survived. The statistics of production are the evidence of this:

	1899-1900	1900-1901	1901-1902
Stamps	175	255	295
Tons crushed	96,077	173,624	249,667
Gold, oz.	55,072	106,588	180,889
Value	£199,634	£383,277	£640,588

This was a fair achievement under severely adverse conditions. It was also a necessary achievement if the Company's and Rhodes's colonizing venture were to survive the war.[41]

In so far as the achievement was due to the increase in the supply of labour, that was essentially immigrant labour. Attempts to attract or force the Rhodesian Africans into the mines, however, continued and became more elaborate and ingenious. Yet these measures, unlike the arrangements for importing labour, were the expression of motives and drives that were more than economic.

One means of encouraging labourers, domestic or foreign, to go to the mines was the improvement of working and living conditions on them. There was room for improvement: low wages, irregular payment, lack of medical facilities especially on small mines, dirty and insanitary compounds. These evils were not general; some mines were much better than others, and the better ones seldom had to complain about the shortage of labour. But in 1901 the government appointed inspectors of native compounds, and by the following year was boasting that most of the evils had been eliminated. Yet it could be argued that this improvement was due less to the need to attract labour—it was the mines themselves that felt the need, and the remedy was open to them—than to pressure from the Colonial Office, which was being prodded by the Aborigines Protection Society and the various tenants of Exeter Hall.[42]

On the other hand the forceful methods of recruitment inherited from the past had a directly economic purpose, even if they failed to achieve it. The native commissioner, Malema, thought that the unrest among Africans, far from being a result of the war, was due entirely to "their being constantly harassed for labour." Assistant Native Commissioner Mullins, reporting on 26 February 1900, was candid: "After I received your order for 20 boys I sent messengers to collect them; when I found they could not get them, I went myself, and noticed directly they saw me, they cleared. All those boys I sent you were caught at beer drinks, this being the only way to get them." In the Ndanga district, a few months later, three messengers trying to recruit labour became impatient. They seized wives and cattle, flogged headmen, and killed fowls. For this the High Court awarded each messenger twenty lashes and two years' hard labour.[43]

The sentence was almost routine; there was no argument about it. There was a great deal of argument about the news complacently reported by the senior native commissioner, Salisbury, in June 1900: that native commissioners on tour constantly brought before chiefs and people the advantages of obtaining money by labour, and that the people were encouraged to tell the NCS which kind of labour—even which mine—they preferred. This sounded too much like the old ways for Chamberlain's liking, and he said so; yet, a year later, it was reported that the native commissioners were still using "direct influence" to obtain labour. In October 1901 Milton was told to instruct them to avoid taking part either directly or indirectly in the recruiting business. The reproof was directed not only at the underlings. H.J. Taylor, chief native commissioner of Matabeleland, whom Milton wanted to appoint to the new post of under-secretary for native affairs, was turned down by Milner and Chamberlain because he had been too keen a labour recruiter.[44]

The effort to keep the hands of officials unsullied was defeated by hard facts. In the middle of 1900 a single Labour Board was substituted for the two bureaux of the preceding years. This was done to simplify the work of importing labourers, and also to keep down wages by removing the competition. The change had little effect on domestic labour; indeed, when it was made the *only* recruiters in Mashonaland were the native commissioners. The new board had separate sections in Salisbury and in Bulawayo, but each Chamber of Mines, as well as the government, was represented on both. After a year of existence the board, having accomplished little or nothing, was divided again, and then abolished on 30 September 1901.

Before, during, and after that year the native commissioners continued to recruit, in spite of Chamberlain's orders to the contrary. The administrator pointed out that if they ceased to do so, and in the absence of a board, recruiting would be taken over by private agencies working for profit, and the last state of the labourer would be worse than the first. There was no point in trying to preserve the Labour Board, as the Colonial Office itself had decided that the importation of labourers must be handled by the government. Using the native commissioners, whose salaries were paid anyway, was cheaper than incurring the extra expense of a Labour Board. Moreover, the Colonial Office felt itself let down on this matter by the resident commissioner. "Sir Marshall Clarke," Frederick Graham wrote, "seems to be wobbling and puts us in a difficult position." On 26 November 1901, Chamberlain gave temporary permission for the old system to continue.[45]

Two years earlier Sir Robert Herbert had remarked that he had "for a long time felt that South Africa must import coloured labour at no distant date; because otherwise the slavery of the natives will become unendurable." In Rhodesia "unendurable slavery" might have been desired by some of the would-be slave-owners, but as a description of the actual position it was an exaggeration. Employers had to use the carrot as well as the stick if they wanted to get and to keep labourers. Of some 9,000 miners employed in Matabeleland in May 1901, more than half had sought work and engaged themselves independently of any recruiting system. In Mashonaland four months later these figures were reported:

Estimated adult male population (African)	59,960
Labourers who sought work independently	9,720
Labourers who sought work through Native Commissioners	18,709
Labourers recruited by Labour Board	3,987

According to Milton, Africans trusted the NCs and preferred to be directed by them. And by 1902 the pressure was relaxed anyway, because the Shangaans were coming again.[46]

That the native commissioners were by this time acting rather as advisers than as a press gang is suggested by these statistics. The pressure now was indirect, and came during the war years to be embodied in a complex of interlocking or mutually supporting laws. How far these were intended primarily to bring labourers to the market, to what extent they did this, and to what extent their purpose may have been a wider social one, can be judged by looking at the measures.

The Native Marriages Ordinance, 1901, belonged to this category. Among cattle-owning Bantu people the payment of cattle by the bridegroom to the bride's father (the payment commonly called *lobola*) had always been the essential means of legalizing a marriage. So it is not surprising that the native commissioners claimed that 95 per cent of the cases brought to them related to this institution. It was more popular with fathers than with sons-in-law, except when the sons-in-law were old men. When H.M. Taberer held an indaba in the Charter district to announce the victory of Paardeberg, and also asked the chiefs if they had any grievances, they replied that their only grievance was that their wives ran away. Taberer said it was their own fault for arranging betrothals, and paying *lobola* in advance, for young girls. How could the girls escape this bondage except by running away? How else, replied the chiefs, could older men get wives?[47]

Lobola was all very well for chiefs and rich men. For the commonalty there was the difficulty that after the rinderpest few young men had any cattle to give. In legislating on this subject the Council therefore had several purposes in mind. Clarifying the law would simplify the work of the courts. Betrothals of children could be prevented. Not least, the custom could be prevented from dying out, as the shortage of cattle threatened to make it do. If there could be no marriage without cattle, and the young man had no great paternal herd to draw upon, he would have to buy cattle himself; to get the money he would have to work for wages. So the Native Marriage Ordinance, 1901, made the payment of *lobola* a necessary requirement for a legal marriage, fixed maximum amounts, and, to prevent former abuses, required the payment to be made within the twelve months preceding the marriage. The parties had to appear before an official to prove that the payment had been made and that the woman was a consenting party. Disputes arising from the contract could be taken to the ordinary courts. Marriages by Christian rites were of course not affected by the ordinance.

The law was effectual because the lost herds were indeed being replaced by purchase, partly from the government which was importing cattle to restock the country. The numbers of large and small stock in African ownership grew as follows:

		1899-1900	1900-1901	1901-1902
Cattle:	Mashonaland	27,682	30,853	39,155
	Matabeleland	8,973	13,073	16,077
	Total	36,655	43,926	55,232
Sheep and goats:	Mashonaland	117,980	130,043	139,246
	Matabeleland	58,242	89,654	119,335
	Total	176,222	219,697	258,581

There was everything to be said for restoring regularity to the institution of marriage. But that this ordinance had any noticeable effect in drawing men to the labour market may be doubted. The law laid down the maximum of five head of cattle for a chief's daughter, four for others, and a maximum average value of £5 per beast; for most bridegrooms, therefore, £20 for a wife. But the elected councillors were soon complaining that no minimum had been prescribed.[48]

Two draft ordinances of 1901 approached the problem from the traditional angle: driving men to work by the old whip of taxation. The Hut Tax Ordinance, amending the original one of 1894, was designed to catch men who were slipping through the net. As Milton bluntly put it, "the object is the imposition of the hut tax upon unmarried male natives who hitherto by herding together in one hut have practically escaped taxation." Every male African over the age of eighteen was to pay (in coin, not in kind) ten shillings in respect of his occupation of every hut used by him during the year. In short, the hut tax was turned into a poll tax. But that it was not expected to increase the supply of labour is shown by the companion measure which was drafted at the same time.

While the hut tax was an important source of revenue, Milton frankly hoped that the Native Taxation Ordinance would not bring in any. It was supposed to be based on one provision of Rhodes's Glen Grey Act, 1894, in the Cape Colony. Every male African capable of work was to pay an annual tax of two pounds (in the Cape, ten shillings); if he had worked within Southern Rhodesia for wages for four months in the year (in the Cape, three months) he would be exempt; if he worked continuously for three years he would then be exempt for life.

This proposal stuck in the throat of the Colonial Office, partly it is true because of "the difficulty of defending it in Parliament." It would have been difficult to defend anywhere. First, the bill did not include the major features of the Glen Grey Act, which were African local self-government and individual land tenure. Second, under that act the tax raised was to be at the disposal of the local African council for its own purposes, but in Rhodesia it was to go into general revenue. If a racially prejudiced observer were unmoved by these considerations, he should have noticed the confused thinking behind the measure. Almost any African could earn £2 by working for a month, or at the most for two. Then why work for four months to avoid paying it? The Rhodesian administration, and the white public behind it, were caught on the horns of this dilemma: being forbidden to use force to get labour they had to use the pressure of taxation; but it was impossible to get imperial consent to an amount of tax that could not be earned in one month. Most Africans able to work for wages were already doing so for one month, which was precisely why the mines were driven to comb the sands of Arabia for the men they needed. Milner and Chamberlain accepted the Hut Tax Ordinance but rejected the other on numerous grounds; no more was heard of it.[49]

Other measures belonging to the same complex and interlocking with those just described were the Pass Law ("Natives Registration Ordinance") and the Masters and Servants Ordinance. Both were amendments of existing laws. The system of passes, which prevailed in the republics but had been abolished in the Cape Colony in 1828, was introduced in Rhodesia rather irregularly in 1893, and in proper form by "the Registration of Natives Regulations, 1895." These provided that an African, upon entering a town, had to obtain from a "Registrar of Natives" a pass to seek work; when he had found work, his contract of service was registered and he received a copy of this; he could not be in the town without one or other of these documents, or away from his employer's premises, or alternatively the "Native Location," between 9 p.m. and 5 a.m. without another pass.

The ordinance of 1901 was based on a recent proclamation of Milner's in the Transvaal, but differed from it almost as significantly as the taxation proposal differed from the Glen Grey Act. The ordinance did in some respects give relief to Africans, for instance by exempting those entering towns on legitimate business other than the search for employment. It made the employer, not the employee, responsible for having the contract of service registered. But in most ways it had quite a different tenor.

The essential purpose of this, as of all pass laws, was to direct labour to where the most influential employers wanted it, and to keep it there in defiance of the workers' preferences. So this ordinance, which applied only to the six principal towns, made the issue of a pass to seek work, or of a contract of service, depend on the registrar's satisfaction that the worker's last contract had been fulfilled and that he had been discharged from it, or else that he had not previously been in employment. The employer had to sign a discharge when the period of contract ended. In the Transvaal, the penalty for refusing to give this was a fine up to £50, or six months' imprisonment. In Rhodesia it was to be a maximum of £2, or fourteen days' imprisonment. By comparison, the African's penalty for travelling without a pass was £2 or one month.

For these reasons Chamberlain delayed his approval, and the ordinance did not become law until November 1902, when the Legislative Council was already debating its amendment and extension. The proposal now was to extend the registration and pass system, which had operated only in six towns, to the whole country. No African would be able to leave his district without a travelling pass or permit to seek work; nor, if he were employed, leave his place of work temporarily without a pass from the employer, or permanently without a discharge. Thus the system would be complete. But not in our period. It was not till the end of 1903 that Lyttelton, the new colonial secretary, allowed the High Commissioner to give his assent to this ordinance, provided that it was amended in certain particulars.[50]

There was no such delay over the Masters and Servants Ordinance, promulgated at the end of 1901, in spite of the qualms in London. Strangely in this context, it was nonracial not only in form but even to some extent in practice. Before it was passed, the Cape Acts of 1856 and 1873 were in force in Rhodesia; the ordinance amended them. Like Cape legislation generally, the acts made no distinction of race. They were concerned mostly with servants in the narrow sense, and there were white servants in Rhodesia. Valets and ladies' maids were brought from England, or engaged there and sent for. The Company report announced a "fair demand for white domestic servants at moderate wages," and some of them were caught in the meshes of the ordinances. But of course almost all servants were black, and masters white; and this law defined servants to include virtually all unskilled workers.

Breach of a contract of service remained as it was in the Cape, but not in Britain, a criminal offence; the fine for a breach by the servant was £1 in the Cape, but £4 in Rhodesia. The Cape law provided that a magistrate or other suitable officer must certify that the contract was understood and entered into voluntarily by both parties; this provision was omitted in Rhodesia. For reasons which have appeared sufficiently in this chapter, servants and other employees were often engaged and brought from outside the country. Under the existing law, when they arrived in Rhodesia at the employer's expense they could repudiate the contract because he had not signed it. It was fair to protect him from this loss, but the ordinance went further: a written undertaking to accept employment in Rhodesia was binding on the employee who signed it abroad, but there was nothing to ensure that the signer understood the conditions, as for example that breach of the contract would be a crime.

The Colonial Office worried about servants recruited in England. The elected members of the Legislative Council had other worries. Grimmer moved an amendment to add up to fifteen cuts with a cane to the other penalties for offences by the servants. He pointed out reassuringly that no magistrate would inflict this punishment on a European, and that Europeans would gladly accept nominal liability to it for the sake of imposing it on African servants. The official majority defeated the motion.

Milner assented to the ordinance, but the power of disallowance remained in London. In the Colonial Office H.B. Cox minuted: "Speaking generally, this ordinance seems to me to show that a very deplorable state of public opinion exists in S. Rhodesia on this question." Chamberlain added: "it will be necessary to keep a very tight hand on Rhodesian legislation." The ordinance was allowed to stand, but on condition that it was amended, as it was in 1902. There were a few ameliorations: if, for instance, a servant were engaged outside the country, a British consul or justice of the peace would be the proper official to see that the parties had understood the contract and entered into it voluntarily.[51]

The attempt by the elected members to introduce the cane was in character. When the new Council met in November 1902 the white public was agitated by the "black peril"—the rape of white women by black men. It was a new phenomenon. A crowd in Bulawayo had tried to lynch a prisoner charged with *attempted* rape, and the whites of that town were enraged by the mild sentence imposed on him by the court. Large and emotional public meetings discussed the question. P. Ross Frames accordingly moved in the Council "for the infliction of the death penalty for rape or attempted rape by natives upon white women." The defeat of Frames's motion was attributed by the *Herald* to the government's inability to defy the Colonial Office, though in fact the officials there were in two minds about the question. The only argument adduced in favour of the proposal was that it might be necessary if mob law were not to take over. Perhaps the administration opposed it merely in the belief that murder was a fate worse than rape.

Frames then returned to the attack with a different proposal: to make carnal intercourse between black men and white women a criminal offence; he said that it was intercourse with white prostitutes that led black men to commit outrages upon white women. As the proposal was based on a Cape act recently passed, the attorney-general refused to accept it until he had seen that act, and the motion fell away for the session.[52]

It may be that the supply of labour from domestic sources was increased by this body of laws, and what labour there was must certainly have been more effectively controlled and retained. But the impression remains that the essential motivation of these measures was to create and preserve a certain social order: white supremacy, black subordination and deference. The economic motive was there too, but it was secondary. The economic object was being attained more effectively by other means.

Southern Rhodesia thus entered its second decade with the same obsessions as had characterized the first. But if many of the concerns of the public and the politicians were a heritage from the nineties, others were new, or at least were old questions in a new guise, and pointed forward to the new century.

A notable example of these was the question of malaria. How much of the history of the country, its invasions, conquests, and colonization, hinged on this scourge has appeared abundantly in these pages. In 1898, with the culminating discoveries of Ronald Ross, Bastianelli, Bignami, and Grassi, the mystery was at last solved. One would have expected this news to have figured prominently in the Rhodesian press within weeks, if not days; but the first public reference in Rhodesia to the new "theory" appeared in the *Bulawayo Chronicle* on 17 October 1900.

The reason for waiting two years to recognize or acknowledge the great discovery appears in the reports that follow over the next twelve months. A belief firmly held for thousands of years could no more be dispelled by one scientific report than could Ptolemaic cosmology in an earlier day. The *Chronicle* in November 1900 could write only of "accumulating evidence," and that "it appears now to be established as a scientific fact." *The Times*, quoted by the *Chronicle*, was complaining of the incredulity of the mass of people. To overcome it, the School of Tropical Medicine conducted an experiment. A mosquito-proof hut was built in the Roman Campagna, the classic land of malaria. The volunteers who occupied it could roam freely during the day, but were confined to the hut from an hour before sunset to an hour after sunrise. None of them caught the fever. Conversely, infected anopheles mosquitoes were brought to England and allowed to bite healthy subjects in a healthy environment; they went down with malaria. Reports continued to come from Italy, where the king and queen took a keen interest in the experiment.

Thus the barrier of incredulity was slowly broken down. But even this life-saving discovery had another side. Hans Sauer, who lectured on the subject with the authority of his professional training, pointed out that as the mosquito was dangerous to Europeans but not to indigenous Africans, who would normally be carriers without having any symptom of the disease, Europeans would have to be as thoroughly segregated from Africans as possible. However that might be, this medical revolution was a major landmark in the lives of the white, and to a small extent of the black, inhabitants of tropical Africa.[53]

The technological revolution represented by railways had already had profound economic, political, and military consequences. But the railway network, built at such a cost in life, health, and financial security, was far from complete when the war put a stop to construction. The great gap was of course between Bulawayo and Salisbury, but Rhodes's Cape-to-Cairo dream was waiting to be realised, and the prosperity of many mines depended on the building of branch lines.

Though the Vryburg-Bulawayo line was in operation again by June 1900, its capacity was restricted by the military use and control of the Cape railways and ports. The building of the link between the two existing termini was therefore begun from Salisbury, at the end of March 1900. The importance of the work is suggested by Rhodes's receiving, in Kimberley on 16 January, a premature message sent through the Boer lines: "Stevens to Rhodes. Board voted twenty thousand pounds earthworks masonry Salisbury Gwelo railway, work starts immediately." The contractor was of course George Pauling. The platelaying from Salisbury began in August, and construction from the Bulawayo end in October.

Though the rails from Salisbury were an extension of the Mashonaland Railway Company's track from Umtali, this new building was financed by Rhodesia Railways, the old Bechuanaland Railway Company, which by a little juggling could just manage to do it. A meeting of the debenture-holders in January 1900 agreed to the issue of another £4,250,000 of debentures to pay for new construction. A year later, new debentures of the Mashonaland Railway, of which the £400,000 allotted to Chartered shareholders were immediately over-subscribed, were issued to pay off a debt to the Chartered Company. They might even be made to stretch further: Hawksley was to be asked "whether it will be permissible for the proceeds of the Debentures to be used for the repayment of the sums advanced by the Chartered Company for the payment of interest on Debentures." If so, all the debts could be cleared off and the balance used to buy, from Rhodesia Railways, the rolling stock already in use—it was on loan from that company. Every penny would be needed if, as the directors later claimed, the interest on the existing debentures was £125,000; the railway handled 20,000 tons a year and would have to charge £6 a ton to be able to pay this interest, but was in fact charging £3 a ton. "Clearing off the debt" was of course one of the old euphemisms; it meant exchanging one creditor for another.[54]

Not that Rhodesia Railways had any capital to spare. Like the Mashonaland Railway, it depended on loans from the Chartered Company to cover current expenditure. At the beginning of 1901, when Pauling signed a contract to build the line from Bulawayo to Wankie for £348,000, the total debt of Rhodesia Railways for construction, including this last sum and excluding the £596,168 already paid, was £1,618,222; and there were other debts for rolling stock and running expenses. Both these companies were still operating on hope and public gullibility.

Nevertheless Rhodesia Railways was called upon to finance further construction. It had originally been intended that the Cape-to-Cairo railway would run from Bulawayo to Gwelo and thence northwards across the Mafungabusi plateau (where coal had been found) to and across the Zambezi. The discovery of coal at Wankie did not immediately affect this plan. The Chartered Company and Rhodesia Railways made an arrangement with the Mashonaland Agency, which owned this coalfield, to build a railway to it, and by April 1900 a survey of the route had been made. But in August Rhodes, speaking at

Gwelo, would say no more than that "if the Wankie coal proved as good as it was reported to be, the main line would go in that direction." The terrain on the Mafungabusi route was found to be difficult, and the Congo Free State authorized the extension of the railway into its territory; but in October the choice of the Wankie route for the main line was still only a probability. By the end of 1902 that line had reached the sixty-mile straight beyond the Gwaai. It was completed to Wankie in September 1903, and to the Victoria Falls on 25 April 1904. Wankie coal and Katanga copper—with the romantic attraction of the Falls for good measure—had decided the route of the main line.

This construction, like that of the line from Bulawayo to Gwelo, was delayed because of the army's control of the Cape railways. "Thousands of tons" of material were said to be waiting at Port Elizabeth for military permission to be forwarded. This problem did not exist on the Beira line, which was therefore used to bring material to Salisbury. The widening of the gauge was completed to Beira, and the first through train arrived there on 8 July 1900—just too late to help the Rhodesia Field Force. Even so, the line from Salisbury to Gwelo was not finished till the end of May 1902. When the extension from Bulawayo was connected with it on 6 October, the main centres of Southern Rhodesia were at last linked, and a railway of standard gauge connected Cape Town with Beira. To make even this belated achievement possible, the Bulawayo Chambers of Mines and of Commerce had agreed, for their members, to give up their railway truckage allowance for fourteen days in favour of railway materials.[55]

One other line was built in 1902, a narrow gauge railway from Salisbury to the Ayrshire mine, completed in August, owned and operated by the mining company and built by Pauling. It was the basis of the future Sinoia branch. Pauling had also signed a contract to build a branch from Gwelo to Selukwe. No work had yet been done on the long-promised Gwanda line.

All this railway building and operation was paid for, as we have seen, by borrowing from the public and from the Chartered Company. But the Chartered Company, which was a shaky concern before 1899, was hard hit by the war. The white politics of Rhodesia during and immediately after the war were shaped largely by this fact, as well as by the perpetual concern with white supremacy, black labour, and the output of the mines.

On 13 October 1900 H. Wilson Fox wrote to Rhodes that the Company would "probably just manage to tide over till next May without selling our De Beers." At the same time he explained the proposal of the directors, following the example of Consolidated Gold Fields, to found a separate company, the Charter Trust, to handle purely financial operations. The distribution of shares and of profits was carefully arranged to benefit both the Chartered Company and its directors. The nominal capital would be £2,000,000. The Chartered Company would in future sell vendor's shares through the Trust, which would also be selling shares itself, so that it would be impossible for the public to know when or whether the BSA Company was selling a particular stock. When the Trust was formed, there would be no need ever to increase the capital of the Chartered Company beyond the present £5,000,000. By the following February Grey could report to Rhodes that the Trust prospectus had been well received.[56]

We now pass to July 1902. The war was over, the raid forgotten by the directors if not by others, and Rhodes and Shippard were dead. Alfred Beit was now invited to return to the board, and Jameson and Sir Lewis Michell (Rhodes's banker) to fill the vacant seats on it. These appointments were made in haste by the old directors, who unanimously waived the rule requiring six weeks' notice and a ballot.[57]

The reason for the haste is not clear, and was not clear to the Colonial Office at the time; but what follows is both more mysterious and much more important.

In September 1902 the new directors, Beit, Jameson, and Michell, arrived in Rhodesia to inspect the estate. One would not expect them, as "new boys" on the board, to make any important decisions independently of their colleagues. But they made the decisions, and there is no evidence that these had been discussed beforehand in St. Swithin's Lane.

They arrived in the country on the eve of the new session of the Legislative Council. It was a new Council too. The second general election had been held in the previous March, but the session postponed till November because some draft ordinances could not be ready earlier. In comparison with the election of 1899 this one was tame. In Mashonaland there were only two candidates. Grimmer refused to stand again because he thought the Council a farce; his supporters nominated Dr. R.J. Wylie in his place. Raleigh Grey allowed his name to go forward, though he was in England at the time and did not attend the session in November. He and Wylie were returned unopposed. In Matabeleland both the former members, Sauer and Hutchinson, stood down. Of the three candidates, J.E. Scott was a strong supporter of the Company, which made his defeat a foregone conclusion. The two elected were P. Ross Frames and C.T. Holland. Frames was no sooner elected than he migrated to the Transvaal, and reappeared only for the session in November. Thus Grimmer had a point.

There were changes on the official side too. When Lawley was appointed governor of Western Australia in 1901, it was decided not to replace him in Bulawayo; Milton, whose appointment was renewed in 1902, became the sole administrator. Judge Vintcent having resigned his seat on the Council, his place was taken ultimately by the new attorney-general, J.G. Kotze, the former chief justice of the South African Republic who had been dismissed by Kruger.[58]

In August and September there had been meetings in Bulawayo to debate a proposal that the charter should be abrogated. A meeting of 750 people voted for abrogation; so did the Chamber of Commerce. The Chamber of Mines opposed it, though admitting the grievances that had provoked the move. Though there was no possibility that the imperial government would heed this suggestion, the discussion was a warning signal to the Company, as also the election in March had been.

When therefore the three visiting directors arrived in Salisbury they were besieged by deputations with grievances, requests, and demands, much as Rhodes had been in his day. The farmers wanted a separate Department of Agriculture; the directors agreed. The Town Council wanted help in various municipal schemes, and was told that the Charter Trust would handle that. The BSA Company did not own the railways (this was true in a sense) so could do nothing about the rates. In a telegram and a letter to the Rhodesia (Bulawayo) Chamber of Mines the directors went further. They promised a new mining law which among other things would reduce the Company's notorious 50 per cent to 30, and in the meantime this proportion would be written into "all future flotations." Postal and telegraph rates would be reduced. A secretary of native affairs, distinct from the administrator (who had hitherto combined that office with his own), would be appointed and would have a seat on the Executive Council. Far outweighing all these concessions, the directors promised a reform in the constitution.[59]

In 1901 the Council had passed a Mines and Minerals Ordinance, which made provisions of some technical importance about the registration of claims and security of title to them, but it was badly drafted and in some ways unenforceable. The details had been discussed in advance with both Chambers of Mines, but when the Bulawayo chamber first saw the text, after the ordinance had been passed, it protested, and petitioned Milner to withhold his assent. Milner, with Milton's concurrence, did so. A more acceptable bill was presented at the session of 1902, but because of prolonged discussions with the Chambers of Mines was held over. To the elected members the most notable feature of this bill was what was *not* in it—any reference to the 50 per cent which the directors had just promised to reduce.

As might be expected, the 1902 session dealt also with the occupation of land. The bill proposed by the government was merely a minor administrative reform, making it possible to have a title changed or modified more cheaply than before. But most landholders still refused to take out any title deeds, because of their objection to the occupation clause included in them. As the surveyor-general refused to make any concession on that point, Ross Frames moved a significant amendment in committee. The bill provided that when land was forfeited it would revert to, and be "re-invested in," the BSA Company. Frames proposed to substitute "the Administration" for the Company. He quoted Rhodes as having said that the land belonged to "the people." When the Company ceased to govern, as it was expected soon to do, Frames wanted the land to belong to the future self-governing colony. The motion was ruled out of order because no motion affecting the property of the Company could be moved without the prior consent of the administrator. But this was the very question that was to be decided, with far-reaching consequences, by the Judicial Committee of the Privy Council during World War I. Another motion by Frames pointed in the same direction: to petition the king to annex Rhodesia to his dominions. This being incompatible with government by the Company, the official majority defeated it.[60]

Many of the old grievances thus still remained at the end of 1902. One, which had been disposed of in the previous year, may be mentioned here: the customs agreement with the Cape Colony, which had aroused so much bitterness in 1899. It was terminated on 15 April 1901. A good excuse had been found. Most goods imported through Cape ports, and the proportion was increasing, were coming through in bond; Southern Rhodesia paid the Cape a 3 per cent transit fee, and collected the customs duty itself; as this meant the employment of a customs staff, Rhodesia might as well collect all the duties. The whole customs system and tariff thus lay open to amendment.[61]

All these matters, though they filled many columns of the press and pages of the official files, were unimportant in comparison with the constitutional change. In his speech at the opening of the session on 6 November Milton made a brief reference to a proposal to enlarge the Legislative Council. On the 20th the attorney-general moved a resolution to ask for the amendment of the order-in-council, so that the Legislative Council would in future consist of the administrator (presiding, and having a casting but not a deliberative vote), the resident commissioner (who had no vote), seven appointed and seven elected members. The latter would be returned not by the two provinces but by four newly delimited divisions. The resolution was passed unanimously and was at once cabled to the board and the Colonial Office ("Most urgent, clear the line"). The three visiting directors had already given their approval. The directors in London gave theirs when they received the news.

The immediate reaction in the Colonial Office gives a few clues to an explanation. It was politically impossible to oppose an increase in popular representation. But the strengthening of the elective element would diminish the power not only of the Company, but of the imperial government, which under the existing system could twist the Company's arm and get measures passed. The new proposal "decreases the security we have for getting any legislation we want passed. Under the new scheme, amending Ordinances directed by the S. of S. will be passed by the Administrator's casting vote, and will not be passed at all if an official has a cold." Moreover, "we are here asked to make a very important and radical alteration in the Constitution of S. Rhodesia in hot haste, without one single word of explanation as to its necessity or as to the reasons which lead to the conclusion that the existing Constitution is not adapted to the circumstances of the Protectorate. I do not see why we should be rushed in this way."

625 War and Peace

The board then offered an explanation:

> Administrator states that the reason for the proposed change in the consti-
> tution of the Legislative Council was the weighty representations which were made to
> the Directors in South Africa by influential sections of the public in Rhodesia, who
> urged that under the present system little public interest is attached to the Council ow-
> ing to the numerical inferiority of the representative members, and that if the propor-
> tion were readjusted the service of the best men would be secured. Mr. Milton further
> says that the terms of the Resolution and the proposed distribution of seats have been
> received throughout the country with practically unanimous approval.

(To judge by press reports, the "influential sections of the public" that made
"weighty representations" meant no more than C.T. Holland, who made the
request to the directors in Bulawayo.) All of this was true, but it cannot have
been the whole truth.[62]

Why should the administration in Salisbury, the visiting directors, and their
London colleagues decide suddenly and with the zeal of converts to reduce
their own control of Rhodesian government and legislation almost to vanishing
point, in favour of the representatives of the "people"? The interests of the
"people" and those of the Company were diametrically opposed on land questions, on mining royalties, on railway rates, and on the larger question of the
division of debts and assets when the time came for the Company to hand over
the government.

When elected representatives were introduced in 1898, the most important
immediate (if not long-term) reason, which Rhodes was frank about, was to
make it harder for the Colonial Office to interfere. The Company called the
settlers to its aid in its conflicts with the imperial government. Was this the motive again in 1902?

Some facts would support that theory. There were issues on which Company
and settlers would be on the same side against Colonial Office "interference":
the recruitment and discipline of labourers, the suppression of troublesome
chiefs and other Africans, taxing Africans to "make them work," and, generally, the whole apparatus of white supremacy that was liable to arouse the opposition of "Exeter Hall." But these issues neither mattered so much to the
Company, nor provoked enough interference from London, to explain the extraordinary step being taken.

The primary interest of the Company was its balance sheet. The biggest item
of expenditure was the police. As the policemen began to return from active
service the future of the force became an important question for debate among
the parties concerned. The Company wanted to reduce its total strength and,
within limits, to substitute black for white policemen. Milton suggested that it
was no longer necessary for the police to have a military character (read: to be
under the command of the commandant-general). A force of 400 whites and

400 blacks would suffice, and they could operate under the Cape Act 12 of 1882.

In the session of 1901 an increase of the strength of the SRV was provided for, but the speeches on both sides made it clear that the purpose of this measure was to make it possible to reduce the police force. Even Sir Marshall Clarke "wobbled" on this question. The men returning from active service, he said, were little interested in ordinary police work. Many were time-expired and would transfer to the new constabulary in the conquered republics. The Ndebele, in spite of Rhodes's promise in 1896, would prefer to be policed by their own people; and so on.

On all this the elected representatives supported the government, but to no avail. The number of white police, Milner said, must be 750. The Cape Act of 1882 would not do, because it placed the force under the governor, and the administrator must not have that position in Rhodesia. The police must continue to be a military force. Chamberlain did not agree that Rhodesia might in emergency, as Milton thought, count on the help of police from the other colonies. Here then was a question, very important to the Company, on which its officials and the elected members stood together against the Colonial Office.[63]

One of the resolutions passed on 20 November, and immediately objected to in London, was that the high commissioner should have the power to amend the constitution further, when asked to do so by the Legislative Council; provided that the ratio of elected to nominated members could not be altered without a motion passed by a three-quarters majority in the Council. The meaning of that was that Company, settlers, resident commissioner, and high commissioner could make an agreement without interference from the Colonial Office. An alliance of that kind had appeared occasionally in the past.

The directors had no cause to love the Colonial Office, which two years earlier had imposed the Supplementary Charter, with its "penal clause," on them. Ever since that date the Company's affairs and administration had been scrutinized in detail, and at many points directed, by the imperial officials. In return, the constitutional proposal was shot at them like a bolt from the blue, originally without any explanation. All these facts produce an impression, but no more than an impression, that the Company men, after chafing in silence under the imperial yoke, seized on the idea of a more popular legislature as a means of casting off the yoke.

But popular representation, after all that had happened in the empire over the last half-century, was a very hot implement to handle. The reason for the note of urgency in the cable from Salisbury had been that Chamberlain was about to leave London on his South African tour, and his approval of a new order-in-council was wanted before he left. He left without giving that approval, because of "the absence of any information as to reasons for urgency of so important a change." But telegrams, including one from Milner who entirely approved of the proposal, followed him on his journey. From Cairo Chamberlain cabled back to London that the desired order-in-council could be prepared at once, with only one added condition: a further constitutional change was not to be made by the high commissioner without the concurrence of the secretary of state.

Arrived in South Africa, Chamberlain lost no time in agreeing to the Rhodesian demand and arranging for its implementation. Milner's confidential dispatch to him explains the position they were both in:

> As you are aware, a feeling has for a long time past been expressed in various quarters in Southern Rhodesia that the inhabitants of the country should be given a greater voice in the management of its affairs. I take it that the present proposals of the Administration are by way of a concession to this feeling. I cannot see that it is in any way to our interest to hinder such a concession being made, and the urgency of the matter from our point of view is constituted by the fact that the Administration, having made their proposals, will undoubtedly lay the whole blame of any delay which may take place in adopting them on the shoulders of His Majesty's Government. They will say, "We are prepared to give the people a greater voice in the management of this country, but, as you see, the Colonial Office has refused to allow it."

Milton had some reason to hope for cooperation by the elected members, or some of them. The violent polemics of the first session had not been repeated. As he reported to Milner,

> The proceedings at each successive session of the Council have been progressively satisfactory to those who wish to see and promote the growth of representative institutions, and . . . I believe the advantages attaching to representation are being increasingly realised, and that by showing a disposition to encourage the people to take a larger share in framing the legislation of the country, the Company is taking a step which will secure to it the assistance of a large majority or even the whole of the inhabitants.

Allowing again for the specialized meaning of "inhabitants" and "people," we cannot be far wrong in thinking that Milton and his officers and the directors had decided that, on balance, the Company would do better by calling the people to its support in opposition to the pressures of Downing Street than by counting on Downing Street to help it to defy the people.

Whether that was the reasoning or not, the most important decision had been taken along the road to an independent Rhodesia under white domination. The decision was not final, but the future would show that the process was very difficult if not impossible to reverse. The new order-in-council was proclaimed on 6 March 1903.[64]

For Rhodesia it was the real opening of the new century, but in describing the constitutional advance we have moved ahead of the events that made 1902 a natural terminal date for this history.

For two years after the relief of Mafeking the war had dragged on, affecting Rhodesia at long range and mostly in its communications and supplies. At last Kitchener's blockhouses, barbed wire, and "drives" had forced the delegates of the commandos to meet the British negotiators at Vereeniging, and on 31 May 1902 the terms agreed upon were signed in Pretoria. The news was not unexpected. It became public the next day, which was a Sunday. The *Bulawayo Chronicle* called it a "glorious First of June." The national anthem was sung in "some" of the churches. The Bulawayo Club hoisted its flag. The Police Band played the national anthem and "Rule, Britannia," at its concert that night. "In the hotels the news was received with an outburst of enthusiastic cheering . . . while jubilant feelings found vent in the National Anthem at more than one dining table." But this was not Mafeking Night. The peace, with its hollow victory, had long been inevitable.[65]

The other event, which made quite a different impact, was the death of Rhodes.

As the time set by the ultimatum in October 1899 was running out, Rhodes had left Cape Town for Kimberley by the last train to get through. The mayor had implored him not to come, but he had to watch over De Beers in the hour of danger; where his treasure was, there was his heart also. He set himself up as the unofficial civilian ruler of the besieged town, the sarcastic critic of its professional defenders, and the would-be military expert in its defence—to the exasperation and fury of Colonel Kekewich and the rest of the army.

Four days after the relief of Kimberley Rhodes addressed an annual general meeting of the De Beers shareholders, to whom he appealed not only for reconciliation with the Boers after the war, but for "equal rights for every civilized man south of the Zambezi." At the request of the Coloured community he afterwards wrote the words on a piece of newspaper, adding the definition: "What is a civilized man? A man whether white or black who has sufficient education to write his name, has some property or works, in fact is not a loafer." Whether the reason was the purifying flame of war or declining health and the approach of death, Rhodes was mellowing in some respects.

He was restless. After a few weeks at Groote Schuur, a few more in England, and two more at Groote Schuur again, he left Cape Town for Beira and Rhodesia on 18 May. This was his longest visit to his new country since 1896; he did not return to the Cape till October. Throughout 1901 he was preoccupied with Cape politics and the intrigues of the Princess Radziwill, except for a shorter visit to Rhodesia in May and June. He laid the foundation stone of a Drill Hall in Bulawayo, and spoke of the coming federation which would be dominated by the North, not by the Cape. His speech at St. John's School was the last recorded speech of his life, and he was not destined to see Rhodesia again.

In England he learned from his heart specialist that his condition was very serious. Accompanied by Jameson, Beit, Metcalfe, his secretary Philip Jourdan, and others of his usual entourage, he sought relief at a shooting lodge in Scotland, and then on a tour through France, Switzerland, Italy, and Egypt. But when he got back to Cape Town on 2 February 1902, he was so obviously dying that he avoided going to the club for fear that his condition would become generally known.[66]

It was a hot summer. Rhodes, gasping for breath, retired to his simple cottage at Muizenberg. Michell heard him say "So little done, so much to do"; but before he died on 26 March his last words, almost inaudible, were some names, thought to be the names of the friends at his bedside.

Of course there were eulogies and tributes from all over the world, and the clichés appropriate to the occasion were exhaustively used. But the position of Rhodes in the country he founded was peculiar, and his relationship to the people he had sent or drawn to it was correctly sensed by the *Bulawayo Chronicle*:

> It is not the great Amalgamator that the people mourn for, not the genius that saved a large empire for the homeland, but it is for the man—the man who had ever an open heart and a generous hand, and whose loss will bring the acutest sorrow into many homes. The people of Rhodesia will feel that they have lost a near relative, because his relation to them was of a peculiar nature. He loved them with a passionate love, and they returned that love as cordially.

Rhodes's body was taken to Groote Schuur, then to lie in state in the Houses of Parliament. On 3 April the remains were taken to St. George's Cathedral for a funeral service conducted by the archbishop; thence to the funeral train which stopped at every significant station for the crowds to pay their respects. Military bands were at the stations to play the Dead March in *Saul*; at small stopping places buglers played the Last Post; as the train passed the little blockhouses in the Karoo their occupants stood to attention with arms reversed. At Kimberley 15,000 people of all races ("marching side by side, absolutely irrespective of social rank, race or colour") filed past the bier for nearly five hours. On the morning of the 8th "a very large crowd" watched the arrival of the train in Bulawayo station.

The coffin was taken to the Drill Hall, where a thousand people, all in mourning dress, gathered on the morning of the 10th for the burial service conducted by the bishop of Mashonaland. The band of the BSAP, with drums muffled in crêpe, a choir of fifty voices, and other clergy supporting the bishop, completed the gathering in the Drill Hall, but when the procession was formed a much larger crowd fell in behind it. The pall-bearers were Pioneers of 1890 and 1893, marching on either side of the gun-carriage. Almost everybody in Rhodesian public life, and many from the other colonies, were in the procession.

These guests and officials followed the cortège to the Matopos in seven special coaches; the public found its own vehicles: "everything in the shape of horse and mule flesh and everything from coaches down to donkey wagons had been requisitioned; the result was literally a town on trek."

The coffin rested for the night at the homestead on Rhodes's farm Sauerdale; the officials and guests spent it at Fuller's hotel, and the public camped on the veld. Early on the morning of the 11th the coffin was taken to the foot of the granite hill which was the place Rhodes had chosen, and called "a view of the world." The grave had already been hewn out of the rock. A team of oxen pulled the gun-carriage to the top. As it passed, two thousand five hundred Africans who had gathered there rose to their feet and murmured "Nkosi!" The public procession followed up the hill to the strains of Chopin's Funeral March. As Bishop Gaul said the words "He cometh up and is cut down as a flower," the coffin was lowered and the slab with the brass plate and the words Rhodes had chosen ("Here lie the remains of Cecil John Rhodes") was moved into place.

The Ndebele indunas and their men then filed past the grave two by two, with "sticks slightly raised as on parade." Gampu headed this procession, followed by Mtshane, who had been the original Ndebele commander in Jameson's War. Mtshane asked to be allowed to recite the praises of the dead, which he did over the grave; the rest passed in silence. The third induna in this procession was Sikhombo, who said that "the bodies of Mzilikazi, the great chief, and of the great white chief now both rest in the Matopos. Their spirits will range the mountains, and they will meet and hold a great Indaba."[67]

On 1 May Col. Frank Rhodes held a smaller indaba at the grave with the principal indunas. Speaking through an interpreter, he officially entrusted the grave to their keeping: "And as a proof that I know the white man and the Matabele will be brothers and friends for ever and ever, I leave my brother's grave in your hands. I charge you to hand down this sacred trust to your sons that come after you from generation to generation; and I know, if you do this, my brother will be pleased." The indunas again paid their tributes to the dead, and promised that they and their children's children would keep their sacred trust.[68]

Rhodes at his death was a director of the Company, but held no public office, in Rhodesia or elsewhere. Yet his body was not in the grave before a cry went up for Jameson to "take his place"; there was an indefinable void that had to be filled. But Jameson had other ideas. He had been elected to the Cape Parliament, and was destined to become prime minister of the old Colony, and president of the Chartered Company.

Few of Rhodes's close friends and associates, or of those who had shared prominently in his imperial venture, chose to make their careers in Rhodesia, though many remained on the board of the Company, or joined it. Maguire became president. Sir Sidney Shippard died, in London, three days after Rhodes. C.D. Rudd, who dominated Consolidated Gold Fields until it went into suspension during the Anglo-Boer War, retired to Scotland and played no further part in South Africa. Hans Sauer retired to England. J.S. Moffat retired to the Cape, but his son H.U. Moffat became premier of Southern Rhodesia, and other members of the family figured prominently in its subsequent history.

Lord Grey became governor-general of Canada. His successor Sir William Milton (knighted in 1903) ruled Southern Rhodesia until 1914. F.C. Selous became a friend of Theodore Roosevelt, hunted with him in Alaska and Canada, took him on an East African safari, and then fought in that country in World War I and was killed there in 1917. Colenbrander survived his adventures with Kitchener's Fighting Scouts, but in 1918 acted the part of Lord Chelmsford in a film about the Zulu War. While attempting to save another man, like Colenbrander thrown from his horse, he was drowned in the swollen Klip River. W.T. Stead drowned too—in the *Titanic*.

Frank ("Matabele") Thompson, though never breaking with Rhodes, disapproved of much of what he did. After helping to get the Rudd Concession, which he had thought of simply as a mining venture, he returned to Cape Town and his wife and family. He had made enough money to take him to Oxford for three years, and he was a member of the Cape Parliament until he left the Progressive Party in 1904. He and Sprigg had been the representatives of the Cape at Edward VII's coronation.

Thompson may be allowed the last word:[69]

> Only once did I again visit Rhodesia. It was in 1904, as a member of the South African Native Affairs Commission. I was standing on the railway platform at Figtree, when I was accosted by one of Lobengula's Indunas. "Ou Tomoson," he said, "how have you treated us, after all your promises, which we believed?"
> I had no answer.

NOTES CHAPTER 15

1 Sir William Butler, *An Autobiography*, pp.440-1; Cd 1791, Q 13586.
2 Butler, *Autobiography*, pp.451-4 (Butler's command did not include Bechuanaland or Rhodesia); A.S. Hickman, *Rhodesia Served the Queen*, pp.59-63, 81; Cd 1791, Q 17953; BSA Co. Govt. Gazette, 6 October 1899 (Govt. Notice 235/1899).
3 CO 879/66/644, no.114, pp.155-6; 68/657, no.77, pp.81-2; CO 417/283/11462, pp.336-45; CO 468/3 (Co. Report, 1898-1900), p.41; Cd 1791, Q 17950; Hickman, *Rhodesia Served the Queen*, p.95.
4 Hickman, *Rhodesia Served the Queen*, pp.131-2, 139-45, 253. E Squadron of the Rhodesia Regiment consisted entirely of Rhodesians.
5 CO 417/276/34717, pp.925, 934-5; Hickman, *Rhodesia Served the Queen*, pp.96-7; *The Times History of the War in South Africa*, vol. IV, pp.203-4.
6 CO 417/283/3848, p.79; Cd 1791, Q 17950; Hickman, *Rhodesia Served the Queen*, pp.187-8, 194, 254-5.
7 CO 417/283/5128, pp.178-9; CO 879/66/644, no.169, encl.1, p.244; Hickman, *Rhodesia Served the Queen*, pp.254-5.

8 co 468/3 (Co. Report 1898-1900), pp.9, 16. The Rhodesia Regiment included 143 men from Mashonaland (co 879/66/644, no.169, p.244).

9 co 879/61/606, no.265 and encls., pp.178-81; no.423, pp.409-10; 63/608, no.21, pp.7-8; 64/634, no.43, encl.5, p.80, encl.6, p.84; no.159, p.194.

10 co 879/64/634, no.43, encl.1, pp.69-72; no.159, encl.1-3, pp.195-202; no.587, encl.1, p.604, encl.7, p.615; co 468/3 (Co. Report 1898-1900), p.9.

11 co 878/64/634, no.16, encls.1, 5, 6, pp.33-6; no.43, encl.5, pp.80-1, encl.6, p.83; no.159, encl.1, pp.193-7; co 417/276/34255, p.907; 34848, pp.972-4; Hickman, *Rhodesia Served the Queen*, pp.123, 303-7; *Bulawayo Chronicle*, 2 December 1899. Charles Duly owned a bicycle shop, which like many others of that day developed into a large motor car business. Duly imported the first car into Rhodesia about October 1902. He took a *Chronicle* reporter and another passenger out in it to show off its performance. After the trip the passengers agreed that "the motor car has come to stay." The car was a 6½ h.p. Gladiator. (*Bulawayo Chronicle*, 8 November 1902.)

12 co 879/56/572, no.668, pp.497-9; 64/634, no.31, pp.47-8; no.159, encl.2, p.198.

13 co 417/276/34103, pp.886-92; 34848, pp.970-6; 308/2687, pp.174-5; 4384, p.181; 309/12947, pp.513, 519; co 879/63/608, no.560, p.180; 66/644, no.112, encl.2, p.153; Colin Harding, *Frontier Patrols*, pp.167-70. Yeomanry were mounted volunteers. The organization dated from the eighteenth century, survived in an inactive way through the nineteenth, and became active again in the Anglo-Boer War. No officers on the active list, or serving NCOs of the army or militia, were attached to the Yeomanry.

14 co 417/308/7490, pp.580, 619; co 879/66/644, no.169, encl.4, p.246.

15 co 879/64/634, no.199, encl.2, p.242; no.391, encl.2, p.388; 68/656, no.53, encl., pp.60-3; *Bulawayo Chronicle* 20 January, 24 February, and 3 March 1900. Hickman, *Rhodesia Served the Queen*, pp.65-6, quotes Plumer's evidence before the Royal Commission on the War in South Africa (Cd 1791), that Nicholson had accumulated enough stocks to feed the whole white population of Rhodesia for eight months. Plumer's memory was at fault here; this statement is not borne out by the contemporary dispatches.

16 co 879/64/634, no.43, encl.4, p.78; no.159, encl.3, p.202; co 468/3 (Co. Report, 1898-1900, p.18); *Bulawayo Chronicle*, 20, 27 January 1900.

17 co 417/283/2395, p.112; 2902, p.148; co 879/68/656, no.53, encl., pp.61-3; co 468/3 (Co. Report 1898-1900, p.9).

18 Sir E. Hertslet, *The Map of Africa by Treaty*, vol. III, p.1024; R.J. Hammond, *Portugal and Africa, 1815-1910*, p.257. Clarke mentioned the "secret treaty"; Chamberlain referred to the Convention of 11 June 1891, and "the Portuguese secret note of the same date," and asked Milner not to mention the latter in communication with the Company. The resources available to me at this point, including the Library of Parliament in Ottawa, have failed to turn up the secret note, but Chamberlain was presumably referring to that and not to the Secret Declaration of 14 October 1899. (co 879/63/608, no.180, p.57, and no.258, p.80.)

19 co 417/283/2395, p.112; 6118, p.210; 8729, pp.306-7; co 879/56/572, no.668, pp.497-9; 63/608, no.323, pp.103-4; no.365, p.116; no.439, p.140.

20 co 879/68/657, no.298, encl.4, p.385; *Bulawayo Chronicle*, 28 April and 12 May 1900.

21 CO 879/68/657, no.58, encl.4, pp. 74-5; no.169, encl.5, p.246; no.204, encl.3, pp.272-4; no.298, encl.3, pp.383-4; 70/662, no.97, p.155; 663, no.196, pp.244-5; CO 417/284/27813, pp.16-23. There is one minor exception, which is mentioned below, to the last statement. The death of the horses gives rise to the question why this did not happen in the units raised earlier. Part of the explanation is that many of the horses of the BSAP, the SRV, and even of the Rhodesia Regiment, were local, acclimatized, and even "salted." But Plumer, who praised the horses brought from the OFS, attributed the health of all of them to care: during the two months of training before the war "the horses themselves were made very fit and we were able to keep that up for the first year . . . and if a horse was ill we . . . considered it a very serious thing." (Plumer's evidence, quoted in Hickman, *Rhodesia Served the Queen*, p.64.)

22 CO 417/276/35364, pp.995-1009 (Postmaster General's report); 283/4587, p.169; 4944, pp.175-7; 5987, pp.205-7; *Bulawayo Chronicle*, 23 December 1899.

23 CO 879/64/634, no.391, encl.10, p.391; no.587, encl.9, p.615; 68/657, no.204, encl.5, pp.274-6.

24 CO 879/56/572, no.668, pp.497-9; 64/634, no.587, encl.1, p.604; CO 417/284/39321, pp.587-91.

25 CO 417/276/34428, pp.908-10; 283/20015, pp.506-10; 319/5309, p.213; 5908, p.276; *Bulawayo Chronicle*, 26 May 1900.

26 CO 417/276/32478, pp.80-1; 34717, p.958; CO 879/66/644, no.112, encl.3, pp.153-4; 70/663, no.18, encl., pp.23-6.

27 CO 417/283/3849, pp.88-108; 4644, pp.127-34; 13205, pp.327-35; Hickman, *Rhodesia Served the Queen*, pp.233-51. For the Derdepoort or Sekwani affair, Blair Hankey, "Black Pawns in a White Man's Game: A Study of the Role of the Non-Whites in the Anglo-Boer War, 1899-1902" (M.A. thesis, Queen's University, 1969), pp.113-50.

28 CO 879/68/656, no.112, encl., pp.177-8; no.118, encl.2, p.191; 69/659, no.78, encls.1, 2, pp.128-9; no.94, encl., p.146; no.142, encl.8, p.191; no.161, encl., pp.248-9; 76/694, no.49 and encls., pp.68-72; no.62, pp.84-6; no.122, encl., pp.165-6; no.142, encl., pp.194-5; 78/702, no.101, p.111; no.307, pp.348-9.

29 *Bulawayo Chronicle*, 13 and 20 March 1901.

30 CO 879/66/644, nos.152, pp.176-8, 153, pp.178-81, 161, pp.214-5, 227, pp.317-9, 265, pp.372-4, 353, pp.545-7; 68/657, no.10, pp.17-9; no.53, encl.1, p.60.

31 *Cape Argus*, 3 April 1900.

32 *Bulawayo Chronicle*, 12 May 1900; *Rhodesia Herald*, 14 and 15 May 1900. See *Bulawayo Chronicle*, leading article of 22 June 1901, for an attack on the Cape and Schreiner. There is a reference to a speech by Rhodes, who said that the Cape had lost its chance and South Africa would be dominated by the "Progressives" of the North. In *Bulawayo Chronicle*, 17 and 25 May 1901, pleas for English to be the only language of instruction in the ex-republics and the only official language in South Africa.

33 *Bulawayo Chronicle*, 26 May 1900.

34 Ibid., 2, 16, and 30 June and 1 September 1900; CO 468/3 (Co. Report 1900-2, p.17).

35 *Bulawayo Chronicle*, 31 January, 25 May, 26 June 1901.

36 CO 879/69/659, no.6, encl., pp.7-8; CO 417/336/1768, pp.10-11; CO 468/3 (Co. Report 1900-2, p.162); *Bulawayo Chronicle*, 7 July and 15 September 1900.

37 CO 879/68/656, no.145, encls.17, 19, pp.236-7; 69/659, no.38, pp.57-8; CO 417/336/1768, pp.2-27; 2288, pp.42-5; CO 468/3 (Co. Report 1900-2, p.18).

38 CO 879/68/656, nos.186, p.304, 196, p.316, 201, p.329, 208, p.334; 69/659, no.53, pp.79-80; no.222, encl., pp.331-4; no.198, pp.298-302; 76/694, no.149, encl.1, pp.200-2; *Bulawayo Chronicle*, 26 October 1900, 4 and 11 January 1901. Another example of "wastage": of 157 labourers sent from Barotseland, all but five deserted on the way (CO 879/68/656, no.145, encl.11, pp.232-4).

39 CO 417/311/27212, pp.196-214; 338/35623, pp.187-94; 345/1402, p.821; 365/45795, p.325; CO 879/69/659, no.6, encl., pp.7-8; *Bulawayo Chronicle*, 19 May, 7, 14, 21, and 28 July 1900; every weekly edition from 13 March to 12 June 1901; 3 July and 7 August 1901.

40 CO 879/71/666, no.100, pp.147-50; 72/680, no.48, encl., pp.53-5 and 49, encl., pp.56-7.

41 CO 468/3 (Co. Report 1900-2, p.17). There is a slight discrepancy between these figures and those quoted in ch. 14, but it is of no consequence.

42 CO 879/68/656, no.71, encl., pp.86-91; no.89, encl., pp.121-2; no.145, encl.11, pp.232-4; CO 417/338/36825, p.357; CO 468/3 (Co. Report 1898-1900, pp.32-3), (Co. Report 1900-2, p.164).

43 CO 879/68/656, no.76, p.105; no.102, encl., Annexure 1, pp.156-7. In the eighteenth century the public houses were favourite places for the press gang in Britain to pick up conscripts for the navy.

44 CO 879/68/656, no.89, encl., pp.120-1; no.91, pp.133-4; 76/694, no.110, encl.1, p.146; 78/702, no.71, pp.76-7; no.152, p.167; CO 417/345/48439, p.148.

45 CO 417/321/40254, p.437; 364/30950, pp.259 ff.; Cd 1200, no.26, pp.82-3; no.38, pp.91-4; *Bulawayo Chronicle*, 2 and 30 June 1900 (Government Notices 102, 103/1900), 3 July 1901.

46 CO 417/276/30765, p.737; *Bulawayo Chronicle*, 3 July 1901. Note the contrast in this matter between an undeveloped country and a developed one, where immigrant workers would be regarded as accentuating, not relieving, the "slavery" of the working class.

47 CO 897/68/656, no.66, encl., pp.78-9; no.89, encl., pp.129-32. The form *lobola* is now used indiscriminately in English in referring to this institution. In the Nguni languages *lobola* is the stem of the verb, but *lobolo* the stem of the noun. The Rhodesian ordinance used the latter form.

48 CO 879/68/656, no.89, pp.123-9; 69/659, no.173, pp.273-5; CO 468/3 (Co. Report 1900-2, p.18). The text of the ordinance is in the *Government Gazette* of 27 December 1901.

49 CO 417/321/42271, pp.606-20; 43035, p.636; 336/4704, pp.117-49; 11503, pp.521-8; CO 879/69/659, nos.32, pp.48-57, 111, p.158, 122, pp.170-2.

50 *Government Gazette*, 26 February 1896 (*sic*, for the Regulations of *1895*); ibid., 21 November 1902; CO 879/69/659, no.168, pp.257-60; 76/694, no.179, pp.227-30; 79/717, no.351 and encls., pp.529-33; no.449, p.687; CO 417/321/42271, pp.606-20; *Rhodesia Herald*, 15 November 1902. Two ordinances on this subject were passed in the session of November 1902: (i) amending the previous ordinance, especially with respect to penalties, as required by Chamberlain; and (ii) the new comprehensive measure described in the text. The ordinance passed in 1901 and gazetted in 1902 also confirmed the existing curfew regulation.

51 CO 417/321/42258, pp.518-30; CO 468/3 (Co. Report 1900-2, p.197).

52 *Bulawayo Chronicle*, 27 September, 4 and 25 October, 15 and 29 November, 6 and 13 December 1902; *Rhodesia Herald*, 24 October, 22 November 1902.

53 More precisely, the reference on 17 October 1900 is the first I have been able to find (*Bulawayo Chronicle*, weekly edition, 19 October 1900). See also ibid., 2 November 1900 and 29 May, 11 September 1901. The malarial mosquito was used as an excuse for racial segregation in Sierra Leone also. (Leo Spitzer, *The Creoles of Sierra Leone: Responses to Colonialism, 1870-1945*, pp.51-63.)

54 Rhodes Papers, Charters, Home Board, nos.36, 57; *Bulawayo Chronicle*, 27 January, 24 March, 25 August 1900; *Rhodesia Herald*, 18 October 1902.

55 Rhodes Papers, Charters, Home Board, Nos.46, 58; Rhodesia Railways, no.112; *Bulawayo Chronicle*, 21 April, 14 July, 25 August, 8 September, 5 October 1900, and 24 May, 7 June, 2 August, 27 September, 11 October, and 26 October 1902; Rhodesia Railways, *Guide to Rhodesia*, p.60.

56 Rhodes Papers, Charters, Home Board, nos.49, 50; Rhodesia Gold Reefs, no.15, encl.; *Bulawayo Chronicle*, 18 October 1902.

57 CO 417/364/28104, pp.136, 139. Art.73 of the Company's deed of settlement permitted the directors to fill vacancies on the board, up to the maximum number fixed by the shareholders; such co-options had to be unanimous; but the six weeks' notice was mandatory, and was simply disregarded in this case.

58 *Bulawayo Chronicle*, 1 and 15 February and the whole of March 1902; 6 and 29 September 1902; *Rhodesia Herald*, 22 February 1902.

59 *Bulawayo Chronicle*, 30 August, 6 September, 4 October 1902; *Rhodesia Herald*, 11 and 18 October 1902; CO 879/78/702, no.380, encl., pp.442-4.

60 CO 879/78/702, no.226 and encls., pp.230-44; *Rhodesia Herald*, 7, 15, 22 November 1902.

61 CO 879/69/659, no.9, pp.9-16; no.147, pp.194-7; *Bulawayo Chronicle*, 3 April 1901.

62 CO 417/345/48597, pp.400-8; 364/48443, pp.357-66; 365/51887, pp.632-3; *Government Gazette*, 7 November 1902; *Rhodesia Herald*, 11 October and 22 November 1902.

63 CO 879/68/656, no.199 and encls., pp.320-6; no.216, pp.339-40; 69/659, no.77, p.128; no.105, pp.151-3; 76/694, no.37, encl.2, pp.52-3; no.106, pp.133-5; no.119, pp.159-61.

64 CO 879/78/702, no.372 and encl., pp.435-6; no.373, p.436; no.384, p.447; no.387, pp.456-7; no.388, p.457; no.389, p.457; no.395, p.471; no.403 and encls., pp.476-7; no.404 and encls., pp.477-9; no.409 and encl., p.481; no.419, pp.496-7; 79/717, no.15, pp.36-7; no.19, pp.43, 45-6; no.121, p.176.

65 *Bulawayo Chronicle*, 7 June 1902.

66 J.G. Lockhart and C.M. Woodhouse, *Rhodes*, pp.439-44, 449, 455-7, 467; Sir Lewis Michell, *The Life of the Rt. Hon. C.J. Rhodes, 1853-1902*, p.276; *Bulawayo Chronicle*, 24 March 1900, 19 June 1901.

67 *Bulawayo Chronicle*, 29 March 1902 (leader of 27 March), 12 April 1902; Lockhart and Woodhouse, *Rhodes*, pp.476-9; Michell, *Rhodes*, pp.310-11; J.G. McDonald, *Rhodes, a Life*, p.390.

68 *Bulawayo Chronicle*, 3 May 1902.

69 Nancy Rouillard, ed., *Matabele Thompson: An Autobiography*, pp.192-3.

636 Rhodes and Rhodesia

I

Common terms in the Bantu languages, chiefly the Nguni group (which includes Zulu, Ndebele, Xhosa), Sotho, and Shona. Note that in these languages nouns are inflected by prefixes. In dictionaries the stem, without prefix, determines the place of the word in alphabetical order. In the following list the word is given in the form, including the prefix, in which it commonly appears in the book, but with cross-reference, where appropriate, to the plural or singular form or stem.

abenhla (plural; stem, enhla). Those from higher up; the second class among the Ndebele, mainly of Sotho-Tswana origin, who were absorbed in the course of the migration by the emigrants from Zululand.

abezansi (plural; stem, zansi). Those from the south; the highest class among the Ndebele, being the original emigrants from Zululand, other Nguni who joined them, and their descendants.

amabutho (plural; singular ibutho). Regiments, and the same units in their civil capacity.

amahole (plural; stem, hole). Pejorative Ndebele term for neighbouring peoples of neither Nguni nor Sotho origin, so mainly Shona or Kalanga; when absorbed into Ndebele society, the lowest class.

amajaha (plural; singular ijaha). Young men; in practice normally young warriors.

dhlodhlo Headring worn by Ndebele (and Zulu) men, after reaching maturity and military capability.

Difaqane Sotho equivalent of Mfecane, q.v.

enhla (stem; plural abenhla). See abenhla.

hole (stem; plural amahole). See amahole.

ibutho (singular; plural amabutho). Regiment, and the same unit in its civil capacity.

ijaha (singular; plural amajaha). Young man; in practice normally a young warrior.

impi An armed party of any size.

indaba Basically "affair"; as used by Europeans, a meeting, discussion (cf. palaver, pow-wow).

induna In Zulu, Ndebele, and some other societies, a civil or military officer.

intaba Hill, mountain

Inxwala Religious festival of the first fruits which inaugurated the year. Europeans used the term "Big Dance," which was in fact only a part (the most important part) of the ceremony.

isigaba (singular; plural izigaba). Chieftaincy, district subject to one of the Ndebele "chiefs" or "great indunas."

isikulu Large Ndebele assembly of indunas and other national leaders.

kudu Large antelope: *Strepsiceros strepsiceros*.

lobola Payment, traditionally in cattle, by bridegroom to bride's father.

Mambo Title of Rozvi emperor; now, more generally, a respectful form of address (Shona).

Mfecane In Nguni languages, "the crushing"—specifically the killings, upheavals, and dispersions caused by the wars of Shaka. (In Sotho, Difaqane).

mhondoro (Shona). Ancestral spirit or its incarnation; originally meant lion, but now obsolete in that sense. In comparison with mudzimu, mhondoro is a spirit concerned with public, national affairs.

mphakathi Inner council of most trusted advisers of Ndebele king.

mudzimu (Shona; singular; plural midzimu). Ancestral spirit. In comparison with mhondoro, mudzimu is a spirit concerned with private and family affairs.

umdanga Central courtyard of Ndebele town.

zansi (stem; plural abezansi). *See* abezansi.

2

Common terms in Dutch, Afrikaans, and South African English.

assegai (S.A. English). African spear.

Boer (Dutch, Afrikaans). Farmer. National appellation of the Afrikaners in the republics.

burger (Dutch, Afrikaans). Citizen; specifically a citizen in his military capacity, under obligation to military service.

commando Generally, a party of armed and mounted citizens summoned to attack or raid an enemy; specifically, those of a district, forming the basic unit of a Boer army.

drift (Dutch). Ford, river crossing.

inspan (Afrikaans and S.A. English). To yoke oxen or horses to a vehicle.

knobkerry (S.A. English). Short thick stick with knobbed head, used as a weapon or missile.

kopje (Dutch; Afrikaans koppie). Hill; literally "little head."

koppie (Afrikaans; Dutch kopje). Hill; literally "little head."

kraal (Afrikaans and S.A. English). Stockaded enclosure, either a village or a fold for animals. (Cf. Spanish corral). In case of a village, not necessarily enclosed.

laager (Dutch). Defendable encampment formed by a circle or rectangle of wagons.

morgen (Dutch, S.A. English). Old Cape land measure, equal to 2.11654 acres, or 0.85655 hectare.

outspan (S.A. English) (Verb). To unyoke oxen or horses from a vehicle. (Noun) Place where wagons or carts are halted and animals unyoked.

pont (Afrikaans and S.A. English). Corruption of pontoon; floating bridge or raft to carry vehicles across a river; moved by pulling on fixed cable spanning river.

poort (Afrikaans). Narrow pass between precipitous mountains.

predikant (Dutch, Afrikaans). Clergyman of the Dutch Reformed Church.

rondavel (Dutch and S.A. English). Circular hut, in imitation of African style, with conical roof, usually of thatch.

Rooinek (Afrikaans). "Redneck"— disparaging term for Englishman or British South African.

skerm (Afrikaans; Dutch scherm). Basically, protection. As used by Europeans of Ndebele military practices, a makeshift shelter.

smelling out (S.A. English). Divination by an isanusi (in Zulu) or magician ("witch-doctor") to identify a witch or sorcerer as the cause of some evil.

spoor (Dutch, Afrikaans). Track, especially the footprints of people or animals.

Staatscourant (Dutch). Government Gazette.

trekgees (Afrikaans). Trek spirit, restless desire to pack and move on.

Uitlander (Dutch, Afrikaans). Foreigner; specifically an immigrant, usually British, into the Transvaal after the opening of the gold mines on the Witwatersrand.

veld (Dutch, Afrikaans and S.A. English). Originally, field. In South African usage, open country, usually grassland, considered either as pasture or with regard to its openness and expanse.

Volksraad (Dutch, Afrikaans: "People's Council"). Legislature of a Boer republic.

voorloper Young boy, African or Coloured, who walks in front of a team of oxen with wagon, leading them by a thong or rein.

3

Names of countries and places. The names used in the book are those of the colonial period. After independence many names were changed, as follows (the list does not include subsequent changes).

COUNTRIES

Colonial	Modern
Basutoland	Lesotho
Bechuanaland	Botswana
Northern Rhodesia	Zambia
Nyasaland	Malawi
Southern Rhodesia	Zimbabwe

PLACES

Colonial	Modern
Belingwe	Mberengwa
Chipinga	Chipinge
Enkeldoorn	Chivhu
Essexvale	Esigodini
Fort Victoria	Masvingo
Gwelo	Gweru
Hartley	Chegutu
Mafeking	Mafikeng
Marandellas	Marondera
Melsetter	Chimanimani
Mtoko	Mutoko
Nuanetsi	Mwenezi
Que Que	Kwekwe
Salisbury	Harare
Shabani	Zvishavane
Sinoia	Chinhoyi
Somabula	Somabhula
Umtali	Mutare
Umvukwes	Mvurwi
Wankie	Hwange

A list of the sources and works actually used for the writing of this book, not a bibliography of the subject. See Preface for reference to this point.

I. PUBLIC RECORDS, UNPUBLISHED

A. Public Record Office, London

(i) CO 417. (Original correspondence between Colonial Office and High Commissioner for South Africa. Series begins January 1884.) Vols.1-90, 97, 99, 100, 101A, 102, 103, 112, 113, 116, 121, 136, 197, 231, 253, 276, 283, 284, 308, 309, 311, 319, 321, 336, 338, 345, 364, 365.

(ii) CO 879. (Colonial Office Confidential Print, Africa, South.) Not published but printed for the use of the cabinet. All the important dispatches in CO 417 are included in this series, but not the successive drafts of the dispatches out from the Office, nor the minutes, written by the officials, on the incoming dispatches and on the drafts of the replies. The whole series up to 1916 is available on microfilm, with the exception (among those used) of one print in too poor a condition to be filmed, viz., CO Confidential Print, Africa, South, 414.

In the following pairs of figures the second is the number of the print, the first the number of the volume in which is is included.
21/274, 22/286, 22/287, 22/297, 23/301, 23/305, 24/317, 26/344, 29/358, 30/369, 30/372, 31/380, 32/392, 33/403, 36/426, 37/439, 37/441, 39/454, 39/459, 40/461, 42/484, 43/491, 43/495, 44/498, 45/505, 47/517, 47/520, 52/552, 53/559, 54/562A, 56/572, 57/574, 61/606, 63/608, 64/634, 66/644, 68/656, 68/657, 69/659, 70/662, 70/663, 71/666, 72/680, 75/686, 76/694, 78/702, 79/717, 86/763.

(iii) CO 537. (Colonial Office files, Supplementary; all Colonies.) Vols. 124B, 127, 130.

(iv) Miscellaneous CO 291. Vol. 26. Foreign Office Confidential Print 179/279, 6178, 6482. BT31/4815/31926 X/K2372 (United Concessions Co.) BSA Co., List of Original Shareholders (formerly in House of Lords Record Office).

B. National Archives of Zimbabwe

(i) BSA Co. Papers, London Office. Series LO3. Out Letters. Series LO5. In Letters.
(ii) BSA Police, Rolls. Victoria Agreement, 1893. B4/2/4.

II. PUBLIC RECORDS, PUBLISHED

(i) Command Papers (included under heading of Parliamentary or Sessional Papers), United Kingdom. ("Blue Books"). The items in these papers were largely identical with those in the Confidential Print, but differed from them in crucial respects. As the Blue Books were published—and very soon after the dates of the papers in them—material too sensitive to be exposed in public was excluded from them, and what remained was carefully edited. Historians writing before the (then) fifty-year rule made the original material available depended essentially on these Command Papers for their Public Records, so were occasionally misled on important points. As several papers were bound together in one volume, they are identified here in two ways, by (a) the number of the Command Paper, beginning with C, and in later series with Cd, Cmd, Cmnd; and (b) the number of the volume, listed under the year and a roman numeral. These papers are indispensable, as material included in them was sometimes omitted from the Confidential Print, with a reference to the Command Paper in which it would be found.
C3914(1884,LVII)
C4190(1884,LVI)

C4194(1884,LVII)
C4213(1884-5,LVII)
C4224(1884-5,LV)
C4251(1884-5,LVII)
C4262(1884-5,LVI)
C4275(1884-5,LVII)
C4310(1884-5,LVII)
C4432(1884-5,LVII)
C4588(1884-5,LVII)
C4643(1886,XLVIII)
C4956(1887,LIX)
C5237(1887,LIX)
C5363(1888,LXXV)
C5524(1888,LXXV)
C5918(1890,LI)
C6370(1890-1,LVII)
C7555(1894,LVII)
277(Treasury Minute, no Command
number; 1894,LVII)
Cd.1200(1902,LXIX)
Cd.1791(1904,XLI)
Cd.8674(1917-8,XXIII)

(ii) Published Records of the BSA Company, on Colonial Office Microfilm.
CO 3/1. Ordinances.
CO 455/1, 455/2. Government Gazettes, 1894-1904.
CO 468/1. Administrative Reports, 1889-1898.
CO 468/3. Administrative Reports, 1899-1902.

(iii) Miscellaneous.
HANSARD, Parliamentary Debates
(United Kingdom)
51-2 Vic., Vol. XI.
52-3 Vic., Vol. I.
CAPE OF GOOD HOPE, Debates, House of
Assembly, 1892.
CAPE OF GOOD HOPE, Votes and Proceedings of House of ASSEMBLY, 1890,
Appendix I, Vol. I.
1898, Appendix I, Vol. II.
SOUTH AFRICAN NATIVE AFFAIRS COMMISSION
(Lagden Commission),
Evidence, Vol. IV.

III. HISTORICAL MANUSCRIPTS
A. *National Archives of Zimbabwe*
Under each of the following headings the identification number, and sometimes the title, refer only to the file or box actually used; the collection may include other files with an additional sequence of numbers.

ADAMS-ACTON, H. Diary (AC 1)
CREWE, P.D. Reminiscences (CR 2)
DAWSON, JAMES Correspondence (DA1/1/1)
FRY, ELLERTON Reminiscences (FR1/4/1)
FRY, IVON Reminiscences (FR2/2/1)
GAMBO [GAMPU] Reminiscences (MISC/GA
2/1/1) (Recorded by C.L. Carbutt)
GRAHAM, M.D. Out Letters (GR 6/1/1)
HOLE, H. MARSHALL Collected Papers (HO
1/3/1, 1/3/4, 1/6/1) including some
papers of James Dawson, and a "key
to the aliases" in *Old Rhodesian
Days*.
JOHNSON, FRANK Correspondence and
Journal (JO 3/1/1 and 3/3/2) Typescript of *Great Days*, including material excised before publication (JO
3/6)
LEASK, THOMAS Agreements (LE 2/2/16-
17)
LOBENGULA Correspondence and other
Papers (LO 1/1/1)
LONDON MISSIONARY SOCIETY Correspondence (LO 6/1/4-5) (Copies; originals
in possession of LMS)
MAXWELL, THOMAS Diary (MA 1/2)
MHLAHLO "Wilson's Last Stand" (Translation of a statement) (MISC/MH
1/1/1)
MOFFAT, JOHN SMITH Political Papers
(Large selection from the MSS. MO 1-
2, edited for publication by the late
Professor J.P.R. Wallis. Never published, but remains in typescript in
the National Archives.)
MOFFAT, RICHARD Reminiscences (MO
4/1/1)
NAPIER, WILLIAM Diary, Nov.-Dec. 1893
(MISC/NA 4/1/1)
NEWTON, SIR FRANCIS Miscellaneous Correspondence (NE 1/1/10)
PIONEER CORPS ASSOCIATION Pioneer
Corps Nominal Rolls (1890, Mashonaland) (PI 2/5)
RUDD, C.D. Correspondence (RU 2/1/1-2)

USHER, W.F. Correspondence (US 1/1/1)

WEALE, M.E. Reminiscences, 1894 (WE 3/2/5)

WESTBEECH, GEORGE. Journal (WE 1/2/1)

WILSON, B. ("Matabele"). Journals (WI 6/2)

WINDRAM, R. FOSTER Matabele Traditions (WI 8/1/1-2) (Records of Oral Interviews)

WOOD, J.G. Journals (WO1/2/1-8)

B. Rhodes House, Oxford

(i) Rhodes Papers.

1. Administrators.

3. Charters (to 1896): 3A/1, 3A/2, 3B.

4. Charters (Home Board).

9. Finance.

10. Gold Fields: 10/1.

19. Rhodesian Gold Reefs.

20. Rhodesia Railways.

(ii) Other. (Abbreviated in notes to RH mss Afr.)

S.4. Some letters of Robert Vavasseur.

S.8. Narrative of Jameson's last meeting with Lobengula, by Howard Pim.

S.71. BSA Co., Charter of Incorporation.

S.73-77. Miscellaneous Papers and Correspondence, BSA Co., 1888-1911. (Notably papers of George Cawston.)

S.226. Ledger Book of James Fairbairn.

t.1. Miscellaneous correspondence of C.J. Rhodes.

t.5. Miscellaneous correspondence of C.J. Rhodes.

C. Miscellaneous locations

COLLECTIONS of private papers.

CHAMBERLAIN, JOSEPH (JO 10/6/1/4). (University of Birmingham)

GREY, FOURTH EARL (University of Durham)

LIPPERT, E. (Archives of Barlow Rand, Johannesburg)

MAUND, E.A. (University of the Witwatersrand)

MILNER, VISCOUNT (New College, Oxford)

SALISBURY, THIRD MARQUESS OF (Hatfield House; formerly at Christ Church, Oxford)

THOMPSON, F.R. ("Matabele"). (In private possession. With the permission of the owners, all the significant papers were photocopied, arranged, and the pages numbered. This copy is in the Douglas Library, Queen's University. The page numbers in the copy, in addition to other identifications, have been given in note references to this collection.)

IV. THESES AND SEMINAR PAPERS

Unpublished when they were consulted. A few have since been published, with or without considerable revision. Where possible, note references to these have been changed to refer to the published books. The latter are listed also below under VIII. In this list and throughout this book "Queen's University" means Queen's University at Kingston, Ontario.

BAKER, DORIS "The British South Africa Company versus the Portuguese in Manicaland and Gazaland, 1889-1892." Queen's University.

BEACH, D.N. "The Rising in South-Western Mashonaland, 1896-7." University of London.

——— "The Politics of Collaboration, South Mashonaland, 1896-7." University of Zimbabwe (Rhodesia), Henderson Seminar Paper 9.

——— "The Adendorff Trek in Shona History." University of Zimbabwe (Rhodesia), Henderson Seminar Paper 14.

——— "Historians and the Shona Empires, Parts I and II. University of Zimbabwe (Rhodesia), Henderson Seminar Papers 19, 20.

——— "The Shona and Ndebele Power." University of Zimbabwe (Rhodesia), Henderson Seminar Paper 26.

BHEBE, N.M.B. "Christian Missions in Matabeleland, 1859-1923." University of London.

CHANAIWA, DAVID "A History of the Nhowe before 1900." University of California.

COBBING, JULIAN "The Ndebele under the Khumalos." University of Lancaster.

HALL, KENNETH O. "Sir Hercules Robinson and South Africa, 1881-1889." Queen's University.

HANKEY, BLAIR "Black Pawns in a White Man's Game: A Study of the Role of the Non-Whites in the Anglo-Boer War, 1899-1902." Queen's University.

HEMKER, ELIZABETH S. "The Role of J.W. Colenbrander in the Occupation and Conquest of Rhodesia, 1893-1896." Queen's University.

KEMP, B.H. "J.W. Colenbrander as Military and Diplomatic Agent in Zululand, Swaziland and Matabeleland, 1879-1896." University of Natal.

KOSMIN, BARRY A. "A Comparative Historical Population Study: The Development of Southern Rhodesian Jewry, 1890-1936." University of Zimbabwe (Rhodesia), Henderson Seminar Paper 17.

MCGILL, D.C. "A History of the Transvaal, 1852-1864." University of Cape Town.

MAYLAM, PAUL. "The Significance of the Disputed Territory in Bechuanaland, 1887-1893." Queen's University.

——— "The British South Africa Company and the Bechuanaland Protectorate, 1889-1899." Queen's University.

PALMER, R.H. "The Making and Implementation of Land Policy in Rhodesia, 1890-1936." University of London.

RENNIE, J.K. "Christianity, Colonialism and the Origins of Nationalism among the Ndau of Southern Rhodesia, 1890-1935." Northwestern University.

REYNOLDS, P.G. "Imperial-Racial Thought in Mid-Victorian England, 1857-1869." Queen's University.

SCHOFFELEERS, J.M. "An Organizational Model of the Mwari Shrines." Typescript. (No date or location.)

TAYLOR, J.J. "The Origins of the Native Department in Southern Rhodesia, 1890-1898." University of Zimbabwe (Rhodesia), Henderson Seminar Paper 7.

VANSTONE, J.P. "Sir Gordon Sprigg: A Political Biography." Queen's University.

V. WORKS OF REFERENCE

BAXTER, T.W. *Guide to the Public Records of Rhodesia, Vol. I, 1890-1923.* Salisbury, 1969. National Archives of Rhodesia (Zimbabwe).

——— and Burke, E.E. *Guide to the Historical Manuscripts in the National Archives of Rhodesia.* Salisbury, 1970. National Archives of Rhodesia (Zimbabwe).

PUBLIC RECORD OFFICE *List of Colonial Office Confidential Print to 1916.* Handbook No. 8. London: H.M.S.O., 1965.

Standard Encyclopedia of Southern Africa Cape Town: Nasionale Opvoedkundige Uitgewery, 1970.

ROSENTHAL, ERIC *Encyclopedia of Southern Africa.* London and New York: Frederick Warne and Co., 1961.

BURDETT, HENRY C. *Burdett's Official Intelligencer.* ("Being a carefully revised précis of all British, American and foreign securities.") 11th year, 1892. 12th year, 1893. London, Spottiswoode and Co.

VI. NEWSPAPERS AND PERIODICALS

(i) Series.

MASHONALAND HERALD, Salisbury. 1891-1892.

RHODESIA HERALD, Salisbury. 1892-1902.

BULAWAYO CHRONICLE (spelt Buluwayo until March 1896). 1894-1902.

CAPE ARGUS, Cape Town. 1884-1902.

THE TIMES, London. 1888-1926.

ZAMBESI MISSION RECORD (Jesuit Mission). Vols. I, II, III.

(ii) Selected issues.

RHODESIA WEEKLY REVIEW, Bulawayo. 28/3/1896.

STAR, Johannesburg. 18/11/1893. 20/1/1894.

STANDARD AND DIGGER'S NEWS, Johannesburg. 13/11/1893, 19 and 20/1/1894.

JOURNAL, Grahamstown. 11/2/1888. 10/3/1888.

CAPE TIMES, weekly edition, Cape Town. 8/11/1897.

ECONOMIST, London. 3/12/1892, 20/1/1894.

VII. ARTICLES

ABRAHAM, D.P. "The Principality of Maungwe: Its History and Traditions." *NADA* (1951).

—— "The Monomotapa Dynasty." *NADA* (1959).

—— "Maramuca: An Exercise in the Combined Use of Portuguese Records and Oral Tradition." *Journal of African History*, II(2) (1961).

ALPERS, EDWARD A. "Dynasties of the Mutapa-Rozwi Complex." *Journal of African History*, XI(2) (1970).

ANON "Unification of the Native Language." *NADA* (1955).

BARNES, J.C. "The 1896 Rebellion in Manicaland." *Rhodesiana*, No.34.

BEACH, D.N. "Kaguvi and Fort Mhondoro." *Rhodesiana*, No.27.

—— "Ndebele Raiders and Shona Power." *Journal of African History*, XV(4) (1974).

BERNHARD, F.O. "Discoverer of Simbabye: The Story of Karl Mauch, Parts I and II." *Rhodesiana*, Nos. 21, 22.

BHEBE, N.M.B. "Some Aspects of Ndebele Relations with the Shona in the Nineteenth Century." *Rhodesian History*, IV (1973).

BHILA, H.H.K. "Manyika's Relationship with the Portuguese and the Gaza-Nguni from 1832 to 1890." *Rhodesian History*, VII (1976).

BURBRIDGE, A., SJ "In Spirit-Bound Rhodesia." *NADA* (1924).

BURKE, E.E. "Lobengula's Seals." *Africana Notes and News*, XI (1955).

—— "Mazoe and the Mashona Rebellion." *Rhodesiana*, No.25.

—— "Fort Victoria to Fort Salisbury, the Latter Part of the Journey of the Pioneer Column in 1890." *Rhodesiana*, No.28.

CARNEGIE, W.A. "Brief Notes on Lobengula and his People." *NADA* (1933).

CAVENDISH, LADY FREDERICK "Five Months in South Africa." *The Living Age* (Boston), vol.185. (Reprinted from *Murray's Magazine*.)

"CHINYANDURA" "The Sinoia Caves — a Historiette." *NADA* (1931).

COBBING, J.R.D. "Lobengula, Jameson and the Occupation of Mashonaland, 1890." *Rhodesian History*, IV (1973).

—— "The Evolution of Ndebele Amabutho." *Journal of African History*, XV(4) (1974).

—— "The Absent Priesthood: Another look at the Rhodesian Risings of 1896-7." *Journal of African History*, XVIII(1) (1977).

COLE, D.T. "Fanagalo and the Bantu Languages in South Africa." *African Studies*, XII(1).

COOKE, C.K. "Lobengula, Second and Last King of the Amandebele: His Final Resting Place and Treasure." *Rhodesiana*, No.23.

DACHS, A.J. "Missionary Imperialism — the case of Bechuanaland." *Journal of African History*, XIII(4) (1972).

DEYO, MARGUERITE. "History of the Mutambara Tribe." *NADA* (1955).

"T.E." "The Story of the Origin of the Name Makoni." *NADA* (1936-7).

EDWARDS, J.A. "The Lomagundi District, a Historical Sketch." *Rhodesiana*, No.7.

EDWARDS, W. "The Wanoe: A Short Historical Sketch." *NADA* (1926).

FORTUNE, G. "A Rozwi Text with Translation and Notes." *NADA* (1956).

—— "Who was Mwari?" *Rhodesian History*, IV (1973).

FRANKLIN, H. "Nyaningwe: Notes on the Chibi Family." *NADA* (1928).

—— "The War of the Tell-Tale between Chiefs Makoni and Mtasa." *NADA* (1938).

"N.G." "Magango Hutari." *NADA* (1933).

GARLAKE, P.S. "Rhodesian Ruins — a Preliminary Assessment of their Style and Chronology." *Journal of African History*, XI(4) (1970).

GELFAND, M. "The Religion of the Mashona." *NADA* (1956).

GUTHRIE, MALCOLM. "Some Developments in the Pre-History of the Bantu Languages." *Journal of African History*, III(2) (1962).

HALKETT, C.H. "With Laing in the Matopos." *Rhodesiana*, No.24.

HICKMAN, A.S. "Norton District and the Mashona Rebellion." *Rhodesiana*, No.3.

HOWLAND, R.C. "The Mazoe Patrol." *Rhodesiana*, No.8.

HOWMAN, ROGER. "Orlando Baragwanath." *Rhodesiana*, No.28.

HUGO, H.C. "The Spirit World of the Mashona." *NADA* (1925).

HURRELL, MRS. A. "The Gwelo Laager, 1896." *Rhodesiana*, No.22.

"H.M.G.J." "Notes on Chiefs Gambo and Sikombo." *NADA* (1925).

"S.J." "Reminiscences of the 1896 Rebellion." *NADA* (1927).

JEFFREYS, M.D.W. Letter, under heading "Hymn Sung — Veterans." Johannesburg *Star* (weekly edition), 8/8/1970.

LIESEGANG, G. "Aspects of Gaza-Nguni History." *Rhodesian History*, VI (1975).

LLOYD, ELAINE. "Mbava." *NADA* (1925).

LYE, WILLIAM F. "The Ndebele Kingdom south of the Limpopo River." *Journal of African History*, X(1) (1969).

"MACHARANGWADA" "*Mudzimu, Shabe, Ngozi*, and other Spirits." *NADA* (1932).

"MAFOHLA" "The Curse of Chigodoro, an Incident in the History of the Vambire Tribe." *NADA* (1928).

MARCONNES, FRANCISQUE, SJ. "The Karangas." *NADA* (1932).

―――― "The Rozvis or Destroyers." *NADA* (1933).

"MARODZI" (translated by F.P.). "The Barozwi." *NADA* (1924).

MORKEL, E.R. "The *Mondoro* or Ancestral Spirit of the Wabuja." *NADA* (1930).

―――― "Spiritualism amongst the Wabudya." *NADA* (1933).

MUDENGE, S.I. "An Identification of the Rozvi and its Implication for the History of the Karanga." *Rhodesian History*, V (1974).

NCUBE, R.M.M. "The True Story *re* Chaminuka and Lobengula." *NADA* (1962).

NEWITT, M.D.D. "The Portuguese on the Zambezi: An Historical Interpretation of the Prazo System." *Journal of African History*, X(1) (1969).

NEWTON, GWENDA "The Go-Between — Jan Grootboom." *Rhodesiana*, No.29.

PALMER, R.H. "Aspects of Rhodesian Land Policy, 1890-1936." Central African Historical Association, Local Series 22.

PHIMISTER, I.R. "Alluvial Gold Mining and Trade in Nineteenth-Century South Central Africa." *Journal of African History*, XV(3) (1974).

POLLETT, HUGH. "The Mazoe Patrol." *Rhodesiana*, No.2.

POSSELT, F.W.T. "Nkulumana: the Disputed Succession." *NADA* (1923).

―――― "Chaminuka the Wizard." *NADA* (1926).

―――― "The Watawara and the Batonga." *NADA* (1929).

RANGER, T.O. "The Re-Writing of African History during the Scramble: The Matabele Dominance in Mashonaland." *African Social Research*, No.4 (December 1967).

―――― "The Meaning of Mwari." *Rhodesian History*, V (1974).

RANKIN, D.J. "The Portuguese in East Africa." *Fortnightly Review*, 1/2/1890.

RICARDE-SEAVER, F.I., and METCALFE, SIR CHARLES. "The British Sphere of Influence in South Africa." *Fortnightly Review*, 1/3/1889.

ROBINSON, K.R. "A History of the Bikita

District." *NADA* (1957).

SEED, H.J., S.J. "A Glimpse of Native History: The Vashawasha." *NADA* (1936-7).

SELOUS, F.C. "Mashunaland and the Mashunas." *Fortnightly Review*, 1/5/1889.

SEYMOUR, LINDSAY F. "The Tradition of the VaMare of Chibi." *NADA* (1940).

SHAW, FLORA "The British South Africa Company." *Fortnightly Review*, 1/11/1889.

SICARD, H. VON "The Origin of Some of the Tribes in the Belingwe Reserve." *NADA* (1948, 1950, 1951, 1952, 1953, 1955).

—— "Rhodesian Sidelights on Bechuanaland History." *NADA* (1954).

—— "The Vuxwa Hills and their Inhabitants." *NADA* (1958).

—— "Mambo Dyembewu." *Proceedings and Transactions of the Rhodesian Scientific Association*, vol.43.

—— "The Derivation of the Name Mashona." *African Studies*, vol.9.

SIGOLA, CHIEF SIMON "How Lobengula Came to Rule the Matabele." *NADA* (1954).

SMITH, ALAN K. "The Peoples of Southern Mozambique: An Historical Survey." *Journal of African History*, XIV(4) (1973).

SMITH, H. STANFORD "Monomotapas." *NADA* (1958).

STIGGER, P. "Volunteers and the Profit Motive in the Anglo-Ndebele War, 1893." *Rhodesian History*, II (1971).

STORRY, J.G. "The Settlement and Territorial Expansion of the Mutasa Dynasty." *Rhodesian History*, VII (1976).

SUMMERS, ROGER. "The Military Doctrine of the Matabele." *NADA* (1955).

TAYLOR, GUY A. "The Matabele Head Ring (Isidhlodhlo) and some Fragments of History." *NADA* (1925).

THACKERAY, R.H. "Henry Hartley, African Hunter and Explorer." *Journal of the Royal African Society*, vol.37 (1938).

THOMPSON, J. BLAKE "Physical Appearances of some Mashona Totemic Groups." *NADA* (1948).

—— and SUMMERS, ROGER. "Mlimo and Mwari: Notes on a Native Religion in Southern Rhodesia." *NADA* (1956).

THOMPSON, LOUIS C. "The Ba-Lemba of Southern Rhodesia." *NADA* (1942).

TIZIRAI, PASKARI "The Story of the Chilimanzi People." *NADA* (1949).

TURTON, J.E.S. "Native History of Salisbury as related by Chari Gwati to J.E.S. Turton." *NADA* (1939).

VAN DER MERWE, D.J. "Some History of the Vakaranga in the Gutu Reserve." *NADA* (1936-7).

—— "The Shona Idea of God." *NADA* (1957).

VAN ONSELEN, C. "Reactions to Rinderpest in Southern Africa." *Journal of African History*, XIII(3) (1972).

[VERSCHOYLE, JOHN.] "Portugal's Aggressions and England's Duty." *Fortnightly Review*, 1/1/1890.

WHEELER, DOUGLAS L. "Gungunyane the Negotiator: A Study in African Diplomacy." *Journal of African History*, IX(4) (1968).

WILLOUGHBY, SIR JOHN "How We Occupied Mashonaland." *Fortnightly Review*, 1/4/1891.

WOODS, G.G.B. "Matabele History and Customs." *NADA* (1929).

—— "Extracts from Customs and History: Amandebele." *NADA* (1931).

(VARIOUS) "Die Groot Trek." Gedenkuitgawe van *Die Huisgenoot*, December 1938.

VIII. BOOKS

AGAR-HAMILTON, J.A.I. *The Native Policy of the Voortrekkers*. Cape Town: Maskew Miller, 1928.

—— *The Road to the North: South Africa, 1852-1886*. London: Longmans, Green, 1937.

ALDERSON, E.A.H. *With the Mounted In-*

fantry and the Mashonaland Field
Force, 1896. London: Methuen,
1898.

AMERY, L.S., ed. The Times History of the
War in South Africa. 7 vols. London:
S. Low, Marston and Co., 1900-
1909.

ANDERSON, ANDREW A. Twenty-Five Years
in a Waggon in the Gold Regions of
Africa. 2 vols. London: Chapman
and Hall, 1887.

ANDREWS, C.F. John White of
Mashonaland. London: Hodder and
Stoughton, 1935.

AXELSON, ERIC Portugal and the Scramble
for Africa, 1875-1891. Johannesburg: Witwatersrand University
Press, 1967.

BADEN-POWELL, R.S.S. The Matabele
Campaign, 1896. London: Methuen,
1901.

BAIÃO, ANTÓNIO; CIDADE, HERNÁNI; and
MÚRIAS, MANUEL, eds. História da
Expansão Portuguesa no Mundo. 3
vols. Lisbon: Editorial Ática, 1940.

BAINES, THOMAS The Gold Regions of
South-Eastern Africa. London: Edward Stanford, 1877.

BAKER, J.N.L. A History of Geographical
Discovery and Exploration. New ed.
London: George G. Harrap, 1937.

BAXTER, T.W., and TURNER, R.W.S. Rhodesian Epic. Cape Town: Howard
Timmins, 1966.

BEAVERBROOK, LORD The Decline and Fall
of Lloyd George. London: Collins,
1963.

BECKER, PETER The Path of Blood: The
Rise and Conquests of Mzilikazi . . .
London: Longmans, Green, 1962.

BERTIN, H. Land Titles in Southern
Rhodesia. Salisbury: Argus Printing
and Publishing Co., 1912.

BLENNERHASSET, ROSE, and SLEEMAN,
LUCY. Adventures in Mashonaland.
London: Macmillan, 1893.

BOGGIE, ALEXANDER From Ox-Wagon to
Railway. Bulawayo: Bulawayo
Times Printing Works, 1897.

BOGGIE, JEANNIE M. Experiences of Rhodesia's Pioneer Women. Bulawayo:

Philpott and Collins, 1938.
—— First Steps in Civilizing Rhodesia.
Bulawayo: Philpott and Collins,
1940.

BOTELHO, JOSÉ JUSTINO TEIXEIRA História
Militar e Política dos Portugueses em
Moçambique, de 1833 aos Nossos
Dias. Lisbon: Centro Tipográfico
Colonial, 1936.

BOWLER, LOUIS P. Facts about the Matabele, Mashonas, and the Middle
Zambesi. Pretoria: B. Gluckstein,
1889.

BROWN, WILLIAM HARVEY On the South
African Frontier. London: Sampson
Low, Marston and Co., 1899.

BRYANT, A.T. Olden Times in Zululand
and Natal. London: Longmans,
Green, 1929.

BUCKLE, G.E., ed. The Letters of Queen
Victoria. 3rd ser., vol. I, 1886-1890.
London: John Murray, 1930.

BULLOCK, CHARLES The Mashona. Cape
Town: J.C. Juta and Co., 1927.

BURKE E.E. The Journals of Carl Mauch,
1869-1872. Transcribed by Mrs. E.
Bernhard, translated by F.O. Bernhard. Salisbury: National Archives
of Rhodesia, 1969.

BURNHAM, F.R. Scouting on Two
Continents. Garden City, N.Y.: Garden City Publishing Co., 1926.

BURTON, R.F. The Lands of Cazembe: Lacerda's Journey to Cazembe in 1798.
Translated and annotated by Captain R.F. Burton, F.R.G.S. (London:
John Murray, 1873.

BUTLER, SIR WILLIAM An Autobiography.
London: Constable, 1911.

CADDICK, HELEN A White Woman in Central Africa. London: T. Fisher Unwin, 1900.

CAIRNS, H.A.C. Prelude to Imperialism:
British Reactions to Central African
Society, 1840-1890. London: Rout-
ledge and Kegan Paul, 1956.

CARNEGIE, DAVID Among the Matabele.
London: Religious Tract Society,
1894.

CARTWRIGHT, A.P. Gold Paved the Way.
London: Macmillan, 1967.

CECIL, LADY GWENDOLEN *The Life of Robert, Marquess of Salisbury*. Vol.IV. London: Hodder and Stoughton, 1932.

CHAMBERS, STRACHEY *The Rhodesians*. London: John Lane, The Bodley Head, 1900.

CHAPMAN, JAMES *Travels in the Interior of South Africa*. 2 vols. London: Bell and Daldy; Edward Stanford, 1868.

CHURCHILL, LORD RANDOLPH *Men, Mines and Animals in South Africa*. London: Sampson Low, Marston and Co., 1892.

COÏLLARD, FRANÇOIS *On the Threshold of Central Africa*. Translated by C.W. Macintosh. London: Hodder and Stoughton, 1897.

COLQUHOUN, ARCHIBALD R. *Matabeleland: The War, and Our Position in South Africa*. London: The Leadenhall Press, n.d.

—— *The Afrikander Land*. London: John Murray, 1906.

—— *Dan to Beersheba: Work and Travel in Four Continents*. London: William Heinemann, 1908.

COLVIN, IAN *The Life of Jameson*. 2 vols. London: Edward Arnold, 1923.

CONSOLIDATED GOLD FIELDS OF SOUTH AFRICA *The Gold Fields*. London: The Consolidated Gold Fields, 1937.

COOK, E.T., and WEDDERBURN, ALEXANDER, eds. *The Complete Works of John Ruskin*. Vol. XX. London: G. Allen, 1906.

COOPER-CHADWICK, J. *Three Years with Lobengula, and Experiences in South Africa*. London: Cassell, 1894.

COUPLAND, REGINALD *Livingstone's Last Journey*. London: Collins, 1945.

COUTINHO, JOÃO DE AZEVEDO *O Combate de Macequece: Notas sôbre algumas Determinantes Proximas e Remotas do Conflito*. 2 vols. or parts. Lisbon: Divisão de Publicações e Biblioteca, Agencia Geral das Colonias, 1935.

CROWE, S.E. *The Berlin West African Conference, 1884-1885*. London: Longmans, Green, 1942.

DACHS, ANTHONY J. *The Papers of John Mackenzie*. Johannesburg: University of the Witwatersrand Press, for African Studies Institute, 1975.

DANEEL, M.L. *The God of the Matopo Hills: An Essay on the Mwari Cult in Rhodesia*. The Hague: Mouton, 1970.

DARTER, ADRIAN *The Pioneers of Mashonaland*. London: Simpkin, Marshall, Hamilton, Kent and Co., 1914.

DAVENPORT, T.R.H. *The Afrikaner Bond: The History of a South African Political Party, 1880-1911*. Cape Town: Oxford University Press, 1966.

DE WAAL, D.C. *With Rhodes in Mashonaland*. Cape Town: J.C. Juta and Co., 1896.

DONOVAN, CAPT. C.H.W. *With Wilson in Matabeleland*. London: Henry and Co., 1894.

DOTSON, FLOYD, and DOTSON, LILLIAN O. *The Indian Minority in Zambia, Rhodesia and Malawi*. New Haven and London: Yale University Press, 1968.

DU PLESSIS, J.S. *Die Ontstaan en Ontwikkeling van die Amp van die Staatspresident in die Zuid-Afrikaansche Republiek, 1858-1902*. In Archives Yearbook for South African History, 1955(I). Pretoria, Government Printer.

D'ERLANGER, BARON E.B. *History of the Construction and Finance of the Rhodesian Transport System*. Privately printed, 1939.

EYBERS, G.W., ed. *Select Documents Illustrating South African Constitutional History*. London: George Routledge and Son, 1918.

FARRANT, JEAN *Mashonaland Martyr: Bernard Mizeki and the Pioneer Church*. Cape Town: Oxford University Press, 1966.

FINDLAY, G.G., and Holdsworth, W.W. *The History of the Wesleyan Methodist Missionary Society*. 5 vols. London: The Epworth Press, 1922.

FINLASON, C.E. *A Nobody in*

Mashonaland. London: George Vickers, 1893.

FITZPATRICK, J. PERCY *Through Mashonaland with Pick and Pen*. Johannesburg, 1892. Reprint. Ad. Donker, 1973.

———— *The Transvaal from Within*. London: Heinemann, 1899.

FLINT, JOHN E. *Sir George Goldie and the Making of Nigeria*. London: Oxford University Press, 1960.

FORT, GEORGE SEYMOUR *Dr. Jameson*. London: Hurst and Blackett, 1918.

FRIPP, CONSTANCE E., and HILLER, V.W., eds. *Gold and the Gospel in Mashonaland, 1888*. [Journals of Bishop Knight-Bruce, edited by Fripp, and of C.D. Rudd, edited by Hiller.] London: Chatto and Windus, 1949.

GALBRAITH, JOHN S. *Mackinnon and East Africa, 1875-1895: A Study in the "New Imperialism"*. Cambridge: Cambridge University Press, 1972.

———— *Crown and Charter: The Early Years of the British South Africa Company*. Berkeley, Los Angeles, London: University of California Press, 1974.

GANN, L.H. *The Birth of a Plural Society*. Manchester: Manchester University Press, 1958.

———— *A History of Southern Rhodesia*. London: Chatto and Windus, 1965.

GARRETT, EDMUND *The Story of an African Crisis*. London: Archibald Constable, 1897.

GARVIN, J.L. *The Life of Joseph Chamberlain*, 3 vols. London: Macmillan, 1932-4. Vol. IV by Julian Amery (1951).

GELFAND, MICHAEL *Mother Patrick and Her Nursing Sisters*. Cape Town: J.C. Juta and Co., 1964.

———— *Tropical Victory: An Account of the Influence of Medicine on the History of Southern Rhodesia, 1890-1923*. Cape Town: J.C. Juta and Co., 1953.

———— *Medicine and Magic of the Mashona*. Cape Town: J.C. Juta and Co., 1956.

———— *Shona Ritual, with Special Reference to the Chaminuka Cult*. Cape Town: J.C. Juta and Co., 1959.

———— *African Background: The Traditional Culture of the Shona-speaking People*. Cape Town: J.C. Juta and Co., 1965.

———— *Shona Religion, with Special Reference to Makorekore*. Cape Town: J.C. Juta and Co., 1962.

GLASS, STAFFORD *The Matabele War*. London: Longmans, Green, 1968.

GRENVILLE, J.A.S. *Lord Salisbury and Foreign Policy: The Close of the Nineteenth Century*. London: University of London, The Athlone Press, 1964.

GREY, ALBERT, FOURTH EARL. *Hubert Hervey, Student and Imperialist: A Memoir*. London: Edwin Arnold, 1899.

HALL, KENNETH O. *Imperial Proconsul: Sir Hercules Robinson and South Africa, 1881-1889*. Kingston, Ontario: The Limestone Press, 1980. (Cf. the same work listed under Theses.)

HAMLEY, R. *The Regiment: The History and Uniform of the B.S.A. Police*. Cape Town: T.V. Bulpin, 1971.

HAMMOND, JOHN HAYS *The Autobiography of John Hays Hammond*. 2 vols. New York: Farrar and Rinehart, 1935.

HAMMOND, R.J. *Portugal and Africa, 1815-1910*. Stanford: Stanford University Press, 1966.

HANNA, A.J. *The Beginnings of Nyasaland and North-Eastern Rhodesia, 1859-1895*. Oxford: The Clarendon Press, 1956.

HARDING, COLIN *Far Bugles*. London: Simpkin, Marshall, 1933.

———— *Frontier Patrols*. London: G. Bell and Sons, 1937.

HARRIS, JOHN H. *The Chartered Millions*. London: Swarthmore Press, n.d.

HEADLAM, CECIL, ed. *The Milner Papers*. 2 vols. London: Cassell, 1931.

HENRY, JAMES A., and SIEPMANN, H.A. *Sixty Years North of the Limpopo: The Story of the Coming of the Stan-*

dard Bank to Rhodesia and Nyasaland. Salisbury: The Standard Bank of South Africa, 1953.

———— The First Hundred Years of the Standard Bank. London: Oxford University Press, 1963.

HERTSLET, SIR EDWARD The Map of Africa by Treaty. 3 vols. London: H.M.S.O., 1909.

HICKMAN, A.S. Men Who Made Rhodesia. Salisbury: British South Africa Company, 1960.

———— Rhodesia Served the Queen. Salisbury: Government of Rhodesia, 1970.

HOFMEYR, J.H. The Life of Jan Hendrik Hofmeyr. Cape Town: Van de Sandt de Villiers, 1913.

HOLE, H. MARSHALL The Making of Rhodesia. London: Macmillan, 1926.

———— Old Rhodesian Days. London: Macmillan, 1928.

———— The Jameson Raid. London: Philip Allan, 1930.

HUGHES, A.J.B. Kin, Caste and Nation among the Rhodesian Ndebele. Manchester: Manchester University Press, for the Rhodes-Livingstone Institute, 1956.

HYATT, S.P. Off the Main Track. London: T. Werner Laurie, n.d.

———— The Old Transport Road. London: Andrew Melrose, 1914.

———— The Diary of a Soldier of Fortune. London: Collins, n.d.

ISAACMAN, ALLEN F. Mozambique: The Africanization of a European Institution: The Zambesi Prazos, 1750-1902. Madison: University of Wisconsin Press, 1972.

JOHNSON, FRANK Great Days. London: G. Bell and Sons, 1940.

JOHNSTON, SIR HARRY The Story of My Life. Indianapolis: The Bobbs-Merrill Co., 1923.

JOHNSTON, JAMES, M.D. Reality versus Romance in South Central Africa. London: Hodder and Stoughton, 1893.

JONES, NEVILLE Rhodesian Genesis. Bulawayo: Rhodesia Pioneers and Early Settlers Society, 1953.

KENNEDY, A.L. Salisbury, 1830-1903: Portrait of a Statesman. London: John Murray, 1953.

KLEIN, HARRY Stage Coach Dust. London: Thomas Nelson, 1937.

KNIGHT, E.F. Rhodesia of To-Day. London: Longmans, Green, 1895.

KNIGHT-BRUCE, G.W.H. Memories of Mashonaland. London: Edward Arnold, 1895.

KRÜGER, D.W. Die Weg na die See. (Published thesis, Potchefstroom University College.) n.p., n.d.

———— Paul Kruger. 2 vols. (Johannesburg: Afrikaanse Pers, 1963.

KUPER, H., HUGHES, A.J.B., and VAN VELSEN, J. The Shona and Ndebele of Southern Rhodesia. Ethnographic Survey of Africa, edited by Daryll Forde: Southern Africa, Part IV. London: International African Institute, 1954.

LAING, MAJOR D. TYRIE. The Matabeleland Rebellion, 1896: With the Belingwe Field Force. London: Dean and Son, n.d.

LEONARD, A.G. How We Made Rhodesia. London: Kegan Paul, Trench, Trübner, 1896.

LEWIS, CECIL, and EDWARDS, G.E. Historical Records of the Church of the Province of South Africa. London: S.P.C.K., 1934.

LINDLEY, M.E. The Acquisition and Government of Backward Territory in International Law. London: Longmans, Green, 1926.

LIVINGSTONE, DAVID Missionary Travels and Researches in South Africa. London: Ward, Lock and Co., 1857.

———— and CHARLES. Narrative of an Expedition to the Zambezi and its Tributaries. London: John Murray, 1865.

LOCKHART, J.G., and WOODHOUSE, C.M. Rhodes. London: Hodder and Stoughton, 1963.

LOUW, A.A. Andrew Louw van Morgenster. Cape Town: N.G. Kerk-Uitgewers, 1965.

LOVEDAY, ARTHUR F. *Three Stages in the History of Rhodesia*. Cape Town: A.A. Balkema, n.d.

LOVETT, RICHARD *The History of the London Missionary Society, 1795-1895*. 2 vols. London: Henry Frowde, 1899.

MCDERMOTT, P.L. *British East Africa or Ibea: A History of the Formation and Work of the Imperial British East Africa Company*. London: Chapman and Hall, 1893.

MCDONALD, J.G. *Rhodes, a Life*. London: Philip Allen, 1927.

MACKENZIE, JOHN. *Ten Years North of the Orange River*. Edinburgh: Edmonston and Douglas, 1871.

—— *Austral Africa, Losing it or Ruling it*. 2 vols. London: Sampson Low, Marston, Searle and Rivington, 1887.

MACKENZIE, W. DOUGLAS. *John Mackenzie, South African Missionary and Statesman*. London: Hodder and Stoughton, 1902.

MAGER, E. *Karl Mauch, Lebensbild eines Afrikareisenden*. Stuttgart: W. Kohlhammer, 1895.

MARTINS, J.P. OLIVEIRA *Portugal em Africa: A Questão Colonial — O Conflicto Anglo-Portuguez*. Porto: Livraria Internacional de Ernesto Chardron. Lugan e Genelioux, Successores, 1891.

MATHERS, E.P. *Zambesia: England's Eldorado in Africa*. London: King, Sell and Railton, 1891.

MATTHEWS, J.W. *Incwadi Yami*. New York: Rogers and Sherwood, 1881.

MAYLAM, PAUL *Rhodes, the Tswana and the British: Colonialism, Collaboration and Conflict in the Bechuanaland Protectorate, 1885-1899*. Westport, Conn., and London: Greenwood Press, 1980. (Cf. the same work listed under Theses.)

MICHELL, SIR LEWIS *The Life of the Rt. Hon. C.J. Rhodes, 1853-1902*. London: Edward Arnold, 1910.

MOFFAT, ROBERT U. *John Smith Moffat, C.M.G., Missionary: A Memoir*. London: John Murray, 1921.

MOHR, EDWARD *To the Victoria Falls of the Zambesi*. Translated by N. D'Anvers. London: Sampson Low, Marston, Searle and Rivington, 1876.

MILLAIS, J.G. *The Life of Frederick Courtenay Selous, D.S.O.* London: Longmans, Green, 1919.

NEWMAN, CHARLES L. NORRIS *Matabeleland and How We Got It*. London: T. Fisher Unwin, 1895.

NOBBS, ERIC A. *Guide to the Matopos*. Cape Town: Maskew Miller, 1924.

O'BRIEN, CONOR CRUISE. *Parnell and His Party, 1880-1890*. Oxford: The Clarendon Press, 1957.

OLIVER, ROLAND *Sir Harry Johnston and the Scramble for Africa*. London: Chatto and Windus, 1957.

OLIVIER, S.P. *Many Treks Made Rhodesia*. Cape Town: Howard Timmins, 1957.

OMER-COOPER, J.D. *The Zulu Aftermath*. London: Longmans, Green, 1962.

PAKENHAM, ELIZABETH *Jameson's Raid*. London: Weidenfeld and Nicolson, 1960.

PALLEY, CLAIRE *The Constitutional History and Law of Southern Rhodesia*. Oxford: The Clarendon Press, 1966.

PAULING, GEORGE *Chronicles of a Contractor*. Facsimile of original edition. Bulawayo: Books of Rhodesia, 1969.

PAVER, B.G. *Zimbabwe Cavalcade*. Rev. ed. London: Cassell, 1957.

PETERMANN, DR. A. *Mittheilungen aus Justus Perthes' Geographischer Anstalt*. Uber wichtige neue Erforschungen auf dem Gesamtgebiete der Geographie. Ergänzungsband VIII, 1873-4. No.37, *Carl Mauch's Reisen im Innern von SüdAfrika, 1865-1872*.

PLUMER, LIEUT.-COL. HERBERT *An Irregular Corps in Matabeleland*. London: Kegan Paul, Trench, Trübner and Co., 1897.

POSSELT, F.W.T. *Fact and Fiction*. Rev. ed. Bulawayo: Rhodesian Printing and Publishing Co., 1942.

POTGIETER, CAREL, and THEUNISSEN, N.H. *Kommandant-Generaal Hendrik Potgieter*. Johannesburg: Afrikaanse Pers, 1938.

PRETORIUS, H.S., and KRÜGER, D.W., eds. *Voortrekker-Argiefstukke, 1829-1849*. Pretoria: Government Printer, 1937.

RADEMEYER, J.I. *Die Land Noord van die Limpopo*. Cape Town: A.A. Balkema, 1949.

RANGER, T.O. *Revolt in Southern Rhodesia, 1896-7*. London: Heinemann, 1967.

RANSFORD, OLIVER *Bulawayo, Historic Battleground of Rhodesia*. Cape Town: A.A. Balkema, 1968.

RHODESIA RAILWAYS *Guide to Rhodesia*. 2nd ed. Bulawayo: Davis and Co., 1924.

RORKE, MELINA *Melina Rorke: Her Amazing Experiences in the Stormy Nineties of South Africa's Story, told by herself*. London: George G. Harrap, 1939.

ROSENTHAL, ERIC., ed. and trans. *The Matabele Travel Letters of Marie Lippert, 1891*. Cape Town: Friends of the S.A. Public Library, 1961.

ROUILLARD, NANCY, ed. *Matabele Thompson, an Autobiography*. London: Faber and Faber, 1936.

RUSSELL, PAUL F. *Man's Mastery of Malaria*. London: Oxford University Press, 1955.

SAUER, HANS *Ex Africa*. London: Geoffrey Bles, 1937.

SCHAPERA, I., ed. *Livingstone's Private Journals, 1851-1853*. London: Chatto and Windus, 1960.

SCHREUDER, D.M. *Gladstone and Kruger*. London: Routledge and Kegan Paul, 1969.

SELOUS, F.C. *A Hunter's Wanderings in Africa*. 5th ed. London: Macmillan, 1907.

—— *Travel and Adventure in South-East Africa*. London: R. Ward and Co., 1893.

—— *Sunshine and Storm in Rhodesia*. London: Rowland Ward and Co., 1896.

SILLERY, ANTHONY *The Bechuanaland Protectorate*. Cape Town: Oxford University Press, 1952.

—— *Founding a Protectorate*. The Hague: Mouton and Co., 1965.

—— *John Mackenzie of Bechuanaland, 1835-1899*. Cape Town: A.A. Balkema, 1971.

SINCLAIR, SHIRLEY *The Story of Melsetter*. Salisbury: M.O. Collins, 1971.

SMITH, EDWIN W. *The Way of the White Fields in Rhodesia*. London: World Dominion Press, 1928.

—— *Great Lion of Bechuanaland*. London: Independent Press, 1957.

SMITH, R.C. *Rhodesia: A Postal History*. Salisbury: R.C. Smith, 1967.

SPITZER, LEO *The Creoles of Sierra Leone: Responses to Colonialism, 1870-1945*. Madison: University of Wisconsin Press, 1974.

STENT, VERE *A Personal Record of Some Incidents in the Life of Cecil Rhodes*. Cape Town: Maskew Miller, n.d.

STOKES, ERIC, and BROWN, RICHARD, eds. *The Zambesian Past*. Manchester: Manchester University Press, 1966.

SUMMERS, ROGER *Zimbabwe: A Rhodesian Mystery*. Johannesburg: Thomas Nelson and Sons, 1965.

—— and PAGDEN, C.W. *The Warriors*. Cape Town: Books of Africa, 1970.

SYKES, FRANK W. *With Plumer in Matabeleland*. London: Archibald Constable and Co., 1897.

TABLER, EDWARD C. *The Far Interior: Chronicles of Pioneering in the Matabele and Mashona Countries, 1847-1879*. Cape Town: A.A. Balkema, 1955.

—— ed. *Zambezia and Matabeleland in the Seventies*. Robins Series, No. 1. London: Chatto and Windus, 1960.

—— *Pioneers of Rhodesia*. Cape Town: C. Struik, 1966.

TANSER, G.H. *A Scantling of Time*. Salisbury: Stuart Manning, 1965.

TAYLOR, C.T.C. *A History of Rhodesian Entertainment*. Salisbury: M.O. Collins (Pvt.), 1968.

653 Bibliography

THEAL, GEORGE MCCALL *The Portuguese in South Africa*. Cape Town: J.C. Juta and Co.; and London: T. Fisher Unwin, 1896.

—— *History of South Africa from 1795 to 1872*. 5 vols. London: Swan, Sonnenschein and Co., 1908.

—— *History of South Africa from 1873 to 1884*. 2 vols. London: George Allen and Unwin, 1919.

THOMAS, THOMAS MORGAN *Eleven Years in Central South Africa*. London: John Snow and Co., 1873.

TREGONNING, K.G. *Under Chartered Company Rule: North Borneo, 1881-1946*. Singapore: University of Malaya Press, 1958.

VAMBE, LAWRENCE *An Ill-Fated People*. London: Heinemann, 1972.

VAN DER MERWE, P.J. *Nog Verder Noord*. Cape Town: Nasionale Boekhandel, 1962.

VAN DER POEL, JEAN *Railway and Customs Policies in South Africa, 1885-1910*. London: Longmans, Green, 1933.

—— *The Jameson Raid*. Cape Town: Oxford University Press, 1951.

VAUGHAN-WILLIAMS, H. *A Visit to Lobengula in 1889*. Pietermaritzburg: Shuter and Shooter, 1947.

VERSCHOYLE, F. ["Vindex"]. *Cecil Rhodes, His Political Life and Speeches, 1881-1900*. London: Chapman and Hall, 1900.

WALKER, ERIC A. *Historical Atlas of South Africa*. Cape Town: Oxford University Press, 1922.

—— *The Great Trek*. London: A. and C. Black, 1948.

—— *A History of Southern Africa*. 3rd ed. London: Longmans, Green, 1957.

WALLER, HORACE, ed. *The Last Journals of David Livingstone*. London: John Murray, 1874.

WALLIS, J.P.R., ed. *The Matabele Journals of Robert Moffat, 1829-1860*. 2 vols. Oppenheimer Series, No. 1. London: Chatto and Windus, 1945.

——, ed. *The Northern Goldfields Diaries of Thomas Baines*. 3 vols. Op-penheimer Series, No. 3. London: Chatto and Windus, 1946.

——, ed. *The South African Diaries of Thomas Leask, 1865-1870*. Oppenheimer Series, No. 8. London: Chatto and Windus, 1954.

——, ed. *The Zambezi Expedition of David Livingstone*. 2 vols. Oppenheimer Series, No. 9. London: Chatto and Windus, 1956.

WARHURST, P.R. *Anglo-Portuguese Relations in South-Central Africa, 1890-1900*. London: Longmans, Green, for the Royal Commonwealth Society, 1962.

WEINTHAL, LEO, ed. *The Story of the Cape to Cairo Railway and River Route, from 1887 to 1922*. 4 vols. London: The Pioneer Publishing Co., 1922-3.

WHEATLEY, HENRY B., F.S.A. *London Past and Present*. Vol. II. London: John Murray, 1891.

WHYTE, FREDERIC *The Life of W.T. Stead*. London: Jonathan Cape, 1925.

WICHMANN, F.A.F. *Die Wordingsgeskiedenis van die ZuidAfrikaansche Republiek, 1838-1860*. In Archives Yearbook for South African History, 1941 (II). Pretoria: Government Printer.

WILLIAMS, BASIL *Cecil Rhodes*. New ed. London: Constable, 1938.

WILLIAMS, SIR RALPH. *How I Became a Governor*. London: John Murray, 1913.

WILLS, W.A., and COLLINGRIDGE, L.T. *The Downfall of Lobengula*. 1894. Reprint. Bulawayo: Books of Rhodesia, 1971.

WILSON, M. and THOMPSON, L.M. eds. *The Oxford History of South Africa*. Vol. I. Oxford: The Clarendon Press, 1969.

WOOD, JOSEPH GARBETT, M.L.A. *Through Matabeleland: The Record of a Ten Months' Trip in an Ox-Wagon through Mashonaland and Matabeleland*. London: Richards, Glanville and Co.; and Grahamstown: Wood Bros., 1893.

352; authority over, 316-18, 323; becomes Rhodesia Mounted Police, 428; Pioneer Column, 164-5, 167, 170, 362, 366

British South Africa Police, 511-12, 515, 516, 532, 590, 591, 595, 596, 604, 626-7, 630

Bronkhorst, J.G.S., 10

Brown, William Harvey, 163, 344, 362, 368, 390, 405, 407, 414, 490, 534, 539

Bruce, A.L., 125, 129

Bruce, Sir George, 307

Brussels Conference, 315, 319, 320

Bryce's store (skirmish), 591

Buchanan, Consul J., 195, 197

Buckingham, Capt., 206

Budjga, 401-2

Bugudwana (ibutho), 275

Bulalima district, 522, 526

Bulawayo, 5, 15, 18, 19, 37-9, 41-2, 44, 55-6, 58-60, 62, 65, 81, 87, 93, 96, 126, 153-6, 159-61, 166, 168-9, 173-5, 181, 216, 226-7, 229-30, 232, 234-6, 250-1, 253, 256, 258-60, 263n41, 265-8, 273, 275-9, 285, 297, 310, 350, 361, 391-2, 396, 406, 408, 415, 425, 428-30, 432-4, 439, 441, 443-6, 448-50, 452, 455-8, 462, 466-7, 477, 485-6, 491, 493, 501, 503, 506-7, 510, 512, 515, 521-2, 526, 543, 555, 559-62, 564, 572-3, 577-9, 581, 583-4, 591-5, 597, 599-603, 606-9, 614, 619-23, 626, 629-30; census, 378-9, 381, 470n39; defence during rebellion, 439, 441, 443-52, 456-7, 470n39; occupied by Company, 276; rail lines connecting, 559, 564-6, 568, 571, 620-2; relocation, 8; urban development, 359-61

Bulawayo Chamber of Commerce, 361, 421, 553, 560, 572, 573, 579, 622, 624

Bulawayo (Rhodesia) Chamber of Mines, 536, 553, 560, 572, 583, 611, 624

Bulawayo Chronicle, 360, 378, 386n18, 391, 421, 429, 433-4, 455, 462, 477, 529, 535, 537, 560, 561, 565, 571, 573, 582, 584, 586n14, 592, 597, 600, 608-9, 620, 629, 630, 633n11, 636n53

Bulawayo Club, 361, 629

Bulawayo Field Force, 226, 446, 512

Bulawayo Sketch, 361

Bulawayo Town Council, 595

Burdett-Coutts, Baroness, 125

Burgers, T.F., 19, 203

Burgher law, 486

Burgin, H.R., 418

Burke, E.E., 171

Burnett, Edward, 36, 129

Burnham, Frederick Russell, 267, 276, 280-2, 284, 287n5, 456, 458-9, 489

Butler, Sir William, 589-90

Buxton, Sir T. Fowell, 107, 129

Caisse des Mines, 57, 97n7

Caldecott, Alfred, 326

Campbell, A.D., 384, 478

Canning, Herbert, 511

"Cape to Cairo" vision, 125, 147n46, 191, 570, 620, 621

Cape Argus, 80, 96, 317, 606

"Cape Boys," 377, 384, 402, 420; Jameson's War, 277; in rebellion, 450, 453, 455, 460, 466-8, 480, 482, 487, 495, 496, 510, 515

Cape Colony, 1, 22, 44, 50n51, 74, 108, 124, 138, 162, 177, 179, 249, 253, 312, 321, 326, 330, 332, 333-4, 373, 377, 384, 466, 523, 527, 531, 537, 539, 543, 556, 559, 577, 579, 590, 594, 600, 605, 610, 616-18, 629, 631-2, 634n32; annexed by Britain, 1, 3; Concession rifles, 89-90, 101n72; Customs Union, 571, 572-4, 580, 625; expansion, 25, 27, 610; German imperialism, 22-3, 28-9, 31; political arrangements for Bechuanaland, 24, 314,

426, 429, 468n3; railway policy, 131-2, 301-3, 559, 563, 570-1, 587n33, 622

Cape Times, 80, 497, 501

Cape Town, 1, 21, 22, 36, 37, 40, 53n111, 63, 72, 80-1, 89, 91, 104-7, 113-15, 140, 151-2, 154-5, 157-8, 163, 203, 208, 218, 240, 253, 255, 317, 344, 348, 371, 392, 416, 428, 430, 432, 433, 452, 454, 455, 463-4, 502, 506, 509, 529, 555, 556, 570, 575, 576, 589, 596, 606, 609, 622, 629, 632

Cape Town Chamber of Commerce, 29, 31

Cardoso, Antonio Mario, 195

Carnegie, David, 15, 84, 110, 154, 398, 505

Carrington, Sir Frederick: African rebellions, 454, 456, 458-64, 466, 510-11, 512, 519n25; Anglo-Boer War, 591, 596-7, 599, 609; Government House Conference, 157; martial law executions, 463-4, 494; Ndebele peace indabas, 496-7, 501-3, 507-8; Pioneer march, 157, 163; prevention of Boer treks, 176, 178-9.

Castens, H.H., 564

Cattle, 8, 87, 109, 139, 168, 226, 229, 284, 373-4, 432-33, 484, 488; African rights to, 336; confiscation from Africans, 285, 374-6, 394-9, 422nn14, 15, 433, 435, 499-500, 615-16; dispute over (1893), 234-7, 239-42, 249-53, 258; raids for, among Africans, 3, 5. See also Lobola; Loot agreements; Rinderpest

Causeway area (Salisbury), 171, 351

Cavendish, Lady Frederick, 106

Cawston, George, 71, 103, 121, 124, 152, 153, 154, 392; amalgamation with Rhodes, 107, 112-15, 117; Anglo-Portuguese treaty, 199; approach for charter,

Jesuits. *See* Roman Catholics
Jews, 355-6
Johannesburg, 42, 66, 89, 173, 175, 232, 353, 366, 426, 428, 430, 434, 495
Johannesburg *Star*, 179, 311
Johnson, Frank W.F., 53n111, 56-7, 97n8, 160, 185n3, 286-7n2, 345, 347, 366-7, 603, 612; Company expeditions to coast, 208-9, 213; contract with Rhodes, 155-6; concession-hunting expeditions, 36-41; land and mining claims, 362-3, 364-5, 368-9, 387n26; Mazoe Valley concession, 151-3; Pioneer Column, 162-5, 172, 206, 295; stake in BSAC, 129; assault scheme, 154-5, 185n8; syndicate, 203, 209, 296, 353, 364-5
Johnston, Sir Harry, 122, 124-6, 147n46, 191, 195, 197, 383, 550
Johnston, Dr James, 348, 357
Joubert, Frans, 10
Joubert, P.J., 21, 34-6, 161
Jourdan, Philip, 629-30
Jubane Hlabangana, 438, 458-9, 474
Judson, Lieut. D., 481
Jules Porges and Company, 124
Juries bill, 579-80

Kafue river, 84, 251
Kaguvi (Gumporeshumba), 475-7, 484, 487, 491, 513, 516, 521-2
Kalanga, 5, 20, 438
Karanga, 5, 457
Keate Award, 18
Kershaw, Maj. F., 459, 462
Kgama (chief of Ngwato), 15, 29, 41, 43, 59-60, 64-5, 74, 82, 87, 112-13, 118-20, 155, 157, 225, 414, 455, 552; accepts British protection, 23, 40, 68; Anglo-Boer War, 595, 603; assists Pioneer Column, 158-9, 164, 170, 172; concession to Johnson, 37-8, 40, 151; deportation of concession

hunters, 40, 60, 73, 182, 322; deputation to England, 426-7; friction with Grobler, 34; Jameson's War, 247-8, 255-6, 265, 275-7; relations with Ndebele, 15, 24-5, 28, 32-3, 40, 65, 232
Khami river, 230, 261n12, 371, 393, 449
Khokhomere, 234, 262n18
Khumalo, Karl, 173, 226-7, 253, 467-8, 472n66, 503-4, 529, 603
Kimberley, 17-18, 27, 30-1, 42, 57, 59, 63, 68, 80, 88-9, 95, 103, 113, 128, 131, 155, 159, 163, 207-8, 216, 301, 304, 308, 326, 347, 364, 377, 383, 402, 407, 414, 452, 454, 581, 593, 621, 629-30
Kimberley Central Company, 36, 58
Kirby, W.F., 253, 255
Kirk, Sir John, 158
Kitchener's Fighting Scouts, 610, 632
Knight, E.F., 349, 358, 364, 370
Knight-Bruce, J.W.H., 55, 73, 74, 79, 81, 212-13, 223n32, 482; activity in Mashonaland, 65-6, 350, 355, 358, 416-18
Knutsford, Lord, 63, 74, 81, 141-2, 302; constitutional position of Rhodesia, 314-15, 320-1, 323; grant of charter, 117, 119-21, 147n30; messages to Lobengula, 108-11, 115, 139, 144; Ndebele deputation, 103-4, 106, 108-11; noncommittal to concessionaires, 57, 63-4, 72, 108; Pioneer Column, 157-8, 162; Rhodesian administration, 412; Rudd Concession, 81, 91, 135, 148n63; vetoes imperial expansion to Matabeleland, 31
Kololo, 2, 13, 193-5, 197
Kopje (Salisbury), 172, 187n41, 351-3, 355, 486

Korekore, 5, 152-3, 475, 522, 604
Kotze, J.G., 623
Kruger, S.J.P.: (1836-87), 4, 9, 19-20, 22, 42; (1888-90), 45-6, 61-2, 73, 104, 131, 161-2, 176, 189; (1891-99), 176-7, 179, 434, 445, 453, 585, 603, 623
Kunzwi (Shona chief), 513-15, 602
Kuruman, 2, 302
Kwena (Tswana tribe), 427

Labouchere, Henry, 149n66, 182, 249, 294, 326, 330, 399
Labour (African), African reactions to, 405-7, 414, 542; conditions, 406, 538-41; dependence of settlers on, 377, 533; farming, 378, 538-41; mining, 377-8, 536-8, 610-13; for Pioneer Column, 164; recruitment, 403-6, 408, 532-3, 535-7, 611-18
Lacerda, Dr. Francisco, 1, 190,
Lagden Commission. *See* South African Native Affairs Commission
Laing, D. Tyrie, 443-4, 448, 460-1, 467, 497
Land, 29, 180-1, 216-17, 219-20, 226; African rights, 335-7, 366, 391-4, 523-7; African tenure types, 524-5; confiscation from Africans, 389-91, 440, 523, 529; grants to whites, 156, 171, 317-18, 366-70, 387n26, 588n51; inability of BSAC to grant, 172-3, 175, 184; as political issue, 558-9, 561, 563, 581-3, 624-5
Land Commission (1894), 335-6, 392-9
Land Survey Regulations (1897), 581, 583
Laurencedale settlement, 368, 373
Lawley, Arthur, 502, 527-9, 537, 549, 555, 564, 566,

404-5, 408, 414-15, 423n27, 432-3, 437, 452-3, 455, 459-60, 462, 465-6, 473, 476-7, 488, 495, 506, 509-10, 512, 515, 521-3, 528, 530, 538-9, 542, 550-1, 554-5, 561-2, 593-4, 597, 600, 610-11, 614, 616; admission of Europeans, 10-11, 19-20; borders of, 15, 73, 232-3; British designs on, 30-4, 44-5, 74, 120, 137-8, 319-21, disposal of land, 156, 248-9, 334-7, 390-2, 394, 523-7, 558-9, 582; invasion and encroachments, 9, 35, 64-5, 68-70, 85-6, 154, 156, 159, 236, 329-30; jurisdiction of Company over, 313-16, 330-1; mineral wealth, 16, 364-6; settlement of Ndebele, 4-5; traders, 55-6. *See also* Ndebele
Matabeleland Company, 17, 112, 130, 148n59, 294-5
Matabeleland Native Labour Bureau, 537-8
Matabeleland Mounted Police, 428, 512
Matabeleland Order-in-Council, 356, 494, 550, 552, 555-7; doubtful legality, 331; negotiations, 331; provisions for government, 331-4, 342n66; provisions regarding Africans, 334-7, 342n71, 392, 400
Matabeleland Regiment (Rhodesia Horse Volunteers), 429-30, 446
Matabeleland Relief Force, 453, 463
Matabele Syndicate, 183-4
Matjesumhlope stream, 359
Matopos, 4-5, 277, 287n9, 391, 394, 408, 435-6, 438-9, 441, 457-9, 500, 504, 507, 521-3, 526-9, 566, 605, 630-1; campaign during rebellion, 449, 452, 460-2, 467-8, 474, 495-7, 503, 506-7, 551
Mauch, Karl, 15-16, 49-50n45, 153

Maund, E.A., 31, 34, 64, 76, 92, 146nn23, 28, 153, 185n3, 226, 253, 262n30, 357, 365; ambivalent relation to Rhodes, 95, 112, 115-16, 130; concession-hunting expeditions, 57-8, 63, 66, 71-2; invasion of Matabeleland, 154; Mazoe Valley, 83, 85, 151; Ndebele deputation, 83-5, 94, 96, 103-6, 149n66; report on Matabeleland, 7, 28, 30; return to Bulawayo, 139-40, Warren embassy to Lobengula, 24-5, 30
Maund, Oakley, 115, 130, 309
Maxim gun, 530; Anglo-Boer War, 592, 598; Jameson's War, 235, 266, 269-70, 273-4, 276, 278-82, 284, 408; Pioneer Column, 164; punitive raids, 412-13; rebellion, 444, 446, 450-1, 455, 485-6, 522
Maxwell, Maj. Thomas, 142, 167, 231, 236, 297, 325
Mazoe district, 390, 403, 409-10, 477, 492, 513-14, 516
Mazoe Patrol, 409, 479-82
Mazoe river, 37-8, 83-5, 105, 112, 151-2, 154, 196, 232, 362, 365
Mazwe (induna), 393, 440, 449, 462
Mazwe (rebel policeman), 492
Mbambeleli (induna), 522-3
Mcheza, 112, 160-1
Melsetter district, 199, 349, 368, 373, 376, 379, 389, 403-4, 415, 418, 420, 423n37, 475, 541, 544, 562-3
Merriman, John X., 89, 610
"Messengers," 532
Metcalfe, Sir Charles, 130, 217, 307, 456, 503, 508, 510, 629
Methodists, 354, 415, 417, 419, 543
Methuen, Maj.-Gen. Paul, 165, 186n31
Mfecane, 2-3

Mfengu (Fingo), 86, 416, 467, 537, 543
Mfezela, 434, 442-3
Mgandane Dlodlo, 236-8, 241-3
Mhasvi (rebel policeman), 479, 481
Mhlaba, 25, 183, 261n12; enquiry into Ndebele succession, 8; execution 229-31, 267, 371, 434; prominence in Ndebele politics, 39; supports Rudd Concession, 86
Mhlahlandlela (ibutho), 237
Mhlahlo, 282-3
Mhluganiswa (induna), 505
mhondoro, 437, 474, 477, 487, 513
Michell, Sir Lewis, 623, 630
midzimu, 437
Mills, Sir Charles, 108, 124, 130, 339n24
Milner, Sir Alfred, 551, 565, 590, 601, 603, 624; administration of Rhodesia, 555-6; 581; African administration, 529, 531-3, 538, 627-8; African labour, 617, 619; cattle and land, 523, 525-6; customs policy, 573; executions and amnesty, 521
Milton, Sir William, 369, 581; administration of Rhodesia, 549, 555, 564, 573, 583, 623-8, 632; Anglo-Boer War, 595, 602-3, 609; labour supply, 533, 538, 611, 614-16; land settlement, 525-6
"Mining Laws," 317-18
Mining Ordinance (1895), 580
Mining Regulations, 364
Minister of mines, 324
Miscegenation, 381-4
Missionaries, 1-2, 9, 12, 35, 56, 158, 344, 368, 379-80, 545n17, 603; attitude to Africans, 419-20, 533-5; Boer antipathy to, 3; Mashonaland, 415-20, 423n33; Matabeleland, 11, 13, 70, 74, 80, 86-8, 166, 252, 414-15; Nyasa region,

121-2, 192-5; precursors of imperialism, 12-13, 15, 20, 74, 414-15, 542; Zimbabwe, 542-4. *See also* Knight-Bruce, J.W.H.; Moffat, R.; Moffat, J.S.; London Missionary Society

Mizeki, Bernard, 416, 418-19, 482, 522

Mkwati, 436-7, 439, 449, 456-7, 460, 474-6, 516

Mlagela (induna), 183, 237

Mlimo, 435-9, 441, 443, 451, 457-8

Mlozi, 194-5

Mlugulu, 39, 84, 110, 434-5, 438-40, 443, 449, 457, 460, 469n16, 529, 605

Mncumbate, 8, 39, 230

Mnyenyezi, 230, 267, 269

Modus vivendi: (1890), 200, 203, 207, 209-10, 212, 214-15, 221n15; (1901), 612

Moffat, H.U., 130, 632

Moffat, John Smith, 13, 15, 56-8, 60-3, 66, 84, 91-2, 94, 96, 110, 115, 125, 140-2, 154, 158, 167-8, 174, 181-3, 226-8, 230, 232-3, 236, 238, 240, 250, 252-3, 255-6, 265, 314, 371; assistant commissioner for protectorate, 34; Company invasion, 154-5, 158; mission to Lobengula, 41, 43-4; involvement with Rudd party, 64-5, 70-1, 74, 81, 93, 96, 103; later career, 632; Ndebele suspicions regarding, 67, 167, 225-6; as queen's representative, 138-40, 143-5; treaty with Lobengula, 44-6, 54nn138, 142, 59, 122, 138, 197, 204-5, 319, 542

Moffat, Richard, 346, 352

Moffat, Robert, 1, 2, 10, 12-13, 34

Mokhuchwane (brother of Kgama), 61

Molimile Molele, 484, 518n15, 543

Molopo river, 24, 34

Monarch mine, 265-6

Montshiwa, 22, 427-8

Moodie, G.B. Dunbar, 206, 368, 371-3, 379, 404

Moodie, Thomas, 372-3

Moore, Henry Clay, 38, 86, 95, 363-9

Morgenster (mission), 415-16, 423n33

Moselekatse. *See* Mzilikazi

Moshete. *See* Moffat, Robert

Mossurize, 196, 204

Mother Patrick, 350

Motloutsi river, 15, 25, 38, 40, 59, 62, 64, 72, 112, 157, 164-5, 167, 172, 226, 232, 247, 257, 259, 265, 350, 454, 466

Motshodi, 312, 568, 595, 603

Mount Hampden, 156-7, 169, 206, 363

Mount Selinda, 196, 349, 416

Mozambique, 2, 118, 121-2, 189-92, 195, 197, 199, 210, 213, 355, 402, 415, 419, 522, 600-1, 605, 611-12

Mozambique Company, 151, 197, 201, 211, 213-15, 219, 305-7

Mpakwe river, 57

mphakathi, 39, 53n124

Mrewa district, 527

Mshete (induna), 140, 167, 173, 175, 181, 183; Ndebele deputation to England, 84-5, 96, 105-9, 139-40, 225; peace mission, 231, 253

Msindazi (induna), 444

Mthethwa, 1-2

Mtini, 449-51

Mtobi, Hezekiah (Anglican priest), 416

Mtoko district, 205, 222n23, 401-2, 417

Mtshane Khumalo (induna), 631; grievances against Company, 393, 395-6, 429; Jameson's War, 269-70, 273, 275, 279, 289; Ndebele peace indabas, 507

Muchemwa (of Mangwende chieftaincy), 483, 522

Mudzimu. *See* Midzimu

Mudzinganyama Jiri Mteveri (Rozvi Mambo), 514

Mugabe (Shona chief), 412

Mungate. *See* Mangwende

Munhumutapa, 5, 437

Musson, George, 89

Mutasa, 5, 171, 203-4, 327, 416, 475; question of allegiance, 198, 201-2, 204-6, 212n16; treaties with BSAC, 200-1, 203-4; Wise-Beningfield Concession, 216-19

Mutekedza, 473, 491, 518n24

Mutola Cirimaunga. *See* Makoni

Mwari, 435-9, 449, 458, 475, 477

Mzila, 192, 196

Mzilikazi, 5, 7, 10-15, 17, 20, 34-5, 44, 47n15, 56, 60, 139, 173, 227, 232, 380, 496, 499, 528, 546n18, 631; Boers, 10-11, 18; Mfecane, 2-3; widow of, 496

Mzingwane district, 432, 446, 526

Mzisi, William, 86

Mzobo (induna), 448

Nagana, 11

Napier, William, 278, 539-40; Jameson Raid; 430-1, 433; Jameson's War, 278, 281-2; rebellion, 445-6, 451, 456

Natal, 1, 4, 5, 8, 16, 18, 25, 38, 43-4, 48n22, 80, 142, 167, 230, 371, 400, 407, 454, 466, 486-7, 539, 554, 585, 594, 605

Natal Land and Colonization Company, 16

Native commissioners, 395-8, 408, 415, 473, 499, 525, 527, 529-32, 537, 542, 556, 602-3; labour recruitment, 391, 403-5; rebellion, 442; tax collection, 401-2

Native Department, 391, 401, 403, 409, 556, 604

Native Labour Bureau, 536-7

"Native locations," 541, 578, 617

Native Marriages Ordinance, 615-16

Native Police, 403, 407-9,